1973

AMERICAN COUNCIL OF LEARNED SOCIETIES

Dictionary
of Scientific
Biography
cSs

DICTIONARY
OF
SCIENTIFIC BIOGRAPHY

PUBLISHED UNDER THE AUSPICES OF
THE AMERICAN COUNCIL OF LEARNED SOCIETIES

The American Council of Learned Societies, organized in 1919 for the purpose of advancing the study of the humanities and of the humanistic aspects of the social sciences, is a nonprofit federation comprising thirty-nine national scholarly groups. The Council represents the humanities in the United States in the International Union of Academies, provides fellowships and grants-in-aid, supports research-and-planning conferences and symposia, and sponsors special projects and scholarly publications.

MEMBER ORGANIZATIONS

AMERICAN PHILOSOPHICAL SOCIETY, 1743
AMERICAN ACADEMY OF ARTS AND SCIENCES, 1780
AMERICAN ANTIQUARIAN SOCIETY, 1812
AMERICAN ORIENTAL SOCIETY, 1842
AMERICAN NUMISMATIC SOCIETY, 1858
AMERICAN PHILOLOGICAL ASSOCIATION, 1869
ARCHAEOLOGICAL INSTITUTE OF AMERICA, 1879
SOCIETY OF BIBLICAL LITERATURE, 1880
MODERN LANGUAGE ASSOCIATION OF AMERICA, 1883
AMERICAN HISTORICAL ASSOCIATION, 1884
AMERICAN ECONOMIC ASSOCIATION, 1885
AMERICAN FOLKLORE SOCIETY, 1888
AMERICAN DIALECT SOCIETY, 1889
AMERICAN PSYCHOLOGICAL ASSOCIATION, 1892
ASSOCIATION OF AMERICAN LAW SCHOOLS, 1900
AMERICAN PHILOSOPHICAL ASSOCIATION, 1901
AMERICAN ANTHROPOLOGICAL ASSOCIATION, 1902
AMERICAN POLITICAL SCIENCE ASSOCIATION, 1903
BIBLIOGRAPHICAL SOCIETY OF AMERICA, 1904
ASSOCIATION OF AMERICAN GEOGRAPHERS, 1904
HISPANIC SOCIETY OF AMERICA, 1904
AMERICAN SOCIOLOGICAL ASSOCIATION, 1905
AMERICAN SOCIETY OF INTERNATIONAL LAW, 1906
ORGANIZATION OF AMERICAN HISTORIANS, 1907
COLLEGE ART ASSOCIATION OF AMERICA, 1912
HISTORY OF SCIENCE SOCIETY, 1924
LINGUISTIC SOCIETY OF AMERICA, 1924
MEDIAEVAL ACADEMY OF AMERICA, 1925
AMERICAN MUSICOLOGICAL SOCIETY, 1934
SOCIETY OF ARCHITECTURAL HISTORIANS, 1940
ECONOMIC HISTORY ASSOCIATION, 1940
ASSOCIATION FOR ASIAN STUDIES, 1941
AMERICAN SOCIETY FOR AESTHETICS, 1942
METAPHYSICAL SOCIETY OF AMERICA, 1950
AMERICAN STUDIES ASSOCIATION, 1950
RENAISSANCE SOCIETY OF AMERICA, 1954
SOCIETY FOR ETHNOMUSICOLOGY, 1955
AMERICAN SOCIETY FOR LEGAL HISTORY, 1956
SOCIETY FOR THE HISTORY OF TECHNOLOGY, 1958

DICTIONARY

OF

SCIENTIFIC BIOGRAPHY

CHARLES COULSTON GILLISPIE

Princeton University

EDITOR IN CHIEF

Volume VIII

JONATHAN HOMER LANE – PIERRE JOSEPH MACQUER

CHARLES SCRIBNER'S SONS · NEW YORK

1 3 5 7 9 11 13 15 17 19 MD/C 20 18 16 14 12 10 8 6 4 2

Printed in the United States of America
Library of Congress Catalog Card Number 69-18090
SBN 684–10119–X (cloth)

Editorial Board

Editorial Staff

Panel of Consultants

Contributors to Volume VIII

The following are the contributors to Volume VIII. Each author's name is followed by the institutional affiliation at the time of publication and the names of articles written for this volume. The symbol † indicates that an author is deceased.

GIORGIO ABETTI
Istituto Nazionale di Ottica
LORENZONI

ERIC J. AITON
Didsbury College of Education
LEIBNIZ

LUÍS DE ALBUQUERQUE
University of Coimbra
LAVANHA; LISBOA

GARLAND E. ALLEN
Washington University
McCLUNG

TOBY A. APPEL
Kirkland College
LEREBOULLET

CORTLAND P. AUSER
Bronx Community College, City University of New York
LARSEN

STANLEY L. BECKER
Bethany College
McCOLLUM

WHITFIELD J. BELL, JR.
American Philosophical Society Library
LEA

LUIGI BELLONI
University of Milan
LARGHI

ENRIQUE BELTRÁN
Mexican Society of the History of Science and Technology
LICEAGA

RICHARD BERENDZEN
Boston University
MAANEN

ALEX BERMAN
University of Cincinnati
LESSON

OLEXA MYRON BILANIUK
Swarthmore College
LICHTENBERG

ASIT K. BISWAS
Department of Environment, Ottawa
LAUSSEDAT

MARGARET R. BISWAS
McGill University
LAUSSEDAT

L. J. BLACHER
Academy of Sciences of the U.S.S.R.
LAVRENTIEV

GEORGE BOAS
Johns Hopkins University
LOVEJOY

WALTER BÖHM
LOSCHMIDT

O. BORŮVKA
Czechoslovak Academy of Sciences
LERCH

GERT H. BRIEGER
Duke University
LOEFFLER

T. A. A. BROADBENT †
MACAULAY; McCOLL; MacMAHON

THEODORE M. BROWN
City College, City University of New York
LOWER

STEPHEN G. BRUSH
University of Maryland
LENNARD-JONES

K. E. BULLEN
University of Sydney
LOVE

VERN L. BULLOUGH
California State University, Northridge
LIND; MACLEAN

IVOR BULMER-THOMAS
LEO; LEODAMAS OF THASOS

WERNER BURAU
University of Hamburg
LUEROTH

JOHN G. BURKE
University of California, Los Angeles
O. LEHMANN; LEONHARD

RICHARD W. BURKHARDT, JR.
University of Illinois
LATREILLE

H. L. L. BUSARD
State University of Leiden
VAN LANSBERGE; LE PAIGE

JEROME J. BYLEBYL
University of Chicago
LAURENS; LEONICENO

ANDRÉ CAILLEUX
Laval University
LAPPARENT; E. A. I. H. LARTET; L. LARTET

KENNETH L. CANEVA
University of Utah
A.-A. DE LA RIVE; C.-G. DE LA RIVE

JEFFREY CARR
University of Leeds
M. LISTER

ETTORE CARRUCCIO
Universities of Bologna and Turin
LORIA

JOHN CHALLINOR
C. LAPWORTH

SEYMOUR L. CHAPIN
California State University, Los Angeles
LE GENTIL DE LA GALAISIÈRE

MARSHALL CLAGETT
Institute for Advanced Study, Princeton
LEONARDO DA VINCI

T. H. CLARK
McGill University
W. E. LOGAN

M. J. CLARKSON
Liverpool School of Tropical Medicine
T. R. LEWIS

E. COUMET
E. LE ROY

MAURICE CRANSTON
London School of Economics
LOCKE

GLYN DANIEL
University of Cambridge
LEAKEY

MAURICE DAUMAS
Conservatoire National des Arts et Métiers
LANGLOIS

AUDREY B. DAVIS
Smithsonian Institution
LIEBERKÜHN

GAVIN DE BEER †
LANKESTER

SALLY H. DIEKE
Johns Hopkins University
J. W. LUBBOCK; C. S. LYMAN

HERBERT DINGLE
LOCKYER

CLAUDE E. DOLMAN
University of British Columbia
J. LISTER

J. G. DORFMAN
Academy of Sciences of the U.S.S.R.
P. P. LAZAREV; P. N. LEBEDEV

SIGALIA DOSTROVSKY
Barnard College
LISSAJOUS

STILLMAN DRAKE
University of Toronto
LE TENNEUR

J. M. EDMONDS
University of Oxford Museum
LHWYD

ix

CONTRIBUTORS TO VOLUME VIII

FRANK N. EGERTON III
University of Wisconsin-Parkside
LOVELL

JON EKLUND
Smithsonian Institution
W. LEWIS

V. A. ESAKOV
Academy of Sciences of the U.S.S.R.
M. P. LAZAREV

C. W. F. EVERITT
Stanford University
F. LONDON; H. LONDON

JOSEPH EWAN
Tulane University
LESQUEREUX

V. A. EYLES
MACCULLOCH

W. M. FAIRBANK
Stanford University
F. LONDON; H. LONDON

W. V. FARRAR
University of Manchester
A. LAPWORTH; LAWES AND GILBERT

GIOVANNI FAVILLI
University of Bologna
LUSTIG

IGNAZIO FAZZARI
University of Florence
LUNA

I. A. FEDOSEYEV
Academy of Sciences of the U.S.S.R.
LEPEKHIN; LOKHTIN

MARTIN FICHMAN
York University
J.-B. LE ROY

KARIN FIGALA
Technische Hochschule München
LONICERUS

N. FIGUROVSKY
Academy of Sciences of the U.S.S.R.
LOVITS

WALTHER FISCHER
LIESGANIG

DONALD FLEMING
Harvard University
J. LOEB

ROBERT FOX
University of Lancaster
N. LEBLANC

EUGENE FRANKEL
Trinity College
H. LLOYD

H.-CHRIST. FREIESLEBEN
LOHSE; LUDENDORFF; LUTHER

HANS FREUDENTHAL
State University of Utrecht
LIE; LOEWNER

BRUNO VON FREYBERG
University of Erlangen-Nuremberg
J. G. LEHMANN

DAVID J. FURLEY
Princeton University
LUCRETIUS

GERALD L. GEISON
Princeton University
J. N. LANGLEY; LOEWI; K. LUCAS

PATSY A. GERSTNER
Dittrick Museum of Historical Medicine
K. N. LANG

OWEN GINGERICH
Smithsonian Astrophysical Observatory
LEAVITT

P. GLEES
University of Göttingen
LEYDIG

THOMAS F. GLICK
Boston University
LEO THE AFRICAN

MARIO GLIOZZI
University of Turin
LEVI-CIVITA

GEORGE GOE
New School for Social Research
LUKASIEWICZ

J. B. GOUGH
Washington State University
C. LE ROY; LESAGE

I. GRATTAN-GUINNESS
Enfield College of Technology
M. P. H. LAURENT

SAMUEL L. GREITZER
Rutgers University
LEMOINE

NORMAN T. GRIDGEMAN
National Research Council of Canada
LOTKA; F.-E.-A. LUCAS

A. T. GRIGORIAN
Academy of Sciences of the U.S.S.R.
LEXELL; LEYBENZON; LYAPUNOV

HENRY GUERLAC
Cornell University
LAVOISIER

THOMAS L. HANKINS
University of Washington
P.-C. LE MONNIER

OWEN HANNAWAY
Johns Hopkins University
LE FEBVRE; L. LEMERY; N. LEMERY

THOMAS HAWKINS
Boston University
LEBESGUE

ROGER HEIM
Muséum National d'Histoire Naturelle
LE DANTEC

JOHANNES HENIGER
State University of Utrecht
LEEUWENHOEK

ARMIN HERMANN
University of Stuttgart
LAUE; LENARD; LUMMER

DIETER B. HERRMANN
Archenhold Observatory, Berlin
LINDENAU

ERWIN N. HIEBERT
Harvard University
MACH

JOEL H. HILDEBRAND
University of California, Berkeley
LATIMER

JOSEPH E. HOFMANN †
LEIBNIZ

HO PENG-YOKE
Griffith University
LI CHIH; LIU HUI

A. HOLLMAN
University College Hospital, London
T. LEWIS

FREDERIC L. HOLMES
University of Western Ontario
LIEBIG

I. B. HOPLEY
Clifton College
LIPPMANN

MICHAEL A. HOSKIN
University of Cambridge
MACLEAR

PIERRE HUARD
René Descartes University
LE DOUBLE; LIEUTAUD; LORRY

WŁODZIMIERZ HUBICKI
Marie Curie-Skłodowska University
LIBAVIUS

AARON J. IHDE
University of Wisconsin, Madison
LEVENE

MARIE JOSÉ IMBAULT-HUART
René Descartes University
LE DOUBLE; LIEUTAUD; LORRY

JEAN ITARD
Lycée Henri IV
P. A. LAURENT; LEGENDRE

R. V. JONES
University of Aberdeen
F. A. LINDEMANN

PAUL JOVET
Centre National de Floristique
L'ÉCLUSE; L'OBEL

SATISH C. KAPOOR
University of Saskatchewan
AUGUSTE LAURENT

B. M. KEDROV
Academy of Sciences of the U.S.S.R.
LENIN; LOMONOSOV

KENNETH D. KEELE
Research Fellow, Wellcome Institute
LEONARDO DA VINCI

A. G. KELLER
University of Leicester
LUSITANUS

MARTHA B. KENDALL
Vassar College
LESLEY

G. B. KERFERD
University of Manchester
LEUCIPPUS

H. C. KING
Royal Ontario Museum
LASSELL

MARC KLEIN
Louis Pasteur University
LAVERAN

FRIEDRICH KLEMM
Deutsches Museum
LINDE

H. KOBAYASHI
Hokkaido University
B. S. LYMAN

MANFRED KOCH
Bergbau Bucherei, Essen
LÖHNEYSS

R. E. KOHLER
University of Pennsylvania
G. N. LEWIS

ELAINE KOPPELMAN
Goucher College
M. LÉVY

SHELDON J. KOPPERL
Grand Valley State College
M. J. L. LE BLANC

FREDERICK KREILING
Brooklyn Polytechnic Institute
LEIBNIZ

A. D. KRIKORIAN
State University of New York at Stony Brook
LIVINGSTON

VLADISLAV KRUTA
Pediatric Research Institute, Brno
LEGALLOIS

GISELA KUTZBACH
University of Wisconsin
JOHN LECONTE; LOOMIS

HENRY M. LEICESTER
University of the Pacific
S. V. LEBEDEV; LE BEL; LE CHÂTELIER

CZESŁAW LEJEWSKI
University of Manchester
LEŚNIEWSKI

JACQUES R. LÉVY
Paris Observatory
LE VERRIER; LYOT

OLGA A. LEZHNEVA
Academy of Sciences of the U.S.S.R.
LENZ

STEN LINDROTH
University of Uppsala
LINNAEUS

ALBERT G. LONG
Hancock Museum
W. H. LANG

RUSSELL McCORMMACH
Johns Hopkins University
LORENTZ

ROBERT M. McKEON
Babson College
LE FÈVRE; J. LEMAIRE; P. LEMAIRE

H. LEWIS McKINNEY
University of Kansas
W. LAWRENCE; JOSEPH LECONTE

MICHAEL S. MAHONEY
Princeton University
LE POIVRE

J. C. MALLET
Centre National de Floristique
L'ÉCLUSE; L'OBEL

NIKOLAUS MANI
Bonn Institute for the History of Medicine
LANGERHANS

AUGUSTO MARINONI
LEONARDO DA VINCI

BRIAN G. MARSDEN
Smithsonian Astrophysical Observatory
LOWELL

KIRTLEY F. MATHER
University of New Mexico
LINDGREN

OTTO MAYR
Smithsonian Institution
LECORNU; H. LORENZ

A. A. MENIAILOV
Academy of Sciences of the U.S.S.R.
LEVINSON-LESSING

DANIEL MERRIMAN
Yale University
M'INTOSH

JÜRGEN MITTELSTRASS
University of Konstanz
LEIBNIZ

A. M. MONNIER
University of Paris
LAPICQUE; MACHEBOEUF

A. M. MONSEIGNY
Muséum National d'Histoire Naturelle
E. A. I. H. LARTET; L. LARTET

DON F. MOYER
Ripon College
S. P. LANGLEY; MACCULLAGH

AXEL V. NIELSEN †
LAU

J. D. NORTH
Museum of the History of Science, Oxford
MACMILLAN

KARL-GEORG NYHOLM
University of Uppsala
LOVÉN

HERBERT OETTEL
LINDELÖF

YNGVE ÖHMAN
Stockholm Observatory
LINDBLAD

OLIVIERO M. OLIVO
University of Bologna
LEVI

RICHARD G. OLSON
University of California, Santa Cruz
LESLIE

C. D. O'MALLEY †
LINACRE

A. PAPLAUSCAS
Academy of Sciences of the U.S.S.R.
LUZIN

JOHN PARASCANDOLA
University of Wisconsin
J. U. LLOYD

FRANKLIN PARKER
West Virginia University
L. LOEB

STUART PIERSON
Memorial University of Newfoundland
LEONHARDI; LYONET

MOGENS PIHL
University of Copenhagen
L. V. LORENZ

DAVID PINGREE
Brown University
LĀṬADEVA; LEO THE MATHEMATICIAN

A. F. PLAKHOTNIK
Academy of Sciences of the U.S.S.R.
LITKE

LUCIEN PLANTEFOL
University of Paris
L.-G. LE MONNIER

GIANLUIGI PORTA
LUCIANI

R. D. F. PRING-MILL
University of Oxford
LULL

P. RAMDOHR
University of Heidelberg
LOSSEN

NATHAN REINGOLD
Smithsonian Institution
LANE

LADISLAO RETI
LEONARDO DA VINCI

R. A. RICHARDSON
University of Western Ontario
MACALLUM

RUTH GIENAPP RINARD
Kirkland College
LIEBERMANN

S. DILLON RIPLEY
Smithsonian Institution
LEVAILLANT

CONTRIBUTORS TO VOLUME VIII

PHILIP C. RITTERBUSH
*Archives of Institutional Change,
Washington, D.C.*
LEIDY

J. M. ROBERTSON
University of Glasgow
K. LONSDALE

ABRAHAM ROBINSON
Yale University
L'HOSPITAL

PAUL G. ROOFE
University of Kansas
LASHLEY

GEORGE ROSEN
Yale University School of Medicine
LUDWIG

CHARLES E. ROSENBERG
University of Pennsylvania
LUSK

B. A. ROSENFELD
Academy of Sciences of the U.S.S.R.
LOBACHEVSKY

K. E. ROTHSCHUH
University of Münster/Westphalia
LOTZE

M. J. S. RUDWICK
University of Cambridge
W. LONSDALE

JULIO SAMSÓ
Universidad Autónoma de Barcelona
LEVI BEN GERSON

RALPH A. SAWYER
University of Michigan
T. LYMAN

WILLIAM L. SCHAAF
Florida Atlantic University
LEURECHON

H. SCHADEWALDT
University of Düsseldorf
LEUCKART

EBERHARD SCHMAUDERER
LUNGE

CECIL J. SCHNEER
University of New Hampshire
LEONARDO DA VINCI

BRUNO SCHOENEBERG
University of Hamburg
LIPSCHITZ

E. L. SCOTT
Stamford High School, Lincolnshire
R. LUBBOCK; D. MACBRIDE

J. F. SCOTT †
MACLAURIN

CAROL SHAMIEH
Boston University
MAANEN

DIANA M. SIMPKINS
Polytechnic of North London
E. W. MACBRIDE

N. SIVIN
Massachusetts Institute of Technology
LI SHIH-CHEN

W. A. SMEATON
University College, London
MACQUER

A. DE SMET
Bibliothèque Royale de Belgique
VAN LANGREN

H. A. M. SNELDERS
State University of Utrecht
H. F. LINK

E. SNORRASON
Rigshospitalet, Copenhagen
LANGE

Y. I. SOLOVIEV
Academy of Sciences of the U.S.S.R.
LUGININ

FRED SOMKIN
Cornell University
J. LUBBOCK

PIERRE SPEZIALI
University of Geneva
L'HUILLIER

FRANS A. STAFLEU
State University of Utrecht
L'HÉRITIER DE BRUTELLE

WILLIAM T. STEARN
British Museum (Natural History)
LINDLEY

C. G. G. J. VAN STEENIS
University of Leiden
LOTSY

LLOYD G. STEVENSON
Johns Hopkins University
MACLEOD

F. STOCKMANS
Free University of Brussels
LIGNIER; LOHEST

CHARLES SÜSSKIND
University of California, Berkeley
LANGMUIR; E. O. LAWRENCE; LODGE

F. SZABADVÁRY
Technical University, Budapest
R. LORENZ

RENÉ TATON
École Pratique des Hautes Études
LIOUVILLE

JEAN THÉODORIDÈS
*Centre National de la Recherche
Scientifique*
LÉGER

D. N. TRIFONOV
Academy of Sciences of the U.S.S.R.
LEBEDINSKY

G. L'E. TURNER
University of Oxford
J. J. LISTER

GEORG USCHMANN
University of Jena
A. LANG

FRANCIS E. VAUGHAN
VEMCO Corporation
LAWSON

J. J. VERDONK
LA ROCHE

THÉODORE VETTER
*Société Française d'Histoire de la
Médecine*
LE CAT

WILLIAM A. WALLACE, O.P.
Catholic University of America
LAX

RAY L. WATTERSON
University of Illinois
LILLIE

EUGENE WEGMANN
LUGEON

ADRIENNE R. WEILL-
BRUNSCHVICG
LANGEVIN

DORA B. WEINER
Manhattanville College
LEURET

JOHN W. WELLS
Cornell University
LESUEUR

GEORGE W. WHITE
University of Illinois
MACLURE

LEONARD G. WILSON
University of Minnesota
LYELL

EDWIN WOLF II
Library Company of Philadelphia
J. LOGAN

A. E. WOODRUFF
Yeshiva University
LARMOR

DENISE WROTNOWSKA
Musée Pasteur
LEVADITI

H. WUSSING
Karl Marx University
C. L. F. LINDEMANN

J. WYART
University of Paris
S.-D. A. LÉVY

A. P. YOUSCHKEVITCH
Academy of Sciences of the U.S.S.R.
LEXELL

BRUNO ZANOBIO
University of Pavia
LUCIANI

DICTIONARY
OF
SCIENTIFIC BIOGRAPHY

DICTIONARY OF
SCIENTIFIC BIOGRAPHY

LANE, JONATHAN HOMER (*b.* Genesee, New York, 9 August 1819; *d.* Washington, D.C., 3 May 1880), *physics.*

Lane left school at the age of eight but acquired enough learning by himself at home to teach in rural schools. In 1839 he entered Phillips Academy at Exeter, New Hampshire. While there, according to his own account, he became interested in what was to be his principal intellectual preoccupation, the experimental determination of absolute zero. He entered Yale, where he was apparently influenced by Denison Olmsted, and graduated in 1846.

After briefly teaching in Vermont, Lane came to Washington, D.C., in 1847 and was employed by the U.S. Coast Survey. He had already published the first of four articles on electricity. In 1848 Lane conferred with Joseph Henry about experiments to determine the speed of propagation of solar light and heat. In that same year, and with Henry's help, he was appointed an examiner in the U.S. Patent Office, where he was closely associated with Charles G. Page. Besides the articles on electricity, which were attempts to provide mathematical formulations for electrical phenomena, Lane published nothing during his years at the Patent Office (but see the comments in the bibliography below). In 1857, he was removed from the Patent Office by a spoils-minded Secretary of the Interior.

From 1857 to 1866, when Lane returned to Washington, his course is obscure, although the Abbe necrology (see below) asserts that he attempted to earn a living as a patent agent. He did attempt to develop his low-temperature apparatus, which was to utilize the expansion of gases for cooling. Failing to gain adequate backing, he went to Franklin, Venango County, Pennsylvania, in 1860, to live with his brother, a blacksmith. Lane expected his brother, who owed him money, to repay the debt by constructing the apparatus, an expectation that was not realized. Abbe also asserts that Lane made a handsome profit from the sale of oil lands in Pennsylvania, which enabled him to return to Washington. This seems unlikely, however, since Henry continued to send him odd computing jobs and even a small grant for the low-temperature experiments, apparently in the belief that Lane needed the money. In 1869 Lane joined the Office of Weights and Measures, the predecessor of the present National Bureau of Standards.

In 1869 Lane read a paper, "On the Theoretical Temperature of the Sun," before the National Academy of Sciences. It was printed in the *American Journal of Science* in the following year. His purpose was to test the adequacy of various current theories of heat by mathematical determinations of the temperature of the sun, on the assumption of a convection system, explicitly based upon James Espy's meteorological theories, for the movement of the photosphere. Lane concluded that none of the theories that assumed that heat was motion provided adequate explanations of his calculated values for the distribution of density, pressure, and temperature in the sun.

The paper gained a modest notoriety because of something it did not demonstrate but which Lane verbally proved to the satisfaction of both Kelvin and Newcomb. According to the latter's autobiography, Lane had given the proof to him prior to 1869 of the "law" by which a gaseous body contracts when it loses heat, but the heat generated by the contraction exceeds the heat lost in order to produce the contraction. Lane did not give the proof in his paper, although it was implicit in the presentation. Kelvin's interest stemmed in part from the possibility that "Lane's law" would contradict his calculation of the age of the earth by changing the quantity of energy available in the sun. Three years after Lane's paper August Ritter independently came to similar conclusions, including an explicit statement of the "paradoxical" law. Interestingly, Ritter also was applying meteorological theory to the study of the sun. Kelvin attempted to remove the supposed difficulty in 1887, for which he was subsequently criticized for "inexactitude" by Emden in 1907.

The principal significance of Lane's article, however, was not the unstated law nor even its testing of current theories of heat but the careful calculation of mass and heat relationships in the sun. The convection model, now discarded, proved useful for arriving at a good first approximation of the structure and energy distribution of the sun, while Lane's work on the structure of a star was a real contribution to the developing evidence of stellar evolution (leading to the Hertzsprung-Russell diagram of 1913).

It is not a wholly easy task to determine what other scientific work Lane actually performed. His bibliography contains only fifteen items, two of which are titles only. His contemporaries reported his unwillingness to rush into publication, this being the presumed reason for the absence of a published account of the work on absolute zero, supposedly completed by 1870. His personal papers in the U.S. National Archives contain several references to what may be published papers (perhaps in nonscientific journals), unpublished papers, or simply drafts or ideas for papers. In 1848, for example, Joseph Henry referred to a Lane paper on solar heat, which is now unknown.

This bibliographic uncertainty is particularly important because the surviving personal papers contain many fragments on proposed experiments and instruments, but since these are often incomplete or unclear, it is difficult to speak about Lane's scientific interests and accomplishments. Most of the fragments display a concern with precision instrumentation, while some clearly indicate Lane's mathematical aptitude. Few of the surviving manuscripts pertain to inventions in the popular sense, and Lane was never issued a patent.

In 1848, Henry called Lane a genuine mathematical physicist. He may indeed have been one. He may also have been a man of ability and overly strong fixations —a crank, as some of his other contemporaries saw him. It is, from the surviving fragments, difficult to decide if Lane was a man whose achievements did not live up to his potential—as his 1870 paper suggests—or a man whose notions surpassed his abilities.

If Lane did not, in fact, achieve his potential, was it his failure, or society's? Mathematical physicists were rare in antebellum America, a fact usually ascribed to a hostile national environment (although mathematical physicists were also relatively rare in European countries). Most of the positions available to Lane were in astronomy and meteorology, and he did work in both fields. Men of promise in his day did not automatically think of the university, nor did universities seek him out.

In Washington, Lane found a small, active, and congenial scientific community that recognized his talents. The Patent Office post, somewhat incongruously, to some extent offered an opportunity for men of scientific interests to earn an income— although they were not given either equipment or time to pursue research. But even time and equipment were provided to Lane, in part by Henry and by the cooperation of government agencies. Even without equipment, he could have pursued theoretical work. Moreover, Henry, Newcomb, Benjamin Peirce, and others provided him with a stimulating intellectual environment.

Newcomb and Cleveland Abbe, in their accounts of Lane, implicitly raise the matter of his personality as a cause for his limited productivity. He is described as gnomelike and living in a garret. His poverty is ascribed to his support of various relatives, but at his death his estate was valued at more than $10,000, of which $8,000 was in gold bonds. If his appearance and style of living were bedraggled, it was hardly due to lack of funds. In writing of him, Lane's contemporaries stressed his "hesitation in speaking," due, perhaps, to a speech defect or to shyness. At any rate, Lane had difficulty in socializing, even in the friendly environment of scientific Washington, where he remained somewhat of an outsider.

When Lane died, five sealed envelopes of priority claims, going back to 1850, remained in the Smithsonian Institution. S. P. Langley, on his arrival in Washington in 1887, prevailed upon Henry's successor, S. F. Baird, to authorize their opening. When this was done, in the presence of Langley and Newcomb, the claims were pronounced worthless. Lane was forgotten and his 1870 paper remained an inexplicable pioneering accident.

BIBLIOGRAPHY

I. ORIGINAL WORKS. A small collection of Lane's personal papers is in the records of the National Bureau of Standards in the U.S. National Archives in Washington, D.C. These contain scientific notes, Lane's accounts of his life and work, and letters both personal and professional. Other records of the National Bureau of Standards contain documents on Lane's activities. Of these the most significant are the reports itemizing the records and papers found in Lane's office in 1879 at the start of his terminal illness. The sealed envelopes are in the "Clippings File" of the Smithsonian Institution Archives. The file account of Lane's estate is in the custody of the Register of Wills of the District of Columbia. Both the account file and the list of Lane records prepared by the Office of Weights and Measures are very useful but frustrating; omnibus listings rather than detailed itemizations occur at a few crucial points. The correspondence in the Lane papers simply adds to the mysteries about him. For example, two different letters indicate that Michael Faraday wrote to Lane, presumably on his electrical work, yet no Faraday letters are in the collection.

II. SECONDARY LITERATURE. Upon Lane's death, J. E. Hilgard, the superintendent of the U.S. Coast and Geodetic Survey issued a statement before the Philosophical Society of Washington on Lane's career, in *Bulletin of the Philosophical Society of Washington*, **3** (8 May 1880), 122–124. This statement and information from W. B. Taylor of the Smithsonian are apparently the principal sources for Cleveland Abbe's "Memoir of Jonathan Homer Lane, 1819–1880," in *Biographical Memoirs. National Academy of Sciences*, **3** (1895), 253–264. There is little evidence for contacts between Abbe and Lane. Abbe read his memoir in 1892, many years after Lane's death and the printed version is replete with errors and doubtful assertions. When Simon Newcomb published his autobiography, *The Reminiscences of an Astronomer* (Boston–New York, 1903); the chapter subheading on Lane was, "A Forgotten Scientist." So forgotten was Lane that the index to the book does not even list him, but the interested reader is directed to pages 245–249.

See also Kelvin, "The Sun's Heat," in the *Proceedings of the Royal Institution of Great Britain*, **12** (1889), 1–21; for the critique of Kelvin, see R. Emden, *Gaskugeln, Anwendungen der Mechanischen Wärmetheorie* ... (Leipzig–Berlin, 1907), 462–469. August Ritter's work originally appeared in various numbers of the *Annalen der Physik und Chemie* and is summed up in his *Anwendungen der mechanischen Wärmetheorie auf kosmologische Probleme* (Leipzig, 1878).

N. REINGOLD

LANG, ARNOLD (*b.* Oftringen, Switzerland, 18 June 1855; *d.* Zurich, Switzerland, 30 November 1914), *zoology.*

Lang was the son of Adolf Lang, a cotton mill owner, who was also enthusiastically engaged in local politics. The family belonged to the Reformed Church.

Lang completed primary school in 1867 and district school in 1870. He then attended the cantonal school in Aarau until 1873. Starting in March 1873 he studied science, especially zoology, in Geneva and then, from 1874 to 1876, in Jena. After receiving the doctorate at Jena (1876), he qualified as privatdocent for zoology at Bern on 26 May 1876. In 1878 and 1879 he was the Swiss representative at the zoological station in Naples, where he remained as an assistant until 1885. In November of that year he went to Jena as privatdocent. In 1886, at the initiative of Ernst Haeckel, he was given the newly created post there of Ritter professor of phylogenetic zoology.

In 1889 he accepted an appointment as full professor of zoology and comparative anatomy at the University of Zurich. In addition, he became professor of zoology at the Eidgenössische Technische Hochschule, took over the directorship of the zoological collections, and founded a zoological institute. Along with his teaching duties, Lang assumed many further responsibilities, including membership on the Zurich school council, and played an active role in Swiss scientific societies. In the last years of his life he successfully campaigned for the rebuilding of the University of Zurich. Poor health forced him to retire on 15 April 1914.

In religious matters Lang characterized himself as an agnostic freethinker. In 1887 he married Jeanne Mathilde Bachelin. They had one son and two daughters. Lang worked intensively, without long periods of relaxation. As a result his arteriosclerotic heart complaint steadily worsened. Humorous and sociable, he was also musically and artistically gifted.

Lang became a corresponding member of the Société des Médecins et Naturalistes de Jassy in 1888 and of the Academy of Natural Sciences of Philadelphia in 1893. Furthermore, he was elected a member of the Royal Society of Sciences at Uppsala in 1901 and *socius extraneus* of the Swedish Academy of Sciences in 1910. Lang was honorary member of many learned societies and received honorary doctorates from both of Zurich's universities.

Lang's interest in zoology was awakened in Geneva by Karl Vogt, who in 1874 gave him a letter of introduction to Haeckel in Jena. At the latter's suggestion Lang translated Lamarck's *Philosophie zoologique* into German. In later writings he repeatedly discussed Lamarck's theory and questions pertaining to the history of the theory of evolution.

Lang's zoological works grew out of his research at Naples under the direction of Dohrn and were devoted to such topics as sessile crustaceans and the comparative anatomy and histology of the nervous system of the platyhelminths. He also wrote a monograph on the polyclads (marine turbellarians). In his popular *Lehrbuch der vergleichenden Anatomie der wirbellosen Tiere* (1888–1894), which was translated into English and French, Lang provided a critical account of the results of his own work and of other original papers on the subject. Through his studies on annelid phylogeny, and especially through his derivation of metamerism and his trophocoel theory of the formation of the entire alimentary canal, Lang participated vigorously in the debate over the problem of the origin of the bodily cavities in general. Moreover, his hybridization experiments with species of the genus *Helix* confirmed Mendel's results. Finally, he established an important basis for experimental genetics with his presentation of the "Anfangsgründe der Biometrik der Variation und Korrelation," which constituted a section of the compilation he published in 1914 under the title *Die experimentelle Vererbungslehre in der Zoologie seit 1900.*

BIBLIOGRAPHY

I. ORIGINAL WORKS. Lang's writings include *Die Polycladen (Seeplanarien) des Golfes von Neapel und der angrenzenden Meeresabschnitte* (Leipzig, 1884); *Mittel und Wege phylogenetischer Erkenntnis* (Jena, 1887); *Lehrbuch der vergleichenden Anatomie der wirbellosen Tiere,* 4 pts. (Jena, 1888–1894; 2nd ed. 1901); *Beiträge zu einer Trophocoeltheorie* (Jena, 1903); *Die experimentelle Vererbungslehre in der Zoologie seit 1900* (Jena, 1914); and "Aus meinem intimen Schuldbuch," in H. Schmidt, ed., *Was wir Ernst Haeckel verdanken,* II (Leipzig, 1914), 259–265.

II. SECONDARY LITERATURE. See E. Haeckel, K. Hescheler, and H. Eisig, *Aus dem Leben und Wirken von Arnold Lang* (Jena, 1916); and G. Uschmann, *Geschichte der Zoologie und der zoologischen Anstalten in Jena 1779–1919* (Jena, 1959), 112–113, 177–182.

GEORG USCHMANN

LANG, KARL NIKOLAUS (*b.* Lucerne, Switzerland, 18 February 1670; *d.* Lucerne, 2 May 1741), *paleontology.*

Lang was a collector of fossils who gave original descriptions of many of the fossils of Switzerland. He was categorically opposed to the idea of their organic origin and particularly argued against the conception of the diluvialists that fossils were animals destroyed in the Flood.

His principal concern was with marine fossils. Confronted with difficulties stemming both from the similarity of these fossils to living animals and their presence on land, especially in the mountains of Switzerland, Lang adopted a view similar to that of Lhwyd. According to Lang the fossils originated from tiny, seminal seeds of living marine animals that were scattered around the earth by the air. Once distributed in this manner the seeds were carried into and through the earth by water. The heat of the earth activated a plastic force inherent in each seed, and the *aura seminalis,* or seminal breeze, gave the seed shape. Because this force was particularly strong in the icy waters and snow of the mountain tops, the fossils were more common in these areas.

Lang's fossil descriptions were used and his theories discussed by Beringer, and Lang is said to have been a colleague of Scheuchzer. Yet the closeness of his relationship with Scheuchzer is open to question since the latter was a diluvialist. Lang's works were well known both in Great Britain and on the Continent but were often severely criticized by diluvialists, one of whom, John Woodward, successfully opposed Lang's membership in the Royal Society of London.

Lang, who studied medicine in Bologna and Rome, held many official medical positions in the forest cantons of Switzerland. He was married to Maria Anna Meyer of Altishofen on 5 November 1708. Lang suffered a stroke in 1733 from which he never fully recovered although he continued to work on his fossil collections with the aid of his son.

BIBLIOGRAPHY

I. ORIGINAL WORKS. For a complete list of Lang's works, see Bachmann (below). His main writings are *Historia lapidum figuratorum Helvetiae, ejusque viciniae, in qua non solum enarrantur omnia eorum genera, species et vires aeneisque tabulis repraesentantur, sed insuper adducuntur eorum loca nativa, in quibus reperiri solent, ut cuilibet facile sit eos colligere modo adducta loca adire libeat* (Venice, 1708); and *Tractatus de origine lapidum figuratorum in quo diffuse disseritur, utrum nimirum sunt corpora marina a diluvio ad montes translata, et tractu temporis petrificata vel an a seminio quodam e materia lapidescente intra terram generentur, quibus accedit accurata diluvii, ejusque in terra effectuum descriptio cum dissertatione de generatione viventium, testaceorum praecipue, plurimorumque corporum, a vi plastica aurae seminalis hinc inde delatae extra consuetum matricem productorum* (Lucerne, 1709).

II. SECONDARY LITERATURE. A biography with a descriptive list of works is Hans Bachmann, "Karl Nikolaus Lang Dr. Phil. et Med. 1670–1741," in *Geschichtsfreund,* **51** (1896), 167–280. Helpful references to Lang's works are in *The Lying Stones of Dr. Beringer, Being His Lithographiae Wirceburgensis,* translated and annotated by Melvin E. Jahn and Daniel J. Woolf (Berkeley–Los Angeles, 1963). A letter from Woodward to Scheuchzer is in Melvin E. Jahn, "Some Notes on Dr. Scheuchzer and on Homo diluvii testis," in Cecil J. Schneer, ed., *Toward a History of Geology* (Cambridge, Mass., 1969), pp. 193–194.

PATSY A. GERSTNER

LANG, WILLIAM HENRY (*b.* Withyham, Groombridge, Sussex, England, 12 May 1874; *d.* Storth, near Milnthorpe, Westmorland, England, 29 August 1960), *botany.*

Lang's father, Thomas Bisland Lang, was a doctor; he died at the age of thirty-four, when his son was only two. His widow, who originally came from Ireland, moved to Bridge of Weir, then a small village fourteen miles from Glasgow, where her husband's parents had lived. Here Lang attended the village school before proceeding to Denniston School in Glasgow and thence to the University of Glasgow in 1889, when he was fifteen. He graduated B.Sc. in 1894 with honors in botany and zoology, and in 1895 M.B., C.M. (medical qualification) with high commendation. Although he registered as a doctor, he never practiced but became junior assistant in botany under Frederick Bower. A year later Lang was awarded a Robert Donaldson scholarship, which enabled him to work under D. H. Scott, keeper of the Jodrell Laboratory at Kew. In the following year Lang returned to Glasgow to become senior assistant in botany, and in 1900 he graduated D.Sc. At that time D. T. Gwynne-Vaughan was the junior assistant. In 1909 Lang left Glasgow to become Barker professor of cryptogamic botany at the University of Manchester. In the following year he married his cousin Elsa Valentine, who died childless in 1957. After retirement in 1940 Lang continued for a time to reside in Manchester, working in the Manchester Museum, but eventually moved to Storth near Milnthorpe in Westmorland, where he died.

Lang's botanical interests were greatly influenced by F. O. Bower, D. H. Scott, and Robert Kidston. Bower occupied the chair of botany at Glasgow University for forty years (1885–1925). According to Lang, Bower was an inspiring teacher, and in a biographical memoir (1949) Lang wrote: "To enter Bower's class for the first time was an arresting experience, as I found in 1890." Both Bower and Scott were greatly influenced by W. C. Williamson, whom they visited in 1889 at Manchester to study his sections of Carboniferous fossil plants. Henceforth Scott was devoted to paleobotany, while Bower determined to study the existing Pteridophyta, especially with regard to the problems of alternation of generations and the origin of a land flora.

Lang's earliest research on apogamous reproduction in ferns was carried out at Kew but had begun in Glasgow as a result of Bower's kindred interest in apospory. Bower favored the view that the sporophyte was a new development from the zygote interpolated between two sexual generations and developed by progressive sterilization. He stated this theory in a paper entitled "On Antithetic as Distinct From Homologous Alternation of Generations in Plants" (1890). D. H. Scott ardently supported the homologous theory, and Lang likewise pointed out that the examples of apogamy he described suggested that the two generations were not as distinct as the antithetic theory supposed.

Lang's interest in alternation of generations led him to investigate apospory in *Anthoceros laevis* and the prothallia in Lycopodiales and Ophioglossales. To obtain specimens he visited Ceylon and Malaya in 1899 and brought back *Helminthostachys zeylanica*,

Ophioglossum pendulum, and *Psilotum*. In these the prothallia are saprophytic by virtue of a symbiotic fungus, whereas in *Lycopodium cernuum* the prothallium has green photosynthetic lobes, a condition Lang regarded as being more primitive. In 1909 Lang published a paper on a theory of alternation of generations based on ontogeny, and as a result a discussion on "alternation" was organized at the Linnean Society.

Apart from two papers on the microsporangia and ovules of *Stangeria paradoxa* (1897, 1900) all of Lang's earlier research was on living cryptogams, including the cone structure of *Lycopodium cernuum* (1908) and the anatomy and morphology of *Botrychium lunaria* (1913) and of *Isoëtes lacustris* (1915). This earlier period of research was abruptly concluded by the unexpected death of D. T. Gwynne-Vaughan, at the age of forty-four, in 1915. The latter had collaborated with Kidston on a study of fossil Osmundaceae; and together they had commenced a series of papers on the Lower Carboniferous flora of Berwickshire, of which only part I (on *Stenomyelon*) was published in 1912. In that year William Mackie, erstwhile schoolmaster and then medical practitioner in Elgin, discovered the plant-bearing cherts of Rhynie in a dry-stone wall during one of his frequent geological excursions to central Aberdeenshire. Kidston took in hand further work to locate the chert bed *in situ* by having trenches dug under the supervision of David Tait of the Geological Survey. According to Crookall (1938), Lang visited Kidston at Stirling in 1915 to discuss the possibility of continuing the investigation of the Lower Carboniferous petrified plants; but it was decided to defer this in order to describe the silicified plants of the Rhynie chert. This they did in five classic papers (1917–1921), and these ancient vascular plants (probably Lower Devonian) have now become familiar to all students of botany under their generic names of *Rhynia*, *Hornea* (now *Horneophyton*), and *Asteroxylon*.

In *Rhynia* and *Hornea* the plants had no roots nor leaves and possessed terminal sporangia. In *Asteroxylon* simple leaves were present, but the vascular traces did not enter the leaves. A new order, Psilophytales, was created for them. Of this joint work D. H. Scott said: "Never was a great discovery more completely and wisely expounded"; and John Walton said it was "the most important contribution of the century to our knowledge of early plant life." Further papers by Kidston and Lang followed on *Hicklingia* and *Palaeopitys* (1923), and on *Nematophyton* and *Pachytheca* (1924).

After Kidston's death in 1924 Lang continued the investigation of pre-Carboniferous plants until about

1945. With Isabel Cookson he described vascular plants from Australia that were apparently of Silurian age (1935), and with W. N. Croft he described Lower Devonian plants from Wales (1942). His last publications were obituaries of J. E. Holloway (1947) and F. O. Bower (1949).

BIBLIOGRAPHY

I. ORIGINAL WORKS. Lang's works include "Studies in the Development and Morphology of Cycadean Sporangia. I. The Microsporangia of *Stangeria paradoxa*," in *Annals of Botany*, **11** (1897), 421–438; "On Apogamy and the Development of Sporangia Upon Fern Prothalli," in *Philosophical Transactions of the Royal Society*, **190B** (1898), 187–238; "The Prothallus of *Lycopodium clavatum* L." in *Annals of Botany*, **13** (1899), 279–317; "Studies in the Development and Morphology of Cycadean Sporangia. II. The Ovule of *Stangeria paradoxa*," ibid., **14** (1900), 280–306; "On Apospory in *Anthoceros laevis*," ibid., **15** (1901), 503–510; "On the Prothalli of *Ophioglossum pendulum* and *Helminthostachys zeylanica*," ibid., **16** (1902), 23–56; "On a Prothallus Provisionally Referred to *Psilotum*," ibid., **18** (1904), 571–577; "On the Morphology of *Cyathodium*," ibid., **19** (1905), 411–426; "On the Sporogonium of *Notothylas*," ibid., **21** (1907), 203–210; "A Theory of Alternation of Generations in Archegoniate Plants Based Upon the Ontogeny," in *New Phytologist*, **8** (1909), 3–12; "Discussion on 'Alternation of Generations' at the Linnean Society," ibid., **8** (1909), 104–116; and "On the Interpretation of the Vascular Anatomy of the Ophioglossaceae," in *Memoirs and Proceedings of the Manchester Literary and Philosophical Society*, **56**, no. 12 (1912), 1–15.

Other papers include "Studies in the Morphology and Anatomy of the Ophioglossaceae. I. On the Branching of *Botrychium lunaria*, with Notes on the Anatomy of Young and Old Rhizomes," in *Annals of Botany*, **27** (1913), 203–242; "Studies in the Morphology and Anatomy of the Ophioglossaceae. II. On the Embryo of *Helminthostachys*," ibid., **28** (1914), 19–37; "Studies in the Morphology and Anatomy of the Ophioglossaceae. III. On the Anatomy and Branching of the Rhizome of *Helminthostachys zeylanica*," ibid., **29** (1915), 1–54; "Studies in the Morphology of Isoëtes. I. The General Morphology of the Stock of *Isoëtes lacustris*," in *Memoirs and Proceedings of the Manchester Literary and Philosophical Society*, **59**, pt. 1 (1915), 1–28; and "Studies in the Morphology of Isoëtes. II. The Analysis of the Stele of the Shoot of *Isoëtes lacustris* in the Light of Mature Structure and Apical Development," ibid., **59**, pt. 2 (1915), 29–56.

"On Old Red Sandstone Plants Showing Structure From the Rhynie Chert Bed, Aberdeenshire," written with R. Kidston, was published in five parts in *Transactions of the Royal Society of Edinburgh;* they are: "Part I. *Rhynia Gwynne-Vaughani*," **51** (1917), 761–784; "Part II. Additional Notes on *Rhynia Gwynne-Vaughani*," **52** (1920), 605–627; "Part III. *Asteroxylon Mackiei*," **52** (1920), 643–680; "Part IV. Restorations of the Vascular Cryptogams,

and Discussion of Their Bearing on the General Morphology of the Pteridophyta and the Origin of the Organization of Land Plants," **52** (1921), 831–854; and "Part V. The Thallophyta Occurring in the Peat-bed; the Succession of the Plants Throughout a Vertical Section of the Bed, and the Conditions of Accumulation and Preservation of the Deposit," **52** (1921), 855–902.

The following articles were published in the *Transactions of the Royal Society of Edinburgh:* "On *Palaeopitys Milleri* M'Nab," written with R. Kidston, **53**, pt. 2 (1923), 409–417; "Notes on Fossil Plants From the Old Red Sandstone of Scotland. I. *Hicklingia Edwardi*, K. and L.," **53** (1923), 405–407, written with R. Kidston; "Notes on Fossil Plants From the Old Red Sandstone of Scotland. II. *Nematophyton Forfarense*, Kidston sp., III. On Two Species of *Pachytheca* (*P. media* and *P. fasciculata*) Based on the Characters of the Algal Filaments," **53** (1924), 603–614, written with R. Kidston.

"Contributions to the Study of the Old Red Sandstone Flora of Scotland" was published in seven parts in *Transactions of the Royal Society of Edinburgh:* "I. On Plant Remains From the Fish-beds of Cromarty" and "II. On a Sporangium-bearing Branch-system From the Stromness Beds," **54** (1925), 253–279; "III. On *Hostimella* (*Ptilophyton*) *Thomsoni*, and Its Inclusion in a new Genus, *Milleria*," "IV. On a Specimen of *Protolepidodendron* From the Middle Old Red Sandstone of Caithness," and "V. On the Identification of the Large 'Stems' in the Carmyllie Beds of the Lower Old Red Sandstone as *Nematophyton*," **54** (1926), 253–279; "VI. On *Zosterophyllum Myretonianum* Penh., and Some Other Plant Remains From the Carmyllie Beds of the Lower Old Red Sandstone," and "VII. On a Specimen of *Pseudosporochnus* from the Stromness Beds," **55** (1927), 448–456; and "VIII. On *Arthrostigma, Psilophyton*, and Some Associated Plant-Remains From the Strathmore Beds of the Caledonian Lower Old Red Sandstone," **57** (1932), 491–521.

See also "Some Fossil Plants of Early Devonian Type From the Walhalla Series, Victoria, Australia," in *Philosophical Transactions*, **219B** (1930), 133–163, written with I. C. Cookson; "On the Spines, Sporangia, and Spores of *Psilophyton princeps*, Dawson, Shown in Specimens from Gaspé," ibid., **219B** (1931), 421–442; "On a Flora, Including Vascular Land Plants, Associated With *Monograptus*, in Rocks of Silurian Age, From Victoria, Australia," ibid., **224B** (1935), 421–449, written with I. C. Cookson; "On the Plant-remains From the Downtonian of England and Wales," ibid., **227B** (1937), 245–291; and "The Lower Devonian Flora of the Senni Beds of Monmouthshire and Breconshire," ibid., **231B** (1942), 131–168, written with W. N. Croft.

See also "Obituary. John Ernest Holloway 1881–1945," in *Obituary Notices of Fellows of the Royal Society*, **5** (1947), 425–444; "Obituary. Frederick Orpen Bower 1855–1948," ibid., **6** (1949), 347–374.

II. SECONDARY LITERATURE. For essential details of Lang's life and work, see E. J. Salisbury, "Obituary. William Henry Lang 1874–1960," in *Biographical Memoirs of the Fellows of the Royal Society*, **7** (1961), 147–160, with a complete bibliography; see also F. O. Bower, "On Antithetic as Distinct From Homologous Alternation of Generations in Plants," in *Annals of Botany*, **4** (1890), 347–370; R. Crookall, "The Kidston Collection of Fossil Plants," in *Memoirs of the Geological Survey of the United Kingdom*, **5** (1938); and R. Kidston and D. T. Gwynne-Vaughan, "On the Carboniferous Flora of Berwickshire. Part 1. *Stenomyelon tuedianum* Kidston," in *Transactions of the Royal Society of Edinburgh*, **48** (1912), 263–271.

ALBERT G. LONG

LANGE, CARL GEORG (*b.* Vordingborg, Denmark, 4 December 1834; *d.* Copenhagen, Denmark, 29 May 1900), *medicine, psychology.*

Lange's father, Frederik Lange, was professor of education at Copenhagen University; his mother, the former Louise Paludan-Müller, came from a learned family.

After graduating from the Copenhagen Metropolitan School in 1853, he studied medicine at Copenhagen University; after receiving the M.D. in 1859 he worked until 1867 as an intern in the medical departments of the Royal Frederiks Hospital and the Almindelig Hospital in Copenhagen. He published studies on ulcerous endocarditis and typhoid fever and an excellent description of the symptomatology and occurrence of rheumatic fever based on 1,900 cases. In 1863 Lange was sent to Greenland and reported on the widespread distribution of tuberculosis there. In 1867–1868 he studied histology in Zurich and experimental physiology in Florence with Moritz Schiff, who in 1856 had demonstrated the vasoconstrictor fibers in the cervical sympathetic segment. Schiff aroused Lange's interest in vasomotor reactions and in neurophysiology. At Florence, Lange published an experimental study concerning curare's influence on the nervous system.

After his return to Copenhagen, Lange was prosector at the Royal Frederiks Hospital and municipal health officer; he also had a private practice. In 1866 he had become coeditor of *Hospitalstidende*, in which many of his pioneer studies were published. In 1866 he was the first to describe acute bulbar paralysis; in 1870 he wrote on symptoms arising from cerebellar tumors; and in 1872 he demonstrated the secondary degeneration of the posterior columns of the spinal cord caused by spinal meningitis, thereby anticipating the later neuron doctrine. His discovery was unnoticed until 1894, when Jean Nageotte made the same findings; it was fully accepted in 1897 in C. W. Nothnagel's *Internal Pathology*. In 1873 Lange published his anatomical-clinical investigations on chronic myelitis, dividing the syndromes into those of the anterior horns with atrophy, in the lateral tracts with paraplegia and in the posterior tracts with root pains and ataxia. It was a very clear and really new point of view—but because it was written in Danish, it did not obtain the distribution and significance it deserved.

From 1869 to 1872 Lange lectured at Copenhagen University on pathology of the spinal cord. The lectures were published as *Forelaesninger over rygmarvens patologi*, which contains physiologically inspired descriptions of the various syndromes of paralysis, sensibility disturbances, and reflex phenomena. There are chapters on pain, hyperesthesia, and eccentric perceptions. His ideas of reflex pain, angina pectoris, and projected pain were later emphasized by Head and Wernøe.

In 1873 Lange failed to obtain the position of physician-in-chief in medicine at the Royal Frederiks Hospital, but 1875 he was appointed lecturer in pathological anatomy and in 1885 became professor of the subject at Copenhagen University. Despite very bad working conditions he continued scientific studies, most of them based on extensive clinical material from his private practice with nervous patients. In 1885 he published *Om Sindsbevaegelser*, a psychophysiological study on vasomotor disturbances and conditioned reflexes during periods of emotional stress. Excitement was the result of vasomotor manifestations and not of mental entities—a theory still known by psychologists as the James-Lange theory.

In 1886 Lange published *Periodiske depressionstilstande*, which separated periodic depressive conditions from the neurasthenic. Since he believed the depressions were caused by uric acid diathesis, his theory was attacked not only by psychiatrists but also by internists. His ideas found several defenders, however, especially in France. In 1899 Lange published *Bidrag til nydelsernes fysiologi*, a study of the pleasurable sensations in emotions. The book met with indignation—his explanations of vasomotor reactions during sympathetic reactions to the perception of beauty disturbed the ideas of aesthetes and philosophers.

As a member of several committees for public hygiene and hospital service and of the City Council, Lange procured reforms in vaccination, school hygiene, hospital buildings, and water supply. He was a member of the board of Medicinsk Selskab and a founder of Biologisk Selskab. As secretary-general of the International Congress of Physicians held at Copenhagen in 1884, he made possible the meeting of such people as Pasteur, Virchow, James Paget, and Donders with the rather provincial Danish medical profession.

BIBLIOGRAPHY

I. ORIGINAL WORKS. A full list of Lange's works is in Knud Faber, *Erindringer om C. Lange*, pp. 61–66. Translations include *Ueber Gemüthsbewegungen. Eine psychologisch-physiologische Studie*, Hans Kurella, trans. (Leipzig, 1887; 2nd ed., 1910); *Les émotions*, G. Dumas, trans. (Paris, 1895; 2nd ed., 1902); *Boden der harnsäure Diathese*, H. Kurella, ed. (Hamburg, 1896); *Sinnesgenüsse und Kunstgenüss*, L. Loewenfeld and H. Kurella, eds. (Wiesbaden, 1903); and *Psychology Classics*, William James, trans. (Boston, 1922).

II. SECONDARY LITERATURE. See Knud Faber, *Erindringer om C. Lange* (Copenhagen, 1927); Edvard Gotfredsen, *Medicinens Historie* (Copenhagen, 1964), pp. 427, 517, 522–523; and P. Bender Petersen, "La description de réflexes conditionnels par C. Lange," in E. Dein, *Sct Hans Hospital 1816–1966* (Copenhagen, 1966), pp. 188–192.

E. SNORRASON

LANGERHANS, PAUL (*b.* Berlin, Germany, 25 July 1847; *d.* Funchal, Madeira, 20 July 1888), *anatomy, pathology.*

Langerhans' father, for whom he was named, was a well-known physician in Berlin; and two younger stepbrothers were also physicians. One of them, Robert (1859–1904), was an assistant to Virchow and later became professor of pathology. Langerhans attended the Gymnasium zum Grauen Kloster in Berlin and graduated at the age of sixteen. From 1865 to 1866 he studied medicine at the University of Jena, where he was much impressed by Haeckel and Gegenbaur. He continued his medical studies in Berlin under K. Bardeleben, E. du Bois-Reymond, R. Virchow, J. Cohnheim, and F. T. von Frerichs. In 1869 he graduated M.D. At Berlin he was particularly influenced by Virchow and Cohnheim, and he became later a close friend of Virchow's. His first important research was done in Virchow's laboratory, where he discovered the cell islands of the pancreas named after him.

In 1870 Langerhans accompanied the geographer Heinrich Kiepert on an expedition to Egypt and Palestine. During the Franco-Prussian War he joined the German army as a physician and worked in a military hospital. After the conclusion of peace he went for a short while to Leipzig to see Ludwig's famous physiological institute and the obstetrical clinics of K. S. F. Crédé. In 1871 he was offered the position of prosector in pathology at the University of Freiburg im Breisgau, where he also became *Privatdozent* in the same year and, later, associate professor. In 1874 tuberculosis of the lung compelled Langerhans to interrupt his academic career. Attempts at cure in Switzerland, Italy, and Germany failed; and in 1875 he settled in Madeira. Its mild climate led to an improvement in his health. In Madeira he later practiced medicine in the capital, Funchal, where he died of a kidney infection.

Langerhans' main scientific achievements consist in his studies of human and animal microscopical anatomy. In this field he was among the first successful investigators to explore the new area of research with novel methods and staining techniques. Langerhans made his first scientific contributions as a medical student in Virchow's laboratory, under the guidance of Virchow and especially of Cohnheim. In 1868 he published a paper on the innervation of the skin; he had used gold chloride as a stain. He was able to show nerve endings in the Malpighian layer of the epidermis and described characteristic oblong bodies with branching processes in the Malpighian layer (later called Langerhans' cells). He believed that these bodies were probably nerve cells, but he did not exclude the possibility that they might be pigment cells (later called dendritic cells).

In his inaugural dissertation (1869) Langerhans immortalized his name by his discovery of characteristic cell islands in the pancreas named for him. The investigations for this work, "Beiträge zur mikroskopischen Anatomie der Bauchspeicheldrüse," were conducted in Virchow's pathology laboratory. The paper presented the first careful and detailed description of the microscopic structure of the pancreas.

Langerhans examined mainly the pancreas of rabbits. He studied fresh tissue and even sought to make microscopic observations of pancreatic tissue in the living animal. His main results were obtained through chemical fixation and maceration. Langerhans injected the pancreatic duct with Berlin blue in order to show the branching and the structure of the excretory system. Examining portions of the fresh gland, he distinguished three zones in the secreting cells: an apical granular zone, the zone of the cell nucleus, and a clear basal zone. In macerated pancreatic tissue he differentiated various types of cells, including small, irregularly polygonal cells without granules. These cells formed numerous spots scattered through the parenchyma of the gland measuring 0.1–0.24 mm. in diameter. Langerhans refrained from making any hypothesis as to the nature and significance of these cells. In 1893 the French histologist G. E. Laguesse named these cell spots "îlots de Langerhans"; the insulin-secreting function of these cells was established later.

Another important contribution, made with F. A. Hoffmann in Virchow's laboratory, dealt with the macrophage system. Langerhans and Hoffmann studied the intravital storage of cinnabar injected intravenously in rabbits and guinea pigs. After the injection they sought the presence of cinnabar in the blood and all the organs except the spleen. They were able to show that cinnabar was taken up by white blood corpuscles but never by the red. They also demonstrated the deposit of cinnabar in fixed cells of the bone marrow, in the capillary system, and in the connective tissue of the liver. This was one of the pioneer investigations that later led to Aschoff's concept of the reticuloendothelial system.

In 1873 Langerhans studied the structure of the skin and its innervation, staining the preparations with osmic acid and picrocarmine. He observed the nerve fibers branching in the interior of Meissner's corpuscles and described the oblong cells lying transversely in these corpuscles. In the report on this study Langerhans described his discovery of the granular cells in the exterior portion of the Malpighian layer (Langerhans' layer, *stratum granulosum*). In 1873 and 1874 Langerhans examined the microscopic structure of the cardiac muscle fibers in vertebrates and of the accessory genital glands of man. One of his last extensive histological papers (1876) was dedicated to the anatomy of the amphioxus.

During his trip to Palestine, Langerhans, stimulated by Virchow's interest in anthropology, made skull measurements and anthropological observations of the population of Palestine. In the last decade of his life, while practicing medicine on Madeira, Langerhans studied the etiology of tuberculosis and cautiously supported Virchow's dualistic view, which differentiated phthisis from tuberculosis. During that time he also published a handbook on Madeira dealing with the climatic and curative properties of that island.

BIBLIOGRAPHY

I. ORIGINAL WORKS. A comprehensive list of Langerhans' anatomical works was compiled by K. Bardeleben, in *Anatomischer Anzeiger*, **3** (1888), 850–851. A partial list is by H. Morrison, in *Bulletin of the Institute of the History of Medicine*, **5** (1937), 266.

On microscopic anatomy see "Ueber die Nerven der menschlichen Haut," in *Virchows Archiv für pathologische Anatomie*, **44** (1868), 325–337; "Zur pathologischen Anatomie der Tastkörper," *ibid.*, **45** (1869), 413–417; "Ueber den Verbleib des in die Circulation eingeführten Zinnobers," *ibid.*, **48** (1869), 303–325; "Beiträge zur mikroskopischen Anatomie der Bauchspeicheldrüse," his inaugural dissertation (Berlin, 1869), repr., with English trans. and introductory essay by H. Morrison in *Bulletin of the Institute of the History of Medicine*, **5** (1937), 259–297; "Ein Beitrag zur Anatomie der sympathischen Ganglien-
zellen," his *Habilitationsschrift* (Freiburg im Breisgau, 1871); "Zur Histologie des Herzens," in *Virchows Archiv für pathologische Anatomie*, **58** (1873), 65–83; "Ueber mehrschichtige Epithelien," *ibid.*, 83–92; "Ueber die accessorischen Drüsen der Geschlechtsorgane," *ibid.*, **61** (1874), 208–228; "Ueber Tastkörperchen und Rete Malpighi," in *Archiv für mikroskopische Anatomie*, **9** (1873), 730–744.

Zoological works include "Zur Entwicklung der Gastropoda opisthobranchia," in *Zeitschrift für wissenschaftliche Zoologie*, **23** (1873), 171–179; and "Zur Anatomie des Amphioxus lanceolatus," in *Archiv für mikroskopische Anatomie*, **12** (1876), 290–348.

A work in pathology is "Zur Aetiologie der Phthise," in *Virchows Archiv für pathologische Anatomie*, **97** (1884), 289–306.

On anthropology see "Ueber die heutigen Bewohner des heiligen Landes," in *Archiv für Anthropologie*, **6** (1873), 39–58, 201–212; and *Handbuch für Madeira* (Berlin, 1885).

II. SECONDARY LITERATURE. The most detailed biographical sketch of Langerhans and evaluation of his work is H. Morrison, in *Bulletin of the Institute of the History of Medicine*, **5** (1937), 259–267, with portrait. See also K. Bardeleben, "Paul Langerhans," in *Anatomischer Anzeiger*, **3** (1888), 850; W. R. Campbell, "Paul Langerhans 1847–1888," in *Canadian Medical Association Journal*, **79** (1958), 855–856; and G. Wolff, "Beiträge berühmter Studenten zur Erforschung des Zuckerstoffwechsels," in *Münchener medizinische Wochenschrift*, **102** (1960), 1203–1208.

NIKOLAUS MANI

LANGEVIN, PAUL (*b*. Paris, France, 23 January 1872; *d*. Paris, 19 December 1946), *physics.*

Langevin, the second son of Victor Langevin, an appraiser-verifier in the Montmartre section of Paris, very early displayed his liking for study. His mother, great-grandniece of the alienist Philippe Pinel, encouraged this inclination; and Langevin was always first in his class from the time he entered the École Lavoisier until he left the École Municipale de Physique et Chimie Industrielles de la Ville de Paris in 1891. (The latter school was established in 1881 by Paul Schützenberger to train engineers.) Langevin's enthusiasm was aroused by his contact with the school's director and by his laboratory work, which was supervised by Pierre Curie.

To further his knowledge Langevin attended the Sorbonne (1891–1893) while teaching a private course and learning Latin on his own. In 1893 he placed first in the competitive entrance examination for the École Normale Supérieure, but he did a year of military service before attending the school. At the École Normale Supérieure he heard the lectures of Marcel Brillouin and undertook research with Jean Perrin (then an *agrégé-préparateur*). Langevin placed first in the competition for the *agrégation* in physical sciences in 1897 and left for Cambridge to spend a year at the Cavendish Laboratory with J. J. Thomson. Under Thomson's direction, he worked on ionization by X rays, in the process discovering, independently of Sagnac, that X rays liberate secondary electrons from metals. Also while at the Cavendish he met J. Townsend, E. Rutherford, and C. T. R. Wilson; all of them soon became friends.

Upon returning to Paris, Langevin established a home (1898). He had four children: Jean (*b.* 1899), André (*b.* 1901)—both of whom became physicists—Madeleine (*b.* 1903), and Hélène (*b.* 1909). Still on scholarship, he was obliged to continue to give private lessons.

During this period the atmosphere in the Paris laboratories was one of intense excitement. At Jean Perrin's laboratory Langevin continued his investigations of the secondary effects of X rays and, on close terms with the Curies, he was present at the birth of the study of radioactivity. Langevin completed his doctoral dissertation in 1902 at the Sorbonne. It dealt with ionized gases and was based on investigations he had begun at Cambridge. After being named *préparateur* to Edmond Bouty at the Sorbonne, Langevin entered the Collège de France in 1902 to substitute for E. E. N. Mascart, whom he replaced in 1909. Meanwhile, he taught also at the École Municipale de Physique et Chimie, succeeding Pierre Curie (1904), and then at the École Nationale Supérieure de Jeunes Filles (Sèvres), replacing Marie Curie, who had been widowed (1906). Langevin loved teaching, and he excelled at it.

In his laboratory at the Collège de France, Langevin continued to study ions in gases, liquids, and dielectrics (1902–1913). In this work he was assisted by his students, including Edmond Bauer, Eugene Bloch, and Marcel Moulin. In his dissertation he had already given a method of calculating the mobility of both positive and negative ions during their passage through a condenser by considering their diffusion and recombination. Moreover, for the first time he communicated his results concerning secondary X rays (1898). Langevin was never in a hurry to publish; his written work is scanty in relation to the extent of his work. Whether it was a question of theory, of experimental results, or even of techniques or apparatus, he spent a long time seeking a simple and clear statement; often his publisher would snatch from him a manuscript filled with changes written in his clear, firm hand.

Langevin's position at the Collège de France was of particular importance to his development, for it freed him to lecture on subjects for which the standard French curriculum had little place. Although he continued after his arrival there to involve himself deeply with the experimental work of students, his own research and teaching turned increasingly to contemporary problems in theoretical physics. For most of the thirty years after he assumed the chair, he was the leading, and at times virtually the only, practitioner and expositor of modern mathematical physics in France. Einstein caught his role and status precisely when he wrote:

> Langevin's scientific thought displayed an extraordinary clarity and vivacity combined with a quick and sure intuition for the essential point. Because of those qualities, his courses exerted a decisive influence on more than a generation of French theoretical physicists. ... It seems to me certain that he would have developed the special theory of relativity if that had not been done elsewhere, for he had clearly recognized its essential points.[1]

The last portion of that evaluation is in part a response to Langevin's first published theoretical papers, presented during 1904 and 1905. They dealt perceptively and authoritatively with a coherent set of current problems developed in the work of Lorentz, Larmor, and Abraham: the concept of electromagnetic mass, its rate of increase with velocity, and the related contraction hypotheses which suggested the impossibility in principle of determining the earth's motion through the ether. Both reports from his students and the speed with which he assimilated the special theory of relativity after 1905 suggest in addition that Langevin's own thoughts, at least on the relation between mass and energy, were developing along lines close to Einstein's before the latter's work appeared in 1905.[2]

That same year is the one in which Langevin published what was perhaps his most original and enduring contribution to physical theory, a quantitative account of paramagnetism and diamagnetism which demonstrated, he said, that it was "possible, using the electron hypothesis, to give precise meaning to the ideas [molecular models] of Ampère and Weber."[3]

To account for paramagnetism Langevin assumed that each molecule had a permanent magnetic moment *m* due to the circulation of one or more electrons. In the absence of an external field, thermal motion would orient the moments of individual molecules at random, so that there would be no net field. An external field, however, would tend to align molecular moments, the extent of the alignment depending both on the field strength and on the intensity of the thermal motion, the latter determined by temperature. Applying Boltzmann's techniques to the problem,

Langevin showed that for low fields the magnetic permeability of a gas should be given by $\mu = m^2N/3kT$, where N is the number of molecules per unit volume, k is Boltzmann's constant, and T is the absolute temperature.

The proportionality of susceptibility to the reciprocal of temperature was, Langevin emphasized, a result which Pierre Curie had found experimentally in 1895. Using the latter's measurement of the proportionality constant, he noted further that the observed susceptibility of oxygen could be accounted for by the orbital motion of even a single electron with velocity $2 \cdot 10^8$ cm/sec. At this time atoms were usually thought to consist of many hundreds of electrons. That so few were needed to explain magnetic properties suggested to Langevin that the electrons with this function might well be the superficial ones, i.e., the valence electrons, which were responsible also for chemical properties. Niels Bohr, whose route to the quantized version of Rutherford's atomic model was deeply influenced by Langevin, was to suggest precisely the same correlation.[4]

The even more puzzling phenomenon of diamagnetism Langevin explained in terms of molecules within which the orbital electronic motions canceled each other, so that no net molecular moment remained. An increasing magnetic field would, however, accelerate the electrons moving in one direction and retard those moving in the other, thus producing a small net moment in a direction opposed to the field. Again Langevin's treatment was quantitative. It predicted that, as Curie had found, diamagnetic susceptibility should be independent of temperature, and it permitted computation of plausible values for the radii of electronic orbits. As a tool for investigating both magnetism and molecular and atomic structure, Langevin's impressive theory was vigorously developed by a number of physicists, especially Pierre Weiss, and Langevin was himself invited to discuss its current state at the famous first Solvay Congress in 1911.

Three years before that, in 1908, Langevin, whose skill in kinetic theory had first been developed when he worked on ionic transport, turned briefly to the theory of Brownian motion developed by Einstein in 1905 and, via a more direct route, by Smoluchowski in 1906. The result was simplified, still-standard treatment which, unlike Smoluchowski's, produced precisely Einstein's formula for the mean-square displacement. Subsequently Langevin took up the subject of thermodynamics and reconsidered its basic notions, starting from theories of Boltzmann and of Planck ("the physics of the discontinuous") in 1913. At the same time he presented "the notions of time, space, and causality" with their relativistic significance. It required much difficult work to arrive at these elucidations; but he presented them simply, sometimes humorously (for example, Jules Verne's cannonball [1911] and Langevin's rocket or cannonball [1912]).

Although Langevin concerned himself with philosophical questions, he did not neglect the technical applications of his work. In 1914 he was called upon to work on ballistic problems and was later requested by Maurice de Broglie, his friend and former student, to find a way of detecting submerged enemy submarines. Lord Rayleigh and O. W. Richardson (1912) had thought of employing ultrasonic waves. In France a Russian engineer, Chilowski, proposed to the navy a device based on this principle; but its intensity was much too weak. In less than three years Langevin succeeded in providing adequate amplification by means of piezoelectricity. His team called the steel-quartz-steel triplet he developed a "Langevin sandwich." Functioning by resonance, it "finally played for ultrasonic waves the same roles as the antenna in radio engineering." Langevin continued to do important work in acoustics and ultrasonics after the war.

Langevin received many honors. In 1915 he was honored by the Royal Society of London, and in 1928 he became a member of that body (he had still not been elected to the Académie des Sciences). He was elected to many other foreign academies and to the Académie de Marine in Paris. His relativistic views still appeared revolutionary: he had invited Michelson and Einstein to speak at the Collège de France as early as 1922. Then came the theories of Louis de Broglie. Langevin, at first surprised, soon became their strongest advocate (1924). The Académie des Sciences elected Louis de Broglie in 1933 and Langevin in 1934. In writing his "Notice," Langevin relived forty years during which he had constantly contributed to deepening our understanding of the universe.

Internationally Langevin's influence became paramount in 1928, when he succeeded H. A. Lorentz as president of the Solvay International Physics Institute, of which he had been a member since 1921. On his initiative a message of sympathy was sent in 1933 to Einstein, who was already being persecuted by the Nazis.

As passionate in his concern for justice as in his quest for truth, in this period Langevin joined various movements supporting victims of fascism and, denouncing the horrors of war, actively participated in campaigns aimed at securing peace. To his mind the same enemy—reaction—opposed the new scientific theories, the modernization of teaching, individual liberty, and the spirit of brotherhood.

When war broke out, Langevin testified in favor of the forty-four Communist deputies excluded from their seats following the signing of the German-Soviet pact. In March–April 1940 he was invited by the navy to direct research on ultrasonic depth finders.

After the departure of the French government from Paris, Langevin again became director of the École Municipale de Physique et Chimie Industrielles (the duties of that office having already been delegated to him); but on 30 October 1940 he was arrested by the Wehrmacht. Dismissed by the Vichy government and imprisoned in Fresnes, he was finally placed under house arrest in Troyes. Messages of sympathy came to him from all over the world. Peter Kapitza invited Langevin to join him in the Soviet Union, but Langevin refused to leave France. Resigned, and surrounded by devoted friends, he resumed his calculations. He then learned of the execution of his son-in-law, the physicist Jacques Solomon (1942), and of the arrest and deportation of his daughter, Hélène Solomon-Langevin (1943). Fearing for his safety, his young friends Frédéric Joliot, H. Moureu, Denivelle, and P. Biquard persuaded Langevin to flee in May 1944. Warmly welcomed in Switzerland, he worked on educational reform for postwar France.

As early as 1904 Langevin had denounced the obstacles to progress found in scientific instruction in the form of "ossifying dogmas" that hinder the recognition of "fruitful principles"—such as rational mechanics vis-à-vis the atomic theory. Faithful to his own thought, he reprinted this article ("L'esprit de l'enseignement scientifique") in 1923. He took up the same theme again in the hope that liberated France would direct its youth along progressive paths in thought and action, and inculcate in them the notions indispensable to philosophers and technicians alike.

After returning to the École Municipale de Physique et Chimie Industrielles in October 1944, Langevin devoted his greatest efforts to educational reforms and to the support of his political friends. His daughter Hélène, returned from Auschwitz, sat in the Assemblée Consultative. He joined her as a member of the Communist Party—several members of which were also members of the government—in the hope of encouraging a brotherhood that capitalism had not succeeded in establishing.

Langevin died following a brief illness. The government, which had made him a grand officer of the Legion of Honor, accorded him a state funeral. His remains were transferred to the Pantheon in 1948, at the same time as those of Jean Perrin.

NOTES

1. A. Einstein, "Paul Langevin," in *La pensée*, **12** (May-June 1947), pp. 13–14.
2. E. Bauer, *L'électromagnétisme hier et aujourd'hui* (Paris, 1949), p. 156 n.
3. P. Langevin, "Magnétisme et théorie des électrons," in *Annales de chimie et de physique*, **5** (1905), 70–127; quotation from end of introduction.
4. Cf. John L. Heilbron and Thomas S. Kuhn, "The Genesis of the Bohr Atom," in *Historical Studies in the Physical Sciences*, **1** (1969), 211–290.

BIBLIOGRAPHY

I. ORIGINAL WORKS. Langevin's writings on X rays and ionization of gas include "Recherches sur les gaz ionisés," his doctoral dissertation (1902), in *Annales de chimie et de physique*, **28** (1903), 289, 433; "Sur les rayons secondaires des rayons de Röntgen," his doctoral dissertation (1902), *ibid.*, p. 500; "Recherches récentes sur le mécanisme du courant électrique. Ions et électrons," in *Bulletin de la Société internationale des électriciens*, 2nd ser., **5** (1905), 615; "Recherches récentes sur le mécanisme de la décharge disruptive," *ibid.*, **6** (1906), 69; "Sur la recombinaison des ions dans les diélectriques," in *Comptes rendus ... de l'Académie des sciences*, **146** (1908), 1011; "Mesure de la valence des ions dans les gaz," in *Radium*, **10** (1913), 113; and "Sur la recombinaison des ions," in *Journal de physique*, 8th ser., **6** (1945), 1.

In the following citations *Physique* refers to *La physique depuis vingt ans* (Paris, 1923). On ions in the atmosphere and particles in suspension, see "Interprétation de divers phénomènes par la présence de gros ions dans l'atmosphère," in *Bulletin des séances de la Société française de physique*, fasc. 4 (19 May 1905), 79; and "Électromètre enregistreur des ions de l'atmosphère," in *Radium*, **4** (1907), 218, written with M. Moulin.

Kinetic theory and thermodynamics are treated in "Sur une formule fondamentale de la théorie cinétique," in *Comptes rendus ... de l'Académie des sciences*, **140** (1905), 35, also in *Annales de chimie et de physique*, 8th ser., **5** (1905), 245; "Sur la théorie du mouvement Brownian," in *Comptes rendus ... de l'Académie des sciences*, **146** (1908), 530; and "La physique du discontinu," in *Les progrès de la physique moléculaire* (Paris, 1914), p. 1, also in *Physique*, p. 189.

On electromagnetic theory and electrons, see "La physique des électrons," in *Rapport du Congrès international des sciences et arts à Saint-Louis* (1904), also in *Physique*, p. 1; "La théorie électromagnétique et le bleu du ciel," in *Bulletin de la Société française de physique*, fasc. 4 (16 Dec. 1910), 80; "Les grains d'électricité et la dynamique électromagnétique," in *Les idées modernes sur la constitution de la matière* (Paris, 1913), p. 54, also in *Physique*, p. 70; and "L'électron positif," in *Bulletin de la Société des électriciens*, 5th ser., **4** (1934), 335.

Writings on magnetic theory and molecular orientation include "Magnétisme et théorie des électrons," in *Annales de chimie et de physique*, 8th ser., **5** (1905), 70; "Sur les biréfringences électrique et magnétique," in *Radium*, **7** (1910), 249; "La théorie cinétique du magnétisme et les magnétons," presented at the Solvay Conference in 1911, in *La théorie du rayonnement et les quanta* (Paris, 1913), also in *Physique*, p. 171; "Sur l'orientation moléculaire," a letter to M. W. Voigt, in *Göttingen Nachrichten*, no. 5 (1912), 589; and "Le magnétisme," in *Sixième Congrès de physique Solvay* (Paris, 1923), p. 352.

The principle of relativity and the inertia of energy are discussed in "Sur l'impossibilité de mettre en évidence le mouvement de translation de la terre," in *Comptes rendus . . . de l'Académie des sciences*, **140** (1905), 1171; "L'évolution de l'espace et du temps," in *Scientia*, **10** (1911), 31, also in *Physique*, p. 265; "Le temps, l'espace et la causalité dans la physique moderne," in *Bulletin de la Société française de philosophie*, **12**, no. 1 (Jan. 1912), 1, also in *Physique*, p. 301; "L'inertie de l'énergie et ses conséquences," in *Journal de physique*, 5th ser., **3** (1913), 553, also in *Physique*, p. 345; "Sur la théorie de la relativité et l'expérience de M. Sagnac," in *Comptes rendus . . . de l'Académie des sciences*, **173** (1921), 831; "La structure des atomes et l'origine de la chaleur solaire," in *Bulletin de l'Université de Tiflis*, **10** (1929); "La relativité," in *Exposés et discussions du Centre de synthèse* (Paris, 1932); "L'oeuvre d'Einstein et l'astronomie," in *L'astronomie*, **45** (1931), 277; "Déduction simplifiée du facteur de Thomas," in *Convegno di fisica nucleare* (Rome, 1931), p. 137; "Espace et temps dans un univers euclidien," in *Livre jubilaire de Marcel Brillouin* (Paris, 1935); and "Résonance et forces de gravitation," in *Annales de physique*, **17** (1942), 261.

On physical chemistry and radioactivity, see "Sur la comparaison des molécules gazeuses et dissoutes," in *Comptes rendus . . . de l'Académie des sciences*, **154** (1912), 594, also in *Procès-verbaux des commissions de la Société française de physique* (19 Apr. 1912), 54; "L'interprétation cinétique de la pression osmotique," in *Journal de chimie-physique*, **10** (1912), 524, 527; and "Sur un problème d'activation par diffusion," in *Journal de physique*, 7th ser., **5** (1934), 57.

Writings on magnitudes and units include "Notions géométriques fondamentales," in *Encyclopédie des sciences mathématiques*, IV, pt. 5, fasc. 1 (1912), 1; and "Sur les unités de champ et d'induction," in *Bulletin de la Société française de physique* (17 Feb. 1922), 33.

Classical and modern mechanics are discussed in "Sur la dynamique de la relativité," in *Procès-verbaux des commissions de la Société française de physique* (15 Dec. 1921), 97, also in *Exposés et discussions du Centre international de synthèse sur la relativité* (Paris, 1932); "Les nouvelles mécaniques et la chimie," in *L'activation et la structure des molécules* (Paris, 1929), p. 550; "La notion de corpuscules et d'atomes," in *Réunion internationale de chimie-physique* (Paris, 1933); and "Sur les chocs entre neutrons rapides et noyaux de masse quelconque," in *Annales de physique*, **17** (1942), 303, also in *Comptes rendus . . . de l'Académie des sciences*, **214** (1942), 517, 867, 889.

On acoustics and ultrasonics, see "Procédés et appareils pour la production de signaux sous-marins dirigés et pour la localisation à distance d'obstacles sous-marins . . .," in *Brevet français*, no. 502.913 (29 May 1916), written with M. C. Chilowski; no. 505.703 (17 Sept. 1918); no. 575.435 (27 Dec. 1923), written with M. C. Florisson; and no. 576.281 (14 Jan. 1924), 1st supp. no. (1 Mar. 1924) and 2nd supp. no. (16 Oct. 1924).

See also "Note sur l'énergie auditive," in *Publications du Centre d'études de Toulon* (25 Sept. 1918); "Émission d'un faisceau d'ondes ultra-sonores," in *Journal de physique*, 6th ser., **4** (1923), 537, written with M. C. Chilowsky and M. Tournier; "Utilisation des phénomènes piézo-électriques pour la mesure de l'intensité des sons en valeur absolue," *ibid.*, 6th ser., **4** (1923), 539, written with M. Ishimoto; "Sondage et détection sous-marine par les ultra-sons," in *Bulletin de l'Association technique maritime et aéronautique*, no. 28 (1924), 407; "La production et l'utilisation des ondes ultra-sonores," in *Revue générale de l'électricité*, **23** (1928), 626; "Sur le mirage ultra-sonore," in *Bulletin de l'Association technique maritime et aéronautique* (1929), 727; "Les ondes ultra-sonores," in *Revue d'acoustique*, **1** (1932), 93, 315; **2** (1933), 288; **3** (1934), 104, with notes by P. Biquard; and "Sur les lois du dégagement d'électricité par torsion dans les corps piézo-électriques," in *Comptes rendus . . . de l'Académie des sciences*, **200** (1935), 1257.

Various technical problems are treated in "Sur la production des étincelles musicales par courant continu," in *Annales des postes, télégraphes et téléphones*, 5th year, no. 4 (1916), p. 404; "Utilisation de la détente pour la production des courants d'air de grande vitesse," in *Procès-verbaux des commissions de la Société française de physique* (20 Feb. 1920), p. 21; "Note sur la loi de résistance de l'air," in *Mémorial de l'artillerie française* (1922), p. 253; "Note sur les effets balistiques de la détente des gaz de la poudre," *ibid.* (1923), p. 3; "Procédé et appareils permettant la mesure de la puissance transmise par un arbre," in *Brevet français* (22 Dec. 1927); "Banc piézo-électrique pour l'équilibrage des rotors," *ibid.* (19 Dec. 1927); "Procédé et dispositif pour la mesure des variations de pression dans les canalisations d'eau ou autre liquide," *ibid.* (6 Aug. 1927), written with R. Hocart; and "L'enregistrement des coups de bélier," in *Bulletin technique de la Chambre syndicale des entrepreneurs de couverture plomberie*, no. 23 (1927), p. 81.

On teaching and pedagogy, see "L'esprit de l'enseignement scientifique," in *L'enseignement des sciences mathématiques et des sciences physiques* (Paris, 1904), also in *Physique*; "Le théorème de Fermat de la loi du minimum de temps en optique géométrique," in *Journal de physique*, ser. 6, **1** (1920), 188; "La valeur éducative de l'histoire des sciences," in *Revue de synthèse*, **6** (1933), 5; "La réorganisation de l'enseignement public en Chine," in *Rapport de la mission d'experts de la Société des Nations*, written with C. H. Becker, M. Falski, and R. H. Tawney (Paris, 1932); "Le problème de la culture générale," in *Discours d'ouverture du Congrès international d'éducation nouvelle, Nice, July 1932*, also in *Full Report of the New Education Fellowship* (London, 1933), p. 73; "L'enseignement en Chine," in *Bulletin de la Société française de pedagogie*, no. 49 (Sept. 1933); and "La Réforme générale de l'enseignement

(Premier rapport sur les travaux de la Commission ministérielle)," in *Bulletin officiel de l'éducation nationale*, no. 23 (15 March 1945), p. 1461.

Other publications include "Notice sur les travaux de Monsieur P. Curie," in *Bulletin des anciens élèves de l'École municipale de physique et chimie industrielles* (Dec. 1904); "Henri Poincaré, le physicien" in *Henri Poincaré* (Paris, 1914), also in *Revue du Mois*, **8** (1913); "Paul Schutzenberger" in *Discours prononcé à l'occasion du centenaire de P. Schutzenberger* (1929); "L'orientation actuelle de la physique," in *L'orientation actuelle des sciences* (Paris, 1930), p. 29; "La physique au Collège de France," in *Volume du centenaire* (Paris, 1932), p. 61; "Ernest Solvay" in *Discours prononcé à l'inauguration du monument d'E. Solvay* (Brussels, 1932); "Paul Painlevé, le savant," in *Les Cahiers rationalistes*, no. 26 (Nov. 1933); "La valeur humaine de la science," preface to *l'Évolution humaine* (Paris, 1933); and "Discours prononcés à l'occasion du cinquantenaire de l'École municipale de physique et chimie industrielles" in *Cinquante années de science appliquée à l'industrie, 1882–1932*.

II. SECONDARY LITERATURE. See P. Biquard, *Paul Langevin, scientifique, éducateur, citoyen* (Paris, 1969), with preface by J. D. Bernal and a bibliography; Louis de Broglie, *Notice sur la vie et l'oeuvre de Paul Langevin* (Paris, 1947); S. Ghiseman, *Paul Langevin* (Bucharest, 1964); *La pensée* (Paris), no. 12 (May–June 1947), spec. no. "In memoriam"; O. A. Staroselskaya Nikitina, *Paul Langevin* (Moscow, 1962); and A. R. Weill, "Paul Langevin," in *Mémorial de l'artillerie française*, fasc. 4 (1946).

See also André Langevin, *Paul Langevin, mon père* (Paris, 1972).

ADRIENNE R. WEILL-BRUNSCHVICG

LANGLEY, JOHN NEWPORT (*b.* Newbury, England, 2 November 1852; *d.* Cambridge, England, 5 November 1925), *physiology, histology.*

Professor of physiology at Cambridge from 1903 until his death, Langley was renowned for his studies of glandular secretion and of the autonomic, or involuntary, nervous system. He was the second son of John Langley, a private schoolmaster at Newbury, who prepared him at home for Exeter Grammar School, where his uncle, Rev. H. Newport, was headmaster. His mother, Mary, was the eldest daughter of Richard Groom, assistant secretary to the Tax Office, Somerset House. In autumn 1871 Langley matriculated with a sizarship at St. John's College, Cambridge, where he later won a scholarship. During his first five terms he read mathematics and history as preparation for a place in the civil service, at home or in India. In May 1873 Langley enrolled in a newly created course in elementary biology offered by Michael Foster, who had come to Cambridge in 1870 as Trinity College praelector in physiology.

Under Foster's inspiration Langley abandoned his former plans and began to read for the natural sciences tripos, in which he took first-class honors in 1874.

Langley graduated B.A. in 1875 and in 1876 succeeded Henry Newell Martin as Foster's chief demonstrator, his salary being paid by Trinity College, where he was elected to a fellowship in 1877. Also in 1877 Langley spent several months in the laboratory of Wilhelm Kühne in Heidelberg, where he studied salivary secretion in the cat. Langley received an M.A. from Cambridge in 1878 and an Sc.D. in 1896. From 1883 to 1903 he was university lecturer in physiology and lecturer in natural science at Trinity College. In 1900 he was named deputy professor to Foster and in 1903 succeeded him as professor of physiology. In 1914 a large new physiological laboratory was built at Cambridge under Langley's direction with funds provided by the Drapers' Company. Upon Langley's death in 1925 the chair passed to Joseph Barcroft.

Elected to fellowship in the Royal Society in 1883 and awarded its Royal Medal in 1892, Langley also served as a member of its Council (1897–1898) and as vice-president (1904–1905). He was president of the Neurological Society of Great Britain in 1893 and president of the physiological section of the British Association in 1899. He was awarded the Baly Medal of the Royal College of Physicians in 1903, the Andreas Retzius medal of the Swedish Society of Physicians in 1912, and honorary doctorates by the universities of Dublin, St. Andrews, Groningen, and Strasbourg. In 1902 he married Vera Kathleen Forsyth-Grant of Ecclesgreig, Kincardineshire, by whom he had one daughter.

Langley's career in research fell into two major phases. From 1875 to 1890 he devoted himself largely to glandular secretion, and from 1890 until his death he worked mainly upon the involuntary nervous system. At the very beginning of his career, however, Langley briefly joined the group of Cambridge researchers who were working in the area of Foster's special interest, the problem of the heartbeat. During the winter of 1874–1875 Foster gave Langley a small amount of the alcoholic extract of jaborandi and asked him to study its physiological action. By October 1875 Langley's focus had narrowed to the effects of the drug on the heart. His major conclusion —that jaborandi altered heart action not by acting on any nervous elements but, rather, by acting directly on the cardiac tissue itself—conformed nicely to Foster's own myogenic view of heart action.[1]

But Langley was quickly distracted from the problem of the heartbeat. One of the most striking effects of jaborandi was to evoke copious secretion from the submaxillary gland. Recognizing in this phenomenon an opportunity to clarify the nature of salivary secretion and of secretion in general, Langley undertook a systematic study of the secretory organs which occupied him for the next fifteen years. In a series of papers remarkable for technical ingenuity and theoretical caution, Langley challenged Rudolf Heidenhain's generally accepted views on the structural changes which take place in secreting glands and on the relationship between glandular secretion and nervous activity.

As early as 1879 Langley had begun to develop the view that gland cells become more granular during rest and less granular during secretion, a conclusion precisely the reverse of Heidenhain's.[2] In making this point Langley emphasized that the structural changes observed in secreting glands are progressive and gradual, with no dramatic turning points discernible in the underlying processes. By 1888 Langley was also prepared to dispute Heidenhain's theory that the salivary glands are supplied not only with secretory nerves but also with "trophic" (metabolic) nerves whose function is to increase the solubility of stored gland substance.[3] With increasing confidence Langley argued that the evidence adduced in support of "trophic" nerves was either unreliable or could more plausibly be ascribed to the effects of local vasomotor nervous action. To the end of his career Langley maintained that the salivary gland, at least, is supplied with but one kind of nerve, which can by itself produce all of the changes observed in glandular secretion.[4]

In the 1880's, although engaged chiefly in these studies on secretion, Langley also undertook studies of the normal anatomy of the dog's brain and of nervous degeneration in the decorticated dog. Although this work from its beginning was related to the celebrated controversy between David Ferrier and Friedrich Goltz over cerebral localization, Langley seems never to have taken a definitive position on the issue.[5] Also in the 1880's Langley devoted himself briefly to the fashionable and controversial subject of hypnotism. Reputedly an accomplished hypnotist himself, chiefly because of his remarkable steely blue eyes, Langley sought to subsume many of the hypnotic phenomena under the physiological concept of irradiated inhibition.[6]

Although Langley's work on glandular secretion had involved him from the outset with problems of sympathetic innervation, his subsequent concentration on the involuntary nervous system was not a direct outgrowth of his work on the secretory nerves. Rather, it had its origin in the discovery that nicotine could selectively interrupt nerve impulses at the sympathetic ganglia. In a joint paper announcing the

discovery in 1889, Langley and William Lee Dickinson emphasized its immense potential as an analytic tool. In particular it seemed to offer an unimpeachable means of distinguishing those nerve fibers which ended in the nerve cells of a ganglion from those which merely ran through the ganglion without being connected with its nerve cells.[7] Although one alumnus of the Cambridge school has claimed in private correspondence that the discovery was really Dickinson's alone and not Langley's,[8] it was certainly Langley who most brilliantly and successfully exploited the new technique. Scarcely six months after the discovery, he had applied it with great success to extending and fortifying his earlier studies on the innervation of the salivary gland.[9] Thereafter the range of his studies expanded dramatically. By using nicotine in concert with more traditional techniques, such as nerve degeneration, Langley was able to map out the plan of much of the involuntary system in exquisite and unprecedented detail. In so doing he built upon the important earlier work of his Cambridge colleague W. H. Gaskell, and their combined contributions made Cambridge for some time the leading center for research on the involuntary nervous system.

Chiefly on histological grounds, Gaskell had established that the "visceral," or involuntary, nerves arise from the central nervous system in three distinct outflows: the cervicocranial, the thoracic, and the sacral. Gaskell's study of the distribution of the gray and white rami had also convinced him that the involuntary system is not essentially independent of the cerebrospinal system, as had been thought. While Langley's work strongly reinforced these fundamental generalizations, it also extended and modified Gaskell's results in several important ways. In the 1890's, at first with Charles Sherrington but mainly alone, Langley charted the distribution of the efferent sympathetic fibers to the skin and their relation to the afferent fibers of the corresponding spinal nerves. In so doing he not only clarified the basis for various pilomotor mechanisms (bristling of hair in cats and dogs, ruffling of feathers in birds) but also contributed importantly to clinical attempts to understand "referred" cutaneous pain in certain visceral diseases.

Moreover, these studies of the pilomotor nerves provided much of the evidence for three of Langley's most original contributions to the histology and physiology of the involuntary nervous system: (1) the conclusion that peripheral ganglia are not collected together according to function, as some had thought, but instead are associated with definite somatic areas, each ganglion being supplied with all of the sympathetic fibers of whatever function (whether inhibitory, motor, or other) which run to its associated area; (2) the discovery that every efferent nerve fiber passes through only one nerve cell on its way to the periphery, a discovery which overturned the hitherto rather casual assumption that such a fiber might run through several nerve cells (or even none), and which therefore had important physiological implications; and (3) his concept of "axon reflexes," developed in opposition to those French workers who followed Claude Bernard in their belief that peripheral ganglia are capable of true reflex action. The issues involved in this dispute are extremely complex, but Langley's basic conclusions were that the supposed ganglionic reflexes take place in the absence of afferent arcs and that they have their origin not in peripheral ganglia but in efferent preganglionic axon processes.

Another of Langley's influential contributions dating from the late 1890's was his successful introduction of a radically new nomenclature for what had been earlier (and loosely) designated the "organic," "vegetative," "sympathetic," "visceral," or "involuntary" nervous system. On the suggestion of Richard Jebb, professor of Greek at Cambridge, Langley proposed instead the term "autonomic,"[10] which still retains its preferred status. Langley thereafter confined the term "sympathetic" to the thoracic outflow of the autonomic system and introduced the term "parasympathetic" to designate its cranial and sacral outflows. By attaching this single name to both the cranial and sacral outflows, Langley wished to emphasize that these nerves belong to a somewhat separate system (which he sometimes called the "oro-anal" system), in that they resemble each other in their action and phylogenetic origin more than they resemble the thoracic (or "sympathetic") nerves. Langley gathered much of the evidence for the existence of this separate, parasympathetic system, although he perhaps tended to minimize the extent to which the idea was already present in Gaskell's earlier work. The importance of "merely" nomenclatural contributions tends to be greatly underrated, but Langley's terminological precision undeniably promoted clarity of thought and conciseness of expression in subsequent literature on the autonomic system. Still other contributions by Langley from the 1890's, perhaps less striking than those already described but characteristically thorough and valuable, were the studies he undertook with H. K. Anderson on the neuromuscular mechanisms of the iris and on the pattern of innervation for the pelvic organs.

Between about 1900 and 1905 Langley's most important new work centered on experimental cross unions of different kinds of nerve fibers. While confirming the functional distinction between efferent and afferent nerve fibers, these cross unions demonstrated the essential functional similarity of all efferent, preganglionic fibers and pointed to the conclusion that the final action of a peripheral nerve fiber depends not on the nature of the fiber itself, nor on the nature of the impulse which it transmits, but on the nature of the tissue in which it ends.

By 1905 Langley had entered perhaps the most fertile phase of his remarkably productive career. The subject to which he now turned was the mode by which nerve impulses or other stimuli are transmitted to various effector cells—whether muscular, glandular, or ganglionic. Here again nicotine and other drugs (especially curare and adrenaline) were utilized as fundamental analytic tools. The background for this new phase of Langley's work was formed in part by his earlier observation that nicotine could stimulate peripheral ganglia even after their preganglionic fibers had degenerated, but, more immediately, by the discovery of adrenalin in 1895 and the revelation soon afterward of its sympathomimetic effects on both normal and denervated muscle or gland cells. That nicotine and adrenalin produced the same effects on denervated as on normal cells raised doubts about the prevailing view that these and other drugs ordinarily act on nerve endings. These doubts were strikingly confirmed by Langley's discovery in 1905 that curare abolishes the slight tonic contractions produced in certain skeletal muscles of the fowl by injection of nicotine. Since this result occurs even after degeneration of the nerve fibers to these muscles, Langley argued that it can only be referred to the mutually antagonistic action of nicotine and curare on striated muscle. And this mutual antagonism could best be understood as the result of a competition between nicotine and curare for some constituent of the muscle substance with which each formed a specific chemical compound.

On grounds such as these Langley was able to suggest in 1906 that every cell connected with an efferent fiber contains a substance responsible for the chief function of that cell (whether contraction, or secretion, or—in the case of nerve cells—the discharging of nerve impulses) as well as other "receptive substances" capable of reacting specifically with chemical bodies (drugs) or sometimes with nervous stimuli. Although the tangled web of issues and influences has yet to be unraveled by historians, it seems clear that Langley's concept of "receptive substances" formed part of the background for later theories of the humoral transmission of nervous impulses[11] and that it provided a stimulus to many subsequent studies in neuromuscular physiology.

Langley himself elaborated his theory in several later studies.

With the advent of World War I, Langley and his depleted staff directed their energies and the facilities of their new laboratory toward studies of more immediate clinical relevance. Special attention was given to means of repairing denervated and atrophied muscle tissue, although Langley's typically cautious and thorough investigation offered little hope to those treating or suffering from such afflictions. His experiments on animals seemed to show that neither electrical stimulation nor massage nor any other physiotherapeutic measures could prevent atrophy in denervated muscle tissue. From the end of the war until his death, Langley worked chiefly on various aspects of vasomotor action, most notably the so-called "antidromic" vasodilatation produced in the hind limb by stimulating certain posterior nerve roots at their entry into the spinal cord. This phenomenon attracted considerable attention because it seemed to offer a unique exception to the Bell-Magendie law of the functional distinction between efferent and afferent fibers. In Langley's view, however, antidromic vasodilatation was produced by metabolites set free in muscle spindle cells by impulses passing down afferent fibers, and was therefore not an exception to the law.

In 1921 Langley gathered the results of much of his research in *The Autonomic Nervous System*, part I. (A projected second part never appeared.) Soon translated into French and German, this work was conceived in part as a rival to Gaskell's posthumous *The Involuntary Nervous System* (1916). Sensitive to suggestions that he had merely followed a path laid out for him by Gaskell, Langley in 1919 wrote a long letter to *Lancet* emphasizing the extent and manner in which his work had gone beyond Gaskell's and pointing to the latter's book as one possible factor impeding proper recognition of his own work. In this letter Langley also emphasized that all of his work on the autonomic system had evolved logically from the studies he had undertaken with Dickinson in 1889 on nicotine and related poisons.[12]

One final contribution of Langley's deserves mention. In 1894 he assumed editorial and financial control of the *Journal of Physiology*, which had acquired both a high reputation and a sizable debt since its founding by Foster in 1878. Besides arranging to pay off the debt and accepting the unsold stock, Langley substituted a policy of fiscal, verbal, and theoretical economy for Foster's rather genial and indulgent editorial policy. From 1894 until his death Langley invested enormous energy and talent in his editorial tasks, although he generously allowed Foster

to retain the official title of editor until the latter's death in 1907.

Under Langley's direction the Cambridge School of Physiology preserved and enhanced the great reputation it had gained under Foster's initial inspiration. Before assuming the professorship Langley had taught only advanced students, but he thereafter followed Foster's example by taking responsibility for the introductory lectures. In the latter capacity he was not notably successful, being both too reserved and too exacting to carry most novices with him. In fact, even a few of his advanced students and colleagues apparently resented his reserve and his alleged egotism; and there is some evidence that personal relationships were consequently strained in the Cambridge physiological laboratory.[13] Like many members of the Cambridge school, Langley was an accomplished athlete; his performances in sprinting, rowing, tennis, and golf were overshadowed by his prodigious talent as a skater. For one of his less avid admirers, this talent was perfectly in keeping with the spirit of Langley's work and character—"brilliant technique on an icy background."[14]

NOTES

1. See J. N. Langley, "The Action of Jaborandi on the Heart," in *Journal of Anatomy and Physiology*, **10** (1876), 187–201; and G. Geison, *Michael Foster*, pp. 377–382.
2. J. N. Langley, "On the Structure of the Serous Glands in Rest and Activity," in *Proceedings of the Royal Society*, **29** (1879), 377–382.
3. See J. N. Langley, "On the Physiology of the Salivary Secretion. Part IV. The Effect of Atropin Upon the Supposed Varieties of Secretory Nerve Fibres," in *Journal of Physiology*, **9** (1888), 55–64, esp. 61–62; and J. N. Langley to E. A. Schäfer, 4 Feb. 1888, Sharpey-Schafer Papers, Wellcome Institute of the History of Medicine.
4. See, for example, J. N. Langley, "Note on Trophic Secretory Fibres to the Salivary Glands," in *Journal of Physiology*, **50** (1916), xxv–xxvi.
5. See E. Klein, J. N. Langley, and E. A. Schäfer, "On the Cortical Areas Removed From the Brain of a Dog, and From the Brain of a Monkey," *ibid.*, **4** (1883), 231–247; J. N. Langley, "The Structure of the Dog's Brain," *ibid.*, 248–285; and "Report on the Parts Destroyed on the Right Side of the Brain of the Dog Operated on by Prof. Goltz," *ibid.*, 286–309; J. N. Langley and C. S. Sherrington, "Secondary Degeneration of Nerve Tracts Following Removal of the Cortex of the Cerebrum in the Dog," *ibid.*, **5** (1884), 49–65; and J. N. Langley and A. S. Grünbaum, "On the Degeneration Resulting From Removal of the Cerebral Cortex and Corpora Striata in the Dog," *ibid.*, **11** (1890), 606–628. In private correspondence Langley did once refer to an apparently fleeting hypothesis of his on the issue of cerebral localization, but the content of this "hypothesis" remains obscure. See J. N. Langley to E. A. Schäfer, 3 Feb. 1884, Sharpey-Schafer Papers, Wellcome Institute of the History of Medicine.
6. See J. N. Langley, "The Physiological Aspect of Mesmerism," in *Proceedings of the Royal Institution of Great Britain*, **11** (1884), 25–43; and J. N. Langley and H. E. Wingfield, "A Preliminary Account of Some Observa-

tions on Hypnotism," in *Journal of Physiology*, **8** (1887), xvii–xxiv.

7. J. N. Langley and W. Lee Dickinson, "On the Local Paralysis of Peripheral Ganglia, and on the Connexion of Different Classes of Nerve Fibres With Them," in *Proceedings of the Royal Society*, **46** (1889), 423–431.

8. W. Langdon-Brown to Donal Sheehan, 11 Mar. 1940, copy deposited in the obituary files, Medical Historical Library, Yale University.

9. J. N. Langley, "On the Physiology of the Salivary Secretion. Part VI. Chiefly Upon the Connection of Peripheral Nerve Cells With the Nerve Fibres Which Run to the Sublingual and Submaxillary Glands," in *Journal of Physiology*, **11** (1890), 123–158.

10. See J. N. Langley, "The Sympathetic and Other Related Systems of Nerves," in *Text-Book of Physiology*, E. A. Schäfer, ed., 2 vols. (Edinburgh–London, 1898–1900), II, 616–696, esp. 659–660.

11. See, e.g., Walter B. Cannon, "The Story of the Development of Our Ideas of Chemical Mediation of Nerve Impulses," in *American Journal of the Medical Sciences*, n.s. **188** (1934), 145–159. According to Henry Dale, however, Langley reacted unfavorably toward, and diverted attention from, the hypothesis of the chemical transmission of nerve impulses as originally proposed by T. R. Elliott in 1904. See H. H. Dale, "T. R. Elliott," in *Biographical Memoirs of Fellows of the Royal Society*, **7** (1961), 53–74, esp. 63–64.

12. J. N. Langley, "The Arrangement of the Autonomic Nervous System," in *Lancet* (31 May 1919), p. 951.

13. Most notably in the letter of Walter Langdon-Brown to Donal Sheehan (see note 8). See also J. F. Fulton to Donal Sheehan, 27 Mar. 1940, copy deposited in obituary files, Medical Historical Library, Yale University. For a rather more favorable view of Langley's personality, see the obituary notices by W. M. Fletcher.

14. Langdon-Brown to Sheehan (note 8).

BIBLIOGRAPHY

I. ORIGINAL WORKS. Of Langley's approximately 170 published research papers, the great majority appeared in the *Journal of Physiology*. A virtually complete bibliography, slightly flawed by occasional errors or omissions in pagination, is given by Walter Morley Fletcher in *Journal of Physiology*, **61** (1926), 16–27. Fletcher did overlook the important letter to *Lancet* cited in note 12 and the obituary notice on Lucas (cited below). The Royal Society *Catalogue of Scientific Papers*, X, 510–511; XVI, 595–596; lists Langley's papers up to 1900.

Langley's major contributions to the physiology of glandular secretion are contained in the six-part article "On the Physiology of the Salivary Secretion," in *Journal of Physiology*, **1** (1878), 96–103, 339–369; **6** (1885), 71–92; **9** (1888), 55–64; **10** (1889), 291–328; and **11** (1890), 123–158. The full measure of those contributions is made clear in Langley's admirable review article "The Salivary Glands," in *Text-Book of Physiology*, E. A. Schäfer, ed., 2 vols. (Edinburgh–London, 1898–1900), I, 475–530.

So extensive and rich was Langley's work on the autonomic nervous system that only a few of his major papers can be listed here. On his studies of the pilomotor nerves, see especially "On Pilomotor Nerves," in *Journal of Physiology*, **12** (1891), 278–291, written with C. S. Sherrington; and "The Arrangement of the Sympathetic Nervous System, Based Chiefly on Observations Upon Pilo-

Motor Nerves," *ibid.*, **15** (1893), 176–244. Langley's work with H. K. Anderson on the innervation of the pelvic and adjoining viscera is described in a seven-part article, *ibid.*, **18** (1895), 67–105; **19** (1895), 71–84, 85–121, 122–130, 131–139; **19** (1896), 372–384; and **20** (1896), 372–406. On the concept of "axon reflexes," see "On Axon-reflexes in the Pre-ganglionic Fibres of the Sympathetic System," *ibid.*, **25** (1900), 364–398.

Langley's concept of "receptive substances" was first announced in "On the Reaction of Cells and of Nerve-Endings to Certain Poisons, Chiefly as Regards the Reaction of Striated Muscle to Nicotine and Curare," *ibid.*, **33** (1905), 374–413. More impressive for its scope and clarity is his Croonian lecture for 1906, "On Nerve-Endings and on Special Excitable Substances in Cells," in *Proceedings of the Royal Society*, **76B** (1906), 170–194. The concept was further developed in a four-part article, "On the Contraction of Muscle, Chiefly in Relation to the Presence of 'Receptive Substances,' " in *Journal of Physiology*, **36** (1907), 347–384; **37** (1908), 165–212, 285–300; and **39** (1909), 235–295.

For Langley's more general accounts of the autonomic nervous system, see his superb article "The Sympathetic and Other Related Systems of Nerves," in *Text-Book of Physiology*, II, 616–696; his presidential address to the physiological section of the British Association, in *Report of the Sixty-Ninth Meeting of the British Association for the Advancement of Science* (London, 1900), pp. 881–892; "The Autonomic Nervous System," in *Brain*, **26** (1903), 1–26; and, of course, his monograph *The Autonomic Nervous System*, pt. 1 (Cambridge, 1921). For a clear and succinct account of the rationale for Langley's nomenclatural innovations, see "The Nomenclature of the Sympathetic and of the Related System of Nerves," in *Zentralblatt für Physiologie*, **27** (1913), 149–152.

For examples of Langley's wartime research on denervated muscle, see "The Rate of Loss of Weight in Skeletal Muscle After Nerve Section With Some Observations on the Effect of Stimulation and Other Treatment," in *Journal of Physiology*, **49** (1915), 432–440, written with Toyojiro Kato; and "Observations on Denervated Muscle," *ibid.*, **50** (1916), 335–344. Langley's major postwar research projects are described in three two-part articles: "Vaso-Motor Centres," *ibid.*, **53** (1919), 120–134, 147–161; "The Secretion of Sweat," *ibid.*, **56** (1922), 110–119, 206–226; and "Antidromic Action," *ibid.*, **57** (1923), 428–446, **58** (1923), 49–69.

Langley also wrote useful obituary articles on four of his Cambridge colleagues—Michael Foster, in *Journal of Physiology*, **35** (1907), 233–246; W. H. Gaskell, in *Proceedings of the Royal Society*, **88B** (1915), xxvii–xxxvi; Arthur Sheridan Lea, *ibid.*, **89** (1916), xxv–xxvii; and Keith Lucas, in *Nature*, **98** (1916), 109. The obituary on Gaskell is noteworthy for its generous assessment of the work of his sometime rival. The range of Langley's interests is indicated in a historiographically undistinguished article, "Sketch of the Progress of Discovery in the Eighteenth Century as Regards the Autonomic Nervous System," in *Journal of Physiology*, **50** (1916), 225–258. Besides his monograph on the autonomic nervous system, Langley's published books were *Practical Histology* (London, 1901; 3rd ed., 1920); and, initially with Michael Foster, *A Course of Elementary Practical Physiology* (London, 1876; 7th ed., 1899); by the 7th ed., L. E. Shore was listed as coauthor.

There is apparently no central repository for Langley's letters or papers, and little seems to have survived. Some ten letters from him to E. A. Schäfer are to be found in the Sharpey-Schafer Papers at the Wellcome Institute of the History of Medicine, London.

II. SECONDARY LITERATURE. For valuable obituary notices, see W. M. Fletcher, in *Journal of Physiology*, **61** (1926), 1–27, which contains a full bibliography; and in *Proceedings of the Royal Society*, **101B** (1927), xxxiii–xli; and C. S. Sherrington, in *Dictionary of National Biography, 1922–1930*, pp. 478–481. For background on some of Langley's research and on his place in the Cambridge school, see Gerald L. Geison, "Michael Foster and the Rise of the Cambridge School of Physiology" (unpublished Ph.D. dissertation, Yale, 1970). His place in the recent history of pharmacological physiology and junctional transmission receives brief attention in Alfred Fessard, "Claude Bernard and the Physiology of Junctional Transmission," in *Claude Bernard and Experimental Medicine*, Francisco Grande and Maurice B. Visscher, eds. (Cambridge, Mass., 1967), pp. 105–123, esp. p. 116; and F. E. Shideman, "Drugs as Tools in the Elucidation of Physiological Mechanisms," *ibid.*, pp. 125–134, esp. pp. 125–127.

GERALD L. GEISON

LANGLEY, SAMUEL PIERPONT (*b.* Roxbury [now part of Boston], Massachusetts, 22 August 1834; *d.* Aiken, South Carolina, 22 February 1906), *astrophysics.*

Langley's parents, Mary Sumner Williams and Samuel Langley, a wholesale merchant of broad interests, traced their ancestry to old and prominent New England families. Langley attended private schools, Boston Latin School, and completed his formal education upon graduation from Boston High School in 1851. From his youth he read extensively in science, literature, and history. Langley had a Puritan morality but was an ardent seeker for religious truth and the nature of the soul, including study of metaphysics, psychology, and psychic phenomena. A bachelor, he was a large man with a florid countenance and robust health but a tendency to be melancholy. Because of a deep-seated shyness, he maintained a front of severe and haughty dignity. He was irascible and often gave offense, but to his intimates he was warmhearted, displaying great charm. Highly respected in scientific circles, he received several scientific honors and honorary degrees.

He was a member of the National Academy of Sciences, on whose council he served; a foreign member of the Royal Society of London, the Royal Society of Edinburgh, and the Accademia dei Lincei of Rome; a correspondent of the Institut de France; and a president of the American Association for the Advancement of Science.

Langley worked as a civil engineer and architect from 1851 to 1864, ranging west to Chicago and St. Louis. After a tour of Europe with his brother John Williams Langley, a chemist, he was an assistant at the Harvard observatory for a year. In 1866 he was appointed assistant professor of mathematics at the Naval Academy and placed in charge of restoring its neglected observatory.

In 1867 Langley was appointed director of the Allegheny Observatory and professor of physics and astronomy at the Western University of Pennsylvania (later University of Pittsburgh). He pioneered in providing standard time signals to railroads; the income from this service helped support the observatory. Langley did his most original work in his twenty years at Pittsburgh.

In January 1887 Langley was appointed assistant secretary, and in November of that year secretary, of the Smithsonian Institution. He did not cease work at Allegheny or take up full-time residence in Washington until 1889, after the death of his Pittsburgh benefactor, William Thaw. Langley then fulfilled the long-held goal of a Smithsonian observatory by founding the Smithsonian Astrophysical Observatory, using private bequests and government support (1890). Besides giving new life to the physical sciences at the Smithsonian, Langley broadened the scope of the institution by beginning what became the National Zoological Park and the National Gallery of Art.

Langley began research on aerodynamics at Pittsburgh in 1887, investigating the pressure on a plane surface inclined to its direction of travel. The results were of minor importance. In 1891 Langley announced that "*Mechanical Flight is possible with engines we now possess,*" on the basis of his prediction that a twenty-pound, one-horsepower steam engine could sustain the flight of a 200-pound airplane at a speed of forty-five miles per hour. In 1896 Langley successfully flew models over the Potomac.

Langley's models were developed in slow stages from bench tests and were designed to be inherently stable. When in 1898, at the request of the War Department, Langley began work on a man-carrying machine, he continued this evolutionary process. His one-quarter (of man-carrying size) model flew very successfully in 1903. The man-carrying airplane did not fly; on two attempts in 1906 the launching apparatus failed. The ridicule of the press, offended by Langley's aloofness, and the mismanaged combination of official secrecy but public testing ended Langley's expensive program.

It has been said that the work of the scientifically respected Langley brought experiments on flight out of the stage of ridicule and into a stage of science. His failure was the occasion for sharp ridicule, however; and the procedures of the Wright brothers were unlike those of Langley because they first mastered the art of flying inherently unstable gliders before adding power. The main line of development of flight followed the work of the Wright brothers and not that of Langley.

It is difficult to agree on what constitutes successful flight of powered, man-carrying, heavier-than-air craft; and there are many motivated by a desire to improve Langley's popular image or to discount the contributions of the Wright brothers in favor of supposed precursors. In 1914, with the support of Smithsonian officials, Glenn Curtiss, a patent opponent of the Wright brothers, barely flew Langley's airplane after significant but unreported modifications. The resulting controversy caused bitter feelings between the Wright brothers and the Smithsonian and did no service to Langley.

Langley's work in astrophysics and infrared spectroscopy was very much in the mainstream of those branches of physics. Although a keen visual observer, Langley made his contribution in the development and application of apparatus and techniques for the measurement of radiation.

Correctly recognizing the need for measurements of the energy of radiation as a function of wavelength, Langley developed a new instrument—the bolometer—between 1879 and 1881 to do this. The bolometer was an ingenious application of the principle— the temperature coefficient of the resistance of metals —being used by William Siemens for the measurement of temperature. It was a Wheatstone bridge with similar narrow platinum strips in opposite arms, one of which was exposed to radiation. With this Langley could measure a temperature difference of $10^{-5°}$ C. in a one-second exposure with an error of less than 1 percent. The bolometer allowed continuous and direct measurement of $E(\lambda)$ versus λ for the full known spectrum of radiation, through what had been delineated (because of the different techniques necessary for measurement before the bolometer) as actinic, visual, and thermal regions.

Langley developed the bolometer to study the solar constant by integrating the energy versus wavelength curves it gave; to study the selective absorption of the earth's atmosphere by repeating measurements for different thicknesses of the atmosphere; and to study the selective absorption of the sun's atmosphere by repeating measurements on various parts of the sun. On his expedition to Mt. Whitney to accomplish this in 1881, Langley discovered significant radiation beyond a wavelength of one micron, which had been thought to be the limit of solar radiation. The superior measurements by means of the bolometer, the newly discovered extent of the solar spectrum, and the new results for selective absorption of the earth's atmosphere were significant contributions to the study of the sun and its effects on the earth.

The dispersion and absorption of prisms depend on wavelength. Grating spectra, although without this disadvantage, are weak and overlap at large wavelengths. Langley's technique was to determine the dispersion and absorption of prisms, rock salt in particular, as a function of wavelength by explicitly using the overlap in grating spectra and the bolometer. The prism was then used in an automatically recording spectrobolometer, which allowed convenient measurement of infrared spectra well beyond previous capability.

The investigations of long wavelengths in the late 1890's which prompted Planck's interpolated radiation law were based, in part, on bolometer measurements. Langley extended measurement of spectra to a five-micron wavelength. The failure of Wein's law was seen beyond a ten-micron wavelength. Langley did some work measuring the spectrum of Leslie cubes— showing, for example, migration of the maximum of radiation intensity as a function of the temperature of the source—but did not study blackbody radiation as such.

In a paper titled "Laws of Nature," Langley expressed his empiricist creed: "[The] practical rule of life [is] that we must act with the majority where our faith does not compel us to do otherwise, [remembering that] we know nothing absolutely or in its essence [and science has authority in matters] only as far as they are settled by evidence and observation alone" ("The Laws of Nature," in *Report of the Board of Regents of the Smithsonian Institution* for 1901 [1902], p. 551).

BIBLIOGRAPHY

I. ORIGINAL WORKS. There are bibliographies of Langley's published works appended to Walcott's memoir of Langley and to the report of the Langley Memorial Meeting (see below). Three major publications—"Researches on Solar Heat and Its Absorption by the Earth's Atmosphere, A Report of the Mount Whitney Expedition,"

Professional Papers of the Signal Service, no. 15 (1884); *Annals of the Astrophysical Observatory of the Smithsonian Institution*, **1** (1900); and "Langley Memoir on Flight," in *Smithsonian Contributions to Knowledge*, **27** (1911)—report most of his work.

II. SECONDARY LITERATURE. Langley prepared some biographical fragments which were used by his very close friend Cyrus Adler for his memoir, "Samuel Pierpont Langley," in *Bulletin of the Philosophical Society of Washington*, **15** (1907), 1–26. Adler contemplated a full biography of Langley, and there may be valuable materials among Adler's papers at the American Jewish Historical Society in New York.

Other notices of Langley are "Samuel Pierpont Langley Memorial Meeting," in *Smithsonian Miscellaneous Collections*, **49** (1907); C. G. Abbot, "Samuel Pierpont Langley," in *Astrophysical Journal*, **23** (1906), 271–283; George Brown Goode, "Samuel Pierpont Langley," in *The Smithsonian Institution: 1846 to 1896*, George Brown Goode, ed. (Washington, D.C., 1896); and C. D. Walcott, "Biographical Memoir of Samuel Pierpont Langley," in *Biographical Memoirs. National Academy of Sciences*, **7** (1917), 247–268.

Autobiographies of Langley's associates containing significant mention of Langley are Charles G. Abbot, *Adventures in the World of Science* (Washington, D.C., 1958); Cyrus Adler, *I Have Remembered the Days* (Philadelphia, 1941); and John A. Brashear, *The Autobiography of a Man Who Loved the Stars*, W. Lucien Scaife, ed. (Boston, 1925).

Among works on the Smithsonian the following, along with the Goode volume listed above, are valuable: Bessie Zaban Jones, *Lighthouse of the Skies, the Smithsonian Astrophysical Observatory: Background and History 1846–1955* (Washington, 1965); and Paul H. Oehser, *Sons of Science: The Story of the Smithsonian Institution and Its Leaders* (New York, 1949).

For Langley's place in the history of flight, see C. G. Abbot, "The 1914 Tests of the Langley 'Aerodrome,'" in *Smithsonian Miscellaneous Collections*, **103**, no. 8 (1942); and Charles H. Gibbs-Smith, *The Aeroplane: An Historical Survey of Its Origins and Development* (London, 1960).

Langley's bolometer work, concerning as it does instrumentation and technique, has not been itself the subject of historical scholarship, although there is perfunctory mention of Langley's contribution in works on astrophysics, infrared spectroscopy, and the prehistory of quantum mechanics.

DON F. MOYER

LANGLOIS, CLAUDE (*b.* France, *ca.* 1700; *d.* France, *ca.* 1756), *instrumentation.*

Documents concerning Langlois's life are rare and fragmentary, but from many accounts we know that between 1730 and 1756 he was the most highly regarded maker of scientific instruments in France and may be considered to have restored this art among the French. He and the other members of his trade provided scientists—at first astronomers—with the means of making highly precise observations during their many astronomical and geodesic missions. At the end of the seventeenth century the British instrument makers had become the undisputed leaders in the opinion of all European scientists, having surpassed Dutch workshops in their specialty—demonstration instruments for physics—and Italian workshops in the field of astronomical instruments (which the Italians had revitalized), and of instrumental optics (which they had created). French workshops were relatively numerous toward the beginning of the eighteenth century and furnished to a still small clientele all the types of instruments known. A few masters, like Nicolas Bion and Michael Butterfield, were better known than their colleagues, but none could be compared with the British competitors. Langlois, around the middle of the eighteenth century, was the first master to establish a firm tradition of precision workmanship in France. In 1730, the earliest date associated with his name, he received his first commission from the Paris observatory, for a wall quadrant of six-foot radius. He must therefore have been quite well known to French astronomers at this period to have merited the confidence represented by their commission. The signature on this instrument indicates that Langlois was established at the sign of the Niveau, probably on the Quai de l'Horloge, where most of the Parisian makers of scientific instruments were located. He was probably about thirty years old to have acquired not only the skill necessary for constructing large observatory wall instruments, but also the commercial foundation that could allow him to engage in such undertakings without serious financial risk. For no matter what price the purchaser paid, the instrument maker's investment in the form of tools, special equipment, and time was considerable in view of the very limited number of instruments of this size that a French workshop could hope to sell. Langlois was in fact the only French instrument maker to have produced such instruments for nearly thirty years. From his workshop came all the kinds of apparatus known at the time, for use in physics laboratories and schools, and by surveyors and navigators. Langlois's innovations in these areas included an improved pantograph that he submitted to the Académie des Sciences for approval.

The result of Langlois's activity seems to have been convincing enough for him to be chosen the official instrument maker of the French astronomers. About 1740 he was named *ingénieur en instruments de mathématiques* by the Academy and along with this title received lodgings at the Louvre, as did all officially designated "artists." This honor apparently reflected the maturing of Langlois's talent and his high reputation among astronomers, notably Cassini II, Cassini de Thury, Camus, Le Monnier, Maupertuis, and the Abbé de Lacaille. During the last twenty-five years of Langlois's life the Paris observatory ordered from him several instruments that were employed, along with English instruments, in the extensive triangulations of the first half of the century. In 1738 he constructed another wall quadrant of three-and-a half-foot radius and a six-foot sector; in 1742 a six-foot portable quadrant with certain features specified by Camus; a large sextant in 1750; and a three-foot portable quadrant in 1756, the year of his death.

In 1733 the Paris Academy decided to organize expeditions to Peru and Lapland to measure a meridian arc of one degree and the length of a seconds pendulum. Langlois was commissioned to construct five quadrants, of which three were taken to Peru and two to Lapland. In 1735 he furnished two standard *toises* established on the basis of the Chatelet *toise*, and each mission took along one standard. The Peru *toise*, also called the Academy *toise*, later replaced the Chatelet *toise* as the official standard. Langlois's successor, his nephew Canivet, was commissioned in 1766 to construct eighty copies, which were distributed to all the provincial *parlements*. Moreover, the Peru *toise* was used in 1793 to determine the length of the four platinum rulers constructed by Étienne Lenoir to measure the bases of Melun and Perpignan for the great meridian triangulation carried out by Delambre and Méchain. Several of Langlois's instruments, the six-foot sector of 1738 and a two-foot quadrant built in 1739, were employed in 1739 and 1740 by Cassini de Thury, Giovanni Domenico Maraldi, and the Abbé de Lacaille for the first series of triangulations undertaken to establish a new map of France. In 1744, Le Monnier entrusted Langlois with the restoration of the meridian gnomon of the Church of St. Sulpice in Paris, laid out twenty years earlier by the clockmaker Sully. The operculum, seventy-five feet above the south portal, was fitted with a lens having a focal length of eighty feet. Langlois placed the long copper plate representing the meridian on the ground; on the terminal obelisk he traced the curve and divisions of the solar pointer as a function of the calendar.

When Langlois died he was succeeded in his post at the Academy by Canivet, whom he had trained, and who in turn was succeeded by one of his own pupils, Lennel. Thus Langlois's workshop, established probably in the first quarter of the eighteenth century, pursued its activity until after 1785. Its founder applied to the construction of astronomical and geodesic instruments traditional methods, the insufficiencies of which were not overcome by English artisans until the 1740's and 1750's. Yet Langlois employed these methods with a skill superior to that of all his compatriots. Having inherited these qualities, his successors were fully prepared to adopt the new English methods. Thus a continuous tradition was established, linking Langlois with the brilliant generation of French instrument makers that flourished from 1780 to 1800 and participated in the establishment of the metric system.

BIBLIOGRAPHY

There are no written works by Langlois; his work survives only in his signed instruments. See G. Bigourdan, *Le système métrique* (Paris, 1901), p. 450; Maurice Daumas, *Les instruments scientifiques aux XVIIᵉ et XVIIIᵉ siècles* (Paris, 1953), p. 420; and C. Wolf, *Recherches historiques sur les étalons de poids et de mesures et les appareils qui ont servi à les construire* (Paris, 1882), p. 84; and *Histoire de l'observatoire* (Paris, 1902), p. 329.

MAURICE DAUMAS

LANGMUIR, IRVING (*b.* Brooklyn, New York, 31 January 1881; *d.* Falmouth, Massachusetts, 16 August 1957), *chemistry, physics.*

Irving Langmuir was the third of four children (all sons) of Charles Langmuir, a New York insurance executive of Scots ancestry, and Sadie Comings Langmuir, the daughter of a professor of anatomy and a descendant, on her mother's side, of the early English settlers who arrived in America on the *Mayflower*. Irving Langmuir alternately attended schools in New York and in Paris, where his father headed the European agencies of the New York Life Insurance Company. Irving was in his last year at the Pratt Institute's manual training high school in Brooklyn in 1898 when his father unexpectedly died at the age of fifty-four of pneumonia contracted during a winter transatlantic crossing. His mother lived to be eighty-seven. Fortunately, Charles Langmuir had provided well for his family, and Irving was able to enter Columbia University. Although deeply interested in science, he chose the more exacting curriculum of the School of Mines. "The course was strong in chemistry," he said later. "It had more physics than the chemical course, and more mathematics than the course in physics—and I wanted all three." He received the degree of metallurgical engineer (equivalent to bachelor of science) in 1903 and decided to enter on a course of postgraduate study in Germany. He hesitated between Leipzig and Göttingen and chose the latter, where he worked under

Walther Nernst on the dissociation of various gases by a glowing platinum wire, research that became the topic of his 1906 doctoral dissertation. The decision for Göttingen very likely had a profound influence on Langmuir's career, for not only was Nernst deeply engaged in the work on thermodynamics that was to earn him the Nobel Prize in 1920, but he was also favorably inclined toward applied research. Nernst had devised a new type of electric lamp that became a great commercial success, in a sense presaging Langmuir's own career in industrial research. At Leipzig, Langmuir would probably have come under the influence of Wilhelm Ostwald and might not have become interested in the problems of molecular and atomic structure that underlie much of his mature work, since Ostwald had little faith in that approach.

Armed with a doctorate from Göttingen, Langmuir returned to America and for a time taught chemistry at Stevens Institute of Technology in Hoboken, New Jersey, but the position gave little scope to his talents. After a summer job at the new research laboratory that the General Electric Company had established in 1901 in Schenectady, New York, he gratefully accepted an offer to stay there permanently. He remained there for forty-one years until his retirement in 1950 and continued as a consultant.

Langmuir's scientific work was extremely varied. During overlapping periods he made major contributions in at least seven fields: chemical reactions at high temperatures and low pressures (1906–1921); thermal effects in gases (1911–1936); atomic structure (1919–1921); thermionic emission and surfaces in vacuum (1913–1937); chemical forces in solids, liquids, and surface films (1916–1943); electrical discharges in gases (1923–1932); and atmospheric science (1938–1955). Much of his work led to technological developments of wide and lasting importance.

His work on chemical reactions at high temperatures and low pressures derived from his dissertation under Nernst, who wanted to understand the equilibrium conditions governing the formation of nitric oxide from air in the vicinity of a hot wire. The scope of the investigation presently came to include other gaseous equilibria. Langmuir was fascinated by the simplicity of the experimental setup, which resembled an incandescent light bulb. The electric lamp of the day was a relatively inefficient device containing a fragile carbon filament and was severely limited in lifetime and power. (Electric street lights used arc lamps.) Tantalum and tungsten filaments were being tried but did not last much longer even in the best available vacuum. Langmuir's first task at General Electric was to find the reason for the short life, which proved to be residual gases adhering to the glass envelope

and other impurities. This research ultimately led to the recognition that filling the lamp with inert gases (a nitrogen-argon mixture worked best) greatly increased both lifetime and efficiency, a discovery that revolutionized the electric-lamp industry. The same studies led to the discovery and understanding of the formation of atomic hydrogen from molecular hydrogen and to a series of other results in the fields of heat transfer and low-pressure phenomena.

Continuing experiments on hot tungsten filaments in various gases, Langmuir turned to a study of heat losses and evaporation from hot filaments. He found that the laws governing the evaporation of tungsten into nitrogen resembled those of heat convection: thin wires lost as much tungsten per unit area as thick wires, but the latter were more efficient, a contradiction that led to the adoption of a lamp filament made from a thin wire tightly coiled into a helix. He also estimated the heat of dissociation of hydrogen and observed various properties of atomic hydrogen, including its adsorption on cold glass walls. The heating effects produced by the recombination of atomic hydrogen later led Langmuir to invent the atomic-hydrogen welding torch, in which an arc between tungsten electrodes in hydrogen produces hydrogen atoms that create heat when they recombine on the metal to be welded.

Of all his major contributions, Langmuir's sortie into atomic structure occupied him for the shortest period (1919–1921). Building upon the ideas of G. N. Lewis, Langmuir suggested a modification in the model of the atom proposed by his idol, Niels Bohr. Although the Lewis-Langmuir theory, called the "octet theory" of chemical valence, ultimately yielded to the quantum-mechanical concepts of chemical bonds, it proved to be astonishingly successful from a practical viewpoint, explaining a great variety of chemical phenomena by essentially classical methods. At this time, Langmuir apparently made a deliberate decision to concentrate his efforts on fields in which such classical methods were likely to yield new results and recognized that atomic structure was not one of them.

Concurrently with these efforts, he was engaged in investigations of thermionic emission and of surfaces in vacuum, two fields that proved of tremendous fundamental and practical importance. Elucidating the phenomenon of space charge (the cloud of charged particles that maintains itself in the interelectrode space) he independently derived for electrons the relationship established previously for ions by C. D. Child. Now known as the Child-Langmuir space-charge equation, the relationship shows that the current between the electrodes is proportional to the voltage raised to the 3/2 power, regardless of the shapes of the electrodes. This law, which underlies the design of a great variety of electron tubes and other devices, was elaborated by Langmuir and his co-workers for several geometrical configurations. At the same time, Langmuir observed that certain admixtures such as thoria, an oxide of thorium (ThO_2), greatly enhanced thermionic emission from tungsten, a result that he correctly ascribed to an effective lowering of the work function by the diffusion of a single layer of thorium atoms to the surface of the tungsten filament. His other studies in this field related to the changes in emission and in ionization produced by the presence of cesium, and were also destined to become of technological importance. A development of more immediate import was his invention of a condensation pump, which produces a good vacuum very quickly with the help of a refrigerant such as liquid nitrogen. This device rapidly came into widespread industrial and laboratory use and continued to dominate the field for decades.

The largest single topic to occupy Langmuir's attention was surface chemistry—the study of chemical forces at interfaces between different substances. He evolved a new concept of adsorption, according to which every molecule striking a surface remains in contact for a time before evaporating, so that a firmly held monolayer is formed. He developed a multitude of experimental techniques for studying surface films on liquids. Turning to solids, he developed the Langmuir adsorption isotherm, an expression for the fraction of surface covered by the adsorbed layer as a function of pressure and the temperature-dependent rates of surface condensation and evaporation. He also characterized the catalytic effect of an adsorbing surface by considering the chemical reaction as occurring in the film, a concept that served to explain many phenomena of surface kinetics that had not been previously understood. It was largely in recognition of this work that Langmuir was awarded the Nobel Prize in chemistry in 1932.

Possibly of even greater lasting significance was his work relating to electric discharges in gases, which derived from an interest in mercury-arc and other gaseous devices used in the control of heavy alternating currents. This effort led to a large body of experimental and analytical research concerned with electron-ion interactions, ionization, oscillations, and other aspects of a space-charge-free ionized gas, the richly complex and inherently unstable medium for which he coined the term "plasma." Subsequent work in such fields as electron physics, magnetohydrodynamics (MHD), and the control of thermonuclear fusion depends heavily on the basic results on plasma first reported in the papers of Langmuir and his associates. In these papers, the concept of electron "temperature" was introduced as well as a method of measuring both it and the ion density by a special electrode, now called the Langmuir probe.

The major field that occupied Langmuir into his retirement years was atmospheric science. Following a lifelong preoccupation with the weather (he was a great outdoorsman, a capable sailor, and an enthusiastic amateur flyer), he studied such phenomena as the regular formation of streaks of seaweed on the wind-blown surface of the sea (windrows), the formation of liquid particles of various sizes in air, and the nucleation of ice crystals in supercooled clouds by "seeding" with solid carbon dioxide particles. This last work, which was based on a discovery of Langmuir's associate V. J. Schaefer, led to the beginnings of artificial weather control, although early efforts at producing rain and diverting storms were marred by much scientific and public controversy regarding the efficacy of cloud seeding.

Langmuir was the first eminent scientist employed by an industrial laboratory to be honored by a Nobel Prize —an aspect of his career that had an impact on the worldwide development of scientific research and that lent a certain cachet to such endeavors. Forward-looking industries everywhere began to appreciate the importance of undirected basic research of a sort previously restricted to universities.

Langmuir's mature life was serene. At the age of thirty-one he married Marion Mersereau of Schenectady; they adopted two children, Kenneth and Barbara. He was close to his brothers and to his many nephews and nieces, several of whom also achieved distinction in scientific fields. Langmuir's elder brother Arthur was a successful industrial chemist, a fact that doubtless influenced young Irving's choice of a career. Moreover, Arthur's enthusiasm for science transmitted itself to Irving through their exceptionally close relationship. Langmuir's interests extended to such diverse fields as the Boy Scout movement, aviation, and music—he was a personal friend of Charles Lindbergh and of the conductor and sound-recording innovator Leopold Stokowski. He also concerned himself with problems of public policy such as the conservation of wilderness areas and control of atomic energy. In 1935 he stood for the city council of Schenectady, N. Y., but failed to be elected. He participated actively in America's scientific war efforts during both world wars: in antisubmarine defense and nitrate production during the first, and in aircraft de-icing and smoke-screen research (both outgrowths of his interest in meteorology) during the second. He worked best with small teams of collaborators. Outstanding among them was Dr. Katherine Blodgett, with whom he worked closely for over thirty years.

In addition to the Nobel Prize, Langmuir received many other honors, among them the Hughes Medal of the Royal Society (1918), the American Rumford Medal (1920), the American Chemical Society's Nichols Medal (1920) and Gibbs Medal (1930), the Franklin Medal (1934), and both Faraday Medals: that of the Chemical Society (1938) and of the Institution of Electrical Engineers (1943). He was granted fifteen honorary degrees. He was a member of the National Academy and a foreign member of the Royal Society and of other bodies. Mount Langmuir in Alaska is named after him, and in 1970 a residential college at the State University of New York at Stony Brook was named Irving Langmuir College in his honor.

BIBLIOGRAPHY

I. ORIGINAL WORKS. Langmuir received 63 patents and published over 200 papers and reports between 1906 and 1956. Virtually all his papers appear in the 12-vol. memorial edition of *The Collected Works of Irving Langmuir*, C. G. Smits, ed. (London–New York, 1960–1962), which is devoted to the following topics: 1. Low-Pressure Phenomena, 2. Heat Transfer—Incandescent Tungsten, 3. Thermionic Phenomena, 4. Electrical Discharge, 5. Plasma and Oscillations, 6. Structure of Matter, 7. Protein Structures, 8. Properties of Matter, 9. Surface Phenomena, 10. Atmospheric Phenomena, 11. Cloud Nucleation, 12. The Man and the Scientist. Scattered throughout are memorial essays by scientists who knew him, including a book-length biography by Albert Rosenfeld, "The Quintessence of Irving Langmuir" in vol. XII, pt. 1, also published separately (New York–Oxford, 1966). In addition to a complete list of Langmuir's own papers, it contains an extensive bibliography of writings about him. Langmuir was also author of *Phenomena, Atoms and Molecules* (New York, 1950).

II. SECONDARY LITERATURE. Tributes are by Sir Hugh Taylor in *Biographical Memoirs of Fellows of the Royal Society*, **4** (1958), 167–184; A. W. Hull in *Nature*, **181** (1958), 148; W. R. Whitney in *Yearbook. American Philosophical Society* (1957), 129–133; and Katherine B. Blodgett in *Vacuum*, **5** (1957), 1–3.

CHARLES SÜSSKIND

LANGREN, MICHAEL FLORENT VAN (*b.* Mechlin or Antwerp, Belgium, *ca.* 1600; *d.* Brussels, Belgium, early May 1675), *engineering, cartography, selenography*.

Very little is known of Van Langren's life. He was the son of Arnold Florent Van Langren, archducal spherographer. His parents, who were Catholics, had left Holland before 1600 for the Spanish Netherlands and finally settled in Brussels in 1611. Like his father, Michael Florent became a royal cosmographer and mathematician. He married Jeanne de Quantere, by whom he had several children.

The primary goal of Van Langren's research was to discover a method of determining longitude at sea. As early as 1621 he attempted to do this by means of lunar observations, basing his procedure on the darkenings and illuminations of the lunar mountains; this approach obviously required good maps of the moon and a precise toponymy. In 1625, at Dunkirk, he presented his method to the archduchess Isabelle. The following year he requested and received assistance to travel to Spain in order to present his method to the king and to call attention to his books *Tábulas astronómicas y hydrográphicas*, which are now lost. The journey lasted from 1631 to 1634; the king promised to finance the publication of his observations. The *Advertencias de Miguel Florencio Van Langren . . . a todos los professores y amadores de la mathemática . . .* appeared in Madrid about 1634.

Van Langren continued his investigations in Brussels, publishing a *Calendarium perpetuum . . .* in 1636 and *La verdadera longitud por mar y tierra . . .* in 1644. Before 15 February 1645 he submitted to the Privy Council a manuscript map of the moon in support of his request for a privilege to publish it (entitled *Luna vel lumina Austriaca Philippica*; it is preserved in Brussels in the Archives Générales du Royaume, Cartes et Plans MS no. 7911). The map, engraved by Van Langren himself, appeared in May 1645. As is indicated by the title, *Plenilunii/Lumina Austriaca Philippica*, it presents the full moon and, as is stated in Van Langren's long legend, it was to be a part of a series of maps showing thirty phases of the moon. These maps, a veritable selenography, were prepared but were never published, owing to the death of Van Langren's patron, Erycius Puteanus, and to the wars. Van Langren also published a text on the comet of 1652, *Repraesentatio partis caeli quam cometa . . . .*

Van Langren also drew geographical maps, several of which have been lost. They included one of a canal from the Meuse to the Rhine (entitled *Fossa Eugeniana* in the first printings and *Fossa Sanctae Mariae* in the following ones [1628]), one of the archdiocese of Mechlin, one of Luxembourg, and one of the three parts of the former duchy of Brabant; the latter three appeared in the *Novus atlas* of W.J. Blaeu. In addition he provided maps and plans for projects for large public works.

In 1640, in Brussels, Van Langren published

Tormentum bellicum trisphaerium, concerning a three-shot cannon. His studies and projects for a port to be constructed at Mardyck, near Dunkirk, date from 1624; and in 1653 he published, again in Brussels, *Description particulière du . . . Banc de Mardijck . . .*, which ran to two editions. His work on the harbor-port of Ostend is set forth in *Profytelijcken middel om . . . de Zee-Haven van Oostende te verbeteren* (Brussels, 1650), in *Briefve description de la ville et havre d'Oostende . . .* (Brussels, 1659), and in *Copies de la VIe, XIe et XIIIe lettre que . . . don Juan d'Austriche a escrit . . . à Michel-Florencio Van Langren . . .* (1667). In 1661 he wrote a short treatise on the cleaning of the canals of Antwerp: *Bewys van de alder-bequaemste ende profytelyckste inventie . . . .* His works concerning Brussels dealt with fortifications, canals, and means of protecting the city from the flooding of the Senne: *Invention et proposition que Michel Florencio Van Langren . . . a faict . . . pour empescher . . . le debordement de la rivière de Senne . . .* (Brussels, 1644), *Eenighe middelen om . . . Brussel van de inondacien . . . te bevryden* (Brussels, 1648), and *Michael Florencio Van Langren . . . sprekende . . . stadt Brussel . . .* (Brussels, 1658).

Van Langren was in contact with most of the scientists of his time, including Erycius Puteanus, Gottfried Wendelin, the French astronomer Boulliau, Barthélémy Petit, the Jesuit Jean Charles de La Faille, and Huygens. He also knew the writings of Hevelius and Riccioli.

As an engineer, a cartographer, and an engraver, Van Langren occupied a leading place in the Spanish Netherlands. As a selenographer he was, like Hevelius, a pioneer. Circumstances did not permit him to develop his talents fully, and only a thorough study of his work will allow us to arrive at a just appreciation of his achievements.

BIBLIOGRAPHY

Eleven of Van Langren's published works are described in *Bibliotheca belgica*, 1st ser., XIII (Ghent–The Hague, 1880–1890), see index; and in *Bibliotheca belgica*, repub. under the direction of M. T. Lenger, III (Brussels, 1964), 674–677.

Secondary literature includes the following: D. Bierens de Haan, "Constantijn Huygens, als waterbouwkundige, Michael Florentz van Langren, in Bouwstoffen voor de geschiedenis der wis- en natuurkundige wetenschappen in de Nederlanden no. XXXIII," in *Verhandelingen der K. akademie van wetenschappen*, sec. 1, **2**, no. 1 (1893); H. Bosmans, "La carte lunaire de Van Langren conservée aux Archives générales du royaume, à Bruxelles," in *Revue des questions scientifiques*, 3rd ser., **4** (1903), 108–139, with facsimile; "Sur un pamphlet concernant les travaux à effectuer au port d'Ostende, publié en 1660 à Bruxelles," in *Revue des bibliothèques et archives de Belgique*, **1** (1903), 287–291; and "La carte lunaire de Van Langren conservée à l'Université de Leyde," in *Revue des questions scientifiques*, 3rd ser., **17** (1910), 248–264, with facsimile; L. Godeaux, *Esquisse d'une histoire des mathématiques en Belgique* (Brussels, 1943), pp. 19–20; J.-C. Houzeau, "Extrait des notes prises à la Bibliothèque royale, à Paris, en mars 1844," in *Bulletin de l'Académie royale . . . de Belgique. Classe des sciences*, **19**, pt. 3 (1852), 498–507; G. des Marez, "Notice sur les documents relatifs à Michel-Florent Van Langren . . . conservés aux Archives de la ville de Bruxelles," in *Revue des bibliothèques et archives de Belgique*, **1** (1903), 371–378, and **2** (1904), 23–31; W. Prinz, "L'original de la première carte lunaire de Van Langren," in *Ciel et terre*, **24** (1903–1904), 99–105, 149–155, with facsimile; Erycius Puteanus, *Honderd veertien Nederlandse brieven aan de astronoom Michael Florent Van Langren*, with intro. by J. J. Moreau (Antwerp–Amsterdam, 1957); A. Quetelet, *Histoire des sciences mathématiques et physiques chez les Belges*, new ed. (Brussels, 1871), pp. 247–253; A. Tiberghien, "Contribution à la bibliographie de M. F. Van Langren. Documents existant à la Bibliothèque royale de Belgique," in *Revue des bibliothèques et archives de Belgique*, **2** (1904), 1–14; and A. Wauters, "Langren (Michel-Florent Van)," in *Biographie nationale . . . de Belgique*, XI (Brussels, 1890–1891), cols. 276–292.

A. DE SMET

LANKESTER, EDWIN RAY (*b.* London, England, 15 May 1847; *d.* London, 15 August 1929), *zoology, natural history.*

The son of Edwin Lankester, M.D., Lankester was educated at St. Paul's School, London; Downing College, Cambridge; and Christ Church, Oxford. After graduating in zoology and geology, he studied at Vienna, Leipzig, and the Zoological Station at Naples. Elected a fellow of Exeter College, Oxford, in 1872, he was two years later appointed professor of zoology at University College, London, a post which he held until 1891, when he was appointed Linacre professor of comparative anatomy at Oxford. While in London he made the acquaintance of an art student at the Slade School, Edwin Stephen Goodrich, whom he inspired with zeal for comparative anatomy. He took him to Oxford; and, through Goodrich, his most distinguished pupil, he spread his teaching in zoology. In 1884 Lankester was foremost in promoting the foundation of the Marine Biological Association, whose laboratory at Plymouth has played a leading part in the training of British biologists. In 1898 Lankester was appointed director of the British Museum (Natural History), but not being suited to administrative work, he retired when he was knighted in 1907. He was elected fellow of the Royal Society in 1875 and corresponding member of the Paris Academy of Sciences in 1899.

Lankester's original researches extended over all major groups of living and fossil animals, from protozoa to mammals. His first paper, on *Pteraspis*, was published when he was sixteen. He demonstrated the fundamental similarities in structure, and therefore the affinities, between spiders, scorpions, and horseshoe crabs. He systematized the field of embryology and introduced the indispensable terms "stomodaeum," "blastopore," and "invagination." A firm supporter and friend of Charles Darwin and of the latter's theories on evolution and natural selection, he distinguished clearly between homology, homoplasy, and analogy of compared organs. Furthermore, he exposed the illogicality of Lamarck's speculations by showing that every character developed by every organism is a response by it to the conditions of its environment. No character is solely inherited or solely acquired; all are, to varying extents, both. Thus the phrase "inheritance of acquired characters" is meaningless.

The strength of Lankester's character and the forcefulness of his personality may be illustrated by his visit to the laboratory of the French neurologist Jean-Martin Charcot, who was experimenting on the power of electric currents (in wire conductors wound round the arms of the subjects) to reinforce suggestion and annul pain. On the order to make electric contact with a battery of storage cells, darning needles were pushed through the arms of young women, who felt nothing. Lankester arrived just before lunchtime and was allowed to wait for Charcot and his team in the laboratory. He employed his time in emptying the acid from all the storage cells, which he then filled with tap water, so that they gave no current. After lunch the experiments were renewed, contacts made, and needles pushed through the arms of the women, who still felt nothing. Lankester then confessed what he had done and, horrified, the team verified that no current flowed. After an awkward silence, Charcot embraced him.

BIBLIOGRAPHY

Lankester's scientific work was published in the journals of the Royal Society and the Palaeontographical Society, and in the *Quarterly Journal of Microscopical Science* (which he edited and brought to a standard of international repute). He contributed numerous articles to the *Encyclopaedia Britannica*, which were reprinted as *Zoological Articles*. He also edited *Treatise on Zoology* (1900–1909), of which 9 vols. appeared; it did much to help the teaching of zoology in English-speaking countries.

After his retirement, Lankester devoted himself to writing books on science for the lay reader: *Science From an Easy Chair* (1908); *Extinct Animals* (1909); *Diversions of a Naturalist* (1915); *Great and Small Things* (1923), which were a great success in introducing the public to scientific progress.

E. S. Goodrich, "Edwin Ray Lankester," in *Proceedings of the Royal Society* (1930), contains a portrait and a bibliography of his scientific papers.

GAVIN DE BEER

LANSBERGE, PHILIP VAN (*b.* Ghent, Belgium, 25 August 1561; *d.* Middelburg, Netherlands, 8 December 1632), *geometry, astronomy.*

On account of the religious troubles of those days his parents Daniel van Lansberge, lord of Meulebeke, and Pauline van den Honingh found themselves obliged to go to France in 1566 and afterward to England, where Philip studied mathematics and theology. He was already back in Belgium in 1579, where he received a call to be a Protestant minister in Antwerp in 1580. After the conquest of Antwerp by Spain on 16 August 1585, Philip left Belgium definitively to establish himself in the Netherlands. He went to Leiden, where he enrolled as a theological student. From 1586 to 1613 he was a Protestant minister at Goes in Zeeland, after which he went to Middelburg, where he died in 1632.

The Danish mathematician Thomas Finck had published an important work, the *Geometriae rotundi*, in Basel in 1583. It is this work that Van Lansberge seems to have followed very closely in his first mathematical study, *Triangulorum geometriae libri IV* of 1591. The first book is devoted to the definitions of the trigonometric functions. Van Lansberge, following Maurice Bressieu, used the term "radius" instead of "sinus totus." The second book contains the method of constructing the tables of sines, tangents, and secants, largely derived from those of Viète and Finck, and the tables themselves, which were used by Kepler in his calculations. The third book is devoted to the solution of plane triangles and is accompanied by numerical illustrations. Van Lansberge's statement and proof of the sine law differs very little from that given by Regiomontanus. The fourth book deals with spherical trigonometry; the first eleven items concern spherical geometry. In the solution of spherical triangles Van Lansberge employs a device similar to that of Bressieu in his *Metrices astronomicae* (Paris, 1581), the marking of the given parts of a triangle by two strokes. Van Lansberge's new proof for the cosine theorem for sides (Book IV, item 17) marks the first time that the theorem appeared in print for angles as well as sides.

But although Van Lansberge may lay claim to the discovery of the theorem for angles, sufficient evidence indicates that this theorem was known to Viète and to Tycho Brahe. On the whole Van Lansberge shows little originality in the content of his trigonometry, but his arrangement of definitions and propositions is less complicated and more systematic than that of Viète and Clavius.

In 1616 Van Lansberge published his *Cyclometriae novae libri II*, which was attacked the same year by Alexander Anderson in his *Vindiciae Archimedis, sive elenchus cyclometriae novae a Philippo Lansbergio nuper editae*. In this book Van Lansberge occupied himself with approximating the ratio between the circumference (Book I), the area (Book II), and the diameter of the circle. He carried the value of π to 28 decimal places by means of a method in which he seems to have joined the quadratrix of the ancients to trigonometric considerations. He thought that he had found a better approximation than that of Ludolf van Ceulen, who had used the Archimedean method of inscribed and circumscribed polygons and had carried the value of π to thirty-five decimal places in 1615. In his *Progymnasmatum astronomiae restitutae de motu solis* (Middelburg, 1619) Van Lansberge taught the probability of the earth's motion according to the Copernican doctrine; the same is true of *Bedenckingen op den dagelyckschen, ende jaerlyckschen loop van den aerdt-kloot* (Middelburg, 1629), translated into Latin by M. Hortensius as *Commentationes in motum terrae diurnum, et annuum* (Middelburg, 1630). Both works were attacked for their Copernican ideas by Morin in his *Famosi et antiqui problematis de telluris motu vel...* (Paris, 1631), and by Libert Froidmond in his *Anti-Aristarchus; sive orbis-terrae immobilis; liber I* (Antwerp, 1631). Although a follower of Copernicus, Van Lansberge did not accept the planetary theories of Kepler altogether. His *Tabulae motuum coelestium perpetuae* (Middelburg, 1632), founded on an epicyclic theory, were much used among astronomers, although they were very inferior to Kepler's Rudolphine tables.

BIBLIOGRAPHY

I. Original Works. Van Lansberge's works were published as *Philippi Lansbergii Astronomi Celebrium Opera Omnia* (Middelburg, 1663).

II. Secondary Literature. A very good biography is by C. de Waard in *Nieuw Nederlandsch biografisch woordenboek* (Leiden, 1912), cols. 775–782. See also the following (listed chronologically): J. E. Montucla, *Histoire des mathématiques*, II (Paris, 1799), 334; D. Bierens de Haan, "Notice sur quelques quadrateurs du cercle dans les Pays-Bas," in *Bullettino di bibliografia e di storia della scienze matematiche e fisiche*, **7** (1874), 120, 121; A. J. van der Aa, *Biographisch woordenboek der Nederlanden*, XI (Haarlem, 1876), 154–157; D. Bierens de Haan, "Bibliographie néerlandaise," in *Bullettino di bibliografia e di storia della scienze matematiche e fisiche*, **15** (1882), 229–231; A. Von Braunmühl, *Vorlesungen über Geschichte der Trigonometrie*, I (Leipzig, 1900), 175, 176, 192; C. de Waard, "Nog twee brieven van Philips Lansbergen," in *Archief vroegere en latere mededelingen ... in Middelburg* (1915), 93–99; H. Bosmans, "Philippe van Lansberge, de Gand, 1561–1632," in *Mathésis; recueil mathématique*, **42** (1928), 5–10; C. de Waard, ed., *Correspondance du M. Mersenne*, II (Paris, 1937), 36, 511–513; and M. C. Zeller, *The Development of Trigonometry From Regiomontanus to Pitiscus* (Ann Arbor., Mich., 1946), 87, 94–97.

H. L. L. Busard

LAPICQUE, LOUIS (*b.* Épinal, France, 1 August 1866; *d.* Paris, France, 6 December 1952), *physiology, anthropology.*

Lapicque's father, a veterinary surgeon, fostered his son's inclination toward natural sciences. At the Paris Medical School, Lapicque displayed an active interest in physics and chemistry, which in those days was rather unusual in medical circles. He was therefore entrusted by the celebrated clinician Germain Sée to organize a small chemical laboratory in the Hôtel-Dieu Hospital, where he investigated the circulation of iron in vertebrates. The amounts of metal to be measured being very small, he tried colorimetric tests. Such tests, despite their sensitivity, were then in disfavor because of their lack of accuracy. Lapicque succeeded in making the thiocyanate test for ferric iron a very precise tool that remained in general use for several decades. He showed that at birth iron is localized mainly in the liver, while there is none in the spleen. When pathological conditions bring severe destruction of red cells, iron accumulates in spleen and liver tissue in the form of a red pigment constituted essentially of colloidal ferric hydroxide. These results were published in his thesis for the doctorate in science. Lapicque's experimental work was then interrupted. A Mme Lebaudy, the wife of a sugar magnate, wanted her son to take a world cruise on her yacht *Semiramis* with a group of dedicated young scientists who might inspire him. The son failed to embark, but the cruise proceeded as planned. Lapicque proved to be an active anthropologist. In the lands of the Indian Ocean he endeavored to measure the anthropological characteristics of the various groups of Negritos. He devised a very useful index: the radius-pelvic ratio, which allowed him to conclude that in ancient times a single Negro race was distributed from Africa to Oceania.

Lapicque made an extensive study of the relation between brain and body weight, a relation discussed by Eugène Dubois, the discover of *Pithecanthropus erectus*. Lapicque, however, generalized this relation. The "exponent of relation" is the same not only between mammals but also between birds. The results appear most strikingly on logarithmic coordinates. The different animal species, even the fossil ones, are represented on parallel lines, the level of each defined by "the coefficient of cephalization," which represents the degree of nervous organization and, in a striking manner, the presumed intelligence of the species. Lapicque also found a precise relation between brain and eye weight.

Lapicque's essential work, however, was in the general physiology of the nervous system. From 1902 he investigated the time factor in nervous processes. From this study he soon derived a fundamental concept: the functional importance of the time factor of nervous electrical excitability. He made it possible to express excitability precisely in terms of "rheobase," an intensity factor, and of "chronaxie," a time factor. Chronaxie represents the functional rapidity of the tissue under investigation. Slow muscles and nerves are characterized by a long chronaxie and fast muscles and nerves by a short one. Furthermore, chronaxie measurements, for the first time, numerically expressed the effects of many agents: for instance, temperature, drugs, and anesthetics. The chronaxies of motor nerves in man could be obtained, thus permitting the evolution of degenerative or regenerative processes to be followed quantitatively. Chronaxie also reveals the fine details of motor organization.

As early as 1907 the concept of the functional role of the time factor of nervous processes, expressed by chronaxie, led Lapicque to theoretical speculations. He postulated that the activation of a chain of nerve cells depended upon the successive electrical stimulation of each cell by the impulse or action potential of the preceding one. By using an electrical stimulus having a shape similar to that of the nerve action potential, he showed that there is such a stimulus of optimal duration defined by the chronaxie of every tissue investigated. In other words, this is selective excitation realized by a tuning between duration of stimulus and chronaxie. Thus Lapicque proposed a theory of nervous processes that was analogous in its principle to the tuning or resonance between two oscillating radio circuits. The theory indicated that transmission of excitation between two nerve cells was optimal when the cells had the same chronaxie. When the

second cell had a long chronaxie, its excitation required iterative activation of the first. In that case the numerical expressions derived by Lapicque are adequate regardless of whether transmission depends on electrical stimulation or, according to modern findings, depends upon liberation of successive "quanta" of a chemical mediator such as acetylcholine. Lapicque's theory was first met with widespread approval and later encountered strong criticism. Yet even in recent years it has provoked much research. It correlated many unexplained results at a time when nervous processes could be investigated only by the indirect methods of electrical stimulation. When the responses of nerve cells and fibers became directly accessible through modern electronics, several predictions based on Lapicque's theory were confirmed. For instance, in 1913 Lapicque and René Legendre had shown that chronaxie of motor fibers or axons is in inverse ratio to their diameter. Thus the velocity of their impulse was assumed to be proportional to their diameter, which was demonstrated by the cathode-ray oscillographic records obtained by Gasser and Erlanger in 1928.

Lapicque's activity was fruitful in many other areas. In nutritional physiology he added to the notion of isodynamic nutrients, developed by Rubner, a new concept: the margin of thermogenesis. His competence in that domain was amply used during World War I by the authorities responsible for the food supply of France. He was the first to advocate, in exceptional circumstances, the reduction of livestock to save grain that could be used for human consumption. This suggestion met with considerable opposition but was finally supported by the government. In connection with saving grain Lapicque found that certain seaweeds (*Laminaria*), collected in the proper season and correctly prepared, made an excellent oat substitute for the feeding of horses. He also investigated the physiology of marine algae. He discovered that ionic exchanges between the cell medium and the surrounding seawater proceed against an osmotic gradient, through the expenditure of metabolic energy. This process, involving an ionic "pump," he named "epictesis," akin to the modern concept of active transport.

As the field surgeon of an infantry regiment, Lapicque devised an adequate defense against the first attacks by poison gas: a filter of loose earth at the entrance of a trench shelter absorbed the gas. Unfortunately, this simple device was inefficient against the mustard gas later used by the German army. Lapicque always showed an unyielding and active opposition to any form of subjugation. In his late seventies he was jailed by the Gestapo for two months during the severe winter of 1941-1942.

Lapicque was an excellent sailor. Every summer he expertly navigated a twenty-ton yawl named *Axone* in the difficult waters off northern Brittany. The members of his laboratory were often on board, enjoying his teaching, which combined physiology and seamanship. He held prestigious teaching posts: associate professor at the Sorbonne in 1899, professor of general physiology at the Muséum d'Histoire Naturelle in 1911, and at the Sorbonne from 1919 to 1936. Both chairs had been Claude Bernard's. Lapicque's activity was not curtailed by his retirement; he studied many problems, such as the density of nerve cells in the various centers. Until his last days he gladly gave his extensive and diverse scientific experience to his students.

BIBLIOGRAPHY

I. ORIGINAL WORKS. Lapicque's writings include *Observations et expériences sur la mutation du fer chez les vertébrés*, his *thèse de sciences* (Paris, 1897); "Unité fondamentale des races d'hommes à peau noire. Indice radio-pelvien," in *Comptes rendus de l'Académie des sciences*, **143** (1906), 81–84; "Échanges nutritifs des animaux en fonction du poids corporel," ibid., **172** (1921), 1526–1529; "Mécanisme des échanges entre la cellule et le milieu ambiant," ibid., **174** (1922), 1490–1492; *L'excitabilité en fonction du temps; la chronaxie, sa signification et sa mesure* (Paris, 1926); "Le poids du cerveau et l'intelligence," in G. Dumas, *Nouveau traité de psychologie*, I (Paris, 1930), 204; "Le problème du fonctionnement nerveux. Esquisse d'une solution," in G. Dumas, *Nouveau traité de psychologie*, I (Paris, 1930), 147–204; and *La machine nerveuse* (Paris, 1943), part of which was written during his imprisonment by the Germans.

II. SECONDARY LITERATURE. See G. Bourguignon, *La chronaxie chez l'homme* (Paris, 1923); and A. Monnier, *L'excitation électrique des tissus. Essai d'interprétation physique* (Paris, 1934).

A. M. MONNIER

LAPLACE, PIERRE SIMON, MARQUIS DE (*b.* Beaumont-en-Auge, Normandy, France, 28 March 1749; *d.* Paris, France, 5 March 1827), *mathematics, astronomy, physics.*

For a detailed study of his life and work, see Supplement.

LAPPARENT, ALBERT-AUGUSTE COCHON DE (*b.* Bourges, France, 30 December 1839; *d.* Paris, France, 4 May 1908), *geology.*

Lapparent was descended from a noble family of the Vendée. His paternal grandfather, Emmanuel,

was a member of the first graduating class of the École Polytechnique (1794); and his father and uncle Henri were students there. Lapparent was admitted with highest standing to the École Polytechnique in 1858, after compiling a good record at the Lycée Bonaparte. He graduated first in his class and then entered the École des Mines, where he studied under Élie de Beaumont. He graduated in 1864, again first in his class.

Lapparent perfected his German and twice traveled in Germany in order to further his studies (1862, 1863). In 1863, in the town of Predazzo in the Tirol, he was the first to describe and name the rock called monzonite. During a stay in Rome in that same year he was enrolled in the Academy of St. Philip Neri, an institution concerned with religious, social, and economic questions. He became its secretary and excelled in summarizing the sometimes confusing discussions of the speakers. An excellent dancer, Lapparent frequented the Monday gatherings held by the Empress Eugénie in 1864. He became an assistant curator (*conservateur-adjoint*) at the École des Mines and, at the request of Achille Delesse, he agreed to edit the reviews of the memoirs on stratigraphy for the *Revue de géologie*. He carried out this task for fifteen years, aided by his knowledge of foreign languages, and acquired a profound knowledge of geology.

From 1865 to 1875 Lapparent supervised the surveying for six maps (scale of 1:80,000) of the Paris Basin. He established the stratigraphy and tectonics of the anticline of the Bray region, recording his findings on structural maps with contour lines. At Mortain he described faults "en échelons." He attributed the origin of the silt of the plateaus to a hypothetical alluvial process; more recent work, however, has tended to stress instead the role of wind (loess) and percolating water. On the other hand, in the controversy over the benches called "rideaux" in the fields of chalky regions, Lapparent presented arguments against their having had a natural origin and for an artificial one, such as ploughing. Since then aerial photographs and the investigations of M. Brochu and A. Agache have fully justified his views.

At the Paris Universal Exposition in 1867 Lapparent was the reporter for the public lectures on the standardization of weights and measures. Following this exposition the idea of a tunnel under the English Channel between England and France, unsuccessfully advanced as early as 1802, was again taken up and an Anglo-French committee was formed. Lapparent was one of the three French geologists assigned to study the project. A total of 7,671 dredgings were carried out at sea, 3,267 of which furnished samples. The continuity of the cretaceous beds on both sides of the Strait of Dover, the good quality of the sixty-meter-thick Cenomanian chalk, and the absence of faults were all demonstrated. The tunnel was possible. For his efforts he was made a member of the Legion of Honor.

Lapparent married in 1868. The marriage brought him happiness, nine children (six of whom survived), and financial independence.

In 1875 the Catholic University (later the Catholic Institute) was founded in Paris. A confirmed Catholic, Lapparent accepted the chair of geology and mineralogy and began his courses in January 1876. In 1879 he had to choose between a career in the Bureau of Mines, where he could look forward to a brilliant future, and remaining at the Catholic Institute, which had very few resources. He opted for the latter.

All the collections—minerals, rocks, fossils—had to be amassed. Lapparent took this task upon himself, without assistance; he was even obliged to write out the labels. He increased his knowledge of rocks considerably and also acquired a more developed taste for the nonabstract, which complemented very well the training—primarily in mathematics and physics—he had received at the École Polytechnique.

Lapparent's teaching was so successful that he received many offers from publishers, and he devoted the rest of his life to writing, especially textbooks. His *Traité de géologie* (Paris, 1882) was the first of its kind to be so well organized and so clear; it went through five editions, each carefully revised and brought up to date. Lapparent's *Cours de minéralogie* (Paris, 1883–1884; 4th ed. 1908) was based on the ideas, then underestimated, of Bravais and of Mallard. He also wrote *Abrégé de géologie* (Paris, 1886; 6th ed., 1907) and *La géologie en chemin de fer* (Paris, 1888), a geological description of the major railway routes of the Paris Basin. In 1889 he published *Précis de minéralogie*, a sixth edition of which came out in 1965. The *Leçons de géographie physique*, which appeared in 1896, is devoted to geomorphology; it is based on the ideas of W. M. Davis and of the American school, which it contributed to popularizing in France. *Le siècle de fer* is a useful collection of lectures and articles. *Science et apologétique* (1905), in which Lapparent attempts to reconcile science and Christianity, is also a plea in favor of science. In nature Lapparent saw, above all, unity, perfection, harmony, and finality.

Those who heard his course lectures and public addresses praised the liveliness of his demonstrations and his brilliant delivery. The successive editions of his treatises show, besides the qualities already mentioned,

his care in constantly keeping his works up to date, his understanding, his lucidity, his mastery of the criticism of publications and ideas, his concern for precise observation, and his deep desire for order and harmony.

Lapparent received many honors. He was president of the Geological Society of France in 1880 and 1900, of the French Mineralogical Society in 1885, and of many other organizations. A member (1897) and later perpetual secretary (1907) of the Academy of Sciences, he was also a member or corresponding member of numerous other academies. He was awarded an honorary doctorate by Cambridge University.

BIBLIOGRAPHY

I. ORIGINAL WORKS. In addition to the works mentioned above, all of which were published in Paris, Lapparent wrote *La formation des combustibles minéraux* (Paris, 1886); *Le niveau de la mer et ses variations* (Paris, 1886); *Les tremblements de terre* (Paris, 1887); and *Leçons de géographie physique* (3rd ed., Paris, 1907).

II. SECONDARY LITERATURE. A. d'Ales, *Études religieuses* (Paris, 1908), p. 511; C. Barrois, "Albert de Lapparent et sa carrière scientifique," in *Revue des questions scientifiques* (July, 1909); A. Lacroix, "Notice historique sur Albert-Auguste de Lapparent," in *Académie des Sciences* (Paris, 1920), with photo; and E. de Margerie, "Albert de Lapparent," in *Annales de Géographie*, **17**, no. 94, 344–347.

ANDRÉ CAILLEUX

LAPWORTH, ARTHUR (*b.* Galashiels, Scotland, 10 October 1872; *d.* Manchester, England, 5 April 1941), *chemistry*.

Lapworth studied chemistry at Mason Science College (later the university), Birmingham, where his father was professor of geology. In 1893 he went to London as a research student at the City and Guilds College, working on naphthalene chemistry under H. E. Armstrong and collaborating with F. S. Kipping in studies on camphor. He, Kipping, and W. H. Perkin, Jr., became related by marrying three sisters. From 1895 to 1900 Lapworth was a demonstrator at the School of Pharmacy, then head of the chemistry department of Goldsmiths' College. In 1909 he left London for Manchester, where he spent the rest of his life, first as senior lecturer in inorganic and physical chemistry, then (1913) as professor of organic chemistry, finally (1922) occupying the senior chair in the department. He was made a fellow of the Royal Society in 1910. The last years of Lapworth's life, even before his retirement in 1935, were clouded by a long and painful illness. Until then he had been a man of many interests, including music, climbing, and what might broadly be called "natural history." He was a reticent and modest person of nonconformist convictions, remembered by his students as friendly although rather remote.

As may be seen from his appointments, Lapworth's knowledge was unusually wide. Although his name is not associated with any single great achievement, he did steady, meritorious work for nearly forty years. In his early work on camphor, he recognized an intramolecular change, related to the pinacol–pinacolone rearrangement, which made possible acceptance of Bredt's structure for camphor. A little later he began the study of reaction mechanisms, notably of cyanohydrin formation and the benzoin rearrangement, which entitles him to be regarded as one of the founders of modern "physical-organic chemistry." He was one of the first to emphasize that organic compounds could ionize either actually or incipiently and that different parts of an organic molecule behave as though they bear electrical charges, either permanently or at the moment of reaction.

With the development of theories of valence based on the electronic structure of the atom, Lapworth was able to refine some speculations about "alternate polarities" into a classification of reactive centers as "anionoid" and "cationoid," the charges being determined by the influence of a "key atom," usually oxygen. In the mid-1920's, when Lapworth elaborated on these concepts with his colleague Robert Robinson, a controversy ensued with C. K. Ingold and his school, who were developing a similar approach to the problems of organic reactivity using a different terminology ("nucleophilic" and "electrophilic" instead of anionoid and cationoid), which eventually gained general acceptance. The controversy, although occasionally sharp, was fruitful; and Lapworth's last paper (1931) bore Ingold's name as a coauthor.

BIBLIOGRAPHY

Lapworth worked by accumulation of detail rather than by publishing "important" papers, but special mention should be made of the following: "On the Constitution of Camphor," in *British Association Report for 1900*, 299–327, which finally pointed the way out of the labyrinth of camphor chemistry; and his two papers on "alternate polarities" in *Memoirs and Proceedings of the Manchester Literary and Philosophical Society*, **64** (1919–1920), no. 3, 16, and *Journal of the Chemical Society*, **121** (1922), 416–427.

The most authoritative notice of Lapworth is Sir Robert Robinson, in *Obituary Notices of Fellows of the Royal Society of London*, **5** (1945–1948), 555–572; repr. without portrait or bibliography, in *Journal of the Chemical Society* (1947), 989–996. See also G. N. Burkhardt, in *Memoirs and Proceedings of the Manchester Literary and Philosophical Society*, **84** (1939-1941), vi–x; and *Nature*, **147** (1941), 769.

W. V. FARRAR

LAPWORTH, CHARLES (*b.* Faringdon, Berkshire, England, 20 September 1842; *d.* Birmingham, England, 13 March 1920), *geology.*

Lapworth's early life was spent in Berkshire and Oxfordshire. In 1864 he became a schoolmaster in southern Scotland. Although his education and scholastic work were purely literary, he soon developed a genius for geological research, in which he engaged intensively during holidays in the surrounding countryside. In 1881 he was appointed to the newly established chair of geology at Mason College (now Birmingham University) and during the first two years there made long and arduous excursions into the northwest of Scotland. His health broke under the strain, and he never fully regained his strength. During his thirty years at Birmingham he taught, lectured, wrote, and advised with fruitful energy and made important contributions to geological knowledge of the English Midlands. He was awarded a Royal Medal by the Royal Society in 1891 and the Wollaston Medal by the Geological Society (its highest honor) in 1899.

Lapworth's investigations into the geology of the Southern Uplands of Scotland in the first phase of his career were epochal because they revolutionized the interpretation of the structure of that important region. A group of fossils, the graptolites, which he used for dating Lower Paleozoic rocks were the means by which he unraveled complicated regional structures. He combined large-scale geological mapping of critical areas with the exhaustive collection of graptolites from the black shale bands (to which they were confined) and the exact discrimination of species to establish his dating method. In the central area, around Moffat, which he studied first, Lapworth found that the numerous shale-band outcrops, which had been thought to represent separate bands at successive horizons in an enormously thick ascending series of strata, were in reality repetitions of a comparatively few bands that were a series of overfolds in which the limbs had become more or less parallel by compaction (isoclinal folding). He demonstrated that the strata, which could be shown to be middle or upper Ordovician and lower Silurian in age, here formed one condensed series only about 250 feet thick (1878). In the Girvan region to the west, the strata, though found to contain graptolite-bearing shale bands, were of quite different lithological types, containing shelly fossils and trilobites. By correlating these bands with the similar bands at Moffat, Lapworth showed that the Girvan rocks, spanning the same time range, were similarly complicated in structure and some twenty times as thick (1882).

From a study and comparison of his own collection of graptolites with collections made in other parts of the world, he tabulated a series of twenty graptolite zones (1879–1880) which seemed to be generally applicable and finally (1889) gave a comprehensive account of the stratigraphy of the Southern Uplands. These results were amplified and confirmed, respectively, in two major works on British paleontology and geology, the *Monograph* of British graptolites (1901–1918) and the Geological Survey *Memoir* on southern Scotland (1899). Lapworth's work inspired research into the working out of the detailed stratigraphy of other British regions by means of the graptolites, particularly by Nicholson and Marr in the English Lake District (1888), Gertrude Elles and Ethel Wood in the Welsh borderland (1900), and O. T. Jones in central Wales (1909).

Meanwhile, Lapworth had proposed (1879) a major classification of the Lower Paleozoic rocks into three systems: Cambrian, Ordovician (a new system), and Silurian. This proposal was so reasonable and convenient on general geological grounds, and provided so satisfactory a solution to the Sedgwick-Murchison controversy over "Cambrian" and "Silurian," that it was immediately and almost universally accepted.

Lapworth's investigations in the Northwest Highlands of Scotland helped to resolve the controversy that was beginning to rage as to the nature of the junction between the Cambrian-Ordovician and the Moinian, a question which affected the interpretation of the structure and history of the entire Scottish Highlands and possibly of other British regions. In the Northwest Highlands there are four main rock groups: gneiss (Lewisian, Pre-Cambrian, in modern terminology and age assignment), overlain unconformably by red sandstone (Torridonian, Pre-Cambrian), overlain unconformably by Cambrian-Ordovician quartzites and limestones, and schists (Moinian) physically overlying the Cambrian-Ordovician with about the same low dip to the east. It had been assumed by Murchison (1858–1860) that there was a conformable upward passage from the Cambrian-Ordovician into the Moinian, but faulting of various kinds had been suggested by Nicol (1861) and Callaway (1881). Lapworth, after painstaking researches (1883), found that the junction was a thrust and that the present character of the Moinian was undoubtedly produced by metamorphism at some post-Ordovician time. He left open the question of the age and character—and thus the correlation—of

the original rocks that had become metamorphosed to form the Moinian. (It is now thought probable that these rocks were the Torridonian.) His interpretation was entirely confirmed and greatly extended by Peach and Horne of the Geological Survey, under the direction of Archibald Geikie. Lapworth's work in both the Uplands and the Highlands impressed him with the importance of tangential stress in the earth's crust throughout geological time.

In the last phase of his career Lapworth, with Birmingham as a center, and using the same insight that he had shown in his work in Scotland, investigated the surrounding rocks, directing his attention chiefly to the Lower Paleozoic inliers. Certain quartzites and sandstones as well as igneous rocks in these inliers were already strongly suspected of being, respectively, Lower Cambrian and Pre-Cambrian. Lapworth found similar rocks in other inliers and confirmed these ages by discovering unmistakable Lower Cambrian fossils, of which the *Olenellus* type of trilobite in Shropshire was particularly important. He mapped much of the Cambrian rocks in north Wales and the Pre-Cambrian, Cambrian, and Ordovician rocks in Shropshire; but his work on the old rocks of Wales and the Midlands was largely left to be carried on by others. Lapworth also did important work on other aspects of Midland geology: the Coal Measures (particularly concealed coalfields), the origin of Permian and Triassic breccias and conglomerates, glaciation, and river history.

BIBLIOGRAPHY

I. ORIGINAL WORKS. Among Lapworth's more important works are "The Moffat Series," in *Quarterly Journal of the Geological Society of London*, **34** (1878), 240–346; "On the Tripartite Classification of the Lower Palaeozoic Rocks," in *Geological Magazine*, **16** (1879), 1–15; "On the Geological Distribution of the Rhabdophora," in *Annals and Magazine of Natural History*, 5th ser., **3** (1879), 245–257, 449–455, **4** (1879), 331–341, **5** (1880), 45–62, 273–285, 358–369, **6** (1880), 16–29, 185–207; "The Girvan Succession," in *Quarterly Journal of the Geological Society of London*, **38** (1882), 537–666; "The Secret of the Highlands," in *Geological Magazine*, **20** (1883), 120–128, 193–199, 337–344; "On the Close of the Highland Controversy," *ibid.*, **22** (1885), 97–106; "On the Discovery of the *Olenellus* Fauna in the Lower Cambrian Rocks of Britain," *ibid.*, **25** (1888), 484–487; "On the Ballantrae Rocks of the South of Scotland and Their Place in the Upland Sequence," *ibid.*, **26** (1889), 20–24, 59–69; "The Geology of South Shropshire," in *Proceedings of the Geologists' Association*, **13** (1894), 297–355, written with W. W. Watts; "A Sketch of the Geology of the Birmingham District," *ibid.*, **15** (1898), 313–416; and *A Monograph of British Graptolites* (London, 1901–1918), of which he was editor; "The Hidden

Coalfields of the Midlands," in *Transactions of the Institution of Mining and Metallurgy*, **33** (1907), 26–50.

II. Secondary Literature. On Lapworth and his work see (listed chronologically) B. N. Peach and J. Horne, *The Silurian Rocks of Britain, Vol. I, Scotland* (*Memoirs of the Geological Survey of Great Britain*, 1899); Anon., "Eminent Living Geologists: Professor Charles Lapworth," in *Geological Magazine*, **38** (1901), 289–303; B. N. Peach, J. Horne *et al.*, *The Geological Structure of the North-West Highlands of Scotland* (*Memoirs of the Geological Survey of Great Britain*, 1907); W. W. W[atts], obituary notice in *Quarterly Journal of the Geological Society of London*, **77** (1921), lv–lxi; W. W. W[atts] and J. J. H. Teall, obituary notice in *Proceedings of the Royal Society*, **92B** (1921), xxxi–xl; W. W. Watts, "The Author of the Ordovician System: Charles Lapworth," in *Proceedings of the Birmingham Natural History and Philosophical Society*, **14** (1921), special suppl.; a revised version in *Proceedings of the Geologists' Association*, **50** (1939), 235–286; W. S. Boulton *et al.*, "The Work of Charles Lapworth," in *Advancement of Science*, **7** (1951), 433–442; and E. B. Bailey, *Geological Survey of Great Britain* (London, 1952).

John Challinor

LA RAMÉE, PIERRE DE. See **Ramus, Petrus.**

LARGHI, BERNARDINO (*b.* Vercelli, Italy, 27 February 1812; *d.* Vercelli, 2 January 1877), *surgery.*

Larghi was the son of Francesco Larghi and Maria de Giudice. He graduated in surgery from the University of Turin in 1833 and in medicine from the University of Genoa in 1836. Returning to Vercelli, he established a dispensary and a small infirmary in his house and began to practice surgery privately. He was so successful that in 1838 he was asked to operate at the St. Andrea Hospital in Vercelli, first in an honorary capacity and from 1844 as head surgeon.

Larghi is known chiefly for his performance of subperiosteal resection before the introduction of antisepsis. The reasons for Larghi's specific interest in this operation require further research; but it appears that earlier biological experiments on the power of the periosteum to regenerate bone were less influential than the brilliant practical results that he obtained. His surgical technique was marked by the extreme care that he took to respect soft paraosteal parts when separating the periosteum from the bone.

In 1845 Larghi performed a resection of the ribs—or actually, an extraction of their bony part—on a twelve-year-old boy suffering from abscess and central caries of the eighth and ninth ribs on the right side. Costal resection until then involved the total removal of the bone with its periosteal covering; it required

that intercostal muscles, nerves, and vessels be cut and thereby introduced the danger of hemorrhage and pneumothorax from pleural perforation. Larghi considered such resection to be more a "demolition" than a surgical procedure. He maintained that the surgeon should not destroy the ribs but, rather, restore and rebuild them, since he believed that nature "strongly thickens the periosteum and for this purpose exudes a gelatinous humor which, working its way between the periosteum and the deteriorated bony part, separates them; this humor awaits only the expulsion of the deteriorated bony part, so that it can occupy the site more properly and be converted to new bone inside the case that generated it." The surgeon's task must therefore be to complete removal of the necrotic bone and to extract it from the thickened periosteal sheath.

Larghi's subsequent works, published in the *Giornale della R. Accademia medico-chirurgica di Torino*, reveal the progress of his techniques for subperiosteal resection and the improvement of his surgical instruments. In May 1852 he extracted the necrotic right hemimandible of a patient, removing the condyle but leaving the articular capsule—as well as the periosteum—in position. The neoarthrosis that formed between the neocondyle of the regenerated mandible and the glenoid cavity suggested to Larghi that other soft parts might be preserved, as shown in his most noted work, *Operazioni sottoperiostee e sottocassulari . . .* (Turin, 1855). After the introduction of antisepsis, subperiosteal resection developed substantially, especially through the work of L. Ollier.

BIBLIOGRAPHY

I. Original Works. Larghi's main works are related to bone surgery and include "Estirpazione o rescissione delle ossa convertita nell'estrazione della loro parte ossea rigenerata dal periostio conservato," in *Giornale delle scienze mediche pubblicato dalla R. Accademia Medico-Chirurgica di Torino*, **28** (1847), 512–520; "Rescissione delle costole convertita nell'estrazione della loro parte ossea," *ibid.*, 521–529; "De l'extraction sous-périostée et de la réproduction des os; extraction sous-périostée des côtes en particulier," in *Gazette médicale de Paris*, **12** (1847), 434–437; "Taglio perpendicolare-longitudinale per le amputazioni delle membre umane," in *Giornale dell Accademia di medicina di Torino*, **5** (1849), 385–398; and "Estrazione e disarticolazione sottoperiostea della porzione destra della mascella inferiore affetta da necrosi," *ibid.*, **17** (1853), 49–62; and "Operazioni sottoperiostee e sottocassulari e guarigione delle malattie delle ossa ed articolazioni per il nitrato d'argento," *ibid.*, **24** (1855), 19–81, 131–169, 302–345, 410–461; **26** (1856), 350–378, 500–506; **27** (1856), 98–130; **31** (1858), 422–428, 467–482; **32** (1858), 225–248;

"Estrazione sotto-cassulo-periostea radio-carpea," *ibid.*, **31** (1858), 299–302; and "Supplemento alle operazioni sotto-periostee e sotto-cassulari," *ibid.*, **7** (1869), 242–356, 373–390, 463–475, 515–523; **8** (1869), 37–62.

II. Secondary Literature. On Larghi's life, see Luigi Belloni, "Dalla osteogenesi periostale alla resezione sotto-periostale, Michele Troja (1775) e Bernardino Larghi (1847)," in *Simposi clinici*, **8** (1971), xxv–xxxii; Enrico Bottini, "Bernardino Larghi. Cenno necrologico," in *Giornale della R. Accademia di medicina di Torino*, 21 d.s. III (1877), 174–185; Carlo Dionisotti, *Notizie biografiche dei Vercellesi illustri* (Biella, 1862), 188–190; and Gabriele Stringa, "Bernardino Larghi," in *Archivio 'Putti' di chirurgia degli organi di movimento*, **5** (1954), 592–599.

Luigi Belloni

LA RIVE, ARTHUR-AUGUSTE DE (*b*. Geneva [then French], 9 October 1801; *d*. Marseilles, France, 27 November 1873), *physics*.

Arthur-Auguste de La Rive was the oldest son of Charles-Gaspard de La Rive and Marguerite-Adelaïde Boissier. In 1826 he married Jeanne-Mathilde Duppa, with whom he had two sons and three daughters. In 1855, five years after his first wife had died, he married the widow of his former colleague George Maurice.

Auguste received his elementary education at home and at the Collège Publique de Genève, passing thence to the Académie de Genève, where his father was an influential professor; from 1816 to 1823 he studied successively letters, philosophy, and law. Although his own interests were primarily scientific, he was still a student of law when, upon the retirement of P. Prevost in November 1822, the chair of physics at the Academy became vacant. Despite the fact that de La Rive had so far published only one minor paper, his father's influence secured him the appointment of professor of general physics on 27 October 1823 at the unusually young age of twenty-two. On 11 November 1823 he was elected to the influential post of secretary of the Sénat Académique, a post he held until 2 August 1836, although as of 4 March 1834 he had technically been secretary of the newly created Corps Académique; in both cases he was known informally simply as secretary of the Academy. When M. Pictet died, his chair was given to de La Rive, who on 1 June 1825 thereby became professor of experimental physics. This change gave him control, as director, of the Academy's physics laboratory, purchased the year before for 40,000 florins.

De La Rive was long a major force, both institutionally and personally, in the affairs of both the Academy and the government, which in oligarchic Geneva were closely connected. In fact it is as a leader of the Swiss scientific community rather than for his own work, which was devoted primarily to the chemical pile, that he is important. From 1832 to 1846 he sat on the Conseil Représentatif, where, as principal author and battle leader, he was instrumental in putting through the educational reforms of 27 January 1834 and 29 May 1835, which created a Conseil d'Instruction Publique to oversee all public education (in the process effectively eliminating the Church as an educational force) and which consolidated the control of the Corps Académique over the Academy. The so-called triumvirate of Auguste de La Rive, David Munier, and Abraham Pascalis effectively ran the Academy during the 1830's and 1840's. When Augustin-Pyramus de Candolle retired in 1835, Auguste became the Academy's chief spokesman. In addition, he was a leader of the antifederalist conservative faction in the Conseil Représentatif, where, especially after the Revolution of 22 November 1841, he found himself forced into an increasingly reactionary position. Similarly, since the late 1830's the Academy had been under severe attack as a reactionary oligarchy, and de La Rive was the opposition's prime target. He retired completely from academic and public life in December 1846, after the political changes in the wake of the Sonderbund Revolution brought into power a liberal government he had bitterly opposed.

He had been rector of the Academy twice, from 1837 to 1840 and from 1843 to 1844. A member since 1822, he was also twice president of the Société de Physique et d'Histoire Naturelle de Genève, in 1845 and 1865. The Paris Académie des Sciences named him one of its eight foreign associates on 11 July 1864; he had been a corresponding member since 6 December 1830.

For a dozen years after the start of his scientific career, de La Rive's favored journal of publication was the Sciences et Arts series of *Bibliothèque universelle des sciences, belles-lettres et arts*, except for his very longest papers, which appeared in *Mémoires de la Société de physique et d'histoire naturelle de Genève*. In 1836 he took over editorship of the former journal and abolished its separate series; the new *Bibliothèque universelle de Genève* was intended for a well-educated but general readership and avoided specialized or technical scientific papers. However, he soon desired a more strictly scientific journal in which to defend his chemical theory of the pile, and from 1841 to 1845 published *Archives de l'électricité. Supplément à la Bibliothèque universelle de Genève*. Finally, in 1846 the literary portion of the *Bibliothèque universelle* was given over to an editorial committee, and de La Rive limited himself to coediting the scientific portion, now published as *Archives des sciences physiques et naturelles. Supplément à la Bibliothèque universelle de Genève*, which enjoyed his collaboration until his death in 1873.

De La Rive made his scientific reputation and consolidated his power in the Academy roughly in the decade before 1835; for an equal length of time thereafter he was the most important figure in the Genevan scientific community, at least as regards local influence and contemporary fame. During this time he was the most powerful personage in the Academy, the editor of Geneva's leading scientific and cultural journal, and a leader of the conservative party in government. He was known as the friend of Ampère, Arago, and especially Faraday, with whom he maintained an extensive correspondence, and as the most dogged defender of the purely chemical theory of the pile.

It was as a critic of Volta's contact theory of the pile, which attributed the production of electricity in the pile to an electromotive force arising from the contact of heterogeneous substances, that de La Rive made his European reputation. He was a scientist of one tenaciously held but imprecisely conceived theory and in this long dispute made no significant original contributions. Neither his experiments, in which his lack of sense for the importance of quantitative measurements contributed to his poor control over his experimental variables, nor his arguments, which tended to be *ad hoc*, were cogent. He placed more weight on supposedly decisive experiments than on theoretical or philosophical considerations, and there is no evidence that, independently of Faraday, he thought to criticize the unreasonableness of the contact force from considerations of causality.

De La Rive's work must be understood in relation to two of Ampère's ideas that decisively shaped his thinking. The first was the absolute distinction between dynamic, or current, and static, or tension, electricity. Hence while a current flowed there could be no tension, and the contact theorists' electromotive force was fundamentally rejected. De La Rive went further than was required by this dichotomy and asserted the nonexistence of the electromotive force in the open pile, where no current flowed but where an electrostatic tension could be measured. (Becquerel and Stefano Marianini, two of his leading critics, defended a modified chemical theory that recognized the existence of an electromotive force but emphasized the necessity of chemical action for the continued production of electricity.) Second, after Ampère, de La Rive pictured the electric current as a series of

decompositions and recompositions of a neutral fluid, the same aether whose greater or lesser vibrations were light and heat and whose positive and negative components were imagined to be variously associated with different chemical elements. These views, which held out the prospect of a unified explanation of electricity, heat, light, and chemical action, determined not only his theory of the pile but also his later work on the vibrations of bodies produced during the passage of electricity and on the light produced by electric arcs, which led to his electric theory of the aurora. In the development of these interconnections his work was largely derivative from that of Félix Savary and, especially, Becquerel, themselves also protégés of Ampère.

The contact theory regarded as its strongest proof experiments which showed that a sensitive electroscope could detect an electric tension between heterogeneous metals held in contact, even when all chemical activity was excluded. De La Rive quite gratuitously explained away these experiments by asserting that carelessness in the thoroughness with which air or water had been excluded had in every case permitted a chemical reaction to take place. The contact theory also made much of the nonproportionality between the apparent chemical activity in the pile and the electricity produced—a problem that bedeviled the chemical theory until Faraday's laws of electrochemical equivalence explained the precise relation between chemical activity and electricity. As a partial solution to this problem de La Rive argued the existence of "countercurrents" within the pile. That is, he allowed that greater chemical activity was accompanied by greater separation of the electric fluids but maintained that the increased conductivity of the more vigorously reacting liquid facilitated their immediate recombination within the pile, with the result that only a fraction of the originally produced electricity passed through the external circuit. In accordance with these views, his solution to the problem of which arrangement of plates and connecting wires produced the greatest current was to require that the resistance of the pile to the recomposition of the separated electricities be "just greater" than the resistance of the external circuit. De La Rive's theory could not explain the increase in tension with an increasing number of couples connected in series. Despite objections to his work—especially by C. H. Pfaff, an ardent contact theorist—he introduced only one significant modification into his theory in that he conceded, following Becquerel, that electricity could be produced not only by chemical means but also by mechanical and thermal actions, although he consistently played down the importance of all but the first.

BIBLIOGRAPHY

I. ORIGINAL WORKS. The most complete bibliography is J. Soret, "Auguste de La Rive. Notice biographique," in *Archives des sciences physiques et naturelles. Supplément à la Bibliothèque universelle et revue suisse*, n.s. **60** (1877), 5–253; the bibliography (pp. 203–222) lists most of his non-scientific publications as well. For his scientific papers, see Royal Society, *Catalogue of Scientific Papers*, II, 212–217; VI, 636; VII, 507–509; and IX, 667. Less extensive but useful is Poggendorff, II, cols. 657–659; and III, 1126. De La Rive's major work was a series of three papers, "Recherches sur la cause de l'électricité voltaïque," in *Mémoires de la Société de physique et d'histoire naturelle de Genève*, **4**, pt. 3 (1828), 285–334; **6**, pt. 1 (1833), 149–208; and **7**, pt. 2 (1836), 457–517; also published separately (Geneva, 1836). The first paper was originally published in slightly different form in *Annales de chimie et de physique*, 2nd ser., **39** (1828), 297–324. Very useful is his "Esquisse historique des principales découvertes faites dans l'électricité depuis quelques années," in *Bibliothèque universelle des sciences, belles-lettres et arts*. Sciences et arts, **52** (1833), 225–264, 404–447; **53** (1833), 70–125, 170–227, 315–352; also published separately (Geneva, 1833). Apart from such separately published memoirs, de La Rive's only book was *Traité d'électricité théorique et appliquée*, 3 vols. (Paris, 1854–1858), translated into English by C. V. Walker as *A Treatise on Electricity, in Theory and Practice*, 3 vols. (London, 1853–1858). The Bibliothèque Publique et Universitaire de Genève preserves six and a half vols. of letters addressed to Auguste, plus a few other items.

II. SECONDARY LITERATURE. The major biography, which also treats his scientific work, is by Soret, cited above, although it is unfortunately often vague with regard to names and dates. Also very useful is Jean-Baptiste-André Dumas, "Éloge historique d'Arthur-Auguste de La Rive," in *Mémoires de l'Académie des sciences de l'Institut de France*, **40** (1876), ix–lix; also published separately (Paris, 1874) and translated into English as "Eulogy on Arthur Auguste de La Rive," in *Smithsonian Annual Report for 1874*, 184–205. See also H. Deonna, "De la Rive," in *Dictionnaire historique et biographique de la Suisse*, II, 648. A great deal of information on his connections with the Academy can be found in Charles Borgeaud, *Histoire de l'Université de Genève*, II, *L'Académie et l'Université du XIXᵉ siècle, 1814–1900* (Geneva, 1934), *passim*. For a detailed examination and estimation of his scientific work, see W. Ostwald, *Elektrochemie. Ihre Geschichte und Lehre* (Leipzig, 1896), *passim*, but especially ch. 12, "Der Kampf zwischen der Theorie der Berührungselektricität und der chemischen Theorie der galvanischen Erscheinungen," pp. 426–492.

KENNETH L. CANEVA

LA RIVE, CHARLES-GASPARD DE (*b.* Geneva, 14 March 1770; *d.* Geneva, Swiss Confederation, 18 March 1834), *physics, chemistry, medicine.*

Nobile Charles-Gaspard de La Rive was the second son of Ami-Jean de La Rive and Jeanne-Elisabeth Sellon. A landowning noble family, the de La Rives had for centuries been prominent members of Geneva's Protestant patriciate. After receiving his primary education at the Collège de Genève, Gaspard entered the Académie de Genève in May 1789 to study law. Although he had studied some natural science, he was still a student of law in August 1794 when the first Genevan Tribunal Révolutionnaire sentenced him to a year's house arrest. However, the relaxation of the Terror after 9 Thermidor freed him to emigrate, whereupon he went to Edinburgh to study medicine. He received his doctorate in 1797 with the publication of his thesis, *Tentamen physiologicum de calore animali*, an unoriginal critique especially of Adair Crawford, in which de La Rive followed his teacher John Allen in attributing animal heat to the combustion in the blood of particles derived from food and oxygen absorbed through the lungs.

De La Rive returned to Geneva late in 1799 and shortly thereafter (probably in 1800) married the well-born Marguerite-Adelaïde Boissier, with whom he had two sons. He soon took charge of the Hospice des Aliénés, where he devoted some thirty years to improving the treatment of the insane. In November 1802 he was named honorary professor (without pay) of pharmaceutical chemistry at the Academy, filling one of the ten new honorary chairs created through the reform efforts of M. Pictet, who wanted a strong faculty of sciences within the Academy. In 1819, as Alexandre Marcet took over instruction in pharmaceutical chemistry, his title became that of honorary professor of general chemistry. He frequently gave series of lectures at the Academy and at the Musée Académique on medicine and, especially after 1818, on experimental chemistry. His well-equipped laboratory was outfitted at his own expense; its doors were always open to visiting scientific dignitaries such as Davy, Arago, and Ampère; and indeed his generosity and personal interest contributed significantly to his contemporary reputation.

On 13 December 1813 he participated in the creation of the reactionary Conseil Provisoire (renamed Conseil d'État in 1814) and remained an active member of the government as *conseiller d'état* until his resignation on 19 June 1818. He was elected *premier syndic* in 1817. On 4 November 1818 the Conseil d'État created an extraordinary seat for him on the Sénat Académique, where he used his considerable influence in support of reforms aimed at freeing the Academy from ecclesiastical control and in strengthening its faculty of science. He authored the *règlement* of 11 November 1818 providing for the conferring of academic degrees by the faculties of science and of letters. Later, during his term as rector of the Academy (November 1823–March 1826), he was the major force behind efforts to transform the Academy into a university and to secure for it the beginnings of state financial support. Most important were the two regulations of 28 November 1825, which consolidated the control of the individual faculties over their own affairs and provided for specialized instruction in the sciences and in letters. He was prominent in the founding and initial funding of the Jardin Botanique in 1817 and of the Société de Lecture in 1818, the latter organized at the urging of A.-P. de Candolle to supplement Geneva's meager libraries.

De La Rive's actual scientific contributions were negligible, both intrinsically and historically. Excepting his work on electricity, his sixteen publications between 1797 and 1833 were predominantly reviews, translations, extracts, and commentaries, with an occasional paper on a minor chemical or medical topic. Perhaps most valuable were his expositions, among the first on the Continent, of Davy's electrochemistry, Dalton's atomic theory, and Berzelius' theory of definite proportions. His work appeared in *Bibliothèque britannique*, Geneva's foremost scientific and literary journal, and in its successor, *Bibliothèque universelle*, both of which enjoyed his editorial collaboration.

De La Rive enjoyed modest contemporary renown as a critical defender of Ampère. He conceived a simple device—his "*flotteur électrique*"—which he believed exhibited the reasonableness of Ampère's theory of magnetism. It consisted of a strip each of copper and zinc, passed through a cork and fastened together at the top to form a ring; when floated on acidulated water near a magnet, the device demonstrated the action of the magnet on a simple current loop. De La Rive believed that certain experiments he performed with it led Ampère to modify his theory—by assuming that the molecular currents in a magnet were progressively more inclined the farther from the axis and the center of the magnet. There is no evidence, however, that the final version of Ampère's theory owed anything to de La Rive's criticisms.[1]

Ampère had shown that a rectangular current loop free to rotate about a vertical axis lying within the plane of the loop would assume a position perpendicular to the magnetic meridian, such that the direction of current in the lower portion of the rectangle was from east to west. Ampère initially attributed this effect to the interaction between east-west currents in the surface of the earth and those in the lower portion of his loop in accordance with his law for the attraction between like-directed currents. De La Rive varied this

experiment by eliminating the lower horizontal segment. In terms of Ampère's earlier deficient explanation, he then expected that the action of the terrestrial currents—if, indeed, such exist—on the remaining upper horizontal portion would rotate the loop 180°; this effect, however, did not occur. The resolution of the difficulty lay in the analysis of the action, on the vertical sides of the loop, of the terrestrial currents—which Ampère now thought had to be located predominantly along the magnetic equator—and in a reconsideration of their action on the horizontal portions. It seems that Ampère had already recognized the deficiency of his original explanation, although de La Rive's criticism spurred him to develop this aspect of his theory in print before he otherwise would have done. De La Rive's experiment was carried somewhat further by his son Auguste, who owed his scientific debut to this controversy.[2]

NOTES

1. The confusion surrounding Gaspard's claims and Ampère's explanations is far out of proportion to the importance of the case. Be that as it may, the relevant sources are Gaspard de La Rive, "Notice sur quelques expériences électro-magnétiques," in *Bibliothèque universelle des sciences, belles-lettres et arts*. Sciences et arts, **16** (1821), 201–203; and "Mémoire sur quelques nouvelles expériences électro-magnétiques et en particulier sur celles de Mr. Faraday," *ibid.*, **18** (1821), 269–286. See also four letters of Ampère's—to S. S. van der Eyk, 12 Apr. 1822; to G. de La Rive, 12 June 1822; to F. Maurice, 6 July 1822; and to Faraday, 10 July 1822—published in *Correspondance du grand Ampère*, L. de Launay, ed., 3 vols. (Paris, 1936–1943), II, 579, 580–582; III, 927; and II, 588, respectively. The letter to de La Rive was originally published as "Extrait d'une lettre de Mr. Ampère au Prof. de La Rive sur des expériences électro-magnétiques," in *Bibliothèque universelle . . .*, **20** (1822), 185–192.

2. The relevant sources are Gaspard de La Rive, "Lettre du Professeur de La Rive à M. Arago (datée le 22 juin 1822), sur des courans galvaniques," in *Annales de chimie et de physique*, 2nd ser., **20** (1822), 269–275; a letter from Ampère to M. Pictet, dated 10 July 1822, published in the former's *Correspondance*, II, 583–585; Auguste de La Rive, "De l'action qu'exerce le globe terrestre sur une portion mobile du circuit voltaïque. (Mémoire lu à la Société de physique et d'histoire naturelle de Genève le 4 septembre 1822)," in *Bibliothèque universelle . . .*, **21** (1822), 29–48 (a footnote to the title adds that "Mr. Ampère, alors à Genève, assistoit à cette séance"). Pp. 29–42 are the memoir proper; pp. 42–47 are Auguste's version of Ampère's verbal explanation of the new experiments; pp. 47–48 describe two other experiments the two did together at Geneva. The version published in *Annales de chimie et de physique*, 2nd ser., **21** (1822), 24–48 ("Mémoire sur l'action qu'exerce . . ."), is the same except that the middle segment (pp. 39–46) has been modified slightly by Ampère; in addition, there follows a note by Ampère on two other new experiments (pp. 48–53).

   On the respective contributions of the two de La Rives, see also Gaspard's letter of 16 Sept. 1822 to Berzelius, in *Jac. Berzelius Bref*, H. G. Söderbaum, ed., 14 vols. in 6 (Uppsala, 1912–1932), VII (= *Strödda Bref (1809–1847)*, III, pt. 2), 60–61; and letters by Ampère to C. J. Bredin, [24] Sept. 1822, and to A. de La Rive, 11–31 Oct. 1822, in his *Correspondance*, II, 509 and 603–604, respectively.

BIBLIOGRAPHY

I. Original Works. Nearly complete bibliographies of Gaspard's scientific works are in Royal Society *Catalogue of Scientific Papers*, II, 217; Poggendorff, II, col. 657; and G. de Fère, "Charles-Gaspard de La Rive," in *Nouvelle biographie générale depuis les temps les plus reculés jusqu'à nos jours*, 46 vols. (Paris, 1853–1866), XXIX, cols. 603–606 (the bibliography, which follows a biography, is extensive but contains many errors). The Bibliothèque Publique et Universitaire de Genève preserves three vols. of MSS containing letters by and to Gaspard and a journal kept during the years 1794 to 1799.

II. Secondary Literature. The most important source is the anonymous "Notice biographique sur M. le prof. G. De La Rive," in *Bibliothèque universelle des sciences, belles-lettres et arts*. Sciences et arts, **55** (1834), 303–338, possibly written by A. Gautier, whose often identically worded obituary notice on Gaspard appeared in *Mémoires de la Société de physique et d'histoire naturelle de Genève*, **10** (1834), xii–xiv. In addition to the biography by de Fère cited above, mention should also be made of A. Maury, "Charles-Gaspard de Larive," in *Biographie universelle (Michaud) ancienne et moderne*, new ed. (Paris, n.d.), XXIII, 264–265. A wealth of information of Gaspard's activities at the Academy is in C. Borgeaud, *Histoire de l'Université de Genève*, II, "L'Académie de Calvin dans l'Université de Napoléon, 1798–1814," and III, "L'Académie et l'Université au XIXe siècle, 1814–1900" (Geneva, 1909–1934), *passim*.

Kenneth L. Caneva

LARMOR, JOSEPH (*b.* Magheragall, County Antrim, Ireland, 11 July 1857; *d.* Holywood, County Down, Ireland, 19 May 1942), *theoretical physics*.

Larmor was the eldest son in a large family. His father gave up farming to become a grocer in Belfast in 1863 or 1864. A shy, delicate, precocious boy, Larmor attended the Royal Belfast Academical Institution; received the B.A. and the M.A. from Queen's University, Belfast; and entered St. John's College, Cambridge, in 1877. In 1880 he was senior wrangler in the mathematical tripos (J. J. Thomson was second), was awarded a Smith's Prize, and was elected fellow of St. John's. For the next five years Larmor was professor of natural philosophy at Queen's College, Galway, then returned as a lecturer to St. John's in 1885. He succeeded Stokes as Lucasian professor in 1903 and retired from the position in 1932. His health deteriorating, he returned to Ireland to spend his final years. He never married.

Larmor became a fellow of the Royal Society in 1892 and served as a secretary from 1901 to 1912. From 1887 to 1912 he served on the council of the London Mathematical Society; he was president of this society in 1914–1915, having been at times vice-president and treasurer. The Royal Society awarded him its Royal Medal in 1915 and its Copley Medal in 1921, and he received the De Morgan Medal of the London Mathematical Society in 1914. Larmor was also awarded many honorary degrees and became a member of various foreign scientific societies. He was knighted in 1909. He represented Cambridge University in Parliament from 1911 to 1922. In his maiden speech in 1912 he defended the unionist position in the debate on Irish home rule. His major concern then and later was for education and the universities. Those who knew him report that Larmor was an unassuming, diffident man who did not readily form close friendships and whose numerous acts of generosity were performed without publicity. In the words of D'Arcy Thompson, "Larmor made few friends, perhaps; but while he lived, and they lived, he lost none."

Larmor's lectures and writings were often obscure, in that he would sketch the broad outlines of his thought without filling in the mathematical details, but this thought was stimulating and creative. He was concerned to stress the physical and geometrical characteristics of a problem rather than the analytical niceties. Of interest in this connection is his "Address on the Geometrical Method," delivered in 1896. In dynamics Larmor was a champion of the principle of least action. An early paper (1884) showed the analogies between diverse physical problems that it can bring to light. The use of the method of least action enables the compression of the basic assumptions involved in constructing a theory into a single function, from which results may be deduced with some guarantee of consistency and completeness. Larmor employed this method in his fundamental works, particularly in electron theory.

Larmor's scientific work centered on electromagnetic theory, optics, analytical mechanics, and geodynamics. As one of the great completers of the edifice of classical mathematical physics he bears comparison with H. A. Lorentz. Like Lorentz, his major work concerned electron theory, that is, the interaction of atomically charged matter and the electromagnetic field. Unlike Lorentz, Larmor did not participate to a large extent as a guide to the newer generation of physicists developing quantum theory and relativity. In general, he maintained a conservative, critical attitude toward the new ideas, particularly examining the possible limitations of the relativity theories.

Larmor's electron theory was a new fusion of electromagnetic and optical concepts. His first paper on electromagnetism, written in 1883, dealt with electromagnetic induction in conducting sheets and solids. In this work he encountered the problem of the effect of the motion of matter through the ether, the central problem leading to relativity and the key concern of his famous book, *Aether and Matter*. Larmor reported on the action of magnetism on light to the British Association for the Advancement of Science in 1893. In this report he discussed the dynamical theory of wave optics which the Irish physicist James MacCullagh had perfected in the 1830's. MacCullagh's treatment had avoided the flaws of other more or less contemporary theories, but MacCullagh had been unable to supplement his mathematical work with a specific mechanical model of the luminiferous ether. His expression for the action function of the ether corresponded to a medium possessing rotational elasticity, however, so that any element of it would resist rotation but otherwise would behave like a liquid. Kelvin's gyrostatic model of the ether, which had been the subject of an article by Larmor, removed the major objection to MacCullagh's theory on grounds of physical unrealizability. Furthermore, in 1880 G. F. FitzGerald had translated MacCullagh's analysis of optical reflection into the language of electromagnetic theory.

Inspired particularly by this last work, Larmor presented his electron theory in three important papers entitled "A Dynamical Theory of the Electric and Luminiferous Medium" in 1894, 1896, and 1898. He combined MacCullagh's type of ether with the electromagnetic field theory by identifying the magnetic force with the rate of displacement of the ethereal medium, and the electric displacement with the absolute rotation of the medium (the curl of the displacement of the ether). At first the permanent Amperian electric currents of material atoms were treated as vortex rings in the ether, thereby introducing Kelvin's vortex theory of the atom, while electric charge was not included integrally in the theory. Two months after the first article in the series was written, however, Larmor added a section incorporating "electrons" into the theory as mobile centers of rotational strain in the ether. In the MacCullagh type of ether such centers of strain would be permanent, possess inertia, and act upon one another as charged particles do.

The second article in the series (written in 1895) developed the theory of electrons foreshadowed in the addendum to the first. The only interaction between the ether and ordinary matter was assumed to be via the discrete electrons (of both signs of charge), and Larmor discussed the relation between a microscopic theory treating the dynamics of the electron and a macroscopic theory in which the current and other variables are treated as statistical averages. The influence of the motion of the matter through the ether on light propagation and the null result of the Michelson-Morley experiment were treated in a fashion similar to that of Lorentz in the same year. A standard of time varying from point to point was introduced, and it was shown that the FitzGerald-Lorentz contraction would arise out of the theory of the equilibrium of charges in a moving ether. Part 3 (written in 1897) dealt further with the effects involving material media, including motion through the ether, optical dispersion, and particularly electrical stresses. Much of this work was incorporated in *Aether and Matter* (published in 1900), which won the Adams Prize at Cambridge in 1898. This book concentrated mainly on the problem of motion of matter through the ether; here we find, perhaps for the first time, the full Lorentz transformations for space and time and for the electromagnetic field *in vacuo*.

Aside from his general version of the electron theory, constructed from a rotationally elastic ether, Larmor is noted for two specific contributions to electrodynamics. He introduced the Larmor precession, which orbiting charges undergo when subjected to a magnetic field, in 1897 in connection with a discussion of the Zeeman effect. In the same article he treated the radiation of an accelerating charge, obtaining the well-known nonrelativistic formula expressing the power radiated as proportional to the square of the product of charge and acceleration.

Larmor was interested in the dynamics of the earth's motion from 1896, when he published a work on the earth's free precession. In 1906 and 1915, with E. H. Hills, he analyzed possible causes of the irregular motion of the earth's axis; among his other articles one concerns irregularities in the earth's rotation and the definition of astronomical time (1915). Among the 104 articles included in Larmor's *Papers* is "Why Wireless Electric Rays Can Bend Round the Earth" (1924), which was of importance for radio communications. He edited several collections of scientific papers besides his own; and he contributed valuable biographical notices of scientists, particularly one of Kelvin (1908). Strongly interested in the history of his subject, he included in his longer papers and as appendixes to his *Papers* very interesting critical summaries of the work that preceded and led to his own research. His own work owed much to "that Scoto-Irish school of physics which dominated the world in the middle of the last century," particularly to W. R. Hamilton, J. MacCullagh, J. C. Maxwell, Kelvin, and G. FitzGerald; and there is little doubt that he considered himself the last follower of this tradition.

BIBLIOGRAPHY

I. ORIGINAL WORKS. Most of Larmor's papers were published in his *Mathematical and Physical Papers*, 2 vols. (Cambridge, 1929). Not included are his later papers on relativity, which are listed in vol. II, and most of his biographical notices. His biography of Kelvin appears in *Proceedings of the Royal Society*, **81A** (1908), i–lxxvi. *Aether and Matter* (Cambridge, 1900) was published separately.

II. SECONDARY LITERATURE. Obituary notices are by E. Cunningham, in *Dictionary of National Biography (1941–1950)*, pp. 480–483; A. S. Eddington, *Obituary Notices of Fellows of the Royal Society of London*, **4** (1942–1943), 197–207; W. B. Morton, in *Proceedings and Report of the Belfast Natural History and Philosophical Society*, 2nd ser., **2**, pt. 3 (1942–1943), 82–90; and D'Arcy W. Thompson, in *Yearbook of the Royal Society of Edinburgh*, **2** (1941–1942), 11–13.

A. E. WOODRUFF

LA ROCHE, ESTIENNE DE (*fl.* Lyons, France, *ca.* 1520), *arithmetic*.

La Roche, known as Villefranche, was born in Lyons. A pupil of Nicolas Chuquet, he taught arithmetic for twenty-five years in the commercial center of his native town and was called "master of ciphers."

La Roche's *Larismetique*, published at Lyons in 1520, was long considered the work of an excellent writer who, early in the sixteenth century, introduced into France the Italian knowledge of arithmetic and useful notations for powers and roots. His fame decreased remarkably in 1880, when Aristide Marre published Chuquet's "Triparty," written in 1484 but preserved only in manuscript. The first part of *Larismetique* was then seen to be mostly a copy of the earlier work, with the omission of those striking features that established Chuquet as an algebraist of the first rank. Chuquet, for example, employed a more advanced notation for powers and he introduced zero as an exponent. It is not clear why La Roche failed to publish the "Triparty." He may have suppressed it in order to claim the credit for himself, or perhaps he thought it too far beyond the comprehension of prospective readers. Nevertheless, through *Larismetique* some of Chuquet's innovations influenced such French arithmeticians as Jean Buteo and Guillaume Gosselin.

The second, and greater, part of La Roche's work has, apart from some geometrical calculations at the end, a commercial character. The author states that as a basis he used "the flower of several masters, experts in the art" of arithmetic, such as Luca Pacioli, supplemented by his own knowledge of business practice. The result was a good but traditional arithmetic that presented an outstanding view of contemporary methods of computation and their applications in trade.

BIBLIOGRAPHY

Larismetique nouellement composee par maistre Estienne de la Roche dict Villefranche natif de Lyon sur le Rosne divisée en deux parties ... (Lyons, 1520) was republished as *Larismetique et geometrie de maistre Estienne de la Roche dict Ville Franche, nouvellement imprimee et des faultes corrigee* ... (Lyons, 1538).

See M. Cantor, *Vorlesungen über Geschichte der Mathematik*, II (Leipzig, 1913), 371–374; and N. Z. Davis, "Sixteenth-Century French Arithmetics on the Business Life," in *Journal of the History of Ideas*, **21** (1960), 18–48. On Chuquet and La Roche, see Aristide Marre, "Notice sur Nicolas Chuquet," in *Bullettino di bibliografia e di storia delle scienze matematiche e fisiche*, **13** (1880), esp. 569–580.

J. J. VERDONK

LARSEN, ESPER SIGNIUS, JR. (*b.* Astoria, Oregon, 14 March 1879; *d.* Washington, D.C., 8 March 1961), *geology*.

The son of a Danish immigrant who had settled in Oregon and had become the first Danish consul in Portland, Larsen attended the local schools. Upon graduation from high school, he did not enter college immediately but worked to ease the financial pressures on the family. Entering the University of California in 1902, Larsen came under the influence of A. C. Lawson and A. S. Eakle while an undergraduate. This led to his taking advanced courses in mathematics and chemistry and contributed to his ultimate decision to make geology and petrology his lifework. After receiving the B.S. degree in 1906, Larsen remained at the university to teach. He left in 1908 but returned to take his doctorate in 1918.

His early studies developed in Larsen the habit of extensive and detailed examination of specimens. He conducted advanced research first as an assistant petrologist in the geophysical laboratory of the Carnegie Institution in Washington, D.C. With H. E. Marwin he developed petrographic techniques, making investigations in optical crystallography and the immersion method of mineral analysis.

In 1909 Larsen was appointed assistant geologist for the U.S. Geological Survey, an association that was one of the most important in his entire professional life. He joined Whitman Cross, who had been studying the volcanic province of the San Juan Mountains of Colorado and New Mexico for fifteen years. Their final report appeared forty-seven years later, in 1956. In Washington, Larsen was associated with F. E. Wright, who pioneered in the development of optical mineralogy. Their joint paper in 1909 was one of the earliest systematic efforts to establish criteria for geological thermometry.

In 1914 Larsen became a full geologist with the U.S. Geological Survey and served until 1923; for the last five years of this period, he headed the petrology section. Upon leaving the Survey, he became professor of petrography at Harvard University, where he remained until 1949. He then returned to the Survey until failing health forced him to reduce his activities in 1958.

Larsen's concern with optical mineralogy led him to assemble and tabulate the optical characteristics of more than 600 nonopaque minerals. Microscopy had been applied intensely to the study of rocks and minerals as early as 1850, with Sorby's development of the thin section technique. It was developed by Zirkel and Rosenbusch in the following years. Larsen extended and refined these early techniques, developing a hollow prism to measure directly the index of refraction of immersion liquids. These methods were refined for the measurement of mineral refraction indexes to three decimal places—until very recently this instrument served as the principal guide to mineral chemistry. Larsen's systematic methods of petrographic microscopy and his catalog-tables of the optical properties of minerals and the interrelationships of their properties with their chemistry were published in 1921. A revised handbook written with H. Berman, *The Microscopic Determination of the Nonopaque Minerals*, appeared in 1934 and remains the single indispensable handbook of optical crystallography.

Larsen's extensive field studies of the San Juans, the southern California batholith, the Idaho batholith, and later the Highwood Mountains of Montana made him a confirmed magmatist. His extensive microscopic studies of the specimens collected during the annual field seasons of nearly half a century reinforced the conclusions he drew in the field. Larsen strongly supported the laboratory investigations of minerals under pressures and high temperatures (phase equilibrium studies) associated with T. Vogt and N. L. Bowen.

Larsen's other major contributions were his development of the concepts of the petrographic province and the variation diagram. He studied the theory of thermal diffusion and applied it to the problem of the cooling of a batholith. He also developed a method of determining the age of igneous rocks using the lead in accessory minerals. His

researches in California's San Diego County batholithic intrusive rocks had led him to examine the radioactivity of zircon. His retirement from Harvard in 1949 enabled him to devote full time in Washington to applying his methods for determining the age of rocks.

Larsen determined that lead would avoid zircon during the crystallization of magma. Therefore the trace amounts of lead found in zircon were of radiogenic origin, and their quantity was a function of the time since crystallization. He separated zircon from large quantities of igneous rock and proceeded to measure the lead in the zircon spectrographically and to determine the α activity. The formula

$$t = C \frac{\text{Pb}}{\alpha}$$

is Larsen's: t = the age of the rock in millions of years; Pb, the lead concentration in parts per million; C = a constant between 2632 and 2013, depending upon the proportion of uranium to thorium; and α, the radioactivity in α counts per milligram of the mineral per hour. When a mineral contained unknown amounts of uranium and thorium, C was obtained by the measurement of the total α activity and a fluorescent analysis of the uranium.

In consequence of such contributions, Larsen was widely recognized as the foremost descriptive and theoretical petrologist in America and was awarded highly prized professional medals by both the Mineralogical and the Geological Societies of America. Perhaps his greatest contribution was in training many of the foremost petrologists of the age, not only in the classroom but also in the field and at the Geological Survey offices. His single-minded concentration on geology led to extreme absentmindedness; nonetheless his kindness and the grave consideration that he infallibly extended to those around him made him the object of an affectionate veneration on the part of his students. Among American geologists over the age of forty, the designation "The Professor" is immediately understood to refer to Larsen.

Larsen was survived by his wife of fifty-one years, the former Eva A. Smith, and for less than a year by the second of his two sons, the petrologist Esper S. Larsen III.

BIBLIOGRAPHY

I. Original Works. Larsen's writings include "Quartz as a Geologic Thermometer," in *American Journal of Science*, 4th ser., **27** (1909), 421–447, written with F. E. Wright; *The Microscopic Determination of the Nonopaque Minerals, Bulletin of the United States Geological Survey* no. 679 (1921), 2nd ed., written with Harry Berman, *ibid.*, no. 848 (1934); "The Igneous Rocks of the Highwood Mountains of Central Montana," in *Transactions of the American Geophysical Union 16th Annual Meeting*, pt. 1 (1935), 288–292, written with C. S. Hurlburt *et al.*; "Some New Variation Diagrams for Groups of Igneous Rocks," in *Journal of Geology*, **46** (1938), 505–520; "Petrographic Province of Central Montana," in *Bulletin of the Geological Society of America*, **51** (1940), 887–948; "Geochemistry," in *50th Anniversary Volume of the Geological Society of America* (Washington, D.C., 1941), pp. 393–413; "Time Required for the Crystallization of the Great Batholith of Southern and Lower California," in *American Journal of Science*, **243A** (1945), 399–416; "Batholith and Associated Rocks of Corona, Elsinore, and San Luis Rey Quadrangles, Southern California," in *Memoirs. Geological Society of America*, **29** (1948), 1–182; "Method for Determining the Age of Igneous Rocks Using the Accessory Minerals," in *Bulletin of the Geological Society of America*, **63** (1952), 1045–1052, written with N. B. Keevil and H. C. Harrison; "Geology and Petrology of the San Juan Region, Southwestern Colorado," in *Professional Papers. United States Geological Survey*, no. 258 (1956), 1–303, written with C. W. Cross; "Lead-Alpha Ages of the Mesozoic Batholiths of Western North America," in *Bulletin of the Geological Society of America*, no. 1070B (1958), 35–62, written with David Gottfried *et al.*; and "A Reconnaissance of the Idaho Batholith and Comparison With the Southern California Batholith," *ibid.*, no. 1070A (1958), 1–33, written with R. G. Schmidt.

II. SECONDARY LITERATURE. See C. S. Hurlburt, Jr., "Esper S. Larsen Jr.," in *American Mineralogist*, **47** (Mar. 1962), 450–459; and W. T. Pecora, "Esper Signius Larsen Jr. 1879–1961," in *Bulletin of the Geological Society of America*, **73** (Apr. 1962), 27–29, followed by a bibliography by Marjorie Hooker, 29–33. See especially the *Festschrift* volume, "Studies in Petrology and Mineralogy," *American Mineralogist*, **35** (1950), 619–958, and the remarkable dedication by J. C. Rabbitt.

CORTLAND P. AUSER

LARTET, ÉDOUARD AMANT ISIDORE HIPPOLYTE (*b.* St.-Guiraud, Gers, France, 15 April 1801; *d.* Seissan, Gers, France, 28 January 1871), *paleontology, prehistory.*

Descended from an old family of landed proprietors established for at least 500 years in the vicinity of Castelnau-Barbarens, Lartet spent his childhood on the family estate of Enpourqueron. While attending the *collège* in Auch, he received from Napoleon I, who was visiting the city, one of the medals awarded to the three most deserving pupils. Lartet went to Toulouse to study law and received his *licence* in 1820. His diploma was signed by Georges Cuvier, who was then a counsellor of state. In 1821 Lartet went to Paris as a probationary lawyer. Already attracted to the natural sciences, however, he attended courses at the Collège de France and visited the Muséum d'Histoire Naturelle. He also enjoyed browsing through the bookstalls along the banks of the Seine in the hope of discovering some rare book on natural history.

Having completed his probationary period, Lartet returned to Gers, where he had been called by his elderly father, who wished to divide his wealth among his children. From this time Lartet lived in the country, managing the property that he had inherited. He often gave free legal advice to the peasants who lived in the vicinity; aware of his interests, they repaid him by bringing him strange objects that they had found during the course of their work: medals, stone axes, shells, bones. One day a peasant brought a fossil tooth that Lartet recognized, after some research, as that of a Mastodon. His vocation was now settled. He hastened to acquire the books necessary to further his knowledge and to guide him in the paleontological research he wished to undertake. Lartet explored the Tertiary terrain of Gers; and toward the end of 1834 he came upon the rich fossil deposit of Sansan, where he was to discover more than ninety genera and species of fossil mammals and reptiles. His son reports: "For fifteen years he made excavations at his own expense and devoted late evenings to the study and classification of this material." Aware of the importance of these discoveries, at the beginning of 1834 Lartet sent Étienne Geoffroy Saint-Hilaire a letter on this subject, one later published in the *Bulletin de la Société géologique de France*.

It was the discovery in 1836 of the first anthropomorphic fossil ape, Pliopithecus, that revealed to Lartet the possibility of discovering human fossil remains. Encouraged by these first results, he continued his investigations with remarkable perseverance, gathering an abundant harvest of fossil remains, many of which were contributed to the Muséum d'Histoire Naturelle in Paris.

Lartet married in 1840 and had one son, Louis, who also became a scientist. In order to supervise his son's education more closely, Lartet decided in 1851 to move to Toulouse, where his son was attending the *lycée*. He remained there for only two years, having resolved to go to Paris, where he would be able to devote himself completely to the work he liked best. With A. Gaudry he investigated the identity of the fossil remains from Pikermi, Greece, and published notes on the paleontology of the Tertiary.

Lartet's memoir on the ancient migrations of the mammals of the Recent period (1858) presaged the turn his career was to take in 1860. He was particularly interested in the discoveries made by Boucher de

Perthes of chipped flint tools in the Somme Valley. Lartet himself had long been concerned with the antiquity of man. His belief in the continuity of life excluded the possibility of a sudden great upheaval that would have interrupted the regular succession of living creatures. His excavations in 1860 at the prehistoric sites of Massat (Ariège) and Aurignac (Haute-Garonne) yielded definite proof of the contemporaneity of man and extinct animal species and enabled him to establish, in 1861, a paleontological chronology based on the study of the large Quaternary mammals. Pursuing his research in this area, in 1863 he explored, along with the wealthy English collector Henry Christy, numerous grottoes in Périgord, particularly La Madeleine, Le Moustier, and Les Eyzies. The discovery of carved and sculpted objects furnished new proof of the existence of prehistoric art. Their finds later enriched the collections of the Musée des Antiquités Nationales in St.-Germain.

On the opening of this museum in 1867, Lartet was made an officer of the Legion of Honor. That same year he presided over the International Congress of Archaeology and Prehistoric Anthropology. In 1865 publication of the *Reliquiae aquitanicae* began in London. This magnificent work was the fruit of Lartet's collaboration with his friend Christy in the excavations in Périgord.

Lartet was named professor of paleontology at the Muséum d'Histoire Naturelle in March 1869; but already afflicted with the disease to which he succumbed two years later, he could not carry out his academic duties and returned to his estate in Gers.

BIBLIOGRAPHY

I. ORIGINAL WORKS. A detailed bibliography of Lartet's writings is in *Vie et travaux de Édouard Lartet* (see below), pp. 77–80. The some 40 titles include *Notice sur la colline de Sansan* (Auch, 1851); "Sur la dentition des proboscidiens fossiles et sur la distribution géographique et stratigraphique de leurs débris en Europe," in *Bulletin de la Société géologique de France*, 2nd ser., **16** (1859), 469–515; "Nouvelles recherches sur la coexistence de l'homme et des grands mammifères fossiles réputés caractéristiques de la dernière période glacière," in *Annales des sciences naturelles*, 4th ser., **15** (1861), 177–253; "Sur des figures d'animaux gravées ou sculptées et autres produits d'art et d'industrie rapportables aux temps primordiaux de la période humaine," in *Revue d'archéologie* (1864), written with H. Christy; and *Reliquiae aquitanicae, Being Contributions to the Archeology and Palaeontology of Perigord* . . ., 2 vols. (London, 1865–1875), written with H. Christy.

II. SECONDARY LITERATURE. *Vie et travaux de Édouard Lartet* (Paris, 1872) is a collection of notices published following his death; of particular interest are those by P. Fischer and E. T. Hamy. Also of value are G. Brégail, *Un éminent paléontologue gersois, Édouard Lartet* (Auch, 1948); Franck Bourdier, *L'art préhistorique et ses essais d'interprétation* (Paris, 1962); E. Cartailhac, "Édouard Lartet. Une féconde découverte à Aurignac," in *Revue du Comminges*, **33** (1918), 55–59; D. Dupuy, *Notice biographique sur Édouard Lartet* (Paris, 1873); and L. Méroc, "Édouard Lartet et son rôle dans l'élaboration de la préhistoire," in *Aurignac et l'aurignacien. Centenaire des fouilles d'Édouard Lartet* (Toulouse, 1963), pp. 7–18.

A. M. MONSEIGNY
A. CAILLEUX

LARTET, LOUIS (*b.* Castelnau-Magnoac, Hautes-Pyrénées, France, 18 December 1840; *d.* Seissan, Gers, France, 16 August 1899), *geology, prehistory*.

Lartet was the son of the paleontologist and student of prehistory Édouard Lartet. After two years at the *lycée* in Toulouse, he continued his studies in Paris, where his family had moved. His father often entertained French and foreign scientists, both at his laboratory and at home; undoubtedly Lartet soon became familiar with the scientific problems discussed at these gatherings.

In 1862 Lartet was named *préparateur* at the Muséum d'Histoire Naturelle. In the same year he accompanied the geologist E. de Verneuil on one of his many trips to Spain. While there Lartet made interesting observations concerning geology and prehistory that were published in the *Bulletin de la Société géologique de France*. Immediately after receiving his *licence ès sciences* he was chosen by de Luynes to participate as a geologist on an expedition that took him from Lebanon to the Red Sea by way of the Jordan Valley and the Dead Sea (February–June 1864). The trip furnished Lartet with the subject of his doctoral dissertation, "Essai sur la géologie de la Palestine et des contrées avoisinantes," which he successfully defended in 1869.

In 1867 and 1868 Lartet was secretary of the International Congresses of Anthropology, held in Paris and London, respectively. Lartet's name, however, remains associated chiefly with the study of the Cro-Magnon deposit, the site of one of the most important discoveries in human paleontology. In April 1868 he was commissioned by the minister of education, Victor Duruy, to verify the authenticity of this discovery.

Apparently the Franco-Prussian War, in which Lartet had served as quartermaster-sergeant, and the death of his father in January 1871 dealt a serious blow to what had promised to be a fruitful career. At the end of the war, Lartet returned to Paris but remained there for only a short time. In 1873 he was named *suppléant* professor of geology at the Faculty of Sciences of Toulouse, and in July 1879 he became a full professor. Nevertheless, teaching apparently did not fulfill his aspirations. He wrote his friend E. T. Hamy in 1882: "I often wish, seeing that we have grown dull as college teachers, to throw off the official livery and return to Paris to resume, like my father, the disinterested study of science. . . ." He was not able to realize this desire. Apart from some observations concerning the geology and prehistory of the Pyrenees, Lartet spent the remainder of his career teaching. He had to retire prematurely because of poor health.

BIBLIOGRAPHY

I. ORIGINAL WORKS. A bibliography of Lartet's writings by J. Canal is in *Bulletin de la Société d'histoire naturelle de Toulouse*, **45**, no. 2 (1912), 87–92. Among his works are "Sur le calcaire à Lychnus des environs de Segura (Aragon)," in *Bulletin de la Société géologique de France*, **20** (1863), 684–698, written with E. de Verneuil; "Mémoire sur une sépulture des anciens troglodytes du Périgord (Cro-Magnon)," in *Annales des sciences naturelles*, Zoologie, 5th ser., **10** (1868), 133–145; "Une sépulture des anciens troglodytes des Pyrénées," in *Comptes rendus hebdomadaires des séances de l'Académie des sciences*, **78** (1874), 1234–1236; and *Exploration géologique de la Mer Morte, de la Palestine et de l'Idumée, comprenant les observations recueillies par l'auteur durant l'expédition du duc de Luynes . . .* (Paris, 1877).

II. SECONDARY LITERATURE. See E. Cartailhac, "Éloge de M. Louis Lartet," in *Mémoires de la Société archéologique du Midi*, **16** (1903–1908), 9–18; and A. Lavergne, "Louis Lartet," in *Revue de Gascogne*, **41** (1900), 177–182.

A. M. MONSEIGNY
A. CAILLEUX

LASHLEY, KARL SPENCER (*b.* Davis, West Virginia, 7 June 1890; *d.* Poitiers, France, 7 August 1958), *psychology, neurophysiology.*

Karl Lashley's ancestry was English, primarily middle class. His father, Charles Gilpin Lashley, was a merchant in Davis, West Virginia, and its mayor and postmaster for many years. Lashley contended that he had received his native endowment from his mother, Maggie Blanche Spencer, a descendant of Jonathan Edwards. She exerted a profound influence upon her only child, encouraging his intellectual pursuits with her own library of 2,000 volumes. As a boy Karl collected various animal and plant specimens on long walks in the country. Throughout his life he formed assorted collections and kept unusual pets.

After receiving his B.A. from West Virginia University in 1910 he was awarded a teaching fellowship in biology at the University of Pittsburgh. He received his Ph.D. in 1914 from Johns Hopkins University under Jennings and Mast. In 1917 Lashley was instructor of psychology at the University of Minnesota; by 1923 he had been promoted to full professor. He remained at Minnesota until 1926, when he joined the staff at the University of Chicago as research psychologist; and he became professor of psychology in 1929. From 1935 to 1955 he was research professor of neuropsychology at Harvard University and, from 1942, director of the Yerkes Laboratories of Primate Biology.

In 1918 Lashley married Edith Ann Baker, an accomplished musician who died in 1948. A son born in 1919 died shortly thereafter. In 1957 he married Claire Imredy Schiller, widow of the Hungarian psychologist Paul Schiller.

Lashley was one of the world's foremost physiological psychologists. His scientific activities may be divided into four distinct periods. In the first (1912–1918) he laid a firm foundation in animal behavior working with lower forms, including their genetic make-up. In the second (1919–1929) his most noted contributions related to his penetrating analysis of the rat brain, in particular cerebral localization and interneuronal connections. His ideas of the learning process emerged from this analysis, culminating in *Brain Mechanisms and Intelligence* (New York, 1964). His theory of the equipotentiality of the cortex attracted world-wide attention and his article "In Search of the Engram" (*The Neuropsychology of Lashley*, pp. 478–505) made him famous. In the third period (1930–1942) he concerned himself primarily with vision, the chief sensory modality in learning. Few other scientific endeavors have equaled this thorough study of vision in relation to learning. In the final period (1941–1958) Lashley was a theorizer, especially on learning. He was also the world's sharpest critic of other theories, and especially of his own. He wrote: "My bricks won't hang together without speculative straw that I know is hooey."

BIBLIOGRAPHY

See Frank A. Beach's memoir of Karl Lashley in *Biographical Memoirs. National Academy of Sciences*, **35** (1961), 163–196. A full and complete bibliography of Lashley's works follows on pp. 196–204. *The Neuropsychology of Lashley*, F. A. Beach, D. O. Hebb, C. T. Morgan, and H. W. Nissen, eds. (New York, 1960), is a collection of Lashley's major publications.

PAUL G. ROOFE

LASSAR-COHN. See **Cohn, Lassar.**

LASSELL, WILLIAM (*b.* Bolton, Lancashire, England, 18 June 1799; *d.* Maidenhead, Berkshire, England, 5 October 1880), *astronomy.*

Lassell served a seven years' apprenticeship with a merchant at Liverpool and then became a brewer. About 1820 he began to construct reflecting telescopes and in 1840 installed a nine-inch Newtonian instrument in a private observatory near Liverpool.

Lassell was the first to design and use machines for surfacing mirrors of speculum metal in which the movement of the polisher closely imitated the circular motion used in polishing by hand. He was also the first to apply Fraunhofer's equatorial mounting to large reflecting telescopes. He mounted both the nine-inch telescope and a fine twenty-four-inch Newtonian, completed in 1846, in that way. With the latter he discovered Neptune's larger satellite, Triton, in 1846; detected Hyperion, the eighth satellite of Saturn (seen simultaneously by W. C. Bond at Harvard College Observatory) in 1848; and confirmed the existence of two satellites of Uranus, Ariel and Umbriel, in 1851.

In 1852 Lassell took the twenty-four-inch telescope to Valletta, Malta, where he expected that the climate would enable him to improve and extend his observational work. He then found that an even larger instrument was desirable, and in 1860 he completed a forty-eight-inch Newtonian telescope supported on a fork-type equatorial mounting. With this instrument, assisted by A. Marth, he searched unsuccessfully for new satellites, discovered 600 new nebulae, and monographed several others.

Upon his return to England in 1864, Lassell settled at Maidenhead, Berkshire. There he resumed his experiments with surfacing machines and constructed an improved form for polishing forty-eight-inch disks. Even so, he did not erect the forty-eight-inch telescope at Maidenhead but relied on the twenty-four-inch until failing eyesight forced him to abandon his studies.

Lassell became a fellow of the Royal Astronomical Society in 1839, received its gold medal in 1849, and was elected its president in 1870. He was elected a fellow of the Royal Society in 1849 and received the Royal Medal in 1858. He was an honorary member of the Royal Society of Edinburgh and the Royal Society of Sciences at Uppsala and held an honorary LL.D. conferred by the University of Cambridge.

BIBLIOGRAPHY

I. ORIGINAL WORKS. For descriptions of machines for polishing specula, see *Monthly Notices of the Royal Astro-nomical Society,* **8** (1848), 197; **9** (1849), 29; **13** (1853), 43; and *Philosophical Transactions of the Royal Society,* **165** (1875), 303; Lassell's telescopes are described in *Memoirs of the Royal Astronomical Society:* the nine-inch reflector, **12** (1842), 265–272; the twenty-four-inch reflector, **18** (1850), 1–25; and the forty-eight-inch reflector, **35** (1866), 1–4. For an account of the Malta observations, see *Memoirs of the Royal Astronomical Society,* **35** (1866), 33–35.

II. SECONDARY LITERATURE. Obituary notices include W. Huggins, in *Proceedings of the Royal Society,* **31** (1880–1881), vii–x; and M. L. Huggins, in *Observatory,* **3** (1880), 587–590. Lassell's activities in telescope-making are discussed in H. C. King, *The History of the Telescope* (London, 1955), pp. 218–224.

H. C. KING

LĀṬADEVA (*fl.* India, *ca.* A.D. 505), *astronomy.*

Lāṭadeva, a pupil of Āryabhaṭa I (*b.* 476), was perhaps originally from Lāṭadeśa in southern Gujarat. He is known primarily through citations in the *Pañcasiddhāntikā* of Varāhamihira (sixth century) and in the commentary on the *Brāhmasphuṭasiddhānta* by Pṛthūdakasvāmin (*ca.* 864); the fragments are collected in O. Neugebauer and D. Pingree, *The Pañcasiddhāntikā of Varāhamihira.*

Lāṭadeva is said by Varāhamihira to have commented on the *Romakasiddhānta* and the *Pauliśasiddhānta,* which represent Greek and Greco-Babylonian astronomical techniques in Sanskrit (see essay in Supplement); he is evidently also responsible for a revision of the *Sūryasiddhānta* whereby it came to conform to the *ārddharātrikapakṣa* of his teacher, Āryabhaṭa I. His epoch for that work was 20/21 March 505.

BIBLIOGRAPHY

All the available material concerning Lāṭadeva and his works will be found in O. Neugebauer and D. Pingree, *The Pañcasiddhāntikā of Varāhamihira* (Copenhagen, 1970), pt. 1, pp. 14–15.

DAVID PINGREE

LATIMER, WENDELL MITCHELL (*b.* Garnett, Kansas, 22 April 1893; *d.* Oakland, California, 6 July 1955), *chemistry.*

Latimer entered the University of Kansas planning to become a lawyer; but finding that he enjoyed mathematics, he sought some subject to which he might apply it. His first contact with chemistry came during his third year at the university. The subject captured his interest, and he decided to become a chemist. He received the B.A. degree from the

University of Kansas in 1915 and served as instructor there from 1915 to 1917. The reputation of G. N. Lewis and his study of some of Lewis' papers led Latimer to Berkeley for graduate study, and he received the Ph.D. degree in 1919. His thesis research was concerned with low-temperature calorimetry and was conducted under the direction of G. E. Gibson. He was retained as a member of the staff and attained full professorship in 1931. Latimer was assistant dean of the College of Letters and Science from 1923 to 1924, dean of the College of Chemistry from 1941 to 1949, and chairman of the department of chemistry from 1945 to 1949.

His first paper, published in 1920 and entitled "Polarity and Ionization From the Standpoint of the Lewis Theory of Valence," written with W. H. Rodebush, was one of Latimer's most important. It contained the first clear recognition of the hydrogen bond as distinct from ordinary dipoles. The properties of numerous substances, including water, are largely determined by hydrogen bonding. The basic idea has found very wide and rapidly increasing application. Linus Pauling, who devotes some fifty pages in *The Nature of the Chemical Bond* to the discussion of examples of hydrogen bonding, states: "I believe that as the methods of structural chemistry are further applied to physiological problems it will be found that the significance of the hydrogen bond for physiology is greater than that of any other single structural feature."

Latimer's 108 scientific contributions are largely concerned with the application of thermodynamics to chemistry. However, he worked on such diverse subjects as dielectric constants, thermoelectric effect and electronic entropy, the ionization of salt vapors, radioactivity, and astrochemical processes involved in the formation of the earth.

Latimer was the first in the United States to liquefy hydrogen and to make measurements in that region of temperature. His leadership had a major influence on the subsequent work of W. F. Giauque, who extended the field to even lower temperatures. Latimer used low-temperature data in conjunction with the third law of thermodynamics to determine the entropies and free energies of aqueous ions. This work supplied much of the material included in his outstanding book, *The Oxidation States of the Elements and Their Potentials in Aqueous Solutions* (1938, 1952). He wrote *A Course in General Chemistry* with W. C. Bray and *Reference Book of Inorganic Chemistry* with J. H. Hildebrand.

Latimer was active on national defense research committees from 1941 to 1945 in the fields of oxygen production, chemical warfare, and plutonium research.

He was director of a Manhattan Engineering District project in the University of California's department of chemistry, involving the chemistry of plutonium, from 1943 to 1947.

He was mainly responsible in the 1930's for initiating a seminar on nuclear chemistry that interested W. F. Libby, G. T. Seaborg, A. C. Wahl, and J. W. Kennedy and helped lay the foundation for the discovery of plutonium. The first separation and identification of plutonium depended on the relative oxidation potentials of the heaviest elements, and Latimer's availability for consultation contributed to the discovery of this extremely important element.

Latimer was a member of the National Academy of Sciences and chairman of the Chemistry Section in 1947–1950, of the American Chemical Society, the Electrochemical Society, the Faraday Society, the American Association for the Advancement of Science, and Sigma Xi. He received the Distinguished Service Award of the University of Kansas in 1948 and the Nichols Medal of the New York Section of the American Chemical Society in 1955. He was elected faculty research lecturer of the University of California in 1953.

Latimer received the Presidential Certificate of Merit for his contributions during World War II.

BIBLIOGRAPHY

A complete bibliography of Latimer's publications is in *Biographical Memoirs of the National Academy of Sciences*, **32** (1958), 230–237.

The following works may be cited from among his 108 publications: "Entropy Changes at Low Temperatures. I. Formic Acid and Urea. A Test of the Third Law of Thermodynamics," in *Journal of the American Chemical Society*, **42** (1920), 1533, written with G. E. Gibson and G. S. Parks; "Polarity and Ionization From the Standpoint of the Lewis Theory of Valence," *ibid.*, 1419, written with W. H. Rodebush; "The Mass Effect in the Entropy of Solids and Gases," *ibid.*, **43** (1921), 818; "A Revision of the Entropies of the Elements," *ibid.*, **44** (1922), 1008, written with G. N. Lewis and G. E. Gibson; "Thermoelectric Force, the Entropy of Electrons and the Specific Heat of Metals at High Temperatures," *ibid.*, 2136; and "The Electrode Potentials of Beryllium, Magnesium, Calcium, Strontium and Barium From Thermal Data," in *Journal of Physical Chemistry*, **31** (1927), 1267.

In the 1930's Latimer published *A Course in General Chemistry*, rev. ed. (New York, 1932; 3rd ed., 1940), written with W. C. Bray; "The Existence of Neutrons in the Atomic Nucleus," in *Journal of the American Chemical Society*, **54** (1932), 2125; "Bond Energies and Mass Defects in Atomic Nuclei," in *Journal of Chemical Physics*, **1** (1933), 133, written with W. F. Libby; "The Action of Neutrons on Heavy Water," in *Physical Review*, **47** (1935),

424, written with W. F. Libby and E. A. Long; "The Entropy of Aqueous Ions and the Nature of the Entropy of Hydration," in *Chemical Reviews*, **18** (1936), 349; "Silver Chromate: Its Heat Capacity, Entropy and Free Energy of Formation. The Entropy and Free Energy of Formation of Chromate Ion," in *Journal of the American Chemical Society*, **59** (1937), 2642, written with W. V. Smith and K. S. Pitzer; *The Oxidation States of the Elements and Their Potentials in Aqueous Solutions* (New York, 1938; 2nd ed., 1952); and "The Free Energy of Hydration of Gaseous Ions and the Absolute Potential of the Normal Calomel Electrode," in *Journal of Chemical Physics*, **7** (1939), 108, written with K. S. Pitzer and C. M. Slansky.

During the 1940's there appeared "The Entropies of Large Ions. The Heat Capacity, Entropy and Heat of Solution of Potassium Chlorplatinate, Tetramethylammonium Iodide and Uranyl Nitrate Hexahydrate," in *Journal of the American Chemical Society*, **62** (1940), 2845, written with L. V. Coulter and K. S. Pitzer; "Ionic Entropies and Free Energies and Entropies of Solvation in Water-Methanol Solutions," *ibid.*, 2019, written with C. M. Slansky; and "The Dielectric Constants of Hydrogen-Bonded Substances," in *Chemical Reviews*, **44** (1949), 59.

In the 1950's Latimer published "The Entropy of Aqueous Solutes," in *Journal of Chemical Physics*, **19** (1951), 1139, written with R. E. Powell; "Methods of Estimating the Entropies of Solid Compounds," in *Journal of the American Chemical Society*, **73** (1951), 1480; "Absolute Entropies in Liquid Ammonia," in *Journal of the American Chemical Society*, **75** (1953), 4147, written with W. L. Jolly; "Heats and Entropies of Successive Steps in the Formation of Al/F_6^{---}," *ibid.*, 1548, written with Jolly; "The Sign of Oxidation-Reduction Potentials," *ibid.*, **76** (1954), 1200; "Symposium on Hydration of Aqueous Ions, Introductory Remarks," in *Journal of Physical Chemistry*, **58** (1954), 513; and "The Complexing of Iron (III) by Fluoride Ions in Aqueous Solution: Free Energies, Heats and Entropies," in *Journal of the American Chemical Society*, **78** (1956), 1827, written with R. E. Connick *et al.*

JOEL H. HILDEBRAND

LATREILLE, PIERRE-ANDRÉ (*b.* Brive-la-Gaillarde, France, 29 November 1762; *d.* Paris, France, 6 February 1833), *entomology, zoology.*

Latreille was the natural son of J.-B.-J. Damazit de Sahuguet, baron d'Espagnac, a high-ranking officer in the French army. The identity of his mother is unknown. He was raised by foster parents, but his father provided for much of his education and in 1778 arranged for him to go to the Collège Cardinal Lemoine in Paris. Latreille received the degree of *maître ès arts* at the University of Paris in 1780. He then prepared for the priesthood and was ordained

in 1786, but his intended ecclesiastical career was cut short by the Revolution.[1] In 1795 he attended the École Normale de Paris.

Frail in constitution throughout his life, Latreille had been encouraged at an early age to pursue natural history as a means of strengthening his health. He took up this activity eagerly, and by the 1790's he had achieved sufficient recognition as a naturalist to be elected an associate, or corresponding, member of the Société d'Histoire Naturelle de Paris (1791), the Société Philomathique de Paris (1795), and the First Class of the Institut de France (1798). Although he was considered one of the foremost entomologists of the day, Latreille spent most of his career in subordinate positions which earned him only a meager existence. In 1798 he went to the Muséum d'Histoire Naturelle in Paris as organizer of its entomological collection. There he officially assumed the role of *aide-naturaliste* in 1805, serving as demonstrator in Lamarck's course in invertebrate zoology. He eventually took over Lamarck's course in 1820, when Lamarck became completely blind. Ill health later forced Latreille to cede some of these responsibilities to Jean Victor Audouin. Following Lamarck's death in 1829, the chair of invertebrate zoology was divided into two, and Latreille became professor in the new chair of entomology. In addition to his work at the Muséum d'Histoire Naturelle, he taught briefly at the École Vétérinaire d'Alfort (1814–1815). He was named a member of the Institut de France in 1814 and received the decoration of the Légion d'Honneur in 1821. Although known primarily for his entomological studies, he wrote on a wide range of zoological subjects as well as ancient geography and chronology.

Latreille's major scientific contribution lay in applying the "natural method" to the classification of the insects, arachnids, and crustaceans. This task was undertaken at a time when entomological knowledge and collections were undergoing a spectacular growth (from an estimated 1,500 specimens in 1789 the collection at the Muséum d'Histoire Naturelle grew to roughly 40,000 specimens representing 22,000 species in 1823).[2] Linnaeus and Fabricius had constructed artificial systems for classifying the insects, the former relying primarily upon the number and configuration of the wings and the latter relying exclusively on the parts of the mouth. Latreille's goal in his first major work, his *Précis* of 1796, was to arrange the genera of insects in their "natural order" by taking numerous characters into consideration. His system was based essentially upon a combination of the characters that Linnaeus and Fabricius had employed.

Latreille's most significant work, the four-volume *Genera crustaceorum et insectorum* (1806–1809), was developed along the same lines. While Latreille praised Cuvier for having founded zoological classification on comparative anatomy, he based his own classificatory work primarily on the consideration of external characters. Nonetheless, as one of his successors remarked more than half a century after the appearance of the *Genera*, the work offered "such an exact exposition of the characters of the insects, arachnids, and crustaceans, and nearly always such a just appreciation of the natural affinities of these animals, that the most modern researches have only added rectifications of a second order."[3]

Unlike such notable predecessors as Réaumur and Fabricius, Latreille presented a balanced approach in his entomological studies, dealing with behavioral and taxonomic problems alike. He also became a self-conscious pioneer in the study of biogeography, observing that temperature alone is insufficient to explain animal distribution and calling attention to the way in which animal distribution is related to the distribution of food sources. Along other lines in the 1820's he advanced theoretical views displaying sympathy with the concept of the unity of plan in the animal kingdom.

Among such strong personalities as Cuvier, Lamarck, Geoffroy Saint-Hilaire, and Blainville, Latreille was a modest, unassuming figure. Although his concerns, as suggested here, were by no means limited to questions of insect classification, he was inclined to leave to others the formulation of broad systems and philosophies. With Étienne Geoffroy Saint-Hilaire he cosigned a report to the Institut that precipitated the famous Cuvier-Geoffroy debate in 1830. The report, on a memoir in which Laurencet and Meyranx had proposed an analogy between the cephalopods and the vertebrates, was, however, written by Geoffroy alone. Latreille, according to a letter he wrote to Cuvier, wished no credit for it, asserting that he himself had given up the idea he had once entertained of considering the invertebrates and vertebrates as constructed upon the same plan.[4]

On another speculative front Latreille's stand was less ambiguous. Although he was for many years Lamarck's assistant and friend, he did not share his mentor's evolutionary views. He found it impossible to conceive of the forms of insects, and in particular their instinctual behavior, as anything other than the evidence of divine wisdom and design. Furthermore, as he remarked on this view of creation shortly before he died: "If we are wrong, do not seek to destroy illusions which are useful rather than harmful to society and which make us happy or console us in the difficult pilgrimage of life."[5]

NOTES

1. Louis de Nussac, *Latreille à Brive*, pp. 25–43, presents in detail the often-told story of how Latreille, imprisoned during the Revolution as a priest who had not preached a sermon, gained his release through the attention focused on him by his chance discovery in his cell of a previously unknown species of beetle.
2. J. P. F. Deleuze, *Histoire et description du Muséum royal d'histoire naturelle* (Paris, 1823), p. 188.
3. Émile Blanchard, *Métamorphoses, moeurs et instincts des insectes* (Paris, 1877), p. 33.
4. Institut de France, MS 3060 (1).
5. Latreille, *Cours d'entomologie*, p. 21.

BIBLIOGRAPHY

I. ORIGINAL WORKS. Latreille's publications total over seventy titles, excluding his contributions to various dictionaries of natural history. A reasonably accurate list of these appears in "Latreille," in *Nouvelle biographie générale* (Paris, 1862), XXIX, 851–854. The entomological titles alone have been compiled by A. Percheron, *Bibliographie entomologique* (Paris, 1837), I, 228–235. Among Latreille's more important works are *Précis des caractères génériques des insectes disposés dans un ordre naturel* (Brive, an v [1796]); *Histoire naturelle, générale et particulière des crustacés et des insectes. Ouvrage faisant suite aux oeuvres de . . . Buffon, rédigé par C. S. Sonnini . . .*, 14 vols. (Paris, 1802–1805); *Genera crustaceorum et insectorum secundum ordinem naturalem in familias disposita*, 4 vols. (Paris, 1806–1909); *Les crustacés, les arachnides et les insectes*, vol. III of Georges Cuvier, *Le règne animal distribué d'après son organisation, pour servir de base à l'histoire naturelle des animaux et d'introduction à l'anatomie comparée* (Paris, 1817)—also vols. IV and V of the 1829 ed.; and *Cours d'entomologie, ou de l'histoire naturelle des crustacés, des arachnides, des myriapodes et des insectes* (Paris, 1831).

The Société Entomologique de France has a collection of Latreille materials numbering 1,637 items, grouped in the following categories: (1) titles and distinctions; (2) MSS of various published scientific works; (3) unpublished works; and (4) scientific correspondence with other entomologists.

II. SECONDARY LITERATURE. There is no full treatment of Latreille's life and scientific work. See Louis de Nussac, *Pierre-André Latreille à Brive de 1762 à 1798* (Paris, 1907); and "Le centenaire de Pierre-André Latreille," in *Archives du Muséum national d'histoire naturelle*, 6th ser., **11** (1934), 1–12; and A. J. L. Jourdan, "Latreille," in *Biographie universelle. Ancienne et moderne*, new ed. (Paris, n.d.), XXIII, 329–331. For a discussion of Latreille's classificatory contributions, see Henri Daudin, *Cuvier et Lamarck, les classes zoologiques et l'idée de série animale (1790–1830)* (Paris, 1926).

RICHARD W. BURKHARDT, JR.

LAU, HANS EMIL (*b*. Odense, Denmark, 16 April 1879; *d*. Usserød, Denmark, 16 October 1918), *astronomy*.

In 1906 Lau received the master's degree at the University of Copenhagen. During the following years he worked at the private Urania Observatory at Frederiksberg, a suburb of Copenhagen. About 1911–1912 he spent a year at the Treptow Sternwarte in Berlin, and after his return to Denmark he built a small private observatory.

In 1905 Lau was awarded a gold medal by Copenhagen University for a discussion of the observations of the bright new star of 1901 and of theories on new stars; he also published an interpretation of a nova spectrum. From his youth Lau worked on the problem of a trans-Neptunian planet (or two planets); and his conclusions must be characterized as sound.

During 1905–1911 Lau made a long series of visual measurements of double stars and did some pioneer work on photographic observations; he discussed the systematic errors of visual observations and made a close determination of the orbit of the system of 70 Ophiuchi; in connection with his reobservation of previously measured optical companions of bright stars he published several discussions of the proper motions and parallaxes of faint stars. He made observations of variable stars, of stars suspected of variability, and of colors of stars; he was also one of the first astronomers to become interested in photographic photometry.

Lau was always an eager observer of the planets, especially of Mars and Jupiter, making drawings of their surfaces and micrometrical determinations of the positions of details on them. His comprehensive descriptions of the yearly changes of the features of Mars and of the clouded world of Jupiter, based on observations collected from a great many observers, must be regarded as exhaustive contemporary discussions of these problems.

Lau never succeeded in obtaining a position at a scientific institution, but his contributions are those of an original and dedicated scientist.

BIBLIOGRAPHY

I. ORIGINAL WORKS. A listing of Lau's works in *Astronomische Nachrichten* is in Poggendorff, V, 711. His writings include "Sur la question des planètes transneptuniennes," in *Bulletin astronomique*, **20** (1903), 251–256; "Sur le spectre des étoiles nouvelles," *ibid.*, **23** (1906), 297–303; "Sur le système de 70 Ophiuchi," *ibid.*, **25** (1908), 139–141, and **26** (1909), 433–456; "Über die Rotation des Planeten Jupiter," in *Astronomische Nachrichten*, **195** (1913),

313–340; "La planète transneptunienne," in *Bulletin de la Société astronomique de France*, **28** (1914), 276–283; "Die periodischen Veränderungen auf dem Mars," in *Astronomische Nachrichten*, **204** (1917), 81–124; and "Untersuchungen über die Farben der Fixsterne," *ibid.*, **205** (1918), 49–70. Lau's measurements of visual double stars are published in a series of papers in *Astronomische Nachrichten*, **169–205** (1905–1918).

II. SECONDARY LITERATURE. There is an obituary by E. Strömgren in *Astronomische Nachrichten*, **208** (1919), 151–152.

AXEL V. NIELSEN

LAUE, MAX VON (*b*. Pfaffendorf, near Koblenz, Germany, 9 October 1879; *d*. Berlin, Germany, 24 April 1960), *theoretical physics*.

After passing the final secondary-school examination in March 1898, Laue began studying physics at the University of Strasbourg, although he was still in military service. In the fall of 1899 he transferred to Göttingen. Under the influence of Woldemar Voigt he chose to specialize in theoretical physics. At the same time he came to prefer optical problems, a preference that was strengthened by the lectures of Otto Lummer which he heard during his three semesters at the University of Berlin. In July 1903, Laue received his doctorate under Max Planck for a dissertation on the theory of interference in plane parallel plates. He then returned for two years to Göttingen, where he passed the state examination to qualify for teaching in the Gymnasiums.

The course that Laue's life was to take was decided in the autumn of 1905, when Planck offered him an assistantship. Laue became Planck's leading and favorite pupil, and the two formed a lifelong friendship. Laue introduced Planck's central concept, entropy, into optics and qualified as university lecturer in 1906 with a work on the entropy of interfering pencils of rays. In the winter semester of 1905–1906 Laue heard Planck's lecture at the Physical Colloquium on the special theory of relativity, which Einstein had just stated. After initial reservations Laue became one of the first adherents of the new theory and, as early as July 1907, presented a proof for it that he drew, characteristically, from optics.

In 1851, after many experiments, Fizeau had discovered a formula for the velocity of light in flowing water that could not be understood in terms of classical physics. Assuming light to be a wave phenomenon in the ether, one could either suppose that the ether does not contribute to the motion of the flowing water, in which case the velocity of light should be $u = c/n$; or one could postulate that the ether is carried along through the motion of the water, in which case the equation ought to be $u = c/n \pm v$. Yet, curiously, the experiments showed partial ether "drag" varying as a specific fraction of the velocity of water — $v(1 - 1/n^2)$ —the Fresnel drag coefficient.

Einstein's special theory of relativity dispensed with the addition or subtraction of the velocities, hitherto assumed to be self-evident, and applied instead a special "addition theorem." In 1907 Laue demonstrated that this theorem readily yields Fizeau's formula with the previously enigmatic Fresnel drag coefficient: $u = c/n \pm v(1 - 1/n^2)$. Laue thereby furnished Einstein's theory with an important experimental proof, which, along with the Michelson-Morley experiment and arguments from group theory, contributed to early acceptance of the theory. Having thus proved himself an expert in relativity theory, in 1910 Laue wrote the first monograph on the subject. He expanded it in 1919 with a second volume on the general theory of relativity; the work went through several editions.

In 1909 Laue became a *Privatdozent* at the Institute for Theoretical Physics, directed by Arnold Sommerfeld, at the University of Munich. Here, in the spring of 1912, Laue had the crucial idea of sending X rays through crystals. At this time scientists were very far from having proved the supposition that the radiation that Roentgen had discovered in 1895 actually consisted of very short electromagnetic waves. Similarly, the physical composition of crystals was in dispute, although it was frequently stated that a regular structure of atoms was the characteristic property of crystals. Laue argued that if these suppositions are correct, then the behavior of X radiation upon penetrating a crystal should be approximately the same as that of light upon striking a diffraction grating; and interference phenomena had been studied by means of the latter arrangement since Fraunhofer. These ideas, which Laue expressed in a discussion with Peter Paul Ewald, were soon being talked about by the younger faculty members. Finally Walter Friedrich, an assistant of Sommerfeld's, and Paul Knipping, a doctoral candidate, began experiments in this field on 21 April 1912. The irradiation of a copper sulfate crystal yielded regularly ordered dark points on a photographic plate placed behind the crystal, the first of what are today called Laue diagrams. On 4 May 1912 Laue, Friedrich, and Knipping announced their success in a letter to the Bavarian Academy of Sciences.

Laue wrote in his autobiography:

> I was plunged into deep thought as I walked home along Leopoldstrasse just after Friedrich showed me this picture. Not far from my own apartment at Bismarckstrasse 22, just in front of the house at Siegfried-strasse 10, the idea for a mathematical explanation of the phenomenon came to me. Not long before I had written an article for the *Enzyklopaedie der mathematischen Wissenschaften* in which I had to re-formulate Schwerd's theory of diffraction by an optical grating (1835), so that it would be valid, if iterated, also for a cross-grating. I needed only to write down the same condition a third time, corresponding to the triple periodicity of the space lattice, in order to explain the new discovery. . . . The decisive day, however, was the one a few weeks later when I could test the theory with the help of another, clearer photograph.

The awarding of the Nobel Prize in physics for 1914 to Laue indicated the significance of the discovery that Albert Einstein called one of the most beautiful in physics. Subsequently it was possible to investigate X radiation itself by means of wavelength determinations as well as to study the structure of the irradiated material. In the truest sense of the word scientists began to cast light on the structure of matter.

Laue was appointed associate professor at the University of Zurich in 1912 and full professor at Frankfurt in 1914. In the latter year Laue's father, an official in the military court system, was elevated to the hereditary nobility. Thus within a few years the unknown *Privatdozent* Max Laue became the world-famous Nobel Prize winner Professor Max von Laue.

During the war Laue worked with Willy Wien in Würzburg on developing electronic amplifying tubes for improving the army's communication techniques. In 1919 he arranged an exchange of teaching posts with Max Born: Born left Berlin to go to Frankfurt and Laue went to the University of Berlin, which he considered his true intellectual home. Here he was again able to be near Planck, his honored teacher and friend.

The new field of X-ray structural analysis that Laue established developed into an important branch of physics and chemistry. The leading researchers in the field were William Henry Bragg and William Lawrence Bragg. Laue himself, a true pupil of Planck's, was interested only in the "great, general principles" and did not concern himself with the study of the structure of individual substances; instead he continued to work on the fundamental theory. Following the preliminary investigations of Charles Galton Darwin and Peter Paul Ewald, Laue expanded his original geometric theory of X-ray interference into the so-called dynamical theory. Whereas the geometric theory dealt with only the interaction between the atoms of the crystal and the incident electromagnetic waves, the dynamical theory took into account the forces between the atoms as well. To be sure, the correction amounted to only a few seconds of arc, but deviations had appeared early in the course of the very precise X-ray spectroscopic measurements.

In the following decades the theory was developed in various directions. When Laue later undertook to provide a comprehensive view of only the principles in *Röntgenstrahl-Interferenzen* (1941), his account ran to 350 pages. After the discovery of electron interference, Laue included this phenomenon in his theory. He did not, however, otherwise participate in the creation or development of quantum theory; and, like Planck, Einstein, de Broglie, and Schrödinger, he was skeptical of the "Copenhagen interpretation."

In 1932 Laue received the German Physical Society's Max Planck Medal. In his acceptance speech Laue presented an important result in the field of superconductivity: the interpretation of a seemingly paradoxical measurement made by W. J. de Haas. Subsequently Laue engaged in a fruitful joint study of this topic with Walther Meissner. Meissner conducted the relevant experiments at the Physikalisch-Technische Reichsanstalt, and Laue acted as theoretical adviser to that institution. Whereas Werner Heisenberg, Fritz London, and Heinz London worked on a quantum theory of superconductivity, Laue characteristically remained within the framework of the classical theory. He applied the purely phenomenological Maxwellian theory to the superconductor and later worked on the thermodynamics of superconductivity.

Laue held positions of exceptional trust at an early age. In 1921, proposed by Max Planck, he became a member of the Prussian Academy of Sciences. Following the establishment of the Emergency-Association of German Science (later the German Research Association), the German physicists elected Laue the representative for theoretical physics. He was chairman of the physics committee and also a member of the electrophysics committee until 1934. Through his solid judgment he directed the available financial resources to the truly important projects and thereby played a not inconsiderable role in the continuance of the "golden age of German physics" even during the economic depression of the Weimar Republic.

Laue's scientific pride did not permit him passively to accept Einstein's dismissal following the Nazi seizure of power. Only two colleagues in the Prussian Academy joined in his protest. As the chairman of the German Physical Society, Laue took issue with the slandering of the theory of relativity as a "worldwide Jewish trick" and gave a highly regarded address at the opening of the physics congress in Würzburg on 18 September 1933. He likened Galileo, the champion of the Copernican world view, to Einstein, the founder of relativity theory, and openly expressed his hope and belief that, as the truth had once before won out against the Church's prohibition, this time it would win out against the National Socialist proscription: "No matter how great the repression, the representative of science can stand erect in the triumphant certainty that is expressed in the simple phrase: And yet it moves."

Although his defense of Einstein had been in vain, Laue did have one success at the end of 1933—in the Prussian Academy. Johannes Stark, Hitler's famous follower, who had become a rabid opponent of modern physical theories, was supposed to be admitted into the Academy at the request of the new regime; and a group of academicians was prepared—reluctantly— to consent to the election. Yet in the session of 11 December 1933 the objections to this choice were set forth so emphatically by Laue, Otto Hahn, and Wilhelm Schlenk that the sponsors withdrew the proposal and Stark was not admitted. On 23 March 1934, Einstein wrote to Laue: "Dear old comrade. How each piece of news from you and about you gladdens me. In fact I have always felt, and known, that you are not only a thinker, but a fine person too."

When Friedrich Schmidt-Ott, the elected president of the German Research Association, was dismissed by the Nazis and replaced by Johannes Stark, Laue was once again the spokesman for the physicists. He wrote to Schmidt-Ott on 27 June 1934: "I heard of your withdrawal from the presidency . . . with deep regret. The overwhelming majority of German physicists, especially the members of the physics committee, share this regret. . . . Under the present circumstances, moreover, I fear that the change in the presidency is the prelude to difficult times for German science, and physics will no doubt have to suffer the first and hardest blow."

In the Research Association, Laue's judgment was no longer asked for; he also lost his position as adviser to the Physikalisch-Technische Reichsanstalt. He continued, however, as professor at the University of Berlin and as deputy director of the Kaiser Wilhelm Institute for Physics. Following his early retirement from teaching in 1943, Laue moved to Württemberg-Hohenzollern; at this time the Kaiser Wilhelm Institute, busy with military research and now under the direction of Werner Heisenberg, was relocated in Hechingen. Although Laue did not participate in the uranium project for the production of atomic energy, he was interned after the war with the atomic physicists by the Allies.

From the beginning Laue stood at the forefront of the rebuilding of German science. In the fall of 1946, working in Göttingen, he created with former colleagues the German Physical Society in the British Zone and in 1950 took part in refounding the League of German Physical Societies, today known as the German Physical Society. Laue played an important part in the reestablishment of the Physikalisch-Technische Bundesanstalt in Brunswick (the successor to the Physikalisch-Technische Reichsanstalt in Berlin) and in the German Research Association, where he was reelected to the physics committee until 1955. At first Laue was active primarily in his former post of deputy director of the Kaiser Wilhelm Institute for Physics at Göttingen. In April 1951, at the age of seventy-one, he took over the directorship of the former Kaiser Wilhelm Institute for Chemistry and Electrochemistry in Berlin-Dahlem. Active up to the end, Laue died in his eighty-first year following an automobile accident. He was mourned by colleagues throughout the world.

BIBLIOGRAPHY

I. ORIGINAL WORKS. Laue's writings were collected in *Gesammelte Schriften und Vorträge*, 3 vols. (Brunswick, 1961), with his autobiography in vol. III. His works include *Die Relativitätstheorie*, 2 vols. (Brunswick, 1911–1919); *Korpuskular- und Wellentheorie* (Leipzig, 1933); *Röntgenstrahl-Interferenzen* (Leipzig, 1941); *Materiewellen und ihre Interferenzen* (Leipzig, 1944); *Geschichte der Physik* (Bonn, 1946); and *Theorie der Supraleitung* (Berlin, 1947).

II. SECONDARY LITERATURE. See the following, listed chronologically: R. Brill, O. Hahn, *et al.,* "Feierstunde zu Ehren von Max von Laue an seinem 80. Geburtstag," in *Mitteilungen aus der Max Planck-Gesellschaft*, **6** (1959), 323–366; Peter Paul Ewald, "Max von Laue," in *Biographical Memoirs of Fellows of the Royal Society*, **6** (1960), 135–156, with bibliography; James Franck, "Max von Laue (1879–1960)," in *Yearbook. American Philosophical Society* (1960), 155–159; Walther Meissner, "Max von Laue als Wissenschaftler und Mensch," in *Sitzungsberichte der Bayerischen Akademie der Wissenschaften zu München* (1960), 101–121; Max Päsler, "Leben und wissenschaftliches Werk Laues," in *Physikalische Blätter*, **16** (1960), 552–567; Peter Paul Ewald, *Fifty Years of X-Ray Diffraction* (Utrecht, 1962), *passim;* Friedrich Herneck, "Max von Laue," in *Bahnbrecher des Atomzeitalters* (Berlin, 1965), pp. 273–326; Paul Forman, "The Discovery of the Diffraction of X-Rays by Crystals," in *Archive for History of Exact Sciences*, **6** (1969), 38–71; and Armin Hermann, "Forschungsförderung der Deutschen Forschungsgemeinschaft und die Physik der letzten 50 Jahre," in *Mitteilungen der Deutschen Forschungsgemeinschaft*, **4** (1970), 21–34, also in *Physik in unserer Zeit*, **2** (1971), 17–23.

Copies of unpublished letters, almost all of them written to Laue, are available at the Deutsches Museum, Munich (Handschriftenabteilung) and at Stuttgart University, in the Department of the History of Science and Technology.

ARMIN HERMANN

LAURENS, ANDRÉ DU (LAURENTIUS) (*b.* Tarascon, near Arles, France, 9 December 1558; *d.* Paris, France, 16 August 1609), *anatomy, medicine.*

Laurens's father was a physician in Arles; his maternal uncle, Honoré Castellan, was an important royal physician. Although their father died when they were young, Laurens and his six brothers all enjoyed successful careers, two becoming archbishops and two becoming royal physicians.

After taking the M.D. at Avignon in 1578, Laurens went to Paris to study under Louis Duret. In 1583 he took another doctorate at Montpellier in order to qualify for the chair of medicine left vacant there in 1582 by the death of Laurent Joubert. After lecturing at Montpellier for about ten years, he left (apparently without relinquishing his chair) to serve as personal physician to the duchess of Uzès; she introduced him at the French court, where he was soon named one of the physicians of Henry IV. In 1596 he became a royal physician in ordinary and in 1600 was designated first physician to Henry's new queen, Marie de Médicis. In 1603 he became chancellor of the University of Montpellier, although he continued to reside at court and delegated his duties to a vice-chancellor. In 1606 he became first physician to the king; he died three years later. In 1601 he had married Anne Sanguin, by whom he had one son.

Laurens's first publication (1593) was a pamphlet in which he attacked the views of Simon Piètre, a prominent Parisian physician, on the foramen ovale of the fetal heart. According to Galen, this orifice permitted blood to pass from the vena cava, through the right and left auricles, and into the pulmonary vein, where it nourished the lungs. Piètre maintained (1593) that the actual function of the foramen was to bring blood from the vena cava into the left ventricle for distribution to the body through the arteries. In his pamphlet Laurens defended Galen's view. Piètre's response led to a further attack by Laurens, and a final defense by Piètre, whose view found little favor until its vindication by William Harvey in *De motu cordis* (1628).

The same Galenic orthodoxy is evident throughout Laurens's *Opera anatomica* (1593). Much of this work was incorporated into the more comprehensive, illustrated *Historia anatomica* (1600), which was one of the most widely used anatomical textbooks of the first half of the seventeenth century. The twelve books of the *Historia* include not only descriptions of the structures, actions, and uses of the parts, but also 178 "controversies" in which are discussed disputed questions generally of a theoretical nature, such as whether there is a natural spirit and whether the brain is the seat of a principal faculty. In his preface Laurens vowed to vindicate Galen from the innumerable calumnies of the moderns as far as truth would permit, and in fact he did support the Galenic position in most of the controversies, upholding, for example, the permeability of the cardiac septum against the pulmonary circuit and other alternatives and rejecting Falloppio's views on the action of the gall bladder.

Laurens's book contains little original material. His anatomical descriptions generally did not improve on those of his predecessors and at times fell short of them. His illustrations were, with few exceptions, borrowed from other works, especially those of Vesalius, as well as Coiter and Varolio; and even many of his controversies were based on earlier works written in the tradition of Peter of Abano's *Conciliator*. Nevertheless, as a textbook the *Historia anatomica* was quite successful. Its anatomical descriptions were concise and lucid, while the controversies provided a comprehensive survey of the various positions in disputed points of anatomy and physiology. Even the orthodoxy of Laurens's views often proved useful to those requiring a foil against which to develop alternative positions. The importance of the book is reflected in its numerous editions, both in Latin and in French, and in the frequency with which it was cited by contemporaries. Many of the controversies were translated into English in Helkiah Crooke's *Mikrokosmographia* (1615), and Theodore Colladon included a detailed critique of the *Historia* in his *Adversaria* (1615).

Laurens also published numerous other medical works, of which the most popular was *Discours de la conservation de la vue*; *des maladies mélancholiques*; *des catarrhes*; *et de la vieillesse* (1594). Intended for a lay audience, the work went through more than twenty editions, and was translated into English, German, Latin, and Italian.

BIBLIOGRAPHY

I. ORIGINAL WORKS. The bibliography in Edouard Turner, "Bibliographie d'André Du Laurens . . . avec quelques remarques sur sa biographie," in *Gazette hebdomadaire de médecine et de chirurgie*, 2nd ser., **17** (1880), 329–341, 381–390, 413–435; and *Études historiques* (Paris, 1876–1885), pp. 209–243, is fairly comprehensive. He accepts *Historia anatomica humani corporis et singularum ejus partium, multis controversiis et observationibus novis illustrata* (Paris, 1600) as the 1st ed., instead of the undated Frankfurt edition, which he dates 1627 rather than 1599 and considers to be a reissue of the Frankfurt edition dated 1600. Turner's list includes the pamphlets exchanged by Piètre and Laurens in 1593. Laurens gives an account of the dispute, including a long extract from Piètre's first tract, in *Historia anatomica*, VIII, controversy 25. *A Discourse of the Preservation of Sight; of Melancholicke Diseases; of Rheumes, and of Old Age*, Richard Surphlett, trans. (London, 1599), was published in facs., with intro. by Sanford V. Larkey (London, 1938).

II. SECONDARY LITERATURE. For biographical information, see Turner, cited above. For a critique of *Historia anatomica*, see M. Portal, *Histoire de l'anatomie et de la chirurgie*, II (Paris, 1770), 147–159.

JEROME J. BYLEBYL

LAURENT, AUGUSTE (or **AUGUSTIN**) (*b.* St.-Maurice, near Langres, Haute-Marne, France, 14 November 1807; *d.* Paris, France, 15 April 1853), *chemistry.*

Jean Baptiste Laurent, who owned a small farm, married Marie-Jeanne Maistre, the daughter of a merchant from Burgundy. Augustin Laurent (who always signed his name as Auguste in later life) was the second of their four children. He received the traditional classical education at the local *collège* in Gray. He passed the entrance examination for the prestigious École des Mines in Paris, as an external student, on 9 December 1826, and received his engineering degree in June 1830. His first publication (1830), written jointly with Arrault, was a thesis submitted in partial fulfillment of the requirements for obtaining a degree; it was written on some of the techniques used in cobalt mines in Germany, which he had visited during his vacation the previous year.

At the beginning of the academic year 1830–1831 he was employed as a laboratory assistant at the École Centrale des Arts et Manufactures by J. B. Dumas. From 1832 to 1834 Laurent worked as chemist for the royal porcelain works at Sèvres, under the direction of Alexandre Brongniart, Dumas's father-in-law. There Laurent developed a method of analyzing silicates by the action of hydrofluoric acid that is still used by chemists.

In 1835 Laurent opened a private school in Paris where he taught chemistry to fee-paying adults. The school was closed after about a year, and its furnishings were sold to pay for the publication of Laurent's doctoral dissertation at the Sorbonne's Faculty of Sciences.

In December 1837 Laurent passed his oral examination and obtained the degree of *docteur-ès-sciences*. His main doctoral thesis developed the principal ideas of his theory of fundamental and derived radicals in organic chemistry.

In 1836–1837 Laurent worked as an analyst for a Paris perfumery owned by a certain Laugier, who regarded him as a partner and associated him with the firm's profits. Laurent received 10,000 francs when he left the perfumery, as his share of the profits.

Laurent was of a very sensitive and nervous disposition, easily discouraged and readily provoked into a quarrel over real or imagined insults. He was also generous and frank and had radical political commitments. A firm adherent of the left-wing republican tradition in France, he was impatient and suspicious of authority. Dumas, who epitomized conventional virtues of the authoritarian and traditionalist kind, was a natural target for Laurent's hostility. Although there is no positive evidence that Dumas tried to harm him, Laurent was persuaded of his senior's malevolence and bad faith. After receiving his doctorate, Laurent became persuaded that Dumas and other university authorities were opposed to the novelty of his ideas in organic chemistry and that he stood no chance of a university appointment in France. Consequently he contemplated abandoning a research career and in 1838 accepted a post as industrial chemist at a ceramics works in Luxembourg. The same year he married Anne-Françoise Schrobilgen, the daughter of an important Luxembourg dignitary.

Laurent's ideas were in fact so easily assimilated by French chemists that by 1839 both the younger chemists as well as their seniors active in research in organic chemistry, including Dumas, had accepted the essentials. Notwithstanding Liebig's exacerbated vanity and nationalism, by 1845 a large group of Germany chemists had also adopted Laurent's views. The same was true of England. Even Berzelius in Sweden, against whose views in organic chemistry Laurent directed most of his work, rendered homage to his genius for experimental work, while dismissing his theoretical assumptions. In his annual report on the development of chemistry during 1843, Berzelius devoted nearly half his account of organic chemistry to a highly complimentary account of Laurent's work; the previous year he had said that Laurent's work on indigo was the best piece of experimental research in vegetable chemistry since Liebig and Wöhler had discovered the benzoyl radical in 1832.

On 30 November 1838 Laurent was appointed to the newly created chair of chemistry at Bordeaux, in his native region. He returned from Luxembourg in early 1839 and occupied this post for the next six years. This was the most productive period of his life, during which he published nearly 100 papers.

During his annual summer vacation visit to his in-laws in 1843, Laurent went to see Liebig in Giessen, where he was well received and established important contacts with the younger German chemists, especially von Hofmann. In the fall of that year he met Gerhardt; by 1844 they were in close contact and their lifelong collaboration had started. Laurent became a *chevalier* of the Légion d'Honneur in 1844.

The first number of the journal jointly edited by Gerhardt and Laurent, *Comptes-rendus mensuels des travaux chimiques*, appeared in February 1845. On 11 August 1845, he was elected a corresponding member of the Académie des Sciences and later that month left Bordeaux for good; he was granted leave of absence with pay until his appointment in 1848 to the post he had long desired, assayer at the Paris Mint. In the meantime he worked at various laboratories at the Collège de France, École Normale, and École des Mines. In 1847 he published his book on crystallography.

Laurent presented his candidature for the chair of chemistry at the Collège de France left vacant by the resignation of Pelouze in November 1850. He was elected by thirteen votes to nine for his rival Balard. But the election had to be ratified by the Académie des Sciences, which preferred Balard (35 to 11). Presumably the hostility of the Academy was dictated by the political disturbances in France in 1851, which aggravated the antagonism of political moderates toward radicals such as Laurent. Having fallen seriously ill, in 1852 he went to recuperate in the south of France but died in Paris of consumption the following year. His family was awarded a state pension. He left the manuscript of *Méthode de chimie*, which was edited by J. Nicklès and published in 1854. Odling published an English version in 1855, and Kekulé offered to translate it into German.

Laurent's career coincided with the attempt to establish organic chemistry as a precise science, clearly distinguishable in its methods and fundamental principles from inorganic chemistry, which had been the main preoccupation of chemists during the previous half century. He was a central figure in the emergence of organic chemistry as a mature science.

A "philosophical" chemist, Laurent realized the need to pass beyond the narrow *ad hoc* theories of limited application adopted by his contemporaries, in order to establish a set of general theoretical principles valid for the whole domain of phenomena studied by organic chemistry. He insisted that an adequate scientific theory had to fulfill three requirements: explanation of all phenomena within the range of the theory; prediction of new and hitherto untested phenomena with its help; and enlargement of the scope of the scientific discipline by the imaginative application of theoretical principles to areas outside its original domain or subject matter.

His earlier contributions to organic chemistry were his thorough and meticulous experimental investigations of naphthalene and its derivatives. The subject had been chosen for him by Dumas, who was studying the reactions of the halogens upon various hydrocarbons (1832). Laurent adapted the existing method for the preparation of naphthalene (developed by Kidd) and succeeded in obtaining a very pure product, at low cost, by the fractional distillation of coal tar. By an extension of this early procedure, he became a major figure in the development of this branch of organic chemistry, the preparation and isolation of compounds by the distillation of coal tar. Using the same method, he and Dumas discovered anthracene (paranaphthalene) in 1832. Upon analysis both naphthalene and anthracene were found to be hydrocarbons containing the same relative proportions of carbon to hydrogen, namely 5:2 ($C = 6$).

The preparation of naphthalene was followed by a study of its reactions with chlorine, bromine, and nitric- and sulfuric-acid anhydrides. Laurent's practice of exhaustively investigating the compounds that a substance formed with each of a small number of reagents—rather than superficially spreading his researches over a very extensive range—was already formed and he never abandoned it. His most striking experimental discoveries were due to this method, such as the eventual preparation of nearly 100 new derivatives of naphthalene with the four reagents mentioned above.

While studying the reactions of naphthalene and its compounds with the halogens and nitric acid, Laurent was from the start characteristically concerned with the construction of an explanatory theory that would account for these phenomena. Like most creative scientists, he generalized his solution to a specific problem through the imaginative use of analogy, leading to the elaboration of the first comprehensive theory adequate for dealing with the whole domain of contemporaneous organic chemistry.

Several factors can be singled out in Laurent's earliest attempt to construct such a theory:

1. *Analogy.* Laurent based his theory upon at least four kinds of analogy drawn from the work of his contemporaries.

a) *Hydrocarbons:* Dumas had affirmed that a hydrocarbon such as ethylene (C_2H_4) acted as an organic radical and gave rise to a whole series of derivative compounds such as alcohol ($C_2H_4 + H_2O$), ether ($2C_2H_4 + H_2O$), and Dutch liquid ($C_2H_4 + Cl_2$). Laurent's study of naphthalene and anthracene, which appeared to contain the same relative proportions of carbon and hydrogen as ethylene and benzene, led him to generalize that all compounds could be understood as derivatives of hydrocarbons analogous to Dumas's series for ethylene.

b) *Substitutions and Additions:* Dumas had also shown that, in a large number of organic reactions, hydrogen was replaced by an equivalent amount of halogens, oxygen, etc. Laurent interpreted the action of the halogens upon naphthalene by applying Dumas's law of substitutions. But the most important demonstration of the truth of this law came from his study of naphthalic acid ($C_{40}H_8O_4 + O_4$; 4-volume formula, $C = 6$). This was formed by treating the following halogen derivative of naphthalene with nitric acid: $C_{40}H_{12}Cl_4 + H_4Cl_4$ (in modern notation $C_{10}H_8Cl_2$).

The reaction was explained by saying that H_4Cl_4 was removed from the radical directly derived from naphthalene (that is, $C_{40}H_{12}Cl_4$, where Cl_4 had replaced H_4 in the hydrocarbon: $C_{40}H_{16}$). But hydrochloric acid had further been added to the halogen derivative of naphthalene ($C_{40}H_{12}Cl_4 + H_4Cl_4$). This additional acid was shown by the reactions of naphthalic acid to remain outside the main radical corresponding to the hydrocarbon. Two analogies were thus involved: one with Dumas's theory of substitution and another based upon the explanation of the additional acid which remained outside of the substituted derivative of naphthalene. Laurent generalized from both and concluded that similar considerations applied to all organic reactions.

c) *Crystallography:* Laurent was greatly influenced by the work of Haüy in crystallography. Haüy had shown that the vast multiplicity of crystalline forms to be discovered in nature were in fact derived from five or six fundamental types of geometrical structure. By the application of a set of mathematical laws it was possible to reconstruct the basic form from which any given crystal was derived. Apart from the essential structure that could be discovered within a crystal, there were external accretions added to the crystal during its growth. A crystal was a unitary structure, and it was only by a feat of abstraction that different parts could be discovered within it. While developing his theory, Laurent closely followed an analogy with Haüy: the basic hydrocarbons from which all organic compounds were derived corresponded to the fundamental crystalline structure; the essential part of a crystal was like that portion of an organic molecule in which substitution occurred, while the additional parts, outside of the main radical, were assimilated to the accidental accretions to the crystal. Even more important than these detailed analogies was Laurent's general supposition, adopted from Haüy (via Baudrimont), that an organic molecule was a unitary structure that could not be interpreted in terms of the predominant dualistic theories of contemporary chemistry.

d) *Isomorphism:* Mitscherlich's law of isomorphism had shown that several substances which crystallized identically possessed similar properties, even though their elementary components were different. From this Laurent concluded that in organic compounds an analogous situation was to be found: it was the position and arrangement of the atoms in a molecule that determined their properties—not their intrinsic natures. Likewise, the properties of organic compounds were dependent upon their position within a "series" into which all such substances were to be naturally classified.

2. *Models*. Laurent wanted to construct a model that would be both a visual aid in understanding his theory and an account of some of the more obvious features of the crystalline forms of the substances studied. There were two kinds of current chemical models upon which he wished to draw, although both were recognized as unsatisfactory in certain important respects. In the first model it was assumed that when two chemical compounds reacted with each other, their molecules retained their original forms and were simply juxtaposed in the resulting combination. The other model was based on the contrary assumption that the original molecules disintegrated completely during the reaction and gave rise to a completely new type of structure. Laurent recognized the force of reasoning behind this second position, especially since it could not be denied that during a reaction there was an internal movement of all the constituents. He suggested however that reactions would be more intelligible if a certain deformation rather than a destruction of the molecular structures of the reactants were assumed.

For organic substances he suggested a pyramidal model that functioned like Haüy's fundamental and derived crystalline structures. Since all organic compounds were ultimately derived from hydrocarbons, Laurent imagined that there was a right-angled pyramid at the center, having as many solid angles and edges as there were atoms of carbon and hydrogen composing the hydrocarbon. The carbon atoms were represented at the angles while the hydrogen atoms occupied the centers of the edges. Attached to the sides of this central structure, although not an integral part of it, there would be other pyramids representing additions to the hydrocarbon, such as water, in Dumas's account of the composition of alcohol or ether ($C_2H_4 + H_2O$ or $2C_2H_4 + H_2O$).

Substitution reactions were represented in this model by the replacement of a hydrogen atom from one of the edges by an equivalent atom, such as chlorine. This obviously meant that for Laurent an electronegative element like a halogen could play a role identical to that of an electropositive element like hydrogen. This idea led to serious personal difficulties

with Berzelius. For in explaining a reaction such as the formation of naphthalic acid, where both substitution and addition occurred in Laurent's model, he assumed that two simultaneous modifications were involved: replacement of the atoms on the edges by their equivalents and attachment of new prisms to the bases. For instance, if four atoms of chlorine acted on the hydrocarbon $C_{12}H_{12}$, two chlorine atoms would replace two of the hydrogen atoms, while the latter combined with the other two chlorine atoms and formed hydrochloric acid, H_2Cl_2, which would attach itself to the bases.

When an equal number of equivalents replaced the atoms of a fundamental radical, the new substance formed had to have a similar formula and composition and the same fundamental properties as the original. In all these reactions it was emphasized that the central nucleus or pyramid retained its structure only as long as the carbon atoms were unaffected. If any of these were removed, the pyramid was destroyed and a wholly different type of product was formed having no relationship to the initial hydrocarbon. As long as the central pyramid was unaffected, the series of compounds belonged to the same family, of which the father was called the fundamental radical and the members to which it gave birth by substitution and addition were called derived radicals.

3. *Rationalism:* The third important influence on Laurent was his unquestioning faith in the rationality of nature. It found expression both in the assumption that nature always follows the simplest means to accomplish the most complicated ends and in the belief that natural phenomena embody mathematical principles. Thus, in his assertion that atoms always combine in simple numerical ratios to form organic compounds Laurent was also influenced by his belief in the uniformity of chemical principles that had to be equally valid both for organic and inorganic chemistry. Now if the laws of multiple proportions and of combining volumes in the latter were to be extended to organic chemistry then all combinations—and not only inorganic ones—occurred in simple numerical ratios. Concretely this meant that the fundamental hydrocarbons from which all organic substances were derived contained carbon and hydrogen in proportions of 1:1, 1:2, 1:3, 2:3, 3:5, · · · · . Another consequence of this rationalistic thinking was Laurent's attempt to give a quasi-mathematical form to his theory, which was stated as a set of formal propositions, an idiosyncrasy that has often occurred in the history of chemistry.

Due to its analogy with Haüy's crystallography, the formal theory was called the theory of fundamental and derived radicals, the former being a hydrocarbon and the latter its substitution and addition products. Among the theory's main tenets was the characterization of the hydrocarbons as neutral substances. The acidity was due to the existence of oxygen as a pyramid suspended outside the nucleus. Laurent maintained that alongside Dumas's law of substitution, the action of the halogens, oxygen, and nitric acid resulted in the formation of the corresponding halogen acid, or water, or nitrous acid, which were sometimes given out and sometimes combined with the new radical that was formed. He based this idea upon his view of acids as being hydrates. Laurent was also concerned to show why compounds containing large proportions of oxygen, such as sugar, gums, and carbon monoxide, were not acidic, surprising as this appeared to those who held that acidity was dependent upon the quantity of oxygen in a substance. This was even more difficult to reconcile with the fact that substances like stearic acid and margaric acids were distinctly acidic in their properties despite the tiny proportion of oxygen that they contained. The explanation Laurent offered was that in the former cases all the oxygen was contained within the fundamental nuclei, while in the latter cases the small quantity of this element was outside them. Thus, these acids were to be written as follows:

$$C_{70}H_{66}O_2 + O \qquad C_{140}H_{134}O_3 + O_2$$
$$\text{(margaric acid)} \qquad \text{(stearic acid)}$$

Both were derived from the hydrocarbon $C_{35}H_{35}$. Similar reasons led to the assertion that when the halogens or hydrogen were located outside the nucleus, the former generated acidic halogen compounds and the latter hydracids or hydrobases. These elements could be removed by the action of alkalis, heat, and other similar agents if they were outside the nucleus, but not when they were part of it. This furnished a simple experimental test for determining their positions.

Organic substances were classified into series defined by the relative numerical proportions of carbon and hydrogen. Given any such compound, it was possible to discover the series to which it belonged by imaginatively reconstructing the fundamental hydrocarbon from which it was derived. Examples of such series were:

a) C:H :: 1:1 which included cetene, tetrene, etherin, methylene, and their respective derivatives.

b) C:H :: 5:2 which included anthracene, naphthalene, and their derivatives.

c) C:H :: 2:1 which included cinnamene, benzogine, benzene, and their derivatives.

d) C:H :: 3:2 which included acetone, metacetone, and chloracetone.

e) C:H :: 5:4 which included pinic and silvic acids, camphene, citrene, and their derivatives.

f) C:H :: 10:7 which included camphor and its derivatives.

If a substance lost a carbon atom during its reactions, then it ceased to belong to the original series and gave rise to one or more compounds in other series.

Laurent's theory, formulated in 1835–1837, had thus succeeded not only in constructing an explanatory model and a set of general rules from which the formation of new organic compounds could be predicted by considering the numerous derivatives of a fundamental hydrocarbon nucleus but he had also furnished the first example of a comprehensive classification of organic compounds. The immediate experimental result that helped to test and confirm this theory was Laurent's discovery of two new hydrocarbons, pyrene and chrysene. Investigating the reactions of these and other similar hydrocarbons with nitric acid, Laurent also succeeded in preparing a new compound with anthracene, anthracenose (anthraquinone). In 1837 he investigated the preparation and properties of fatty acids and showed that the results coincided with those predicted on the basis of his theory.

In 1842 Laurent investigated the action of bromine on camphor and discovered that a compound was formed having a remarkable property: when this compound was heated or treated with an alkali it directly gave off bromine and not hydrobromic acid. Laurent had previously asserted that the theory of hydracids was correct in that when a halogen or oxygen acted upon a hydrocarbon, half of the element replaced an equivalent amount of hydrogen in the hydrocarbon nucleus. The other half united with the hydrogen given off during substitution, forming the corresponding acid or water; and this could combine with the derivative radical as an addition product located outside the central radical. It followed that, upon heating or reacting with potash, this acid or water was given off, a fact Laurent thought had been confirmed by all his previous work. But the behavior of the compound formed by camphor and bromine had disproved this, since bromine and not hydrobromic acid was given off. This observation was of special importance to him, for it involved modifying his theory in several important respects. First, he had to admit the correctness of the hydrogen theory of acids, due to Davy and Dulong, rather than the theory that the acids were hydrates, which he had hitherto maintained. Second, he had to abandon Dumas's theory of ethers and their halogen products. An ether did not contain water, nor did its halogen compounds contain a halogen acid; in both cases the fundamental radical was directly combined to oxygen or a halogen.

This result was of such importance to Laurent, involving, as it did, a modification of some of his essential ideas, that he had to obtain further experimental confirmation. The new experiments upon naphthalene and its compounds fully confirmed the predictions based on the view that in superchlorates or superbromides the additional chlorine and bromine existed outside the central nucleus as halogens and not as hydracids. There was still the need to prove that oxygen existed as such and not as water in similar cases. The proof was furnished by experiments upon the benzoyl series.

Ammonium sulfide was made to react with bitter almond oil, and the new compound obtained corresponded to the sulfide of the oil (*hydrure de sulfobenzoïle*):

$$\text{bitter almond oil} \quad C^{28}H^{12} + O^2$$
$$\text{new sulfide formed} \quad C^{28}H^{12} + S^2.$$

Various products were obtained upon distillation of this sulfide of benzoyl, including a new hydrocarbon, first discovered by Laurent, which he named stilbene. It resembled naphthalene in its properties, and its composition was represented by bitter almond oil minus oxygen, $C^{28}H^{12}$, or in four volumes $C^{56}H^{24}$. On reacting with chromic acid, this substance gave the desired addition product in which the hydrocarbon nucleus combined directly with oxygen (located outside the center) rather than with water; bitter almond oil or benzoic acid were the oxidation products of stilbene. ($C^{56}H^{24}$ had thus formed $C^{28}H^{12} + O^2$, an oxide—not a hydrate.)

Alongside this discovery another important influence led Laurent to modify his original theory. This was his work on crystallography in which he attempted to prove that the compounds derived by substitution from a fundamental radical were all isomorphic. He had already suggested this for the naphthalene series in 1837 and had continued to collect experimental evidence for it. The influence of the arrangement and order of the atoms in an organic molecule thus appeared to be of far greater importance in determining its properties than Laurent had previously realized. He thus insisted that the substitution derivatives of a fundamental hydrocarbon radical were distinguishable not only by their composition but also by the order in which the elements were introduced into them. For instance, if the fundamental radical were $C^{32}H^{32}$, and four of its hydrogen atoms were replaced by two chlorine and two bromine atoms, the resulting products would then be two different derived radicals, $C^{32}H^{28}Br^2Cl^2$ and $C^{32}H^{28}Cl^2Br^2$.

Laurent also pointed out (a factor that was to have an important development under the designation "mixed types" in the theories of Williamson and others) that complicated fundamental radicals were in fact due to additions of simpler ones; conversely, simpler fundamental radicals could be obtained by successive subtractions from a more complicated one. In fact it was possible to discover the internal arrangement of simpler radicals that were combined to form a complex one. Here a change from Laurent's original model was involved; instead of a single pyramid at the center, the nucleus was a complicated structure of several pyramids. For example, the following series all contained the last fundamental radical ($C^{24}H^{12}$) or one of its derivatives as a constituent part:

coumalic series	C^{40}	benzoic series	C^{28}
anisic series	C^{32}	salicylic series	C^{28}
phthalic series	C^{32}	anthracenic series	C^{28}
cinnamic series	C^{32}	aniline series	C^{28}
hippuric series	C^{32}	chloranilic series	C^{24}
indigo series	C^{32}	benzic series	C^{29}
estragon oil	C^{40}	phenic series	C^{29}

It was possible to transform these series into simpler ones and thereby to discover the simpler radicals of which their fundamental radicals were formed. Estragon oil, for example (derived radical $C^{40}H^{24}O^2$), was composed of three simpler radicals: C^8H^8, $C^{24}H^{12}$, $C^8H^4O^2$.

The modified theory was accompanied by a new method of classification. Laurent criticized (1844) the prevalent schemes in organic chemistry, derived as they were mainly from the dualistic classification of compounds into acids, bases, and the salts they engendered. He said that the same organic substance, for example, the same vegetable oils, could in fact be simultaneously considered as an essence or a fatty body, and a base or a salt, depending upon the characteristics singled out. The best classification for him would have been one in which the only substances grouped together were those that could be mutually transformed into each other, for instance, acetic and chloracetic acids. Unfortunately, this principle of mutual generation could not be applied in the vast majority of cases, so that another, more indirect, set of criteria had to be sought.

Laurent suggested two such criteria that could serve as mutual checks upon the position of an organic compound within a classificatory scheme (constancy in the number of carbon atoms in all members of the same group) and the existence of a fundamental radical from which all compounds in the same group were to be derived. Likening his classificatory principles to those of botany, he predicted that while external characteristics were of no help in taxonomy, the need to classify plants according to their generating principles—from seed to tree, flower, fruit—would eventually lead to the discovery of an embryonic cell or a nucleus that was reduplicated within each member of a botanical family. Fundamental radicals were similar to such nuclei, since they were reduplicated as a stable structure in all the members of a series in organic chemistry. This analogy has led to Laurent's theory being referred to as the "nucleus" theory.

In this later classification Laurent pointed out that the fundamental nuclei in organic chemistry did not necessarily have to be hydrocarbons but could contain any number of primary constituents and carbon.

Organic chemistry for Laurent comprised five types of structures.

1. Fundamental radicals. These were groups of atoms which fulfilled the same functions as the nonmetallic elements. From these, by equivalent substitution, derived radicals were formed which also played the same role as nonmetallic elements. For example:

$$\begin{array}{ll} \text{fundamental radical} & C_{32}H_{32} = R \\ \text{derived radical} & C_{32}H_{30}Cl_2 = R' \\ \text{derived radical} & C_{32}H_{28}Cl_4 = R'' \\ \text{derived radical} & C_{32}H_{20}Cl_{12} = R'''. \end{array}$$

2. Derived and fundamental radicals combined with elements to form chlorides, oxides, sulfides, etc. represented by: aR, bR, cR, $\cdots$; aR', bR', cR', $\cdots$; aR'', bR'', cR'', $\cdots$.

3. An excess of oxygen transformed the radical into an acid, that is, under the influence of oxygen in excess, an equivalent of hydrogen underwent a modification of properties that made it easy for a metal to replace it. Depending upon the quantity of oxygen, various kinds of weak organic acids were formed when this element combined with the radical:

$$\begin{array}{l} \text{oxides OR, OR', OR'', OR''', } \cdots; \\ \text{monobasic acids } O_2R, O_4R, O_4R', \cdots; \\ \text{polybasic acids } O_6R, O_6R', O_8R, \cdots. \end{array}$$

4. Organic metals. Hydrogen played the same role as a metal in organic chemistry, because the addition of hydrogen to a radical resulted in the formation of compounds that behaved identically to metals in inorganic chemistry.

5. Complex types. Radicals of two or more different types sometimes combined to form more complicated structures. For example, formiobenzoic acid, $C_{16}H_8 + O_6$, in spite of the six atoms of oxygen was monobasic, because it was formed by the combination of two different compounds: $C_{14}H_6 + O_6$ (bitter almond oil) $+ C_2H_2 + O_4$ (monobasic formic acid).

Laurent wanted to introduce a consistent nomenclature into organic chemistry, rather similar to Lavoisier's reform of the nomenclature of inorganic chemistry. His attempt was eminently rational but came too soon to be effective. Although Laurent's ideas were to be the basis—acknowledged or unacknowledged—of later structural organic chemistry, his views needed to be supplemented by a clear recognition of the idea of valence and chemical bond before a complete reform of the basis of organic chemistry was to be possible.

Laurent tried various types of nomenclatures; this was necessitated by the growing number of organic compounds discovered by him and his contemporaries. Some idea of a later version of his attempted reform can be gathered from the following:

Hydrocarbons. These were to have names ending in "ene" for the fundamental radicals: benzene, stilbene, etc.

Derived radicals. If oxygen replaced the hydrogen in a fundamental radical, then the progressive substitution products had names ending in the same order as the vowels:

$$\begin{array}{ll} \textit{palène} & C_4H_4 \\ \textit{palase} & C_4H_2O \\ \textit{palèse} & C_4O_2. \end{array}$$

If chlorine, bromine, $\cdots$, were substituted then the prefixes chlo-, bro-, $\cdots$, were to be added:

$$\begin{array}{ll} \textit{chlopalase} & C_4H_2Cl_2 \\ \textit{chlopalèse} & C_4Cl_4. \end{array}$$

Additional products. If the fundamental or derived radicals combined with an equivalent hydrogen, forming an organic metal, the ending "ene" was changed to "um":

$$\begin{array}{llll} \textit{palène} & C_4H_4 & \textit{palum} & H_4(C_4H_4) \\ \textit{chlopalase} & C_2H_2Cl_2 & \textit{chlopalasum} & H_4(C_4H_2Cl_2) \end{array}$$

If oxygen combined with the organic metals to give acids, the ending was changed to "ique":

$$\begin{array}{llll} \textit{palène} & C_4H_4 & \text{acid } \textit{palique} & (C_4H_4)\,H_4 + O_4 \\ \textit{palase} & C_4H_2O & \text{acid } \textit{palasique} & (C_4O)\,H_4 + O_4 \end{array}$$

In *Méthode de chimie* Laurent gave a more detailed and systematic account of the ideas on theoretical chemistry and classification that he had been developing. Among other important discoveries the following two are especially noteworthy.

1. *Reform of atomic weights.* Laurent pointed out that the formulas of organic compounds needed to be reduced to half their accepted values, that is, two-volume formulas were to replace four-volume formulas. In arriving at this conclusion he had been

influenced by Gerhardt. Laurent also recognized that the molecules of the elements hydrogen, chlorine, etc. were biatomic.

2. *The benzene ring.* Chemical compounds, represented on a geometrical model, were taken to form complete polyhedra. In a substitution reaction with a simple element, such as the replacement of hydrogen by chlorine in naphthalene, one of the edges of the original polyhedron occupied by a hydrogen atom was supposed to be removed; and the resulting complex could be stable only if the original polyhedron was immediately reformed by the substituted chlorine edge. When the substitution occurred in a complex radical the situation was even more complicated. Here two complete polyhedra were originally present, as, for example, in the action of ammonia upon benzoyl chloride (C_7H_5ClO). During the reaction both polyhedra lost an edge, respectively due to the removal of hydrogen in ammonia and chlorine in benzoyl chloride, the amide (NH_2) and benzoyl radical being left in the end product. These were two incomplete polyhedra, each of which functioned as a missing edge for the other. The model taken by Laurent for these compounds was, significantly, a hexagon in each case and the substitution was represented thus: $Bz = C_6H_5O$; $A = NH_2$

benzoyl chloride   ammonia   Bz   A

The two-faced Cl and H were removed during the reaction, and the polyhedron BzA was formed as a result.

Laurent constructed numerous other models of the same kind for different types of chemical reactions; but the fact that compounds of the benzene series were already envisaged as hexagonal, coupled with the view that the reinstatement of the edge was prompted by the requirement for chemical stability in the residual compounds, is especially significant for its obvious parallels with Kekulé's later views on the structure of benzene.

BIBLIOGRAPHY

An excellent bibliography, listing 216 of Laurent's publications, is J. Jacques, "Essai bibliographique sur l'oeuvre et la correspondance d'Auguste Laurent," in *Archives. Institut grand-ducal de Luxembourg*. Section des sciences naturelles, physiques et mathématiques, **22** (1955), 11–35. Laurent's doctoral diss. was published as *Recherches diverses de chimie organique. Sur la densité des argiles cuites à diverses températures* (Paris, 1837); a rare work, it may be consulted at the Faculté de Pharmacie and at the Bibliothèque de l'Institut, Paris. His two books are *Précis de cristallographie suivi d'une méthode simple d'analyse au chalumeau* (Paris, 1847); and *Méthode de chimie* (Paris, 1854). There is no worthwhile secondary literature.

SATISH C. KAPOOR

LAURENT, MATTHIEU PAUL HERMANN (*b.* Echternach, Luxembourg, 2 September 1841; *d.* Paris, France, 19 February 1908), *mathematics, higher education.*

Laurent's father, Auguste, was a noted chemist. After his father's death in 1853, Laurent was sent to the École Polytechnique in Paris and the École d'Application at Metz. He rose to the rank of officer but resigned in 1865 and took his *docteur-ès-sciences* at the University of Nancy with a thesis on the continuity of functions of a complex variable. In 1866 he became *répétiteur* at the École Polytechnique but returned to active military service during the Franco-Prussian War. He resigned to resume the post of *répétiteur* at the École Polytechnique, and in 1871 he was appointed actuary for the Compagnie d'Assurance de l'Union. In 1874 he married Berthe Moutard; in 1883 he became an *examinateur* at the École Polytechnique, and in 1889 he was appointed professor at the École Agronomique in Paris. In 1905 he was made an officer of the Legion of Honor.

Although Laurent's output comprised about thirty books and several dozen papers, his importance lies mainly in the teaching rather than in the development of mathematics. His papers dealt primarily with problems in analysis (especially relating to infinite series, elliptic functions, and Legendre polynomials), the theory of equations, differential equations and their solution, analytic geometry and the theory of curves, and the theory of substitutions and elimination. In the latter field he made one of his most useful contributions by extending some of the known techniques of eliminating variables to find the solutions to equations. Laurent was also noteworthy in developing statistical and interpolation formulas for the calculation of actuarial tables, annuities, and insurance rates; and he gave the name "chremastatistics" to subjects such as insurance and economics. He was a founding member of the Société des Actuaires Français and from 1903 was responsible for the mathematical section of the *Grande encyclopédie*, to which he contributed over 130 articles. He was a member of the editorial boards of the *Journal des mathématiques pures et appliquées* and of the *Nouvelles* annales des mathématiques, contributing articles especially to the latter.

Laurent's first textbook was the short *Traité des séries* (1862), one of the first works devoted entirely to the convergence as well as the summation of series; it was followed by *Traité des résidus* (1865). (It was Pierre Alphonse Laurent who was responsible, in 1843, for the Laurent series.) Of Laurent's later works, the comprehensive seven-volume *Traité d'analyse* (1885–1891) is notable. It is divided into two parts, of two and five volumes respectively, on the differential and integral calculus, and includes not only the standard treatments of the derivative and the integral and their applications to geometry but also substantial sections on the theory of functions, determinants, and elliptic functions. The last three volumes are devoted entirely to the solution and application of ordinary and partial differential equations. Laurent's other books deal with probability, arithmetic and algebra, rational mechanics, and statistics and its applications in economics. In 1895 he published *Traité d'arithmétique* under the names of his friends C. A. Laisant and Émile Lemoine, since arithmetic was part of the curriculum of the École Polytechnique, and he was not allowed as an examiner to publish the work under his own name.

BIBLIOGRAPHY

I. ORIGINAL WORKS. In addition to works mentioned in the text, the following are worthy of note: *Traité du calcul des probabilités* (Paris, 1873); *Théorie élémentaire des fonctions elliptiques* (Paris, 1882); *Traité d'algèbre* (Paris, 1867; 5th ed., 1894); *Traité de mécanique rationnelle*, 2 vols. (Paris, 1889); *Théorie des jeux de hasard* (Paris, 1893); *Théorie des assurances sur la vie* (Paris, 1895); *Opérations financières* (Paris, 1898); *L'élimination* (Paris, 1900); *Petit traité d'économie politique* (Paris, 1902); *Traité de perspective* [intended for artists and draftsmen] (Paris, 1902); *Appendice sur les résidus ...* (Paris, 1904); *Théorie des nombres ordinaires et algébriques* (Paris, 1904); *La géométrie analytique* (Paris, 1906); and *Statistique mathématique* (Paris, 1908), his last book. A substantial number of his papers on statistical and related matters were published in *Bulletin trimestriel de l'Institut des actuaires français*.

II. SECONDARY LITERATURE. The most comprehensive source of bibliographical and biographical information is a 63-page pamphlet published in 1909 under the title *Hermann Laurent 1841–1908. Biographie—bibliographie*. This work is, however, extremely rare; and a fairly substantial amount of information may be gleaned from Poggendorff, IV, 844; V, 713. A notice on Laurent appeared in the *Grande encyclopédie*, XXI, 1038.

I. GRATTAN-GUINNESS

LAURENT, PIERRE ALPHONSE (*b.* Paris, France, 18 July 1813; *d.* Paris, 2 September 1854), *mathematics, optics.*

In 1832, after studying for two years at the École Polytechnique, Laurent graduated among the highest in his class, receiving the rank of a second lieutenant in the engineering corps. When he left the École d'Application at Metz he was sent to Algeria, where he took part in the Tlemcen and Tafna expeditions. He returned to France and participated in the study leading to the enlargement of the port of Le Havre. Laurent spent about six years in Le Havre directing the difficult hydraulic construction projects. His superiors considered him a promising officer; they admired his sure judgment and his extensive practical training.

In the midst of these technical operations Laurent composed his first scientific memoirs. Around 1843 he sent to the Académie des Sciences a "Mémoire sur le calcul des variations." The Academy had set the following problem as the subject of the Grand Prize in the mathematical sciences for 1842: Find the limiting equations that must be joined to the indefinite equations in order to determine completely the maxima and minima of multiple integrals. The prize was won by Pierre Frédéric Sarrus, then dean of the Faculty of Sciences of Strasbourg. A memoir by Delaunay was accorded an honorable mention. Laurent submitted his memoir to the Academy after the close of the competition but before the judges announced their decision. His entry presented great similarities to Sarrus's work. Although some of Laurent's methods could be considered more inductive than rigorous, Cauchy, in his report of 20 May, concluded that the piece should be approved by the Academy and inserted in the *Recueil des savants étrangers*. Laurent's work was never published, however, while Delaunay's memoir appeared in the *Journal de l'Ecole polytechnique* in 1843, and Sarrus's in the *Recueil des savants étrangers* in 1846.

A similar fate befell Laurent's "Extension du théorème de M. Cauchy relatif à la convergence du développement d'une fonction suivant les puissances ascendantes de la variable x." The content of this paper is known only through Cauchy's report to the Academy in 1843. Characteristically, Cauchy spoke more about himself than about the author. He stated his own theorem first:

Let x designate a real or imaginary variable; a real or imaginary function of x will be developable in a convergent series ordered according to the ascending powers of this variable, while the modulus of the variable will preserve a value less than the smallest of the values for which the function or its derivative ceases to be finite or continuous.

While carefully examining the first demonstration of this theorem, Laurent recognized that Cauchy's analysis could lead to a more general theorem, which Cauchy formulated in his report in the following way:

> Let x designate a real or imaginary variable; a real or imaginary function of x can be represented by the sum of two convergent series, one ordered according to the integral and ascending powers of x, and the other according to the integral and descending powers of x; and the modulus of x will take on a value in an interval within which the function or its derivative does not cease to be finite and continuous.

Cauchy thought Laurent's memoir merited approval by the Academy and inclusion in the *Recueil des savants étrangers*, but it too was not published. One can gain an idea of Laurent's methods by his study published posthumously in 1863.

Meanwhile Laurent abandoned research in pure mathematics and concentrated on the theory of light waves. The majority of his investigations in this area appeared in notes published in the *Comptes rendus hebdomadaires des séances de l'Académie des sciences*. Laurent summarized the principal ideas of his research in a letter to Arago. He declared that the theory of polarization was still at the point where Fresnel had left it. He criticized Cauchy's method of finding differential equations to explain this group of phenomena and asserted that the equations were purely empirical. He rejected the use of single material points in determining the equations of motion of light, and employed instead a system combining the spheroids and a system of material points. Cauchy responded vigorously to Laurent's claim that he had thereby proved that the molecules of bodies have finite dimensions.

When Jacobi, a correspondent of the Academy since 1830, was elected a foreign associate member in 1846, Cauchy nominated Laurent for Jacobi's former position, but he was not elected. A short time later Laurent was promoted to major and called to Paris to join the committee on fortifications. While carrying out his new duties, he continued his scientific research. He died in 1854 at the age of forty-two, leaving a wife and three children.

His widow arranged for two more of his memoirs to be presented to the Academy of Sciences. One, on optics, *Examen de la théorie de la lumière dans le système des ondes*, was never published, despite Cauchy's recommendation that it be printed in the *Recueil des savants étrangers*. The other did not appear until

1863, when it was published in the *Journal de l'Ecole polytechnique*. Designating the modulus of a complex number as X and its argument as p, Laurent proposed to study the continuous integrals of the equation

$$dF/dx = 1/(x \sqrt{-1}) \cdot dF/dp,$$

where F is a function of the form $\varphi + \psi \sqrt{-1}$ subject to the condition $F(x, \pi) = F(x, -\pi)$, and which, together with its first order partial derivatives, remains finite and continuous for all x and all p relative to the points of the plane included between two closed curves A and B, each of which encircles the origin of the system of coordinates. If C is a curve encircling the origin, contained between A and B and represented by the polar equation

$$X = P(p), \quad \text{with} \quad P(\pi) = P(-\pi),$$

Laurent demonstrated that the integral

$$I = \int_{-\pi}^{+\pi} dp \, F(P, p)(\sqrt{-1} + 1/P \cdot dP/dp)$$

is independent of the curve C, that is, of the function P. He thus showed that the first variation of I is identically zero when C undergoes an infinitely small variation. He arrived at the same result, moreover, by calculating a double integral following a procedure devised by Cauchy. Laurent deduced his theorem from it by a method analogous to the one Cauchy had employed to establish his own theorem. He showed that if ρ_1 and ρ_2 are the radii of two circles centered at the origin and tangent respectively to the curves A and B, then at every polar coordinate point (X, p) situated in the annulus delimited by these circles:

$$F(X, p)$$

$$= \frac{1}{2\pi} \sum_{0}^{\infty} X^n e^{np\sqrt{-1}} \int_{-\pi}^{+\pi} dp' \, F(\rho_2, p') \frac{1}{\rho_2^n e^{np'\sqrt{-1}}}$$

$$+ \frac{1}{2\pi} \sum_{0}^{\infty} \frac{1}{X^n e^{np\sqrt{-1}}} \int_{-\pi}^{+\pi} dp' \, F(\rho_1, p') \, \rho_1^n e^{np'\sqrt{-1}}.$$

In the memoir he applied these results to the problem of the equilibrium of temperatures in a body and to the phenomenon of elasticity.

BIBLIOGRAPHY

I. ORIGINAL WORKS. Among Laurent's writings are "Mémoire sur la forme générale des équations aux différentielles linéaires et à coëfficients constants, propre à représenter les lois des mouvements infiniment petits d'un système de points matériels, soumis à des forces d'attraction ou de répulsion mutuelle," in *Comptes rendus hebdomadaires des séances de l'Académie des sciences*, **18** (1844), 294–297; "Equations des mouvements infiniment petits d'un système de sphéroïdes soumis à des forces d'attraction ou de répulsion mutuelle," *ibid.*, 771–774; "Sur la nature des forces répulsives entre les molécules," *ibid.*, 865–869; "Sur la rotation des plans de polarisation dans les mouvements infiniment petits d'un système de sphéroïdes," *ibid.*, 936–940; "Sur les fondements de la théorie mathématique de la polarisation mobile," *ibid.*, **19** (1844), 329–333; "Mémoire sur les mouvements infiniment petits d'une file rectiligne de sphéroïdes," *ibid.*, 482–483; and "Note sur les équations d'équilibre entre des forces quelconques, appliquées aux différents points d'un corps solide libre," in *Nouvelles annales de mathématiques*, IV (1845), 9–14.

See also "Note sur la théorie mathématique de la lumière," in *Comptes rendus hebdomadaires des séances de l'Académie des sciences*, **20** (1845), 560–563, 1076–1082, 1593–1603; "Observations sur les ondes liquides," *ibid.*, **20** (1845), 1713–1716; "Sur les mouvements atomiques," *ibid.*, **21** (1845), 438–443; "Sur les mouvements vibratoires de l'éther," *ibid.*, 529–553; "Recherches sur la théorie mathématique des mouvements ondulatoires," *ibid.*, 1160–1163; "Sur la propagation des ondes sonores," *ibid.*, **22** (1846), 80–84; "Sur les ondes sonores," *ibid.*, 251–253; and "Mémoire sur la théorie des imaginaires, sur l'équilibre des températures et sur l'équilibre d'élasticité," in *Journal de l'École polytechnique*, **23** (1863), 75–204.

II. SECONDARY LITERATURE. For information on Laurent's work, see the following articles in Augustin Cauchy, *Oeuvres complètes*, 1st ser., VIII (Paris, 1893): "Rapport sur un mémoire de M. Laurent qui a pour titre: Extension du théorème de M. Cauchy relatif à la convergence du développement d'une fonction suivant les puissances ascendantes de la variable x (30 Octobre 1843)," pp. 115–117; "Rapport sur un mémoire de M. Laurent relatif au calcul des variations (20 Mai 1844)," pp. 208–210; and "Observations à l'occasion d'une note de M. Laurent (20 Mai 1844)," pp. 210–213.

See also "Mémoire sur la théorie de la polarisation chromatique (27 Mai 1844)," *ibid.*, XI (Paris, 1899), 213–225; and "Rapport sur un mémoire de M. Laurent, relatif aux équations d'équilibre et de mouvement d'un système de sphéroïdes sollicités par des forces d'attraction et de répulsion mutuelles (31 Juillet 1848)," *ibid.*, pp. 73–75; and "Rapport sur deux mémoires de M. Pierre Alphonse Laurent, chef de bataillon du Génie (19 Mars 1855)," *ibid.*, XII (Paris, 1900), pp. 256–258.

For further reference, see Joseph Bertrand, "Notice sur les travaux du Commandant Laurent, lue en Avril 1860 à la séance annuelle de la Société des Amis des Sciences," in *Éloges académiques* (Paris, 1890), pp. 389–393; and I. Todhunter, *A History of the Calculus of Variations* (1861), pp. 476–477.

JEAN ITARD

LAUSSEDAT, AIMÉ (*b.* Moulins, France, 19 April 1819; *d.* Paris, France, 18 March 1907), *photogrammetry*.

After graduating from the École Polytechnique in 1840, Laussedat joined the Engineer Corps of the French army. He spent some years working on the fortifications of Paris and along the Spanish border, then taught courses in astronomy and geodesy at the École Polytechnique. In 1856 he was made professor of geodesy, and in 1873 he became professor of geometry at the Conservatoire des Arts et Métiers. He was promoted to colonel in the Engineer Corps in 1874 and retired as an officer in 1879. Laussedat became the director of studies at the École Polytechnique in 1880, and in 1881 succeeded Hervé-Mangon as director of the Conservatoire des Arts et Métiers. He was a member of the council of the Paris observatory, and during the siege of Paris (1870–1871) presided over the commission charged with the establishment of a department of visual communication. In 1894 he was elected a member of the Académie des Sciences.

Laussedat's main contribution was in the field of photogrammetry. From about 1849 he carried out extensive investigations on the use of photography to prepare topographic maps. In 1858 he used a glass-plate camera, supported by a string of kites, for aerial photography. He also prepared some maps from photographs taken from balloons (during a photographic trip in a balloon called *L'Univers*, he broke his leg). Laussedat abandoned his experiments on aerial photography with kites and balloons about 1860, primarily because it was extremely difficult to take enough photographs from one air station to cover the entire area visible from that station.

Laussedat made considerable use of ground photography by means of a phototheodolite (a combination of theodolite and camera). In 1859 he announced to the Académie des Sciences that he had successfully prepared topographic maps from the photographs taken with this instrument. His new technique was critically examined by two members of the Academy, Pierre Daussy and P. A. Laugier, and was found to be completely satisfactory. Laussedat exhibited the first known phototheodolite at the Paris Exposition of 1867, along with a map of Paris he had prepared with it. The map compared favorably with those prepared with the aid of conventional surveying instruments.

In spite of the ridicule he received from many of his contemporaries, Laussedat conducted further research on the use of photographs to prepare topographic maps. He successfully developed a new method of mathematical analysis to convert overlapping perspective views into orthographic projections in one plane. Laussedat discussed the results of his many years of research in *Recherches sur les instruments, les méthodes et le dessin topographiques.* The book was highly acclaimed, and some of the principles he laid down are still in use. Because of his manifold contributions to the field of aerial photography, he is often called the "father of photogrammetry."

BIBLIOGRAPHY

Laussedat's writings include *Expériences faites avec l'appareil à mesurer les bases appartenant à la Commission de la carte d'Espagne* (Paris, 1860); *Leçons sur l'art de lever les plans* (Paris, 1861); *Recherches sur les instruments, les méthodes et le dessin topographiques,* 3 vols. (Paris, 1898–1903); and *La délimitation de la frontière franco-allemande* (Paris, 1901). See also "Sur le progrès de l'art de lever les plans à l'aide de la photographie en Europe et en Amérique," in *Comptes rendus . . . des séances de l'Académie des sciences,* Session of 6 Feb. 1896.

ASIT K. BISWAS
MARGARET R. BISWAS

LAVANHA, JOÃO BAPTISTA (*b.* Portugal, *ca.* 1550; *d.* Madrid, Spain, 31 March 1624), *cosmography, mathematics.*

Lavanha was appointed professor of mathematics at Madrid in 1583. (At that time Spain and Portugal were united under Philip II.) From 1587 he served as chief engineer and several years later became chief cosmographer; although provisionally named to this post in 1591, he did not actually assume its duties until 1596. Responsible for the technical aspects of navigation, he maintained in Lisbon a chair for the teaching of mathematics to sailors and pilots. He also inspected the maps and instruments used in navigation prepared in the cartography workshops and supervised the construction of astrolabes, quadrants, and compasses. In addition he was placed in charge of the examinations required of all who wished to become pilots, cartographers, or instrument makers for the navy.

The best-known of Lavanha's works is undoubtedly the *Regimento nautico* (1595; 2nd ed., 1606), which contains important texts for pilots, including rules for determining latitude and tables of the declination of the sun, corrected by Lavanha himself. Around 1600 Lavanha was the first to prepare tables of azimuths at rising and setting for the observation of magnetic declination by taking the rhumb line of the rising or setting of the sun with the magnetic compass.

As an engineer Lavanha carried out fieldwork for the tracing of topographical maps, the most important

of which is the map of the kingdom of Aragon (1615–1618); to determine the coordinates of the fundamental points of the map Lavanha used a goniometer of his own design. This instrument was later perfected and proved very useful in surveying.

BIBLIOGRAPHY

I. ORIGINAL WORKS. The *Regimento nautico* underwent two eds. during the author's lifetime (see text). Lavanha's other works are "Tratado da arte de navegar," library of the National Palace, Madrid, MS 1910; still unpublished, this MS contains Lavanha's lectures given at Madrid in 1588; *Naufrágio de nau S. Alberto* (Lisbon, 1597); *Itinerário do reino de Aragon* (Zaragoza, 1895), which contains the notes taken by Lavanha during his travels in the course of preparing the topographical map of Aragon; "Descripción del universo," National Library, Madrid, MS 9251, a brief and carefully done treatise on cosmography dedicated to the crown prince and dating from 1613; *Quarta década da Ásia* (Madrid, 1615), a new ed. of the work of the same title by João de Barros, rev. and completed by Lavanha; and *Viagem da catholica real magestade del rey D. Filipe N. S. ao reyno de Portugal e relação do solene recebimento que nelle se lhe fez* (Madrid, 1622), an account of the festivities held in honor of the visit of Philip II to Portugal. Lavanha also wrote on history and the nobility.

II. SECONDARY LITERATURE. See Armando Cortesão, *Cartografia e cartógrafos portugueses dos séculos XVI e XVII,* II (Lisbon, 1935), 294–361; and Sousa Viterbo, *Trabalhos nauticos, dos Portugueses nos séculos XVI e XVII* (Lisbon, 1898), pp. 171–183.

LUÍS DE ALBUQUERQUE

LAVERAN, CHARLES LOUIS ALPHONSE (*b.* Paris, France, 18 June 1845; *d.* Paris, 18 May 1922), *medicine, biology, parasitology.*

Laveran studied medicine in Strasbourg, attending simultaneously the École Impériale du Service de Santé Militaire and the Faculté de Médecine, which in the 1860's were both well-known medical schools. His doctoral dissertation, defended at Strasbourg in 1867, dealt with experimental research on the regeneration of nerves; it is still worth consulting. Laveran served as military physician in the Franco-Prussian War. In 1874, after a competitive examination, he was named *professeur agrégé* at the École du Val de Grâce. From 1878 to 1883 he served in Algeria. During this period he carried out research on malaria, first at Bône and then at Constantine, where on 6 November 1880, at the military hospital, he discovered the living agent of malaria. Malarial fevers had afflicted men since antiquity, and their causes had been explained by the most varied and most contradictory hypotheses (see Hackett and Manson-Bahr). In his Nobel address he gave a precise and detailed account of his discovery.

Laveran, transferred to Paris, left the malaria-infested regions; and the discovery that its vector is the mosquito was made by Sir Ronald Ross, who always admitted having been put on this track by the work of Manson and of Laveran.

Laveran's discovery was greeted without enthusiasm. The military authorities did not recognize his merits, and he was not promoted. After having held the post of professor of military hygiene at the École du Val de Grâce from 1884 to 1894 and having filled several temporary administrative positions at Lille and Nantes, he left the army in 1896 to enter the Pasteur Institute, which "was proud to welcome independent spirits desiring to undertake disinterested research" (Roux). From 1897 Laveran carried out research on parasitic blood diseases in man and animals. In 1907 he was awarded the Nobel Prize for his work on pathogenic protozoans. He used the prize money to organize a laboratory at the Pasteur Institute for tropical medicine, which bears his name. In 1908 he founded the Société de Pathologie Exotique and was its president for twelve years. The Academy of Sciences, which had acknowledged his talents in 1889 with a major prize, elected him a member in 1901. He later became a member and president of the Academy of Medicine. He published the results of his numerous investigations not only in notes and memoirs but also in voluminous monographs remarkable for both the precision of their texts and the excellence of their illustrations.

Laveran was described by his friends Calmette and Émile Roux. He was cold and distant to those who did not know him and was a tenacious and solitary worker. Yet in his private life he was known for his cheerful disposition and was devoted to literature and the fine arts. His family consisted not only of his wife and sister, but also of his colleagues at the Pasteur Institute to whom he was attached by bonds of friendship.

BIBLIOGRAPHY

I. ORIGINAL WORKS. Laveran's writings include "Recherches expérimentales sur la régénération des nerfs" (Strasbourg, 1867), his M.D. thesis; *Traité des maladies et épidémies des armées* (Paris, 1875); "Sur un nouveau parasite trouvé dans le sang de plusieurs malades atteints de fièvre palustre," in *Bulletin de l'Académie de Médecine*, 2nd ser., **9** (1880), 1268; "Deuxième note relative à un nouveau parasite trouvé dans le sang de malades atteints de la fièvre palustre," *ibid.*, p. 1346; "Description d'un nouveau parasite découvert dans le sang de malades atteints d'impaludisme," in *Comptes rendus hebdomadaires des séances de l'Académie des sciences*, **93** (1881), 627; *Nature parasitaire des accidents de l'impaludisme, description d'un nouveau parasite trouvé dans le sang des malades atteints de fièvre palustre* (Paris, 1881); *Nouveaux éléments de pathologie et de clinique médicales*, 2nd ed., rev. and enl., 2 vols. (Paris, 1883), written with S. Teissier—see "Paludisme," p. 92; *Du paludisme et de son hématozoaire* (Paris, 1891); "Protozoa as Causes of Diseases," in *Nobel Lectures, Physiology or Medicine 1901–1921* (Amsterdam, 1967), pp. 257–274; *Trypanosomes et trypanosomiases*, 2nd ed., rev. (Paris, 1912), written with F. Mesnil; and *Leishmanioses-Kala-Azar-Bouton d'Orient, Leishmaniose américaine* (Paris, 1917).

II. SECONDARY LITERATURE. See A. Calmette, "Le professeur Laveran," in *Bulletin de la Société de pathologie exotique*, **15**, no. 6 (1922), 373–378; I. Fischer, *Biographisches Lexikon der hervorragenden Aerzte der letzten fünfzig Jahre*, II (Berlin, 1933), p. 873; L. W. Hackett, *Malaria in Europe, an Ecological Study* (Oxford, 1937), p. 109; P. Manson-Bahr, "The Story of Malaria: The Drama and Actors," in *International Review of Tropical Medicine*, **2** (1963), 329–390; R. Ross, *Nobel Lectures, Physiology or Medicine 1901–1921* (Amsterdam, 1967), pp. 19–119; J. L. Rouis, *Histoire de l'École impériale du Service de santé militaire instituée en 1856 à Strasbourg* (Nancy, 1898); E. Roux, "Jubilé de M. le pr. Laveran," in *Annales de l'Institut Pasteur*, **29** (1915), 405–414; and "A. Laveran," *ibid.*, **36**, no. 6 (1922), 459–461; and Edmond and Étienne Sergent and L. Parrot, *La découverte de Laveran* (Paris, 1929).

MARC KLEIN

LAVOISIER, ANTOINE-LAURENT (*b.* Paris, France, 26 August 1743; *d.* Paris, 8 May 1794), *chemistry, physiology, geology, economics, social reform.*

Remarkable for his versatility, as scientist and public servant, Lavoisier was first of all a chemist of genius, justly remembered for his discovery of the role of oxygen in chemical reactions and as the chief architect of a reform of chemistry, a reform so radical that he himself spoke of it early on as a "revolution" in that science. Yet Lavoisier also had a lifelong interest in geology and developed some original notions of stratigraphy; he was a pioneer in scientific agriculture, a financier of ability who holds a respected if minor place in the history of French economic thought, and a humanitarian and social reformer who used his position as a scientific statesman and landowner to alleviate the evils of society. His death on the guillotine in his fifty-first year, with creative powers still undiminished, has marked him, with the obvious exceptions of Louis XVI and Marie Antoinette, as the outstanding martyr to the excesses of the Reign of Terror during the French Revolution.

Lavoisier was a Parisian through and through and a child of the Enlightenment. Born in 1743, in the midreign of Louis XV and in the last year of the administration of Cardinal Fleury, his boyhood coincided with the flowering of the philosophic movement in France. The *Traité de dynamique*, which was to make d'Alembert's reputation, was published in the year of Lavoisier's birth. Voltaire's *Lettres philosophiques* had appeared ten years earlier (1733). Lavoisier was eight years old when the first volume of the *Encyclopédie* appeared and ten when Diderot, in his *Interprétation de la nature*, proclaimed that the future of science lay not in mathematical studies but in experimental physics—exemplified by the discoveries of Benjamin Franklin—and in chemistry.

Lavoisier's family, originally from Villers-Cotterets, a forest-encircled town some fifty miles north of Paris, was of humble, doubtless of peasant, origin.[1] His earliest recorded ancestor, a certain Antoine Lavoisier, was a courier of the royal postal service *(chevaucheur des écuries du roi)* who died in 1620; a son, another Antoine, rose to be master of the post at Villers-Cotterets, a position of some distinction. Three generations later Lavoisier's grandfather, still another Antoine, served as solicitor *(procureur)* at the bailiff's court of Villers-Cotterets and married Jeanne Waroquier, the daughter of a notary from nearby Pierrefonds. Their only son, Jean-Antoine, Lavoisier's father, was sent to Paris to study law. In 1741, still a mere fledgling in his profession, Jean-Antoine inherited the estate, as well as the *charge* of solicitor at the Parlement of Paris, of his uncle Jacques Waroquier. The following year he married Émilie Punctis, the well-dowered daughter of an attorney *(avocat)* at the Paris law courts. Their first child, Antoine-Laurent, the subject of this sketch, and a younger sister who was to die in her teens, were both born in the house in the cul-de-sac Pecquet (or Pecquay) which had been the residence of the old solicitor.[2] Here Lavoisier spent the first five years of his life, until the death of his mother in 1748. This bereavement led Jean-Antoine to move the two children to the house of his recently widowed mother-in-law, Mme Punctis, in the rue du Four near the church of St. Eustache.[3] In this house, tenderly cared for by an adoring maiden aunt, Mlle Constance Punctis, Lavoisier spent his childhood, his school days, and his young manhood until his marriage.

Lavoisier received his formal education in the Collège des Quatre Nations, a remarkable school— among its alumni were the physicist and mathema-

tician d'Alembert, the astronomer J. S. Bailly, and the painter David—founded by the will of Cardinal Mazarin and so commonly called the Collège Mazarin. In the autumn of 1754, shortly after his eleventh birthday, Lavoisier was enrolled as a day student *(externe)* in the splendid building that today houses, under its gilded dome, the constituent academies of the Institut de France. At Mazarin, Lavoisier gained a sound classical and literary training, earned more than his share of literary prizes, and received the best scientific education available in any of the Paris schools. The course of study at Mazarin covered nine years; after the class of rhetoric, devoted to language and literature, and before the two years of philosophy, came a full year devoted to mathematics and the sciences under the tutelage of the distinguished astronomer Lacaille, famed for his expedition to the Cape of Good Hope and his charting of the stars of the southern hemisphere. We can gather something of Lacaille's teaching from his elementary books on mathematics, mechanics, optics, and astronomy. More than a trace of this training is to be found in Lavoisier's earliest scientific memoir, a highly precise description of an aurora borealis visible at Villers-Cotterets in October 1763. Observing it on a clear night, he showed his familiarity with Flamsteed's star table, carefully locating the streamers with respect to the visible stars and measuring their azimuth and altitude with a compass provided with an alidade.[4]

In 1761, rather than complete the class of philosophy leading to the baccalaureate of arts, Lavoisier transferred to the Faculty of Law; faithful, for the moment at least, to the family tradition, he received his baccalaureate in law in 1763 and his licentiate the following year.

Yet already his interest had turned to science, which he pursued in extracurricular fashion while carrying on his legal studies. Lavoisier may have received some further instruction from Lacaille in the intimacy of the latter's observatory at the Collège Mazarin, but only for a short while, for Lacaille died late in 1762. In the summer of 1763, and again the following year, Lavoisier accompanied the distinguished botanist Bernard de Jussieu on his *promenades philosophiques* in the Paris region.[5] Yet Jussieu's influence was probably slight—botany held little attraction for Lavoisier—whereas Lacaille's teaching helps account for Lavoisier's quantitative bent of mind, his lifelong interest in meteorological phenomena, and the barometric observations he made throughout his career.

Lavoisier's family and friends were soon aware that science had captivated the young man and was luring him away from the law. In an early letter (dated

March 1762) Lavoisier was addressed by a family friend as "mon cher et aimable mathématicien"; and the same correspondent expressed concern that his young friend's health might suffer from his intense application to the various branches of science.[6] It is better, he continued—and Lavoisier would surely have disagreed—to have a year more on earth than a hundred years in the memory of men. Clearly, Lavoisier already displayed the boundless energy and wide-ranging curiosity that was to characterize him all his life; indeed another family friend, the geologist Jean-Étienne Guettard, described him in these years as a young man whose "natural taste for the sciences leads him to want to know all of them before concentrating on one rather than another."[7] Yet it was Guettard who exerted the greatest influence upon Lavoisier and focused the young man's attention upon geology and mineralogy, and also, since it was an indispensable ancillary science, upon chemistry; for Guettard believed that to be "a mineralogist as enlightened as one can be," it was important to learn enough chemistry to be able to analyze, and so help to identify and classify, rocks and minerals.[8]

It was probably at Guettard's suggestion that Lavoisier attended the course in chemistry given by Guillaume François Rouelle.[9] A brilliant and flamboyant lecturer and a vivid popularizer, Rouelle filled his lecture hall at the Jardin du Roi with a mixed audience of students, young apothecaries, society folk, and such well-known men of letters as Diderot, Rousseau, and the economist Turgot. Besides Lavoisier, the leading French chemists of at least two generations were introduced to the subject by Rouelle. Included in Rouelle's course was a series of lectures on mineralogical problems; besides describing the physical and chemical properties of mineral substances, Rouelle touched upon his own rather special theory of geological stratification.

Accordingly, persuaded that these lectures provided the best—if not the only—instruction in mineralogy and the chemistry of minerals, Lavoisier followed them faithfully, probably in 1762–1763. If he attended the showy lectures at the Jardin du Roi, he almost certainly followed the private—and perhaps more technical—course Rouelle taught in his apothecary shop on the rue Jacob, near St. Germain des Prés.

Under Guettard's guidance geology absorbed Lavoisier's attention in these years. As early as 1763 he began his collection of rock and mineral specimens; and with Guettard he explored the region around Villers-Cotterets, where he was accustomed to vacation with relatives.

For some time, indeed since 1746, Guettard had nurtured a plan for a geologic and mineralogic atlas of France. It did not receive official support until 1766, when it was commissioned and funded by the royal government; but even earlier Guettard enlisted young Lavoisier as a collaborator. In repeated excursions in northern France—to Mézières and Sedan, through Normandy to the coast at Dieppe—the two men collected specimens, noted outcroppings, drew sections, and described the principal strata, assembling material for the atlas. Their intensive exploration and mappings continued until 1770, by which time they had completed and printed sixteen regional quadrangles, using symbols to designate the rock formations and mineral deposits.

The most extensive of these joint expeditions, and the most venturesome, was a trip through the Vosges Mountains and parts of Alsace and Lorraine in 1767. Accompanied by Lavoisier's servant, Lavoisier and Guettard traveled on horseback for four months, often under trying, if not actually hazardous, conditions. The letters Lavoisier exchanged with his father and his adoring aunt during this long absence from Paris have largely survived; and Lavoisier's own warm, affectionate epistles are very nearly the only letters among the many extant in which we glimpse his personal feelings.

Lavoisier's special contribution to this venture, as to the other expeditions, was to add a quantitative character to their observations. He used the barometer systematically to measure the heights of mountains and the elevations and inclinations of strata, intending to use the results for drawing type sections; and he collected samples of mineral and spring waters to be analyzed in the field or shipped back to Paris. Nor was all this deemed of purely practical value: by 1766 he had outlined a research program of experiments and observations that should lead him, in the language of the day, to a "theory of the earth," that is, to an understanding of the changes that had altered the surface of the globe.

For the most part, Lavoisier's early theories of stratification were derived from Guettard and Rouelle or from his reading of Buffon's *Théorie de la terre* of 1749. Guettard, of a largely practical turn of mind, described the geology of France in terms of three *bandes* differing in their lithology. Rouelle distinguished the *terre ancienne*, the granitic and schistose formations in which fossils apparently were absent, from the generally horizontal, sedimentary strata rich in fossils, which he called the *terre nouvelle*. The strata of the *terre nouvelle*, he believed, had been deposited when the sea covered all or most of the continent of Europe. Accepting Rouelle's division (although often using Guettard's terms), Lavoisier at first assumed that there had been only a single epoch in which the present continents were submerged. But he soon observed that the *terre nouvelle* was composed of two different kinds of strata: fine-grained, calcareous beds (pelagic beds), such as would result from a slow deposition in the open sea, and littoral deposits of rougher, abraded, and pebblelike material, formed at beaches and coastlines. These had been distinguished by his predecessors, but it was Lavoisier who noted that littoral and pelagic beds sometimes seemed to alternate with each other. As early as October 1766 he came to the radical conclusion—which greatly extended his conception of geologic time—that there may have been a succession of epochs marked by a cyclically advancing and retreating sea. In the regions he knew best there was not a single *terre nouvelle* but, rather, three different pelagic formations laid down at different times. Even the *terre ancienne* was not truly primitive rock; it was more likely, he remarked at one point, to be composed of littoral beds formed very long ago *(bancs littoraux beaucoup plus anciennement formés)*.

Lavoisier never lost interest in these geological problems, although after 1767 his opportunities for fieldwork markedly diminished; he continued, as far as innumerable distractions permitted, to be associated with the atlas project until 1777, the year when Antoine Monnet was officially put in charge of it. But it was not until 1788 that Lavoisier presented his theory of stratification to the Academy.

Lavoisier's earliest chemical investigation, his study of gypsum, was mineralogical in character; begun in the autumn of 1764, it was intended as the first paper in a series devoted to the analysis of mineral substances. This systematic inventory was to be carried out, not by the method of J. H. Pott—who exposed minerals to the action of fire—but by reactions in solution, by the "wet way." "I have tried to copy nature," Lavoisier wrote. "Water, this almost universal solvent . . . is the chief agent she employs; it is also the one I have adopted in my work."[10] Using a hydrometer, he determined with care the solubility of different samples of gypsum (samples of selenite, or *lapis specularis*, some supplied by Guettard and Rouelle). He made similar measurements with calcined gypsum (plaster of Paris). Analysis convinced him that this gypsum was a neutral salt, a compound of vitriolic (sulfuric) acid and a calcareous or chalky base. Not content with having shown by analysis the composition of the gypsum, Lavoisier completed his proof by a synthesis following, as he said, the way that nature had formed the gypsum. He further demonstrated that gypsum, when transformed by strong heating into plaster of Paris, gives off a vapor, which he showed to be pure water, making up about a quarter of the weight of gypsum. Conversely, when plaster of Paris is mixed with water and turns into a solid mass, it avidly combines with water. Using the expression first coined by Rouelle, he called this the "water of crystallization."

This first paper, which in so many respects embodies the quantitative methods Lavoisier was to employ in his later work, had in fact been largely anticipated by others, notably by Marggraf, who had already discovered the composition of gypsum and shown that it contained water *(phlegm)*. Yet Lavoisier's work was more thorough; and his paper, his first contribution to the Academy of Sciences (read to the Academy on 25 February 1765), appeared in 1768 in what was usually called the *Mémoires des savants étrangers*, an Academy organ which published some of the papers read to that body by nonmembers, often by those who, like Lavoisier, aspired to membership.[11]

At the age of twenty-one Lavoisier was already an aspirant; to be sure, the time had passed when men of that tender age were readily admitted to the Academy as *élèves* or *adjoints*. Yet Lavoisier had friends in the Academy, and his father and his aunt were not averse to pulling such strings as came to hand. Meanwhile, the young man laid siege to the Academy from another angle. He resolved in 1764 to compete for the prize offered by the lieutenant general of police, and to be judged by the Academy, for the best method of improving the street lighting of Paris. The effort he put into this inquiry was prodigious; he attempted, as A. N. Meldrum put it, to exhaust the subject—theoretically, practically, and even (as he was to do so often in later inquiries) historically. He sought the best available material for lamp wicks and the combustible; he determined what shape—whether parabolic, hyperbolic, or elliptical—made the best reflectors; he recommended how lanterns should be suspended to give the best illumination; and much else, although there was practically no chemistry involved. Lavoisier did not win the contest—indeed nobody did, for the prize was divided into smaller awards; but a gold medal, specially authorized by the king, was presented to him at the Easter public session of the Academy on 9 April 1766, a month after he had read to that body a second paper on gypsum.

Later that month Lavoisier's supporters in the Academy entered his name in the list of candidates for the place of *adjoint chimiste* that had fallen vacant. Needless to say, Lavoisier, at the age of twenty-two, was the youngest postulant. The winner, Louis Cadet de Gassicourt, like most of the others, was some ten years his senior. Nevertheless, Lavoisier's confidence was unabated; just prior to this election he drafted two similar letters, to be signed by one or more of his friends in the Academy; one was addressed to Mignot de Montigny (the president of the Academy for that year), the other to the perpetual secretary, Grandjean de Fouchy. Both letters urged the Academy to create a new division or class of *physique expérimentale*.[12] If Lavoisier hoped to make room for himself in this rigidly structured and exclusive body, nothing came of this early example of his ambition and overwhelming self-confidence; the letters probably were never sent. But that Lavoisier was serious about the importance of experimental physics we need hardly doubt; he thought of himself, then and later, as a *physicien*, an experimental physicist, even more than as a chemist. Only when his investigations dealt with the reactive or combinatorial behavior of substances (as in the paper on gypsum) did Lavoisier speak of doing chemistry. When, on the other hand, he investigated the physical "instruments" that bring about or influence chemical change—water, elastic fluids like air, imponderable fluids like heat or electricity—this was physics; he was wont, characteristically, to refer to Boyle and Priestley as *physiciens*, not as chemists. There is further proof of his sincerity; in 1785, when the Academy of Sciences underwent its last reorganization before the Revolution—and this was largely Lavoisier's achievement—a *classe de physique générale* was finally established.

Lavoisier was not easily discouraged. In 1767, during his trip through the Vosges with Guettard, he received optimistic news from his father about his chances of election. Indeed, he seems to have taken his success for granted. On the title page of a copy of Agricola's *De re metallica*, which he purchased in Strasbourg in September, he wrote confidently: "Antonius Laurentius Lavoisier Regiae Scientiarum Academiae Socius anno 1767."[13]

In the spring of 1768 Lavoisier read to the Academy of Sciences a paper on hydrometry describing an accurate instrument of the constant-immersion type which he had designed. This was followed by the reading of a long paper on the analysis of samples of water he had collected in the course of his travels with Guettard. Then, as now, Europeans ascribed remarkable curative properties to the waters of various spas; and already there had grown up a large medico-chemical literature on mineral waters. Before Lavoisier, these were the only waters commonly analyzed. The method employed was first to identify by qualitative analysis the principal salt in a given sample; the concentration of this salt was then determined by evaporating a certain volume of water to dryness and weighing the solid residue. Lavoisier distrusted this method, for the salt could be lost by decrepitation, spattering, volatilization, or in some cases by de-

composition. His method was to determine the concentration of the characteristic salt by making specific-gravity measurements of the water sample with his improved hydrometer, a method which was, of course, limited to waters containing a single salt. Typically, Lavoisier did not concern himself with the analysis of mineral waters—which, he wrote, were important for only a small number of privileged persons—but with the potable waters used by society as a whole: waters from springs, wells, and rivers. He analyzed some samples in the field, but the best of his many measurements were made at the virtually constant temperature of the deep cellars of the Paris astronomical observatory.

Water, as we have seen, fascinated Lavoisier; he spoke of it as *l'agent favori de la nature* and as the chief agent in shaping the earth, producing all its crystal forms (including the diamond!). Analysis of waters ought to give some clue, he believed, to the kinds of hidden strata through which water flowed before emerging as a spring or river. The tables that accompanied this paper reveal his objective: the first table lists his analyses of water found in the inclined granitic and schistose strata of the Vosges Mountains, where all of his samples were more or less rich in Glauber's salt (hydrated sodium sulfate). The second table, analyzing water samples collected in the *bande calcaire*, disclosed a marked quantity of selenite or gypsum, with traces of sea salt.

Lavoisier's election to the Academy followed shortly upon the reading of this paper. The Academy's vote was divided between Lavoisier and Gabriel Jars, a mining engineer for the royal government, with Lavoisier receiving a slight majority. When, according to established practice, the two top names were submitted to the king's minister, the Comte de St. Florentin, Jars was designated *adjoint chimiste* but a special dispensation was accorded Lavoisier, who was admitted, to the great joy of his father and his aunt, as *adjoint chimiste surnuméraire*.

Shortly before his election, in March 1768, Lavoisier entered the Ferme Générale, a private consortium that collected for the government such indirect imposts as the tax on tobacco and on salt (the *gabelle*), as well as customs duties and taxes on produce entering Paris. Having inherited a considerable fortune from his mother, he now invested a substantial portion of his capital by assuming a third of the interest of the farmer-general, François Baudon, in a lease *(bail)* negotiated under the name of a certain Jean d'Alaterre. Some of Lavoisier's future colleagues in the Academy of Sciences feared these responsibilities would detract from his scientific work. Others, like the astronomer Lalande, supported Lavoisier by arguing that his increased wealth made it unnecessary for him to seek other ways of earning a living. Indeed, so the story goes, one mathematician remarked, "Fine. The dinners he will give us will be that much better."

For the next few years, much of Lavoisier's time was taken up with journeys, as a traveling inspector (*tourneur*), on behalf of the Ferme Générale. One of these expeditions, from July to November 1769, took him across Champagne to inspect tobacco factories and check on the deployment of brigades assigned to catch smugglers. The early months of 1770 found him at Lille in Flanders; in August he was in Amiens, where he read a paper on the mineralogy of France (especially Picardy) at a public session of the Academy of Amiens. In the same year, again combining scientific work with his official travels, he presented a memoir on the water supply of Rouen to the academy of that city.

In 1771 Lavoisier married Marie Anne Pierrette Paulze, the only daughter of a farmer-general, Jacques Paulze. The discrepancy of age was notable: Lavoisier was twenty-eight, his bride not quite fourteen. Although the marriage was childless, it was happy and harmonious, a bourgeois marriage singularly devoid, it would seem, of anything other than fidelity and mutual esteem. Mme Lavoisier trained herself to be her husband's collaborator: she learned English (which he did not read), studied art with the painter David, and became a skilled draftsman and engraver. The thirteen copperplate illustrations in her husband's *Traité élémentaire de chimie* are her work; they are signed "Paulze Lavoisier sculpsit." In 1775, when Lavoisier was appointed a commissioner of the Royal Gunpowder Administration (Régie des Poudres et Salpêtres), to serve in effect as scientific director, the couple took up residence in the Paris Arsenal.[14] Here Lavoisier equipped a fine laboratory where most of his later scientific work was carried out. Mme Lavoisier often assisted him, recording the results of experiments; and as his hostess to visiting scientific celebrities, and at weekly gatherings of his scientific colleagues, she proved an indefatigable promoter of the "new chemistry" and her husband's renown.

As Lavoisier himself insisted, concern for the public welfare was at least as important in directing his attention to the problem of water supply for Paris as was scientific curiosity. One of his earliest publications (in the *Mercure de France* for October 1769) was a reply to a certain Father Félicien de St. Norbert who had opposed a much-discussed plan to bring to Paris, by an open canal, the waters of the Yvette, a tributary of the Orge River. The plan had been proposed by an engineer, Antoine de Parcieux, who in memoirs read to the Academy of Sciences defended the feasibility of the project. The potability of the water of the

Yvette and its purity seemed attested by experiments performed under the separate auspices of the Academy of Sciences and the Faculty of Medicine. Since these analyses involved weighing the solid residue obtained by evaporation to dryness, the question arose at the Academy whether it was true that water, on distillation, could be in part transmuted into earth; if so— and several early chemists believed this to be the case—then the method of evaporating to dryness was undependable. The transmutation problem was discussed by the physicist J. B. Le Roy in a memoir presented at the Easter public meeting of the Academy in 1767. Le Roy did not believe that water could be changed into earth, but suggested instead that earth is somehow essential to the nature of water, or intimately associated with it, and that during distillation water and earth pass over together into the receiver. Nevertheless, the doctrine of transmutation had the authority of J. B. Van Helmont and of Robert Boyle, each of whom believed he had shown by experiment that the nutrition and growth of plants can only be attributed to water. Experiments like theirs were performed by various eighteenth-century scientists, chief among them the German physician Johann Theodor Eller, who found support for this doctrine by an experiment in which earth appeared to be formed when water was subjected to violent and prolonged shaking in a closed vessel and by experiments, performed with hyacinth bulbs, similar to the plant experiments of Van Helmont and Boyle.

This question, which had engaged so many distinguished scientists, Lavoisier was to solve, not long after his election to the Academy of Sciences, by means of an experiment that was to make his name widely known and satisfy that craving for public recognition which was already a marked aspect of his character. He began in the late summer of 1768 with attempts to obtain distilled water of the highest purity for use as a standard in his hydrometric measurements. Pure rain water, he found, when repeatedly distilled, always left behind a small solid residue, yet with no appreciable change in its specific gravity. It occurred to him that the solid matter might have been produced during the distillation, perhaps from the glass, some of which might have been dissolved by the boiling water. To settle the question, he placed the sample of water, which he had repeatedly distilled, in a carefully cleaned and weighed glass vessel called a pelican, a vessel so designed that water-vapor condensed in a spherical cap, then descended to the bottom through two handle-like tubes, only to be vaporized once more. Before placing the apparatus on a sand-bath, he weighed the pelican with its contained water (obtaining thereby, by difference, the weight of water). He began the refluxing on 24 October 1768, continuing it for 101 days. After a few weeks he noted the appearance of particles of solid matter. When he stopped the experiment on 1 February 1769, he weighed the apparatus, finding no appreciable change in weight. Then transferring the water and the solid matter to another glass container, Lavoisier dried the pelican, reweighed it and found it significantly lighter. When he weighed the earthy particles, and evaporated the water to dryness, weighing the solid residue, he found the total amount of the solid matter roughly equal to the loss in weight of the pelican. Clearly, the earthy material (silica) had been dissolved from the glass and was not the result of a transmutation of the water.

This well-known experiment demonstrates Lavoisier's experimental ingenuity and those gravimetric procedures that were to characterize his later work. The research was written up and initialed (paraphé) by the secretary of the Academy early in 1769; yet the paper was not read until November 1770. Lavoisier's discovery, presented in a public session, was promptly noted by the press; but impatient to see the results in print and unwilling to await the leisurely publication of the Histoire et mémoires of the Academy, Lavoisier profited from the establishment of a new scientific journal, the Abbé Rozier's Observations sur la physique, sur l'histoire naturelle, et sur les arts. A reference to Lavoisier's experiment appeared in a note in the first number of this journal (July 1771), and an extended summary was published in the second (August) number. Lavoisier's full account did not appear in the Histoire et mémoires until 1773.

This famous experiment may have had a practical aim, but its theoretical significance was probably foremost in Lavoisier's mind: water, he had shown, was not transmuted into earth and was probably an unchangeable element. We now know that as early as 1766 Lavoisier had begun to speculate about the nature of the traditional four elements, stimulated by two papers of J. T. Eller published in the Memoirs of the Berlin Academy. In these papers Eller rejected the doctrine of four elements and defended instead the notion that the true principles of nature were the "active" elements, fire and water. Water, as Eller believed he had shown by experiment, could produce earth. Lavoisier's experiment had pretty well disposed of this contention. But more interesting to Lavoisier was Eller's suggestion that air was the result of a combination of water with the matter of fire. This identification of water vapor with air can best be understood in the light of eighteenth-century theories about air and vapors. Air was the elastic body par excellence, playing its role (in combustion, for example) as a

physical rather than a chemical agent. Vapors, on the other hand, were not thought to be inherently elastic but to be foreign particles dispersed and dissolved in air, just as particles of salt are dissolved in water. Nevertheless, scientists (Wallerius and Eller among them) had shown that water could evaporate in a vacuum, where there was no air into which the particles of water could be dissolved. Moreover, the increase in barometric pressure in the receiver of an air pump after the evaporation of water suggested to Eller that the water had been transformed into air by combining with the matter of fire.

In May 1766, Lavoisier jotted down two notes inspired by a rapid reading of Eller's papers; these, he noted, struck him as "very well done." In the first of his notes he recorded Eller's notion that air might not be an element but a combination of water with the matter of fire. In his second note he developed his own theory, ignoring Eller's identification of water vapor with air. Instead, he suggested that air, by being combined with the matter of fire, might be a fluid in a permanent state of expansion. The elements, Lavoisier wrote, enter into the composition of all bodies; but this combination does not take place in the same manner in all bodies. There is a great similarity between the aerial fluid and the igneous fluid. Both lose a part of their (characteristic) properties when they combine with bodies. It is known, for example, that air when combined ceases to be elastic and occupies a space infinitely less than when it was free.

This last comment is a clear allusion to the work of Stephen Hales, who, in a long chapter of his Vegetable Staticks, had demonstrated that air could exist "fixed" in a wide variety of animal, vegetable and mineral substances. Hales's book had been translated in 1735 by Buffon, and Lavoisier doubtless first learned of Hales's experiments on "fixed air" from the lectures of Rouelle. But he may have been impelled by a reference in one of Eller's papers to turn directly to the Vegetable Staticks. In the years that followed, Lavoisier was to puzzle over this problem of the elements, with his attention focused increasingly upon the fixation of air and the possibility that the aeriform state resulted from the combination of some base with the matter of fire.

A key idea drawn from his reading of Hales was that the effervescence produced in various chemical reactions was not merely the result of the thermal agitation accompanying the reaction, or "fermentation," but was instead the sudden release of "fixed air." In 1768 Lavoisier called attention to a phenomenon (observed long before by the chemist E. F. Geoffroy) that certain effervescent reactions produce a cooling effect.[15] This appeared to refute the belief that effervescences were simply the result of strong intestine motion of particles and that the heat, as some scientists believed, observed in other effervescent reactions was the result of friction. Moreover, it supported his notion that the air so released combined with the "matter of fire." Not long afterward, sometime between 1769 and 1770, Lavoisier became familiar with another phenomenon that supported his notion that air might be a combination of a base with the "matter of fire."

The observation of the Scots physician William Cullen (and of Lavoisier's compatriot Antoine Baumé) that when highly volatile liquids like ether or alcohol are vaporized, they produce a pronounced drop in temperature, was strong support for this theory, for the simplest explanation was that the change from liquid to vapor was accompanied by the absorption of heat or the "matter of fire." In 1771—as yet unaware of Joseph Black's unpublished discoveries concerning latent heat—Lavoisier observed that when ice melts, although heat is steadily applied to it, the temperature of an ice-water mixture remains unchanged. Clearly, "fire" becomes "fixed," unable to affect the thermometer.

All these scattered bits of evidence were given clear meaning when Lavoisier encountered—just when, we are not certain—a remarkable article entitled "Expansibilité" in the *Encyclopédie* of Diderot and d'Alembert. The author of this anonymous article was the economist, philosopher, and public servant Turgot. Turgot defined "expansibilité," a word he seems to have coined, to mean unlimited elasticity, like that of air. But to Turgot not merely air, but all vapors, are expansible, a property they acquire when heat, or the subtle matter of fire, enters bodies and weakens the attractive forces binding the particles together. Common air is simply a particular vapor, or what Lavoisier would have called an aeriform fluid; if it were possible to lower the temperature sufficiently, it should be possible to liquefy it. And Turgot made the remarkable suggestion, later taken up by Lavoisier, that all substances are in principle capable of existing in any of the three states of matter—as solid, liquid, or acriform fluid (gas)—depending upon the amount of the matter of fire combined with them. Sometime before the summer of 1772 Lavoisier had drafted an incomplete but remarkable memoir which he called "Système sur les éléments" and which outlined a covering theory—if we may call it that—which was henceforth to guide his own investigations and his interpretation of the findings of others. The elements, notably water, air, and fire, can exist in either of two forms, fixed or free. In the crystals of certain salts,

water is fixed as "water of crystallization." Air is not only fixed in many substances but even enters into the composition of mineral substances. The same is true of "phlogiston or the matter of fire." But how, he asks, can air, a fluid capable of such remarkable expansion, be fixed in solid substances and occupy such a small space? The answer is his *théorie singulière*, according to which water exists in the atmosphere as a vapor in which the particles are combined with the fine, elastic particles of the matter of fire; and the air we breathe is not a simple substance but a special kind of fluid combined with the matter of fire.

Up to this point, these were only private speculations which Lavoisier set down in several unpublished drafts. He had performed no experiments, and the theory derived entirely from his reading and the inferences he drew from the discoveries of others. But in the course of 1772 some new facts came to Lavoisier's attention and led to his famous first experiments on combustion, the dramatic first steps toward his "revolution in chemistry."

This revolution has often been summed up as Lavoisier's overthrow of the phlogiston theory (his new chemistry was later called the antiphlogistic chemistry), but this is only part of the story. His eventual recognition that the atmosphere is composed of different gases that take part in chemical reactions was followed by his demonstration that a particular kind of air, oxygen gas, is the agent active in combustion and calcination. Once the role of oxygen was understood—it had been prepared before Lavoisier, first by Scheele in Sweden and then independently by Priestley in England—the composition of many substances, notably the oxyacids, could be precisely determined by Lavoisier and his disciples. But the discovery of the role of oxygen was not sufficient of itself to justify abandoning the phlogiston theory of combustion. To explain this process, Lavoisier had to account for the production of heat and light when substances burn. It is here that Lavoisier's theory of the gaseous state, and what for a time was his theory of the elements, came to play a central part.

At this point, we may ask what Lavoisier could have known about the work of the British pneumatic chemists other than Stephen Hales. The answer would seem to be "very little." Of Joseph Black, often described as a major influence upon him, Lavoisier clearly knew nothing at first hand until 1773 or perhaps late 1772, for Black's famous *Essay on Magnesia Alba* was for long unavailable in French. Yet Black's major achievements were summarized in the French translation (1766) of David MacBride's *Experimental Essays on Medical and Philosophical Subjects*, a work strongly indebted to Hales and

Black, and chiefly concerned with the possible medical uses of Black's "fixed air" (carbon dioxide). Although Lavoisier had the book in his library, there is no evidence that he was impressed by it. On the other hand Jean Bucquet, a physician and chemist whom Lavoisier admired, and who later became his collaborator, had his interest in the chemistry of air aroused by MacBride's book. In his *Introduction à l'étude des corps naturels tirés du règne mineral* (2 vols., Paris, 1771), Bucquet remarks that air is found in almost all bodies in nature, in almost all minerals, although perhaps not in metals. He discusses the rival views of J. F. Meyer and MacBride on the causticity of alkalis and quicklime, and describes the precipitation of calcareous matter when "fixed air" is passed through limewater.

The famous paper of Henry Cavendish on "fixed air" long remained unknown, and it was some time before Joseph Priestley's work could serve as a stimulus to inquiries about different kinds of air. In March 1772, Priestley reported to the Royal Society the experiments that later appeared in the first volume of his *Observations on Different Kinds of Air*, a work only published late in 1772. Some faint echoes of his discoveries did reach the French chemists during the spring; what especially attracted their attention was Priestley's discovery that vitiated air is restored by the gaseous exchange of plants, and his report that an English physician had cured putrid fever by the rectal administration of "fixed air." It was not, however, these vague reports that made Frenchmen aware of Priestley's activity, but rather his first publication on gases, a modest pamphlet entitled *Directions for Impregnating Water with Fixed Air*, which appeared in June 1772 and was soon translated into French. Here again it was the presumed medical use of such artificial soda water that accounts for the impression it made. Yet we can only conclude that in 1772 the book by Stephen Hales was the predominant influence in interesting Lavoisier in the chemical role of air.

Early in 1772, at all events before June of that year, there appeared a book by the provincial lawyer and chemist Louis Bernard Guyton de Morveau, which conclusively proved that the well-known gain in weight of lead and tin when they are calcined is not a peculiarity of those metals, but that all calcinable metals become heavier when transformed into a calx; moreover, this increase has a definite upper limit characteristic of each metal. Guyton sought to explain these results by invoking a fanciful variation of the phlogistic hypothesis, but Lavoisier saw at once that the fixation of air might be the cause. By August he had devised an experiment to determine the role that air might play in chemical reactions involving metals.

Was air absorbed by or released from a metal when exposed to the strong heat of a burning glass? Perhaps it would be possible to answer this question by using an apparatus devised by Stephen Hales (his pedestal apparatus) which enabled the amount of air released or absorbed to be measured. Soon after, however, Lavoisier learned that a Paris pharmacist, Pierre Mitouard, had reported that when phosphorus was burned to form the acid, air seemed to be absorbed.

In the early autumn of 1772 Lavoisier carefully verified this report. He burned weighed quantities of phosphorus and sulfur and discovered that the acids produced weighed more than the starting materials and absorbed, notably in the case of sulfur, "a prodigious amount of air." Soon after, using a modification of Hales's pedestal apparatus, he heated minium (red lead) in the presence of charcoal in a closed vessel and observed that a large amount of air was given off. This discovery struck him as "one of the most interesting of those that have been made since the time of Stahl."[16] Accordingly, he followed the common practice of the Academy of Sciences to assure priority and recorded these results in a famous sealed note *(pli cacheté)* deposited with the secretary of the Academy.

These experiments confirmed Lavoisier's suspicions that air, or some constituent of air, played an important role in the processes of combustion and calcination. In the autumn of 1772 he set himself to read everything that had been published on aeriform fluids. Translations were soon made available (probably through the indefatigable transmitter of scientific gossip Jean Hyacinthe Magellan) not only to Lavoisier but also to such of his fellow chemists in France as Bucquet, Hilaire-Marin Rouelle (the brother of Lavoisier's teacher), and the pharmacist Pierre Bayen, all of whom investigated, late in 1772 and in early 1773, the production and properties of Black's "fixed air."[17]

On 20 February 1773, Lavoisier opened a new research notebook (the first of his famous *registres de laboratoire*) with a memorandum announcing his intention to embark on a "long series of experiments" on the elastic fluid emitted from bodies during various chemical reactions and on the air absorbed during combustion. The subject was obviously so important— "destined," as he put it, "to bring about a revolution in physics and chemistry"—that he proposed in the succeeding months to repeat all the early experiments and to extend his own. The results, both of his reading and of his experimentation, were presented to the Academy of Sciences in the spring and summer of 1773—the *pli cacheté* was opened on 5 May—and formed the substance of his first book, the *Opuscules physiques et chimiques*, which was published in January 1774.

Also in 1774 two French chemists, Pierre Bayen and Cadet de Gassicourt, investigated the peculiar behavior of red calx of mercury *(mercurius calcinatus per se)*. From this substance, they claimed, the metal could be regenerated without the addition of a reducing agent rich in phlogiston, like charcoal, simply by heating it to a higher temperature. Was this true? And was this "red precipitate of mercury," as Lavoisier called it, a true calx?[18] Early in the autumn of 1774 the subject was discussed at the Academy of Sciences, and Lavoisier was made a member of a committee to examine this question. But before the inquiry could be made, there occurred an episode about which much ink has been spilt.

In October the English chemist Joseph Priestley, during a visit to Paris, dined with Lavoisier and a group of other French scientists. Priestley told the assembled guests that in the previous summer he had obtained a new kind of air by heating the "red precipitate of mercury." The air was poorly soluble in water, and in it a candle burned more brightly than in common air. Priestley had, in fact, prepared oxygen; but at the moment he thought he had found a species of nitrous air (nitric oxide), a gas he had discovered earlier.

Since Lavoisier, not long after, turned to investigate this new air, Priestley may be pardoned for believing that Lavoisier was simply following his clue. Many scholars have accepted Priestley's claim, but it is certainly not true.[19] Lavoisier and the other members of the Academy committee were already familiar with the "red precipitate of mercury" and reported in November that it was reduced without addition. If this substance was a true calx, Lavoisier did not need Priestley's disclosure to know that an air would be released when it was reduced. Indeed, Pierre Bayen, one of the first to call attention to the strange behavior of the red precipitate, had actually found that a gas was given off on reduction, although he erred in claiming that it was Joseph Black's "fixed air."

Lavoisier took up this question seriously in the early months of 1775. He collected the air produced by the reduction of mercury calx and tested it, not to see if it had the properties of Priestley's new air, which did not immediately occur to him, but to determine whether or not it was "fixed air," first by passing the gas through limewater (which it did not precipitate), then by seeing whether it would extinguish a flame. He recorded in his notebook that "far from being extinguished," the flame burned more brightly than in air.[20] He concluded that the air was "not only common air . . . but even more pure than the air in which we live."

At the public session of the Academy on 26 April 1775, Lavoisier described his discoveries in a paper entitled "Mémoire sur la nature du principe qui se combine avec les métaux pendant leur calcination, et qui en augmente le poids." Determined as usual to bring out his results as soon as possible and aware that the *Histoire et mémoires* of the Academy was several years behind schedule, Lavoisier published this classic paper (in its first version) in the May issue of Rozier's *Observations sur la physique*.

Meanwhile, Priestley was not idle. With a new sample of the red precipitate purchased in Paris, he again took up the investigation soon after his return to England. Various tests, carried out early in 1775, convinced him that he had not prepared nitrous air but had discovered a new gas "between four and five times as good as common air." A firm advocate of the phlogiston theory, he assumed—because this gas supported combustion so much better than common air—that it must be a better receptacle for phlogiston, had less phlogiston already in it, and should be called "dephlogisticated air." Priestley published these experiments and his conclusion in the second volume of his *Experiments and Observations on Different Kinds of Air*, which appeared before the end of 1775.

If Lavoisier owed little or nothing to Priestley's earlier disclosure, his indebtedness to Priestley at this point in time is undeniable. Advance sheets of Priestley's volume reached Paris by December,[21] and Lavoisier saw at once the significance of the new facts they contained. He set to work to confirm and extend Priestley's work; preparing once more the air from the mercury calx, he referred to it in his laboratory notebook as "the dephlogisticated air of M. Prisley [*sic*]."[22] He noted that calcining mercury would be a way of analyzing atmospheric air into its chief components. So in April he studied the residual air left after prolonged calcination of mercury, which of course was mainly nitrogen; and although he found that like Black's "fixed air" it did not support combustion, yet it did not precipitate limewater. He followed this analysis, according to his custom, by a synthesis: he mixed five parts of the residual air with one part of "dephlogisticated air" and found that a candle burned in it about as brightly as in common air. The highly respirable property of "dephlogisticated air" now commanded his attention. At the Château de Montigny, with his friend Trudaine de Montigny, Lavoisier carried out experiments on the respiration of birds, confirming that they lived much longer in the new gas than in common air and showing that in both cases they vitiated the air by producing Black's "fixed air."

When in 1778 Lavoisier reread to the Academy of Sciences his classic paper of three years earlier and published it in the Academy's *Mémoires*, he revised it without making it clear that he had changed his conclusions—and, indeed, recast the paper—because of what he had learned from Priestley's book and from his own subsequent experiments. Priestley, to be sure, is not mentioned. But Lavoisier no longer described the air produced by reducing mercury calx (without addition) as highly pure atmospheric air; now he called it "the purest part of the air" or "eminently respirable air." This air, he also showed, combines with carbon to produce Black's "fixed air," which he was soon to call, since it was known to be weakly acidic and to combine with alkalis and alkaline earths to form what we call the carbonates, "chalky aeriform acid" *(acide crayeux aériforme)*.

Lavoisier's activity during these years was prodigious; his scientific productivity was at its peak, and the experiments that he performed alone or with his collaborator, Jean Bucquet, contributed to round out his theory. Several main lines of inquiry were pursued simultaneously: the properties of aeriform fluids, the mystery of vaporization and heat, the role of "eminently respirable air" in combustion and respiration, and the formation of acids. This last was to add a new dimension to his oxygen theory.

Considerable progress had been made during the eighteenth century toward understanding the behavior of acids.[23] Rouelle, Lavoisier's teacher, had confirmed that salts were combinations of an acid with certain substances that served as a "base" (alkalis, earths, and metals); and he had shown that certain salts were genuinely neutral while others contained an excess of acid. New acids, too, were identified; beginning with his preparation of tartaric acid in 1770, the great Swedish chemist Carl Wilhelm Scheele added nearly a dozen organic acids to the roster of new chemical individuals, as well as preparing acids from such metals as arsenic and tungsten.

As to the cause of acidity, various theories were current—for example, Newton's doctrine that acids were substances "endued with a great attractive force, in which their activity consists," a theory favored by Macquer and Guyton de Morveau. Lavoisier, on the other hand, thought in more traditional terms and believed it possible to identify the "constituent principles" of acids and bases, just as his predecessors had analyzed salts into their two major constituents. One widely held notion was that there was one fundamental or "universal" acid, of which the individual acids were simply modifications. Various acids were nominated for this distinction, including vitriolic (sulfuric) acid and Black's "fixed air," which Bergman called the "aerial acid."

The sharp, fiery taste of acids led to a confusion of acidity with the causticity of such substances as corrosive sublimate or quicklime. Joseph Black had argued that the causticity of quicklime was an inhering property that was masked when the lime combined with "fixed air." A chemist and apothecary of Osnabrück, J. F. Meyer (1705–1765), attacked Black's theory and argued that mild alkalis become caustic when they take up an oily acid, *acidum pingue*, as he believed limestone does when it is burned to quicklime. The calxes of metals, Meyer thought, might contain *acidum pingue*. This imaginary protean substance, closely related to fire and light, was also the "universal primitive acid" of which all other acids were modifications.

As early as 1766, Lavoisier was familiar with Meyer's theory, for in his notes on Eller's memoirs he makes a passing reference to *acidum pingue*. When he wrote the *Opuscules* in 1773, Lavoisier had not definitely decided in favor of Black's theory rather than Meyer's; both theories of causticity were presented on their merits, although Lavoisier wrote of Meyer's book that it contained a "multitude of experiments, most of them well made and true," and noted that the theory of *acidum pingue* explains "in the most natural and simple fashion" the gain in weight of metals on calcination. Should Meyer's ideas be adopted, the result would be nothing less than a new theory directly contrary to that of Stahl.[24]

It is likely that Lavoisier at first shared the widespread notion that a universal acid, whether or not it was an *acidum pingue*, was to be found in the atmosphere and that this primitive acid gave rise to all the particular acids known to the chemist. His important step forward was to abandon the notion, essentially tautological, that an acid gave rise to acids and to suggest that an identifiable chemical substance, in fact an aeriform fluid or gas, played this universal role of acid-former. Yet before the autumn of 1772 Lavoisier did not suspect that air entered into the composition of acids. When air was released in the reaction between an acid and a metal, as in the production of "inflammable air" (hydrogen), Lavoisier believed that it came from the metal. In his August Memorandum of 1772 he wrote that "air enters into the composition of most minerals, even of metals, and in great abundance." Yet his experiments with phosphorus and sulfur convinced him that when they were burned to form the acids, air was absorbed. In the *Opuscules* of 1774 Lavoisier could remark that phosphoric acid was "in part composed of air, or at least of an elastic substance contained in air."

He did not return to the subject until two years later. On 20 April 1776, Lavoisier read to the Academy one of his most brilliant papers, a memoir entitled "Sur l'existence de l'air dans l'acide nitreux." Referring back to his experiments on phosphorus and sulfur, and his conclusion that air entered into the composition of the acids resulting from the combustion of these substances, he was led to consider the nature of acids in general and to conclude that all acids were in great part made up of air; that this substance was common to all of them; and, further, that they were differentiated by the addition of "principles" characteristic of each acid. When he "applied experiment to theory," Lavoisier was able to confirm his suspicion that it was the "purest portion of the air," Priestley's dephlogisticated air, that entered without exception into the composition of acids, and especially of nitric acid, which was particularly deserving of study because of the importance of saltpeter (potassium nitrate) in the making of gunpowder.

The experiments were as follows. When a known quantity of nitric acid was heated with a weighed amount of mercury, the resulting product was a white mercurial salt (mercuric nitrate); this decomposed to form the red oxide, yielding nitric oxide *(air nitreux)*. On further heating, the red oxide, as Lavoisier already knew, decomposed, producing metallic mercury and the "air better than common air," or "eminently respirable air." Lavoisier was careful to separate the different gaseous fractions by collecting the air under different bell jars over water. According to his practice, the analysis was followed by a synthesis: by bringing together the nitric oxide and the "pure air" in the presence of a small amount of water, he was able to regenerate nitric acid.

Almost exactly a year later, on 21 March 1777, Lavoisier read a memoir to the Academy of Sciences in which he showed that phosphorus burned in air combines with the "eminently respirable air" to form phosphoric acid. When this air is used up, the remaining air, which he called *mofette atmosphérique* (nitrogen), does not support combustion or sustain life. In the same paper he showed that sulfur takes up "eminently respirable air" in the formation of vitriolic acid.

In 1779 Lavoisier brought together the results of all this work in an important paper (published in 1781) entitled "Considérations générales sur la nature des acides." Here are set forth his conclusions that since "eminently respirable air" is a constituent of so many acids, it may play the role of "universal acid" or, rather, of the "acidifiable principle." When combined with carbonaceous substances or charcoal, this air forms chalky acid (carbon dioxide); with sulfur,

vitriolic acid; with nitric oxide, nitric acid; with phosphorus, phosphoric acid. When combined with metals, on the other hand, it forms calxes (oxides). Nevertheless, it was the acid-forming characteristic that impressed him; he therefore proposed to call the acidifying principle or base of "eminently respirable air" the "oxygen principle" *(principe oxigine)*, that is, the "begetter of acids." What he soon called "vital air"[25] he described, faithful to his conception of aeriform fluids, as a combination of the "matter of fire" with a base, the "principe oxigine." By 1787, when the collaborative *Nomenclature chimique* was published, *oxigine* had become *oxygène*. In the meantime he had extended the application of his oxygen theory of acids and had discovered that there existed related acids that differed only in the proportion of oxygen they contained, as for example sulfurous and sulfuric acids; the higher the degree of oxygenation, he discovered, the stronger was the acid produced. In a paper published in 1785 Lavoisier made an equally important contribution by proving that the solution of metals in acids was a form of calcination: a calcination by the "wet way" *(par la voie humide)*. The metal combines with a quantity of the *principe oxigine* approximately equal to that which it is capable of removing from the air in the course of ordinary calcination.

Scholars have generally pointed to Lavoisier's theory of acids as perhaps his major error, or at least as a rash induction. From his analysis of a number of the oxyacids (carbonic, sulfuric, nitric) and certain organic acids (oxalic and acetic), all shown to contain oxygen, he argued that all acids must be so constituted, although he readily admitted that muriatic (hydrochloric) acid had not been shown to contain oxygen, which indeed it does not. Lavoisier explained this away by assuming that so far it had resisted further analysis.

Besides oxygen, other gases interested Lavoisier (the term "gas" was soon to replace the word "air" or the phrase "aeriform fluid"),[26] and none more than the "inflammable air" produced by the action of weak acids on iron or copper. In September 1777 with Bucquet he burned this "inflammable air" to see whether, as Bucquet expected, "fixed air" was produced, as was the case in the combustion of carbon. The limewater test was negative. What, then, was the product formed?

After the death of Bucquet, Lavoisier repeated this experiment in the winter of 1781–1782, using what he called a gasholder or pneumatic chest *(caisse pneumatique)* to store the oxygen and maintain a steady flow into a bottle filled with "inflammable air." Persuaded that some acid should be formed when the two gases were burned together, he was surprised when once more he failed to detect any product or even a trace of acidity. Convinced that something must have been produced, since the basic article of scientific faith, on which his quantitative procedures were based, was that matter is neither created nor destroyed in chemical reactions, Lavoisier determined to carry out the experiment "with more precision and on a larger scale." To this end, assisted by his younger colleague, the mathematician Laplace, he designed a combustion apparatus in which streams of the two gases, each stored in a pneumatic chest, could be brought together in a double nozzle and burned together.

Before this new apparatus was completed, Lavoisier used the first pneumatic chest in a spectacular experiment in which a stream of oxygen, directed into a hollowed-out piece of charcoal, burned at such a high temperature that it melted platinum, a recently described metal that had resisted fusion even at the temperature of the great burning glass of Trudaine. Lavoisier reported his success at the public session of the Academy of Sciences on 10 April 1782. Early in June, and at considerable expense, he transported his equipment to the Academy and demonstrated, in the presence of a visiting Russian grand duke (traveling incognito as the Comte du Nord), the melting of a small mass of platinum by what Benjamin Franklin, another observer, called a fire "much more powerful than that of the strongest burning mirror," indeed the "strongest fire we yet know."[27]

Lavoisier's combustion apparatus was ready by June 1783 and was immediately put to historic use. In that month the Academy of Sciences was visited by the assistant of Henry Cavendish, Charles Blagden, a physician and scientist who the following year was to become the secretary of the Royal Society. Blagden, so the familiar account runs, informed Lavoisier and some other members of the Academy of Sciences that Cavendish had obtained pure water when he had detonated a mixture of "inflammable air" and "dephlogisticated air" in a closed vessel. As Blagden recalled this event, the French scientists replied that they had already heard about such experiments as repeated by Joseph Priestley but doubted that the weight of water, as Cavendish claimed, was equal to the weight of the gases used. They believed, rather, that the water was already contained in, or united to, the gases used. Nevertheless, Blagden's disclosure supported what they had already learned. Accordingly, Lavoisier and Laplace put into action the newly completed combustion apparatus. On 24 June 1783, in the presence of Blagden and several academicians, they burned substantial amounts of the dry gases and obtained enough of the liquid product so that it could be tested. It did not give an acid reaction with litmus

or syrup of violets, precipitate limewater, or give a positive test with any of the known reagents; it appeared to be "as pure as distilled water." In reporting on these experiments, Lavoisier confessed that it was not possible to be certain of the exact quantity of the gases that were burned; but, he argued, since in physics, as in mathematics, the whole is equal to the sum of its parts, and since only water and nothing else was formed, it seemed safe to conclude that the weight of the water was the sum of the weights of the two gases from which it was produced.

With the return of the Academy in November from its vacation, Lavoisier read at the public meeting an account of his experiments, making the historic announcement that water was not a simple substance, an element, but a compound of the *principe oxigine* with what he proposed to call the "aqueous inflammable principle" *(principe inflammable aqueux)*, that is, hydrogen. A summary of these results appeared anonymously in the December issue of Rozier's journal.[28] A draft of this summary in Lavoisier's hand, recently identified in the archives of the Academy of Sciences, proves beyond a doubt that he was the author.[29] The fuller and more elaborate memoir, published after Lavoisier had begun extensive work with J. B. M. Meusnier, appeared in the Academy's *Mémoires* in 1784.[30]

The summer and autumn of 1783 riveted public attention, and that of the scientific community (including that shrewd American observer, Benjamin Franklin), upon the dramatic success of the first lighter-than-air flights. Soon after the pioneer demonstrations by the Montgolfier brothers came the historic exploit of the Marquis d'Arlandes and Pilatre de Rozier, who made the earliest manned free ascent. The hot air "aerostats," as the balloons were called, could be made to rise or descend only by varying the intensity of the fire of straw or other light combustible which caused hot air to rise into the open bottom of the balloon.

A quite different, and far more promising, solution was soon proposed and demonstrated by J. A. C. Charles, a free-lance teacher of physics. With his assistants, the brothers Robert, he launched an unmanned balloon that had been laboriously filled with "inflammable air." On 1 December, Charles and the younger Robert took off from the Tuileries in a basket *(nacelle)* lifted by a hydrogen-filled balloon twenty-six feet in diameter; they rose to the height of 300 fathoms: driven by a southeast wind, they covered a distance of nine leagues before an uneventful descent. Then Charles went aloft alone, rose to the height of nearly 1,700 fathoms, showing physicists, Lavoisier wrote, "how one can rise up to the clouds to study the causes of meteors."[31] What particularly impressed Lavoisier was the complete control Charles and Robert had over their machine, using bags of sand to slow the ascent of the balloon and descending by venting hydrogen.

Meanwhile, the Academy of Sciences appointed a standing committee to find measures for improving balloons, by determining the best shape, ways of maneuvering them, and above all by finding "a light gas, easy to obtain and always available, and which would be cheap" with which to fill the balloons. The committee included, besides the Academy's officers, physicists like J. B. Le Roy, Mathurin Brisson, and Coulomb, and chemists like Berthollet and Lavoisier, who—as he habitually did when serving on committees—became its secretary. Attached to this group was J. B. M. Meusnier, a young officer on leave from the Corps of Engineers. A graduate of the military engineering school at Mézières, he had been since 1776 a corresponding associate (correspondant) of the Academy of Sciences. The ease with which "inflammable air" had been obtained from the decomposition of water convinced Lavoisier that this was the route to follow in obtaining in quantity the cheap, light gas sought by the committee. In this inquiry, carried out in his laboratory at the Arsenal, Lavoisier had the invaluable assistance of Meusnier. In March 1784 they produced a small amount of the inflammable air by plunging a red-hot iron into water; later that month they successfully decomposed water by passing it drop by drop through an incandescent gun barrel. In this fashion Meusnier and Lavoisier prepared eighty-two pints of the light, inflammable air, and on 29 March they repeated this experiment in the presence of members of the standing committee. Meusnier presented the results of this joint effort to the Academy on 21 April; the full memoir was published soon after.

Steps were now taken to carry out with high precision a really large-scale decomposition of water into its constituent gases and its synthesis. Meusnier radically redesigned Lavoisier's gasholders (caisses pneumatiques) to allow the volume of gas and the rate of outflow to be measured with accuracy. These earliest "gasometers," as well as a combustion flask for the large-scale synthesis of water, were the work of the instrument maker Pierre Mégnié.

The experiments were carried out at the Arsenal on 27 and 28 February 1785, in the presence of members of a special evaluation committee of the Academy and other invited guests. For the decomposition experiment, water was percolated through a gun barrel filled with iron rings; the inflammable air was collected in bell jars over water in a pneumatic trough, from which it was transferred to a gasometer.

In one experiment the volume of the gas (expressed in weight equivalents of water) was found to be equal to well over 335 livres of water. These experiments, in the opinion of Daumas and Duveen, exceeded all previous chemical investigations in "the perfection of the equipment used, the scale upon which the work was carried out, and the importance of the conclusions to be derived from the results."[32] On 19 March, Berthollet, who had followed these experiments closely, wrote to Blagden of the recent keen interest "in the beautiful discovery of Mr. Cavendish on the composition of water," remarking that "Mr. Lavoisier has tried to bring to this matter all the accuracy of which it is capable."[33] Water, all but a few intransigent opponents were obliged to admit, was not the irreducible "element" it had always been thought to be but a compound of the oxygen principle with the inflammable air that was soon to be baptized "hydrogen," the begetter of water.

The demonstration of the compound nature of water put the capstone on Lavoisier's oxygen theory of combustion. For a number of years Lavoisier had been reluctant to come out openly in opposition to the phlogiston theory, nor had he been in a hurry to publish his speculations about the nature of "aeriform fluids" or gases.[34] Not enough evidence was at hand to support his theory that gas was only a state which substances acquire when they are combined with a sufficient amount of the "matter of fire." His studies of heat were inspired by a desire to support what came to be called his "caloric" theory.

In the spring of 1777 Lavoisier had enlisted the cooperation of his young colleague at the Academy, Laplace, in experiments on the vaporization of water, ether, and alcohol in the evacuated receiver of an air pump.[35] These experiments convinced Lavoisier that under proper conditions of temperature and pressure, these fluids could be converted into vapors which, like air, existed "in a state of permanent elasticity." Emboldened by these results, Lavoisier presented in November 1777 the substance of one of his most famous papers, "Mémoire sur la combustion en général," the earliest announcement of his theory of combustion and his first, albeit cautious, assault on the phlogiston theory.

When Lavoisier resumed his collaboration with Laplace in 1781, the two soon undertook (1782–1783) a famous series of experiments, using a piece of apparatus—the ice calorimeter—and a technique, both suggested by Laplace.[36] With this contrivance the heat given off by hot bodies when they cooled, by exothermic chemical reactions, or by animals placed within the apparatus, was measured by the amount of water produced by the melting of ice.

With their calorimeter Lavoisier and Laplace determined the specific heats of various substances, the heats of formation of different compounds, and measured the heat produced by a guinea pig confined for several hours in their apparatus. Laplace read an account of these experiments to the Academy on 18 June 1783; their classic joint "Mémoire sur la chaleur" was published as a pamphlet later that summer and, essentially unaltered, in the *Histoire et mémoires* of the Academy in 1784. For Lavoisier, certain of these experiments on heat were convincing proof of his theory of vaporization, which held that gases owe their aeriform, elastic state to their combination with a large amount of the "matter of fire"; and so the heat and light given off during combustion must come from the fire matter released from the "vital air" (oxygen gas) when the oxygen principle combines with a combustible substance.

It has been argued that Lavoisier's caloric theory merely transferred the phlogiston from the combustible to the "vital air," and there is something to this view. Like phlogiston, the fire matter was a weightless fluid (or at least too tenuous to be weighed); nevertheless, unlike phlogiston, which defied measurement, both the intensity (the temperature) and the extensive measure of the fire (the heat produced in a given period of time) could be precisely measured. These calorimetric experiments, together with the work on water, seemed to Lavoisier to complete the evidence for his theory of combustion; and in 1786 he published his definitive attack on the old theory, "Réflexions sur le phlogistique." A brilliant dialectical performance, rightly called "one of the most notable documents in the history of chemistry,"[37] it is a closely reasoned refutation not only of Stahl but also of those latter-day phlogistonists, such as Macquer and Antoine Baumé, who had tried to modify Stahl's hypothesis in the light of the new experimental evidence.

The "Réflexions" was a personal manifesto, but it did not serve to convince all French scientists. Some, like Baumé, like Joseph Priestley, remained recalcitrant to the end. But the most tireless antagonist was the physician and naturalist Jean Claude de La Métherie. Lavoisier's exact contemporary (he was born in September 1743), he was a prolific author of generally wordy, often slovenly works on natural history, natural philosophy, geology, and chemistry. Never admitted to the Academy of Sciences, he yet occupied an influential position, for in 1785 he became editor of Rozier's old journal, the *Observations sur la physique*. La Métherie, a devoted and uncritical disciple of Priestley, was violently opposed to Lavoisier's theories; the *Observations*, therefore,

which had once been so hospitable to Lavoisier, became—to a degree—the journal of the opposition.

The years 1785–1789 nevertheless brought a number of able chemists into Lavoisier's camp: Claude Berthollet, who had been converted when he closely followed the work on the decomposition and synthesis of water; Antoine de Fourcroy, the student of Lavoisier's former collaborator Bucquet; and Guyton de Morveau. These men, forming with Lavoisier and his wife what we might call the "antiphlogistic task force," set out to convert the scientific world to the "new chemistry." The instruments they employed were several and well-selected—intended to attract the young and the uncommitted.

First of all, to persuade a new generation of chemists to join their ranks and to complete what Lavoisier had envisaged since 1773—a revolution in chemistry—these men brought out a collaborative work, the *Méthode de nomenclature chimique* (1787). Originally suggested by Guyton de Morveau to eliminate the confused synonymy of chemistry, and prefaced by a memoir of Lavoisier, it emerged as a complete break with the past. In effect the scheme was based upon the new discoveries and theories, a fact that led the aging Joseph Black to complain that to accept the new nomenclature was to accept the new French theories. In a series of tables the *Nomenclature* listed the elements (*substances non décomposées*), that is, those bodies that had not been, or perhaps could not be, decomposed. Fifty-five in number, these simple bodies included light and Lavoisier's "matter of fire," now called "caloric"; the elementary gases: oxygen, nitrogen (*azote*), and "inflammable air," now called hydrogen; carbon, sulfur, and phosphorus; the sixteen known metals; a long list of organic "radicals" (i.e. acidifiable bases); and the as yet undecomposed alkaline earths and alkalis. Compounds were designated, as chemists have done ever since, so as to indicate their constituents: the metallic calxes were now called oxides; the salts were given names indicating the acid from which they are formed (sulfates, nitrates, carbonates, and so on). The *Nomenclature*—translated into English, German, Italian, and Spanish—was extremely influential and widely read.

A second expression of the collective effort was a French translation of Richard Kirwan's 1787 *Essay on Phlogiston*. This translation, made by Mme Lavoisier, was published in 1788, the year after the *Nomenclature chimique*, and was copiously annotated with critical notes by members of the task force: the chemists Guyton de Morveau, Berthollet, and Fourcroy; the physicists and mathematicians Monge and Laplace; and, of course, Lavoisier himself.

A third and most important instrument was the establishment of a new scientific journal, edited—and dominated—by the votaries of the "new chemistry." The first number of this journal, the *Annales de chimie*, appeared in 1789, the year of the Revolution. Its editors were, besides Lavoisier, his early disciples— Guyton, Berthollet, Fourcroy, and Monge—with the addition of three new recruits: the Strasbourg metallurgist the Baron de Dietrich, Jean-Henri Hassenfratz, and Pierre Auguste Adet.

Constituting still another, and much underestimated, vehicle for diffusing the new ideas were the later editions of Fourcroy's *Élémens d'histoire naturelle et de chimie.*[38] Of this immensely popular work a third edition, completely recast in terms of the "new chemistry," was published toward the end of 1788. A fourth edition appeared in 1791 and a fifth in 1793; it was translated into English, Italian, German, and Spanish. Its influence cannot be exaggerated, for it was one of the richest compendia of up-to-date chemical fact before the appearance of Thomas Thomson's *System of Chemistry* (1802). It was, moreover, the first work to present the whole of chemistry, as then known, in the light of Lavoisier's doctrines and according to the new nomenclature.

The last—and the best-known—of the propaganda instruments was Lavoisier's classic book, *Traité élémentaire de chimie* (1789). The culmination of Lavoisier's achievement, it grew out of the *Nomenclature*—indeed, it was a sort of justification of it. Neither a general reference work nor a technical monograph, this small work was a succinct exposition of Lavoisier's discoveries (and those of his disciples) and an introduction to the new way of approaching chemistry. Significantly, it begins, after the famous "Discours préliminaire," with an exposition of that theory of vaporization and the states of matter which had guided Lavoisier throughout much of his scientific career.

The "Discours préliminaire," a defense of the new chemistry with its new nomenclature, is also a short essay on scientific pedagogy, and on the proper method of scientific inquiry. The most widely read of Lavoisier's writings, it opens with quotations from the *Logique* (1780) of the Abbé de Condillac: language is the instrument of analysis; we cannot think without using words; the art of reasoning depends upon a well-made language *(l'art de raisonner se réduit à une langue bien faite)*. The *Traité*, Lavoisier remarks in this prefatory essay, grew out of his work on the nomenclature which, "without my being able to prevent it," developed into an element of chemistry. This must be taken with a grain of salt, for in notes set down in 1780–1781 Lavoisier had already outlined an elementary treatise, to be prefaced with two preliminary *discours*, one of which closely resembles the "Discours préliminaire" of 1789 and was intended to treat the application of logic to the physical sciences, especially chemistry. The notes for this preface, with page reference to the *Logique* in the margin, cite the same passages from Condillac that Lavoisier eventually used in print.

The epistemological and psychological assumptions Lavoisier outlines in the "Discours préliminaire" of 1789 are the commonplaces of eighteenth-century thought, found not only in Condillac, but in d'Alembert and in Rousseau's *Emile*: at birth, the mind is a *tabula rasa*; all our ideas come from the senses; analysis—that shibboleth of the Enlightenment—is the only way to truth; even a small child analyzes his experience; nature, through deprivation and pain, corrects his errors in judgment.

The beginning student of physical science must follow the path nature uses in forming the ideas of a child. His mind must be cleared of false suppositions, and his ideas should derive directly from experience or observation. But a scientific Emile is not promptly corrected by nature through the pleasure-pain principle; men are not punished for the hypotheses they invent, which their amour-propre leads them to elaborate and cling to. Because the imagination and reason must be held in check, we must create an artificial nature through the use of experiment.

Lavoisier gives numerous examples of the speculative notions that often hamper the progress of chemistry. He derides the order commonly followed in works on chemistry, which begin by treating the elements of bodies *(principes des corps)* and explaining tables of affinity. This latter branch of chemistry he acknowledges to be important (perhaps the best calculated to make chemistry eventually a true science), but it is not fully warranted by experiment, and is unsuited to an elementary treatise. As to the elements, all we can say about their nature and number amounts to mere metaphysical talk. And if by elements we mean those simple, indivisible particles *(molécules)* that bodies are made of, it is likely that we know nothing about them. Even the existence of his cherished caloric fluid, although it explains the phenomena of nature in a very satisfactory manner, is a mere hypothesis.

The chief operation of chemistry is to determine by analysis and synthesis the composition of the various substances found in nature; chemistry advances toward its goal by dividing, subdividing, and subdividing still again. If we mean by the elements of bodies the limit reached by this subdivision, then all the substances we are unable to decompose are to us as the elements out of which the other substances are made. In the *Traité* these substances are called *substances simples*; yet Lavoisier confesses: "We cannot be certain that what we regard today as simple is really so; all that we can say is that such a substance is the actual limit reached by chemical analysis, and that, in the present state of our knowledge, it cannot be further subdivided."

When we compare the table of *substances simples* in the *Traité* with that given in the *Nomenclature* two years earlier, we note some interesting changes. First, the list has been drastically reduced and now contains only thirty-three substances. Nineteen organic radicals and the three alkalis (potash, soda, and ammonia) have been eliminated, and with some justification. There was increasing evidence that the organic radicals could be broken down—in the *Traité* Lavoisier himself reports the composition of the "acetic radical"—and the case of the alkalis was similar. In 1785 Berthollet had shown that ammonia consists only of hydrogen and nitrogen, and presumably Lavoisier believed that potash and soda would also turn out to be compounds of familiar substances.

Both in the *Nomenclature* and the *Traité* the tables of undecomposed or simple substances are divided into subgroups, five in the first case, four (with the elimination of the alkalis) in the second. But in both tables the first subgroup is distinguished from the rest. In the *Nomenclature* this is made up of light, caloric, oxygen, and hydrogen. In the *Traité*, nitrogen *(azote)* has been added, and here for the first time these substances are described surprisingly as "simple substances which belong to the three kingdoms and which one can consider as the elements of bodies." It is curious that these five substances appear to Lavoisier to have more claim to the status of elements than other simple bodies, for example sulfur, phosphorus, carbon, or the metals.

The principal justification is revealed in a note Lavoisier set down in 1792 where he writes: "It is not enough for a substance to be simple, indivisible, or at least undecomposed for us to call it an element. It is also necessary for it to be abundantly distributed in nature and to enter as an essential and constituent principle in the composition of a great number of bodies." Wide distribution, and its presence in a great number of compounds, qualifies a substance to be called an element. Gold, on the other hand, is a simple substance, yet it is not an element. But there is something more to Lavoisier's conception of an element: he specifically notes that such a substance "enters as an essential and constituent principle" in compound bodies. In the older chemistry, from which Lavoisier is unable to free himself completely,

the elements—the four elements of Aristotle, the *tria prima* of Paracelsus, and so on—were thought of as the bearers and the causes of the distinctive qualities of bodies into which they enter. As we saw in discussing his theory of acids, Lavoisier had strong ties to this "chemistry of principles." So in his first subgroup the substances deserving to be called elements act in this special way. Thus caloric is the "principle" that accounts for a body's physical state. Oxygen, of course, conveys acidity. Hydrogen is the producer of water, that essential substance found in all the realms of nature. But what of light and of nitrogen? Lavoisier never quite satisfied himself about the nature of light, but he knew from the work of Ingenhousz and Sennebier that light plays an essential part in the gaseous chemistry of vegetation, a matter to which he alluded in a remarkable speculative paper he published in 1788. Nitrogen, to be sure, is everywhere in the earth's atmosphere and is widely distributed in animal and vegetable substances. But was this sufficient reason for Lavoisier to elevate it to the dignity of an "element" of the first subgroup? Quite possibly he gave it this higher status because he tended to think, on the basis of Berthollet's analysis of ammonia, that nitrogen might be the "principle" of all alkalis, what Fourcroy would have liked to call "alkaligène."

Lavoisier's *Traité*, albeit an elementary textbook, contains important material much of which he had not previously published, notably his pioneer experiments on the combustion analysis of organic compounds and on the phenomenon of alcoholic fermentation, which impressed him as "one of the most striking and the most extraordinary" effects observed by the chemist. He was aware that the combustion of substances of vegetable origin, such as sugar and alcohol, yielded water and carbon dioxide; but he was convinced that these compounds did not exist preformed in the substances burned—which, however, do contain the elements hydrogen, oxygen, and carbon. Lavoisier's first combustion analyses involved burning various oils in a rather complicated apparatus shown in one of the plates of the *Traité*. A simpler contrivance was devised for the combustion of highly volatile substances like alcohol and ether. In his analysis of alcohol he determined the ratio of hydrogen to carbon by weight to be 3.6 to 1, not far from the correct value of 4 to 1.

Like his immediate predecessors—Macquer, for example—Lavoisier distinguished three kinds of fermentation: vinous or spirituous fermentation, acid or acetous fermentation (such as produces acetic acid), and putrid fermentation. He did not speculate about the underlying cause of these processes, although he took for granted the existence of some sort of "ferment," but confined himself to the chemical changes. Vinous or alcoholic fermentation, marked by a violent intestine motion, he saw to be a chemical reaction involving rearrangement of the three essential organic "principles": oxygen, hydrogen, and carbon. He assumed an equality or "equation"[39] between the amount of these elements in the original sugar and the amount in the end products: alcohol, carbon dioxide, and acetic acid. His experiments seemed to bear out his assumption. His data, however, were wholly unreliable, although the end result was correct. As Arthur Harden put it: "The research must be regarded as one of those remarkable instances in which the genius of the investigator triumphs over experimental deficiencies." The numbers reveal grave errors, and "it was only by a fortunate compensation of these that a result as near the truth was attained."[40]

In describing his work on fermentation in chapter XIII of the *Traité*, Lavoisier stated most clearly his principle of the conservation of matter in chemical reactions:

> Nothing is created either in the operations of the laboratory, or in those of nature, and one can affirm as an axiom that, in every operation, there is an equal quantity of matter before and after the operation; that the quality and quantity of the principles are the same, and that there are only alterations and modifications. On this axiom is founded the whole art of making experiments in chemistry: we must suppose in all of them a true equality or equation between the principles of the body one examines, and those that we extract [*retire*] by analysis.[41]

Despite his prolonged interest in the chemistry of respiration, which had preoccupied him on and off since his earliest work on combustion, Lavoisier deliberately omitted all references to the subject in his *Traité élémentaire de chimie*. When in his earliest experiments on different kinds of air Lavoisier exposed small animals to these gases, it was less to explore the phenomenon of respiration than to characterize the gases. He was already aware that "fixed air" asphyxiated animals and that atmospheric air, "corrupted and infected" by the respiration of man or animals, takes on the character of "fixed air." In his *Opuscules physiques et chimiques*, where he summarized Priestley's experiments and recounted his own, Lavoisier advanced a physical, rather than a chemical, explanation of respiration. The role of atmospheric air, he then believed, is to inflate the lungs; "fixed air" is unable to do this because, being highly soluble in water, it is taken up by the moisture of the lungs "and suddenly loses its elasticity." In an atmosphere

of "fixed air," therefore, the action of the lung is suspended and the animal suffocates.[42]

It was only after his first experiments with "dephlogisticated air" (oxygen) and his discovery that, far from killing animals, this gas "seemed, on the contrary, better fitted to sustain their respiration"[43] than ordinary air, that Lavoisier turned to the problem of respiration: it had now become a problem of physiological chemistry. His earliest experiments were carried out at the Château de Montigny with his friend Trudaine de Montigny during the Academy's vacation (October 1776).[44] He read the results at the Easter public session on 9 April 1777, under the title "Mémoire sur les changements que le sang éprouve dans les poumons et sur le mécanisme de la respiration."[45] By this time he could assert that respiration involved only the *air éminemment respirable* (oxygen), and that the remainder of the air is purely passive, entering and leaving the lung unchanged. In the course of respiration animals take in the *air éminemment respirable*, which is either converted into *acide crayeux aériforme* (carbon dioxide) or is exchanged in the lung, the oxygen being absorbed and an approximately equal volume of carbon dioxide being supplied by the lung. Lavoisier tended to favor the first alternative. Indeed, in that same year, in his "Mémoire sur la combustion en général," he suggests in a concluding paragraph that this reaction is similar to the combustion of carbon and must be accompanied by the release of a certain amount of the matter of fire. This, he points out, may account for the production of animal heat.[46] A persuasive argument seemed to him to be that, just as the calcination of mercury and lead results in red powders, so the absorption of oxygen gives a bright red color to arterial blood.

The calorimeter provided a new instrument for the quantitative study of animal heat and the verification of Lavoisier's combustion theory of respiration. In a famous experiment with Laplace they measured the heat produced by a guinea pig exhaling a given amount of carbon dioxide, comparing this figure with the heat of formation of the same amount of carbon dioxide produced by burning carbon in an atmosphere of oxygen. But the results showed a significant discrepancy: more heat was produced by the guinea pig than by the burning of carbon. It was soon discovered that the experimental animals gave off less carbon dioxide than the intake of oxygen had led them to expect. In a paper read before the Royal Society of Medicine in February 1785, Lavoisier argued that either some of the oxygen unites with the blood or it combines with hydrogen to form water.[47] Although not fully convinced, Lavoisier favored the second alternative;

and in his last experiments, carried out in cooperation with Armand Seguin, he assumed that both carbon dioxide and water were produced. The collaborative work was begun in 1789 and reported to the Academy late in 1790 and in 1791. These experiments were more genuinely physiological than Lavoisier's early ones. Lavoisier and Seguin found that the quantity of oxygen consumed increases with the temperature and is greater during digestion and exercise. The combustion, according to their findings, occurs in the lung, more specifically in its tubules, into which the blood secretes a "humor" composed of carbon and hydrogen. Understandably, the pressure of events during the Revolution left Lavoisier little time for scientific work; experiments begun collaboratively were in some cases left for Seguin to complete. Our most vivid record of these last experiments are the drawings made by Mme Lavoisier showing Seguin, his face covered by a mask, breathing air or oxygen to determine the amount consumed when at rest or at work.

The range of Lavoisier's activity is hard for lesser talents and less rigidly disciplined personalities to comprehend. To carry on his multifarious public responsibilities without neglecting his beloved science required a rigid and inflexible schedule. Mme Lavoisier tells us that he rose at six in the morning, worked at his science until eight and again in the evening from seven until ten. The rest of the day was devoted to the business of the Ferme Générale, the Gunpowder Administration, and meetings of the Academy of Sciences and of its numerous special committees. One day a week, his *jour de bonheur*, he devoted entirely to scientific experiments.[48]

Lavoisier rose steadily in the hierarchy of the Academy of Sciences. In August 1772 he was promoted to the rank of associate *(associé chimiste)*; he reached the top rank of *pensionnaire* in 1778. He served on a number of those committees set up at the request of the royal government to investigate matters of public concern. Among the most notable of these committees were those formed to investigate the condition of the prisons and hospitals of Paris and one, on which Lavoisier served with Benjamin Franklin, charged with investigating Mesmer's cures by what he called "animal magnetism."

Nor were his responsibilities confined to his official duties. Lavoisier's father, shortly before his death, purchased one of those honorific offices that carried with it the privilege of hereditary nobility. The title devolved on Lavoisier in 1775, and not long afterward he purchased the country estate of Fréchines, near Blois. Here he carried on agricultural experiments, chiefly concerned with the improvement of livestock, which he reported to the Royal Agricultural Society of Paris (to which he had been elected in 1783) and to the government's Committee on Agriculture, established soon after by Calonne, the minister of finance *(contrôleur général)*.

In sympathy with much of the criticism leveled against the *Ancien Régime*, Lavoisier shared many of the ideas of the *philosophes* and was closely associated with Pierre Samuel Dupont de Nemours and other physiocrats. Politically liberal, and almost certainly a Freemason, he took an active part in the events leading to the Revolution. In 1787 he was chosen a representative of the third estate at the provincial assembly of the Orléanais, the province in which he was a landowner. He served on the important standing committee *(bureau)* that dealt with social conditions and agriculture; he wrote reports on the *corvée*, on charitable foundations, and on trade; and he was responsible for many far-reaching proposals: schemes for old-age insurance, charity workshops to give employment to the poor, and tax reform.

When, after a lapse of nearly two centuries, the famous Estates-General was brought into being once again to deal with France's mounting problems, Lavoisier was chosen as alternate deputy for the nobility of Blois; as secretary, he drafted their bill *(cahier)* of grievances, a remarkably liberal document that embodied many of his earlier proposals. Although he never served in the National Assembly, multiple activities occupied him during the years of the Revolution. He was elected to the Commune of Paris and took his turn with the National Guard. He joined the most moderate of the revolutionary clubs, the short-lived Society of 1789. For this self-appointed planning group, whose members included Condorcet, the economist Pierre Samuel Dupont de Nemours, and the famous Abbé Sieyès, Lavoisier prepared his important paper on the *assignats*, pointing to the problems inherent in issuing paper money. Because of his mastery of financial matters, he was made a director of the Discount Bank (Caisse d'Escompte), established in 1776 by his friend Turgot; became an administrator of the national treasury; and in 1791 published a long report on the state of French finances. In the same year he brought out a classic statistical study of the agricultural resources of the country.[49] For the recently created Advisory Bureau for the Arts and Trades (Bureau de Consultation des Arts et Métiers) he helped draft, along with others, an elaborate scheme for the reform of the national educational system of France, based largely, to be sure, on ideas already put forward by Condorcet.

Unhappy at the leftward thrust of the Revolution, Lavoisier nevertheless remained loyal to his country.

In these critical years he was active in the Academy of Sciences, (he served as its treasurer from 1791 until the abolition of that body), and took an important part in the most enduring of its accomplishments: the establishment of the metric system of weights and measures.[50] Until his arrest he was engaged, in collaboration with the crystallographer René-Just Haüy, in establishing the metric unit of mass (the gram). Together they measured with high precision the weight of a given volume of distilled water at different temperatures.

Despite his eminence and his services to science and to France, Lavoisier was the target of increasingly violent attacks by radical journalists like Jean-Paul Marat. One after another the institutions with which Lavoisier had been associated changed form or were abolished. He was removed from his post in the Gunpowder Administration in 1791 but remained at the Arsenal until 1793, when he severed all connections with the *Régie*. That year brought the Reign of Terror, the abolition of the Discount Bank and the suppression of all the royal learned societies, including the Academy of Sciences.

In 1791 the National Assembly had abolished the unpopular Ferme Générale and set up a committee of experts from it (which did not include Lavoisier) charged with liquidating its affairs. This committee made slow progress and was accused of delaying tactics. On 24 December 1793 an order went out for the arrest of all the farmers-general. Lavoisier and his father-in-law were imprisoned with the others. All were tried by the Revolutionary Tribunal on the morning of 8 May 1794. They were convicted and executed on the guillotine that same afternoon. The story is told that Lavoisier appealed at his trial for time to complete some scientific work and that the presiding judge replied, "The Republic has no need of scientists." The story is apocryphal.[51] Authentic, however, is the remark attributed to Lagrange, the day after Lavoisier's execution: "It took them only an instant to cut off that head, and a hundred years may not produce another like it."

NOTES

1. For Lavoisier's genealogy, see Edouard Grimaux, *Lavoisier*, 2nd ed., p. 326.
2. Now the rue Pecquay. See Jacques Hillairet, *Dictionnaire historique des rues de Paris*, 3d ed. (Paris, 1966), II, 250. The Turgot plan of Paris (1739) shows the cul-de-sac "Pequet" opening from the rue des Blancs-Manteaux, not far from the Palais Soubise (the present Archives Nationales). By Piganiol de la Force it was called "Cul-de-sac Pequai ou de Novion dans la rue des Blancs-Manteaux," in *Description de Paris* (Paris, 1742), 427.
3. Grimaux erroneously called it the rue du Four Saint-Eustache; its name was simply rue du Four, or rue du Four-Saint Honoré, although to distinguish it from the rue du Four on the Left Bank, letters to residents were sometimes addressed "rue du Four St. Honoré près St. Eustache." It is now the rue de Vauvilliers, running from the rue Saint Honoré to the rue Coquillière.
4. Not published in Lavoisier's lifetime, the piece on the aurora is printed in *Oeuvres de Lavoisier*, IV, 1–7.
5. Lavoisier papers, archives of the Academy of Sciences, dossier 424. Cited by Rhoda Rappaport in "Lavoisier's Geologic Activities," in *Isis*, **58** (1968), 377.
6. *Oeuvres de Lavoisier—Correspondance*, fasc. I, 1–3.
7. Guettard, "Mémoire qui renferme des observations minéralogiques," cited by Rappaport, *loc. cit.*, p. 376.
8. Guettard, "Mémoire sur la manière d'étudier la minéralogie," cited by Rappaport, ibid.
9. For a general appraisal of Rouelle and his course in chemistry, see Rhoda Rappaport, "G.-F. Rouelle: An Eighteenth-Century Chemist and Teacher," in *Chymia*, **6** (1960), 68–101.
10. *Oeuvres de Lavoisier*, III, 112.
11. The full title of this publication is *Mémoires de mathématique et de physique, présentés à l'Académie royale des sciences, par divers savans et lûs dans ses assemblées.*
12. These unsigned letters, which have puzzled scholars, are printed in *Oeuvres de Lavoisier—Correspondance*, fasc. I, 7–10, repr. from *Oeuvres de Lavoisier*, IV, 561–563.
13. The Agricola title page, with Lavoisier's inscription, is reproduced as pl. I of Denis I. Duveen, *Bibliotheca alchemica et chemica* (London, 1949). The book itself is now in the Lavoisier Collection at Cornell University.
14. For the early history of the powder industry in France, see Régis Payan, *L'évolution d'un monopole: L'industrie des poudres avant la loi du 13 fructidor an V* (Paris, 1934). The *régie* was established by Turgot to replace the earlier *ferme*. See Douglas Dakin, *Turgot* (London, 1939), 164–166; and Edgar Faure, *La disgrâce de Turgot* (Paris, 1961), 108–110.
15. In a paper entitled "De la manière de composer des feux d'artifices colorés en bleu et en jaune," deposited as a sealed note on 14 May 1768. See *Oeuvres de Lavoisier—Correspondance*, fasc. I, 107–108. A significant reference by Lavoisier to the ideas of Hales about the fixation of air appeared in a paper of the same year. See J. B. Gough, "Lavoisier's Early Career in Science," in *British Journal for the History of Science*, **4** (1968), 52–57. More detailed early references to Hales's experiments are given in Lavoisier's "Sur la nature de l'eau," published in 1773, and in his *Opuscules physiques et chimiques* of 1774.
16. This famous phrase appears in Lavoisier's *pli cacheté* of 1 Nov. 1772. Repro. in Henry Guerlac, *Lavoisier—The Crucial Year* (Ithaca, N.Y., 1961), 227–228. In an important paper Robert E. Kohler, Jr., noting that Lavoisier's words suggest surprise, argues that the experiments on phosphorus and sulfur were simply to determine whether air enters into the composition of acids, as the Abbé Rozier had suggested, and were not guided by a primary interest in calcination. Only after his work on phosphorus and sulfur was Lavoisier led to wonder whether the addition of air might not explain the increase in weight of metallic calxes. This indeed is what Lavoisier tells us. See Kohler's "The Origin of Lavoisier's First Experiments on Combustion," in *Isis*, **63** (1972), 349–355.
17. The first of these translations, a *précis raisonné* of a memoir by a follower of Joseph Black, N. J. von Jacquin, was published in Rozier's *Observations sur la physique* in February 1773. Translations of Joseph Black's classic paper on magnesia alba, Joseph Priestley's "Observations on Different Kinds of Air," and Daniel Rutherford's paper on mephitic air (nitrogen) appeared in the spring and early summer in the same journal.
18. On this question, see a paper by C. E. Perrin, "Prelude to Lavoisier's Theory of Calcination—Some Observations on *mercurius calcinatus per se*," in *Ambix*, **16** (1969), 140–151.

19. In September 1774 the Swedish chemist Scheele communicated to Lavoisier a method of making oxygen by heating a preparation of silver carbonate. This letter was not published in *Oeuvres de Lavoisier—Correspondance*, fasc. II. See Uno Boklund, "A Lost Letter From Scheele to Lavoisier," in *Lychnos* (1957), 39–62. Boklund virtually accused the French scholars, including René Fric, of suppressing the letter so as to give all credit to Lavoisier, although he was aware that Grimaux had published this letter long before, as "Une lettre inédite de Scheele à Lavoisier," in *Revue générale des sciences pures et appliquées*, 1 (1890), 1–2. In any case Lavoisier seems to have been too preoccupied with other matters to follow up Scheele's suggestion.
20. M. Berthelot, *La révolution chimique*, 264–265.
21. See letters of Magellan (or Magalhaens) to Lavoisier in *Oeuvres de Lavoisier—Correspondance*, fasc. II, 504–508.
22. Berthelot, *op. cit.*, p. 271.
23. Much of this section is dependent upon Maurice Crosland's article "Lavoisier's Theory of Acidity," in press.
24. *Oeuvres de Lavoisier*, I, 482.
25. In a paper published in the *Histoire et mémoires* of the Academy in 1784, Lavoisier adopted, at the suggestion of Condorcet, the term *air vital* for what he had previously called (after Priestley) "dephlogisticated air" or "eminently respirable air." *Oeuvres de Lavoisier*, II, 263.
26. Originally a term used by Van Helmont to signify "a Spirit that will not coagulate," it was applied particularly to noxious vapors like firedamp. In the 1st ed. (1766) of his *Dictionnaire de chimie*, P. J. Macquer applied the term to "the volatile invisible parts which escape from certain bodies," for example, "the noxious vapors which rise from burning charcoal, and from matters undergoing spirituous fermentations." But in the 2nd ed. (1778) of the *Dictionnaire* he applied the word generally to aeriform fluids. See, for example, the articles "Gas ou air déphlogistiqué" and "Gas méphytique ou air fixe." In the same year Jean Bucquet included in his *Mémoire sur la manière dont les animaux sont affectés par différens Fluides Aériformes* an introductory section entitled "Histoire abrégé des différens Fluides aériformes ou Gas." The spelling used by both men is "gas," not "gaz." It is possible that this generalized use of the term "gas" may have been influenced by the second edition (1777) of James Keir's trans. of the first ed. of Macquer's *Dictionnaire* to which Keir appends *A Treatise on the Various Kinds of Permanently Elastic Fluids, or Gases*. A MS French translation of this treatise survives among Lavoisier's papers.
27. *Writings of Benjamin Franklin*, Albert Henry Smyth, ed., VIII (1906), 314.
28. *Observations sur la physique*, 23 (1783), 452–455. The paper is entitled "Extrait d'un mémoire lu par M. Lavoisier, à la séance publique de l'Académie royale des sciences, du 12 novembre, sur la nature de l'eau."
29. By C. E. Perrin. See his "Lavoisier, Monge and the Synthesis of Water," to appear in *British Journal for the History of Science*.
30. *Oeuvres de Lavoisier*, II, 334–359. Lavoisier notes that certain additions were made relative to the work done with Meusnier.
31. *Ibid.*, III, 733. See Benjamin Franklin's letters to Sir Joseph Banks, *Writings of Benjamin Franklin*, IX (1906), 79–85, 105–107, 113–117, and 119–121. On 16 September 1783 Franklin wrote to Richard Price: "All the Conversation here at present turns upon the Balloons fill'd with light inflammable Air, and the means of managing them, so to give men the Advantage of Flying." *Ibid.*, pp. 99–100.
32. Maurice Daumas and Denis I. Duveen, "Lavoisier's Relatively Unknown Large-Scale Decomposition and Synthesis of Water," in *Chymia*, 5 (1959), 126–127.
33. *Ibid.*, 127.
34. Two anonymous attacks on the phlogiston theory published in Rozier's *Observations sur la physique* in 1773 and 1774 have been widely attributed to Lavoisier—for example, by Berthelot, McKie, and Duveen. For arguments against Lavoisier's authorship and suggestions of likely alternatives, see Carleton Perrin, "Early Opposition to the Phlogiston Theory: Two Anonymous Attacks," in *British Journal for the History of Science*, 5 (1970), 128–144.
35. Henry Guerlac, "Laplace's Collaboration With Lavoisier," in *Actes du XII*ᵉ *Congrès international d'histoire des sciences, Paris, 1968*, III B (Paris, 1971), 31–36.
36. Mme Lavoisier's drawing of the ice calorimeter is given in pl. VI of Lavoisier's *Traité élémentaire de chimie*. Two versions have survived and are in the collection of the Conservatoire des Arts et Métiers in Paris. It has not been possible to determine with certainty which of Lavoisier's artisans built the calorimeters, but it was probably a tinsmith named Naudin. See Maurice Daumas, *Lavoisier théoricien et expérimentateur* (1955), p. 142 and notes, and the illustrations in his "Les appareils d'expérimentation de Lavoisier," in *Chymia*, 3 (1950), 45–62, fig. 3.
37. Douglas McKie, *Antoine Lavoisier* (London–Philadelphia, 1935), p. 220.
38. For Fourcroy, and his relations with Lavoisier, see W. A. Smeaton, *Fourcroy, Chemist and Revolutionary, 1755–1809* (Cambridge, 1962).
39. J. R. Partington calls this the first use of the word "equation" in our modern sense of "chemical equation." Lavoisier's example is: must of grapes = carbonic acid + alcohol. See Partington's *History of Chemistry*, III, 480.
40. Arthur Harden, *Alcoholic Fermentation* (London, 1911), p. 3. Partington has remarked (*History of Chemistry*, III, p. 376) that Lavoisier "aimed at accurate results, but seldom achieved them." Guichard (*Essai historique sur les mesures en chimie* [Paris, 1937], 54–60), after examining Lavoisier's numerical results, judged his precision extremely variable; indeed in the later, more complicated experiments the accuracy was less than in the earliest ones. Yet Lavoisier repeatedly stressed the importance of quantitative accuracy. In the *Traité* he writes: "La détermination du poids des matières et des produits, avant et après les expériences, étant la base de tout ce qu'on peut faire d'utile et d'exact en chimie, on ne saurait y apporter trop d'exactitude" (*Oeuvres de Lavoisier*, I, 251); elsewhere he writes "Rien n'est supposé dans ces explications, tout est prouvé, le poids et la mesure à la main" (*ibid.*, V, 270).
41. *Oeuvres de Lavoisier*, I, 101. The axiom that matter is neither created nor destroyed originated with the atomists of antiquity. It was clearly stated by Mariotte in his *Essai de logique* (1678) and was a common assumption of eighteenth-century scientists. But Lavoisier deserves credit for applying it specifically to the operations of the chemist and for spelling out a law of the conservation of matter in chemical reactions.
42. *Ibid.*, 520–521, 625–627.
43. "Mémoire sur la nature du principe qui se combine avec les métaux pendant leur calcination, et qui en augmente le poids," in *Observations sur la physique*, 5 (1775), 433.
44. Berthelot, *op. cit.*, 290–291.
45. Cited from the *Procès-verbaux* of the Academy of Sciences by Maurice Daumas, in *Lavoisier, théoricien et expérimentateur*, p. 38. Daumas says this remained unpublished, yet it was almost certainly published, with the inevitable modifications, in 1780 as "Expériences sur la respiration des animaux." See *Oeuvres de Lavoisier*, II, 174–183.
46. *Ibid.*, 232.
47. "Altérations qu'éprouve l'air respiré," *ibid.*, 676–687.
48. Charles C. Gillispie, "Notice biographique de Lavoisier par Madame Lavoisier," in *Revue d'histoire des sciences et de leurs applications*, 9 (1956), 57.
49. *Résultats extraits d'un ouvrage intitulé: De la richesse territoriale du royaume de France* (Paris, 1791). Together with other of Lavoisier's economic writings this is printed in G. Schelle and E. Grimaux, *Lavoisier—statique agricole et*

projets de réformes (Paris, 1894). See also Oeuvres de Lavoisier, VI, 403–463.

50. For Lavoisier's role in the attempts to reform the Academy, and the political struggles within that body, see Roger Hahn, *The Anatomy of a Scientific Institution* (Berkeley–Los Angeles, 1971), especially chapters 8 and 9.

51. J. Guillaume, "Un mot légendaire: 'La République n'a pas besoin de savants,' " in *Révolution française*, **38** (1900), 385–399, and *Études révolutionnaires*, 1st ser. (Paris, 1908), pp. 136–155.

BIBLIOGRAPHY

I. ORIGINAL WORKS. For a bibliography of Lavoisier's papers—academic, scientific, and in popular periodicals—and his major and minor separate works, consult Denis I. Duveen and Herbert S. Klickstein, *A Bibliography of the Works of Antoine Laurent Lavoisier, 1743–1794* (London, 1954), and Duveen's *Supplement* (London, 1965).

Lavoisier's published articles, some hitherto unpublished papers, and two of his major books are printed in *Oeuvres de Lavoisier*, 6 vols. (Paris, 1862–1893). The first 4 vols. were edited by the distinguished chemist J. B. Dumas, the last 2 vols. by Edouard Grimaux, Lavoisier's principal biographer. Much, but by no means all, of Lavoisier's surviving correspondence through 1783 has appeared in *Oeuvres de Lavoisier—Correspondance*, 3 fascs. (Paris, 1955–1964), edited by the late René Fric under the auspices of the Académie des Sciences. A further fasc. completed before the death of M. Fric is due to appear. The editing of this work leaves much to be desired; many letters, some quite important, have been overlooked; for a scathing appraisal of fasc. I, see A. Birembaut, "La correspondance de Lavoisier," in *Annales historiques de la Révolution française*, **29** (Oct.–Dec. 1957), 340–351.

Lavoisier's major books are four in number. His *Opuscules physiques et chimiques* (Paris, 1774) was intended to be the first of a series of vols. containing the results of his investigations. The later vols. never materialized. A posthumous reissue of the 1st ed. was published in 1801; the *Opuscules* was trans. with notes and an appendix by Thomas Henry as *Essays Physical and Chemical* (London, 1776). A German trans. by C. E. Weigel appeared as vol. I of his 5-vol. collection entitled *Lavoisier physikalisch-chemische Schriften* (Greifswald, 1783–1794). The remaining 4 vols. contain German versions of a number of Lavoisier's scientific papers (the last 2 vols. were the work of H. F. Link).

Méthode de nomenclature chimique, proposée par MM. de Morveau, Lavoisier, Bertholet [sic] & de Fourcroy. On y a joint un nouveau système de caractères chimiques, adaptés à cette nomenclature, par MM. Hassenfratz & Adet (Paris, 1787). There is a 2nd printing of this 1st ed.; the 2nd ed. appeared in 1789, as vol. III of the 2nd ed. of Lavoisier's *Traité élémentaire de chimie*. It is entitled *Nomenclature chimique, ou synonymie ancienne et moderne, pour servir à l'intelligence des auteurs*. There is an English trans. of this collaborative work by James St. John (London, 1788); an Italian version by Pietro Calloud (Venice, 1790); and a German trans. by Karl von Meidinger (Vienna, 1793).

Various abridgments and tabular versions of the new nomenclature appeared in English, German, and Italian. The chief agent for transmitting the new chemistry to Germany was Christoph Girtanner (1760–1800), who in 1791 brought out a German version of the *Nomenclature chimique* and the next year his *Anfangsgründe der antiphlogistischen Chemie* (Berlin, 1792). For the reception of Lavoisier's work in Italy, see Icilio Guareschi, "Lavoisier, sua vita e sue opere," in *Supplemento annuale alla Enciclopedia di chimica scientifica e industriale*, **19** (Turin, 1903), 307–469, esp. 452–455.

In 1778 Lavoisier proposed to devote a 2nd vol. of his *Opuscules* to setting forth a *système général* of chemistry expounded in a rational and deductive fashion, according to the *méthode des géomètres*. Such a work was never written; but this method was used in his most famous book, the *Traité élémentaire de chimie* (Paris, 1789), a book that in fact grew out of the work on the chemical nomenclature and first appeared in a single volume; a 2nd printing in 2 vols. appeared in the same year, as did a 2nd ed. An influential English trans. by Robert Kerr appeared as *Elements of Chemistry, in a New Systematic Order, Containing All the Modern Discoveries* (Edinburgh, 1790). There are several later eds. of Kerr's trans. The *Traité* appeared in German, translated by S. F. Hermbstadt (Berlin–Stettin, 1792); in Dutch, by N. C. de Fremery (Utrecht, 1800); in Italian, by Vincenzo Dandolo (Venice, 1791); and in Spanish, by Juan Manuel Munarriz (Madrid, 1798).

About 1792 Lavoisier planned a complete ed. of his memoirs in 8 vols.; also to be included were papers by some of his disciples. The posthumous *Mémoires de chimie*, printed in 2 vols. for Mme Lavoisier from incomplete proofs partially corrected by Lavoisier, is all that resulted from this project. The vols. are undated (there are no title pages, only half titles), and they were not commercially published; Mme Lavoisier presented copies to selected institutions and individuals. Although Duveen assigns the year 1805 to this work, it was circulating two years earlier—when, as J. R. Partington has shown, Berthollet quoted it by vol. and pg. The *Mémoires*, not repr. in the *Oeuvres*, includes reprints and revisions of previously published papers, as well as hitherto unpublished results, such as experiments carried out toward the close of his collaboration with Laplace in 1783–1784 on problems related to heat. There are several papers by Lavoisier's latter-day collaborator, Armand Seguin.

The chief repository of Lavoisier manuscripts is the Académie des Sciences in Paris, in whose archives one can consult Lavoisier's laboratory notebooks and some twenty *cartons* containing drafts of scientific papers, academy reports, and so on. There are important letters in the Collection de Chazelles in the city library of Clermont-Ferrand, and other manuscripts, notably letters, in the possession of Count Guy de Chabrol. Microfilms of the letters and other documents in the Fonds Chabrol are available in the archives of the Académie des Sciences, as is also a xerographic copy of the second laboratory notebook *(registre)* for the period 9 September 1773 to

5 March 1774. This had been given by François Arago to the library of Perpignan, and for a time was believed lost. See the *Comptes rendus des séances de l'Académie des sciences*, **135** (1902), 549–557 and 574–575. There are scattered documents in various provincial libraries in France, notably Orléans, and important material in the Archives Nationales, chiefly dealing with the period of the Revolution. The Bibliothèque Nationale has little to offer, except Fr. nouv. acq. 5153, which is an account of Lavoisier's repetition of his classic early experiments before an Academy committee. The Lavoisier Collection in the Olin Library of Cornell University was originally assembled by Denis I. Duveen. Besides a number of manuscripts, many books from Lavoisier's own library with his *ex libris*, this includes the most nearly complete assemblage of the books and pamphlets published by Lavoisier, and in nearly all the known editions and variants.

II. SECONDARY LITERATURE. The earliest biographical sketches of Lavoisier appeared in the early days of the Directory: Joseph Jérôme Lalande, "Notice sur la vie et les ouvrages de Lavoisier," in *Magasin encyclopédique*, **5** (1795), 174–188, English trans. in *Philosophical Magazine*, **9** (1801), 78–85; and Antoine François de Fourcroy, *Notice sur la vie et les travaux de Lavoisier* (Paris, 1796). Other early sketches are Thomas Thomson, "Biographical Account of M. Lavoisier," in *Annals of Philosophy*, **2** (1813), 81–92; and Georges Cuvier, "Lavoisier," in L. G. Michaud, ed., *Biographie universelle*, new ed. (Paris, 1854–1865), XXIII, 414–418, based in part on information, much of it inaccurate, supplied by Lavoisier's widow. See Charles C. Gillispie, "Notice biographique de Lavoisier par Madame Lavoisier," in *Revue d'histoire des sciences et de leurs applications*, **9** (1956), 52–61. The standard biography is Edouard Grimaux, *Lavoisier 1743–1795, d'après sa correspondance, ses manuscrits, ses papiers de famille et d'autres documents inédits* (Paris, 1888; 2nd ed., 1896; 3rd ed., 1899). No trans. was ever published, and most subsequent biographies have relied heavily upon Grimaux—for example, Mary Louise Foster, *Life of Lavoisier* (Northampton, Mass., 1926); J. A. Cochrane, *Lavoisier* (London, 1931); and Douglas McKie, *Antoine Lavoisier* (London–New York, 1952). For a general appraisal of this literature, see Henry Guerlac, "Lavoisier and His Biographers," in *Isis*, **45** (1954), 51–62. A readable study, which makes use of some recent research, is Léon Velluz, *Vie de Lavoisier* (Paris, 1966). Short but informative is Lucien Scheler, *Lavoisier et le principe chimique* (Paris, 1964).

There have been a number of general investigations of Lavoisier's work in chemistry. The pioneer study is surely the IVe Leçon of J.-B. Dumas, *Leçons sur la philosophie chimique professées au Collège de France* (Paris, n.d., but certainly 1836, the year the lectures were delivered). A second edition, an unaltered reprint, appeared in 1878. Still valuable, especially for its excerpts and paraphrases from Lavoisier's laboratory notebooks, is Marcelin Berthelot, *La révolution chimique—Lavoisier* (Paris, 1890, 2nd ed., 1902). Douglas McKie, *Antoine Lavoisier, the Father of Modern Chemistry* (Philadelphia, 1935), owes

much to the pioneer work of Andrew Norman Meldrum (see below). In the same year appeared Hélène Metzger's classic *La philosophie de la matière chez Lavoisier* (Paris, 1935). Worth consulting is Sir Harold Hartley, "Antoine Laurent Lavoisier, 26 August 1743–8 May 1794," in *Proceedings of the Royal Society*, **189A** (1947), 427–456. Extremely valuable for the use made of the *procès-verbaux* of the Academy of Sciences and other unpublished documents relating to Lavoisier's work is Maurice Daumas, *Lavoisier, théoricien et expérimentateur* (Paris, 1955). An elaborate treatment of Lavoisier's achievements is given by J. R. Partington, *A History of Chemistry*, III, ch. IX. A general review of the state of Lavoisier studies is given by W. A. Smeaton, "New Light on Lavoisier: The Research of the Last Ten Years," in *History of Science*, **2** (1963), 51–69.

For eighteenth-century chemical theory before Lavoisier the classic studies are Hélène Metzger, *Les Doctrines chimiques en France du début du XVIIe à la fin du XVIIIe siècle* (Paris, 1923) and her *Newton, Stahl, Boerhaave et la doctrine chimique* (Paris, 1930). The technological background is described in Henry Guerlac, "Some French Antecedents of the Chemical Revolution," in *Chymia*, **5** (1959), 73–112. For Lavoisier's teacher of chemistry, see Rhoda Rappaport, "G. F. Rouelle: An Eighteenth-Century Chemist and Teacher," *ibid.*, **6** (1960), 68–101, and her "Rouelle and Stahl—The Phlogistic Revolution in France," *ibid.*, **7** (1961), 73–102. A different emphasis is found in Martin Fichman, "French Stahlism and Chemical Studies of Air, 1750–1779," in *Ambix*, **18** (1971), 94–122.

Studies of special aspects of Lavoisier's chemical research abound. For the early stages of his career, see A. N. Meldrum, "Lavoisier's Early Work on Science, 1763–1771," in *Isis*, **19** (1933), 330–363; **20** (1934), 396–425; and his "Lavoisier's Work on the Nature of Water and the Supposed Transmutation of Water Into Earth (1768–1773)," in *Archeion*, **14** (1932), 246–247. These studies have been corrected or amplified by Henry Guerlac, "A Note on Lavoisier's Scientific Education," in *Isis*, **47** (1956), 211–216; by Rhoda Rappaport, "Lavoisier's Geologic Activities, 1763–1792," *ibid.*, **58** (1968), 375–384; and by J. B. Gough, "Lavoisier's Early Career in Science, an Examination of Some New Evidence," in *British Journal for the History of Science*, **4** (1968), 52–57, who was the first to identify (correcting Daumas) Lavoisier's notes from Eller and to see their significance for Lavoisier's theory of heat and vaporization. Consult also W. A. Smeaton, "*L'avant-coureur*, the Journal in Which Some of Lavoisier's Earliest Research Was Reported," in *Annals of Science*, **13** (1957), 219–234. This article actually appeared in 1959. There is useful information in E. McDonald, "The Collaboration of Bucquet and Lavoisier," in *Ambix*, **13** (1966), 74–84.

For Lavoisier's first experiments on combustion, the pioneer work of A. N. Meldrum, *The Eighteenth Century Revolution in Science—The First Phase* (Calcutta–London–New York, n.d. [1930]), is classic. See too his "Lavoisier's Three Notes on Combustion: 1772," in *Archeion*, **14** (1932), 15–30; also Max Speter, "Die entdeckte Lavoisier-Note vom 20 Oktober 1772," in *Zeitschrift für angewandte Chemie*, **45** (1932); his "Kritisches über die Entstehung von Lavoisiers System," *ibid.*, **39** (1926), 578–582; and his article "Lavoisier," in Gunther Bugge, ed., *Das Buch der grossen Chemiker* (Berlin, 1929), I, 304–333. For new light on the famous sealed note, see Henry Guerlac, "A Curious Lavoisier Episode," in *Chymia*, **7** (1961), 103–108. For the research leading up to Lavoisier's investigations in the autumn of 1772, see Guerlac, *Lavoisier—The Crucial Year* (Ithaca, N.Y., 1961), where the basic documents are reproduced in the app. For a reassessment see Robert E. Kohler, Jr., "The Origin of Lavoisier's First Experiments on Combustion," in *Isis*, **63** (1972), 349–355. The discovery of oxygen, and the influence of Priestley upon Lavoisier, are treated by Meldrum, *Eighteenth Century Revolution in Science*, chap. 5; by Sir Philip Hartog, "The Newer Views of Priestley and Lavoisier," in *Annals of Science*, **5** (1941), 1–56; and by Sidney J. French, "The Chemical Revolution—The Second Phase," in *Journal of Chemical Education*, **27** (1950), 83–88. C. E. Perrin, "Prelude to Lavoisier's Theory of Calcination—Some Observations on Mercurius Calcinatus per se," in *Ambix*, **16** (1969), 140–151, casts new light on Lavoisier's possible debt to Priestley and to Pierre Bayen.

For the stages in the preparation of Lavoisier's most famous book see Maurice Daumas, "L'élaboration du *Traité de Chimie* de Lavoisier," in *Archives internationales d'histoire des sciences*, **29** (1950), 570–590. For Lavoisier's attitude towards affinity theories see Daumas, "Les conceptions sur les affinités chimiques et la constitution de la matière," in *Thalès* (1949–1950), 69–80. Both these papers discuss unpublished notes for a work Lavoisier did not live to undertake seriously, to be entitled "Cours de chimie expérimentale" or "Cours de philosophie expérimentale." A provocative paper on the famous "Discours préliminaire" is Robert Delhez, "Révolution chimique et Révolution française: *Le Discours préliminaire* au *Traité élémentaire de chimie* de Lavoisier," in *Revue des questions scientifiques*, **143** (1972), 3–26.

Lavoisier's early theory of the elements and of the aeriform state of matter has been the focus of recent investigations. Guerlac, in "A Lost Memoir of Lavoisier," in *Isis*, **50** (1959), 125–129, attempts to reconstruct the character of a supposedly lost memoir by Lavoisier. This document was published with other *inédits* by René Fric, "Contribution à l'étude de l'évolution des idées de Lavoisier sur la nature de l'air et sur la calcination des métaux," in *Archives internationales d'histoire des sciences*, **12** (1959), 125–129, actually published 1960. Further contributions are Maurice Crosland, "The Development of the Concept of the Gaseous State as a Third State of Matter," in *Proceedings of the 10th International Congress of the History of Science* II (Paris, 1962), 851–854; J. B. Gough, "Nouvelle contribution à l'étude de l'évolution des idées de Lavoisier sur la nature de l'air et sur la calcination des métaux," in *Archives internationales d'histoire des sciences*, **22** (1969), 267–275, publishes a draft by Lavoisier entitled "De l'élasticité et de la formation des fluides élastiques," dated end of Feb. 1775. See also Robert Siegfried, "Lavoisier's View of the Gaseous State and Its Early Application to Pneumatic Chemistry," in *Isis*, **63** (1972), 59–78. The most exten-

sive treatment of this aspect of Lavoisier's work is Gough's Ph.D. dissertation, "The Foundations of Modern Chemistry: The Origin and Development of the Concept of the Gaseous State and Its Role in the Chemical Revolution of the Eighteenth Century" (Cornell University, June 1971). Robert J. Morris has criticized, with some justice, Guerlac's narrow interpretation of Lavoisier's "Système sur les élémens" of the summer of 1772 but denies that it was in fact a system of the elements. See R. J. Morris, "Lavoisier on Air and Fire: The Memoir of July 1772," in *Isis*, **60** (1969), 374–377; and Guerlac's reply, *ibid.*, 381–382.

Closely related to the problem of the aeriform state is Lavoisier's caloric theory, a matter discussed cursorily in most accounts of his work. But recent work has reopened the question. Henry Guerlac, "Laplace's Collaboration With Lavoisier," in *Actes du XIIᵉ Congrès international d'histoire des sciences; Paris, 1968*, III B (Paris, 1971), 31–36, is an abstract of a forthcoming study of the collaborative experiments of Lavoisier and Laplace on heat. Robert Fox, *The Caloric Theory of Gases, From Lavoisier to Regnault* (Oxford, 1971), has a long first chapter entitled "The Study of Gases and Heat to 1800." An important study is Robert J. Morris, "Lavoisier and the Caloric Theory," in *British Journal for the History of Science*, **6** (1972), 1–38.

For Lavoisier's instrument makers see Maurice Daumas, *Les instruments scientifiques aux XVIIᵉ et XVIIIᵉ siècles* (Paris, 1953). Descriptions of surviving pieces of Lavoisier's apparatus are given in P. Truchot, "Les instruments de Lavoisier. Relation d'une visite à La Canière (Puy-de-Dôme) où se trouve réunis les appareils ayant servi à Lavoisier," in *Annales de chimie et de physique*, 5th ser., **18** (1879), 289–319; also Maurice Daumas, "Les appareils d'expérimentation de Lavoisier," in *Chymia*, **3** (1950), 45–62; and chs. 5 and 6 of Daumas, *Lavoisier, théoricien et expérimentateur*; and Graham Luske, "Mementoes of Lavoisier, Notes on a Trip to Château de la Canière," in *Journal of the American Medical Association*, **85** (1925), 1246–1247. An attempt to evaluate the quantitative precision of Lavoisier's experiments is made by M. Guichard, *Essai historique sur les mesures en chimie* (Paris, 1937), 53–72.

On the synthesis and decomposition of water, the fullest account is in J. R. Partington, *History of Chemistry*, III, 325–338, 436–456. Maurice Daumas and Denis Duveen, "Lavoisier's Relatively Unknown Large-Scale Decomposition and Synthesis of Water, February 27 and 28, 1785," in *Chymia*, **5** (1959), 113–129, discuss in detail the experiments of Meusnier and Lavoisier that were never formally published, and were described only in the account printed in the obscure *Journal polytype des sciences et des arts* of 26 Feb. 1786; repr. in *Oeuvres de Lavoisier*, V, 320–339. C. E. Perrin, in an article in press entitled "Lavoisier, Monge and the Synthesis of Water," accounts for the apparent coincidence of the synthesis of water by Lavoisier and Laplace and by Gaspard Monge in the summer of 1783 by suggesting a knowledge (prior to the disclosure by Blagden of Cavendish's results) of Priestley's repetition of Cavendish's experiment.

For the pioneer balloon experiments, the most elaborate contemporary source is Barthélemy Faujas de Saint-Fond, *Description des expériences de la machine aérostatique de MM. Montgolfier . . . suivie de mémoires sur le gaz inflammable etc.*, 2 vols. (Paris, 1783–1784). Gaston Tissandier, *Histoire des ballons et des aéronautes célèbres* (Paris, 1887), is an admirable account, superbly illustrated. The report of the first commission on the Montgolfier balloons (composed of Le Roy, Tillet, Brisson, Cadet de Gassicourt, Lavoisier, Bossut, Condorcet, and Desmarest) appeared first as a pamphlet in 1784 and later in the *Mémoires* of the Academy of Sciences. It is repr. in *Oeuvres de Lavoisier*, III, 719–735, and in *Extraits des mémoires de Lavoisier concernant la météorologie et l'aéronautique* (Paris, 1926), published by the Office National Météorologique de France.

A brief account of Lavoisier's work on organic analysis is given in Ferenc Szabadváry, *History of Analytical Chemistry* (Oxford–London, 1966), pp. 284–287. His studies of alcoholic fermentation are described in P. Schutzenberger, *Les fermentations*, 5th ed. (Paris, 1889), pp. 14–15; Carl Oppenheimer, *Ferments and Their Actions*, trans. from the German by C. Ainsworth Mitchell (London, 1901), pp. 3–4; and Arthur Harden, *Alcoholic Fermentation* (London, 1911), pp. 2–3.

For Lavoisier's geology see Pierre Comte, "Aperçu sur l'oeuvre géologique de Lavoisier," in *Annales de la Société géologique du Nord*, 69 (1949), 369–375; A. V. Carozzi, "Lavoisier's Fundamental Contribution to Stratigraphy," in *Ohio Journal of Science*, 65 (1965), 71–85; Rhoda Rappaport, "The Early Disputes Between Lavoisier and Monnet, 1777–1781," in *British Journal for the History of Science*, 4 (1969), 233–244; "Lavoisier's Geologic Activities, 1763–1792," in *Isis*, 58 (1968), 375–384; "The Geological Atlas of Guettard, Lavoisier, and Monnet," in Cecil J. Schneer, ed., *Towards a History of Geology* (Cambridge, Mass., 1969), pp. 272–287; and "Lavoisier's Theory of the Earth," to appear in *British Journal for the History of Science*.

On the new nomenclature, see M. P. Crosland, *Historical Studies in the Language of Chemistry* (London, 1962), chs. 3–8. See also Denis I. Duveen and Herbert S. Klickstein, "The Introduction of Lavoisier's Chemical Nomenclature Into America," in *Isis*, 45 (1954), 278–292, 368–382; and H. M. Leicester, "The Spread of the Theory of Lavoisier in Russia," in *Chymia*, 5 (1959), 138–144. For Britain and Germany, see Crosland, *Historical Studies . . .*, pp. 193–206, 207–210.

Lavoisier's physiological writings, notably on respiration, are discussed in Charles Richet, "Lavoisier et la chaleur animale," in *Revue scientifique*, 34 (1884), 141–146; Alphonse Milne-Edwards, *Notice sur les travaux physiologiques de Lavoisier* (Paris, 1885); G. Masson, ed., *Lavoisier, la chaleur et la respiration, 1770–1789* (Paris, 1892); M. J. Rosenthal, "Lavoisier et son influence sur les progrès de la physiologie," in *Revue scientifique*, 47 (1891), 33–42; J. C. Hemmeter, "Lavoisier and the History of the Physiology of Respiration and Metabolism," in *Johns Hopkins Hospital Bulletin*, 29 (1918), 254–264; Graham

Lusk, "A History of Metabolism," in L. F. Barker, ed., *Endocrinology and Metabolism* (New York, 1922), III, 3–78—a section of this history is devoted to Lavoisier, pp. 19–30; R. Foregger, "Respiration Experiments of Lavoisier," in *Archives internationales d'histoire des sciences*, 13 (1960), 103–106; and Everett Mendelsohn, *Heat and Life* (Cambridge, Mass., 1964), 134–139, 146–165, which discusses Lavoisier's work perceptively. Charles A. Culotta, "Respiration and the Lavoisier Tradition: Theory and Modification, 1777–1850," in *Transactions of the American Philosophical Society*, n.s. 62 (1972), 3–40, is the most recent study. See also John F. Fulton, Denis I. Duveen, and Herbert S. Klickstein, "Antoine Laurent Lavoisier's Réflexions sur les effets de l'éther nitreux dans l'économie animale," in *Journal of the History of Medicine and Allied Sciences*, 8 (1953), 318–323; W. A. Smeaton, "Lavoisier's Membership of the Société Royale de Médecine," in *Annals of Science*, 12 (1956), 228–244; and Denis I. Duveen and H. S. Klickstein, "Antoine Laurent Lavoisier's Contributions to Medicine and Public Health," in *Bulletin of the History of Medicine*, 29 (1955), 164–179.

For Lavoisier's role in the improvement of saltpeter production and gunpowder manufacture, see Robert P. Multhauf, "The French Crash Program for Saltpeter Production, 1776–94," in *Technology and Culture*, 12 (1971), 163–181. The gunpowder situation in America at the outbreak of the Revolution, and the aid received from France, is described by Orlando W. Stephenson, "The Supply of Gunpowder in 1776," in *American Historical Review*, 30 (1925), 271–281. More than half of vol. V of the *Oeuvres de Lavoisier* is devoted to his papers on saltpeter and the work for the Régie des Poudres. See also J. R. Partington, "Lavoisier's Memoir on the Composition of Nitric Acid," in *Annals of Science*, 9 (1953), 96–98. The relations between Franklin and Lavoisier are described by H. S. van Klooster, "Franklin and Lavoisier," in *Journal of Chemical Education*, 23 (1946), 107–109; and by Denis I. Duveen and H. S. Klickstein, "Benjamin Franklin (1706–1790) and Antoine Laurent Lavoisier (1743–1794)," in *Annals of Science*, 11 (1955), 103–128, 271–302, and 13 (1957), 30–46. See also Claude A. Lopez, "Saltpetre, Tin and Gunpowder: Addenda to the Correspondence of Lavoisier and Franklin," in *Annals of Science*, 16 (1960), 83–94. For a remarkable letter from Lavoisier to Franklin, see René Fric, "Une lettre inédite de Lavoisier à B. Franklin," in *Bulletin historique et scientifique de l'Auvergne*, 9 (1924), 145–152.

On Lavoisier as a financier and economic theorist, Eugène Daire and Gustave de Molinari, *Mélanges d'économie politique*, I (Paris, 1847), 577–580, contains a "Notice sur Lavoisier," followed by two of his essays in political economy. See also G. Schelle and E. Grimaux, *Lavoisier—statistique agricole et projets de réformes* (Paris, 1894); and R. Dujarric de la Rivière, *Lavoisier économiste* (Paris, 1949). For Lavoisier's relations with Pierre Samuel Dupont de Nemours and Pierre's son, see Bessie Gardner Du Pont, *Life of Éleuthère Irénée du Pont from Contemporary Correspondence* (11 vols., Newark, Delaware, 1923–

1926), *passim*, I, 141–145, and R. Dujarric de la Rivière, *E. I. Du Pont de Nemours, élève de Lavoisier* (Paris, 1954), esp. 157–158.

For Lavoisier's interest in agriculture, see Henri Pigeonneau and Alfred de Foville, *L'administration de l'agriculture au controle générale des finances (1785–1787). Procès-verbaux et rapports* (Paris, 1882); and Louis Passy, *Histoire de la Société nationale d'agriculture de France*, I, *1761–1793* (Paris, 1912), which is all that appeared. André J. Bourde, *The Influence of England on the French Agronomes, 1750–1789* (Cambridge, 1953); and *Agronomie et agronomes en France au XVIIIe siècle*, 3 vols. (Paris, 1967), provide the essential background with incidental references to Lavoisier. See also W. A. Smeaton, "Lavoisier's Membership of the Société Royale d'Agriculture and the Comité d'Agriculture," in *Annals of Science*, 12 (1956), 267–277.

Lavoisier's role as an officer of the Academy of Sciences, before and during the French Revolution, bulks large in Roger Hahn, *The Anatomy of a Scientific Institution, the Paris Academy of Sciences, 1666–1803* (Berkeley–Los Angeles, 1971). There are glimpses of Lavoisier and his wife in Arthur Young's *Travels in France*, the best (and fully annotated) ed. of which is the French trans. by Henri Sée, *Voyages en France en 1787, 1788 et 1789*, 3 vols. (Paris, 1931), espec. I, pp. 189–191; in Beatrix Cary Davenport, ed., *A Diary of the French Revolution by Gouverneur Morris, 1752–1816* (Boston, 1939); in V. A. Eyles, "The Evolution of a Chemist, Sir James Hall," in *Annals of Science*, 19 (1963), 153–182; and in J. A. Chaldecott, "Scientific Activities in Paris in 1791," *ibid.*, 24 (1968), 21–52.

Grimaux gives much useful information about Mme Lavoisier, her education, her marriage, and her contributions to her husband's career in his *Lavoisier*, 2nd ed., pp. 35–44; for the genealogy of her family and an account of her life after Lavoisier's execution, see the appendixes to the same work, pp. 330–336. Worth consulting is Denis I. Duveen, "Madame Lavoisier, 1758–1836," in *Chymia*, 4 (1953), 13–29. Mme Lavoisier's major contribution to the campaign for the new chemistry was her (anonymous) trans. of Richard Kirwan's *Essay on Phlogiston* (London, 1784); the French version, *Essai sur le phlogistique* (Paris, 1788), has notes by the translator and extensive critical commentary by Guyton de Morveau, Laplace, Monge, Berthollet, Fourcroy, and Lavoisier himself. Grimaux (*op. cit.*, p. 42) speaks of her "traductions inédites de Priestley, Cavendish, Henry, etc." Her last effort along these lines is her trans. of Kirwan's "Strength of Acids and the Proportion of Ingredients in Neutral Salts," in *Proceedings of the Royal Irish Academy*, 4 (1790), 3–89. It appeared in *Annales de chimie*, 14 (1792), 152, 211, 238–286.

Lavoisier's role in the French Revolution, his imprisonment, and his execution have produced a substantial, and sometimes controversial, literature. See, for example, Denis I. Duveen, "Antoine Laurent Lavoisier (1743–1794), a Note Regarding His Domicile During the French Revolution," in *Isis*, 42 (1951), 233–234; and "Antoine Laurent

Lavoisier and the French Revolution," in *Journal of Chemical Education*, 31 (1954), 60–65; 34 (1957), 502–503; 35 (1958), 233–234, 470–471. See also Marguerite Vergnaud, "Un savant pendant la Révolution," in *Cahiers internationaux de sociologie*, 17 (1954), 123–139; Denis I. Duveen and Marguerite Vergnaud, "L'explication de la mort de Lavoisier," in *Archives internationales d'histoire des sciences*, 9 (1956), 43–50; Denis I. Duveen, "Lavoisier Writes to Fourcroy From Prison," in *Notes and Records. Royal Society of London*, 13 (1958), 59–60; and "Lavoisier Writes to His Wife From Prison," in *Manuscripts*, 10 (fall 1958), 38–39; and Denis I. Duveen and H. S. Klickstein, "Some New Facts Relating to the Arrest of Antoine Laurent Lavoisier," in *Isis*, 49 (1958), 347–348. On the problem of whether Fourcroy interceded on behalf of Lavoisier, see G. Kersaint, "Fourcroy a-t-il fait des démarches pour sauver Lavoisier?" in *Revue générale des sciences pures et appliquées*, 65 (1958), 151–152; and his "Lavoisier, Fourcroy et le scrutin épuratoire du Lycée de la rue de Valois," in *Bulletin. Société chimique de France* (1958), 259. For a comment on Kersaint's article, see Maurice Daumas, "Justification de l'attitude de Fourcroy pendant la Terreur," in *Revue d'histoire des sciences et de leurs applications*, 11 (1958), 273–274.

Other aspects of Lavoisier's career during the Revolution are mentioned by Henry Guerlac, "Some Aspects of Science During the French Revolution," in *Scientific Monthly*, 80 (1955), 93–101, repr. in Philipp G. Frank, ed., *The Validation of Scientific Theories* (Boston, 1957), 171–191; J. Guillaume, "Lavoisier anti-clérical et révolutionnaire," in *Révolution française*, 26 (1907), 403–423, repr. in *Études révolutionnaires*, 1st ser. (Paris, 1908), 354–379; Lucien Scheler, *Lavoisier et la Révolution française. II. Le journal de Fourgeroux de Bondaroy* (Paris, 1960), ed. with the collaboration of W. A. Smeaton. See also Smeaton's "The Early Years of the Lycée and the Lycée des Arts. A Chapter in the Lives of A. L. Lavoisier and A. F. de Fourcroy," in *Annals of Science*, 11 (1955), 257–267; 12 (1956), 267–277; and his "Lavoisier's Membership of the Assembly of Representatives of the Commune of Paris, 1789–1790," *ibid.*, 13 (1957), 235–248. For the text of letters seized at Lavoisier's house on 10 and 11 Sept. 1793, see Douglas McKie, "Antoine Laurent Lavoisier, F.R.S.," in *Notes and Records of the Royal Society*, 7 (1949), 1–41.

For the educational proposals attributed to Lavoisier, see Harold J. Abrahams, "Lavoisier's Proposals for French Education," in *Journal of Chemical Education*, 31 (1954), 413–416; and his "Summary of Lavoisier's Proposals for Training in Science and Medicine," in *Bulletin of the History of Medicine*, 32 (1958), 389–407. That Lavoisier was by no means the sole author of the *Réflexions sur l'instruction publique* has been shown by K. M. Baker and W. A. Smeaton, "The Origins and Authorship of the Educational Proposals Published in 1793 by the *Bureau de Consultation des Arts et Métiers* and Generally Ascribed to Lavoisier," in *Annals of Science*, 21 (1965), 33–46.

HENRY GUERLAC

LAVRENTIEV, BORIS INNOKENTIEVICH (*b.* Kazan, Russia, 13 August 1892; *d.* Moscow, U.S.S.R., 9 February 1944), *histology.*

Lavrentiev graduated from the Medical Faculty of Kazan University in 1914. From then until 1920 he was an army doctor, and in 1921 he became a prosector in the department of histology of Kazan University. In 1925 he was sent for a year to Utrecht to work in the neurohistological laboratory under J. Boecke. From 1927 to 1929 Lavrentiev was professor of histology at the Veterinary Faculty of the Zootechnical Institute in Moscow, then head of the department of histology at the First Moscow Medical Institute from 1929 to 1932. He headed the morphology department of the All-Union Institute of Experimental Medicine in Leningrad (it moved in 1934 to Moscow), at the same time holding the chair of histology at the Second Moscow Medical Institute. From 1941 to 1943, when the Institute of Experimental Medicine was evacuated to Tomsk, Lavrentiev was its acting director. In 1943 he continued his scientific work and teaching in Moscow. He was elected corresponding member of the Soviet Academy of Sciences in 1939.

The work of Lavrentiev and his collaborators was in the experimental study of the histophysiology of the autonomic nervous system. Their experiments with resection of ganglions and section of nerves, as well as their subsequent study by means of silver impregnation that adopted the Bielschowsky-Gross method (with Lavrentiev's modification), allowed investigation of the phenomena of degeneration and regeneration of the lost nerve connections and changes in synapses, autonomic ganglia, and the nerve endings in tissues and organs. On the basis of his research Lavrentiev supported the concept of the trophic effect of the nervous system and the theory of its neuronal structure. Lavrentiev demonstrated the existence and functions of interneuron bonds (synapses) not only on histological sections but also intravitally on the isolated heart of the frog, and he established that synapses ensure relative independence of neurons while connecting them in an integral system. In his work on the sensitive innervation of internal organs and the morphology of interoceptors, Lavrentiev suggested a classification of such receptors and determined the origin and localization of the sensitive neurons supplying internal organs.

BIBLIOGRAPHY

I. ORIGINAL WORKS. Lavrentiev's writings include "Innervatsionnye mekhanizmy (sinapsy), ikh morfologia i patologia" ("Innervation Mechanisms [Synapses], Their Morphology and Pathology"), in *Transactions of the 1st Histological Conference* (Moscow, 1934); "Gistofiziologia innervatsionnykh mekhanizmov (sinapsov)" ("The Histology of Innervation Mechanisms [Synapses]"), in *Fiziologichesky zhurnal SSSR*, **21**, nos. 5–6 (1936), 858–859; "Nekotorye voprosy teorii stroenia nervnoy tkani" ("Some Problems of the Theory of the Structure of Nervous Tissue"), in *Arkhiv biologicheskikh nauk*, **48**, nos. 1–2 (1937), 194–210; "Chuvstvitelnaya innervatsia vnutrennikh organov" ("The Sensitive Innervation of Internal Organs"), in *Zhurnal obshchei biologii*, **4**, no. 4 (1943), 232–249; "Morfologia antagonisticheskoi innervatsii v avtonomnoi nervnoi sisteme" ("The Morphology of Antagonistic Innervation in the Autonomic Nervous System"), in *Morfologia avtonomnoy nervnoy sistemy* ("The Morphology of the Autonomic Nervous System"), 2nd ed. (Moscow, 1946); and "Chuvstvitelnaia innervatsia vnutrennikh organov" ("The Sensitive Innervation of Internal Organs"), in *Morfologia chuvstvitelnoy innervatsii vnutrennikh organov* ("Morphology of the Sensitive Innervation of Internal Organs") (Moscow, 1948), 5–21.

II. SECONDARY LITERATURE. See N. G. Feldman, *B. I. Lavrentiev* (Moscow, 1970); A. N. Mislavsky, "Pamyati B. I. Lavrentieva" ("In Memory of B. I. Lavrentiev"), in *Zhurnal obshchei biologii*, **5**, no. 4 (1944), 199–204; E. K. Plechkova, "Boris Innokentievich Lavrentiev," in *Lyudi russkoy nauki. Biologia . . .* ("Men of Russian Science. Biology . . ."; Moscow, 1963), 448–456; and A. A. Zavarzin, "Pamyati B. I. Lavrentieva," in *Morfologia avtonomnoy nervnoy sistemy* ("Morphology of the Autonomic Nervous System"), 2nd ed. (Moscow, 1946), 7–12.

L. J. BLACHER

LAWES, JOHN BENNET (*b.* Rothamsted, near Harpenden, Hertfordshire, England, 28 December 1814; *d.* Rothamsted, 31 August 1900); and **GILBERT, JOSEPH HENRY** (*b.* Hull, England, 1 August 1817; *d.* Harpenden, England, 23 December 1901), *agricultural chemistry.*

Lawes was educated at Eton and Oxford; he left without taking a degree, although he had cultivated an amateur's taste for chemistry and pharmacy. In 1834 he inherited the manor and estate of Rothamsted; and two years later, becoming interested in the problems of a neighboring landowner, he began his agricultural experiments. Having seen that ground bones, or "mineral phosphates," were highly effective as manures on some fields but useless on the majority, Lawes was able to devise a method—treatment with acids—that made them universally effective. (Acids convert insoluble tricalcium phosphate into more soluble monocalcium salt, a process that acidic soils perform naturally.) Despite the opposition of his mother, who was bitterly opposed to "trade," he acquired a factory at Deptford Creek and in the summer of 1843 began the manufacture of "superphosphate," using the profits to finance further experiments at Rothamsted. In the same year he engaged Gilbert to assist him in this work, especially in the performance of chemical analyses; and a rough laboratory was improvised in a converted barn. Gilbert, although partly blinded by a gun accident when a boy, had studied chemistry at Glasgow University and University College, London, and, for a short time, under Liebig at Giessen. The collaboration of Lawes and Gilbert lasted for more than fifty years, and together they built Rothamsted into a world-famous institution. In character they were complementary: Lawes was the organizer, the man of affairs, impatient of detail, dealing in large ideas and general principles; Gilbert was a laboratory chemist, methodical and fussily accurate, a diligent attender of scientific meetings.

In 1840, Liebig published *Die organische Chemie in ihre Anwendung auf Agricultur und Physiologie*—translated into English in the same year by Lyon Playfair—which expounded his belief that manures were effective only by virtue of their mineral content and that nitrogenous and humus-forming manures were unnecessary and wasteful. These views were set out with such clarity and force, and Liebig's authority was so great, that they were widely believed, although they ran counter to most farming experience and were based on the slenderest experimental evidence. Lawes and Gilbert, in a long series of carefully planned field experiments, were able to show by 1851 that, as far as nitrogen was concerned, Liebig was in error, although they did not solve the puzzle of the nitrogen balance of leguminous plants. During this study they evolved the "chessboard" system of random plots for field trials on the fields of Broadbalk and Barnfield.

During the 1850's the financial basis of Rothamsted was in danger because of the widespread pirating of the superphosphate patent. Lawes spent much of this decade in protracted lawsuits; but his eventual victory enabled him to extend his experiments to long-term studies of grassland economy, animal feeding, and water balance. His work on the agricultural utilization of sewage led to Lawes being appointed to membership of a Royal Commission in 1857.

As must be inevitable in such lengthy projects a certain stagnation eventually became obvious. This was due partly to Gilbert's innate conservatism, which, as he grew older, hardened into intolerance of younger chemists and new ideas. Rather than collaborate with younger colleagues, he built up over the years a corps of village boys, each highly skilled in one operation of analytical chemistry. His iron rule over this little empire fitted in well with Lawes's paternalistic supervision of his manor. But Lawes began to feel that he had to make innovations, and in 1876 he appointed Robert Warington as his personal assistant. Gilbert took this as a deliberate affront, and personal relations were never quite easy at Rothamsted again; for lack of cooperation, Warington achieved little.

Lawes sold the superphosphate business in 1872, although he then had other interests in the manufacture of tartaric and citric acids. In 1889 he put Rothamsted under the control of the Lawes Agricultural Trust, with an endowment of £100,000, so that its work would not cease with his death (unlike the parallel enterprise of Boussingault in France); it continues to the present day. He was elected fellow of the Royal Society in 1854 and was made a baronet in 1882; Gilbert was elected fellow of the Royal Society in 1860 and was knighted in 1893.

BIBLIOGRAPHY

I. ORIGINAL WORKS. The work of Lawes and Gilbert was published entirely in the form of papers, under both joint and separate authorship, mostly in the *Journal of the Royal Agricultural Society*. After their deaths a summary of their work, incorporating much previously unpublished material, was written by A. D. Hall: *The Book of the Rothamsted Experiments* (London, 1905). Their collected papers (not quite complete) were published as *The Rothamsted Memoirs on Agricultural Chemistry and Physiology*, 7 vols. (London, 1893–1899).

II. SECONDARY LITERATURE. There are several obituary notices, including (Lawes) *Proceedings of the Royal Society*, **75** (1905), 228; *Journal of the Chemical Society*, **79** (1901), 890; *Nature*, **62** (1900), 467; *Journal of the Royal Agricultural Society*, **61** (1900), 511; (Gilbert) *Proceedings of the Royal Society*, **75** (1905), 237; *Journal of the Chemical Society*, **81** (1902), 625; *Nature*, **65** (1902), 205; *Journal of the Royal Agricultural Society*, **62** (1901), 347. E. Grey, *Rothamsted Experiment Station: Reminiscences, Tales, and Anecdotes 1872–1922* (Harpenden, 1922), is exactly described by its title. The best account of their work is in E. J. Russell, *A History of Agricultural Science in Great Britain, 1620–1954* (London, 1966). Both of these books, and many of the obituary notices, include portraits.

W. V. FARRAR

LAWRENCE, ERNEST ORLANDO (*b.* Canton, South Dakota, 8 August 1901; *d.* Palo Alto, California, 27 August 1958), *physics*.

Lawrence was the elder son of Carl Gustav Lawrence, a Wisconsin-born educator whose father,

Ole Hundale Lavrens (also a teacher), emigrated from Telemark in Norway to the Wisconsin Territory in 1846. His mother, Gunda Jacobson Lawrence, was also a teacher and of Norwegian ancestry. Lawrence's father was a graduate of the University of Wisconsin who successively served as city, county, and state superintendent of public education in South Dakota, and in 1919 became president of a teacher's college.

As a boy, Lawrence attended public schools in Canton, South Dakota, and in Pierre, the state capital. His best friend was Merle A. Tuve, another teacher's son who also became a well-known physicist (he measured, with Gregory Breit, the height of the ionosphere in 1925). Lawrence finished high school at sixteen and attended Saint Olaf College, a small Lutheran college in Northfield, Minnesota, on a scholarship for a year. He transferred to the University of South Dakota, where he first became interested in physics under the guidance of the professor of electrical engineering, Lewis E. Akeley, who recognized his student's unusual aptitude for science. After graduating with high honors in 1922, Lawrence enrolled at the University of Minnesota for postgraduate studies, mainly at the urging of Merle Tuve, who had preceded him to Minneapolis.

After earning a master's degree at Minnesota under the direction of W. F. G. Swann with an experimental confirmation of the theory of induction in an ellipsoid rotating in a magnetic field, Lawrence followed Swann to the University of Chicago, where he came into contact with A. A. Michelson, H. A. Wilson, Leigh Page, Arthur Compton, and Niels Bohr. In 1924 Lawrence followed Swann to Yale, where he completed his doctoral dissertation, a study of the photoelectric effect in potassium vapor. He remained at Yale as a research fellow and then assistant professor, quickly gaining a reputation as a brilliant experimenter, mainly in photoelectricity.

In 1928, at twenty-seven, Lawrence was offered an associate professorship at the University of California in Berkeley and startled fellow physicists by accepting —exchanging a famous old university for a little-known state university in the Far West. Its subsequent world renown as a center of research was due to a considerable extent to the primacy of its physics faculty, which came to rank with those of Cambridge and (in an earlier day) Göttingen among the world's finest. That phase began with the tenure of Lawrence and his contemporaries, among whom were Samuel Allison, R. B. Brode, and J. R. Oppenheimer. Within two years Lawrence, at twenty-nine, had become a full professor.

With his first graduate students, Niels E. Edlefsen and M. Stanley Livingston, Lawrence developed his invention of a circular accelerator, later called the cyclotron, in the shape of a flat circular can cut in two

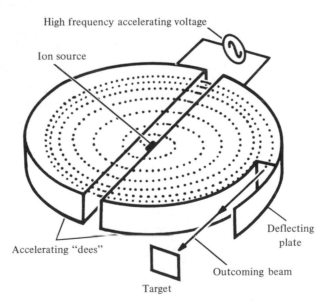

FIGURE 1. The circular accelerator.

94

along a diameter and placed inside a vacuum chamber. A high-frequency oscillator is connected between the two D-shaped halves, and charged particles are introduced near the center. The particles are constrained to travel in a circular path by a magnetic field along the axis of the can. With proper synchronization, the oscillating field serves to impart successive accelerations to each particle as it repeatedly crosses the boundary between the two halves, sending it on an ever-widening path with increasing velocity as it spirals outward. When it approaches the wall, it can be deflected through an opening toward a target, which it hits with a high velocity, producing nuclear disintegrations. Lawrence conceived the idea after seeing the illustrations for an article by the Norwegian-born engineer Rolf Wideröe elaborating a linear, rather than a circular, acceleration scheme proposed by the Swedish physicist Gustaf A. Ising.

The cyclotron was the first in a family of circular particle accelerators that made high acceleration energies available with relatively small instruments. Once the principle was proved, progress was swift. The unavailability of a sufficiently strong magnet was an obstacle that Lawrence characteristically overcame by persuading the Federal Telegraph Co. to donate an eighty-ton iron core originally intended for a radio arc generator but no longer needed. With this magnet and a cyclotron chamber 27.5 inches in diameter, Lawrence and his associates were able to produce energies of millions of electron volts. This achievement ushered in the era of high-energy physics and made possible the disintegration of atomic nuclei, artificial isotopes, and the discovery of new elements. Biomedical applications include radioactive tracers and uses in cancer therapy. One of the first results of major importance, the disintegration of lithium, was achieved at Berkeley as early as 1932, that *annus mirabilis* of modern physics which also saw the earlier disintegration of lithium by John Cockcroft and E. T. S. Walton, and the discovery of deuterium by H. C. Urey, of the neutron by James Chadwick, and of the positron by C. D. Anderson, each later honored by a Nobel Prize. In addition to lithium, many heavier nuclei were disintegrated in the Berkeley cyclotron, which was unique in that respect—no other machine could then do it. These disintegrations proved that nearly every nuclear reaction takes place if there is sufficient energy for it, a result of great importance in the development of nuclear physics. They also permitted accurate determination of the binding energy of various nuclei and, by comparison of the measured reaction energies (the masses were measured in a mass spectrograph), a complete verification of Einstein's law relating energy and mass.

World renown followed quickly. Lawrence was invited to his first Solvay Congress at thirty-two, was elected to the National Academy of Sciences at thirty-three, became director of his Radiation Laboratory at thirty-five, and in 1939 received the Nobel Prize, the first American associated with a state university to do so. (He had already received, in 1937, the Comstock Prize of the National Academy of Sciences and the Royal Society's Hughes Medal.) He was named director of what became known as the Radiation Laboratory ("Rad Lab") at Berkeley.

Lawrence was one of the American physicists who helped set up another "Radiation Laboratory" at the Massachusetts Institute of Technology in 1940; but that name disguised the laboratory's real function, the development of centimetric radar. He actively recruited young scientists for the laboratory but did not go himself, for with America's entry into World War II, an even larger project appeared on the horizon: the "Manhattan Project" to develop a nuclear or "A" (atomic) fission bomb.

Fearful that German scientists might be the first to develop such a weapon, other scientists, led by refugees from Nazism, proposed such a development to the U.S. government. The Berkeley Rad Lab, and Lawrence and Oppenheimer personally, were destined to play major roles in these endeavors. The Rad Lab helped devise a method of obtaining fissionable materials. A thirty-seven-inch cyclotron was converted into a mass spectograph for the purpose. The electromagnetic separation method devised at Berkeley was later used in a large laboratory (known as Y-12) at Oak Ridge, Tennessee, which provided the separated U^{235} for the Hiroshima atomic bomb. Oppenheimer became director of the laboratory at Los Alamos, New Mexico, where the first bombs were produced.

In 1945, with World War II ended by fission bombs dropped on Hiroshima and Nagasaki, the Rad Lab returned to predominantly scientific pursuits, including the construction of a 184-inch cyclotron (actually a new type of accelerator, the synchrocyclotron, based on a principle formulated by E. M. McMillan). The Los Alamos Scientific Laboratory, still managed by the University of California, continued in weapons research. Lawrence was actively involved in the subsequent controversy about the advisability of developing another, more destructive weapon, the thermonuclear-fusion or "H" (hydrogen) bomb. Its advocates (among whom the Hungarian-born physicist Edward Teller was the most prominent) prevailed. Oppenheimer was against it, and his long friendship with Lawrence ended over their deep disagreements on the desirable defense posture of the United States. The final break came when Oppenheimer, in a *cause célèbre*, lost the security clearance he needed as a government consultant.

In addition to the laboratory at Los Alamos, a second laboratory for research on nuclear weapons was started at Livermore, California, under the sponsorship of Lawrence and Edward Teller. This laboratory was at first a branch of the Rad Lab. Research at the Berkeley site was limited to basic science. During these years, larger and more efficient accelerators were designed and constructed there, and for a long time the Rad Lab had the highest energies and a near-monopoly of the type of results depending on them. Machines that could accelerate particles to energies of billions of electron volts (BeV—hence the name of one of them, the "bevatron") were constructed. It was by means of the bevatron that the antiproton was discovered by Emilio Segrè and Owen Chamberlain, and the properties of mesons were explored in detail, which led to a general understanding of strongly interacting particles. Lawrence also created the style of "big science"; large-scale physics started in Berkeley and set the pattern around the world in such later organizations as the Brookhaven National Laboratory in New York, the Centre Européen Pour la Recherche Nucléaire (CERN) in Switzerland, and the National Accelerator Laboratory in Illinois. Lawrence remained personally involved throughout and suffered no lessening of his inventive genius (among other devices, he invented a novel type of color television tube at this time); but increasing demands on him as a government and industrial consultant often took him away from Berkeley. Among these endeavors was his participation, at the request of President Eisenhower, in the Conference of Experts to Study the Possibility of Detecting Violations of a Possible Agreement on Suspension of Nuclear Tests in Geneva in the summer of 1958. It proved to be his last contribution. Exhausted and plagued by recurrent ulcerative colitis, he was flown home for an operation, which he did not survive.

Lawrence married Mary (Molly) Kimberly Blumer, daughter of the dean of Yale's medical faculty, in 1932; he had first met her when she was a schoolgirl of sixteen. They had two sons and four daughters. He was very close to his younger brother John, a physician who was associated with him professionally as director of a biophysics laboratory founded at Berkeley for the purpose of exploiting biomedical applications of nuclear physics. Another close associate was E. M. McMillan, who succeeded to the directorship of the Rad Lab. Several other associates achieved great prominence, including Luis Alvarez, Owen Chamberlain, Glenn Seaborg, and Emilio Segrè, each of whom later received a Nobel Prize, as did McMillan.

Lawrence's name is commemorated in the two Rad Lab sites, now known as the Lawrence Berkeley Laboratory and the Lawrence Livermore Laboratory; and in the Lawrence Hall of Science, a Berkeley museum and research center devoted to the improvement of science education. Annual Lawrence Awards are given to young scientists honored by the U.S. Atomic Energy Commission (AEC), and the transuranium element 103, discovered at Berkeley, was named Lawrencium. Lawrence was a member of the National Academy of Sciences, a foreign member of the Swedish Academy, an honorary member of the Soviet Academy, and the recipient of countless honorary degrees and other awards from institutions all over the world.

BIBLIOGRAPHY

I. ORIGINAL WORKS. A complete list of Lawrence's publications follows the article by Luis W. Alvarez in *Biographical Memoirs. National Academy of Sciences*, **41** (1970), 251–294. Lawrence's papers are in the Bancroft Library on the Berkeley campus of the University of California.

II. SECONDARY LITERATURE. A biography commissioned by the University of California and based on hundreds of interviews and a large store of written materials is Herbert Childs, *An American Genius: The Life of Ernest Lawrence* (New York, 1968). Lawrence's role in the beginnings of the atomic age is described in several book-length studies, among which vol. I of the AEC-sponsored history by R. G. Hewlett and O. E. Anderson Jr., *The New World: 1939–1946* (New York, 1962), is the most detailed. There are also journalistic accounts, not uniformly flattering to Lawrence, such as those by Robert Jungk, *Heller als tausend Sonnen* (Stuttgart, 1956), trans. by James Cleugh as *Brighter Than a Thousand Suns* (New York, 1960); and Nuel Pharr Davis, *Lawrence and Oppenheimer* (New York, 1968).

For an authoritative account of the development of the cyclotron, see M. Stanley Livingston, "History of the Cyclotron (Part I)," in *Physics Today*, **12** (Oct. 1959), 18–23; and Edwin M. McMillan (Part II), *ibid.*, 24–34.

CHARLES SÜSSKIND

LAWRENCE, WILLIAM (*b.* Cirencester, Gloucestershire, England, 16 July 1783; *d.* London, England, 5 July 1867), *anatomy, physiology, surgery.*

The son of William Lawrence, chief surgeon of Cirencester, and Judith Wood, Sir William Lawrence was a distinguished and gifted surgeon who was active at St. Bartholomew's Hospital in London for sixty-five years. His honors were numerous. In addition to serving as president of the Royal College of Surgeons for two terms (1846, 1855), he was also president of the Medical and Chirurgical Society of London (1831), surgeon extraordinary, and then sergeant-surgeon to Queen Victoria (1858). On 30 April 1867 a baronetcy was conferred upon him.

Lawrence was educated in a private school in his home town until 1799, when he was apprenticed to Dr. John Abernethy, assistant surgeon at St. Bartholomew's Hospital and one of the most popular medical teachers of his day. Only two years later, Lawrence was appointed Abernethy's demonstrator in anatomy, a post which he held for twelve years. Despite his youth, he soon acquired a reputation as an excellent teacher of anatomy and earned his diploma from the Royal College of Surgeons in 1805. He was elected assistant surgeon at St. Bartholomew's and fellow of the Royal Society in 1813. From 1814 to 1826 he was surgeon to the London Infirmary for Curing Diseases of the Eye (later the London Ophthalmic Infirmary and then the Royal Ophthalmic Hospital). He was appointed surgeon to the Royal Hospitals of Bridewell and Bethlehem in 1815 and was surgeon to St. Bartholomew's Hospital from 1824 to 1865.

After his nomination as professor of anatomy and surgery in 1815 by the Royal College of Surgeons, Lawrence delivered lectures to that body (1816–1818) on comparative anatomy, physiology, and the natural history of man. In 1829 he succeeded Abernethy at St. Bartholomew's as lecturer on surgery, a position he held until 1862. Although he had opposed the administration of the College of Surgeons, Lawrence was elected over two senior members to their council (1828) and later to the position of examiner (1840–1867), and was Hunterian orator in 1834 and 1846. His extensive private medical practice and lecturing at a private school of medicine on Aldersgate Street until 1829 were additional requirements on his time. He published many articles, particularly in *Lancet*, *Medical Gazette*, and *Transactions of the Medical and Chirurgical Society*. His *Lectures on Surgery Delivered in St. Bartholomew's Hospital* was published in 1863; unfortunately, by then his techniques had been superseded and the lectures obviously were out of date.

The earliest recognition of Lawrence's abilities occurred in 1806 when the College of Surgeons awarded him the Jacksonian Prize for his essay on ruptures. Published the following year as *A Treatise on Hernia*, the work became a standard reference and appeared in French (1818) and Italian (1820) translations. Dedicated to Abernethy, it is an excellent example of lucid exposition and thorough mastery of the subject.

Lawrence was one of the most distinguished English eye surgeons of his day. His private practice and his experiences as surgeon to the London Ophthalmic Infirmary laid the foundations for his *Treatise on the Venereal Diseases of the Eye* (1830). His lengthy *Treatise on the Diseases of the Eye* (1833) is an expanded version of his lectures on anatomy, physiology, and diseases of the eye delivered before the London Ophthalmic Infirmary and displays his outstanding abilities as an observer of diseases and as a practicing pathologist.

Although the Greeks had observed diseases of the eye and Celsus had summarized all examples known to his time, ophthalmology was largely in the hands of quacks and charlatans from the sixteenth to the eighteenth centuries. With the establishment of the Vienna school of ophthalmology in the latter half of the eighteenth century, the discipline entered its modern phase. In 1805 the London Ophthalmic Infirmary was established, and in 1810 students were admitted for observation and instruction. Lawrence was, therefore, one of its pioneering surgeons and produced one of the earliest reliable treatises in English on ophthalmology, "the equal of any work on the subject that appeared for many years."

Of a much more controversial nature were Lawrence's lectures presented before the Royal College of Surgeons from 1816 through 1818. In 1814, immediately preceding his presentation, Abernethy had delivered a series of anatomical lectures before that august body. The first two lectures, discussing his interpretation of John Hunter's views on life, were published in the same year. Reviewers were critical of Abernethy's somewhat obscure efforts, and Lawrence himself used his appointment to the college as a platform to criticize severely Hunter's vitalism as expounded by Abernethy. Dedicated to Blumenbach, whose *Short History of Comparative Anatomy* he had translated in 1807, Lawrence's *Lectures on Physiology* drew upon the works of various Continental authors, especially French, to expound his belief that the laws of physics and chemistry apply to organic nature. Nevertheless, physiological phenomena involve exceedingly complex systems: "We cannot expect to discover the true relations of things, until we rise high enough to survey the whole field of science, to observe the connexions of the various parts and their mutual influence." To compare the vital principle to magnetism, electricity, or galvanism, however, was unacceptable; extreme reductionism overlooked the complexities of the situation. Lawrence preferred a balanced view of life, encompassing as much scientific data as possible. Nevertheless, his belief that all mental activity was a function of the brain—not of an immortal, immaterial soul—cut to the heart of the theological establishment, which considered his "materialism" tantamount to atheism because he denied that the human soul existed beyond the body.

Lawrence's lectures, especially those published in 1819, generated severe criticism from Abernethy, theologians, physiologists, and his senior colleagues at the college. Although insisting he would not be silenced, he was compelled to withdraw his book within a month of its release by the threat of losing his position as surgeon at the Bridewell and Bethlehem hospitals. One contemporary observed, however, that Lawrence was not sincerely anxious for the matter to be dropped, for the book was still available from the publisher, "though at an advanced price." Indeed, the book went through ten subsequent editions (essentially printings), one of which was a pirated edition that James Smith brought out in 1822. Lawrence's attempt to prevent publication failed when Lord Eldon ruled in Chancery Court that parts of the work seemed to be "directed against the truth of the Scripture" and therefore could not be copyrighted. That various editions were subsequently printed suggests that Lawrence secretly urged their publication or was disinclined to go to court over the matter. It is clear, however, that his earlier suppression of his book was unrelated to the Chancery Court case.

While Lawrence has been described as an English medical evolutionist—another forerunner of Darwin—he maintained that man is "separated by a broad and clearly defined interval from all other animals," even the great apes. Although the evolutionist A. R. Wallace alluded to him with approbation in 1845, Lawrence had referred only to human variation which could explain the existence of different races of man: "The diversities of physical and moral endowment which characterize the various races of man, must be analogous in their nature, causes, and origin, to those which are observed in the rest of animal creation; and must therefore be explained on the same principles" (*Lectures on Physiology* [1822], p. 233). The different races of man had arisen through the ordinary process of variation observed in animals. Lawrence was no more an evolutionist, however, than many other English scientists like Blyth, Prichard, or Lyell, who also made highly suggestive remarks but failed to conclude that species evolve as well as vary. Lawrence's perceptive observations on inheritance do not make him a legitimate precursor of Darwin and Wallace.

Although an excellent lecturer and surgeon, and an outstanding member of the English medical community, Lawrence was not a creative thinker. In many ways his ideas were conservative. Had his *Lectures on Physiology* (1819) been published in France, instead of England, they would not have created the stir they did. We may conclude that his reputation did not rest on a single brilliant discovery, but rather on a lifetime of distinguished work in many areas of medicine and biology.

BIBLIOGRAPHY

I. ORIGINAL WORKS. In addition to works cited in the text, Lawrence published *An Introduction to Comparative Anatomy and Physiology; Being the Two Introductory Lectures Delivered at the Royal College of Surgeons on the 21st and 25th of March, 1816* (London, 1816); *Lectures on Physiology, Zoology, and the Natural History of Man, Delivered at the Royal College of Surgeons* (London, 1819); and *The Hunterian Oration Delivered at the Royal College of Surgeons* (London, 1834); also his later lecture (London, 1846).

II. SECONDARY LITERATURE. On Lawrence's life, see W. R. LeFanu, "Past Presidents: Sir William Lawrence, Bart.," in *Annals of the Royal College of Surgeons of England*, 25 (1959), 201–202; [W. S. Savory], "Sir William Lawrence, Bart.," in *St. Bartholomew's Hospital Reports*, 4 (1868), 1–18; and Norman Moore, *The History of St. Bartholomew's Hospital*, II (London, 1918), pp. 660–663.

For his work on ophthalmology see Burton Chance, "Sir William Lawrence in Relation to Medical Education with Special Reference to Ophthalmology in the Early Part of the Nineteenth Century," in *Annals of Medical History*, 8 (1926), 270–279.

On physiology see June Goodfield-Toulmin, "Blasphemy and Biology," in *Rockefeller University Review*, 4 (1966), 9–18; and "Some Aspects of English Physiology: 1780–1840," in *Journal of the History of Biology*, 2 (1969), 283–320; and Owsei Temkin, "Basic Science, Medicine, and the Romantic Era," in *Bulletin of the History of Medicine*, 37 (1963), 97–129.

For anthropology see C. D. Darlington, *Darwin's Place in History* (Oxford, 1959), pp. 19–24, 100–101; Peter G. Mudford, "William Lawrence and *The Natural History of Man,*" in *Journal of the History of Ideas*, 29 (1968), 430–436; and Kentwood D. Wells, "Sir William Lawrence (1783–1867), A Study of Pre-Darwinian Ideas on Heredity and Variation," in *Journal of the History of Biology*, 4 (1971), 319–361.

H. LEWIS McKINNEY

LAWSON, ANDREW COWPER (*b*. Anstruther, Scotland, 25 July 1861; *d*. San Leandro, California, 16 June 1952), *geology.*

The eldest of ten children of William Lawson and Jessie Kerr, Andrew was educated in public schools in Hamilton, Ontario. He received a bachelor's degree in 1883 from the University of Toronto, the master's degree in 1885, and the doctorate from the Johns Hopkins University in 1888. In 1890, after seven years with the Geological Survey of Canada, he joined the geology department of the University of California at Berkeley, where he was active for sixty years.

Lawson was raised a devout Calvinist. Through his studies he became an active opponent of dogma and gave up his religious beliefs, but he never effected a complete emotional adjustment to the change. In 1889 Lawson married Ludovika von Jansch, of Brünn, Moravia, who bore him four sons. She died in 1929. In 1931 he married Isabel R. Collins of Ottawa. He was survived by her and their one son and by two sons by his first wife. A man of powerful physique and dynamic drive, he continued working effectively well into his ninetieth year. Lawson served many learned and cultural societies with distinction and was, in 1926, president of the Geological Society of America. His achievements brought honors and recognition.

Lawson's studies of isostasy over the three decades 1920–1950 have drawn special attention to its importance in diastrophism. In a number of general theoretical papers he developed the logical consequences of isostatic adjustment as an important factor in orogenesis, indeed in some instances as the determinative agent in the elevation of lofty mountains and the depression of deep troughs and basins. Widely distributed field evidence in support of his findings is presented in these writings and others following, eighteen papers in all, showing the importance of isostasy in the development of such features as the Sierra Nevada, the Great Valley of California, the Mississippi delta, and the Cordilleran shield.

From time to time for some forty years Lawson turned his attention to the region northwest of Lake Superior, and in thirty-five papers he presented a great body of new information and revised the correlation of the pre-Cambrian rocks over a large part of North America. In his early studies about Lake of the Woods and Rainy Lake he found that the Laurentian, previously regarded as the oldest known formation and comprising metamorphosed sediments, was a granite intrusive into metamorphosed volcanic and sedimentary rocks which he called Keewatin. Underlying these he found another sedimentary series which he named Coutchiching and recognized as the oldest rocks in the region. His report of 1887 on these findings was published only after much controversy. Returning to this area in 1911, Lawson recognized two periods of batholithic invasion, the oldest being

termed Laurentian and the younger Algoman, each followed by a great period of peneplanation. The resulting surfaces, termed the Laurentian peneplain and the Eparchean peneplain respectively, afforded references for the correlation of the invaded formations, and for the subsequently deposited sedimentary beds, over vast areas.

In Berkeley, Lawson initiated a systematic investigation of the geology of the western coastal area and established the *Bulletin of the Department of Geology*, for publishing papers relating to this work. Along with this undertaking, assisted by various students, Lawson carried out the preparation of the San Francisco Folio, which included five quadrangles in the San Francisco Bay region. This work was published by the U. S. Geological Survey in 1914. At his death, the *Bulletin* comprised twenty-eight volumes of from 400 to 600 pages each.

As chairman of the Department of Geology at the university for more than twenty years, Lawson was diligent in promoting its growth while continuing his own research work. For three years he was, at the same time, dean of the College of Mining, where he established instruction and research in petroleum engineering, the first program of the kind in any American university.

After the California earthquake of 18 April 1906, Lawson supervised the preparation of a report by the State Earthquake Investigation Commission. It included two volumes and an atlas comprising 500 pages and for many years it was the most informative treatise published on any earthquake; and it led to many new developments, one of the more important being the initiation of the elastic rebound theory of the dynamics of earthquakes by H. F. Reid. Lawson's continued activity in this field brought about the organization of the Seismological Society of America; the founding of the *Bulletin* of this society; the construction in Berkeley, in 1911, of the most complete seismograph station in America; the formulation of a plan, later carried out with the help of the Carnegie Institution of Washington, for an extensive network of seismograph stations in California; and the establishment at the University of California, in 1927, of the first professorship in seismology in the United States.

As a mining consultant Lawson not only visited most of the mining camps in North America, but worked in many from time to time over a period of years. At the same time, he was also a consultant in a number of construction engineering projects, including the Golden Gate bridge.

His sharp wit, dynamic personality, and sound thinking marked Lawson as a man feared in debate and revered in counsel. As an architect and skilled workman he put up several fireproof and earthquake-resistant buildings in the vicinity of his home. He collected paintings and wrote fifty-five poems expressing inner thoughts of considerable variety, from the light and cheerful to the profound and philosophical.

BIBLIOGRAPHY

A complete bibliography of all Lawson's 114 works is included in the biography by Francis E. Vaughan, *Andrew C. Lawson, Scientist, Teacher, Philosopher* (Glendale, Calif. 1970).

The following are representative: "The Archean geology of the region north-west of Lake Superior," in *Fourth International Geological Congress, London, 1888. Compte Rendu* (1891), 130–152; "The Cordilleran Mesozoic revolution," in *Journal of Geology*, **1** (1893), 579–586; "The Eparchean interval; a criticism of the use of the term Algonkian," in *University of California Publications, Department of Geology, Bulletin*, **3** (1902), 51–62; "The California earthquake of April 18, 1906," written with others, the report of the State Earthquake Investigation Commission, which is *Carnegie Institution of Washington Publication No. 87;* "The Archean geology of Rainy Lake restudied," which is *Geological Survey of Canada, Memoir 40;* "A standard scale for the pre-Cambrian rocks of North America," in *Twelfth International Geological Congress, Toronto, 1913. Compte Rendu* (1914), 349–370; "Ore deposition in and near intrusive rocks by meteoric waters," in *University of California Publications, Department of Geology, Bulletin*, **8** (1914), 219–242; "The spirit of science," in *University of California Chronicle*, **22** (1920), 143–161; "The geological implications of the doctrine of isostasy," in *National Research Council, Bulletin*, **8**, pt. 4, no. 46 (1924); "The classification and correlation of the pre-Cambrian rocks," in *University of California Publications, Department of Geological Sciences, Bulletin*, **19**, no. 11 (1930), 275–293.

FRANCIS E. VAUGHAN

LAX, GASPAR (*b*. Sariñena, Aragon, Spain, 1487; *d*. Zaragoza, Spain, 23 February 1560), *mathematics, logic, natural philosophy.*

After studying the arts and theology in Zaragoza, Lax taught in Paris in 1507 and 1508 at the Collège de Calvi, also known as the "Little Sorbonne." He transferred to the Collège de Montaigu, where he continued to teach and to study under the Scottish master John Maior; in 1517 he returned to the Collège de Calvi. Lax had an agile mind and an excellent

memory, but he became so engrossed with the logical subtleties of the nominalist school that he was soon known as "the Prince of the Parisian *sophistae*." A prolific writer, he turned out a series of ponderous tomes on *exponibilia, insolubilia,* and other topics of terminist logic. His student, the humanist Juan Luis Vives, later reported that he heard Lax and his colleague, John Dullaert of Ghent, moan over the years they had spent on such trivialities. Lax taught at Paris until 1523; possibly he returned to Spain in 1524, along with his countryman Juan de Celaya, when foreigners were asked to leave the university. In 1525 he taught mathematics and philosophy at the *studium generale* of Zaragoza. He remained there until his death, at which time he was vice-chancellor and rector.

Lax achieved greater fame as a mathematician than as a logician or as a philosopher. He published his *Arithmetica speculativa* and *Proportiones* at Paris in 1515 (Villoslada adds to these a *De propositionibus arithmeticis*, same place and date). The first is described by D. E. Smith as "a very prolix treatment of theoretical arithmetic, based on Boethius and his medieval successors" (p. 121). The *Proportiones* is a more compact and formalistic treatment of ratios, with citations of Euclid, Jordanus, and Campanus; unlike most sixteenth-century treatises on ratios, however, it does not deal with the velocities of motion in the Mertonian and Parisian traditions. Possibly Lax treated this interesting topic in his *Quaestiones phisicales,* printed at Zaragoza, 1527, according to early lists. (I have searched extensively for this, with no success.)

BIBLIOGRAPHY

None of Lax's works is translated from the Latin, and copies of the originals are rare; positive microfilms of the *Arithmetica speculativa* and various logical works are obtainable from the Vatican Library.

A brief general treatment of Lax is in R. G. Villoslada, S.J., *La universidad de Paris durante los estudios de Francisco de Vitoria (1507–1522)*, Analecta Gregoriana XIV (Rome, 1938), pp. 404–407 and *passim*. See also Hubert Élie, "Quelques maîtres de l'université de Paris vers l'an 1500," in *Archives d'histoire doctrinale et littéraire du moyen âge*, **18** (1950–1951), 193–243, esp. 214–216.

Lax's logical and philosophical thought is treated by Marcial Solana, *Historia de la filosofía española, Época del Renacimiento (siglo XVI)* (Madrid, 1941), III, 19–33. His arithmetic is described in D. E. Smith, *Rara arithmetica* (Boston–London, 1908), p. 121.

WILLIAM A. WALLACE, O.P.

LAZAREV, MIKHAIL PETROVICH (*b.* Vladimir, Russia, 14 November 1788; *d.* Vienna, Austria, 23 April 1851), *navigation, oceanography.*

Lazarev was trained in both theoretical and practical navigation. From 1799 to 1803 he studied with P. Y. Gamaleya and G. A. Sarychev at the Naval Academy in St. Petersburg, then volunteered as a seaman in the British Navy. From 1808 he served on various military ships in the Baltic Sea. In 1813 he made the first of his three voyages around the world, commanding the *Suvorov.* This expedition lasted until 1813, and among its discoveries was a group of coral islands in the South Pacific that are now called the Suvorov atoll. In 1819 Lazarev was named commander of the sloop *Mirny*, the second ship of Bellinsgauzen's two-year expedition to the Antarctic. (For a complete account of this venture, which was organized to collect astronomical, hydrographical, and ethnographical data, and to map new lands and report on specifically polar phenomena, see the article on F. F. Bellinsgauzen, I, 594–595.) From 1822 to 1825 Lazarev was commander of the frigate *Kreyser*; he was promoted to admiral in 1843.

On all three of his voyages, Lazarev and his assistants were concerned with correcting navigational maps; they further determined precisely the locations of many islands discovered by themselves or by earlier explorers. Lazarev also made depth soundings of coastal waters (as, for example, those of Novo Arkhangel'sk and San Francisco Bay), observed local relief features, and determined the height of mountains. His measurements and observations were very accurate; on the voyage of the *Mirny*, he determined the height of Mt. Egmont in New Zealand to be 8,232 feet (it is actually 8,260 feet), while the meteorological data that he recorded on the *Kreyser* were of such high quality that they were published by the Naval Ministry in 1882.

Lazarev was an honorary member of the Russian Geographical Society and of Kazan University. One of the first Soviet Antarctic stations was named for him, as were a chain of Antarctic mountains, a great Antarctic trough, a group of mountains in the Tuamotu Archipelago, and several capes and harbors.

BIBLIOGRAPHY

I. ORIGINAL WORKS. Lazarev wrote *Meteorologicheskie nablyudenia, proizvodivshiesya vo vremya krugosvetnogo plavania fregata "Kreyser" pod komandoy kapitana II ranga Lazareva 1-go v 1822, 1823, 1824, 1825 godakh* ("Meteorological Observations, Made During the Voyage Around the World of the Frigate *Kreyser* Under the Command of Captain, Second Rank, Lazarev in 1822, 1823, 1824, 1825"; St. Petersburg, 1882); and *Dokumenty . . .*, 3 vols. (Moscow, 1952–1961).

II. SECONDARY LITERATURE. On Lazarev and his work see I, 595, and M. I. Belov, "Shestaya chast sveta otkryta russkimi moryakami (novye materialy . . .)" ("The Sixth Part of the World Discovered by Russian Sailors [New Materials . . .]"), in *Izvestiya Vsesoyuznogo geograficheskogo obshchestva*, **94**, no. 2 (1962), 105–114; V. A. Esakov *et al.*, *Russkie okeanicheskie i morskie issledovania v XIX-nach. XX v.* ("Russian Oceanic and Sea Investigations in the Nineteenth and Early Twentieth Centuries"; Moscow, 1964), pp. 53–69; M. I. Firsov, *Pervootkryvatel golubogo kontinenta* ("Discoverer of the Blue Continent"; Vladimir, 1963); K. I. Nikulchenkov, *Admiral Lazarev. 1788–1851* (Moscow, 1956); [P. M. Novoselsky], *Yuzhny polyus. Iz zapisok byvshego morskogo ofitsera* ("The South Pole. From the Notes of a Former Naval Officer"; St. Petersburg, 1853); B. Ostrovsky, *Lazarev* (Moscow, 1966), with bibliography pp. 174–175; A. V. Sokolov and E. G. Kushnarev, *Tri krugosvetnykh plavania M. P. Lazareva* ("M. P. Lazarev's Three Voyages Around the World"; Moscow, 1951); and N. N. Zubov, *Otechestvennye moreplavateli—issledovateli morey i okeanov* ("National Navigators and Investigators of the Seas and Oceans": Moscow, 1954), pp. 168–179; and "Mikhail Petrovich Lazarev," in *Otechestvennye fiziko-geografy i puteshestvenniki* ("National Physical Geographers and Travelers"; Moscow, 1959), pp. 193–197.

V. A. ESAKOV

LAZAREV, PETR PETROVICH (*b.* Moscow, Russia, 14 April 1878; *d.* Alma-Ata, U.S.S.R., 24 April 1942), *physics, biophysics, geophysics.*

Lazarev's father was a civil engineer. Upon graduation from the Gymnasium in Moscow, Lazarev entered the Medical Faculty of Moscow University, from which he graduated with distinction in 1901. In 1902 he passed the examinations for the academic degree of doctor of medicine and became an assistant in the ear clinic at Moscow University. Lazarev became deeply interested in the physical and mathematical sciences while he was still a student, and in 1903 he passed the examination for the entire course of study in the Faculty of Physics and Mathematics without ever having attended classes there.

While working in the ear clinic, Lazarev completed his first two research papers on the activity of the sensory organs. In the first paper he demonstrated experimentally that the phases of overtones do not influence the reception of sound. This helped to serve as an argument in favor of Helmholtz' resonance theory of hearing. In the second paper Lazarev demonstrated a distinct connection between auditory and visual sensations: the audibility of a sound is intensified by the simultaneous stimulation of the eyes by light.

In 1903–1905 Lazarev attended the weekly colloquiums of P. N. Lebedev and conducted several unofficial physical experiments in his laboratory. This work served to initiate a close friendship and scientific collaboration that lasted until Lebedev's death in 1912. In 1907 Lazarev passed his master's examinations and became an assistant professor at the Faculty of Physics and Mathematics of Moscow University. In 1911 he defended his master's dissertation on the temperature discontinuity at the gas-solid boundary. This topic, which arose from a research project conducted by Lebedev on the sensitivity of vacuum thermoelements, possessed great importance as a new experimental confirmation of the kinetic theory of gases. From that time on, Lazarev became Lebedev's chief assistant and the independent head of a group of researchers concerned with molecular and chemical physics.

In 1912 Lazarev defended his doctoral dissertation, "Vytsvetanie krasok i pigmentov v vidimom svete" ("The Fading of Colors and Pigments in Visible Light"). In this work Lazarev first established the connection between the quantity of matter decomposed under the influence of light and the light energy absorbed, as well as the dependence of the speed of a reaction upon the length of the light wave and the influence of oxygen on fading. This work, which is now acknowledged as one of the fundamental investigations of prequantum photochemistry, led to a series of investigations both abroad and in Russia.

In 1911 a significant number of professors and teachers left Moscow University as a protest against the reactionary actions of the minister of education, L. A. Kasso. Among them were Lazarev, Lebedev, and the majority of their colleagues. A short time later Lebedev's laboratory work was transferred to a small private institution, Shanyavsky City University. After Lebedev's death in April 1912, the supervision of his laboratory was entrusted to Lazarev. During the following years he began to concentrate his scientific interests on biophysics of the sense organs and the theory of nerve excitation. Guided by several experimental works of J. Loeb, Lazarev established his ion theory of nerve excitation. As a basis for his experimental law of excitation, Lazarev accepted Loeb's formula $C_1/(C_2 + b) =$ constant (where C_1 is the concentration of ions which give rise to the excitation of nerves and muscles, C_2 is the concentration of ions which depress this excitation, and b is a constant). In his theory Lazarev proceeded from the proposition that the coagulation of colloidal albuminous particles initiates the excitation process. The stability of the system is determined by the sign of the charge of the ions present in the solution. Lazarev produced many experimental research papers and, on the basis of extensive experimental material obtained by his collaborators, proposed the basic laws of ion theory for the excitation of living tissue. This theory has in significant measure retained its importance in modern biophysics.

Lazarev placed Loeb's formula at the base not only of nerve and muscle excitation theory but of peripheral vision theory as well. Lazarev was one of the first to raise the question of the photochemical interpretation of the phenomena of eye adaptation, and he produced a series of works in support of this conception. In proposing that ions are the products of the photochemical decomposition of visual purple, Lazarev constructed the mathematical theory of the laws of peripheral vision under various conditions. He also formulated on these principles a theory of hearing and taste. Lazarev occupied himself with these questions for the rest of his life.

Lazarev's activity was not limited to scientific research. From the beginning of World War I he participated in organizing medical aid for the front. He organized the production of medical thermometers, created the central diagnostic X-ray clinic for Moscow hospitals and a mobile X-ray section for the hospitals of the Moscow guberniya, and personally concerned himself with the training of physicians in roentgenology.

In 1917, shortly before the February Revolution, Lazarev was elected a full member of the Russian Academy of Sciences. He supported the October Revolution, and shortly afterward organized the first special scientific research institute for physics and biophysics in Russia. During the Civil War, Lazarev organized a laboratory in which he worked out the theoretical and practical problems of light and sound concealment and camouflage. In 1918 Lazarev, commissioned by the Soviet government, became the head of research into the Kursk Magnetic Anomaly. Before the Revolution, geomagnetic investigations in the region of the anomaly were conducted by E. J. Leyst. His investigations led him to suggest that enormous deposits of iron ore were to be found there, but geological prospecting did not support this view. The geomagnetic maps compiled by Leyst were stolen after his death.

Lazarev began all the work anew and established widespread geophysical and geological prospecting surveys which, in 1919, revealed the presence of enormous reserves of iron ore near the surface. He personally played a large part in implementing the geophysical calculations and initiated new investigations and geophysical methods of prospecting. He devoted much attention to scientific literature and was the founder of the journal *Uspekhi fizicheskikh nauk*.

BIBLIOGRAPHY

Many of Lazarev's more than 500 published works are in *Izbrannye sochinenia* ("Selected Works"), vols. II and III (Moscow–Leningrad, 1950)—vol. I has not yet been published.

On Lazarev or his work, see the following (listed chronologically): E. V. Shpolsky, "Petr Petrovich Lazarev (1878–1942)," in *Uspekhi fizicheskikh nauk*, **27** no. 1 (1945), 1–12; T. P. Kravets, "Tvorchesky put akademika P. P. Lazareva" ("The Creative Path of Academician P. P. Lazarev"), *ibid.*, 13–21; B. V. Deryagin, "O rabotakh akad. P. P. Lazareva v oblasti biologicheskoy fiziki" ("On the Works of Academician P. P. Lazarev in the Area of Biological Physics"), suppl. to *Issledovania po adaptatsii P. P. Lazareva* ("Studies in Adaptation by P. P. Lazarev"; Moscow–Leningrad, 1947); and S. V. Kravkov, "Petr Petrovich Lazarev (K desyatiletiyu so dnya smerti)" ("Petr Petrovich Lazarev [On the Tenth Anniversary of His Death]"), in *Uspekhi fizicheskikh nauk*, **46**, no. 4 (1952), 441–449.

J. G. DORFMAN

LEA, ISAAC (*b.* Wilmington, Delaware, 4 March 1792; *d.* Philadelphia, Pennsylvania, 8 December 1886), *malacology*.

The fifth son of James Lea, a Quaker merchant of Wilmington, Isaac attended the local academy with the idea of becoming a physician; but at the age of fifteen he went to work in the Philadelphia mercantile business of his brother John, who eventually made him a partner. In Philadelphia, Lea formed a lifelong friendship with Lardner Vanuxem, with whom he roamed the countryside collecting minerals, rocks, and fossils. They were both elected to the Academy of Natural Sciences of Philadelphia in 1815; and in 1818 Lea published in its *Journal* his first scientific paper, "An Account of the Minerals at Present Known to Exist in the Vicinity of Philadelphia." The study of geology led to the study of shells, and Lea spent several years studying the collections of freshwater mollusks that Major Stephen Long had sent to the Academy from the Ohio River and that his brother Thomas Lea had gathered for him near Cincinnati. In 1827 he published, in *Transactions of the American Philosophical Society*, "A Description of Six New Species of the Genus Unio." Thereafter he devoted most of his scientific attention to "this truly seducing branch of Nat: Hist:." His *Contributions to Geology* (Philadelphia, 1833), a descriptive catalogue principally of specimens of the Tertiary formations at Claiborne, Alabama, firmly established his reputation. Its text was distinguished by care and judgment; and its typography and illustrations, Roderick Murchison told the author, had "quite the stamp of being issued by one of the best workshops of Europe."

The subject was well chosen, for although mollusks abounded in American rivers, scarcely anyone had searched for them there. An acute and accurate observer, during a long lifetime Lea collected, identified, and described, chiefly in papers to the Academy of Natural Sciences and the American Philosophical Society, 1,842 species of some fifty genera of freshwater and terrestrial mollusks. "I sometimes fear I take up too much room in the Society's Transactions," he once half-apologized, "but it is a great matter to have new objects of Natural History well illustrated—it saves hundreds of mistakes which in time might otherwise occur." In addition to shells, Lea figured the embryonic forms of thirty-eight species of *Unio* and described the soft parts of another 234. His *Synopsis of the Family of Naïades* (Philadelphia–London, 1836; 4th ed. 1870) classified the synonymy of the Unionidae, until then in great confusion. He also investigated physiological questions, such as mollusks' sensitivity to light and differences due to sex. Lea ordered 250 reprints of each paper, bound them up from time to time with title page and introduction as *Observations on the Genus Unio* (13 vols., 1827–1874), and presented them to institutions and individuals. "Your intelligent perseverance with consummate skill & taste have reared a brilliant monument in this part of conchology," the elder Silliman told him in 1860 in acknowledging one of these volumes. Lea's bibliography, compiled in 1876, contained 279 titles.

Lea's personal collection was steadily augmented by gifts from other naturalists—among them Jeffries Wyman, Charles M. Wheatley, Bishop Stephen Elliott, Gerard Troost, John LeConte, and Dr. John Kirk, who accompanied Livingstone to Lake Nyassa. After seeing Lea's cabinet in 1846, Agassiz declared "that all which European naturalists have written on this subject must be revised." Captain Frederick Marryat pronounced it "certainly the most interesting [museum] I saw in the States" and a principal reason why Philadelphia, not Boston, must be considered "the most scientific city in the Union." In his later years Lea turned to the study of crystals and is said to have been the first in America to engage in microscopic mineralogy.

Unlike those of some contemporaries, Lea's disputes with fellow scientists were never acrimonious. He thought Rafinesque's descriptions "very imperfect"; and in a "rectification" of T. A. Conrad's errors and omissions, he asserted his own claims to priority in discoveries (1854). His report on the footprints of the reptile *Sauropus primaevus* in the Old Red Sandstone was disputed by Agassiz, who asserted that no air-breathing animals had existed earlier than the new Red Sandstone. Lea maintained his position in a carefully argued and illustrated monograph, which he ultimately reproduced in elephant folio, with a lithograph of the footprint in actual size. Of some importance then, the matter is of less concern now that fossils of air-breathers have been found in other formations.

Lea was a striking example of the self-taught amateur who by single-minded attention to a limited subject makes a comprehensive, basic, and lasting contribution to knowledge. He expressed the spirit that guided him in 1826: "To scrutinize the first cause is vain; we must make ourselves acquainted with the effects and compare them. In this we have ample room to engage all our faculties." Lea served as president of the Academy of Natural Sciences, vice-president of the American Philosophical Society (where he was also chairman of the finance and publications committees), and president of the American Association for the Advancement of Science. He received an honorary LL.D. from Harvard in 1852 and was a member or fellow of a score of foreign academies. On visits to England and Europe in 1832 and 1852–1853 he was warmly received by Alexander von Humboldt, William Buckland, Charles Lyell, Roderick Murchison, and Adam Sedgwick; and he inspected and named specimens of Unionidae in the British Museum, the Jardin des Plantes, and private collections.

Lea did his scientific work at the end of days filled with business and social obligations. Having joined Mathew Carey's publishing firm in 1821 after his marriage to Carey's daughter Frances Anne, he eventually became president, but retired in 1851. He was rich, with the obligations that wealth entails. Commenting on several unexpected family deaths that left him in 1845 responsible for the children of four relatives, he exclaimed to J. C. Jay, "God knows when I shall have leisure to pursue my wishes in our beautiful branch of Science." Of his three children, M. Carey Lea was a pioneer in photochemistry; and Henry Charles Lea, whose first published paper was on shells, became, after retiring from the publishing firm, the historian of the Inquisition. Lea bequeathed his collection, numbering nearly 10,000 specimens, to the National Museum, Washington.

BIBLIOGRAPHY

I. ORIGINAL WORKS. Lea's contributions are analyzed in Newton P. Scudder, *Published Writings of Isaac Lea, LL.D., Bulletin. United States National Museum*, no. 23 (Washington, D.C., 1885). The Academy of Natural Sciences of Philadelphia and the American Philosophical Society Library possess correspondence used in this sketch. Lea's journals of foreign travel are available on film at the American Philosophical Society Library.

II. SECONDARY LITERATURE. The principal biographical sketch is by Newton P. Scudder, introducing Lea's *Published Writings*, cited above. For other data see "A Sketch of the History of Conchology in the United States," in *American Journal of Science and Arts*, 2nd ser., **33** (1862), 161–180; W. H. Dall, "Isaac Lea, LL.D.," in *Science*, **8** (17 Dec. 1886), 556–558; Joseph Leidy, "Biographical Notice," in *Proceedings of the American Philosophical Society*, **24** (1887), 400–403; and W. J. Youmans, *Pioneers of Science in America* (New York, 1896), 260–269.

WHITFIELD J. BELL, JR.

LEAKEY, LOUIS SEYMOUR BAZETT (*b.* Kabete, Kenya, 7 August 1903; *d.* London, England, 1 October 1972), *archaeology, human paleontology, anthropology.*

Leakey was the son of Canon Leakey of the Church Missionary Society in Kenya and was brought up with the native Kikuyu. After attending Weymouth College he went to St. John's College, Cambridge, from which he graduated in archaeology and anthropology and took his Ph.D. in African prehistory. He then became a research fellow of the college and, in 1966, an honorary fellow. His interests in prehistory and ethnology were stimulated by M. C. Burkitt and A. C. Haddon. He was a member of the British Museum East African Expedition to Tanganyika in 1924 and from 1926 led his own East African archaeological research expeditions. Leakey's important discoveries about the prehistory of East Africa and his discovery of early hominids were published in *The Stone Age Cultures of Kenya* (1931), *The Stone Age Races of Kenya* (1935), and *Stone-Age Africa* (1936).

His archaeological and paleontological work did not detract from his interest in Kenya and its politics, an interest which his close association with the Kikuyu made him particularly well equipped to pursue, as can be seen from his autobiographical *White African* (1937). The results of his research for the Rhodes Trustees into the customs of the Kikuyu tribe (1937–1939) are in press. At the outbreak of World War II he was in charge of special branch 6 of the Criminal Investigation Department in Nairobi; he continued as a handwriting expert to the department until 1951.

At the end of the war he returned to his archaeological and paleontological researches, as curator of the Coryndon Memorial Museum, Nairobi (1945–1961), and later as honorary director of the National Centre of Prehistory and Paleontology in Nairobi, and on behalf of various research foundations. He founded the Pan-African Congress on Prehistory, of which he was general secretary (1947–1951) and president (1955–1959). On periods of leave during the war Leakey and his second wife, the former Mary Douglas Nicol, discovered the Acheulean site of Olorgesailie in the Rift Valley. He continued his researches after the war. His work on the Miocene deposits of western Kenya produced among other discoveries the almost complete skull of *Proconsul africanus*, the earliest ape yet found.

Financed largely by the National Geographic Society of Washington, Leakey and his family, beginning in 1959, undertook large-scale work at Olduvai. There, in their first season, Mary Leakey found the skull of *Australopithecus (Zinjanthropus) boisei*; and in 1960 their son Jonathan discovered the first remains of *Homo habilis,* a hominid dated by the potassium-argon method at 1.7 million years. Also in 1960 Leakey discovered the skull of one of the makers of the Acheulean culture at Olduvai, which he named *Homo erectus*. These remarkable researches have been published and are still being published in a series of books entitled *Olduvai Gorge*. After his death his work was continued by his wife and his son Richard, who just before his father's death was able to show him the remains of a human being found on the shores of Lake Rudolf below a tufa dated at 2.6 million years.

Charles Darwin speculated that Africa might be the continent where man had emerged; and Leakey's fieldwork seems to have shown this guess to be a sound one. After his death the Kenya authorities established a museum and research institute which they propose to call The Louis Leakey Memorial Institute for African Prehistory.

A man of very wide interests and a great lover of both domestic and wild animals, Leakey was a trustee of the National Parks of Kenya and of the Kenya Wild Life Society and president of the East African Kennel Club. An enthusiastic and inspiring teacher, he was keen to demonstrate flint knapping, a technique he had learnt from Llewellyn Jewitt's account of the methods used by the nineteenth-century flint forger Edward Simpson, and from watching the knappers at Brandon in Suffolk. He

traveled extensively, lecturing to large European and American audiences, and worked tirelessly to disseminate knowledge of his discoveries. His enthusiasm, it was claimed, often carried him to extremes. Although intolerant of opposing views that he considered ill-informed, he realized that, in his field, it was necessary to be a competent archaeologist, human paleontologist, zoologist, anatomist, and geologist— and hardly anyone could be expert in all of them. Many of his discoveries were controversial but his persistence and faith were amply justified. No one has hitherto contributed more to the direct discovery of early man and his ancient culture.

BIBLIOGRAPHY

A complete list of Leakey's published works will appear in his biography, now being written by Sonia Cole. On his early life, see *White African* (1937); a sequel is in press.

In addition to works cited in the text, Leakey's books include *Adam's Ancestors* (London, 1934); *Kenya: Contrasts and Problems* (London, 1936); *The Miocene Hominoidea of East Africa* (London, 1951), written with W. E. Le Gros Clark; *Olduvai Gorge* (Cambridge, 1951); *Mau Mau and the Kikuyu* (London, 1952); *Animals in Africa* (London, 1953), a book of photographs by Ylla to which Leakey contributed the text; and *Defeating Mau Mau* (London, 1954).

GLYN DANIEL

LEAVITT, HENRIETTA SWAN (*b.* Lancaster, Massachusetts, 4 July 1868; *d.* Cambridge, Massachusetts, 12 December 1921), *astronomy*.

Miss Leavitt was one of seven children of George Roswell Leavitt, a prominent Congregationalist minister, and Henrietta Swan Kendrick Leavitt. Both parents were of colonial stock, and their daughter held to the stern virtues of her Puritan ancestors.

Miss Leavitt found her first real opportunity to study astronomy at what is now Radcliffe College, from which she received an A.B. in 1892. She spent an additional year as an advanced student and, after a period of travel, became a volunteer research assistant at the Harvard College Observatory. In 1902, after receiving a permanent position there, she rapidly advanced from an assistant who measured the brightness of variable stars on photographic plates to chief of the photographic photometry department.

During the 1880's and 1890's Edward Pickering, the director of the Harvard College Observatory, had embarked on an extensive program for the determination of visual stellar magnitudes. By 1907 the importance of photographic magnitudes had become apparent, especially because by then it was realized that the photographic plate had a greater sensitivity to blue than the eye. Pickering consequently announced plans to establish a standard photographic sequence based on stars near the north celestial pole. According to S. I. Bailey (1922), Miss Leavitt carried out the plan with "unusual originality, skill and patience"; 299 plates from thirteen telescopes were compared to determine standards with a brightness range of six million (fourth to twenty-first magnitudes). This "north polar sequence" was eventually published as volume 27, number 3 of the *Annals of Harvard College Observatory* (1917). An extension of this research was given in number 4 of the same volume, in which Miss Leavitt supplied secondary magnitude standards for the forty-eight "Harvard standard regions" devised by Pickering. A similar work presented magnitude standards for the Astrographic Catalogue (*Annals of Harvard College Observatory*, **85**, no. 1, 1919; nos. 7 and 8, published posthumously, 1924–1926). The north polar sequence and its subsidiary magnitudes provided the standards for most statistical investigations of the Milky Way system until about 1940.

Miss Leavitt's most famous discovery, the period-luminosity relation of the Cepheid variable stars, originated in her study of the variables in the Magellanic Clouds, made on plates taken at the Harvard southern station in Arequipa, Peru. In the memoir "1777 Variables in the Magellanic Clouds" (*Annals of Harvard College Observatory*, **60**, no. 4 [1908]), she derived periods for sixteen of them and remarked, "It is worthy of notice . . . that the brighter variables have longer periods." In 1912 she extended the analysis to twenty-five stars and, in spite of considerable scatter in the data, found that the apparent magnitude decreased linearly with the logarithm of the period (*Circular. Astronomical Observatory of Harvard College*, no. 173). This relation was seized upon by Shapley at the Mount Wilson Observatory, who calibrated the absolute magnitudes of the Cepheid variables, thereby making it a basic tool for ascertaining the size of the Milky Way galaxy and its distance to other galaxies. To Miss Leavitt's contemporaries, however, her more obvious contribution was her discovery of 2,400 variable stars, about half of those known at the time.

Dorrit Hoffleit has written that although Miss Leavitt was not accorded the honors and publicity of her colleagues Williamina Fleming and Annie Cannon, she was fully as deserving. "Her most important work required greater understanding and even more

meticulous care, and was more desperately needed by other astronomers of the time, even though it lacked the glamour and popular appeal of the newly opened field of stellar spectroscopy." Like Miss Cannon, she was extremely deaf. Deeply conscientious and religious, she was devoted to her work and her family, sharing her mother's home in Cambridge after her father's death in 1911. She died there of cancer in 1921.

BIBLIOGRAPHY

Miss Leavitt's principal contributions appeared in the *Annals of Harvard College Observatory* and *Circular. Astronomical Observatory of Harvard College*.

See the obituary by Solon I. Bailey in *Popular Astronomy*, **30** (1922), 197–199; and the biography by Dorrit Hoffleit in *Notable American Women* (Cambridge, Mass., 1971).

OWEN GINGERICH

LEBEDEV, PETR NIKOLAEVICH (*b*. Moscow, Russia, 8 March 1866; *d*. Moscow, 1 April 1912), *physics*.

Lebedev's father, Nikolay Vasilievich, a prosperous merchant, tried to guide his son into the same path by sending him to commercial school and then to a *Realschule*. After completing his secondary education, Lebedev entered the Moscow Highest Technical School. Convinced, however, that the career of an engineer was not for him, in 1887 he entered one of the best schools of physics in western Europe, at Strasbourg University, to work under A. Kundt. In 1888 Kundt moved to Berlin University; Lebedev could not follow him because he lacked the prerequisite diploma from a classical Gymnasium. At the suggestion of Friedrich Kohlrausch, Lebedev wrote "Ob izmerenii dielektricheskikh postoyannykh parov i o teorii dielektrikov Mossotti-Klauziusa" ("On the Measurement of the Dielectric Constants of Vapors and on the Theory of Dielectrics of Mossotti and Clausius"), in which he experimentally confirmed this theory. In the fall of 1891 he returned to Moscow; and at the invitation of A. G. Stoletov, then head of the department of physics at Moscow University, became a teacher there. In 1900 he defended his dissertation, "Eksperimentalnoe issledovanie ponderomotornogo deystvia voln na rezonatory" ("An Experimental Investigation of the Ponderomotive Action of Waves on Resonators"), for which he was awarded the doctorate in physical and mathematical sciences. Lebedev subsequently became professor of physics at Moscow University.

In his dissertation Lebedev posed the problem of studying the action of light waves on molecules in the simplest form. In view of the impossibility of investigating the effect on individual molecules, he tried to observe the influence of electromagnetic waves on a schematic molecule, using a resonator suspended from a twisted thread, which had its own period of vibration. Lebedev extended this research to hydrodynamic and acoustical waves. It appeared that the ponderomotive actions of waves completely different in nature were subject to the same laws. In investigating electromagnetic waves Lebedev encountered their similarity to light waves. He succeeded in constructing an extremely small vibrator, which allowed him to obtain waves from four to six millimeters long—100 times shorter than the waves studied by H. Hertz and ten times shorter than those studied shortly before by Righi. The small size of the apparatus allowed Lebedev to study, for the first time, the double refraction of electromagnetic waves in natural crystals of rhombic sulfur. His work "O dvoynom prelomlenii luchey elektricheskoy sily" ("On the Double Refraction of the Rays of Electric Force," 1895), established him as an excellent experimenter. Lebedev's success in obtaining short waves was not surpassed until thirty years later, by A. A. Glagoleva-Arkadieva and, independently, by M. A. Levitskaya.

As early as 1891 Lebedev became seriously interested in the pressure of light. He turned his attention to the fact that since the force of gravity is proportional to the volume of a body whereas light pressure must be proportional to its surface, it may be asserted that in a particle of cosmic dust the forces of light pressure pushing the particle away from the sun will be equal to the force of gravity attracting it toward the sun. Lebedev used this theory to explain why comets' tails always point away from the sun. His hypothesis was considered correct until the discovery of the solar wind, which creates substantially greater pressure than the sun's light.

Around 1898, Lebedev began experimental research on light pressure. Although its presence had been predicted by Maxwell's theory, it had not been detected experimentally before Lebedev. He first undertook research on the pressure of light on solid bodies. Because of the weakness of the effect itself and the considerable number of possible side effects, this experimental problem presented very great difficulties: if a body that is supposed to react to light pressure is placed in a gas, the warming of the body by the light will inevitably cause convection currents and thus set the body in motion. If the body is placed in a vacuum (in practice, in gas at very low pressure), the so-called radiometric effect will occur. As a result of the uneven warming of the front and back of the body, the molecules of gas hitting the body from the front will be repulsed more forcefully than those striking the back, thereby exerting greater pressure. By extremely ingenious methods Lebedev succeeded in completely eliminating these side effects and not only detected the pressure of light but also measured it and showed the correctness of Maxwell's quantitative theory. "Opytnoe issledovanie svetovogo davlenia" ("An Experimental Investigation of the Pressure of Light") was read by Lebedev at the International Congress of Physicists at Paris in 1899 and was published in 1901.

In connection with the study of processes in gas, Lebedev first considered the advantages of measuring radiant energy with vacuum thermocouples (1902).

He began the second, more difficult, phase of his research by studying the pressure of light on gases and completed this work in 1910. The attempts of other scientists to repeat Lebedev's research on light pressure were unsuccessful until the 1920's, when physicists developed new vacuum techniques.

Lebedev subsequently began to study the origin of terrestrial magnetism, seeking to relate it to the earth's rotation. He did not live to complete this and some other research.

Lebedev was one of many professors who in 1911 left Moscow University in protest against the illegal violation of the university's autonomy by the minister of education, L. A. Kasso. Deprived of his laboratory, he was offered chairs at a number of universities, including some abroad, and a campaign was begun to gather private funds to build him a laboratory. But the shock of these events affected his health and led to his sudden death.

Lebedev's activity was not limited to scientific research. He created an important school of Russian physics, which produced such scientists as P. P. Lazarev, T. P. Kravets, S. I. Vavilov, and V. K. Arkadiev, who have played a major role in the development of Soviet physics.

BIBLIOGRAPHY

Lebedev's writings have been brought together in three books: *Sobranie sochineny* ("Collected Works"; Moscow, 1913), with "Biografichesky ocherk" ("Biographical Sketch"), pp. vii–xxiii; *Izbrannye sochinenia* ("Selected Works"), A. K. Timiryazev, ed. (Moscow, 1949), with Timiryazev's foreword and biographical sketch, pp. 11–32; and *Sobranie sochineny*, in the series Klassikov Nauki (Moscow, 1963), which includes T. P. Kravets, "Petr Nikolaevich Lebedev," pp. 391–405; and N. A. Kaptsov, "Rol Petra Nikolaevicha Lebedeva v sozdanii nauchno-issledovatelskikh kadrov" ("The Role of Petr Nikolaevich Lebedev in the Development of Personnel for Scientific Research"), pp. 406–412.

J. G. DORFMAN

LEBEDEV, SERGEI VASILIEVICH (*b.* Lublin, Poland, 13 July 1874; *d.* Leningrad, U.S.S.R., 2 May 1934), *chemistry.*

Lebedev was the son of a priest. When he was eight, his father died and the family moved to Warsaw, where he received his Gymnasium training. In 1895 he entered the University of St. Petersburg, where he studied organic chemistry with Favorsky. Upon graduation in 1900 he was employed by the Institute of Communications to study the steel of railroad rails. However, wishing to return to academic work, in 1906 he spent some time at his own expense at the Institut Pasteur and the Sorbonne in Paris. After returning to St. Petersburg he began independent study of the chemistry of unsaturated hydrocarbons, a subject to which he devoted the rest of his life.

His extensive investigations of the conditions and products of polymerization of divinyl hydrocarbons led to his dissertation in 1913, for which he received the Tolstoy Prize. He became a docent at the university and, in 1915, professor of chemistry at the Women's Pedagogical Institute. In 1917 he was named professor of chemistry at the Military Medical Academy, where he remained until his death. He found the laboratory at this institution in very poor condition and succeeded in building it into one of the best organic laboratories in the Soviet Union. He continued his researches on many types of unsaturated compounds, investigating both their polymerization and hydrogenation. During World War I he began studies on the chemistry of petroleum. In 1925 he organized a petroleum laboratory at Leningrad University, where he found that the pyrolysis of petroleum hydrocarbons produced diethylene compounds such as he had previously studied.

In 1926, realizing that a severe shortage of rubber existed in the Soviet Union, he began the work for which he is best known. His earlier studies on polymerization had often yielded rubberlike polymers, and an ample source of divinyl was then available from petroleum. He gathered a group of seven chemists (five of them his students) to investigate the production of synthetic rubber. The work was at first carried on only in the chemists' spare time. They soon found a better method for producing divinyl from alcohol. In 1927 they obtained a form of synthetic rubber by polymerizing divinyl in the presence of sodium. In 1928 the petroleum laboratory at the

university was converted to a laboratory for synthetic rubber. By 1930 the process was being carried out in an experimental plant. Full factory production began in 1932–1933. The polymer had a structure different from that of natural rubber, but Lebedev showed that it was a fully satisfactory substitute.

Lebedev received many honors in the Soviet Union. He was made a corresponding member of the Academy of Sciences in 1928 and a member in 1932. He received the Order of Lenin in 1931. A laboratory for the study of high molecular-weight compounds was founded under his direction at the Academy of Sciences, although his plans for its development were cut short by his death in 1934.

BIBLIOGRAPHY

I. ORIGINAL WORKS. There is a bibliography of Lebedev's scientific papers in *Zhurnal obshchei khimii*, **5** (1935), 15–17. The monograph reporting his early work and foreshadowing his work on rubber is *Issledovannie v oblasti polimerizatsii dvuetilenovykh uglevodorodov* ("Studies in the Field of the Polymerization of Diethylene Hydrocarbons") (St. Petersburg, 1913).

II. SECONDARY LITERATURE. A biography and critical evaluation of his scientific work is A. I. Yakubchik, "Akademik S. V. Lebedev," in *Zhurnal obshchei khimii*, **5** (1935), 1–14. Further biographical references are given in *Bolshaya sovetskaya entsiklopedia* ("Great Soviet Encyclopedia"), 2nd ed., XXIV (1953), 381–382.

HENRY M. LEICESTER

LEBEDINSKY, VYACHESLAV VASILIEVICH (*b.* St. Petersburg, Russia [now Leningrad, U.S.S.R.], 1 September 1888; *d.* Moscow, U.S.S.R., 12 December 1956), *chemistry.*

A student of Chugaev, Lebedinsky graduated in 1913 from St. Petersburg University and was retained by Chugaev in the department of inorganic chemistry to prepare for a teaching career. From 1920 to 1935 he was a professor at Petrograd (later Leningrad) University, and from 1935 to 1952 at the Moscow Institute of Fine Chemical Technology and at the Moscow Institute of Non-Ferrous Metals and Gold. Lebedinsky's scientific work was done in the Platinum Section of the Commission for the Study of Productive Forces (from 1916), at the Institute for the Study of Platinum and Precious Metals (1918–1934) in Leningrad, and at the Institute of General and Inorganic Chemistry of the Academy of Sciences in Moscow.

Lebedinsky's basic works were related to the study of the chemistry of complex compounds, chiefly rhodium and iridium. His studies of the complex compounds of rhodium won worldwide recognition. From the six possible forms of the ammonium derivative of trivalent rhodium he synthesized compounds corresponding to the four forms $Me_2[RhX_5NH_3]$, $Me[RhX_4(NH_3)_2]$, $[RhX_3(NH_3)_3]$, and $[RhX_2(NH_3)_4]X$, where X is an anion. His research on the ammonium compounds of rhodium and iridium led Lebedinsky to draw the important conclusion that the compounds containing an odd number of ammonia molecules in the inner sphere are the more stable and more easily synthesized; whereas, in the case of pyridine compounds, those containing an even number of molecules of ammonia are more easily synthesized. Study of the chemical compounds of rhodium enabled Lebedinsky to show that they possess a regularity of transinfluence.

Lebedinsky was one of the first to undertake work on the synthesis of complex compounds of rhenium and obtained its compound with ethylenediamine, with rhenium in the form of a cation.

Lebedinsky developed a new industrial method for obtaining pure rhodium and took part in the work of the refining commission. He carried out valuable investigations on processing wastes from refineries to extract precious metals, separating precious metals from weak solutions and salts, and developing the technology of extracting precious metals from copper-nickel sludge. In 1946 Lebedinsky was elected a corresponding member of the Soviet Academy of Sciences.

BIBLIOGRAPHY

I. ORIGINAL WORKS. Lebedinsky's writings include "Novye kompleksnye soedinenia rodia" ("New Complex Compounds of Rhodium"), in *Zhurnal Russkago fiziko-khimicheskogo obshchestva*, **48** (1916), 1955, written with L. A. Chugaev; "Novy ryad ammiachnykh soedineny rodia" ("A New Series of Ammonia Compounds of Rhodium"), in *Izvestiya Instituta po izucheniyu platiny i drugikh blagorodnykh metallov*, no. 2 (1933); and "O nekotorykh novykh kompleksnykh soedineniakh renia" ("On Certain New Complex Compounds of Rhenium"), in *Zhurnal obshchei khimii*, **13** (1943), 253, written with B. N. Ivanov-Emin.

II. SECONDARY LITERATURE. See O. E. Zvyagintsev, "Vyacheslav Vasilievich Lebedinsky," in *Zhurnal neorganicheskoi khimii*, **2** (1957), 1713.

D. N. TRIFONOV

LE BEL, JOSEPH ACHILLE (*b.* Pechelbronn, Bas-Rhin, France, 24 January 1847; *d.* Paris, France, 6 August 1930), *chemistry.*

Le Bel was one of those solitary workers who make a single outstanding contribution to science and then retire into semiobscurity for the rest of a long life. His contribution was the statement of the relation of stereochemical structure to optical activity in organic compounds.

He came from a wealthy family that controlled petroleum workings at Pechelbronn, and he himself was active in managing them during the first part of his life. He was educated at the École Polytechnique, and after serving as assistant to Balard, the discoverer of bromine, in 1873 he began to work in the laboratory of Wurtz. At this time van't Hoff was also working with Wurtz, and he and Le Bel announced the same theory almost simultaneously. Van't Hoff's paper appeared in Dutch in September 1874, and Le Bel's was published in French in November of the same year; however, there is no evidence that either was influenced by the other. Each arrived at his conclusion independently at this time probably because organic chemistry had reached a point at which such a theory had become essential to further progress. The structural theory, which had so well explained many types of isomerism, had failed completely to account for optical isomers.

Between 1848 and 1853 Pasteur had shown the significance of nonsuperposable mirror images in optically active crystals, but this idea had not been extended to molecular structures even after Kekulé had explained the structures of organic compounds in terms of the tetravalence of carbon. In 1874 Le Bel, starting from the views of Pasteur, and van't Hoff, starting from the more rigid ideas of Kekulé, arrived independently at the theory that when the four substituents around a carbon atom are different— that is, when the carbon compound is asymmetric— molecular mirror images must exist and they must show opposite optical activities. Both Le Bel and van't Hoff used this idea to explain many cases in which such isomerism did or did not occur. Van't Hoff subsequently shifted his interest to physical chemistry, in which he made his most important contributions; but Le Bel continued to work as an organic chemist. For a time he divided his work between his industrial activities at Pechelbronn and his chemical studies in Paris, but after 1889 he sold his petroleum interests and retired to carry on his favorite work privately in Paris. He continued to investigate optical activity. In 1891 he believed that he had found evidence for optical isomers in compounds of pentavalent nitrogen; such isomerism was later conclusively established by Pope in England.

Le Bel never held an academic appointment nor did he ever have any students. He served as president of the Société Chimique de France in 1892, and his work received general recognition in England. A conflict with members of the Académie des Sciences delayed his membership until 1929, near the end of his life. In his later years he devoted himself chiefly to paleontological and philosophical studies and to botanical work in his extensive garden.

BIBLIOGRAPHY

I. ORIGINAL WORKS. Le Bel's works have been reprinted as *Vie et oeuvres de J.-A. Le Bel*, Marcel Delépine, ed. (Paris, 1949). His theory was explained in "Sur les relations qui existent entre les formules atomiques des corps organiques et le pouvoir rotatoire de leurs dissolutions," in *Bulletin de la Société chimique de Paris*, **22** (1874), 337–347.

II. SECONDARY LITERATURE. Aside from the biography by Delépine listed above, there are short obituaries by W. J. Pope in *Journal of the Chemical Society* (1930), 2789–2791; and by E. Wedekind in *Zeitschrift für angewandte Chemie*, **43** (1930), 985–986.

HENRY M. LEICESTER

LEBESGUE, HENRI LÉON (*b*. Beauvais, France, 28 June 1875; *d*. Paris, France, 26 July 1941), *mathematics*.

Lebesgue studied at the École Normale Supérieure from 1894 to 1897. His first university positions were at Rennes (1902–1906) and Poitiers (1906–1910). At the Sorbonne, he became *maître de conférences* (in mathematical analysis, 1910–1919) and then *professeur d'application de la géométrie à l'analyse*. In 1921 he was named professor at the Collège de France and the following year was elected to the Académie des Sciences.

Lebesgue's outstanding contribution to mathematics was the theory of integration that bears his name and that became the foundation for subsequent work in integration theory and its applications. After completing his studies at the École Normale Supérieure, Lebesgue spent the next two years working in its library, where he became acquainted with the work of another recent graduate, René Baire. Baire's unprecedented and successful researches on the theory of discontinuous functions of a real variable indicated to Lebesgue what could be achieved in this area. From 1899 to 1902, while teaching at the Lycée Centrale in Nancy, Lebesgue developed the ideas that he presented in 1902 as his doctoral thesis at the Sorbonne. In this work Lebesgue began to develop his theory of integration which, as he showed, includes within its scope all the bounded discontinuous functions introduced by Baire.

The Lebesgue integral is a generalization of the integral introduced by Riemann in 1854. As Riemann's theory of integration was developed during the 1870's and 1880's, a measure-theoretic viewpoint was gradually introduced. This viewpoint was made especially prominent in Camille Jordan's treatment of the Riemann integral in his *Cours d'analyse* (1893) and strongly influenced Lebesgue's outlook on these matters. The significance of placing integration theory within a measure-theoretic context was that it made it possible to see that a generalization of the notions of measure and measurability carries with it corresponding generalizations of the notions of the integral and integrability. In 1898 Émile Borel was led through his work on complex function theory to introduce radically different notions of measure and measurability. Some mathematicians found Borel's ideas lacking in appeal and relevance, especially since they involved assigning measure zero to some dense sets. Lebesgue, however, accepted them. He completed Borel's definitions of measure and measurability so that they represented generalizations of Jordan's definitions and then used them to obtain his generalization of the Riemann integral.

After the work of Jordan and Borel, Lebesgue's generalizations were somewhat inevitable. Thus, W. H. Young and G. Vitali, independently of Lebesgue and of each other, introduced the same generalization of Jordan's theory of measure; in Young's case, it led to a generalization of the integral that was essentially the same as Lebesgue's. In Lebesgue's work, however, the generalized definition of the integral was simply the starting point of his contributions to integration theory. What made the new definition important was that Lebesgue was able to recognize in it an analytical tool capable of dealing with—and to a large extent overcoming—the numerous theoretical difficulties that had arisen in connection with Riemann's theory of integration. In fact, the problems posed by these difficulties motivated all of Lebesgue's major results.

The first such problem had been raised unwittingly by Fourier early in the nineteenth century: (1) If a bounded function can be represented by a trigonometric series, is that series the Fourier series of the function? Closely related to (1) is (2): When is the term-by-term integration of an infinite series permissible? Fourier had assumed that for bounded functions the answer to (2) is Always, and he had used this assumption to prove that the answer to (1) is Yes.

By the end of the nineteenth century it was recognized—and emphasized—that term-by-term integration is not always valid even for uniformly bounded series of Riemann-integrable functions, precisely because the function represented by the series need not be Riemann-integrable. These developments, however, paved the way for Lebesgue's elegant proof that term-by-term integration is permissible for any uniformly bounded series of Lebesgue-integrable functions. By applying this result to (1), Lebesgue was able to affirm Fourier's conclusion that the answer is Yes.

Another source of difficulties was the fundamental theorem of the calculus,

$$\int_a^b f'(x)\, dx = f(b) - f(a).$$

The work of Dini and Volterra in the period 1878–1881 made it clear that functions exist which have bounded derivatives that are not integrable in Riemann's sense, so that the fundamental theorem becomes meaningless for these functions. Later further classes of these functions were discovered; and additional problems arose in connection with Harnack's extension of the Riemann integral to unbounded functions because continuous functions with densely distributed intervals of invariability were discovered. These functions provided examples of Harnack-integrable derivatives for which the fundamental theorem is false. Lebesgue showed that for bounded derivatives these difficulties disappear entirely when integrals are taken in his sense. He also showed that the fundamental theorem is true for an unbounded, finite-valued derivative f' that is Lebesgue-integrable and that this is the case if, and only if, f is of bounded variation. Furthermore, Lebesgue's suggestive observations concerning the case in which f' is finite-valued but not Lebesgue-integrable were successfully developed by Arnaud Denjoy, starting in 1912, using the transfinite methods developed by Baire.

The discovery of continuous monotonic functions with densely distributed intervals of invariability also raised the question: When is a continuous function an integral? The question prompted Harnack to introduce the property that has since been termed absolute continuity. During the 1890's absolute continuity came to be regarded as the characteristic property of absolutely convergent integrals, although no one was actually able to show that every absolutely continuous function is an integral. Lebesgue, however, perceived that this is precisely the case when integrals are taken in his sense.

A deeper familiarity with infinite sets of points had led to the discovery of the problems connected with the fundamental theorem. The nascent theory of infinite sets also stimulated an interest in the meaningfulness of the customary formula

$$L = \int_a^b [1 + (f')^2]^{1/2}$$

for the length of the curve $y = f(x)$. Paul du Bois-Reymond, who initiated an interest in the problem in 1879, was convinced that the theory of integration is indispensable for the treatment of the concepts of rectifiability and curve length within the general context of the modern function concept. But by the end of the nineteenth century this view appeared untenable, particularly because of the criticism and counterexamples given by Ludwig Scheeffer. Lebesgue was quite interested in this matter and was able to use the methods and results of his theory of integration to reinstate the credibility of du Bois-Reymond's assertion that the concepts of curve length and integral are closely related.

Lebesgue's work on the fundamental theorem and on the theory of curve rectification played an important role in his discovery that a continuous function of bounded variation possesses a finite derivative except possibly on a set of Lebesgue measure zero. This theorem gains in significance when viewed against the background of the century-long discussion of the differentiability properties of continuous functions. During roughly the first half of the nineteenth century, it was generally thought that continuous functions are differentiable at "most" points, although continuous functions were frequently assumed to be "piecewise" monotonic. (Thus, differentiability and monotonicity were linked together, albeit tenuously.) By the end of the century this view was discredited, and no less a mathematician than Weierstrass felt that there must exist continuous monotonic functions that are nowhere differentiable. Thus, in a sense, Lebesgue's theorem substantiated the intuitions of an earlier generation of mathematicians.

Riemann's definition of the integral also raised problems in connection with the traditional theorem positing the identity of double and iterated integrals of a function of two variables. Examples were discovered for which the theorem fails to hold. As a result, the traditional formulation of the theorem had to be modified, and the modifications became drastic when Riemann's definition was extended to unbounded functions. Although Lebesgue himself did not resolve this infelicity, it was his treatment of the problem that formed the foundation for Fubini's proof (1907) that the Lebesgue integral does make it possible to restore to the theorem the simplicity of its traditional formulation.

During the academic years 1902–1903 and 1904–1905, Lebesgue was given the honor of presenting the Cours Peccot at the Collège de France. His lectures, published as the monographs *Leçons sur l'intégration* . . . (1904) and *Leçons sur les séries trigonométriques* (1906), served to make his ideas better known. By

1910 the number of mathematicians engaged in work involving the Lebesgue integral began to increase rapidly. Lebesgue's own work—particularly his highly successful applications of his integral in the theory of trigonometric series—was the chief reason for this increase, but the pioneering research of others, notably Fatou, F. Riesz, and Fischer, also contributed substantially to the trend. In particular, Riesz's work on L^p spaces secured a permanent place for the Lebesgue integral in the theory of integral equations and function spaces.

Although Lebesgue was primarily concerned with his own theory of integration, he played a role in bringing about the development of the abstract theories of measure and integration that predominate in contemporary mathematical research. In 1910 he published an important memoir, "Sur l'intégration des fonctions discontinues," in which he extended the theory of integration and differentiation to n-dimensional space. Here Lebesgue introduced, and made fundamental, the notion of a countably additive set function (defined on Lebesgue-measurable sets) and observed in passing that such functions are of bounded variation on sets on which they take a finite value. By thus linking the notions of bounded variation and additivity, Lebesgue's observation suggested to Radon a definition of the integral that would include both the definitions of Lebesgue and Stieltjes as special cases. Radon's paper (1913), which soon led to further abstractions, indicated the viability of Lebesgue's ideas in a much more general setting.

By the time of his election to the Académie des Sciences in 1922, Lebesgue had produced nearly ninety books and papers. Much of this output was concerned with his theory of integration, but he also did significant work on the structure of sets and functions (later carried further by Lusin and others), the calculus of variations, the theory of surface area, and dimension theory.

For his contributions to mathematics Lebesgue received the Prix Houllevigue (1912), the Prix Poncelet (1914), the Prix Saintour (1917), and the Prix Petit d'Ormoy (1919). During the last twenty years of his life, he remained very active, but his writings reflected a broadening of interests and were largely concerned with pedagogical and historical questions and with elementary geometry.

BIBLIOGRAPHY

Lebesgue's most important writings are "Intégrale, longueur, aire," in *Annali di matematica pura ed applicata*, 3rd ser., **7** (1902), 231–359, his thesis; *Leçons sur l'intégration et la recherche des fonctions primitives* (Paris, 1904;

2nd ed., 1928); *Leçons sur les séries trigonométriques* (Paris, 1906); and "Sur l'intégration des fonctions discontinues," in *Annales scientifiques de l'École normale supérieure*, 3rd ser., **27** (1910), 361–450. A complete list of his publications to 1922 and an analysis of their contents is in Lebesgue's *Notice sur les travaux scientifiques de M. Henri Lebesgue* (Toulouse, 1922). Lebesgue's complete works are being prepared for publication by l'Enseignement Mathématique (Geneva).

Biographical information and references on Lebesgue can be obtained from K. O. May, "Biographical Sketch of Henri Lebesgue," in H. Lebesgue, *Measure and the Integral*, K. O. May, ed., (San Francisco, 1966), 1–7. For a discussion of Lebesgue's work on integration theory and its historical background, see T. Hawkins, *Lebesgue's Theory of Integration: Its Origins and Development* (Madison, Wis., 1970).

THOMAS HAWKINS

LE BLANC, MAX JULIUS LOUIS (*b.* Barten, East Prussia [now Poland], 26 May 1865; *d.* Leipzig, Germany, 31 July 1943), *chemistry*.

Le Blanc received his chemical education at the universities of Tübingen, Munich, and Berlin, where in 1888 he became privatdocent with A. W. Hofmann in organic chemistry. In 1891 he went to Wilhelm Ostwald's institute at Leipzig and wrote his inaugural essay, "On the Electromotive Force of Polarization."

In 1896 he left his position as extraordinary professor at Leipzig to become the director of the electrochemical division of the Höchster Farbenfabriken. Five years later he accepted a call to the chair of physical chemistry at the technical institute at Karlsruhe, and in 1906 he became director of the physical chemical institute at Leipzig. He was personally responsible for much of the building and equipping of these two institutions. After his retirement in 1934 he remained a participant in scientific affairs mainly through his service to the Sächsische Akademie der Wissenschaften zu Leipzig.

Most of Le Blanc's chemical studies involved the phenomenon of electrochemical polarization: the nature of the decomposition voltage of aqueous solutions of electrolytes and the groundwork for the understanding of the processes occurring at the electrodes in electrolysis. Noting that the decomposition potentials of many aqueous solutions of salts were nearly the same (1.7 volts), he concluded that the electrode processes were identical and that hydrogen and oxygen gas were discharged at the electrodes.

In 1891 Le Blanc introduced the concept of overvoltage, the amount by which the decomposition potential is higher than the calculated value. This phenomenon has been most studied with hydrogen, where the effect is significant. The introduction of the hydrogen electrode is perhaps his most important contribution to science. In 1893 he observed that if a stream of hydrogen gas is allowed to flow over the surface of a platinized platinum electrode, it behaves like an electrode of hydrogen gas, with the platinum having no effect.

Interested in industrial chemistry, Le Blanc developed a process for the electrochemical regeneration of chromic acid, which found extensive use in the manufacture of dyes. During World War I he worked on a method of reclaiming rubber. He wrote several highly successful textbooks, including *Lehrbuch der Elektrochemie*.

BIBLIOGRAPHY

I. ORIGINAL WORKS. Le Blanc's major textbook, *Lehrbuch der Elektrochemie* (Leipzig, 1895), went through twelve German eds., the latest appearing in 1925. This work was translated into French, and into English as *Elements of Electrochemistry*, Willis R. Whitney, trans. (London, 1896); and *A Textbook of Electrochemistry*, W. R. Whitney and John W. Brown, trans. (New York, 1907). *Die Darstellung des Chroms und seiner Verbindungen mit Hilfe des elektrischen Stroms* (Halle, 1902) appeared in English as *The Production of Chromium and Its Compounds by the Aid of the Electric Current*, Joseph W. Richards, trans. (Easton, Pa., 1904). Most of Le Blanc's important research on electrode processes is reported in "Die elektromotorischen Kräfte der Polarisation," in *Zeitschrift für physikalische Chemie*, **8** (1891), 299; **12** (1893), 333; the hydrogen electrode is discussed in the second paper.

II. SECONDARY LITERATURE. A listing of Le Blanc's more than one hundred publications and a short biographical sketch is in M. Volmer, "Max Le Blanc als Forscher und Lehrer," in *Zeitschrift für Elektrochemie und angewandte physikalische Chemie*, **41** (1935), 309–314. Care must be taken in using this bibliography, as only the first of a series of several papers with the same title is listed. Karl Bonhoeffer has written two short biographical notes: "Max Le Blanc zum 26.5.1935," in *Forschungen und Fortschritte*, **11** (1935), 191–192; and "Max Le Blanc," *ibid.*, **19** (1943), 371–372. The two 1935 sketches honored Le Blanc on his seventieth birthday, and the third is a brief obituary notice.

SHELDON J. KOPPERL

LEBLANC, NICOLAS (*b.* Ivoy-le-Pré, France, 6 December 1742; *d.* Paris, France, 16 January 1806), *chemistry*.

From 1751 Leblanc was brought up as an orphan in Bourges. Influenced by his guardian, who was a doctor, he went to the École de Chirurgie in Paris and in 1780 entered the service of the duc d'Orléans (the future Philippe Égalité) as a surgeon. The patronage of the Orléans family, which lasted until the duke was guillotined in November 1793, gave Leblanc the opportunity for research. He began with a study of crystallization, the results of which were later incorporated in his book *Cristallotechnie* (1802). But the most important work dating from this period was that which led him in 1789 to the discovery of the Leblanc process for the artificial preparation of soda. Although it was developed industrially, the discovery brought Leblanc neither happiness nor prosperity, and he eventually committed suicide.

During the late eighteenth century there were strong incentives to devise a new method for the preparation of soda. It was observed that it might soon become impossible to meet the growing industrial demand for soda from the traditional sources, such as potash, which was obtained from wood ashes, or from coastal shrubs like barilla, imported from Spain. In the 1770's and 1780's a number of alternative methods were developed, and between 1783 and 1788 the Académie des Sciences showed its interest by offering a prize for the best method of preparing soda from salt. Although no prize was awarded, by the time Leblanc made his discovery in 1789 several establishments were manufacturing artificial soda in France, if only as a by-product.

In Leblanc's method, sodium sulfate is prepared by the action of sulfuric acid on the salt from seawater and is then converted to soda by calcination with limestone and charcoal. It is not clear how Leblanc discovered the method, for there was no obvious precedent in the processes then in use; and the precise mechanism of the reaction was still obscure over a century later. In fact in 1810, in an article disputing Leblanc's claim to the discovery, J. J. Dizé even maintained that at first Leblanc had prepared sodium sulfide, mistaking it for soda, and that the correct process was developed only in subsequent researches undertaken by Leblanc and Dizé jointly, with guidance from Jean Darcet, the agent of the duc d'Orléans. Unfortunately there is no way of confirming or disproving Dizé's account, but it seems probable that the credit for the discovery should go to Leblanc. In any event, such was the decision of a commission specially appointed by the Académie des Sciences in 1856.

Once made, the discovery was quickly applied. In 1790 the duc d'Orléans, Leblanc, Dizé, and Henri Shée formed a company; and between 1791 and 1793, with capital provided by the duke, a factory was established at St.-Denis. But regular production never began. In 1793 work was abandoned because of the wartime shortage of sulfuric acid, and early in 1794 the factory was nationalized as property of the executed duc d'Orléans. Some months later details of Leblanc's process (with details of all the other known processes for the manufacture of soda) were published by the Committee of Public Safety in the interests of the war effort. Although Leblanc very soon began to seek compensation for his losses, it was several years before his many letters and petitions had any effect, and even when control of the factory was provisionally returned to him in 1800, pending a definitive ruling on his claims, he did not succeed in reviving it through lack of capital. His hope was always that the final settlement of his claims would give him the capital he needed. However, when a settlement was eventually made, in November 1805, the award announced fell far short of his expectations, and two months later, in despair and ill health, Leblanc shot himself.

BIBLIOGRAPHY

I. ORIGINAL WORKS. Leblanc's only major publication is *De la cristallotechnie, ou sur les phénomènes de la cristallisation* (Paris, 1802). For references to the surviving MS material see the article by C. C. Gillispie cited below.

II. SECONDARY LITERATURE. The standard biography, *Nicolas Leblanc, sa vie, ses travaux, et l'histoire de la soude artificielle* (Paris, 1884), is by Leblanc's grandson, Auguste Anastasi. Despite some useful documentation, it is uncritical and has set the tone for most subsequent biographical sketches, nearly all of which reflect Anastasi's undue reverence for Leblanc. The most useful of the derivative sketches are P. Baud, "Les origines de la grande industrie chimique en France," in *Revue historique,* **174** (1934), 1–18; and R. E. Oesper, "Nicolas Leblanc (1742–1806)," in *Journal of Chemical Education,* **19** (1942), 567–572, and **20** (1943), 11–20. An important reappraisal is C. C. Gillispie, "The Discovery of the Leblanc Process," in *Isis,* **48** (1957), 152–170, which uses MS material to show Leblanc as the victim less of misfortune than of his own difficult personality. The article also reexamines the circumstances of the discovery. A more favorable view of Leblanc appears in J. G. Smith, "Studies of Certain Chemical Industries in Revolutionary and Napoleonic France" (Leeds University, Ph.D. thesis, 1970). For the deliberations of the 1856 commission, see L. J. Thenard *et al.,* "Rapport relatif à la découverte de la soude artificielle," in *Comptes rendus hebdomadaires des séances de l'Académie des sciences,* **42** (1856), 553–578.

ROBERT FOX

LE BOUYER DE FONTENELLE, BERNARD. See Fontenelle, Bernard Le Bouyer de.

LE CAT, CLAUDE-NICOLAS (*b.* Blérancourt, Picardy, France, 6 September 1700; *d.* Rouen, France, 21 August 1768), *surgery, anatomy, physiology, biomechanics.*

Le Cat was the son of Claude Le Cat, a surgeon, and Anne-Marie Méresse, the daughter of a surgeon. Despite this family tradition, he himself was committed to an ecclesiastical career before taking up the study of surgery with his father. Following this early training he took courses under Winslow at the Écoles de Médecine in Paris and attended the lectures of Boudou at the Hôtel-Dieu, Le Dran at La Charité, and Duvernay at the Jardin Royal. In 1729 Le Cat was appointed physician and surgeon to the archbishop of Rouen, where he settled permanently, becoming chief surgeon at the Hôtel-Dieu there in 1731. On 29 January 1733 he received the M.D. at Rheims and then took the master's degree in surgery.

From the beginning of his surgical practice Le Cat devoted himself enthusiastically to operating for vesicular stones. He invented or perfected several instruments for lithotomy, one of which, a combined gorget and cystotome, he defended in a vigorous polemic with Jean Baseilhac, celebrated as a lithotomist under his name in religion, Frère Côme. Always open to technical innovation, he also operated on lachrimal fistula through the nasal passage and employed the method of reduction and Daviel's new method of extraction to treat cataracts. One of his procedures foreshadowed the modern method of diaphysectomy.

In 1736 Le Cat established a school for anatomy and surgery in Rouen. He was an early advocate of the union of medicine and surgery and adopted an anatomico-clinical method whereby his students participated in his researches, including animal vivisections. In 1737 he was appointed royal demonstrator in surgery, and gave courses in experimental physics as well as therapeutics, anatomy, and physiology.

Le Cat's medical investigations led him to a theory whereby malignant fevers represent the internalization of external diseases of a herpetic nature, while disease itself is directly attributable to a qualitative or quantitative loss of nervous fluid. Le Cat never fully formulated this hypothesis; like his theories on the cause of menstruation, prolonged pregnancy, and "spontaneous combustion" in human beings (and, indeed, like the works of many of his contemporaries), his theory of disease lacked coherence. More clearly realized was his biomechanic notion of the organism as a hydraulic machine, wherein he drew an analogy between the animal economy and a system of pipes and tubes. Such a view brought Le Cat into conflict with Haller, especially in respect to the latter's ideas of irritability and sensibility, both of which Le Cat thought to be purely mechanical effects.

The *Traité des sens*, Le Cat's most important work, grew as much out of his researches in physics as in physiology. In it Le Cat presented a theory of the propagation of light contrary to that of Newtonian attraction. He further reported on the pigmented choroid coat of the eye and assigned it a common embryonic origin with the pigment of the skin. Other of his writings further demonstrate the breadth of his interests, which encompassed geophysics, astronomy, conchology, geology, embryology and teratology, electricity, literature, the fine arts, and archaeology. But in an age shaped by Descartes, Borelli, and Bellini, Le Cat must be remembered primarily, with Vaucanson and Quesnay, as one of the first adherents of a mechanistic approach to physiology.

Le Cat was a man of his times. Philosophically, he was a neo-Cartesian and believed in the union of the soul and the body. A devout Catholic throughout his life, he was a friend of the Abbé Nollet, Fontenelle, and Voltaire; he strongly opposed the ideas of Rousseau. He was a founding member of the Rouen Académie des Sciences, and a member of a number of other learned societies, both in France and elsewhere. Louis XV granted him titles of nobility and the rank of *écuyer* in recognition of his services.

In 1742, when he was forty-two years old, Le Cat married Marie-Marguerite Champossin, a girl of thirteen. Their only daughter, Charlotte-Bonne, married the surgeon Jean-Pierre David, who succeeded Le Cat in all his offices.

BIBLIOGRAPHY

I. ORIGINAL WORKS. Among Le Cat's principal works that were published separately are his dissertation, *Sur le balancement d'un arc-boutant de l'église Saint-Nicaise* (Rheims, 1724); *Dissertation sur le dissolvant de la pierre, et en particulier sur celui de Melle Stephens* (Rouen, 1739); *Traité des sens en particulier* (Rouen, 1740; repr. Amsterdam, 1744); *Remarques sur les mémoires de l'académie de chirurgie. "Lettres d'un chirurgien de Paris à un chirurgien de province, son élève"* (Amsterdam, 1745); *Réfutation du discours du citoyen de Genève qui a remporté le prix de l'Académie de Dijon, en l'année 1750 sous le nom d'un académicien de la même ville* (London, 1751); *Éloge de M. de Fontenelle* (Rouen, 1759); *Nouveau système sur la cause de l'évacuation périodique du sexe* (Amsterdam, 1765); *Traité de l'existence, de la nature et des propriétés du fluide des nerfs et principalement de son action dans le mouvement musculaire suivi des dissertations sur la sensibilité des méninges, des tendons ...* (Berlin, 1765); *Traité de la couleur de la peau humaine en général, de celle des*

nègres en particulier et de la métamorphose d'une de ces couleurs en l'autre, soit de naissance, soit accidentellement (Amsterdam, 1765); *Parallèle de la taille latérale de M. Le Cat avec celle du lithotome caché suivi de deux dissertations: I. Sur l'adhérence des pierres dans la vessie; II. Sur quelques nouveaux moyens de briser la pierre* (Amsterdam, 1766); *Lettre de M. Le Cat à M. Maître ès arts et en chirurgie de Paris sur les avantages de la réunion du titre de Dr. en médecine avec celui de maître en chirurgie et sur quelques abus dans l'un et l'autre art, 11 juin 1762* (Amsterdam, 1766); *Traité des sensations et des passions en général et des sens en particulier* (La Chapelle, 1767); *La théorie de l'ouïe* (La Chapelle, 1768); *Cours abrégé d'ostéologie* (Rouen, 1768); and *Mémoire posthume sur les incendies spontanés de l'économie animale* (Paris, 1813).

The three-volume collected *Oeuvres physiologiques* (Paris, 1767–1768) comprise *Traité des sensations et des passions en général*, *Traité des sens*, and *La théorie de l'ouïe*; an early work, *Description d'un homme automate dans lequel on verra exécuter les principales fonctions de l'économie animale, la circulation, la respiration, les sécrétions, & au moyen desquels on peut déterminer les effets méchaniques de la saignée, & soumettre au joug de l'expérience plusieurs phénomènes intéressants qui n'en paroissent pas susceptibles*, presented to the Académie de Rouen in 1744, appears to have been lost.

In addition to the above, Le Cat published a number of articles and memoirs in both French and foreign journals. His manuscripts may be found in the Bibliothèque Municipale, Rouen; Bibliothèque Municipale, Caen; Académie des Sciences, Belles-lettres, et Arts de Rouen, Rouen; Bibliothèque de la Faculté de Médecine, Paris; Collection of Dr. Jean, Rouen; Archives de l'Académie Royale de Chirurgie, Bibliothèque de l'Académie Nationale de Médecine, Paris; Bibliothèque Nationale, Paris; and Bibliothèque Municipale, Bordeaux.

II. SECONDARY LITERATURE. On Le Cat and his work see the anonymous "Précis de la vie & des travaux de M. Le Cat, écuyer, docteur en médecine, & chirurgien en chef de l'hôtel-dieu de Rouen ...," in *Journal des beaux-arts et des sciences*, **4** (1768), 312–340; and "Éloge de Monsieur Le Cat," in *Mercure de France* (2 Apr. 1769), 151–170; Louis Antoine, "Éloge de Monsieur le Cat," in E. Dubois, ed., *Éloges lus dans les séances publiques de l'Académie royale de chirurgie, de 1750 à 1792* (Paris, 1889), pp. 129–159; Ballière-Delaisment, *Éloge de Monsieur Le Cat* (Rouen, 1769); L. Boucher, "Notice sur les débuts de Claude-Nicolas Le Cat," in *Précis analytique des travaux de l'Académie des sciences, belles-lettres, et arts de Rouen* (1901); Valentin, *Éloge de Monsieur le Cat* (Rouen, 1769); A. Doyon and L. Liaigre, "Méthodologie comparée du biomécanisme et de la mécanique comparée," in *Dialectica*, **10** (1956), 292–335; André Girodie, "Le chirurgien Claude-Nicolas Le Cat de Blérancourt. Amateur d'art et chevalier de l'Arc," in *Bulletin de la Société d'histoire de Haute Picardie*, **6** (1928), 51–67; Merry Delabost, "Souvenirs épars. À propos de portraits de deux amis chirurgiens de l'Hôtel-Dieu, membres de l'Académie de Rouen," in *Précis analytique des travaux de l'Académie des sciences,* *belles-lettres, et arts de Rouen* (1909–1910), 247–256; Gustave Pawlowski, "Claude-Nicolas Le Cat, célèbre chirurgien, ses lettres d'annoblissement et sa descendance," in *Revue d'histoire nobiliaire*, **1** (1882), 109–128; and Théodore Vetter, *Claude-Nicolas Le Cat (1700–1768). Chirurgien de province au siècle des lumières.*

THÉODORE VETTER

LE CHÂTELIER, HENRY LOUIS (*b.* Paris, France, 8 October 1850; *d.* Miribel-les-Échelles, Isère, France, 17 September 1936), *chemistry, metallurgy.*

On his father's side Le Châtelier came from a line of scientists and technologists, while his mother's ancestors were artists, sculptors, architects, and geographers. His maternal grandfather, Pierre Durand, operated lime kilns and was a friend of Louis Vicat, a specialist in synthetic cements. Two of Le Châtelier's uncles were engineers, one was an architect, and one a specialist in African affairs who helped to form French governmental policy in this field. His father Louis was inspector general of mines for France and the engineer responsible for building much of the French railway system. A strong republican, he resigned when Napoleon III became emperor and thereafter acted as advisor in the construction of railroads in Austria and Spain. He was associated with Deville in establishing an aluminum industry in France and with W. Siemens in building the first open-hearth steel furnace. The leading chemists of France frequently visited his home.

Thus young Le Châtelier grew up in an atmosphere in which science and technology met on equal terms. Even in his youth he was allowed to work for a time in Deville's laboratory. He later said that his contacts with these friends of his father were important influences in shaping his career and establishing his reputation as a chemist. The other significant influence on his life was his mother, who raised her children according to a strict schedule and instilled in them a sense of order and discipline reinforced by the somewhat rigid training obtained in French technical schools. It is not surprising that due to their father's activities all the children in the family were associated with scientific or technological employment throughout their lives or, in view of his mother's strictness, that Henry remained a scientific and political conservative. All his life he was more interested in confirming natural laws than in overthrowing them.

Le Châtelier attended a military academy in Paris for a short time before enrolling at the Collège Rollin, from which he received his Litt.B. in 1867 and his B.S. in 1868. In 1869 he entered the École Polytech-

nique. Even in his student days he showed his originality and his feeling for the importance of an experimental rather than a theoretical approach to science. With some of his fellow students he designed a course in physics based entirely on the positivism of Comte and eliminating all abstract entities such as force.

His studies were interrupted by the Franco-Prussian War, in which he served as a lieutenant in the army. He resumed his academic work in 1871, enrolling in the École des Mines, as he planned to make a career in government administration. After graduation in 1873 he spent several years traveling, chiefly in North Africa in connection with a government plan to create an inland sea in that region. In 1875 he took up the duties of a mining engineer at Besançon. He married Geneviève Nicolas in 1876, and their seven children carried on the family traditions. The three sons became engineers, the four daughters married into the same profession.

In 1877 Le Châtelier's career underwent a sharp change. Daubrée, the director of the École des Mines, did not know him personally, but he did know his father and had noted that the son had done well in chemistry while in the school. He therefore offered Le Châtelier the position of professor of general chemistry. He accepted the offer and remained at the institution until his retirement in 1919. At first he taught only chemistry but later added metallurgy to his subjects. He received the degree of Doctor of Physical and Chemical Science in 1887, at which time his title was changed to professor of industrial chemistry and metallurgy. In the same year he accepted the chair of chemistry at the Collège de France and retained the post until 1908. In 1907 he succeeded Moissan as professor of general chemistry at the Sorbonne and held the chair until becoming an honorary professor in 1925. In this post he was able to direct the researches of graduate students. During his active years between 1908 and 1922 he directed the work of more than a hundred students, twenty-four of whom received their doctorates under his supervision. His lectures were very popular, and several were afterward published as books.

Le Châtelier was always interested in the organization of science, especially in relation to its industrial applications. In particular, he attended many international congresses devoted to industrial problems. During his life he held increasingly important positions on a large number of commissions and boards to advise the government on scientific and technical questions. Among these were the Commission on Explosives, the National Science Bureau, the Commission on Weights and Measures, the Commission on Standardization of Metallic Products, the Commission on Inventions, and the Committee for the Control of French Monetary Circulation. In 1916 President Wilson appointed him advisor in the establishment of the National Research Council in the United States.

In 1907 he was appointed inspector general of mines and became a member of the Académie des Sciences. He received medals and honors from almost every French scientific and engineering society and from numerous foreign countries including Poland, Russia, England, and the United States. He also held honorary doctorates from the universities of Aix-la-Chapelle (Aachen), Manchester, Louvain, and Madrid and the Technical University of Denmark.

In his later years Le Châtelier devoted himself to writing on philosophical and social questions, an activity which he continued until his death at his country estate at the age of almost eighty-six.

The research activities of Le Châtelier were many and varied, and at first glance it would seem that there was little relation between some of them. Yet, as is often the case with scientists, there was continuity, and it is possible to see how one line of study led to another.

When he first assumed an academic position he was somewhat at a loss as to what research he should undertake. His grandfather had made a collection of different types of hydraulic cements, and he decided an investigation of these might be profitable. For simplicity he began first to study the setting of plaster of Paris, which had originally been investigated by Lavoisier and Payen. They believed that during the burning of gypsum, anhydrous calcium sulfate was formed, and that in setting, the gypsum was immediately regenerated. In his first paper on the subject (1882) Le Châtelier found that the gypsum could be burned at a lower temperature than Payen had called for and that the product formed was not the anhydrous salt but a hemihydrate. In the setting process it formed a supersaturated solution around the particles of gypsum, from which new crystals of gypsum precipitated to form an interlocking mass. This work showed him the importance of compound formation in complex mixtures, and much of his subsequent work in various fields involved the detection of such compounds.

He next turned his attention to the problem of the setting of cements composed of calcium silicates. He found it better first to study barium ortho and metasilicates which he could easily synthesize in their pure form. The anhydrous forms of these salts, formed by fusion, set with water to form a barium metasilicate hexahydrate. The same changes occurred with the

calcium silicates, in all cases giving rise to the essential setting compound, which was $3CaO \cdot SiO_2$. Other components of the cements merely acted as fluxes. Since alumina was always present in cements, Le Châtelier next studied a series of calcium aluminates, preparing the pure salts synthetically. These compounds also showed the phenomenon of setting, but the products were less stable than were the silicates. A mixture of silicates and aluminates hydrolyzed to form the stable compound and calcium hydroxide. As was the case with plaster of Paris, a supersaturated solution of calcium salts precipitated the stable component in the form of interlocking crystals. Le Châtelier determined the effect of changing the ratio of lime or magnesia to silica or alumina and determined the conditions under which disintegration of the cement occurred. He also studied the setting of cements under varied conditions in air, water, or seawater. He carried out analogous studies on ceramics and glass. Published in 1887 as his doctoral thesis, the work on cements has been called a classic of inorganic chemistry.

In all these studies he was guided equally by the intrinsic scientific interest of the reactions and their practical value to users of cements. He never recognized a distinction between pure and applied science, and many of his most fruitful ideas came from industrial problems.

In the course of his studies on the silicates he had to use very high temperatures, the measurement of which was difficult with the instruments then available. Gas thermometers were inaccurate above 500°C. Platinum-iron and platinum-palladium thermocouples had been introduced, but Regnault, after careful study, had concluded that they gave widely varying results and should not be considered in any accurate work. Le Châtelier saw that the difficulty lay in the diffusion of one metal into the other at high temperatures and in lack of uniformity of the wires. After a series of studies he was able to show that a thermocouple consisting of platinum and a platinum-rhodium alloy gave accurate and reproducible results. He also introduced the custom of using the boiling points of naphthalene and sulfur and the melting points of antimony, silver, copper, gold, and palladium as standard fixed points in the calibration of his thermocouples. Since that time these thermocouples have been used successfully in all high-temperature work. He also made a number of studies of optical pyrometers which were useful in his day but have since been superseded by other methods.

A number of serious mine disasters led the French government in 1882 to ask the École des Mines to investigate their cause and prevention. In association with the professor of metallurgy, Mallard, Le Châtelier took up these problems. The two men first studied the temperature of ignition, speed of propagation of the flame, and conditions for explosion of mixtures of hydrogen, methane, and carbon monoxide with air. Later these same factors were investigated in other gases and gas mixtures. The study of the combustion of acetylene resulted in development of the oxyacetylene torch and its use in welding. In the course of their study they determined accurately for the first time the specific heats of a number of gases at high temperatures. Their results subsequently proved very useful in the study of combustion in industrial furnaces. During his investigations of mining problems Le Châtelier made a number of improvements in miners' safety lamps and, together with Mallard, discovered several explosives that were safer than those in use at the time.

Le Châtelier then began to apply his earlier studies to events that occurred in the blast furnace. Industrialists had been puzzled by the reaction of iron oxides with carbon monoxide in the furnace. It was believed that the products should be iron and carbon dioxide. However, the gases emerging from the furnace still contained a considerable amount of carbon monoxide. Some industrialists believed that this was due to incomplete mixing of the reactants, but increasing the height of the furnace for better mixing did not help. Le Châtelier realized that the carbon monoxide formed carbon dioxide and carbon in a reversible reaction, for which the iron oxides acted as a catalyst.

His studies at high temperatures, both with the silicates and the combustion of gases, and the study of reactions in the blast furnace combined to interest Le Châtelier in the conditions needed for equilibrium in chemical reactions. His friend Deville had shown that in many reversible reactions dissociation occurred, and this emphasized the importance of studying equilibrium conditions. In his studies on the effect of temperature on such equilibria, van't Hoff had concluded that all equilibria between two different states of matter (systems) are displaced by a lowering of the temperature toward that of the system whose formation develops heat.

Le Châtelier took up the study of these phenomena and in 1884 was able to announce the famous generalization that bears his name, the Le Châtelier principle: "Every system in stable chemical equilibrium submitted to the influence of an exterior force which tends to cause variation either in its temperature or its condensation (pressure, concentration, number of molecules in the unit of volume) in its totality or only in some one of its parts can undergo only those interior modifications which, if they occur alone, would produce a change of temperature, or of condensation, of a sign contrary to that resulting from the exterior force." He stated it more simply in his summary article in the *Annales des mines* of 1888: "Every change in one of the factors of an equilibrium occasions a rearrangement of the system in such a direction that the factor in question experiences a change in the sense opposite to the original change." In this paper he illustrated his principle for a number of equilibria involving pressure, temperature, and electromotive force. As was usual with him, he applied the principle to practical studies, working out equilibrium conditions for gas furnaces and gaseous reactions.

Another result of his blast furnace studies was his investigation of the behavior of various gas mixtures. His student Boudouard worked out the conditions for the carbon monoxide reaction when catalyzed by iron oxide. Other gas mixtures were also tested. The most interesting results came from a study of the reaction of nitrogen and hydrogen in the presence of an iron catalyst in an attempt to synthesize ammonia. Le Châtelier worked out the theoretically correct conditions of temperature and pressure and the amount of catalyst needed as early as 1900. Unfortunately, when he tested his calculations in the laboratory, the gas mixture contained some air, and an explosion resulted. Unaware of the cause of this at the time, he abandoned the experiments, and it was left for Haber to accomplish the ammonia synthesis on a commercially practical scale after 1905.

Le Châtelier was greatly interested in thermodynamics. In the course of his work on equilibrium in reversible systems he discovered the work of J. W. Gibbs. He recognized that the highly abstract mathematical form of its presentation had prevented most chemists from understanding its chemical applications, and he did his best to spread knowledge of these in France. In spite of his efforts chemists did not accept it quickly, but he himself utilized it in the rest of his work. Some of his calculations anticipated the Nernst heat theorem. He applied his knowledge in this field to his studies of glasses and glazes, and investigated the properties of refractory materials and slags.

Le Châtelier's association with Mallard introduced him to metallurgy, and although he hesitated at first to work in this field, feeling that he knew too little of it, he gradually began to introduce lectures on the subject into his chemical course and was soon actively carrying on metallurgical research and lecturing on the subject, as he did for the rest of his life. Therefore, after 1887 he assumed the title of professor of metallurgy in addition to his other titles at the École des Mines.

Mallard asked him to study allotropic modifications in certain minerals. Having decided that a good approach was to investigate the expansion of the minerals with increasing temperature, he designed an efficient dilatometer for this purpose. With it he demonstrated that quartz, instead of expanding evenly with temperature, showed a break in its expansion curve at definite temperatures. These corresponded to formation of different allotropic modifications. He then applied the idea of using physical methods for detecting chemical changes to the study of metals and especially of alloys. Most chemists at this time believed that alloys were simply indefinite mixtures of the component metals. Le Châtelier disproved this by studies at higher temperature than had previously been used, employing his dilatometer and using measurements of electrical conductivity and freezing-point-composition diagrams. He was particularly successful in demonstrating the existence of inter-metallic compounds by employing the latter method. In 1895 he pointed out that there were two parts to the study of alloys: determination of the chemical constitution, including formation of intermetallic compounds, solid solutions, and allotropic modifications; and the physical structure or arrangement of the several kinds of crystals in the alloys.

Much of his metallurgical work was concerned with the chemistry and metallurgy of iron and steel. It had been believed that the hardness of quenched steel was due to the retention of a hard variety of iron stable at high temperatures and retained by rapid cooling. Le Châtelier showed that the solid solution which was stable at high temperatures broke up upon cooling into two phases, iron and iron carbide. He pointed out that this process was analogous to crystallization of two phases from a liquid solution. Quenching prevented this separation. The hard form of iron was thus a solid solution of carbon in the low-temperature allotropic form of iron the formation of which was not prevented during the rapid cooling. The data from Le Châtelier's paper were later used by Roozeboom to construct the first equilibrium diagram for this series. This was the earliest application of the phase rule to a metallic system. Through Roozeboom's work the value of phase rule studies was finally recognized by industrial chemists.

Le Châtelier was always interested in the advancement of the science of metallurgy in France. Realizing the lack of a good textbook, he arranged for the committee on alloys that he had organized to publish a volume, *Contribution à l'étude des alliages,* containing papers by leading French metallurgists. Several of Le Châtelier's own contributions were included. For a long time it was the only really good textbook on metallurgy available in France. Le Châtelier was also aware that, while both England and Germany had special metallurgical journals, none existed in France. Therefore in 1904 he founded the *Revue de métallurgie,* which he edited until 1914. In the publication of this journal he was aided by his daughters, especially Geneviève, who died in 1923, the only one of his children who did not survive him.

One article printed in this journal concerned the high-speed steel tools developed in the United States by the industrial engineer F. W. Taylor. Thinking that they had been discovered accidentally, Le Châtelier entered into correspondence with Taylor and was relieved to discover that they were the result of a truly scientific study. He thus became aware of the work of Taylor, the father of scientific management, who stressed the application of scientific methods in the operation of factories and industrial concerns. Le Châtelier was greatly impressed by Taylor's ideas and devoted much time in his later years to advocating the introduction of the Taylor system into French industry. His book *Le Taylorisme,* published in 1928, was devoted to an effort to increase the efficiency of French workmen. As part of the desired program he recommended a more liberal status for factory workers, and he became interested in political economy.

During World War I, Le Châtelier served as advisor to the government on many military matters. He was influential in a metallurgical study of the heat treatment of shell cases. After the war he gradually withdrew from extensive laboratory work, although he continued to publish short notes on scientific subjects. His writings were always influential and clearly show his interest in the industrial applications of science. Thus *Leçons sur le carbone,* published from his lectures at the Sorbonne, opens with a discussion of the meaning of science and scientific laws. He then describes the various forms of carbon, leading up to a discussion of fuels and metallic carbides. The industrial uses of these materials are described. A survey of oxides of carbon and the carbonates leads to a consideration of the laws of equilibrium, including a description of his own work. The book concludes with a section on atomic and molecular weights, although Le Châtelier avoids descriptions in atomic terms. Historical examples are given throughout.

After World War I Le Châtelier became increasingly concerned with sociological and philosophical questions. In his lectures he had always stressed the importance of general principles rather than merely listing chemical compounds and their properties. He was sometimes accused of teaching physics rather than chemistry. Nevertheless he could not accept theories that appeared to him to lack experimental foundation. As he had avoided the concept of force in physics during his student days, so in later life he avoided the use of atomic theory as much as possible. Since he worked almost entirely with inorganic compounds, he was not concerned with questions of structure, and so was able to consider atoms merely as useful pedagogic tools without deciding whether or not they actually existed.

After his retirement he spent much time in consideration of problems of intellectual and moral education. He stressed the importance of literature and Latin as part of a general education and campaigned for restraint of political expenditures and better coordination of science and industry. Le Châtelier's last paper, on which he was working at the time of his death, was entitled "Morals and Human Affairs."

BIBLIOGRAPHY

I. Original Works. There is a complete bibliography in *Revue de métallurgie*, **34** (1937), 145–160. A bibliography of Le Châtelier's scientific work is in *Bulletin de la Société chimique de France*, 5th ser., **4** (1937), 1596–1611. The complete form of the Le Châtelier principle is given in "Recherches expérimentales et théoriques sur les équilibres chimiques," in *Annales des mines et des carburants*, 8th ser., **13** (1888), 157–380. The studies on cements are described in the doctoral thesis *Recherches expérimentales sur la constitution des mortiers hydrauliques* (Paris, 1887).

II. Secondary Literature. The most complete survey of Le Châtelier's life and work is the Jan. 1937 special issue, "À la mémoire de Henry Le Châtelier 1850–1936," of *Revue de métallurgie*, **34** (1937), 1–160. Full biographies with emphasis on the scientific work are C. H. Desch, "The Le Châtelier Memorial Lecture," in *Journal of the Chemical Society* (1938), 139–150; and P. Pascal, "Notice sur la vie et les travaux de Henry Le Châtelier," in *Bulletin de la Société chimique de France*, 5th ser., **4** (1937), 1557–1596. A shorter and more personal biography is R. E. Oesper, "The Scientific Career of Henry Louis Le Châtelier," in *Journal of Chemical Education*, **8** (1931), 442–461.

HENRY M. LEICESTER

LECLERC. See **Buffon, Georges-Louis Leclerc, Comte de.**

L'ÉCLUSE (CLUSIUS), CHARLES DE (*b*. Arras, France, 19 February 1526; *d*. Leiden, Netherlands, 1609), *botany.*

Known to botanists by the Latinized name of Clusius, L'Écluse was the son of Michel de l'Escluse,

lord of Watènes and councillor at the provincial court of Artois, and of Guillièmine Quineault. The elder son in a rich and respectable family, he had a happy childhood and received a substantial education. Amiable and charming, he possessed a lively and penetrating intelligence and was a man of few words. He may have owed his serious nature and sad disposition to his delicate health. His interests were many: objets d'art, antiquities, the history of customs and of peoples. Although he lived in the company of the wealthy and powerful, L'Écluse remained unaffected and without prejudice. Firm in his philosophical and religious convictions, he suffered along with his family the effects of anti-Protestant persecutions. In 1571 he returned his share of the estate to his father, who had just been stripped of his fortune.

L'Écluse was trained as a lawyer and in 1548 received his *licence* in law from the University of Louvain. His interest in botany was not awakened until 1551, when he went to Provence and began gathering plants for the garden of his teacher, Guillaume Rondelet, a professor at the University of Montpellier. L'Écluse's excellent knowledge of Latin allowed him to write and to translate several works in natural science; he did not merely translate the works of his contemporaries but often expanded and even corrected them.

The first book on which L'Écluse collaborated, Rondelet's *De piscibus marinis libri XVIII*, which he wrote up entirely from the great ichthyologist's notes, appeared in 1554. Since his translations contain considerable original work, it is worth citing the most important of them:

Histoire des plantes (1557) is the French version of Dodoens' *Cruydeboeck;* this translation, mentioned by Gaspard Bauhin in his *Pinax*, can be considered a second edition of the original work.

Aromatum et simplicium aliquot medicamentorum apud iodos nascentium historia (1567) is taken from Garcia del Huerto's *Coloquios dos simples.*

For Jacques Amyot's *Vie des hommes illustres grecs et romains* (1568), L'Écluse translated the biographies of Hannibal and Scipio Africanus from Latin into French.

De simplicibus medicamentis ex occidentali India delatis quorum in medicina usus est (1574) is the translation of a work by the Seville physician Nicolas Monardes on the medicinal plants of the West Indies, to which L'Écluse added a supplement in 1582.

Aromatum et medicamentorum in orientali India nascentium liber (1582) is the translation of *Tractado de las drogas y medicinas de las Indias orientales* by Cristóbal Acosta.

A Latin translation of the accounts of Pierre Belon's voyage to the Orient and the Middle East appeared in 1589.

A complete edition of the three translations concerning the medicinal plants of the Indies appeared in 1593.

In addition, L'Écluse composed *Aliquot notae in garciae aromatum historiam* (1582) from the notes on the western coasts of America furnished by Francis Drake upon the return of his famous expedition to the Pacific.

Long periods spent in Provence, Spain, and Austria-Hungary enabled L'Écluse to make numerous botanical observations, on the basis of which he wrote accounts of the floras of these regions that are still valuable. L'Écluse's first entirely original work, *Rariorum aliquot stirpium per Hispanias observatarum historia* (1576), was prepared from notes collected during his travels in Spain in 1564–1565. It contains admirable engravings executed under the author's supervision, either from sketches or from specimens he had collected. These plates, paid for by the publisher Plantin, were also used to illustrate the works of Dodoens and Lobel. L'Écluse's flora of Hungary and Austria was published in 1583 and is still consulted for its descriptions of Alpine plants. *Rariorum plantarum historia* (1601) records approximately 100 new species; *Exoticorum libri decem* (1605) is an important work on exotic flora and includes everything that L'Écluse published on the subject. These two works contain all of L'Écluse's original contributions in botany and natural history and are still often consulted. They are sometimes found bound as a single work.

Honoring the promise that had been made to L'Écluse, Plantin's sons-in-law and successors published his works posthumously, in 1611, under the title *Curae posteriores*. There is also the 1644 folio volume of the works of Dodoens and L'Écluse, several copies of which contain colored plates.

The last sixteen years of L'Écluse's life brought him great satisfaction. Appointed in 1593 by the trustees of the University of Leiden to succeed Dodoens, he held the chair of botany until his death in 1609. It may justly be said that Leiden had become the botanical center for the whole of Europe. L'Écluse's communications to his many correspondents regarding exchanges of plants and documents allow us to reconstruct the state of botany in that period, especially in the Low Countries.

BIBLIOGRAPHY

I. ORIGINAL WORKS. L'Écluse's first original work was a "petit recueil auquel est contenue la description d'aucune gomme et liqueurs, provenant tant des arbres que des herbes . . .," appended to his trans. of Dodoens' *Cruydeboeck* as *Histoire des plantes* (Antwerp, 1557). It was followed by *Rariorum aliquot stirpium per Hispanias observatarum historia* (Antwerp, 1576), a flora of Spain that L'Écluse considered his first original work; *Aliquot notae in garciae aromatum historia* (Antwerp, 1582), collected notes on American flora; and *Rariorum aliquot stirpium, per Pannoniam, Austriam et vicinas quasdam provincias observatarum* (Antwerp, 1583). *Rariorum plantarum historia* (Antwerp, 1601) was an authoritative collection that included descriptions of European plants as well as of foreign ones—including the potato; a concluding treatise on mushrooms is also of interest.

L'Écluse's works were collected as *Exoticorum libri decem*, 3 vols. (Leiden, 1605), which also included 3 new chapters; a French trans. by Antoine Colin, as *Des drogues, espicèries et de medicamens simples*, was published at Lyons in 1602 (2nd ed., 1619). *Curae posteriores* (Leiden, 1611) was published posthumously by Plantin.

For bibliographical details of L'Écluse's translations, see *British Museum General Catalogue of Printed Books*, CXXXII, cols. 786–787; additional information may be found in *Nouvelle biographie générale*, XXX (Paris, 1862), cols. 220–221; and Michaud, *Biographie universelle*, new ed., XXIII, 534–535.

II. SECONDARY LITERATURE. On L'Écluse and his work, see L. Legré, *La botanique en Provence au XVIe siècle*, V (Marseilles, 1901); and C. J. É. Morren, *Charles de l'Escluse, sa vie et ses oeuvres* (Liége, 1875). See also C. F. A. Morren, in *Belgique horticole*, **3** (1853), v xix; and *Bulletin. Société royale de botanique de Belgique*, **1** (1862), 14–15.

P. JOVET
J. C. MALLET

LECONTE, JOHN (*b*. near Savannah, Georgia, 4 December 1818; *d*. Berkeley, California, 29 April 1891), *physics, natural history*.

LeConte was the son of the Georgia plantation owner Louis LeConte and Ann Quarterman. The family provided a stimulating scientific environment. John Eatton LeConte, Louis' brother, and his son, John Lawrence, were important entomologists; Louis was a competent amateur botanist, and John LeConte and his brother Joseph, his closest scientific associate throughout his life, were among the most respected scientists of the South before the Civil War.

In 1835 LeConte entered Franklin College of the University of Georgia. After graduating in 1838 he studied medicine at the College of Physicians and Surgeons of New York and received his degree in 1841. Upon the death of his father he returned to Savannah with his wife, Josephine Graham of New York. After four years of a modest medical practice LeConte was appointed professor of chemistry and natural history at Franklin College. In 1855 he taught chemistry at the College of Physicians and Surgeons, and in 1856 he and his brother Joseph accepted professorships in physics and chemistry, respectively, at South Carolina College. During the Civil War both worked for the Confederate government in the production of niter and other chemicals. Choosing to leave the South after the war, they were appointed professors at the newly founded University of California in 1869 on the recommendation of Joseph Henry. As senior faculty member, LeConte became acting president in 1869 and again in 1875, and was president from 1876 to 1881. He held the chair of physics until his death.

Typical of early and mid-nineteenth-century scientists, he developed a wide-ranging interest in several branches of science. Most of his publications were in medicine and physics, but he also published on physiology, botany, astronomy, and geophysics. That he made no major contributions to scientific knowledge was perhaps partly due to this diversity. Many of his papers centered on criticizing the work of others. LeConte disliked and avoided experiments, collecting facts and observations for his studies mostly from the literature. In his career as a professor of physics he stressed general principles rather than their applications. This attitude won him respect among his colleagues, at a time when basic science was not generally appreciated. Preoccupation with administrative duties and personal problems severely hampered his scientific activity during his years at California.

Most important among his early papers was an article on the nervous system of the alligator. He promoted the use of statistics as a quantitative approach to medical research. His reputation as a physicist stemmed largely from his discovery of the sensitive flame in 1858, providing a method of visualizing the effects of sound waves. His 1864 paper on the velocity of sound clarified certain misconceptions concerning Laplace's theory. He also investigated the nature of sound shadows in water. Influenced by the work of John Tyndall and Jacques-Louis Soret he provided an explanation for the color of lakes in terms of selective reflection.

BIBLIOGRAPHY

I. ORIGINAL WORKS. LeConte's most important works include "Experiments Illustrating the Seat of Volition in the Alligator or Crocodilus Lucius of Cuvier," in *New York Journal of Medicine and the Collateral Sciences*, **5** (1845), 335–347; "Statistical Researches on Cancer," in *Southern Medical and Surgical Journal*, n.s. **2** (1846), 257–

293; "On the Influence of Musical Sounds on the Flame of a Jet of Coal Gas," in *American Journal of Science*, 2nd ser., **23** (1858), 62–67; "On the Adequacy of Laplace's Explanation to Account for the Discrepancy Between the Computed and the Observed Velocity of Sound in Air and Gases," in *Philosophical Magazine*, 4th ser., **26** (1864), 1–32; "On Sound Shadows in Water," *ibid.*, 5th ser., **13** (1882), 98–113; and "Physical Studies of Lake Tahoe," in *Overland Monthly and Out West Magazine*, 2nd ser., **2** (1884), 41–52.

An almost complete MS for a college textbook on physics was destroyed during the Civil War along with most of his other early papers. The largest collection of his papers is the John LeConte Papers, Bancroft Library, University of California. This collection also contains an eight-page autobiography, "Sketch of John LeConte." Other MSS are at the South Carolina Library, University of South Carolina. The bulk of LeConte's letters are found in the papers of correspondents. See Lewis R. Gibbes Papers, Library of Congress, and Benjamin Peirce Papers, Harvard University Archives.

II. SECONDARY LITERATURE. A dissertation by J. S. Lupold, *From Physician to Physicist: The Scientific Career of John LeConte, 1818–1891* (University of South Carolina, 1970), 264, contains valuable bibliographical and biographical information. Joseph LeConte, "Biographical Memoir of John LeConte, 1818–1891," in *Biographical Memoirs. National Academy of Sciences*, **3** (1895), 371–393, includes a selected bibliography and an evaluation of his most important scientific papers. William LeConte Stevens, "Sketch of Professor John LeConte," in *Popular Science Monthly*, **36** (1889), 112–113, contains a complete bibliography of LeConte's works.

GISELA KUTZBACH

LECONTE, JOSEPH (*b*. Liberty County, Georgia, 26 February 1823; *d*. Yosemite Valley, California, 5 July 1901), *natural history, physiology, geology*.

LeConte was the fifth of seven children. His mother died when he was three, and the boy acquired his love of science from his father, Joseph LeConte, an erudite man who had once studied medicine. LeConte received his early education on his father's plantation and at a neighboring school in Liberty County before going (in January 1839) to Franklin College of the University of Georgia, from which he was graduated in 1841. LeConte studied medicine for a brief period in 1842 with a physician, Dr. Charles West, in Macon, Georgia. In 1843–1844, he took the intensive four-month winter medical course at the College of Physicians and Surgeons, New York, N.Y., but broke off his studies to undertake a trip to the headwaters of the Mississippi and to the Great Lakes. On this trip his interest in geology was intensified, although he subsequently finished his medical studies, taking his degree in 1845.

In 1850 LeConte abandoned the medical practice that he had established in Macon and went to Harvard to study zoology and geology with Louis Agassiz. With Agassiz he made scientific expeditions to Florida, to the fossiliferous areas of New York, and to the Massachusetts shores. In June 1851 he and three other students received the first degrees conferred by the newly established Lawrence Scientific School at Harvard. LeConte then began his academic career, teaching various sciences at Oglethorpe University, Georgia; Franklin College, University of Georgia; and South Carolina College, Columbia, South Carolina, a tenure that was interrupted by the Civil War, when LeConte served the Confederacy first as a government arbitrator and then as a chemist. In 1866 he returned briefly to teach at what had been renamed the University of South Carolina, but found Reconstruction policies to be intolerable. Consequently, he and his brother John joined the newly founded University of California in 1869. LeConte was appointed professor of geology and natural history and did his most important scientific work during his tenure there. LeConte became the first president of that institution.

LeConte published books and articles on a wide range of subjects, including various aspects of geology, binocular vision, physiology (especially glycogenic function of the liver), and evolution. Some of his most substantial contributions to geology included his views on the structure and origin of mountain ranges, the genesis of metals, crucial periods in the history of the earth, the demonstration of the great importance of the Ozarkian (Sierran) epoch, and the great lava flood of the northwest. His ideas became widely known through the publication of his *Elements of Geology* (1878), which offered a scholarly combination of principles (dynamical geology) and elements (historical and structural geology) with extensive treatment of American geology.

LeConte's work on vision culminated in his 1881 book *Sight*, which combined excellent experiments with perceptive observations (although devoid of mathematics). This, together with his physiological work on the liver, was further elaborated in his *Outlines of the Comparative Physiology and Morphology of Animals* (1900), which represents a summary of many of his biological ideas. LeConte himself described his work in evolution as "philosophical," since he contributed no new facts. Nevertheless, his books on the subject had a general, popular influence in reconciling science and religion, being designed to make evolution palatable to both clergymen and scientists who were frightened by the apparent materialism and possible impious implications of evolutionary doctrines.

LeConte enjoyed many academic honors, including an LL.D. from Princeton. In 1847 he married Bessie Nisbet; they had three daughters and one son. He died of a heart attack while on a geological expedition.

BIBLIOGRAPHY

I. ORIGINAL WORKS. LeConte's scientific books are *Religion and Science. A Series of Sunday Lectures on the Relation of Natural and Revealed Religion, or the Truths Revealed in Nature and Scripture* (New York, 1873), which went into many editions; *Elements of Geology: A Text-Book for Colleges and for the General Reader* (New York, 1878; 5th ed., revised and partially rewritten by Herman LeRoy Fairchild, 1903); *Sight: An Exposition of the Principles of Monocular and Binocular Vision* (New York, 1881; 2nd ed., 1897); *A Compend of Geology* (New York, 1884; rev. ed., 1898); *Evolution and Its Relation to Religious Thought* (New York, 1888; 2nd ed. as *Evolution: Its Nature, Its Evidences, and Its Relation to Religious Thought*, 1891); and *Outlines of Comparative Physiology and Morphology of Animals* (New York, 1900).

See also his autobiographical writings, *The Autobiography of Joseph LeConte*, William Dallam Armes, ed. (New York, 1903); *'Ware Sherman. A Journal of Three Month's Personal Experiences in the Last Days of the Confederacy*, with "Introductory Reminiscence" by his daughter Caroline LeConte (Berkeley, 1937); *A Journal of Ramblings Through the High Sierra of California by the University Excursion Party* (San Francisco, 1875; repr. [1960]).

Manuscript materials are at the University of North Carolina Library, Southern Historical Collection (Elizabeth [Furman] Talley papers and Joseph LeConte papers); University of Michigan, Michigan Historical Collections (Alexander Winchell papers); Duke University Library (Benjamin Leonard Covington Wailes papers); University of South Carolina, South Caroliniana Library (Joseph LeConte papers); Henry E. Huntington Library, San Marino, California (Charles Russell Orcutt correspondence); and the University of California, Berkeley, Bancroft Library.

II. SECONDARY LITERATURE. The most comprehensive account of LeConte and his work is Eugene W. Hilgard, "Biographical Memoir of Joseph LeConte, 1823–1901," in *Biographical Memoirs. National Academy of Sciences*, 6 (1909), 147–218, with bibliography, 212–218. A summary of some of his geological work is George P. Merrill, *The First One Hundred Years of American Geology* (New Haven, 1924), 344–345, 364–368.

H. LEWIS MCKINNEY

LECOQ DE BOISBAUDRAN. See **Boisbaudran, Paul Émile Lecoq de.**

LECORNU, LÉON FRANÇOIS ALFRED (*b*. Caen, France, 13 January 1854; *d*. St.-Aubin-sur-Mer, Calvados, France, 13 November 1940), *mechanics, mechanical engineering.*

Lecornu proved an exceptional student at the secondary school in Caen; in his final year he won the prize of honor in the annual *concours général* and easily passed the competitive entrance examinations for both the École Normale Supérieure and the École Polytechnique. He entered the latter in 1872 but two years later transferred to the École Supérieure des Mines. After graduating he joined the Corps des Mines and began to pursue two careers simultaneously —one professional, the other academic.

His first engineering assignments were in Rennes and in Caen. In 1893, when he returned to Paris, he was promoted to chief engineer in charge of the technical supervision of the railroads of western France. He rose in the Corps des Mines to the rank of inspector general first class and retired in 1924.

In 1880 Lecornu received a *doctorat ès sciences* from the Sorbonne with his dissertation, "Sur l'équilibre des surfaces flexibles et inextensibles." In 1881 he joined the faculty of Caen as associate professor. After his move to Paris he was appointed *répétiteur* at the École Polytechnique (1896) and professor of mechanics at the École des Mines (1900) and at the École Polytechnique (1904). After retiring from the latter in 1927, he continued to teach at the École Nationale Supérieure d'Aéronautique until 1934.

The tenor of Lecornu's original work in mechanics is the application of the classical methods to the analysis of a variety of engineering problems. In his dissertation he established the relationship between the stresses and the geometrical characteristics of deformed surfaces. Applying his general theory to an ellipsoidal surface, he was able to determine the conditions of rupture of air balloons. A similar approach was used to analyze the stability of rotating millstones. Other representative studies are his papers on pendulums of variable length, on inertial errors in the steam engine indicator, on speed regulation, and on the dynamics of gear teeth.

Much of Lecornu's writing was expository and didactic and was characterized by an informal, popular style. He wrote a number of textbooks on mechanics and mechanical engineering, and edited the multivolume *Encyclopédie de mécanique appliquée* (Paris, 1924). In 1910 Lecornu was elected a member of the mechanics section of the Académie des Sciences, which he served as president in 1930. He received the Prix Poncelet (1900) and the Prix Montyon (1909), and was a commander of the Legion of Honor.

Lecornu also had two minor avocations: geology (he published extensively while a mining engineer in Normandy) and the piano.

BIBLIOGRAPHY

I. ORIGINAL WORKS. Lecornu's books are *Régularisation du mouvement dans les machines* (Paris, 1898); *Les régulateurs des machines à vapeur* (Paris, 1904); *Dynamique appliquée* (Paris, 1908); *Théorie des moteurs legers* (Paris, 1911); *Cours de mécanique, professé à l'École Polytechnique*, 3 vols. (Paris, 1914–1918); *La mécanique: les idées et les faits* (Paris, 1918); *Théorie mécanique de l'élasticité* (Paris, 1929); and *Propriétés générales des machines* (Paris, 1930). Incomplete bibliographies of his scientific papers are given in Poggendorff, IV, 855; V, 721; and VI, 1485; and in Royal Society *Catalogue of Scientific Papers*, X, 544–545; and XVI, 664–665.

II. SECONDARY LITERATURE. The principal source on Lecornu is the obituary by H. Vincent, in *Comptes rendus hebdomadaires des séances de l'Académie des sciences*, **211** (1940), 493–498. Additional facts and a portrait are in N. Imbert, ed., *Dictionnaire national des contemporains*, I (Paris, 1936), 378. The catalog of the Bibliothèque Nationale lists also a *Notice sur les travaux scientifiques de M. Léon Lecornu* (Paris, 1896).

OTTO MAYR

LE DANTEC, FÉLIX (*b*. Plougastel-Daoulas, France, 16 January 1869; *d*. Paris, France, 6 June 1917), *biology.*

Le Dantec, whose father was a naval physician and friend of Ernest Renan, was exceptionally precocious. He performed brilliantly on the entrance examination for the École Normale Supérieure; during his stay there he was influenced by C. Hermite and J. Tannery, who cultivated his penchant for mathematics. Suddenly attracted to the natural sciences, he made the acquaintance of A. Giard, who, through his unrelenting critical sense, freed Le Dantec from intellectual rigidity. Pasteur appointed him laboratory assistant at the Institut Pasteur in 1888, and sent him first to Laos and then to Brazil, where he founded a laboratory for the study of yellow fever. Le Dantec then gave free rein to the wide-ranging interests of an insatiably curious mind. In 1891 he defended a doctoral thesis on intracellular digestion in the protozoans, followed by numerous scientific and philosophical works that attest to the fruitfulness and brilliance of his intellect. Although an atheist, Le Dantec was always open to religious discussion. He was appointed lecturer at the University of Lyons in 1893, assistant lecturer in 1899, and full professor of general biology at the Sorbonne in 1908.

Le Dantec's gifts for generalization bore the mark of his mathematical training. His biological work began with a study of bacteria. He held that their physiological activity could be interpreted in the symbolic terms of a chemical equation and that elemental life was explicable by the existence of a specific substance that was only transmitted through heredity. He thus sought to reconstruct biology in accordance with the precise language of chemistry, eliminating any anthropomorphism. His logic led him to Lamarckian principles of adaptation and to the inheritance of acquired characteristics, which were the basis of his law of functional assimilation. For Le Dantec protoplasm grows by living; life and growth are a single phenomenon. Stasis produces erosion, destruction, and death. Starting from this conception he explained the law of natural selection and considered psychological and social questions. Conscience, he believed, is nonexistent: men are puppets, subject solely to the laws of mechanics.

Le Dantec's work survives only for its flashes of insight and its clarity. Although he constructed a precarious system based on facts obtained at second hand, his vigorous attacks on anthropomorphism, his passion for truth, his noble character, and his veneration of science explain his being described as a secular saint.

BIBLIOGRAPHY

I. ORIGINAL WORKS. Among Le Dantec's more important works are *La matière vivante* (Paris, 1895); *Théorie nouvelle de la vie* (Paris, 1896); *La sexualité* (Évreux, 1899); *L'unité dans l'être vivant* (Paris, 1902); *Traité de biologie* (Paris, 1903); *Science et conscience* (Paris, 1908); and *La science de la vie* (Paris, 1912).

Among his philosophical works are *L'athéisme* (Paris, 1907); and his last work, *Le problème de la mort et la conscience universelle* (Paris, 1917).

II. SECONDARY LITERATURE. On Le Dantec and his work, see G. Bonnet, *La morale de Félix Le Dantec* (Poitiers, 1930); C. Pérez, *Félix Le Dantec* (1918); and E. Rabaud, "Félix Le Dantec," in *Bulletin biologique* (1917).

ROGER HEIM

LE DOUBLE, ANATOLE FÉLIX (*b.* Rocroi, France, 14 August 1848; *d.* Tours, France, 22 October 1913), *anatomy*.

Le Double moved to Tours when still a child and never left that city; he died there, asphyxiated by carbon monoxide from a faulty stove. Le Double was a nonresident (1871) and a resident medical student (1873) in the Parisian hospitals and earned his medical degree at the University of Paris in 1873. He was a surgeon at the Hospice Général in Tours from 1879 to 1885, when he was appointed professor of anatomy. He then gave up the practice of medicine in order to devote his time to anatomical research. His career was crowned by his election as a corresponding, and then as a national associate member of the Académie de Médecine (1907).

Le Double was greatly interested in anomalies of the components of the human body including the muscles (1897), bones (1903), and hair. From his numerous statistics he attempted to derive general considerations valid for all observed cases. According to him, anomalies are not sports of nature occurring by mere chance. Defending the opposite thesis, he reaffirmed the conception of those anatomists who regarded anomalies as variations from a normal type and as subject to certain laws, including (1) the correlative and inverse balancing of the skull and face; (2) the correlation of cranial and brain volumes, especially the volume of the frontal lobes; (3) when several anomalies are observed in the same individual they are usually found in organs that have the same embryologic origin and that develop synchronously; (4) regardless of their type or location, variations in no way represent an anatomical indication of degeneracy, insanity, or criminality; (5) variations are indexes of human evolution: some are atavistic remnants of a previous evolutionary stage (reverse theromorphic variations), while others point to the form that such variations may take in adapting to a new environment (progressive or adaptive anomalous variations); (6) an anatomically aberrant organ is more subject to pathological processes than any other.

Between 1880 and 1883 Le Double published in Dechambre's *Dictionnaire encyclopédique des sciences médicales* twenty-four articles on the muscles of the trunk. In *Rabelais anatomiste et physiologiste* (1899), which was often plagiarized, Le Double asserted that Rabelais was the first before Fabricius Hildanus to have described tracheal deformations brought on by goiter and to have given the symptomatology of venereal sarcocele and of mercurial stomatitis. Le Double also indicated that Rabelais knew of the scabies-causing mite and exterminated it. However, not all his claims for Rabelais have been substantiated.

BIBLIOGRAPHY

I. ORIGINAL WORKS. No complete bibliography of Le Double's works has been compiled. A list of 24 works may be found in the *Catalogue général* of the Bibliothèque

Nationale, Paris, XCII, cols. 407–410; the Royal Society *Catalogue of Scientific Papers*, X, 547; XVI, 668–669; lists 35 papers written up to 1900. In addition Le Double was author of *Fatale histoire* (Tours, 1892), under the pseudonym F. du Pleix; *Les velus* (Paris, 1912), written with F. Houssay; and *Bossuet, anatomiste et physiologiste* (Paris, 1913).

II. SECONDARY LITERATURE. On Le Double and his work, see (listed chronologically) *Gazette médicale du Centre*, **11** (1906), 129–133, with photograph; R. Mercier, "A. F. Le Double," in *Paris médical*, **12**, supp. (1912–1913), 935; *Semana médica* (Buenos Aires), **20**, pt. 2 (1913), 1611–1614; *Répertoire de médecine internationale*, **3** (1913), 24; L. Dubreuil-Chambardel, "Le professeur Le Double," in *Gazette médicale du Centre*, **18** (1913), 257–258; *Bulletin de l'Académie de médecine*, **70** (1913), 288–290; L. Dubreuil-Chambardel and Faix, "Le professeur Le Double," in *Aesculape*, **3** (1913), 271–272, with portrait; F. Baudoin, "Le professeur Le Double," in *Annales medico-chirurgicales du centre* (1913), 505–508, with photograph; C. de Varigny, "L'oeuvre du Dr. Le Double," *ibid.*, 172–176; 185–187; J. Renault, "Un anatomiste philosophe: Félix Anatole Le Double," in *Gazette médicale du Centre*, **18** (1914), 285–288; F. Houssay, "Anatole Félix Le Double et l'école tourangelle des variations anatomiques," *ibid.*, **19** (1914), 14–16; "Le Double," in *Biographisches Lexikon der hervoragenden Ärzte der letzen fünfzig Jahre*, II (Berlin–Vienna, 1933), 879–880; and C. Mentré, *Rabelais et l'anatomie* (Nancy, 1970), diss.

PIERRE HUARD
MARIE JOSÉ IMBAULT–HUART

LEEUWENHOEK, ANTONI VAN (*b.* Delft, Netherlands, 24 October 1632; *d.* Delft, 26 August 1723), *natural sciences, microscopy*.

Leeuwenhoek was the son of Philips Thoniszoon, a basket-maker, and Margriet Jacobsdochter van den Berch. He took his surname ("Lion's Corner") from the corner house near the Leeuwenpoort ("Lion's Gate") at Delft, which was owned by his father. The family belonged to the prosperous middle class of artisans, brewers, and lesser public officials, which was typical of the Golden Age of the Dutch Republic.

His father died at an early age, in 1638, and Leeuwenhoek was sent to the grammar school of Warmond, a village near Leiden. For some time afterwards he lived with a relative in Benthuizen, then, in 1648, moved to Amsterdam, where he was apprenticed to a cloth merchant. Returning to Delft, Leeuwenhoek began a career as a shopkeeper. On 29 July 1654, he married Barbara de Mey, daughter of Elias de Mey, a serge merchant from Norwich, England. They had five children, of whom only one, their daughter Maria, survived her father.

In 1660 Leeuwenhoek took up a new career as a civil servant with an appointment as usher to the aldermen of the municipality of Delft. In 1666 his wife died, and two years later Leeuwenhoek made one of the only two foreign trips that he took in his lifetime, visiting the chalk hills of Gravesend and Rochester in Kent, England. (His other occasion for travel abroad was a journey that he made to Antwerp in 1698 to see the Jesuit scholar Daniel Papenbroek.) Upon his return to Delft in 1669 he was appointed surveyor to the court of Holland.

Leeuwenhoek remarried on 25 January 1671. His second wife was Cornelia Swalmius, the daughter of Johannes Swalmius, a Calvinist minister at Valkenburg, near Leiden. She died in 1694; the one child of this marriage did not survive infancy. In the meantime Leeuwenhoek continued to advance in the service of the city of Delft, being made chief warden of the city in 1677 and, because of his mathematical skills, wine-gauger (or inspector of weights and measures) in 1679. The income and emoluments from these offices made him financially secure, especially in his old age, when the municipality, in gratitude for his scientific achievements, granted him a pension.

Leeuwenhoek's scientific life may be said to have begun in about 1671, when he was thirty-nine years old. At that time, developing the idea of the glasses used by drapers to inspect the quality of cloth, he constructed his first simple microscopes or magnifying glasses, consisting of a minute lens, ground by hand from a globule of glass, clamped between two small perforated metal plates. To this apparatus he fixed a specimen holder that revolved in three planes. From these beginnings Leeuwenhoek went on to grind about 550 lenses in his lifetime. Although always secretive about his technique, he achieved lenses of increasing quality, of which the best that survives, in the University Museum of Utrecht, has a linear magnifying power of 270 and a resolving power of 1.4 μ. (From his recorded observations it may be surmised that he must have actually made lenses of 500 power, with a resolution of 1.0 μ.) Whatever his methods, Leeuwenhoek's instruments were not surpassed until the nineteenth century.

To his work in lens-grinding Leeuwenhock brought a good pair of eyes, mathematical exactitude, great patience, and even greater manual dexterity. These same qualities, together with a keen, practical intellect, served him in the exploration of the whole field of natural science that occupied him in fifty years of continuous work. Strictly speaking, his scientific training was incomplete—he never attended a university—and he was limited by his lack of skill in classical and foreign languages. He was, however, able to rely upon such friends as de Graaf and Constantijn Huygens (as well as upon professional translators) to aid him. He derived much of his scientific knowledge from Dutch authors—for example, Cornelis Bontekoe on medicine and Swammerdam on insects—and from Dutch translations of standard works, or, indeed, from the illustrations of books that he was not otherwise able to read (Hooke on microscopy, Grew on plant anatomy, and Redi on insects). He gained new information, too, from correspondence with the Royal Society (which had to be translated) and from conversations with visiting scholars.

Still, Leeuwenhoek remained in relative scientific isolation. One consequence of this was that he was not always fully acquainted with the researches and theories of his fellow scientists, and so could not incorporate their sometimes valuable suggestions into his own work. But he was thus able to work with full independence and to make a sharp distinction between the empiricism and speculation that marked the sometimes chaotic world of seventeenth-century science. Leeuwenhoek apparently regarded speculation as an academic occupation and therefore out of his domain, and this attitude permitted him a certain degree of detachment. He usually set out his observations fully, as facts, and only then, in a separate section, allowed himself to wonder what these facts might mean. (This caution is perhaps the reason that he did not publish a definitive work on microscopy.)

Leeuwenhoek's chief area of endeavor was the microscopical investigation of organic and inorganic structures. His most important contributions were made in the field of general biology; his studies in other branches of science were largely excursions in the interest of solving fundamental biological problems. Leeuwenhoek's method was based upon two presuppositions: that inorganic and organic nature are generally similar, and that all living creatures are similar in form and function. To demonstrate these similarities he attempted to study as many types as possible of any given group of organisms and then to generalize from this data; by drawing analogies between animals and plants, he sometimes succeeded in overcoming highly difficult problems in the interpretation of microscopic structures. Leeuwenhoek followed the Cartesian method in trying to apply his somewhat primitive knowledge of the laws of physics to living nature (and thereby exhibited some bias against chemical explanations).

Leeuwenhoek made his most important discovery early in his scientific career, in 1674, when he recognized the true nature of microorganisms. Starting from the assumption that life and motility are iden-

tical, he concluded that the moving objects that he saw through his microscope were little animals. He recorded these observations in his diary, and two years later, in a letter of 9 October 1676, communicated them to the Royal Society, where they caused a sensation. (Indeed, such was the disbelief of some of the fellows of that body that Leeuwenhoek felt obliged to procure written attestations to the reliability of his observations from ministers, jurists, and medical men.) Leeuwenhoek subsequently described, in about thirty letters to the Royal Society, many specific forms of microorganisms, including bacteria, protozoa, and rotifers, as well as his incidental discovery of ciliate reproduction. It was necessary to devise a scale by which to measure this formerly invisible new world, and Leeuwenhoek therefore developed a practical system of micrometry, utilizing as standards a grain of coarse sand (870μ), a hair from his beard (100μ), a human erythrocyte (7.2μ), and bacteria in pepper-water ($2-3 \mu$).

Microscopy, however, was only a tool that Leeuwenhoek put at the service of his two lifelong scientific concerns: his study of sexual reproduction, which was designed to refute the theory of spontaneous generation, and his study of the transport system of nutrients in plants and animals. He was drawn to the investigation of animal reproduction when, in 1677, a medical student, Johan Ham, of Arnhem, told him that he had seen animalcules in human seminal fluid. Ham presumed that these little animals had been generated by putrefaction; Leeuwenhoek, however, supposed them to be a normal component of semen throughout the animal kingdom. In the course of forty years, he described the spermatozoa of arthropods, mollusks, fishes, amphibians, birds, and mammals.

Such a persuasion led Leeuwenhoek to a new definition of the fertilization process. Having observed the spermatozoa, he was able to proceed beyond the prevalent notion that fertilization occurred from vapors arising out of the seminal fluid and to postulate that the spermatozoa actually penetrated the egg (although he was not able to observe this process). Assuming that the fast-moving spermatozoa were the origin of all new animal life (since he equated life with motility), he went on to state that the new life was nourished by the egg and the uterus. He thus denied any generative role to the motionless (and therefore lifeless) egg, and placed himself in direct opposition to those who, like Harvey in the *De generatione* of 1651, held the egg to be the source of all new life. Leeuwenhoek thus arrived at an animalculist theory of reproduction. A critical case in point was that of reproduction in mammals. The ovists thought that the follicle (discovered by de

Graaf and named after him) was, in fact, the egg, while Leeuwenhoek pointed out that it was impossible for the entire follicle to pass through the narrow fallopian tube to the uterus. (It is interesting to note that the actual mammalian egg was not found until 1826, when K. E. von Baer discovered it, and that the ovist-animalculist controversy persisted until 1875, when Hertwig demonstrated that fertilization represents the fusion of the nuclei of the spermatozoon and the egg.)

A corollary of Leeuwenhoek's theory of reproduction was his denial, following in the footsteps of Swammerdam and Redi, of the Aristotelian theory of generation, whereby some animals were thought to originate from the putrefaction of organic matter. In particular the Aristotelians held that certain tiny animals—such as insects and intestinal worms—were very primitive in structure and were generated in this way. In a series of investigations Leeuwenhoek demonstrated the complex structure of mites, lice, and fleas, and described their copulation and life cycles. His studies took him as far as the problem of reproduction in the eel and in intestinal parasites.

Since he believed all living forms to be functionally similar to one another, Leeuwenhoek also made extensive investigations of reproduction in plants. In a letter of 12 October 1685 he drew upon his studies of the seeds of angiosperms to explain his theory of plant reproduction: since motionless plants could not copulate, each individual had to provide for its own propagation. The embryonic plant was therefore the source of new life; the endosperm was the primary nutritive uterus and the earth the secondary nutritive uterus for the seed of the plant. Since he considered the flower to be the beautiful but functionless ornament of the plant, Leeuwenhoek did not investigate the anthers and ovaries.

Leeuwenhoek endeavored to draw an analogy between the animal system and the plant system when he took up his second important area of investigation, the system of nutrient transport. He minutely analyzed the transport canals, particularly their walls, the transport media (as, for example, blood), and the nutritive matter to be moved. Having no concept of the cell, he imagined the system to be composed of pipes or vessels.

In his studies of animals, Leeuwenhoek distinguished among what he called air vessels, intestinal tubes, chyle vessels, blood vessels, and nerve tubes. He was, however, not always able to interpret their functions, and he was not always successful in drawing analogies within the animal systems. For example, although he was aware of the morphological similarity of the cartilaginous rings in the bronchia of mammals and

the chitinous spiral in the trachea of insects, he chose to consider the trachea a blood vessel surrounding the intestinal tube.

Leeuwenhoek was particularly attentive to the blood vessels and the blood. Harvey had described the circulation of the blood in 1628, while Malpighi discovered the capillaries in 1661 and, in 1665, observed the corpuscles for the first time (although he wrongly identified them as fat globules). Leeuwenhoek, unaware of Malpighi's work, effectively rediscovered the blood corpuscles, in 1674, and the blood capillaries (in 1683). He went on to describe and measure the erythrocytes and their nuclei in fishes, amphibians, and mammals, and further investigated the walls of the blood vessels. (In the course of these studies Leeuwenhoek devised an ingenious apparatus —his famous "eel-spy"—to demonstrate the corpuscles and blood circulation in the tail of a live eel.) Nevertheless, Leeuwenhoek did not fully understand the function of the blood. Although he recognized it as the means whereby food particles were moved from the intestinal tube to the tissues, he rejected, on the basis of air-pump experiments, the notion that it might also serve to transport air.

Leeuwenhoek's work coincided again with that of Malpighi (as well as that of Grew) in the area of plant anatomy. Indeed, the three must be considered the founders of that study. Leeuwenhoek brought remarkable insight to the three-dimensional structure of the root, stem, and leaf, and illustrated his findings with radial, tangential, and cross sections of those organs. He considered plant tissue to be composed of a complex of tubes surrounded by other tissues made up of globules (cells), but his terminology is often unclear because he only rarely understood the function of the structures that he identified.

For example, in a long letter to the Royal Society of 12 January 1680, Leeuwenhoek described the elements that make up several kinds of wood. It is clear that he here considered all vertical and horizontal woody tracts to be sap-transporting vessels, in opposition to Grew, who distinguished between air vessels and sap vessels. Leeuwenhoek had observed the cross-walls of the rays and sieve tubes in plants on many occasions, and had drawn elaborate diagrams of them. He now interpreted them as being valves, analogous to those in animal veins, and was thus led to formulate a theory whereby the sap was moved from valve to valve by purely mechanical means. Twelve years later, however, in a letter of 12 August 1692, he changed his mind and, in a lengthy comparison of microscopic structures in plants and animals, arrived at something very close to Grew's theory. He now assumed the horizontal and vertical tracts in plants to be air tubes, and the secondary thickenings of these elements and the intercellular spaces between them to be sap vessels.

It was through letters—more than 300 of them, written to private scientists and amateurs in both Holland and other countries—that Leeuwenhoek made his work known. He wrote exclusively in Dutch, but had a few of his letters translated for the benefit of his correspondents. Primarily, though, he was indebted to the Royal Society of London for the publication of his views, and 190 of his letters are addressed to that body.

Leeuwenhoek's correspondence with the Royal Society began, through the intermediacy of de Graaf, one of the Society's Dutch correspondents, with his letter of 28 April 1673. This initial communication convinced the fellows of the great significance of his microscopic findings, and the Society prepared English translations or summaries of his letters for their *Philosophical Transactions* (1673–1724). It is apparent from the few letters to Leeuwenhoek that survive that he must have exchanged letters with the Royal Society on a regular basis, and that his London correspondents encouraged him to investigate new fields. Leeuwenhoek, in return, transmitted in each letter an exact account of the state of these studies. (It is sometimes perplexing to the modern reader, who may be unaware of the interaction of Leeuwenhoek and the Royal Society, to try to surmount the seeming lack of order in the sequence of subjects treated in the letters.)

Beginning in 1679, the French journal *Recueil d'expériences et observations sur le combat qui procède du mélange des corps* published Leeuwenhoek's letters, translating them from the *Philosophical Transactions*, and French summaries of them, drawn from the same source, appeared in the *Journal des sçavans*. Latin extracts were made and published in the *Acta eruditorum*, beginning in 1682.

Leeuwenhoek himself did not publish his work until 1684, when he brought out some of his letters in Dutch; from 1685 onward he also published Latin translations. He initially edited, reprinted, and reissued some of his letters separately or in groups of two or three, a practice that has resulted in some bibliographical confusion. From 1687 he adopted a more systematic course of publication, however, and in 1718 he brought out a collected edition of his letters in Dutch, followed in 1722 by a Latin edition. (In 1932, in commemoration of the tercentenary of Leeuwenhoek's birth, the Royal Academy of Sciences of Amsterdam and the *Nederlands Tijdschrift voor Geneeskunde* undertook a complete critical edition of all of his letters.)

Leeuwenhoek's scientific achievements were recognized during his lifetime by both his colleagues and the public. In 1680 he was elected a fellow of the Royal Society of London; in 1699 he was appointed a correspondent of the Paris Académie des Sciences; and in 1716 the Louvain College of Professors awarded him a silver medal. In addition to the pension that it gave him, the municipality of Delft made him special awards upon the publication of several of his books. The increasing number of learned and eminent visitors from several countries eventually caused Leeuwenhoek to demand introductory letters; his guests included kings and princes, among them Peter the Great, James II, Frederick the Great, Elector August II of Saxony, and the Grand Duke Cosimo III of Tuscany. In his old age, Leeuwenhoek became a legend; to his displeasure, his fellow townsmen reverently referred to him as a magician.

Four pictures of Leeuwenhoek made during his lifetime remain. He is a figure in Cornelis de Man's *Anatomy Lesson of Dr. Cornelis 'sGravesande*, painted in 1681 and now in the Old and New Hospital, Delft. In 1686 Johannes Verkolje made two portraits of him; one is a painting (now in the National Museum of the History of Science, Leiden), showing Leeuwenhoek holding his diploma of fellowship in the Royal Society, while the other is a mezzotint engraving in which the subject is seen handling one of his small microscopes. Another engraving was made by Jan Goeree in about 1707, and shows Leeuwenhoek in his old age.

BIBLIOGRAPHY

I. ORIGINAL WORKS. A complete list of the many editions of Leeuwenhoek's works appears as an appendix to A. Schierbeek's biography, cited below.

His own collected Dutch edition, the *Brieven* or *Werken*, consists of four (sometimes five) volumes: I. *Brieven, Geschreven aan de Wyt-vermaarde Koninglijke Wetenschap-zoekende Societeit, tot Londen in Engeland*, 10 pts. (Leiden–Delft, 1684–1694), with a *Register* (Leiden, 1695)—the title page of each part gives a more substantial idea of its contents; II. *Vervolg Der Brieven, Geschreven aan de Wyt-vermaarde Koninglijke Societeit in Londen* (Leiden, 1688), *Tweede Vervolg Der Brieven* (Delft, 1689), *Derde Vervolg Der Brieven* (Delft, 1693), and *Vierde Vervolg Der Brieven* (Delft, 1694); III. *Vijfde Vervolg Der Brieven, Geschreven aan verscheide Hoge Standspersonen En Geleerde Luijden* (Delft, 1696), *Sesde Vervolg Der Brieven* (Delft, 1697), and *Sevende Vervolg Der Brieven* (Delft, 1702); IV. *Send-Brieven* (Delft, 1718).

His Latin edition also consists of four volumes: I. *Arcana Natura Detecta* (Leiden, 1722), *Continuatio Epistolarum* (Leiden, 1715), and *Continuatio Arcanorum Naturae*

Detectorum (Leiden, 1722); II. *Opera Omnia, Seu Arcana Naturae* (Leiden, 1722); III. *Epistolae ad Societatem Regiam Anglicam* (Leiden, 1719); IV. *Epistolae Physiologicae Super compluribus Naturae Arcanis* (Delft, 1719).

The only comprehensive English translation of the letters is Samuel Hoole, *The Select Works of Antony van Leeuwenhoek*, 2 vols. (London, 1798–1807), which, however, omits all references to animal reproduction.

The Collected Letters of Antoni van Leeuwenhoek, edited by the Leeuwenhoek Commission of the Royal Academy of Sciences of Amsterdam, presently comprises eight volumes (Amsterdam, 1939–1967) of 118 letters written between 1673 and 1692.

II. SECONDARY LITERATURE. The most important recent works on Leeuwenhoek are C. Dobell, *Antony van Leeuwenhoek and His "Little Animals"* (London–Amsterdam, 1932; 2nd ed., New York, 1958); and A. Schierbeek, *Antoni van Leeuwenhoek. Zijn Leven en Zijn Werken*, 2 vols. (Lochem, 1950–1951), of which a concise English version is *Measuring the Invisible World. The Life and Works of Antoni van Leeuwenhoek FRS* (London–New York, 1959).

JOHANNES HENIGER

LE FEBVRE, NICAISE (*b.* Sedan, France, *ca.* 1610; *d.* London, England, 1669), *pharmacy, chemistry.*

Nicaise Le Febvre (variously spelled Le Fèvre, Le Févre, Le Febure and sometimes incorrectly given the Christian name Nicolas) was born in the important Huguenot center of Sedan in the Ardennes. His father, Claude Le Febvre, was a Protestant apothecary from Normandy who had settled in Sedan during the Wars of Religion; his mother, Françoise de Beaufort, came from a local family of physicians and apothecaries. Following preliminary schooling in the pedagogium of the Calvinist academy of Sedan, Nicaise became an apprentice in his father's shop in 1625. Before he completed his training his father died, and the direction of his education was taken over by Abraham Duhan, a doctor of medicine and professor of philosophy at the academy. After qualifying as a master apothecary Le Febvre continued in his father's business until 1646–1647; he then moved to Paris, where he initially enjoyed the patronage of his coreligionist, the physician Samuel du Clos. Le Febvre soon began to offer private courses in pharmaceutical chemistry. In 1652 he obtained the *privilège* of a royal apothecary and distiller and was appointed demonstrator in chemistry at the Jardin du Roi after the departure of William Davison. Among those attending his courses were a number of English royalist emigrés; and following the restoration of Charles II in 1660, Le Febvre was invited to England as royal professor of chemistry and apothecary to the

king's household. He was established in a laboratory in St. James's Palace, which he furnished with supplies from France. Le Febvre was admitted to the Royal Society in November 1661 on the nomination of Sir Robert Moray. His name also appears on the list of registered fellows drawn up at the reorganization of the Society in May 1663. He was an active member and in 1664 was appointed to the chemical committee of the society. Le Febvre died in London in the spring of 1669 and was buried in the parish of St. Martin-in-the-Fields.

Le Febvre's principal contribution to the literature of science is his textbook, the *Traicté de la chymie* (Paris, 1660). This work has a pivotal position in the series of French chemical teaching manuals of the seventeenth century. Its theoretical content, based largely on Paracelsus, Helmont, and Glauber, represents the culmination of the iatrochemical tradition in this series of French texts; its practical content and organization, however, were very closely followed by Nicolas Lemery in his *Cours de chymie* (1675), the most successful textbook of the late seventeenth century employing a corpuscular-mechanist interpretation. In his prefatory dedication to his fellow apothecaries, Le Febvre asserts the superiority of contemporary German pharmaceutical works to their French counterparts: in particular he cites the work of Johann Christian Schröder and Johann Zwelfer. Le Febvre's own text contains a significant infusion of mid-century German influences.

The theoretical introduction to the *Traicté* is an individualistic but interesting synthesis of chemical philosophy. For Le Febvre chemistry is a practical science of natural things with three main branches: philosophical chemistry, which seeks to understand the causes of natural and cosmological phenomena that are beyond the manipulative skill of the chemist to control or reproduce; iatrochemistry or medical chemistry, which seeks to apply the knowledge of natural phenomena acquired from philosophical chemistry to the practice of medicine; and pharmaceutical chemistry, which has as its sole object the preparation of remedies according to the directives of those versed in iatrochemistry. Thus chemistry is both science and art, "a knowledge of Nature itself reduced to operation."

Le Febvre's chemical theory is eclectic, drawing on Neoplatonic, Paracelsian, Helmontian, and Aristotelian ideas. The origin of all natural things is a homogeneous spirit, referred to as the universal spirit, which circulates throughout the cosmos. It is one in essence but threefold in nature. Being at once hot, moist, and dry, it is also known under the names of the three Paracelsian principles, sulfur, mercury, and salt. Individual chemical substances are generated and corporified out of this universal spirit by the action of specifying ferments present in the material matrices in which the spirit is entrapped. In this theoretical schema the four Aristotelian elements of fire, air, water, and earth are not considered as material components of chemical composition but as the four principal cosmogonic regions or matrices in which specification of the universal spirit takes place. Thus, fire is the matter of the heavens, and the stars are the specific ferments moving in this element whence the universal spirit always returns to take on its most perfect idea or form. Air is the first general matrix in which the universal spirit, emanating from the stars in the form of light, is corporified. This first corporeal form of the spirit is a hermaphroditic salt which is then absorbed successively by the other two matrices of water and earth; there it is specificated into the diverse forms of the mineral, vegetable, and animal kingdoms.

In addition to this theoretical discussion of principles and elements which belongs properly to philosophical, or "scientific," chemistry, Le Febvre recognizes five elements or principles which are the products of analysis by fire and belong to the art of chemistry. These elements are water or phlegm, spirit or mercury, sulfur or oil, salt, and earth. There is a limit to the resolution of mixt bodies, as further refinement would remove the specifying idea and corporifying matrix, thus resolving everything into the universal spirit. The art of chemistry resides precisely in refining and purifying the components of mixt bodies by repeated solutions and coagulations so that they may act more efficaciously—without simultaneously resolving everything into the universal spirit.

Following a brief description of the principal operations of the art, Le Febvre gives a description of apparatus illustrated with figures. The most notable illustration depicts an operator carrying out a calcination of antimony by means of a burning lens. In the text Le Febvre draws attention to the gain in weight following calcination which he attributes to the fixation of solar rays in the metal. This mode of calcining antimony had previously been described by Hamerus Poppius in *Basilica antimonii* (1618). Le Febvre's extensive list of chemical preparations, which forms the bulk of the text, are arranged under the headings of the three kingdoms of nature.

Le Febvre's other published work was a description of the preparation of Sir Walter Raleigh's great cordial, a polypharmaceutical preparation which, according to John Evelyn, he prepared before King Charles II in 1662.

BIBLIOGRAPHY

I. ORIGINAL WORKS. The various eds. of the *Traicté de la Chymie* are listed in J. R. Partington, *A History of Chemistry*, III (London, 1962), 17–18. The 1st ed. (Paris, 1660) was followed by five eds. in French, two of which (1669, 1696) were published in Leiden. The last French ed. (1751) was enlarged by one Du Moustier, Apothicaire de la Marine (actually the Abbé Lenglet du Fresnoy). An English trans. by P. D. C. Esq. first appeared as *A Compendious Body of Chemistry* (London, 1662). Subsequent English eds. appeared in London in 1664 and 1670 as *A Compleat Body of Chemistry*. A German trans. entitled *Chymischer Handleiter* appeared at Nuremberg in 1672. Subsequent German eds. are reported for 1675, 1676, 1685, and 1688. J. Ferguson, *Bibliotheca chemica*, II (Glasgow, 1906), 18, reports a Latin ed. in 2 vols. (Besançon, 1737).

Le Febvre's discourse on Sir Walter Raleigh's cordial was *A Discourse upon Sir Walter Rawleigh's Great Cordial . . . Rendered into English by Peter Belon* (London, 1664). A French version appeared in London in 1665.

G. Goodwin, "Le Fevre," in *Dictionary of National Biography*, XXXII (London, 1892), 399; and the *British Museum General Catalogue* ("Lefèvre, Nicolas") wrongly attribute to him "Disputatio de myrrhata potione," in J. Pearson, *Critici sacri*, IX (1660). The author of this work was Nicolas Le Fèvre (d. 1612), a French theologian. The French translator of Sir Thomas Browne, *La réligion du médecin* (The Hague, 1688), is yet another Nicolas Le Fevre. On these false attributions see the Dorveaux articles below.

II. SECONDARY LITERATURE. The "Avant-propos" of the *Traicté de la chymie* contains autobiographical reminiscences which are the principal source for Le Febvre's early life. Further background on his origins is in J. Villette, "Un procès entre un chirurgien et des médecins sedanais en 1646," in *Revue d'Ardenne et d'Argonne*, **10** (1903), 1–16. The most detailed and accurate biographical notice is P. Dorveaux, "L'apothicaire LeFebvre Nicaise, dit Nicolas," in *Proceedings of the Third International Congress of the History of Medicine, London, 1922* (Antwerp, 1923), 207–212. Substantially the same article appeared in *Bulletin de la Société d'histoire de la pharmacie*, no. 42 (May 1924), 345–356. See also J. P. Contant, *L'enseignement de la chimie au Jardin Royal des Plantes de Paris* (Paris, 1952), 88–90; J. R. Partington, *A History of Chemistry*, III (London, 1962), 17–24; and G. Goodwin (cited above). The best discussion of Le Febvre's textbook remains H. Metzger, *Les doctrines chimiques en France du début du XVIIe à la fin du XVIIe siècle* (Paris, 1923; repr. 1969), 62–82.

OWEN HANNAWAY

LE FÈVRE (or **LE FÈBVRE**), **JEAN** (*b*. Lisieux, France, 9 April 1652[?]; *d*. Paris, France, 1706), *astronomy*.

Le Fèvre's origins remain uncertain, although tradition has it that he started life as a weaver.

Scholars have confused him with an instrument maker having the same surname. Not until the age of thirty did he appear in the French scientific community as the friend of a certain Father Pierre, an amateur astronomer slightly older than Le Fèvre who had studied humanities in Lisieux and was professor of rhetoric at the Collège de Lisieux in Paris. Father Pierre, an associate of Picard and of P. de La Hire, recommended his friend to Picard, who, after testing Le Fèvre's ability to calculate astronomical tables, assigned him the task of doing the calculations for the *Connaissances des temps*. Through Picard's influence and probably that of La Hire, Le Fèvre became a member of the Académie des Sciences a few months later. After Picard's death he continued the more pedestrian aspects of Picard's work by calculating astronomical tables, by publishing the *Connaissances des temps*, by making a few astronomical observations, and by assisting La Hire in surveying.

Soon after La Hire published his *Tabulae astronomicae* . . . (Paris, 1687), Le Fèvre accused him of stealing his astronomical tables and publishing them as his own. Le Fèvre's ill feeling toward his colleague and mentor smoldered until 1700, when it erupted again after La Hire's son, Gabriel-Philippe, had published *Ephemerides ad annum 1701* (Paris, 1700). In the original preface to the *Connaissances des temps* for 1701, Le Fèvre, who probably resented not having been named the Academy's official publisher of ephemerides, let his anger flame and treated the La Hires rudely. The French government, which took offense at this, had the original preface replaced by one praising the La Hires and transferred permission to publish the *Connaissances des temps* from Le Fèvre to the Académie des Sciences. In 1701 the government succeeded in having Le Fèvre excluded from the Academy for having failed to attend meetings regularly, as required by the rules. During the remaining few years of his life Le Fèvre seems to have continued publishing ephemerides under the pseudonym of J. de Beaulieu.

BIBLIOGRAPHY

I. ORIGINAL WORKS. Le Fèvre published the *Connaissances des temps* from 1685 to 1701 and may also have published it during 1682–1684. J.-J. Le Français de Lalande, *Bibliographie astronomique* (Paris, 1803), pp. 341–343, gives the preface to the *Connaissances des temps* that Le Fèvre was obliged to delete. Le Fèvre also published *Ephémérides pour les années 1684 et 1685, calculées pour le méridien de Paris* . . . (Paris, 1684). The following, published under the pseudonym J. de Beaulieu, may be by Le Fèvre: *Ephémérides des mouvements célestes pour l'an de grâce 1702* . . . (Paris, 1702); *Ephémérides des mouvements célestes depuis l'an 1702 jusqu'à 1715* . . . (Paris, 1703), republished with the title *Eph. . . . 1703 . . . 1714 . . .;* and *État du ciel pendant l'année 1706* . . . (Paris, 1706). Lalande, *op. cit.*, p. 349 identifies Beaulieu as being Charles Desforges; yet it seems reasonable to identify Beaulieu as Le Fèvre if a remark of the *Journal des sçavans* for 1703, p. 274, is interpreted in the context of the confrontation between Le Fèvre and the La Hires. Le Fèvre's MSS are at the Académie des Sciences.

II. SECONDARY LITERATURE. Amédée Tissot, *Étude biographique sur Jean Le Fèvre* . . . (Paris, 1872), gives the most complete biographical survey; M. J. Delacourtie, "L'astronome Jean Le Fèvre," in *Bulletin de la Société historique de Lisieux* (1951–1952), 43–48, accurately summarizes Tissot's study. Both studies fail to give scholarly references, although Tissot states that he used Le Fèvre's MSS, which he had found in the archives of the Académie des Sciences. They confuse a certain Le Fèvre, "Ingénieur pour les instruments de mathématique," who appeared in the Paris scientific community around 1702 and whose activity continued well after Le Fèvre's death, with Le Fèvre—Lalande and the *Journal des sçavans* (see its indexed table of contents) do not make this error. The *Histoire de l'Académie royale des sciences* for 1700, 2nd ed. (Paris, 1761), pp. 109–111, reports on the accuracy of Le Fèvre's tables—Tissot, *op. cit.*, p. 63, erroneously states that this occurred in 1703; the same work for 1686–1699 (Paris, 1733), p. 74, gives an account of a fireball observed by Le Fèvre. Lalande, *op. cit.*, pp. 312–314, details Le Fèvre's activities during the period 1682–1685. Michaud, *Biographie universelle* . . ., XXIII (Paris, 1819), 546, gives a good account of Le Fèvre's life. Bonaventure d'Argonne's gossipy *Mélanges d'histoire et de littérature*, 4th ed. (Paris, 1725), I, 145, refers to Le Fèvre's humble origins. C. Wolf, *Histoire de l'observatoire de Paris* . . . (Paris, 1902), pp. 221–222, mentions Le Fèvre in connection with the surveying of France. Lalande, *op. cit.*, pp. 341–344; J. Bertrand, *L'Académie des sciences et les académiciens* . . . (Paris, 1869), pp. 55–58, 297–298; and *Histoire de l'Académie royale des sciences* for 1701, 2nd ed. (Paris, 1743), pp. 113–114, document Le Fèvre's quarrel with the La Hires. *Histoire de l'Académie royale des sciences* for 1700, 2nd ed. (Paris, 1761), pp. 129–130, recounts that the Academy commissioned G.-P. de La Hire to draw up new astronomical tables. *Journal des sçavans* for 1702, pp. 212–216, and for 1703, pp. 270–274 discusses ephemerides.

ROBERT M. MCKEON

LEGALLOIS, JULIEN JEAN CÉSAR (*b.* Cherrueix, near Dol, France, 1 February 1770; *d.* Paris, France, 10 February 1814), *physiology.*

Legallois was the first of the great French physiologists who based their conclusions on animal experiments. (He was followed by Magendie, Flourens,

Claude Bernard, and Brown-Séquard, among others.) He is chiefly remembered as the first to localize the respiratory center in the medulla and as one of those who anticipated the internal secretions.

Legallois was the son of a Breton farmer who is said to have worked his land himself. The boy's mother died when he was very young, but his father secured him a good education. His father died when Legallois was thirteen and a student at the Collège de Dol; he received a modest inheritance that he used to further his education. He won first prize in rhetoric at Dol and then began to study medicine at Caen. His career, however, was interrupted once by illness and again, after he recovered, by his involvement as a student leader in an armed movement in support of the federalists. After the defeat of his party, Legallois returned home to escape punishment but was denounced by a relative and fled to Paris. There he remained unnoticed among the crowd of young men trying to learn medicine in the hospitals after the abolition of the medical faculties.

Denounced a second time, Legallois braved his fate, and presented himself to the Comité des Poudres et Salpêtres. He proved himself satisfactory to the committee and was sent to organize and direct the manufacture of gunpowder in his native district. The following year, after the foundation of the École de Santé, Legallois, who had distinguished himself by his accomplishments, was delegated by the district committee to go to Paris as a wage-earning student. Besides medicine he studied Greek, Italian, and English, graduating in 1801. His dissertation was addressed to the question of whether blood is identical in all vessels through which it flows. In it Legallois pointed out that although blood is identical in all the arteries, it changes as it passes through the various organs and thus one organ may by its products influence all the others. This dissertation revealed Legallois's interest in experimental physiology and was widely appreciated as a model of physiological discussion.

Even before his graduation Legallois had acquired great experience in practical medicine through working in hospitals for some ten years. While preparing his dissertation he realized the importance of experimental inquiry. For this reason he devoted much of his energy after he qualified to physiological research, although he had no official position in that field. For about ten years he served as physician to the poor of the twelfth civil district of Paris. He wrote two medico-historical surveys (one on the discovery of galvanism and one on the chronology of Hippocrates) and a review of data on the contagious nature of yellow fever. He then began a long series of physiological experiments to determine the conditions basic to maintaining the life of any part of the body or, indeed, of the organism as a whole—in short, what he called "the principle of life."

A clinical observation led him to speculate about how long a newborn, fully developed fetus might live without breathing. He was inspired in part by the experiments made by Lavoisier and Laplace in connection with the generation of animal heat and its relation to respiratory exchange, but soon he noticed that life closely depends on two functions, those of the nervous system and the circulation of the blood. Having noted that the interruption of circulation at some specific point led to the death of the part of the body affected, and that stoppage of the heart caused the death of the whole animal, Legallois formed his remarkable idea that it should be possible to maintain life by a sort of injection, "and if there be a continuous supply of arterial blood, natural or artificially prepared—provided such a procedure be possible—life of any portion could be indefinitely maintained. . ., even in the head after decapitation, with all the functions proper to the brain." He pointed out in this way life could be reestablished in a part reduced to a state of apparent death after the cessation of circulation. At a time when profuse bloodletting was the therapeutic procedure of choice, Legallois's idea of revival (or "resurrection," as he called it) through bringing arterial blood to the tissues was an outstanding one. Although he reached his conclusion from physiological experiments, the technique was developed and applied in practical medicine only much later.

In spite of his severe myopia and short, thick fingers, Legallois was very skillful in experiments on living animals. His general approach was equally important. He recognized both the possibilities and the limitations of the experimental method as well as the conditions that must be observed to reach valid results. He therefore stressed the importance of the choice of animals and the necessity of the controls being of the same species, sex, and age, writing that "The greatest harm to experimental physiology was the negligence of researchers in the choice of experimental animals [which] they took . . . as they fell into their hands without attention to . . . species or age, and compared the results of experiments made in this manner as though they had compared animals of the same species and of the same age." Legallois thought that life depended on the impression of blood on the brain and the spinal cord, or on a principle resulting from this impression; death was therefore due to the extinction of that principle and might be only partial if the extinction were incomplete.

It had already been well accepted that locomotion and motility in general depend on the brain, which determines and regulates all animal functions. Legallois, however, concluded from his experiments that the principle of sensation and motility could only reside in the spinal cord, and that the brain is not the unique origin of nervous power. One of his most important achievements was the demonstration of the metameric organization of the spinal cord, by which each segment serves as a center of a specific region, coordinating its sensory and motor activity. "If instead of destroying spinal cord we divide it into its transverse sections, parts of the body corresponding to each spinal-cord segment conserve sensation and motility, but without harmony and each one independent of the others as if the sections were made across the whole body of the animal. In short, there are as many centers of sensation as there are spinal segments." The brain thus regulates the movements of the body without supplying the immediate principle; this originates in the spinal cord. The brain acts on the spinal cord in the same way that the spinal cord acts on the muscles, the white matter of the brain being composed of filaments which end in the gray matter of the cord. This gray matter, the origin of the spinal nerves, is the seat of the principle of life.

The mechanics of respiration—those movements which make possible the entry of air into the lungs—depend immediately on the brain; since life is maintained by respiration, the life of the animal depends on the brain, through the medium of the spinal cord. Legallois then, in 1812, convincingly demonstrated that respiratory movements originate in a small area of the medulla oblongata near the occipital foramen and near the level of the origin of the vagus nerves. Indeed, if the cranium of a young rabbit is opened and the brain cut off in serial transverse slices, beginning at the stem, the whole of the cerebrum and of the cerebellum—as well as a part of medulla—can be removed; and respiration ceases suddenly only when the lesion reaches the level of the vagus nerves. This effect is not due to the elimination of the vagi, since in an adult animal respiration goes on (although in a somewhat modified form) for a long time after their transsection.

Legallois was the first to draw attention to variations according to age in the respiratory reactions to the excitation of the central nervous system of animals of the same species. "Repetition of the same experiments on animals of various ages could throw light on many questions in physiology," he wrote.

Legallois was cautious in drawing conclusions from his experiments. In dealing with complex phenomena he tried to isolate the elementary features and thus to determine the general laws of nature. His experiments were remarkable in the diversity and ingenuity of their design and arranged in a logical sequence. Legallois's unshakable belief in the supreme importance of observations and well-performed experiments, together with his reserve in interpreting his data, indicate that he was a scientist of great stature.

Legallois died prematurely, about a year after his appointment to the great hospital and asylum of Bicêtre in the outskirts of Paris. He used to walk there from his home every day and in winter, after one such walk, contracted peripneumonia. Well aware of the physiological role of the blood, he refused the usual treatment of the time, bleeding, objecting that his inflammation was of "adynamic" nature, a theory to which some of his biographers believed that he fell victim. Legallois's notion was, however, sound, although several decades had to pass before the disastrous practice of therapeutic bloodletting was abandoned.

BIBLIOGRAPHY

I. ORIGINAL WORKS. Legallois's works were posthumously collected and edited by his son Eugène as *Oeuvres de J. J. C. Legallois avec des notes de M. Pariset*, 2 vols. (Paris, 1824; 2nd ed., 1830). His most important and best-known work, *Expériences sur le principe de la vie, notamment sur celui des mouvements du coeur, et sur le siège de ce principe* (Paris, 1812), was translated into English by N. Nancrede and J. Nancrede as *Experiments on the Principle of Life and Particularly on the Principle of the Motion of the Heart, and on the Seat of This Principle* (Philadelphia, 1813).

His other works include *Le sang est-il identique dans tous les vaisseaux qu'il parcourt?* (Paris, 1802), his M.D. diss.; *Recherches chronologiques sur l'Hippocrate* (Paris, 1804); *Recherches sur la contagion de la fièvre jaune* (Paris, 1805); several articles in the *Dictionnaire des sciences médicales;* and the posthumous *Fragments d'un mémoire sur le temps durant lequel les jeunes animaux peuvent être, sans danger, privés de la respiration* (Paris, 1834).

II. SECONDARY LITERATURE. There is a biographical notice in Legallois's *Oeuvres*, I, 1–11; and an anonymous "Notice biographique sur M. Legallois," in *Bulletin et mémoires de la Société de la Faculté de médecine de Paris*, 4 (1814–1815), 105–109. See also the article on Legallois in *Dictionnaire des sciences médicales, biographie médicale*, V (Paris, 1822), 565–566; G. Canguilhem, *La formation du concept de réflexe aux XVIIᵉ et XVIIIᵉ siècles* (Paris, 1955); E. Clark and C. D. O'Malley, *The Human Brain and Spinal Cord* (Berkeley–Los Angeles, 1968); A. Dechambre, in *Dictionnaire encyclopédique des sciences médicales*, 2nd ser., II (Paris, 1876), 138–139; P. Huard, "César Legallois (1770–1814) découvre en 1811 le principe de la résuscitation," in *Histoire de la médecine*, 4 (1954), 23–25; M. Neuburger, *Die historische Entwicklung der experimentellen Gehirn- und Rückenmarksphysiologie von Flourens* (Stuttgart, 1897); and J. Sourry, *Système nerveux central. Structure et fonctions* (Paris, 1899).

The reports of the National Institute of France on *Expériences sur le principe de la vie* and on Legallois's other experiments are trans. in A. P. W. Philip, *An Experimental Inquiry Into the Laws of the Vital Functions* (London, 1817; Philadelphia, 1818).

VLADISLAV KRUTA

LEGENDRE, ADRIEN-MARIE (*b*. Paris, France, 18 September 1752; *d*. Paris, 9 January 1833), *mathematics*.

Legendre, who came from a well-to-do family, studied in Paris at the Collège Mazarin (also called Collège des Quatre-Nations). He received an education in science, especially mathematics, that was unusually advanced for Paris schools in the eighteenth century. His mathematics teacher was the Abbé Joseph-François Marie, a mathematician of some renown and well-regarded at court. In 1770, at the age of eighteen, Legendre defended his theses in mathematics and physics at the Collège Mazarin. In 1774 Marie utilized several of his essays in a treatise on mechanics.

Legendre's modest fortune was sufficient to allow him to devote himself entirely to research. Nevertheless he taught mathematics at the École Militaire in Paris from 1775 to 1780.

In 1782 Legendre won the prize of the Berlin Academy. The subject of its competition that year concerned exterior ballistics: "Determine the curve described by cannonballs and bombs, taking into consideration the resistance of the air; give rules for obtaining the ranges corresponding to different initial velocities and to different angles of projection." His essay, which was published in Berlin, attracted the attention of Lagrange, who asked Laplace for information about the young author. A few years later the Abbé Marie and Legendre arranged for Lagrange's *Mécanique analytique* (Paris, 1788) to be published and saw it through the press.

Meanwhile, Legendre sought to make himself better known in French scientific circles, particularly at the Académie des Sciences. He conducted research on the mutual attractions of planetary spheroids and on their equilibrium forms. In January 1783 he read a memoir on this problem before the Academy; it was published in the *Recueil des savants étrangers* (1785). He also submitted to Laplace essays on second-degree indeterminate equations, on the properties of continued fractions, on probabilities, and on the rotation of bodies subject to no accelerating force. As a result, on 30 March 1783 he was elected to the Academy as

an *adjoint mécanicien*, replacing Laplace, who had been promoted to *associé*.

Legendre's scientific output continued to grow. In July 1784 he read before the Academy his "Recherches sur la figure des planètes." Upon the publication of this memoir, he recalled that Laplace had utilized his works in a study published in the *Mémoires de l'Académie des sciences* for 1782 (published in 1784) but written after his own, which allowed "M. de Laplace to go more deeply into this matter and to present a complete theory of it." The famous "Legendre polynomials" first appeared in these 1784 "Recherches."

The "Recherches d'analyse indéterminée" (1785) contains, among other things, the demonstration of a theorem that allows decision on the possibility or impossibility of solution of every second-degree indeterminate equation; an account of the law of reciprocity of quadratic residues and of its many applications; the sketch of a theory of the decomposition of numbers into three squares; and the statement of a theorem that later became famous: "Every arithmetical progression whose first term and ratio are relatively prime contains an infinite number of prime numbers."

In 1786 Legendre presented a study on the manner of distinguishing maxima from minima in the calculus of variations. The "Legendre conditions" set forth in this paper later gave rise to an extensive literature. Legendre next published, in the *Mémoires de l'Académie* for 1786, two important works on integrations by elliptic arcs and on the comparison of these arcs; here can be found the rudiments of his theory of elliptic functions.

In the works cited above, Legendre had marked off his favorite areas of research: celestial mechanics, number theory, and the theory of elliptic functions. Although he did take up other problems in the course of his life, he always returned to these subjects.

Legendre's career at the Academy proceeded without any setbacks. On the reorganization of the mechanics section he was promoted to *associé* (1785). In 1787, along with Cassini IV and Méchain, he was assigned by the Academy to the geodetic operations undertaken jointly by the Paris and Greenwich observatories. On this occasion he became a fellow of the Royal Society. His work on this project found expression in the "Mémoire sur les opérations trigonométriques dont les résultats dépendent de la figure de la terre." Here are found "Legendre's theorem" on spherical triangles:

> When the sides of a triangle are very small in relation to the radius of the sphere, it differs very little from a

rectilinear triangle. If one subtracts from each of its angles a third of the excess of the sum of the three angles over [the sum of] two right angles, the angles, diminished in this manner, may be considered those of a rectilinear triangle whose sides are equal in length to those of the given triangle.

This memoir also contains his method of indeterminate corrections:

In these calculations there exist some elements that are susceptible to a slight uncertainty. In order to make the calculation only once, and in order to determine the influence of the errors at a glance, I have supposed the value of each principal element to be augmented by an indeterminate quantity that designates the required correction. These literal quantities, which are considered to be very small, do not prevent one from carrying out the calculation by logarithms in the usual manner.

In the *Mémoires de l'Académie* for 1787 Legendre published an important theoretical work stimulated by Monge's studies of minimal surfaces. Entitled "L'intégration de quelques équations aux différences partielles," it contains the Legendre transformation. Given the partial differential equation

$$R \frac{\partial^2 z}{\partial x^2} + S \frac{\partial^2 z}{\partial x \, \partial y} + T \frac{\partial^2 z}{\partial y^2} = 0.$$

Set $\partial z / \partial x = p$ and $\partial z / \partial y = q$. Suppose R, S, T are functions of p and q only. Legendre is concerned with the plane tangent to the surface being sought: $z = f(x, y)$. The equation of this plane being $pX + qY - Z - v = 0$, he shows that v satisfies the equation

$$R \frac{\partial^2 v}{\partial q^2} - S \frac{\partial^2 v}{\partial p \, \partial q} + T \frac{\partial^2 v}{\partial p^2} = 0.$$

Later, in volume II of his *Traité des fonctions elliptiques* (1826), Legendre employed an analogous procedure to demonstrate "the manner of expressing every integral as an arc length of a curve." If $\int p d\omega$ is the integral in question (p being a function of ω), he shows that the arc length of the envelope of the family of straight lines $x \cos \omega + y \sin \omega - p = 0$ is equal to $\int p d\omega + p'$, where p' is the derivative of p with respect to ω.

In 1789 and 1790 Legendre presented his "Mémoire sur les intégrales doubles," in which he completed his analysis of the attraction of spheroids; a study of the case of heterogeneous spheroids; and some investigations of the particular integrals of differential equations.

In April 1792 Legendre read before the Academy an important study on elliptic transcendentals, a more systematic account of material presented in his first works on the question, dating from 1786. The academies were suppressed in August 1793; consequently he published this study himself, toward the end of the same year, in a quarto volume of more than a hundred pages.

The times were difficult for everyone and for Legendre in particular. He may even have been obliged to hide for a time. In any case his "small fortune" disappeared, and he was obliged to find work, especially since he had married a girl of nineteen, Marguerite Couhin. He later wrote to Jacobi:

I married following a bloody revolution that had destroyed my small fortune; we had great problems and some very difficult moments, but my wife staunchly helped me to put my affairs in order little by little and gave me the tranquillity necessary for my customary work and for writing new works that have steadily increased my reputation.

On 13 April 1791 Legendre had been named one of the Academy's three commissioners for the astronomical operations and triangulations necessary for determining the standard meter. His colleagues were Méchain and Cassini IV, who four years earlier had participated with him in the geodetic linking of the Paris and Greenwich meridians. On 17 March 1792, however, Legendre had requested to be relieved of this assignment. In ventôse *an* II (February–March 1794) the Commission of Public Instruction of the department of Paris appointed him professor of pure mathematics at the short-lived Institut de Marat, formerly the Collège d'Harcourt. During 1794 he was head of the first office of the National Executive Commission of Public Instruction (the second section, Sciences and Letters). He had eight employees under him and was expected to concern himself with weights and measures, inventions and discoveries, and the encouragement of science.

A tireless worker, during this same period Legendre published his *Éléments de géométrie*. This textbook was to dominate elementary instruction in the subject for almost a century. On 29 vendémiaire *an* II (20 October 1793) the Committee of Public Instruction, of which Legendre soon became senior clerk, commissioned him and Lagrange to write a book entitled *Éléments de calcul et de géométrie*. Actually his work must already have been nearly finished. He had probably been working on it for several years, encouraged perhaps by Condorcet, who stated in 1791, in his *Mémoires sur l'instruction publique:* "I have often spoken of elementary books written for children and for adults, of works designed to serve as guides for teachers. . . . Perhaps it is of some use to mention here that I had conceived the project for these works and prepared the means necessary to execute them. . . ."

In the meantime the decimal system had been adopted for the measurement of angles; and the survey offices, under the direction of Prony, undertook to calculate the sines of angles in ten-thousandths of a right angle, correct to twenty-two decimal places; the logarithms of sines in hundred-thousandths of a right angle, correct to twelve decimal places; and the logarithms of numbers from 1 to 200,000, also to twelve decimal places. In 1802 Legendre wrote: "These three tables, constructed by means of new techniques based principally on the calculus of differences, are one of the most beautiful monuments ever erected to science." Prony had them drawn up rapidly through a division of labor that permitted him to employ people with low qualifications. The work was prepared by a section of analysts headed by Legendre, who devised new formulas for determining the successive differences of the sines. The other sections had only to perform additions. This collective work resulted in two completely independent copies of the tables, which were mutually verified by their identity. These manuscript tables were deposited at the Bureau des Longitudes. An explanatory article appeared in the *Mémoires de l'Institut* (1801).

Legendre figured neither among the professors of the *écoles normales* of *an* III nor among those of the École Polytechnique. He did, however, succeed Laplace, in 1799, as examiner in mathematics of the graduating students assigned to the artillery. He held this position until 1815, when he voluntarily resigned and was replaced by Prony. He was granted a pension of 3,000 francs, equal to half his salary. He lost it in 1824 following his refusal to vote for the official candidate in an election for a seat in the Institute.

Legendre was not one of the forty-eight scholars selected in August 1795 to form the nucleus of the Institut National, but on 13 December he was elected a resident member in the mathematics section. In 1808, upon the creation of the University, he was named a *conseiller titulaire*. A member of the Legion of Honor, he also obtained the title of Chevalier de l'Empire—a minor honor compared with the title of count bestowed on his colleagues Lagrange, Laplace, and Monge. When Lagrange died in 1813, Legendre replaced him at the Bureau des Longitudes, where he remained for the rest of his life.

We now return to Legendre's scientific publications. The first edition of his *Essai sur la théorie des nombres* appeared in 1798. In it he took up in a more systematic and more thorough fashion the topics covered in his "Recherches" of 1785.

His *Nouvelles méthodes pour la détermination des orbites des comètes* (1806) contains, in a supplement, the first statement and the first published application of the method of least squares. Gauss declared in his *Theoria motus corporum coelestium* (1809) that he himself had been using this method since 1795. This assertion, which was true, infuriated Legendre, who returned to the subject in 1811 and 1820.

Legendre had been dismayed once before by Gauss: in 1801 the latter attributed to himself the law of reciprocity of quadratic residues, which Legendre had stated in 1785. Later, in 1827, Legendre wrote to Jacobi: "How has M. Gauss dared to tell you that the majority of your theorems [on elliptic functions] were known to him and that he had discovered them as early as 1808? This excessive impudence is unbelievable in a man who has sufficient personal merit not to have need of appropriating the discoveries of others."

Both Legendre in his indignation and Gauss in his priority claims were acting in good faith. Gauss considered that a theorem was his if he gave the first rigorous demonstration of it. Legendre, twenty-five years his senior, had a much broader and often a hazier sense of rigor. For Legendre, a belated disciple of Euler, an argumentation that was merely plausible often took the place of a proof. Consequently all discussion of priority between the two resembled a dialogue of the deaf.

In "Analyse des triangles tracés sur la surface d'un sphéroïde" (read before the Institute in March 1806), in which he considered the triangles formed by the geodesics of an ellipsoid of revolution, Legendre generalized his theorem concerning spherical triangles. Gauss provided a much broader generalization of this theorem in 1827, in his "Disquisitiones generales circa superficies curvas."

Legendre brought out the second edition of *Essai sur la théorie des nombres* in 1808. He later wrote two supplements to it (1816, 1825).

The "Recherches sur diverses sortes d'intégrales définies" (1809) continued an early study of Eulerian integrals—the term is Legendre's—in particular of the "gamma function." The earlier work appeared in 1793, in *Mémoire sur les transcendantes elliptiques*. The investigations of 1809 were, in turn, revised, completed, and enlarged in later works devoted to elliptic functions (1811, 1816, 1817, 1826).

Volume I of the *Exercices de calcul intégral* (1811) contains a majority of the results that Legendre obtained in the study of elliptic integrals. Volume III was published in 1816. Volume II, which includes the important numerical tables of the elliptic integrals, appeared in 1817.

In 1823 Legendre published "Recherches sur quelques objets d'analyse indéterminée et particulièrement sur le théorème de Fermat" in *Mémoires de l'Académie*. It contains a beautiful demonstration of the impossibility of an integral solution of the equation $x^5 + y^5 = z^5$, followed by an examination of more complicated cases of the theorem. This memoir was reproduced as the second supplement to the *Essai sur la théorie des nombres* (1825).

In 1825 and 1826, in *Traité des fonctions elliptiques*, Legendre took up once more and developed the essential aspects of his 1811 work, including applications to geometry and mechanics. In 1827, however, Jacobi informed Legendre of his own discoveries in this area. The latter, inspired by the contributions of his correspondent and by those of Abel, published three supplements to his *Théorie des fonctions elliptiques* (the title of volume I of the *Traité*) in rapid succession (1828, 1829, 1832).

In May 1830 the third edition of Legendre's *Théorie des nombres* appeared. In this two-volume work he developed the material of the *Essai* of 1808, adding new thoughts inspired, to a large extent, by Gauss. Jacobi drew his attention to a weak point in his reasoning, and on 11 October 1830 Legendre presented a corrected memoir that appeared in 1832 in the Academy's *Mémoires*. Shortly before his death he referred to this memoir as a necessary complement and conclusion to his *Traité* and expressed the need for printing it at the end of that work. His wish was not fulfilled.

The "Réflexions sur différentes manières de démontrer la théorie des parallèles ou le théorème sur la somme des trois angles du triangle" appeared in the *Mémoires* in 1833. Legendre had already sent a separately printed copy of it to Jacobi at the end of June 1832.

Legendre died on 9 January 1833, following a painful illness. His health had been failing for several years. His wife, who died in December 1856, made a cult of his memory and until her death displayed a naïve, religious respect for everything that had belonged to him. She left to the village of Auteuil (now part of Paris) the last country house in which they had lived. They had no children.

We shall now return to the three main fields treated in Legendre's works: number theory, elliptic functions, and elementary geometry—more particularly, the theory of parallel lines.

Number Theory. In the introduction to the second edition of his *Théorie des nombres* (1808) Legendre exhibited an admirable concern for rigor. For example, he demonstrated the commutativity of the product of integers by a technique related to Fermat's method of infinite descent. A direct disciple of Euler and Lagrange, he, like them, made frequent use of the algorithm of continued fractions, as much to solve first-degree indeterminate equations as to show that Fermat's equation $x^2 - Ay^2 = 1$ always admits an integral solution.

Moreover, Legendre followed Lagrange step by step in the study of quadratic forms, a study that he completed in some respects. He showed, for example, that every odd number not of the form $8k + 7$ is the sum of three squares. (He had shown this imperfectly as early as 1785 and in a nearly satisfactory manner in 1798.) On the basis of this result, Cauchy, in 1812, demonstrated Fermat's theorem for the case of polygonal numbers.

Legendre's principal contribution was the law of reciprocity of quadratic residues. He stated it as early as 1785, when he produced a very long and imperfect demonstration of it. In 1801 Gauss subjected it to a thorough criticism and was able to declare that he was the first to have demonstrated the proposition rigorously. In 1808, while preserving his first exposition, improved in 1798, Legendre adopted the proof given by his young critic. In 1830 he added to it that of Jacobi, which he found superior.

We have already mentioned Legendre's contributions to the study of Fermat's great theorem concerning the impossibility of finding an integral solution of the equation $x^n + y^n + z^n = 0$. In this connection he had met Dirichlet, a young mathematician of great promise.

A very skillful calculator, Legendre furnished valuable tables listing the quadratic and linear divisors of quadratic forms and the least solutions of Fermat's equation $x^2 - Ay^2 = \pm 1$. For the latter table, published in 1798 and reproduced in a much abridged form in 1808, he later (1830) utilized the corrections made by the Danish mathematician C. F. Degen.

Legendre should be considered a precursor of analytic number theory. His law of the distribution of prime numbers, outlined in 1798 and made more precise in 1808, took the following form: If y is the number of prime numbers less than x, then $y = \dfrac{x}{\log x - 1.08366}$. He found it, he stated, by induction. In 1830 he pointed out again that it had been found through induction and that "it remains to demonstrate it a priori"; and he developed some observations on this subject in a manner similar to Euler's. About 1793 Gauss intuited the law of the asymptotic distribution of prime numbers, which could have occurred to any attentive reader of Euler. But it was Legendre who first drew attention to this remarkable law, which was not truly demonstrated until 1896 (by Charles de la Vallée Poussin and Jacques Hadamard).

On the other hand, Legendre thought he had demonstrated, as early as 1785, that in every arithmetic progression $ax + b$ where a and b are relative primes, there is an infinite number of primes. He even specified that in giving to b the $\varphi(a)$ values prime to a and less than this number ($\varphi(a)$ being Euler's indicatrix), the prime numbers are distributed almost equally among the $\varphi(a)$ distinct progressions. These propositions were first rigorously demonstrated by Dirichlet in 1837.

Giving a rather broad scope to number theory, Legendre sought in 1830 to present Abel's conceptions concerning the algebraic solution of equations. Legendre thought it had been convincingly proved that such a solution is in general impossible for degrees higher than the fourth. He was also interested in the numerical solution of equations. In particular he studied the separation of roots and their expansion as continued fractions. In 1808 he presented a demonstration of the fundamental theorem of algebra that was quite analogous to that given by J. R. Argand in 1806. These essentially correct analytical demonstrations required only a few restatements to be made rigorous.

It should be noted that in 1806 Legendre's attitude toward Argand was very understanding. He did not publicly adopt the latter's ideas on the geometric representation of complex numbers; but thanks to the letter that he wrote to François Argand concerning his brother's discovery, that discovery was not lost, and in 1813 it reached a large audience through Gergonne's *Annales*.

In note 4 of his *Éléments de géométrie*—a note included in the first editions of the work—Legendre, by employing the algorithm of continued fractions, established Lambert's theorem (1761): the ratio of the circumference of a circle to its diameter is an irrational number. He improved this result by showing that the square of this ratio is also irrational, and added: "It is probable that the number π is not even included in the algebraic irrationals, but it appears to be very difficult to demonstrate this proposition rigorously."

Much attracted throughout his life by number theory, Legendre was well aware of the difficulties it presents and in his last years experienced a sort of disenchantment with it. For example, in 1828 he wrote to Jacobi: "I would advise you not to give too much time to investigations of this nature: they are very difficult and are often fruitless."

Number theory, of course, does not constitute the most significant portion of his *oeuvre*. Instead, he should be considered the founder of the theory of elliptic functions. MacLaurin and d'Alembert had studied integrals expressible by arcs of an ellipse or a hyperbola. Fagnano had shown that to any given ellipse or hyperbola two arcs the difference of which equals an algebraic quantity can be assigned in an infinite number of ways (1716). He had also demonstrated that the arcs of Bernoulli's lemniscate $(x^2 + y^2)^2 = a^2(x^2 - y^2)$ can be multiplied and divided algebraically like the arcs of a circle. This was the first demonstration of the use of the simplest of the elliptic integrals, the one later designated by Legendre as $F(x)$ and considered by him to govern all the others.

In 1761 Euler had found the complete algebraic integral of a differential equation composed of two separate but similar terms, each of which is integrable only by arcs of conics: $\dfrac{dx}{R(x)} + \dfrac{dy}{R(y)} = 0$, R being the square root of a fourth-degree polynomial. This discovery, made almost by chance, allowed Euler to compare—in a more general manner than had ever been done previously—not only arcs of the same conic section or lemniscate but also, in general, all the transcendentals $\displaystyle\int \dfrac{P\,dx}{R}$, where P is a rational function of x and R is the square root of a fourth-degree polynomial.

In 1768 Lagrange undertook to incorporate Euler's discovery into the ordinary procedures of analysis and, in 1784 and 1785, he presented a general method for finding the integrals $\displaystyle\int \dfrac{P\,dx}{R}$ by approximation. Meanwhile, John Landen had demonstrated in 1775 that every arc of a hyperbola can be measured by two arcs of an ellipse. As a result of this memorable discovery the term "Landen's theorem" was applied not only to this result but also to the first known transformation of elliptic integrals.

Such was the state of research in the theory of elliptic transcendentals in 1786, when Legendre published his works on integration by elliptic arcs. The first portion of these, written before he had become aware of Landen's discoveries, contained new ideas concerning the use of elliptic arcs, notably a method of avoiding the use of hyperbolic arcs by replacing them with a suitably constructed table of elliptic arcs. He then gave a new demonstration of Landen's theorem and proved by the same method that every given ellipse is part of an infinite sequence of ellipses, related in such a way that by the rectification of two arbitrarily chosen ellipses the rectification of all the others is obtained. With this theorem it was possible to reduce the rectification of a given ellipse to that of two others differing arbitrarily little from a circle.

But this topic, and the theory of elliptic transcendentals in general, required a more systematic treatment. This is what Legendre, who was virtually alone in his interest in the problem, attempted to provide in his "Mémoire sur les transcendantes elliptiques" (1793). He proposed to compare all functions of this type, classify them into different species, reduce each one to the simplest possible form, evaluate them by the easiest and most rapid approximations, and create a sort of algorithm from the theory as a whole.

Later research having enabled him to perfect this theory in several respects, Legendre returned to it in the *Exercices* of 1811. On this occasion he gave his theory a trigonometric appearance. Setting $\Delta = \sqrt{1 - c^2 \sin^2 \varphi}$, with $0 \leqslant c \leqslant 1$, he calls c the modulus of the function. The integral being taken from 0 to φ, φ is called its amplitude; $\sqrt{(1 - c^2)} = b$ is the complement of the modulus. The simplest of the elliptic transcendentals is the integral of the first kind: $F(\varphi) = \int \frac{d\varphi}{\Delta}$. The integral of the second kind, which is representable by an elliptic arc of major axis 1 and eccentricity c, takes the form $E(\varphi) = \int \Delta d\varphi$. The integral of the third kind is

$$\Pi(\varphi) = \int \frac{d\varphi}{(1 + \eta \sin^2 \varphi) \Delta},$$

with parameter n. Every elliptic integral can be expressed as a combination of these three types of transcendentals.

Let φ and ψ be two variables linked by the differential equation

$$\frac{d\varphi}{\sqrt{1 - c^2 \sin^2 \varphi}} + \frac{d\psi}{\sqrt{1 - c^2 \sin^2 \psi}} = 0.$$

The integral of the equation is $F(\varphi) + F(\psi) = F(\mu)$, μ being an arbitrary constant. Euler's theorem gives

$$\cos \varphi \cos \psi - \sin \varphi \sin \psi \sqrt{1 - c^2 \sin^2 \mu} = \cos \mu.$$

Thus it allows μ to be found algebraically, such that $F(\varphi) + F(\psi) = F(\mu)$, and then $F(\varphi)$ to be multiplied by an arbitrary number, whole or rational. From these observations Legendre deduced many consequences for each of the three kinds of integrals.

Furthermore, by designating the integral of the first kind with modulus c and amplitude φ as $F(c, \varphi)$, Legendre was able, with the aid of Landen's theorem, to establish the transformation later called quadratic.

Thus, if $\sin(2\varphi' - \varphi) = c \sin \varphi$ and if $c' = \frac{2 \sqrt{c}}{1 + c}$, then $F(c', \varphi') = \frac{1 + c}{2} F(c, \varphi)$. Through repeated use of this transformation Legendre constructed and

published (1817) his tables of elliptic functions. In 1825 he wrote:

> To render the theory wholly useful it remained to construct a series of tables by means of which one could find, in every given case, the numerical value of the functions. These tables have finally been constructed, after a multitude of investigations undertaken with a view toward discovering the methods and formulas most suitable to diminishing the length and difficulty of the calculations.

The work Legendre published in 1826, volume II of *Traité des fonctions elliptiques*, contains nine of these tables. The last one is "the general table of the functions F and E for each [sexagesimal] degree of the amplitude φ and of the angle of the modulus θ ($\sin \theta = c$) to ten decimal places for θ less than 45° and nine for θ between 45° and 90°." He wrote to Jacobi regarding these enormous computations that he carried out unassisted: "My goal has always been to introduce into calculation new elements that one can work with in arbitrary numbers, and I devoted myself to an exceedingly long and tedious task in order to construct the tables, a task I do not hesitate to believe is as considerable as that of Briggs's great tables."

Volume II of the *Traité* (1826) includes material on the construction of elliptic functions that is of the greatest interest from the point of view of numerical analysis. In particular Legendre presents a symbolic calculus, inspired by Lagrange, linking the expansion of a function by Taylor's formula with the calculation of its finite differences of various orders. Other investigations of this topic may be found in the analogous studies by Arbogast and Kramp, and by the students of Hindenburg. The same volume of the *Traité* lists—to twelve decimal places—the logarithms of the values of the gamma function $\Gamma(x)$ when x varies in thousandths of an integer and ranges from 1 to 2 inclusively.

In the meantime, around 1825, chance led Legendre to examine two functions F linked by relationships between their moduli, on the one hand, and their amplitudes, on the other—relationships that do not arise in the context of Landen's transformation. In generalizing these relationships Legendre discovered a new transformation closely related to the trisection of the function F. This trisection necessitated the solution of a ninth-degree algebraic equation. The new transformation reduced this solution to that of two third-degree equations.

In 1827, however, Jacobi (whose correspondence with Legendre, always of the greatest scientific and human interest, continued until 1832) communicated to Legendre his own discoveries and also informed him of Abel's. Legendre's attitude in the face of the discoveries of his young rivals was remarkable for its enthusiasm and forthrightness. In the foreword to volume III of his *Traité* he announced:

A young geometer, M. Jacobi of Koenigsberg, who was not aware of the *Traité* [but who, it should be added, was familiar, like Abel, with the *Exercices* of 1811], has succeeded, through his own investigations, in discovering not only the second transformation, which is related to the number 3, but a third related to the number 5, and he has already become certain that there must exist a similar one for every given odd number.

Legendre also drew attention to Abel's memoirs and analyzed their content. Legendre's first two supplements are devoted primarily to Jacobi's works but also to those of Abel, which contained the first appearance of modern elliptic functions, the inverse functions of the Legendre integrals. Legendre discussed their extension to the complex domain and their double periodicity in his usual somewhat ponderous style. The third supplement deals mainly with Abel and his great theorem. Legendre concluded his work on 4 March 1832: "We have only touched the surface of this subject, but it may be supposed that it will be steadily enriched by the works of mathematicians and that eventually it will constitute one of the most beautiful parts of the analysis of transcendental functions."

In 1869 Charles Hermite made the following judgment concerning Legendre's writings: "Legendre, who for so many reasons is considered the founder of the theory of elliptic functions, greatly smoothed the way for his successors; it is the fact of the double periodicity of the inverse function, immediately discovered by Abel and Jacobi, that is missing and that gave such a restrained analytical character to his *Traité des fonctions elliptiques.*"

Legendre's *Éléments de géométrie* long dominated elementary instruction in the subject through its numerous editions and translations. Quite dogmatic in its presentation, this work marked a partial return to Euclid in France. The notes that accompany and enrich the text still have a certain interest. The text itself, virtually unchanged since the first edition, does not take into account the various contributions made by Monge's disciples. The *Éléments* is above all a typical example of the difficulties encountered by the advocates of non-Euclidean geometries in their struggle to gain acceptance for their conceptions. The first published work of János Bolyai dates from 1832 and is thus contemporary with "Réflexions . . . sur la théorie des parallèles . . .," in which Legendre

recalled the efforts (all unsuccessful although he was not convinced of this) that he made between 1794 and 1823 to demonstrate Euclid's postulate. Let us first mention two very positive achievements that date from 1800. First: "The sum of the three angles of a rectilinear triangle cannot be greater than two right angles," a proposition he arrived at, of course, by accepting all the axioms, theorems, and postulates preceding the parallel postulate in Euclid's *Elements.* Second: "If there exists a single triangle in which the sum of the angles is equal to two right angles, then in any triangle the sum of the angles will likewise be equal to two right angles."

Yet, aside from these beautiful theorems, demonstrated in an impeccable manner, hardly anything but paralogisms are to be found. Like all the disciples of Newton, Legendre believed in absolute space and in the "absolute magnitude" of the sides of a rectilinear triangle. Taking up again a favorite idea of Lagrange's, outlined by the latter in volume 2 of the *Mémoires de Turin* (1761), he utilized (1794) the "law of homogeneous magnitudes" to establish the theorem of the sum of the angles of a triangle. Suppose a triangle is given with a side a and the adjacent angles B and C. The triangle is then well defined. The third angle A is therefore a function of the given quantities: $A = \varphi(B, C, a)$. But A, B, and C are pure numbers and a is a length. Now, by solving the equation $A = \varphi(B, C, a)$ with a as the unknown, the equation $a = f(A, B, C)$ is obtained "from which it would result that the side a is equal to a pure number without dimension, which is absurd." The law of homogeneous magnitudes therefore requires that this length disappear from the formula at the start and thus that $A = \varphi(B, C)$. By considering a right triangle and its altitude it is easily found that $A + B + C = \pi$.

Until the end of his life Legendre remained convinced of the value of this reasoning, and his other attempts at demonstration held only a purely pedagogical interest for him. They all failed because he always relied, in the last analysis, on propositions that were "evident" from the Euclidean point of view. Among these are the following: two convex contours of opposed concavities intersect at a finite distance; from a point within an angle a straight line cutting the two sides can always be drawn; and through three nonaligned points a circumference of a circle can always be passed.

At the end of his *Réflexions*, Legendre even adopted the pseudodemonstration of Louis Bertrand involving infinite spaces of various orders; and he thought he had improved it by what was actually an even more obscure argument. His virtuosity in spherical geometry and spherical trigonometry did not free him from a blind belief in absolute Euclidean space. "It is nevertheless certain," he wrote in 1832, "that the theorem on the sum of the three angles of the triangle should be considered one of those fundamental truths that are impossible to contest and that are an enduring example of mathematical certitude."

Let us conclude this study by emphasizing the transitional character of Legendre's works, which, in time as well as in spirit, are neither completely of the eighteenth century nor of the nineteenth. His scientific activity, extending from about 1770 to the end of 1832, was divided equally between the two centuries. He was a first-rate disciple of Lagrange and above all of Euler. His writings, like theirs, treat both abstract mathematics and the application of mathematics to the system of the world. Yet his boundless confidence in the powers of abstract science bespeaks a certain naïveté. In 1808 he wrote: "It is remarkable that from integral calculus an essential proposition concerning prime numbers can be deduced." The law in question was that of the distribution of the primes, and his remark is very pertinent. He added: "All the truths of mathematics are linked to each other, and all means of discovering them are equally admissible." One can easily agree with him on this point. But he went further, and here he makes one smile: "Consequently we were led to consider functions in order to demonstrate various basic theorems of geometry and mechanics."

Number theory was a sound and difficult school of logic for Legendre, as for all mathematicians who have worked in that field. Yet on several occasions, as in his studies of Eulerian integrals, he employed disconcerting arguments. For example, having established for positive integral values a certain relationship in which the gamma function occurs, he declares that the relationship is true for every value of this variable because the two members of the relationship are continuous functions. Elsewhere he elaborates on his reasoning: the two members are reduced to the same expression, which he works out; it is an extremely divergent (in the modern sense of the term) series. Still another time he employs an "infinite constant."

Consequently Legendre's writings rapidly became obsolete. Nevertheless he remains a marvelous calculator, a skillful analyst, and, in sum, a good mathematician. In both the theory of elliptic functions and number theory he raised questions that were fruitful subjects of investigation for mathematicians of the nineteenth century.

BIBLIOGRAPHY

I. ORIGINAL WORKS. Legendre's writings are *Theses mathematicae ex analysi, geometria, mecanica exerptae, ex collegio Mazarinaeo* (Paris, 1770); Abbé Marie, *Traité de mécanique* (Paris, 1774), which includes several passages by Legendre; *Recherches sur la trajectoire des projectiles dans les milieux résistants* (Berlin, 1782); "Recherches sur la figure des planètes," in *Mémoires de l'Académie des sciences* for 1784, pp. 370 ff.; "Recherches d'analyse indéterminée," *ibid.* for 1785, pp. 465–560; "Mémoire sur la manière de distinguer les maxima des minima dans le calcul des variations," *ibid.* for 1786, pp. 7–37, and 1787, 348–351; German trans. in Ostwalds Klassiker der exacten Wissenschaften, no. 47; "Mémoires sur les intégrations par arcs d'ellipse et sur la comparaison de ces arcs," in *Mémoires de l'Académie des sciences* for 1786, pp. 616, 644–673; "Mémoire sur l'intégration de quelques équations aux différences partielles," *ibid.* for 1787, pp. 309–351; "Mémoire sur les opérations trigonométriques dont les résultats dépendent de la figure de la terre," *ibid.* for 1787, pp. 352 ff.; "Mémoire sur les intégrales doubles," *ibid.* for 1788, pp. 454–486; "Recherches sur les sphéroïdes homogènes," *ibid.* for 1790; and "Mémoire sur les intégrales particulières des équations différentielles," *ibid.* for 1790.

Works published after the establishment of the republic are *Mémoire sur les transcendantes elliptiques* (Paris, 1793); *Éléments de géométrie, avec des notes* (Paris, 1794; 12th ed., 1823), new ed. with additions by A. Blanchet (Paris, 1845; 21st ed., 1876)—these eds. often depart from Legendre's text; English trans. by John Farrar (Cambridge, Mass., 1819) and other English eds. until 1890; German trans. by A. L. Crelle (Berlin, 1822); Romanian trans. by P. Poenaru (Bucharest, 1837); *Essai sur la théorie des nombres* (Paris, 1798; 2nd ed., 1808; with supps., 1816, 1825; 3rd ed., 2 vols., Paris, 1830) and German trans. by Maser as *Zahlentheorie* (Leipzig, 1893); *Méthodes analytiques pour la détermination d'un arc de méridien, par Delambre et Legendre* (Paris, 1799); "Nouvelle formule pour réduire en distances vraies les distances apparentes de la lune au soleil ou à une étoile," in *Mémoires de l'Institut national des sciences et arts*, **6** (1806), 30–54; and *Nouvelles méthodes pour la détermination des orbites des comètes . . .* (Paris, 1806).

Subsequent works are "Analyse des triangles tracés sur la surface d'un sphéroïde," in *Mémoires de l'Institut national des sciences et arts*, **7**, pt. 1 (1806), 130–161; "Recherches sur diverses sortes d'intégrales définies," *ibid.* (1809), pp. 416–509; "Méthode des moindres carrés pour trouver le milieu le plus probable entre les résultats de différentes observations," *ibid.*, pt. 2 (1810), 149–154, with supp. (Paris, 1820); "Mémoire sur l'attractions des ellipsoïdes homogènes," *ibid.*, pt. 2 (1810), pp. 155–183, read 5 Oct. 1812; *Exercices de calcul intégral*, 3 vols. (Paris, 1811–1817); "Sur une méthode d'interpolation employée par Briggs dans la construction de ses grandes tables trigonométriques," in *Connaissance des temps ou des mouvements célestes pour 1817*, **10** (Paris, 1815), 219–222; "Méthodes diverses pour faciliter l'interpolation des grandes tables trigonométriques," *ibid.*, pp. 302–331; and "Recherches sur quelques objets d'analyse indéterminée et particulièrement sur le théorème de Fermat," in *Mémoires de l'Académie des sciences*, n.s. **6** (1823), 1–60.

Traité des fonctions elliptiques et des intégrales eulériennes, avec des tables pour en faciliter le calcul numérique was published in 3 vols. (Paris, 1825–1828); vol. I contains the theory of elliptic functions and its application to various problems of geometry and mechanics; vol. II contains the methods of constructing the elliptical tables, a collection of these tables, the treatise on Eulerian integrals, and an appendix; and vol. III includes various supplements to the theory of Eulerian functions. The three supplements are dated 12 Aug. 1828, 15 Mar. 1829, and 4 Mar. 1832.

Legendre's last works are "Note sur les nouvelles propriétés des fonctions elliptiques découvertes par M. Jacobi," in *Astronomische Nachrichten*, **6** (1828), cols. 205–208; "Mémoire sur la détermination des fonctions Y et Z qui satisfont à l'équation: $4(x^n - 1) = (x - 1)(Y^2 \pm nZ^2)$," in *Mémoires de l'Académie des sciences*, **11** (1832), 81–99, read 11 Oct. 1830; and "Réflexions sur différentes manières de démontrer la théorie des parallèles ou le théorème sur la somme des trois angles du triangle," *ibid.*, **12** (1833), 367–410.

For Legendre's mathematical correspondence with Jacobi, see C. G. J. Jacobi, *Gesammelte Werke*, I (Berlin, 1881), 386–461. For his correspondence with Abel, see N. H. Abel, *Mémorial publié à l'occasion du centenaire de sa naissance*, pt. 2 (Oslo, 1902): pp. 77–79 (Legendre's letter to Abel, 25 Oct. 1828), pp. 82–90 (Abel's letter to Legendre, 25 Nov. 1828), and pp. 91–93 (Legendre's letter to Abel, 16 Jan. 1829).

II. SECONDARY LITERATURE. On Legendre and his work, see Élie de Beaumont, "Éloge historique d'Adrien-Marie Legendre, lu le 25 mars 1861," in *Mémoires de l'Académie des sciences*, **32** (1864), xxxvii–xciv; J. B. J. Delambre, *Rapport historique sur les progrès des sciences mathématiques depuis 1789, et sur leur état actuel* (Paris, 1810), pp. 7–10, 34, 46–96, 135–137, in which S. F. Lacroix was responsible for everything concerning pure mathematics; A. Birembaut, "Les deux déterminations de l'unité de masse du système métrique," in *Revue d'histoire des sciences et de leurs applications*, **12**, no. 1 (1958), 24–54; C. D. Hellman, "Legendre and the French Reform of Weights and Measures," in *Osiris*, **1** (1936), 314–340; Jacob, "A. M. Legendre," in Hoefer, ed., *Nouvelle biographie générale*, XXX (Paris, 1862), cols. 385–388; Gino Loria, *Storia delle matematiche*, 2nd ed. (Milan, 1950), pp. 768–770; Maximilien Marie, *Histoire des mathématiques*, X (Paris, 1887), 110–148; L. Maurice, "Mémoire sur les travaux et les écrits de M. Legendre," in *Bibliothèque universelle des sciences, belles-lettres et arts. Sciences et arts* (Geneva), **52** (1833), 45–82; and E. H. Neville, "A Biographical Note," in *Mathematical Gazette*, **17** (1933), 200–201.

See also N. Nielsen, *Géomètres français sous la Révolution* (Copenhagen, 1929), pp. 166–174; Maurice d'Ocagne, *Histoire abrégée des mathématiques* (Paris, 1955), pp. 182–187; Parisot, "Legendre," in Michaud, ed., *Biographie universelle ancienne et moderne*, XXIII, 610–615; Poggendorff, I, cols. 1406–1407; Denis Poisson, "Discours prononcé aux funérailles de M. Legendre . . .," in *Moniteur*

universel (20 Jan. 1833), p. 162; J. M. Querard, "Legendre, Adrien-Marie," in *France littéraire*, **5** (1833), 94–95; A. Rabbe, *Biographie universelle et portative des contemporains*, III (Paris, 1834), 234–235; L. G. Simons, "The Influence of French Mathematicians at the End of the Eighteenth Century Upon the Teaching of Mathematics in American Colleges," in *Isis*, **15**, no. 45 (Feb. 1931), 104–123; D. E. Smith, "Legendre on Least Squares," in *A Source Book in Mathematics* (New York, 1929), pp. 576–579; I. Todhunter, *A History of the Progress of the Calculus of Variations* (Cambridge, 1861), ch. 9, pp. 229–253; A. Aubry, "Sur les travaux arithmétiques de Lagrange, de Legendre et de Gauss," in *Enseignement mathématique*, **11** (1909), 430–450; and Ivor Grattan-Guinness, *The Development of the Foundations of Mathematical Analysis from Euler to Riemann* (Cambridge, Mass., 1970), pp. 29, 36–41.

JEAN ITARD

LE GENTIL DE LA GALAISIÈRE, GUILLAUME-JOSEPH-HYACINTHE-JEAN-BAPTISTE (*b.* Coutances, France, 12 September 1725; *d.* Paris, France, 22 October 1792), *astronomy*.

Following early schooling in his native city, Le Gentil, the only son of a none-too-wealthy Norman gentleman, went to Paris to study theology. While pursuing that course he also attended Delisle's lectures at the Collège Royal on astronomy, to which he soon found himself more attracted. An introduction to Jacques Cassini at the observatory in 1748 definitely established this change in direction by bringing Le Gentil an offer of lodgings there and observational training under Cassini de Thury and G. D. Maraldi. He was soon engaged in a regular, well-rounded program of celestial observations.

Having obtained the support of important members of the Academy of Sciences and having demonstrated, as early as 1749, his acquired skill and promise through the discovery of a nebula, a drawing of which he presented to them, Le Gentil was elected to the Academy in 1753. During the succeeding six years his contributions to its *Mémoires* ranged from historical concerns with the saros, through observational and descriptive papers, to studies that combined his own observations with those of others to perfect existing theory and quantitative evaluation of orbit inclinations and the obliquity of the ecliptic.

The turning point in Le Gentil's career was his commission to observe the 1761 transit of Venus at Pondicherry, India. Because the English had captured that settlement just as he arrived (in 1760), Le Gentil was obliged to witness the transit from shipboard, without any possibility for scientifically significant observations. Since another transit of Venus was to take place in 1769, Le Gentil resolved to remain in the East in order to complete his mission. He used the intervening years to collect vast amounts of material on Indian astronomy and to make numerous excursions, from Madagascar to Manila, during the course of which he amassed observations on a broad spectrum of phenomena. Although his own calculations showed that the latter site would be excellent for observing the transit of 3 June 1769, the Academy ordered him back to Pondicherry for that purpose. The decision was unfortunate, since Manila was very clear that day, while at Pondicherry a cloud obscured the sun precisely during the crucial period. It was thus an extremely disappointed Le Gentil who returned to Paris two years later after an absence of eleven and a half years.

Problems of a different sort now confronted him. Le Gentil's relatives, believing him dead, had begun a division of his estate; and the Academy, some members of which apparently interpreted his absence as undertaken for personal enrichment, had relegated him to "veteran" status. Both problems were soon solved: the former by legal actions which, however, did not return stolen monies and left him responsible for court costs; and the latter by his reinstatement in 1772 as an associate and, a decade later, by his supernumerary promotion to the pensionary level. Le Gentil married and moved back to the observatory, and was soon dividing his time between attention to the only offspring of his marriage, a daughter, and to his writings, most of which were based on the materials that he had brought back from the East.

Le Gentil's major work was the two-volume *Voyage dans les mers d'Inde* . . . (1779–1781). The first volume was devoted to India and, after a discussion of the customs and religion of its inhabitants, dealt at considerable length with the history of Brahman astronomy. Le Gentil's largely conjectural contention of that science's great antiquity was disputed by many contemporaries and was rejected by virtually all later scholars. On the other hand, his personal astronomical observations—as well as those dealing with geography, meteorology, and physics—were securely based and of more lasting importance. His instruments having been verified at the outset, Le Gentil's latitude and longitude determinations inspired confidence; his newly calculated table of refractions for the torrid zone, even without barometer and thermometer readings, was a decided improvement over existing values and a remarkable anticipation of later ones. His solstitial observations confirmed his earlier conclusions about the diminution of the obliquity of the ecliptic.

The second volume of the *Voyage* was devoted to the Philippines, Madagascar, and the Mascarenes. Except for the difference in locale, the absence of a historical section, and greater emphasis on geography and navigation, it conveyed the same sort of useful information as did the first.

Some of these materials were abstracted and offered to the Academy as memoirs during the 1770's, while the *Voyage* was in preparation. Even after its publication, however, Le Gentil continued to exploit his Indian data, sometimes combining them with observations made after his return. Papers of the 1780's dealing with refraction and the obliquity of the ecliptic were representative of this type, and a group of historical offerings during the same period were largely restatements of his claims for Indian astronomy, occasionally buttressed by "evidence" from Gothic zodiacs in and near Paris. The most important of his totally new productions were a memoir on tides that Le Gentil had observed on the coasts of Normandy and a paper alleging certain advantages of binocular over monocular instruments. Neither work was responsible for any basic advance.

The reconstruction of the observatory displaced Le Gentil from his lodgings in 1787, and he never returned—nor did the Academy ever fill the vacancy created by his death in 1792.

BIBLIOGRAPHY

I. ORIGINAL WORKS. Le Gentil's major work was *Voyage dans les mers de l'Inde (1760–1771), fait par ordre du roi, à l'occasion du passage de Vénus, sur le disque du soleil, le 6 Juin 1761, & le 3 du même mois 1769,* 2 vols. (Paris, 1779–1781). His only other non-Academic publication dealt with the transit of Venus and was written before his departure: "Mémoire de M. Le Gentil, au sujet de l'observation qu'il va faire, par ordre du roi, dans les Indes orientales, du prochain passage de Vénus pardevant le soleil," in *Journal des sçavans* (Mar. 1760), 137–139. Except for his 1749 "Mémoire sur une étoile nébuleuse nouvellement découverte à côté de celle qui est au-dessus de la ceinture d'Andromède," in vol. II (1755) of the so-called *Savants étrangers* series, all of his other publications were contributions to the *Mémoires*. These included a paper on the inequalities noticed in the movements of Jupiter and Saturn and tables of the oppositions of those planets with the sun that he had read to the Academy as a nonmember and that had been destined for the same *Savants étrangers* volume. Having attained membership before the latter was printed, however, he withdrew it from the printing office, made some changes in it, reread it to the Academy, and placed it in the *Mémoires* for 1754.

Inasmuch as Quérard provides a nearly complete chronological listing of forty papers in the *Mémoires* from 1752 through 1789 (with none between 1760 and 1770, because of Le Gentil's absence), there is no need to repeat long titles here. It has, however, been thought appropriate to indicate the years in which Le Gentil offered various types of memoirs. His historical studies began with two papers on the saros (1756), in which he rejected Halley's explanation of that period and substituted a fanciful scheme of his own; continued with three memoirs on various aspects of Indian astronomy (1772, pt. 2)—the antiquity of which he specifically insisted upon in a later work (1784); and ended by treating the origin of the zodiac and related matters (1782, two in 1785, two in 1788, 1789), again with frequent claims for Indian primacy.

Le Gentil's purely observational works of the 1750's dealt with determinations of the apparent diameter of the sun (1752, 1755) and of the earth's shadow during lunar eclipses (1755), and recorded such transient and permanent phenomena as nebulae (1759), a variable star (1759), rainbows (1757), lunar occultations of a star (1753) and Venus (1753), a lunar eclipse (1755), and inferior conjunctions of Venus (1753) and Mercury (1753). The latter, as with the observations of oppositions of Jupiter and Saturn (see above), were combined with remarks of theoretical interest.

More important efforts in the realm of theory were Le Gentil's researches into the obliquity of the ecliptic (1757) and his three-part study of the principal orbital elements of the superior planets (one part in 1757, two in 1758). In addition to the abstract items of the 1770's—the most important of which were two papers on horizontal refraction in the torrid zone (1774)—during that period he offered remarks on the temperature of the cellars of the Paris observatory (1774), an observation of a lunar eclipse (1773, with Bailly), and a memoir on the disappearance of Saturn's ring (1775). Although he thereafter reported both specifically astronomical and various general physical observations: for instance, on the intense cold of late 1783 and on the prevailing winds of Paris (both in 1784), the works noted in the text were far more important contributions: those on refraction (1789), the obliquity of the ecliptic (1783), tides (1782), and binocular instruments (1787).

II. SECONDARY LITERATURE. In his series of annual histories of astronomy from 1781 to 1802, J. J. de Lalande almost always offered brief notices of astronomers who died during those years; his succinct treatment of Le Gentil may be most conveniently consulted in his *Bibliographie astronomique* . . . (Paris, an XI [1803]), p. 722. During Condorcet's absence from the Academy in 1792, the writing of an "official" *éloge* fell to the vice-secretary, J. D. Cassini (IV); the product was published in his *Mémoires pour servir à l'histoire des sciences et à celle de l'Observatoire royal de Paris* (Paris, 1810), pp. 358–372. That rather laudatory and uncritical account should be supplemented by J. B. J. Delambre's trenchant analysis of Le Gentil's most important works in *Histoire de l'astronomie au dix-huitième siècle* (Paris, 1827), pp. 688–709; Delambre had earlier criticized Le Gentil's ideas about Indian astronomy in his *Histoire de l'astronomie ancienne* (Paris, 1817), I, 511–514.

As mentioned above, a nearly complete listing of Le Gentil's offerings in the *Mémoires*, although virtually nothing else, is available in J. M. Quérard, *La France littéraire* . . ., V (Paris, 1833), 95–96. The subsequent treatments in J. F. Michaud, ed., *Biographie universelle*, XXIII, 618–619; and in Niels Nielsen, *Géomètres français du dix-huitième siècle* (Paris, 1935), pp. 266–269, are flawed by minor errors. More specifically concerned with Le Gentil's voyage and its outcome are Alfred Lacroix, *Figures de savants*, III (Paris, 1938), 169–176; and, more important, Harry Woolf, *The Transits of Venus* (Princeton, 1959), esp. pp. 126–130, 151–156.

SEYMOUR L. CHAPIN

LÉGER, URBAIN-LOUIS-EUGÈNE (*b*. Loches, France, 7 September 1866; *d*. Grenoble, France, 7 July 1948), *zoology, protistology, hydrobiology.*

Léger, the son of Urbain-Louis Léger, a schoolteacher, and Marie-Eugénie Tretois, spent his childhood in Touraine. At the Faculty of Science of Poitiers he studied natural science, for which he received his *licence*, and, under the direction of Aimé Schneider, prepared his thesis for the *doctorat-ès-sciences* on the subject of the Gregarines (parasitic protozoans of invertebrates). He defended the thesis, for which he himself engraved the plates, in Paris on 27 February 1892 under the chairmanship of G. Bonnier. He was then appointed *préparateur* and then *chef de travaux* of zoology in Marion's laboratory at the Faculty of Sciences at Marseilles. He completed his medical studies and in 1895 defended his doctoral thesis in medicine on the histology of senile arteries before the Faculty of Medicine of Montpellier.

In 1898 Léger was appointed deputy lecturer and in 1904 professor of zoology at the Faculty of Sciences in Grenoble. He was appointed to the same post at the School of Medicine in 1910 and remained in Grenoble until his death.

While at Marseilles, Léger was married to Juliette Baraton, by whom he had three sons: Jacques, Jean, and Louis. He was the recipient of many honors: twice laureate of the Institute (Prix Serres, 1920; Prix Petit d'Ormoy, 1933); corresponding member of the Academy of Agriculture (1927); corresponding member of the Academy of Sciences (1928); officer of the Legion of Honor (1929); member of the Masaryk Academy of Prague; and member of the Romanian Academy of Sciences.

Léger's scientific output was considerable, comprising approximately 300 publications, which can be divided into two major groups: those on protistology and those on hydrobiology and pisciculture. In protistology Léger studied primarily parasitic species: Sporozoa (Gregarinida and Coccidia), Cnidosporidia, Flagellatae, and Ciliata. His researches on the

Gregarinida, done for the most part in collaboration with O. Duboscq, yielded data concerning their morphology, cytology, sexuality, life cycle, and their effect on the host. The papers on *Stylocephalus* and *Porospora* have become classics. Furthermore, Léger was interested in the Trichomycetes, curious parasites of arthropods which possess plantlike characteristics.

Léger began his piscicultural investigations in 1901. In 1909 he published a monograph on the fishes of Dauphiné, which was followed by numerous studies dealing with the physicochemical and biological factors of fresh waters and with the parasites and pathology of fishes. He also recommended attempts, which were successful, to introduce char in Alpine Lakes and rainbow trout in Madagascar.

At once a great researcher and a brilliant teacher, Léger was a cultivated artist—he was a watercolorist—and a direct and friendly man. His influence on his many pupils and his work in science give him a prominent place among French biologists of the first half of the twentieth century.

BIBLIOGRAPHY

I. ORIGINAL WORKS. Léger's principal works are *Recherches sur les Grégarines* (Poitiers, 1892); "Recherches sur les artères séniles," in *Annales de la Faculté des sciences de Marseille* (1895); "Nouvelles recherches sur les Polycystidées parasites des arthropodes terrestres, "*ibid.*, **6** (1896); "Essai sur la classification des Coccidies et description de quelques espèces nouvelles," in *Bulletin du Muséum d'histoire naturelle de Marseille*, **1** (1898), 71–123; "Les grégarines et l'épithélium intestinal chez les Trachéates," in *Archives de parasitologie*, **6** (1902), 377–473, with O. Duboscq; "Recherches sur les Myriapodes de Corse et leurs parasites," in *Archives de zoologie expérimentale et générale* (ser. 43), **1** (1903), 307–358, with Duboscq and H. Brolemann; "La reproduction sexuée chez les *Stylorhynchus*," in *Archiv für Protistenkunde*, **3** (1904), 303–357; "Nouvelles recherches sur les Grégarines et l'épithélium intestinal des Trachéates," *ibid.*, **4** (1904), 335–383, with Duboscq; "Étude sur la sexualité des Grégarines," *ibid.*, **17** (1909), 19–134, with Duboscq; "Poissons et Pisciculture dans le Dauphiné," in *Travaux du Laboratoire de pisciculture de l'Université de Grenoble*, **2** (1909); "Les Porosporides et leur évolution," in *Travaux de la Station zoologique de Wimereux*, **9** (1925), 126–139, with Duboscq; and "Contribution à la connaissance des Eccrinides," in *Archives de zoologie expérimentale et générale*, **86** (1948), 29–144, with Duboscq and O. Tuzet.

II. SECONDARY LITERATURE. M. Caullery, "Notice nécrologique sur M. Louis-Urbain-Eugène Léger (1866–1948)," in *Comptes rendus hebdomadaires des séances de l'Académie des sciences*, **277** (1948), 101–102; A. Dorier, "Discours prononcé aux obsèques du Professeur Léger," in *Travaux du Laboratoire d'hydrobiologie et de pisciculture de l'Université de Grenoble*, **9–11** (1948), 38–40; and *Hommage à Louis Léger 1866–1948* (Grenoble, 1949).

J. THÉODORIDÈS

LEHMANN, JOHANN GOTTLOB (*b.* Langenhennersdorf, near Pirna, Germany, 4 August 1719; *d.* St. Petersburg, Russia [now Leningrad, U.S.S.R.], 22 January 1767), *medicine, chemistry, metallurgy, mineralogy, geology.*

Lehmann was the son of Martin Gottlob Lehmann, a prosperous gentleman farmer, and Johanna Theodora Schneider. His early education was largely at the hands of private tutors, although he did attend the Fürstenschule, in Schulpforta, for one semester in 1735 before ill health forced him to withdraw. In 1738 he matriculated as a medical student at the University of Leipzig; the following year he transferred to the University of Wittenberg, where he studied with the anatomist Abraham Vater. He received the M.D. in 1741, with a dissertation on the nervous papillae.

Lehmann then went to Dresden to practice medicine, but soon, having become acquainted with the natural scientists resident there, discovered his real field of interest to be mining and metallurgy. Saxony, a mining center, was an ideal place to take up that subject, and Lehmann became engrossed in all aspects of it. He was particularly concerned with the origins and distribution of ore deposits and with the chemical composition of various ores. He made field trips, among them one to Bohemia, to further his knowledge, and by 1750, the year in which he left Dresden for Berlin, he had become known for his writings on mines and mining.

Christlob Mylius, a scientist and a friend of Lehmann's, wrote that Lehmann initially came to Berlin in connection with the establishment of the state porcelain factory there. If such were the case, he did not participate in this enterprise for long, since shortly after his arrival he received an official commission to study mining procedures in the Prussian provinces and to make recommendations for their improvement. He spent several years on this project, mostly in the Harz. In August 1754 Lehmann was appointed *Bergrat;* he served as director of copper mining and of the Bureau of Mines in Hasserode, where he also established a smelter and factory for manufacturing blue pigment from cobalt from a neighboring mine. In 1755 and 1756 Lehmann traveled in Silesia in his official capacity.

In 1756, too, Lehmann settled in Berlin, having married Maria Rosina von Grünroth. He had been a member of the Royal Prussian Academy of Sciences since 1754, and his work in the capital was done largely under the auspices of that body. Lehmann thus entered into a period of extraordinary scientific activity, publishing his researches in chemistry, geology, and mineralogy. Of these, the most important and lasting were his geological studies. In geology Lehmann emphasized the importance of geological strata in determining the history of the earth; he was also one of the first to seek physico-chemical explanations for the origin of mineral deposits within the context of that history. (His new notion of the composition of the earth further enabled him to reach a theory of the propagation of earthquakes as being dependent on the "inner structure of the surface of the earth.")

In his *Versuch einer Geschichte von Flötz-Gebürgen* of 1756, Lehmann, in discussing sedimentary rocks, described and compared sequences of strata on the basis of his own novel observations. Recognizing that the older strata were formed by the action of water, he developed the laws governing the formation of mountains, making a distinction between what he called "Ganggebürge"—a mountain formed of veined rock—and "Flötzgebürgen," mountains formed of stratified rock. These are now called *Unterbau* and *Oberbau* (substructure and superstructure), respectively. Drawing upon his observations, Lehmann was to draw up the first geological profile. In it he demonstrated that rocks do not lie next to each other in a haphazard way, but rather are formed in historical sequence. He thus may be considered the founder of stratigraphy; his attempt to establish the laws underlying the formation of the earth provided the basis for modern geology.

Lehmann's work in chemistry—which, indeed, constituted the greatest part of his researches—is today primarily of historical value. In his studies of rocks and ores he sought to determine their composition and metallurgical properties, and he suggested a system of classification based upon chemical composition (in contrast to Agricola's classification by external characteristics and Linnaeus' classification by crystal form). He analyzed many minerals for the first time; these analyses led to the discovery of new metals, including cobalt and tungsten. Lehmann's *Cadmiologia* of 1760 dealt specifically with cobalt ores, treating their occurrence, mineralogy, and chemistry, and the technology necessary to their mining and commercial use. But because he was limited to the techniques of quantitative analysis, Lehmann was able to make no fundamental and lasting contribution to the development of chemistry.

Mining technology was the framework into which Lehmann fitted all his research. He consciously sought to introduce into mining new scientific findings from all the natural sciences to enrich the technology that had evolved over the centuries. An uncompromising empiricist, Lehmann brought this point of view to his work in the field, in the mine, and in the laboratory. Following in the steps of Karl Friedrich Zimmermann, Lehmann advocated the establishment of specialized research institutions; he envisioned a technical teaching and research institute that would be the equal in prestige of the established universities. He was rewarded in his efforts by the founding of the Freiberg Bergakademie in 1765.

In 1760 Lehmann was invited to St. Petersburg by the Imperial Academy of Sciences. He accepted the following year, and in July 1761 left Berlin for Russia, where he took up a post as professor of chemistry at the University of St. Petersburg and director of the Academy's natural history collection. He also continued his researches and, in the five and one-half years that remained to him, made thirty-seven reports to the Academy on the composition of minerals, the smelting of ores, the composition of soils and peats, the commercial manufacture of alum, fossil remains, and the geological structure of both specific regions and of the whole earth. He proposed the establishment of a governmental department to supervise the exploration of Russia's mineral resources through a cartographical survey of geological relationships. (In this Lehmann was ahead of his time; two years after his death Catherine the Great commissioned the first of several Siberian explorations, giving Pallas the particular charge of conducting geological and orographic observations.) Lehmann's death, at forty-seven, was caused by a bilious fever, and not by arsenic poisoning, as rumored.

BIBLIOGRAPHY

I. Original Works. Bruno von Freyberg gives a list of 112 titles in *Johann Gottlob Lehmann, ein Arzt, Chemiker, Metallurg, Bergmann, Mineraloge und grundlegender Geologe*, cited below. In particular, see *Dissertatio de consensu partium corporis humani occasione spasmi singularis in manu eiusque digitis ex hernia observati* (Wittenberg, 1741); "Sammlung einiger mineralischer Merkwürdigkeiten des Plauischen Grundes bey Dressden," in *Neue Versuche nützlicher Sammlungen* (1749, 580–597); *Abhandlung von Phosphoris* (Dresden–Leipzig, 1750); *Kurtze Nachricht vom Erbbereiten* (Dresden–Leipzig, 1750); *Kurtze Einleitung in einige Theile der Bergwerks-Wissenschaft* (Berlin, 1751); "Ohnmassgeblicher Vorschlag, auf was Art und Weise man zu einer genaueren Entdeckung der unter der Erde verborgenen Dinge, oder kurz zu sagen, zu einer unterirdischen Erdbeschreibung gelangen könne," in *Physika-*

lische Belustigungen, **2** (1752), 27–42; *Abhandlung von den Metallmüttern* (Berlin, 1753); *Versuch einer Geschichte von Flötz-Gebürgen* (Berlin, 1756); *Physicalische Gedanken von denen Ursachen derer Erdbeben* (Berlin, 1757); "Histoire du Chrysoprase de Kosemitz," in *Histoire de l'Académie de Berlin,* **11** (1757), 202–214; *Kurzer Entwurf einer Mineralogie* (Berlin, 1758); *Cadmiologia,* pt. 1 (Berlin, 1760); *Probierkunst* (Berlin, 1761); *Physikalisch-chymische Schriften* (Berlin, 1761); *Specimen orographiae generalis tractus montium primarios globum nostrum terraqueum pervagantes* (St. Petersburg, 1762); *Cadmiologia,* pt. 2 (Königsberg–Leipzig, 1766); *De nova minerae plumbi specie crystallina rubra* (St. Petersburg, 1766); "Historia et examen chymicum lapidis nephritici," in *Novi commentarii Academiae* [of St. Petersburg], **10** (1766), 381–412; "De vitro fossili naturali sive de Achate Islandico," *ibid.,* **12** (1768), 356–367; "De Cupro et Orichalco magnetico," *ibid.,* 368–390; and "Specimen Oryctographiae Stara-Russiensis et lacus Ilmen," *ibid.,* 391–402.

II. Secondary Literature. Works about Lehmann include Bruno von Freyberg, *Die geologische Erforschung Thüringens in älterer Zeit* (Berlin, 1932); *Neues über Johann Gottlob Lehmann* (Erlangen, 1948); and *Johann Gottlob Lehmann, ein Arzt, Chemiker, Metallurg, Bergmann, Mineraloge und grundlegender Geologe,* vol. I of Erlanger Forschungen B, (Erlangen, 1955); W. von Gümbel, "Johann Gottlob Lehmann," in *Allgemeine deutsche Biographie,* XVIII (Leipzig, 1883), 140–141; and Hans Prescher, "Johann Gottlob Lehmann (1719–1767). Zum 200. Todestage des bedeutenden Bergmanns, Metallurgen und Begründers der modernen Erdgeschichtsforschung," in *Der Anschnitt,* **19** (1967), 9–18. See also Poggendorff, I, 1409–1416.

Bruno von Freyberg

LEHMANN, OTTO (*b.* Konstanz, Germany, 13 January 1855; *d.* Karlsruhe, Germany, 17 June 1922), *crystallography, physics.*

Lehmann discovered liquid crystals; substances which behave mechanically as liquids but display many of the optical properties of crystalline solids.

Lehmann's father had been a professor of science and mathematics at the Gymnasium in Freiburg im Breisgau and was particularly interested in the mathematical manifestations of organic nature. He sought to develop mathematical formulas for such phenomena as the geometric forms of the leaves of plants, and his interests stimulated the scientific bent of his son. Lehmann received his doctorate from the University of Strasbourg in 1876 and taught in secondary schools at Freiburg im Breisgau and Mulhouse from 1876 to 1883. In the latter year he became *Dozent* and in 1885 associate professor of physics at the Technische Hochschule at Aachen; in 1888 he was named associate professor at the Tech-

nische Hochschule at Dresden; and in 1889 he succeeded Heinrich Hertz as professor of physics at the Technische Hochschule at Karlsruhe. He remained in this post until his death.

Lehmann's early scientific interest and experimentation were concerned with electric discharges in rarefied gases, but he soon turned his attention to the study of the fine structure of matter as revealed under the microscope. His first major work describing his studies was *Molekularphysik, mit besonderer Berüchtsichtigung mikroskopischer Untersuchung und Anleitung zu solchen* (1888–1889).

In 1888 the Austrian botanist Friedrich Reinitzer noticed that the solid compound cholesteryl benzoate seemed to have two distinct melting points, becoming a cloudy liquid at 145° C. and turning clear at 179° C. Reinitzer's observation came to Lehmann's attention, and he immediately began research on this and other organic substances displaying the same property. He determined in 1889 that the cloudy intermediate phase contained areas that possessed a molecular structure similar to that of solid crystals, and he called this phase "liquid crystal." In 1922 G. Friedel suggested the term "mesomorphic" to include Lehmann's liquid crystals as well as any state of matter intermediate between the amorphous and crystalline states; however, the term "liquid crystal" is still employed.

Lehmann published his results in two major works: *Flüssige Krystalle* (1904) and *Die neue Welt der flüssigen Krystalle und deren Bedeutung für Physik, Chemie, Technik und Biologie* (1911). His results astonished and perplexed the scientific world, since he demonstrated that the fluidity of many organic substances is not only equal to or greater than water but that they also display the double refracting properties of crystals, some being twice as birefringent as calcite.

Lehmann's work stimulated much research in this area as well as studies to find technical applications of the phenomenon, and these efforts are still continuing.

BIBLIOGRAPHY

I. Original Works. Lehmann's chief publications are *Molekularphysik, mit besonderer Berüchtsichtigung mikroskopischer Untersuchung und Anleitung zu solchen,* 2 vols. (Leipzig, 1888–1889); *Krystallanalyse, oder die chemische Analyse durch Beobachtung der Krystallbindung mit Hülfe des Mikroskops* (Leipzig, 1891); *Elektrizität und Licht* (Brunswick, 1895); *Die elektrische Lichterschein* (Halle, 1898); *Flüssige Krystalle* (Leipzig, 1904); and *Die neue Welt der flüssigen Krystalle und deren Bedeutung für Physik, Chemie, Technik und Biologie* (Leipzig, 1911). In addition, he published approximately 120 articles in scientific journals.

II. SECONDARY WORKS. Obituary notices are in *Physikalische Zeitschrift*, **24** (1923), 289–291; and *Zeitschrift für technische Physik*, **4** (1923), 1.

JOHN G. BURKE

LEIBENSON, LEONID S. See **Leybenzon, Leonid S.**

LEIBNIZ, GOTTFRIED WILHELM (*b*. Leipzig, Germany, 1 July 1646; *d*. Hannover, Germany, 14 November 1716), *mathematics, philosophy, metaphysics*.

Leibniz was the son of Friedrich Leibniz, who was professor of moral philosophy and held various administrative posts at the University of Leipzig. His mother, Katherina Schmuck, was also from an academic family. Although the Leibniz family was of Slavonic origin, it had been established in the Leipzig area for more than two hundred years, and three generations had been in the service of the local princes.

Leibniz attended the Nicolai school, where his precocity led his teachers to attempt to confine him to materials thought suitable to his age. A sympathetic relative recognized his gifts and aptitude for self-instruction, and on the death of Friedrich Leibniz, in 1652, recommended that the boy be given unhampered access to the library that his father had assembled. By the time he was fourteen, Leibniz had thus become acquainted with a wide range of classical, scholastic, and even patristic writers, and had, in fact, begun that omnivorous reading that was to be his habit throughout his life. (Indeed, Leibniz' ability to read almost anything led Fontenelle to remark of him that he bestowed the honor of reading on a great mass of bad books.)

At the age of fifteen Leibniz entered the University of Leipzig, where he received most of his formal education, although that institution was at that time firmly entrenched in the Aristotelian tradition and did little to encourage science. In 1663 he was for a brief time a student at the University of Jena, where Erhard Weigel first taught him to understand Euclidean geometry. Leibniz continued his studies at Altdorf, from which he received the doctorate in 1666, with a dissertation entitled *Disputatio de casibus perplexis*. He was invited to remain at that university, but chose instead, during the second half of 1667, to undertake a visit to Holland.

Leibniz reached Mainz, where, through the offices of the statesman J. C. von Boyneburg, he met the elector Johann Philipp von Schönborn, who asked him into his service. Leibniz worked on general legal problems, developed his program for legal reform of the Holy Roman Empire, wrote (anonymously) a number of position papers for the elector, and began a vast correspondence that by 1671 had already brought him into contact with the secretaries of the Royal Society of London and the Paris Academy of Sciences, as well as with Athanasius Kircher in Italy and Otto von Guericke in Magdeburg. He also began work on his calculating machine, a device designed to multiply and divide by the mechanical repetition of adding or subtracting. In 1671 Pierre de Carcavi, royal librarian in Paris, asked Leibniz to send him this machine so that it could be shown to Colbert. The machine was, however, only in the design stage at that time (although a model of it was built in 1672 and demonstrated to the Academy three years later).

In the winter of 1671–1672, Leibniz and Boyneburg set forth a plan to forestall French attacks on the Rhineland. By its terms, Louis XIV was to conquer Egypt, create a colonial empire in North Africa, and build a canal across the isthmus of Suez—thereby gratifying his imperial ambitions at no cost to the Netherlands and the German states along the Rhine. Leibniz was asked to accompany a diplomatic mission to Paris to discuss this matter with the king. He never met Louis, but he did immerse himself in the intellectual and scientific life of Paris, forming a lifelong friendship with Christiaan Huygens. He also met Antoine Arnauld and Carcavi. The official mission came to nothing, however, and in December 1672 Leibniz' patron and collaborator Boyneburg died.

In January 1673 Leibniz went to London with a mission to encourage peace negotiations between England and the Netherlands; while there he became acquainted with Oldenburg, Pell, Hooke, and Boyle, and was elected to the Royal Society. The mission was completed, but the elector Johann Philipp had died, and his successor showed little interest in continuing Leibniz' salary, especially since Leibniz wanted to return to Paris. Leibniz arrived in the French capital in March 1673, hoping to make a sufficient reputation to obtain for himself a paid post in the Academy of Sciences. Disappointed in this ambition, he visited London briefly, where he saw Oldenburg and Collins, and in October 1676 left Paris for Hannover, where he was to enter the service of Johann Friedrich, duke of Brunswick-Lüneburg. En route, Leibniz stopped in Holland, where he had scientific discussions with Jan Hudde and Leeuwenhoek, and, at The Hague between 18 and 21 November, conducted a momentous series of conversations with Spinoza.

By the end of November Leibniz had arrived in Hannover, where he was initially a member of the duke's personal staff. He acted as adviser and librarian, as well as consulting on various engineering projects. (One of these, a scheme to increase the yield of the Harz silver mines by employing windmill-powered pumps, was put into operation in 1679, but failed a few years later, through no fault of the engineering principles involved.) Leibniz was soon formally appointed a councillor at court, and when Johann Friedrich died suddenly in 1679 to be succeeded by his brother Ernst August (in March 1680), he was confirmed in this office. Sophia, the wife of the new duke, became Leibniz' philosophical confidante; Ernst August commissioned him to write a genealogy of the house of Brunswick, *Annales imperii occidentes Brunsvicenses*, to support the imperial and dynastic claims of that family. Leibniz' researches on this subject involved him in a series of scholarly travels; his princely support opened the doors of archives and libraries, and he was enabled to meet and discuss science with eminent men throughout Europe.

Leibniz left Hannover in October 1687 and traveled across Germany; in Munich he found an indication that the Guelphs were related to the house of Este, an important point for his genealogy. In May 1688 he arrived in Vienna; in October of that year he had an audience with Emperor Leopold I, to whom he outlined a number of plans for economic and scientific reforms. He also sought an appointment at the Austrian court, which was granted only in 1713. He then proceeded to Venice and thence to Rome. He hoped to meet Queen Christina, but she had died; he did become a member of the Accademia Fisico-matematica that she had founded. In Rome, too, Leibniz met the Jesuit missionary Claudio Filippo Grimaldi, who was shortly to leave for China as mathematician to the court of Peking; Grimaldi awakened in Leibniz what was to become a lasting interest in Chinese culture. Returning north from Rome, Leibniz stopped in Florence for a lively exchange on mathematical problems with Galileo's pupil Viviani; in Bologna he met Malpighi.

On 30 December 1689 Leibniz reached Modena, his ultimate destination, and set to work in the ducal archives which had been opened to him. (Indeed, he threw himself into his genealogical research with such fervor that he afflicted himself with severe eyestrain.) He interrupted his work long enough to arrange a marriage between Rinaldo d'Este of Modena and Princess Charlotte Felicitas of Brunswick-Lüneburg (celebrated on 2 December 1695), but by February 1690 he was able to prove the original relatedness of the house of Este and the Guelph line, and his research was complete. He returned to Hannover, making various stops along the way; his efforts were influential in the elevation of Hannover to electoral status (1692) and earned Leibniz himself an appointment as privy councillor.

Elector Ernst August died in January 1698 and his successor, Georg Ludwig, although urging Leibniz to complete the history of his house, nevertheless declined to make any other use of his services. Leibniz found support for his project in other courts, however, particularly through the patronage of Sophia Charlotte, daughter of Ernst August and Sophia and electress of Brandenburg. At her invitation Leibniz went to Berlin in 1700, in which year, on his recommendation, the Berlin Academy was founded. Leibniz became its president for life. Sophia Charlotte died in 1705; Leibniz made his last visit to Berlin in 1711. He persisted in his efforts toward religious, political, and cultural reforms, now hoping to influence the Hapsburg court in Vienna and Peter the Great of Russia. In 1712 Peter appointed him privy councillor, and from 1712 to 1714 he served as imperial privy councillor in Vienna.

On 14 September 1714 Leibniz returned to Hannover; he arrived there three days after Georg Ludwig had left for England as King George I. Leibniz petitioned for a post in London as court historian, but the new king refused to consider it until he had finished his history of the house of Brunswick. Leibniz, plagued by gout, spent the last two years of his life trying to finish that monumental work. He died on 14 November 1716, quite neglected by the noblemen he had served. He never married.

FREDERICK KREILING

LEIBNIZ: Physics, Logic, Metaphysics

The special problems for any comprehensive treatment of the scientific investigations of Leibniz arise, on the one hand, from the fact that essential parts of his work have not been edited and, on the other hand, from the universality of his scientific interests. In view of this diversity of interests and the fragmentary, or rather encyclopedic, character of his work, the expositor is confronted with the task of achieving, at least in part, what Leibniz himself, following architectonic principles (within the framework of a *scientia generalis*), was unable to accomplish.

Leibniz is a striking example of a man whose universal interests (in his case ranging from physics through theory of law, linguistic philosophy, and historiography to particular questions of dogmatic theology) hindered rather than aided specialized scientific work. On the other hand, this broad interest, insofar as it remained oriented in architectonic principles, led to a concentration on methodological questions. In relation to the structure of a science, these are more important than concrete results. The position of Leibniz at the beginning of modern science is analogous to that of Aristotle at the beginning of ancient science. Leibniz' universality is comparable with that of Aristotle, different only in that it did not, as Aristotle's, remain grounded in essentially unchanged metaphysical distinctions but evolved by degrees from an encyclopedic multiplicity of interests. Consequently, in the strict sense in which there is an Aristotelian system, there is no Leibnizian system but rather a marked metaphysical and methodological concern that systematically expresses variations on the same theme in the various special fields (such as physics and logic) and underlies Leibniz' quest to establish a unified system of knowledge.

Leibniz' autobiographical statement in a letter to Rémond de Montmort in 1714 explains how, at the age of fifteen, though accepting the mechanical philosophy, his search for the ultimate grounds of mechanism led him to metaphysics and the doctrine of entelechies. This indicates the early orientation of Leibniz' thought towards the ideas of the *Monadologie*. Instead of setting out his philosophy systematically in a *magnum opus*, Leibniz presented piecemeal clarifications of his views in works that, in various ways, were inspired by the publications of others. After reading the papers of Huygens and Wren on collision and the *Elementorum philosophiae* of Hobbes, Leibniz composed his *Hypothesis physica nova*, consisting of two parts, *Theoria motus abstracti* and *Theoria motus concreti*, which in 1671 he presented respectively to the Paris Academy of Sciences and the London Royal Society. At this time, Leibniz owed more to Descartes, whose work he knew only at second hand, than he was later willing to admit. Closer study of the philosophy of Descartes led Leibniz to a more decisive rejection.

In 1686 he published in the *Acta eruditorum* a criticism of Descartes's measure of force, *Brevis demonstratio erroris memorabilis Cartesii et aliorum circa legem naturae*, which started a controversy with Catalan, Malebranche, and Papin lasting until 1691. Also in 1686 Leibniz sent to Arnauld, for his comments, an essay entitled *Discours de métaphysique*, in which he developed the ideas of the later *Théodicée*. The tracts entitled *De lineis opticis*, *Schediasma de resistentia medii*, and *Tentamen de motuum coelestium causis*, published in the *Acta eruditorum* in 1689, were hurriedly composed by Leibniz after he had read the review of Newton's *Principia* in the same journal, in an attempt to obtain some credit for results which he

had derived independently of Newton. In 1692, at the instigation of Pelisson, Leibniz wrote an *Essay de dynamique*, which was read to the Paris Academy by Philippe de la Hire, and in 1695 there appeared in the *Acta eruditorum* an article entitled *Specimen dynamicum*, which contained the clearest exposition of Leibniz' dynamics.

Leibniz' *Nouveaux essais sur l'entendement humain*, completed in 1705 but not published during his lifetime, presented a detailed criticism of Locke's position. By adding *nisi ipse intellectus* to the famous maxim, *Nihil est in intellectu quod non prius fuerit in sensu* (wrongly attributed to Aristotle by Duns Scotus[1]), Leibniz neatly reversed the application of the principle by Locke. According to Leibniz, the mind originally contains the principles of the various ideas which the senses on occasion call forth.

In 1710 Leibniz published his *Essais de Théodicée sur la bonté de Dieu, la liberté de l'homme et l'origine du mal*, a work composed at the instigation of Sophia Charlotte, with whom Leibniz had conversed concerning the views of Bayle. In response to a request from Prince Eugene for an abstract of the *Théodicée*, Leibniz in 1714 wrote the *Principes de la nature et de la grâce fondées en raison* and the *Monadologie*. When in 1715 Leibniz wrote to Princess Caroline of Wales, criticizing the philosophical and theological implications of the work of Newton, she commissioned Samuel Clarke to reply. The ensuing correspondence, containing Leibniz' most penetrating criticism of Newtonian philosophy, was published in 1717.

Rational Physics (Protophysics). In his efforts to clarify fundamental physical principles, Leibniz followed a plan which he called a transition from geometry to physics through a "science of motion that unites matter with forms and theory with practice."[2] He sought the metaphysical foundations of mechanics in an axiomatic structure. The *Theoria motus abstracti*[3] offers a rational theory of motion whose axiomatic foundation *(fundamenta praedemonstrabilia)* was inspired by the indivisibles of Cavalieri and the notion of *conatus* proposed by Hobbes. Both the word *conatus* and the mechanical idea were taken from Hobbes,[4] while the mathematical reasoning was derived from Cavalieri. After his invention of the calculus, Leibniz was able to replace Cavalieri's indivisibles by differentials and this enabled him to apply his theory of *conatus* to the solution of dynamical problems.

The concept of *conatus* provided for Leibniz a path of escape from the paradox of Zeno. Motion is continuous and therefore infinitely divisible, but if motion is real, its beginning cannot be a mere nothing.[5] *Conatus* is a tendency to motion, a mind-like quality having the same relation to motion as a point to space (in Cavalieri's terms) or a differential to a finite quantity (in terms of the infinitesimal calculus). *Conatus* represents virtual motion; it is an intensive quality that can be measured by the distance traversed in an infinitesimal element of time. A body can possess several *conatuses* simultaneously and these can be combined into a single *conatus* if they are compatible. In the absence of motion, *conatus* lasts only an instant,[6] but however weak, its effect is transmitted to infinity in a plenum. Leibniz' doctrine of *conatus*, in which a body is conceived as a momentary mind, that is, a mind without memory, may be regarded as a first sketch of the philosophy of monads.

Mathematically, *conatus* represents for Leibniz accelerative force in the Newtonian sense, so that, by summing an infinity of *conatuses* (that is, by integration), the effect of a continuous force can be measured. Examples of *conatus* given by Leibniz are centrifugal force and what he called the solicitation of gravity. Further clarifications of the concept of *conatus* are given in the *Essay de dynamique* and *Specimen dynamicum*, where *conatus* is compared with static force or *vis mortua* in contrast to *vis viva*, which is produced by an infinity of impressions of *vis mortua*.

Physics (Mechanical Hypothesis). Leibniz soon recognized that the idea of *conatus* could not by itself explain the results of the experiments of Huygens and Wren on collision. Since in the absence of motion *conatus* lasts only an instant, a body once brought to rest in a collision, Leibniz explains, could not then rebound.[7] A new property of matter was needed and this was provided for Leibniz by the action of an ether. As conceived by Leibniz in his *Theoria motus concreti*,[8] the ether was a universal agent of motion, explaining mechanically all the phenomena of the visible world. This essentially Cartesian notion was adopted by Leibniz following a brief attachment to the doctrine of physical atomism defended in the works of Bacon and Gassendi. Leibniz did not, however, become a Cartesian, nor did he aim to construct an entirely new hypothesis but rather to improve and reconcile those of others.[9]

A good example of the way in which Leibniz pursued this goal is provided by the planetary theory expounded in his *Tentamen de motuum coelestium causis*. In this work, Leibniz combined the mechanics of *conatus* and inertial motion with the concept of a fluid vortex to give a physical explanation of planetary motion on the basis of Kepler's analysis of the elliptical orbit into a circulation and a radial motion. Leibniz' harmonic vortex accounted for the circulation while the variation in distance was explained by the combined action of the centrifugal force arising from the circulation and the solicitation of gravity. This solicitation he held to be the effect of a second independent vortex of the kind imagined by Huygens, to whom he described Newton's attraction as "an immaterial and inexplicable virtue," a criticism he made public in the *Théodicée* and repeated in the correspondence with Clarke.

Although Leibniz' planetary theory could be described as a modification of that of Descartes, he did not acknowledge any inspiration from this source. Attributing the idea of a fluid vortex to Kepler and also, but incorrectly, the idea of centrifugal force, Leibniz claimed that Descartes had made ample use of these ideas without acknowledgment. Leibniz had already, in a letter to Arnauld,[10] rejected the Cartesian doctrine that the essence of corporeal substance is extension. One reason that led him to this rejection was the theological problem of transubstantiation which he studied at the instigation of Baron Boyneburg,[11] but the most important dynamical reason was connected with the relativity of motion. As explained by Leibniz in the *Discours de métaphysique*,[12] since motion is relative, the real difference between a moving body and a body at rest cannot consist of change of position. Consequently, as the principle of inertial motion precludes an external impulse for a body moving with constant speed, the cause of motion must be an inherent force. Another argument against the Cartesian position involves the principle of the identity of indiscernibles. From this principle it follows that, besides extension, which is a property carried by a body from place to place, the body must have some intrinsic property which distinguishes it from others. According to Leibniz, bodies possess three properties which cannot be derived from extension: namely, impenetrability, inertia, and activity. Impenetrability and inertia are associated with *materia prima*, which is an abstraction, while *materia secunda* (the matter of dynamics) is matter endowed with force.

Since, for Leibniz, force alone confers reality to motion, the correct measure of force becomes the central problem of dynamics. Now Descartes had measured what Leibniz regarded as the active force of bodies, that is, the cause of their activity, by their quantity of motion. But, as Leibniz remarked in a letter of 1680,[13] Descartes's erroneous laws of collision implied that his basic principle of the conservation of motion was false. In 1686 Leibniz published his criticism of the Cartesian principle of the conservation of motion in his *Brevis demonstratio erroris mirabilis Cartesii*, thereby precipitating the *vis viva* controversy. According to Leibniz, Descartes had incorrectly generalized from statics to dynamics. In statics or virtual motion, Leibniz explains, the force is as the velocity but when the body has acquired a finite velocity and the force has become live, it is as the square of the velocity. As Leibniz remarked on several occasions, there is always a perfect equation between cause and effect, so that the force of a body in motion is measured by the product of the mass and the height to which the body could rise (the effect of the force). Using the laws of Galileo, this height was shown by Leibniz to be proportional to the square of the velocity, so that the force *(vis viva)* could be expressed as mv^2.

Since *vis viva* was regarded by Leibniz as the ultimate physical reality,[14] it had to be conserved throughout all transformations. Huygens had shown that, in elastic collision, *vis viva* is not diminished. The *vis viva* apparently lost in inelastic collision Leibniz held to be in fact simply distributed among the small parts of the bodies.[15]

Leibniz discovered the principle of the conservation of momentum, which he described as the "quantité d'avancement."[16] Had Descartes known that the quantity of motion is preserved in every direction (so that motion is completely determined, leaving no opportunity for the directing influence of mind), Leibniz remarks, he would probably have discovered the preestablished harmony. But in Leibniz' view, the principle of the conservation of momentum did not correspond to something absolute, since two bodies moving together with equal quantities of motion would have no total momentum. Leibniz' discovery of yet another absolute quantity in the concept of *action* enabled him to answer the Cartesian criticism that he had failed to take time into account in his consideration of *vis viva*. In his *Dynamica de potentia et legibus naturae corporeae*, Leibniz made an attempt to fit this new concept into his axiomatic scheme.

Although succeeding generations described the *vis viva* controversy as a battle of words, there can be no doubt that Leibniz himself saw it as a debate about the nature of reality. Referring to his search for a true dynamics, Leibniz remarked in 1689 that, to escape from the labyrinth, he could find "no other thread of Ariadne than the evaluation of forces, under the supposition of the metaphysical principle that the total effect is always equal to the complete cause."[17]

Scientia Generalis. According to the usual distinctions, the position that Leibniz took in physics, as well as in other fundamental questions, was rationalistic, and to that extent, despite all differences in detail, was related to Descartes's position. Evident confirmation of this may be seen in Leibniz' controversy with Locke; although he does not explicitly defend the Cartesian view, he uses arguments compatible with this position.

It is often overlooked, however, that Leibniz was always concerned to discuss epistemological issues as questions of theoretical science. For example, while Locke speaks of the origins of knowledge, Leibniz speaks of the structure of a science which encompasses that particular field. Thus Leibniz sees the distinction between necessary and contingent truths, so important in the debate with Locke, as a problem of theoretical science which transcends any consideration of the historical alternatives, rationalism and empiricism. Neither an empiricist in the sense of Locke nor yet a rationalist in the sense of Descartes, Leibniz saw the refutation of the empiricist's thesis (experience as the nonconceptual basis of knowledge) not as the problem of a rational psychology as it was then understood (in Cartesian idiom, the assumption of inborn truths and ideas) but as a problem that can be resolved only within the framework of a general logic of scientific research. Nevertheless, he shares with Descartes one fundamental rationalistic idea, namely the notion (which may be discerned in the Cartesian *mathesis universalis)* of a *scientia generalis*. In connection with his theoretical linguistic efforts towards a *characteristica universalis*, this thought appears in Leibniz as a plan for a *mathématique universelle*.[18]

Inspired by the ideas of Lull, Kircher, Descartes, Hobbes, Wilkins, and Dalgarno, Leibniz pursued the invention of an alphabet of thought *(alphabetum cogitationum humanarum)*[19] that would not only be a form of shorthand but a formalism for the creation of knowledge itself. He sought a method that would permit "truths of reason in any field whatever to be attained, to some degree at least, through a calculus, as in arithmetic or algebra."[20] The program of such a *lingua philosophica* or *characteristica universalis* was to proceed through lists of definitions to an elementary terminology encompassing a complete encyclopedia of all that was known. Leibniz connected this plan with others that he had, such as the construction of a general language for intellectual discourse and a rational grammar, conceived as a continuation of the older *grammatica speculativa*.

While Leibniz' programmatic statements leave open the question of just how the basic language he was searching for and the encyclopedia were to be connected (the *characteristica universalis*, according to other explanations, was itself to facilitate a compendium of knowledge), a certain *ars combinatoria*, conceived as part of an *ars inveniendi*, was to serve in the creation of the lists of definitions. As early as 1666, in Leibniz' *Dissertatio de arte combinatoria*, the *ars inveniendi* was sketched out under the name *logica inventiva* (or *logica inventionis*) as a calculus of concepts in which, in marked contrast to the traditional theories of concepts and judgments, he discusses the possibility of transforming rules of inference into schematic deductive rules. Within this framework there is also a complementary *ars iudicandi*, a mechanical procedure for decision making. However, the thought of gaining scientific propositions by means of a calculus of concepts derived from the *ars combinatoria* and a mechanical procedure for decision making remained lodged in a few attempts at the formation of the "alphabet." Leibniz was unable to complete the most important task for this project, namely, the proof of its completeness and irreducibility, nor did he consider this problem in his plans for the *scientia generalis*, a basic part of which was the "alphabet," the *characteristica universalis* in the form of a *mathématique universelle*.

The *scientia generalis* exists essentially only in the "tables of contents," which are not internally consistent terminologically and thus admit of additions at will. Nevertheless, it is clear that Leibniz was thinking here of a structure for a general methodology, consisting, on the one hand, of partial methodologies concerning special sciences such as mathematics, and on the other hand, of procedures for the *ars inveniendi*, such as the *characteristica universalis;* taken together, these were probably intended to replace traditional epistemology as a unified conceptual armory. This was by no means impracticable, at least in part. For example, the analytical procedures in which arithmetical transformations occur independently of the processes to which they refer, employed by Leibniz in physics, may be construed as a partial realization of the concept of a *characteristica universalis*.

Formal Logic. Leibniz produced yet another proof of the feasibility of his plan for schematic operations with concepts. Besides the infinitesimal calculus, he created a logical calculus *(calculus ratiocinator, universalis, logicus,* or *rationalis)* that was to lend the same certainty to deductions concerning concepts as that possessed by algebraic deduction. Leibniz stands here at the very beginning of formal logic in the modern sense, especially in relation to the older syllogistics, which he succeeded in casting into the form of a calculus. A number of different steps may be distinguished in his program for a logical calculus. In 1679 various versions of an arithmetical calculus appeared that permitted a representation of a conjunction of predicates by the product of prime numbers assigned to the individual predicates. In order to solve the problem of negation—needed in the syllogistic modes—negative numbers were introduced for the nonpredicates of a concept. Every concept was assigned a pair of numbers having no common factor,

in which the factors of the first represented the predicates and the factors of the second represented the nonpredicates of the concept. Because this arithmetical calculus became too complex, Leibniz replaced it in about 1686 by plans for an algebraic calculus treating the identity of concepts and the inclusion of one concept in another. The components of this calculus were the symbols for predicates, $a, b, c, \ldots$ *(termini)*, an operational sign $-$ *(non)*, four relational signs $\subset, \not\subset, =, \neq$ (represented in language by *est, non est, sunt idem* or *eadem sunt, diversa sunt)* and the logical particles in vernacular form. To the rules of the calculus *(principia calculi)*—as distinct from the axioms *(propositiones per se verae)* and hypotheses *(propositiones positae)* which constitute its foundation —belong the principles of implication and logical equivalence and also a substitution formula. Among the theses *(propositiones verae)* that can be proved with the aid of the axioms and hypotheses, such as $a \subset a$ (reflexivity of the relation $\subset$) and $a \subset b$ et $b \subset c$ implies $a \subset c$ (transitivity of $\subset$), is the proposition $a \subset b$ et $d \subset c$ implies $ad \subset bc$. This was called by Leibniz the "admirable theorem" *(praeclarum theorema)* and appears again, much later, with Russell and Whitehead.[21]

Leibniz extended this algebraic calculus in various ways, first with a predicate-constant *ens* (or *res*), which may be understood as a precursor of the existential quantifier, and secondly with the interpretation of the predicates as propositions instead of concepts. Inclusion between concepts becomes implication between propositions and the new predicate-constant *ens* appears as the truth value *(verum)*, intensionally designated as *possibile*. These discourses were concluded in about 1690 with two calculi[22] in which a transition is made from an (intensional) logic of concepts to a logic of classes. The first, originally entitled *Non inelegans specimen demonstrandi in abstractis* (a "plus-minus calculus"), is a pure calculus of classes (a dualization of the thesis of the original algebraic calculus) in which a new predicate-constant *nihil* (for *non-ens*) is introduced. The second calculus (a "plus calculus") is an abstract calculus for which an extensional as well as an intensional interpretation is expressly given. Logical addition in the "plus-minus calculus" is symbolized by $+$. In the "plus calculus," logical addition, as well as logical multiplication in the intensional sense, is symbolized by $\oplus$, while the relational sign $=$ *(sunt idem* or *eadem sunt)* is replaced by ∞ and the sign $\neq$ by *non* $A \infty B$. Furthermore, subtraction appears in the "plus-minus calculus," symbolized by $-$ or $\ominus$, and also the relation of incompatibility *(incommunicantia sunt)* together with its negation *(com-*

municantia sunt or *compatibilia sunt).* For example, one of the propositions of the calculus states: $A - B = C$ holds exactly, if and only if $A = B + C$, and B and C are incompatible; in modern notation

$$a \sqsubset b = c \wedge (b \subset a) \leftrightarrow a = (b \vee c) \wedge (b \mid c).$$

(The condition $b \subset a$ is implicit in Leibniz' use of the symbol —).

If we disregard a few syntactical details and observe that Leibniz' work gives an approximation to a complete interpretation of the elements of a logical calculus (including the rules for transformation), we see here for the first time a formal language and thus an actual successful example of a *characteristica universalis.* It is true that Leibniz did not make sufficient distinction between the formal structure of the calculus and the interpretations of its content; for example, the beginnings of the calculus are immediately considered as axiomatic and the rules of transformation are viewed as principles of deduction. Yet it is decisive for Leibniz' program and our appreciation of it that he succeeded at all, in his logical calculus, in the formal reconstruction of principles of deduction concerning concepts.

General Logic. Leibniz' general logical investigations play just as important a role in his systematic philosophy as does his logical calculus. Most important are his analytical theory of judgment, the theory of complete concepts on which this is based, and the distinction between necessary and contingent propositions. According to Leibniz' analytical theory of judgment, in every true proposition of the subject-predicate form, the concept of the predicate is contained originally in the concept of the subject *(praedicatum inest subiecto).* The *inesse* relation between subject and predicate is indeed the converse of the universal-affirmative relation between concepts, long known in traditional syllogisms *(B inest omni A* is the converse of *omne A est B).*[23] Although it is thus taken for granted that subject-concepts are completely analyzable, it suffices, in a particular case, that a certain predicate-concept can be considered as contained in a certain subject-concept. Fundamentally, there is a theory of concepts according to which concepts are usually defined as combinations of partials, so that analysis of these composite concepts *(notiones compositae)* should lead to simple concepts *(notiones primitivae* or *irresolubiles).* With these, the *characteristica universalis* could then begin again. When the predicate-concept simply repeats the subject-concept, Leibniz speaks of an identical proposition; when this is not the case, but analysis shows the predicate-concept to be contained implicitly in the subject-concept, he speaks of a virtually identical proposition.

The distinction between necessary propositions or truths of reason *(vérités de raisonnement)* and contingent propositions or truths of fact *(vérités de fait)* is central to Leibniz' theory of science. As contingent truths, the laws of nature are discoverable by observation and induction but they have their rational foundation, whose investigation constitutes for Leibniz the essential element in science, in principles of order and perfection. Leibniz replaces the classical syllogism, as a principle of deduction, by the principle of substitution of equivalents to reduce composite propositions to identical propositions. Contingent propositions are defined as those that are neither identical nor reducible through a finite number of substitutions to identical propositions.

All contingent propositions are held by Leibniz to be reducible to identical propositions through an infinite number of steps. Only God can perform these steps, but even for God, such propositions are not necessary (in the sense of being demanded by the principle of contradiction). Nevertheless, contingent propositions, in Leibniz' view, can be known *a priori* by God and, in principle, also by man. For Leibniz, the terms *a priori* and *necessary* are evidently not synonymous. It is the principle of sufficient reason that enables us (at least in principle) to know contingent truths *a priori.* Consequently, the deduction of such truths involves an appeal to final causes. On the physical plane, every event must have its cause in an anterior event. Thus we have a series of contingent events for which the reason must be sought in a necessary Being outside the series of contingents. The choice between the possibles does not depend on God's understanding, that is to say, on the necessity of the truths of mathematics and logic, but on his volition. God can create any possible world, but, being God, he wills the best of all possible worlds. Thus the contingent truths, including the laws of nature, do not proceed from logical necessity but from a moral necessity.

Methodological Principles. Logical calculi and the notions mentioned under "General Logic" belong to a general theory of foundations that also encompasses certain important Leibnizian methodological principles. The principle of sufficient reason *(principium rationis sufficientis,* also designated as *principium nobilissimum)* plays a special role. In its simplest form it is phrased "nothing is without a reason" *(nihil est sine ratione),* which includes not only the concept of physical causality *(nihil fit sine causa)* but also in general the concept of a logical antecedent-consequent relationship. According to Leibniz, "a large part of metaphysics [by which he means rational theology], physics, and ethics" may be constructed on this proposition.[24] Viewed methodologically, this means that, in the principle of sufficient reason, there is a teleological as well as a causal principle; the particular import of the proposition is that both principles may be used in the same way for physical processes and human actions.

Defending the utility of final causes in physics (in opposition to the view of Descartes), Leibniz explained that these often provided an easier path than the more direct method of mechanical explanation in terms of efficient causes.[25] Leibniz had himself in 1682 used a variation of Fermat's principle in an application of his method of maxima and minima to the derivation of the law of refraction. Closely associated with the principle of sufficient reason is the principle of perfection *(principium perfectionis* or *melioris)*. In physics, this principle determines the actual motion from among the possible motions, and in metaphysics leads Leibniz to the idea of "the best of all possible worlds." The clearest expression of Leibniz' view is to be found in his *Tentamen anagogicum*,[26] written in about 1694, where he remarks that the least parts of the universe are ruled by the most perfect order. In this context, the idea of perfection consists in a maximum or minimum quantity, the choice between the two being determined by another architectonic principle, such as the principle of simplicity. Since the laws of nature themselves are held by Leibniz to depend on these principles, he supposed the existence of a perfect correlation between physical explanations in terms of final and efficient causes.

In relation to Leibniz' analytical theory of judgment and his distinction between necessary and contingent propositions, the principle of sufficient reason entails that, in the case of a well-founded connection between, for example, physical cause and physical effect, the proposition that formulates the effect may be described as a logical implication of the proposition that formulates the cause. Generalized in the sense of the analytical theory of truth and falsehood that Leibniz upholds, this means: "nothing is without a reason; that is, there is no proposition in which there is not some connection between the concept of the predicate and the concept of the subject, or which cannot be proved *a priori.*"[27] This logical sense of the principle of sufficient reason contains also (in its formulation as a *principium reddendae rationis*) a methodological postulate; propositions are not only capable of being grounded in reasons (in the given analytical manner) but they must be so grounded (insofar as they are formulated with scientific intent).[28]

In addition to the principle of sufficient reason, the principle of contradiction *(principium contradictionis)*

and the principle of the identity of indiscernibles *(principium identitatis indiscernibilium)* are especially in evidence in Leibniz' logic. In its Leibnizian formulation, the principle of contradiction, $\neg(A \wedge \neg A)$, includes the principle of the excluded middle, $A \vee \neg A$ *(tertium non datur)*: "nothing can be and not be at the same time; everything is or is not."[29] Since Leibniz' formulation rests on a theory according to which predicates, in principle, can be traced back to identical propositions, he also classes the principle of contradiction as a principle of identity. The principle of the identity of indiscernibles again defines the identity of two subjects, whether concrete or abstract, in terms of the property that the mutual replacement of their complete concepts in any arbitrary statement does not in the least change the truth value of that statement *(salva veritate)*. Two subjects s_1 and s_2 are different when there is a predicate P that is included in the complete concept S_1 of s_1 but not in the complete concept S_2 of s_2, or vice versa. If there is no such predicate, then because of the mutual replaceability of both complete concepts S_1 and S_2, there is no sense in talking of different subjects. This means, however, that the principle of the identity of indiscernibles, together with its traditional meaning ("there are no two indistinguishable subjects"[30]), is synonymous with the definition of logical equality ("whatever can be put in place of anything else, *salva veritate*, is identical to it"[31]).

Metaphysics (Logical Atomism). Since the investigations of Russell and Couturat, it has become clear that Leibniz' theory of monads is characterized by an attempt to discuss metaphysical questions within a framework of logical distinctions. On several occasions, however, Leibniz himself remarks that dynamics was to a great extent the foundation of his system. For example, in his *De primae philosophiae emendatione et de notione substantiae*, Leibniz comments that the notion of force, for the exposition of which he had designed a special science of dynamics, added much to the clear understanding of the concept of substance.[32] This suggests that it was the notion of mechanical energy that led to the concept of substance as activity. Again, it is in dynamics, Leibniz remarks, that we learn the difference between necessary truths and those which have their source in final causes, that is to say, contingent truths,[33] while optical theory, in the form of Fermat's principle, pointed to the location of the final causes in the principle of perfection.[34] Even the subject-predicate logic itself, which forms the rational foundation of Leibniz' metaphysics, seems to take on a biological image, such as the growth of a plant from a seed, when Leibniz writes to De Volder that the present state of a substance must involve its future states and vice versa. It thus appears that physical analogies very probably provided the initial inspiration for the formation of Leibniz' metaphysical concepts.

In the preface to the *Théodicée*, Leibniz declares that there are two famous labryrinths in which our reason goes astray; the one relates to the problem of liberty (which is the principal subject of the *Théodicée*), the other to the problem of continuity and the antinomies of the infinite. To arrive at a true metaphysics, Leibniz remarks in another place, it is necessary to have passed through the labyrinth of the continuum.[35] Extension, like other continuous quantities, is infinitely divisible, so that physical bodies, however small, have yet smaller parts. For Leibniz, there can be no real whole without real unities, that is, indivisibles,[36] or as he expresses it (repeating a phrase used by Nicholas of Cusa[37]), being and unity are convertible terms.[38] Now the real unities underlying physical bodies cannot be mathematical points, for these are mere nothings. As Leibniz explains, "only metaphysical or substantial points . . . are exact and real; without them there would be nothing real, since without true unities *[les véritables unités]* a composite whole would be impossible."[39] Within the narrower framework of physics, such unities can be understood as the concept of mass-points, but they are meant in the broader sense of the classical concept of substance, to the consideration of which Leibniz had in 1663 devoted his first philosophical essay, *Dissertatio metaphysica de principio individui*. Leibniz' metaphysical realities are unextended substances or monads (a term he used from 1696), whose essence is an intensive quality of the nature of force or mind.

Leibniz consciously adheres to Aristotelian definitions, when he emphasizes that we may speak of an individual substance whenever a predicate-concept is included in a subject-concept, and this subject-concept never appears itself as a predicate-concept. A concept fulfilling this condition may thus be designated as an individual concept *(notion individuelle)* and may be construed as a complete concept, that is, as the infinite conjunction of predicates appertaining to that individual. If a complete subject-concept were itself to appear as a predicate-concept, then according to the principle of the identity of indiscernibles, the predicated individual would be identical to the designated individual. This result of Leibniz is a logical reconstruction of the traditional ontological distinction between substance and quality.

The definition of individual concepts, according to which individual substances are denoted by complete concepts, leads also to the idea, central to the theory of monads, that each monad or individual substance represents or mirrors the whole universe. What Leibniz means is that, given a particular subject, all other subjects must appear, represented by their names or designations, in at least one of the infinite conjunction of predicates constituting the complete concept of that particular subject.

Leibniz describes the inner activity which constitutes the essence of the monad as perception.[40] This does not imply that all monads are conscious. The monad has perception in the sense that it represents the universe from its point of view, while its activity is manifested in spontaneous change from one perception to another. The attribution of perception and appetition to the monads does not mean that they can be sufficiently defined in terms of physiological and psychological processes, although Leibniz does compare them to biological organisms; he was, of course, familiar with the work of Leeuwenhoek, Swammerdam, and Malpighi on microorganisms, which seemed to confirm the theory of preformation demanded by the doctrine of monads. Once again, the logical basis for the theory of perception is that the concept of the monad's inner activity must occur in the concept of the individual monad; for everything that an individual substance encounters "is only the consequence of its notion or complete concept, since this notion already contains all predicates or events and expresses the whole universe."[41]

Within the framework of this conceptual connection between a theory of perception and a theory of individual concepts, sufficient room remains for physiological and psychological discussion and here Leibniz goes far beyond the level of debate in Locke and Descartes. In particular, Leibniz distinguishes between consciousness and self-consciousness, and again, between stimuli which rise above the threshold of consciousness and those that remain below it; he even observes that the summation of sub-threshold stimuli can finally lead to one that emerges over the threshold of consciousness, a clear hint of the existence of the unconscious.

Since, for Leibniz, the real unities constituting the universe are essentially perceptive, it follows that the real continuum must also be a continuum of perception. The infinite totality of monads represent or mirror the universe, of which each is a part, from all possible points of view, so that the universe is at once continuous and not only infinitely divisible but actually divided into an infinity of real metaphysical atoms.[42] As these atoms are purely intensive unities, they are mutually exclusive, so that no real interaction between them is possible. Consequently, Leibniz needed his principle of the preestablished harmony (which, he claimed, avoided the perpetual intervention of God involved in the doctrine of occasionalism) to explain the mutual compatibility of the internal activities of the monads. Leibniz thus evaded the antinomies of the continuum by conceiving reality not as an extensive plenum of matter bound by physical relations but as an intensive plenum of force or life bound by a preestablished harmony.

The monads differ in the clarity of their perceptions, for their activity is opposed and their perceptions consequently confused to varying degrees by the *materia prima* with which every created monad is endowed. As with the *materia prima* of dynamics, that of the monads is thus associated with passivity. Only one monad, God, is free of *materia prima* and he alone perceives the world with clarity, that is to say, as it really is.

Physical bodies consist of infinite aggregates of monads. Since such aggregates form only accidental unities, they are not real wholes and consequently, in Leibniz' view, not possessed of real magnitude. It is in this sense that Leibniz denies infinite number while admitting the existence of an actual infinite. When an aggregate has one dominant monad, the aggregate appears as the organic body of this monad. Aggregates without a dominant monad simply appear as *materia secunda*, the matter of dynamics. Bodies as such are therefore conceived by Leibniz simply as phenomena, but in contrast to dreams and similar illusions, well-founded phenomena on account of their consistency. For Leibniz then, the world of extended physical bodies is just a world of appearance, a symbolic representation of the real world of monads.

From this doctrine it follows that the forces involved in dynamics are only accidental, or derivative, as Leibniz terms them. The real active force, or *vis primitiva*, which remains constant in each corporeal substance, corresponds to mind or substantial form. Leibniz does not, however, reintroduce substantial forms as physical causes;[43] for in his view, physical explanations involve a *vis derivativa* or accidental force by which the *vis primitiva* or real principle of action is modified.[44] One monad, having more *vis primitiva*, represents the universe more distinctly than another, a difference that can be expressed by the terms active and passive, though there is, of course, no real interaction. In the world of phenomena, this relation is symbolized in the notion of physical causality. The laws of nature, including the principle of the conservation of *vis viva*, thus have relevance only at the phenomenal level, though they symbolize, on the metaphysical plane, an order manifested through the realization of predicates of individual substances in accordance with the preestablished harmony.

In the early stages of the formulation of his meta-

physics, Leibniz located the unextended substances, that he later called monads, in points.[45] This presupposed a real space in which the monads were embedded, a view that consideration of the nature of substance and the difficulties of the continuum caused him soon to abandon. In his *Système nouveau*,[46] written in 1695, Leibniz described atoms of substance (that is, monads) as metaphysical points, but the mathematical points associated with the space of physics he described as the points of view of the monads. Physical space, Leibniz explains, consists of relations of order between coexistent things.[47] This may be contrasted with the notion of an abstract space, which consists of an assemblage of possible relations between possible existents.[48] For Leibniz then, space is an assemblage of relations between the monads. By locating the points of space in a quality of the monads, namely their points of view, Leibniz makes space entirely dependent on the monads. Space itself, however, is not a property of the monads, for points are not parts of space. In the sense of distance between points, space is a mere ideal thing, the consideration of which, Leibniz remarks, is nevertheless useful.[49] Distances between points are representations of the differences of the points of view of the monads. Owing to the preestablished harmony, these relations are compatible, so that space is a well-founded phenomenon, an extensive representation of an intensive continuum. Similarly time, as the order of noncontemporaneous events,[50] is also a well-founded phenomenon.

Leibniz' objections to the kind of absolute real space and time conceived by Newton are expressed most completely in his correspondence with Clarke. Real space and time, Leibniz argues, would violate the principle of sufficient reason and the principle of the identity of indiscernibles. For example, a rotation of the whole universe in an absolute space would leave the arrangement of bodies among themselves unchanged, but no sufficient reason could be found why God should have placed the whole universe in one of these positions rather than the other. Again, if time were absolute, no reason could be found why God should have created the universe at one time rather than another.[51]

From the ideal nature of space and time, it follows that motion, in the physical sense, is also ideal and therefore relative.[52] Against Newton, Leibniz maintains the relativity not only of rectilinear motion but also of rotation.[53] Yet Leibniz is willing to admit that there is a difference between what he calls an absolute real motion of a body and a mere change in its position relative to other bodies. For it is the body in which the cause of motion (that is, the active force) resides that is truly in motion.[54] Now it is evidently the *vis primitiva* that Leibniz has in mind, since consideration of the *vis derivativa (conatus* or *vis viva)* does not serve to identify an absolute motion, so that we may interpret Leibniz as saying that true absolute motion appertains to the metaphysical plane, where it can be perceived only by God. Indeed all bodies have an absolute motion in this sense, for since all monads have activity, all aggregates have *vis viva*. The world of phenomena is therefore conceived by Leibniz as a world of bodies in absolute motion (rest being a mere abstraction) but a world in which only relative changes of position can be observed.

The theory of monads may be seen as a sustained effort to present, in "cosmological" completeness, a systematic unified structure of knowledge on the basis of a logical reconstruction of the concept of substance. Insofar as the central assertion, namely, that because there are composite "substances," there must be simple substances, is not only a cosmological and metaphysical statement, but in addition, an assertion of the priority of synthetic over analytic procedures, his efforts retain their original methodological meaning. As revealed in his plan for a *characteristica universalis*, analysis, for Leibniz, implies synthesis, but a synthesis that must begin with irreducible elements. Where there are no such elements, neither analysis nor synthesis is possible within the framework of Leibniz' constructive methodology. This means that Leibniz, in the course of his protracted efforts to define an individual substance, moved from physical atomism to logical atomism in the modern sense, as represented by Russell. Leibniz believed that he had proved the thesis of an unambiguously defined world, in which the physico-theological theme running through the mechanistic philosophy of his age might once again be seen as a metaphysics in the classical sense.

Influence. The thought of Leibniz influenced the history of philosophy and science in two ways; first, through the mediocre systematization of Christian Wolff known as the "Leibnizo-Wolffian" philosophy, and secondly, through the significance of particular theories in the history of various sciences. While the tradition of the Leibnizo-Wolffian philosophy ended with Kant, the influence of particular theories of Leibniz lasted through the nineteenth and into the twentieth century.

The controversy with Newton and Clarke was not conducive to the reception of Leibniz' work in physics and hindered the objective evaluation of important contributions such as his law of radial acceleration. The *vis viva* controversy arose as a direct result of Leibniz' criticism of Descartes and concerned not only the measure of force but also the nature of force itself. While 'sGravesande and d'Alembert (in his *Traité de mécanique*) judged the dispute to be merely a semantic argument, Kant in 1747 *(Gedanken von der wahren Schätzung der lebendigen Kräfte)* made an ineffective attempt at reconciliation. Leibnizian dynamics was developed further by Bošković, who transformed the concept of dynamic force in the direction of a concept of relational force.

Within the framework of rational physics, Kant contributed some essential improvements, such as the completion of the distinction between necessary and contingent propositions by means of the concept of the synthetic *a priori* and clarification of the principle of causality. Leibniz' protophysical plan, however, remained intact. It was continued later by Whewell, Clifford, Mach, and Dingler, to mention only a few. Insofar as the fundamental concepts of space and time were concerned, the Newtonian ideas of absolute space and time at first prevailed over the Leibnizian ideas of relational space and time. Kant also tried here to mediate between the ideas of Leibniz and Newton, but his own suggestion (space as the origin of the distinction between a nonreflexible figure and its mirror image, such as a pair of gloves) strongly resembled the Newtonian concept of absolute space. Modern relativistic physics has turned the scales in favor of the ideas of Leibniz.

Among the methodological principles of Leibniz, only the principle of sufficient reason has played a prominent role in the history of philosophy. Wolff, disregarding Leibniz' methodological intentions, tried to prove it by ontological means *(Philosophia sive ontologia);* Kant reduced it essentially to the law of causality and in 1813 Schopenhauer drew on it for the elucidation of his four conditions of verification *(Über die vierfache Wurzel des Satzes vom zureichenden Grunde)*. On the other hand, the methodological project of a *characteristica universalis* together with the ensuing development of logical calculi has played a most significant role in the history of modern logic. In 1896 Frege, recalling Leibniz, described his *Begriffsschrift* of 1879 as a *lingua characterica* (not just a *calculus ratiocinator*), thus distinguishing it from the parallel efforts of Boole and Peano. De Morgan and Boole tried to carry out what Scholz has described as the "Leibniz program" of the development of a logical algebra of classes. This connection between logic and mathematics, evident also in Peirce and Schröder, was once again weakened by Frege, Peano, and Russell, whose work (especially that of Frege) nevertheless bears the inescapable influence of Leibniz; for even where the differences are greatest, the development of modern logic can be traced back to Leibniz. In this connection, it is fortunate that (in the absence of any publications of Leibniz) there is a tradition of correspondence beginning with letters between Leibniz, Oldenburg, and Tschirnhaus. The emphasis here, as exemplified in the logic theories of Ploucquet, Lambert, and Castillon, is on the intensional interpretation of logical calculi.

While there is an affinity between the theory of monads and Russell's logical atomism, a direct influence of the more metaphysical parts of the theory of monads on the history of scientific thought is difficult to prove. Particular results, such as the biological concept of preformation (accepted by Haller, Bonnet, and Spallanzani) or the discovery of sensory thresholds, though related to the theory of monads in a systematic way, became detached from it and followed their own lines of development. Yet the term "monad" played an important role with Wolff, Baumgarten, Crusius, and, at the beginning, with Kant (as exemplified in his *Monadologica physica* of 1756), then later with Goethe and Solger as well. Vitalism in its various forms, including the "biological romanticism" of the nineteenth century (the Schelling school), embraced in general the biological interpretation of the theory of monads, but this did not amount to a revival of the metaphysical theory. It is more likely that vitalism simply represented a reaction against mechanism, a tradition to which Leibniz also belonged.

NOTES

1. Duns Scotus, *Questiones super universalibus Porphyrii* (Venice, 1512), Quest. 3.
2. L. Couturat, ed., *Opuscules et fragments inédits de Leibniz* (Paris, 1903; Hildesheim, 1966), p. 594.
3. G. W. Leibniz, *Sämtliche Schriften und Briefe*, VI, 2, pp. 258–276.
4. T. Hobbes, *Elementorum philosophiae* (London, 1655), sectio prima: de corpore, pars tertia, cap. 15, §2 and §3.
5. *Sämtliche Schriften und Briefe*, VI, 2, p. 264.
6. *Ibid.*, p. 266.
7. *Ibid.*, p. 231.
8. *Ibid.*, pp. 221–257.
9. *Ibid.*, p. 257.
10. *Sämtliche Schriften und Briefe*, II, 1, p. 172.
11. *Ibid.*, pp. 488–490.
12. G. W. Leibniz, *Die philosophischen Schriften*, C. I. Gerhardt, ed., IV, p. 444; cf. p. 369.
13. *Sämtliche Schriften und Briefe*, II, 1, p. 508.
14. P. Costabel, *Leibniz et la dynamique* (Paris, 1960), p. 106.
15. G. W. Leibniz, *Mathematische Schriften*, C. I. Gerhardt, ed., VI, pp. 230–231. The manuscript called *Essay de dynamique* by Gerhardt is not earlier than 1698.
16. P. Costabel, *op. cit.*, p. 105.
17. *Ibid.*, p. 12.
18. *Sämtliche Schriften und Briefe*, VI, 6, p. 487.
19. L. Couturat, *op. cit.*, p. 430.
20. *Die philosophischen Schriften*, VII, p. 32.
21. *Principia mathematica*, *3. 47.
22. *Die philosophischen Schriften*, VII, pp. 228–247. Cf. L. Couturat, *op. cit.*, pp. 246–270.
23. *Sämtliche Schriften und Briefe*, VI, 1, p. 183.
24. *Die philosophischen Schriften*, VII, p. 301.
25. *Ibid.*, IV, pp. 447–448.
26. *Ibid.*, VII, pp. 270–279.
27. *G. W. Leibniz, Textes inédits*, G. Grua, ed. (Paris, 1948), I, p. 287.
28. *Die philosophischen Schriften*, VII, p. 309. Cf. L. Couturat, *op. cit.*, p. 525.
29. L. Couturat, *op. cit.*, p. 515.
30. *Sämtliche Schriften und Briefe*, VI, 6, p. 230.
31. *Die philosophischen Schriften*, VII, p. 219.
32. *Ibid.*, IV, p. 469.
33. *Ibid.*, III, p. 645.
34. *Ibid.*, IV, p. 447.
35. *Mathematische Schriften*, VII, p. 326.
36. *Die philosophischen Schriften*, II, p. 97.
37. Nicholas of Cusa, *De docta ignorantia*, Bk. II, ch. 7.
38. *Die philosophischen Schriften*, II, p. 304.
39. *Ibid.*, IV, p. 483.
40. *Principes de la nature et de la grâce*, A. Robinet, ed., p. 27.
41. *Discours de métaphysique*, G. le Roy, ed., p. 50.
42. *Die philosophischen Schriften*, I, p. 416.
43. *Ibid.*, II, p. 58.
44. *Mathematische Schriften*, VI, p. 236.
45. *Die philosophischen Schriften*, II, p. 372.
46. *Ibid.*, IV, p. 482.
47. *Ibid.*, IV, p. 491. Cf. II, p. 450.
48. *Ibid.*, VII, p. 415.
49. *Ibid.*, VII, p. 401.
50. *Mathematische Schriften*, VII, p. 18.
51. *Die philosophischen Schriften*, VII, p. 364.
52. *Ibid.*, II, p. 270. Cf. *Mathematische Schriften*, VI, p. 247.
53. *Mathematische Schriften*, II, p. 184.
54. *Die philosophischen Schriften*, VII, p. 404. Cf. IV, p. 444 and L. Couturat, *op. cit.*, p. 594.

JÜRGEN MITTELSTRASS
ERIC J. AITON

LEIBNIZ: Mathematics

Leibniz had learned simple computation and a little geometry in his elementary studies and in secondary schools, but his interest in mathematics was aroused by the numerous remarks on the importance of the subject that he encountered in his reading of philosophical works. In Leipzig, John Kuhn's lectures on Euclid left him unsatisfied, whereas he received some stimulation from Erhard Weigel in Jena. During his student years, he had also cursorily read introductory works on Cossist algebra and the *Deliciae physico-mathematicae* of Daniel Schwenter and Philipp Harsdörffer (1636–1653) with their varied and mainly practical content. At this stage Leibniz considered himself acquainted with all the essential areas of mathematics that he needed for his studies in logic, which attracted him much more strongly. The very modest specialized knowledge that he then possessed is reflected in the *Dissertatio de arte combinatoria*

(1666); several additions are presented in the *Hypothesis physica nova* (1671).

In accord with the encyclopedic approach popular at the time, Leibniz limited himself primarily to methods and results and considered demonstrations nonessential and unimportant. His effort to mechanize computation led him to work on a calculating machine which would perform all four fundamental operations of arithmetic.

Leibniz was occupied with diplomatic tasks in Paris from the spring of 1672, but he continued the studies (begun in 1666) on the arithmetic triangle which had appeared on the title page of Apianus' *Arithmetic* (1527) and which was well known in the sixteenth century; Leibniz was still unaware, however, of Pascal's treatise of 1665. He also studied the array of differences of the number sequences, and discovered both fundamental rules of the calculus of finite differences of sequences with a finite number of members. He revealed this in conversation with Huygens, who challenged his visitor to produce the summation of reciprocal triangular numbers and, therefore, of a sequence with infinitely many members. Leibniz succeeded in this task at the end of 1672 and summed further sequences of reciprocal polygonal numbers and, following the work of Grégoire de St.-Vincent (1647), the geometric sequence, through transition to the difference sequence.

As a member of a delegation from Mainz, Leibniz traveled to London in the spring of 1673 to take part in the unsuccessful peace negotiations between England, France, and the Netherlands. He was received by Oldenburg at the Royal Society, where he demonstrated an unfinished model of his calculating machine. Through Robert Boyle he met John Pell, who was familiar with the entire algebraic literature of the time. Pell discussed with Leibniz his successes in calculus of differences and immediately referred him to several relevant works of which Leibniz was not aware—including Mercator's *Logarithmotechnia* (1668), in which the logarithmic series is determined through prior division, and Barrow's *Lectiones opticae* (1669) and *Lectiones geometricae* (1670). (Barrow's works were published in 1672 under the single title *Lectiones opticae et geometricae.*)

Leibniz became a member of the Royal Society upon application, but he had seriously damaged his scientific reputation through thoughtless pronouncements on the array of differences, and still more through his rash promise of soon producing a working model of the calculating machine. Leibniz could not fully develop the calculator's principle of design until 1674, by which time he could take advantage of the invention of direct drive, the tachometer, and the stepped drum.

Through Oldenburg, Leibniz received hints, phrased in general terms, of Newton's and Gregory's results in infinitesimal mathematics; but he was still a novice and therefore could not comprehend the significance of what had been communicated to him. Huygens referred him to the relevant literature on infinitesimals in mathematics and Leibniz became passionately interested in the subject. Following the lead of Pascal's *Lettres de "A. Delonville"* [= *Pascal*] *contenant quelques unes de ses inventions de géométrie* (1659), by 1673 he had mastered the characteristic triangle and had found, by means of a transmutation—that is, of the integral transformation, discovered through affine geometry,

$$\frac{1}{2} \int_0^x \left[y(\bar{x}) - x \frac{dy}{dx}(\bar{x}) \right] \cdot d\bar{x},$$

for the determination of a segment of a plane curve—a method developed on a purely geometrical basis by means of which he could uniformly derive all the previously stated theorems on quadratures.

Leibniz' most important new result, which he communicated in 1674 to Huygens, Oldenburg, and his friends in Paris, were the arithmetical quadrature of the circle, including the arc tangent series, which had been achieved in a manner corresponding to Mercator's series division, and the elementary quadrature of a cycloidal segment (presented in print in 1678 in a form that concealed the method). Referred by Jacques Ozanam to problems of indeterminate analysis that can be solved algebraically, Leibniz also achieved success in this area by simplifying methods, as in the essay on

$$x + y + z = p^2, \; x^2 + y^2 + z^2 = q^4$$

(to be solved in natural numbers). Furthermore, a casual note indicates that at this time he was already concerned with dyadic arithmetic.

The announcement of new publications on algebra provoked Leibniz to undertake a thorough review of the pertinent technical literature, in particular the Latin translation of Descartes's *Géométrie* (1637), published by Frans van Schooten (1659–1661) with commentaries and further studies written by Descartes's followers.

His efforts culminated in four results obtained in 1675: a more suitable manner of expressing the indices (*ik* in lieu of a_{ik}, for instance); the determination of symmetric functions and especially of sums of powers of the solutions of algebraic equations; the construction of equations of higher degree that can be represented by means of compound radicals; and ingenious attempts to solve higher equations algorithmically by means of radicals, attempts that were not recognized as fruitless because of the computational difficulties involved. On the other hand, Leibniz succeeded in demonstrating the universal validity of Cardano's formulas for solving cubic equations even when three real solutions are present and in establishing that in this case the imaginary cannot be dispensed with. The generality of these results had been frequently doubted because of the influence of Descartes. Through this work Leibniz concluded that the sum of conjugate complex expressions is always real (cf. the well-known example $\sqrt{1 + \sqrt{-3}} + \sqrt{1 - \sqrt{-3}} = \sqrt{6}$). The theorem named for de Moivre later proved this conclusion to be correct.

In the fall of 1675 Leibniz was visited by Tschirnhaus, who, while studying Descartes's methods (which he greatly overrated), had acquired considerable skill in algebraic computation. His virtuosity aroused admiration in London, yet it did not transcend the formal and led to a mistaken judgment of the new results achieved by Newton and Gregory. Tschirnhaus and Leibniz became friends and together went through the unpublished scientific papers of Descartes, Pascal, and other French mathematicians. The joint studies that emerged from this undertaking dealt with the array of differences and with the "harmonic" sequence $\cdots$, 1/5, 1/4, 1/3, 1/2, 1/1 and was treated by Leibniz as the counterpart of the arithmetic triangle. They then considered the succession of the prime numbers and presented a beautiful geometric interpretation of the sieve of Eratosthenes—which, however, cannot be recognized from the remark printed in 1678 that the prime numbers greater than three must be chosen from the numbers $6n \pm 1$.

When Roberval died in 1675 Leibniz hoped to succeed him in the professorship of mathematics established by Pierre de la Ramée at the Collège de France and also to become a member of the Académie des Sciences. Earlier in 1675 he had demonstrated at the Academy the improved model of his calculating machine and had referred to an unusual kind of chronometer. He was rejected in both cases because his negligence had cost him the favor of his patrons. Nevertheless, his thorough, critical study of earlier mathematical writings resulted in important advances, especially in the field of infinitesimals. He recognized the transcendence of the circular and logarithmic functions, the basic properties of the logarithmic and other transcendental curves, and the correspondence between the quadrature of the circle and the quadrature of the hyperbola. In addition, he considered questions of probability.

In the late autumn of 1675, seeking a better understanding of Cavalieri's quadrature methods (1635),

Leibniz made his greatest discovery: the symbolic characterization of limiting processes by means of the calculus. To be sure, "not a single previously unsolved problem was solved" by this discovery (Newton's disparaging judgment in the priority dispute); yet it set out the procedure to be followed in a suggestive, efficient, abstract form and permitted the characterization and classification of the applicable computational steps. In connection with the arrangement in undetermined coefficients, Leibniz sought to clarify the conditions under which an algebraic function can be integrated algebraically. In addition he solved important differential equations: for example, the tractrix problem, proposed to him by Perrault, and Debeaune's problem (1638), which he knew from Descartes's *Lettres* (III, 1667); and which required the curve through the origin determined by

$$\frac{dy}{dx} = \frac{x - y}{a}.$$

He established that not every differential equation can be solved exclusively through the use of quadratures and was immediately cognizant of the far-reaching importance of symbolism and technical terminology.

Leibniz only hinted at his new discovery in vague remarks, as in letters to Oldenburg in which he requested details of the methods employed by Newton and Gregory. He received some results in reply, especially concerning power series expansions—which were obviously distorted through gross errors in copying—but nothing of fundamental significance (Newton's letters to Leibniz of June and October 1676, with further information on Gregory and Pell supplied by Oldenburg). Leibniz explained the new discovery to him personally, but Tschirnhaus was more precisely informed. He did not listen attentively, was troubled by the unfamiliar terminology and symbols, and thus never achieved a deeper understanding of Leibnizian analysis. Tschirnhaus also had the advantage of knowing the answer, written in great haste, to Newton's first letter, where Leibniz referred to the solution of Debeaune's problem (as an example of a differential equation that can be integrated in a closed form) and hinted at the principle of *vis viva*. Leibniz also included the essential elements of the arithmetical quadrature of the circle; yet it was derived not by means of the general transmutation but, rather, through a more special one of narrower virtue. Tschirnhaus did not know that the preliminary draft of this letter contained an example of the method of series expansion through gradual integration (later named for Cauchy [1844] and Picard [1890]) and, in any case, he would not have been able to understand and fully appreciate it. On the other hand, he did see and approve the definitive manuscript (1676) on the arithmetical quadrature of the circle. This work also contains the proof by convergence of an alternating sequence with members decreasing without limit; the rigorous treatment of transmutation and its application to the quadrature of higher parabolas and hyperbolas; the logarithmic series and its counterpart, the arc tangent series, and its numerical representation of $\frac{\pi}{4}$ (Leibniz series); and the representation of $\frac{ln\,2}{4}$ and $\frac{\pi}{8}$ through omission of members of the series

$$\sum_{n=2}^{\infty} \frac{1}{(n-1)(n+1)} = \frac{3}{4}.$$

The planned publication did not occur and subsequently the paper was superseded by Leibniz' own work as well as by that of others, particularly the two Bernoullis and L'Hospital.

Since there was no possibility of obtaining a sufficiently remunerative post in Paris, Leibniz entered the service of Hannover in the fall of 1676. He traveled first to London, where he sought out Oldenburg and the latter's mathematical authority, John Collins. He presented them with papers on algebra, which Collins transcribed and which were transmitted to Newton. A longer discussion with Collins was devoted primarily to algebraic questions although dyadics were also touched upon. Leibniz also made excerpts from Newton's letters and from the manuscript of his *De analysi per aequationes numero terminorum infinitas* (1669), which had been deposited with the Royal Society, and from the extracts procured by Collins of letters and papers of Gregory, only a small selection of which Leibniz had obtained earlier. He then went to Amsterdam, where he called on Hudde, who informed him of his own mathematical works.

In the intellectually limited atmosphere of Hannover there was no possibility of serious mathematical discussion. His talks with the Cartesian A. Eckhardt (1678–1679) on Pythagorean triangles with square measures and related questions were unsatisfying. The correspondence with Oldenburg provided an opportunity, in the early summer of 1677, to communicate the determination of tangents according to the method of the differential calculus, but this exchange ended in the autumn with Oldenburg's death. Huygens was ill and Tschirnhaus was traveling in Italy. Thus, in the midst of his multitudinous duties at court, Leibniz lacked the external stimulus needed to continue his previous studies on a large scale. Instead, he concentrated on symbological investigations, his first detailed draft in dyadics, and studies

on pure geometric representation of positional relations without calculation, the counterpart to analytic geometry. Only after the founding of the *Acta eruditorum* (1682) did Leibniz present his mathematical papers to the public. In 1682 he published "De vera proportione circuli ad quadratum circumscriptum in numeris rationalibus" and "Unicum opticae, catoptricae et dioptricae principium," concise summaries of the chief results of the arithmetical quadrature of the circle and a hint regarding the derivation of the law of refraction by means of the extreme value method of the differential calculus. These revelations were followed in 1684 by the method of determining algebraic integrals of algebraic functions, a brief presentation of the differential calculus with a hint concerning the solution of Debeaune's problem by means of the logarithmic curve, and further remarks on the fundamental ideas of the integral calculus.

In 1686 Leibniz published the main concepts of the proof of the transcendental nature of $\int \sqrt{a^2 \pm x^2} \cdot dx$ and an example of integration, the first appearance in print of the integral sign (the initial letter of the word *summa*).

Yet Leibniz did not attract general attention until his public attack on Cartesian dynamics (1686–1688) by reference to the principle of the conservation of *vis viva*, with the dimensions mv^2. In the subsequent controversy with the Cartesians, Leibniz put forth for solution a dynamic problem that was also considered by Huygens (1687) and Jakob Bernoulli (1690): Under what conditions does a point moving without friction in a parallel gravitational field descend with uniform velocity? In this connection, Bernoulli raised the problem of the catenary, which was solved almost simultaneously by Leibniz, Huygens, and Johann Bernoulli (published 1691) and which introduced for debate a series of further subjects of increasing difficulty, stemming primarily from applied dynamics. Two are particularly noteworthy: The first was the determination, requested by Leibniz in 1689, of the isochrona paracentrica. Under what conditions does a point moving without friction under constant gravity revolve with uniform velocity about a fixed point? This problem was solved by Leibniz, Jakob Bernoulli, and Johann Bernoulli (1694). The second was the determination, requested by Johann Bernoulli, of the conditions under which a point moving without friction in a parallel gravitational field descends in the shortest possible time from one given point to another given point below it. This problem, called the brachistochrone, was solved in 1697 by Leibniz, Newton, Jakob Bernoulli, and Johann Bernoulli.

The participants in these investigations revealed only their results, not their derivations. The latter are found, in the case of Leibniz, in the posthumous papers or, in certain instances, in the letters exchanged with Jakob Bernoulli (from 1687), Rudolf Christian von Bodenhausen (from 1690), L'Hospital (from 1692), and Johann Bernoulli (from 1693). These letters, like the papers on pure mathematics that Leibniz published in the scientific journals, were usually hastily written in his few free hours. They were not always well edited and are far from being free of errors. Yet, despite their imperfections, they are extraordinarily rich in ideas. In part the letters were written to communicate original ideas, which were only occasionally pursued later; most of them, however, are drawn from earlier papers or brief notes. The following ideas in the correspondence should be specially mentioned:

(a) The determination of the center of curvature for a point of a curve as the intersection of two adjacent normals (1686–1692). Leibniz erroneously assumed that the circle of curvature has, in general, four neighboring points (instead of three) in common with the curve. It was only after some years that he understood, through the detailed explanation of Johann Bernoulli, the objections made by Jakob Bernoulli (from 1692). He immediately admitted his error publicly and candidly, as was his custom (1695–1696).

(b) The determination of that reflecting curve in the plane by which a given reflecting curve is completed in such a way that the rays of light coming from a given point are rejoined, after reflection in both curves, in another given point (1689).

(c) A detailed presentation of the results of the arithmetical quadrature of the circle and of the hyperbola, combined with communication of the power series for the arc tangent, the cosine, the sine, the natural logarithm, and the exponential function (1691).

(d) The theory of envelopes, illustrated with examples (1692, 1694).

(e) The treatment of differential equations through arrangement in undetermined coefficients (1693).

(f) The determination of the tractrix for a straight path and, following this, a mechanical construction of the integral curves of differential equations (1693), the earliest example of an integraph.

In 1694 Leibniz expressed his intention to present his own contributions and those of other contemporary mathematicians uniformly and comprehensively in a large work to be entitled *Scientia infiniti*. By 1696 Jakob Bernoulli had provided him with some of his own work and Leibniz had composed headings

for earlier notes and selected some essential passages, but he did not get beyond this preliminary, unorganized collection of material. Much of his time was now taken up defending his ideas. Nieuwentijt, for example (1694–1696), questioned the admissibility and use of higher differentials. In his defense, Leibniz emphasized that his method should be considered only an abbreviated and easily grasped guide and that everything could be confirmed by strict deductions in the style of Archimedes (1695). On this occasion he revealed the differentiation of exponential functions such as x^x, which he had long known.

Even the originality of Leibniz' method was called into doubt. Hence, in 1691, Jakob Bernoulli, who was interested primarily in results and not in general concepts, saw in Leibniz' differential calculus only a mathematical reproduction of what Barrow had presented in a purely geometrical fashion in his *Lectiones geometricae*. He also failed to realize the general significance of the symbolism. In England it was observed with growing uneasiness that Leibniz was becoming increasingly the leader of a small but very active group of mathematicians. Moreover, the English deplored the lack of any public indication that Leibniz—as Newton supposed—had taken crucial suggestions from the two great letters of 1676. Representative material from these letters was in Wallis' *Algebra* (1685), and it was expanded in the Latin version (Wallis' *Opera*, II [1693]). Fatio de Duillier, who shortly before had seen copies of Newton's letters and other unpublished writings on methods of quadrature (1676), became convinced that in the treatment of questions in the mathematics of infinitesimals Newton had advanced far beyond Leibniz and that the latter was dependent on Newton. Since 1687 Fatio had been working with Huygens, who did not think much of Leibniz' symbolism, on the treatment of "inverse" tangent problems—differential equations—and in simple cases had achieved a methodical application of integrating factors.

In the preface to Volume I of Wallis' *Opera*, which did not appear until 1695, it is stated that the priority for the infinitesimal methods belongs to Newton. Furthermore, the words are so chosen that it could have been—and in fact was—inferred that Leibniz plagiarized Newton. Wallis, in his concern for the proper recognition of Newton's merits, was unceasing in his efforts to persuade Newton to publish his works on this subject. Beyond this, he obtained copies of several of the letters exchanged between Leibniz and Oldenburg in the years 1673 to 1677 and received permission from Newton and Leibniz to publish the writings in question. He included them in Volume III of his *Opera* (1699). The collection he assembled was based not on the largely inaccessible originals but, rather, on copies in which crucial passages were abbreviated. As a result, it was possible for the reader to gain the impression that Newton possessed priority in having obtained decisive results in the field of infinitesimals (method of tangents, power series in the handling of quadratures, and inverse tangent problems) and that Leibniz was guilty of plagiarism on the basis of what he had taken from Newton. Fatio pronounced this reproach in the sharpest terms in his *Lineae brevissimi descensus investigatio* (1699).

Leibniz replied in 1700 with a vigorous defense of his position, in which he stressed that he had obtained only results, not methods, from Newton and that he had already published the fundamental concepts of the differential calculus in 1684, three years before the appearance of the material that Newton referred to in a similar form in his *Principia* (1687). On this occasion he also described his own procedure with reference to de Moivre's theorem (1698) on series inversion through the use of undetermined coefficients. Leibniz made his procedure more general and easier to grasp by the introduction of numerical coefficients (in the sense of indices). The attack subsided because Fatio, who was excitable, oversensitive, and given to a coarse manner of expression, turned away from science and became a fervent adherent of an aggressive religious sect. He was eventually pilloried.

Wallis' insinuations were repeated by G. Cheyne in his *Methodus* (1703) and temperately yet firmly rebutted in Leibniz' review of 1703. Cheyne's discussion of special quadratures was probably what led Newton to publish the *Quadratura curvarum* (manuscript of 1676) and the *Enumeratio linearum tertii ordinis* (studies beginning in 1667–1668) as appendices to the *Optics* (1704). Newton viewed certain passages of Leibniz' review of the *Optics* (1705) as abusive attacks and gave additional material to John Keill, who, in a paper published in 1710, publicly accused Leibniz of plagiarism. Leibniz' protests (1711) led to the establishment of a commission of the Royal Society, which decided against him (1712) on the basis of the letters printed by Wallis and further earlier writings produced by Newton. The commission published the evidence, together with an analysis that had been published in 1711, in a *Commercium epistolicum* (1713 edition).

The verdict reached by these biased investigators, who heard no testimony from Leibniz and only superficially examined the available data, was accepted without question for some 140 years and was influential into the first half of the twentieth century. In the light of the much more extensive material now available, it is recognized as wrong. It can be understood only in the nationalistic context in which the controversy took place. The continuation of the quarrel was an embarrassment to both parties; and, since it yielded nothing new scientifically, it is unimportant for an understanding of Leibniz' mathematics. The intended rebuttal did not materialize, and Leibniz' interesting, but fragmentary, account of how he arrived at his discovery (*Historia et origo calculi differentialis* [1714]) was not published until the nineteenth century.

The hints concerning mathematical topics in Leibniz' correspondence are especially fascinating. When writing to those experienced in mathematics, whom he viewed as competitors, he expressed himself very cautiously, yet with such extraordinary cleverness that his words imply far more than is apparent from an examination of the notes and jottings preserved in his papers. For instance, his remarks on the solvability of higher equations are actually an anticipation of Galois's theory. Frequently, material of general validity is illustrated only by simple examples, as is the case with the schematic solution of systems of linear equations by means of number couples (double indices) in quadratic arrangement, which corresponds to the determinant form (1693).

In several places the metaphysical background is very much in evidence, as in the working out of binary numeration, which Leibniz connected with the creation of the world (indicated by 1) from nothingness (indicated by 0). The same is true of his interpretation of the imaginary number as an intermediate entity between Being and Not-Being (1702). His hope of being able to make a statement about the transcendence of π by employing the dyadic presentation (1701) was fruitless yet interesting, for transcendental numbers can be constructed out of infinite dual fractions possessing regular gaps (an example in the decimal system was given by Goldbach in 1729). The attempts to present $\sum_{n=1}^{r} \frac{1}{n}$ (reference in 1682, recognized as false in 1696) and $\sum_{n=1}^{\infty} \frac{1}{n^2}$ (1696) in closed form were unsuccessful, and the claimed rectification of an arc of the equilateral hyperbola through the quadrature of the hyperbola (1676) was based on an error in computation. Against these failures we may set the importance of the recognition of the correspondence between the multinomial theorem (1676) and the continuous differentiation and integration with fractional index that emerged from this observation. During this period (about 1696) Leibniz also achieved the general representation of partial differentiation; the reduction of the differential equation

$$a_{00} + a_{10}x + (a_{01} + a_{11}x)y' = 0$$

by means of the transformation

$$x = p_{11}u + p_{12}v, \; y = p_{21}u + p_{22}v;$$

the solution of

$$y' + p(x)y + q(x) = 0$$

and

$$(y')^2 + p(x)y' + q(x) = 0$$

through series with coefficients in number couples; and the reduction of the equation, which had originated with Jakob Bernoulli,

$$y' = p(x)y + q(x)y^n$$

to

$$y' = P(x)y + Q(x).$$

Leibniz' inventive powers and productivity in mathematics did not begin to slow until around 1700. The integration of rational functions (1702–1703) was, to be sure, an important accomplishment; but the subject was not completely explored, since Leibniz supposed (Johann Bernoulli to the contrary) that there existed other imaginary units besides $\sqrt{-1}$ (for example, $\sqrt[4]{-1}$) which could not be represented by ordinary complex numbers. The subsequent study, which was not published at the time, on the integration of special classes of irrational functions also remains of great interest. The discussion with Johann Bernoulli on the determination of arclike algebraic curves in the plane (1704–1706) resulted in both a consideration of relative motions in the plane and an interesting geometric construction of the arclike curve equivalent to a given curve. This construction is related to the optical essay of 1689 and to the theory of envelopes of 1692–1694, but it cannot readily be grasped in terms of a formula (1706). The remarks (1712) on the logarithms of negative numbers and on the representation of $\sum(-1)^n$ by $1/2$ can no longer be considered satisfactory. The description of the calculating machine (1710) indicates its importance but does not give the important details; the first machines of practical application were constructed by P. M. Hahn in 1774 on the basis of Leibniz' ideas.

Leibniz accorded a great importance to mathematics because of its broad interest and numerous applications. The extent of his concern with mathematics is evident from the countless remarks and notes in his posthumous papers, only small portions of which have been accessible in print until now, as well as from the exceedingly challenging and suggestive influential comments expressed brilliantly in the letters and in the works published in his own lifetime.

Leibniz' power lay primarily in his great ability to distinguish the essential elements in the results of others, which were often rambling and presented in a manner that was difficult to understand. He put them in a new form, and by setting them in a larger context made them into a harmoniously balanced and comprehensive whole. This was possible only because in his reading Leibniz was prepared, despite his impatience, to immerse himself enthusiastically and selflessly in the thought of others. He was concerned with formulating authoritative ideas clearly and connecting them, as he did in so exemplary a fashion in the mathematics of infinitesimals. Interesting details were important—they occur often in his notes—but even more important were inner relationships and their comprehension, as this term is employed in the history of thought. He undertook the work required by such an approach for no other purpose than the exploration of the conditions under which new ideas emerge, stimulate each other, and are joined in a unified thought structure.

JOSEPH E. HOFMANN

BIBLIOGRAPHY

I. ORIGINAL WORKS. The following volumes of the *Sämtliche Schriften und Briefe*, edited by the Deutsche Akademie der Wissenschaften in Berlin, have been published: Series I (*Allgemeiner politischer und historischer Briefwechsel*), vol. 1: 1668–1676 (1923; Hildesheim, 1970); vol. 2: 1676–1679 (1927; Hildesheim, 1970); vol. 3: 1680–1683 (1938; Hildesheim, 1970); vol. 4: 1684–1687 (1950); vol. 5: 1687–1690 (1954; Hildesheim, 1970); vol. 6: 1690–1691 (1957; Hildesheim, 1970); vol. 7: 1691–1692 (1964); vol. 8: 1692 (1970); Series II (*Philosophischer Briefwechsel*), vol. 1: 1663–1685 (1926); Series IV (*Politische Schriften*), vol. 1: 1667–1676 (1931); vol. 2: 1677–1687 (1963); Series VI (*Philosophische Schriften*), vol. 1: 1663–1672 (1930); vol. 2: 1663–1672 (1966); vol. 6: *Nouveaux essais* (1962).

Until publication of the *Sämtliche Schriften und Briefe* is completed, it is necessary to use earlier editions and recent partial editions. The most important of these editions are the following (the larger editions are cited first): L. Dutens, ed., *G. W. Leibnitii opera omnia*, 6 vols. (Geneva, 1768); J. E. Erdmann, ed., *G. W. Leibniz. Opera philosophica quae extant latina gallica germanica omnia* (Berlin, 1840; Aalen, 1959); G. H. Pertz, ed., *G. W. Leibniz. Gesammelte Werke*, Part I: *Geschichte*, 4 vols. (Hannover,

1843–1847; Hildesheim, 1966); A. Foucher de Careil, ed., *Leibniz. Oeuvres*, 7 vols. (Paris, 1859–1875; Hildesheim, 1969); C. I. Gerhardt, ed., *G. W. Leibniz. Mathematische Schriften*, 7 vols. (Berlin–Halle, 1849–1863; Hildesheim, 1962). An index to the edition has been compiled by J. E. Hofmann (Hildesheim, 1971); C. I. Gerhardt, ed., *Die philosophischen Schriften von G. W. Leibniz*, 7 vols. (Berlin, 1875–1890; Hildesheim, 1960–1961); G. E. Guhrauer, ed., *G. W. Leibniz. Deutsche Schriften*, 2 vols. (Berlin, 1838–1840; Hildesheim, 1966); J. G. Eckhart, ed., *G. W. Leibniz. Collectanea etymologica* (Hannover, 1717; Hildesheim, 1970); A. Foucher de Careil, ed., *Lettres et opuscules inédits de Leibniz* (Paris, 1854; Hildesheim, 1971); A. Foucher de Careil, ed., *Nouvelles lettres et opuscules inédits de Leibniz* (Paris, 1857; Hildesheim, 1971); C. Haas, ed. and tr., *Theologisches System* (Tübingen, 1860; Hildesheim, 1966); C. L. Grotefend, ed., *Briefwechsel zwischen Leibniz, Arnauld und dem Landgrafen Ernst von Hessen-Rheinfels* (Hannover, 1846); C. I. Gerhardt, ed., *Briefwechsel zwischen Leibniz und Christian Wolff* (Halle, 1860; Hildesheim, 1963); E. Bodemann, ed., *Die Leibniz-Handschriften der Königlichen öffentlichen Bibliothek zu Hannover* (Hannover, 1889; Hildesheim, 1966); and *Der Briefwechsel des G. W. Leibniz in der Königlichen öffentlichen Bibliothek zu Hannover* (Hannover, 1895; Hildesheim, 1966); C. I. Gerhardt, ed., *Der Briefwechsel von G. W. Leibniz mit Mathematikern* (Berlin, 1899; Hildesheim, 1962); L. Couturat, ed., *Opuscules et fragments inédits de Leibniz* (Paris, 1903; Hildesheim, 1966); E. Gerland, ed., *Leibnizens nachgelassene Schriften physikalischen, mechanischen und technischen Inhalts* (Leipzig, 1906); H. Lestienne, ed., *G. W. Leibniz. Discours de métaphysique* (Paris, 1907, 2nd ed., 1929; Paris, 1952); I. Jagodinskij, ed., *Leibnitiana elementa philosophiae arcanae de summa rerum* (Kazan, 1913); P. Schrecker, ed., *G. W. Leibniz. Lettres et fragments inédits sur les problèmes philosophiques, théologiques, politiques de la réconciliation des doctrines protestantes (1669–1704)* (Paris, 1934); G. Grua, ed., *G. W. Leibniz. Textes inédits*, 2 vols. (Paris, 1948); W. von Engelhardt, ed. and tr., *G. W. Leibniz. Protogaea*, in *Leibniz. Werke* (W. E. Peuckert, ed.), vol. I (Stuttgart, 1949); A. Robinet, ed., *G. W. Leibniz. Principes de la nature et de la grâce fondés en raison. Principes de la philosophie ou monadologie. Publiés intégralement d'après les manuscrits de Hanovre, Vienne et Paris et présentés d'après des lettres inédits* (Paris, 1954); and *Correspondance Leibniz-Clarke. Présentés d'après les manuscrits originales des bibliothèques de Hanovre et de Londres* (Paris, 1957); G. le Roy, ed., *Leibniz. Discours de métaphysique et correspondance avec Arnauld* (Paris, 1957); O. Saame, ed. and tr., *G. W. Leibniz. Confessio philosophi. Ein Dialog* (Frankfurt, 1967); J. Brunschwig, ed., *Essais de Théodicée sur la bonté de Dieu, la liberté de l'homme et l'origine du mal* (Paris, 1969).

There are translations of single works, especially into English and German. English translations (including selections): *Philosophical Works*, G. M. Duncan, ed. and tr. (New Haven, 1890); *The Monadology and Other Philosophical Writings*, R. Latta, ed. and tr. (Oxford, 1898); *New Essays Concerning Human Understanding*, A. G. Langley, ed. and tr. (Chicago, 1916, 1949); *Discourse on Metaphysics*, P. G. Lucas and L. Grint, ed. and tr. (Manchester, 1953; 2nd ed. 1961); *Philosophical Writings*, M. Morris, ed. and tr. (London, 1934, 1968); *Theodicy*, E. M. Huggard and A. Farrer, ed. and tr. (London, 1951); *Selections*, P. P. Wiener, ed. (New York, 1951; 2nd ed. 1971); *Philosophical Papers and Letters*, L. E. Loemker, ed. and tr., 2 vols. (Chicago, 1956; 2nd ed. Dordrecht, 1969); *The Leibniz-Clarke Correspondence*, H. G. Alexander, ed. (Manchester, 1956); *Monadology and Other Philosophical Essays*, P. and A. Schrecker, ed. and tr. (Indianapolis, 1965); *Logical Papers*, G. H. R. Parkinson, ed. and tr. (Oxford, 1966); *The Leibniz-Arnauld Correspondence*, H. T. Mason, ed. and tr. (Manchester–New York, 1967); *General Investigations Concerning the Analysis of Concepts and Truths*, W. H. O'Brian, ed. and tr. (Athens, Ga., 1968).

German translations (including selections) are *Handschriften zur Grundlegung der Philosophie*, E. Cassirer, ed., A. Buchenau, tr., 2 vols. (Hamburg, 1904; 3rd ed. 1966); *Neue Abhandlungen über den menschlichen Verstand*, E. Cassirer, ed. and tr. (3rd ed., 1915; Hamburg, 1971); the same work, edited and translated by H. H. Holz and W. von Engelhardt, 2 vols. (Frankfurt, 1961); *Die Theodizee*, A. Buchenau, ed. and tr. (Hamburg, 2nd ed., 1968); *Schöpferische Vernunft*, W. von Engelhardt, ed. and tr. (Marburg, 1952); *Metaphysische Abhandlung*, H. Herring, ed. and tr. (Hamburg, 1958); *Fragmente zur Logik*, F. Schmidt, ed. and tr. (Berlin, 1960); *Vernunftprinzipien der Natur und der Gnade. Monadologie*, H. Herring, ed., A. Buchenau, tr. (Hamburg, 1960); *Kleine Schriften zur Metaphysik*, H. H. Holz, ed., 2 vols. (Frankfurt–Vienna, 1966–1967).

Bibliographical material on the works of Leibniz and the secondary literature can be found in E. Ravier, *Bibliographie des oeuvres de Leibniz* (Paris, 1937; Hildesheim, 1966), additional material in P. Schrecker, "Une bibliographie de Leibniz," in *Revue philosophique de la France et de l'Étranger*, **126** (1938), 324–346; Albert Rivaud, *Catalogue critique des manuscrits de Leibniz Fasc. II (Mars 1672–Novembre 1676)* (Poitiers, 1914–1924; repr. New York–Hildesheim, 1972); K. Müller, *Leibniz-Bibliographie. Verzeichnis der Literatur über Leibniz* (Frankfurt, 1967). Bibliographical supplements appear regularly in *Studia Leibnitiana. Vierteljahresschrift für Philosophie und Geschichte der Wissenschaften*, K. Müller and W. Totok, eds., **1** (1969); G. Utermöhlen, "Leibniz-Bibliographie 1967–1968," **1** (1969), 293–320; G. Utermöhlen and A. Schmitz, "Leibniz-Bibliographie. Neue Titel 1968–1970," **2** (1970), 302–320; A. Koch-Klose and A. Hölzer, "Leibniz-Bibliographie. Neue Titel 1969–1971," **3** (1971), 309–320.

II. Secondary Literature. The literature on Leibniz' philosophy and science is so extensive that a complete presentation cannot be given. In the following selection, more recent works have been preferred, especially those which may provide additional views on the philosophy and science of Leibniz.

H. Aarsleff, "Leibniz on Locke and Language," in *American Philosophical Quarterly*, **1** (1964), 165–188; E. J. Aiton, "The Harmonic Vortex of Leibniz," in *The Vortex Theory of Planetary Motions* (London–New York, 1972); and "Leibniz on Motion in a Resisting Medium," in *Archive for History of Exact Sciences*, **9** (1972), 257–274; W. H. Barber, *Leibniz in France. From Arnauld to Voltaire* (Oxford, 1955); Y. Belaval, *Leibniz critique de Descartes* (Paris, 1960); and *Leibniz. Initiation à sa philosophie* (Paris, 1962; 3rd ed. 1969); A. Boehm, *Le "vinculum substantiale" chez Leibniz. Ses origines historiques* (Paris, 1938; 2nd ed. 1962); F. Brunner, *Études sur la signification historique de la philosophie de Leibniz* (Paris, 1950); G. Buchdahl, *Metaphysics and the Philosophy of Science. The Classical Origins—Descartes to Kant* (Oxford, 1969); P. Burgelin, *Commentaire du* Discours de métaphysique de Leibniz (Paris, 1959); H. W. Carr, *Leibniz* (London, 1929, 1960); E. Cassirer, *Leibniz' System in seinem wissenschaftlichen Grundlagen* (Marburg, 1902; Darmstadt, 1962); P. Costabel, *Leibniz et la dynamique. Les textes de 1692* (Paris, 1960); L. Couturat, *La logique de Leibniz* (Paris, 1901; Hildesheim, 1961); L. Davillé, *Leibniz historien. Essai sur l'activité et les méthodes historiques de Leibniz* (Paris, 1909); K. Dürr, *Neue Beleuchtung einer Theorie von Leibniz. Grundzüge des Logikkalküls* (Darmstadt, 1930); K. Dürr, "Die mathematische Logik von Leibniz," in *Studia philosophica*, **7** (1947), 87–102; K. Fischer, *G. W. Leibniz. Leben, Werke und Lehre* (Heidelberg, 5th ed. 1920, W. Kabitz, ed.); J. O. Fleckenstein, *G. W. Leibniz. Barock und Universalismus* (Munich, 1958); G. Friedmann, *Leibniz et Spinoza* (Paris, 2nd ed. 1946, 3rd ed. 1963); M. Gueroult, *Dynamique et métaphysique leibniziennes suivi d'une note sur le principe de la moindre action chez Maupertuis* (Paris, 1934, 1967); G. E. Guhrauer, *G. W. Freiherr von Leibniz. Eine Biographie*, 2 vols. (Wrocław, 1846; Hildesheim, 1966); G. Grua, *Jurisprudence universelle et théodicée selon Leibniz* (Paris, 1953); and *La justice humaine selon Leibniz* (Paris, 1956); H. Heimsoeth, *Die Methode der Erkenntnis bei Descartes und Leibniz*, 2 vols. (Giessen, 1912–1914); A. Heinekamp, *Das Problem des Guten bei Leibniz* (Bonn, 1969); K. Hildebrandt, *Leibniz und das Reich der Gnade* (The Hague, 1953); H. H. Golz, *Leibniz* (Stuttgart, 1958); K. Huber, *Leibniz* (Munich, 1951); J. Jalabert, *La théorie leibnizienne de la substance* (Paris, 1947); J. Jalabert, *Le Dieu de Leibniz* (Paris, 1960); J. Guitton, *Pascal et Leibniz* (Paris, 1951); M. Jammer, *Concepts of Force. A Study in the Foundations of Dynamics* (Cambridge, Mass., 1957); W. Janke, *Leibniz. Die Emendation der Metaphysik* (Frankfurt, 1963); H. W. B. Joseph, *Lectures on the Philosophy of Leibniz*, J. L. Austin, ed. (Oxford, 1949); W. Kabitz, *Die Philosophie des jungen Leibniz. Untersuchungen zur Entwicklungsgeschichte seines Systems* (Heidelberg, 1909); F. Kaulbach, *Die Metaphysik des Raumes bei Leibniz und Kant* (Cologne, 1960); R. Kauppi, *Über die leibnizsche Logik. Mit besonderer Berücksichtigung des Problems der Intension und der Extension* (*Acta Philosophica Fennica XII;* Helsinki, 1960); W. Kneale and M. Kneale, *The Development of Logic* (Oxford, 1962); L. Krüger, *Rationalismus und Entwurf einer universalen Logik bei Leibniz* (Frankfurt, 1969); D. Mahnke, "Leibnizens Synthese von Universalmathematik und Individualmetaphysik," in *Jahrbuch für Philosophie und phänomenologische Forschung*, **7** (1925), 305–612 (repr. Stuttgart, 1964); G. Martin, *Leibniz. Logik und Metaphysik* (Cologne, 1960; 2nd ed., Berlin, 1967; English tr. by P. G. Lucas and K. J. Northcott from the 1st ed. : *Leibniz. Logic and Metaphysics* (Manchester–New York, 1964); J. T. Mertz, *Leibniz* (Edinburgh–London, 1884; repr. New York, 1948); R. W. Meyer, *Leibniz and the 17th Century Revolution* (Glasgow, 1956); J. Mittelstrass, *Neuzeit und Aufklärung. Studien zur Entstehung der neuzeitlichen Wissenschaft und Philosophie* (Berlin, 1970); J. Moreau, *L'universe leibnizien* (Paris–Lyons, 1956); K. Müller and G. Krönert, *Leben und Werk von G. W. Leibniz. Eine Chronik* (Frankfurt, 1969); E. Naert, *Leibniz et la querelle du pur amour* (Paris, 1959); E. Naert, *Mémoire et conscience de soi selon Leibniz* (Paris, 1961); G. H. R. Parkinson, *Logic and Reality in Leibniz' Metaphysics* (Oxford, 1965); G. H. R. Parkinson, *Leibniz on Human Freedom* (*Studia Leibnitiana Sonderheft 2;* Wiesbaden, 1970); C. A. van Peursen, *Leibniz* (Baarn, 1966), tr. into English by H. Hoskins (London, 1969); H. Poser, *Zur Theorie der Modalbegriffe bei G. W. Leibniz* (*Studia Leibnitiana Suppl. VI;* Wiesbaden, 1969); N. Rescher, "Leibniz' Interpretation of His Logical Calculi," in *Journal of Symbolic Logic*, **19** (1954), 1–13; N. Rescher, *The Philosophy of Leibniz* (Englewood Cliffs, N.J., 1967); W. Risse, *Die Logik der Neuzeit II: 1640–1780* (Stuttgart, 1970); A. Robinet, *Malebranche et Leibniz. Relations personelles* (Paris, 1955); A. Robinet, *Leibniz et la racine de l'existence* (Paris, 1962); B. Russell, *A Critical Exposition of the Philosophy of Leibniz* (Cambridge, 1900; 2nd ed., London, 1937); H. Schiedermair, *Das Phänomen der Macht und die Idee des Rechts bei G. W. Leibniz* (*Studia Leibnitiana Suppl. VII;* Wiesbaden, 1970); H. Scholz, "Leibniz" (1942), reprinted in H. Scholz, *Mathesis universalis*, H. Hermes, F. Kambartel and J. Ritter, eds. (Basel, 1961); L. Stein, *Leibniz und Spinoza. Ein Beitrag zur Entwicklungsgeschichte der leibnizischen Philosophie* (Berlin, 1890); G. Stieler, *Leibniz und Malebranche und das Theodizeeproblem* (Darmstadt, 1930); W. Totok and C. Haase, eds., *Leibniz. Sein Leben, sein Wirken, seine Welt* (Hannover, 1966); A. T. Tymieniecka, *Leibniz' Cosmological Synthesis* (Assen, 1964); P. Wiedeburg, *Der junge Leibniz, das Reich und Europa*, pt. I, 2 vols. (Wiesbaden, 1962).

E. Hochstetter, ed., *Leibniz zu seinem 300 Geburtstag 1646–1946*, 8 pts. (Berlin, 1946–1952); G. Schischkoff, ed., *Beiträge zur Leibniz-Forschung* (Reutlingen, 1947); E. Hochstetter and G. Schischkoff, eds., *Zum Gedenken an den 250 Todestag von G. W. Leibniz* (*Zeitschrift für philosophische Forschung*, **20**, nos. 3–4 (Meisenheim, 1966), 377–658; and *Zum Gedenken an den 250 Todestag von G. W. Leibniz* (*Philosophia naturalis*, **10**, no. 2 (1968), 134–293); *Leibniz (1646–1716). Aspects de l'homme et de l'oeuvre (Journées Leibniz, organis. au Centre Int. de Synthèse, 28–30 mai 1966)* (Paris, 1968); *Studia Leibnitiana Supplementa*, vols. I-V *(Akten des Int. Leibniz-Kongresses Hannover, 14–19 November 1966)* (Wiesbaden, 1968–1970).

LEIDY, JOSEPH (*b.* Philadelphia, Pennsylvania, 9 September 1823; *d.* Philadelphia, 30 April 1891), *biology.*

A descriptive scientist of unusual range, Leidy made contributions of lasting value in human anatomy, parasitology, protozoology, and paleontology of mammals and reptiles.

Leidy was the second son and third child of Philip Leidy, a Philadelphia hatter and member of a family of mechanics and artisans who immigrated to Bucks County, Pennsylvania, from Wittenberg in the early eighteenth century, and Catherine Mellick, of Columbia County, Pennsylvania, following whose death in 1823 Philip Leidy married her cousin Christiana T. Mellick of Philadelphia. Joseph Leidy attended a private day school and was influenced to study natural history by a visiting lecturer on minerals. This early taste deepened under the guidance of a nearby horticulturist and during rambles in the countryside. A little book of drawings of shells accompanied by both scientific and common names, done by Leidy when he was ten, may be seen at the Academy of Natural Sciences of Philadelphia. Encouraged by his stepmother to become a student of anatomy, he matriculated at the University of Pennsylvania, where Paul B. Goddard introduced him to microscopy and supervised his dissertation on the comparative anatomy of the vertebrate eye, for which he was awarded the M.D. in 1844.

Leidy failed in an effort to build a private medical practice and seemed much better suited to close study. In the words of his biographer, W. S. W. Ruschenberger:

> It may truly be said that Dr. Leidy was born to be a naturalist. To his innate ability to perceive the minutest variations in the forms and color of things was united artistic aptitude of a high order. These natural faculties, in continuous exercise almost from his infantile days, and his love of accuracy, enabled him to detect minute differences and resemblances of all objects, and to correctly describe and portray them [p. 147].

His acuteness was exemplified by his noticing minute specks in a slice of pork he was eating, and thus discovering that *Trichinella spiralis*, known to be a parasite of man, infested the raw flesh of pigs and that it could be killed by boiling. In 1853 Leidy was appointed professor of anatomy at the University of Pennsylvania. He published a widely admired manual on human anatomy in 1861 and served during the Civil War as an army surgeon, performing many autopsies. In 1864 he married Anna Harden of Louisville, Kentucky; they adopted one daughter.

Leidy seems to have had an unusual degree of patience that allowed him to observe organisms for longer than was strictly necessary in order to publish a description. When writing up the discovery of an unusual planarian in a spring in Pennsylvania, he added notes on behavior and feeding habits and conducted experiments on its capacity for regeneration. In 1848 he commenced studies on the intestinal flora and fauna of healthy animals, an intricate and difficult subject which prompted reflections on spontaneous generation and the origin of life. Leidy found no difficulty in step-by-step reasoning from close study of intestinal microorganisms to considerations of life in the universe, and he offered a calmly worded suggestion that all life had evolved from comparably simple circumstances. His discovery in 1848 that the larval eye persisted into the adult stage of the Cirripedia attracted the attention of Charles Darwin and exemplified Leidy's capacity for detail, for these organs are very minute and rudimentary.

In 1848 Leidy was elected to the Academy of Natural Sciences of Philadelphia, then the foremost American institution for the deposit of paleontological specimens. In 1847 he described the fossil remains of the horse in America with the accuracy and minuteness that became his hallmarks. Charles Lyell urged Leidy to devote himself to paleontology. Spencer Baird turned over to him the vertebrate paleontology collections of the Smithsonian Institution and by 1855 Leidy had inspected most of the important finds from the American West. He proved to be a talented and perceptive comparative anatomist, writing meticulous descriptions of fossil mammals that have endeared him to subsequent workers. One typical appraisal is that he was "a paleontologist's paleontologist," whose monographs eschewed speculation and laid the foundation for understanding the diverse North American fossil vertebrates. "The Extinct Mammalian Fauna of Dakota and Nebraska" (1869), probably his greatest single work, was thought by Henry Fairfield Osborn to be "with the possible exception of Cope's *Tertiary Vertebrata*, the most important paleontological work which America has produced." The infant science of paleontology became embroiled in controversy among its promoters; and Leidy, who had no appetite for acrimony, gradually shifted his interests to protozoology.

Leidy devoted the years 1874 to 1878 to studies of freshwater Protozoa in a diverse array of habitats, ranging from the Uinta Mountains of Utah to the bogs of the Southeast. His monograph *Fresh-Water Rhizopods of North America* (1879), illustrated with superb lithographs of his field drawings, was the equal of any previous work in the field, constituting a remarkable portrayal of the diversity of unicellular life in microhabitats.

Leidy was a devoted worker who missed only five days in thirty-eight years as professor of anatomy, and his steadfastness contributed greatly to the strength of the institutions he served. He was president of the Academy of Natural Sciences for the last ten years of his life and in 1885 became president of the Wagner Free Institute of Science and director of its museum. His lectures there were popular discourses revealing an unaffected humanity—the quality that prompted him, while visiting the fish market in search of scientific specimens, to tell fish sellers the scientific names of uncommon varieties for them to copy onto their signs for the public.

His dislike for the controversies that beset vertebrate paleontology did not prevent Leidy from seeking the wider scientific implications of facts that he regarded as established. He drew connections from observations of parasites to concepts of contagion or primordial origins of life, for example, and exercised great powers of observation. His perceptions were marked by sober appreciation of the vastness and diversity of life, as in these comments on the Bridger Basin in Utah:

> The utter desolation of the scene, the dried-up watercourses, the absence of any moving object, and the profound silence which prevailed, produced a feeling that was positively oppressive. When I then thought of the buttes beneath my feet, with their entombed remains of multitudes of animals forever extinct, and reflected upon the time when the country teemed with life, I truly felt that I was standing on the wreck of a former world [*Contributions to the Extinct Vertebrate Fauna of the Western Territories*, pp. 18–19].

BIBLIOGRAPHY

I. ORIGINAL WORKS. Leidy's writings include "A Flora and Fauna Within Living Animals," in *Smithsonian Contributions to Knowledge*, **5** (1853); "The Ancient Fauna of Nebraska, a Description of Extinct Mammalia and Chelonia From the Mauvaises Terres of Nebraska," *ibid.*, **6** (1854); "Cretaceous Reptiles of the United States," *ibid.*, **14** (1865); "The Extinct Mammalian Fauna of Dakota and Nebraska . . .," which is *Journal of the Academy of Natural Sciences of Philadelphia*, 2nd ser., **7** (1869); *Contributions to the Extinct Vertebrate Fauna of the Western Territories*, Report of the U.S. Geological Survey of the Territories (Washington, D.C., 1873); and *Fresh-Water Rhizopods of North America, ibid.* (Washington, D.C., 1879).

MS collections in the Academy of Natural Sciences, Philadelphia, include diaries and correspondence and a 373-page typescript of excerpts from these prepared by Joseph Leidy, Jr., covering the period 1823–1869. Medical correspondence is at the College of Physicians, Philadelphia.

II. SECONDARY LITERATURE. See W. S. W. Ruschenberger, "A Sketch of the Life of Joseph Leidy, M.D., L.L.D.,"

in *Proceedings of the American Philosophical Society*, **30** (1892), 135–184, with bibliography; and Joseph Leidy, Jr., ed., "Researches in Helminthology and Parasitology by Joseph Leidy," in *Smithsonian Miscellaneous Collections*, **46**, no. 1477 (1904), with bibliography.

PHILIP C. RITTERBUSH

LEMAIRE, JACQUES (*fl.* Paris, France, 1720–1740), and **PIERRE** (*fl.* Paris, 1733–1760), *instrument making.*

A member of the Société des Arts and an associate of its president, the clockmaker Julien Le Roy, Jacques Lemaire built sundials, many of which Le Roy had designed. He invented the front-view reflecting telescope, which Herschel developed so advantageously in giant telescopes and which does away with the auxiliary mirror used to project the image onto the eyepiece of the Newtonian reflecting telescope. He developed a mechanical device that permits several screws to be advanced at once by turning a single screw.

Lemaire's son, Pierre, who carried on the tradition of excellence and inventiveness established in his father's workshop, and who had all sorts of scientific instruments made in the family shop, enjoyed the reputation of being the outstanding French compass maker. He was the first Frenchman to construct the Hadley octant and thereafter proudly used an image of it as his ensign, which had been a lodestone. He worked closely with the academicians Duhamel du Monceau and La Condamine, who inspired him.

A great variety of instruments possessed by the Académie des Sciences came from the Lemaire workshop, which, with that of Langlois, kept alive in France a tradition of quality precision-instrument making in spite of the impediments caused by the craft guild system of the *ancien régime*.

BIBLIOGRAPHY

I. ORIGINAL WORKS. Jacques Lemaire's front-view reflecting telescope of 1728 is described in *Machines et inventions approuvées par l'Académie royale des sciences . . .*, VI (Paris, 1735), 61–63; his device of 1726 for advancing several screws is in *ibid.*, IV (Paris, 1735), 179–180, and in *Histoire de l'Académie des sciences* for 1726 (1728), p. 17.

Pierre Lemaire's work on compasses is described by Duhamel du Monceau, who did experiments with Pierre, in *Mémoires de l'Académie des sciences* for 1745 (1749), pp. 181–193; a description of his compass, inspired by Hadley's quadrant and by a proposal made in 1733 by La Condamine, is in *Histoire de l'Académie des sciences* for 1747 (1752), p. 126, and in *Machines et inventions approu-*

vées par l'Académie royale des sciences ..., VII (Paris, 1777), 361–367.

Instruments constructed by the Lemaires may be found at the Conservatoire National des Arts et Métiers, Paris; at the Musées Royaux d'Art et d'Histoire, Brussels; in the Mensing Collection at the Adler Museum, Chicago; at the National Maritime Museum, Greenwich; at the Musée de la Marine, Paris; and at the British Museum, London. The inventory of instruments possessed by the Académie des Sciences before the French Revolution is at the Archives Nationales, Paris, F^{14} 1274.

II. Secondary Literature. La Condamine's proposal and test of Pierre Lemaire's compass are found in *Mémoires de l'Académie des sciences* for 1733 (Paris, 1735), 446–456, and for 1734 (Paris, 1736), 597–599. Pierre Lemaire's address is mentioned in *ibid.* for 1734, 599; *ibid.* for 1745, 181; J. B. N. D. d'Apres de Mannevillette, *Le nouveau quartier anglois ou description et usage d'un nouvel instrument pour observer la latitude sur mer* (Paris, 1739), p. 46; H. Michel, *Introduction à l'étude d'une collection d'instruments anciens de mathématiques* (Antwerp, 1939), p. 96.

J.-A. Nollet, *Art des expériences* (Paris, 1770), I, 247–248, praises Pierre Lemaire's compasses. M. Daumas, *Les instruments scientifiques aux XVIIe et XVIIIe siècles* (Paris, 1953), offers a comprehensive survey that permits the reader to situate the Lemaires in the context of their times.

Robert M. McKeon

LEMERY, LOUIS (*b.* Paris, France, 25 January 1677; *d.* Paris, 9 June 1743), *chemistry, anatomy, medicine.*

Louis Lemery was the eldest son of the chemist Nicolas Lemery. Attracted at first to the legal profession, he finally gave in to his father's wishes and went on to a distinguished career in science and medicine which undoubtedly benefited in part from the reputation of his father. Educated at the Collège d'Harcourt, he proceeded to the Faculty of Medicine of Paris where he graduated M.D. in 1698. In 1700 he was admitted to the Academy of Sciences of Paris, as an *élève* of first the botanist Tournefort and then (from 1702) of his father. In 1712 he was elevated to the rank of *associé*, and in 1715, when his father took the *vétérance*, Louis succeeded him as *chimiste pensionnaire*. Between 1707 and 1710 he occasionally deputized for Guy-Crescent Fagon in the chemistry courses at the Jardin du Roi; he shared these duties with Claude Berger and E. F. Geoffroy. When Fagon resigned from the chemistry chair at the Jardin in 1712, however, Geoffroy was chosen over Lemery for the post. Lemery succeeded Geoffroy in this position in 1730.

Lemery was a physician at the Hôtel Dieu from 1710 to his death, a *médecin du roi* from 1722, and personal physician to Louis XV's cousin, the Princesse de Conti, in whose salon he composed many of his scientific works. He married Catherine Chapot in 1706, and one daughter survived from the marriage.

The bulk of Lemery's scientific writings were published in the *Mémoires de l'Académie royale des sciences.* They dealt mainly with problems of chemical analysis, especially of organic materials, and with fetal anatomy and the origin of monsters. In an early series of papers published between 1705 and 1708 he contested E. F. Geoffroy's view that iron could be synthesized from certain vegetable oils and mineral earths, and also that iron found in the ashes of plants was a product of the combustion.

Lemery's most important observations on organic analysis are contained in four papers published in 1719–1721. These represent a reevaluation of the Academy's long-standing project on the analysis of plants. In the first paper Lemery argued that fire is too destructive a tool for the analysis of organic materials, reducing them all to the same indiscriminate end products—a view his father had suggested in his textbook of 1675. In the subsequent papers, however, it became clear that he had no alternatives to offer to the traditional method of distillation analysis. Consequently he argued for a controlled use of this technique and stated that the important thing in such analysis is not to seek the ultimate principles of organic materials, but to seek only proximate principles. Lemery applied these considerations to the saline constituents of plants and animals, attempting to analyze them in terms of their acid and alkaline components. He concentrated on the ammoniacal and nitrate salts, drawing on the results of an earlier paper (1717) on the formation of niter, in which he had criticized the views of Mayow. In a 1709 paper on the nature of fire and light, he contested traditional Cartesian views and argued that fire and light were distinctive chemical fluids.

Lemery's anatomical papers dealt with the circulation of the blood in the fetal heart and with the origin of monsters. On this latter topic he disputed the emboîtement views of the Academy's anatomists, Duverney and Winslow, that monsters derived from monstrous embryos; Lemery argued instead that they were the product of purely accidental factors influencing the development of normal embryos in the womb.

In addition to his Academy memoirs, Lemery published two monographs. His *Traité des alimens* (1702) is a dictionary of edibles with a description of their nutritional value in terms of chemico-mechanical principles. His *Dissertation sur la nourriture des os* (1704) arose out of a protracted dispute with Nicolas Andry, whose *Traité de la génération des vers dans le corps de l'homme* Lemery had criticized severely in the

Journal de Trévoux. In this work Lemery maintained that part of the marrow had a nutritional function in young bones.

BIBLIOGRAPHY

I. ORIGINAL WORKS. Lemery's works include *Traité des alimens où l'on trouve par ordre, et séparément la différence & le choix qu'on doit faire de chacun d'eux en particulier* (Paris, 1702; 2nd ed., Paris, 1705, repr. 1709; 3rd ed., 2 vols., Paris, 1755, trans. by D. Hay as *A Treatise of All Sorts of Foods* . . . (London, 1745); Lemery's three letters on N. Andry's book on the generation of worms appeared first in the *Journal de Trévoux,* beginning in November 1703; see also *Dissertation sur la nourriture des os: où l'on explique la nature & l'usage de la Moelle. Avec trois lettres sur le livre de la génération des vers dans le corps de l'homme* (Paris, 1704). Lemery's many presentations to the Academy of Sciences are to be found in the *Histoire* and *Mémoires* of the Academy between 1702 and 1740. A complete listing is given in J. M. Quérard, *La France littéraire,* V (Paris, 1833), 141–142; *Nouvelle biographie générale,* XIII (Paris, 1862), cols. 603–604, lists the more important papers, while Poggendorff, I, col. 1418, cites the principal chemical papers.

II. SECONDARY LITERATURE. The principal source for Lemery's life is the *éloge* by Dortous de Marain in *Histoire de l'Académie royale des sciences pour l'année 1743–1746,* 195–208; see also J. P. Contant, *L'enseignement de la chimie au jardin royal des plantes de Paris* (Paris, 1952), 57–60; and J. A. Hazon, ed., *Notice des hommes les plus célèbres de la Faculté de Médecine en l'Université de Paris* (Paris, 1778), 195–198.

Lemery's contributions to organic analysis at the Academy of Sciences are discussed in F. L. Holmes, "Analysis by Fire and Solvent Extractions: the Metamorphosis of a Tradition," in *Isis,* **62** (1971), 129–148; some aspects of Lemery's chemistry are discussed in H. Metzger, *Les doctrines chimiques en France du début du XVIIe à la fin du XVIIIe siècle* (Paris, 1923, repr. 1969), pp. 341–420; and in J. R. Partington, *A History of Chemistry,* III (London, 1962), 41–42.

OWEN HANNAWAY

LEMERY, NICOLAS (*b.* Rouen, France, 17 November 1645; *d.* Paris, France, 19 June 1715), *chemistry, pharmacy.*

Nicolas Lemery was the fifth of seven children born to Julien Lemery, a Protestant attorney in the Parlement of Normandy, and his second wife, Susan Duchemin. When Nicolas was eleven years old his father died, leaving a widow and four surviving children. Shortly before his fifteenth birthday he was indentured as an apprentice apothecary to his uncle Pierre Duchemin in Rouen. After serving six years with his uncle, in 1666 he went to Paris, where he became a boarding student of Christopher Glaser, then demonstrator in chemistry at the Jardin du Roi. Apparently Lemery did not find Glaser a compatible teacher, and this arrangement lasted only two months. He then embarked on a six-year period of travel and study. Few details survive of this period in his life. He is known to have visited Lyons and Geneva and to have spent a considerable part of the time between 1668 and 1671 in Montpellier, where he resided with a young Protestant master apothecary, Henri Verchant. In the summer of 1670 he was registered as a student of pharmacy in Montpellier and was permitted to attend the courses on "simples" and anatomy given at the Faculty of Medicine for such students. According to Fontenelle, he also taught chemistry courses to Verchant's students that attracted members of the medical faculty and other notables of the town.

In 1672 Lemery returned to Paris, where he associated with members of the household of Louis, prince of Condé (le Grand Condé). He attended the conferences of the Abbé Bourdelot, the prince's physician, and worked in the laboratory of the prince's apothecary Bernadin Martin. This connection no doubt introduced Lemery to the fashionable intellectual circles of Paris. In 1674 he secured his professional status by purchasing the office of apothecary to the king and *grand prévôt* of France, thus circumventing the legal obstacles in the path of a Protestant seeking admission to the guild of apothecaries of Paris. During the next seven years he established a highly successful pharmaceutical business, specializing in patent medicines. In addition, he gained a considerable reputation as a teacher of chemistry by his private courses. These courses not only catered to the professional needs of pharmacy apprentices but also attracted a large audience from fashionable Parisian society interested in semipopular scientific expositions. The textbook of his course, the *Cours de chymie* (1675), enjoyed unprecedented success for such a work, selling, as Fontenelle comments, like a work of romance or satire.

Beginning in 1681, however, increasing religious intolerance in France introduced a period of considerable anxiety in Lemery's life. He was required to dispose of his office as privileged apothecary to the king, and in 1683 proceedings were set in train to close his laboratory and shop. These events prompted him to go to England in 1683, perhaps in anticipation of securing a position there. Disappointed, however, he returned within the year to France, where he acquired an M.D. degree at the University of Caen in order to reestablish his professional status following the loss of his position as privileged apothecary. He continued his teaching in increasingly difficult circumstances until the revocation of the Edict of Nantes in 1685, when as a Protestant he lost all his professional and legal rights. Early in the following year he abjured his religion and was received, together with his family, into the Roman Catholic church. Shortly thereafter he was granted permission to reestablish his laboratory and shop on condition that he take no apprentices, following opposition from the Paris guild of apothecaries on the grounds that he had forfeited his right as an apothecary by qualifying as a physician. Lemery devoted the next twelve years largely to pharmacy, publishing at the end of this period his *Pharmacopée universelle* (1697) and the *Traité des drogues simples* (1698). In 1699 he was admitted to the reorganized Academy of Sciences as associate chemist, and in November of the same year he succeeded Claude Bourdelin as *chimiste pensionnaire*. His subsequent scientific work was associated almost exclusively with the Academy. He died in 1715.

Lemery's scientific career fell into three phases: the first (1674–1683) was dominated by his successful teaching career and the publication of his *Cours de chymie;* the second (1686–1698) saw the reestablishment of his pharmaceutical business following his conversion to Catholicism and culminated in the publication of his *Pharmacopée universelle* and *Traité des drogues simples;* and the third period (1699–1715) was dominated by his association with the Academy of Sciences, which resulted in the publication of several memoirs in the Academy's journal and a monograph on antimony entitled *Traité de l'antimoine* (1707).

Lemery's teaching and textbook on chemistry, the *Cours de chymie*, owed their success to his clear and entertaining presentation of chemistry in corpuscular-mechanist terms. His adoption of mechanical modes of explanation brought the French chemical teaching tradition out of its earlier Paracelsian-Helmontian inheritance into the mainstream of contemporary Cartesian natural philosophy. His originality, however, should not be exaggerated; his presentation of chemistry remained wedded to the pharmaceutical goals of the teaching tradition established at the Jardin du Roi, and in practical content and organization his text follows very closely the works of his predecessors Nicaise Le Febvre and Christopher Glaser. The sources of his mechanism are unclear, as there is no formal philosophical or methodological introduction to his chemistry. They were probably largely Cartesian in influence. He was a close friend of the Cartesian Pierre-Sylvain Régis, who lectured on Cartesian natural philosophy in Lemery's laboratory in 1680; but the atomism of Gassendi also probably influenced him, and he mentions François Bernier's redaction of Gassendi's philosophy in the 1690 edition of the *Cours de chymie.*

But Lemery cannot be said to have developed a thoroughgoing Cartesian or atomistic theory of matter. Rather he introduced his explanations of chemical reactions in terms of particle shape and movement on an *ad hoc* basis, appealing to a naive empiricism which stressed the visual imagination, bolstered in some instances by microscopic observation. Thus the best way to explain the nature of salts, according to Lemery, is to attribute shapes to their constituent particles which best answer to all the effects they produce. Acid salts must have sharp pointed particles because of their sharp taste and, even more convincingly, because they solidify in the form of sharp pointed crystals. Contrariwise, alkalis are composed of earthy solid particles whose interstitial pores are so shaped as to admit entry of the spiked particles of acid. For reaction to take place between a particular acid and alkali, there must be an appropriate relationship between the size of the acid spikes and alkaline pores. Effervescence is produced in some acid-alkaline reactions by the expulsion of fire particles entrapped in the pores of the alkalis. Lemery also deduced the shapes of particles from the alleged physiological action of chemical substances in conformity with then current iatrophysical doctrines.

As a common origin for all salts Lemery suggests the fossil or gem salt (common salt) which is formed from an acid liquor flowing in veins in the earth. The acid liquor insinuates itself into the pores of stones and after concoction for several years forms this primogenital salt. All salts are derived from this fossil salt, with the exception of saltpeter, which derives its acidity directly from acid particles in the atmosphere. He tentatively suggests, however, that the acid liquor responsible for the formation of fossil salt may derive its acidity, like saltpeter, from the acid particles in the atmosphere. Vegetable salts in their turn are derived from terrestrial salt by absorption into the plant. Lemery's discussion of vegetable salts leads him to an interesting critique of analysis by fire. He recognizes three species of vegetable salt: the acid or essential salt crystallized directly from the juice of plants; the volatile alkaline salt produced by distilling macerated and fermented seeds and fruits; and the alkaline fixed salt derived from the ashes of combusted plant materials. Of the three, only the first type is preexistent in plants; the other two are products of the action of fire. In discussing the production of the alkaline volatile salt of plants by heating, Lemery concludes that it must be admitted that fire destroys and confounds most things which it dissects, and there is no occasion to believe that it yields substances in their natural state. The probity of fire as a tool in vegetable analysis became a subject of much discussion and debate in the Academy of Sciences in Lemery's lifetime and subsequently.

Lemery, however, was not disposed to renounce analysis by fire entirely: he still finds a place in his chemistry for the five iatrochemical principles of salt, sulfur, mercury, water, and earth based on fire analysis. His retention of these principles reveals a curious tension in Lemery's chemistry between his innovative mechanist approach and its traditional iatrochemical framework. He states that he would like to believe that these principles are found in all mixt bodies but acknowledges that the existence of all five can be demonstrated only in animal and vegetable bodies: they cannot be separated so readily from minerals, and not even two of them can be extracted from gold and silver. Consequently, in spite of his initial discussion of them, the principles play a limited role in his subsequent exposition. Nevertheless, he is insistent that experimentally determined principles have a place in chemistry as an antidote to purely hypothetical mechanical theories of matter—one must proceed from the demonstrable products of chemical analysis to the shapes of particles and not vice versa. In spite of the drift of his arguments, Lemery, however, is unable or unwilling to formulate a new set of empirically determined principles based on a wider range of analysis than that of fire.

Lemery's chief contributions to pharmacy were his two complementary works, the *Pharmacopée universelle* and the *Traité des drogues simples*. These are alphabetically arranged lists of composites and simples respectively, giving the source, virtues, doses, and therapeutic action of the various medicaments. They represent a comprehensive dictionary of pharmaceuticals. Their chief rival was Pierre Pomet's *Histoire générale des drogues* (1694).

His last major work was *Traité de l'antimoine* (1707), which contained the results of his investigation into the properties and preparations of mineral antimony, his chosen topic of research on admission to the Academy of Sciences in 1699. It is a thorough and systematic collection of preparations of antimony arranged according to technique of preparation, but it does not depart in spirit or style from the section on antimony in the *Cours de chymie*. He also published in the *Mémoires* of the Academy papers on the physical and chemical explanations of subterranean fires, earthquakes, hurricanes, thunder, and lightning (1700), which he attributed to the spontaneous

reaction of iron and sulfur, and on the analysis of camphor (1705), honey (1706), cows' urine (1707), and experiments on corrosive sublimate (1712). All are of minor importance, and his last researches in the Academy suffer comparison with the work of the other chemists, Guillaume Homberg, E. F. Geoffroy, and his son Louis Lemery.

The elder Lemery invites comparison with his older English contemporary Robert Boyle. Both were advocates of an eclectic mechanical philosophy and were firmly convinced of the contributions chemistry had to make to that philosophy. Lemery's vision of chemistry, however, was much more limited due to his professional commitment to pharmacy and to his inheritance of a well-established textbook tradition which was largely pharmaceutically oriented. He was perhaps inhibited by overriding professional concerns from attempting to integrate his chemistry more fully into the new scientific philosophy in the manner of Boyle. Also the opportunity to do so within the broader scientific environment of the Academy of Sciences came late in his life, and by that time his interests and outlook were set. Two of Lemery's sons followed their father's interest in chemistry, and both became members of the Academy. The elder, Louis Lemery (Lemery *le fils*, 1677–1743), succeeded his father as *chimiste pensionnaire* in 1715. A younger son, Jacques Lemery (Lemery *le jeune*, 1677/1678–1721), was an associate of the Academy from 1715, publishing several memoirs on phosphorus before his early death.

BIBLIOGRAPHY

I. ORIGINAL WORKS. There is no wholly satisfactory guide to the numerous editions of Lemery's works; most useful are J. Roger, *Les médecins normands du XIIe au XIXe siècle* (Paris, 1890), 53–55; A. J. J. Vandevelde, "L'oeuvre bibliographique de Nicolas Lemery," in *Bulletin des sociétés chimiques Belges*, **30** (1921), 153–166; and J. R. Partington, *A History of Chemistry*, III (London, 1962), 29–31.

More than thirty eds. of the *Cours de chymie* (Paris, 1675) have been recorded. Eleven separate eds. appeared which claimed to have been revised and corrected by the author himself, the last of these being the 11th (Leiden, 1716), reissued in Paris in 1730. Other eds. in French were published at Amsterdam, Leiden, Lyons, Brussels, and Avignon between 1682 and 1751. The last French ed. was edited by Théodore Baron (Paris, 1756), who added many notes in an effort to update it in conformity with current phlogistic theory; this ed. was reissued in Paris in 1757. The *Cours* was also translated into Latin, German, Dutch, Italian, Spanish, and English. The English translations were by Walter Harris (London, 1677, 1686, from the 1st and 5th French eds. respectively) and by James Keill (London, 1698, 1720, from the 8th and 11th French eds. respectively).

The *Pharmacopée universelle* (Paris, 1697) appeared in at least five subsequent eds. from Paris, Amsterdam, and The Hague. The last ed. was in two vols., Paris 1763–1764. The *Traité universel des drogues simples* (Paris, 1698) appeared in at least five eds. to 1759. The 3rd (Amsterdam, 1716) and subsequent eds. have the title *Dictionnaire ou traité universel des drogues simples*. It was translated into Italian, German, Dutch, and English.

The *Traité de l'antimoine* (Paris, 1707) was translated into German and Italian.

A work entitled *Recueil de curiositez rares et nouvelles des plus admirables effets de la nature et de l'art* by a Sieur d'Emery, although sometimes attributed to Nicolas Lemery, is not generally considered to be by him.

Lemery's contributions to the Paris Academy of Sciences are to be found in its *Histoires* and *Mémoires* (1699–1712).

II. Secondary Literature. Fontenelle's *éloge*, in *Histoire de l'Académie royale des sciences* for 1715 (Paris, 1717), pp. 73–82, remains an important source for Lemery's life. It is not without error, however, and should be supplemented by P. Dorveaux, "Apothicaires membres de l'Académie royale des sciences, VI. Nicolas Lemery," in *Revue d'histoire de la pharmacie*, **19** (1931), 208–219. J. Roger, *Les médecins normands du XIIe au XIX siècle* (Paris, 1890), 47–55, repeats several of Fontenelle's errors but includes two unpublished letters of Lemery from the 1660's. P.-A. Cap, *Études biographiques pour servir à l'histoire des sciences. Première série, chimistes-naturalistes* (Paris, 1857), 180–226, is a romanticized account of Lemery's life based largely on Fontenelle but gives useful genealogical information. See also E. and E. Haag, *La France protestante*, VI (Paris, 1856), 538–544. Lemery's chemistry is discussed in J. R. Partington, *A History of Chemistry*, III (London, 1962), 28–41; J. Read, *Humour and Humanism in Chemistry* (London, 1947), 116–123; and most fully by H. Metzger, *Les doctrines chimiques en France du début du XVIIe à la fin du XVIIIe siècle* (Paris, 1923; repr. 1969), 281–338, and *passim*.

Owen Hannaway

LEMOINE, ÉMILE MICHEL HYACINTHE (*b.* Quimper, France, 22 November 1840; *d.* Paris, France, 21 December 1912), *mathematics*.

Lemoine can be characterized as an amateur mathematician and musician whose work was influential in both areas. Like a number of other famous French mathematicians, he was educated at the École Polytechnique in Paris, from which he was graduated in 1860. He taught there but was forced to resign after five or six years because of poor health. Subsequently he was a civil engineer, and he eventually became chief inspector for the department of gas supply in Paris. His avocations remained mathematics and music.

In 1860, while he was still at the École Polytechnique, Lemoine and other teachers formed a chamber music group, nicknamed "La Trompette." Camille Saint-Saëns wrote pieces for it.

Lemoine's major mathematical achievements were in geometry. He and John Casey are generally credited with having founded the newer geometry of the triangle.

In 1873, at the meeting of the Association Française pour l'Avancement des Sciences held in Lyons, Lemoine presented a paper entitled "Sur quelques propriétés d'un point remarquable du triangle." In this paper he called attention to the point of intersection of the symmedians of a triangle and described some of its more important properties. He also introduced the special circle named for him.

The point of concurrence of the symmedians of a triangle is called the Lemoine point (in France), the Grebe point (in Germany, after E. W. Grebe), or, most generally, the symmedian point. The last term was coined by the geometer Robert Tucker, of the University College School in London, in the interest of uniformity and amity. It is generally symbolized by K.

The symmedian point had appeared in the work of geometers before Lemoine, but his was the first systematic exposition of some of its interesting properties. Lemoine's concern with the problem of simplifying geometric constructions led him to develop a theory of constructions, which he called geometrography. He presented this system at the meeting of the Association Française pour l'Avancement des Sciences that was held at Oran, Algeria, in 1888.

Briefly, Lemoine reduced geometric constructions to five elementary operations: (1) placing a compass end on a given point; (2) placing a compass end on a given line; (3) drawing a circle with the compass so placed; (4) placing a straightedge on a given point; (5) drawing a line once the straightedge has been placed. The number of times any one of these five operations was performed he called the "simplicity" of the construction. The number of times operation (1), (2), or (4) was performed he called the "exactitude" of the construction. By a suitable examination of the operations involved in a construction, it is usually possible to reduce the simplicity. For example, it is possible to reduce the simplicity of the construction of a circle tangent to three given circles (Apollonius' problem) from over 400 steps to 199 steps.

This system had a mixed reception in the mathematical world. It appears to help reduce the number of steps required for constructions but generally requires more geometrical sophistication and inge- nuity on the part of the constructor. It is now generally ignored.

Lemoine also wrote on local probability and on transformations involving geometric formulas. Con- cerning these transformations, he showed that it is always possible, by a suitable exchange of line seg- ments, to derive from one formula a second formula of the same nature. Thus, from the formula for the radius of the incircle of a triangle, it is possible to derive formulas for the radii of the excircles of the same triangle.

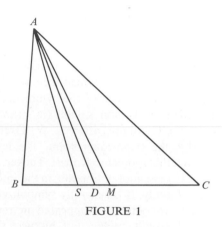

FIGURE 1

His mathematical work ceased after about 1895, but Lemoine's interest in the field continued. In 1894 he helped C. A. Laisant to found the periodical *Intermédiare des mathématiciens* and was its editor for many years.

Lemoine's reputation rests mainly on his work with the symmedian point. Briefly (see Figure 1), if, in triangle *ABC*, cevian *AM* is the median from vertex *A* and cevian *AD* is the bisector of the same angle,

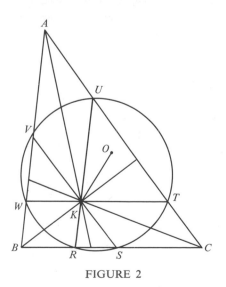

FIGURE 2

then cevian *AS*, which is symmetric with *AM* in respect to *AD*, is the symmedian to side *BC*. Among the results presented by Lemoine were that the three symmedians of a triangle are concurrent and that each symmedian divides the side to which it is drawn in the ratio of the squares of the other two sides.

If (see Figure 2) lines are drawn through the given symmedian point *K* parallel to the sides of the given triangle, these lines meet the sides of the triangle in six points lying on a circle. This circle is called the first Lemoine circle. The center of the circle is the midpoint of the line segment, *OK*, joining the circum- center and symmedian point of the triangle. The distances of *K* from the sides of the triangle are proportional to the lengths of the sides. The line segments cut from the sides by the first Lemoine circle have lengths proportional to the cubes of the sides. If antiparallels are drawn to the sides through *K*, they meet the sides of the triangle in six concyclic points. The circle thus determined, called the second Lemoine circle, has its center at *K*. Since their intro- duction by Lemoine, many properties of the sym- median point and the Lemoine circles have been discovered.

BIBLIOGRAPHY

I. ORIGINAL WORKS. Lemoine's papers are listed in Poggendorff, III, 793; IV, 864; V, 727–728; and in the Royal Society *Catalogue of Scientific Papers*, VIII, 200– 201; X, 560–561; XVI, 699–700. See esp. "Note sur un point remarquable du plan d'un triangle," in *Nouvelles annales de mathématiques*, 2nd ser., **12** (1873), 364–366; "Quelques questions de probabilités résolues géométrique- ment," in *Bulletin de la Société mathématique de France*, **11** (1883), 13–25; and "Sur une généralisation des pro- priétés relative au cercle de Brocard et au point de Le- moine," in *Nouvelles annales de mathématiques*, 3rd ser., **4** (1885), 201–223, repr. as "Étude sur le triangle et certains points de géométrographie," in *Proceedings of the Edin- burgh Mathematical Society*, **13** (1895), 2–25.

II. SECONDARY LITERATURE. On Lemoine and his work see *La grande encyclopédie*, XXI (Paris, n.d.), 1197; F. Cajori, *A History of Mathematics*, 2nd ed. (London, 1919), 299–300; J. L. Coolidge, *A History of Geometrical Methods* (Oxford, 1940), p. 58, and *passim;* and R. A. Johnson, *Modern Geometry* (Boston–New York, 1929), *passim.*

SAMUEL L. GREITZER

LE MONNIER, LOUIS-GUILLAUME (*b.* Paris, France, 27 June 1717; *d.* Montreuil, France, 7 Septem- ber 1799), *botany, physics.*

Le Monnier was the son of Pierre Le Monnier, professor of philosophy at the Collège d'Harcourt and member of the Académie des Sciences; his older brother was the distinguished astronomer Pierre-Charles Le Monnier. Le Monnier's scientific career was quite unusual. He is considered a botanist because this was the category of his membership in the Académie Royale des Sciences and, later, of his associate membership in the Institute, and because he was a professor at the Jardin du Roi. Yet on the basis of his very slight written work, which dates mainly from his youth, the title of physicist would be much more appropriate.

In 1739, at the age of twenty-two, Le Monnier accompanied Cassini de Thury and Lacaille on a mission to extend the meridian of the observatory of Paris into the South of France. His publications from this time (in *Suite des Mémoires de l'Académie* [1740]) contain accounts of purely physical experiments (observations of mercury in barometers in the mountains of Auvergne, in the Canigou, and elsewhere), descriptions of mines and mineral springs, and the results of his botanizing.

It was with the publication of the manuscript containing his observations made in the South of France that Le Monnier started his botanical career. In the province of Berry he noted diseased wheat on which the growths of ergot were an inch and a half long. He collected plants and drew up floras, some of twenty pages: for Berry, the mountains of Auvergne, Roussillon, and the mountains of the diocese of Narbonne. He noted interesting ecological trends, finding similarities between the mountain plants and the plants of Lapland described by Linnaeus. Although he did not publish anything after 1752, he continued his work as a botanist; the evidence can be found in the archives of the Museum of Natural History and of the Academy of Sciences.

In 1741 Le Monnier presented a memoir to the Academy entitled "Sur le rapport de différents degrés de fluidité des liquides." Utilizing an original method, he presented measurements of the flow-times of a series of liquids through the same orifice. Le Monnier pointed out the importance of the "specific gravity" of these liquids. In 1744 and 1747 he carried out analyses—simultaneously physical, chemical, and medical—of the mineral waters of Mont d'Or and Barège.

In 1746, following the famous Leyden jar experiment, he published "Recherches sur la communication de l'électricité." Simplifying Musschenbroek's apparatus, he verified the facts previously reported and established important new results: conducting bodies become charged with electricity as a function of their surface area, not of their mass; water is one of the best conductors of electricity. In this field Le Monnier

found himself the rival of the Abbé Nollet, who did not welcome any challenge to this authority. It was to Le Monnier, however, that Diderot assigned the two articles "Aimant" and "Aiguille aimantée" in the first volume of the *Encyclopédie*. Furthermore Le Monnier communicated to the Academy certain results "concerning the perfect resemblance recently observed between electric matter and that of thunder" ("Observations sur l'électricité de l'air" in *Mémoires de l'Académie royale des sciences* [1752]), and six months later published his method of studying storms and his own findings, which confirmed Franklin's.

In the *Mémoires de l'Académie royale des sciences* he signed his works "par M. Le Monnier, Médecin" to distinguish them from those of his father and of his brother, with whom he sat in the Academy for fourteen years. It was both as a physician and as a botanist that he published his observations, "Sur les pernicieux effets d'une espèce de champignons appelée par les botanistes, *Fungus mediae magnitudinis totus albus* Vaillant n° 17."

But all these efforts were, for him, peripheral: his own science was botany, and we should be no more astonished to find him in 1745 taking Linnaeus botanizing in the forest of Fontainebleau with Antoine and Bernard de Jussieu than to see him as a botanist at the Academy. If we are to believe G. Cuvier, "he could have been one of our most famous botanists," but, prevented by timidity, he wrote nothing; this timidity was due to the "unjust criticisms to which his first memoirs were subjected"—and Cuvier is undoubtedly referring to the criticisms of the Abbé Nollet.

Le Monnier first practiced medicine in the hospital of Saint-Germain-en-Laye. Subsequently he was chief physician of the Hanoverian army (1756) and then first physician in ordinary both to Louis XV and to Louis XVI. He became first physician to the latter in 1788. Through kindness he also dispensed medical care to the poor.

His practical work as a botanist is worth mentioning. While still young he met Louis de Noailles at the latter's garden. He enjoyed organizing de Noailles's park, which contained rare trees and a botanical garden. One day there he fainted from excitement in the presence of Louis XV, who gave him a post as botanist and placed him in charge of the botanical garden of the Trianon. Owing to his credit at court and at the Academy, Le Monnier obtained, through the help of diplomats and of botanists sent abroad on missions, a considerable number of plants which he raised in nurseries and which he gladly gave to plant-lovers. There are many examples of his work still in existence in Paris and he enriched French horticulture with many species of rhododendron and Kalmia, the long-flowered *Mirabilis Jalapa*, the pink-flowered locust, flowering dogwood (*Cornus florida*), and many other plants. He advocated the use of humus for plants liking an acid soil.

In Montreuil, near Versailles, Le Monnier lived on the property of the Comtesse de Marsan, governess of the royal children. He had saved her life in a serious illness and her interest in botany helped him in his career.

He also had an apartment in the Tuileries and on 10 August 1792, during the attack on the palace, his life was miraculously saved by an unknown individual. Destitute, he retired to Montreuil, where he lived a miserable existence on the income from an herbalist's shop which he opened. After the death of his wife in 1793 he was cared for with devotion by a niece, who eventually married him.

BIBLIOGRAPHY

I. ORIGINAL WORKS. Le Monnier published the following papers: "Monnier (M. Le) Médecin. Ses observations d'histoire naturelle faites dans les provinces méridionales de la France pendant l'année 1739," in *Suite des Mémoires de l'Académie* (1740), 111–235; "Sur le rapport des différens degrés de fluidité des liquides," in *Histoire de l'Académie des Sciences* (1741), 11–17; "Examen des eaux minérales du Mont d'Or," in *Mémoires de l'Académie des Sciences* (1744), 157–169; "Recherches sur la communication de l'électricité," *ibid.* (1746), 447–464; "Examen de quelques fontaines minérales de la France," *ibid.* (1747), 259–271; "Sur les pernicieux effets d'une espèce de champignons, appelée par les botanistes, *Fungus mediae magnitudinis totus albus* Vaillant n° 17," *ibid.* (1749), 210–223; and "Observations sur l'électricité de l'air," *ibid.* (1752), 233–243. He also wrote the articles "Aiguille aimantée" and "Aimants" for *Encyclopédie ou Dictionnaire raisonné des Sciences, des Arts et des Métiers*, I (1751), 199–202, 214–223. A large number of MSS are preserved in the Bibliothèque Centrale of the Muséum d'Histoire Naturelle.

II. SECONDARY LITERATURE. Two early biographies are G. Cuvier, "Notice sur la vie et les ouvrages du C^en Lemonnier," in *Mémoires de l'Institut National des Sciences et des Arts*, **3** (an IX), 101–117, and A. N. Duchesne, "Éloge historique du Cit. Lemonnier, Médecin," in *Magasin encyclopédique* (1799), 489–500.

L. PLANTEFOL

LE MONNIER, PIERRE-CHARLES (*b.* Paris, France, 20 November 1715; *d.* Herils, Calvados, France, 3 April 1799), *astronomy.*

Le Monnier's father, for whom he was named, was professor of philosophy at the Collège d'Harcourt and a member of the Académie des Sciences. His brother was Louis-Guillaume Le Monnier, also a member of the Academy, professor of botany at the Jardin du Roi and *premier médecin ordinaire* to Louis XV. In 1763 he married a Mlle. Cussy from a prominent Norman family and had three daughters, one of whom married the mathematician Lagrange. A second daughter married his brother, Louis-Guillaume Le Monnier.

Le Monnier was presented to Louis XV by the duc de Noailles and remained a great favorite of the king, before whom he made important observations of the transits of Venus (1761) and Mercury (1753) across the face of the sun. The king in turn procured for him some of the best astronomical instruments in France. At that time the English instruments were superior to the French ones. He obtained a telescope by Short and two excellent quadrants by Bird and Sisson. He also constructed a great meridian at the church of Saint Sulpice in 1743.

Le Monnier began his astronomical career early with the assistance of his father. In 1732 J. P. Grandjean de Fouchy allowed him to observe at the Rue des Postes in Paris, and his first work was on the equation of the sun. In 1735 Le Monnier presented an elaborate lunar map to the Academy of Sciences and was admitted as *adjoint géomètre* on 23 April 1736, at the age of twenty. He rose to *pensionnaire* by 1746, became professor at the Collège Royal, and was admitted to the Royal Society, the Berlin Academy, and the Académie de la Marine.

Le Monnier's career was launched when he accompanied Clairaut and Maupertuis on their 1736 expedition to Lapland to measure a degree of an arc of meridian. Le Monnier had indicated his skill by observations made in 1731 on the opposition of Saturn, and his youth and vigor were an asset on such a hazardous and demanding voyage. In addition to surveying the degree of meridian, he made observations to calculate atmospheric refraction at various latitudes and in different seasons.

Of all his diverse interests, Le Monnier's work on lunar motion was the most extensive and the most important. In the first edition of the *Principia*, Newton had shown that the principal inequalities of the moon could be calculated from his law of universal gravitation; and in the second edition he applied these calculations to the observations of John Flamsteed. His methods, however, added little to the theory that Jeremiah Horrocks had suggested long before. Flamsteed calculated new tables based on Horrocks' theory incorporating Newton's corrections, but he did not publish them. They appeared for the first time in Le Monnier's *Institutions astronomiques*

(1746), his most famous work. It was basically a translation of John Keill's *Introductio ad veram astronomiam* (London, 1721) but with important additions and with new tables of the sun and moon. The book, the first important general manual of astronomy in France, later was largely replaced by the textbooks of Lalande and Lacaille.

Le Monnier supported the view of Edmond Halley that the irregularities of the moon's motion could be discovered by observing the moon regularly through an entire cycle of 223 lunations (the saros cycle of approximately eighteen years and eleven days), with the assumption that the irregularities would repeat themselves throughout each cycle. Le Monnier and James Bradley began such a series of observations, Le Monnier continuing his work for fifty years. During the 1740's Clairaut, d'Alembert, and Euler were working in competition to create a satisfactory mathematical lunar theory, which demanded an approximate solution to the three-body problem. In the ensuing controversy d'Alembert was seconded by Le Monnier, and he used Le Monnier's *Institutions astronomiques* as the basis for his tables. In 1746 Le Monnier presented a memoir to the Academy describing his observations of the inequalities in the motion of Saturn caused by the gravitational attraction of Jupiter, and he persuaded the Academy to choose as its prize question for 1748 the problem of providing a satisfactory theory to explain the observed inequalities. Euler entered the contest, used Le Monnier's data, and won the prize. His results were important for lunar theory, because an explanation of the perturbations of Saturn also required a treatment of the three-body problem.

The best lunar tables of the eighteenth century were those of Tobias Mayer, which were based on Euler's theory but with the magnitude of the predicted perturbations taken from observations. Le Monnier, however, adhered stubbornly to the task of correcting Flamsteed's tables even while confessing the superiority of Mayer's. Le Monnier's stubbornness is explained in part by his admiration for English methods in astronomy. In addition to his study of lunar motion he published *La théorie des comètes* (1743), which was largely a translation of Halley's *Cometography* but with several additions, constructed the first transit instrument in France at the Paris observatory, corresponded with James Bradley, and was the first to apply Bradley's discovery of the earth's nutation to correcting solar tables. He traveled to England in 1748 and observed an annular eclipse of the sun in Scotland. An indefatigable observer, Le Monnier undertook a star catalog and in 1755 produced a map of the zodiacal stars. His records show no fewer than twelve observations of Uranus, but he never identified it as a planet. He also wrote on navigation, magnetism, and electricity.

His most prominent pupil was Jérôme Lalande. Lalande attended Le Monnier's lectures in mathematical physics at the Collège Royale and with Le Monnier's strong recommendation and assistance went to Berlin in 1751 to make measurements of the moon simultaneous with those by Lacaille at the Cape of Good Hope, the purpose being to determine the lunar parallax. Le Monnier allowed Lalande to take his best quadrant on the journey. Soon afterward, however, the two men quarreled, partly because of Lalande's growing attachment to Lacaille, whom Le Monnier saw as a bitter foe. Le Monnier's irascibility led him into frequent controversy. He worked continually until 10 November 1791, when an attack of paralysis ended his career as a practicing astronomer.

BIBLIOGRAPHY

I. ORIGINAL WORKS. The most important works by Le Monnier are *Histoire céleste ou recueil de toutes les observations astronomiques faites par ordre du roy, avec un discours préliminaire sur le progrès de l'astronomie* (Paris, 1741); *La théorie des comètes, où l'on traite du progrès de cette partie de l'astronomie avec des tables pour calculer les mouvements des comètes, du soleil et des principales étoiles fixes* (Paris, 1743); *Institutions astronomiques ou leçons élémentaires d'astronomie . . . précédées d'un essai sur l'histoire de l'astronomie* (Paris, 1746); *Observations de la lune, du soleil et des étoiles fixes pour servir à la physique céleste et aux usages de la navigation . . .*, 4 vols. (Paris, 1751–1773); *Nouveau zodiaque réduit à l'année 1755 avec les autres étoiles dont la latitude s'étend jusqu'à 10 degrés au nord et au sud de l'écliptique . . .* (Paris, 1755); *Astronomique nautique lunaire, où l'on traite de la latitude et de la longitude en mer de la période saros* (Paris, 1771); *Mémoires concernant diverses questions d'astronomie, de navigation, et de physique lus et communiqués à l'Académie royale des sciences*, 3 vols. (Paris, 1781–1788); and many contributions to the *Mémoires* of the Académie des Sciences.

II. SECONDARY LITERATURE. A long and highly critical analysis of Le Monnier's works appears in J. B. J. Delambre, *Histoire de l'astronomie au dix-huitième siècle* (Paris, 1827), pp. 179–238. A more favorable account is in Jérôme Lalande, *Bibliographie astronomique avec l'histoire de l'astronomie depuis 1781 jusqu'à 1802* (Paris, 1803), pp. 819–826. Biographical information is in Michel Robida, *Ces bourgeois de Paris. Trois siècles de chronique familiale, de 1675 à nos jours* (Paris, 1955). An account of the expedition to Lapland is in Pierre Brunet, *Maupertuis, étude biographique*, I (Paris, 1929), pp. 33–64; Le Monnier's involvement in the controversy over lunar theory is described in an unpublished paper by Craig B. Waff, "The

Introduction of the Theory of Universal Gravitation Into Lunar Theory: Après le système du monde"; and in Thomas L. Hankins, *Jean d'Alembert: Science and the Enlightenment* (Oxford, 1970), pp. 28–42.

THOMAS L. HANKINS

LENARD, PHILIPP (*b*. Pressburg, Austria-Hungary [now Bratislava, Czechoslovakia], 7 June 1862; *d.* Messelhausen, Germany, 20 May 1947), *physics*.

Lenard was the son of a wealthy wine maker and wholesaler. His mother, the former Antonie Baumann, died young, and Lenard, an only child, was raised by an aunt who subsequently married his father.

Lenard was at first educated at home, but when he was nine he entered the cathedral school in Pressburg and later the Realschule. For him mathematics and physics were "oases in the desert" of other subjects, and he studied these two subjects by himself with the aid of college textbooks. In addition, he carried out chemistry and physics experiments on his own. He once devoted his summer vacation entirely to study of the new field of photography.

In his unpublished autobiography Lenard wrote, "When school days ended, a painful void came into my life." His father, who wanted him to carry on the wine business, permitted him, after long arguments, to continue his studies, but only at the Technische Hochschulen in Vienna and Budapest; moreover, he was to occupy himself primarily with the chemistry of wine. After a few dreary semesters Lenard joined his father's business.

In the summer of 1883, Lenard used the savings from a year of work for a trip to Germany. In Heidelberg he met Robert Bunsen, a figure who had long been a "secret object of worship." Bunsen's lectures were a revelation to Lenard, who was now firmly resolved to become a scientist; he matriculated at Heidelberg in the winter semester 1883–1884.

Lenard studied physics for four semesters at Heidelberg and two at Berlin. From Helmholtz he received the idea for his dissertation: "Über die Schwingungen fallender Tropfen." He began work on it at Berlin in the summer of 1885 and completed it at Heidelberg in 1886. He received his doctorate summa cum laude and thereupon became an assistant to Quincke at Heidelberg.

Since Lenard still returned to Pressburg on university vacations, he was now able to devote greater effort to the work he had begun while a student with his Gymnasium teacher Virgil Klatt. Their joint undertaking opened up for Lenard an important field of research, phosphorescence, in which he carried out

investigations for more than forty years. As Klatt gradually withdrew from the work, Lenard played an increasingly larger role. When, toward the end of his life, three volumes of his planned four-volume *Wissenschaftliche Abhandlungen* were published, the entire second volume was devoted to this topic. As early as 1889 he had discovered that phosphorescence is caused by the presence of very small quantities of copper, bismuth, or manganese in what were previously thought to be pure alkaline earth sulfides.

After three years as an assistant at Heidelberg, Lenard spent half a year in England, where he worked in the electromagnetic and engineering laboratories of the "City and Guilds of the London Central Institution." Afterward he was an assistant for a semester at Breslau and then came to Bonn on 1 April 1891 to work in the same capacity under Hertz, who was already famous for his discovery of electromagnetic waves. Lenard was a great admirer of Hertz, yet his hypersensitivity, which later became pathological, caused him to feel neglected and pushed aside even by Hertz. When Hertz died unexpectedly on 1 January 1894, at the age of thirty-six, Lenard took charge of the publication of the three-volume *Gesammelte Werke*. He had to sacrifice much time for this task, especially for the *Prinzipien der Mechanik*, which, although complete, required editing. More than two decades later Lenard published a literary monument to Hertz in *Grosse Naturforscher*. In the meantime, however, Lenard had developed his racial ideology and he felt obliged to reveal that he had detected a split personality in Hertz, whose father's family was Jewish. Hertz's theoretical works, especially the *Prinzipien der Mechanik*, seemed to Lenard a characteristic product of his Jewish inheritance.

Lenard qualified as a lecturer in 1892 with a work on hydroelectricity, but he was principally engaged in continuing the cathode ray experiments that Hertz had begun. Cathode rays had been Lenard's favorite topic since 1880, when he had read Sir William Crookes's paper "Radiant Matter or the Fourth Physical State."

Lenard utilized Hertz's discovery that thin metal sheets transmit cathode rays, and at the end of 1892 he constructed a tube with a "Lenard window." With this device he was able to direct the rays out of the discharge space and into either open air or a second evacuated space, where they could be further examined independently of the discharge process. As Lenard said later, "For the first time completely pure experiments were now possible."

Like Jean Perrin, Willy Wien, and J. J. Thomson, Lenard established that cathode rays consist of negatively charged particles. In harsh priority disputes, especially with Thomson, Lenard claimed, on the basis of his 1898 publication "Über die electrostatischen Eigenschaften der Kathodenstrahlen," to have made the first "incontestable, convincing determination of what were soon called 'electrons.'"

In order to prove absorption Lenard utilized a phosphorescent screen that lit up as soon as it was struck by cathode rays:

> If we employ a phosphorescent screen, we find that it shines dazzlingly when placed right next to the window; ... at a distance of about 8 cm the screen remains completely dark; obviously air at full atmospheric pressure is not at all permeable to cathode rays, not nearly as much as it is, for example, to light. Therefore, these rays must be extraordinarily short, so short that the molecular structure of matter, which vanishes in comparison with light waves—which are after all very small—becomes very appreciable in comparison with them. Naturally it then becomes possible, with the aid of these rays, to obtain information concerning the constitution of molecules and atoms [*Über Kathodenstrahlen*, p. 10].

Lenard was in fact able to infer from the absorption of the cathode rays by matter the correct conclusion that the effective center of the atom is concentrated in a tiny fraction of the atomic volume previously accepted in the kinetic theory of gases. Lenard's "dynamide" was an important predecessor of the atomic model of Rutherford, who in 1910–1911, on the basis of the deflections of α particles, drew the same conclusion as Lenard had earlier from the scattering of electrons.

Following Roentgen's discovery of X rays at the end of 1895, Lenard was deeply depressed that he, in the course of his constant experimenting with cathode ray tubes, had not achieved this success himself. Moreover, before the discovery was made, Lenard had provided Roentgen, at the latter's request, with a "reliable" tube and Roentgen did not reveal whether or not the discovery was made with this tube. Thus Lenard felt that his contribution should have been acknowledged in Roentgen's "Über eine neue Art von Strahlen." The affair left a permanent scar, and Lenard never used the term *Röntgenstrahlen*, although it became standard usage in Germany. He spoke only of "high frequency radiation."

At Hertz's untimely death, Lenard was also obliged to act as director of the laboratory. At the initiative of Friedrich Theodor Althoff, of the Prussian Ministry of Education, he obtained his first offer of a tenured position, an associate professorship at Breslau (October 1894). Since hardly any possibility of experimental work existed at Breslau, Lenard gave up this post after a year in favor of a nontenured lectureship at the Technische Hochschule in Aachen—as an assistant to Adolph Wüllner.

In October 1896 Lenard accepted an offer of an extraordinary professorship at Heidelberg. Two years later he went to Kiel—as a full professor and director of the physics laboratory. After a few years he was able to build a new laboratory. In 1902 Lenard succeeded in discovering important properties of the photoelectric effect. He found that as the intensity of the light increases the number of electrons set free rises, but their velocity remains unaffected: the velocity depends solely on the wavelength. The interpretation of this relationship was provided in 1905 by Albert Einstein's hypothesis of light quanta.

In 1905 Lenard received the Nobel Prize in physics for his cathode ray experiments; and in 1907 he succeeded Quincke as professor and director of the physics and radiology laboratory at the University of Heidelberg. Once more a new laboratory was constructed, on a splendid site on Philosophenweg, above the city; it was completed just before the outbreak of World War I. (The laboratory was renamed the Philipp Lenard Laboratory in 1935.)

In 1909, Adolf von Harnack, in the famous memorandum which led to the founding of the Kaiser Wilhelm Society, called Lenard the "most celebrated scientist" in the field of physical research. The initiated had a different opinion. In the summer of 1910, Einstein wrote to his friend Johann Jakob Laub, who was working as Lenard's assistant at Heidelberg: "Lenard must be very 'unevenly developed' in many things. His recent lecture on the abstruse ether [*Über Äther und Materie* (Heidelberg, 1910)] seems to me almost infantile. Moreover, the investigation that he has forced upon you . . . borders very closely on the ludicrous. I am sorry that you have to waste your time with such stupidities."

In August 1914 Lenard was swept along by the wave of patriotism and nationalism. Most scientists eventually found their way back to a more sober view, but Lenard persisted in his position of supernationalism. He composed the libelous *England und Deutschland zur Zeit des grossen Krieges*, in which he asserted that the work of German researchers was systematically hidden and plagiarized by their British colleagues. Congratulating Stark on the new advances on the effect that he had discovered, Lenard wrote (14 July 1915) with anger (which Stark shared) about the Dutch physicists whose sympathies were with the Allies: "Knowledge of the atoms is thus progressing well. That this now can happen among us cannot be put forth even by the 'neutralists' themselves as an English achievement."

After Germany's defeat Lenard felt himself called upon, as a teacher, to incite student youth against the ruling parties of the Weimar Republic, whom he despised for their democratic and antimilitaristic views. His final lecture for 1919 ended with the words: "We are a dishonorable nation, because we are a disarmed nation. He who does not offer resistance is worth nothing. To whom do we owe our dishonor? To the present rulers. Work, as I believe you will, so that next year we will have another government."

After the murder of Walther Rathenau, a state funeral and full cessation of work was decreed for 27 June 1922. Lenard protested by having the physics laboratory remain open. After the Heidelberg memorial service, where it became known that Lenard had stated he would not give his students time off because of a dead Jew, a crowd of hundreds of angry students and workers, led by the future Social Democratic Reichstag deputy, Carlo Mierendorff, stormed the laboratory. Lenard was taken into protective custody by police officials called to the scene and was released a few hours later. The incident attracted great attention throughout the country, and passionate stands were taken on both sides.

Lenard's anti-Semitism and nationalism increased. He attributed the turmoil in the newspapers about the general theory of relativity to an agreement between Einstein and the Jewish press. When the so-called Arbeitsgemeinschaft deutscher Naturforscher zur Erhaltung reiner Wissenschaft, founded by nationalistic and anti-Semitic demagogues, began a slander campaign against Einstein in Berlin in the summer of 1920, Lenard volunteered to head the movement.

The growing conflict broke into the open on 9 September 1920 at the eighty-sixth conference of the Deutsche Naturforscher und Ärzte in Bad Nauheim. The debate over the general theory of relativity turned into a dramatic duel between Einstein and Lenard. As Max Born recounted it, Lenard directed "sharp, malicious attacks against Einstein, with an unconcealed anti-Semitic bias." Fortunately, Max Planck, who was presiding over the debate, was able to prevent an uproar.

Along with personal antagonisms, another cause of Lenard's deep dissatisfaction—which often expressed itself in unusual aggression—was that mathematically difficult theories were attaining a decisive position in physics. Lenard, whose strength lay in experimentation, could not and did not want to follow this path. His anti-Semitism, joined with this disinclination for the new physical theories, led him to contrast the "dogmatic Jewish physics" with a pragmatic "German physics," in which experiments were paramount. In

1936–1937 Lenard published four volumes of experimental physics with the title *Deutsche Physik*, based on his lectures of the preceding decades. The preface begins with the author's war cry:

> "German physics?" one will ask.—I could also have said Aryan physics or physics of the Nordic man, physics of the reality explorers, of the truth seekers, the physics of those who have founded natural science.— "Science is and remains international!" someone will reply to me. He, however, is in error. In reality science, like everything man produces, is racially determined, determined by blood.

Only a very few of his colleagues (notably Stark) took Lenard's side, and his efforts remained, despite the support of the Third Reich, fruitless.

Lenard was among the ealiest adherents of National Socialism, and on 29 February 1924 he concluded his lectures for the winter semester with a reference to Hitler as the "true philosopher with a clear mind"; on 8 May his appeal to Hitler, cosigned by Stark, appeared in the *Grossdeutsche Zeitung;* and on 19 December of the same year he expressed the hope, also in a lecture, that Hitler would soon be released from prison. On 15 May 1926 Lenard traveled to a party meeting in Heilbronn, in order to meet Adolf Hitler in person. Further meetings followed, and throughout his life Hitler prized, even revered, this Nobel laureate who, unlike the other German scientists who treated Hitler as someone only half educated, had followed him unconditionally from the beginning.

Lenard became Hitler's authority in physics, teaching him, as Albert Speer reports in his memoirs, that in nuclear physics and relativity theory the Jews exercised a destructive influence. Hitler thus occasionally referred to nuclear physics as "Jewish physics," which resulted in delays in support for nuclear research. This ideological blindness and the expulsion of Jewish scientists from the Third Reich could only have had a damaging, perhaps fatal, effect on any German efforts to develop nuclear weapons—despite the early commanding lead of German physics.

After World War II, Lenard was not arrested (he was eighty-three), but he left Heidelberg, probably on orders, to live in the small village of Messelhausen, where he died.

BIBLIOGRAPHY

I. Original Works. For Lenard's writings, see *Über Kathodenstrahlen* (Leipzig, 1906; 2nd ed., Leipzig, 1920); *Über Äther und Materie* (Heidelberg, 1910; 2nd ed., Heidelberg, 1911); *England und Deutschland zur Zeit des grossen Krieges* (Heidelberg, 1914); *Über Relativitätsprinzip, Äther,*

Gravitation (Leipzig, 1918; 3rd ed., Leipzig, 1921); *Über Äther und Uräther* (Leipzig, 1921; 2nd ed., Leipzig, 1922); "Kathodenstrahlen," in *Handbuch der Experimentalphysik*, **14**, pt. 1 (Leipzig, 1927), written with August Becker; "Phosphoreszenz und Fluoreszenz," in *Handbuch der Experimentalphysik*, **23**, pt. 1 (Leipzig, 1928), written with Ferdinand Schmidt and Rudolf Tomaschek; and "Lichtelektrische Wirkung," in *Handbuch der Experimentalphysik*, **23**, pt. 2 (Leipzig, 1928), written with August Becker.

For further reference, see *Grosse Naturforscher. Eine Geschichte der Naturforschung in Lebensbeschreibungen* (Munich, 1929; 4th ed., Munich, 1941); *Deutsche Physik*, 4 vols. (Munich–Berlin, 1936–1937); *Wissenschaftliche Abhandlungen aus den Jahren 1886–1932*, 3 vols. (Leipzig, 1942–1944); and "Erinnerungen eines Naturforschers" (unpublished typewritten MS, completed in 1943. There is a copy in the Lehrstuhl für Geschichte der Naturwissenschaften und Technik der Universität Stuttgart); some of Lenard's instruments are in the possession of the Deutsches Museum in Munich. A list of them can be found in the Museum's library under no. 1962 B 350.

II. SECONDARY LITERATURE. For information on Lenard's life and work, see August Becker, ed., *Naturforschung im Aufbruch. Reden und Vorträge zur Einweihungsfeier des Philipp Lenard-Institutes der Universität Heidelberg am 14. u. 15. Dezember 1935* (Munich, 1936), also including Johannes Stark, "Philipp Lenard als deutscher Naturforscher," pp. 10–15; *Philipp Lenard, der deutsche Naturforscher. Sein Kampf um nordische Forschung ... Herausgegeben im Auftrag des Reichstudentenführers* (Munich-Berlin, 1937); "Philipp Lenard, der Vorkämpfer der Deutschen Physik," in *Karlsruher Akademische Reden*, **17** (Karlsruhe, 1937); and *Zum 80. Geburtstag von ... Philipp Lenard und zum 70. Geburtstag von Reichspostminister Dr. Ing. e.h. Wilhelm Ohnesorge* (Vienna, 1942).

See also Ernst Brüche and H. Marx, "Der Fall Philipp Lenard—Mensch und 'Politiker,'" in *Physikalische Blätter*, **23** (1967), 262–267; Carl Ramsauer, *Physik-Technik-Pädagogik. Erfahrungen und Erinnerungen* (Karlsruhe, 1949), pp. 102, 106–119; "Zum zehnten Todestag. Philipp Lenard 1862–1947," in *Physikalische Blätter*, **13** (1957), 219–222; Charlotte Schmidt-Schönbeck, "300 Jahre Physik und Astronomie an der Universität Kiel," Ph.D. dissertation (University of Kiel, 1965); and Franz Wolf, "Zur 100. Wiederkehr des Geburtstages von Philipp Lenard," in *Naturwissenschaften*, **49** (1962), 245–247.

ARMIN HERMANN

LENIN (ULYANOV), VLADIMIR ILYICH (*b.* Simbirsk, Russia [now Ulyanovsk, U.S.S.R.], 22 April 1870; *d.* Gorki, near Moscow, U.S.S.R., 21 January 1924), *politics, statesmanship, philosophy.*

Lenin's paternal grandfather was a peasant and a serf. His father, Ilya Nicolaevich, was an inspector of public schools in Simbirsk, and his mother, Maria

Alexandrovna Blank, a well-educated woman. His character and outlook were strongly influenced by his family, by the political and social environment in which he was brought up, and by the progressive traditions of Russian literature. An elder brother, Alexander, was executed in 1887 for an attempt on the life of the Czar Alexander III. In 1887 Lenin graduated from the Gymnasium with a gold medal and entered the University of Kazan. He was soon expelled for participating in the student movement and arrested. He then began the study of Marxism, seeing in it the ideological weapon for liberation of the Russian proletariat. In 1891 he succeeded brilliantly in the examination for the faculty of law at the University of St. Petersburg.

This notice will be concerned only with the place of natural science and its philosophy in Lenin's work and thought. It is convenient to divide his career into three periods. The first (1893–1905) includes his work in St. Petersburg, his Siberian exile in the village of Shushenskoye, where he married Nadezhda Konstantinova Krupskaya, and his first residence abroad from 1900 to 1905. The second (1905–1917) includes his participation in the revolutionary events of 1905–1907, followed by his second and longer residence abroad from 1908 to 1917. The third (1917–1924) includes the February and October revolutions and the early years of the Soviet state.

Throughout the first period of his life, Lenin studied seriously about natural science with emphasis on its history and on the parallels to be made out between developments in natural and social science. He devoted particular attention to the Darwinian theory of evolution, to chemistry, and to psychology, with a view to substantiating and developing a scientific method applicable to the analysis and generalization of factual material. He adopted the name Lenin in 1901, as a literary pseudonym in the first instance.

It was after 1907, however, during his exile in Switzerland that Lenin gave himself most intensively to scientific reading. The positivist philosophies of Ernst Mach and Richard Avenarius were then arousing interest among the Russian intelligentsia. Lenin considered them to be merely varieties of subjective idealism, and directed a book, *Materialism and Empiriocriticism* (1909), against them and their Russian followers. The argument is a defense and a development of dialectical materialism, the philosophical theory of Marx and Engels.

In preparation for that work, Lenin studied hundreds of writings on natural science and philosophy, concentrating now on physics, and reading widely in the literature in English, French, German, and Italian, as well as Russian. He frequented the libraries of Geneva and Paris, and traveled to London to work, like Marx before him, in the reading room of the British Museum. In the course of his studies, he formed the view that a revolution in science had begun around the turn of the century, marked by Roentgen's discovery of X rays, the isolation of radium, the identification of the electron, and the transformation of chemical elements in early atomic physics. Traditional notions about the structure and physical properties of matter and the modes of motion had thus been vitiated. It was henceforth quite impossible to hold that atoms were indivisible, elements immutable, mass invariant, and the laws of classical mechanics universally valid. Experiment showed the contrary.

Nevertheless, changes in scientific comprehension of matter offered no justification for the views of idealists and the energeticists, who made the error of referring matter to electricity while separating motion from matter and declaring motion to be immaterial. Philosophical materialism, Lenin argued, does not presuppose admitting any specific physical theory of the structure of matter as a compulsory requirement. He showed that all physical notions are relative and changeable—and yet their relativity and changeability fails to lead to a conclusion that matter may disappear or be transferred into something spiritual or immaterial. That atoms turn out to be divisible is not to be taken as a derogation of the objective existence of matter. Indeed, Lenin predicted ever further penetration of science into matter, stating that the electron is as inexhaustible as the atom, and therefore could no more be regarded as the least structural unit of matter than could the atom itself. In Lenin's view, modern physics illustrated the dialectical nature of human cognition, and it substantiated materialism. Certain physicists who adopted idealistic notions in this crisis of the old views of matter failed to understand the point. Their errors, in Lenin's view, were a feature of the revolutionary disintegration of previous basic orthodoxies in physics. Lenin indicated that overcoming the difficulties and resolving the crisis required replacing obsolete metaphysical materialism with dialectical materialism.

During his years in Bern early in the war Lenin concentrated his studies on Hegel's philosophy as well as on the history of science and technology, which he thought the most pertinent aspect of history for verifying the operation of the dialectical method. His notes on these studies were the direct continuation of *Materialism and Empiriocriticism*. They were published after his death under the title *Philosophical Notebooks* (1929–1930), for once involved in the events of the Revolution in Russia, he had no time to finish the treatise on dialectics he had conceived and already begun.

As head of the Soviet state, Lenin took a direct part in the organization of science, higher education, and cultural life. Technological problems of the energy supply had interested him even during the years of exile, when among his scientific interests was a study of the possibility of converting mineral coal deposits into gas for urban and industrial use. Now in April 1918 he formed a plan according to which the Russian Academy of Sciences should take an active part in constructing a new socialist economy. His most immediate concerns were with seeking out new mineral resources within Soviet Russia and devising a scheme for electrifying the whole country.

The Civil War in Russia (1918–1920) impeded putting these ideas into effect for a time, but at the end of 1920 Lenin drew together leading scientists and engineers in preparing a detailed project for electrification under a famous slogan: "Communism is Soviet power plus the electrification of the whole country." His speeches and writings of that period emphasize the importance of developing science and technology for the benefit of all humanity, and not of a privileged class. It was his view that science is a force making for peace and welfare in a time of inevitable revolutionary change. He kept himself informed of developments in science, and never disputed technical findings or theory on dogmatic grounds. Lenin admired Einstein as one of the great reformers of natural science and considered the theory of relativity to be entirely consistent with the dialectical progress of knowledge. He ardently advocated union between progressive scientists and Marxist philosophers. His article "On the Significance of Militant Materialism" (1922) was dedicated to that subject.

BIBLIOGRAPHY

I. ORIGINAL WORKS. Lenin's works have been collected in several editions, all published in Moscow: 1st ed., 20 vols. (1920–1926); 2nd and 3rd eds., 30 vols. (1925–1932); 4th ed., 45 vols. (1941–1957); and 5th ed., complete in 55 vols. (1958–1965). Translations include that into English of the 4th ed., as *Collected Works*, 45 vols. (Moscow–London, 1960–1970), with index to the complete works (1969–1970). Archive materials and manuscripts are listed in *Leninskye zborniki* ("Lenin Collections"), 37 collections, 39 vols. (Moscow, 1924–1970).

Lenin's works on science include *Materializm i empiriocrititsizm* ("Materialism and Empiriocriticism"), in several eds. (Moscow, 1909–1969), translated into several languages, including English (Moscow, 1970); *O nauke i vysshem obrazovanii* ("On Science and Higher Education"); 1st ed., Moscow, 1967; 2nd ed., 1971); and V. V. Adoratsky, ed., *Filosofskye tetradi*, which first appeared as vols. IX and XII (Moscow, 1929, 1930) of *Leninskye zborniki* (most recent separate edition, Moscow, 1969), and which was translated into several languages, including into French as *Cahiers philosophiques* (Paris, 1955).

II. SECONDARY LITERATURE. On Lenin and his scientific work, see the collections *Organizatsia nauki v pervye gody sovetskoy vlasti (1917–1925)*. M. S. Bastrakova *et al.*, eds., *Sbornik dokumentov* ("Organization of Science in the First Years of Soviet Power [1917–1925]. A Collection of Documents"; Leningrad, 1968); M. E. Omelyanovsky, ed., *Lenin i sovremenoye estestvoznanie* ("Lenin and the Contemporary Natural Sciences"; Moscow, 1969), English trans. in press; P. N. Pospelov, ed., *Lenin i Akademia nauk. Sbornik dokumentov* ("Lenin and the Academy of Sciences. A Collection of Documents"; Moscow, 1969); A. V. Koltsov, ed., *V. I. Lenin i problemi nauki* ("V. I. Lenin and Problems of Science"; Leningrad, 1969); and M. V. Keldysh *et al.*, eds., *Lenin i sovremennaya nauka* ("Lenin and Contemporary Science"; Moscow, 1970).

See also B. M. Kedrov, *Lenin i revolutsia v estestvoznanii XX veka* ("Lenin and the Revolution in the Natural Sciences in the Twentieth Century"; Moscow, 1969); and *Lenin i dialektika estestvoznania XX veka* ("Lenin and the Dialectics of the Natural Sciences in the Twentieth Century"; Moscow, 1971), trans. into French as Boniface Kedrov, *Dialectique, logique, gnoséologie: leur unité* (Moscow, 1970); and P. V. Kopnine, *Filosofskye idei V. I. Lenina i logika* ("Philosophical Ideas of V. I. Lenin and Logic"; Moscow, 1969); *Dialektika kak logika poznania. Opyt logiko-gnoseologitcheskogo issledovania* ("Dialectics as Logic and the Theory of Cognition. The Logical and Gnosiological Analysis"; Moscow, 1973).

Biographies include *Vladimir Ilyich Lenin. Biograficheskaya khronika 1870–1921* ("Vladimir Ilyich Lenin. A Biographical Chronicle 1870–1921"), written under the direction of G. N. Gorshkov, 3 vols. (Moscow, 1970–1972); *Vladimir Ilyich Lenin. Biografia*, written under the direction of P. N. Pospelov (1st ed., Moscow, 1960; 5th ed., 1972); K. A. Ostroukhova *et al.*, *V. I. Lenin. Kratkyi biograficheskiyi otcherk* ("V. I. Lenin. A Short Biography"; 1st ed., Moscow, 1960; 7th ed., written under the direction of G. D. Obytchkin, 1972); G. N. Golykov *et al.*, eds., *Vospominania o Vladimire Ilyiche Lenine* ("Recollections of V. I. Lenin"), 5 vols. (Moscow, 1968–1970); and, especially, N. K. Krupskaya, *O Lenine* ("On Lenin"; Moscow, 1971).

B. M. KEDROV

LENNARD-JONES, JOHN EDWARD (*b.* Leigh, Lancashire, England, 27 October 1894; *d.* Stoke-on-Trent, England, 1 November 1954), *theoretical physics, theoretical chemistry*.

As one of the first scientists to make a career of theoretical physics and theoretical chemistry, Lennard-Jones was an outstanding example of a type that has now become familiar in the physical sciences. His genius was not to make fundamental discoveries or to conduct crucial experiments but to realize quickly the potentialities of new theories proposed by other scientists and, by ingenious and painstaking calculations, to develop them to the stage where they could be applied quantitatively to a wide range of experimental data. His major contributions were in three closely related areas: the determination of interatomic and intermolecular forces; the quantum theory of molecular structure; and the statistical mechanics of liquids, gases, and surfaces.

Until the age of thirty-one his name was John Edward Jones. He studied mathematics at Manchester University, where he began his research career under the direction of Sir Horace Lamb, with work on the theory of sound. After serving in the Royal Flying Corps during World War I, he returned to Manchester as lecturer in mathematics. Jones became interested in the kinetic theory of gases through his contact with Sydney Chapman, who was then the professor of mathematics and natural philosophy at the university. In 1916 Chapman had published a new method for calculating the transport coefficients of a gas (viscosity, thermal conductivity, and diffusion) for various kinds of molecular force laws. In 1922 Jones extended this work to rarefied gases. He then went to Cambridge University, where he received his Ph.D. in 1924, and worked with R. H. Fowler, who was at that time developing quantum statistical mechanics. In 1925 he married Kathleen Mary Lennard and changed his own name to Lennard-Jones. In the same year he was elected reader in mathematical physics at the University of Bristol; he was later the first occupant of the chair of theoretical physics there.

The work for which Lennard-Jones is now best known—his determination of a semiempirical interatomic force law—was based on Chapman's gas theory and the Heisenberg-Schrödinger quantum mechanics, together with an analysis of experimental data on the properties of gases and solids. In 1924 he proposed to represent interatomic forces by the general formula

$$F(r) = -\frac{a}{r^n} + \frac{b}{r^m},$$

where *r* is the distance between the centers of two atoms. (Negative values of the function correspond to an attractive force, positive values to a repulsive force.) He attempted to determine the constants *a*, *b*, *n*, and *m* for various gases by comparing theoretical and experimental values of transport coefficients and virial coefficients (the latter being obtained from the pressure-volume-temperature relationships). In addition, X-ray diffraction data on the equilibrium interatomic distances in the solid state were used.

Lennard-Jones's first results led to values of about 5 for n and 14 or 15 for m, for the noble gases. Quantum-mechanical calculations by S. C. Wang, J. C. Slater, R. Eisenschitz, and F. London (1927–1930) indicated that n, the exponent for the long-range attractive force, should be 7 rather than 5. As a result Lennard-Jones adopted the value $n = 7$ and then, primarily for reasons of mathematical convenience, chose $m = 13$; the experimental data could be fitted equally well by several values of m. The potential energy function corresponding to this force law is

$$V(r) = -\frac{A}{r^6} + \frac{B}{r^{12}};$$

and this function, first proposed in 1931, is now generally known as the Lennard-Jones potential, or sometimes more specifically as the Lennard-Jones (6,12) potential, to distinguish it from the general form proposed earlier.

It was already evident by 1931 that quantum-mechanical calculations led to an exponential form for the short-range repulsive force; thus an alternative potential function, $V(r) = -Ar^{-6} + Be^{-kr}$, was advocated by J. C. Slater and later by R. A. Buckingham; it is generally known as the (exp, 6) potential. Extensive calculations of transport coefficients and virial coefficients of gases for these two potential functions led to the conclusion, by 1955, that both were about equally satisfactory. More recent research has shown that neither is really adequate for describing molecular and atomic interactions at very short or very long distances. Nevertheless, the Lennard-Jones potential continues to be used in many statistical mechanical calculations.

In 1932 Lennard-Jones was appointed to the new Plummer chair of theoretical chemistry at Cambridge University. As the first officially recognized "theoretical chemist" in England (or perhaps in the world), he quickly established himself as a leader in applying quantum mechanics to numerous aspects of the structure and properties of molecules. Many of his students are still actively pursuing research in this area, and Lennard-Jones must therefore be given much of the credit for introducing the discipline of quantum chemistry into Britain. His own research papers, in the 1930's and in the early 1950's, dealt with the molecular orbital method, in which calculations are based on trial wave functions chosen to reflect the structure and symmetry of the molecule as a whole, in contrast with the "valence bond" method, advocated by Linus Pauling and others, in which

atomic wave functions are taken as the starting point. Lennard-Jones also pioneered the use of mechanical computers in quantum-mechanical calculations as early as 1939.

In 1937–1939 Lennard-Jones and A. F. Devonshire published a series of papers on critical phenomena and the equation of state of liquids and dense gases. Their theory was based on a "cell model" in which each molecule is assumed to move only within a small volume, where it is acted on by a force field determined by the average positions of its neighbors. While this model would seem to attribute a solidlike structure to the system, it was found to give approximately correct results for the behavior of gases and liquids near the critical point and thus stimulated considerable work by other theorists who attempted to improve the model.

Lennard-Jones used his considerable administrative talents not only in his academic positions but also as chief superintendent of armament research for the Ministry of Supply during World War II. In 1953 he accepted the position of principal at the newly founded University College of North Staffordshire, Keele, but he was prevented from carrying out his plans for that institution by his death in 1954.

BIBLIOGRAPHY

I. ORIGINAL WORKS. A partial list of Lennard-Jones's publications is given in the memoir by N. F. Mott (cited below). The following corrections should be made in the list:

1926. "The Forces Between Atoms and Ions." Pt. II of this paper has B. M. Dent as coauthor.

1927. "The Equation of State of a Gaseous Mixture." W. R. Cook is coauthor.

1934. "Energy Distribution in Molecules in Relation to Chemical Reactions." The discussion remark by Lennard-Jones begins on p. 242, not 239.

1936. "The Interaction of Atoms and Molecules With Solid Surfaces." Pts. III and IV have A. F. Devonshire as coauthor; pt. V is by Devonshire alone and therefore should not be listed here.

1937. (Same title). Pts. VI and VII have A. F. Devonshire as coauthor.

The following papers should be added to Mott's list: "Calculation of Surface-Tension From Intermolecular Forces," in *Transactions of the Faraday Society*, **36** (1940), 1156–1162, written with J. Corner; "Critical and Co-operative Phenomena. VI. The Neighbour Distribution Function in Monatomic Liquids and Dense Gases," in *Proceedings of the Royal Society*, **178**A (1941), 401–414, written with J. Corner; "The Education of the Man of Science (Discussion Remarks)," in *Advancement of Science*, **4** (1948), 318–319; "Implications of the Barlow Report (Discussion Remarks)," *ibid.*, **5**, no. 17 (1948), 7–8; "The

Molecular Orbital Theory of Chemical Valency. XIV. Paired Electrons in the Presence of Two Unlike Attracting Centers," in *Proceedings of the Royal Society*, **218A** (1953), 327–333, written with A. C. Hurley; and "New Ideas in Chemistry," in *Advancement of Science*, **11** (1954), 136–148, repr. in *Scientific Monthly*, **80** (Mar. 1955), 175–184.

II. SECONDARY LITERATURE. Short obituary notices on Lennard-Jones were published by C. A. Coulson in *Nature*, **174** (1954), 994–995; and by A. M. Tyndall in *Proceedings of the Physical Society of London*, **67A** (1954), 1128–1129, **67B** (1954), 916–917. An article by N. F. Mott, with bibliography and portrait, appeared in *Biographical Memoirs of Fellows of the Royal Society*, **1** (1955), 175–184. His work on interatomic forces and statistical mechanics is discussed by S. G. Brush, "Interatomic Forces and Gas Theory From Newton to Lennard-Jones," in *Archive for Rational Mechanics and Analysis*, **39** (1970), 1–29; and by J. O. Hirschfelder, C. F. Curtiss, and R. B. Bird, *Molecular Theory of Gases and Liquids* (New York, 1954).

STEPHEN G. BRUSH

LENZ, EMIL KHRISTIANOVICH (Heinrich Friedrich Emil) (*b*. Dorpat, Russia [now Tartu, Estonian S.S.R.], 24 February 1804; *d*. Rome, Italy, 10 February 1865), *physics, geophysics*.

Lenz's father, senior secretary of the Dorpat magistracy, died in 1817, leaving his widow and two sons in straitened circumstances.

After graduating from secondary school with highest honors in 1820, Lenz entered Dorpat University. At the university he studied chemistry under his uncle, J. E. F. Giese, and physics under G. F. Parrot, who had founded the physics department and its physical cabinet and was the first rector of the university. Soon Parrot recommended the nineteen-year-old student to Admiral I. F. Krusenstern as a geophysical observer during Kotzebue's second scientific voyage around the world (1823–1826) on the sloop *Predpriatie*.

In 1828 Lenz was elected junior scientific assistant of the St. Petersburg Academy of Sciences. In 1829–1830 he traveled in southern Russia, where he participated in an ascent of Mt. Elbrus in the Caucasus and determined its height, conducted magnetic observations at Nikolayev according to Humboldt's program of simultaneous observations, initiated accurate measurements of variations in the level of the Caspian Sea by setting up a surveying rod in Baku, and took samples of petroleum and natural gas. In 1830 he was elected associate academician and in 1834 a full academician.

In the spring of 1831 Lenz began his investigations of electromagnetism, which he continued until 1858.

At the same time he lectured on physics at the Naval Military School (1835–1841), the Artillery Academy (1848–1861), the Central Pedagogical Institute (1851–1859), and the University of St. Petersburg (1836–1865), where from 1840 to 1863 he was dean of the physics and mathematics department and later the first rector to be elected by the professoriat in accordance with the new statutes of the university. Lenz died of an apoplectic stroke while on vacation. In 1830 he had married A. P. Helmersen, sister of the geologist G. P. Helmersen; they had seven children. Robert became a physicist and headed the physics department of the St. Petersburg Technological Institute. Lenz's students A. S. Savelyev, F. F. Petrushevsky, F. N. Shvedov, and M. P. Avenarius became university professors. His physics textbook for secondary schools ran to thirteen editions, and that on physical geography for higher military educational institutions ran to four.

Lenz's services as an expert were frequently enlisted to solve scientific and engineering problems. Many decorations were conferred on him, and he held the rank of privy councillor. He was an honorary member of many Russian universities, the Physical Society in Frankfurt am Main, and the Berlin Geographical Society, and was corresponding member of the Turin Academy of Sciences. His papers were published in the *Mémoires* and *Bulletin* of the St. Petersburg Academy of Sciences and, as a rule, in Poggendorff's *Annalen* at the same time. Some papers were also published in England, France, and Switzerland.

Lenz's name survives in the history of physics as the result of his discovery of two fundamental physical laws—soon seen as special cases of the law of conservation of energy—and a great many empirical quantitative relationships of electromagnetic, electrothermal, and electrochemical phenomena; his development of precise measuring methods, instruments, and standards; and his investigations of the theoretical principles of electrical engineering. All three of these aspects of his work can be found in almost any of his publications. His application of Ohm's law and Gauss's method of least squares and his graphical representation of various laws have distinguished his work from the scientific papers of most of his contemporaries.

In November 1833, Lenz read his paper ("Ueber die Bestimmung der Richtung der durch elektrodynamische Vertheilung erregten galvanischen Ströme") before the St. Petersburg Academy. It established Lenz's law, relating the phenomena of induction to those of the ponderomotive interaction of currents and magnets discovered by Oersted and Ampère. Lenz's law states that the induced current is in such a direction as to oppose, by its electromagnetic action, the motion of the magnet or coil that produces the induction. F. Neumann's derivation of the mathematical expression for the electromotive force of induction (1846) and Helmholtz's proof of the law of conservation of energy for electromagnetic phenomena (1847) were based on Lenz's law. This law also includes the principle of invertibility of motor and generator, which Lenz demonstrated on Pixii's magnetoelectric machine in 1838. The same law explains the phenomenon of armature reaction, discovered by Lenz in 1847 in his experiments with Störer's machine. This enabled Lenz to disprove W. Weber's incorrect hypothesis that the failure of current to increase with increased armature speeds was due to delay in the rate of magnetization of the iron, and to indicate the necessity of providing brushes at the neutrals of the machine. Continuing his experiments with Störer's machine, Lenz devised a method for plotting curves showing the phase relationship between current and magnetization (1853–1858).

Independently of Joule and with greater accuracy, in 1842–1843 Lenz established the law of the thermal action of a current, appreciating that the quantity of heat obtained was limited by the chemical processes of the battery. In 1838 he gave a visual and conclusive proof of J. C. A. Peltier's discovery by freezing water with an electric current on a layer of bismuth and antimony.

Lenz worked out the theoretical and practical aspects of the ballistic method of measuring electrical and magnetic quantities (1832) on the basis of his conception of the instantaneous, impactlike effect of induction current. Employing this method, he was able to make the first quantitative investigation of the induction phenomena themselves. (He established that the induced electromotive force in a coil is the sum of the electromotive force in each turn and does not depend upon the diameter of the turns, the thickness of the wire, or the metal of which it is made.) He also made a quantitative comparison of the resistivity of wire of different metals, established the laws of temperature dependence of resistivity in quadratic form for eight metals, derived the square-law variation of the attractive force of electromagnets with the magnetization current (under the conditions of the experiment, the magnetic field was proportional to the magnetic induction), and plotted curves showing the intensity distribution of magnetization along an iron core of a coil of finite length. The last of these measurements was made by Lenz as a member of a special committee which investigated the possibility of using Jacobi's electric motor for propelling ships. In their joint investigations (1837–1840) it was shown that the magnetization of electromagnets and,

consequently, the available power of the motor depend upon the amount of zinc dissolved in the battery. Therefore all hopes of obtaining "free work" by means of electromagnets had to be abandoned.

In 1844 Lenz deduced the law of the branching of currents in a system of parallel-connected elements with arbitrary electromotive forces and resistances—four years before the publication of Kirchhoff's more general laws.

Lenz's most significant investigation in electrochemistry, conducted with A. S. Savelyev (1844–1846), established the additivity of electrode potentials in a galvanic cell; the existence of a series of electrode potentials at the metal-electrolyte boundary, similar to the Volta series; and the additivity laws of the electromotive forces of polarization on the cathode and anode, as well as of the electromotive forces of polarization and initial electrode potential of each electrode.

In the first half of the nineteenth century, data were being accumulated in geophysics; and the main problem was to ensure their reliability. This work was done by Lenz in his own observations and in the instructions he drew up for expeditions of the Russian Geographic Society, which he helped to organize in 1845.

During the voyage of the *Predpriatie*, Lenz's use of instruments, invented by Parrot for determining the specific gravity and temperature of seawater to a depth of about two kilometers, yielded results that were not excelled in accuracy by the *Challenger* expedition or on the voyages of S. O. Makarov on the *Vityaz* at the end of the nineteenth century.

Lenz also discovered and correctly explained the existence of salinity maximums in the Atlantic and Pacific oceans north and south of the equator, the greater salinity of the Atlantic in comparison with the Pacific, and the decreasing salinity of the Indian Ocean encountered in traveling east. He noted that at definite latitudes, water at the ocean's surface is warmer than the air above it; and he found two maximums and two minimums of barometric pressure in the tropics.

BIBLIOGRAPHY

I. ORIGINAL WORKS. Some of Lenz's works were collected as *Izbrannie trudy* ("Selected Works"; Moscow, 1950), with articles by T. P. Kravetz, L. S. Berg, and K. K. Baumgart and a bibliography of 251 items. This collection does not include the following important works: "Ueber die Gesetze, nach welchen der Magnet auf eine Spirale einwirkt, wenn es ihr plötzlich genähert oder von ihr entfernt wird, und über die vortheilhafteste Konstruktion der Spiralen zu magneto-elektrischem Behufe," in *Mémoires de l'Académie impériale des sciences de St.-Pétersbourg*, 6th ser., **2** (1833), 427–457, also in R. Taylor, ed., *Scientific Memoirs*, I (London, 1837), 608–630; "Ueber einige Versuche im Gebiete der Galvanismus," in *Bulletin scientifique de l'Académie impériale des sciences de St.-Pétersbourg*, **3**, no. 21 (1838), cols. 321–326, also in *Annals of Electricity, Magnetism and Chemistry*, **3** (1838), 380–385; *Rukovodstvo k fizike, sostavlennoe dlya russkikh gimnazy* ("Manual of Physics, Prepared for Russian Secondary Schools"; St. Petersburg, 1839; 13th ed., Moscow, 1870); "Ueber galvanische Polarisation und elektromotorische Kraft in Hydroketten," in *Bulletin de la classe physico-mathématique de l'Académie impériale des sciences de St.-Pétersbourg*, **5** (1847), 1–28; and *Fizicheskaya geografia. S prilozheniem osobennogo atlasa* ("Physical Geography. With Special Atlas Appended"; St. Petersburg, 1851; 4th ed., 1865), also translated into Swedish (Kuopio, Finland, 1854).

II. Secondary Literature. On Lenz or his work, see W. K. Lebedinsky, "E. K. Lenz kak odin iz osnovateley nauki ob elektromagnetisme" ("E. K. Lenz as One of the Founders of the Science of Electromagnetism"), in *Elektrichestvo*, nos. 11–12 (1895), 153–161; O. A. Lezhneva, "Die Entwicklung der Physik in Russland in der ersten Hälfte des 19. Jahrhunderts," in *Sowjetische Beiträge zur Geschichte der Naturwissenschaften* (Berlin, 1960); O. A. Lezhneva and B. N. Rzhonsnitsky, *Emil Khristianovich Lenz* (Moscow–Leningrad, 1952), which has a bibliography of 114 titles; and W. M. Stine, "The Contribution of H. F. E. Lenz to the Science of Electromagnetism," in *Journal of the Franklin Institute*, **155** (Apr.–May 1903), 301–314, 363–384.

OLGA A. LEZHNEVA

LEO (*fl.* Athens, first half of fourth century B.C.), *mathematics*.

Leo was a minor mathematician of the Platonic school. All that is known of him comes from the following passage in the summary of the history of geometry reproduced in Proclus' commentary on the first book of Euclid's *Elements*:[1]

> Younger than Leodamas [of Thasos] were Neoclides and his pupil Leo, who[2] added many things to those discovered by their predecessors, so that Leo was able to make a collection of the elements more carefully framed both in the number and in the utility of the things proved, and also found *diorismoi*, that is, tests of when the problem which it is sought to solve is possible and when not.

Proclus' source immediately adds that Eudoxus of Cnidus was "a little younger than Leo"; and since he has earlier made Leodamas contemporary with Archytas and Theaetetus, this puts the active life of Leo in the first half of the fourth century B.C. It is not stated in so many words that he lived in Athens; but since all the other persons mentioned belonged to the Platonic circle, this is a fair inference.

Leo had been preceded in the writing of *Elements* by Hippocrates of Chios. His book has not survived and presumably was eclipsed by Euclid's. He is the first Greek mathematician who is specifically said to have occupied himself with conditions of the possibility of solutions of problems; but the Greek word[3] does not necessarily mean that he discovered or invented the subject—and indeed it is clear that there must have been *diorismoi* before his time. From the earliest days it must have been realized that a triangle could be constructed out of three lines only if the sum of two was greater than the third, as is explicitly stated in Euclid I.22. This was certainly known to the Pythagoreans, and the more sophisticated *diorismos* in Euclid VI.28 is also probably Pythagorean: a parallelogram equal to a given rectilineal figure can be "applied" to a given straight line so as to be deficient by a given figure only if the given figure is not greater than the parallelogram described on half the straight line and is similar to the defect.[4] There is also a *diorismos* in the second geometrical problem in Plato's *Meno*; and if its latest editor, R. S. Bluck, is right in dating that work to about 386–385 B.C., it probably preceded Leo's studies.[5] Nevertheless, Leo must have distinguished himself in this field to have been so singled out for mention by Eudemus, if he is Proclus' ultimate source; it is probable that he was the first to recognize *diorismoi* as a special subject for research, and he may have invented the name.[6]

NOTES

1. Proclus, *In primum Euclidis*, Friedlein ed., pp. 66.18–67.1.
2. The Greek word is in the plural.
3. It is εὑρεῖν, which in its primary sense means no more than "to find." T. L. Heath, *A History of Greek Mathematics* (Oxford, 1921), I, 303, 319, takes it to mean that Leo "invented" *diorismoi*—which he rightly regards as an error—but this is to read too much into the word in this context.
4. The problem is equivalent to the solution of the quadratic equation

$$ax - (b/c)x^2 = A,$$

which has a real root only if

$$A \not> (c/b) \cdot (a^2/4).$$

See T. L. Heath, *The Thirteen Books of Euclid's Elements*, 2nd ed. (Cambridge, 1925; repr. Cambridge–New York, 1956), II, 257–265.
5. See R. S. Bluck, *Plato's Meno* (Cambridge, 1961), pp. 108–120, for the date and app., pp. 441–461, for a discussion of this much-debated problem with full documentation.
6. Primarily signifying "definition," διορισμός came to have two technical meanings in Greek mathematics: (1) the particular

enunciation of a Euclidean proposition, that is, a closer definition of the thing sought in relation to a particular figure; and (2) an examination of the conditions of possibility of a solution. Pappus uses the word in the latter sense only, but Proclus knows both meanings (*In primum Euclidis*, Friedlein ed., pp. 202.2–5, 203.4, 9–10). It is easy to see how one meaning merges into the other. See T. L. Heath, *The Thirteen Books of Euclid's Elements*, I, 130–131; and Charles Mugler, *Dictionnaire historique de la terminologie géométrique des grecs*, pp. 141–142.

IVOR BULMER-THOMAS

LEO THE AFRICAN, also known as **al-Ḥasan ibn Muḥammad al-Wazzān al-Zayyātī al-Gharnāṭī** (*b.* Granada, Spain, *ca.* 1485; *d.* Tunis, Tunisia, after 1554), *geography.*

Leo was born in Granada, some five years before the fall of the kingdom and his family's exile to Fez, where he was educated. His geographical knowledge was based on the medieval Islamic geographical corpus and on direct observation gleaned from four journeys (as reconstructed by Mauny): (1) from Fez to Constantinople in 1507–1508; (2) to Timbuktu in 1509–1510 or the following year; (3) to Timbuktu again, and thence to Egypt via Lake Chad in 1512–1514; and (4) a final sojourn (1515–1518) as ambassador from Morocco to the Ottoman court, which took him to Constantinople and then Egypt, Arabia, and Tripoli, where he was captured by Italian pirates, transported to Italy, and given as a slave to Pope Leo X. Leo was converted to Catholicism under the aegis of the pope, whose name he took upon baptism. In 1529 he returned to Tunis and was reconverted to Islam.

In Italy, Leo wrote his geographical treatise, *Della descrittione dell'Africa*, in Italian (although doubtless it was based on Arabic notes or drafts). The *Descrittione* is divided into nine books, with the first devoted to generalities about Africa and its people and the next five to a description of North Africa. Book VII added measurably to what little had been known of the upper Niger and other regions bordering the Sahara on the south. Book VIII describes Egypt. The ninth book (of most interest to historians of science because of fresh data presented by Leo and his discussion of the limitations of Pliny's knowledge of Africa) is an essay on the rivers, animals, minerals, and plants of Africa.

The *Descrittione* was a substantial addition to the impoverished knowledge of African geography inherited from the Middle Ages. A treatise of practical geography, giving distances between places in miles, it belongs to the traditional Islamic geographical genre of "routes and provinces" (*masālik wa-mamālik*).

It was much consulted by makers of maps and portolanos (as in the maps of Africa of Ramusio [1554], Luchini [1559], and Ortelius [1570], and the Mediterranean portolano of W. Barentszoon [1596]) for 200 or more years after publication and was, in consequence, one of the few works composed in the postmedieval Islamic world which had influence in Europe.

BIBLIOGRAPHY

I. ORIGINAL WORKS. Leo's treatise, *Della descrittione dell'Africa et delle cose notabili che quivi sono*, was first published in G. B. Ramusio, ed., *Navigationi e viaggi*, I (Venice, 1550), 1–103. An inexact Latin trans. by Jean Fleurian, *De totius Africae descriptione* (Antwerp, 1556), was the source of John Pory's English trans., *A Geographical Historie of Africa* (London, 1600; facs. ed., Amsterdam–New York, 1969), which was reedited by Robert Brown for the Hakluyt Society: *The History and Description of Africa*, 3 vols. (London, 1896; repr. New York, 1963). The standard modern critical ed. is *Description de l'Afrique*, A. Epaulard, trans., 2 vols. (Paris, 1956).

II. SECONDARY LITERATURE. The fullest treatment of Leo's life and work is provided by Louis Massignon, *Le Maroc dans les premières années du XVIe siècle. Tableau géographique d'après Léon l'Africain* (Algiers, 1905), which is concerned solely with the Moroccan portion of his work. Two brief but important summaries are Massignon's entry in *Encyclopaedia of Islam*, III (Leiden, 1936), 22; and Angela Codazzi, "Leone Africano," in *Enciclopedia italiana di scienze, lettere ed arti*, XX (Rome, 1933), 899. For specific aspects of Leo's work, see Codazzi, "Dell'unico manoscritto conosciuto della 'Cosmografia dell'Africa' di Giovanni Leone l'Africano," in *International Geographical Congress (Lisbon, 1949). Comptes rendus*, IV (Lisbon, 1952), 225–226; Raymond Mauny, "Notes sur les 'Grands Voyages' de Léon l'Africain," in *Hespéris*, 41 (1954), 379–394; and Robert Brunschvig, "Léon l'Africain et l'embouchure du Chélif," in *Revue africaine* (Algiers), 79 (1936), 599–604.

THOMAS F. GLICK

LEO THE MATHEMATICIAN, also known as **Leo the Philosopher** (*b.* Constantinople[?], *ca.* 790; *d.* Constantinople[?], after 869), *mathematics, astronomy.*

Leo, who is often confused both by medieval and modern scholars with Emperor Leo VI the Wise (886–912) and with the patrician Leo Choerosphactes (*b. ca.* 845–850; *d.* after 919), belonged to a prominent Byzantine family, as is indicated by the fact that his cousin, John VII Morocharzianus the Grammarian, had been patriarch (837–843). The rather conflicting sources attest that Leo obtained a rudimentary education in rhetoric, philosophy, and arithmetic from a scholar on the island of Andros but that his more advanced knowledge of these subjects, and of geometry, astronomy, and astrology was gained through his own researches among the manuscripts that he found in monastic libraries.

In the 820's Leo began to give private instruction at Constantinople; one of the students who had read Euclid's *Elements* with him was captured by the Arab army in 830 or 831, and his enthusiastic report of his master's accomplishments caused the caliph al-Ma'mūn (813–833) to invite Leo to Baghdad. The Byzantine emperor Theophilus (829–842), learning of this invitation, responded by charging Leo with the task of providing public education at the Church of the Forty Martyrs in Constantinople. While he was in Theophilus' service, Leo supervised the construction of a series of fire-signal stations between Loulon, located north of Tarsus and close to the Arab border, and the capital. A message could be transmitted over these stations in less than an hour; by establishing theoretically synchronized chronometers at either end, Leo was able to provide for the transmission of twelve different messages depending on the hour at which the first fire was lit.

From the spring of 840 until the spring of 843 Leo served as archbishop of Thessalonica, a post he received presumably because of his political influence rather than his holiness. He was promptly deposed when the iconodule Methodius I succeeded his iconoclast cousin John as patriarch in 843. Leo apparently returned to private teaching in Constantinople until about 855, when he was appointed head of the "Philosophical School" founded by Caesar Bardas (*d.* 866) in the Magnaura Palace, where arithmetic, geometry, and astronomy, as well as grammar and philosophy, were taught. The last notice of him is in a chronicle recording an astrological prediction that he made in Constantinople in 869.

From ninth-century manuscripts Leo is known to have been involved in the process of transcribing texts written in majuscule script into minuscule; this activity may well have included some editorial work, although its nature and extent are uncertain. In any case, he was connected with the transcription of at least some of the *Tetralogies* of Plato's works, of the larger part of the corpus of Archimedes' works, and of Ptolemy's *Almagest*; it is likely that he was also concerned with the collection of mathematical and astronomical writings known as the *Little Astronomy*. Arethas' copy of Euclid's *Elements* contains, at VI.5, a "school note" by Leo on the addition and subtraction of fractions, in which he uses the Greek alphabetical symbols for numbers as the denominators. Finally,

from some of his poems preserved in the *Palatine Anthology*, it is known that he possessed copies of the *Mechanics* of Cyrinus and Marcellus, the *Conics* of Apollonius, the *Introduction* of the astrologer Paul of Alexandria, the romance of Achilles Tatius, as well as works of Theon on astronomy and Proclus on geometry.

His own surving scientific works are astrological. His "Scholia on the Hourly Motion," which claims to correct an error in an example given in Porphyrius' commentary on Ptolemy's *Apotelesmatics*, in fact refers to one in Pancharius' commentary on Ptolemy III 11, 8–11, as cited by Hephaestio of Thebes, *Apotelesmatics* II 11, 39–40 (Pingree, p. 124); his solution is absurdly taken from an entirely different example in the anonymous commentary on Ptolemy III 11, 10 (Wolf, p. 114). This proves that his technical mastery of astrology was very shaky indeed. His treatise "On the Solar Eclipse in the Royal Triplicity" is lifted from Lydus' *On Omens* 9 (Wachsmuth, pp. 19–21) and from Hephaestio I 21, 12–32 (Pingree, pp. 54–62). The short works on political astrology attributed to him in some manuscripts seem to be derived from the eleventh-century Byzantine translation of an Arabic astrological compendium of one Aḥmad, in which they are II 123–125. It is at present impossible to judge the authenticity of the other brief tracts on divination by thunder, earthquakes, the lords of the weekdays, and the gospels and psalms that are found in Byzantine manuscripts, but skepticism seems to be called for.

It remains, then, that Leo was important for his role in the transmission of Greek scientific literature and in the restoration of Byzantine learning after a long period of decline. He made few, if any, original contributions to science.

BIBLIOGRAPHY

I. ORIGINAL WORKS. 1. A homily delivered at Thessalonica on 25 March 842, is in V. Laurent, ed., *Mélanges Eugène Tisserant*, II (Vatican City, 1964), 281–302.

2. "Scholia on the Hourly Motion," F. Cumont, ed., in *Catalogus codicum astrologorum graecorum* (hereafter cited as *CCAG*), I (Brussels, 1898), p. 139.

3. "On the Solar Eclipse in the Royal Triplicity," F. C. Hertlein, ed., in *Hermes*, 8 (1874), 173–176; cf. F. Boll in *CCAG*, VII (Brussels, 1908), 150–151.

4. Twelve poems in the *Palatine Anthology* (IX 200–203, 214, 361, and 578–581; XV 12; and XVI [*Planudean Anthology*] 387 C). IX 1–358 was edited by P. Waltz (Paris, 1957), and XV by F. Buffière (Paris, 1970); the rest may be found in the ed. by F. Dübner, 2 vols. (Paris, 1864–1877).

5. A group of poems was attributed to Leo and edited by J. F. Boissonade, in *Anecdota graeca*, II (Paris, 1830), 469 ff.; the first, on old age, may indeed be his.

The following are of doubtful authenticity:

6–7. "How to Know the Lengths of the Reigns of Kings and Rulers, and What Happens in Their Reigns" and "On the Appearance of the Ruler," F. Cumont, ed., in *CCAG*, IV (Brussels, 1903), 92–93; it has been noted previously that these are taken from Aḥmad.

8. "Thunder Divination According to the Course of the Moon," an unpublished treatise found on fols. 1–2 of A 56 sup. in the Ambrosian Library, Milan. The index to *CCAG*, III (Brussels, 1901), incorrectly ascribes to Leo that text edited by A. Martini and D. Bassi on pp. 25–29.

9. "Divination From the Holy Gospel and Psalter," on fols. 28v–30 of Laurentianus graecus 86, 14, Florence.

10. "On a Sick Man," a treatise on medical astrology preserved on fols. 137v–138 of Vaticanus graecus 952.

11. A work on astrological predictions from the lords of the weekdays, accompanied by a "portrait" of Leo, on fols. 284v–285v of codex 3632 of the University Library, Bologna.

12. "Earthquake Omens," A. Delatte, ed., *CCAG*, X (Brussels, 1924), 132–135, is attributed to the Emperor Leo (Leo VI the Wise); but the attribution could possibly be a mistake for Leo the Mathematician.

13. "Gnomic Sayings," M. A. Šangin, ed., in *CCAG*, XII (Brussels, 1936), 105.

14. A poem edited by P. Matranga, *Anecdota graeca*, II (Rome, 1850), 559, is sometimes—and probably erroneously—ascribed to Leo; it follows some pieces by Leo's student Constantine, attacking him for studying pagan science, *ibid.*, 555–559.

II. SECONDARY LITERATURE. The best source is now P. Lemerle, *Le premier humanisme byzantin* (Paris, 1971), pp. 148–176; Lemerle gives references to almost all the earlier literature and is weak only in his discussion of Leo's astrological tracts.

DAVID PINGREE

LEO SUAVIUS. See **Gohory, Jacques.**

LEODAMAS OF THASOS (*b.* Thasos, Greece; *fl.* Athens, *ca.* 380 B.C.), *mathematics.*

Leodamas is treated as a contemporary of Plato in the summary of the history of geometry which Proclus reproduces in his commentary on the first book of Euclid's *Elements:*

> At this time also lived Leodamas of Thasos, Archytas of Tarentum and Theaetetus of Athens, by whom the theorems were increased in number and brought together in a more scientific grouping.[1]

Thasos, the birthplace of Leodamas, is an island in the northern Aegean off the coast of Thrace; but it would appear from the linking of his name with that of Archytas and Theaetetus that he spent his productive years in the Academy at Athens. This association with Archytas and Theaetetus suggests that he must have been a considerable mathematician; but the only other fact known about him is that Plato, according to Diogenes Laertius, "explained" ($\epsilon i\sigma\eta\gamma\dot{\eta}\sigma\alpha\tau o$) to him the method of analysis[2] or, according to Proclus, "communicated" ($\pi\alpha\rho\epsilon\delta\dot{\epsilon}\delta\omega\kappa\epsilon\nu$) it to him.[3] Proclus describes analysis as carrying that which is sought up to an acknowledged first principle; he says it is the most elegant of the methods handed down for the discovery of lemmas in geometry, and he adds that by means of it Leodamas discovered many things in geometry.[4] These passages have led some to suppose that Plato invented the method of mathematical analysis, but this is possibly due to confusion with Plato's emphasis in the *Republic* on philosophical analysis. Mathematical analysis is clearly the same as reduction, of which Hippocrates had given a notable example in the reduction of the problem of doubling the cube to that of finding two mean proportionals; and the method must have been in use even earlier among the Pythagoreans.[5]

NOTES

1. Proclus, *In primum Euclidis*, Friedlein ed. (Leipzig, 1873, repr. Hildesheim, 1967), p. 66.14–18.
2. Diogenes Laertius, III.24. If this sentence is to be read in conjunction with the one preceding, Diogenes' authority is Favorinus.
3. Proclus, *op. cit.*, p. 211.21–22.
4. The fact that at this point Proclus waxes so eloquent about the merits of analysis is regarded by T. L. Heath, in *A History of Greek Mathematics*, I (Oxford, 1921), 120, as proof that he could not himself have been the author of the summary of geometry, and it is virtually certain that the ultimate source of this part of the summary is Eudemus.
5. In the same passage Diogenes Laertius, relying on Favorinus, attributes to Plato the first use of the word "element"— which is obviously untrue, since Democritus must have used it before him.

BIBLIOGRAPHY

See Kurt von Fritz, "Leodamas," in Pauly-Wissowa, Supp. VII (Stuttgart, 1940), cols. 371–373.

IVOR BULMER-THOMAS

LEONARDO DA VINCI (*b.* Vinci, near Empolia, Italy, 15 April 1452; *d.* Amboise, France, 2 May 1519), *anatomy, technology, mechanics, mathematics, geology.*

The reader may find helpful a preliminary word of explanation on the treatment being given the work of

Leonardo da Vinci. The range of his knowledge was such as to recommend individual treatment of specific areas, but it is not that which is exceptional about the article that follows, for other articles in this *Dictionary* have been divided among several scholars specializing in appropriate disciplines. But the case of Leonardo is *sui generis* even in the context of the Renaissance, hospitable though its climate was to the growth of personal legends. It would be well to agree, before trying to penetrate Leonardo's sensibility, that it is anachronistic to ask whether he was a "scientist" and, although we may use the word "science" for convenience, it is largely irrelevant to wonder what he contributed toward its development. Strictly speaking, a thing cannot be a contribution unless it is known; and until the notebooks came to light, much was rumored but very little known of Leonardo's work except for his surviving paintings and (perhaps) certain features of his engineering practice, together with the well-founded tradition that he was learned in anatomy.

Rather than attributing this or that "discovery" to Leonardo, the interesting matter is to learn what Leonardo knew and how he knew it. It is to fulfill that purpose that the present article was composed. The task is important because it measures the scope of an extraordinary intellect and sensibility. Beyond that, it is rewarding because the study of Leonardo enables us to estimate what could be known at that particular juncture. Indeed, the opportunity is unique in the history of science, at least in its extent, for scientists and philosophers who advance their subjects by completing and communicating their work normally obscure in the process the elements with which they began. Not so Leonardo, whose art in drawing and artlessness in writing open windows to the knowledge latent in the civilization of the Renaissance.

The editors consider that they have been fortunate in persuading Dr. Kenneth D. Keele to write an introductory section on the lineaments of Leonardo's career together with a more detailed treatment of his studies in anatomy and physiology. Drs. Ladislao Reti, Marshall Clagett, Augusto Marinoni, and Cecil Schneer then develop in comparable detail the aspects of Leonardo's work that pertain to technology and engineering, to the science of mechanics, to mathematics, and to geology.

CHARLES C. GILLISPIE

LIFE, SCIENTIFIC METHODS, AND ANATOMICAL WORKS

Leonardo da Vinci was the illegimate son of Piero da Vinci, a respected Florentine notary, and a peasant girl named Caterina. The year that Leonardo was born, his father was rapidly married off to a girl of good family, Albiera di Giovanni Amadori. Genetically it is of some interest that Piero's youngest legitimate son, Bartolommeo, an enthusiastic admirer of his half-brother Leonardo, deliberately repeated his father's "experiment" by marrying a woman of Vinci and, as Vasari relates, "prayed God to grant him another Leonardo." In fact he produced Pierino da Vinci, a sculptor of sufficient genius to win himself the name of "Il Vinci" long before he died at the age of twenty-two.

Young Leonardo's education at Vinci was conventionally limited to reading and writing. His early manifested gifts for music and art induced his father to apprentice him, about 1467, to Andrea del Verrocchio, in whose workshop he studied painting, sculpture, and mechanics. During this period in Florence, Leonardo's activities appear to have been directed predominantly toward painting and sculpture; the earliest of his pictures still extant, the "Baptism of Christ," was painted in collaboration with Verrocchio in 1473. The "Adoration of the Magi" was still incomplete when he left for Milan in 1482, to enter the employ of Ludovico Sforza (Ludovico il Moro), duke of Milan. In his application to Ludovico, Leonardo revealed that a great deal of his attention had already been devoted to military engineering; only in concluding did he mention his achievements in architecture, painting, and sculpture, which could "well bear comparison with anyone else."

Leonardo lived at Milan in the duke's service until 1499. During these years his interest in the problems of mechanics and the physics of light grew steadily while his artistic output reached a peak in the fresco "The Last Supper" (1497) and in the clay model of his great equestrian statue of Francesco Sforza (1493). The notebooks of this period show the increase of his interest in mathematics, the physics of light, the physiology of vision, and numerous mechanical problems, including those of flight. Four projects for books—separate treatises on painting, architecture, mechanics, and the human figure—appear in his notes. These studies were to occupy him for the rest of his life. During his last years in Milan he collaborated with the mathematician Luca Pacioli on his *Divina proportione*; Leonardo drew the figures for the first book.

After the capture of the duke of Milan by the French, Leonardo left for Venice, eventually returning to Florence. He then entered the service of Cesare Borgia and was employed for about a year as chief inspector of fortifications and military engineer in the Romagna. Following this he was responsible for an unsuccessful attempt to divert the Arno near Pisa. While in Florence he began the portrait "Mona Lisa" and also the ill-fated fresco "Battle of Anghiari." During these years in Florence, from 1500 to 1506, Leonardo began his systematic researches into human anatomy. Mathematics and the mechanical sciences, too, increasingly occupied his time; and he began to couple his study of the problem of human flight with intensive research on bird flight and meteorology. His studies on the movement of water, a lifelong preoccupation, were later compiled into the *Treatise on the Movement and Measurement of Water*.

In June 1506 Leonardo returned to Milan, where Charles d'Amboise, the French governor, showed him the keenest appreciation he had yet experienced. During this period he produced most of his brilliant anatomical drawings, perhaps stimulated for a short while by the young Pavian anatomist Marcantonio della Torre. Leonardo had now come to feel that mathematics held the key to the "powers" of nature; and his work in hydrology, geology, meteorology, biology, and human physiology was increasingly devoted to a search for the geometrical "rules" of those powers through visual experience, experiment, and reason.

After the French were expelled from Milan in 1513, Leonardo left for Rome, hoping that the Medici Pope Leo X and his brother Giuliano would provide him with encouragement and a good working environment. Nothing came of this hope; and in 1516 he resumed the French liaison, this time with Francis I, with whom he traveled to Amboise in 1516. He died there after a stroke.

Problems of Evaluating Leonardo's Scientific Thought. There are many different opinions concerning Leonardo's stature as a scientist. The essential reason that this is so lies in the grossly abbreviated form in which his work has come down to posterity. Leonardo himself noted that "abbreviators of works do harm to knowledge . . . for certainty springs from a complete knowledge of all the parts which united compose the whole" (*Windsor Collection*, fol. 19084r, in I. A. Richter, *Selections . . .*, p. 3). Unhappily, his extant notes are both abbreviated and confused. It is therefore necessary to assess these defects before evaluating Leonardo's work in the history of science.

The Losses of Leonardo's Manuscripts. Although Leonardo clearly intended to write treatises on painting, architecture, mechanics, and anatomy, he brought none to publication. Two known works are published under his name, the *Treatise on Painting* and *Treatise on the Movement and Measurement of Water*; both were compiled after his death from his notes. These remain of great value, although their respective compilers, Francesco Melzi and Luigi Arconati, constructed them according to their own ideas, rather than Leonardo's. The great mass of surviving data consists of some 6,000 sheets of Leonardo's manuscript notes. It is difficult to estimate what proportion of the whole these represent. Reti has calculated that 75 percent of the material used by Melzi for his compilation of the *Treatise on Painting* has since been lost. If only a corresponding proportion of Leonardo's scientific notes are extant, this is indeed a severe truncation. The qualitative loss is probably even greater, since there is no trace of a number of "books" to which Leonardo frequently referred in his notes as "completed," and which he used as references, among them an "Elements of Mechanics," and a "Book on Water"—not to mention fifteen "small books" of anatomical drawings.

Sources of Confusion in the Notes. The notes that remain are in great confusion, in part because Leonardo himself made no effort to integrate them, and in part because after his death they underwent almost every conceivable kind of disarrangement and mutilation—as is illustrated by the great scrapbook of sheets composing the *Codex Atlanticus*. Thus the thousands of pages that do survive resemble the pieces of a grossly incomplete jigsaw puzzle.

FIGURE 1. The diversity of subjects on a single page of Leonardo's notes, of which this is an example, raises problems of interpretation (*Windsor Collection*, fol. 12283. Reproduced by gracious permission of Her Majesty Queen Elizabeth II).

Leonardo's mode of expressing himself often challenges interpretation. Apart from his "mirror" script, he habitually presented his thoughts visually, sometimes covering an astonishing range of phenomena with very few words, as in *Windsor Collection*, fol. 12283 (Figure 1). This page contains segments of circles, a geometrical study for the "rule of diminution" of a straight line when curved, a study of curly hair (with a note on its preparation), and drawings of grasses curling around an arum lily, an old man with curly hair, trees, billowing clouds, rippling waves in a pool, a prancing horse, and a screw press. All can be seen as studies of curves, viewed from different aspects, each of which is developed in detail in various parts of his notes. The sheet provides a good example of Leonardo's visual approach to any problem—by integration—a mode which has until recently been frowned upon by orthodox science. Interpretation of the meaning of many of the drawings must necessarily be speculative; but it is always dangerous to call any drawing a "doodle," since some of Leonardo's most interesting scientific concepts appear as casual, small, inartistic figures.

A further source of confusion in Leonardo's notes derives from his habit of periodically returning to the same subject. This often resulted in incompatible statements in different notes, which Leonardo himself recognized, referring in 1508 to his notes as "a collection without order taken from many papers . . . for which O reader blame me not because the subjects are many, and memory cannot retain them . . . because of the long intervals between one time of writing and another" (*Codex Arundel*, fol. 1r).

Leonardo's thinking was intensely progressive during these "long intervals" of time. A note made in 1490 may therefore differ markedly from one on the same subject from 1500 or 1510. With this understanding, contradictory statements can often be transformed into sources of comprehension if they can be dated—a means of tracing the progress of Leonardo's thought that has only recently become available.

In 1936, with the facsimile production of the Forster codices, it was thought that publication of extant Leonardo notes was complete. Nevertheless, in 1967 two further codices, containing 340 folios, were found in Madrid. These still await publication; and one wonders how many more will be found.

Leonardo's Scientific Method. Leonardo lived at a time when theology was the queen of the sciences. Theological thinking emphasizes the divine incomprehensibility and mystery of natural phenomena; even the Neoplatonic thought of Leonardo's contemporary Marsilio Ficino focused on a direct, revealed link between the mind of man and God and was not concerned with the visual exploration of natural phenomena. Leonardo, on the other hand, declared that faith that is the foundation of all science: there is a logic in natural phenomena detectable by the senses and comprehensible to the mathematical logic of the human mind. Beyond this he postulated God as the creator of all.

Leonardo felt his way to his scientific outlook through his study of the theory of painting, which led him to analyze visual phenomena. As he declared,

> Painters study such things as pertain to the true understanding of all the forms of nature's works, and solicitously contrive to acquire an understanding of all these forms as far as possible. For this is the way to understand the Creator of so many admirable things, and this is the way to love such a great Inventor. In truth great love is born of great knowledge of the thing that is loved [*Treatise on Painting*, para. 80].

For Leonardo the world of nature was created by God, and the science or theory of painting "is a subtle invention which with philosophical and ingenious speculation takes as its theme all the various kinds of forms, airs and scenes, plants, grasses and flowers which are surrounded by light and shade. And this truly is a science and the true-born daughter of Nature" (MS *Ashburnham* 2038, fol. 20r, in E. MacCurdy, *Notebooks*, II, 229).

Science for Leonardo was basically visual: "The eye, the window of the soul, is the chief means whereby the understanding can most fully and abundantly appreciate the infinite works of Nature; and the ear is second" (MS *Ashburnham* 2038, fol. 20r, in E. MacCurdy, *Notebooks*, II, 227). He asserted his belief that the patterns of natural phenomena can conform with the patterns of form created in the human mind—"Painting compels the mind of the painter to transform itself into the very mind of Nature to become an interpreter between Nature and the art. It explains the causes of Nature's manifestations as compelled by its laws. . ." (*Treatise on Painting*, para. 55). These are "laws of necessity the artificer of nature—the bridle, the law and the theme" (*Codex Forster*, III, fol. 43v); while "Necessity constrains all effects to the direct result of their causes" (*Codex Atlanticus*, fol. 345v-b). For Leonardo these causes, effects, and laws could be expressed visually in the form of a geometry that includes the movement of things as well as their resting forms.

Leonardo's Mathematics of Science. Leonardo defined science as "that mental analysis which has its origin in ultimate principles beyond which nothing in nature can be found which is part of that science" (*Treatise on Painting*, para. 1). Geometry was such a science, in which "the point is that than which nothing can be smaller. Therefore the point is the first principle of geometry and nothing in nature or the human mind can be the origin of the point" (*ibid.*). He differentiated between the "natural" point, which has the characteristics of an atom, and the "conceptual" point of geometry: "The smallest natural point is larger than all mathematical points, because a natural point is a continuous quantity and as such is infinitely divisible, while the mathematical point is indivisible, having no quantity" (quoted from J. P. Richter, *Literary Works of Leonardo*, 44). In this way he linked geometry with physics and denied the term "science" to any investigation that is not capable of "mathematical" demonstration, such as the so-called sciences that "begin and end in the mind" and are "without the test of experience." He proclaimed the necessity for both geometry and experience, taking as his example astronomy, which was all "visual lines, which enclose all the different shapes of bodies created by nature, and without which the art of geometry is blind" (*Treatise on Painting*, para. 15). Thus, via geometry, human experience could interpret nature.

Leonardo divided his inquiry into three coincident parts: the geometry of vision, the geometry of nature, that is, physics or "natural philosophy," and pure geometry. His investigation of vision was the first of his physiological researches; it pertained primarily to perception and derived largely from the traditional concept of a cone of vision. (Pure geometry—that is, Euclidean geometry—is discussed in the mathematics section, below.)

The Geometry of Vision. Without the test of visual experience there could be no science for Leonardo, for "the observer's mind must enter into nature's mind" (*Treatise on Painting*, para. 40). The problem of vision involved his concept of the spread of light from its source. This he conceived of by analogy to the transverse wave-spread set up by dropping a stone into a still pond. "Just as a stone flung into water becomes the centre and cause of many circles . . . so

any object placed in the luminous atmosphere diffuses itself in circles and fills the surrounding air with images of itself" (MS *A*, fol. 9r). These images spread out in circles from the surfaces of the object with steady diminution of power to the eye (Figure 2). As pond waves spread by the power of percussion, so the light wave varies in power with the force of percussion and inversely with its distance in the form of an infinite number of pyramids (like perspective), diminishing as they approach the eye (Figure 3). The

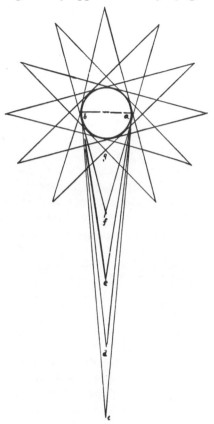

FIGURE 3. The pyramidal spread of light from a luminous object, *ab*, in all directions. "The circle of equidistant converging rays of the pyramid will give angles, and objects to the eye of equal size" (MS *Ashburnham* 2038, fol. 6b).

pyramidal form which Leonardo used to represent this decline of power has the characteristic that

> . . . if you cut the pyramid at any stage of its height by a line equidistant from its base you will find that the proportion of the height of this section from its base to the total height of the pyramid will be the same as the proportion between the breadth of this section and the breadth of the whole base [MS *M*, fol. 44r].

Leonardo thus represented the power of percussion by the base or diameter of a cone or pyramid, and its

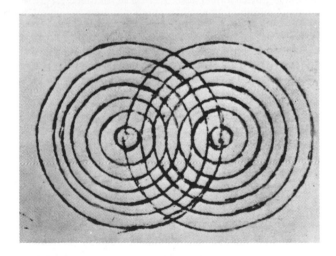

FIGURE 2. The intersection of waves produced by two stones dropped into a pond. Leonardo used this as an analogy for the spread of all powers produced by percussion, in which he included light and sound (MS *A*, fol. 61r).

decline by its breadth at any height of the pyramid. When the spreading light image reaches the pupil, it finds not a point but a circle, which in its turn contracts or expands with the power of light reaching it and forms the base of another cone or pyramid of light rays directed by refraction through the lens system of the eye to the optic nerve (Figure 4). The image then travels via the central foramen up the nerve to the "imprensiva" of the brain, wherein the percussion is impressed. Here it joins with the impressions made by the "percussions" from the nerves that serve the senses of hearing, smell, touch, and pain—all of which are activated by similar percussive mechanisms following similar pyramidal laws.

Thus in the imprensiva a spatiotemporal verisimilitude of the external environment is produced, while a truly mathematical, geometrically conditioned model of reality is experienced by the "senso commune" in

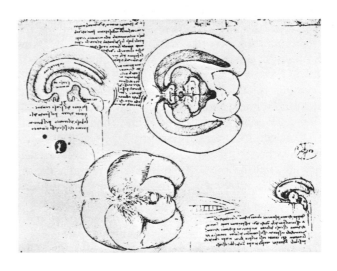

FIGURE 5. Wax casts of the cerebral ventricles. In the figure at left the lateral ventricle is labeled "imprensiva"; the third ventricle, "senso commune"; and the fourth ventricle, "memoria" (*Quaderni d'anatomia*, fol. 7r. Reproduced by gracious permission of Her Majesty Queen Elizabeth II).

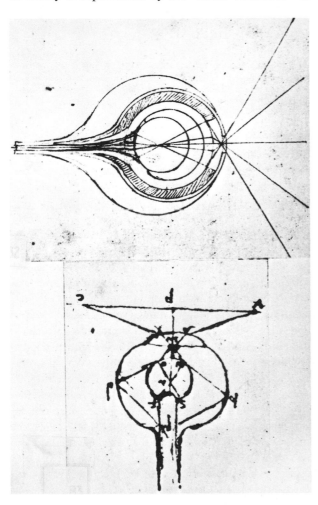

FIGURE 4. The dioptrics of the lens system of the eye. In the upper figure rays are shown crossing once at the pupil and again in the lens, to which the optic nerve is in apposition (*Codex Atlanticus*, fol. 337r-a). Below, rays are reflected from the retina, which acts as a mirror (MS *D*, fol. 10).

the third ventricle where all these sensations come together (Figure 5). "Experience therefore does not ever err, it is only your judgment that errs in promising itself results which are not caused by your experiments" (*Codex Atlanticus*, fol. 154r). Leonardo later located the imprensiva in the lateral ventricles of the brain when he discovered them. "Memory" and "judgment" he located in the fourth and third ventricles, respectively. Thus his distinction between sensory "experience" and "judgment" have physiological as well as psychological connotations.

Leonardo recognized that errors of sensory observation can occur. He attributed these to "impediments"—the resulting experience "partaking of this impediment in a greater or less degree in proportion as this impediment is more or less powerful."

The Geometry of Nature. The pyramidal form that Leonardo imposed upon the propagation of visual images he further applied to the propagation of the four "powers" of nature: "movement, force, weight, and percussion." He saw it as perspectival, i.e., simple, pyramidal proportion. It was in this form, therefore, that he quantified these powers, whether dealing with light and vision, as above, or with other forms of the powers of nature, as, for example, weights, levers, the movements of water, and power transmission in machines, including the human heart or limbs. For example, he described the force of a spring as "pyramidal because it begins at a point or instant and with each degree of movement and time it acquires size and speed" (MS *G*, fol. 30r); he further described the movement of compound pulleys as "pyramidal since it proceeds to slowness with uniform diminution of uniformity down to the last rope" (*ibid.*, fol. 87v); see mechanics section, below. Such phrasing is reminiscent of the terminology of the Merton School and reminds one that the names "Suisset" and "Tisber" occur in Leonardo's notes.

Leonardo's close relationship with Luca Pacioli in Milan strongly stimulated his interest in mathematics. At this time he made an intensive study of algebra and the "manipulation of roots," describing algebra as "the demonstration of the equality of one thing with another" (MS *K*, II, fol. 27b). He does not, however, appear to have applied this concept of algebraic equations to his scientific work. On the other hand, he did apply square roots to the calculation of wingspan in relation to the weight of the human flying machine. His formula ran thus: "If a pelican of weight 25 pounds has a wingspan of 5 braccia, then a man of weight 400 pounds will require a wingspan of $\sqrt{400} = 20$ braccia" (*Codex Atlanticus*, fol. 320r-b). This calculation was made about the time of his final attempt at flight (1504). Leonardo never applied the inverse-square law to any "power" or "force."

Leonardo's Methods of Observation and Experiment. Leonardo's acquisition of "experience" was remarkable for three main methods: measurement, models, and markers. From about 1490, when he concluded that the "powers" of nature had geometrical relationships, Leonardo attempted to quantify his observations and experiments. Measurement entered into all his observations; measurements of weights, distances, and velocities. His notes from about this time contain descriptions of hodometers, anemometers, and hygrometers, as well as balances of various ingenious types.

In general one is struck, however, by the crudity of his measurements of both space and time. He rarely mentioned any spatial measurement other than the braccio (approximately twenty-four inches). For small intervals of time, such as the heart rate, he used musical tempi. Here he explained, "of which tempi an hour contains 1080" (*Quaderni d'anatomia*, II, 11r). For timing he used sandglasses and water clocks. Although he certainly did not invent the balance, he did use balances in a highly original way—for example, by placing a man in one pan and observing whether the downward movement of a levered wing to which he was attached would raise him or not, and by weighing objects at different temperatures.

Models were Leonardo's favorite form of experi-

mental demonstration. He used them particularly for observations of the flow of water or blood currents. Perhaps his smallest model was a glass cast of an aorta with its valves (Figure 6); the largest was one of

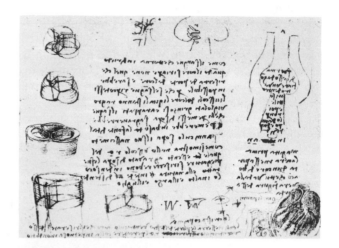

FIGURE 6.   Upper right, a glass cast of an aorta with instructions for casting. The figures on the left margin are also schemes for aortic models (*Quaderni d'anatomia*, II, fol. 12r. Reproduced by gracious permission of Her Majesty Queen Elizabeth II).

the Mediterranean, which he built to demonstrate the effects of the rivers entering it.

Markers were another favorite method for visualizing the movements of water, both in Leonardo's models and in actual rivers. His models for this purpose consisted of tanks with three glass sides through which he could view the seeds, bits of paper, or colored inks used as markers; he had a special set of floats, each designed to be suspended at a different depth. With such observations and experiments he accumulated an enormous mass of data regarding the directions and velocities of water movements, their angles of reflection, the effects of percussion, and the movements of suspended solids. He traced the movements of sand and stones in water and their mode of deposition, as well as the action of water on surrounding surfaces—for instance, the erosion of river banks. He also applied these results to such problems as the movement of lock gates or aortic valves. He extended the marker method to the other "elements," particularly to the movement of solid bodies in air, including projectiles, dust, and "birds" (models).

Leonardo frequently advocated the repetition of experiments, "for the experiment might be false whether it deceived the investigator or not" (MS *M*, fol. 57r). If a confirmed experiment did not agree with a suggested mathematical "rule," he discarded the rule. By this means, and clearly to his surprise, he had to reject the Aristotelian "rule" that "if a power moves a mobile object with a certain speed, it will move half this mobile object twice as swiftly." By experiment Leonardo tested the rule, comparing the movements of "atoms" of dust in air with those of large objects fired from a mortar; and from his observations he drew a moral—mistrust those who have used nothing but their imagination and have not verified their statements by experiment. For Leonardo mathematical rules had to give way to experimental verification or refutation.

Leonardo applied his experimental or mathematical results only to visual space. Unlike such medieval antecedents as Oresme, he refused to quantify such abstract qualities as beauty or glory; he specifically stated that geometry and arithmetic "are not concerned with quality, the beauty of nature's creations, or the harmony of the world" (*Treatise on Painting*, para. 15). He honored the precept that these are fields for the creative arts rather than for the creative sciences.

Leonardo's "Rules." Not only did Leonardo advocate repetition of experiments, but he performed experiments in series, each repeated with one slight variation to resemble continuous change. For example, on investigating flight with model birds, he wrote: "Suppose a suspended body resembling a bird and that the tail is twisted to different angles. By means of this you will be able to derive a general rule as to the various movements of birds occasioned by bending their tails" (MS *L*, fol. 61v). Demonstrating the distribution of weight of a beam suspended by two cords, he wrote: "I make my figures so that you shall know all the cases that are placed under one simple rule" (*Codex Atlanticus*, fol. 274r-b). The statement is carried out in the following three pages of patient depiction of all the variable distributions of weight (*ibid.*, fols. 274r-b, r-a, v-b).

Thus by repeated observation, repeated experiment, and calculatedly varying his experiments, Leonardo built up quantitative data into limited generalized "rules." "These rules," he wrote, "are the causes of making you know the true from the false" (*ibid.*, fol. 119v-a). Since the rule is mathematical in form, he averred, "There is no certainty where one cannot apply any of the mathematical sciences" (MS *G*, fol. 96v); and clearly it follows that "No man who is not a mathematician should read the elements of my work" (*Windsor Collection*, fol. 19118v, in I. A. Richter, *Selections* . . ., p. 7).

The Four Powers. Leonardo's notes contain long debates on the nature of movement, weight, force, and percussion, all in the context of the Aristotelian elements of earth, air, fire, and water. From this debate emerged the statement: "Weight, force, together with percussion, are to be spoken of as the producers of movement as well as being produced by it" (*Codex Arundel*, fol. 184v). He finally saw weight as an accidental power produced by a displaced element "desiring" to return to its natural place in its own element. Thus "gravity" and "levity" were two aspects of the same drive. Force was caused by violent movement stored within bodies. Sometimes Leonardo called force "accidental weight," using the Aristotelian meaning of "accidental." Movement of an object from one point to another could be natural, accidental, or participating. Impetus was derived movement arising from primary movement when the movable thing was joined to the mover. He defined percussion as "an end of movement created in an indivisible period of time, because it is caused at the point which is the end of the line of movement" (*Codex Forster*, III, fol. 32r. in I. A. Richter, *Selections* . . ., p. 77).

This remarkable simplification of his experiences of "nature" was applied by Leonardo to all fields of investigation and practical creation, that is, to science and its derived art of invention. Clearly these four powers were both derived from, and most applicable to, mechanics. "Mechanics is the paradise of mathematical science because here one comes to the fruits of mathematics" (MS *E*, fol. 8v). This statement was generalized when Leonard asserted: "Proportion is not only found in numbers and measurements but also in sounds, weights, times, spaces, and whatsoever powers there be" (MS *K*, 497, Ravaisson-Mollien). From these two statements his essentially integrative approach to all problems can be glimpsed. In each field of investigation he built up, from quantitative observation and experiment, defined mathematical "rules" which he applied to the particular problem occupying him. For example, with regard to the flight of the bird, when discussing the problem of its being overturned, he set out the forces concerned and then stated: "This is proved by the first section of the Elements of Machines which shows how things in equilibrium which are percussed outside their center of gravity send down their opposite sides . . ." (*Codex on Flight* . . ., fol. 8r). He continued, "And in this way it will return to a position of equilibrium. This is proved by the fourth of the third, according to which that object is more overcome that is acted on by the greater forces; also by the fifth of the third, according to which a resistance is weaker the farther it is from its fixed point" (*ibid.*, fol. 9r). In this way Leonardo's "rules" were built into the structure of his thought about all the powers of nature, imparting a remarkable consistency in all fields, whether mechanics, light, sound, architecture, botany, or human physiology. Unfortunately, the books to which he refers in this way, showing how he reached these generalizations, have been lost.

Leonardo's Achievements in Science. Leonardo's achievements in art and science depended primarily on his remarkable acuity of vision, and his particular sensitivity to the geometrical consequences of that vision. These gifts he combined with the creative technology of the engineer and the artist. These creative aspects emerge in his achievements in scientific technology.

Mathematics. Leonardo's approach to mathematics was predominantly physical. Even when appearing abstract, as in his "Book on Transmutation" (of forms), his practical object was revealed by his reference to the metalworker or sculptor. Typical of his contribution to mathematics were proportional and parabolic compasses. His explorations of the properties of the pyramid were, as is to be expected, thorough. As a result of an experimental investigation of the center of gravity of a tetrahedron, he discovered that the center of gravity is at "a quarter of the axis of that pyramid" (MS *F*, fol. 51r). (For his development of pure mathematics, see the section on mathematics.)

Mechanics. (Here brief mention is made only of the main areas studied by Leonardo. For fuller development of these, see the section on mechanics.) Leonardo's point of departure for statics was Archimedes' work on the lever, of the principles of which he had some understanding. His appreciation that equilibrium of a balance depends arithmetically upon the weights and their distances from the fulcrum gave him many examples of pyramidal (arithmetical) proportion.

Leonardo never quite reached the concepts of mass or inertia, as opposed to weight. He still used the "halfway" concept of impetus when he said, "All moved bodies continue to move as long as the impression of the force of their motors remains in them" (*Codex on Flight . . .*, fol. 12r). This is as near as he came to Newton's first law. And although Leonardo disproved the Aristotelian relationship between force, weight, and velocity, he did not reach the concept of acceleration resulting from action of the force on a moving body. Newton's third law, however, Leonardo did state clearly in his concrete way and apply persistently. For example, "An object offers as much resistance to the air as the air does to the object" (*Codex Atlanticus*, fol. 381v-a). And after a repetition of this statement he added: "And it is the same with water, which a similar circumstance has shown me acts in the same way as air" (*Codex Atlanticus*, fol. 395r). One can see here the process by which he built up to one of his "rules"—Newton's third law.

Gravity for Leonardo was the force of weight which is exerted "along a central line which with straightness is imagined from the thing to the center of the world" (MS *I*, fol. 22v). In his investigations of it Leonardo dropped weights from high towers. For example, he dropped two balls of similar weight together and observed at the bottom whether they still touched (MS *M*, fol. 57r). From such experiments he noted: "In air of uniform density the heavy body which falls at each degree of time acquires a degree of movement more than the degree of preceding time . . . the aforesaid powers are all pyramidal, seeing that they commence in nothing and proceed to increase in degrees of arithmetical proportion" (*ibid.*, fol. 44r). He concluded that the velocity is proportional to the time of fall but, incorrectly, that the distance of fall is also proportional directly to the time, not to its square.

Leonardo appreciated and used the concepts of resolving and compounding of forces. He described the parallelogram of forces, although he did not draw it, in analyzing the flight of the bird (*Codex on Flight*, fol. 5r); and he resolved the movement of a weight down an inclined plane into two components (MS *G*, fol. 75r). Such movement led him to study friction, a force which, like so many others, he divided into simple and compound. Leonardo appreciated the importance of the pressure or weight factor and the nature of the surface and their independence of area. Thus, for "a polished smooth surface" he found a coefficient of friction of 0.25. He was aware that such friction produces heat.

Hydrodynamics. All the "rules" described above were carried into Leonardo's studies of the movement of water. Here two phenomena received particular attention: wave formation and eddies. He found the velocity of flow of water to be inversely proportional to the dimension of the passage, whether rivers or blood vessels are being discussed. Currents of water, as observed by his marker experiments, percussed so that the angles of incidence and reflection were equal, similar to those made by bouncing balls. The formation of the transverse wave from the percussion of a stone in water was similarly explained. The cohesion of a drop of water against the force of gravity led Leonardo to postulate a force "like that of a magnet," which was also responsible for capillary attraction. The extent of his studies of water is reflected in the *Codex Leicester*, where he draws "732 conclusions as to water" (*Codex Leicester*, fol. 26v).

LEONARDO DA VINCI

Cosmology. Water, more than the other elements, led Leonardo to compare "the greater and the lesser world." The macrocosm–microcosm analogy was very real to him, since he believed that similar laws governed both the cosmos and the body of man. He considered at one time, for example, that the movement of the waters of the earth, particularly to the tops of mountains, was analogous to the movement of blood to the head, both being produced by heat. At first he postulated that water was drawn up by the heat of the sun; later he suggested that the heat arose from subterranean fires, from volcanos in the earth. He posited such subterranean fires as an analogy to the human heart, which he saw not only as the percussor of blood to the periphery but also as a source of heat to the body through the friction of the blood in its chambers (Figure 7).

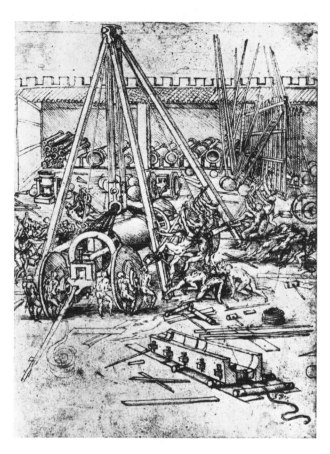

FIGURE 8. "The Arsenal," one of the many studies of the external powers of the human body, here being exerted to create a power transformation into the projectile force of a cannon (*Windsor Collection*, fol. 12647. Reproduced by gracious permission of Her Majesty Queen Elizabeth II).

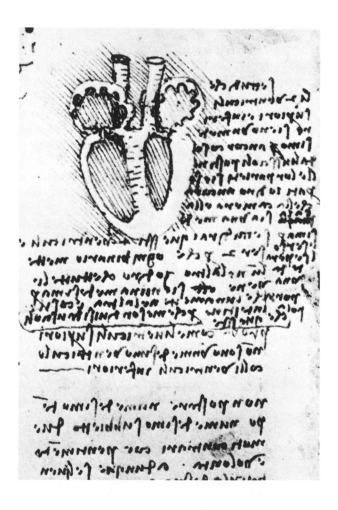

FIGURE 7. The heart as a percussion and heat-producing instrument. Blood from the atria, above, is propelled into the ventricles, below, from which part of the blood is propelled into the blood vessels and part back into the atria, producing heat by friction (*Quaderni d'anatomia*, II, fol. 3v. Reproduced by gracious permission of Her Majesty Queen Elizabeth II).

Leonardo saw the land of the world as emerging from its surrounding element of water by a process of growth. Mountains, the skeleton of the world, were formed by destructive rain, frost, and snow washing the soft earth down into the rivers. Where large landslides occurred, inland seas were formed, from which the waters eventually broke through gorges to reach the sea, their "natural" level. No better summary of Leonardo's neptunist concept of these geological changes can be found than the background of his "Mona Lisa."

Biology. From about 1489 to 1500 Leonardo investigated the physiology of vision and the external powers of the human body. During this period he applied the principles of the "four powers"—movement, force, weight, and percussion—to every conceivable human activity. Many of the drawings of men in action found in the *Treatise on Painting* date from this period, during which he also completed a book, now lost, on the human figure. He drew men sitting, standing, running, digging, pushing, pulling, and so on, all with such points of reference as the center of gravity or the leverage of the trunk and limbs. These simple movements he elaborated into studies of men at work and so to the transformation of human power into machines at work, the field of many of his technological inventions (Figure 8). (For Leonardo's development of this field, see the section on technology.)

Anatomy. Leonardo later investigated the internal powers of the human body. He described his approach to human anatomy and physiology in a passage headed "On Machines":

> Why Nature cannot give movement to animals without mechanical instruments is shown by me in this book, *On the Works of Motion Made by Nature in Animals.* For this I have set out the rules on the 4 powers of nature without which nothing can through her give local motion to these animals. Therefore we shall first describe this local motion, and how it produces and is produced by each of the other three powers. . . .

He then briefly defined these powers (*Quaderni d'anatomia*, I, fol. 1r) and added an admonition: "Arrange it so that the book of the elements of mechanics with examples shall precede the demonstration of the movement and force of man and other animals, and by means of these you will be able to prove all your propositions" (*Anatomical Folio A*, fol. 10r).

As usual, Leonardo gave intense thought to his methods of approaching the problem of man the machine. "I shall describe the function of the parts from every side, laying before your eyes the knowledge of the whole healthy figure of man in so far as it has local motion by means of its parts" (*Quaderni d'anatomia*, I, fol. 2r). He applied his gift of visual artistry and his concepts of the four powers to the human body with results that remain unique. The mechanics of the musculoskeletal system were displayed and explained, such complex movements as pronation and supination being correctly analyzed and demonstrated.

In his anatomical writings Leonardo, always fastidious, noted his intense dislike of "passing the night hours in the company of corpses, quartered and flayed, and horrible to behold."

Human Anatomy. On several occasions Leonardo laid out comprehensive plans for demonstrating the anatomy of the human body. In all of them he put great stress on the necessity for presenting the parts of the body from all sides. He stated, moreover, that each part must be dissected specifically to demonstrate vessels, nerves, or muscles:

> . . . you will need three [dissections] in order to have a complete knowledge of the veins and arteries, destroying all the rest with very great care; three others for a knowledge of the membranes, three for the nerves, muscles and ligaments, three for the bones and cartilages . . . . Three must also be devoted to the female body, and in this there is a great mystery by reason of the womb and its fetus.

Leonardo thus hoped to reveal "in fifteen entire figures . . . the whole figure and capacity of man in so far as it has local movement by means of its parts" (*Quaderni d'anatomia*, I, fol. 2r). His extant anatomical drawings show that he was in fact able to carry out a large part of this extensive program.

In addition to conventional methods of dissection, Leonardo brought to his study of anatomy his own particular skill in modelmaking. He discovered the true shape and size of the cerebral ventricles through making wax casts of them, and he came to appreciate the actions of the ventricles of the heart and the aortic valves by making casts of the cardiac atria and ventricles and glass models of the aorta.

Since his approach was primarily mechanical, Leonardo regarded the bones of the skeleton as levers and their attached muscles as the lines of force acting upon them. A firm knowledge of these actions could not be reached without a detailed demonstration of the shapes and dimensions of both bones and muscles. About 1510, Leonardo executed for this purpose a series of drawings, which constitute a large part of the collection *Anatomical Folio A*. Here he systematically illustrated all the main bones and muscles of the body, often accompanying the drawings with mechanical diagrams to show their mode of action. In these drawings Leonardo frequently adopted the technique of representing muscles by narrow bands, corresponding to what he called their "lines of force" (Figure 9), thus facilitating demonstration of their mechanical powers. Since an understanding of the mode of articulation of joints is clearly necessary to an appreciation of their movements in leverage, Leonardo illustrated these structures by an exploded view, whereby the joint surfaces are separated and the surrounding tendons of muscles are severed to show their exact lines of action in moving the joints. Such illustrations permitted Leonardo to demonstrate, for example, the subtleties of the movements of the upper cervical spine and the shoulder joint.

Possibly because the visual sense was so overwhelmingly important to him, Leonardo appears to have made his earliest anatomical studies on the optic nerves, cranial nerves, spinal cord, and peripheral nervous system. In the course of these studies he traced back the optic nerves, beautifully illustrating the optic chiasma and the optic tracts. In his attempts to elucidate the central distribution of sensory tracts in the brain, he injected the cerebral ventricles with wax, thereby ascertaining and demonstrating their approximate shape, size, and situation. On this discovery he based his own mechanical theory of sensation through percussion.

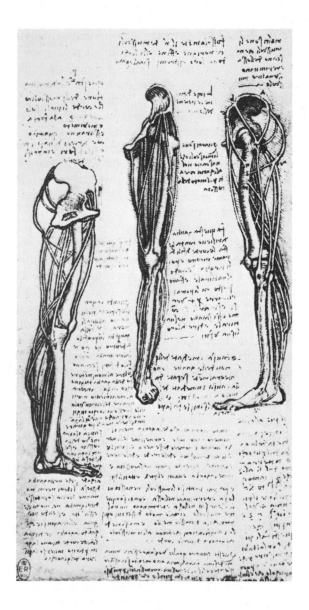

FIGURE 9. The muscles of the leg, one of the many studies of the internal powers of the human body; here the accurately dissected muscles are represented by their "central lines of force," showing their mechanical leverage on the joints (*Quaderni d'anatomia*, V, fol. 4r. Reproduced by gracious permission of Her Majesty Queen Elizabeth II).

Leonardo conceived the eye itself to be a camera obscura in which the inverted image, formed by light penetrating the pupil, is reinverted by the action of the lens. By constructing a glass model of the eye and lens, into which he inserted his own head with his own eye in the position corresponding to that of the optic nerve, he came to the conclusion that the optic nerve was the sensitive visual receptor organ. Here his own experimental brilliance deceived him.

On pithing a frog he noted, "The frog instantly dies when the spinal cord is pierced, and previous to this it lived without head, heart, bowels, or skin. Here therefore it would seem lies the foundation of movement and life" (*Quaderni d'anatomia*, V, fol. 21v). He here contradicted both Aristotelian and Galenic concepts, and opened the way for his own mechanical theory of sensation and movement.

Leonardo's interest in the alimentary tract arose with his dissection of the "old man" in the Hospital of Santa Maria Nuova in Florence. From this dissection he made drawings of the esophagus, stomach, liver, and gallbladder, and drew a first approximation of the distribution of the coils of small and large intestines in the abdomen. Perhaps most notable of all was a detailed sketch of the appendix (its first known representation) accompanied by the hypothesis that it served to take up superfluous wind from the bowel. The heat necessary for digestive coction of the food, Leonardo held, was derived from the heat of the heart—not from the liver, as the Galenists stated. The movement of food and digested products down the bowel was, in Leonardo's view, brought about by the descent of the diaphragm and the pressure produced by contraction of the transverse muscles of the abdomen. Since he did not vivisect, he did not observe peristalsis. Always aware of the necessity of feedback mechanisms to preserve the equilibrium of life, Leonardo was greatly concerned with the fate of superfluous blood, since blood was thought to be continuously manufactured by the liver. Superfluous blood, Leonardo thought, was dispersed through the bowel, contributing largely to the formation of the feces.

Leonardo understood in principle the mechanism of respiration, clearly described by Galen. Describing the movements of the ribs, he wrote, ". . . since there is no vacuum in nature the lung which touches the ribs from within must necessarily follow their expansion; and the lung therefore opening like a pair of bellows draws in the air" (*Anatomical Folio A*, fol. 15v). He considered, however, that the most powerful muscle of inspiration is the diaphragm, the "motor of food and air," as he called it, since by its descent it draws in air and presses food down the gut. After a long debate Leonardo decided that expiration is mostly passive, induced by the diaphragm rising with contraction of the abdominal muscles, and subsidence of the ribs.

Leonardo's studies of the heart and its action occupy more anatomical sheets than those of any other organ. By tying off the atria and ventricles and injecting them with air (later wax), he obtained an accurate idea of their shape and volume. He thus came to recognize that the atria are the contracting chambers of the heart which propel blood into the ventricles, a discovery to which he devoted pages of discussion and verification because it was entirely opposed to Galenic physiology. He applied the same technique to the root of the aorta to discover the aortic sinuses, subsequently named after the anatomist Antonio Maria Valsalva. Having established the shape and position of the valve cusps, Leonardo applied the same marker technique which he used so often in his studies of rivers and water currents. To a glass model of the aorta, containing the aortic valve ring and cusps of an ox, he attached the ventricle (or a bag representing it), which he squeezed so that water passed through the valve. The water contained the seeds of panic grass, which served to demonstrate the directional flow of the currents passing the valve cusps. From these experiments Leonardo showed that the aortic valve cusps close in vertical, not horizontal, apposition—that is, from the side, by pressure of eddying currents, not from above, by direct reflux. Although much modern evidence confirms this view, such action has not yet been directly visualized through angiocardiography.

Other features of Leonardo's study of the anatomy of the heart include his detailed demonstration of the coronary vessels and of the moderator band which some have named after him. By observation of the movements of the "spillo," the instrument that slaughterers used to pierce the heart of a pig, Leonardo deduced the relation of systole to the production of the pulse and apex beat. He considered that the force of cardiac percussion propelling the blood was exhausted by the time the blood reached the periphery of the body, however, and thus missed the Harveian concept of its circulation.

Although his drawings of the kidney, ureter, and bladder are relatively sophisticated, Leonardo's mechanistic physiology did not take him far beyond Galen's views on urology. He saw the kidney as acting as a kind of filter, as did Vesalius after him. His representation of the uterus as a single cavity marks a great advance, particularly in his drawing of a five-month *fetus in utero*, although even in this drawing Leonardo showed the cotyledons of the bovine uterus.

His drawings of male and female genitalia that pertain to coitus show an austere emphasis on procreation that is perhaps reflected in his comment: "The act of procreation and the members employed therein are so repulsive that if it were not for the beauty of the faces and the adornments of the actors and the pent-up impulse, nature would lose the human species" (*Anatomical Folio A*, fol. 10r).

Comparative Anatomy. Although Leonardo concentrated his anatomical investigations on the human body, he by no means confined them to that field. From the artistic point of view, he was equally interested in the structural mechanics of the horse; and from the point of view of the ever-present problem of flying, the anatomy of the bird and bat took priority.

There are scattered through Leonardo's extant notebooks illustrations and notes on the anatomy of horses, birds, bats, oxen, pigs, dogs, monkeys, lions, and frogs. Most of these were studies undertaken to solve particular "power" problems. His anatomy of the horse, however, forms an important exception, for Lomazzo, Vasari, and Rubens all refer to the existence of Leonardo's "book on the anatomy of the horse," which has since been lost. Possible remnants of it remain in some of the drawings of the proportions of the horse in the Royal Library, Windsor, the *Codex Huygens*, and the musculoskeletal sketches in MS *K*, folios 102r and 109v. But perhaps the best-known comparative study of the hind limbs of the horse and the legs of man has come down to us in his drawing on *Quaderni d'anatomia*, V, fol. 22r, where he wrote: "Show a man on tiptoe so that you may compare man with other animals."

In a number of cases Leonardo repeated Galen's mistakes in substituting animal for human parts. These mistakes diminished as his increasing knowledge of anatomy revealed to him surprising variation of form in organs serving similar physiological functions. He then turned to such variations to gain knowledge of the function. Such was the basis of his numerous studies of the shapes of the pupils of the eye in men, cats, and different birds. And it was by dissection of the lion that Leonardo came to say:

> I have found that the constitution of the human body among all the constitutions of animals is of more obtuse and blunt sensibilities, and so is formed of an instrument less ingenious and of parts less capable of receiving the power of the senses. I have seen in the leonine species how the sense of smell forming part of the substance of the brain descends into a very large receptacle to meet the sense of smell. . . . The eyes of the leonine species have a great part of the head as their receptacle, so that the optic nerves are in immediate conjunction with the brain. With man the contrary is

seen to be the case, for the cavities of the eye occupy a small part of the head, and the optic nerves are thin, long and weak [*Anatomical Folio B*, fol. 13v].

That Leonardo appreciated the importance of these studies in comparative anatomy is evinced in his note "Write of the varieties of the intestines of the human species, apes, and such like; then of the differences found in the leonine species, then the bovine, and lastly the birds; and make the description in the form of a discourse" (*Anatomical Folio B*, fol. 37r). His awareness of homologous structures was most pronounced in relation to the limbs, the form and power of which in both man and animals were of outstanding artistic and scientific importance to him. "Anatomize the bat, study it carefully and on this construct your machine," he enjoins on MS *F*, folio 41v. Comparing the arm of man and the wing of the bird, he pointed out: "The sinews and muscles of a bird are incomparably more powerful than those of man because the whole mass of so many muscles and of the fleshy parts of the breast go to aid and increase the movement of the wings, while the breastbone is all in one piece and consequently affords the bird very great power" (*Codex on Flight . . .*, fol. 16r). To elucidate this problem he embarked on a comparative mechanical anatomy of the proportions of the wings of the bat, the eagle, and the pelican, and the arm of man. He even reduced the forelimb to a three-jointed model of levers representing humerus, forearm, and hand, manipulating this artificial limb by pulley mechanisms. He was clearly using comparative anatomy as a means of solving the great problem of human flight.

Such comparisons led Leonardo to suggest repeatedly that he should represent the hands and feet of "the bear, monkey, and certain birds" in order to see how they differ from those of man. Examples of such completed work are scattered in the notes.

From such studies Leonardo came to realize the anatomical significance of "the movements of animals with four feet, amongst which is man, who likewise in his infancy goes on four feet, and who moves his limbs crosswise, as do other four-footed animals, for example the horse in trotting" (MS *E*, fol. 16r; *Codex Atlanticus*, fol. 297r).

From such steps Leonardo reached the generalization: "All terrestrial animals have a similarity of their parts, that is their muscles, nerves and bones, and these do not vary except in length and size, as will be demonstrated in the book of Anatomy. . . . Then there are the aquatic animals which are of many varieties, concerning which I shall not persuade the painter that there is any rule, since they are of almost infinite variety, as are insects" (MS *G*, fol. 5v). "Man

differs from animals," concludes Leonardo, "only in what is accidental, and in this he is divine. . . ." (*Anatomical Folio B*, fol. 13v). After referring to skill in drawing, knowledge of the geometry of the four powers, and patience as being necessary for completing his anatomical researches, he finally wrote of his work: "Considering which things whether or no they have all been found in me, the hundred and twenty books which I have composed will give their verdict, yes or no. In these I have not been hindered either by avarice or negligence, but only by want of time. Farewell" (*Quaderni d'anatomia*, I, fol. 13r).

Botany. Leonardo's botanical studies developed, as it were, in miniature along lines similar to those of his anatomy, with the important difference that in this field he had no predecessors like Galen and Mondino to aid (or impede) his personal observations. These studies commenced in his early years with representation of the external forms of flowering plants, and it was not long before evidence appeared of his interest in plant physiology. About 1489, on a page containing two of his most beautiful designs for cathedrals, he presented a series of four botanical diagrams, one being described by the words: "If you strip off a ring of bark from the tree, it will wither from the ring upwards and remain alive from there downwards" (MS *B*, fol. 17v). Experiments and observations on the movement of sap and growth of plants and trees continued. They reached a climax about 1513, when he was in Rome. Many of these are gathered together in MS *G* and book VI of the *Treatise on Painting*. For many years Leonardo saw movement of sap in the plant as analogous to the movement of blood in the animal and water in the living earth. It is drawn upward by the heat of the sun and downward by its own "natural" weight:

Heat that is poured into animated bodies moves the humours which nourish them. The movement made by this humour is the conservation of itself. The same cause moves the water through the spreading veins of the earth as that which moves the blood in the human species. . . . In the same way so does the water that rises from the low roots of the vine to its lofty summit and falling through the severed branches upon the primal roots mounts anew [*Codex Arundel*, fols. 234r, 235].

Incidentally, he postulated this same mechanism for the absorption of food from the human intestine by the portal veins.

Leonardo described an experiment with a gourd:

The sun gives spirit and life to plants and the earth nourishes them with moisture. In this connection I once made an experiment of leaving only one very small root on a gourd and keeping it nourished with water and the gourd brought to perfection all the fruits that it could produce, which were about sixty. And I set myself diligently to consider the source of its life; and I perceived that it was the dew of the night which penetrated abundantly with its moisture through the joints of its great leaves to nourish this plant with its offspring, or rather seeds which have to produce its offspring. . . . The leaf serves as a nipple or breast to the branch or fruit which grows in the following year [MS *G*, fol. 32v].

Thus Leonardo reached a concept of the necessity of sunlight "giving spirit and life" through its leaves to a plant, while the moisture of its sap came from both root and leaf. He also perceived upward and downward movement of sap. He located the cambium when he stated: "The growth in thickness of trees is brought about by the sap which in the month of April is created between the 'camicia' [cambium] and the wood of the tree. At that time this cambium is converted into bark and the bark acquires new cracks" (*Treatise on Painting*, pt. VI, McMahon ed., p. 893).

Appreciating this seasonal growth of wood from the cambium, Leonardo came to recognize its part in the annual ring formation in trees. He wrote: "The age of trees which have not been injured by men can be counted in years by their branching from the trunk. The trees have as many differences in age as they have principal branches. . . . The circles of branches of trees which have been cut show the number of their years, and also show which years were wetter or drier according to their greater or lesser thickness . . ." (*ibid.*, p. 900). In these words Leonardo showed himself to be the originator of dendrochronology.

Leonardo's observation on the growth of the tree trunk and the patterns of its branches and leaves, combined with his views on plant nutrition, initiated his study of phyllotaxy:

> The lower trunks of trees do not keep their roundness of size when they approach the origin of their branches or roots. And this arises because the higher and lower branches are the organs [membra] by which the plants (or trees) are nourished; that is to say, in summer they are nourished from above by the dew and rain through the leaves and in winter from below through the contact which the earth has with their roots. . . . Larger branches do not grow toward the middle of the tree. This arises because every branch naturally seeks the air and avoids shadow. In those branches which turn to the sky, the course of the water and dew descends . . . and keeps the lower part more humid than the upper, and for this reason the branches have more abundant nourishment there, and therefore grow more [*ibid.*, p. 885].

Thus the trunk of the tree, being most nourished, is the thickest part of the tree. Leonardo saw here the mechanical implications of the force of winds on trees: "The part of the tree which is farthest from the force which percusses it is most damaged by this percussion because of its greater leverage. Thus nature has provided increased thickness in that part, and most in such trees as grow to great heights like pines" (*Codex Arundel*, fol. 277v). Leonardo asserted that the branch pattern of a plant or tree follows its leaf pattern: "The growth of the branches of trees on their principal trunk is like that of the growth of their leaves, which develop in four ways, one above the other. The first and most general is that the sixth leaf above always grows above the sixth below; and the second is for the third pair of leaves to be above the third pair below; the third way is that for the third leaf to be above the third below" (*Treatise on Painting*, McMahon ed., p. 889). This whole pattern of trunk, branch, and leaf Leonardo saw as designed to catch maximum sun, rain, and air—the leaves and branches were arranged "to leave intervals which the air and sun can penetrate, and drops that fall on the first leaf can also fall on the fourth and sixth leaves, and so on" (*ibid.*).

"All the flowers that see the sun mature their seed and not the others, that is, those that see only the reflection of the sun" (MS *G*, fol. 37v). And of seeds he wrote, "All seeds have the umbilical cord which breaks when the seed is ripe; and in like manner they have matrix [uterus] and secundina [membranes], as is shown in herbs and seeds that grow in pods" (*Quaderni d'anatomia*, III, fol. 9v). These words, written on a page of drawings of the infant in the womb, vividly reveal Leonardo's integrating mode of thought.

KENNETH D. KEELE

TECHNOLOGY

A statistical analysis of his extant writings suggests that technology was the most important of Leonardo's varied interests. Indeed, it is revealing to compare the volume of his technological writings with that of his purely artistic work. Of his paintings, fewer than ten are unanimously authenticated by art scholars. This evident disinclination to paint, which even his contemporaries remarked upon, contrasts strongly with the incredible toil and patience that Leonardo lavished upon scientific and technical studies, particularly in geometry, mechanics, and engineering.

Documentary evidence indicates that in his appointments Leonardo was always referred to not only as an artist but also as an engineer. At the court of Ludovico il Moro he was "Ingeniarius et pinctor," while Cesare Borgia called him his most beloved

"Architecto et Engegnero Generale" (1502). When Leonardo returned to Florence, he was immediately consulted as military engineer and sent officially "a livellare Arno in quello di Pisa e levallo del letto suo" (1503).[1] In 1504 he was in Piombino, in the service of Jacopo IV d'Appiano, working on the improvement of that little city-state's fortifications.[2] For Louis XII he was "notre chier et bien aimé Léonard de Vinci, notre paintre et ingénieur ordinaire" (1507).[3] When in Rome, from 1513 to 1516, his duties clearly included technical work, as documented by drafts of letters to his patron Giuliano de' Medici, found in the *Codex Atlanticus*. Even his official burial document refers to him as "Lionard de Vincy, noble millanois, premier peinctre et ingenieur et architecte du Roy, mescanichien d'Estat ..." (1519).[4] The surviving notebooks and drawings demonstrate Leonardo's lifelong interest in the mechanical arts and engineering.

Leonardo's scientific and technological activities were well known to his early biographers, even if they did not approve of them. Paolo Giovio's short account on Leonardo's life (*ca.* 1527) contains a significant phrase: "But while he was thus spending his time in the close research of subordinate branches of his art he carried only very few works to completion."

Another biographer, the so-called "Anonimo Gaddiano" or "Magliabechiano," writing around 1540, said that Leonardo "was delightfully inventive, and was most skillful in lifting weights, in building waterworks and other imaginative constructions, nor did his mind ever come to rest, but dwelt always with ingenuity on the creation of new inventions."

Vasari's biography of Leonardo, in his *Lives of the Painters, Sculptors and Architects* (1550; 2nd ed., 1568), reflects the widespread sentiments of his contemporaries who were puzzled by the behavior of a man who, unconcerned with the great artistic gifts endowed upon him by Providence, dedicated himself to interesting but less noble occupations.

Vasari's testimony concerning Leonardo's widespread technological projects (confirmed by Lomazzo) is important in assessing the influence of Leonardo on the development of Western technology:

> He would have made great profit in learning had he not been so capricious and fickle, for he began to learn many things and then gave them up ... he was the first, though so young, to propose to canalise the Arno from Pisa to Florence. He made designs for mills, fulling machines, and other engines to go by water. ... Every day he made models and designs for the removal of mountains with ease and to pierce them to pass from one place to another, and by means of levers, cranes and winches to raise and draw heavy weights; he devised a method for cleansing ports, and to raise water from great depths, schemes which his brain never ceased to evolve. Many designs for these motions are scattered about, and I have seen numbers of them. ... His interests were so numerous that his inquiries into natural phenomena led him to study the properties of herbs and to observe the movements of the heavens, the moon's orbit and the progress of the sun.

(It is characteristic of Leonardo's contemporary critics that Vasari, giving an account of Leonardo's last days, represents him as telling Francis I "the circumstances of his sickness, showing how greatly he had offended God and man in not having worked in his art as he ought.")

Lomazzo, in his *Trattato della pittura* (Milan, 1584), tells of having seen many of Leonardo's mechanical projects and praises especially thirty sheets representing a variety of mills, owned by Ambrogio Figino, and the automaton in the form of a lion made for Francis I. In his *Idea del tempio della pittura* (Milan, 1590), Lomazzo mentions "Leonardo's books, where all mathematical motions and effects are considered" and of his "projects for lifting heavy weights with ease, which are spread over all Europe. They are held in great esteem by the experts, because they think that nobody could do more, in this field, than what has been done by Leonardo." Lomazzo also notes "the art of turning oval shapes with a lathe invented by Leonardo," which was shown by a pupil of Melzi to Dionigi, brother of the Maggiore, who adopted it with great satisfaction.

Leonardo's actual technological investigations and work still await an exhaustive and objective study. Many early writers accepted all the ingenious mechanical contrivances found in the manuscripts as original inventions; their claims suffer from lack of historical perspective, particularly as concerns the work of the engineers who preceded Leonardo. The "inventions" of Leonardo have been celebrated uncritically, while the main obstacle to a properly critical study lies in the very nature of the available evidence, scattered and fragmented over many thousands of pages. Only in very recent times has the need for a chronological perspective been felt and the methods for its adoption elaborated.[5] It is precisely the earliest—and for this reason the least original—of Leonardo's projects for which model makers and general authors have shown a predilection. On the other hand, the preference for these juvenile projects is fully justified: they are among the most beautiful and lovingly elaborated designs of the artist-engineer. The drawings and writings of MS *B*, the *Codex Trivulzianus*, and the earliest folios of the *Codex Atlanticus* date from this period (*ca.* 1478–1490). Similar themes in the almost contemporary manuscripts of Francesco di Giorgio Martini offer ample opportunity to study Leonardo's early reliance on traditional technological schemes (Francesco di Giorgio himself borrowed heavily from Brunelleschi and especially from Mariano di Jacopo, called Taccola, the "Archimedes of Siena"); the same comparison serves to demonstrate Leonardo's originality and his search for rational ways of constructing better machines.

While he was still in Florence, Leonardo acquired a diversified range of skills in addition to the various crafts he learned in the workshop of Verrocchio, who was not only a painter but also a sculptor and a goldsmith. Leonardo must therefore have been familiar with bronze casting, and there is also early evidence of his interest in horology. His famous letter to Ludovico il Moro, offering his services, advertises Leonardo's familiarity with techniques of military importance, which, discounting a juvenile self-confidence, must have been based on some real experience.

Leonardo's true vocation for the technical arts developed in Milan, Italy's industrial center. The notes that he made during his first Milanese period (from 1481 or 1482 until 1499) indicate that he was in close contact with artisans and engineers engaged in extremely diversified technical activities—with, for example, military and civil architects, hydraulic engineers, millers, masons and other workers in stone, carpenters, textile workers, dyers, iron founders, bronze casters (of bells, statuary, and guns), locksmiths, clockmakers, and jewelers. At the same time that he was assimilating all available traditional experience, Leonardo was able to draw upon the fertile imagination and innate technological vision that, combined with his unparalleled artistic genius in the graphic rendering of the most complicated mechanical devices, allowed him to make improvements and innovations.

From about 1492 on (as shown in MS *A*; *Codex Forster*; *Codex Madrid*, I; MS *H*, and a great number of pages of the *Codex Atlanticus*), Leonardo became increasingly involved in the study of the theoretical background of engineering practice. At about that time he wrote a treatise on "elementi macchinali" that he returned to in later writings, citing it by book and paragraph. This treatise is lost, but many passages in the *Atlanticus* and *Arundel* codices may be drafts for it. *Codex Madrid*, I (1492–1497), takes up these matters in two main sections, one dealing with matters that today would be called statics and kinematics and another dedicated to applied mechanics, especially mechanisms.

Our knowledge of the technical arts of the fourteenth to sixteenth centuries is scarce and fragmentary. Engineers were reluctant to write about their experience; if they did, they chose to treat fantastic possibilities rather than the true practices of their time. The books of Biringuccio, Agricola, and, in part, Zonca are among the very few exceptions, although they deal with specialized technological fields. The notes and drawings of Leonardo should therefore be studied not only to discover his inventions and priorities, as has largely been done in the past, but also—and especially—for the insight they give into the state of the technical arts of his time. Leonardo took note of all the interesting mechanical contrivances he saw or heard about from fellow artists, scholars, artisans, and travelers. Speaking of his own solutions and improvements, he often referred to the customary practices. Thus his manuscripts are among the most important sources for medieval and Renaissance technology. In all other manuscripts and books of machines by authors of the periods both preceding and following Leonardo, projects for complete machines are presented, without any discussion of their construction and efficiency.[6] The only exception previous to the eighteenth-century authors Sturm, Leupold, and Belidor is represented by the work of Simon Stevin, around 1600.

As far as the evidence just mentioned shows, the mechanical engineering of times past was limited by factors of two sorts: various inadequacies in the actual construction of machines produced excessive friction and wear, and there was insufficient understanding of the possibilities inherent in any mechanical system. Leonardo's work deserves our attention as that of the first engineer to try systematically to overcome these shortcomings; most important, he was the first to recognize that each machine was a composition of certain universal mechanisms.

In this, as in several other respects, Leonardo anticipated Leupold, to whom, according to Reuleaux, the foundations of the science of mechanisms is generally attributed.[7] Indeed, of Reuleaux's own list of the constructive elements of machines (screws, keys or wedges, rivets, bearings, plummer blocks, pins, shafts, couplings, belts, cord and chain drives, friction wheels, gears, flywheels, levers, cranks, connecting rods, ratchet wheels, brakes, pipes, cylinders, pistons, valves, and springs), only the rivets are missing from Leonardo's inventories.

In Leonardo's time and even much later, engineers were convinced that the work done by a given prime mover, be it a waterwheel or the muscles of men or animals, could be indefinitely increased by means of suitable mechanical apparatuses. Such a belief led fatally to the idea of perpetual motion machines, on whose development an immense amount of effort was wasted, from the Middle Ages until the nineteenth century. Since the possibility of constructing a perpetual motion machine could not, until very recent times, be dismissed by scientific arguments, men of science of the first order accepted or rejected the underlying idea by intuition rather than by knowledge.

Leonardo followed the contemporary trend, and his earliest writings contain a fair number of perpetual motion schemes. But he gave up the idea around 1492, when he stated "It is impossible that dead [still] water may be the cause of its own or of some other body's motion" (MS *A*, fol. 43r), a statement that he later extended to all kinds of mechanical movements. By 1494 Leonardo could say that

> . . . in whatever system where the weight attached to the wheel should be the cause of the motion of the wheel, without any doubt the center of the gravity of the weight will stop beneath the center of its axle. No instrument devised by human ingenuity, which turns with its wheel, can remedy this effect. Oh! speculators about perpetual motion, how many vain chimeras have you created in the like quest. Go and take your place with the seekers after gold! [*Codex Forster*, II₂, fol. 92v].

Many similar statements can be found in the manuscripts, and it is worth noting that Leonardo's argument against perpetual motion machines is the same that was later put forth by Huygens and Parent.

Another belief common among Renaissance engineers was that flywheels (called "rote aumentative") and similar energy-storing and equalizing devices are endowed with the virtue of increasing the power of a mechanical system. Leonardo knew that such devices could be useful, but he also knew that their incorporation into a machine caused an increase in the demand of power instead of reducing it (*Codex Atlanticus*, fol. 207v-b; *Codex Madrid*, I, fol. 124r).

A practical consequence of this line of thought was Leonardo's recognition that machines do not perform work but only modify the manner of its application. The first clear formulation of this was given by Galileo,[8] but the same principle permeates all of Leonardo's pertinent investigations. He knew that mechanical advantage does not go beyond the given power available, from which the losses caused by friction must be deducted, and he formulated the basic concepts of what are known today as work and power. Leonardo's variables for these include force, time, distance, and weight (*Codex Forster*, II₂, fol. 78v; *Codex Madrid*, I, fol. 152r). One of the best examples is folio 35r of *Codex Madrid*, I, where Leonardo compares the performance of two lifting systems;

the first is a simple windlass moved by a crank, capable of lifting 5,000 pounds; the second is also moved by a crank, but a worm gear confers upon it a higher mechanical advantage, raising its lifting capacity to 50,000 pounds. Leonardo affirms that operators of both machines, applying twenty-five pounds of force and cranking with the same speed, will have the load of 50,000 pounds raised to the same height at the end of one hour. The first instrument will raise its load in ten journeys, while the second will lift it all at once. The end result, however, will be the same.

In the same codex Leonardo established rules of general validity: "Among the infinite varieties of instruments which can be made for lifting weights, all will have the same power if the motions [distances] and the acting and patient weights are equal" (*Codex Madrid*, I, fol. 175r). Accordingly, "It is impossible to increase the power of instruments used for weight-lifting, if the quantity of force and motion is given" (*ibid.*, fol. 175v).

That Leonardo had an intuitive grasp of the principle of the conservation of energy is shown in many notes dispersed throughout the manuscripts. He tried to measure the different kinds of energy known to him (muscle power, springs, running and falling water, wind, and so forth) in terms of gravity—that is, using dynamometers counterbalanced by weights, anticipating Borelli and Smeaton. He even tried to investigate the energetic equivalent of gunpowder, weighing the propellant and the missile and measuring the range. The missile was then shot from a crossbow spanned with a given weight, which was then correlated with the quantity of gunpowder used in the first experiment (*ibid.*, fol. 60r).

Leonardo was aware that the main impediment to all mechanical motions was friction. He clearly recognized the importance of frictional resistance not only between solid bodies but also in liquids and gases. In order to evaluate the role of friction in mechanical motions, he devised ingenious experimental equipment, which included friction banks identical to those used by Coulomb 300 years later. From his experiments Leonardo derived several still-valid general principles—that frictional resistance differs according to the nature of the surfaces in contact, that it depends on the degree of smoothness of those surfaces, that it is independent of the area of the surfaces in contact, that it increases in direct proportion to the load, and that it can be reduced by interposing rolling elements or lubricating fluids between the surfaces in contact. He introduced the concept of the coefficient of friction and estimated that for "polished and smooth" surfaces the ratio F/P was 0.25, or one-fourth of the weight. This value is reasonably accurate for hardwood on hardwood, bronze on steel, and for other materials with which Leonardo was acquainted.[9]

Leonardo's main concern, however, was rolling friction. Realizing that lubrication alone could not prevent rapid wear of an axle and its bearing, Leonardo suggested the use of bearing blocks with split, adjustable bushings of antifriction metal ("three parts

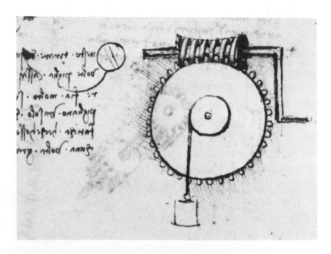

FIGURE 1. Worm gear, shaped to match the curve of the toothed wheel it drives. Designed by Leonardo in 1495 (*Codex Madrid*, I, 17v). It was reinvented by the English engineer Henry Hindley, *ca.* 1740.

of copper and seven of tin melted together"). He was also the first to suggest true ball and roller bearings, developing ring-shaped races to eliminate the loss due to contact friction of the individual balls in a bearing. Leonardo's thrust bearings with conical pivots turning on cones, rollers, or balls (*ibid.*, fol. 101v) are particularly interesting. He also worked persistently to produce gearings designed to overcome frictional resistance. Even when they are not accompanied by geometrical elaborations, some of his gears are unmistakably cycloidal. Leonardo further introduced various new gear forms, among them trapezoidal, helical, and conical bevel gears; of particular note is his globoidal gear, of which several variants are found in the *Codex Atlanticus* and *Codex Madrid*, I, one of them being a worm gear shaped to match the curve of the toothed wheel it drives, thus overcoming the risk inherent in an endless screw that engages only a single gear tooth (*ibid.*, fols. 17v–18v). This device was rediscovered by Henry Hindley around 1740.

Leonardo's development of complicated gear systems was not motivated by any vain hope of obtaining limitless mechanical advantages. He warned the makers of machines:

The more wheels you will have in your instrument, the more toothing you will need, and the more teeth, the greater will be the friction of the wheels with the spindles of their pinions. And the greater the friction, the more power is lost by the motor and, consequently, force is lacking for the orderly motion of the entire system [*Codex Atlanticus*, fol. 207v-b].

Leonardo's contribution to practical kinematics is documented by the devices sketched and described in his notebooks. Since the conversion of rotary to alternating motion (or vice versa) was best performed with the help of the crank and rod combinations, Leonardo sketched hundreds of them to illustrate the kinematics of such composite machines as sawmills, pumps, spinning wheels, grinding machines, and blowers. In addition he drew scores of ingenious combinations of gears, linkages, cams, and ratchets, designed to transmit and modify mechanical movements. He used the pendulum as an energy accumulator in working machines as well as an escapement in clockwork (*Codex Madrid*, I, fol. 61v).

Although simple cord drives had been known since the Middle Ages, Leonardo's belt techniques, including tightening devices, must be considered as original. His manuscripts describe both hinged link chains and continuous chain drives with sprocket wheels (*ibid.*, fol. 10r; *Codex Atlanticus*, fol. 357r-a).

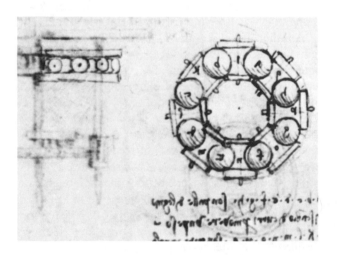

FIGURE 2. Antifriction balls designed by Leonardo for a ball bearing. Reinvented in 1920 (*Codex Madrid*, I, 101v).

Leonardo's notes about the most efficient use of prime movers deserve special attention. His particular interest in attaining the maximum efficiency of muscle power is understandable, since muscle power represented the only motor that might be used in a flying machine, a project that aroused his ambition as early as 1487 and one in which he remained interested until the end of his life. Since muscles were also the most common source of power, it was further important to establish the most effective ways to use them in performing work.

Leonardo estimated the force exerted by a man turning a crank as twenty-five pounds. (Philippe de La Hire found it to be twenty-seven pounds, while Guillaume Amontons, in similar experiments, confirmed Leonardo's figure; in 1782 Claude François Berthelot wrote that men cannot produce a continuous effort of more than twenty pounds, even if some authors admitted twenty-four.)[10] Such a return seemed highly unsatisfactory. Leonardo tried to find more suitable mechanical arrangements, the most remarkable of which employ the weight of men or animals instead of muscle power. For activating pile drivers (*Codex Leicester*, fol. 28v [*ca.* 1505]) or excavation machines (*Codex Atlanticus*, fols. 1v-b, 331v-a), Leonardo used the weight of men, who by running up ladders and returning on a descending platform, would raise the ram or monkey. Leonardo used the same system for lifting heavier loads with cranes, the counterweight being "one ox and one man"; lifting capacity was further increased by applying a differential windlass to the arm of the crane (*ibid.*, fol. 363v-b [*ca.* 1495]).

Until the advent of the steam engine the most popular portable prime mover was the treadmill, known since antiquity. Leonardo found the conventional type, in which men walk inside the drum, in the manner of a squirrel cage, to be inherently less efficient than one employing the weight of the men on the outside of the drum. While he did not invent the external treadmill, he was the first to use it rationally—the next scholar to analyze the efficiency of the treadmill mathematically was Simon Stevin (1586).

Leonardo also had very clear ideas about the advantages and the limitations of waterpower. He rejected popular hydraulic perpetual motion schemes, "Falling water will raise as much more weight than its own as is the weight equivalent to its percussion. . . But you have to deduce from the power of the instrument what is lost by friction in its bearings" (*ibid.*, fol. 151r-a). Since the weight of the percussion, according to Leonardo, is proportional to height, and therefore to gravitational acceleration ("among natural forces, percussion surpasses all others . . . because at every stage of the descent it acquires more momentum"), this represents the first, if imperfect, statement of the basic definition of the energy potential $Ep = mgh$.

Leonardo describes hydraulic wheels on many pages of his notebooks and drawings, either separately or as part of technological operations. He continually sought improvements for systems currently in use. He evaluated all varieties of prime movers, vertical as well as horizontal, and improved on the traditional Lombard mills by modifying the wheels and their races and introducing an adjustable wheel-raising device (MS *H*; *Codex Atlanticus*, fols. 304r-b, v-d [*ca.* 1494]).

In 1718 L. C. Sturm described a "new kind" of mill constructed in the Mark of Brandenburg, "where a lot of fuss was made about them, although they were not as new as most people in those parts let themselves be persuaded. . . ." They were, in fact, identical to those designed by Leonardo for the country estate of Ludovico il Moro near Vigevano around 1494.

It is noteworthy that in his mature technological projects Leonardo returned to horizontal waterwheels for moving heavy machinery (*Codex Atlanticus*, fol. 2r-a and b [*ca.* 1510]), confirming once more the high power output of such prime movers. His papers provide forerunners of the reaction turbine (*Codex Forster*, I₂) and the Pelton wheel (*Codex Madrid*, I, fol. 22v); drawings of completely encased waterwheels appear on several folios of the *Codex Atlanticus*.

There is little about wind power in Leonardo's writings, probably because meteorological conditions limited its practical use in Italy. Although it is erroneous to attribute the invention of the tower mill to Leonardo (as has been done), the pertinent sketches are significant because they show for the first time a brake wheel mounted on the wind shaft (MS *L*, fol. 34v). (The arrangement reappears, as do many other ideas of Leonardo's, in Ramelli's book of 1588 [plate cxxxiii].) Windmills with rotors turning on a vertical shaft provided with shield walls are elaborated on folios 43v, 44r, 74v, 75r, and 55v of *Codex Madrid*, II; and there can be no doubt that Leonardo became acquainted with them through friends who had seen them in the East.

In contrast with Leonardo's scant interest in wind power, he paid constant attention to heat and fire as possible sources of energy. His experiments with steam are found on folios 10r and 15r of the *Codex Leicester*. His approximate estimation of the volume of steam evolved through the evaporation of a given quantity of water suggests a ratio 1 : 1,500, the correct figure being about 1 : 1,700. Besson in 1569 still believed that the proportion was 1 : 10, a ratio raised to 1 : 255 in the famous experiments of Jean Rey; it was not until 1683 that a better estimate— 1 : 2,000—was made by Samuel Morland. Leonardo's best-known contribution to the utilization of steam power was his "Architronito" (MS *B*, fol. 33r), a steam cannon. The idea is not as impractical as generally assumed, since steam cannons were used in the American Civil War and even in World War II (Holman projectors). It was Leonardo, and not Branca (1629), who described the first impulse turbine moved by a jet of steam (*Codex Leicester*, fol. 28v).

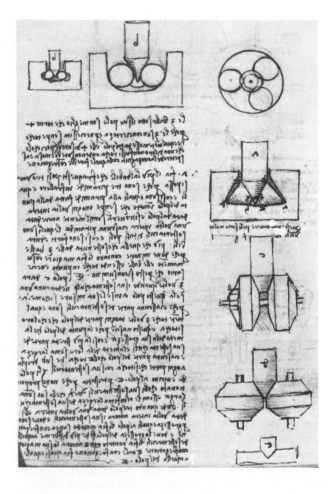

FIGURE 3. Ring-shaped race for a ball bearing with independent separation devices, *ca.* 1494 (*Codex Madrid*, I, 20v). Reinvented in the eighteenth century.

One of Leonardo's most original technological attempts toward a more efficient prime mover is the thermal engine drawn and described on folio 16v of MS *F* (1508–1509), which anticipates Huygens' and Papin's experiments. In 1690 Papin arrived at the idea of the atmospheric steam engine after Huygens' experiments with a gunpowder engine (1673) failed to give consistent results. Leonardo's atmospheric thermal motor, conceived "to lift a great weight by means of fire," like those of Huygens and Papin, consisted of cylinder, piston, and valve, and worked in exactly the same way.[11]

Leonardo's studies on the behavior and resistance of materials were the first of their kind. The problem was also attacked by Galileo, but an adequate treatment of the subject had to wait until the eighteenth century. One of Leonardo's most interesting observations was pointed out by Zammattio and refers to the bending of an elastic beam, or spring. Leonardo recognized clearly that the fibers of the beam are lengthened at the outside of the curvature and shortened at the inside. In the middle, there is an area which is not deformed, which Leonardo called the "linea centrica" (now called the neutral axis). Leonardo suggested that similar conditions obtained in the case of ropes bent around a pulley and in single as well as intertwisted wires (*Codex Madrid*, I, fols. 84v, 154v). More than two centuries had to pass before this model of the internal stresses was proposed again by Jakob Bernoulli.

Leonardo's notebooks also contain the first descriptions of machine tools of some significance, including plate rollers for nonferrous metals (MS *I*, fol. 48v), rollers for bars and strips (*Codex Atlanticus*, fol. 370v-b; MS *G*, fol. 70v), rollers for iron staves (*Codex Atlanticus*, fol. 2r-a and b), semiautomatic wood planers (*ibid.*, fol. 38v-b), and a planer for iron (*Codex Madrid*, I, fol. 84v). His thread-cutting machines (*Codex Atlanticus*, fol. 367v-a) reveal great ingenuity, and their principle has been adopted for modern use.

Not only did Leonardo describe the first lathe with continuous motion (*ibid., fol.* 381r-b) but, according to Lomazzo, he must also be credited with the invention of the elliptic lathe, generally attributed to Besson (1569). Leonardo described external and internal grinders (*ibid.*, fols. 7r-b, 291r-a) as well as disk and belt grinding machines (*ibid.*, fols. 320r-b, 380v-b, 318v-a). He devoted a great deal of attention to the development of grinding and polishing wheels for plane and concave mirrors (*ibid.*, fols. 32r-a, 396v-f, 401r-a; *Codex Madrid*, I, fol. 163v, 164r; MS *G*, fol. 82v, for examples). Folio 159r-b of the *Codex Atlanticus* is concerned with shaping sheet metal by stamping (to make chandeliers of two or, better, four parts). The pressure necessary for this operation was obtained by means of a wedge press.

Leonardo's interest in water mills has already been mentioned. Of his work in applied hydraulics, the improvement of canal locks and sluices (miter gates and wickets) is an outstanding example. He discussed the theory and the practice of an original type of centrifugal pump (MS *F*, fols. 13r, 16r) and the best ways of constructing and moving Archimedean screws. Some of these methods were based on coiled pipes (MS *E*, fols. 13v, 14r) like those seen by Cardano at the waterworks of Augsburg in 1541.

Leonardo left plans for a great number of machines which were generally without parallel until the eighteenth and nineteenth centuries. Some of these are the improved pile drivers (*Codex Forster*, II, fol. 73v; MS *H*, fol. 80v; *Codex Leicester*, fol. 28v) later described by La Hire (1707) and Belidor (1737), a cylindrical bolter activated by the main drive of a grain mill (*Codex Madrid*, I, fols. 21v, 22r), and a mechanized wedge press (*ibid.*, 46v, 47r), which in the eighteenth century became known as the Dutch press. Particularly original are Leonardo's well-known canal-building machines, scattered through the *Codex Atlanticus*—in Parsons' opinion, "had Leonardo contributed nothing more to engineering than his plans and studies for the Arno canal, they alone would place him in the first rank of engineers for all time." The knowledge that most of those projects were executed in the Romagna during Leonardo's service with Cesare Borgia makes little difference.

Leonardo also designed textile machinery. Plans for spinning machines, embodying mechanical principles which did not reappear until the eighteenth century, are found on folio 393v-a of the *Codex Atlanticus*, as well as in the *Codex Madrid*, I (fols. 65v, 66r). The group represented in the *Codex Atlanticus* includes ropemaking machines of advanced design (fol. 2v-a and b), silk doubling and winding machines (fol. 36v-b), gig mills whose principle reappears in the nineteenth century (fols. 38r-a, 161v-b, 297r-a), shearing machines (fols. 397r-a, 397v-a), and even a power loom (fols. 317v-b, 356r-a, 356v-a).

Leonardo was also interested in the graphic arts and in 1494 presented details of the contemporary printing press, antedating by more than fifty years the first sensible reproduction of such an instrument. Even earlier (around 1480) he had tried to improve the efficiency of the printing press by making the motion of the carriage a function of the motion of the pressing screw. Leonardo's most interesting innovation in this field, however, was his invention of a technique of relief etching, permitting the printing of text and illustration in a single operation (*Codex Madrid*, II, fol. 119r [1504]). The technique was reinvented by William Blake in 1789 and perfected by Gillot around 1850.[12]

Leonardo's work on flight and flying machines is too well known to be discussed here in detail. The most positive part of it consists of his studies on the flight of birds, found in several notebooks, among them *Codex on Flight* . . .; MSS *K*, *E*, *G*, and *L*; *Codex Atlanticus*; and *Codex Madrid*, II, etc. Leonardo's flying machines embody many interesting mechanical features, although their basic conception as ornithopters makes them impractical. Only later did Leonardo decide to take up gliders, as did Lilienthal 400 years later. Although the idea of the parachute and of the so-called helicopter may antedate Leonardo, he was the first to experiment with true airscrews.

Leonardo's interest in chemical phenomena (for example, combustion) embraced them as such, or in relation to the practical arts. He made some inspired projects for distillation apparatus, based on the "Moor's head" condensation system that was universally adopted in the sixteenth century. Descriptions of water-cooled delivery pipes may also be found among his papers, as may a good description of an operation for separating gold from silver (*Codex Atlanticus*, fol. 244v [*ca.* 1505]). Some of the most original of the many practical chemical operations that are described in Leonardo's notebooks are concerned with making decorative objects of imitation agate, chalcedony, jasper, or amber. Leonardo began with proteins—a concentrated solution of gelatin or egg-white—and added pigments and vegetable colors. The material was then shaped by casting in ceramic molds or by extrusion; after drying, the objects were polished and then varnished for stability (MS *I*, fol. 27v; MS *F*, fols. 42r, 55v, 73v, 95v; MS *K*, fols. 114–118). By laminating unsized paper impregnated with the same materials and subsequently drying it, he obtained plates "so dense as to resemble bronze"; after varnishing, "they will be like glass and resist humidity" (MS *F*, fol. 96r). Leonardo's notes thus contain the basic operations of modern plastic technology.[10]

Of Leonardo's projects in military engineering and weaponry, those of his early period are more spectacular than practical. Some of them are, however, useful in obtaining firsthand information on contemporary techniques of cannon founding (*Codex Atlanticus*, fol. 19r-b) and also provide an interesting footnote on the survival, several centuries after the introduction of gunpowder, of such ancient devices as crossbows, ballistae, and mangonels. Leonardo did make some surprisingly modern suggestions; he was a stout advocate (although not the inventor) of breech-loading guns, he designed a water-cooled barrel for a rapid-fire gun, and, on several occasions, he proposed ogive-headed projectiles, with or without directional fins. His designs for wheel locks (*ibid.*, fols. 56v-b, 353r-c, 357r-a) antedate by about fifteen years the earliest known similar devices, which were constructed in Nuremberg. His suggestion of prefabricated cartridges consisting of ball, charge, and primer, which occurs on folio 9r-b of the *Codex Atlanticus*, is a very early (*ca.* 1480) proposal of a system introduced in Saxony around 1590.

Several of Leonardo's military projects are of importance to the history of mechanical engineering because of such details of construction as the racks used for spanning giant crossbows (*ibid.*, fol. 53r-a and b [*ca.* 1485]) or the perfectly developed universal joint on a light gun mount (*ibid.*, fol. 399v-a [*ca.* 1494]).

Leonardo worked as military architect at the court of Ludovico il Moro, although his precise tasks are not documented. His activities during his short stay in the service of Cesare Borgia are, however, better known. His projects for the modernization of the fortresses in the Romagna are very modern in concept, while the maps and city plans executed during this period (especially that of Imola in *Windsor Collection*, fol. 12284) have been called monuments in the history of cartography.

One of the manuscripts recently brought to light, *Codex Madrid*, II, reveals an activity of Leonardo's unknown until 1967—his work on the fortifications of Piombino for Jacopo IV d'Appiano (1504). Leonardo's technological work is characterized not only by an understanding of the natural laws (he is, incidentally, the first to have used this term) that govern the functioning of all mechanical devices but also by the requirement of technical and economical efficiency. He was not an armchair technologist, inventing ingenious but unusable machines; his main goal was practical efficiency and economy. He continually sought the best mechanical solution for a given task; a single page of his notes often contains a number of alternative means. Leonardo abhorred waste, be it of time, power, or money. This is why so many double-acting devices—ratchet mechanisms, blowers, and pumps—are found in his writings. This mentality led Leonardo toward more highly automated machines, including the file-cutting machine of *Codex Atlanticus,* folio 6r-b, the automatic hammer for gold-foil work of *Codex Atlanticus*, folios 8r-a, 21r-a, and 21v-a, and the mechanized printing press, rope-making machine, and power loom, already mentioned.[14]

According to Beck, the concept of the transmission of power to various operating machines was one of the most important in the development of industrial machinery. Beck thought that the earliest industrial application of this type is found in Agricola's famous *De re metallica* (1550) in a complex designed for the mercury amalgamation treatment of gold ores.[15] Leonardo, however, described several projects of the same kind, while on folios 46v and 47r of *Codex Madrid*, I, he considered the possibility of running a complete oil factory with a single power source. No fewer than five separate operations were to be performed in this combine—milling by rollers, scraping, pressing in a wedge press, releasing the pressed material, and mixing on the heating pan. This project is further remarkable because the power is transmitted by shafting; the complex thus represents a complete "Dutch oil mill," of which no other record exists prior to the eighteenth century.

Leonardo's interest in practical technology was at its strongest during his first Milanese period, from 1481 or 1482 to 1499. After that his concern shifted from practice to theory, although on occasion he resumed practical activities, as in 1502, when he built canals in the Romagna, and around 1509, when he executed works on the Adda River in Lombardy. He worked intensively on the construction of concave mirror systems in Rome, and he left highly original plans for the improvement of the minting techniques in that city (1513–1516). He was engaged in hydraulic works along the Loire during his last years.

NOTES

1. Luca Beltrami, *Documenti e memorie riguardanti la vita e le opere di Leonardo da Vinci* (Milan, 1919), nos. 66, 117, 126, 127.
2. *Codex Madrid*, II, *passim*.
3. Beltrami, op. cit., no. 189.
4. Beltrami, op. cit., no. 246.
5. G. Calvi, *I manoscritti di Leonardo da Vinci* (Bologna, 1925); A. M. Brizio, *Scritti scelti di Leonardo da Vinci* (Turin, 1952); Kenneth Clark, *A Catalogue of the Drawings of Leonardo da Vinci at Windsor Castle* (Cambridge, 1935; 2nd rev. ed., London, 1968–1969); C. Pedretti, *Studi Vinciani* (Geneva, 1957).
6. Kyeser (1405), Anonymous of the Hussite Wars (*ca.* 1430), Fontana (*ca.* 1420), Taccola (*ca.* 1450), Francesco di Giorgio (*ca.* 1480), Besson (1569), Ramelli (1588), Zonca (1607), Strada (1617–1618), Veranzio (*ca.* 1615), Branca (1629), Biringuccio (1540), Agricola (1556), Cardano (1550), Lorini (1591), Böckler (1661), Zeising (1607–1614).
7. F. Reuleaux, *The Kinematic of Machinery* (New York, 1876; repr. 1963); R. S. Hartenberg and J. Denavit, *Kinematic Synthesis of Linkages* (New York, 1964).
8. G. Galilei, *Le meccaniche* (*ca.* 1600), trans. with intro. and notes by I. E. Drabkin and Stillman Drake as *Galilei on Motion and on Mechanics* (Madison, Wis., 1960).
9. G. Canestrini, *Leonardo costruttore di macchine e veicoli* (Milan, 1939); L. Reti, "Leonardo on Bearings and Gears," in *Scientific American*, **224** (1971), 100.
10. E. S. Ferguson, "The Measurement of the 'Man-Day,'" in *Scientific American*, **225** (1971), 96. The writings of La Hire and Amontons are in *Mémoires de l'Académie . . .*, **1** (1699).
11. L. Reti, "Leonardo da Vinci nella storia della macchina a vapore," in *Rivista di ingegneria* (1956–1957).
12. L. Reti, "Leonardo da Vinci and the Graphic Arts," in *Burlington Magazine*, **113** (1971), 189.
13. L. Reti, "Le arti chimiche di Leonardo da Vinci," in *Chimica e l'industria*, **34** (1952), 655, 721.
14. B. Dibner, "Leonardo: Prophet of Automation," in C. D. O'Malley, ed., *Leonardo's Legacy* (Berkeley–Los Angeles, 1969).
15. T. Beck, *Beiträge zur Geschichte des Maschinenbaues* (Berlin, 1900), pp. 152–153.

LADISLAO RETI

MECHANICS

Although Leonardo was interested in mechanics for most of his mature life, he would appear to have turned more and more of his attention to it from 1508 on. It is difficult to construct a unified and consistent picture of his mechanics in detail, but the major trends, concepts, and influences can be delineated with some firmness.[1] Statics may be considered first, since this area of theoretical mechanics greatly attracted him and his earliest influences in this field probably came from the medieval science of weights. To this he later added Archimedes' *On the Equilibrium of Planes*, with a consequent interest in the development of a procedure for determining the centers of gravity of sundry geometrical magnitudes.

In his usual fashion Leonardo absorbed the ideas of his predecessors, turned them in practical and experiential directions, and developed his own system of nomenclature—for example, he called the arms of balances "braccia" while in levers "lieva" is the arm of the lever to which the power is applied and "contralieva" the arm in which the resistance lies. Influenced by the Scholastics, he called the position of horizontal equilibrium the "sito dell'equalità" (or sometimes the position "equale allo orizzonte"). Pendent weights are simply "pesi," or "pesi attacati," or "pesi appiccati"; the cords supporting them—or, more generally, the lines of force in which the weights or forces act or in which they are applied—are called "appendicoli." Leonardo further distinguished between "braccia reali o linee corporee," the actual lever arms, and "braccia potenziali o spirituali o semireali," the potential or effective arms. The potential arm is the horizontal distance to the vertical (that is, the "linea central") through the center of motion in the case of bent levers, or, more generally, the perpendicular distance to the center of motion from the line of force about the center of motion. He often called the center of motion the "centro del circunvolubile," or simply the "polo."

The classical law of the lever appears again and again in Leonardo's notebooks. For example, *Codex Atlanticus*, folio 176v-d, states, "The ratio of the weights which hold the arms of the balance parallel to the horizon is the same as that of the arms, but is an inverse one." In *Codex Arundel*, folio 1v, the law appears formulaically as $W_2 = (W_1 \cdot s_1)/s_2$: "Multiply the longer arm of the balance by the weight it supports and divide the product by the shorter arm, and the result will be the weight which, when placed on the shorter arm, resists the descent of the longer arm, the arms of the balance being above all basically balanced."

A few considerations that prove the influence of the medieval science of weights upon Leonardo are in order. The medieval science of weights consisted essentially of the following corpus of works:[2] Pseudo-Euclid, *Liber de ponderoso et levi*, a geometrical treatment of basic Aristotelian ideas relating forces, volumes, weights, and velocities; Pseudo-Archimedes, *De ponderibus Archimenidis* (also entitled *De incidentibus in humidum*), essentially a work of hydrostatics; an anonymous tract from the Greek, *De canonio*, treating of the Roman balance or steelyard by reduction to a theoretical balance; Thābit ibn Qurra, *Liber karastonis*, another treatment of the Roman balance; Jordanus de Nemore, *Elementa de ponderibus* (also entitled *Elementa super demonstrationem ponderum*), a work existing in many manuscripts and complemented by several reworked versions of the late thirteenth and the fourteenth centuries, which was marked by the first use of the concept of positional gravity *(gravitas secundum situm)*, by a false demonstration of the law of the bent lever, and by an elegant proof of the law of the lever on the basis of the principle of virtual displacements; an anonymous *Liber de ponderibus* (called, by its modern editor, Version P), which contains a kind of short Peripatetic commentary to the enunciations of Jordanus; a *Liber de ratione ponderis*, also attributed to Jordanus, which is a greatly expanded and corrected version of the *Elementa* in four parts and is distinguished by a more correct use of the concept of positional gravity, by a superb proof of the law of the bent lever based on the principle of virtual displacements, by the same proof of the law of the straight lever given in the *Elementa*, and by a remarkable and sound proof of the law of the equilibrium of connected weights on adjacent inclined planes that is also based on the principle of virtual displacements—thereby constituting the first correct statement and proof of the inclined plane law—and including a number of practical problems in statics and dynamics, of which the most noteworthy are those connected with the bent lever in part III; and Blasius of Parma, *Tractatus de ponderibus*, a rather inept treatment of the problems of statics and hydrostatics based on the preceding works.

The whole corpus is marked methodologically by its geometric form and conceptually by its use of dynamics (particularly the principle of virtual velocities or the principle of virtual displacements in one form or another) in application to the basic statical problems and conclusions inherited from Greek antiquity. Leonardo was much influenced by the corpus' general dynamical approach as well as by particular conclusions of specific works. Reasonably conclusive evidence exists to show that Leonardo had read Pseudo-Archimedes, *De canonio*, and Thābit ibn Qurra, while completely conclusive evidence reveals his knowledge of the *Elementa*, *De ratione ponderis*, and Blasius. It is reasonable to suppose that he also saw the other works of the corpus, since they were so often included in the same manuscripts as the works he did read.

The two works upon which Leonardo drew most heavily were the *Elementa de ponderibus* and the *Liber de ratione ponderis*. The key passage that shows decisively that Leonardo read both of them occurs in *Codex Atlanticus*, folios 154v-a and r-a. In this passage, whose significance has not been properly recognized before, Leonardo presents a close Italian translation of all the postulates from the *Elementa* (E.01–E.07) and the enunciations of the first two propositions (without proofs), together with a definition that precedes the proof of proposition E.2.[3] He then shifts to the *Liber de ratione ponderis* and includes the enunciations of all the propositions of the first two parts (except R2.05) and the first two propositions of the third part.[4] It seems likely that Leonardo made his translation from a single manuscript that contained both works and, after starting his translation of the *Elementa*, suddenly realized the superiority of the *De ratione ponderis*. He may also have translated the rest of part III, for he seems to have been influenced by propositions R3.05 and R3.06, the last two propositions in part III, and perhaps also by R3.04 in passages not considered here (see MS *A*, fols. 1r, 33v). Another page in *Codex Atlanticus*, folio 165v-a and v-c, contains all of the enunciations of the propositions of part IV (except for R4.07, R4.11–12, and R4.16). The two passages from the *Codex Atlanticus* together establish that Leonardo had complete knowledge of the best and the most original work in the corpus of the medieval science of weights.

The passages cited do not, of course, show what Leonardo did with that knowledge, although others do. For example in MS *G*, folio 79r, Leonardo refutes the incorrect proof of the second part of proposition E.2 (or of its equivalent, R1.02). The proposition states: "When the beam of a balance of equal arm lengths is in the horizontal position, if equal weights are suspended [from its extremities], it will not leave the horizontal position, and if it should be moved from the horizontal position, it will revert to it."[5] The second part is true for a material beam supported from above, since the elevation of one of the arms removes the center of gravity from the vertical line through the fulcrum and, accordingly, the balance beam returns to the horizontal position as the center of gravity seeks the vertical. The medieval proof in E.2 and R1.02, however, treats the balance as if it were a theoretical balance (with weightless beam) and attempts to show that it would return to the horizontal position. Based on the false use of the concept of positional gravity, it asserts that the weight above the line of horizontal equilibrium has a greater gravity according to its position than the weight depressed below the line, for if both weights tended to move downward, the arc on which the upper weight would move intercepts more of the vertical than the arc on which the lower weight would tend to move. Leonardo's refutation is based on showing that because the weights are connected, the actual arcs to be compared are oppositely directed and so have equal obliquities—and thus the superior weight enjoys no positional advantage. In MS *E*, folio 59r, Leonardo seems also to give the correct explanation for the return to horizontal equilibrium of the material beam.

A further response to the *Liber de ratione ponderis* is in *Codex Atlanticus*, folio 354v-c, where Leonardo again translates proposition R1.09 and paraphrases proposition R1.10 of the medieval work: "The equality of the declination conserves the equality of the weights. If the ratios of the weights and the obliquities on which they are placed are the same but inverse, the weights will remain equal in gravity and motion" ("La equalità della declinazione osserva la equalità de' pesi. Se le proporzioni de' pesi e dell' obbliqua dove si posano, saranno equali, ma converse, essi pesi resteranno equali in gravità e in moto"). The equivalent propositions from the *Liber de ratione ponderis* were "R1.09. Equalitas declinationis identitatem conservat ponderis" and "R1.10. Si per diversarum obliquitatum vias duo pondera descendant, fueritque declinationum et ponderum una proportio eodum ordine sumpta, una erit utriusque virtus in descendendo."[6] While Leonardo preserved R1.09 exactly in holding that positional weight on the incline is everywhere the same as long as the incline's declination is the same, his rephrasing of R1.10 indicates that he adopted a different measure of "declination."

R. Marcolongo believed that Leonardo measured obliquity by the ratio of the common altitude of the inclines to the length of the incline (that is, by the sine of the angle of inclination), while Jordanus had measured obliquity by the length of the incline that intercepts the common altitude (that is, by the cosecant of the angle).[7] Thus, if p_1 and p_2 are connected weights placed on the inclined planes that are of lengths l_1 and l_2, respectively, with common altitude h, then, according to Marcolongo's view of Leonardo's method, $p_1/p_2 = (h/l_2)/(h/l_1)$, and thus $p_1/p_2 = l_1/l_2$, as Jordanus held. Hence, if Marcolongo is correct, Leonardo had absorbed the correct exposition of the inclined plane problem from the *Liber de ratione ponderis*. Perhaps he did, but it is not exhibited in this passage, for the figure accompanying the passage (Figure 1), with its numerical designations of 2 and 1

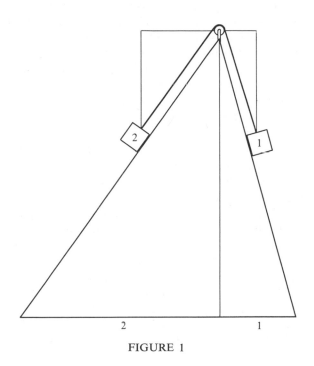

FIGURE 1

on the bases cut off by the vertical, shows that Leonardo believed the weights on the inclines to be inversely proportional to the tangents of the angles of inclination rather than to the sines—and such a solution is

clearly incorrect. The same incorrect solution is apparent in MS *G*, folio 77v, where again equilibrium of the two weights is preserved when the weights are in the same ratio as the bases cut off by the common altitude (thus implying that the weights are inversely proportional to the tangents).

Other passages give evidence of Leonardo's vacillating methods and confusion. One (*Codex on Flight*, fol. 4r) consists of two paragraphs that apply to the same figure (Figure 2). The first is evidently an explanation of a proposition expressed elsewhere (MS *E*, fol. 75r) to the effect that although equal weights balance each other on the equal arms of a balance, they do not do so if they are put on inclines of different obliquity. It states:

> The weight *q*, because of the right angle *n* [perpendicularly] above point *e* in line *df*, weighs 2/3 of its natural weight, which was 3 pounds, and so has a residual force ["che resta in potenzia"] [along *nq*] of 2 pounds; and the weight *p*, whose natural weight was also 3 pounds, has a residual force of 1 pound [along *mp*] because of right angle *m* [perpendicularly] above point *g* in line *hd*. [Therefore, *p* and *q* are not in equilibrium on these inclines.]

The bracketed material has been added as clearly implicit, and so far this analysis seems to be entirely correct. It is evident from the figure that Leonardo has applied the concept of potential lever arm (implying static moment) to the determination of the component of weight along the incline, so that $F_1 \cdot dn = W_1 \cdot de$, where F_1 is the component of the natural weight W_1 along the incline, *dn* is the potential lever arm through which F_1 acts around fulcrum *d*, and *de* is the lever

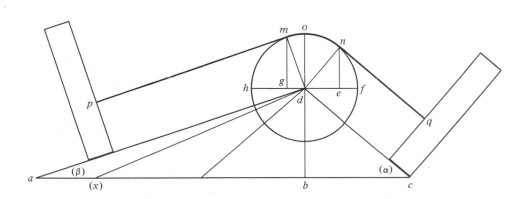

FIGURE 2

arm through which W_1 would act when hanging from n. Hence, $F_1 = W_1 \cdot (de/dn) = W_1 \cdot \sin \angle dne$. But $\angle dne = \angle \alpha$, and so we have the correct formulation $F_1 = W_1 \cdot \sin \alpha$. In the same way for weight p, it can be shown that $F_2 = W_2 \cdot \sin \beta$. And since Leonardo apparently constructed $de = 2df/3$, $dg = hd/3$, and $W_1 = W_2 = 3$, obviously $F_1 = 2$ and $F_2 = 1$ and the weights are not in equilibrium.

In the second paragraph, which also pertains to the figure, he changes p and q, each of which was initially equal to three pounds, to two pounds, and one pound, respectively, with the object of determining whether the adjusted weights would be in equilibrium:

> So now we have one pound against two pounds. And because the obliquities *da* and *dc* on which these weights are placed are not in the same ratio as the weights, that is, 2 to 1 [the weights are not in equilibrium]; like the said weights [in the first paragraph?], they alter natural gravities [but they are not in equilibrium] because the obliquity *da* exceeds the obliquity *dc*, or contains the obliquity *dc*, $2\frac{1}{2}$ times, as is demonstrated by their bases *ab* and *bc*, whose ratio is a double sesquialterate ratio [that is, 5:2], while the ratio of the weights will be a double ratio [that is, 2:1].

It is abundantly clear, at least in the second paragraph, that Leonardo was assuming that for equilibrium the weights ought to be directly proportional to the bases (and thus inversely proportional to the tangents); and since the weights are not as the base lines, they are not in equilibrium. In fact, in adding line $d[x]$ Leonardo was indicating the declination he thought would establish the equilibrium of p and q, weights of two pounds and one pound, respectively, for it is obvious that the horizontal distances $b[x]$ and bc are also related as 2 : 1. This is further confirmation that Leonardo measured declination by the tangent.

Assuming that both paragraphs were written at the same time, it is apparent that Leonardo then thought that both methods of determining the effective weight on an incline—the method using the concept of the lever and the technique of using obliquities measured

FIGURE 3. (Note: The horizontal base line and the continuation of the line from point *c* beyond the pulley wheel to the balance beam are in Leonardo's drawing but should be deleted.)

by tangents—were correct. A similar confusion is apparent in his treatment of the tensions in strings. But there is still another figure (Figure 3), which has accompanying it in MS *H*, folio 81(33)v, the following brief statement: "On the balance, weight *ab* will be as weight *cd*." If Leonardo was assuming that the weights are of the same material with equal thickness and, as it seems in the figure, that they are of the same width, with their lengths equal to the lengths of the vertical and the incline, respectively, thus producing weights that are proportional to these lengths, then he was indeed giving a correct example of the inclined-plane principle that may well reflect proposition R1.10 of the *Liber de ratione ponderis*. There is one further solution of the inclined-plane problem, on MS *A*, folio 21v, that is totally erroneous and, so far as is known, unique. It is not discussed here; the reader is referred to Duhem's treatment, with the caution that Duhem's conclusion that it was derived from Pappus' erroneous solution is questionable.[8]

As important as Leonardo's responses to proposition R1.10 are his responses to the bent-lever proposition, R1.08, of the *Liber de ratione ponderis*. In *Codex Arundel*, folio 32v, he presents another Italian translation of it (in addition to the translation already noted in his omnibus collection of translations of the enunciations of the medieval work). In this new translation he writes of the bent-lever law as "tested": "Tested. If the arms of the balance are unequal and their juncture in the fulcrum is angular, and if their termini are equally distant from the central [that is, vertical] line through the fulcrum, with equal weights applied there [at the termini], they will weigh equally [that is, be in equilibrium]"—or "Sperimentata. Se le braccia della bilancia fieno inequali, e la lor congiunzione nel polo sia angulare, se i termini lor fieno equalmente distanti alla linea central del polo, li pesi appiccativi, essendo equali, equalmente peseranno," a translation of the Latin text, "R1.08. Si inequalia fuerint brachia libre, et in centro motus angulum fecerint, si termini eorum ad directionem hinc inde equaliter accesserint, equalia appensa, in hac dispositione equaliter ponderabunt."[9] Other, somewhat confused passages indicate that Leonardo had indeed absorbed the significance of the passage he had twice translated.[10]

More important, Leonardo extended the bent-lever law beyond the special case of equal weights at equal horizontal distances, given in R1.08, to cases in which the more general law of the bent lever—"weights are inversely proportional to the horizontal distances"—is applied. He did this in a large number of problems to which he applied his concept of "potential lever arm." The first passage notable for this concept is in

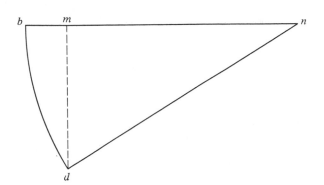

FIGURE 4. (Note: This is the essential part of a more detailed drawing.)

MS *E*, folio 72v, and probably derives from proposition R3.05 of the *Liber de ratione ponderis*.[11] Here Leonardo wrote (see Figure 4): "The ratio that space *mn* has to space *nb* is the same as the ratio that the weight which has descended to *d* has to the weight it had in position *b*. It follows that, *mn* being 9/11 of *nb*, the weight in *d* is 9/10 (! 9/11) of the weight it had in height *b*." In this passage *n* is the center of motion and *mn* is the potential lever arm of the weight in position *d*. His use of the potential lever arm is also illustrated in

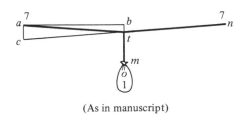

(As in manuscript)

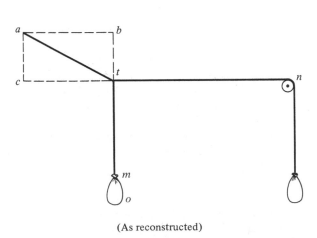

(As reconstructed)

FIGURE 5

a passage that can be reconstructed from MS *E*, folio 65r, as follows (Figure 5). A bar *at* is pivoted at *a*; a weight *o* is suspended from *t* at *m* and a second weight acts on *t* in a direction *tn* perpendicular to that of the first weight. The weights at *m* and *n* necessary to keep the bar in equilibrium are to be determined. In this determination Leonardo took *ab* and *ac* as the potential lever arms (and so labeled them), so that the weights *m* and *n* are inversely proportional to the potential lever arms *ab* and *ac*. The same kind of problem is illustrated in a passage in *Codex Atlanticus*, folio 268v-b, which can be summarized by reference to Figure 6. Cord *ab* supports a weight *n*, which is

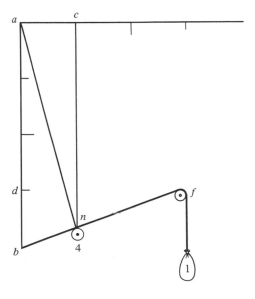

FIGURE 6

pulled to the position indicated by a tangential force along *nf* that is given a value of 1 and there keeps *an* in equilibrium. The passage indicates that weight 1, acting through a distance of four units (the potential lever arm *an*), keeps in equilibrium a weight *n* of 4, acting through a distance of one unit (the potential counterlever *ac*). A similar use of "potential lever arm" is found in problems like that illustrated in Figure 7, taken from MS *M*, folio 40r. Here the potential lever arm is *an*, the perpendicular drawn from the line of force *fp* to the center of motion *a*. Hence the weights suspended from *p* and *m* are related inversely as the distances *an* and *am*. These and similar problems reveal Leonardo's acute awareness of the proper factors of horizontal distance and force determining the static moment about a point.

The concept of potential lever arm also played a crucial role in Leonardo's effort to analyze the tension

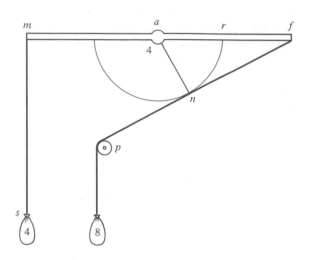

FIGURE 7

in strings. Before examining that role, it must be noted that Leonardo often used an incorrect rule based on tangents rather than sines, a rule similar to that which he mistakenly applied to the problem of the inclined plane. An example of the incorrect procedure appears in MS *E*, folio 66v (see Figure 8):

The heavy body suspended in the angle of the cord divides the weight to these cords in the ratio of the angles included between the said cords and the central [that is, vertical] line of the weight. Proof. Let the angle of the said cord be *bac*, in which is suspended heavy body *g* by cord *ag*. Then let this angle be cut in the position of equality [that is, in the horizontal direction] by line *fb*. Then draw the perpendicular *da* to angle *a*

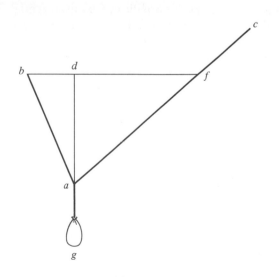

FIGURE 8

and it will be in the direct continuation of cord *ag*, and the ratio which space *df* has to space *db*, the weight [that is, tension] in cord *ba* will have to the weight [that is, tension] in cord *fa*.

Thus, with *da* the common altitude and *df* and *db* used as the measures of the angles at *a*, Leonardo is actually measuring the tensions by the inverse ratio of the tangents. This same incorrect procedure appears many times in the notebooks (for instance, MS *E*, fols. 67v, 68r, 68v, 69r, 69v, 71r; *Codex Arundel*, fol. 117v; MS *G*, fol. 39v).

In addition to this faulty method Leonardo in some instances employed a correct procedure based on the concept of the potential lever arm. In *Codex Arundel*, folio 1v, Leonardo wrote that "the weight 3 is not distributed to the real arms of the balance in the same [although inverse] ratio of these arms but in the [inverse] ratio of the potential arms" (see Figure 9).

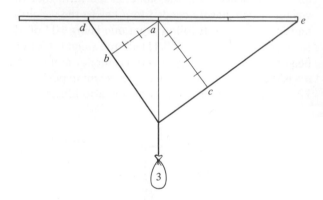

FIGURE 9

The cord is attached to a horizontal beam and a weight is hung from the cord. In the figure *ab* and *ac* are the potential arms. This is equivalent to a theorem that could be expressed in modern terms as "the moments of two concurrent forces around a point on the resultant are mutually equal." Leonardo's theorem, however, does not allow the calculation of the actual tensions in the strings. By locating the center of the moments first on one and then on the other of the concurrent forces, however, Leonardo discovered how to find the tensions in the segments of a string supporting a weight. In *Codex Arundel*, folio 6r (see Figure 10), he stated:

Here the potential lever *db* is six times the potential counterlever *bc*. Whence it follows that one pound placed in the force line "appendiculo" *dn* is equal in power to six pounds placed in the semireal force line

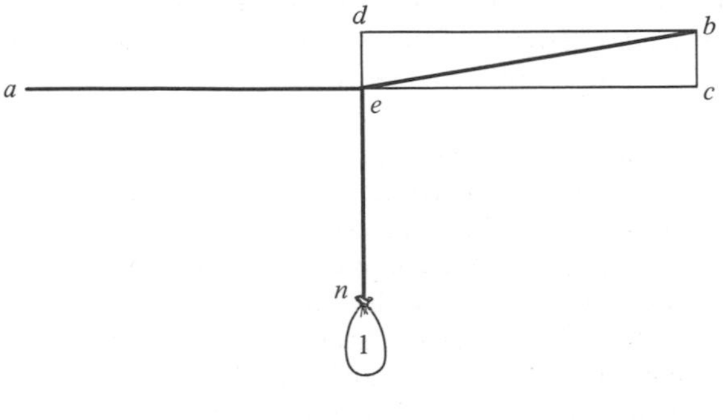

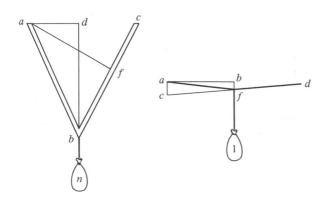

FIGURE 10

ca, and to another six pounds of power conjoined at b. Therefore, the cord aeb by means of one pound placed in line dn has the [total] effect of twelve pounds.

All of which is to say that Leonardo has determined that there are six pounds of tension in each segment of the cord. The general procedure is exhibited in MS E, folio 65r (see Figure 11). Under the figure is the caption "a is the pole [that is, fulcrum] of the angular balance [with arms] ad and af, and their force lines ['appendiculi'] are dn and fc." This applies to the figure on the left and indicates that af and da are the lever arms on which the tension in cb and the weight hanging at b act. Leonardo then went on to say: "The greater the angle of the cord which supports weight n in the middle of the cord, the smaller becomes the potential arm [that is, ac in the figure on the right] and the greater becomes the potential counter-arm [that is, ba] supporting the weight." Since Leonardo has drawn the figure so that ab is four times ac and has marked the weight of n as 1, the obvious implication is that the tension in cord df will be 4.

In these last examples the weight hangs from the center of the cord. But in Codex Arundel, folio 6v, the same analysis is applied to a weight suspended at a point other than the middle of the cord (Figure 12).

Here the weight n is supported by two different forces, mf and mb. Now it is necessary to find the potential levers and counterlevers of these two forces bm and fm. For the force [at] b [with f the fulcrum of the potential lever] the [potential] lever arm is fe and the [potential] counterlever is fa. Thus for the lever arm fe the force line ["appendiculo"] is eb along which the motor b is applied; and for the counterlever fa the force line is an, which supports weight n. Having arranged the balance of the power and resistance of motor and weight, it is necessary to see what ratio lever fe has to counterlever fa; which lever fe is 21/22 of counterlever fa. Therefore b suffers 22 [pounds of

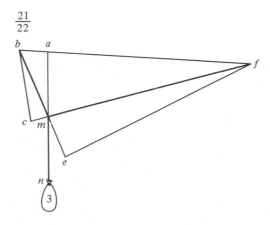

FIGURE 12. (Note: There is some discrepancy between Leonardo's text and the figure as concerns the relative length of the lines.)

tension] when n is 21. In the second disposition [with b instead of f as the fulcrum of a potential lever], bc is the [potential] lever arm and ba the [potential] counterlever. For bc the force line is cf along which the motor f is applied and weight n is applied along force line an. Now it is necessary to see what ratio lever bc has to counterlever ba, which counterlever is 1/3 of the lever. Therefore, one pound of force in f resists three pounds of weight in ba; and 21/22 of the three pounds in n, when placed at b, resist twenty-two placed in ba. ... Thus is completed the rule for calculating the unequal arms of the angular cord.

In a similar problem in Codex Arundel, folio 4v, Leonardo determined the tensions of the string segments; in this case the strings are no longer attached or fixed to a beam but are suspended from two pulley wheels from which also hang two equal weights (Figure 13). Here abc is apparently an equilateral

FIGURE 11

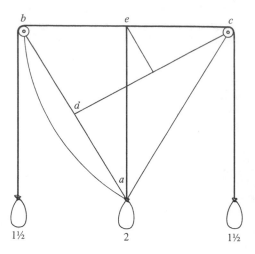

FIGURE 13

triangle, *cd* is the potential arm for the tension in string *ba* acting about fulcrum *c* and *ec* is the potential counterlever through which the weight 2 at *a* acts. If an equilateral triangle was intended, then, by Leonardo's procedure, the tension in each segment of the string ought to be $2/\sqrt{3} = 1.15$, rather than 1.5, as Leonardo miscalculated it. It is clear from all of these examples in which the tension is calculated that Leonardo was using a theorem that he understood as: "The ratio of the tension in a cord segment to the weight supported by the cord is equal to the inverse ratio of the potential lever arms through which the tension and weight act, where the fulcrum of the potential bent lever is in the point of support of the other segment of the cord." This is equivalent to a theorem in the composition of moments: "If one considers two concurrent forces and their resultant, the moment of the resultant about a point taken on one of the two concurrent forces is equal to the moment of the other concurrent force about the same point." The discovery and use of this basic concept in analyzing string tensions was Leonardo's most original development in statics beyond the medieval science of weights that he had inherited. Unfortunately, like most of Leonardo's investigations, it exerted no influence on those of his successors.

Another area of statics in which the medieval science of weights may have influenced Leonardo was that in which a determination is made of the partial forces in the supports of a beam where the beam itself supports a weight. Proposition R3.06 in the *Liber de ratione ponderis* states: "A weight not suspended in the middle [of a beam] makes the shorter part heavier according to the ratio of the longer part to the

shorter part."[12] The proof indicates that the partial forces in the supports are inversely related to the distances from the principal weight to the supports. In *Codex Arundel*, folio 8v (see Figure 14), Leonardo arrived at a similar conclusion:

> The beam which is suspended from its extremities by two cords of equal height divides its weight equally in each cord. If the beam is suspended by its extremities at an equal height, and in its midpoint a weight is hung, then the gravity of such a weight is equally distributed to the supports of the beam. But the weight which is moved from the middle of the beam toward one of its extremities becomes lighter at the extremity away from which it was moved, or heavier at the other extremity, by a weight which has the same ratio to the total weight as the motion completed by the weight [that is, its distance moved from the center] has to the whole beam.

Leonardo also absorbed the concept, so prevalent in the medieval science of weights (particularly in the *De canonio*, in Thābit ibn Qurra's *Liber karastonis*, and in part II of the *Liber de ratione ponderis*), that a

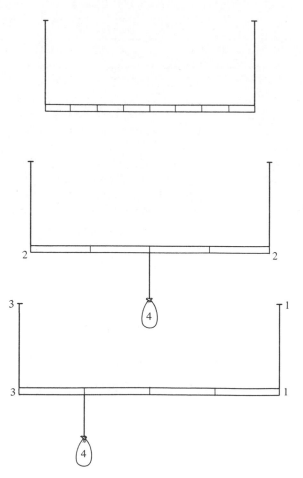

FIGURE 14

segment of a solid beam may be replaced by a weight hung from the midpoint of a weightless arm of the same length and position. For example, see Leonardo's exposition in MS *A*, folio 5r (see Figure 15):

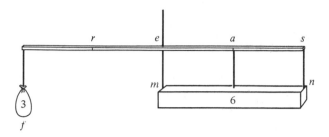

FIGURE 15

If a balance has a weight which is similar [that is, equal] in length to one of its arms, the weight being *mn* of six pounds, how many pounds are to be placed in *f* to resist it [that is, which will be in equilibrium with it]? I say that three pounds will suffice, for if weight *mn* is as long as one of its arms, you could judge that it may be replaced in the middle of the balance arm at point *a;* therefore, if six pounds are in *a*, another six pounds placed at *r* would produce resistance to them [that is, be in equilibrium with them], and, if you proceed as before in point *r* [but now] in the extremity of the balance, three pounds will produce the [necessary] resistance to them.

This replacement doctrine was the key step in solving the problem of the Roman balance in all of the above-noted tracts.[13]

The medieval science of weights was not the only influence upon Leonardo's statics, however, since it may be documented that he also, perhaps at a later time, read book I of Archimedes' *On the Equilibrium of Planes*. As a result he seems to have begun a work on centers of gravity in about 1508, as may be seen in a series of passages in *Codex Arundel*. Since these passages have already been translated and analyzed in rather complete detail elsewhere,[14] only their content and objectives will be given here. Preliminary to Leonardo's propositions on centers of gravity are a number of passages distinguishing three centers of a figure that has weight (see *Codex Arundel*, fol. 72v): "The first is the center of its natural gravity, the second [the center] of its accidental gravity, and the third is [the center] of the magnitude of this body." On folio 123v of this manuscript the centers are defined:

The center of the magnitude of bodies is placed in the middle with respect to the length, breadth and thickness of these bodies. The center of the accidental gravity of these bodies is placed in the middle with respect to

the parts which resist one another by standing in equilibrium. The center of natural gravity is that which divides a body into two parts equal in weight and quantity.

It is clear from many other passages that the center of natural gravity is the symmetrical center with respect to weight. Hence, the center of natural gravity of a beam lies in its center, and that center would not be disturbed by hanging equal weights on its extremities. If unequal weights are applied, however, there is a shift of the center of gravity, which is now called the center of accidental gravity, the weights having assumed accidental gravities by their positions on the unequal arms. The doctrine of the three centers can be traced to Scholastic writings of Nicole Oresme, Albert of Saxony, Marsilius of Inghen (and, no doubt, others).[15] In all of these preliminary considerations Leonardo assumed that a body or a system of bodies is in equilibrium when supported from its center of gravity (be it natural or accidental). It should also be observed that Leonardo assumed the law of the lever as being proved before setting out to prove his Archimedean-like propositions.

The first Archimedean passage to note is in *Codex Arundel*, folio 16v, where Leonardo includes a series of statements on equilibrium that is drawn in significant part from the postulates and early propositions of book I of *On the Equilibrium of Planes*. His terminology suggests that when Leonardo wrote this passage, he was using the translation of Jacobus Cremonensis (*ca.* 1450).[16]

More important than this passage are the propositions and proofs on centers of gravity, framed under the influence of Archimedes' work, which Leonardo specifically cites in a number of instances. The order for these propositions that Leonardo's own numeration seems to suggest is the following:

1. *Codex Arundel*, folio 16v, "Every triangle has the center of its gravity in the intersection of the lines which start from the angles and terminate in the centers of the sides opposite them." This is proposition 14 of book I of *On the Equilibrium of Planes*, and Leonardo included in his "proof" an additional proof of sorts for Archimedes' proposition 13 (since that proposition is fundamental for the proof of proposition 14), although the proof for proposition 13 ignores Archimedes' superb geometrical demonstration. Depending, as it does, on balance considerations, Leonardo's proof is more like Archimedes' second proof of proposition 13. Leonardo's proof of proposition 14 is for an equilateral triangle, but at its end he notes that it applies as well to scalene triangles.

2. *Codex Arundel*, folio 16r: "The center of gravity of any two equal triangles lies in the middle of the

line beginning at the center of one triangle and terminating in the center of gravity of the other triangle." This is equivalent to proposition 4 of *On the Equilibrium of Planes*, but Leonardo's proof differs from Archimedes' in that it merely shows that the center of gravity is in the middle of the line because the weights would be in equilibrium about that point. Archimedes' work is here cited (under the inaccurate title of *De ponderibus*, since the Pseudo-Archimedean work of that title was concerned with hydrostatics rather than statics).

3. *Codex Arundel*, folio 16r: "If two unequal triangles are in equilibrium at unequal distances, the greater will be placed at the lesser distance and the lesser at the greater distance." This is similar to proposition 3 of Archimedes' work. Leonardo, however, simply employed the law of the lever in his proof, which Archimedes did not do, since he did not offer a proof of the law until propositions 6 and 7.

4. *Codex Arundel*, folio 17v: "The center of gravity of every square of parallel sides and equal angles is equally distant from its angles." This is a special case of proposition 10 of *On the Equilibrium of Planes*; but Leonardo's proof, based once more on a balancing procedure, is not directly related to either of the proofs provided by Archimedes.

5. *Codex Arundel*, folio 17v: "The center of gravity of every corbel-like figure [that is, isosceles trapezium] lies in the line which divides it into two equal parts when two of its sides are parallel." This is similar to Archimedes' proposition 15, which treated more generally of any trapezium. Leonardo made a numerical determination of where the center of gravity lies on the bisector. Although his proof is not close to Archimedes', like Archimedes he used the law of the lever in his proof.

6. *Codex Arundel*, folio 17r: "The center of gravity of every equilateral pentagon is in the center of the circle which circumscribes it." This has no equivalent in Archimedes' work. The proof proceeds by dividing the pentagon into triangles that are shown to balance

about the center of the circle. Again Leonardo used the law of the lever in his proof, much as he had in his previous propositions. The proof is immediately followed by the determination of the center of gravity of a pentagon that is not equilateral, in which the same balancing techniques are again employed. Leonardo here cited Archimedes as the authority for the law of the lever, and the designation of Archimedes' proposition as the "fifth" is perhaps an indication that he was using William of Moerbeke's medieval translation of *On the Equilibrium of Planes* instead of that of Jacobus Cremonensis, in which the equivalent proposition is number 7. Although these exhaust those propositions of Leonardo's that are directly related to *On the Equilibrium of Planes*, it should be noted that Leonardo used the same balancing techniques in his effort to determine the center of gravity of a semicircle (see *Codex Arundel*, fols. 215r-v).

It should also be noted that Leonardo went beyond Archimedes' treatise in one major respect—the determination of centers of gravity of solids, a subject taken up in more detail later in the century by Francesco Maurolico and Federico Commandino. Two of the propositions investigated by Leonardo may be presented here to illustrate his procedures. Both propositions concern the center of gravity of a pyramid and appear to be discoveries of Leonardo's. The first is that the center of gravity of a pyramid (actually, a regular tetrahedron) is, at the intersection of the axes, a distance on each axis of 1/4 of its length, starting from the center of one of the faces. (By "axis" Leonardo understood a line drawn from a vertex to the center of the opposite face.) In one place (*Codex Arundel*, fol. 218v) he wrote of the intersection of the pyramidal axes as follows: "The inferior [interior?] axes of pyramids which arise from [a point lying at] 1/3 of the axis of their bases [that is, faces] will intersect in [a point lying at] 1/4 of their length [starting] at the base."

Despite the confusion of singulars and plurals as well as of the expression "inferior axes," the prop-

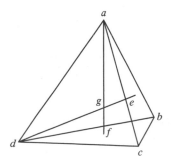 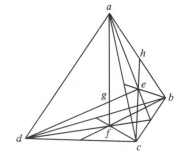 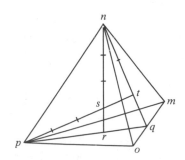

FIGURE 16

osition is clear enough, particularly since Leonardo provided both the drawing shown in Figure 16 and its explanation and, in addition, the intersection of the pyramidal axes is definitely specified as the center of gravity in another passage (fol. 193v): "The center of gravity of the [pyramidal] body of four triangular bases [that is, faces] is located at the intersection of its axes and it will be in the 1/4 part of their length." The proof of this is actually given on the page of the original quotation about the intersection of the axes (fol. 218v), but only as a proof following a more general statement about pyramids and cones:

> The center of gravity of any pyramid—round, triangular, square, or [whose base is] of any number of sides—is in the fourth part of its axis near the base. Let the pyramid be *abcd* with base *bcd* and apex *a*. Find the center of the base *bcd*, which you let be *f*, then find the center of face *abc*, which will be *e*, as was proved by the first [proposition]. Now draw line *af*, in which the center of gravity of the pyramid lies because *f* is the center of base *bcd* and the apex *a* is perpendicularly above *f* and the angles *b*, *c* and *d* are equally distant from *f* and [thus] weigh equally so that the center of gravity lies in line *af*. Now draw a line from angle *d* to the center *e* of face *abc*, cutting *af* in point *g*. I say for the aforesaid reason that the center of gravity is in line *de*. So, since the center is in each [line] and there can be only one center, it necessarily lies in the intersection of these lines, namely in point *g*, because the angles *a*, *b*, *c* and *d* are equally distant from this *g*.

As noted above, the proof is given only for a regular tetrahedron, none being given for the cone or for other pyramids designated in the general enunciation. It represents a rather intuitive mechanical approach, for Leonardo abruptly stated that because the angles *b*, *c*, and *d* weigh equally about *f*, the center of gravity of the base triangle, and *a* is perpendicularly above *f*, the center of gravity of the whole pyramid must lie in line *af*. This is reminiscent of Hero's demonstration of the equilibrium of a triangle supported at its center with equal weights at the angles. This kind of reasoning, then, seems to be extended to the whole pyramid by Leonardo at the end of the proof in which he declared that each of the four angles is equidistant from *g* and, presumably, equal weights at the angles would therefore be in equilibrium if the pyramid were supported in *g*. It is worth noting that a generation later Maurolico gave a very neat demonstration of just such a determination of the center of gravity of a tetrahedron by the hanging of equal weights at the angles.[17] Finally, one additional theorem (without proof), concerning the center of gravity of a tetrahedron, appears to have been Leonardo's own discovery (*Codex Arundel*, fol. 123v):

> The pyramid with triangular base has the center of its natural gravity in the [line] segment which extends from the middle of the base [that is, the midpoint of one edge] to the middle of the side [that is, edge] opposite the base; and it [the center of gravity] is located on the segment equally distant [from the termini] of the [said] line joining the base with the aforesaid side.

Despite Leonardo's unusual and imprecise language (an attempt has been made to rectify it by bracketed additions), it is clear that he has here expressed a neat theorem to the effect that the center of gravity of the tetrahedron lies at the intersection of the segments joining the midpoint of each edge with the midpoint of the opposite edge and that each of these segments is bisected by the center of gravity. Again, it is possible that Leonardo arrived at this proposition by considering four equal weights hung at the angles. At any rate the balance procedure, whose refinements he learned from Archimedes, no doubt played some part in his discovery, however it was made.

Leonardo gave considerable attention to one other area of statics, pulley problems. Since this work perhaps belongs more to his study of machines, except for a brief discussion in the section on dynamics, the reader is referred to Marcolongo's brief but excellent account.[18]

Turning to Leonardo's knowledge of hydrostatics, it should first be noted that certain fragments from William of Moerbeke's translation of Archimedes' *On Floating Bodies* appear in the *Codex Atlanticus*, folios 153v-e, 153r-b, and 153r-c.[19] These fragments (which occupy a single sheet bound into the codex) are not in Leonardo's customary mirror script but appear in normal writing, from left to right. Although sometimes considered by earlier authors to have been written by Leonardo, they are now generally believed to be by some other hand.[20] Whether the sheet was once the property of Leonardo or whether it was added to Leonardo's material after his death cannot be determined with certainty—at any rate, the fragments can be identified as being from proposition 10 of book II of the Archimedean work. Whatever Leonardo's relationship to these fragments, his notebooks reveal that he had only a sketchy and indirect knowledge of Archimedean hydrostatics, which he seems to have drawn from the medieval tradition of *De ponderibus Archimenidis*. Numerous passages in the notebooks reveal a general knowledge of density and specific weight (for instance, MS *C*, fol. 26v, MS *F*, fol. 70r; MS *E*, fol. 74v). Similarly, Leonardo certainly knew that bodies weigh less in water than in air (see MS *F*, fol. 69r), and in one passage (*Codex Atlanticus*, fol. 284v) he proposed to measure the relative resistance of water as compared with air by plunging the weight on one arm of a balance held in aerial equilibrium into water and then determining how much extra weight must be added to the weight in the water to maintain the balance in equilibrium. See also MS *A*, folio 30v: "The weight in air exhibits the truth of its weight, the weight in water will appear to be less weight by the amount the water is heavier than the air."

So far as is known, however, the principle of Archimedes as embraced by proposition 7 of book I of the genuine *On Floating Bodies* was not precisely stated by Leonardo. Even if he did know the principle, as some have suggested, he probably would have learned it from proposition 1 of the medieval *De ponderibus Archimenidis*. As a matter of fact, Leonardo many times repeated the first postulate of the medieval work, that bodies or elements do not have weight amid their own kind—or, as Leonardo put it (*Codex Atlanticus*, fol. 365r-a; *Codex Arundel*, fol. 189r), "No part of an element weighs in its element" (cf. *Codex Arundel*, fol. 160r). Still, he could have gotten the postulate from Blasius of Parma's *De ponderibus*, a work that Leonardo knew and criticized (see MS *Ashburnham* 2038, fol. 2v). It is possible that since Leonardo knew the basic principle of floating bodies—that a floating body displaces its weight of liquid (see *Codex Forster* II₂, fol. 65v)—he may have gotten it directly from proposition 5 of book I of *On Floating Bodies*. But even this principle appeared in one manuscript of the medieval *De ponderibus Archimenidis* and was incorporated into John of Murs' version of that work, which appeared as part of his widely read *Quadripartitum numerorum* of 1343.[21] So, then, all of the meager reflections of Archimedean hydrostatics found in Leonardo's notebooks could easily have been drawn from medieval sources, and (with the possible exception of the disputed fragments noted above) nothing from the brilliant treatments in book II of the genuine *On Floating Bodies* is to be found in the great artist's notebooks. It is worth remarking, however, that although Leonardo showed little knowledge of Archimedean hydrostatics he had considerable success in the practical hydrostatic questions that arose from his study of pumps and other hydrostatic devices.[22]

The problems Leonardo considered concerning the hydrostatic equilibrium of liquids in communicating vessels were of two kinds: those in which the liquid is under the influence of gravity alone and those in which the liquid is under the external pressure of a piston in one of the communicating vessels. In connection with problems of the first kind, he expressly and correctly stated the law of communicating vessels in *Codex Atlanticus*, folio 219v-a: "The surfaces of all liquids at rest, which are joined together below, are always of equal height." Leonardo further noted in various ways that a quantity of water will never lift another quantity of water, even if the second quantity is in a narrower vessel, to a level that is higher than its own, whatever the ratio between the surfaces of the two communicating vessels (*Codex Atlanticus*, fol. 165v)—although he never gave, as far as can be seen, the correct explanation: the equality of the air pressure on both surfaces of the water in the communicating vessels. In some but not all passages (see *Codex Leicester*, fol. 25r; *Codex Atlanticus*, fol. 321v-a) Leonardo did free himself from the misapplication to hydrostatic equilibrium of the principle of the equilibrium of a balance of equal arms bearing equal weights (*Codex Atlanticus*, fol. 206r-a; *Codex Arundel*, fol. 264r). His own explanations are not happy ones, however. He also correctly analyzed the varying levels that would result if, to a liquid in a U-tube, were added a specifically lighter liquid which does not mix with the initial liquid (see Figure 17). In MS *E*, folio

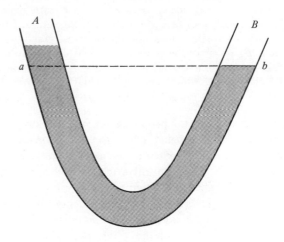

FIGURE 17

74v, he indicated that if the specific weight of the initial liquid were double that of the liquid added, the free surface of the heavier liquid in limb *B* would be at a level halfway between the level of the free surface of the lighter liquid and the surface of contact of the two liquids (the last two surfaces being in limb *A*).

In problems of the second kind, in which the force of a piston is applied to the surface of the liquid in one of the communicating vessels (Figure 18), despite some passages in which he gave an incorrect or only partially true account (see MS *A*, fol. 45r; *Codex Atlanticus*, fol. 384v-a), Leonardo did compose an entirely correct and generally expressed applicable statement or rule (*Codex Leicester*, fol. 11r). Assuming the tube on the right to be vertical and cylindrical, Leonardo observed that the ratio between the pressing weight of the piston and the weight of water in the tube on the right, above the upper level of the water in the vessel on the left, is equal to the ratio between the area under pressure from the piston and the area

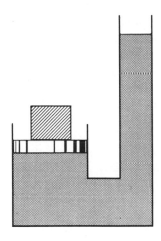

FIGURE 18

of the tube on the right (see *Codex Atlanticus*, fols. 20r, 206r-a, 306v-c; *Codex Leicester*, fol. 26r). And indeed, in a long explanation accompanying the rule in *Codex Leicester*, folio 11r, Leonardo approached, although still in a confused manner, the concept of pressure itself (a concept that appears in no other of his hydrostatic passages, so far as is known) and that of its uniform transmission through a liquid. Leonardo did not, however, generalize his observations to produce Pascal's law, that any additional pressure applied to a confined liquid at its boundary will be transmitted equally to every point in the liquid. Incidentally, the above-noted passage in *Codex Leicester*, folio 11r, also seems to imply a significant consequence for problems of the first kind: that the pressure in an enclosed liquid increases with its depth below its highest point.

Any discussion of Leonardo's knowledge of hydrostatics should be complemented with a few remarks regarding his observations on fluid motion. From the various quotations judiciously evaluated by Truesdell, one can single out some in which Leonardo appears as the first to express special cases of two basic laws of fluid mechanics. The first is the principle of continuity, which declares that the speed of steady flow varies inversely as the cross-sectional area of the channel. Leonardo expressed this in a number of passages, for example, in MS *A*, folio 57v, where he

stated: "Every movement of water of equal breadth and surface will run that much faster in one place than in another, as [the water] may be less deep in the former place than in the latter" (compare MS *H*, fol. 54(6)v; *Codex Atlanticus*, fols. 80r-b, 81v-a; and *Codex Leicester*, fols. 24r and, particularly, 6v). He clearly recognized the principle as implying steady discharge in *Codex Atlanticus*, folio 287r-b: "If the water is not added to or taken away from the river, it will pass with equal quantities in every degree of its breadth [length?], with diverse speeds and slownesses, through the various straitnesses and breadths of its length."

The second principle of fluid motion enunciated by Leonardo was that of equal circulation. In its modern form, when applied to vortex motion, it holds that the product of speed and length is the same on each circle of flow. Leonardo expressed it, in *Codex Atlanticus*, folio 296v-b, as:

> The helical or rather rotary motion of every liquid is so much the swifter as it is nearer to the center of its revolution. This that we set forth is a case worthy of admiration; for the motion of the circular wheel is so much the slower as it is nearer to the center of the rotating thing. But in this case [of water] we have the same motion, through speed and length, in each whole revolution of the water, just the same in the circumference of the greatest circle as in the least. . . .

It could well be that Leonardo's reference to the motion of the circular wheel was suggested by either a statement in Pseudo-Aristotle's *Mechanica* (848A)—that on a rotating radius "the point which is farther from the fixed center is the quicker"—or by the first postulate of the thirteenth-century *Liber de motu* of Gerard of Brussels, which held that "those which are farther from the center or immobile axis are moved more [quickly]. Those which are less far are moved less [quickly]."[23] At any rate, it is worthy of note that Leonardo's statement of the principle of equal circulation is embroidered by an unsound theoretical explanation, but even so, one must agree with Truesdell's conclusion (p. 79): "If Leonardo discovered these two principles from observation, he stands among the founders of western mechanics."

The analysis can now be completed by turning to Leonardo's more general efforts in the dynamics and kinematics of moving bodies, including those that descend under the influence of gravity. In dynamics Leonardo often expressed views that were Aristotelian or Aristotelian as modified by Scholastic writers. His notes contain a virtual flood of definitions of gravity, weight, force, motion, impetus, and percussion:

1. MS *B*, folio 63r: "Gravity, force, material motion and percussion are four accidental powers

with which all the evident works of mortal men have their causes and their deaths."

2. *Codex Arundel*, folio 37r: "Gravity is an invisible power which is created by accidental motion and infused into bodies which are removed from their natural place."

3. *Codex Atlanticus*, folio 246r-a: "The power of every gravity is extended toward the center of the world."

4. *Codex Arundel*, folio 37v: "Gravity, force and percussion are of such nature that each by itself alone can arise from each of the others and also each can give birth to them. And all together, and each by itself, can create motion and arise from it" and "Weight desires [to act in] a single line [that is, toward the center of the world] and force an infinitude [of lines]. Weight is of equal power throughout its life and force always weakens [as it acts]. Weight passes by nature into all its supports and exists throughout the length of these supports and completely through all their parts."

5. *Codex Atlanticus*, folio 253r-c: "Force is a spiritual essence which by accidental violence is conjoined in heavy bodies deprived of their natural desires; in such bodies, it [that is, force], although of short duration, often appears [to be] of marvelous power. Force is a power that is spiritual, incorporeal, impalpable, which force is effected for a short life in bodies which by accidental violence stand outside of their natural repose. 'Spiritual,' I say, because in it there is invisible life; 'incorporeal' and 'impalpable,' because the body in which it arises does not increase in form or in weight."

6. MS *A*, folio 34v: "Force, I say to be a spiritual virtue, an invisible power, which through accidental, external violence is caused by motion and is placed and infused into bodies which are withdrawn and turned from their natural use. . . ."

On the same page as the last Leonardo indicated that force has three "offices" ("ofizi") embracing an "infinitude of examples" of each. These are "drawing" ("tirare"), "pushing" ("spignere"), and "stopping" ("fermare"). Force arises in two ways: by the rapid expansion of a rare body in the presence of a dense one, as in the explosion of a gun, or by the return to their natural dispositions of bodies that have been distorted or bent, as manifested by the action of a bow.

Turning from the passages on "force" to those on "impetus," it is immediately apparent that Leonardo has absorbed the medieval theory that explains the motion of projectiles by the impression of an impetus into the projectile by the projector, a theory outlined in its most mature form by Jean Buridan and repeated by many other authors, including Albert of Saxony, whose works Leonardo had read.[24] Leonardo's

dependence on the medieval impetus theory is readily shown by noting a few of his statements concerning it:

1. MS *E*, folio 22r: "Impetus is a virtue ["virtù"] created by motion and transmitted by the motor to the mobile that has as much motion as the impetus has life."

2. *Codex Atlanticus*, folio 161v-a: "Impetus is a power ["potenzia"] of the motor applied to its mobile, which [power] causes the mobile to move after it has separated from its motor."

3. MS *G*, folio 73r: "Impetus is the impression of motion transmitted by the motor to the mobile. Impetus is a power impressed by the motor in the mobile. . . . Every impression tends toward permanence or desires to be permanent."

In the last passage Leonardo's words are particularly reminiscent of Buridan's "inertia-like" impetus. On the other hand, Buridan's quantitative description of impetus as directly proportional to both the quantity of prime matter in and the velocity of the mobile is nowhere evident in Leonardo's notebooks. In some passages Leonardo noted the view held by some of his contemporaries (such as Agostino Nifo) that the air plays a supplementary role in keeping the projectile in motion (see *Codex Atlanticus*, fol. 168v-b): "Impetus is [the] impression of local motion transmitted by the motor to the mobile and maintained by the air or the water as they move in order to prevent a vacuum" (cf. *ibid.*, fol. 219v-a). In *Codex Atlanticus*, folio 108r-a, however, he stressed the role of the air in resisting the motion of the projectile and concluded that the air gives little or no help to the motion. Furthermore, in *Codex Leicester*, folio 29v, he gives a long and detailed refutation of the possible role of the air as motor, as Buridan had before him. And not only is it the air as resistance that weakens the impetus in a projectile; the impetus is also weakened and destroyed by the tendency to natural motion. For example, in MS *E*, folio 29r, Leonardo says: "But the natural motion conjoined with the motion of a motor [that is, arising from the impetus derived from the motor] consumes the impetus of the motor."

Leonardo also applied the impetus theory to many of the same inertial phenomena as did his medieval predecessors—for instance, to the stability of the spinning top (MS *E*, fol. 50v), to pendular and other kinds of oscillating motion (*Codex Arundel*, fol. 2r), to impact and rebound (*Codex Leicester*, fols. 8r, 29r), and to the common medieval speculation regarding a ball falling through a hole in the earth to the center and rising on the other side before falling back and oscillating about the center of the earth (*Codex Atlanticus*, fol. 153v-b). In a sense, all of these last are embraced by the general statement in MS

E, folio 40v: "The impetus created in whatever line has the power of finishing in any other line."

In the overwhelming majority of passages, Leonardo applied the impetus theory to violent motion of projection. In some places, however, he also applied it to cases of natural motion, as did his medieval predecessors when they explained the acceleration of falling bodies through the continuous impression of impetus by the undiminished natural weight of the body. For example, in *Codex Atlanticus,* folio 176r-a, Leonardo wrote: "Impetus arises from weight just as it arises from force." And in the same manuscript (fol. 202v-b) he noted the continuous acquisition of impetus "up to the center [of the world]." Leonardo was convinced of the acceleration of falling bodies (although his kinematic description of that fall was confused); hence, he no doubt believed that the principal cause of such acceleration was the continual acquisition of impetus.

One last aspect of Leonardo's impetus doctrine remains to be discussed—his concept of compound impetus, defined in MS *E,* folio 35r, as that which occurs when the motion "partakes of the impetus of the motor and the impetus of the mobile." The example he gave is that of a spinning body moved by an external force along a straight line. When the impetus of the primary force dominates, the body moves along a simple straight line. As that impetus dies, the rotary motion of the spinning body acts with it to produce a composite-curved motion. Finally, all of the impetus of the original motion is dissipated and a simple circular motion remains that arises only from the spinning body. A series of passages (*Codex Arundel,* fols. 143r–144v) are further concerned with the relationship of transversal and natural motions, which, if the passages and diagrams have been understood correctly, concur to produce resultant composite motions. It appears later in the same manuscript (fol. 147v) that Leonardo thought that the first part of a projectile path was straight until the primary impetus diminished enough for the natural motion to have an effect:

> The mobile is [first] moved in that direction ["aspetto"] in which the motion of its motor is moved. The straightness of the transversal motion in the mobile lasts so long as the internal power given it by the motor lasts. Straightness is wanting to the transversal motion because [that is, when] the power which the mobile acquired from its motor diminishes.

A beautiful instance of compound motion upon which Leonardo reported more than once is that of an arrow or stone shot into the air from a rotating earth, which arrow or stone would fall to the ground with rectilinear motion with respect to the rotating earth because it receives a circular impetus from the earth. But with respect to a stationary frame, the descent is said to be spiral, that is, compounded of

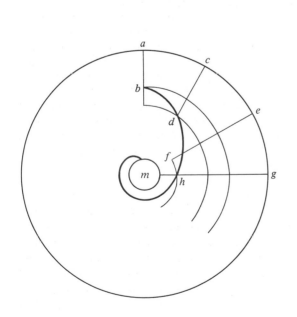

(As in manuscript)

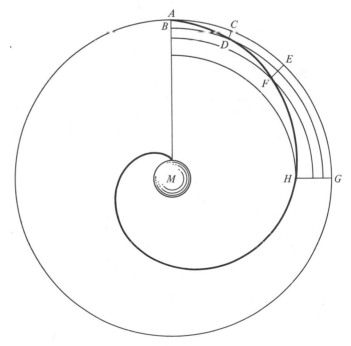

(Reconstructed)

FIGURE 19

rectilinear and circular motions. The longer of the passages in which Leonardo described this kind of compound motion is worth quoting (MS *G*, fol. 55r; see Figure 19):

> On the heavy body descending in air, with the elements rotating in a complete rotation in twenty-four hours. The mobile descending from the uppermost part of the sphere of fire will produce a straight motion down to the earth even if the elements are in a continuous motion of rotation about the center of the world. Proof: let *b* be the heavy body which descends through the elements from [point] *a* to the center of the world, *m*. I say that such a heavy body, even if it makes a curved descent in the manner of a spiral line, will never deviate in its rectilinear descent along which it continually proceeds from the place whence it began to the center of the world, because when it departs from point *a* and descends to *b*, in the time in which it has descended to *b*, it has been carried on to [point] *d*, the position of *a* having rotated to *c*, and so the mobile finds itself in the straight line extending from *c* to the center of the world, *m*. If the mobile descends from *d* to *f*, the beginning of motion, *c*, is, in the same time, moved from *c* to *f* [!*e*]. And if *f* descends to *h*, *e* is rotated to *g;* and so in twenty-four hours the mobile descends to the earth [directly] under the place whence it first began. And such a motion is a compounded one.
>
> [In margin:] If the mobile descends from the uppermost part of the elements to the lowest point in twenty-four hours, its motion is compounded of straight and curved [motions]. I say "straight" because it will never deviate from the shortest line extending from the place whence it began to the center of the elements, and it will stop at the lowest extremity of such a rectitude, which stands, as if to the zenith, under the place from which the mobile began [to descend]. And such a motion is inherently curved along with the parts of the line, and consequently in the end is curved along with the whole line. Thus it happened that the stone thrown from the tower does not hit the side of the tower before hitting the ground.

This is not unlike a passage found in Nicole Oresme's *Livre du ciel et du monde*.[25]

In view of the Aristotelian and Scholastic doctrines already noted, it is not surprising to find that Leonardo again and again adopted some form of the Peripatetic law of motion relating velocity directly to force and inversely to resistance. For example, MS *F*, folios 51r-v, lists a series of Aristotelian rules. It begins "1⁰ if one power moves a body through a certain space in a certain time, the same power will move half the body twice the space in the same time. . . ." (compare MS *F*, fol. 26r). This law, when applied to machines like the pulley and the lever, became a kind of primitive conservation-of-work principle, as it had been in antiquity and the Middle Ages. Its sense was

that "there is in effect a definite limit to the results of a given effort, and this effort is not alone a question of the magnitude of the force but also of the distance, in any given time, through which it acts. If the one be increased, it can only be at the expense of the other."[26] In regard to the lever, Leonardo wrote (MS *A*, fol. 45r): "The ratio which the length of the lever has to the counterlever you will find to be the same as that in the quality of their weights and similarly in the slowness of movement and in the quality of the paths traversed by their extremities, when they have arrived at the permanent height of their pole." He stated again (*E*, fol. 58v):

> By the amount that accidental weight is added to the motor placed at the extremity of the lever so does the mobile placed at the extremity of the counterlever exceed its natural weight. And the movement of the motor is greater than that of the mobile by as much as the accidental weight of the motor exceeds its natural weight.

Leonardo also applied the principle to more complex machines (MS *A*, fol. 33v): "The more a force is extended from wheel to wheel, from lever to lever, or from screw to screw, the greater is its power and its slowness." Concerning multiple pulleys, he added (MS *E*, fol. 20v):

> The powers that the cords interposed between the pulleys receive from their motor are in the same ratio as the speeds of their motions. Of the motions made by the cords on their pulleys, the motion of the last cord is in the same ratio to the first as that of the number of cords; that is, if there are five, the first is moved one braccio, while the last is moved 1/5 of a braccio; and if there are six, the last cord will be moved 1/6 of a braccio, and so on to infinity. The ratio which the motion of the motor of the pulleys has to the motion of the weight lifted by the pulleys is the same as that of the weight lifted by such pulleys to the weight of its motor. . . .

It is not difficult to see why Leonardo, so concerned with this view of compensating gain and loss, attacked the speculators on perpetual motion (*Codex Forster* II₂, fol. 92v): "O speculators on continuous motion, how many vain designs of a similar nature have you created. Go and accompany the seekers after gold."

One area of dynamics that Leonardo treated is particularly worthy of note, that which he often called "percussion." In this area he went beyond his predecessors and, one might say, virtually created it as a branch of mechanics. For him the subject included not only effects of the impacts of hammers on nails and other surfaces (as in MS *C*, fol. 6v; MS *A*, fol.

53v) but also rectilinear impact of two balls, either both in motion or one in motion and the other at rest (see the various examples illustrated on MS *A*, fol. 8r), and rebound phenomena off a firm surface. In describing impacts in *Codex Arundel*, folio 83v, Leonardo wrote: "There are two kinds ["nature"] of percussion: the one when the object [struck] flees from the mobile that strikes it; the other when the mobile rebounds rectilinearly from the object struck." In one passage (MS *I*, fol. 41v), a problem of impacting balls is posed: "Ball *a* is moved with three degrees of velocity and ball *b* with four degrees of velocity. It is asked what is the difference ["varietà"] in such percussion [of *a*] with *b* when the latter ball would be at rest and when it [*a*] would meet the latter ball [moving] with the said four degrees of velocity."

In some passages Leonardo attempted to distinguish and measure the relative effects of the impetus of an object striking a surface and of the percussion executed by a resisting surface. For example, in *Codex Arundel*, folio 81v, he showed the rebound path as an arc (later called "l'arco del moto refresso") and indicated that the altitude of rebound is acquired only from the simple percussion, while the horizontal distance traversed in rebound is acquired only from the impetus that the mobile had on striking the surface, so that "by the amount that the rebound is higher than it is long, the power of the percussion exceeds the power of the impetus, and by the amount that the rebound's length exceeds its height, the percussion is exceeded by the impetus."

What is perhaps Leonardo's most interesting conclusion about rebound is that the angle of incidence is equal to that of rebound. For example, in *Codex Arundel*, folio 82v, he stated: "The angle made by the reflected motion of heavy bodies becomes equal to the angle made by the incident motion." Again, in MS *A*, folio 19r (Figure 20), he wrote:

> Every blow struck on an object rebounds rectilinearly at an angle equal ["simile"] to that of percussion. This proposition is clearly evident, inasmuch as, if you would strike a wall with a ball, it would rise rectilinearly at an angle equal to that of the percussion. That is, if

the ball *b* is thrown at *c*, it will return rectilinearly through the line *cb* because it is constrained to produce equal angles on the wall *fg*. And if you throw it along line *bd*, it will return rectilinearly along line *de*, and so the line of percussion and the line of rebound will make one angle on wall *fg* situated in the middle between two equal angles, as *d* appears between *m* and *n*. [See also *Codex Atlanticus*, fol. 125r-a.]

The transfer, and in a sense the conservation, of power and impetus in percussion is described in *Codex Leicester*, folio 8r:

> If the percussor will be equal and similar to the percussed, the percussor leaves its power completely in the percussed, which flees with fury from the site of the percussion, leaving its percussor there. But if the percussor—similar but not equal to the percussed—is greater, it will not lose its impetus completely after the percussion but there will remain the amount by which it exceeds the quantity of the percussed. And if the percussor will be less than the percussed, it will rebound rectilinearly through more distance than the percussed by the amount that the percussed exceeds the percussor.

Leonardo is here obviously groping for adequate laws of impact.

The last area to be considered is Leonardo's treatment of the kinematics of moving bodies, especially the kinematics of falling bodies. In *Codex Arundel*, folio 176v, he gave definitions of "slower" and "quicker" that rest ultimately on Aristotle:[27] "That motion is slower which, in the same time, acquires less space. And that is quicker which, in the same time, acquires more space." The description of falling bodies in respect to uniform acceleration is, of course, more complex. It should be said at the outset that Leonardo never succeeded in freeing his descriptions from essential confusions of the relationships of the variables involved. Most of his passages imply that the speed of fall is not only directly proportional to the time of fall, which is correct, but that it is also directly proportional to the distance of fall, which is not. In MS *M*, folio 45r, he declared that "the gravity [that is, heavy body] which descends freely, in every degree of time, acquires a degree of motion, and, in every degree of motion, a degree of speed." If, like Duhem, one interprets "degree of motion," that is, quantity of motion, to be equivalent not to distance but to the medieval impetus, then Leonardo's statement is entirely correct and implies only that speed of fall is proportional to time of fall. One might also interpret the passage in MS *M*, folio 44r, in the same way (see Figure 21):

> Prove the ratio of the time and the motion together with the speed produced in the descent of heavy bodies

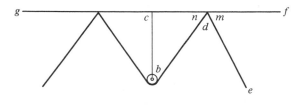

FIGURE 20

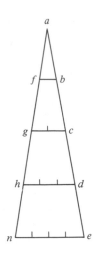

FIGURE 21

by means of the pyramidal figure, for the aforesaid powers ["potenzie"] are all pyramidal since they commence in nothing and go on increasing by degrees in arithmetic proportion. If you cut the pyramid in any degree of its height by a line parallel to the base, you will find that the space which extends from the section to the base has the same ratio as the breadth of the section has to the breadth of the whole base. You see that [just as] *ab* is 1/4 of *ae* so section *fb* is 1/4 of *ne*.

As in mathematical passages, Leonardo here used "pyramidal" where "triangular" is intended.[28] Thus he seems to require the representation of the whole motion by a triangle with point *a* the beginning of the motion and *ne* the final speed, with each of all the parallels representing the speed at some and every instant of time. In other passages Leonardo clearly coordinated instants in time with points and the whole time with a line (see *Codex Arundel*, fols. 176r-v). His triangular representation of quantity of motion is reminiscent of similar representations of uniformly difform motion (that is, uniform acceleration) in the medieval doctrine of configurations developed by Nicole Oresme and Giovanni Casali; Leonardo's use of an isosceles triangle seems to indicate that it was Casali's account rather than Oresme's that influenced him.[29] It should be emphasized, however, that in applying the triangle specifically to the motion of fall rather than to an abstract example of uniform acceleration, Leonardo was one step closer to the fruitful use to which Galileo and his successors put the triangle. Two similar passages illustrate this—the first (MS *M*, fol. 59v) again designates the triangle as a pyramidal figure, while in the second, in *Codex Madrid* I, folio 88v (Figure 22)[30] the triangle is divided into sixteen

equally spaced sections. Leonardo explained the units on the left of the latter figure by saying that "these unities are designated to demonstrate that the excesses of degrees are equal." Lower on the same page he noted that "the thing which descends acquires a degree of speed in every degree of motion and loses a degree of time." By "every degree of motion" he may have meant equal vertical spaces between the parallels into which the motion is divided. Hence, this phrase would be equivalent to saying "in every degree of time." The comment about the loss of time merely emphasizes the whole time spent during the completion of the motion.

All of the foregoing comments suggest a possible, even plausible, interpretation of Leonardo's concept of "degree of motion" in these passages. Still, one should examine other passages in which Leonardo seems also to hold that velocity is directly proportional to distance of fall. Consider, for example, MS *M*, folio 44v: "The heavy body ["gravità"] which descends, in every degree of time, acquires a degree of motion more than in the degree of time preceding, and similarly a degree of speed ["velocità"] more than

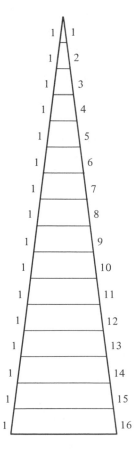

FIGURE 22

232

```
1  2  3  4  5  6  7  8  9  10
o  o  o  o  o  o  o  o  o  o
o  ·  ·  ·  ·  ·  ·  ·  ·  ·
   o  ·  ·  ·  ·  ·  ·  ·  ·
      o  ·  ·  ·  ·  ·  ·  ·
         o  ·  ·  ·  ·  ·  ·
            o  ·  ·  ·  ·  ·
               o  ·  ·  ·  ·
                  o  ·  ·  ·
                     o  ·  ·
                        o  ·
                           o
```

FIGURE 23

in the preceding degree of motion. Therefore, in each doubled quantity of time, the length of descent ["lunghezza del discenso"] is doubled and [also] the speed of motion." The figure accompanying this passage (Figure 23) has the following legend: "It is here shown that whatever the ratio that one quantity of time has to another, so one quantity of motion will have to the other and [similarly] one quantity of speed to the other." There seems little doubt from this passage that Leonardo believed that in equal periods of time, equal increments of space are being acquired. One last passage deserves mention because, although also ambiguous, it reveals that Leonardo believed that the same kinds of relationships hold for motion on an incline as in vertical fall (MS *M*, fol. 42v): "Although the motion be oblique, it observes, in its every degree, the increase of the motion and the speed in arithmetic proportion." The figure (Figure 24) indicates that the motion on the incline is represented by the triangular section *ebc*, while the vertical fall is represented by *abc*. Hence, with this figure Leonardo clearly intended that the velocities at the end of both vertical and oblique descents are equal (that is, both are represented by *bc*) and also that the velocities midway in these descents are equal (that is, *mn = op*). The figure also shows that the times involved in acquiring the velocities differ, since the altitude of △*ebc* is obviously greater than the altitude of △ *abc*.

So much, then, for the most important aspects of Leonardo's theoretical mechanics. His considerable dependence on earlier currents has been noted, as has his quite significant original extension and development of those currents. It cannot be denied, however, that his notebooks, virtually closed as they were to his successors, exerted little or no influence on the development of mechanics.

NOTES

1. The many passages from Leonardo's notebooks quoted here can be found in the standard eds. of the various MSS. Most of them have also been collected in Uccelli's ed. of *I libri di meccanica*. The English trans. (with only two exceptions) are my own.
2. The full corpus has been published in E. A. Moody and M. Clagett, *The Medieval Science of Weights* (Madison, Wis., 1952; repr., 1960). Variant versions of the texts have been studied and partially published in J. E. Brown, "The 'Scientia de ponderibus' in the Later Middle Ages" (dissertation, Univ. of Wis., 1967).
3. Moody and Clagett, *op. cit.*, pp. 128–131. Incidentally, the definition that precedes the proof is the sure sign that Leonardo translated the postulates and first two enunciations from the *Elementa* rather than from version P (where the enunciations are the same), since the definition was not included in Version P.
4. *Ibid.*, pp. 174–207.
5. *Ibid.*, pp. 130–131.
6. *Ibid.*, pp. 188–191. Leonardo's translation of these same propositions in *Codex Atlanticus*, fols. 154v-a–r-a, is very literal: "La equalità della declinazione conserva la equalità del peso. Se per due vie di diverse obliquità due pesi discendano, e sieno medesimo proporzione, se della d[ecli-nazione] de' pesi col medesimo ordine presa sarà ancora una medesima virtù dell'una e d[ell'altra in discendendo]." The bracketed material has been added from the Latin text.
7. Marcolongo, *Studi vinciani*, p. 173.
8. Duhem, *Les origines de la statique*, I, 189–190.
9. Moody and Clagett, *op. cit.*, pp. 184–187. Leonardo's more literal translation of Rl.08 in *Codex Atlanticus*, fol. 154v-a, runs: "Se le braccia della libra sono inequali e nel centro del moto faranno un angolo, s'e' termini loro s'accosteranno parte equalmente alla direzione, e' pesi equali in questa disposizione equalmente peseranno."
10. Marcolongo, *op. cit.*, p. 149, discusses one such passage (*Codex Arundel*, fol. 67v); see also pp. 147–148, discussing the figures on MS *Ashburnham* 2038, fol. 3r; and *Codex Arundel*, fol. 32v (in the passage earlier than the one noted above in the text).
11. Moody and Clagett, *op. cit.*, pp. 208–211.
12. *Ibid.*, pp. 210–211.
13. *Ibid.*, pp. 64–65, 102–109, 192–193.
14. Clagett, "Leonardo da Vinci . . .," pp. 119–140.
15. *Ibid.*, pp. 121–126.
16. *Ibid.*, p. 126.
17. Archimedes, *Monumenta omnia mathematica, quae extant . . . ex traditione Francisci Maurolici* (Palermo, 1685), *De*

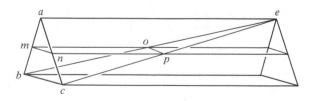

FIGURE 24

momentis aequalibus, bk. IV, prop. 16, pp. 169–170. Maurolico completed the *De momentis aequalibus* in 1548.

18. Marcolongo, *op. cit.,* pp. 203–216.
19. See Clagett, "Leonardo da Vinci . . .," pp. 140–141. That
account is here revised, taking into account the probability
that the fragments were not copied by Leonardo.
20. *Ibid.,* p. 140, n. 65, notes the opinion of Favaro and Schmidt
that the fragments are truly in Leonardo's hand. But Carlo
Pedretti, whose knowledge of Leonardo's hand is sure and
experienced, is convinced they are not. Arredi, *Le origini
dell'idrostatica,* pp. 11–12, had already recognized that the
notes were not in Leonardo's hand.
21. M. Clagett, *The Science of Mechanics in the Middle Ages*
(Madison, Wis., 1959; repr., 1961), pp. 124–125.
22. Here Arredi's account is followed closely.
23. Clagett, *The Science of Mechanics,* p. 187.
24. *Ibid.,* chs. 8–9.
25. *Ibid.,* pp. 601–603.
26. Hart, *The Mechanical Investigations,* pp. 93–94.
27. Clagett, *The Science of Mechanics,* pp. 176–179.
28. Clagett, "Leonardo da Vinci . . .," p. 106, quoting MS *K,*
fol. 79v.
29. M. Clagett, *Nicole Oresme and the Medieval Geometry of
Qualities* (Madison, Wis., 1968), pp. 66–70.
30. I must thank L. Reti, editor of the forthcoming ed. of the
Madrid codices, for providing me with this passage.

MARSHALL CLAGETT

MATHEMATICS

Leonardo's admiration for mathematics was uncon-
ditional, and found expression in his writings in such
statements as "No certainty exists where none of the
mathematical sciences can be applied" (MS *G,* fol.
96v). It is therefore useful to consider the development
of his mathematical thought, drawing upon the whole
of his manuscripts in order to reconstruct its principal
stages; such a study will also serve to illustrate the
sources for much of his work.

Leonardo particularly valued the rigorous logic
implicit in mathematics, whereby the mathematician
could hope to attain truth with the same certitude as
might a physicist dealing with experimental data.
(Students of the moral and metaphysical sciences, on
the other hand, had no such expectation, since they
were forced to proceed from unascertainable and
infinitely arguable hypotheses.) His predilection did
not, however, presuppose a broad mathematical
culture or any real talent for calculation. Certainly,
his education was that of an artisan rather than a
mathematician, consisting of reading, writing, and
the practical basics of calculus and geometry, together
with the considerable body of practical rules that
had been accumulated by generations of craftsmen
and artists.

The effects of his early education may be seen in
Leonardo's literary style (he preferred aphorisms and
definitions to any prolonged organic development of
ideas) and in his mathematics, which contains grave
oversights not entirely due to haste. An example of
the latter is his embarrassment when confronted with
square and cube roots. In *Codex Arundel* (fol. 200r)
he proposed, as an original discovery, a simple
method for finding all roots "both irrational and
rational," whereby the "root" is defined as a fraction
of which the numerator alone is multiplied by itself
one or two times to find the square or cubic figure.
Thus the square root of 2 is obtained by multiplying
2/2 by 2/2 to find 4/2, or simply 2; while the cube root
of 3 is reached by taking $3/9 \times 3/9 \times 3/9 = 27/9$, or 3.
He applied this erroneous method several times in his
later work; however absurd they might be, Leonardo
seems to have been prouder of his discoveries in
mathematics than in any other field.

When he was in his late thirties, Leonardo began to
try to fill the gaps in his education and took up the
serious study of Latin and geometry, among other
subjects. At the same time he began to write one or
more treatises. He wished to write for scientists,
although scholars of the period were not prepared to
admit the knowledge possessed by an artist as science.
(An illustration of this occurs in Alberti's definition
of the "principles" of geometry, in which he stated
that he could not use truly scientific terms because he
was addressing himself to painters.) It was only after
Leonardo entered the Sforza service in Milan and
became associated with philosophers and men of
letters on a basis of mutual esteem that he took up his
theory of the supremacy of painting. This theory was
in part incorporated into the *Treatise on Painting*
compiled by Leonardo's disciple Francesco Melzi,
who, however, omitted Leonardo's definitions of the
geometric "principles" of point, line, and area—
definitions that Leonardo had drawn up with great
care, since he wished them to be read by mathematicians rather than artists.

As a painter, Leonardo was, of course, concerned
with proportion and also with "vividness of the
actions" (this is how he translated Ficino's definition
of beauty as "actus vivacitas"). In his pursuit of the
latter, Leonardo inclined toward physics, seeking
motions that could be studied experimentally.
Perspective, too, had an important place in the
treatise on painting, but Leonardo was more concerned
with aerial perspective (chiaroscuro) than with linear.
MS *C* (1490) is rich in geometrical drawings, although
limited to the depiction of the projection of rays of
light; it contains no organic system of theorems.

Aside from those in MS *C,* the pages dedicated to
geometry in other early manuscripts are few; there are
nine in MS *B* (*ca.* 1489) and nineteen in MS *A* (1492).
The prevalent matter in all of these is the division of
the circumference of the circle into equal parts, a
prerequisite for the construction of polygons and for

various other well-known procedures. The notes set down are not connected with each other and represent elementary precepts that were common knowledge to all "engineers." Because of these limitations, it is impossible to accept Caversazzi's thesis concerning MS *B*, folios 27v and 40r, wherein Leonardo explained how to divide a circumference into equal parts by merely "opening the compass"; Caversazzi sees this as an "exquisite geometric discovery," one that may be applied to solve Euclidean problems of the first and second degree. But since at this time Leonardo had not yet begun to study Euclid, it is probable that he was referring to precepts known to all draftsmen.

Seven pages are devoted to geometry in *Codex Forster* III (1493–1495) and, again, these contain only elementary formulas, expressed in language more imaginative than scientific (the volume of a sphere, for example, is described as "the air enclosed within a spherical body"). Only in *Codex Forster* II$_1$, written between 1495 and 1497, are there the first signs of a concentrated interest in geometrical problems, particularly those that were deeply to concern Leonardo in later years—lunes and the equivalence of rectilinear and curvilinear surfaces. An additional seventeen pages of this manuscript are devoted to the theory of proportion.

The two manuscripts that mark the close of Leonardo's first sojourn in Milan MS *M* and MS *I*—are of far greater importance. The first thirty-six pages of MS *M* contain translations of Euclid ("Petitioni" and "Conceptioni") as well as derivations of propositions 1–42 (with a few omissions) of book I of the *Elements*, together with a group of propositions from the tenth book. Propositions 43–46 of book I appear in the first sixteen folios of MS *I* (which must for that reason be considered as being of a later date than MS *M*), as do propositions 1–4 and 6–10 of book II, selections from book III, and occasional references to book X. These evidences of Leonardo's systematic study of Euclid may be related to his friendship and collaboration with Luca Pacioli.

Leonardo must have read the *Elements* and acquired some deeper knowledge of geometry before undertaking the splendid drawings of solid bodies with which he illustrated the first book of Pacioli's *Divina proportione*. His interest in this work is probably reflected in the pages of *Codex Forster* II$_1$ on proportion; it would also explain his study of the tenth book of the *Elements*, the book least read because of its difficulty and its practical limitation to the construction of regular polygons. Pacioli was thus responsible for arousing Leonardo's enthusiasm for geometry and for introducing him to Euclid's work; indeed, he may

have helped him read Euclid, since the text would have been extremely difficult for a man as relatively unlettered as Leonardo. (It is interesting to note that MS *I* also contains some first principles of Latin, copied from Perotti's grammar.) Pacioli's influence on Leonardo was probably also indirect, through his *Summa arithmetica* and perhaps through his translation of the *Elements*.

That Leonardo had at hand the Latin text of the *Elements* of 1482 or 1491 can be seen through the identity of some of his drawings with those texts as well as by certain verbal correspondences. At the same time, his method was not to transcribe sentences from the text he was studying but to attempt to present geometrical ideas graphically. Each page of his geometrical notes represents an aid to memorizing Euclid's text, rather than a compendium; hence it is not always easy to trace the specific passages studied. For example, Leonardo would often begin with a sketch, a number, or occasionally a word which he must have used initially to impress upon his mind some of the intricacies of Euclid's theses and later to recall the whole content. In MS *M*, folio 29v, three figures appear: a point and a line; the same point and line with an additional transversal line; and two parallel lines joined by the transversal, the original point having disappeared. The correspondence with the Euclidean thesis, together with the coincidence of similar notes on the preceding and following pages to propositions 27, 28, 29, 30, and 32, respectively, prove this to be Euclid's book I, proposition 31.

Notes on Euclid's first books also appear in certain folios of the *Codex Atlanticus*, where they are set out in better order and in a more complete form. On folio 169r-b, for instance, the "Petitioni" and "Conceptioni" are presented symbolically, while on folio 177v-a proposition 1.7 is transformed into a series of thirteen drawings.

Leonardo continued to work with Pacioli after they both left Milan in 1499. In the *Codex Atlanticus* he stated that he would learn "the multiplication of roots" from his friend "master Luca" (fol. 120r-d), and he had in fact transcribed all the rules for operations with fractions from the *Summa arithmetica* (fol. 69, a–b). Pietro da Novellara recorded in 1503 that Leonardo was neglecting painting in favor of geometry; this activity is reflected in MS *K*, *Codex Madrid*, II, and *Codex Forster* I$_1$, as well as in many folios of the *Codex Atlanticus*.

Two-thirds of MS *K*$_1$ (1504) are devoted to Euclid. From folio 15v to folio 48v Leonardo copied, in reverse order, almost all the marginal figures of books V and VI of the *Elements*. He transcribed none of the text, although the drawings are accompanied by unmistakable signs of his contemplation of the theory of proportion. MS K_2 contains notes similar to those in MS M and MS I; here they refer to the whole of the second book of the *Elements*, to a few propositions of books I, II, and III, and to nine of the first sixteen definitions of book V.

Leonardo's interest in the theory of proportion is further evident in *Codex Madrid*, II, folios 46v–50, in which he summarizes and describes the treatise "De proportionibus et proportionalitatibus" that is part of Pacioli's *Summa arithmetica*. A drawing on folio 78 of the same manuscript, graphically illustrating all the various kinds of proportions and proportionalities, is also taken from Pacioli's book, while Euclid reappears in the last five pages of the manuscript proper. In the latter portion Leonardo transcribed, in an elegant handwriting, the first pages of an Italian version of the *Elements*, the author of which is not known (the list of Leonardo's books cites only "Euclid, in Italian, that is, the first three books"). Folio 85r contains the ingenious illustration of Euclid's so-called algorithm (VII.2, X.2–3) that is repeated in more detail in *Codex Atlanticus*, folio 207r-b.

It is thus clear from manuscript sources that from the time that Leonardo began to collaborate with Pacioli on the *Divina proportione*, he concentrated on books I and II of Euclid—an indispensable base—and on books V and VI, the theory of proportion that had also been treated by Pacioli in the *Summa arithmetica*. The few references to book X deal with the ratios of incommensurate quantities; therefore there can be no doubt that the subject of proportions and proportionalities remained a constant center of Leonardo's interest.

There is no evidence of a similar study of the last books of Euclid, but it must not be forgotten that about two-thirds of Leonardo's writings have been lost. There is, moreover, no lack of practical applications of the propositions of the last books in Leonardo's writings. But *Codex Madrid,* II, is of particular importance because it demonstrates that Leonardo, after conducting a modest study of Euclid from approximately 1496 to 1504, began to conduct ambitious personal research. Having copied out the first pages of the *Elements* as, perhaps, a model, Leonardo wrote on folios 111r and 112r two titles indicative of the plan of his work, "The Science of Equiparation" and "On the Equality of Unequal Areas." For this new science he wrote on folio 107v a group of "Petitioni" and "Conceptioni" based upon Euclid's. Here Leonardo's chief concern lay in the squaring of curvilinear surfaces, which he generally divided into "falcates" (triangles with one, two, or three curved sides) and "portions" (circular segments formed by an arc and a chord, which could also be the side of a polygon inscribed in a circle). He carried out the transformation of these figures into their rectilinear equivalents by various means, some of which (such as superimposition and motion, or rotation) were mechanical.

The use of mechanical solutions, rarely accepted by Euclid, may perhaps be attributable to Leonardo's engineering background; he would almost seem to have recognized the unorthodoxy of his procedures in applying to himself Giordano's words: "This method is not simply geometrical but is subordinated to, and participates in, both philosophy and geometry, because the proof is obtained by means of motion, although in the end all mathematical sciences are philosophical speculations" (*Codex Madrid*, II, fol. 107r). Leonardo noted, however, that the squaring of curvilinear surfaces could be accomplished by more orthodox geometrical methods, provided the curved sides of the figure form parts of circles proportional among themselves (*Codex Atlanticus*, fol. 139v-a).

It is a short step from squaring falcates to squaring the circle, and Leonardo proposed several solutions to the latter problem. Again, some of them were mechanical and were suggested to him by studying Vitruvius. These consist in, for example, measuring the rectilinear track left by a wheel of which the width is one-quarter of the wheel's diameter (MS G, fol. 61r; also MS E, fol. 25v, where the width of the wheel that makes "a complete revolution" is mistakenly given as being equal to the radius). The circumference is obtained by winding a thread around the wheel, then withdrawing and measuring it (MS K, fol. 80r).

Leonardo was also well acquainted with the method for the "quadratura circuli per lunulas," which he knew from the *De expetendis et fugiendis rebus* of Giorgio Valla. A drawing corresponding to this method appears in MS K, folio 61r. (The identity of "Zenophont" or "Zenophonte," a mathematician criticized by Leonardo on the previous page of the same manuscript, is probably resolvable as Antiphon,

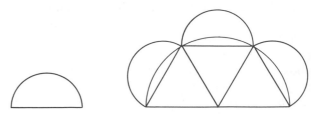

FIGURE 1. The quadratura circuli per lunulas.

whose method of quadrature was also criticized by Valla.)

Leonardo of course knew Archimedes' solution to squaring the circle; Clagett has pointed out that he both praised and criticized it without ever having understood it completely. He accepted Archimedes' first proposition, which establishes the equivalence of a circle and a rectangular triangle of which the shorter sides are equal to the radius and the circumference of the circle, respectively; he remained unsatisfied with the third proposition, which fixes the approximate ratio between the circumference (taken as an element separating two contiguous classes of polygons) and the diameter as 22:7. Leonardo tried to take this approximation beyond the ninety-six-sided polygon; it is in this attempt at extension ad infinitum that the value of his effort lies.

Valla provided Leonardo with a starting point when, in describing the procedure of squaring "by lunes," he recommended "trapezium dissolvatur in triangula." Leonardo copied Valla's drawing, dividing the trapezium inscribed in a semicircle into three triangles; he extended the concept in MS K, folio 80r, in which he split the circle into sixteen triangles, rectified the circumference, then fitted the triangles together like gear teeth, eight into eight, to attain a rectangle equivalent to the circle. He took a further step in *Codex Madrid*, II, folio 105v, when departing from Euclid II.2 (circles are to each other as the squares of their diameters), he took two circles, having diameters of 1 and 14, respectively, and divided the larger into 196 sectors, each equivalent to the whole of the smaller circle.

In *Codex Atlanticus*, folio 118v-a, Leonardo dealt with circles of the ratio 1:1,000 and found that when the larger was split into 1,000 sectors, the "portion" (the difference between the sector and the triangle) was an "imperceptible quantity similar to the mathematical point." By logical extension, if each sector were "a millionth of its circle, it would be a straight portion" or "almost plane, and thus we would have carried out a squaring nearer the truth than Archimedes'" (*Codex Madrid*, II, fol. 105v). In *Codex Arundel*, folio 137v, Leonardo squared the two diameters, writing "one by one is one" and "one million by one million is one million"; his disappointment in seeing that the squares did not increase suggested the variant "four million by four million is sixteen million" (that he corrected his error in *Codex Atlanticus*, fol. 118r-a, writing "a million millions," reveals a poor grasp of calculation).

Leonardo was clearly proud of his discovery of the quadrature, and in *Codex Madrid*, II, folio 112r he recorded the exact moment that it came to him—on the night of St. Andrew's day (30 November), 1504, as hour, light, and page drew to a close. In actual fact, however, Leonardo's discovery amounted only to affirming the equivalence of a given circle to an infinitesimal part of another without calculating any measure; to have made the necessary calculations, he would have had to use Archimedes' formula 22:7, which he rejected. Leonardo characterized Archimedes' method of squaring as "ben detta e male data" (*Codex Atlanticus*, fol. 85r-a), that is, "well said and badly given." It would seem necessary to describe his own solution simply as "detta," not "data."

The presumed discovery on St. Andrew's night did, however, encourage Leonardo to pursue his geometrical studies in the hope of making other new breakthroughs. MS K_3, MS F, and a large number of pages in the *Codex Atlanticus* demonstrate his continuous and intense work in transforming sectors, "falcates," and "portions" into rectilinear figures. Taking as given that curved lines must have equal or proportional radii, Leonardo practiced constructing a series of squares doubled in succession, in which he inscribed circles proportioned in the same way; to obtain quadruple circles, he doubled the radii. To obtain submultiple circles, he divided a square constructed on the diameter of the circle into the required number of rectangles, transforming one into a square and inscribing the submultiple circle therein. In order to double the circle, however, instead of using the diagonal of the square constructed on the diameter, he turned to arithmetic calculus to increase proportionally the measure of the radius, adopting a ratio of 1:3/2, which is somewhat greater than the true one of $1:\sqrt{2}$. To obtain a series of circles doubling one another, he divided the greatest radius into equal parts, forgetting that arithmetic progression is not the same as geometric (*Codex Madrid*, II, fols. 117v, 132).

Alternating with the many pages in the *Codex Atlanticus* devoted to the solution of specific problems are others giving the fundamental rules of Leonardo's new science of comparison. Within the same sphere falls a group of pages in *Codex Madrid*, II, which are concerned with transforming rectilinear figures into other equivalent figures or solids into other solids. These sections of the two collections, presumably together with pages that are now lost, are preparatory to the short treatise on stereometry contained in *Codex Forster* I_1 (1505) and entitled "Book on Transformation, That Is, of One Body Into Another Without Decrease or Increase of Substance." In his study of this treatise, Marcolongo judges it to be suitable "for draftsmen more skilled in handling rule, square, and compass than in making numerical calculations"—Leonardo's viewpoint was often that of the engineer.

One of the problems to which Leonardo chose to apply his new science was that of how to transform a parallelepiped into a cube, or how to double the volume of a cube and then insert two proportional means between two segments. In the *Summa arithmetica*, Pacioli had solved the problem and had described how to find the cube root of 8 by geometrical methods, although he provided no geometrical demonstrations. Leonardo, in *Codex Atlanticus*, folio 58r, stated that if the edge of a cube is 4, the edge of the same cube doubled will be 5 plus a fraction that is "inexpressible and easier to make than to express." By 1504 Leonardo also possessed Valla's book, which gave the solution of the problem, with numerous demonstrations from the ancients. Leonardo copied various figures from Valla (in *Codex Arundel*, fols. 78r–79v, where the last one is, however, Pacioli's) and transcribed a vernacular translation of the part of Valla's book referring to the demonstrations of Philoponus and Parmenius. (That, having the Latin text at hand, Leonardo felt the need to translate or to have translated the two pages that interested him confirms his difficulty in reading Latin directly— Clagett and Marcolongo have both pointed out many mistakes in the translation of this passage which, if uncorrected, distort the text.)

Leonardo repeatedly expressed his dissatisfaction with the solution reported by Valla. He particularly objected to having to make the rule swing until the compass has fixed two points of intersection; this "negotiation," he stated (*Codex Atlanticus*, fol. 218v-b), seemed to him "dubious and mechanical." Since Valla attributed this procedure to Plato, Leonardo further stated, in MS *F* (1508), folio 59r, that "the proof given by Plato to the inhabitants of Delo is not geometrical." He continued to look for other, more truly "geometrical," means to double the cube or find the cube root.

In folios 50v–59v of MS *F* and in the similar folios 159r-a and b of the *Codex Atlanticus*, Leonardo tried, in opposition to the "ancient system," to resolve the problem by decomposing and rebuilding a cube; he further attempted to apply Pythagoras' theorem by substituting three cubes for three squares constructed on the sides of a right triangle. Since every square is equal to half the square constructed on its diagonal, he attempted to halve each cube with a diagonal cut, on the assumption that the face of a doubled cube could be obtained through manipulating the rectangular face formed by the cut. He arranged nine cubes in the form of a parallelepiped upon which he analyzed the diagonals that he supposed to represent the square

and cube roots, respectively (*Codex Atlanticus*, fols. 159r-b, 303r-b; *Windsor Collection*, fol. 19128). He forgot, however, that the progression of squares and cubes does not correspond to the natural series of numbers. Although he studied the proportions between the areas that "cover" a cube and those of the same cube doubled, he realized that he could not apply "the science of cubes based on surfaces, but based on bodies [volumes]" (*Codex Arundel*, fol. 203r). He was thus aware that his formulation of the problem was inaccurate.

Leonardo finally arrived at a solution. He recorded in *Codex Atlanticus*, folios 218v-b, 231r-b, that in order to "avoid the difficulty of the mechanical system" taught by Plato and other ancients, he had

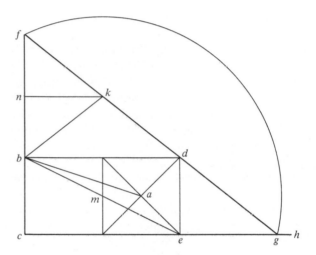

FIGURE 2. $bc : eg = eg : bf = bf : bd$
$eg = fk = kd = kb$
$ab = bf$ (*Codex Atlanticus*, 218v-b).

eliminated the compass and the imprecise movement of the rule in favor of placing two sides of the rectangle in the ratio $b = 2a$ (thereby unknowingly reestablishing the ratio used in the Greek text). Step by step, then, his procedure was to join two faces of a cube to make a rectangle, connect the upper-left angle to the center of the right square, then carry the line obtained to the upper extension of side a; from the extreme point thus reached, he drew a line that, touching the upper-right angle of the rectangle, cut the extension of its base. On this line Leonardo was able to determine the measure of the edge of the doubled cube, a measure that is to be found four times in the figure thus constructed. His results are reasonably accurate; with $a = 2$, Leonardo obtained a cube root for 16 as little as 0.02967 in excess of its true value.

Leonardo was unable to demonstrate the truth of his "new invention" save through criticism of the "mechanical test" of the compass, which after "laborious effort" helped the ancients to discover the proportional means—whereas now, Leonardo claimed, "without effort I use it to confirm that my experiment was confirmed by the ancients"—which, he added, "could not be done before our time." What Leonardo had discovered was that the third proportional number, used to determine the second, coincides with a line that can be more accurately constructed inside the rectangle; he thereby simplified the classical procedure without in any way discussing its scientific demonstrations, which he took for granted. He must, however, have checked his results experimentally and judged them with his unerring eye.

Other pages of the *Codex Atlanticus* contain summaries of problems to be solved, as, for example, folio 139r-a, which is entitled "Curvilinear Geometrical Elements." This, together with other titles—"On Transformation," folio 128r-a; "Book on Equation," folio 128r-a; and "Geometrical Play" ("De ludo geometrico"), folios 45v-a, 174v-b, 184v-c, and 259v-a —including the previously mentioned "Science of Equiparation"—might suggest that Leonardo had actually written systematic books and treatises that are now lost. But it is known that he cherished projects that he did not complete; and it is unlikely that he composed treatises using methods and forms different from those set out in, for example, *Codex Forster* I_2. The titles of treatises projected but unwritten do provide some record of the stages of his mathematical work, in addition to which Leonardo has recorded some specific dates for his successes.

Leonardo's discovery on St. Andrew's night has already been mentioned; in the same manuscript, *Codex Madrid*, II, on folio 118r, he further mentioned that a certain invention had been given to him "as a gift on Christmas morning 1504." In *Windsor Collection*, folio 19145, he claimed to have discovered, after prolonged research, a way of squaring the angle of two curved sides on Sunday, 30 April 1509. (Folio 128r-a of the *Codex Atlanticus*, the beginning of the "Book of Equation," is concerned with the squaring of a "portion" of a single curved side and promises a second book devoted to the new procedure.)

Although the last discovery is exactly dated, Leonardo's explanation of it is not very clear. (This is often the case in Leonardo's work, since the manuscripts are marked by incomplete and fragmentary discussions, geometrical figures unaccompanied by any explanation of the construction, and the bare statements of something proved elsewhere.) His accomplishment is, however, apparent—he had learned how to vary a "portion" in infinite figures,

decomposing and rebuilding it in many different ways. The examples drawn on the *Windsor Collection* page cited reappear, with variations, in hundreds of illustrations scattered or collected in the *Codex Atlanticus*. The reader can only be dismayed by their complexity and monotony.

The mathematical pages of the *Codex Atlanticus* (to which all folio numbers hereafter cited refer) provide an interesting insight into the late developments of Leonardo's method. On folio 139r-a, among other places, he confirmed his proposal to vary "to infinity" one or more surfaces while maintaining the same quantity. It is clear that he received from the elaboration of his geometric equations the same pleasure that a mathematician derives from the development of algebraic ones. If, at the beginning of his research on the measure of curvilinear surfaces, his interest would seem to have been that of an engineer, his later work would seem to be marked by a disinterested passion for his subject. Indeed, the title of the last book that he planned— "Geometrical Play," or "De ludo geometrico"—which he began on folio 45v-a and worked on up to the last years of his life, indicates this.

For example, one of Leonardo's basic exercises consists of inscribing a square within a circle, then joining the resultant four "portions" in twos to get

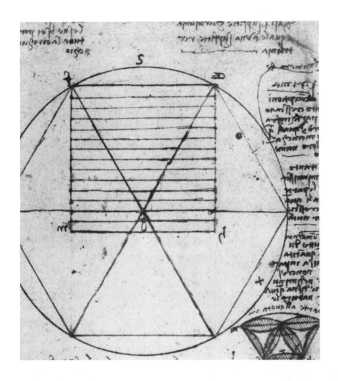

FIGURE 3. The square of proportionality (*Codex Atlanticus*, 111v-b).

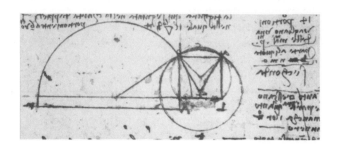

FIGURE 4. (*Codex Atlanticus*, 111v-b).

"bisangoli." The "bisangles" can then be broken up, subdivided, and distributed within the circumference to create full and empty spaces which are to each other as the inscribed square is to the four "portions" of the circumscribed circle. An important development of this is Leonardo's substitution of a hexagon for the square, the hexagon being described as the most perfect division of the circle (fols. 111v-a and b [Figs. 3, 4]). This leaves six "portions" for subsequent operations, and Leonardo recommended their subdivision in multiples of six. (On the splendid folio 110v-a [Fig. 5], he listed and calculated the first fifty multiples of six, but through a curious oversight the product of 34×6 is given as 104, rather than 204; and all the following calculations are thus incorrect.)

To obtain the exact dimensions of submultiple "portions," Leonardo devised the "square of proportionality" (fol. 107v-a), which he constructed on the side of the hexagon inscribed within the circle and then subdivided into the required number of equal rectangles. He next transformed one such rectangle into the equivalent square, the side of which is the radius of the submultiplied circle, the side of the corresponding inscribed hexagon, and the origin or chord of the minor "portions." These were then joined in pairs ("bisangoli"), combined into rosettes or stars, and distributed inside the circumference of the circle in a fretwork of full and empty spaces, of which the area of all full spaces is always equal to that of the six greater "portions" and the area of all the empty spaces to the area of the inscribed hexagon. The result is of undoubted aesthetic value and may be taken as the culmination of the geometrical adventure that began for Leonardo with Pacioli's *Divina proportione*.

Although Leonardo remained faithful throughout his life to the idea of proportion as the fundamental structure of reality, the insufficient and inconstant rigor of his scientific thesis precludes his being considered a mathematician in the true sense of the word. His work had no influence on the history of math-

ematics; it was organic to his reflections as an artist and "philosopher" (as he wished to call himself and as he was ultimately called by the king of France). In his geometrical research he drew upon Archimedes and the ancients' doctrine of lunes to develop the most neglected parts of Euclid's work—curvilinear angles, the squaring of curvilinear areas, and the infinite variation of forms of unaltered quantity. Thus, in Leonardo's philosophy, does nature build and infinitely vary her forms, from the simplest to the most complex; and even the most complex have a rational structure that defines their beauty. It was Leonardo's profound intuition that "Necessity . . . bridle and eternal rule of Nature" must have a mathematical foundation and that the infinite forms found in nature must therefore be the infinite variations of a fundamental "equation."

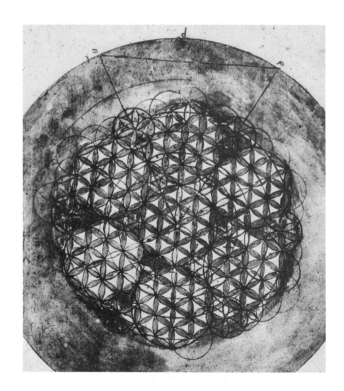

FIGURE 5. (*Codex Atlanticus*, 110v-a).

Leonardo thus expressed a Pythagorean or Platonic conception of reality, common to many artists of the Renaissance. It was at the same time a revolutionary view, inasmuch as it identified form as function and further integrated into the concept of function the medieval notion of substance. Leonardo did not formulate his conception of reality in the abstract terms of universal scientific law. Rather, as the purpose of his painting was always to render the most subtle designs of natural structures, his last geometric constructions were aimed at discovering the mathematical structure of nature.

AUGUSTO MARINONI

GEOLOGY

In the later years of his life Leonardo da Vinci described the configuration of the earth's crust as the result of actual processes, principally fluvial, operating over immense periods of time—a system of geology which Duhem described as "perhaps his most complete and lasting invention" (Duhem, II, p. 342).

For Leonardo, the study of the great world was related to the study of man. "Man is the model of the world" (*Codex Arundel*, fol. 156v; De Lorenzo, p. 8), he wrote, ". . . called by the ancients a microcosm . . ., composed like the earth itself, of earth, water, air and fire; as man contains within himself bones, the supports and armature of the flesh, the world has rocks, the supports of the earth: as man has in him the lake of blood which the lungs swell and decrease in breathing, the body of the earth has its oceanic sea which also swells and diminishes every six hours in nourishing the world" (MS *A*, fol. 55v).

Leonardo's geologic perceptions date back to his earliest apprenticeship in Florence. Horizontally stratified rocks in the foreground and pyramidal peaks above a background sea in the *Baptism of Christ* (Uffizi, Florence), which he worked on with his master Verrocchio in 1472, reflect the influence of Van Eyck on Florentine landscape conventions (Castelfranco, p. 472).

Leonardo's earliest dated work (1473), probably drawn in the field, is a sketch of the valley of the Arno (Uffizi). It displays similar characteristics— horizontal strata with waterfalls in the right foreground, and eroded hills above a broad alluvial valley behind.

In subsequent drawings and paintings, rocks may be thrown into cataclysmic contortions but at the same time are folded and fractured realistically. (Leonardo's infrequent mentions of earthquakes [*Codex Leicester*, fol. 10v], volcanoes [*Codex Arundel*, fol. 155r; and Richter, 1939], and internal heat betray a lack of firsthand familiarity with Italy from Naples south. His idea of catastrophe was of storm, avalanche, and flood, and his apocalyptic essays do not alter the essential actualism of his system. He pointedly neglects the plutonist orogenic ideas of Albertus Magnus for the gradualist-neptunism of Albert of Saxony [Duhem, II, p. 334].) The cliffs rising from a harbor in the background to the

Annunciation (Uffizi) are not unlike views from above Lake Como or Lake Maggiore in the gathering mists. But the ultimate expression of Leonardo's visual apprehension of topography and the true measure of the extent of his journey from the first sketch of 1473 is in the Windsor drawings of the Alps above the plains of the Po (*Windsor Collection*, folios 12410, 12414). They were done in the final years of his life in Italy at about the same time that he formulated his geologic system (Calvi, p. xiii, places the composition of the geologic notes in Tuscany before his Alpine studies). In these notes Leonardo boldly rejected Judeo-Christian cosmology for the secular naturalism of the classical tradition as demonstrated by natural processes and by the actual configuration of the material world. Leonardo estimated that 200,000 years were required for the Po to lay down its plain ([Muentz, p. 34]; he had clearly abandoned the Judeo-Christian time scale for one that was two to three orders of magnitude greater [cf. Duhem, II, p. 335; and Richter, p. 915]).

In Leonardo's system, the highest peaks of the Alps and the Apennines were former islands in an ancient sea. Mountains are continually eroded by winds and rains. Every valley is carved by its river, which is proven by the concordance of the stratigraphic column across the valley walls (*Codex Leicester*, fol. 10r) and the proportionality of river size to valley breadth (*Codex Atlanticus*, fol. 321b). The foothills and plains made by alluvial deposition continually extend the area of land at the expense of the sea. Mountains made lighter by erosion rise slowly to maintain the earth's center of gravity at the center of the universe, bringing up petrified marine strata with their accompanying fauna and flora to be eroded into mountains in their turn.

Such great lakes as the Black Sea are impounded by the collapse of mountains and then, as streams breach the barriers, they drain down one into the other. In this way the Arno was seen to be cutting through its own flood plain, the Po to have filled in the great north Italian triangle from the Alps and Apennines to Venice, and the Nile from Memphis to Alexandria. The Mediterranean itself, the "greatest of rivers," is being filled by the expanding deltas of its tributaries. When the future extension of the Nile erodes through the barrier of the Pillars of Hercules, it will drain what remains of the Mediterranean. Its bottom, relieved of the weight of the superincumbent sea, will rise isostatically (not to be confused with the modern concept of isostasy) to become the summits of mountains.

Just as Leonardo turned to dissection to study anatomy, so he dissected the earth—first in Milan during the years that he spent with Ludovico Sforza (il Moro); later as architect and engineer-general to Cesare Borgia and in land reclamation in Tuscany and for Leo X—for a period of 33 years from 1482 until 1515. Excavations for canals, moats, and roadways in Lombardy, Tuscany, Emilia, and the Romagna were carried out under his direct supervision during most of his career. He constructed plans and relief maps requiring exact measurements as well as lithologic and structural insight. His designs for surveying and drafting instruments; his numerous sketches, notes, and calculations of costs, manpower, and time; and his meticulous plans of machines for excavation and hydraulic controls all attest to the extent of his occupation with practical geology. The maps themselves—"bird's-eye" topographic constructions, relief maps, and outline plans of drainage and culture—are the geological analogues of his anatomical drawings, transcending sixteenth-century technics and science.

Leonardo was familiar with classical geological traditions through the works of Albertus Magnus and Cecco d'Ascoli, Vincent of Beauvais, Ramon Lull, Isidore of Seville, Jan de Mandeville, and, above all, Albert of Saxony. Yet his demonstrations of the organic origins of fossils *in situ*, the impossibility of the biblical deluge, and the natural processes of petrifaction are based on meticulous observations— for example, of growth lines on shells (*Codex Leicester*, fol. 10a; Richter, p. 990).

"When I was casting the great horse at Milan. . . .," he wrote, "some countrymen brought to my workshop a great sack of cockles and corals that were found in the mountains of Parma and Piacenza" (*Codex Leicester*, fol. 9v). Was it his experience with the process of casting that led him ultimately to discuss the origins of the fossils and their casts; of worm tracks; *glossopetrae*; fragmented and complete shells; paired and single shells; leaves; tufa; and conglomerates? Did this casting experience lead to a discussion of the relationship of velocity of flow to the sedimentary gradation from the mountains to the sea, of coarse gravels and breccias to the finest white potter's clay?

Leonardo also observed and discussed turbidity currents (*Codex Leicester*, fol. 20r); initial horizontality (MS *F*, fol. 11v); the relationship of sedimentary textures to turbulence of flow, graded bedding, the formation of evaporites (*Codex Atlanticus*, fol. 160); and the association of folded strata with mountains (*Codex Arundel*, fol. 30b, Richter, 982). After numerous false starts, he arrived at an understanding of the hydrologic cycle (MS *E*, fol. 12a and Richter, 930); he dismissed the Pythagorean identification of the forms of the elements with the Platonic solids (MS *F*

and Richter, 939); and he recorded the migration of sand dunes (MS *F*, fol. 61a and Richter, 1087).

After the period as engineer with Cesare Borgia, Leonardo had returned to Florence, then proceeded to Rome, and finally found sanctuary in Milan in 1508. Here he made the geologic notes of MS *F* under the heading *De mondo ed acque*. It is from this period also that the red chalk Windsor drawings of the Alps date, reflecting his interest in, and excursions into, the nearby Alps (Clark, p. 134).

Leonardo brought not only his experience and his scientific principles to his landscapes, but also his sense of fantasy (Castelfranco, p. 473). The foreground of the two versions of the *Virgin of the Rocks* (Louvre and National Gallery) appears to be alternately horizontal, vertical, and horizontal strata, with caves widening into tunnels so that the roofs form natural bridges, some of them falling in. Such hollowing out from underneath and falling in of the back is the same mechanism used by Nicholas Steno in his *Prodromus* of 1669 to account for the inclination of strata.

Duhem has argued cogently that Leonardo's ideas were transmitted through Cardano and Palissy to the modern world. There are many similarities which suggest a connection also with the highly influential *Telliamed* of Benoit de Maillet (1749). The notebooks were in part accessible well in advance of the modern development of a natural geology. G. B. Venturi's studies of the geologic material in the notebooks were published in 1797 when catastrophic views of earth history were dominant. This was the year of birth of Charles Lyell, whose *Principles of Geology* in 1830 first formally established actualism as geologic orthodoxy. (In later editions of the *Principles*, Lyell wrote that his attention was called to the Venturi studies by H. Hallam. G. Libri's notes on Leonardo's geology also date to the decade of Lyell's *Principles*. By contrast, the diluvial doctrine which Leonardo had demolished was seriously defended by William Buckland in his *Reliquiae diluvianae* as late as 1823, and catastrophism persisted well into the second half of the nineteenth century.)

Unfortunately, Leonardo rarely if ever sketched an indubitable fossil. He discussed but never illustrated the vivid Lake Garda *ammonitico rosso*—a Jurassic red marble with striking spiral ammonites used extensively in Milan. Leonardo's realistic strata, especially in the *Virgin and St. Anne* of the Louvre, closely resemble these limestones as they weather in the Milanese damp. How is it possible that his "ineffable left hand" traced no illustrations of his comments— those comments which in their freshness, their simplicity, and vivid detail are a warranty of firsthand observation and an actualistic geologic position not achieved again for centuries? "The understanding of times past and of the site of the world is the ornament and the food of the human mind," he wrote (*Codex Atlanticus*, fol. 365v).

CECIL J. SCHNEER

BIBLIOGRAPHY

Arbitrary Collections

1.	*Codex Atlanticus*	1478–1518
2.	*Windsor Collection*	1478–1518
3.	*Codex Arundel*	1480–1518

Notebooks

4.	*Codex Forster*, I_2 (fols. 41–55)	1480–1490
5.	MS *B*	ca. 1489
6.	*Codex Trivulzianus*	ca. 1489
7.	MS *C*	1490
8.	*Codex Madrid*, II (fols. 141–157)	1491–1493
9.	MS *A*	1492
10.	*Codex Madrid*, I	1492–1497
11.	*Codex Forster*, II_1, II_2, III	1493–1495
12.	MS *H*	1493–1494
13.	MS *M*	ca. 1495
14.	MS *I*	1495–1499
15.	MS *L*	1497; 1502–1503
16.	*Codex Madrid*, II (fols. 1–140)	1503–1505
17.	MS K_1	1504
18.	MS K_2	1504–1509
19.	*Codex Forster*, I_1	1505
20.	*Codex on Flight* . . .	1505
21.	*Codex Leicester*	ca. 1506
22.	MS *D*	ca. 1508
23.	MS *F*	1508–1509
24.	MS K_3	1509–1512
25.	*Anatomical Folio A*	ca. 1510
26.	MS *G*	1510–1516
27.	MS *E*	1513–1514

Note: Not all scholars are in agreement as to the years given above. It is, however, a matter of plus or minus one or two years.

I. ORIGINAL WORKS. Published treatises (compilations) are *Treatise on Painting* (abr.), pub. by Rafaelle du Fresne (Paris, 1651), complete treatise, as found in *Codex Urbinas latinus* 1270, trans. into English, annotated, and published in facs. by Philip A. McMahon (Princeton, 1956); and *Il trattato del moto e misura dell'acqua* . . ., pub. from *Codex Barberinianus* by E. Carusi and A. Favoro (Bologna, 1923).

Published MSS are *Codex Atlanticus*, facs. ed. (Milan, 1872 [inc.], 1894–1904), consisting of 401 fols., each containing one or more MS sheets (*Codex* is in the Biblioteca Ambrosiana, Milan); MSS *A–M* and *Ashburnham* 2038 and 2037 (in the library of the Institut de France), 6 vols., Charles Ravaisson-Mollien, ed. (Paris, 1881–1891), consisting of 2,178 facs. reproducing the 14 MSS in the Institut de France and Bibliothèque Nationale, with transcription and French trans.; *Codex Trivulzianus*, transcription and annotation by Luca Beltrami (Milan, 1891), containing 55 fols.; *Codex on the Flight of Birds*, 14 fols. pub. by Theodore Sabachnikoff, transcribed by Giovanni Piumati, translated by C. Ravaisson-Mollien (Paris, 1893, 1946); *The Drawings of Leonardo da Vinci at Windsor Castle*, cataloged by Kenneth Clark, 2nd ed., rev. with the assistance of Carlo Pedretti (London, 1968), containing 234 fols.: repros. of all the drawings at Windsor, including the anatomical drawings (notes are not transcribed or translated where this has been done in other works—such as the selections of J. P. Richter, *Anatomical Folios A* and *B*, and the *Quaderni d'anatomia*; see below); *Dell'anatomia fogli A*, pub. by T. Sabachnikoff and G. Piumati (Turin, 1901); *Dell'anatomia fogli B*, pub. by T. Sabachnikoff and G. Piumati (Turin, 1901); *Quaderni d'anatomia*, 6 vols., Ove C. L. Vangensten, A. Fonahn, and H. Hopstock, eds. (Christiania, 1911–1916), all the anatomical drawings not included in *Folios A* and *B; Codex Leicester* (Milan, 1909), 36 fols., pub. by G. Calvi with the title *Libro originale della natura peso e moto delle acque* (*Codex* is in the Leicester Library, Holkham Hall, Norfolk); *Codex Arundel*, a bound vol. marked *Arundel 263*, pub. by the Reale Commissione Vinciana, with transcription (Rome, 1923–1930), containing 283 fols. (*Codex* is in British Museum); and *Codex Forster*, 5 vols., 304 fols., pub. with transcription by the Reale Commissione Vinciana (Rome, 1936) (*Codex* is in the Victoria and Albert Museum, London).

MSS are J. P. Richter, *The Literary Works of Leonardo da Vinci*, 2 vols. (London, 1970), containing a transcription and English translation of a wide range of Leonardo's notes—used as a reference work in Clark's *Catalogue of the Drawings at Windsor Castle;* and E. MacCurdy, *The Notebooks of Leonardo da Vinci*, 2 vols. (London, 1939; 2nd ed., 1956), the most extensive selection of Leonardo's notes.

II. SECONDARY LITERATURE. The following works can be used to obtain a general picture of Leonardo's scientific work: Mario Baratta, *Leonardo da Vinci ed i problemi della terra* (Turin, 1903); Elmer Belt, *Leonardo the Anatomist* (Lawrence, Kan., 1955); Girolamo Calvi, *I manoscritti di Leonardo da Vinci* (Rome, 1925); B. Dibner, *Leonardo da Vinci, Military Engineer* (New York, 1946), and *Leonardo da Vinci, Prophet of Automation* (New York, 1969); Pierre Duhem, *Études sur Léonard de Vinci* (Paris, 1906–1913; repr. 1955); Sigrid Esche-Braunfels, *Leonardo da Vinci, das anatomische Werk* (Basel, 1954); Giuseppe Favoro, *Leonardo da Vinci, i medici e la medicina* (Rome, 1923), and "Leonardo da Vinci e l'anatomia," in *Scientia*, no. 6 (1952), 170–175; Bertrand Gille, *The Renaissance Engineers* (London, 1966); I. B. Hart, *The World of Leonardo da Vinci* (London, 1961); L. H. Heydenreich, *Leonardo da Vinci* (Berlin, 1944), also trans. into English (London, 1954); K. D. Keele, *Leonardo da Vinci on the Movement of the Heart and Blood* (London, 1952); "The Genesis of Mona Lisa," in *Journal of the History of Medicine*, **14**

(1959), 135; and "Leonardo da Vinci's Physiology of the Senses," in C. D. O'Malley, ed., *Leonardo's Legacy* (Berkeley–Los Angeles, 1969); E. MacCurdy, *The Mind of Leonardo da Vinci* (New York, 1928); J. P. McMurrich, *Leonardo da Vinci, the Anatomist* (Baltimore, 1930); Roberto Marcolongo, *Studi vinciani: Memorie sulla geometria e la meccanica di Leonardo da Vinci* (Naples, 1937); and A. Marinoni, "The Manuscripts of Leonardo da Vinci and Their Editions," in *Leonardo saggi e ricerche* (Rome, 1954).

See also C. D. O'Malley, ed., *Leonardo's Legacy—an International Symposium* (Berkeley–Los Angeles, 1969); C. D. O'Malley and J. B. de C. M. Saunders, *Leonardo da Vinci on the Human Body* (New York, 1952); Erwin Panofsky, *The Codex Huygens and Leonardo da Vinci's Art Theory* (London, 1940); A. Pazzini, ed., *Leonardo da Vinci. Il trattato della anatomia* (Rome, 1962); Carlo Pedretti, *Documenti e memorie riguardanti Leonardo da Vinci a Bologna e in Emilia* (Bologna, 1953); *Studi vinciani* (Geneva, 1957); and *Leonardo da Vinci on Painting—a Lost Book (Libro A)* (London, 1965); *Raccolta vinciana*, "Commune di Milano, Castello Sforzesco," I–XX (Milan, 1905–1964); Ladislao Reti, "Le arti chimiche di Leonardo da Vinci," in *Chimica e l'industria*, **34** (1952), 655–721; "Leonardo da Vinci's Experiments on Combustion," in *Journal of Chemical Education*, **29** (1952), 590; "The Problem of Prime Movers," in *Leonardo da Vinci, Technologist* (New York, 1969); and "The Two Unpublished Manuscripts of Leonardo da Vinci in Madrid," *ibid.*; I. A. Richter, *Selections From the Notebooks of Leonardo da Vinci* (Oxford, 1962); Vasco Ronchi, "Leonardo e l'ottica," in *Leonardo saggi e ricerche* (Rome, 1954); George Sarton, *Léonard de Vinci, ingénieur et savant. Colloques internationaux* (Paris, 1953), pp. 11–22; E. Solmi, *Scritti vinciani*, papers collected by Arrigo Solmi (Florence, 1924); K. T. Steinitz, *Leonardo da Vinci's Trattato della pittura* (Copenhagen, 1958); Arturo Uccelli, *I libri di meccanica di Leonardo da Vinci nella ricostruzione ordinata da A. Uccelli* (Milan, 1940); Giorgio Vasari, *Lives of the Painters and Architects* (London, 1927); and V. P. Zubov, *Leonardo da Vinci*, trans. from the Russian by David H. Kraus (Cambridge, Mass., 1968).

The remainder of the bibliography is divided into sections corresponding to those in the text: Technology, Mechanics, Mathematics, and Geology.

Technology. On Leonardo's work in technology, the following should be consulted: T. Beck, *Beiträge zur Geschichte des Maschinenbaues*, 2nd ed. (Berlin, 1900), completed in *Zeitschrift des Vereines deutscher Ingenieure* (1906), 524–531, 562–569, 645–651, 777–784; I. Calvi, *L'architettura militare di Leonardo da Vinci* (Milan, 1943); G. Canestrini, *Leonardo costruttore di macchine e veicoli* (Milan, 1939); B. Dibner, *Leonardo da Vinci, Military Engineer* (New York, 1946); F. M. Feldhaus, *Leonardo der Techniker und Erfinder* (Jena, 1922); R. Giacomelli, *Gli scritti di Leonardo da Vinci sul volo* (Rome, 1936); C. H. Gibbs Smith, "The Flying Machine of Leonardo da Vinci," in *Shell Aviation News*, no. 194 (1954); *The Aeroplane* (London, 1960); and *Leonardo da Vinci's Aeronautics*

(London, 1967); B. Gille, *Engineers of the Renaissance* (Cambridge, Mass., 1966); I. B. Hart, *The Mechanical Investigations of Leonardo da Vinci* (London, 1925; 2nd ed., with a foreword by E. A. Moody, Berkeley–Los Angeles, 1963), and *The World of Leonardo da Vinci* (London, 1961); *Léonard de Vinci et l'expérience scientifique au XVI siècle* (Paris, 1952), a collection of articles; *Leonardo da Vinci* (New York, 1967), a collection of articles originally pub. in 1939; R. Marcolongo, *Leonardo da Vinci artista-scienziato* (Milan, 1939); W. B. Parsons, *Engineers and Engineering in the Renaissance* (Baltimore, 1939; 2nd ed., Cambridge, Mass., 1968); L. Reti, "Leonardo da Vinci nella storia della macchina a vapore," in *Rivista di ingegneria* (1956–1957); L. Reti and B. Dibner, *Leonardo da Vinci, Technologist* (New York, 1969); G. Strobino, *Leonardo da Vinci e la meccanica tessile* (Milan, 1953); C. Truesdell, *Essays in the History of Mechanics* (New York, 1968); L. Tursini, *Le armi di Leonardo da Vinci* (Milan, 1952); A. Uccelli, *Storia della tecnica . . .* (Milan, 1945), and *I libri del volo di Leonardo da Vinci* (Milan, 1952); A. P. Usher, *A History of Mechanical Inventions*, rev. ed. (Cambridge, Mass., 1954); and V. P. Zubov, *Leonardo da Vinci* (Cambridge, Mass., 1968).

Mechanics. Particularly useful as a source collection of pertinent passages on mechanics in the notebooks is A. Uccelli, ed., *I libri di meccanica . . .* (Milan, 1942). The pioneer analytic works were those of P. Duhem, *Les origines de la statique*, 2 vols. (Paris, 1905–1906), and *Études sur Léonard de Vinci* (Paris, 1906–1913; repr. 1955). These works were the first to put Leonardo's mechanical works into historical perspective. Their main defect is that a full corpus of Leonardo's notebooks was not available to Duhem. They are less successful in interpreting Leonardo's dynamics. Far less perceptive than Duhem's work is F. Schuster's treatment of Leonardo's statics, *Zur Mechanik Leonardo da Vincis* (Erlangen, 1915), which also suffered because the sources available to him were deficient. A work that ordinarily follows Schuster (and Duhem) is I. B. Hart, *The Mechanical Investigations of Leonardo da Vinci* (London, 1925; 2nd ed., with foreword by E. A. Moody, Berkeley–Los Angeles, 1963). It tends to treat Leonardo in isolation, although the 2nd ed. makes some effort to rectify this deficiency. The best treatment of Leonardo's mechanics remains R. Marcolongo, *Studi vinciani: Memorie sulla geometria e la meccanica di Leonardo da Vinci* (Naples, 1937). It is wanting only in its treatment of Leonardo's hydrostatics and the motion of fluids. For a brief but important study of Leonardo's hydrostatics, see F. Arredi, *Le origini dell'idrostatica* (Rome, 1943), pp. 8–16. For an acute appraisal of Leonardo's mechanics in general and his fluid mechanics in particular, see C. Truesdell, *Essays in the History of Mechanics* (New York, 1968), pp. 1–83, esp. 62–79. Finally, for the influence of Archimedes on Leonardo, see M. Clagett, "Leonardo da Vinci and the Medieval Archimedes," in *Physis*, **11** (1969), 100–151, esp. 108–113, 119–140.

Mathematics. The most thorough study of Leonardo's mathematical works was carried out in the first part of the twentieth century by R. Marcolongo, whose most important writings are: "Le ricerche geometrico-meccaniche di Leonardo da Vinci," in *Atti della Società italiana delle scienze, detta dei XL*, 3rd ser., **23** (1929), 49–100; *Il trattato di Leonardo da Vinci sulle trasformazioni dei solidi* (Naples, 1934); and *Leonardo da Vinci artista-scienziato* (Milan, 1939). The cited article of C. Caversazzi, "Un'invenzione geometrica di Leonardo da Vinci," is in *Emporium* (May 1939), 317–323. Important articles are M. Clagett, "Leonardo da Vinci and the Medieval Archimedes," in *Physis*, **11** (1969), 100–151; and C. Pedretti, "The Geometrical Studies," in K. Clark, *The Drawings of Leonardo da Vinci at Windsor Castle*, 2nd ed., rev. (London, 1968), I, xlix–liii; and "Leonardo da Vinci: Manuscripts and Drawings of the French Period, 1517–1518," in *Gazette des beaux-arts* (Nov. 1970), 185–318.

The following studies by A. Marinoni provide a detailed analysis of some of Leonardo's works: "Le operazioni aritmetiche nei manoscritti vinciani," in *Raccolta vinciana*, XIX (Milan, 1962), 1–62; "La teoria dei numeri frazionari nei manoscritti vinciani. Leonardo e Luca Pacioli," *ibid.*, XX (Milan, 1964), 111–196; and "L'aritmetica di Leonardo," in *Periodico di matematiche* (Dec. 1968), 543–558. See also Marinoni's *L'essere del nulla* (Florence, 1970) on the definitions of the "principles" of geometry in Leonardo, and "Leonardo da Vinci," in *Grande antologia filosofica* (Milan, 1964), VI, 1149–1212, on the supposed definition of the principle of inertia.

Geology. On Leonardo's work in geology, see the following: Mario Baratta, *Leonardo da Vinci ed i problemi della terra* (Turin, 1903); *I disegni geografici di Leonardo da Vinci conservati nel Castello di Windsor* (Rome, 1941); Girolamo Calvi, *Introduction, Codex Leicester* (Rome, 1909); Giorgio Castelfranco, "Sul pensiero geologico e il paesaggio di Leonardo," in Achille Marazza, ed., *Saggi e Ricerche* (Rome, 1954), app. 2; Kenneth Clark, *Leonardo da Vinci* (Baltimore, 1963); Giuseppe De Lorenzo, *Leonardo da Vinci e la geologia* (Bologna, 1920); Pierre Duhem, *Études sur Léonard de Vinci*, 3 vols. (Paris, 1906–1913; repr. 1955); Eugène Muentz, *Leonardo da Vinci, Artist, Thinker, and Man of Science* (New York, 1898); and J. P. Richter, ed., *The Notebooks of Leonardo da Vinci* (New York, 1970).

LEONARDO OF PISA. See **Fibonacci, Leonardo.**

LEONHARD, KARL CÄSAR VON (*b.* Rumpenheim bei Hanau, Germany, 12 September 1779; *d.* Heidelberg, Germany, 23 January 1862), *mineralogy, geology*.

Early in his career, Leonhard adhered to the teachings of Werner but later deserted neptunism for volcanism. As the founding editor of the *Taschenbuch für die gesammte Mineralogie*, Leonhard earned a place among the foremost mineralogists of his time. His prolific writings contributed to the rise of popular interest in geology during the nineteenth century.

In 1797 Leonhard attended the University of Marburg; and in 1798 he went to the University of Göttingen, where his interest in mineralogy was awakened by Johann Friedrich Blumenbach. Because of his early marriage, however, he had to abandon his original intention to study mineralogy under Werner at Freiberg, and he took a position as an assessor in the bureau of land taxes in Hanau. Nevertheless, he corresponded with Werner, Voigt, and von Buch at Freiberg concerning geology and mineralogy, and he devoted his spare time to pursuing these studies. Beginning in 1803 he traveled frequently through Thuringen and Saxony to study the geology of these areas. From 1805 to 1810 he published his three-volume *Handbuch einer allgemeinen topographischen Mineralogie*, in which he took Werner's position on neptunism. Despite the Napoleonic campaigns of this period, Leonhard visited the Austrian Alps and the Salzkammergut, meeting Friedrich Mohs in Vienna and von Moll in Munich. In 1806 he collaborated with K. F. Marx and H. Kopp on *Systematisch tabellarische Übersicht und Charakteristik der Mineralien*, and in 1807 he originated the *Taschenbuch für die gesammte Mineralogie*. This journal soon attained prominence and received widespread support from German scientists, and it made Leonhard's name known throughout Europe. In 1830 the name of the journal was changed to the *Jahrbuch für Mineralogie, Geognosie, Geologie und Petrefaktenkunde*, and from 1833 to 1862 it appeared as the *Neues Jahrbuch für Mineralogie, Geognosie, Geologie und Petrekfaktenkunde*. It remains one of the foremost German scientific journals. From 1811 to 1821 Leonhard also edited the *Allgemeines Repertorium der Mineralogie*.

In 1809 Leonhard became a counselor and adviser in the bureau of mines of the Grand Duchy of Frankfurt, and in 1811 he was appointed the chief of land administration for this regime. In 1813 he was named inspector general and privy councillor of this portion of Napoleon's Confederation of the Rhine. Considered to be a friend of the French, Leonhard was stripped of his offices after the restoration and was forced to take another position as assessor. In 1815, however, he was called to Munich to teach in the academy, and in 1818 he was appointed professor of mineralogy at the University of Heidelberg, a position he held until his death. In an article concerning the instruction of science and medicine at Heidelberg, which appeared in Christian Karl André's *Hesperus* in 1831, Leonhard was described as having an astonishing fund of information concerning minerals and fossils and their classification. The article complained, however, that his approach was completely practical, that his knowledge was limited to the physical properties of minerals, that he completely neglected mathematics and chemistry, and that he used barbaric terminology in his lectures and gesticulated endlessly.

In 1817 Leonhard, together with J. K. Kopp and K. L. Gärtner, published *Propädeutik der Mineralogie*, considered at the time the most instructive source work in mineralogy. In 1818 he wrote *Zu Werners Andenken* as a tribute to his old friend; but that same year he also published *Zur Naturgeschichte der Vulkane*, in which he announced his change of allegiance from neptunism to volcanism because of the increasing evidence forthcoming from the study of basalt.

Leonhard's *Charakteristik der Felsarten* (1823) was the most complete work on petrology that appeared in the early nineteenth century. Although written primarily from a mineralogical point of view, the work also contained information concerning the occurrence of various kinds of rocks. Leonhard attempted to divide rocks into four classes: (1) rocks composed of unlike constituents; (2) rocks that are apparently uniform; (3) derivative or fragmented rocks; and (4) friable rocks. He based these distinctions on visible examination, so that his divisions were arbitrary and to a large extent unsatisfactory.

Leonhard's travels in Auvergne, Bohemia, and other volcanic areas, resulted in *Die Basaltgebilde* (1832). This work was a comprehensive study and conclusively proved the volcanic origin of basalt both with respect to its geological occurrence and to the appearance of the areas where the basalt contacted other rocks. The book aided substantially in the victory of volcanism.

Beginning in 1833 Leonhard turned his attention to the popularization of mineralogy and geology. His first effort, published that year, was *Geologie oder Naturgeschichte der Erde*, and in 1845–1847 he produced a three-volume work entitled *Taschenbuch für Freunde der Geologie* and, in 1846, *Naturgeschichte des Steinreichs*. His last scientific work, *Die Hüttenerzeugnisse als Stützpunkte geologischer Hypothesen*, appeared in 1858.

Leonhardite, $2(Ca_2Al_4Si_8O_{24} \cdot 7H_2O)$, an aluminosilicate of calcium, was named in honor of Leonhard by Blum in 1843.

BIBLIOGRAPHY

I. ORIGINAL WORKS. Leonhard was a prolific writer. His chief works are *Handbuch einer allgemeinen topogra-*phischen Mineralogie, 3 vols. (Frankfurt, 1805–1809); *Die Form-Verhältnisse und Grupperungen der Gebirge* (Frankfurt, 1812), written with P. E. Jasson; *Mineralogische Studien* (Nuremberg, 1812), written with C. J. Selb; *Propädeutik der Mineralogie* (Frankfurt, 1817), written with J. K. Kopp and K. L. Gärtner; *Zu Werners Andenken* (Frankfurt, 1818); *Zur Naturgeschichte der Vulkane* (Frankfurt, 1818); *Handbuch der Oryktognosie* (Heidelberg, 1821); *Charakteristik der Felsarten* (Heidelberg, 1823); *Die Naturgeschichte des Mineralreichs* (Heidelberg, 1825), 2nd ed. *Grundzüge der Geognosie und Geologie* (Heidelberg, 1831); *Agenda geognostica* (Heidelberg, 1829); *Die Basaltgebilde* (Stuttgart, 1832); *Geologie oder Naturgeschichte der Erde*, 5 vols. (Heidelberg, 1833); *Lehrbuch der Geognosie und Geologie* (Heidelberg, 1835); *Naturgeschichte des Steinreichs* (Heidelberg, 1846); *Taschenbuch für Freunde der Geologie*, 3 vols. (Heidelberg, 1845–1847); *Aus unserer Zeit in meinem Leben*, 2 vols. (Stuttgart, 1854–1856); and *Die Hüttenerzeugnisse als Stützpunkt geologischer Hypothesen* (Heidelberg, 1858). Leonhard also published about 30 articles in scientific journals.

II. SECONDARY LITERATURE. See *Allgemeine deutsche Biographie*, XVIII (Leipzig, 1883), 308–311; *Aus der Geschichte der Universität Heidelberg und ihrer Fakültaten* (Heidelberg, 1961); and "Obituary, K. C. von Leonhard," in *American Journal of Science*, 2nd ser., 33 (1862), 453.

JOHN G. BURKE

LEONHARDI, JOHANN GOTTFRIED (*b*. Leipzig, Saxony, 18 June 1746; *d*. Dresden, Saxony, 11 January 1823), *chemistry, medicine, pharmacy*.

Leonhardi's father, a physician, inspired a love of learning in his young son. After studying at home under various tutors Leonhardi enrolled in the local lyceum, and there completed his training in the classical languages. In 1764 he entered the University of Leipzig, where in the course of his studies in philosophy and science he heard Johann Heinrich Winkler lecture on physics and Karl Wilhelm Pörner on chemistry. He began to read medicine under Christian Gottlieb Ludwig. He received his baccalaureate in 1767. Continuing his work in medicine, for which he had an "innate love," he delivered his "lectures for the License" in 1769 on the structure and function of the conglobate glands (that is, glands of simple structure, such as the lymphatics). He was awarded a master's degree in 1770 and the baccalaureate in medicine the following year with a dissertation *De resorptionis in corpore humano praeter naturam impeditae causis atque noxis* (Leipzig, 1771).

Remaining at Leipzig as *Privatdozent*, Leonhardi lectured on medicine and chemistry. He became extraordinary professor of medicine in 1781. In 1782 he moved to the University of Wittenberg (at that time still in Saxony) as professor of medicine; in 1791 he accepted the post of personal physician and councillor to the elector of Saxony, Friedrich Augustus III. Leonhardi was also given a seat in the Dresden public health council. Although he retained his professorship at Wittenberg, he arranged for a deputy to lecture in his place. In 1815 he became a knight of the Königliche Sächsische Civil-Verdienstorden. Despite almost constant ill health during the last decade or so of his life, Leonhardi managed to continue his favorite work of editing and translating.

Leonhardi did little original research. The bulk of his writings consists of summaries, compilations, and translations. He also wrote a number of short, academic, and unoriginal medical discourses. His chief accomplishment was *Chymisches Wörterbuch . . . übersetzt und mit Anmerkungen und Zusätzen vermehrt*, 6 pts. (Leipzig, 1781–1783), his authoritative translation of Pierre-Joseph Macquer's *Dictionnaire de chimie*. Leonhardi's well-received and widely used version amounted to a new, expanded edition, approximately two and a half times the length of the original, to which Leonhardi himself contributed about 150 new articles. The abundant annotation shows him to have been in complete command of the chemical literature of his day; the references are given exactly and the commentary in the notes is clear, factual, and comprehensive. Judging by these excellent notes, Leonhardi's primary interest appears to have been the qualitative analysis of inorganic substances, especially those of actual or potential industrial value. He followed the current controversies on the nature of combustion and the "airs" with great interest and published a summary of recent pneumatic discoveries as *Aerologie* (1781). The notational underbrush grows thickest in the less theoretical parts of the *Dictionnaire*. Like Macquer he was not a reductionist; he did not find it helpful to devise premature theories about the ultimate constituents of things. Leonhardi adhered to the phlogiston theory until the early 1790's. Leonhardi's was not a creative mind, but it was surely a disciplined and well-stocked one.

BIBLIOGRAPHY

I. Original Works. This list contains those of Leonhardi's works which are either (1) of special interest for chemistry or (2) not listed in the *British Museum Catalogue of Printed Books* or in the *Index Catalogue of the Surgeon General's Office, U.S. Army* (1st ser.). The latter catalogue has a nearly complete list of Leonhardi's medical works.

1. *Observationes quasdam chemicas proponit praelectionesque suas aestivas . . .* (Leipzig, 1775).

2. "Versuch einer Anleitung zu gemeinnütziger ökonomischen Prüfung der sämtlichen Gewässer in Sachsen," in *Schriften der Leipziger Oekonomischen Societät*, **6** (1784).

3. "Chymische Untersuchung des ächten Braunschweigischen Grüns," *ibid.*

4. *Vinorum alborum metallici contagii suspectorum docimasiae curae repetitae et novae* (Wittenberg, 1787).

5. *Programma de tubarum uterinarum morbis pauca quaedam* (Wittenberg, 1788).

6. *Physiologia muci primarum viarum* (Wittenberg, 1789).

7. *De succorum humanorum salibus dulcibus* (Leipzig, 1790).

8. Letters to the editor, Crell's *Chemische Annalen* (1789), pt. 2, 423–424; (1790), pt. 2, 126–128; (1794), pt. 1, 177–178.

Translations, editions, introductions:

9. D. P. Loyard, *Versuch über einen tollen Hundebiss*, with notes by Leonhardi (Leipzig, 1778).

10. *Herrn Peter Joseph Macquers Chymisches Wörterbuch, oder allgemeine Begriffe der Chemie nach alphabetischer Ordnung, aus dem Französischen nach der zweiten Ausgabe übersetzt und mit Anmerkungen und Züsatzen vermehrt*, 6 vols. (Leipzig, 1781–1783); 2nd ed., 7 vols. (Leipzig, 1788–1791); 3rd ed., prepared by J. B. Richter, 3 vols. (Leipzig, 1806–1809); separate publication of Leonhardi's notes and additions: *Neue Zusätze und Anmerkungen zu Macquers Chymischen Wörterbuch erster Ausgabe*, 2 vols. (Leipzig, 1792).

11. *Aerologie physico-chemicae recentioris primae linae* (Leipzig, 1781); expanded and translated as *Kurzer Umriss der neuern Entdekkungen über die Luftgattungen* (Graz, 1783).

12. *C. W. Scheeles . . . Chemische Abhandlung von der Luft und dem Feuer . . .*, 2nd ed. (Leipzig, 1782), contains notes by Leonhardi which were incorporated into the Baron de Dietrich's *Supplément au Traité Chimique de l'Air et du Feu de M. Scheele . . .* (Paris, 1785). C. G. Kayser, *Vollständiges Bücher-Lexicon* (Leipzig, 1834–1838), lists a third German ed. (1788).

13. *Schwedisches Apothekerbuch*, translated from the 2nd (Latin) ed. and annotated by Leonhardi (Leipzig, 1782).

14. Pierre Bayen, *Untersuchungen über das Zinn, und Beantwortung der Frage: Ob Man sich ohne Gefahr zu ökonomischen Gebrauche der zinnernen Gefässe bedienen könne ? . . . Aus dem Französischen übersetzt; herausgegeben und mit Anmerkungen begleitet D. Johann Gottfried Leonhardi . . .* (Leipzig, 1784).

15. A. F. L. Dörffurt, *Abhandlung über den Kampher, mit Vorrede von J. G. Leonhardi* (Wittenberg, 1793).

16. *Pharmacopoea Saxonica* (Dresden, 1820).

II. Secondary Literature. See J. Ferguson, *Bibliotheca chemica*, II (Glasgow, 1906), 28, and the literature cited there; L. F. F. Flemming, *De vita et meritis beati Joh. Gottfr. Leonhardi* (Dresden, 1823)—the author was unable to locate this in preparing the above article; Michaud, *Biographie universelle*, XXIV, 185–186; and J. R. Partington, *A History of Chemistry*, III (London, 1961), 81–82, 493–494, 616–619. Leonhardi's sketch of his early life is in A. G. Plaz, *Panegyrin medicam* (Leipzig, 1771), xii–xv. I am indebted to Dr. John B. Blake of the U.S. National

Library of Medicine for calling this reference to my attention. For reviews of the *Wörterbuch*, see *Annales de chimie*, **4** (1790), 289; **11** (1791), 204; **12** (1792), 110.

STUART PIERSON

LEONICENO, NICOLÒ (*b.* Vicenza, Italy, 1428; *d.* Ferrara, Italy, 9 June 1524), *medicine, philology.*

Leoniceno's father, Francesco, a physician, was from an ancient noble family of Vicenza; his mother, Madalena, was the daughter of Antonio Loschi, a humanist and secretary of Pope Alexander V. At Vicenza, Leoniceno received thorough training in Latin and Greek from Ognibene de' Bonisoli and then studied philosophy and medicine at Padua, taking his doctorate around 1453. Little is known of his activities during the following decade, except that he is said to have traveled to England; by 1462 he was back at Padua, possibly as a teacher. In 1464 he was called to teach at the University of Ferrara, where he remained for the rest of his ninety-six years, except for a year at Bologna (1508–1509). He did not marry.

Under the celebrated Guarino da Verona, Ferrara had become a major center for the study of classical literature, and Leoniceno took his place there as one of the leading Greek scholars of his age. (He is sometimes confused with the contemporary Hellenist Nicolò Leonico Tomeo.) Among Leoniceno's friends and correspondents were other major figures in the revival of ancient learning, including Pico della Mirandola, Giorgio Valla, Politian, Ermolao Barbaro, and Erasmus.

At Ferrara, Leoniceno taught mathematics, then Greek philosophy, and finally medicine, in which area he made his most important contribution. The teaching in European medical schools at this time was ultimately derived from the Greek physicians, especially Galen, but as interpreted and systematized by the Arabic authors. In the several stages of textual transmission, translation, and interpretation that separated European Arabist medicine from the original Greek sources, considerable distortion and corruption had been introduced; but it was obscured by the poor quality of such translations of genuine Galenic works as were generally available. Humanists had long ridiculed the Arabist medical tradition for its "barbarous" Latinity and the sterility of its scholastic disputations, but not until the late fifteenth century were serious attempts made to provide an alternative by reviving Greek medicine in its pristine form. Leoniceno was one of the chief pioneers in this effort to recover and edit the works of the Greek physicians and to prepare faithful Latin translations, and he was the first to develop this new approach into a serious rival to the established Arabist tradition. Under his leadership Ferrara became the main center for studying the revived Galenic medicine, and from there the movement spread to the other Italian medical schools and then to the rest of Europe. Among Leoniceno's students were Giovanni Manardi, Antonio Musa Brasavola, and Lodovico Bonacciolo; and others who were influenced by him included Giovanni Battista da Monte (Montanus), Thomas Linacre, and Leonhard Fuchs.

In accordance with the general humanist credo, Leoniceno placed great emphasis on the study of individual words and their meanings as the key to understanding the works of the Greek medical authorities. In his preface to his translations of Galen (1508) he cited examples of how an error in transcribing or translating a single word could distort the meaning of an entire passage; and in other works he sought to demonstrate that the words of the Greek physicians had been so often misconstrued by the Arabists as to make the resulting medical system a menace to human life. In his tracts on the errors of Pliny he cited numerous mistakes made by the Arabists in the identification of medicinal herbs described by the Greeks, and he also pointed out many corruptions, both terminological and factual, introduced into Galenic anatomy by Ibn Sīnā, Mondino de' Luzzi, and Benedetti. He based the latter criticisms in part on such Galenic treatises as the *Anatomical Procedures* and *Whether Blood is Naturally Contained in the Arteries* that were not generally available for another generation. In his treatise on syphilis he discussed similar errors in the naming and identification of diseases.

On the more constructive side, Leoniceno supplied the texts for the first genuine Galenic works to be published in Greek (1500) and published Latin translations of eleven Galenic treatises, beginning with the *Ars medica* (1508) and the *Commentary on the Aphorisms of Hippocrates*, together with the *Aphorisms* themselves (1509). He was very proud of these translations and in 1522 published a lengthy apologia against three men, each of whom had criticized his translation of only a single word or phrase. He also translated into Latin and Italian a number of works by nonmedical authors.

In 1497 Leoniceno published the first scholarly treatise on syphilis, a very influential work that went through numerous editions during the following century. He tried to show that although the disease had only recently appeared in Europe, it had occurred at various times in the remote past and was therefore not an essentially new disease.

Leoniceno's work *On the three ordered doctrines according to the opinion of Galen* (1508) was of some importance in the discussion of method during the sixteenth century. At the beginning of *Ars medica* Galen had stated that there are three ways of teaching a subject in an orderly manner: analysis, synthesis, and the explication of definitions. The medieval commentators had sought, with somewhat confusing results, to relate these three ways to the various methods of demonstration and dialectic referred to by Plato, Aristotle, and other authors. Leoniceno showed that as an exegesis of the *Ars medica* the entire discussion was pointless, because Galen was referring simply to didactic techniques and not to methods of philosophic inquiry or demonstration. His clarification of this point seems to have been widely accepted, although around 1517 a professor at Padua (possibly Ludovico Carenzio) defended the medieval authors, leading an anonymous Roman disciple of Leoniceno (or possibly Leoniceno himself) to publish a refutation.

In 1490 Leoniceno inaugurated a famous controversy on the errors of Pliny the elder. In that year he sent to Politian a critique of Ibn Sīnā, in which he noted in passing that Pliny seemed to have confused the two herbs ivy and cistus because of the similarity of their Greek names (κισσός and κίσθος); Politian commended Leoniceno's castigation of Ibn Sīnā but politely challenged his criticism of Pliny. Leoniceno responded with a tract, *On the errors of Pliny and others in medicine* (1492), in which he not only defended his original point but charged Pliny with many other errors stemming from verbal confusion. This work provoked an indirect response from Barbaro in support of Pliny and a direct attack on Leoniceno by the Ferrarese lawyer Pandolfo Collenuccio. Others joined in the fray on both sides, with Leoniceno himself contributing three additional tracts in 1493, 1503, and 1507, the latter in response to Alessandro Benedetti. (Leoniceno's tracts were apparently circulated in manuscript before being printed.)

This polemic was primarily an internal dispute among humanists, in contrast to Leoniceno's attacks on the Arabists. Pliny's *Natural History* was avowedly a compilation from earlier sources, chiefly Greek, and Leoniceno charged that he had often garbled the information that he transcribed. The controversy stemmed from the reluctance of some humanists to admit that an authentic Roman, who wrote in "eloquent" Latin and was fluent in Greek, could have made the same kinds of linguistic errors as the despised "barbarous" authors. To soften the blow Leoniceno sought to show that the Arabs had made even worse errors than Pliny in interpreting the Greeks and that the medieval Latin authorities were

worse still. However, this argument did not placate his opponents, who thought that textual emendation and sympathetic interpretation would absolve Pliny of Leoniceno's charges. In this assumption they were partly justified, since some of the errors that Leoniceno singled out were in fact due to corruptions of the text he had used, and some of his interpretations of Pliny were unnecessarily harsh. Collenuccio also objected strongly to Leoniceno's assumption that the testimony of the Greek authorities, unconfirmed by observation, was an adequate standard of the truth of Pliny's statements, but the immediate outcome of the dispute, as of most of Leoniceno's work, was to enhance the authority of the Greeks at the expense of their Roman, Arabic, and medieval Latin followers. (Leoniceno eventually concluded that Celsus had similarly misinterpreted the Greek medical writers on whom he had relied.) Serious criticism of the Greeks themselves, based on independent observation and reasoning, was to begin a generation later, but it was to take many generations to overthrow completely the Hellenist tradition in medicine that Leoniceno had done so much to establish.

BIBLIOGRAPHY

I. ORIGINAL WORKS. *De Plinii et aliorum in medicina erroribus* (Ferrara, 1492) is the first of Leoniceno's tracts on Pliny; *De Plinii, & plurimum aliorum medicorum in medicina erroribus* (Ferrara, 1509) contains all four, as do subsequent eds. His other works are *Libellus de epidemia, quam vulgo morbum gallicum vocant* (Venice–Milan–Leipzig, 1497); *De tiro seu vipera* and *De dipsade et pluribus aliis serpentibus* (Venice, ca. 1497), both repr. as *De serpentibus* (Bologna, 1518); *De virtute formativa* (Venice, 1506); *In libros Galeni e greca in latinam linguam a se translatos prefatio communis. Ejusdem in artem medicinalem Galeni ... prefatio. Galeni ars medicinalis Nicolao Leoniceno interprete. ... Ejusdem de tribus doctrinis ordinatis secundum Galeni sententiam opus* (Venice, 1508), repr. with *Galeni in aphorismos Hippocratis, cum ipsis aphorismis, eodem Nicolao Leoniceno interprete* (Ferrara, 1509); *Medici Romani Nicolai Leoniceni discipuli antisophisia [antisophista]* (Bologna, 1519), of uncertain authorship; and *Contra obtrectatores apologia* (Venice, 1522). Most of Leoniceno's works went through one or more subsequent editions; all except his translations, the *Prefatio communis*, and the *Prefatio in artem medicinalem* are included in *Opuscula*, D. A. Leennium, ed. (Basel, 1532). A facs. of the first ed. of *De morbo gallico*, with intro., is included in K. Sudhoff, *The Earliest Printed Literature on Syphilis*, adapted by C. Singer, Monumenta Medica, III (Florence, 1925). Loris Premuda edited *De Plinii ... erroribus*, with intro. and Italian trans. (Milan–Rome, 1958). R. J. Durling, "A Chronological Census of Renaissance Editions and Translations of Galen," in *Journal of the Warburg and Courtauld*

Institutes, **24** (1961), 230–305, lists Leoniceno's trans. of Galen, p. 297. P. O. Kristeller gives references to Italian archival material about Leoniceno in *Iter italicum,* 2 vols. (London–Leiden, 1963–1967).

II. SECONDARY LITERATURE. The only full-length study is D. Vitaliani, *Della vita e delle opere di Nicolò Leoniceno Vicentino* (Verona, 1892); see also Premuda's intro. to his ed. of *De Plinii . . . erroribus.* On the Galenic revival and Leoniceno's role in it, see Durling's intro. to his "Chronological Census," esp. p. 236. On Leoniceno's influence, esp. in Germany, see Luigi Samoggia, *Le ripercussioni in Germania dell' indirizzo filologico-medico leoniceniano della scuola Ferrarese per opera di Leonardo Fuchs,* Quaderni de Storia Della Scienza e Della Medicina, IV (Ferrara, 1964). On method, see N. W. Gilbert, *Renaissance Concepts of Method* (New York, 1960), pp. 102–104. On the errors of Pliny, see Lynn Thorndike, *A History of Magic and Experimental Science,* IV (New York, 1934), 593–610; A. Castiglioni, "The School of Ferrara and the Controversy on Pliny," in E. A. Underwood, ed., *Science, Medicine, and History* (London, 1953), I, 269–279; and F. Kudlien, "Zwei medizinisch-philologische Polemiken am Ende des 15. Jahrhunderts," in *Gesnerus,* **22** (1965), 85–92.

JEROME J. BYLEBYL

LE PAIGE, CONSTANTIN (*b.* Liège, Belgium, 9 March 1852; *d.* Liège, 26 January 1929), *mathematics.*

Le Paige, the son of Jeanne Jacques and Constantin Marie Le Paige, received his secondary education at Spa and Liège. After taking a course in mathematics with V. Falisse, he entered the University of Liège in 1869, where he attended the lectures of E. Catalan, to whom we owe a special form of determinants, the so-called circulants. After his graduation on 28 July 1875, Le Paige began teaching the theory of determinants and higher analysis at the university. He was appointed extraordinary professor of mathematics in 1882, and ordinary professor in 1885, which post he retained until his retirement in 1922; he was appointed professor emeritus in 1923. His wife was the former Marie Joséphine Ernst.

Le Paige began work at a time when the theory of algebraic forms, initiated by Boole in 1841 and developed by Cayley and Sylvester in England, Hermite in France, and Clebsch and Aronhold in Germany, had drawn the attention of the geometers. This theory studies the properties of such forms, which remain unchanged under linear substitutions. Le Paige's investigations touched mainly upon the geometry of algebraic curves and surfaces, and the theory of invariants and involutions. He coordinated and generalized the extensions which at that time had been tried. His best-known achievement was the construction of a cubic surface given by nineteen points. Starting from the construction of a cubic surface given by a straight line, three groups of three points on a line, and six other points, Le Paige comes to the construction of a cubic surface given by three lines and seven points. From this he proceeds to the construction of a cubic surface given by a line, three points on a line, and twelve other points, and by means of the construction of a cubic surface given by three points on a line and sixteen other points, he arrives at a surface given by nineteen points.

Steiner's theorem, that a conic section can be generated by the intersection of two projective pencils, had been extended by Chasles to plane algebraic curves. Le Paige also studied the generation of plane cubic and quartic curves, and the construction of a plane cubic curve given by nine points is presented in his memoir "Sur les courbes du troisième ordre" (*Mémoires de l'Académie royale de Belgique,* 43 [1881] and 45 [1882]), written with F. Folie.

Besides writing on algebraic geometry, Le Paige was also a historian of mathematics. He published the correspondence of Sluse, canon of Liège, with Pascal, Huygens, Oldenburg, and Wallis. His "Notes pour servir à l'histoire des mathématiques dans l'ancien pays de Liège" (*Bulletin de l'Institut archéologique liègeois,* 21 [1890]), devotes a large section to the Belgian astronomer Wendelin, and in "Sur l'origine de certains signes d'opération" (*Annales de la Société scientifiques de Bruxelles,* 16 [1891–1892]) Le Paige explains the origin of the symbols of operation. After his appointment as director of the Institut d'Astrophysique de Cointe-Slessim in 1897 Le Paige wrote a number of astronomical treatises.

Le Paige was elected a member of the Royal Academy of Sciences of Belgium in 1885. His international reputation is attested by the following partial list of his affiliations: member of the Royal Society of Sciences of Liège (1878) and of the Royal Society of Bohemia; corresponding member of the Pontificia Accademia dei Nuovi Lincei (1881) and of the Royal Academy of Sciences of Lisbon (1883); and honorary member of the Mathematical Society of Amsterdam (1886).

BIBLIOGRAPHY

In addition to the works mentioned in the text, Le Paige published the following astronomical works: "Sur la réduction au lieu apparent. Termes dus à l'aberration," in *Mémoires de la Société royale des Sciences de Liège,* 3 (1901); and "Étude sur les visées au bain de mercure," *ibid.*

A fuller account of Le Paige's work and a complete list of his publications is given in L. Godeaux, "Notice sur Constantin le Paige," in *Annuaire de l'Académie royale de Belgique,* **105** (1939), 239–270.

H. L. L. BUSARD

LEPEKHIN, IVAN IVANOVICH (*b.* St. Petersburg, Russia [now Leningrad, U.S.S.R.], 21 September 1740; *d.* St. Petersburg, 18 April 1802), *geography, natural history.*

Lepekhin's father, Ivan Sidorovich Lepekhin, was a guardsman in the Semenovsky regiment. The soldiers of this regiment were entitled to send their children to the Gymnasium and University attached to the St. Petersburg Academy; and in the spring of 1751, the ten-year-old Lepekhin was accepted at the Gymnasium. He studied there, at state expense, until January 1760, when he was accepted as a student at the University. He remained at the University for two and a half years, studying the humanities and chemistry, but he wanted most of all to study the broader discipline of natural history which was not taught there. Lepekhin therefore asked for and received permission to study at a foreign university. His request was granted and in November 1762 he enrolled at the University of Strasbourg.

At Strasbourg, Lepekhin devoted himself to practical anatomy, physiological experiments on living animals, and medicine. In his free time, he collected and studied plants and insects in the vicinity of Strasbourg and compiled lists of local birds and fish. In the summer of 1766 he defended his dissertation on the formation of vinegar ("Specimen de acetificatione") and received the doctorate in medicine.

Lepekhin returned to St. Petersburg in the fall of 1767 and the following June was elected an adjunct of the Academy. In April of 1771 he was made academician in the department of natural history.

Lepekhin is known mainly as the leader of one of the five expeditions organized by the Academy in 1768 to study the natural resources of Russia and to collect ethnographic and economic data. In the first three years the expedition, which consisted of Lepekhin and six companions, traveled from Moscow to Simbirsk (Ulyanovsk), Samara (Kuibyshev), Saratov, Tsaritsyn (Volgograd), Gurev, Orenburg, Ekaterinburg (Sverdlovsk), and Tyumen. They were to proceed as far as Tobolsk and then to return to St. Petersburg. At Tyumen, where he spent the third winter, Lepekhin was granted permission to travel instead into northern European Russia—to the area around the White Sea. In 1772 the expedition left Tyumen and traveled to Archangel via Verkhoture and Veliki Ustyug. From Archangel they explored the White Sea coast, the Solovetskiye Islands, and the Kanin Peninsula. They then returned to St. Petersburg by way of Kholmogory, Kargopol, and Ladoga. In 1773 Lepekhin led a nine-month expedition to investigate Byelorussia.

From 1774 to 1802 Lepekhin was head of the Botanical Garden of the Academy of Sciences, and from 1777 to 1794 of the Gymnasium. From 1783 until his death he was the permanent secretary of the Russian Academy, created in the same year for work in the area of Russian literature (it was active until 1841, when it merged with the Petersburg Academy of Sciences as the Section of Russian Language and Literature). He participated in the compilation and publication of a six-volume *Dictionary of the Russian Academy* and directed its organization.

Along with his substantial administrative work in the two academies, Lepekhin systematically published articles devoted to the description of the new species of animals and plants he had discovered during his travels. He wrote forty-four articles (excluding the articles on physiology) in Latin, Russian, and French. But Lepekhin's chief scientific work was his four-volume *Diaries of a Journey Through Various Provinces of the Russian State* (1771–1805). The first three volumes were translated into German in 1774–1783, and published in 1784 in French in Lausanne. These publications enhanced Lepekhin's scientific reputation abroad. In 1776 he was elected a member of the Berlin Academy and several newly discovered plants and insects were named by German scientists in his honor.

The *Diaries* are a rich collection of natural science and ethnographic information relating to the Volga area, the Urals and adjacent northwestern Kazakhstan and western Siberia, and northern European Russia. Lepekhin gave special attention to the description of more than 300 species of animals and their habits and distribution. With great care he described more than 100 birds and 117 insect species. What is important about the *Diaries* is that they not only described different species but also gave whole zoological maps of broad areas, which was an innovation.

In the *Diaries* much attention was given also to plants. Many unknown plants of the Urals and the northern tundra were described, and much information was collected about plants useful to man and ways of cultivating them. Along with factual data the *Diaries* contain a number of interesting general observations. Concerning the question of the variability of the earth's surface, Lepekhin thoroughly rejected the widespread belief that changes in the earth's surface were the result of catastrophic floods. Like Lomonosov, with whose *O sloyakh zemnykh* ("On the Layers of the Earth") he became acquainted while still a student in Strasbourg, Lepekhin considered that the changes were the result of the slow influence of water and underground fire and were still taking place. To explain the presence of marine fossils in layers of rock, he said, "There was once ocean floor upon which now are built famous cities, and populous towns . . ." (*Diaries*, III, p. 36).

Speaking of the origin of the Ural Mountains, Lepekhin came to the correct idea of the hydrologic cycle in nature, aligning himself with those natural scientists "Who by ocean vapors, which are the source of rivers, determine the circulation of the atmosphere" (*Diaries*, II, p. 144). In a number of places in the *Diaries* Lepekhin closely approached an understanding of the possibility of change caused by external conditions. He described many deposits of useful fossils, and in particular he noted the phenomena of oil in several places between the Urals and the Volga. To Lepekhin's many contributions to science must be added his ten-volume Russian edition of Buffon's *Histoire naturelle* (St. Petersburg, 1789–1808). Lepekhin himself translated volumes V–X, and Volume I in collaboration with Rumovsky.

BIBLIOGRAPHY

I. ORIGINAL WORKS. See I. I. Lepekhin, *Dnevnye zapiski puteshestvia po raznym provintsiam Rossyskogo gosudarstva* ("Diaries of a Journey Through Various Provinces of the Russian State"; pts. 1–4, St. Petersburg, 1771–1805).

II. SECONDARY LITERATURE. For information on Lepekhin's life, see N. G. Fradkin, *Akademik I. I. Lepekhin i ego puteshestvia po Rossii v 1768–1773 gg* ("Academician I. I. Lepekhin and His Journeys Through Russia in 1768–1773"; Moscow, 1953); T. A. Lukina, *Ivan Ivanovich Lepekhin* (Moscow–Leningrad, 1965); N. Ya. Ozeretskovsky, "Zhizn I. I. Lepekhina" ("Life of I. I. Lepekhin"), in *Zhurnal departamenta narodnogo prosveshchenia*, no. 11 (1822), 281–288; V. A. Polenov, "Kratkoe zhizneopisanie I. I. Lepekhina" ("A Short Description of the Life of I. I. Lepekhin"), in *Trudy Rossyskoy Akademii*, pt. 2 (1840), 205–215; and M. I. Sukhomlinov, "I. I. Lepekhin," in *Istoria Rossyskoy Akademii*, no. 2 (1875), 157–299.

I. A. FEDOSEEV

LE POIVRE, JACQUES-FRANÇOIS (*fl.* France, early eighteenth century), *mathematics.*

A minor figure in the early history of projective geometry, Le Poivre is known only by his short treatise, *Traité des sections du cylindre et du cône considérées dans le solide et dans le plan, avec des démonstrations simples & nouvelles* (Paris, 1704). According to the review of this work in the *Journal des sçavans*, he lived in Mons and worked on the treatise for three years; nothing more is known about him.

Aimed both at presenting the conic sections in a form readily understandable to the novice and at offering new results to specialists, the *Traité* is divided into two parts. The first examines the ellipse by means of the parallel projection of a circle from one plane to another and, by inversion of the projection, within the same plane. Although primarily interested here in the tangent properties of the curve, Le Poivre also proves several theorems concerning its conjugate axes in a much simpler way than had been achieved earlier.

Part 2 is more interesting for its greater generality. Here Le Poivre generates the conic sections by means of the central projection of a circle. Taking a circle as base and a point S (at first assumed to be off the plane of the circle) as summit, he draws two parallel lines ab and DE in the plane of the circle (see Fig. 1).

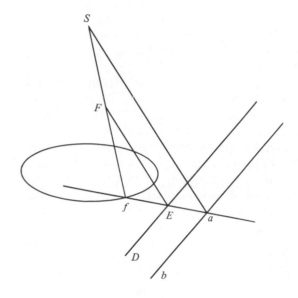

FIGURE 1

He then draws through any point f on the circle an arbitrary line intersecting DE at E and ab at a. Having drawn Sa, he draws EF parallel to it and intersecting Sf at F. Point F, he then shows, lies on a conic section, the precise nature of which depends on the location of line ab: if ab lies wholly outside the circle, the section is an ellipse; if ab is tangent to the circle, the section is a parabola; if ab cuts the circle, the section is a hyperbola. The theorems that he goes on to prove are nevertheless independent of the specific position of ab and hence apply to conic sections in general.

If one views ab and DE as the intersections of two parallel planes with the plane of the circle, and Sf as an element of the cone determined by point S and the circle, then Le Poivre's construction reduces to that of Apollonius. But the construction itself does not rely on that visualization of a solid, nor does it require that S in fact be off the plane of the circle.

Hence the theorems also hold for central projections in the same plane.

In reviewing Le Poivre's *Traité* for the *Acta eruditorum*, Christian Wolff spoke warmly of its elegance and originality. The anonymous reviewer of the *Journal des sçavans*, however, insisted on Le Poivre's omission of several important conic properties, in particular the focal properties, and on the extent to which he had failed to go beyond (or even to equal) the methods of Philippe de La Hire. In fact, Le Poivre's method of central projection is essentially that employed by La Hire in Part 2 of his *Nouvelle méthode en géométrie, pour les sections des superficies coniques et cylindriques* (Paris, 1673). Whether independent of La Hire or not, Le Poivre's work was apparently lost in his shadow, not to be brought to light again until Michel Chasles's survey of the history of geometry in 1837.

BIBLIOGRAPHY

Le Poivre's *Traité* is quite rare. The above description of it is taken from the reviews in the *Acta eruditorum* (Mar. 1707), 132–133 (the identification of Wolff as reviewer is from a contemporary marginal in the Princeton copy); and the *Journal des sçavans*, **32** (1704), 649–658. Chasles, who felt that Le Poivre belonged in a class with Desargues, Pascal, and La Hire, discusses his work in pars. 31–34 of ch. 3 of the *Aperçu historique sur l'origine et le développement des méthodes en géométrie, particulièrement de celles qui se rapportent à la géométrie moderne* (Brussels, 1837); German trans. by L. A. Sohncke (Halle, 1839; repr. Wiesbaden, 1968). The entry for Le Poivre in the *Nouvelle biographie générale*, XXX (Paris, 1862), 852, stems entirely from Chasles.

MICHAEL S. MAHONEY

LERCH, MATHIAS (*b.* Milínov, near Sušice, Bohemia, 20 February 1860; *d.* Sušice, Czechoslovakia, 3 August 1922), *mathematics*.

Lerch studied mathematics in Prague and, in 1884 and 1885, at the University of Berlin under Weierstrass, Kronecker, and Lazarus Fuchs. In 1886 he became a *Privatdozent* at the Czech technical institute in Prague and in 1896 full professor at the University of Fribourg. He returned to his native country in 1906, following his appointment as full professor at the Czech technical institute in Brno. In 1920 Lerch became the first professor of mathematics at the newly founded Masaryk University in Brno. He died two years later, at the age of sixty-two. In 1900 he received the grand prize of the Paris Academy for his *Essais sur le calcul du nombre des classes de formes quadratiques binaires aux coefficients entiers* [199].

Of Lerch's 238 scientific writings, some of which are quite comprehensive, 118 were written in Czech. About 150 deal with analysis and about forty with number theory; the rest are devoted to geometry, numerical methods, and other subjects. Lerch's achievements in analysis were in general function theory, general and special infinite series, special functions (particularly the gamma function), elliptic functions, and integral calculus. His works are noteworthy with regard to methodology. In particular he described and applied to concrete questions new methodological principles of considerable importance: the principle of the introduction of an auxiliary parameter for meromorphic functions [203] and the principle of most rapid convergence [210]. Lerch's best-known accomplishments include the Lerch theory on the generally unique solution φ of the equation $J(a) = \int_0^\infty \exp(-ax)\ \varphi(x)\ dx$—[73, 180]—which is fundamental in modern operator calculus; and the Lerch formula [101, 105, 116, 124], obtained originally from the theory of Malmsténian series, for the derivative of the Kummerian trigonometric development of $\log \Gamma(v)$:

$$\sum_{k=1}^{\infty} \sin(2k + 1)\ v\pi \cdot \log \frac{k}{k+1}$$
$$= (\log 2\pi - \Gamma'[1]) \sin v\pi$$
$$+ \frac{\pi}{2} \cos v\pi + \frac{\Gamma'(v)}{\Gamma(v)} \sin v\pi\ (0 < v < 1).$$

BIBLIOGRAPHY

I. ORIGINAL WORKS. A complete, chronological bibliography of Lerch's scientific works was published by J. Škrášek in *Czechoslovak Mathematical Journal*, **3** (1953), 111–122. The numbers in text in square brackets refer to works so numbered in Škrášek's listing.

II. SECONDARY LITERATURE. An extensive discussion of Lerch's work in mathematical analysis was published by O. Borůvka *et al.* in *Práce Brněnské základny Československé akademie věd*, **29** (1957), 417–540. A detailed biography of Lerch can be found in an article by L. Frank in *Časopis pro pěstování matematiky*, **78** (1953), 119–137.

O. BORŮVKA

LEREBOULLET, DOMINIQUE-AUGUSTE (*b.* Épinal, France, 19 September 1804; *d.* Strasbourg, France, 5 October 1865), *zoology, embryology*.

Lereboullet was the son of an employee in the administration of indirect taxation at Épinal. After obtaining baccalaureates in letters and sciences at the Collège de Colmar, he spent a year at the University of Freiburg. There he studied German and was introduced to German science, a subject that he later analyzed, over a period of nearly thirty years, for the *Gazette médicale de Paris*. Returning to France, he studied medicine at Strasbourg, then in 1832 obtained permission to study the cholera epidemic at Paris. The data that he thus gathered was incorporated in the thesis with which he obtained the M.D. in the same year.

He immediately entered the Faculty of Sciences at Strasbourg as *préparateur* for G. L. Duvernoy, a friend and former collaborator of Cuvier. When in 1838 Duvernoy was appointed to Cuvier's chair at the Collège de France, Lereboullet (who had in 1837 received the licentiate and in 1838 the doctorate in natural science) succeeded him at Strasbourg in the chair of zoology and animal physiology.

Lereboullet had begun his zoological work by studying the comparative anatomy of vertebrates. His doctoral thesis dealt with the comparative anatomy of the respiratory system, while in another early work, which was awarded a prize by the Academy of Sciences, he examined the comparative anatomy of the genital organs in vertebrates. It was perhaps indicative of the German influence on his work that Lereboullet then took up the study, novel to France, of comparative histology. His memoir on the cellular structure of the liver, for which be was awarded the Portal Prize by the Academy of Medicine in 1851, described how cells are altered in the common pathological condition known as *foie gras*.

In 1849 Lereboullet began his celebrated research in comparative embryology. Having learned to fertilize fish eggs artificially, he was able to examine microscopically the earliest phases of development. In 1853 the Academy of Sciences proposed for competition the problem of comparing the development of a vertebrate with a mollusk or an articulate and Lereboullet chose as research subjects the pike, the perch, and the crayfish. Although he was paid for his work the Academy did not find it adequate to the problem, which was reset in 1856. This time Lereboullet studied the trout, the lizard, and the pond snail, and concluded his memoir with generalizations that satisfied the Academy, which awarded him the prize in 1857.

In his memoir Lereboullet had analyzed all phases of development, beginning with the unfertilized egg. He concluded that the unfertilized egg in all of his subjects appeared to be similar in the first three of Cuvier's four embranchments, but that soon after fertilization the paths of development separated, each embranchment manifesting its own proper characteristics. Finding himself in accord with von Baer

and Henri-Milne Edwards, Lereboullet argued against the doctrine of unity of type and against E. R. A. Serres' recapitulation theory.

While studying the pike, Lereboullet noticed the frequent occurrence of monstrosities. Geoffroy Saint-Hilaire had previously claimed that monsters could be produced at will by the use of external agents, and the Academy set the problem of whether determined monstrosities could be experimentally produced by known physical agents for the subject of a competition in 1860. Lereboullet had begun to make teratological experiments in 1852. He subjected nearly 300,000 pike eggs to such disturbing agents as heat, cold, running water, and brushing, and carefully tabulated his results, noting that neither the fact nor the agent of perturbation had an effect on the number or type of abnormality that occurred. He concluded that abnormalities were most probably inherent in the structure of the germ, rather than caused by outside agents.

Lereboullet divided monsters into two groups (single and double) and seven classes, which he attributed to modifications in the blastodermic thickening and the embryonic bond. He recognized that the thickened edge of the blastoderm—the embryonic ring—gives rise to all embryonic structures and suggested that double monsters develop from two separate points in the blastodermic thickening. For these experiments the Academy gave Lereboullet the Alhumbert Prize, which he shared with Camille Dareste, although they had arrived at opposite theoretical conclusions.

In describing the earliest phases of animal development Lereboullet divided the elements constituting the fertilized egg into plastic elements (deriving from the germinative vesicle) that would eventually produce the cells of "animal life" and nutritive elements (deriving from the vitellus) that would produce the organs of "vegetative life." His work was precisely observed and factual. As a member of the *école de Cuvier*, he avoided theory and rejected the hypotheses of spontaneous generation, unity of type, recapitulation, multiple origin of the human species, and transformism.

Lereboullet was a modest and religious man. He was married; two of his sons later became doctors. He was active in several scientific societies, directed the Museum of Natural History of Strasbourg, and acted as dean of the Faculty of Sciences from 1861 until his death.

BIBLIOGRAPHY

I. ORIGINAL WORKS. A complete list of Lereboullet's publications may be found in Hergott, *Notice sur le docteur*

Lereboullet (Strasbourg, 1866); an incomplete list is in Beaunis, "A. Lereboullet," in *Gazette médicale de Paris* (1865), 797–806. The Royal Society *Catalogue of Scientific Papers*, III, VIII, contains a list of his memoirs. His major publications were *Choléra-morbus observé à Paris et dans le département de la Meuse pendant l'année 1832* (Strasbourg, 1832), his M.D. diss.; *Anatomie comparée de l'appareil respiratoire dans les animaux vertébrés* (Strasbourg, 1838), his D.Sc. diss.; "Recherches sur l'anatomie des organes génitaux des animaux vertébrés," in *Nova acta academiae naturae curiosorum*, **23** (1851), 1–228, also published separately (Breslau, 1851); "Mémoire sur la structure intime du foie et sur la nature de l'altération connue sous le nom de *foie gras*," in *Mémoires de l'Académie de médecine*, **17** (1853), 387–501; "Recherches d'embryologie comparée sur le développement du brochet, de la perche et de l'écrevisse, Académie des Sciences," in *Mémoires présentés par divers savants étrangers*, **17** (1862), 447–805, also published separately (Paris, 1862); "Recherches d'embryologie comparée sur le développement de la truite, du lézard et du limnée," in *Annales des sciences naturelles*, 4th ser., **16** (1861), 113–196; **17** (1862), 89–157; **18** (1862), 87–211; **19** (1863), 5–130; **20** (1863), 5–58, also published separately (Paris, 1863); "Recherches sur les monstruosités du brochet observées dans l'oeuf et sur leur mode de production," *ibid.*, 4th ser., **20** (1863), 5th ser., **1** (1864). "Anatomie philosophique," in *Dictionnaire encyclopédique des sciences médicales*, contains a good summary of Lereboullet's scientific methodology and of his views on contemporary scientific theories.

II. SECONDARY LITERATURE. There is no adequate or readily available biography of Lereboullet. The two most complete accounts of his life and work are listed above. For evaluations of Lereboullet's embryological work see J. Oppenheimer, "Historical Introduction to the Study of Teleostean Development," in *Osiris*, **2** (1936), 124–148, esp. 142–148; and "Some Historical Relationships Between Teratology and Experimental Embryology," in *Bulletin of the History of Medicine*, **42** (1968), 145–159, esp. 151–154.

TOBY A. APPEL

LE ROY, CHARLES (*b.* Paris, France, 12 January 1726; *d.* Paris, 10 December 1779), *physics, meteorology, medicine.*

Le Roy was a member of a distinguished family. His father, Julien, was a celebrated horologist. One of his older brothers, Jean-Baptiste, was an eminent physicist and a member of the Paris Academy of Sciences, and his younger brother, Julien-David, was a noted architect and historian of architecture. Charles received his medical education at the University of Montpellier. After traveling extensively in Italy, he returned to Montpellier as a member of the Faculty of Medicine.

Le Roy was a member of the Royal Academy of Sciences at Montpellier and a corresponding member of the Paris Academy of Sciences. In 1777 he returned to Paris, where he practiced medicine until his death in 1779.

Although a physician and teacher of medicine, Le Roy made his most important scientific contribution in physics. In 1751 he published a theory of evaporation that was to dominate discussions of the topic for more than forty years.

In the early eighteenth century, theories of evaporation were usually couched in the idiom of the prevailing mechanical philosophy. Many theories ascribed the "elevation" of vapors in the air to the specific legerity of water particles. Some scientists believed that the molecules of a liquid could be expanded by heat until their density became less than that of the atmosphere, at which point they would rise into the air rather like vacuum-filled balloons. Followers of Descartes thought that during evaporation "subtile matter" infiltrated particles of a liquid, thus reducing their specific gravity and causing them to rise into the ambient air. Other theories, especially those formulated by the followers of Newton, depended upon the concept of attractive forces acting at a distance. Desaguliers, for example, thought that evaporation was caused by atmospheric electricity attracting water particles into the air.

The problem with these early mechanical theories was that they were based upon untestable hypotheses concerning the behavior of submicroscopic particles. To invent an explanation of this kind, it was necessary only to conceive a plausible mechanism and present it as fact. To be sure, such mechanical conceptions could not be disproved—but they could not be proved either.

The value of Le Roy's theory was in its radically different approach to the problem of evaporation. Rather than attempting to deduce an explanation from an imagined account of the behavior of unseen particles, he presented instead a simple analogy between observable phenomena. Vapors, he said, are to the air as dissolved salts are to water. Le Roy made no attempt to explain the mechanism of solution itself, which he considered beyond the capabilities of the science of his day. It was sufficient merely to show that the phenomena of solution and evaporation were analogous and thus avoid useless debate over alternative mechanical hypotheses. All empirical generalizations concerning evaporation and vapors could be accounted for by referring to the analogous generalizations concerning the behavior of solution. For example, the fact that improved circulation and constant renewing of the air increases the rate of evaporation is analogous to the fact that stirring a liquid increases the rate at which salts dissolve in it. Heating will also increase the rates of both evaporation and dissolution, whereas cooling will retard both processes. Furthermore, just as a liquid may be saturated with a salt, so too may the atmosphere be saturated with water; and just as cooling a saturated solution will cause precipitation of the dissolved salt, so too will cooling a saturated atmosphere cause precipitation of water. In fact, the use of the word "precipitation" in meteorological contexts seems to be a linguistic remnant of Le Roy's once-popular theory.

The major weakness of Le Roy's solution theory of vapors was its inability to explain convincingly the widely known phenomenon of evaporation *in vacuo*. Clearly, liquids could not dissolve themselves in mere nothing. Le Roy's attempted explanation of this anomaly was farfetched. He knew from Stephen Hales's famous experiments that water contained a large quantity of dissolved air. Le Roy supposed that when water was placed in a vacuum apparatus, the air came out of it and dissolved the very water in which it had itself previously been dissolved.

There is nothing to indicate that Le Roy undertook any but the most casual experiments to substantiate his theory. He seems to have derived most of his empirical generalizations from everyday observation and from the writings of others. Indeed, the theory itself was probably anticipated by other scientists, some of whom Le Roy mentioned in his articles. Le Roy's version of the solution theory was, however, the most clearly and completely developed, and through its publication in the *Encyclopédie* it became widely known and accepted despite its one rather obvious weakness. Other versions of the theory were subsequently published in Britain by Benjamin Franklin and Henry Home, Lord Kames.

Although the solution theory of vapors has proved untenable, Le Roy nevertheless performed an invaluable service to science. By clearing away the arcane mechanisms that had been conceived by his predecessors and presenting instead a clear, testable hypothesis, he prepared the way for the important advancements in the theory of evaporation made by Lavoisier and Dalton. In particular, by focusing on the anomaly of evaporation *in vacuo*, he directed attention to a phenomenon that was to prove a key to the understanding of the gaseous state. In his insistence on the use of analogy instead of mechanism, he anticipated a mode of scientific explanation that was to prove remarkably fruitful in the hands of more thoughtful experimentalists, and notably in Lavoisier's. Finally, the theory itself was, for its time, a good one. It proved useful in most instances and

provided an acceptable conceptual framework for dealing with many phenomena in the realms of meteorology, physics, and chemistry. The theory also provided a criterion for distinguishing true vapors from smokes and exhalations: true vapors, like true solutions, are perfectly transparent; whereas smokes and exhalations, like liquid suspensions, are cloudy.

In addition to his work on evaporation, Le Roy also communicated to the Academy a number of other observations. While traveling in Italy, he experimented on the asphyxiating gas produced in the Grotto del Cane, near Naples, and he attempted to provide an explanation for marine phosphorescence in the Mediterranean Sea. During his tenure at the Faculty of Medicine at Montpellier, he wrote extensive treatises on mineral waters, physiology, medicine, and chemistry.

BIBLIOGRAPHY

I. ORIGINAL WORKS. Le Roy's principal works are "Mémoire sur l'élévation et la suspension de l'eau dans l'air," in *Histoire et mémoires de l'Académie Royale des Sciences* (1751), pp. 481–518; "Évaporation," in *Encyclopédie*, VI (Paris, 1756), pp. 123–130; and *Mélanges de physique et de médecine* (Paris, 1771).

II. SECONDARY LITERATURE. For biographical references, see the *éloges* cited in *Nouvelle biographie générale*, XXX (Paris, 1862), 892; and L. Dulieu, "Un Parisien professeur à l'Université de Medecine de Montpellier: Charles Le Roy (1726–1779)," in *Revue d'histoire des sciences et leurs applications*, 6 (1953), 50–59. On eighteenth-century theories of evaporation, see S. A. Dyment, "Some Eighteenth Century Ideas Concerning Aqueous Vapor and Evaporation," in *Annals of Science*, 2 (1937), 465–473; and J. B. Gough, "Nouvelle contribution à l'évolution des idées de Lavoisier sur la nature de l'air et sur la calcination des métaux," in *Archives internationales d'histoire des sciences*, 22, no. 89 (July-Dec. 1969), 267–275. On the solution theory, see Benjamin Franklin, "Physical and Meteorological Observations, Conjectures, and Suppositions," in *Letters and Papers on Philosophical Subjects* (London, 1769); and Lord Kames's article on evaporation in *Essays and Observations, Physical and Literary, Read Before a Society in Edinburgh*, III (Edinburgh, 1772), pp. 80 ff.

J. B. GOUGH

LE ROY, ÉDOUARD (*b*. Paris, France, 18 June 1870; *d*. Paris, 9 November 1954), *mathematics, philosophy.*

Le Roy's father worked for the Compagnie Transatlantique for several years and then established his own business outfitting ships in Le Havre. Le Roy studied at home under the guidance of a tutor and was admitted in 1892 to the École Normale Supérieure. He became an *agrégé* in 1895 and earned a doctor of science degree in 1898; his thesis attracted the attention of Henri Poincaré. Until 1921 he taught mathematics classes that prepared students for the leading scientific schools. From 1924 to 1940 he was *chargé de conférences* at the Faculty of Sciences in Paris.

Although trained as a mathematician, Le Roy's enthusiastic discovery of the "new philosophy" of Bergson, to which he devoted a book in 1912, led him to teach philosophy. Bergson appointed Le Roy his *suppléant* in the chair of modern philosophy at the Collège de France (1914–1920). Named professor in 1921, Le Roy taught there until 1941; several of his published works are transcriptions of his courses. He was elected to the Académie des Sciences Morales et Politiques in 1919, and he entered the Académie Française as Bergson's successor in 1945.

A Catholic and a scientist, Le Roy had, in his youth, put forth theses in the philosophy of religion and the philosophy of science that provoked lively polemics. In "Qu'est-ce qu'un dogme?" (*La quinzaine*, 16 Apr. 1905) he emphasized the opposition between dogma and the body of positive knowledge. Dogma, he asserted, has a negative sense: it excludes and condemns certain errors rather than determining the truth in a positive fashion. Above all a dogma has a practical sense—that is its primary value.

Le Roy was thus involved in the quarrels precipitated by "modernist philosophy," which was condemned in the encyclical *Pascendi* by Pope Pius X in 1907, and his *Le problème de Dieu* (1929) was placed on the Index in June 1931. In the philosophy of science, Le Roy had proclaimed, in articles in *Revue de métaphysique et de morale* (1899, 1900), that facts are less established than constituted and that, far from being received passively by the mind, they are to some extent created by it. These paradoxical statements excited a certain interest through Poincaré's criticism of them in *La valeur de la science* (Paris, 1906, ch. 10).

While wishing to defend and justify the Bergsonian notion of creative evolution, Le Roy set forth his own philosophy of life, a "doctrine of authentically spiritualist inspiration" that sought a "restoration of finality" and respected the idea of creation. Le Roy's views were similar in many ways to those of his friend Teilhard de Chardin. According to Le Roy, there exists at the basis of life—as the major cause of its changes and progress—a psychic factor, a genuine power of invention. To recapture the activity of this factor one must consider the sole contemporary being —that is, Man—in which the power of creative evolution is still vital. Man must be observed in his capacity as inventor in order to return, by means of retrospective analogy, to the paleontological past. Biosphere and noosphere are the great moments of evolution. At the origin of the noosphere we must conceive a phenomenon *sui generis* of vital transformation affecting the entire biosphere: hominization. Humanity then appears as a new order of reality, sustaining a relationship with the lower forms of life analogous to that between these lower forms and inanimate matter. Man then no longer seems a paradoxical excrescence but becomes the key to transformist explanations. According to the "lesson that emerges from Christianity," man's intuition of a spiritual beyond and the ideal of an interior and mystic life show that we must form a concept of *Homo spiritualis* distinct from *Homo faber* and *Homo sapiens.*

In analyzing the history and philosophy of science, Le Roy likewise accorded a central position to the notion of invention, itself intimately linked to that of intuition, since intuitive thought is always, to some extent, inventive. True mathematical intuition is operative intuition; and the analyst should everywhere attempt to bring to consciousness the operative action perceived in its dynamic indivisibility. The transition from physics to microphysics clearly illuminates "the primary role of a factor of inventive energy in the innermost recesses of thought." Reason itself is in a state of becoming and must gradually be invented.

What will regulate this invention? An absolutely primary foundation must be sought which will be indisputable in every regard and, at the same time, dynamic and vital. Synthesizing twenty-five years of teaching, Le Roy in the *Essai d'une philosophie première*, his last course at the Collège de France, presented the major steps of such a search, the chief concern of which is to satisfy "the demands of idealism."

BIBLIOGRAPHY

I. ORIGINAL WORKS. Le Roy's principal publications are "Sur l'intégration des équations de la chaleur," in *Annales scientifiques de l'École normale supérieure*, **14** (1897), 379–465, and *ibid.*, **15** (1898), 9–178, his doctoral diss.; *Dogme et critique* (Paris, 1906); *Une philosophie nouvelle: Henri Bergson* (Paris, 1912); *L'exigence idéaliste et le fait de l'évolution* (Paris, 1927); *Les origines humaines et l'évolution de l'intelligence* (Paris, 1928); *La pensée intuitive*, 2 vols. (Paris, 1929–1930); *Le problème de Dieu* (Paris, 1929); and *Introduction à l'étude du problème religieux* (Paris, 1944).

After Le Roy's death his son, Georges Le Roy, published the lectures his father had given at the Collège de France as *Essai d'une philosophie première, l'exigence idéaliste et l'exigence morale*, 2 vols. (Paris, 1956–1958); and *La pensée mathématique pure* (Paris, 1960). The "Notice bibliographique," in *Études philosophiques* (Apr. 1955), 207–210, records many of Le Roy's works.

II. SECONDARY LITERATURE. See the following, listed chronologically: S. Gagnebin, *La philosophie de l'intuition. Essai sur les idées de Mr Édouard Le Roy* (Paris, 1912); L. Weber, "Une philosophie de l'invention. M. Édouard Le Roy," in *Revue de métaphysique et de morale*, **39** (1932), 59–86, 253–292; F. Olgiati, *Édouard Le Roy e il problema di Dio* (Milan, 1929); J. Lacroix, "Édouard Le Roy, philosophe de l'invention," in *Études philosophiques* (Apr. 1955), 189–205; G. Maire, "La philosophie d'Edouard Le Roy," *ibid.*, **27** (1972), 201–220; M. Tavares de Miranda, *Théorie de la vérité chez Édouard Le Roy* (Paris–Recife, Brazil, 1957); and G. Bachelard, *L'engagement rationaliste* (Paris, 1972), 155–168.

Biographical information is in E. Rideau, "Édouard Le Roy," in *Études*, no. 245 (April 1945), 246–255; and in the addresses delivered at the Académie Française by A. Chaumeix at the time of Le Roy's reception on 18 Oct. 1945, in *Institut de France, Publications diverses*, no. 18 (1945); and by H. Daniel-Rops when he succeeded Le Roy at the Academy, *ibid.*, no. 8 (1956).

On Le Roy's religious philosophy, see the article by E. Rideau cited above and A.-D. Sertillanges, *Le christianisme et les philosophes*, II (Paris, 1941), 402–419.

In an app. to *Bergson et Teilhard de Chardin* (Paris, 1963), pp. 655–659, M. B. Madaule discusses Le Roy's friendship with Teilhard, the large area of agreement in their views, and their correspondence.

Concerning the polemic with Poincaré, the ways in which Le Roy weakened his first statements, and his final homage to Poincaré, see J. Abelé, "Le Roy et la philosophie des sciences," in *Études*, no. 284 (April 1955), 106–112.

M. Serres discusses Le Roy's *La pensée mathématique pure* in "La querelle des anciens et des modernes," in his *Hermès ou la communication* (Paris, 1968), pp. 46–77. While terming the work a "monument of traditional epistemology," he shows how Le Roy, in applying his method of analysis to a mathematics that was already outdated, failed completely to consider "modern mathematics."

E. COUMET

LE ROY, JEAN-BAPTISTE (*b.* Paris, France, 15 August 1720; *d.* Paris, 21 January 1800), *physics, scientific instrumentation.*

Son of the renowned clockmaker Julien Le Roy, Jean-Baptiste Le Roy was one of four brothers to achieve scientific prominence in Enlightenment France; the others were Charles Le Roy (medicine and chemistry), Julien-David Le Roy (architecture), and Pierre Le Roy (chronometry). Elected to the Académie Royale des Sciences in 1751 as *adjoint géomètre*, Le Roy played an active role in technical as well as

administrative aspects of French science for the next half-century. He was elected *pensionnaire mécanicien* in 1770 and director of the Academy for 1773 and 1778, and became both a fellow of the Royal Society and a member of the American Philosophical Society in 1773.

Le Roy's major field of enquiry was electricity, a subject on which European opinion was much divided at mid-century. The most prominent controversy engaged the proponents of the Abbé Nollet's doctrine of two distinct streams of electric fluids (outflowing and inflowing) and the partisans of Benjamin Franklin's concept of a single electric fluid. This debate intensified in France in 1753 with an attack on Franklin's views by Nollet. Le Roy, later a friend and correspondent of Franklin, defended his single-fluid theory and offered considerable experimental evidence in support thereof. He played an important role in the dissemination of Franklin's ideas, stressing particularly their practical applications, and published many memoirs on electrical machines and theory in the annual *Histoires* and *Mémoires* of the Academy and in the *Journal de physique.*

A regular contributor to the *Encyclopédie*, Le Roy wrote articles dealing with scientific instruments. The most important of these included comprehensive treatments of "Horlogerie," "Télescope," and "Électromètre" (in which Le Roy claimed priority for the invention of the electrometer). He also promoted the use of lightning rods in France, urged that the Academy support technical education, and was active in hospital and prison reform. After the Revolutionary suppression of royal academies, Le Roy was appointed to the first class of the Institut National (*section de mécanique*) at its formation in 1795.

BIBLIOGRAPHY

I. ORIGINAL WORKS. Le Roy wrote no extended treatise on electricity. His more important publications include "Mémoire sur l'électricité, où l'on montre par une suite d'expériences qu'il y a deux espèces d'électricités, l'une produite par la condensation du fluide électrique, & l'autre par sa raréfaction," in *Mémoires de l'Académie royale des sciences* (1753), 447–474; "Mémoire sur un phénomène électrique intéressant et qui n'avoit pas encore été observé; ou sur la différence des distances auxquelles partent les étincelles entre deux corps métalliques de figures différentes, selon que l'un de ces deux corps est électrifié, & que l'autre lui est présenté," *ibid.* (1766), 541–546; "Mémoire sur les verges ou barres métalliques, destinées à garantir les édifices des effets de la foudre," *ibid.* (1770), 53–67; "Mémoire sur une machine à électriser d'une espèce nouvelle," *ibid.*, pt. 1 (1772), 499–512; and "Mémoire sur la forme des barres ou des conducteurs métalliques destinées à préserver les édifices des effets de la foudre, en transmettant son feu à la terre," *ibid.* (1773), 671–686.

For Le Roy's ideas on hospitals, see *Précis d'un ouvrage sur les hôpitaux, dans lequel on expose les principes résultant des observations de physique et de médecine qu'on doit avoir en vue dans la construction de ces édifices, avec un projet d'hôpital disposé d'après ces principes* (Paris, n.d.).

II. SECONDARY LITERATURE. There is no biography of Le Roy. Details concerning his life and work can be found in Louis Lefèvre-Gineau, *Funérailles du citoyen le Roy* (Paris, 1801); and F. Hoefer, ed., *Nouvelle biographie générale*, XXX (1859), 891. Franklin's letters to Le Roy are in Albert Henry Smyth, ed., *The Writings of Benjamin Franklin*, 10 vols. (New York, 1905–1907), *passim.*

MARTIN FICHMAN

LESAGE, GEORGE-LOUIS (*b.* Geneva, Switzerland, 13 June 1724; *d.* Geneva, 9 November 1803), *physics.*

Lesage's father, also named George-Louis, was a distinguished teacher of mathematics and physics as well as a moral philosopher and theologian. Born in Conches, in Normandy, of a notorious Huguenot family, he was exiled to England at the age of eight to escape the religious persecutions in France. He married Anne-Marie Camp in 1722 and settled in Geneva shortly before the birth of his only son.

The elder Lesage instructed his son in the classics and the rudiments of mathematics and science. At the *collège* in Geneva Lesage studied physics with Jean-Louis Calandrani and mathematics with Gabriel Cramer.

Lesage wanted to become a philosopher; but his father, desiring that he should find more remunerative employment, determined instead that his son should become a physician. Lesage reluctantly attended medical school at Basel. After a brief sojourn in Paris, he returned to Geneva and attempted to take up the practice of medicine. The city authorities intervened— as the son of an immigrant, Lesage was not qualified. At first he tried to raise the money to purchase bourgeois status by entering the prize essay contest of the Paris Academy of Sciences. He failed and thus gave up medicine entirely and became a teacher of mathematics.

Lesage's reputation derived largely from his efforts to explain mechanistically the cause of gravitational phenomena. Although Newton's law had finally been accepted by Continental scientists, it still presented serious intellectual difficulties. Every particle of matter in the universe supposedly attracted every other inversely as the squares of the distances separating them and directly as the products of their masses. Many found it inconceivable, however, that lumps of inanimate matter could somehow divine the presence of their neighbors, measure the appropriate distances and masses, and attract each other across the intervening space. The absurdity of such a notion was manifest, especially to Continental scientists imbued with the precepts of the Cartesian mechanical philosophy. Yet Newton's law of gravity had been verified in innumerable instances and without exception. In the minds of most eighteenth-century scientists, the validity of the Newtonian law was unquestionable; but because of their commitment to the mechanical philosophy, they generally—albeit often tacitly—assumed that some underlying impulsive mechanism was responsible for the so-called Newtonian attraction. Newton himself had attempted to provide mechanical explanations of his law but without much success.

Inspired by Lucretius' *De rerum natura* and doubtless also by the pervasive climate of Cartesianism, Lesage set about the formidable task of explaining the Newtonian law of attraction in terms of the mechanical philosophy. His basic system rested upon his conception of "otherworldly particles" (*particules ultramondaines*), so-called because of their exemption from the law of gravity. These gravitational particles were presumed to be extremely small Lucretian atoms that moved in every direction and at very high velocity. Any isolated mass of ordinary matter (its atoms were presumed to be much larger than those composing the gravitational fluid) would not be moved by the impacts of the gravitational particles since they would impinge on it from all directions at once. (Lesage did allow for slight oscillation caused by temporary imbalance of forces, rather like the Brownian motion of particles in a gas or liquid.) Two masses of ordinary matter, however, would block some of the particles coming from either direction along the lines connecting the parts of one with those of the other. Each mass, in effect, would cast a kind of "gravitational shadow" on the other; and the resulting disequilibrium of force would impel the two bodies together, thus giving the illusion of an attraction between the masses. The greater the distance between the two bodies, the less intense would be the effect of the mutual gravitational shadow. Indeed, Lesage maintained that it would vary inversely as the square of the distance, in accordance with the Newtonian law. Similarly, the larger the mass of the body, the more gravitational particles would be intercepted and the greater would be the disequilibrium of force. To make the impulsive force vary with the mass rather than with the surface area of the body was always the most difficult problem faced by those who attempted to adduce mechanical explanations of the Newtonian law. By making his bodies extremely porous and quite large relative to their constituent atoms, Lesage was able at least to achieve an approximation of the proper relation between mass and gravitational force.

Using this ingenious mechanism, Lesage attempted to explain not only gravitation but also chemical affinity and corporeal cohesion. His system was not widely accepted among his contemporaries. It was too burdened with *ad hoc* assumptions, and because certain parameters (the size of the various atoms and the mean free path of the particles composing the gravitational fluid) could not be established, his theory was not subject to rigorous mathematical analysis. In short, his theory was not unlike the clever but untestable mechanical hypotheses that had burdened physics in the previous century. As a result Lesage's work was less criticized than neglected.

Despite this neglect and despite the fact that he published relatively little in his lifetime (although he did, in fact, write a great deal) Lesage acquired a fairly extensive reputation, largely through his correspondence with the great natural philosophers and mathematicians of his age. He was elected a correspondent of the Paris Academy of Sciences on 28 February 1761, and after the reorganization of the Academy became a first-class corresponding member on 12 September 1803.

BIBLIOGRAPHY

The only major work published during Lesage's lifetime was his *Essai de chimie mécanique* (Rouen, 1758), the main source for his explanation of Newtonian attraction.

On Lesage's life and work, see Pierre Prévost, *Notice de la vie et des écrits de George-Louis Le Sage de Genève* (Geneva, 1805), which contains an extensive and detailed biography, pp. 1–184; a list of his shorter published articles and letters, pp. 91–95; a list of his many unpublished large works and an account of their contents, pp. 95–101; "Lucrèce Neutonien," one of Lesage's many MS works on gravitation, with a conveniently succinct exposition of his system; and a portion of Lesage's large correspondence with contemporary scientists, philosophers, and mathematicians, pp. 189–502.

J. B. GOUGH

LESLEY, J. PETER (*b*. Philadelphia, Pennsylvania, 17 September 1819; *d*. Milton, Massachusetts, 1 June 1903), *geology*.

Fourth in a line of Peter Lesleys and first son of Peter III and Elizabeth Oswald Allen, Peter Lesley was a delicate, introverted, and bookish youngster. He entered the University of Pennsylvania at fifteen and graduated Phi Beta Kappa in 1838. Frail health frustrated his plans to continue directly in school studying for the Presbyterian ministry, so at his father's urging he sought outdoor employment. He joined the first state survey of Pennsylvania, directed by Henry Darwin Rogers, and passed the years 1838–1841 surveying the bituminous and anthracite coal regions.

Although he was untrained and inexperienced when he entered fieldwork, his insights into the complicated geology of the state won him Rogers' praise. When in 1841 the survey was abandoned for lack of funds, Lesley returned to his studies at Princeton Theological Seminary. He maintained contact with Rogers, however, and when the Seminary was in recess he helped him with the preparation of maps and sections for the final survey report.

Lesley was licensed to preach by the Philadelphia Presbytery in 1844 and took up pastoral work the following year after traveling in Europe. He began his brief career in the ministry as an avowed conservative on questions of religious doctrine. Subsequent exposure to the liberal opinions of Rogers, Agassiz, Emerson, Lyell, and other associates in Boston, where he had gone to assist Rogers, radicalized the young clergyman to such an extent that he gave up the ministry altogether and became a geologist in 1852.

His first book, *A Manual of Coal and Its Topography*, has been called "the most important matter of the decade, geographically considered" (Davis [1919], 183). It is an attempt to group the Appalachian coal beds systematically, to correlate them with coal measures in Europe and elsewhere, and to emphasize the importance of topographical geology in Pennsylvania. Lesley proffered a catastrophic explanation of Appalachian landforms, although in later works, when his break with the ministry was not so fresh, this approach was replaced by uniformitarianism.

His second major work, *The Iron Manufacturers' Guide* (1859), contains information and statistics on ironworks as well as a detailed geological discussion of iron deposits in Pennsylvania and elsewhere. The preface is notable for its intemperate personal attack on Rogers, who, Lesley felt, had failed to credit his young apprentices on the first state survey. Accusing Rogers of scientific theft and labeling him an "imposture," Lesley sought to rectify the indignity of being mentioned only briefly in Rogers' preface.

When in 1873 he himself became director of the second state survey, Lesley was careful to see that each fieldworker be given due credit for his work. He often altered field reports and maps or added footnotes to his apprentices' texts before sending them to press; he felt that doing so would clarify the material and protect the authors from unfavorable criticism. Lesley's practice caused understandable consternation among his staff. As director of the survey he examined every line, map, and illustration in the seventy-seven volumes of text and thirty-four atlases. Lesley attempted to distill all this for the final summary, but his health broke under the strain and he was forced to delegate responsibility to others.

Although christened Peter Lesley, he disliked his first name and in 1850 added the initial "J." from "Junior" and began signing his work "J. P. Lesley." Toward the end of his life he reverted to J. Peter Lesley.

BIBLIOGRAPHY

I. Original Works. Lesley's most important contributions are *A Manual of Coal and Its Topography* (Philadelphia, 1856); *The Iron Manufacturers' Guide to Furnaces, Forges and Rollings Mills of the United States* (New York, 1859); and the *Second Geological Survey of Pennsylvania Report*: *A Historical Sketch of Geological Explorations in Pennsylvania and Other States* (Harrisburg, Pa., 1876); and *Final Report: A Summary Description of the Geology of Pennsylvania*, 3 vols. (1892–1895).

II. Secondary Literature. A two-volume biography was edited by his eldest daughter, Mary Lesley Ames, as *Life and Letters of Peter and Susan Lesley* (New York, 1909). For biographical notices see W. M. Davis, "Biographical Memoir of J. P. Lesley," in *Biographical Memoirs. National Academy of Sciences*, 8 (1919), 152–240; P. Frazer, "J. Peter Lesley," in *American Geologist*, 32 (1903), 133–136; A. Geikie, "Notice of J. P. Lesley," in *Quarterly Journal of the Geological Society of London*, 60 (1904), xlix–lv; B. S. Lyman, "Biographical Sketch of J. Peter Lesley," in *Transactions of the American Institute of Mining Engineers*, 34 (1903), 726–739; G. P. Merrill, "Peter Lesley," in *Dictionary of American Biography;* and J. J. Stevenson, "Memoir of J. Peter Lesley," in *Bulletin of the Geological Society of America*, 15 (1904), 532–541.

Martha B. Kendall

LESLIE, JOHN (*b.* Largo, Scotland, 16 April 1766; *d.* Coates, near Cupar, Fife, Scotland, 3 November 1832), *natural philosophy.*

Leslie was one of three sons born to a poor cabinetmaker, Robert Leslie, and his wife, Anne Carstairs. At the age of thirteen he entered the University of St. Andrews, where he studied mathematics under Nicholas Vilant, who also taught John Playfair and James Ivory. In 1785, Leslie went to Edinburgh to continue his studies with Joseph Black, John Robison, and the moral philosopher Dugald Stewart, from whom he derived a continuing interest in the philosophy and history of science. From 1790 to 1804, when his major work, *An Experimental Inquiry Into the Nature and Propagation of Heat*, appeared, Leslie supported himself by working as a science tutor to Thomas Wedgwood, son of the Etruria potter, Josiah, and by writing for the *Monthly Review*. Leslie became professor of mathematics at the University of Edinburgh in 1805, over the protests of the local clergymen that his acceptance of Hume's notions of causality made him an atheist; and in 1819 he was promoted to the chair of natural philosophy. Throughout his life Leslie refused membership in all British scientific societies because he felt slighted when the Royal Society of London refused his first communication in 1791, but he was made a corresponding member of the Paris Académie Royale des Sciences in 1820 and was knighted in 1832 for his scientific work.

Leslie's *Experimental Inquiry* (1804) established several fundamental laws of heat radiation: that the emissivity and absorptivity for any surface are equal, that the emissivity of a surface increases with the decrease of reflectivity, and that the intensity of heat radiated from a surface is proportional to the sine of the angle of the rays to the surface. The book also played a major role in the early nineteenth-century argument about whether heat was a form of matter or a mode of motion. Leslie's experiments showed that heat, unlike light, was not directly transmitted through transparent solids. Since Leslie embraced a corpuscular theory, he incorrectly interpreted the apparent blockage of heat radiation as evidence that heat was composed of particles much larger than those of light. He borrowed from James Hutton the basic notion that heat was a compound formed by the union of light particles with ordinary particles of matter. François Delaroche later showed that Leslie's failure to detect direct transmission of heat through solids was a result of using only low-temperature heat sources whose radiation was absorbed by the solid screens. In the meantime, Leslie's puzzling experimental results had stimulated further investigations of diathermancy and the nature of radiant heat.

Although Leslie is best known for his heat studies, his interests were wide-ranging. In 1791, for example, he wrote a paper which analyzed the leakage of static electricity from charged bodies through different conducting paths. First he theorized that the quantity of electricity conducted to ground per unit time I would be proportional to the instantaneous intensity of the source—that is, the quantity of electricity per unit volume at any moment V—where it joined the conductor. In addition, he argued that the amount communicated per unit time would be a function of the composition of the conductor ρ, that it would be proportional to the cross-sectional area of the conductor α, and that it would be inversely proportional to the length L of the conductor. In modern symbols, $I = V\rho(\alpha/L)$. Next he provided a limited confirmation of his theory by varying the length, composition, and cross sections of conductors discharging a bank of Leyden jars. Finally, he showed geometrically that one could replace a series of conducting segments of varying compositions, lengths, and cross sections with a single equivalent conductor, and he suggested that similar geometrical methods could be used to simplify "more intricate cases" such as those in which parallel conductors were used simultaneously to produce the discharge. Thus he prefigured many of Georg Ohm's considerations of voltaic electricity.

His systematic study, begun in 1793, of temperature-density relations in gases allowed him to propose a widely discussed formula for the decrease of temperature with increasing height in the atmosphere. In 1800, he announced the discovery of the wet- and dry-bulb hygrometer and provided an essentially correct theory of how the instrument operates. In 1802 he presented the first correct interpretation of capillary action, thus stimulating the work of Thomas Young and James Ivory. Finally, in 1810, Leslie showed that it was possible to attain very low temperatures by evaporating water in the presence of a desiccant in an evacuated receiver, thus providing the principle exploited by Ferdinand Carré in creating the first laboratory ice machines.

In his theoretical work Leslie emphasized the need for systematic explanations; he had little patience with the English love of what he called "dull empiricism." In conformity with this deep interest in theoretical schemes, Leslie was a principal proponent of the point atomist theory of Bošković.

BIBLIOGRAPHY

I. ORIGINAL WORKS. Leslie wrote ten book-length works, twenty-one journal articles, at least thirty-seven reviews, and sixteen encyclopedia articles. His most important books are *An Experimental Inquiry Into the Nature and Propagation of Heat* (London, 1804); *A Short Account of Experiments and Instruments Depending on the Relations of Air to Heat and Moisture* (Edinburgh, 1813); and *The Philosophy of Arithmetic* (Edinburgh, 1817). Leslie's important historical sketch of the exact sciences in the eighteenth century is most widely available in Dugald Stewart, Sir James Mackintosh, John Playfair, and John Leslie, *Dissertations on the History of Metaphysical and Ethical, and of Mathematical and Physical Science* (Edinburgh, 1835).

His more important articles include "Description of a Hygrometer and Photometer," in Nicholson's *Journal of Natural Philosophy*, **3** (1800), 461–467; "On Capillary Action," in *Philosophical Magazine*, **14** (1802), 193–205; "Méthode nouvelle de produire et d'entretenir la congelation," in *Annales de chimie et de physique*, **78** (1811), 177–182; "On Heat and Climate," in *Annals of Philosophy*, **14** (1819), 5–27, first read to the Royal Society of London in 1793; and "Observations on Electrical Theories," in *Edinburgh Philosophical Journal*, **11** (1824), 1–39, read to the Royal Society of Edinburgh in 1792.

II. SECONDARY LITERATURE. The only significant published biographical sketch is Macvey Napier, "Leslie, Sir John," in *Encyclopaedia Britannica*, 7th ed. (1842), VIII, 242–252. For more detailed information and bibliography see Richard Olson's thesis, "Sir John Leslie: 1766–1832; A Study of the Pursuit of the Exact Sciences in the Scottish Enlightenment" (Harvard, 1967).

RICHARD G. OLSON

LEŚNIEWSKI, STANISŁAW (*b*. Serpukhov, Russia, 18 March 1886; *d*. Warsaw, Poland, 13 May 1939), *philosophy of mathematics*.

After studying philosophy at various German universities, Leśniewski received the Ph.D. under Kazimierz Twardowski at Lvov in 1912. From 1919 until his death he held the chair of philosophy of mathematics at the University of Warsaw and, with Jan Łukasiewicz, inspired and directed research at the Warsaw school of logic. As a student Leśniewski studied the works of John Stuart Mill and Edmund Husserl, but through the influence of Łukasiewicz he soon turned to mathematical logic and began to study the *Principia* and the writings of Gottlob Frege and Ernst Schröder. A thorough and painstaking analysis of Russell's antinomy of the class of all those classes which are not members of themselves led Leśniewski to the construction of a system of logic and of the foundations of mathematics remarkable for its originality, elegance, and comprehensiveness. It consists of three theories, which he called prototheic, ontology, and mereology.

The standard system of prototheic, which is the most comprehensive logic of propositions, is based on a single axiom; and the functor of equivalence, "if and only if," occurs in it as the only undefined term. The directives of prototheic include (1) three rules of inference: substitution, detachment, and the distribution of the universal quantifier; (2) the rule of protothetical definition; and (3) the rule of protothetical extensionality. Prototethic presupposes no more fundamental theory, whereas all other deductive theories which are not parts of protothetic must be based on it or on a part of it.

Ontology is obtained by subjoining ontological axioms to protothetic, adapting the directives of protothetic to them, and allowing for a rule of ontological definition and a rule of ontological extensionality. The standard system of ontology is based on a single ontological axiom, in which the functor of singular inclusion, the copula "is," occurs as the only undefined term. Ontology comprises traditional logic and counterparts of the calculus of predicates, the calculus of classes, and the calculus of relations, including the theory of identity.

By subjoining mereological axioms to ontology and adapting the ontological directives to them, we obtain mereology, which is a theory of part-whole relations. The standard system of mereology, with the functor "proper or improper part of" as the only undefined term, can then be based on a single mereological axiom. No specifically mereological directives are involved. While ontology yields the foundations of arithmetic, mereology is the cornerstone of the foundations of geometry.

Leśniewski formulated the directives of his systems with unprecedented precision. In the art of formalizing deductive theories he has remained unsurpassed. Yet the theories that he developed never ceased for him to be interpreted theories, intended to embody a very general, and hence philosophically interesting, description of reality.

BIBLIOGRAPHY

I. ORIGINAL WORKS. Leśniewski's writings include "O podstawach matematyki" ("On the Foundations of Mathematics"), in *Przegląd filozoficzny*, **30** (1927), 164–206; **31** (1928), 261–291; **32** (1929), 60–101; **33** (1930), 77–105, 142–170, with a discussion of the Russellian antinomy and an exposition of mereology; "Grundzüge eines neuen Systems der Grundlagen der Mathematik," in *Fundamenta mathematicae*, **14** (1929), 1–81, which gives an account of the origin and development of protothetic and contains the statement of protothetical directives; "Über die Grundlagen der Ontologie," in *Comptes rendus des séances de la Société des sciences et des lettres de Varsovie*, Cl. III, **23** (1930), 111–132, containing the statement of the directives of ontology; "Über Definitionen in der sogenannten Theorie der Deduktion," *ibid.*, **24** (1931), 289–309, with the statement of the rules of inference and the rule of definition for a system of the classical calculus of propositions; and *Einleitende Bemerkungen zur Fortsetzung meiner Mitteilung u.d. T. "Grundzüge eines neuen Systems der Grundlagen der Mathematik"* (Warsaw, 1938), which includes a discussion of certain problems concerning protothetic. The last two works are available in an English trans. in Storrs McCall, ed., *Polish Logic 1920–1939* (Oxford, 1967), pp. 116–169, 170–187. *Grundzüge eines neuen Systems der Grundlagen der Mathematik § 12* (Warsaw, 1938) offers the deduction of an axiom system of the classical calculus of propositions from a single axiom of protothetic.

II. SECONDARY LITERATURE. See T. Kotarbiński, *La logique en Pologne* (Rome, 1959); C. Lejewski, "A Contribution to Leśniewski's Mereology," in *Polskie towarzystwo naukowe na obszyźnie. Rocznik*, **5** (1955), 43–50; "A New Axiom of Mereology," *ibid.*, **6** (1956), 65–70; "On Leśniewski's Ontology," in *Ratio*, **1** (1958), 150–176; "A Note on a Problem Concerning the Axiomatic Foundations of Mereology," in *Notre Dame Journal of Formal Logic*, **4** (1963), 135–139; "A Single Axiom for the Mereological Notion of Proper Part," *ibid.*, **8** (1967), 279–285; and "Consistency of Leśniewski's Mereology," in *Journal of Symbolic Logic*, **34** (1969), 321–328; E. C. Luschei, *The Logical Systems of Leśniewski* (Amsterdam, 1962), a comprehensive and reliable presentation of the foundations of the systems constructed by Leśniewski; J. Słupecki, "St. Leśniewski's Protothetics," in *Studia logica*, **1** (1953), 44–112; "S. Leśniewski's Calculus of Names," *ibid.*, **3** (1955), 7–76, which concerns ontology; "Towards a Generalised Mereology of Leśniewski," *ibid.*, **8** (1958), 131–163; B. Sobociński, "O kolejnych uproszczeniach aksjomatyki 'ontologji' Prof. St. Leśniewskiego" ("On Successive Simplifications of the Axiom System of Prof. S. Leśniewski's 'Ontology'"), in *Fragmenty filozoficzne* (Warsaw, 1934), pp. 144–160, available in English in Storrs McCall, ed., *Polish Logic 1920–1939* (Oxford, 1967), pp. 188–200; "L'analyse de l'antinomie Russellienne par Leśniewski," in *Methodos*, **1** (1949), 94–107, 220–228, 308–316; **2** (1950), 237–257; "Studies in Leśniewski's Mereology," in *Polskie towarzystwo naukowe na obczyźnie. Rocznik*, **5** (1955), 34–43; "On Well-Constructed Axiom Systems," *ibid.*, **6** (1956), 54–65; "La génesis de la escuela polaca de lógica," in *Oriente Europeo*, **7** (1957), 83–95; and "On the Single Axioms of Protothetic," in *Notre Dame Journal of Formal Logic*, **1** (1960), 52–73; **2** (1961), 111–126, 129–148, in progress; and A. Tarski, "O wyrazie pierwotnym logistyki," in *Przegląd filozoficzny*, **26** (1923), 68–89, available in English in A. Tarski, *Logic, Semantics, Metamathematics* (Oxford, 1956), pp. 1–23, important for the study of protothetic.

CZESŁAW LEJEWSKI

LESQUEREUX, LEO (*b.* Fleurier, Neuchâtel, Switzerland, 18 November 1806; *d.* Columbus, Ohio, 25 October 1889), *botany, paleontology*.

The earliest authority in the United States on fossil plants and its second-ranking bryologist, Lesquereux was an expatriate from the political revolution of

1847–1848, as were Louis Agassiz and Arnold Guyot. Lesquereux was of French Huguenot ancestry, the only son of V. Aimé and Marie Anne Lesquereux. His father was an unlettered manufacturer of watch springs. His well-read mother wished him to become a Lutheran minister. At the age of ten he suffered a near-fatal fall that brought on partial deafness. After two years at the *collège* of Neuchâtel, where he was a classmate of Guyot, he taught French at Eisenach with the intention of entering a university later. In 1830 he married Sophia von Wolffskel von Reichenberg, daughter of a general attached to the court of Saxe-Weimar; they had four sons and a daughter. Lesquereux discontinued his teaching because of his growing deafness and returned to Neuchâtel and the engraving of watchcases. It was probably while convalescing from a prolonged illness there that he became interested in mosses. He told Henry Bolander that he owed his enthusiasm for mosses to Wilhelm Schimper, whom he called *facile princeps bryologorum*. In an effort to enhance the nation's fuel supply the Swiss government offered a prize for an essay on the formation of peat bogs, and Lesquereux won. His essay, on the peat bogs of the Jura (1844), attracted the notice of Louis Agassiz, who was then at Neuchâtel.

Discouraged by the political ferment of the times and encouraged by Agassiz, Lesquereux and his family took steerage passage for Boston, arriving in September 1848. Agassiz at once employed him in classifying plants that he had collected on his 1848 expedition to Lake Superior. W. S. Sullivant, the country's leading bryologist and a well-to-do businessman of Columbus, Ohio, urged Lesquereux to work with him in the preparation of *Musci boreali-americani* (1856; 2nd ed., 1865) and *Icones muscorum* (1864). Lesquereux supplemented his income by a small jewelry business. In 1849 he toured the southern states for Sullivant and began writing a series of twenty-seven "Lettres écrites d'Amérique destinées aux émigrants," articles rich in commentary on American mores that were published in Neuchâtel's *Revue suisse*. Sullivant and Lesquereux began a *Manual of the Mosses of North America*, but it was interrupted by Sullivant's death in 1873 and by Lesquereux's failing eyesight. Lesquereux then enlisted Thomas Potts James to assist with the microscopic examinations; and the 447-page *Manual*, describing about 900 species, was published under their authorship (Boston, 1884) two years after James's death. Lesquereux's later years were spent naming fossils.

His first paleobotanical publication was a monograph of Carboniferous fossils of Pennsylvania (1854), followed by another on Illinois (1863), from which the locality of Mazon Creek became a classic. From 1867 to 1872 he organized the fossils that had accumulated at Harvard's Museum of Comparative Zoology; this was his only institutional affiliation. This engagement contributed to his monumental three-volume *Coal Flora of Pennsylvania* (1879–1884). Later R. D. Lacoe of Pittston, Pennsylvania, engaged Lesquereux as a semipensioner to organize his large private collection of fossils, which he bequeathed to the National Museum (now the National Museum of Natural History) in Washington, D.C.

BIBLIOGRAPHY

I. ORIGINAL WORKS. No thoroughly satisfactory bibliography of Lesquereux's publications has appeared; imperfect but useful are those by McCabe and Smith, cited below, and John M. Nickles, "Geologic Literature on North America, 1785–1918," in *Bulletin of the United States Geological Survey*, no. 746 (1923), 654–656. The essay that attracted Agassiz was published as part of "Quelques recherches sur les marais tourbeux en général," in *Neuchâtel Société des Sciences Naturelles, Mémoires*, 3 (1844), 1–138. *Lettres écrites d'Amérique* (Neuchâtel, 1849) was published in an enlarged ed. (Neuchâtel, 1853). The Lesquereux-James correspondence (1857–1881) of 270 letters, bound in 3 vols., is at Farlow Cryptogamic Laboratory, Harvard University; and 58 letters (1862–1872) to Henry Nicholas Bolander are at the Bancroft Library, Berkeley, California. An autobiographical letter was published as a pref. to Lesquereux's posthumous "Flora of the Dakota Group," in *Monographs of the U.S. Geological Survey*, 17 (1892), 1–400, reprinted in *Isis*, 34 (1942), 97–98. There is no catalog of his type specimens, figures, or cited specimens (2,460 in all), but according to W. C. Darrah, quoted in Sarton (see below), 1,415 specimens having the "status of types" are at the Botanical Museum, Harvard. His flowering plants, preserved in the British Museum (Natural History) and elsewhere, are numbered for example "Lx. 121" but lack date of collecting.

II. SECONDARY LITERATURE. Some authors give Charles as his first name, but he never used it in his letters or writings, as noted by G. P. Merrill, in *Dictionary of American Biography* XI (New York, 1933), 188–189. J. Peter Lesley, who met Lesquereux in 1851, wrote the most detailed account of his earlier life, in *Biographical Memoirs. National Academy of Sciences*, 3 (1895), 187–212, although the date of Lesquereux's death given there, 20 Oct., is an error. Heretofore unpublished facts regarding his parents, portraits, collections, and publications are presented with charm by George Sarton, in *Isis*, 34 (1942), 97–108; but Sarton's fig. 6 of a page of "MS preface to Manual of Mosses" is in the hand of Asa Gray and not of Lesquereux. Sereno Watson's handwriting appears on p. 18 ff. Both Gray and Watson edited the *Manual* MS. According to Charles R. Barnes, in *Botanical Gazette*, 15 (1890), 16–19, mementos of Lesquereux were presented to the Musée d'Histoire Naturelle at Neuchâtel. The sketch by Annie M. Smith, in *Bryologist*, **12** (1909), 75–78, includes a portrait; as does that of L. R. McCabe, in *Popular Science Monthly*, **30** (1887), 835–840, which is based on an interview with Lesquereux. Charles H. Sternberg, *Life of a Fossil Hunter* (New York, 1909), pp. 21–25, published Lesquereux's letter of 14 Apr. 1875 in facs. Additional biographical notes will be found in W. C. Darrah, "Leo Lesquereux," in *Harvard University Botanical Museum Leaflets*, **2** (1934), 113–119; and in Andrew Denny Rodgers, III, *Noble Fellow, William Starling Sullivant* (New York, 1940), pp. 191–204, and *passim*.

JOSEPH EWAN

LESSON, RENÉ-PRIMEVÈRE (*b*. Cabane-Carée, Rochefort, France, 20 March 1794; *d*. Rochefort, 28 April 1849), *natural history, scientific exploration*.

The son of a navy clerk of modest means, Lesson had had little formal education when in 1809, not yet sixteen years old, he entered the naval medical school of Rochefort. Lesson was largely self-taught in natural history, which became a lifelong passion. In 1811, he was conscripted into the navy as a third-class auxiliary surgeon, serving on several French ships and seeing action against the British. He qualified as *officier de santé* in 1816, competed successfully for third-class navy pharmacist that same year, and was promoted to second-class pharmacist in 1821. By this time, Lesson had also made a botanical survey of the Rochefort region, which was published much later (*Flore Rochefortine*, 1835). Lesson would probably have remained an obscure naturalist had he not embarked in 1822 on the corvette *Coquille* for a voyage of scientific exploration and discovery which dramatically altered his life and brought him into national prominence.

On 11 August 1822, the *Coquille* sailed from Toulon, commanded by Duperrey with J.-S.-C. Dumont d'Urville second in command and responsible for acquisitions in botany and entomology. The other two naturalists, Garnot and Lesson, also served as medical officers; Garnot's fieldwork covered mammals and birds, while Lesson was assigned fish, mollusks, crustaceans, zoophytes, and geology. Among the places visited by the *Coquille* were Tenerife, Brazil, the Falkland Islands, Chile, Peru, Tahiti, New Ireland, the Moluccas, and Australia, where Garnot was forced by illness to leave the expedition in January 1824, and Lesson assumed his scientific and medical duties. The *Coquille* proceeded to New Zealand, the Caroline Islands, New Guinea, Java,

Mauritius, Réunion, and St. Helena, finally landing at Marseilles on 24 March 1825.

On 18 July 1825, Cuvier and Latreille reported to the Academy of Sciences on the expedition's zoological data and collections, which had been deposited at the Museum of Natural History in Paris. Lesson and Garnot were praised for bringing back hitherto unknown species of birds, reptiles, fish, mollusks, and crustaceans. Lesson was also cited for his remarkable colored illustrations of fish and mollusks and for his valuable aid to Dumont d'Urville for the insect collection. A later report on the voyage of the *Coquille*, made by Arago to the Academy on 22 August 1825, mentioned 330 geological specimens brought back by Lesson.

For Lesson, the four years of leave in Paris from 1825 to 1829 were his most productive scientifically. He wrote furiously, published the results of his voyage, studied, and made friends with outstanding naturalists and scientists of the capital. Upon his return to Rochefort he taught botany at the naval medical school and in 1831 was made professor of pharmacy. A succession of promotions culminated in 1835 with his appointment as the top-ranking navy pharmacist (*premier pharmacien en chef*) for Rochefort. In 1833 he was elected a corresponding member of the Academy of Sciences.

Lesson occupies a prominent place among French naturalist-voyagers of the period, namely F. Péron, Quoy, Gaimard, Garnot, Dumont d'Urville, and C. Gaudichaud-Beaupré. Lesson's numerous publications encompassed virtually all aspects of natural history, and included some archaeology, ethnography, and folklore, but his most important contributions were to zoology. Particularly significant was his work in ornithology, especially his writings on hummingbirds and birds of paradise.

BIBLIOGRAPHY

I. ORIGINAL WORKS. Among Lesson's more important publications are *Manuel de mammalogie, ou histoire naturelle des mammifères . . .* (Paris, 1827); *Manuel d'ornithologie, ou description des genres et des principales espèces d'oiseaux . . .*, 2 vols. (Paris, 1828); *Voyage médical autour du monde, exécuté sur la corvette du Roi la Coquille . . .* (Paris, 1829); *Zoologie du voyage autour du monde . . .* (Paris, 1829), written with P. Garnot, and with F.-E. Guérin-Méneville for the entomological part; *Histoire naturelle des oiseaux-mouches . . .* (Paris, 1829–1830); *Histoire naturelle des colibris . . .* (Paris, 1830–1831); *Les trochilidées, ou colibris et les oiseaux-mouches . . .* (Paris, 1830–1831); *Manuel d'histoire naturelle médicale et de pharmacographie . . .* (Paris, 1833); *Manuel d'ornithologie domestique, ou guide de l'amateur des oiseaux de volière . . .* (Paris,

1834); and *Histoire naturelle des oiseaux de paradis . . . et des épimaques* (Paris, 1835).

For additional listings of Lesson's publications, see *Catalogue général des livres imprimés de la Bibliothèque Nationale*, XCVI (Paris, 1929), 409–415; and British Museum, *General Catalogue of Printed Books*, CXXXV (London, 1962), 834–835. A comprehensive bibliography of Lesson's articles is given in Royal Society, *Catalogue of Scientific Papers (1800–1863)*, III, 971–975.

II. Secondary Literature. A detailed account of Lesson's life and work is given by Louis Rallet, "Un naturaliste saintongeais: René-Primevère Lesson (1794–1849)," in *Annales de la Société des sciences naturelles de la Charente-Maritime*, n.s. **3** (May, 1953), 77–131.

Other sources include John Dunmore, *French Explorers of the Pacific*, vol. II, *The Nineteenth Century* (Oxford, 1969), 109–155, and *passim; Nouvelle biographie générale*, J. C. F. Hoefer, ed., XXIX, 972–974; and J. Léonard, *Les officiers de santé de la marine française de 1814 à 1835* (Paris, 1967), 129–133, 236–237, and *passim*. Brief biographies can be found in *Biographie universelle, ancienne et moderne*, L. G. Michaud and J. F. Michaud, eds., new ed., XXIV, 330–331; and *La Grande encyclopédie*, XXII, 103.

Alex Berman

LESUEUR, CHARLES-ALEXANDRE (*b.* Le Havre, France, 1 January 1778; *d.* Le Havre, 12 December 1846), *natural history*.

Since his father was an officer in the Admiralty, Lesueur was readily accepted at the age of nine at the École Royale Militaire at Beaumont-en-Auge. From 1797 to 1799 he was *sous-officier* in the Garde Nationale at Le Havre. He had early shown remarkable talent in sketching, and in 1800 his great opportunity came when the expedition to Australia and Tasmania of the corvettes *Géographe* and *Naturaliste* (1800–1804), under the command of Nicolas Baudin, was fitted out and sailed from Le Havre. Lesueur shipped as apprentice helmsman but was soon placed in charge of drawing natural history subjects. His relations with the naturalist François Péron were close throughout the long voyage, and through their efforts more than 100,000 zoological specimens, including at least 2,500 new species, were brought back to Paris. The official report of the expedition, written by Péron and Lesueur, was completed later by Claude de Freycinet. Unfortunately Péron died in 1810 before the natural history results were completed, and few of the more than 1,500 of Lesueur's beautiful drawings were ever published. He later took them to America and eventually back to Le Havre, where they survived World War II.

In 1815 Lesueur met in Paris the geologist William Maclure, with whom he sailed for America on 15

August as a paid companion and naturalist. They spent a year in the West Indies on the way, where, among other novelties, Lesueur found many new species of fish, corals, and other marine organisms, some of which he described a few years later. In May 1816 they arrived in New York and immediately set out on a long trip through New England, New York, Pennsylvania, New Jersey, and Maryland. On the journey Maclure reexamined in more detail the geology he had studied some years earlier, and Lesueur assiduously collected fossils (which he probably understood better than anyone else in America at the time), fishes, mollusks, and insects.

For the next nine years Lesueur resided in Philadelphia, where he established himself as naturalist-engraver and teacher of drawing, earning a precarious living. He enjoyed his association with other Philadelphia naturalists, such as Thomas Say, Gerard Troost, and George Ord, to whom he brought his wide knowledge of tropical marine faunas. He soon became a member of the American Philosophical Society and an enthusiastic supporter of the newly founded Academy of Natural Sciences of Philadelphia.

In 1825 Lesueur left for Robert Owen's settlement at New Harmony, Indiana, in Maclure's "Boatload of Knowledge." Although New Harmony's utopian dream soon faded, Lesueur remained there many years, beginning a great work on the fishes of North America—one of several extensive projects that never materialized. An indifferent writer and a compulsive wanderer, Lesueur spent much time on long trips down the Ohio and took four long trips down the Mississippi to New Orleans. In 1837 he descended that river for the last time and returned to France on 27 July 1837, after an absence of twenty-two years. After eight years in Paris he was appointed curator of the newly established Muséum d'Histoire Naturelle du Havre, where he died on 12 December 1846.

In spite of his literary failings, Lesueur's explorations in the Mississippi valley contributed much to the zoology and paleontology of that poorly known area. He was the first to collect and study the fishes of the North American interior and published twenty-nine papers on them as well as others on reptiles, crustaceans, and other organisms. The record he left bears witness to "his quick and agile pencil and his clumsy and encumbered pen."

BIBLIOGRAPHY

I. Original Works. A list of Lesueur's publications is appended to the memoir by Ord (below).

II. Secondary Literature. See Gilbert Chinard, "The American Sketchbooks of C.-A. Lesueur," in *Proceedings of the American Philosophical Society*, **93** (1933), 114–118, with portrait, bust, and sketch; Jean Guiffry, ed., *Dessins de Ch.-A. Lesueur executés aux États-Unis de 1816 à 1837* (Paris, 1933), with 50 plates and reproductions of many of Lesueur's American sketches; E.-T. Hamy, "Les voyages du naturaliste Ch. Alex. Lesueur dans l'Amérique du Nord (1815–1837)," in *Journal de la Société des Américanistes de Paris*, **5** (1904), with 17 plates and 14 figures; and *The Travels of the Naturalist Charles A. Lesueur in North America, 1815–1837*, H. F. Raup, ed. (Kent, Ohio, 1968), with 26 illustrations and 4 maps; Waldo G. Leland, "The Lesueur Collection of American Sketches in the Museum of Natural History at Havre, Seine-Inférieure," in *Mississippi Valley Historical Review*, **10** (1923), 53–78, which lists American notes and sketches then in Le Havre; Mme Adrien Loir, *C.-A. Lesueur, artiste et savant français en Amérique de 1816–1839* (Le Havre, 1920), with 42 figures; André Maury, "C.-A. Lesueur, voyageur et peintre-naturaliste Havrais," in *French-American Review*, **1** (1948), 161–171, with portrait and 8 illustrations; George Ord, "A Memoir of Charles Alexandre Lesueur," in *American Journal of Science*, 2nd ser., **8** (1849), 189–216, a lengthy account of the *Géographe* and *Naturaliste* expedition by Lesueur's closest American friend, with a list of Lesueur's published writings.

JOHN W. WELLS

LE TENNEUR, JACQUES-ALEXANDRE (*b.* Paris, France; *d.* after 1652), *mathematics, physics.*

Described as a patrician of Paris on the title page of his principal book, little else is known of Le Tenneur, friend of Mersenne and correspondent of Gassendi. Probably a resident of Paris until the mid-1640's, he was at Clermont-Ferrand (near Puy-de-Dôme) late in 1646, and in 1651 he was counselor to a provincial senate. C. De Waard identifies him as counselor to the Cour des Aydes of Guyenne, but without indicating dates.

All modern authorities agree in attributing to Le Tenneur the *Traité des quantitez incommensurables*, whose author identified himself on its title page only by the letters I.N.T.Q.L.[1] Mersenne mentioned the *Traité* as in preparation on 15 January 1640 and sent a copy to Haak on 4 September, indicating that it was "by one of my friends." It was directed against Stevin's *L'arithmétique* (Leiden, 1585; ed. A. Girard, 1625), particularly opposing Stevin's treatment of unity as a number. Although Le Tenneur's arguments now seem elementary and conservative, they go to the heart of the foundations of algebra, standing as a final attempt to preserve the classical Greek separation of arithmetic from geometry that Descartes abandoned in 1637. The basic question is whether the unit may properly be considered as divisible. Against Stevin's

affirmative answer, Le Tenneur took the view that this would in effect either merely substitute a different unit or deny the existence of any unit relevant to the problem at hand. The bearing of this analysis on the problems of indivisibles and infinitesimals that were then coming to the fore is evident; but a rapid and widespread acceptance of algebraic geometry doomed the classic distinctions, and the book was neglected. Aware of Viète's work and of the need to give symbolic treatment to incommensurables in the classic sense, Le Tenneur included a paraphrase of book X of Euclid's *Elements*, in which he gave the symbolic operations for each proposition. The book ends with an essay, addressed to the Académie Française, proposing that French should be used in science and outlining methods for the coining of terms, reminiscent of Stevin's earlier argument for the use of Dutch.

In January 1648 Mersenne wrote to Le Tenneur asking him to perform the barometric experiment at Puy-de-Dôme later done by F. Perier at Pascal's request. Le Tenneur, who had moved to Tours, replied that it could not be done in winter and expressed the view that, in any event, the level of mercury would not be changed by the ascent.

The importance of Le Tenneur to the history of science, however, depends on another book, *De motu naturaliter accelerato . . .* (1649), in which he showed himself to be the only mathematical physicist of the time who understood precisely Galileo's reasoning in rejecting the proportionality of speeds in free fall to the distances traversed. This subject was hotly debated in the late 1640's between Gassendi and two Jesuits, Pierre Cazré and Honoré Fabri. In 1647 Fermat, who had previously questioned the validity of Galileo's odd-number rule for distances traversed, wrote out for Gassendi a rigorous demonstration of the impossibility of space proportionality, believing that Galileo had deliberately withheld his own. Le Tenneur, who appears not to have seen Fermat's proof, perceived and illustrated the nature of Galileo's use of one-to-one correspondence between the speeds in a given fall from rest and those in its first half.

Le Tenneur's interest in the matter began with a request from Mersenne for a discussion of Cazré's *Physica demonstratio* (1645), which in turn had arisen from his letters to Gassendi opposing the latter's *De motu impresso a motore translato* of 1642. Le Tenneur's critique of Cazré took the form of a *Disputatio physico-mathematicus* sent in manuscript form to Mersenne, probably in mid-1646, and also sent to Cazré or forwarded to him by Mersenne. Gassendi published his own reply to Cazré as *De proportione qua gravia decidentia accelerantur* (1646) and sent a copy to Le Tenneur. Writing on 24 November 1646 to acknowledge this gift, Le Tenneur sent Gassendi a copy of his *Disputatio*. Gassendi replied on 14 December, and on 16 January 1647 Le Tenneur wrote him that Mersenne had mentioned some other Jesuit than Cazré. This was Honoré Fabri, whose *Tractatus physicus de motu locali* (1646) acknowledged the correctness of Galileo's rules for sensible distances only, explaining this in terms of the space–proportionality of insensible quanta of impetus. Baliani had (also in 1646) advanced a similar hypothesis. Two days later, Le Tenneur wrote that Cazré had meanwhile replied to his earlier *Disputatio* and sent the reply to Gassendi with his own rebuttal.

On 12 April 1647 Le Tenneur wrote out a refutation of Fabri's position in the form of a long letter to Mersenne. Fabri contended that the hypotenuse in Galileo's triangle was in ultimate reality a discrete step function (a denticulated line, as he called it) and that the space quanta traversed in true physical instants progressed as the positive integers rather than as the observed odd numbers. Le Tenneur opposed any analysis by physical instants (the medieval *minima naturalia*) on the grounds that if indivisible, such instants implied Galileo's law, whereas if divisible, they fell under Galileo's phrase "in any parts of time" and excluded Fabri's hypothetical increments of velocity added discretely (*simul*).

Mersenne appears to have communicated this letter to Fabri, who published it as an appendix to a new book in 1647, with critical comments. Finally, Le Tenneur wrote out a long reply to Fabri and composed a further treatise of his own in support of Galileo's laws against all his opponents. On 1 January 1649 he submitted it to Gassendi with the idea of publishing it together with his previous writings on the subject if Gassendi approved. Gassendi had meanwhile moved to Aix-en-Provence for his health and did not receive the material until Easter. His enthusiastic letter of endorsement was sent to Le Tenneur on 17 May 1649 and was included as the final item in *De motu accelerato*.

Of all the participants in this wordy dispute, only Le Tenneur correctly reconstructed Galileo's original argument. His book is of further interest for its inclusion of a strictly mathematical derivation of Galileo's odd-number rule by the young Christiaan Huygens, which had been sent by his father to Mersenne. Le Tenneur published it together with a postil predicting great things from Huygens. *De motu accelerato* is of further historical importance for its refutation of Fabri's dictum that no physical instant could be identical with a mathematical point in time, the last stand of orthodox Aristotelian physics and impetus theory against the continuity concept introduced by Galileo. Even Descartes had rejected the idea that in reaching any given speed from rest, a body must first have passed through every lesser speed. His letters to Mersenne on this point may have been the occasion for its having been called to the attention of Le Tenneur.

The only other books by Le Tenneur related to controversies with Jean-Jacques Chifflet over French history and royal genealogy. He sent one of these to Gassendi and in an accompanying letter seems to have considered himself more a historian than a scientist, despite his valuable if neglected contributions to fundamental issues of mathematics and physics in the seventeenth century.

NOTE

1. The attribution, although probably correct, is not yet certain. No early reference to this book includes more than the family name of the author, and the title page suggests the possibility that there may have been an I. N. (or J. N.) Le Tenneur; Gassendi mentioned a brother of Jacques-Alexandre who has not been identified. In the preface, the author expressed his intention of identifying himself after hearing comments on his book; if the same author wrote *De motu accelerato* (1649) mention of the earlier book would be expected in it. Moreover, the vigorous argument for the use of French hardly fits J.-A. Le Tenneur, who thereafter published only in Latin.

BIBLIOGRAPHY

I. ORIGINAL WORKS. Le Tenneur's writings are *Traité des quantitez incommensurables* (Paris, 1640); *De motu naturaliter accelerato tractatus physico-mathematicus* (Paris, 1649), one section of which had appeared under the author's initials in H. Fabri (P. Mousnier, ed.), *Metaphysica demonstrativa* (Lyons, 1647); *Veritas vindicata adversus . . . Joan. Jac. Chifletii* (Paris, 1651); and *De sacra ampulla remensi tractatus apologeticus adversus Joan. Jac. Chifletum* (Paris, 1652). Some correspondence between Gassendi and Le Tenneur was published in Gassendi, *Opera omnia*, VI (Lyons, 1658). See Adam and Tannery, eds., *Oeuvres de Descartes*, V (Paris, 1903); L. Brunschvig and P. Boutroux, eds., *Oeuvres de B. Pascal*, II (Paris, 1908). Some of Le Tenneur's letters are preserved at Vienne, France, and at the Bibliothèque Nationale, Paris.

II. SECONDARY LITERATURE. For references to and notes about Le Tenneur see *Correspondance du P. Marin Mersenne*, P. Tannery and C. De Waard, eds., IX–XI; most letters between the two men have not yet been published and were not accessible for this article. See also H. Brown, *Scientific Organization in 17th Century France* (New York, 1967), pp. 54–56; S. Drake in *Isis*, **49** (1958), 342–346; **49** (1958), 409–413; *British Journal of the History of Science*, **5** (1970), 34–36; and *Galileo Studies* (Ann Arbor, Mich., 1970), 235–236; W. E. K. Middleton, *History of the*

Barometer (Baltimore, 1964), 40, which gives references to papers on the Pascal controversy published by Felix Matthieu in the *Revue de Paris* (1906).

STILLMAN DRAKE

LE TONNELIER DE BRETEUIL. See **Châtelet, Gabrielle-Émilie Le Tonnelier de Breteuil, Marquise du.**

LEUCIPPUS (*fl.* Greece, fifth century B.C.), *philosophy.*

The first of the Greek atomists, Leucippus was probably the founder of the school of Abdera, whose most famous exponent was Democritus. Although at the end of the fourth century B.C. Epicurus denied that there had ever been any such person as Leucippus, the evidence of Aristotle is sufficient to establish that he existed and that he was earlier in date than Democritus. Aristotle treated his theories as providing a logical alternative to those of Parmenides, and a later tradition actually made him a pupil of Zeno, of the school of Parmenides. This, taken with the late chronology for Democritus, has led some scholars to date Leucippus' activity as late as 430 B.C. But neither the chronology of Democritus nor the relationship of Leucippus to Parmenides is in any way certain. Leucippus probably came from Miletus in Ionia and may have brought knowledge of the physical theories of the Ionians with him to Abdera in Thrace, either sometime after its refoundation as a colony about 500 B.C. (when it soon became an important city in the Persian system of government in Thrace) or sometime after its accession to the Athenian league in the period after 478.

By the fourth century B.C. Leucippus' basic doctrines and probably his writings as well seem to have become incorporated into a kind of corpus of atomist writings, the whole of which was attributed to his more famous pupil and successor, Democritus. Therefore, at many points it is no longer possible to distinguish what originated with Leucippus from what may have been added by Democritus. But Theophrastus attributed to Leucippus a *Megas diakosmos* ("Great World System") later listed among Democritus' writings, and one quotation is preserved from a work *On Mind*. (For the origins of atomism and the theories given in the Democritean corpus, see Democritus.)

As the last writer in a position to distinguish Leucippus' views from those of Democritus, Theophrastus makes it clear that the essentials of atomism were already held by Leucippus. Both

matter and void have real existence. The constituents of matter are elements infinite in number and always in motion, with an infinite variety of shapes, completely solid in composition. We can be sure that a great deal more of Democritus' doctrine was also to be found in Leucippus, but we cannot say how much more.

On the other hand, we have preserved from Theophrastus a summary of Leucippus' account of the creation of physical worlds that is ascribed to him alone, so that it is likely to be correct in essentials. The earth and stars originated from a single whirl of colliding bodies, cut off from the infinite. The further details, which are strongly reminiscent of earlier Ionian cosmologies, include a doctrine of a surrounding membrane that has a typical early biological sound.

BIBLIOGRAPHY

The fragments and testimonia are collected in H. Diels and W. Kranz, *Die Fragmente der Vorsokratiker*, 6th ed., II (Berlin, 1952). For translation and discussion of the more important texts, see G. S. Kirk and J. E. Raven, *The Presocratic Philosophers* (Cambridge, 1957); and for more extended treatments, see C. Bailey, *The Greek Atomists and Epicurus* (Oxford, 1928); and W. K. C. Guthrie, *History of Greek Philosophy*, II (Cambridge, 1965), ch. 8.

G. B. KERFERD

LEUCKART, KARL GEORG FRIEDRICH RUDOLF (*b.* Helmstedt, Germany, 7 October 1822; *d.* Leipzig, Germany, 6 February 1898), *zoology, parasitology.*

Leuckart, whose father owned a printing plant, attended the Gymnasium in Helmstedt. His uncle, Friedrich Sigismund Leuckart, who was professor of zoology at Freiburg im Breisgau, made a strong impression on him and awakened his love for zoology. As a student he collected insects and soon decided to become a zoologist. At this period, however, he could do so only by obtaining a medical education, since there were no faculties of natural science. Consequently, in 1842 Leuckart began medical studies at the University of Göttingen. He soon came into contact with the distinguished zoologist Rudolf Wagner, with whom he formed a lifelong friendship. Wagner encouraged Leuckart to undertake independent research and made him an assistant in his institute in 1845, after Leuckart had passed the state medical examination. Leuckart's dissertation (*De monstris eorumque causis et ortu*), published in the same year, won a university prize; and Wagner immediately gave him an additional post as his lecture assistant. At the end of 1847 Leuckart qualified as a zoology lecturer at Göttingen with a lecture entitled "Naturgeschichte mit besonderer Berücksichtigung des Menschen und der Tiere." The following year Leuckart went on his first scientific expedition, to the German North Sea coast to study marine invertebrates. His investigations led to the establishment of the phylum Coelenterata.

In 1850, at the age of twenty-eight, Leuckart was appointed associate professor of zoology at the University of Giessen, to which Justus von Liebig and the anatomist and embryologist Theodor Bischoff were attracting many young researchers. Leuckart took his place among this illustrious company and later called his years in Giessen the happiest and most scientifically productive of his life. Here he met his wife, the daughter of a royal privy councillor, and conducted the investigations (1850–1869) on human and animal parasites that brought him world fame. In 1869 Leuckart accepted an offer from the University of Leipzig to succeed Eduard Pöppig, who had distinguished himself mainly as a geographer and world traveler. The facilities at his disposal were at first inadequate, but in 1880 he was given a new zoological institute constructed according to his plans and furnished with laboratories, a museum, and a library. Zoologists from all over the world came to the institute as guest researchers. Leuckart's outstanding skill as a teacher and his clear delivery brought him many students who later held chairs of zoology not only at German universities but also in England, France, Italy, Sweden, Russia, Switzerland, Japan, and the United States. The *Festschrift* published on his seventieth birthday includes contributions by more than 130 former students and co-workers.

Leuckart was named a privy councillor by the king of Saxony and was awarded an honorary Ph.D. by the University of Giessen in 1861. He was an honorary member of the Imperial Academy of Sciences of St. Petersburg and received the highest Prussian and Bavarian orders: Pour le Mérite für Künste und Wissenschaften and Maximilianorden. In 1873 he became dean of the philosophical faculty and in 1877–1878 was rector of the University of Leipzig. His powers gradually diminished, and the accidental death of his son Rudolf, a very promising chemist, and of a daughter, after a long illness, pained him deeply and affected his creative ability in his later life. He died of a stroke, following an attack of bronchitis.

Leuckart's first scientific work, which he began in 1847–1848, was the division of Cuvier's Radiata into Coelenterata and Echinodermata (terms of his own devising). The result marked the beginning of a new period of scientific zoology, that of animal systematics based on subtle morphological investigations. His division of the Metazoa into six principal phyla—Coelenterata, Echinodermata, Annelida, Arthropoda, Mollusca, and Vertebrata—is still considered classic, although it provoked considerable opposition when it was first proposed. For example, in 1848 the physiologist Carl Ludwig greeted with sarcasm the morphological point of view that Leuckart presented in his first book, *Über die Morphologie und die Verwandtschaftsverhältnisse der wirbellosen Tiere:* "It would have to be considered a good sign for German science if this book found no readers." Against this, the distinguished anatomist Heinrich Rathke wrote to Leuckart: "I hope not only that [your publication] finds many readers but also—should this happen—that it will be considered a sign of German science."

In *Die anatomisch-physiologische Übersicht des Tierreichs*, published jointly with Carl Georg Bergmann in 1852, Leuckart placed greater emphasis on the physiological approach that ultimately enabled him to discover the developmental process of many parasites. He was especially interested in the sexual organs of the lower animals and in parthenogenesis, as well as in polymorphism, a term he originated. This research was summarized in the article "Zeugung" in Rudolf Wagner's *Handwörterbuch der Physiologie* (IV, 1853). Leuckart's primary interest, however, was parasitology, a subject then being established. His studies of the *Pentastomum*, *Taenia*, liver fluke, and, most notably, *Trichina spiralis* were epoch-making. In opposition to Küchenmeister's view, Leuckart was able to show that *Taenia saginata* occurs only among cattle and *Taenia solium* only among pigs.

In 1860 Leuckart and Friedrich Albert von Zenker simultaneously discovered the *Trichina*, and an unpleasant priority dispute began. Although Leuckart's publication did appear shortly before Zenker's, there is no doubt today that Zenker made the decisive discovery first. Both works, following the initiative of Rudolf Virchow, led to the world's first meat inspection law. Leuckart carried out fundamental investigations of the Acanthocephalata and of *Onchocerca volvulus*, an organism responsible for *onchocerciasis*, which is still epidemic in central Africa. Leuckart also established the protozoan class Sporozoa and the order Coccidia. Many of his conclusions, derived from detailed investigations, were not confirmed until after his death; among these was the course of development of the roundworm *Ascaris lumbricoides* and the tapeworm *Diphyllobothrium latum*, which was first clarified in 1916 but had been correctly predicted by Leuckart.

The fruit of Leuckart's research in parasitology, the two-volume *Die menschlichen Parasiten und die von ihnen herrührenden Krankheiten*, was never completed; the aging Leuckart did not find the strength to finish it. Nevertheless, it has become a classic of parasitology, along with *Berichte über die Leistungen der niederen Thiere* (founded by Carl Theodor von Siebold), which Leuckart edited from 1848 to 1879 and which is a valuable source of information for mid-nineteenth-century zoological literature. Summing up his life-work, Leuckart wrote: "It is not possible for man, as a thinking being, to close his mind to the knowledge that he is ruled by the same power as is the animal world. Like the despised worm he lives in dependence upon external commands, and like the worm he perishes, even when he has shaken the world through the power of his ideas."

BIBLIOGRAPHY

I. ORIGINAL WORKS. A list of the 115 zoological species, genera, and orders that Leuckart named, as well as a complete bibliography of his scientific publications, is in O. Taschenberg, "Rudolf Leuckart," in *Leopoldina* (1899), 63–66, 89–94, 102–112. His most important works are *Beiträge zur Kenntniss wirbelloser Thiere* (Brunswick, 1847), written with Heinrich Frey; *Über die Morphologie und die Verwandtschaftsverhältnisse der wirbellosen Thiere* (Brunswick, 1848); "Ist die Morphologie denn wirklich so ganz unberechtigt?" in *Zeitschrift für wissenschaftliche Zoologie*, **2** (1850), 271–275; *Über den Polymorphismus der Individuen oder die Erscheinungen der Arbeitstheilung in der Natur* (Giessen, 1851); *Anatomisch-physiologische Übersicht des Thierreichs* (Stuttgart, 1852), written with C. G. Bergmann; *Die Blasenbandwürmer und ihre Entwicklung* (Giessen, 1856); *Untersuchungen über Trichina spiralis* (Leipzig–Heidelberg, 1860; 2nd ed., 1866); *Die menschlichen Parasiten und die von ihnen herrührenden Krankheiten*, 2 vols. (Leipzig–Heidelberg, 1863–1876; 2nd ed., 1879–1894 [completed by Gustav Brandes]; 3rd ed., 1886–1901), also translated into English (Edinburgh–Philadelphia, 1886); "Organologie des Auges. Vergleichende Anatomie," in C. F. von Graefe and E. T. Saemisch, eds., *Handbuch der gesamten Augenheilkunde*, II (Leipzig, 1875), pp. 145–301; and "Zur Entwicklungsgeschichte des Leberegels," in *Archiv für Naturgeschichte*, **48** (1882), 80–119.

II. SECONDARY LITERATURE. See R. Blanchard, "Notices biographiques: Rodolphe Leuckart," in *Archives de parasitologie*, **1** (1898), 185–190; O. Bütschli, "Die wichtigsten biographischen Daten aus dem Leben Rudolf Leuckarts," in *Zoologisches Zentralblatt*, **6** (1899), 264–266; J. V. Carus, "Zur Erinnerung an Rudolf Leuckart," in *Sitzungsberichte der K. Sächsischen Gesellschaft für Wissenschaften*, Math.-phys. Kl. (1898), 49–62; C. Grobben, "Rudolf Leuckart," in *Verhandlungen der Zoologische-botanischen Gesellschaft in Wien*, **48** (1898), 241–243; L. Grosse, "Leuckart in seiner Bedeutung für Natur- und Heilkunde," in *Jahresberichte*

der Gesellschaft für Natur- und Heilkunde in Dresden (1898), 93–96; R. von Hanstein, "Rudolf Leuckart," in *Naturwissenschaftliche Rundschau*, **13** (1898), 242–246; A. Jacobi, "Rudolf Leuckart," in *Zentralblatt für Bakteriologie, Parasitenkunde, Infektionskrankheiten und Hygiene*, 1st Section, **23** (1898), 1073–1081; H. A. Kreis, "Rudolf Leuckart, der Begründer der modernen Parasitologie," in *CIBA-Zeitschrift* (Basel), **5** (1937), 1755–1757; G. Olpp, *Hervorragende Tropenärzte in Wort und Bild* (Munich, 1932), pp. 236–240, an especially detailed biography; and the unsigned "Rudolf Leuckart," in *Nature*, **57** (1898), 542.

H. SCHADEWALDT

LEURECHON, JEAN (*b.* Bar-le-Duc, France, *ca.* 1591; *d.* Pont-à-Mousson, France, 17 January 1670), *mathematics.*

Leurechon was a Jesuit who taught theology, philosophy, and mathematics in the cloister of his order at Bar-le-Duc, Lorraine. Very little is known of his personal life. In his earlier years he wrote several tracts on astronomy and an inconsequential work on geometry.

Leurechon is remembered chiefly for his collection of mathematical recreations, some of which were published under other names. Issued at a time when interest in recreational mathematics was rapidly rising, this work obviously appealed to popular fancy, for it passed through some thirty editions before 1700. Based largely on the work of Bachet de Méziriac, it included, besides many original problems, some taken from Cardano. It served in turn as a foundation for the works of Mydorge, Ozanam, Montucla, and Charles Hutton. For the most part Leurechon borrowed only Bachet's simpler and easier problems, completely bypassing the more significant sections. Leurechon's work was characterized by Montucla as "a pathetic jumble" and by D. E. Smith as "a poor collection of trivialities."

BIBLIOGRAPHY

I. ORIGINAL WORKS. Leurechon's tracts on astronomy include *Pratiques de quelques horloges et du cylindre* (Pont-à-Mousson, 1616); *Ratio facillima describendi quamplurima et omnis generis horologia brevissimo tempore* (Pont-à-Mousson, 1618); and *Discours sur les observations de la comète de 1618* (Paris–Rheims, 1619). His work on geometry was *Selectae propositiones in tota sparsim mathematica pulcherrime proposita* (Pont-à-Mousson, 1622).

His collection of mathematical recreations, published under the pseudonym Hendrik van Etten, was *La récréation mathématique ou entretien facétieux sur plusieurs plaisants problèmes, en fait arithmétique . . .* (Pont-à-Mousson, 1624); 2nd ed., rev. and enl. (Paris, 1626). Many subsequent eds. and translations appeared: the first English trans., by William Oughtred, was *Mathematicall Recreations* (London, 1633).

II. SECONDARY LITERATURE. On Leurechon and his work, see Moritz Cantor, *Vorlesungen über Geschichte der Mathematik*, II (Leipzig, 1913), 673–674; 768–769; and Poggendorff, I, 1438. See also H. Zeitlinger, *Bibliotheca chemico-mathematica* (London, 1921), I, 61; II, 536.

WILLIAM L. SCHAAF

LEURET, FRANÇOIS (*b.* Nancy, France, 30 December 1797; *d.* Nancy, 6 January 1851), *psychiatry, public health, comparative anatomy.*

Leuret's education was achieved against the wishes of his father, a baker, who wanted his three sons to follow a trade. With his mother's persistent support, François was sent to a seminary. After an older brother, an army doctor, died in the Napoleonic Wars, François went to Paris to study medicine. In 1818, his father having cut off all funds, he enlisted in the army, a career that suited him ill. Stationed at St.-Denis, he walked to Paris daily to attend medical lectures, notably those of Jean-Étienne Esquirol at the Salpêtrière Hospital. His friend Ulysse Trélat secured a scholarship at Charenton, enabling Leuret to study further with Esquirol and with Spurzheim, and to work in the laboratories at Charenton and Alfort. He published several papers (1824, 1825) and earned his medical doctorate in 1826 with a thesis on changes in the blood. He spent the next twenty years in practice, research, writing, and as medical director of the private Maison de Santé du Gros Caillou in Paris. Late in 1839, Leuret was finally appointed psychiatrist in chief at Bicêtre, succeeding Guillaume Ferrus, whose assistant he had been since 1836. But Leuret was ill and died eleven years later of what seems to have been congestive heart failure. He attained only minor official distinctions and in an unsuccessful bid for the Paris Academy of Medicine in 1836 won only one vote out of 134. His decorations included the Legion of Honor and the Cholera Medal.

Leuret's early research in physiological chemistry and comparative anatomy resulted in a major book (1839), in which he elaborated the latest microscopic and differential staining techniques. The materials for a second volume were published by Gratiolet in 1857, on the initiative of Leuret's friend, the publisher J.-B. Baillière. After receiving his M.D. degree, Leuret practiced medicine in Nancy until 1829, when Esquirol appointed him editor of the newly founded *Annales d'hygiène publique et de médecine légale*. This excellent and influential journal attracted the contributions of concerned physicians, philanthropists, lawyers, and public officials. Leuret's editorial hand is evident in the sections "Correspondence," "Bibliography," and "Varia," and he contributed major papers on cholera (1831), on the Parisian poor (1836), and on his trip through northern Germany and to St. Petersburg where he visited poorhouses and insane asylums (1838).

Psychiatry was Leuret's major concern. Beginning with the comparative anatomy of the nervous system, he soon focused on psychosomatic and mental illness. His opposition to phrenology appears in two devastating book reviews in the *Annales* (1836) and a sarcastic account of Gall's visit to the Salpêtrière (1840). Like his heroes Philippe Pinel and Esquirol, Leuret was committed to "moral," that is, psychological, therapy. At Bicêtre, he introduced the teaching of academic subjects, dance, gymnastics, and music. He instituted a common dining hall and continued Pinel's practice of manual work in the fields. He argued somewhat paradoxically that, confronted with uncooperative patients, the psychiatrist may have to "attack and badger" in order to effect a cure ([1838], 553). He made frequent use of punitive cold showers and dousings, controversial methods that he justified at length in *Du traitement moral de la folie* (1840).

Leuret's major contribution as a teacher, therapist, and writer was his opposition to the prevalent tendency to find correlations between morbid brain anatomy and mental illness.

BIBLIOGRAPHY

I. ORIGINAL WORKS. A complete bibliography of Leuret's works is in Ulysse Trélat, "Notice sur François Leuret," in *Annales d'hygiène publique et de médecine légale*, **45** (1851), 241–263. Works cited in the text are *Mémoire sur l'altération du sang* (Paris, 1826); "Mémoire sur l'épidémie, désignée sous le nom de choléra-morbus," in *Annales d'hygiène publique et de médecine légale*, **6** (1831), 313–472; "Notice sur les indigents de la ville de Paris," *ibid.*, **15** (1836), 294–358; "Notice historique sur A. J. B. Parent-Duchatelet," *ibid.*, **16** (1836), v–xxi; "Notice sur quelques-uns des établissements de bienfaisance du nord de l'Allemagne et de St. Pétersbourg," *ibid.*, **20** (1838), 346–406; "Mémoire sur le traitement moral de la folie," in *Mémoires de l'Académie royale de médecine de Paris*, **7** (1838), 552–576; *Anatomie comparée du système nerveux considéré dans ses rapports avec l'intelligence*, 2 vols. (Paris, 1839–1857), vol. II edited by Pierre Gratiolet; and *Du traitement moral de la folie* (Paris, 1840).

II. SECONDARY LITERATURE. On Leuret and his work, see A. Brierre de Boismont, "Notice biographique sur François Leuret, médecin-en-chef de l'hospice de Bicêtre," in *Annales medico-psychologiques*, **3** (1851), 512–527; and U. Trélat, "Notice sur François Leuret," in F. Leuret and P. Gratiolet, *Anatomie comparée du système nerveux*, I (Paris, 1839), xiii–xxx.

See also the biographies in A. Dechambre, *Dictionnaire encyclopédique des sciences médicales*, 2nd ser., II (Paris, 1869), 403–404; A. Hirsch, *Biographisches Lexikon der hervorragenden Ärzte aller Zeiten und Völker*, 2nd ed., III (Berlin, 1931), 759–760; and R. Semelaigne, *Aliénistes et philanthropes* (Paris, 1912), 482–484.

Dora B. Weiner

LEVADITI, CONSTANTIN (*b.* Galaţi, Romania, 19 July 1874; *d.* Paris, France, 5 September 1953), *medicine, bacteriology.*

Orphaned at the age of eight, Levaditi was raised by an aunt in the port city of Galaţi. This stimulating environment heightened the sense of independence and initiative that he owed to his naturally lively intelligence. This aunt later entrusted him to his other aunt, a laundress at the Branconvan Hospital in Bucharest, where he completed his secondary schooling and medical studies. In 1895 he was accepted into the laboratory of Victor Babès. There he found his lifework: scientific research, particularly on the actinomycotic form of the tubercle bacillus. In 1898 Levaditi worked in Paris with Charles Bouchard and also with Albert Charrin at the Collège de France. Then, at Frankfurt am Main, he studied with Paul Ehrlich, whose views on chemotherapy profoundly influenced him. Admitted in 1900 to the Pasteur Institute, he served as assistant to Élie Metchnikoff in his work on phagocytosis and syphilis. Soon, however, he began to devote himself to his own research.

Levaditi received the M.D. at Paris in 1902. He became head of the laboratory of the Pasteur Institute in 1910 and in 1926 its *chef de service*. Throughout this period he trained numerous students and disciples. Entering World War I as a volunteer, he attained the rank of captain and was detached to serve with the ambulances of la Panne. In this capacity he worked on developing an antitetanus vaccine and studied streptococcus in wounds. After the war he resumed his work at the Pasteur Institute, adding new projects to those already in progress. After 1932 Levaditi divided his time between the Pasteur Institute and the Alfred Fournier Institute, which was the center for the French National League Against Venereal Diseases. After retiring from the Pasteur Institute in 1940, he devoted his efforts to the latter organization until his death at the age of seventy-nine.

In 1903 Levaditi married a Romanian woman who bore him two children. His son, Jean C. Levaditi, became head of the department of histopathology at the Pasteur Institute.

Levaditi became a naturalized French citizen in 1907. He was a member of many French and foreign academies, including the Académie de Médecine, to which he was named in 1928. He was commander of the Legion of Honor and received many prizes, including Cameron Prize (Edinburgh) in 1928, the Paul Ehrlich Prize in 1931, and eight prizes from the Académie des Sciences of Paris.

Levaditi published more than 1,200 notes, articles, and monographs. His penetrating intuition, enhanced by his power of reasoning and remarkable technical knowledge, enabled him to stay informed about new developments; by isolating these developments from their original context in order to set them against his own conceptions, he produced an immense body of work. Thus he noticed that the origin of a group of viral diseases whose agent he named ultravirus was still unknown. This group provided the connecting link for all his investigations, which were outwardly dissimilar (for instance, neurotropic skin diseases).

Levaditi dominated the study of syphilis in his time. After the discovery of the *Treponema pallidum* by Fritz Schaudinn and Paul-Erich Hoffmann, he studied it, using the silver-salt staining method, in the livers of newborn congenital syphilitics. He demonstrated that to supplement the Wassermann-Bordet reaction, a normal liver could be used for diagnosis, thus pioneering the study of antigens. Following Benjamin Sauton, he, Robert Sazerac, and Louis Fournier applied bismuth therapy to syphilis, and achieved results with metallotherapy. He was put in charge of Wassermann serum diagnosis at the Pasteur Institute. Levaditi also used stovarsol (Fourneau 190) in syphilis therapy, after its discovery by Fourneau, Jacques and Thérèse Tréfouël, and Navarro-Martin.

Inspired by Pasteur's work on rabies, Levaditi carried out important experiments on lethargic encephalitis. With Karl Landsteiner he established that the poliomyelitis virus is an ultravirus. During the epidemics in Sweden in 1913 and in Alsace in 1930 he was in charge of committees of assistance. In 1930 Louis Pasteur Vallery-Radot wrote that in France, Levaditi was "the instigator of all research on the etiology of poliomyelitis."

From 1936 to 1940 Levaditi studied the sulfamides and their derivatives. Beginning in 1946 he turned to antibiotics and their mechanisms, which he examined through experimentation on animals. He wrote several important monographs soon after the discovery of each new antibiotic. Levaditi continued his studies of viruses and of chemotherapeutic action on bacteria until his death. A major result of this dedicated effort was his discovery of what are today called the interference phenomena.

BIBLIOGRAPHY

I. ORIGINAL WORKS. Bibliographies of monographs and articles by Levaditi are his *Travaux de médecine expérimentale, 1897–1931. Ectodermoses neurotropes, neuroprotozooses, syphilis, chimiothérapie et chimioprévention, phagocytose, immunité, érythème polymorphe, rhumatisme, ergostérol irradié* (Paris, 1931); and *Titres et travaux. Microbiologie, pathologie humaine et animale, chimiothérapie. 1897–1951* (Paris, 1952).

His writings include *La leucocytose et ses granulations* (Paris, 1902); *La nutrition dans ses rapports avec l'immunité* (Paris, 1904); *La réaction des anticorps syphilitiques dans la paralysie générale et le tabès* (Paris, 1906), written with A. Marie; *La syphilis* (Paris, 1909), written with F. Roché; *Traitement de la paralysie générale par injection du sérum salvarnisé dans la dure-mère cérébrale* (Paris, 1913), written with A. Marie et T. Martel; *Étude sur le tréponème de la paralysie générale* (Paris, 1919), written with A. Marie; *Les ectodermoses neurotropes, poliomyélite, encéphalite, herpès* (Paris, 1922), with preface by E. Roux; "Vaccine pure cérébrale, virulence pour l'homme," in *Comptes rendus hebdomadaires des séances de l'Académie des sciences*, **174** (1922), 248–252, written with S. Nicolau; *Étude de l'action thérapeutique sur la syphilis* (Paris, 1923), written with R. Sazérac; *Le bismuth dans le traitement de la syphilis* (Paris, 1924); *L'herpès et le zona* (Paris, 1926); *Travaux de microbiologie et de pathologie humaines et animales. 1897–1933* (Paris, 1933); *Prophylaxie de la syphilis* (Paris, 1936); *Traité des ultravirus des maladies humaines et animales*, 2 vols. (Paris, 1943–1948); *La pénicilline et ses applications thérapeutiques* (Paris, 1945); *Précis de virologie médicale* (Paris, 1945); *La streptomycine et ses applications thérapeutiques, principalement dans la tuberculose* (Paris, 1946); *Les antibiotiques autres que la pénicilline* (Paris, 1950); and *Le chloramphénicol et ses applications thérapeutiques* (Paris, 1951).

II. SECONDARY LITERATURE. On Levaditi and his work, see R. Dujarric de La Rivière, *Souvenirs* (Périgueux [1962]), pp. 136–137; E. Iftimovici, *C. Levaditi* (Bucharest, 1960); P. Lépine, "Constantin Levaditi (1874–1953)," in *Presse médicale*, **71** (1953), 1455; and "C. Levaditi, 1874–1953," in *Annales de l'Institut Pasteur*, **85** (1953), 355; L. Pasteur Vallery Radot, "La poliomyélite épidémique," in *Revue des deux mondes*, **9** (1930), 899–914; E. Roux, "Rapport sur les travaux de M. le Docteur C. Levaditi. Sur les spirochètes en général et le *Treponema pallidum* en particulier," in *Comptes rendus hebdomadaires des séances de l'Académie des sciences*, **145** (1907), 1025.

DENISE WROTNOWSKA

LEVAILLANT (LE VAILLANT), FRANÇOIS (*b.* Paramaribo, Netherlands Guiana [now Surinam], 1753; *d.* La Noue, near Sézanne, France, 22 November 1824), *natural history.*

The son of a wealthy trader from the vicinity of Metz who had become French consul in the Dutch colony, Levaillant presumably acquired a love of travel and exploration from his family. At the age of ten he went with them to Holland and later spent two years in Germany and seven in the French countryside, where he developed a love of hunting, began to study birds, and learned taxidermy. While visiting Paris in 1777 he became a devotee of the cabinets and collections of natural history and resolved to explore the remotest part of the globe. Having fixed on Africa as the least-known continent, he sailed from Holland for the Cape of Good Hope on 19 December 1779, arriving there on 29 March 1781. While he was hunting near the Bay of Saldanha, his boat was attacked by a British flotilla, and he lost his personal effects except for his gun, ten ducats, and the light clothes he was wearing. The colonists, however, outfitted him for his first tour of the interior, a six-month circular trip up from the east into the veld. His second trip, in 1783, lasted nearly a year and was attended with great physical difficulty as he traveled north along the left bank of the Orange River into land occupied by warring tribes. Protected by his faithful Hottentot retinue, Levaillant managed to hunt with the savage Hausa and to bring back his collections relatively unscathed. Returning to France in 1784 he was imprisoned for a time but survived the Revolution and retired to a small estate at La Noue, near Sézanne in Champagne. Here he wrote the books that have survived controversy and accusations of substitute authorship. Although his ornithological work consists essentially of magnificent illustrated books, devoid of scientific terminology, they were among the first to reveal to Frenchmen (and later Germans and Englishmen) the wonders of Africa and of the tropics. Levaillant was the first Frenchman to bring a giraffe to the Jardin des Plantes. Through his books and collections he popularized the wonders of the exotic fauna in which he had delighted. Decorated under the Empire with the Legion of Honor, he died at his country estate in 1824. In his best-known book, *Voyages de F. Le Vaillant dans l'intérieur de l'Afrique*, he mentions two of his African friends: Klaas, a Hottentot companion for whom Klaas' cuckoo is named; and "the fair" Narine, an African maiden (whose relationship to the explorer has always been thought romantic) for whom the lovely Narina trogon is named. Levaillant's ornithological production was great, though unscientific. His principal work was the magnificent *Histoire naturelle des oiseaux d'Afrique;* the general artistic supervisor is thought to have been Jean-Baptiste Audubert.

BIBLIOGRAPHY

I. ORIGINAL WORKS. Levaillant's writings are *Voyages de F. Le Vaillant dans l'intérieur de l'Afrique 1781–1785* (Paris, 1790); *Histoire naturelle des oiseaux d'Afrique,* 6 vols. (Paris, 1796–1812); *Histoire naturelle d'une partie d'oiseaux nouveaux et rares de l'Amérique et des Indes* (Paris, 1801); *Histoire naturelle des perroquets,* 2 vols. (Paris, 1801–1805), with 73 plates colored under the supervision of Barraband, supp. vols. added by Alexandre Bourjot-Saint-Hilaire (1837–1838) and Charles de Souancé (1857–1858); and *Histoire naturelle des oiseaux de paradis at des rolliers,* 2 vols. (Paris, 1801–1806).

II. SECONDARY LITERATURE. See Andrew Crichton, "Memoir of Le Vaillant," in William Swainson, *Birds of Western Africa,* pt. 2 (Edinburgh, 1845), pp. 17–31; and J. H. Ogilvie, *A Bibliography of Le Vaillant's Voyages and Oiseaux d'Afrique* (Johannesburg, 1962).

S. DILLON RIPLEY

LEVENE, PHOEBUS AARON THEODOR (*b.* Sagor, Russia, 25 February 1869; *d.* New York, N. Y., 6 September 1940), *biochemistry.*

An American biochemist who carried out extensive research on conjugated proteins, Levene was particularly noted for his pioneering work on nucleoproteins and their component nucleic acids. He was the second of eight children of a custom shirtmaker, Solom Michael Levene and the former Etta Brick. The family moved to St. Petersburg in 1873 so the children might attend private schools and the classical academy. Upon graduation from the latter in 1886, Phoebus was admitted to the Imperial Military Medical Academy in St. Petersburg, where chemistry was taught by Borodin and his son-in-law, Alexander Dianin. Because of growing anti-Semitism the Levene family emigrated to New York in 1891, but Phoebus returned to the medical academy and received his M.D. in the fall of that year.

He then undertook medical practice in New York's Lower East Side but was concurrently enrolled as a special student in the chemistry department of the Columbia University School of Mines. In 1896 he became associate in physiological chemistry at the recently opened laboratories of the Pathological Institute of the New York State Hospitals. He soon contracted tuberculosis and, while recovering in a sanitarium at Saranac Lake, decided to abandon the practice of medicine and devote his life to biochemical

research. At various times in the next decade he served at the Pathological Institute and at the Saranac Lake Laboratory for the Study of Tuberculosis, where he worked on the chemistry of the tubercle bacillus. Interspersed were periods of study with Edmund Drechsel in Bern, Albrecht Kossel in Marburg, and Emil Fischer in Berlin. At Marburg he became interested in nucleic acids, and at Berlin he applied Fischer's new ester fractionation procedure to the determination of the amino acids in gelatin. In 1905 Simon Flexner selected him to head the biochemical studies at the newly created Rockefeller Institute for Medical Research, where he worked until his retirement in 1939.

Levene was an intense, hard-driving scientist. He was thin, of short stature, and had penetrating, dark-brown eyes, close-cropped mustache, and a stern expression. He liked to work in the laboratory and managed to do so while supervising a staff of postdoctoral students and assistants, many of them from foreign countries. He conferred daily with his associates, keeping in close touch with the progress of their research and making suggestions reflecting his broad familiarity with the literature. An accomplished linguist, he addressed his foreign students in their native tongues. He spoke excellent German and French, but his English always had a heavy Russian accent.

In 1919 he met Anna M. Erickson at Saranac Lake. She was born in Montana but was then a member of the Norwegian Lutheran Colony in Evanston, Illinois. They were married in 1920. There were no children. Their home reflected Levene's interest in music (he played the violin), contemporary art, and literature. Although a gracious host in a social setting, Levene never permitted social affairs to interfere with his scientific activities. His political views were liberal; he supported the Kerensky government, but was unsympathetic to the Bolsheviks.

Of particular importance in his career was his pioneering work on the nucleic acids. Although discovered in 1871, little was known about them in 1900 except that they were present in nucleoproteins, and contained phosphoric acid groups associated with nitrogenous and nonnitrogenous material. Levene showed the presence in cells of two principal types. One, obtained readily from yeast, he showed to be composed of four nucleosides in which he identified the hitherto unknown sugar D-ribose. The optical isomer, L-ribose, had recently been synthesized in Europe, and Levene showed his sugar to be identical except for direction of optical rotation. He also synthesized the hypothetical hexose sugars, D-allose and D-altrose, from D-ribose.

In subsequent work Levene identified four nucleotides from yeast nucleic acid and showed the presence of phosphoric acid, ribose, and a nitrogenous base (either a purine or a pyrimidine). He was able to show that nucleic acids are high polymers composed of the four nucleotides. Related work on thymus nucleic acid showed a similar composition, but the identity of the sugar remained elusive until Levene identified it in 1929, twenty years after the identification of ribose, as 2-deoxy-D-ribose. His laboratory established the sequence of units in the nucleotides, worked out the ring structures of the sugars, and established the position of attachment of the bases and phosphate units on the sugars. Levene died four years before RNA and DNA were recognized to play a principal role in transmission of hereditary information.

Besides his work on the ribose sugars, Levene undertook work on the glycoproteins in 1900, isolating nitrogenous sugars from the mucoids. The structures of these hexosamines could be established only after extensive synthetic studies on sugars and amino sugars. His identification of chondrosamine as 2-amino-2-deoxy-D-galactose and chitosamine as 2-amino-2-deoxy-D-glucose was later confirmed by the work of Haworth and his associates. In his studies of sugar Levene made important contributions to the understanding of the Walden inversion.

Other research dealt with the lipids. Levene showed that lecithin isolated from different parts of the body contains different fatty acids; that sphingomyelins prepared from various organs are identical; and that "kerasinic acid" from the cerebroside, kerasin, is identical with lignoceric acid.

Levene was a skilled laboratory worker who utilized simple apparatus with great effectiveness. Because of his medical training he carried out animal experiments with unusual skill. His more than 700 publications reveal a great diversity of research interests, yet they reflect an integration revealing a deep understanding of the problems involved in unraveling the chemistry of living processes. His early work resulted in the isolation of specific proteins. It was necessary to develop improved analytical procedures to unravel their composition. He complemented analysis with synthesis in attacking such problems. Early work on the racemization of synthetic diketopiperazines led him to conclude that protein structure was explainable by classical valence theory. While his isolation of propylglycine anhydride from a gelatin hydrolysate challenged the new polypeptide theory of protein structure, the problem was ultimately resolved. His work on protein structure quickly led to studies of the nonprotein constituents of conjugated proteins (nucleoproteins, lipoproteins, glycoproteins) and thereby to the studies of sugars, lipids, and nucleic acids.

Levene was a charter member of the American Society of Biological Chemists, the National Academy of Sciences, and of numerous other American and foreign societies. In 1931 he received the Willard Gibbs Medal of the American Chemical Society and in 1938 was awarded the William H. Nichols Medal of the New York section of the same society.

BIBLIOGRAPHY

I. ORIGINAL WORKS. A bibliography of Levene's publications is appended to the biography by D. D. Van Slyke and W. A. Jacobs (see below). Most appeared in the *Journal of Biological Chemistry*. Levene published fragmentary results rapidly, rather than waiting until a major area of research was completed. His books are *Hexosamines, Their Derivatives, and Mucins and Mucoids* (New York, 1922); *Hexosamines and Mucoproteins* (New York, 1925); and *Nucleic Acids* (New York, 1931).

II. SECONDARY LITERATURE. There are no extensive biographies of Levene. The best short biography of him as a person is Melville L. Wolfram, "Phoebus Aaron Theodor Levene," in Eduard Farber, ed., *Great Chemists* (New York, 1961), pp. 1313–1324. Wolfram served as a postdoctoral fellow in Levene's laboratory and obtained personal information about the family background from Alexander, the younger brother of Phoebus. He gives Aaron as the father's name and has much information on Levene's Russian name and its transliteration. There is also some personal material in D. D. Van Slyke and W. A. Jacobs, "Phoebus Aaron Theodor Levene," *Biographical Memoirs. National Academy of Sciences*, **23** (1945), 75–126. Other sketches are R. Stuart Tipson, "Phoebus Aaron Theodor Levene, 1869–1940," in *Advances in Carbohydrate Chemistry*, **12** (1957), 1–12; and Lawrence W. Bass, "American Contemporaries, P. A. Levene," in *Industrial and Engineering Chemistry. News edition*, **12** (1934), 105.

AARON J. IHDE

LE VERRIER, URBAIN JEAN JOSEPH (*b.* Saint-Lô, France, 11 March 1811; *d.* Paris, France, 23 September 1877), *astronomy, celestial mechanics, meteorology.*

Le Verrier, whose family came from Normandy, attended secondary school in his native city and then in Caen. The family's finances were modest; and his father, an estate manager, sold his house in order to send Le Verrier to Paris to prepare for the École Polytechnique. Admitted in 1831, he graduated as *élève-ingénieur* of the state tobacco company and for two years studied at the specialized school of tobacco manufacture. He then resigned to pursue chemical research under Gay-Lussac.

In 1837 Le Verrier married the daughter of his former mathematics professor. He gave private lessons to support himself and applied for the position of *répétiteur de chimie* at the École Polytechnique. Having already published two well-received memoirs on combinations of phosphorus, he was accepted— as *répétiteur d'astronomie*.

Le Verrier was already interested in astronomy; his first publication (1832) had dealt with shooting stars and had led to his first contact with the astronomer royal, George Airy. Henceforth, Le Verrier devoted himself exclusively to astronomy. In 1837 he began to study the most general problem of celestial mechanics, the stability of the solar system. The perturbations of the major axes of the orbits had been treated, but Laplace had failed to obtain significant results for the eccentricities and inclinations. Extending Laplace's calculations by carrying the approximations much further and by making a more complete analytical study, Le Verrier derived in 1839 and 1840 precise limits for the eccentricities and inclinations of the seven planets, given the masses accepted at the time. For Jupiter, Saturn, and Uranus he demonstrated that stability is acquired without restriction.

Le Verrier next turned to the theoretical study of Mercury, the existing tables of which did not agree well with observation, and then to the identification of periodic comets. His progress in the analytic theory of perturbations was recognized by the Académie des Sciences; he became a member in January 1846, while engaged in the work that led him to the discovery of Neptune.

Until 1846 there was no theory of Uranus that permitted its movements to be represented satisfactorily. In 1821 Bouvard had constructed tables that, abandoning the older positions, adhered very closely to recent observations. Yet twenty years later a discrepancy of two minutes had already been observed, and several astronomers suggested that it might result from the attraction of an unknown planet. In 1845 Arago presented the problem to Le Verrier, who began by establishing a precise theory of Uranus. He then demonstrated that its observed perturbations could not be explained as the effect of the actions of Jupiter and Saturn, whatever modifications might eventually be made in the values assigned to the masses of those planets. He began to search for signs of an unknown disturbing planet. Finally, in a third memoir on the subject, appearing on 31 August 1846, Le Verrier fixed the exact position of the unknown planet and gave its apparent diameter.

Le Verrier communicated the result of his investigations to several astronomers who had powerful instruments at their disposal. Among them was J. G. Galle, at the Berlin observatory, who was notified by Le Verrier on 23 September. Two days later he wrote to Le Verrier: "The planet whose position you indicated *really exists*. The same day I received your letter I found a star of the eighth magnitude that was not recorded on the excellent Carta Hora XXI (drawn by Dr. Bremiker). . . . The observation of the following day confirmed that it was the planet sought." The map to which Galle referred had just reached him. The object observed was fifty-two minutes from the position predicted by Le Verrier. First called Le Verrier's planet, it was eventually named Neptune.

The English astronomer J. C. Adams had independently carried out a study essentially equivalent to Le Verrier's, although less elaborate, and had sent it to Airy. Having disregarded it until apprised of Le Verrier's second memoir on the subject, Airy then initiated a series of similar observations. Unfortunately, the Greenwich observatory did not possess a sufficiently accurate star map; thus identification of the planet required an effort that was not made until after the announcement of Galle's observation.

While Le Verrier, Airy, and Adams were establishing friendly relations at this period, a sharp polemic over the priority in this discovery was being conducted by French and English journalists. A short while later French and American scientists contested the role of Le Verrier's work and claimed that the discovery was due solely to chance. This assertion was based on the fact that at the end of several months, observations had shown that the elements of Neptune's orbit were quite different from those predicted by Le Verrier. Sir John Herschel explained the error of Le Verrier's opponents as follows: "The axis and excentricity are intellectual objects . . ., useful to represent to the mind's eye the general relations of the planet to space and time. The direct object of the enquiry was to say whereabouts in space at the present moment is the disturbing body. . . ." In fact, the perturbations of Uranus by Neptune are great only when these planets are at least approximately in heliocentric conjunction; and, for these times, their analysis furnishes the position then occupied by Neptune but not the totality of its orbit.

This successful application of mathematical analysis helped to make the public and governments aware of the importance of scientific research in general. Encouraged, in 1847 Le Verrier conceived the project "of embracing in a single work the whole of the planetary system," that is, of constructing theories and tables of the planets and determining their masses in a uniform manner while simultaneously taking into account all the mutual perturbations. This work, which he did not complete until a month before his death, occupies more than 4,000 pages of the *Annales de l'Observatoire de Paris.*

Le Verrier began by establishing the expansion of the perturbing force in its most general form—an expansion extended to the seventh power of the eccentricities and inclinations, and including 469 terms dependent on 154 special functions. This work, carried out in 1849, was the basis of later investigations. Le Verrier then turned to the first four planets, from Mercury to Mars, the theory and tables of which he completed in 1861. Between 1870 and 1877 he treated the other four planets.

Le Verrier's theories are literal and therefore permit interpretations of broad scope. But in elaborating them he did not adhere rigorously to his initial plan: the mutual perturbations of the big planets were too large for them all to undergo complete analytical expansions, and it was necessary to resort to interpolation procedures; for the other planets a uniform treatment was not possible, and certain constants had to be determined separately on the basis of isolated effects in which they played a preponderant role. On the whole, the ensemble represents a considerable advance in the determination of both the masses of the planets and their orbits.

Le Verrier hoped that his work would lead to further discoveries analogous to that of Neptune. His project of 1847 states that he wished to "put everything in harmony if possible and, if it is not, to declare with certainty that there exist still unknown causes of perturbations, the sources of which would then and only then be recognizable." He knew by 1843 that the observed motion of Mercury would not agree with theory. In 1859 he showed that Mercury moves as if an unknown agent produced an advance of its perihelion of about thirty-eight seconds per century. He then put forth the hypothesis of the perturbing action of an intramercurial planet—or, rather, of a group of such planets; the dimensions of a single perturbing body—on the order of those of Mercury—ruled out the possibility of this body having remained unobserved. The hypothesis was not confirmed by the observations conducted for this purpose. No satisfactory explanation was found until 1916, when Karl Schwarzschild, applying the theory of general relativity to celestial mechanics, demonstrated that the only notable correction in the orbits in relation to the Newtonian theory was an advance in the perihelia. This advance is very slight, except in the case of Mercury where it attains forty-three seconds per century. Hence the disagreement pointed out by Le Verrier ultimately became the most celebrated proof of the validity of Einstein's theory.

Le Verrier was one of the founders of modern meteorology. In 1854 the minister of war requested him to study the cyclone that struck the fleets besieging Sevastopol. His systematic inquiry in Europe and Asia enabled him to determine the path of the cyclone. Occupied during this period with the reorganization of the meteorological observation service of the Paris observatory, Le Verrier conceived "the project of a vast meteorological network designed to warn sailors of approaching storms." The greatest difficulty lay in securing the cooperation of the various telegraphic services. By 1857 the project was sufficiently advanced for distribution of a daily bulletin giving the atmospheric conditions at fourteen French and five foreign stations. In England, Robert Fitzroy took the lead in the practical application of the method, and succeeded in 1859 in establishing a storm warning and signaling center for British ports, something that Le Verrier obtained for France and continental Europe in 1863. The predictions were based on the examination of wind charts and isobars. The bulletin prepared by the Paris observatory, which became international in 1872, was sent to all European capitals; it was furnished twice a day when the situation was unsettled, and special telegrams were sent in case of severe storms. Le Verrier also organized a network of stations to report on thunderstorms. When he died, the various meteorological services were reorganized as the Bureau Central Météorologique de France.

Authoritarian and easily offended, but possessed of absolute integrity in scientific matters, Le Verrier conducted his projects like battles—in which, however, he displayed more emotion than strategy. As a result, in the course of his career he acquired the friendship and often the admiration of the greatest foreign scientists while quarreling with most of his French colleagues, who were in more direct contact with him. His dispute with Arago began, paradoxically, because the latter wished to name the new planet for Le Verrier.

Appointed director of the Paris observatory in 1854, following the death of Arago, Le Verrier successively lost the confidence of all its members. They reproached him especially for prohibiting them from taking the initiative and doing private work and for devoting to astronomy only a tenth of the available funds. His management was so contested that he was dismissed in 1870. Reinstated in 1873, after the death of his successor and enemy Charles-Eugène Delaunay, he was then prudent enough to devote all his activity to celestial mechanics. For the first time in his life he trained a student, J. B. Gaillot, who completed the theories of Jupiter and Saturn, which Le Verrier had not had the opportunity to treat thoroughly.

Le Verrier succumbed to the effects of a liver disease that caused him great discomfort during his last five years and affected his already difficult disposition. The fatal progress of this disease has been attributed to the intensity of his scientific work. His other responsibilities included a chair of celestial mechanics at the Sorbonne, created for him after the discovery of Neptune, and, beginning in 1849, a chair of astronomy. He occupied himself as well with the observatory of Marseilles, which was established at his initiative as a branch of the Paris observatory. In 1849 Le Verrier was elected deputy from La Manche, after a campaign in which he affirmed his Catholic faith and his conservative ideas. Three years later he was named to the Imperial Senate, and he remained a senator until the end of the Empire. He was a member of most of the scientific academies of Europe and had the distinction of twice receiving the gold medal of the Royal Astronomical Society of London (1868, 1876).

BIBLIOGRAPHY

I. Original Works. A complete list of Le Verrier's publications is in Institut de France, *Centenaire de la naissance de U. J. J. Le Verrier* (Paris, 1911), pp. 93–128. Most of his scientific work was presented in the form of notes (totaling 230) in the *Comptes rendus . . . de l'Académie des sciences* between 1835 and 1878. His studies in chemistry are "Sur les combinaisons du phosphore avec l'hydrogène," in *Annales de chimie*, **60** (1835), 174–194; and "Sur les combinaisons du phosphore avec l'oxygène," *ibid.*, **65** (1837), 18–35. The notes relating to the discovery of Neptune are in *Comptes rendus . . . de l'Académie des sciences*, **21** (1845), 1050–1055; **22** (1846), 907–918; **23** (1846), 428–438, 657–659; and **27** (1848), 208–210, 273–279, 304, 325–332. The organization of the meteorological investigations is set forth in *Historique des entreprises météorologiques de l'Observatoire impérial de Paris. 1854–1867* (Paris, 1868). All the memoirs on the theories and tables of the planets were published in *Annales de l'Observatoire impérial de Paris. Mémoires*, **1–9** (1855–1868), and then in the *Annales de l'Observatoire national de Paris. Mémoires*, **10** (1874) to **14**, no. 2 (1877).

II. Secondary Literature. See the following, listed chronologically: C. Pritchard, "Address . . . Gold Medal," in *Monthly Notices of the Royal Astronomical Society*, **28** (1868), 110–122; J. C. Adams, "Address . . . Gold Medal," *ibid.*, **36** (1876), 232–246; J. B. Dumas *et al.*, "U. J. Le Verrier. Discours prononcés aux funérailles," in *Comptes rendus . . . de l'Académie des sciences*, **85** (1877), 580–596; J. R. Hind, "Le Verrier," in *Monthly Notices of the Royal Astronomical Society*, **38** (1878), 155–168; J. Bertrand, "Éloge historique de Le Verrier," in *Annales de l'Observa-*

toire de Paris. Mémoires, **15** (1880), 3–22; F. Tisserand, "Les travaux de Le Verrier," *ibid.*, 23–43; E. Mouchez, F. Tisserand, and O. Struve, *Discours prononcés à l'occasion de la cérémonie d'inauguration de la statue de Le Verrier . . .* (Paris, 1889), pp. 15–41; Sir Robert Ball, *Great Astronomers* (London, 1895), pp. 335–353; Institut de France, *Centenaire de la naissance de U. J. J. Le Verrier* (Paris, 1911), and *Exposition Le Verrier et son temps. Catalogue* (Paris, 1946), both containing extensive documentation; A. Danjon, "Le Verrier créateur de la météorologie," in *La météorologie* (1946), 363–382.

See also F. Tisserand, "Notice sur les planètes intramercurielles," in *Annuaire publié par le Bureau des longitudes* for 1882, pp. 729–772; and, on the discovery of Neptune, R. Grant, *History of Physical Astronomy* (London, 1852), pp. 123–210.

Jacques R. Lévy

LEVI BEN GERSON (*b.* Bagnols, Gard, France, 1288; *d.* 20 April 1344), *mathematics, astronomy, physics, philosophy, commentary on the Bible and the Talmud.*

Levi was also called RaLBaG (a monogram of Rabbi Levi ben Gerson) by the Jewish writers and Gersoni, Gersonides, Leo de Bannolis or Balneolis, Leo Judaeus, and Leo Hebraeus (not to be confused with Leone Ebreo [*d.* 1521/1535], author of the *Dialoghi d'Amore*) by Latin writers. He lived in Orange and Avignon, which were not affected by the expulsion of the Jews from France in 1306 by the order of King Philip the Fair. He seems to have maintained good relations with the papal court—the Latin translations of *De sinibus, chordis et arcubus* and *Tractatus instrumenti astronomie* were dedicated to Clement VI in 1342—and with eminent French and Provençal personalities: his *Luḥot* and *De harmonicis numeris* were written at the request of a group of Jews and Christian noblemen and at the request of Philip of Vitry, bishop of Meaux, respectively. It has been insinuated, without foundation, that he embraced Christianity. It is possible that he practiced medicine, although the evidence is scant. He probably knew neither Arabic nor Latin and thus had to base his work on available Hebrew translations.

In 1321 or 1322 Levi finished the *Sefer ha mispar* ("Book of Number"), also called *Ma'aseh ḥosheb* ("Work of the Computer"; see Exodus 26:1). It deals with general principles of arithmetic and algebra and their applications to calculation: summations of series and combinatorial analysis (permutations and combinations). He used mathematical induction in his demonstrations earlier than Francesco Maurolico (1575) and Pascal (*ca.* 1654). He explained place value notation, but instead of figures, he uses Hebrew letters according to their numerical value, as well as sexagesimal fractions.

In 1342 Levi wrote *De harmonicis numeris*, of which only the Latin translation survives. Its purpose was to demonstrate that, except for the pairs 1-2, 2-3, 3-4, and 8-9, it is impossible for two numbers that follow each other to be composed of the factors 2 and 3.

Levi's trigonometrical work is in *De sinibus, chordis et arcubus* (dated 1343) based on the Hebrew text of his *Sefer Tekunah*. He uses chords, sines, versed sines, and cosines but no tangents (known in Europe since 1126). Following Ptolemaic methods, he calculated sine tables with great precision. He also formulated the sine theorem for plane triangles; this theorem had been known in the Orient since the end of the tenth century, but it is not clear whether Levi rediscovered it independently or knew it through Jābir ibn Aflaḥ (twelfth century).

Levi wrote two geometrical works: a commentary on books I–V of Euclid's *Elements* that used the Hebrew translation by Moses ibn Tibbon (Montpellier, 1270)—an attempt to construct a geometry without axioms—and the treatise *Ḥibbur ḥokmat ha-tishboret* ("Science of Geometry"), of which only a fragment has been preserved.

The greatest work by Levi ben Gerson is philosophical in character. It is entitled *Milḥamot Adonai* ("The Wars of the Lord") and is divided into six books. The fifth book deals with astronomy and is composed of three treatises, the first of which is known as *Sefer Tekunah* ("Book of Astronomy"). Completed in 1328 and revised in 1340, it was translated into Latin in the fourteenth century. It is divided

into 136 chapters and includes two works that are frequently found separately in the manuscripts: the *Luḥot* (chapter 99), astronomical tables calculated for the meridian of Ezob (Izop; Orange) in 1320, and his description of the construction and use of the instrument called the Jacob's staff (chapters 4-11). Levi treated this instrument not only in the chapters mentioned (which were translated into Latin by Peter of Alexandria in 1342) but also in two Hebrew poems. In these versions it is called *kelī* ("instrument") and *megalleh 'amūqqōt* ("secretum revelator"; see Job 12:22); on the other hand, one of these two poems bears the subtitle "'al ha-maqel" ("Concerning the Staff") and in it he refers to Jacob's staff (Genesis 32:10). This is the origin of the expression *baculus Jacobi*, used in some Latin manuscripts, and of the misunderstanding that he wanted to attribute his invention to someone called Jacob. The instrument is also called *baculus geometricus, baculus astronomicus,* or *balestilha*. It consists of a graduated rod and a plate that moves along the rod perpendicular to it. In order to measure an angle, the observer must look at both ends of the plate. The angle α is determined solving triangle *ABC*. This instrument helped Levi in his attempts to determine the center of vision in the eye; unfortunately the experiment was not sufficiently precise and Levi concluded that the center of vision is in the crystalline lens, thus agreeing with Galen and Ibn al-Haytham.

Levi's astronomical system began with a critique of the *Almagest* and of al-Biṭrūjī's *Kitāb al-hay'a* (translated into Hebrew in the thirteenth century). His principal sources were al-Battānī (whom he could have known through Abraham bar Ḥiyya), the *Islāḥ al-Majisṭī* of Jābir ibn Aflaḥ (translated by Moses ibn Tibbon in 1274), Ibn Rushd, and Abraham ibn 'Ezra. He followed the doctrine of al-Farghānī (Hebrew translation by Jacob Anaṭoli, *ca.* 1231–1235) concerning the motion of the solar apogee. He rejected the planetary systems of Ptolemy and al-Biṭrūjī because he did not feel that they conformed with the data obtained by observation, as in the variations in the apparent sizes of the planets. Thus Levi observed that, according to Ptolemy, the apparent size of Mars must vary sixfold while, according to his own observations, it varies twice. The Ptolemaic epicycles also did not agree with observations (accepting the one of the moon would imply that we see both sides alternately). In the same way Levi rejected the theory of the trepidation of the equinoxes. This theoretical work was accompanied by many years of well-defined observation (1321–1339) in which Levi used his staff and the camera obscura. The use of the camera obscura in astronomy dates back to Ibn

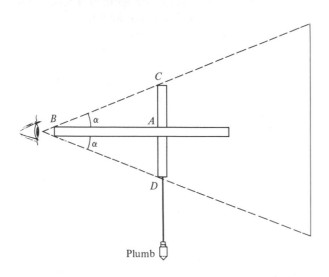

FIGURE 1. Jacob's staff.

al-Haytham and was known in Europe in the second half of the thirteenth century; Levi is distinguished for his careful instructions on how the observations should be performed and for his explanation of the theoretical basis of the camera obscura.

The planetary system conceived by Levi contains a mixture of technical considerations with others of a metaphysical character. He postulates the existence of forty-eight spheres, some concentric with the earth and others not. The movement is transmitted from the innermost sphere to the outermost by means of an intermediate nonresistant fluid. The stars are affixed to the last sphere of their own system, and each sphere or system of spheres is moved by an immaterial intelligence. The number of spirits that move the heavens is, then, forty-eight or eight. Within this general framework, Levi investigated particularly the sun and the moon. His lunar model eliminated the use of epicycles; its results were practically equivalent to those of Ptolemy's model at syzygy and quadrature (where Levi believed them to be adequate enough) but an entirely new correction was introduced by him at the octants (where Ptolemaic theory could not be accepted because of systematic discrepancies with observation): there is no evidence to suggest a relationship between Levi and Tycho Brahe concerning the latter's discovery of variation (an inequality that reaches its maximum at octant). It is also clear that Levi's model represented the two first lunar inequalities better than Ptolemy's model did. Finally he eliminated practically all the variations in lunar distance from the earth, for which he rightly criticized Ptolemy's model.

The movements of the planets were less extensively dealt with (chapters 103–135). Levi carefully studied the controversial question concerning the places of Venus and Mercury with respect to the sun (chapters 129–135) without arriving at any definitive conclusion. Finally, one of his greatest contributions to medieval astronomy was his extraordinary enlargement of the Ptolemaic universe—for example, the maximum distance of Venus (Ptolemy, 1,079 earth radii; Levi, 8,971,112 earth radii); the distance of the fixed stars from the center of the earth (Ptolemy, 20,000 earth radii; Levi, $159 \times 10^{12} + 6,515 \times 10^8 + 1,338 \times 10^4 + 944$ earth radii); and the diameter of first-magnitude stars (Ptolemy, $4.5 + 1/20$ earth radii; Levi, more than 328×10^8 earth radii).

A few astrological treatises of Levi have been preserved, including a prediction addressed to Pope Benedict XII in 1339 and his *Prognosticon de conjunctione Saturni et Jovis (et Martis) a.D. 1345*, left unfinished at his death (the Latin translation by Peter of Alexandria and Solomon ben Gerson, Levi's brother, is extant). This conjunction of the three superior planets was also the subject of predictions by John of Murs and Firminus de Bellavalle (Firmin de Beauval). At the outbreak of the black plague of 1348 the conjunction was believed, retrospectively, to be the celestial cause that had corrupted the air.

Levi's work was influential in Europe until the eighteenth century. In the fourteenth century his astronomical tables were used by Jacob ben David Yomtob in constucting his own tables (Perpignan, 1361). It influenced the astrological work of Symon de Covino (*d.* 1367), as well as the astronomical work of Immanuel ben Jacob of Tarascon (*fl. ca.* 1340–1377). In the fifteenth century the *Sefer Tekunah* was praised by Abraham Zacuto (*ca.* 1450–1510); and the treatise *De sinibus* was the model for the *De triangulis* of Regiomontanus (1464; published 1533). The latter, as well as his disciples Bernhard Walther (1430–1504) and Martin Behaim (*d.* 1507), used the Jacob's staff, and it continued to be widely used in navigation, with various improvements, until the middle of the eighteenth century. In the seventeenth century Kepler wrote to his friend Johannes Ramus, asking him to send a copy of the *Sefer Tekunah* to him. There is also a curious cosmographical treatise written in Hebrew by an unknown Roman Jew who cites Levi as being among the greatest authors of the past.

BIBLIOGRAPHY

I. ORIGINAL WORKS. Gerson Lange, *Die Praxis des Rechners* (Frankfurt, 1909), contains an edited German trans. of the *Ma'aseh Hosheb;* Joseph Carlebach, *Lewi als Mathematiker* (Berlin, 1910), has an ed. of the *De numeris harmonicis* on pp. 125–144. Maximilian Curtze, "Die Abhandlungen des Levi ben Gerson über Trigonometrie und den Jacobstab," in *Bibliotheca mathematica*, 2nd ser., **12** (1898), 97–112, is a Latin trans. of the *De sinibus* and the *Tractatus instrumenti astronomie*. The eds. of the *Milḥamot Adonai* do not include the *Sefer Tekunah*, which traditionally is considered as a separate work. On the latter see Ernest Renan, "Les écrivains juifs français du XIVe siècle," in *Histoire littéraire de la France*, XXXI (Paris, 1893), 586–644—see esp. pp. 624–641, the Hebrew and Latin texts of the intro. and table of contents of the *Sefer Tekunah;* see also Baldassarre Boncompagni, "Intorno ad un trattato d'aritmetica stampato nel 1478," in *Atti dell'Accademia Pontificia dei Nuovi Lincei* (1863), 741–753, a textual study of three Latin MSS from the above-mentioned work plus some short . fragments. Goldstein ("Levi ben Gerson's Lunar Model" quoted below) gives an English translation of the significant passages concerning Levi's lunar theory. On the MSS of the *Sefer Tekunah*, as well as the remaining unpublished works by Levi, see Moritz Steinschneider, *Mathematik bei den*

Juden (Leipzig, 1893–1899; Frankfurt, 1901; Hildesheim, 1964).

II. SECONDARY LITERATURE. See F. Cantera Burgos, *El judío salamantino Abraham Zacut. Notas para la historia de la astronomía en la España medieval* (Madrid, n.d.), pp. 53, 55, 153, 189–190; Pamela H. Espenshade, "A Text on Trigonometry by Levi ben Gerson," in *Mathematics Teacher*, **60** (1967), 628–637; Bernard R. Goldstein, "The Town of Ezob/Aurayca," in *Revue des études juives*, **126** (1967), 269–271; "Preliminary Remarks on Levi ben Gerson's Contributions to Astronomy," in *Proceedings of the Israel Academy of Sciences and Humanities*, **3**, no. 9 (1969), 239–254; *Al-Biṭrūjī: On the Principles of Astronomy*, I (New Haven–London, 1971), 40–43; "Levi ben Gerson's Lunar Model," in *Centaurus*, **16** (1972), 257–283; and "Theory and Observation in Medieval Astronomy," in *Isis*, **63** (1972), 39–47; Isidore Loeb, "La ville d'Hysope," in *Revue des études juives*, **1** (1880), 72–82; D. C. Lindberg, "The Theory of Pinhole Images in the Fourteenth Century," in *Archives for History of Exact Sciences*, **6** (1970), 299–325, esp. pp. 303 ff.; José M. Millás Vallicrosa and David Romano, *Cosmografía de un judío romano del siglo XVII* (Madrid–Barcelona, 1954), pp. 20, 33, 65, 70, 76–77, 85, 87; B. A. Rosenfeld, "Dokazatelstva piatogo postulata Evklida srednevekovykh matematikov Khasana Ibn al-Khaisana i Lva Gersonida" ("The Proofs of Euclid's Fifth Postulate by the Medieval Mathematicians Ibn al-Haytham and Levi ben Gerson"), in *Istoriko-matematicheskie issledovaniya*, **11** (1958), 733–782; George Sarton, *Introduction to the History of Science*, III (Baltimore, 1947–1948), 594–607, and the bibliography given there—see also pp. 129, 886, 1116, 1516, 1518; and Lynn Thorndike, *A History of Magic and Experimental Science*, III (New York–London, 1934), 38, 303–305, 309–311.

JULIO SAMSÓ

LEVI, GIUSEPPE (*b*. Trieste, Austria-Hungary, 14 October 1872; *d*. Turin, Italy, 3 February 1965), *human anatomy, histology, embryology.*

Levi's father, Michele Levi, was a wealthy Jewish financier whose family had financially helped the Austrian administration; his mother, Emma Perugia, was from Pisa. In spite of being brought up conservatively Levi became an enthusiastic Irredentist. He completed his secondary education in Trieste; and when his father died, the family moved to Florence, where he studied medicine and surgery, graduating in 1895. He became an assistant at a psychiatric clinic in Florence (1896–1898); then in Berlin (1898–1899) at the Institute of Anatomy directed by O. Hertwig; and returned in 1900 to Florence, to the Institute of Anatomy, as an assistant to Chiarugi. Later that year Levi obtained the chair of anatomy at the University of Sassari, then at the

University of Palermo in 1914, and finally that at the University of Turin, where he remained from 1919 until 1938. Dismissed from the university because of the fascist racial laws, he obtained a post at the University of Liège (1938–1941). He was reinstated into the Italian university system in 1945 and retired in 1947, subsequently becoming director of the Center for Studies on Growth and Senility of the National Research Council. Levi was married to Lidia Tinzi, a Catholic. The couple had five children.

Levi was a member, from 1926, of the Accademia dei Lincei; of the Accademia dei XL from 1933, of the Academy of Sciences of Bologna from 1945; and of many other Italian and foreign academies and scientific societies. He held honorary doctorates from the universities of Liège, Montevideo, and Santiago (Chile); he also received the royal prize of the Accademia dei Lincei in 1923 and a gold medal "dei Benemeriti" of the Scuola della Cultura e dell'Arte.

In 1896–1898, while an assistant in the psychiatric clinic, Levi was interested less in the patients than in morphology. He conducted studies on the structure of the nucleus of nerve cells, epoch-making studies that were fully understood and confirmed only fifty years later (H. Hydén, 1945). He also investigated the Nissl substance, which he did not consider exclusive to the nerve cell, a notion also confirmed much later.

While Levi was working with Chiarugi, he carried out important morphological and histogenetic studies on the comparative anatomy of the dorsal and ventral hippocampus nerve, completing previous observations by Elliot Smith, and on the morphology of the chondrocranium of man and other mammals. In a monograph on the spinal ganglia of over fifty vertebrate species, he illustrated the significance of the fenestrated apparatus of the ganglion cells and the size relationships between those cells and the body of the animal. He concluded that the size of neurons is proportional to the size of the body (Levi's law), in contrast with Driesch's law, which states that the size of the cells remains constant in both the variable and the stable elements. In 1921–1925 Levi further extended the study of the development mechanism which controls the dimensions and the number of supercellular units (the histomers of Heidenhain) during the growth of the body, in relation to the rate of growth and the length of life.

At Sassari, Levi studied the morphology of chondriosomes by normal histological methods; and later, using Harrison's method to study the behavior of mitochondria in cultured live cells, he concluded that there is no relation between mitochondria and secretion granules and that they do not transform themselves into paraplasm or myofibrils.

Levi was one of the pioneers in cultivating tissues *in vitro*, a line of research he pursued at the University of Palermo from 1914 to 1919. He confirmed the cytologic studies of Warren and Margaret Lewis and extended his observations to elements from various tissues, studying the changes that the tissues undergo while being placed in culture. He demonstrated the existence of neurofibrils in the live elements, a finding confirmed by the electron microscope (F. Schmitt, Fernandez Moran, Palay, and Bairati).

Levi continued to develop this line of research at the University of Turin and initiated a number of students into the field. In 1934 he published an extensive monograph, "Explantation," a documentation and discussion of the first twenty-five years of study on cultivation of tissues *in vitro*. Of particular interest are further observations by him and his students on the interdependence relationships of neurons grown *in vitro*, on the regeneration *per primam* of axons *in vitro*, and on the differentiation of neurons in the spinal ganglia of the chicken embryo. With this method he also confirmed the acute observations of Flemming and Boveri on the fibrillar structure of neurons. In 1927 he began an extensive plan of research on the morphological aspects of the aging of tissues and organs.

Levi's treatise on histology is marked by extreme individuality and progressiveness; it ran to four Italian (1927–1954) and two Spanish editions. Levi's knowledge of the field, his remarkable memory, his quick intuition, and his grasp of modern concepts and techniques made him for many years Italy's leading authority in biology. He was opposed to any racial or religious bigotry and did not approve of the Zionist movement. His sense of dignity and of independence, his social ideas, and his faith in the spiritual freedom of man made him a strenuous opponent of Fascism, under which he suffered persecution and imprisonment. He was strict, honest, loyal, intolerant of vulgarity and mediocrity; a severe and exacting, yet affectionate and generous teacher. Eight of his students became professors of human anatomy, histology, or embryology. Until the end of his life he retained his extraordinary memory and clarity of mind, and continued his keen interest in the progress of biological research. He died at the age of ninety-two, after a long and painful illness.

BIBLIOGRAPHY

I. ORIGINAL WORKS. Levi's writings include "Su alcune particolarità di struttura del nucleo delle cellule nervose,"
in *Rivista di Patologia nervosa e mentale*, **1** (1896), 141–149; "Contributo alla fisiologia della cellula nervosa," *ibid.*, 169–180; "Ricerche sulla capacità proliferativa della cellula nervosa," *ibid.*, 385–386; "Ricerche citologiche comparate sulla cellula nervosa dei vertebrati," *ibid.*, **2** (1897), 1–43; "Sulla cariocinesi delle cellule nervose," *ibid.*, **3** (1898), 97–112; "Sulle modificazioni morfologiche delle cellule nervose di animali a sangue freddo durante l'ibernazione," *ibid.*, 443–459; "Beitrag zum Studium der Entwicklung des Primordialcranium des Menschen," in *Archiv für mikroskopische Anatomie und Entwicklungsmechanik*, **55** (1900), 341–414; "Ueber die Entwicklung und Histogenese der Amnioshornformation," *ibid.*, **64** (1904), 389–404; "Morfologia e minuta struttura dell'ippocampo dorsale," in *Archivio italiano di anatomia e di embriologia*, **3** (1904), 438–484; "Sull'origine filogenetica della formazione ammonica," *ibid.*, 234–247; the three-part "Studi sulla grandezza delle cellule. I. Ricerche comparative sulla grandezza delle cellule dei mammiferi," *ibid.*, **5** (1906), 291–358; "II. Le variazioni dell'indice plasmatico-nucleare durante l'intercinesi," *ibid.*, **10** (1911), 545–554; and "III. Le modificazioni della grandezza cellulare e nucleare e dell'indice plasmatico-nucleare durante i precoci periodi dell'ontogenesi dei mammiferi," in *Ricerche di biologia dedicate al Prof. A. Lustig* (Florence, 1914), pp. 1–26; "Cenni sulla costituzione e sullo sviluppo dell'uncus dell'ippocampo nell'uomo," in *Archivio italiano di anatomia e di embriologia*, **8** (1909), 535–562; "Contributo alla conoscenza del condrocranio dei mammiferi," in *Monitore zoologico italiano*, **20** (1909), 159–174; and "Il comportamento dei condriosomi durante i più precoci periodi dello sviluppo dei mammiferi," in *Archiv für Zellforschung*, **13** (1915), 471–524.

See also "Per la migliore conoscenza del fondamento anatomico e dei fattori morfogenetici della grandezza del corpo," in *Archivio italiano di anatomia e di embriologia*, supp. **18** (1921), 316–434; "Wachstum und Körpergrösse," in *Ergebnisse der Anatomie und Entwicklungsgeschichte*, **26** (1925), 87–342; *Trattato di istologia* (Turin, 1927; 4th ed., 1954); "Gewebezüchtung," in Tibor Péterfi, ed., *Methodik der wissenschaftlichen Biologie*, I (Berlin, 1928), pp. 494–558; *Fisiopatologia della vecchiaia*, I, *Istologia sieroterapico* (Milan, 1933); "Explantation, besonders die Struktur und die biologischen Eigenschaften der in vitro gezüchteten Zellen und Gewebe," in *Ergebnisse der Anatomie und Entwicklungsgeschichte*, **31** (1934), 125–707; and his revision and enlargement of Giulio Chiarugi's *Trattato di anatomia dell'uomo*, 9th ed. (Milan, 1959).

II. SECONDARY LITERATURE. For further information on Levi's life and work consult the following biographical and bibliographical sources: Rodolfo Amprino, "Giuseppe Levi," in *Acta anatomica*, **66** (1967), 1–44, which includes a complete bibliography; and Oliviero M. Olivo, "Commemorazione del socio Giuseppe Levi," in *Atti dell'Accademia nazionale dei Lincei. Rendiconti*, 8th ser., **40** (1966), 954–972, with a bibliography. See also *Annuario Accademia Nazionale dei XL* (1961), pp. 49–66.

OLIVIERO M. OLIVO

LEVI-CIVITA, TULLIO (*b.* Padua, Italy, 29 March 1873; *d.* Rome, Italy, 20 December 1941), *mathematics, mathematical physics.*

The son of Giacomo Levi-Civita, a lawyer who from 1908 was a senator, Levi-Civita was an outstanding student at the *liceo* in Padua. In 1890 he enrolled in the Faculty of Mathematics of the University of Padua. Giuseppe Veronese and Gregorio Ricci Curbastro were among his teachers. He received his diploma in 1894 and in 1895 became resident professor at the teachers' college annexed to the Faculty of Science at Pavia. From 1897 to 1918 Levi-Civita taught rational mechanics at the University of Padua. His years in Padua (where in 1914 he married a pupil, Libera Trevisani) were scientifically the most fruitful of his career. In 1918 he became professor of higher analysis at Rome and, in 1920, of rational mechanics. In 1938, struck by the fascist racial laws against Jews, he was forced to give up teaching.

The breadth of his scientific interests, his scruples regarding the fulfillment of his academic responsibilities, and his affection for young people made Levi-Civita the leader of a flourishing school of mathematicians.

Levi-Civita's approximately 200 memoirs in pure and applied mathematics deal with analytical mechanics, celestial mechanics, hydrodynamics, elasticity, electromagnetism, and atomic physics. His most important contribution to science was rooted in the memoir "Sulle trasformazioni delle equazioni dinamiche" (1896), which was characterized by the use of the methods of absolute differential calculus that Ricci Curbastro had applied only to differential geometry. In the "Méthodes de calcul différentiel absolus et leurs applications," written with Ricci Curbastro and published in 1900 in *Mathematische Annalen*, there is a complete exposition of the new calculus, which consists of a particular algorithm designed to express geometric and physical laws in Euclidean and non-Euclidean spaces, particularly in Riemannian curved spaces. The memoir concerns a very general but laborious type of calculus that made it possible to deal with many difficult problems, including, according to Einstein, the formulation of the general theory of relativity.

Although Levi-Civita had expressed certain reservations concerning relativity in the first years after its formulation (1905), he gradually came to accept the new views. His own original research culminated in 1917 in the introduction of the concept of parallelism in curved spaces that now bears his name; it furnishes a simple law for transporting a vector parallel to itself along a curve in a space of n dimensions. With this new concept, absolute differential calculus, having absorbed other techniques, became tensor calculus, now the essential instrument of the unitary relativistic theories of gravitation and electromagnetism. Two of the concept's many applications and generalizations were in the "geometry of paths," which extends the concept of Riemannian variety, and in the theory of spaces with affine and projective connections, which is used with the geometry for a complete representation of electromagnetic phenomena in the framework of general relativity.

In studying the stability of the phenomena of motion, Levi-Civita used a general method, which, by means of a periodic solution of a first-order differential system, restores stability or instability to the study of certain point transformations. He ascertained that periodic solutions, in a first approximation of apparent stability, prove instead to be unstable. Another of Levi-Civita's contributions to analytical mechanics was the general theory of stationary motions, in which moving bodies passing the same spot always do so at the same speed. The theory enabled him to find with a uniform method all the known cases of stationary motion and also to discover new ones.

From 1906 Levi-Civita's memoirs in hydrodynamics, his favorite field, deal with the resistance of a liquid to the translational motion of an immersed solid; he resolved the problem through the general integration of the equations for irrotational flows past a solid body, allowing for the formation of a cavity behind it. His general theory of canal waves originated in a memoir written in 1925.

In related memoirs (1903–1916) Levi-Civita contributed to celestial mechanics in the study of the three-body problem: the determination of the motion of three bodies, considered as reduced to their centers of mass and subject to mutual Newtonian attraction. In 1914–1916 he succeeded in eliminating the singularities presented at the points of possible collisions, past or future. His results furnished a rigorous solution to the classic problem—which, by indirect method and by transcending dynamic equations, Karl F. Sundmann had reached in 1912, as Levi-Civita himself admitted.

His research in relativity led Levi-Civita to mathematical problems suggested by atomic physics, which in the 1920's was developing outside the traditional framework: the general theory of adiabatic invariants, the motion of a body of variable mass, the extension of the Maxwellian distribution to a system of corpuscles, and Schrödinger's equations.

BIBLIOGRAPHY

I. ORIGINAL WORKS. All of Levi-Civita's memoirs and notes published between 1893 and 1928 were collected in his *Opere matematiche. Memorie e note*, 4 vols. (Bologna, 1954–1960). Other works include *Questioni di meccanica classica e relativistica* (Bologna, 1924), also in German trans. (Berlin, 1924); *Lezioni di calcolo differenziale assoluto* (Rome, 1925); *Lezioni di meccanica razionale*, 2 vols. (Bologna, 1926–1927; 2nd ed., 1930), written with Ugo Amaldi; and *Fondamenti di meccanica relativistica* (Bologna, 1928).

II. SECONDARY LITERATURE. See the following, listed chronologically: Corrado Segre, "Relazione sul concorso al premio reale per la matematica, del 1907," in *Atti dell'Accademia nazionale dei Lincei. Rendiconti delle sedute solenni*, **2** (1908), 410–424; Albert Einstein, "Die Grundlage der allgemeinen Relativitätstheorie," in *Annalen der Physik*, 4th ser., **49** (1916), 769; "Tullio Levi-Civita," in *Annuario della Pontificia Accademia delle Scienze*, **1** (1936–1937), 496–511, with a complete list of his memberships in scientific institutions and of his academic honors; and Ugo Amaldi, "Commemorazione del socio Tullio Levi-Civita," in *Atti dell'Accademia nazionale dei Lincei, Rendiconti. Classe di scienze fisiche, matematiche e naturali*, 8th ser., **1** (1946), 1130–1155, with a complete bibliography.

MARIO GLIOZZI

LEVINSON-LESSING, FRANZ YULEVICH (*b.* St. Petersburg, Russia, 9 March 1861; *d.* Leningrad, U.S.S.R, 25 October 1939), *geology, petrography.*

An academician of the Soviet Academy of Sciences from 1925 (and a corresponding member since 1914), Levinson-Lessing was the son of a well-known doctor. He married Varvara Ippolitovna Tarnovskaya, who was his colleague in the Commission for Scientific Education, in 1919. Their son Vladimir, an art critic, became a well-known specialist on European art.

Levinson-Lessing spent his childhood in St. Petersburg and received his secondary education there. At St. Petersburg University he studied under the petrographer A. A. Inostrantsev. He graduated in 1883 and remained there to prepare for a teaching career. Undoubted influences on Levinson-Lessing in the first years of his scientific career were his teacher and colleague, the pioneer soil scientist V. V. Dokuchaev, and V. I. Vernadsky. Under this influence he concentrated on the chemistry of inorganic nature. Levinson-Lessing maintained lifelong ties with soil science, had a continuing interest in its problems, and headed various soil institutions.

Ten years after graduating from the university, during which period he had synthesized his work in regional petrography and marked out new paths in its theoretical structure, Levinson-Lessing became professor of mineralogy at the University of Yurev (Tartu).

Working from 1902 to 1930 at the Polytechnical Institute in Leningrad, Levinson-Lessing organized the first laboratory of experimental petrography in Russia, and then a geochemical section. From a division of mineralogy he created petrography, which has become an independent field of knowledge. His main areas of concentration were the analysis of the crust of the earth, the penetration of its depths, and the clarification of the structure of mountains and rocks and their accompanying ore deposits.

Levinson-Lessing developed the idea of the separation or differentiation of magma, placed it on a factual basis, and transformed it into a scientific theory. Having firmly established magma as a complex silicate solution differing from aqueous solutions by its considerable viscosity and susceptibility to intense supercooling, he advanced the doctrine of two ancestral magmas, granite and basalt, that had played a primary role in the creation of the rock of the earth's core. From them came all igneous rocks, the various compositions of which are caused by differing mixtures of these magmas, by the melting and assimilation of previously existing rocks, by fractional crystallization, and by gravity settling. All these processes together create the phenomenon of magmatic differentiation. Igneous rocks after the Precambrian era are primarily the result of the melting of particular parts of the earth's solid crust. Only older igneous rocks had the ancestral granite and gabbroic magmas as their sources.

Levinson-Lessing's regional petrographic works were the basis for the development of theoretical petrology. His expeditions in Karelia (now the Karelo-Finnish S.S.R.), the Urals, the Caucasus, Transcaucasia, the Crimea, the Khibiny Mountains, and eastern Siberia enabled him to approach the solution of the problems of petrographic formations and origin. In 1888 he advanced the idea of the Olonets diabasic formation, which was productively developed in the theory of formations. His trips to Italy and his ascent of Vesuvius with A. Rittmann provided an impetus for the creation in 1935 of the volcanological station at Kamchatka, where Soviet volcanology developed.

Classifying and systematizing igneous rocks occupied Levinson-Lessing throughout his career. In 1898 he proposed the first rational chemical classification of rocks. In his works he depended on physical and chemical research methods, using them to solve such problems as the differentiation of magma and the genesis and classification of rocks and ore deposits.

An active participant in the International Geological Congress, Levinson-Lessing corresponded with the most distinguished geologists and petrographers of western Europe and the United States. At the seventh session of the Congress, Levinson-Lessing was elected to the commission on the classification of igneous rock. For the eighth session, which took place in 1900, he prepared the *Petrographic Dictionary*. At the Paris meeting of the Commission on Petrographic Nomenclature he presented a report and his own additions. He also participated in the twelfth, fourteenth, and seventeenth sessions. At the last session the Permanent Commission on Petrography, Mineralogy, and Geochemistry was organized, with Levinson-Lessing as president.

Levinson-Lessing was a historian of petrography and the natural sciences whose works are well-known both in the Soviet Union and abroad; his monographs *Uspekhi petrografii v Rossii* ("The Progress of Petrography in Russia"; 1923) and *Vvedenie v istoriyu petrografii* ("Introduction to the History of Petrography"; 1936) and many biographical sketches of well-known scientists reveal a tireless researcher in the history of science. A historical approach to the solution of basic scientific problems characterized Levinson-Lessing and appeared in many of his works, particularly in the important "Problema genezisa magmaticheskikh porod i puti k ee razresheniyu" ("The Problem of the Genesis of Magmatic Rock and the Means of Solving It"; 1934).

Analyzing the phenomena of rock formation, the centuries-long changes in shorelines and volcanoes, Levinson-Lessing concluded that different parts of the earth's crust rise and fall simultaneously. Mountains were formed by these movements, and plastic or liquid magma was transferred at depth, serving as the source of magmatic and volcanic phenomena. Bringing together all that was known at the beginning of the twentieth century regarding the formation of mountains, he asserted that systems arose after prolonged sinking followed by slow uplift. Folded mountain chains were formed at the borders of the continents and seas. The sinking of some blocks in the sea was accompanied by rising of the adjoining lands. Sinking and rising were kept more or less equal by the warping of separate blocks of the earth's crust. Levinson-Lessing believed that volcanoes accompany uplifts of parts of the earth's crust and that a major factor in their eruption is the pressure on lava exerted by the sinking of other blocks. He considered the fluctuation of lava levels in the volcanoes of the Hawaiian Islands to be an especially clear example, believing that the lakes of lava form the upper parts of columns of liquid lava going down to subterranean lava reservoirs. These columns of lava would be in hydrostatic equilibrium.

For Levinson-Lessing science not only collects and describes facts but also compares them, penetrates into their essence, and structures them in broad generalizations. In his article "Rol fantazii v nauchnom tvorchestve" ("The Role of Fantasy in Scientific Creativity") he described scientific creativity as consisting of three main elements: the empirical, which provides a basis; scientific fantasy, or the creative idea; and the testing and investigation of the creative idea through logical analysis and experiment. All three elements are necessary, he believed, for scientific creativity and progress. The development and flowering of science requires a harmonious combination of observations, experiments, and ideas; induction and deduction together; a combination of concrete facts, perceived externally, and intuitive forms, which arise subjectively.

BIBLIOGRAPHY

I. ORIGINAL WORKS. Many of Levinson-Lessing's writings are in *Izbrannye trudy* ("Selected Works"), 4 vols. (Moscow–Leningrad, 1944–1955). Among his works are "Olonetskaya diabazovaya formatsia" ("Olonets Diabasic Formation"), in *Trudy Imperatorskago S.-Peterburgskago obshchestva estestvoispytatelei*, Otdelenie geologii i mineralogii, **19** (1888); "Issledovania po teoreticheskoy petrografii v svyazi s ucheniem izverzhennykh porod tsentralnogo Kavkaza" ("Research in Theoretical Petrography in Connection with the Theory of Igneous Rock of the Central Caucasus"), *ibid.*, **26** (1898); "Sferolitovye porody Mugodzhar" ("Spherulite Rocks of Mugodzhar"), *ibid.*, **33**, no. 5 (1905); "Sushchestvuet li mezhdu intruzivnymi i effuzivnymi porodami razlichie v khimicheskom sostave" ("Is There a Difference in Chemical Composition Between Intrusive and Effusive Rocks?"), in *Izvestiya S.-Peterburgskago politekhnicheskago instituta Imperatora Petra Velikago* (1906), nos. 1–2; "Polveka mikroskopii v petrografii" ("A Half Century of Microscopy in Petrography"), *ibid.*, **10** (1908); "O samom yuzhnom mestopozhdenii platiny na Urale" ("On the Most Recent Platinum Deposits in the Urals"), *ibid.*, **13** (1910); and *Vulkany i lavy Tsentralnogo Kavkaza* ("Volcanoes and Lava of the Central Caucasus"; St. Petersburg, 1913).

Later works are *Uspekhi petrografii v Rossii* ("The Progress of Petrography in Russia"; Petrograd, 1923); "Rol fantazii v nauchnom tvorchestve" ("The Role of Fantasy in Scientific Creativity"), in *Peterburgskoe nauchnoe khimiko-tekhnicheskoe izdatelstvo* (1923), 36–50; "Professor Aleksandr Aleksandrovich Inostrantsev," in *Izvestiya Geologicheskago komiteta za 1919 g.*, **38**, no. 3 (1924); "Trappy Tuluno-Udinskogo i Bratskogo rayonov v vostochnoy Sibiri" ("Diabases of the Tulun-Udinsky and Bratsky Regions in Eastern Siberia"), in *Trudy Soveta po izucheniyu proizvoditelnykh sil*, Seriya sibirskaya, no. 1 (1932); "Problema genezisa magmaticheskikh porod i puti k ee razresheniyu" ("The Problem of the Genesis of Magmatic Rock and the Means of Solving It"), in *Izdatel-*

stvo Akademii nauk SSSR (1934); "O svoeobraznom tipe differentsiatsii v vartolite Yalguby" ("On a Peculiar Type of Differentiation in Variolite of Yalguba"), in *Trudy Petrina Akademii nauk SSSR*, no. 5 (1935); *Vvedenie v istoriyu petrografii* ("Introduction to the History of Petrography"; Leningrad, 1936); "Spornye voprosy sistematiki i nomenklatury izverzhennykh porod" ("Controversial Questions of Systematization and Nomenclature of Igneous Rocks"), in *Doklady Akademii nauk SSSR*, **21**, no. 3 (1938); and "Problemy magmy" ("Problems of Magma"), in *Uchenye zapiski Leningradskogo gosudartstvennogo universiteta*, **3**, no. 17 (1937), also in *Izvestiya Akademii nauk SSSR*, Seriya geologicheskaya, no. 1 (1939).

II. SECONDARY LITERATURE. See I. M. Asafova and O. V. Isakova, *Franz Yulevich Levinson-Lessing* (Moscow, 1941); D. S. Belyankin, "Akademik F. Y. Levinson-Lessing v trudakh ego po teoreticheskoy petrografii" ("Academician F. Yu. Levinson-Lessing in His Works on Theoretical Petrography"), in *Izvestiya Akademii nauk SSSR*, Seriya geologicheskaya (1945), no. 1, pp. 18–27; A. S. Ginzberg, "Znachenie petrograficheskikh rabot. F. Y. Levinson-Lessinga dlya russkoy i mirovoy nauki" ("The Significance of the Petrographical Work of F. Y. Levinson-Lessing in Russian and World Science"), *ibid.* (1952), no. 5, pp. 7–11; S. S. Kuznetsov, "Krupny russky ucheny F. Y. Levinson-Lessing" ("The Great Russian Scientist F. Y. Levinson-Lessing"), in *Vestnik Leningradskogo gosudarstvennogo universiteta* (1948), no. 5, pp. 128–144; P. I. Lebedev, *Akademik F. Y. Levinson-Lessing kak teoretik petrografii* ("Academician F. Y. Levinson-Lessing as a Theoretician of Petrography"; Moscow–Leningrad, 1947); B. L. Lichkov, "Idei F. Y. Levinson-Lessinga o vekovykh kolebaniakh zemnoy kory v svete sovremennykh vozzreny" ("The Ideas of F. Y. Levinson-Lessing on Secular Oscillations of the Earth's Crust in the Light of Contemporary Views"), in *Ocherki po istorii geologicheskikh znanii*, no. 5 (1965), pp. 248–259; A. A. Polkanov, "F. Y. Levinson-Lessing kak petrograf-myslitel" ("F. Y. Levinson-Lessing as a Petrographic Thinker"), in *Izvestiya Akademii nauk SSSR*, Seriya geologicheskaya, no. 4 (1950), pp. 25–27; and D. I. Shcherbakov, "Rol F. Y. Levinson-Lessinga v razvitii uchenia o rudnykh mestorozhdenia" ("The Role of F. Y. Levinson-Lessing in the Development of the Theory of Ore Deposits"), *ibid.*, no. 3 (1961), pp. 55–60.

A. A. MENIAILOV

LÉVY, MAURICE (*b*. Ribeauvillé, France, 28 February 1838; *d*. Paris, France, 30 September 1910), *mathematics, engineering.*

Maurice Lévy had a distinguished career as a practicing engineer, teacher, and researcher. He studied at the École Polytechnique from 1856 to 1858 and at the École des Ponts et Chaussées. After graduating he served for several years in the provinces

and continued his studies. In 1867 he was awarded the *docteur ès sciences* and in 1872 was assigned to the navigation service of the Seine in the region of Paris. In 1880 he became chief government civil engineer and, in 1885, inspector general. At the same time Lévy pursued an academic career. From 1862 to 1883 he served as *répétiteur* in mechanics at the École Polytechnique. In 1875 he was appointed professor of applied mechanics at the École Centrale des Arts et Manufactures, and in 1885 he became professor of analytic and celestial mechanics at the Collège de France. Lévy was elected to the Académie des Sciences in 1883 and served as president of the Société Philomatique in 1880.

Lévy's research ranged over projective and differential geometry, mechanics, kinematics, hydraulics, and hydrodynamics. Of his two theses, the first, influenced by the work of Gabriel Lamé, deals with orthogonal curvilinear coordinates; the second is on the theory and application of liquid motion. He often returned to the question of elasticity, and his writings on the subject include a book published in 1873. His other works include theoretical treatises on energy and hydrodynamics, as well as more practical ones on boat propulsion.

Lévy considered his most significant work to be that on graphical statics (1874), which was an attempt to apply the methods of projective geometry, particularly the theory of geometric transformations, to problems of statics. It was directed toward engineers and was very popular, going through three editions.

BIBLIOGRAPHY

I. ORIGINAL WORKS. A complete bibliography is in Poggendorff, III, 804–805; IV, 876–877; and V, 737. Lévy's two theses are "Sur une transformation des coordonnées curvilignes orthogonales, et sur les coordonnées curvilignes comprenant une famille quelconque de surfaces du second ordre," in *Journal de l'École polytechnique*, **26** (1870), 157–200; and *Essai théorique et appliqué sur le mouvement des liquides*, published separately (Paris, 1867). His books are *Étude d'un système de barrage mobile* (Paris, 1873); *Application de la théorie mathématique de l'élasticité à l'étude de systèmes articulés* (Paris, 1873); *La statique graphique et ses applications aux constructions*, with atlas (Paris, 1874; 2nd ed., 4 vols., Paris, 1886–1888; 3rd ed., 1913–1918); *Sur le principe d'énergie* (Paris, 1890), written with G. Pavie; *Étude des moyens mécanique et électrique de traction des bateaux, Partie I: Halage funiculaire* (Paris, 1894); *Théorie des marées* (Paris, 1898); and *Éléments de cinématique et de mécanique* (Paris, 1902).

II. SECONDARY LITERATURE. There is very little available beyond the article in *La grande encyclopédie*, XXII,

148; and the obituary by Émile Picard in *Comptes rendus hebdomadaires des séances de l'Académie des sciences*, **151** (1910), 603–606.

ELAINE KOPPELMAN

LÉVY, SERVE-DIEU ABAILARD (called **ARMAND**) (*b*. Paris, France, 14 November 1795; *d*. le Pecq, near Saint-Germain, France, 29 July 1841), *mineralogy*.

Lévy's father, a Florentine Jew, was an itinerant merchant who, on one of his trips to France, married a Parisian Catholic, Céline Mailfert. Their son's birth records bear the unusual given names Serve-Dieu Abailard, which also appear on his death certificate, but Lévy called himself, more simply, Armand. It is under this name that he appears on the membership list of the Geological Society of London, beginning in 1824.

Lévy completed his secondary studies in Paris, at the Lycée Henri IV, and won the *concours général* in mathematics, a competition for the best students from all French *lycées* and *collèges*. He passed the entrance examination for the École Normale Supérieure in 1813 and graduated in 1816 with the title of *agrégé* in mathematical sciences. As it was difficult for a Jew to obtain a university position in France, he decided to leave the country and accept the post of professor at the Collège Royal of Île Bourbon (now Île de la Réunion) in the Indian Ocean. He embarked at Rochefort in 1818; the vessel was shipwrecked near Plymouth, an event that determined Lévy's scientific career. For the next two years he supported himself by giving mathematics lessons and in 1820 met a rich mineral merchant, Henry Heuland, who had just sold a large collection of minerals to Charles Hampden Turner. Lévy was hired to make an inventory of it and to produce a descriptive catalog. In 1822, in London, he married Harriet Drewet, who was nineteen; they had several children.

In 1827 the work for which Heuland had commissioned Lévy was finished; and it was decided that, for reasons of economy, the catalog would be printed in Belgium. Lévy therefore moved to Brussels to supervise the printing of the text and the engraving of the illustrations. He was also appointed reader at the University of Liège, teaching analytical mechanics, astronomy, crystallography, and mineralogy. On 3 April 1830 he was elected a member of the Académie des Sciences et Belles-lettres of Brussels. After the July Revolution of 1830 he returned to Paris as a lecturer in mathematics at the École Normale Supérieure and professor at the Collège Royal Charlemagne (1831).

A short while after his return to France, Lévy's wife died. In 1838 he married Amélie Rodriguez Henriquez, the sister of his close friend, the mathematician Olinde Rodriguez. They had two daughters, the elder of whom married Alexandre Bertrand, curator of the Musée de Saint-Germain and brother of the mathematician Joseph Bertrand.

Lévy was a man of great frankness and exquisite politeness. If he was sometimes touchy, even with his friends, it was because he had been the object of racial and religious prejudice. During his stay in England, Lévy became friendly with Wollaston and Herschel, and he was a member of the council of the Geological Society of London from 1826 to 1828. In France he had powerful defenders in Arago, Poisson, Charles Dupin, and the mineralogists Brochant, Brongniart, and Beudant. Des Cloizeaux considered himself Lévy's student. Lévy died of a ruptured aneurysm at the age of forty-five.

Lévy became a mineralogist apparently by necessity rather than by vocation. While a student at the École Normale Supérieure, he undoubtedly took the mineralogy courses given by Haüy. He used the latter's methods and perfected his system of notation in the illustrations of the Heuland collection catalog. The Haüy-Lévy notation or, as it is sometimes called, the Lévy crystallographic notation is still used.

From a morphological point of view, a crystal is characterized by its "primitive form," a parallelepiped the symmetry of which represents the symmetry of the crystal. Haüy had shown that all the plane surfaces of a crystal can be envisaged as "rational truncations" on the vertices and edges of the primitive solid. Lévy designated the vertices by vowels, the edges by consonants, and the planes by these vowels and consonants modified by a coefficient (a simple fraction) indicating their slope. For example, all the vertices of the cube are designated by the letter a, and the regular octahedron, which derives from the cube, by a^1. It is easy to pass from Lévy's notation to the crystallographic notation devised by W. H. Miller, which is now in general use.

In describing the Heuland collection and in measuring surface angles of its specimens with a goniometer, Lévy discovered important new mineral species: forsterite, babingtonite, brochantite, roselite, brookite, herschelite, phillipsite and beudantite. He also gave precise descriptions of the crystalline forms of eudialyte, wagnerite, and euclase. In addition, he named several minerals that were subsequently recognized as varieties of previously described species: turnerite, a variety of monazite; bucklandite, a variety of allanite; königite, a variety of brochantite; mohsite, a variety of ilmenite; and humboldtite, a variety of datolite.

While studying the zinc-bearing minerals of La Vieille-Montagne, in Belgium, Lévy discovered an important new zinc silicate which he named willemite. The results of his research were published post-humously in the *Annales des mines* (1843) through the efforts of Des Cloizeaux.

BIBLIOGRAPHY

See M. A. Lacroix, "A. Lévy (1795–1841)," in *Bulletin de la Société française de minéralogie et de cristallographie*, **42**, no. 3 (1919), 122.

J. WYART

LEWIS, GILBERT NEWTON (*b.* West Newton, Massachusetts, 25 October 1875; *d.* Berkeley, California, 23 March 1946), *physical chemistry*.

Lewis received his primary education at home from his parents, Frank Wesley Lewis, a lawyer of independent character, and Mary Burr White Lewis. He read at age three and was intellectually precocious. In 1884 his family moved to Lincoln, Nebraska, and in 1889 he received his first formal education at the university preparatory school. In 1893, after two years at the University of Nebraska, Lewis transferred to Harvard, where he obtained his B.S. in 1896. After a year of teaching at Phillips Academy in Andover, Lewis returned to Harvard to study with the physical chemist T. W. Richards and obtained his Ph.D. in 1899 with a dissertation on electrochemical potentials. After a year of teaching at Harvard, Lewis made the pilgrimage to Germany, the center of physical chemistry, and studied with W. Nernst at Göttingen and with W. Ostwald at Leipzig. Upon his return to Harvard in 1901, he was appointed instructor in thermodynamics and electrochemistry. In 1904 Lewis was granted a leave of absence and became a chemist with the Bureau of Weights and Measures in Manila. After one year (a year he seldom spoke of) he joined the group of progressive young physical chemists around A. A. Noyes at the Massachusetts Institute of Technology.

Most of Lewis' lasting interests originated during his Harvard years. The most important was thermo-dynamics, a subject in which Richards was very active at that time. Although most of the important thermo-dynamic relations were known by 1895, they were seen as isolated equations, and had not yet been ratio-nalized as a logical system, from which, given one relation, the rest could be derived. Moreover, these relations were inexact, applying only to ideal chemical systems. These were two outstanding problems of theoretical thermodynamics. In two long and am-bitious theoretical papers in 1900 and 1901, Lewis tried to provide a solution. He proposed the new idea of "escaping tendency" or *fugacity* (a term he coined), a function with the dimensions of pressure which expressed the tendency of a substance to pass from one chemical phase to another. Lewis believed that fugacity was the fundamental principle from which a system of real thermodynamic relations could be derived. This hope was not realized, though fugacity did find a lasting place in the description of real gases.

Lewis' early papers also reveal an unusually advanced awareness of J. W. Gibbs's and P. Duhem's ideas of free energy and thermodynamic potential. These ideas were well known to physicists and mathematicians, but not to most practical chemists, who regarded them as abstruse and inapplicable to chemical systems. Most chemists relied on the familiar thermodynamics of heat (enthalpy) of Berthelot, Ostwald, and Van't Hoff, and the calorimetric school. Heat of reaction is not, of course, a measure of the tendency of chemical changes to occur, and Lewis realized that only free energy and entropy could provide an exact chemical thermodynamics. He derived free energy from fugacity; he tried, without success, to obtain an exact expression for the entropy function, which in 1901 had not been defined at low temperatures. Richards too tried and failed, and not until Nernst succeeded in 1907 was it possible to calculate entropies unambiguously. Although Lewis' fugacity-based system did not last, his early interest in free energy and entropy proved most fruitful, and much of his career was devoted to making these useful concepts accessible to practical chemists.

At Harvard, Lewis also wrote a theoretical paper on the thermodynamics of blackbody radiation in which he postulated that light has a pressure. He later revealed that he had been discouraged from pursuing this idea by his older, more conservative colleagues, who were unaware that W. Wien and others were successfully pursuing the same line of thought. Lewis' paper remained unpublished; but his interest in radiation and quantum theory, and (later) in relativity, sprang from this early, aborted effort. From the start of his career, Lewis regarded himself as both chemist and physicist.

A third major interest that originated during Lewis' Harvard years was valence theory. In 1902, while trying to explain the laws of valence to his students, Lewis conceived the idea that atoms were built up of a concentric series of cubes with electrons at each corner. This "cubic atom" explained the cycle of eight elements in the periodic table and was in accord with the widely accepted belief that chemical bonds were formed by transfer of electrons to give each atom a complete set of eight. This electrochemical theory of valence found its most elaborate expression in the work of Richard Abegg in 1904, but Lewis' version of this theory was the only one to be embodied in a concrete atomic model. Again Lewis' theory did not interest his Harvard mentors, who, like most American chemists of that time, had no taste for such speculation. Lewis did not publish his theory of the cubic atom, but in 1916 it became an important part of his theory of the shared electron pair bond.

Extremely bright and precocious as a young man, Lewis was also shy and lacking in self-confidence. His ideas were unorthodox and singular, perhaps owing in part to his unusual education. He was disappointed and resentful that his talents were not appreciated, especially by Richards. In 1928 he refused a call to Harvard and in 1929 refused an honorary degree.

Lewis remained at M.I.T. for seven years and there laid the foundations for his important work in thermodynamics. It was well-known that the equilibrium position of any chemical system could in theory be predicted from free-energy data—an invaluable aid to both pure and applied chemistry. But existing free-energy data were mostly unreliable, contradictory, and spotty. Existing methods for measuring free energies were imperfect. In practice, application of thermodynamics to chemistry was extremely difficult even for the specialist. Early in his career Lewis began to pursue this neglected opportunity. In Manila, he determined the oxygen-water electromotive potential, a key datum for many chemical reactions. At M.I.T. he systematically studied the free energy of formation of compounds of oxygen, nitrogen, the halogens, sulfur, and the alkali metals. Particularly important was his measurement of the free energy of formation of simple organic compounds, beginning in 1912 with ammonium cyanate and urea. Lewis realized that the most fruitful use of free-energy data would be in complex organic reactions, an insight that was borne out in the 1920's and 1930's.

In 1907 Lewis set forth a new system of thermodynamics based on the new concept of activity. A function with the dimensions of concentration, activity expresses the tendency of substances to cause change in chemical systems. Lewis derived activity by generalizing the idea of fugacity, but also emphasized that it could be derived directly from free energy, since change in free energy is proportional to change in activity. Lewis showed that in terms of activity, all the familiar thermodynamic equations for ideal systems became "perfectly exact and general"

for real systems. He also defined the important new concept of partial molal properties and a more exact form of Nernst's equation for the potential of a single concentration cell. Both ideas proved very useful in treating real chemical systems.

Like fugacity, the conception of activity never played the central theoretical role that Lewis thought it would; but it proved indispensable for treating deviations from ideal behavior in real solutions. In general, Lewis' main contribution to thermodynamics was not in grand theory but, rather, in its practical applications to real systems. He made chemists aware of the importance of hydration of ions and clarified the theory of liquid boundary potentials and conductivity, all of which derived from the practical necessities of measuring free-energy data. His definition of ionic strength (1921) allowed the systematization of activity data. Lewis set new standards of experimental accuracy and reliability; to a fertile but unorganized field he began to bring new clarity and order.

Lewis' other theoretical interests also flourished at M.I.T. The publication of Einstein's theory of relativity (1905) and his mass-energy equation renewed Lewis' interest in his early speculations on radiation. He derived the mass-energy equation from his early idea of the pressure of light without using the principle of relativity (1908). This striking concurrence of his view with Einstein's convinced Lewis of the value of his youthful ideas and made him one of the very few early supporters of Einstein and relativity in America. A second paper with Richard Tolman (1912), deriving Einstein's equation from conservation laws and the principle of relativity, illustrates Lewis' delight in the bizarre paradoxes of relativity theory that most people found so profoundly disturbing: Lewis was an iconoclast and reveled in the overthrow of long-established ideas.

In 1912 Lewis accepted an offer to become dean and chairman of the College of Chemistry at the University of California at Berkeley. The chemistry department was badly run-down, and Lewis was given generous financial support and a free hand to recruit new faculty and to initiate reforms. With him he brought William Bray, Richard Tolman, and Joel Hildebrand, all of whom became distinguished teachers and authors; their textbooks trained the first generation of American chemists who rivaled the products of German universities. The most advanced ideas of German physical chemistry—above all, thermodynamics—still neglected at most American universities, were familiar at Berkeley.

Lewis himself taught no courses—he was always uneasy speaking before a large group—but his influence was felt everywhere. The curriculum was reformed, and introductory courses became models of clarity. Lewis kept the teaching load light and encouraged original research among both his colleagues and his students. No one was permitted to become a narrow specialist, and speculation and free discussion were encouraged. Lewis presided over weekly research conferences where the latest topics were discussed with the utmost freedom by professors and students alike. Lewis had missed this progressive, cooperative "spirit of research" in his student days at Harvard, and its results can be seen in the reputation that his department quickly attained and in the roster of fine chemists it turned out. Lewis' reform and modernization of chemical education set the standard for American chemistry and is one of his most important and enduring achievements.

At Berkeley, Lewis' work on thermodynamics grew more intense. In a long paper of 1913 he summarized and brought up to date the theory and methods for calculating free-energy data. The great utility of a complete table of free energies for predicting chemical behavior, he asserted, made the collection of such data "an imperative duty of chemistry." In the next seven years Lewis published a series of lengthy papers, many in collaboration with Merle Randall, systematically collecting and reworking all the known free-energy data for each element. Especially important is a compendium of entropy data (1917) and an empirical verification of Nernst's third law. All this material became the body of his book on thermodynamics (1923). Next to Nernst and Fritz Haber, Lewis was probably the most important figure in chemical thermodynamics at that time; and his clear, systematic organization of data was second to none.

Equally fruitful was Lewis' theoretical achievement in valence theory. In 1913 Bray and Lewis proposed a dualistic theory of valence which distinguished two distinctly different kinds of bond: the familiar polar bond formed by electron transfer, as in Na^+Cl^-, and a nonpolar bond that did not involve electron transfer. The polar theory, exemplified by J. J. Thomson's popular book *The Corpuscular Theory of Matter* (1907), was then at the peak of its popularity. Bray and Lewis were the first to challenge the view that all bonds, even those in the inert hydrocarbons, were polar; and their heresy was not well received. But other dissenters soon appeared. In 1914 Thomson himself postulated a nonpolar bond involving two electrons and two tubes of force. In 1915 Lewis saw in manuscript a paper by Alfred Parson, an English graduate student visiting Berkeley for a year, that postulated a two-electron nonpolar bond and also a cubic octet very similar to Lewis' cubic atom. This

striking coincidence apparently revived Lewis' interest in his early speculations on atomic structure and valence. Lewis probably derived the shared electron pair bond from a combination of the novel and suggestive theories of Parson and Thomson with his own model of the cubic atom.

Early in 1916 Lewis published his germinal paper proposing that the chemical bond was a pair of electrons shared or held jointly by two atoms. The cubic atom was an integral part of Lewis' theory of molecular structure. In terms of cubic atoms, the single bond was represented by two cubes with a shared edge, or more simply by double dots (Figure 1), a convention that has been universally adopted.

FIGURE 1. The Cl_2 molecules in terms of Lewis' cubic atoms and electron pairs.

According to the octet rule, for a molecule to be stable, each atom must be surrounded by four pairs of electrons that are either shared or free pairs. From this simple idea Lewis derived structures for the halogen molecules, the ammonium ion, and the oxyacids, all of which had proved insoluble for previous theories of valence. Lewis conceived polar bonds simply as unequally shared electron pairs. Since complete transfer of electrons was only the extreme case of polarity, Lewis abandoned his earlier dualistic view. The polar theory became a special case of Lewis' more general and unified theory.

Lewis' theory of the shared-pair bond received no notice in 1916, and he followed it up with only one further paper on color in molecules with "odd" or unpaired electrons (1916). His cubic or "static" atom appeared to be inconsistent with the physicists' view of the atom, based mainly on spectroscopy, which demanded moving electrons, as in Bohr's planetary model (1913). The physicists' "dynamic" atom, however, failed to explain the rigid stereochemistry of carbon compounds. This apparent paradox was much disputed in 1919–1923, and Lewis vigorously defended the static atom against Bohr's atom in a lecture to the Physical Society in 1916 and in his book *Valence* (1923).

By 1916 World War I had halted scientific work in Europe, and in January 1918 Lewis went to France as a major in the Chemical Warfare Service. There he organized the Gas Defense School to train gas officers, and proved so excellent an organizer that he was decorated for his service upon his return in September 1918.

In the spring of 1919 the cubic atom and the shared-pair bond were taken up by Irving Langmuir, who was already famous for his invention of the gas-filled electric lamp and his theory of surface absorption. His dramatic lecture on the new theory of the atom, delivered to the American Chemical Society in April 1919 and often repeated by request elsewhere, suddenly kindled the interest of American chemists. In a series of long papers and lectures in 1919–1921 Langmuir elaborated Lewis' theory so successfully that the Lewis-Langmuir theory, or the Langmuir theory as it was known to many, was talked of everywhere and soon was widely accepted. Lewis was resentful that Langmuir received so much of the credit for the ideas that he had originated. Langmuir always acknowledged his debt to Lewis but felt that he had added enough on his own to warrant the compound name. An exchange of polite but outspoken letters in 1919–1920 probably did not clear the air, but some years later Lewis and Langmuir were again on friendly terms.

Langmuir abruptly ceased publishing on valence in 1921, probably realizing the superiority of the increasingly sophisticated Bohr theory. Lewis, however, continued to support the static atom in a lecture to the Faraday Society in 1923 and in his *Valence and the Structure of Atoms and Molecules* (1923). The conflict between the static and dynamic atoms soon disappeared with the introduction of directed orbitals, and the cubic atom quickly became obsolete. But the shared-pair bond proved to be one of the most fruitful ideas in the history of chemistry. *Valence* became the textbook of the first generation of chemists for whom the chemical bond was more than a simple line. For the first time mechanisms of complex organic reactions could be explained in terms of shifting electron pairs; and in England a new school of physical-organic chemistry was formed by A. Lapworth, M. Lowry, R. Robinson, and others. In the late 1920's the shared-pair bond was the starting point for the new quantum chemistry of E. Schrödinger, H. London, L. Pauling, and others, which transformed Lewis' germinal idea into a quantum mechanical theory of molecular structure.

In 1923 Lewis also published, with Merle Randall, *Thermodynamics and the Free Energy of Chemical Substances.* This extremely influential textbook was for several generations the clearest and simplest presentation of chemical thermodynamics. Its summaries of reliable free-energy data made readily accessible to chemists, even to the novice, the powerful tools of thermodynamics. Once the luxury of specialists, after 1923 thermodynamics was increasingly regarded as an indispensable part of chemical education and research.

For Lewis 1923 marked an end to two of his most abiding interests. He had had enough of collecting free-energy data; and in organic and quantum chemistry, where the shared-pair theory proved most fruitful, Lewis was not at home. He thus found himself at loose ends; and for the next ten years he occupied himself almost exclusively with his third early interest, the theory of radiation and relativity. He tried to derive the laws of quantum radiation by thermodynamic reasoning from the law of microscopical reversibility. He proposed that light does not emit to all space but only to a receiver and that in the space-time manifold, emitter and receiver are in "virtual contact." Such entrancing paradoxes of space and time formed the bulk of his Silliman lectures of 1925 and the resulting book, *The Anatomy of Science* (1926). The decade 1923–1933 was certainly the least successful period of Lewis' career. He was a good enough mathematician to follow the contemporary developments in relativity and quantum theory, but he remained an amateur and an outsider. His novel ideas, stemming from youthful inspiration and his bent for thermodynamic reasoning, remained out of touch with the best professional thought. Lewis styled himself an *enfant terrible* and enjoyed shocking people with his unorthodox views. The profound revolution in physics in the 1920's encouraged his taste for paradoxes; it was clear that some cherished beliefs would be brought down. Anything seemed possible, and it was difficult to distinguish brilliant ideas from absurd ones. A letter from Einstein to Lewis suggests that even he took Lewis' ideas seriously; but in retrospect it is clear that Lewis was out of his depth.

Lewis probably sensed this, for in 1933 he abruptly abandoned theorizing to exploit an unexpected opportunity in a field quite new to him, the separation of isotopes. Deuterium had been discovered in 1932 by Harold Urey, who noted that it might be isolated on a large scale by fractional electrolysis of water. Lewis had been trying to separate oxygen isotopes when he realized that deuterium, being twice the size of ordinary hydrogen, would be easier and more interesting to obtain. In 1933 he succeeded in obtaining nearly pure heavy water and in the next two years rushed out, against intense competition, twenty-eight reports on deuterium chemistry, including several in collaboration with E. O. Lawrence on the nuclear reactions of deuterium in the cyclotron. Since deuterium was markedly different from hydrogen, Lewis foresaw a whole new chemistry of deutero compounds with distinct and unusual properties. But by 1934 these high hopes had apparently paled, for Lewis abruptly ceased work on heavy water. Covalent carbon-deuterium bonds are in fact not easy to make, and deutero compounds are not very different from ordinary compounds.

It is precisely these properties that make deuterium an ideal tracer for studying organic, and especially biochemical, reactions; but Lewis was not prepared to exploit this opportunity. He carried out several studies on the lethal effect of heavy water on germinating plant seeds and on living creatures, but he did not realize how deuterium could be used to study the microchemistry of living tissue. Lewis also tried to follow up the nuclear physics of deuterium in 1936–1937, but this attempt ended in failure when a report on the refraction of neutrons by wax had to be withdrawn as an experimental error. Again Lewis was not at home in either of the fields opened up by his own work.

In 1938 Lewis finally hit upon a fruitful combination of theory and experiment in photochemistry. He had long been interested in the theory of colored compounds. In 1914 he identified two different forms of the indicator methylene blue, and in 1916 his idea of the shared-pair bond led him to propose that color was due to the presence of "odd" electrons. (His work on color had won him the Nichols Medal in 1921.) The occasion for his return to this subject was an important lecture on the theory of acids and bases at the Franklin Institute in 1938. According to his generalized theory of acids and bases proposed in 1923, bases were molecules having free electron pairs to donate, whereas acids were electron-poor molecules that could accept an extra pair. The idea of a general base had been widely accepted; but because of the prevailing proton theory of acidity, Lewis' conception of acids had not. His 1938 lecture did much to make the Lewis acid an important part of chemical theory.

Many of the Lewis acids, such as the triphenyl-carbonium salts, exist in a variety of different-colored forms. Lewis proposed that these forms were of two distinct "electromeric" types which differed only in the distribution of electrons in the molecule. Neutralization of one kind required energy of activation, while the other was neutralized spontaneously. Ironically, the concept of electromerism had been an important

part of the abandoned electrochemical theory of valence, which Lewis' shared-pair bond and Pauling's theory of resonance hybrids had rendered obsolete. Despite its outmoded terminology, Lewis' theory of electromeric states proved extremely fruitful. Photochemistry was already becoming a popular field in the 1930's, but like thermodynamics in 1910 it lacked a solid theoretical foundation. In a long review in 1939 Lewis and Melvin Calvin summarized the known facts in terms of their elaborate theory of color. There followed a series of fine experimental papers on fluorescence and phosphorescence spectra and on photochemical reactions in rigid media.

Lewis separated two emission bands in phosphorescence spectra, which he associated with "electromeric" excited states. From one, emission was delayed, that is, it required energy of activation; from the other, emission was instantaneous. At first Lewis had consciously avoided quantum mechanical interpretations, preferring a more classical chemical approach. But by 1943 his kinetic and optical studies of phosphorescence had led him to believe that the two electromeric states were in fact the singlet and triplet states of quantum theory. This striking conclusion, which was confirmed in several important papers in 1944–1945 with Calvin and Michael Kasha, was the starting point for the rapid development of photochemistry.

These were Lewis' last papers. He died in 1946 while carrying out an experiment on fluorescence. Thus at the end of his career Lewis again found a field that combined theoretical interest and practical opportunities; to photochemistry he was able to bring the same rigor of experiment and vigor of imagination that characterized the best work of his early years.

BIBLIOGRAPHY

I. ORIGINAL WORKS. Lewis' principal writings are "Outlines of a New System of Thermodynamic Chemistry," in *Proceedings of the American Academy of Arts and Sciences*, **43** (1907), 259–293; "The Atom and the Molecule," in *Journal of the American Chemical Society*, **38** (1916), 762–785; *Thermodynamics and the Free Energy of Chemical Substances* (New York, 1923), written with M. Randall; *Valence and the Structure of Atoms and Molecules* (New York, 1923; repr. New York, 1965); "The Isotope of Hydrogen," in *Journal of the American Chemical Society*, **55** (1933), 1297–1300; "Acids and Bases," in *Journal of the Franklin Institute*, **226** (1938), 293–318; and "Phosphorescence and the Triplet State," in *Journal of the American Chemical Society*, **66** (1944), 2100–2109, written with M. Kasha.

Two boxes of Lewis' correspondence and some MS notes from his student years are in the Lewis Archive,

University of California, Berkeley. The Harvard Archives contain Lewis' Harvard records and a brief correspondence with T. W. Richards.

II. SECONDARY LITERATURE. J. H. Hildebrand, "Gilbert N. Lewis," *Biographical Memoirs. National Academy of Sciences*, **31** (1958), 209–235, includes a complete bibliography. See also W. F. Giauque, "Gilbert N. Lewis," in *Yearbook. American Philosophical Society* for 1946, pp. 317–322; A. Lachmann, *Borderland of the Unknown* (New York, 1956); and R. E. Kohler, "The Origin of G. N. Lewis's Theory of the Shared Pair Bond," in *Historical Studies in the Physical Sciences*, **3** (1971), 343–376. The relation between Lewis and Langmuir is discussed in R. E. Kohler, "Irving Langmuir and the Octet Theory of Valence," *ibid.*, **4** (1972).

R. E. KOHLER

LEWIS, THOMAS (*b.* Cardiff, Wales, 26 December 1881; *d.* Rickmansworth, England, 17 March 1945), *physiology, cardiology, clinical science.*

Thomas Lewis' parents were Welsh. His father, Henry Lewis, was a prominent coal mining engineer from a long line of Monmouthshire yeomen. The family was well-to-do, and Lewis was educated at home until the age of sixteen by his mother and a private tutor. His upbringing was Methodist and his father, to whose encouragement and stimulus he owed much, was a widely read and clearheaded man with a library of several thousand volumes. However, the young Lewis had no interest in books and spent every spare moment in sporting activities and in the local fields and woods.

He took up medicine because he hoped that by becoming a doctor he might emulate the skill of the family physician, who was an expert conjurer. After preclinical work at University College, Cardiff, where he was encouraged in critical thought and research by the physiologist Swale Vincent, in 1902 he entered University College Hospital, London, his medical home for the rest of his life. He graduated M.B., B.S. (university gold medal) in 1905, M.D. in 1907, and was elected fellow of the Royal College of Physicians in 1913. He became a fellow of the Royal Society of London in 1918 and was knighted in 1921. Of his numerous national and foreign distinctions none was more significant than the Copley Medal of the Royal Society (1941), which had previously been awarded to only one clinician, Lord Lister. In 1916 Lewis was appointed physician on the staff of the Medical Research Committee (later Council), which, as he later said, broke the ice in Great Britain as the first full-time research post in clinical medicine. Also in 1916 he married Lorna Treharne James of Merthyr

Tydfil, Glamorgan, Wales; they had two daughters and one son.

A man of outstanding intellect with an enormous capacity for unrelenting hard work, Lewis remained in full mental vigor until the end of his life, although he sustained a myocardial infarct at the age of forty-five. At the time of a second attack eight years later he said to Sir Arthur Keith, "Another arrow from the same quiver, my friend, and one of them will get me in the end." He died from a fourth attack at the age of sixty-three.

Lewis' career in medical research began while he was still a student, with the publication of papers on the hemolymph glands that later became standard works. But his interest in cardiac physiology, stimulated by a year in E. H. Starling's laboratory, came from his work with Leonard Hill on the influence of respiration on the venous and arterial pulses. This association inevitably led him into contact with James Mackenzie, whose great work, *The Study of the Pulse*, had appeared in 1902. Their meeting in 1908 began a friendship that profoundly influenced Lewis' life. Mackenzie urged him to study the irregular action of the heart, and Lewis acquired the new Einthoven string galvanometer, set it up in the medical school basement, and plunged into his investigations on the spread of the excitatory processes in the dog heart, coupled with bedside and electrocardiographic studies on clinical arrhythmias. In 1909 he showed that Mackenzie's "irregular irregularity" of the heart was due to atrial fibrillation. Only two years later *The Mechanism of the Heart Beat* was published, and this scholarly scientific monograph soon became the bible of electrocardiography. In the foreword to the second edition (1920) Lewis set forth his scientific credo in a passage which illustrates the simplicity and clarity of his writing:

> Inexact method of observation, as I believe, is one flaw in clinical pathology to-day. Prematurity of conclusion is another, and in part follows from the first; but in chief part an unusual craving and veneration for hypothesis, which besets the minds of most medical men, is responsible. The purity of a science is to be judged by the paucity of its recorded hypothesis. Hypothesis is the heart which no man with right purpose wears willingly upon his sleeve.

Lewis' work from 1908 to 1925 gave him a complete mastery of all aspects of the electrophysiology of the heart, the human electrocardiogram, and clinical disorders of the heartbeat. It included his famous hypothesis of circus movement as the mechanism of atrial fibrillation. Much of this work, done with a succession of talented young men, of whom the first were Paul D. White of Boston and Jonathan Meakins of Montreal, was published in the journal *Heart*, which Lewis founded with Mackenzie's help in 1909.

World War I interrupted these studies in 1914, just after Lewis' return from America, where he had delivered the Herter lectures in Baltimore and the Harvey lecture in New York. Fortunately his talents were harnessed to a study of the condition known to the military as D.A.H. (deranged action of the heart), which was causing a serious loss of manpower at the front. His work at the Military Heart Hospitals led to its redefinition as the effort syndrome, with "a system of graded drills employed remedially and as a means of justly grading soldiers for supposed affections of the heart." This was the foundation of his later insistence on judging the state of the heart from the patient's exercise tolerance rather than on the then fashionable method of assessing cardiac murmurs. He was also involved in the problems of diagnosis and prognosis in organic heart disease and with R. T. Grant instituted an unsurpassed follow-up over ten years of 1,000 soldiers with valvular disease.

By 1925 Lewis had had enough of his elaborate electrocardiographic work and, believing that "the cream was off," he returned to observations on the cutaneous vessels which he had started during the war. He was also influenced by a growing belief that man, not animals, was the proper subject for hospital-based research. A series of observations on the vascular reaction of the skin to various injuries led to his description of the red line, flare, and wheal so produced as the triple response, with the postulate that the original stimulus acts by damaging the tissues, which produce a histaminelike compound that Lewis called the H-substance. This work was gathered together in 1927 in his monograph *The Blood Vessels of the Human Skin and Their Responses*. A notable feature of these experiments which became a hallmark of his later work was that they were carried out with the simplest apparatus, as was his brilliant elucidation of Trousseau's phenomenon in tetany using only two blood-pressure cuffs. In parallel with this laboratory work he was engaged in a study of Raynaud's disease and other maladies affecting blood flow to the limbs and digits.

Lewis' third, and last, period began with his work on pain. One suspects that this subjective phenomenon taxed even his unique research talents to the utmost. Certainly, the summary of his researches published as the monograph *Pain* (1942) lacks the sparkle of his earlier writings. Nevertheless, much was accomplished. The separateness of superficial and deep pain was emphasized. The double pain response to a single stimulus distinguished two systems of pain nerves in skin. Factor P was proposed as the cause of pain in ischemic limb muscle and possibly in heart muscle as well, in angina pectoris. The pain of visceral disease and referred pain in general were investigated experimentally by the injection of hypertonic saline into the interspinal ligaments. The curious hyperalgesia of damaged skin, "erythralgia," led to the uncharacteristically weak hypothesis of the nocifensor system of nerves.

Lewis' worldwide fame as a teacher came from a number of books written for a wider audience than was reached by his scientific papers and monographs. The first, in 1912, was *Clinical Disorders of the Heart Beat*, followed in 1913 by *Clinical Electrocardiography*. Both went through several editions and must have been a godsend to clinicians trying to understand the then novel methods of investigating the heart. However, Lewis grudged the time spent on them, writing only from a sense of duty to the profession. His best-known book, *Diseases of the Heart* (1933), was widely translated. *Clinical Science, Illustrated by Personal Experiences* (1934) recounted his methods of attack upon clinical problems such as intermittent claudication and bacterial endocarditis. *Vascular Disorders of the Limbs* (1936) is still a most useful acount. His last book, *Exercises in Human Physiology* (1945), demonstrates his interest in medical education and presents a detailed account of simple experiments that students may make on themselves.

At University College Hospital he worked constantly in the wards and in the out-patient department. His superb clinical teaching emphasized a meticulous examination of the patient followed by a penetrating analysis of the relationship of the symptoms and signs to the underlying hemodynamic and pathological disturbances. Few students other than his clinical clerks attended his rounds, however, the majority preferring didactic presentations. At his regular medical school lectures he displayed his interest in the history of medicine, especially the French physicians of the nineteenth century.

Lewis' most important contribution to medicine may have been his concept of clinical science, his insistence that progress in medicine would come chiefly from scientific studies on living men in health and disease, rather than from the basic science laboratories and from animal experimentation. With controlled investigation of patients now basic to much of medicine, it is difficult to relive the time when Lewis, almost alone, fought for the creation of established career posts in medical research, now numbered in the tens of thousands. This must have been the most difficult period of his life and he signaled it in 1930 by renaming his own department the Department of Clinical Research and by founding the Medical Research Society, and in July 1933 by changing the title of *Heart* to *Clinical Science*.

BIBLIOGRAPHY

A complete bibliography of Lewis' twelve books and 229 scientific papers is in the notice by A. N. Drury and R. T. Grant, in *Obituary Notices of Fellows of the Royal Society of London*, **5** (1945), 179–202. See also *American Heart Journal*, **29** (1945), 419–420; *British Medical Journal* (1945), **1**, 461–463, 498; *Lancet* (1945), **1**, 419–420; *University College Hospital Magazine*, **30** (1945), 36–39; and *British Heart Journal*, **8** (1946), 1–3.

A collection of papers by his former pupils and collaborators is in *University College Hospital Magazine*, **40** (1955), 63–74.

A. HOLLMAN

LEWIS, TIMOTHY RICHARDS (*b.* Llanboidy, Carmarthenshire, Wales, 31 October 1841; *d.* Southampton, England, 7 May 1886), *tropical medicine.*

Timothy Lewis, the second son of William Lewis, was born at Llanboidy but spent his early years at Crinow, a small village in Pembrokeshire, to which his family removed while he was still in his infancy. There he received his early education, first at the village school until he was ten years old, and later at a private grammar school recently opened in the locality by the Reverend James Morris, which he attended until he was fifteen. He then became apprenticed to a local pharmacist with whom he remained for four years, before moving to London. He became a compounder of medicines at the German Hospital in Dalston, London, where he became proficient in German. At the same time he attended lectures in human medicine at University College, London, where his skill in the laboratory as a chemist was quickly recognized. Subsequently, in the hospital's wards, his intelligence and attention to detail were so marked that he was awarded the Fellowes silver medal for clinical medicine in 1866. He completed his studies at the Medical School of the University of Aberdeen, from which he received the degree of M.B. with honors in 1867.

Immediately after qualifying he applied for a commission in the army medical department and was placed first in the entrance examination for the Army Medical School at Netley, near Southampton, his name again appearing at the head of the list at the completion of the four-month course. He was commissioned successively as assistant surgeon (31 March 1868), surgeon (1 March 1873), and surgeon major (31 March 1880), and for three years before his death in 1886 he held the post of assistant professor of pathology at the Army Medical School in Netley.

Little was known of the etiology of disease, and the imagination of many investigators ran riot in hypothesis and speculation. Lewis' work, collected and reprinted in 1888 in a commemorative volume, reveals the power of his critical examination and judgment, which enabled him to refute the wilder claims of some of his contemporaries, including such outstanding workers as Hallier, Koch, and Pasteur.

After completing the course at Netley, Lewis and D. D. Cunningham, the two best students of the session, were sent to study in Germany before proceeding to India to investigate the causation of cholera. They published a series of papers, together and singly, of which Lewis' first work, issued in 1870, on the microscopic objects found in the stools of patients with cholera, contains the first authentic account of amoebas from the human intestine. The delicate drawings (108 in all) demonstrate the care and exactitude of his observations. His interests were extremely wide, and over the next fourteen years his studies ranged over cholera, leprosy, fungal diseases, Oriental sore, bladder worms of pigs and cattle, and the diets of prisoners in Indian jails. His detailed descriptions of the blood parasites of man and animals constitute his most significant contribution to knowledge and exercised a fundamental influence over the attitude of his contemporaries to the etiology of disease. His two reports on the nematode hematozoa of man and animals (1874) contain the first account of microfilariae in human blood and revealed its connection with chyluria and elephantiasis. Lewis named the hematozoon *Filaria sanguinis hominis* (F.S.H.), later known as *Filaria bancrofti*. This work was originally published as an appendix to the annual report of the sanitary commissioner with the government of India and was not readily obtainable outside India. Manson, however, stumbled across it in the British Museum while on leave from China and, realizing its significance, carried out experiments on the life history of F.S.H. on his return to China in 1875. As a result he was able in 1877 to describe its development in mosquitoes.

In 1878 and 1884 Lewis published two reports on blood parasites of man and animals, including microfilariae, spirochetes in relapsing fever, and trypanosomes in the blood of rats, which was subsequently named *Trypanosoma lewisi* by Kent in 1880.

Two weeks before his death, Lewis was recommended by the council of the Royal Society for election as one of the fellows for 1886, but he did not live to be elected. He died of pneumonia contracted, his notebook suggests, by accidentally inoculating himself during his experiments.

Lewis' meticulous search for pathogenic organisms in blood, feces, and urine, and his knowledge of organisms which are normally present without producing disease, unquestionably bore fruit in the discoveries of subsequent workers. As Dobell rightly pointed out, "Lewis was, like Manson, a pioneer."

BIBLIOGRAPHY

Lewis' writings were brought together in W. Aitken, G. E. Dobson, and A. E. Brown, eds., *Physiological and Pathological Researches: Being a Reprint of the Principal Scientific Writings of the Late T. R. Lewis* (London, 1888). For his journal articles, see Royal Society *Catalogue of Scientific Papers*, X, 584; XII, 445; and XVI, 761.

Obituaries appeared in *British Medical Journal* (26 June 1886), 1242–1243; *Lancet* (22 May 1886), 993; and *Nature*, **34** (1886), 76–77, with bibliography. See also C. Dobell, "T. R. Lewis," in *Parasitology*, **14** (1922), 413–416.

M. J. CLARKSON

LEWIS, WILLIAM (*b.* Richmond, Surrey, England, 1708; *d.* Kingston, Surrey, England, 21 January 1781), *chemistry, pharmacy, chemical technology.*

Born into a brewing family in the environs of London, Lewis had an early opportunity to observe rudimentary chemical technology. By the time he had spent some five years at Oxford (1725–1730) and graduated M.B. from Cambridge in 1731, he had acquired a definite interest in the chemical arts. He was giving public lectures in chemistry "with a View to the Improvement of Pharmacy, Trades and the Art itself" at least as early as 1737. Within a few years he had established sufficient reputation to be elected a member of the Royal Society in October 1745, and he remained a part of the London scientific scene for the rest of his life.

Whatever Lewis learned at Newtonian Oxford and Cambridge was supplemented and shaped by later editorial labors on authors less devoted to the mechanical philosophy. His practical bent was nurtured by his 1746 edition of George Wilson's venerable *Compleat Course of Chemistry* and by his abridgment in the same year of the Edinburgh *Medical Essays*. The latter included many articles reflecting the long-term interests of the Edinburgh physicians in the practical chemistry associated with materia medica and mineral waters. Lewis' own interest in applied

chemistry never waned, and, after he moved westward out of London proper to the village of Kingston in 1746, he continued to work on pharmacy and materia medica, gradually expanding his interests to include other areas of chemical technology.

That his plan for a broadly based attack on problems in applied chemistry was formed fairly early is suggested by his published pamphlet of 1748 proposing a periodical entitled *Commercium philosophico-technicum*. As planned, this new publication was to examine various manufacturing processes systematically, through laboratory studies where necessary, and to eliminate wasteful procedures and products. Lewis was far from alone in these interests. Many men of commerce and learning felt the need for the practical improvements in the arts that were promised but never delivered by the enthusiasts of the new mechanical philosophy. Indeed, this period saw the rise of several groups interested in such improvements, notably the Royal Society of Arts (founded 1754) and the Lunar Society of Birmingham. Lewis himself had a broad circle of acquaintances with similar outlooks, and he availed himself of their opinions of his projects on a number of recorded occasions.

While his broad plan for applied chemistry was thus being formulated, Lewis kept up his pharmaceutical activities. He had agreed to produce a new English pharmacopoeia and, perhaps as preparation for this task, translated the fourth Latin edition of the *Edinburgh Pharmacopoeia* and published it in 1748.

One of the most significant events in Lewis' life occurred in 1750, when he began his lifelong association with Alexander Chisholm. Searching for an intelligent and educated assistant for his numerous projects, Lewis found one, appropriately enough, in a London bookstore. Their careers, until Lewis' death, were inseparably entwined; to speak of one is to speak of the other. Chisholm, who in 1743 had graduated M.A. from Marischal College, Aberdeen, was an able linguist, competent in Latin and Greek and in the German and Swedish vernaculars. Indeed, it is believed that the translation of Caspar Neumann's chemical lectures was done by Chisholm.

Lewis' long-standing interest in materia medica and his studies of previous works in pharmacy, including his translation of the *Edinburgh Pharmacopoeia*, culminated in 1753 with the publication of *The New Dispensatory*, which was based on Quincy's *Complete English Dispensatory*. Careful and systematic, like all of Lewis' works, the *New Dispensatory* was highly praised by that archcritic William Cullen as the only English pharmacopoeia that "made any improvement on the Materia Medica . . . ." The work went through many editions before and after Lewis' death, and its spirit was retained in the form and arrangement of Andrew Duncan's *Edinburgh New Dispensatory* (1803), which survived well into the nineteenth century.

Perhaps no work better shows Lewis' abilities as an experimentalist than his series of researches on platinum during the 1750's. Although others had attacked this intractable metal before him, using a number of standard metallurgical techniques, Lewis succeeded where others had failed through his careful systematic approach and the clever use of chemical analogy. Well-versed in the trends of his time, Lewis quickly turned to acids to get the metal into solution. Noting certain similarities between platinum and gold, Lewis defined the new metal in terms of an old one whose chemistry was relatively well understood. In his knowledge of solution chemistry and his ability to employ it imaginatively, Lewis showed himself to be in the forefront of eighteenth-century experimental chemistry. For this effort and for his already substantial contributions to pharmacy and materia medica Lewis was awarded the Copley Medal of the Royal Society in 1754.

Attracted by the empiricism bias of the work of the German chemist and apothecary Caspar Neumann, Lewis published in 1759 a translation with both additions and abridgments of Neumann's chemical lectures. Neumann's approach presents a strong contrast to George Wilson's stark collection of recipes; for the former, although cautious as a theoretician, was a follower of Georg Ernst Stahl, and thus his work employed the complex of ideas associated with the "inflammable principle"—phlogiston. Much has been made of Lewis' description of Neumann as "biassed by no theory and attached to no opinions." That Lewis would hold such an opinion would literally mean that he had never read Neumann, for there is no possible doubt where the latter's theoretical sympathies lay. What Lewis undoubtedly objected to was the preconceived and—to him as well as to other practical chemists like Robert Dossie— ill-conceived notions of the corpuscularians. Like most of his contemporaries, Lewis felt free to accept or reject the various dicta associated with the phlogiston concept. His interests lay in the determination of chemical composition, a task that Stahl and such followers as Neumann were certainly better equipped to handle than the Newtonian chemists. Lewis himself used the other pillar of phlogiston chemistry—affinity —with ease, even though, like many others, he was not overly concerned with the corpuscular details of this theory.

Certainly Lewis' most ambitious work was the *Commercium philosophico-technicum*, which appeared in sections over the period 1763–1765. He divided the book into seven topics that by no means form a complete survey of chemical technology of this period. The topics included such diverse headings as the chemistry of gold, vitrification, expansion and contraction of bodies with change in temperature, blowing air into furnaces by the force of falling water, methods of producing the color black, and a summation of Lewis' studies on platinum. While these topics differed widely in their immediate applicability to technology, as a group they demonstrated forcefully the possibility of relating chemical knowledge to a wide variety of industrial problems.

Although Lewis was prolific, his general way of working was slow and methodical. He read extensively, took notes and made additions to them from his own experience, and even conducted new experiments to confirm or deny the claims of others. But it must not be assumed that his only virtue was his systematic methodology. His skepticism about the "mechanical philosophy" was in itself a philosophical position, one which was shared by a substantial number of his contemporaries. In his later works, and particularly in the highly empirical *Commercium philosophico-technicum*, he eschewed a simple empirical approach— such as descriptions of manufactures or histories of processes—for one that was based on the "invariable properties of matter." What Lewis avoided was a dependence on the sterile mechanical philosophy that promised so much and produced so little in chemistry.

BIBLIOGRAPHY

I. Original Works. Lewis' works are *A Course of Practical Chemistry in Which are Contained All the Operations Described in Wilson's Complete Course of Chemistry* (London, 1746); *Medical Essays & Observations*, published by a society in Edinburgh, in six volumes, abridged and disposed under general heads (2 vols., London, 1746); *Pharmacopoeia of the Royal College of Physicians of Edinburgh* (London, 1748); *Proposals for Printing, by Subscription, Commercium philosophico-technicum or The Philosophical Commerce of the Arts* (London, 1748); *Oratio in theatro Sheldoniano, habilo idibus Aprilis* (Oxford, 1749); *An Answer to the Serious Inquiry Into Some Proceedings Relating to the University of Oxford* (London, 1751); *The New Dispensatory . . . Intended as a Correction and Improvement of Quincy* (London, 1753; 6th ed., 1799); "Experimental Examination of a White Metallic Substance . . .," in *Philosophical Transactions*, **48**, pt. 2 (1754), 638–689; "Experimental Examination of Platina," *ibid.*, **50**, pt. 1 (1757), 148–166; *The Chemical Works of Caspar Neumann* (London, 1759); *Experimental History of the Materia Medica* (London, 1761; 3rd ed., 1769); *Commercium philosophico-technicum or The Philosophical Commerce of Arts: Designed as an Attempt to Improve Arts, Trades and Manu-*

factures (London, 1763–1765); *Experiments and Observations on American Potashes* (London, 1767); and the posthumous *A System of the Practice of Medicine, From the Latin of Dr. Hoffmann By the Late William Lewis* (London, 1783).

II. Secondary Literature. See F. W. Gibbs, "William Lewis, M.B., F.R.S. (1708–1781)," in *Annals of Science*, **8** (1952), 122–151; Edward Kremers, "William Lewis," in *Journal of the American Pharmaceutical Association*, **20** (1931), 1204–1209; and Nathan Sivin, "William Lewis (1708–1781) As A Chemist," in *Chymia*, **8** (1962), 63–88.

Jon Eklund

LEXELL, ANDERS JOHAN (*b.* Äbo, Sweden [now Turku, Finland], 24 December 1740; *d.* St. Petersburg, Russia, 11 December 1784), *mathematics, astronomy*.

Lexell was the son of Jonas Lexell, a city councillor and jeweler, and his wife, Magdalena Catharina Björckegren. He graduated from the University of Äbo in 1760 as bachelor of philosophy and became assistant professor of Uppsala Nautical School in 1763 and professor of mathematics in 1766. Invited to work at the St. Petersburg Academy of Sciences on the recommendation of the Swedish astronomer P. W. Wargentin in 1768, he was appointed adjunct in 1769 and professor of astronomy in 1771. IIis research soon made him well-known. In 1775 the Swedish government offered him a professorship at the University of Äbo which would permit him to proceed with his work in St. Petersburg until 1780; but Lexell preferred to remain in Russia. He spent 1780–1782 traveling in Western Europe; and his letters to J. A. Euler, permanent secretary of the Academy, contain valuable information on scientific life in Germany, France, and England. (These letters are kept at the Archives of the U.S.S.R. Academy of Sciences, Leningrad.)

After Leonhard Euler's death in 1783, Lexell for a short time held Euler's professorship of mathematics, but Lexell himself died the following year. Lexell was a member of the Academy of Sciences in Stockholm, the Society of Sciences in Uppsala (1763), and a corresponding member of the Paris Académie des Sciences (1776).

At St. Petersburg Lexell immediately became one of the closest associates of Leonhard Euler. Under the famous mathematician's supervision he and W.-L. Krafft and J. A. Euler helped to prepare Euler's *Theoria motuum lunae, nova methodo pertractata* (1772) for publication. Euler's influence upon Lexell's scientific activity was considerable; but the latter's works were carried out independently.

On 3 June 1769 the St. Petersburg Academy conducted observations of the transit of Venus at many sites in Russia. Lexell took an active part in the organization and processing of the observations. Using L. Euler's method he calculated (1) the solar parallax to be $8''.68$ (compared to today's value of $8''.80$). No less interesting was Lexell's determination of the orbits of the 1769 comet (2) and especially of the comet discovered in 1770 by Messier (3). Lexell established the period of the latter on its elliptical orbit as five and a half years; this was the first known short revolution-period comet. Passing near Jupiter and its satellites the comet exerted no influence upon their motion; Lexell thus concluded that the masses of comets are rather small in spite of their enormous sizes. Lexell's comet, which had not been observed before 1770, has not been seen again; probably it lost its gaseous coat and become invisible. Still more important was Lexell's investigation of the orbit of the moving body discovered by W. Herschel on 13 March 1781 and initially regarded as a comet. Lexell's calculations showed that this heavenly body was a new planet (Uranus), nearly twice as far from the sun as Saturn (4). Moreover, Lexell pointed out that perturbations in the new planet's motion could not be explained by the action of the known members of the solar system and stated the hypothesis that they must be caused by another, more remote planet. This hypothesis proved correct when Neptune was discovered in 1846 on the basis of the calculations of J. Adams and U. Le Verrier.

Lexell's mathematical works are devoted to problems of analysis and geometry. Following Euler he elaborated the method of integrating factor as applied to higher order differential equations (1771). He gave a solution of linear systems of second order differential equations with constant coefficients (1778, 1783); suggested a classification of elliptic integrals (1778); calculated integrals of some irrational functions by reducing them to integrals of rational functions (1785).

Lexell for the first time constructed a general system of polygonometry (5), e.g., of trigonometrical solution of plane n-gons on the given $2n - 3$ sides and angles between them, provided that at least $n - 2$ elements are sides. These investigations formed a natural sequel to and generalization of the works on trigonometrical solution of quadrangles published shortly before by J.-H. Lambert (1770), J. T. Mayer (1773), and S. Björnssen (1780). Lexell based solutions of all the problems on two principal equations obtained when the sides of a polygon are projected on the two normal (to one another) axes situated in its plane, provided that one of them coincides with some side. From these equations he deduced others effective in the solution of triangles and quadrangles on certain given elements, suggested analogous formulae for pentagons, hexagons, and heptagons and stated considerations relevant to classification and solution of problems in the general case. He also considered, though in less detail, the problem of solution of *n*-gons on diagonals and on angles they form with sides. After Lexell polygonometry was also worked out by S. L'Huillier (1789).

Lexell considerably enriched spherical geometry and trigonometry. Especially brilliant is his theorem discovered no later than 1778 but published only in 1784: the geometric locus of the vertices of spherical triangles with the same base and equal area are arcs of two small circles whose extremities are points diametrically opposite to the extremities of the common base (6).

In his two articles which were published posthumously (7, 8), Lexell established other properties of small circles on the sphere and deduced a number of new propositions of spherical trigonometry in which he generalized Heron's and Ptolemy's theorems for the sphere and suggested elegant formulae for defining the radii of circumference of circles inscribed in spherical triangles or quadrangles and circumscribed about them. Works by St. Petersburg academicians N. Fuss and F. T. Schubert on spherical geometry and trigonometry were close to these investigations.

Five unpublished papers on geometry by Lexell are preserved in the Archives of the Academy of Sciences in Leningrad (18).

BIBLIOGRAPHY

I. ORIGINAL WORKS.

1. *Disquisitio de investiganda vera quantitate parallaxeos Solis ex transitu Veneris ante discum solis anno 1769* (St. Petersburg, 1772).

2. *Recherches et calculs sur la vraie orbite elliptique de la comète de l'an 1769 et son temps périodique* (St. Petersburg, 1770), written with L. Euler.

3. *Réflexions sur le temps périodique des comètes en général et principalement sur celui de la comète observée en 1770* (St. Petersburg, 1772).

4. *Recherches sur la nouvelle planète découverte par Mr Herschel* (St. Petersburg, 1783).

5. "De resolutione polygonorum rectilineorum," in *Novi Commentarii Ac. Sc. Petropolitanae*, **19** (1774), 1775, 184–236; **20** (1775), 1776, 80–122.

6. "Solutio problematis geometrici ex doctrina sphaericorum," in *Acta Ac. Sc. Petropolitanae*, **5**, 1 (1781), 1784, 112–126.

7. "De proprietatibus circulorum in superficie sphaerica descriptorum," *ibid.*, **6**, 1 (1782), 1786, 58–103.

8. "Demonstratio nonnullorum theorematum ex doctrina sphaerica," *ibid.*, **6**, 2 (1782), 1786, 85–95.

II. SECONDARY LITERATURE.

9. "Précis de la vie de M. Lexell," in *Nova acta Ac. Sc. Petropolitanae*, **2** (1784), 1788, 12–15.

10. J.-C. Poggendorf, *Biographisch-Literarisches Handwörterbuch zur Geschichte der exacten Wissenschaften*, I (Leipzig, 1863), 1444–1446, contains bibliography. (See also 13.)

11. *Nordisk Familjebok Konversationslexikon och realencyklopedi*, IX (Stockholm, 1885), 1189–1191.

12. M. Cantor, *Vorlesungen über Geschichte der Mathematik*, IV (Leipzig, 1908), see Index.

13. O. V. Dinze and K. I. Shafranovski, *Matematika v izdaniakh Akademii nauk* ("Mathematical Works Published by Academy of Sciences") (Moscow–Leningrad, 1936).

14. *Svenska män och kvinnor. Biografisk uppslagswork*, IV (Stockholm, 1948), 553.

15. *Istoria Akademii nauk SSSR* ("History of the Academy of Sciences of the U.S.S.R."), I (Moscow–Leningrad, 1958), see Index.

16. V. I. Lysenko, "Raboty po poligonometrii v Rossii XVIII v." ("Works on Polygonometry in Russia in the XVIII Century"), in *Istorico-matematicheskie issledovania*, **12** (1959), 161–178.

17. *Idem*, "O rabotakh peterburgskikh akademikov A. I. Lexella, N. I. Fussa u F. I. Shuberta po sfericheskoi geometrii i sfericheskoi trigonometrii" ("On the Works of Petersburg Academicians A. I. Lexell, N. I. Fuss, and F. T. Schubert on Spherical Geometry and Trigonometry"), in *Trudy Instituta istorii estestvoznania i tekhniki*, **34** (1960), 384–414.

18. *Idem*, "O neopublikovannykh rukopisiakh po geometrii akademikov A. I. Lexella i N. I. Fussa" ("On the Unpublished Works of Academicians A. I. Lexell and N. I. Fuss on Geometry"), in *Voprosy istorii estestvoznania i tekhniki*, **9** (1960), 116–120.

19. *Idem*, "Iz istorii pervoi peterburgskoi matematicheskoi shkoly" ("On the History of the First Mathematical School in St. Petersburg"), in *Trudy Instituta istorii estestvoznania i tekhniki*, **43** (1961), 182–205.

20. A. P. Youschkevitch, *Istoria matematiki v Rossii do 1917 goda* ("History of Mathematics in Russia Until 1917") (Moscow, 1968), see Index.

A. T. GRIGORIAN
A. P. YOUSCHKEVITCH

LEYBENZON, LEONID SAMUILOVICH (*b*. Kharkov, Russia, 26 June 1879; *d*. Moscow, U.S.S.R., 15 March 1951), *mechanical engineering, geophysics*.

The son of a physician, Leybenzon graduated in 1897 from the Tula classical Gymnasium. He then entered the physics and mathematics section of Moscow University. In 1901 he graduated from the university and in 1906 from the Moscow Higher Technical School. While still a student, he went, on the recommendation of his teacher Zhukovsky, as a mechanical engineer to the Aerodynamics Institute in Kuchino (1904). Here he helped to build the first wind tunnel in Russia and a machine for testing propellers. He also constructed two-component aerodynamic scales, built models, and worked out the first methods of aerodynamic and structural design of the airplane, following Zhukovsky's instructions.

In 1915 he defended his dissertation for a master's degree in applied mathematics at Moscow University, "K teorii bezbalochnykh pokryty" ("Toward a Theory of Ribless Covering"), and in 1916 was made professor of mechanics at Yurev University. In 1917 Leybenzon presented his dissertation for a doctorate in applied mathematics, "O prilozhenii metoda garmonicheskikh funktsy Tomsona k boprosu obvstoychivosti szhatyh sfericheskoy i tsilindricheskoy uprugikh obolochek" ("On the Application of the Method of Harmonic Functions of Thomson to the Question of the Stability of Compressed Spherical and Cylindrical Elastic Membranes"). From 1919 to 1929 Leybenzon was professor of applied mechanics at Tbilisi Polytechnical Institute and University.

In 1921 Leybenzon became professor at the Polytechnical Institute in Baku. At that time he began his remarkable activity in the science and technology of petroleum. In 1922 he returned to Moscow and was made head of the Department of Applied Mechanics at Moscow University. In 1933 Leybenzon was elected corresponding member of the Academy of Sciences of the U.S.S.R. and in 1943 active member.

The range of Leybenzon's scientific interests was extraordinarily wide. He did extensive research in aerodynamics, elasticity theory, hydraulics, and geophysics. In the theoretical section of the Central Aerohydrodynamic Institute from 1933 to 1936, Leybenzon was concerned with airplane design, with the theory of the border layer, and gas dynamics. His works on the theory of hydrodynamic lubrications and the theory of evaporation of liquid drops in a gas current are of great significance. The important transformations given by Leybenzon for the basic equations of gas dynamics of Chaplygin should also be noted.

Leybenzon contributed to elasticity theory and resistance of materials. He gave a method of determining the position of the center of a curve and presented an interesting theorem on the circulation of tangent stress on a curve. He also demonstrated a general method for softening or relaxing border conditions. He deserves credit for the development of methods of approximating the determination of the turning moment into the theory of torsion and the setting of upper and lower limits to its size.

Leybenzon's scientific research and his many years

of teaching the theory of elasticity culminated in notable monographs and textbooks. Among them are *Kurs teorii uprugosti* ("Course in the Theory of Elasticity"; 1942), *Elementy matematicheskoy teorii plastichnosti* ("Elements of the Mathematical Theory of Plasticity"; 1943), and *Variatsionnye metody resheniya zadach teorii uprugosti* ("Variational Methods of Solving Problems in the Theory of Elasticity"; 1943).

Leybenzon's work on the production of petroleum was also of great significance. In 1932 he published a fundamental investigation, "Priblizhennaya dinamicheskaya teoria glubokogo nasosa" ("An Approximating Dynamic Theory of the Deep Pump"). His "Podzemnaya gidravlika vody, nefti i gaza" ("Underground Hydraulics of Water, Petroleum and Gas"; 1934) provided a scientific basis for the rational development of petroleum and gas deposits. His works laid the foundation for the development of the theory of filtration of aerated liquids. Leybenzon had a direct role in the planning and building of the first Soviet pipelines from Baku to Batumi and from Groznyy to Tuapse. A large part of his work was in geophysics, particularly the application of the elasticity theory to the study of the structure of the earth.

BIBLIOGRAPHY

I. ORIGINAL WORKS. For Leybenzon's works, see *Sobranie trudov* ("Collected Works"), 4 vols. (Moscow, 1951–1955): I. *Teoria uprugosti* ("Theory of Elasticity"; 1951); II. *Podzemnaya gidrogazodinamika* ("Underground Gas Dynamics"; 1953); III. *Neftepromyslovaya mekhanika* ("Mechanics of the Petroleum Industry"; 1955); and IV. *Gidrodinamika. Geofizika* ("Hydrodynamics. Geophysics"; 1955).

II. SECONDARY LITERATURE. For information on Leybenzon's life, see L. I. Sedov, "Osnovnye daty zhizni i deyatelnosti L. S. Leybenzona" ("Basic Facts in the Life and Work of L. S. Leybenzon"), in *Uspekhi matematicheskikh nauk*, 7 (1952), 127–134; and B. N. Yurev, "Leonid Samuilovich Leybenzon," in *Izvestiya Akademii nauk SSSR. Otdelenie tekhnicheskikh nauk* (1949), no. 8, 1138–1142.

A. T. GRIGORIAN

LEYDIG, FRANZ VON (*b.* Rothenburg-ob-der-Tauber, Germany, 21 May 1821; *d.* Rothenburg-ob-der-Tauber, 13 April 1908), *comparative anatomy.*

One of three children, Leydig was the only son of Melchior Leydig, a Catholic and a minor public official, and his wife Margareta, a Protestant. Leydig shared his father's religion as well as his hobbies, the elder Leydig being a keen gardener and beekeeper. Leydig himself later recalled that these childhood interests established his lifelong concern with botany and zoology. At the age of twelve the boy acquired a simple microscope, at which he spent most of his free time. (A few years later, during his studies at Würzburg, a local doctor lent him a more sophisticated instrument.)

Beginning in 1840 Leydig studied medicine at the universities of Würzburg and Munich. He received his doctorate in medicine at Würzburg and became an assistant in the department of physiology, teaching also histology and developmental anatomy under Kölliker. He qualified as a university lecturer in 1849, and as extraordinary professor in 1855. In the winter of 1850–1851, Leydig made a trip to Sardinia, where he became aware of the rich marine life that was to become the subject of some of his most important researches. This journey, coupled with his early preoccupation with microscopy, determined the course of his life's work.

In 1857 Leydig was appointed full professor of zoology at the University of Tübingen and published his *Lehrbuch der Histologie des Menschen und der Tiere*, his outstanding contribution to morphology. In his introduction to the *Lehrbuch*, Leydig reviewed the crucial developments in the history of histology, including the discovery and definition of the cell by Purkyně, Valentin, and Schwann, the last of whom described it as a vesicle containing a nucleus (1839). Leydig paid further tribute to other contemporary anatomists, particularly Johannes Müller for his work on glands and for the emphasis that he properly placed upon the significance of the cellular doctrine for pathology. Leydig's book was published at about the same time as other general treatments of similar subjects—most notably Kölliker's *Handbuch der Gewebelehre des Menschen* (1852) and Gerlach's *Handbuch der allgemeinen und speciellen Gewebelehre des menschlichen Körpers* ... (1848). The *Lehrbuch*, however, gives the best account of the rapid growth of comparative microscopical anatomy in the two decades following Schwann's discoveries.

In addition to its historical importance, Leydig's *Lehrbuch* is significant for his description in it of a large secretory cell, found in the epidermis of fishes and larval Amphibia. This mucous cell is peculiar in that it does not pour its secretions over the surface of the epithelium; Leydig believed that its function was to lubricate the skin, and the cell now bears his name.

Chief among Leydig's other discoveries is the interstitial cell, a body enclosed within a smooth endoplastic reticulum and containing lipid granules and crystals, that occurs in the seminiferous tubules and in the mediaseptum and connective-tissue septa of the testes. These cells are believed to produce the male hormone testosterone, which determines male secondary sexual characteristics. Leydig described the interstitial cells in his detailed account of the male sex organs, "Zur Anatomie der männlichen Geschlechtsorgane und Analdrüsen der Säugetiere," published in 1850:

> The comparative studies of the testis resulted in the discovery of cells surrounding the seminiferous tubules, vessels, and nerves. These special cells are present in small numbers where they follow the course of the blood vessels, but increase in mass considerably when surrounding seminiferous tubules. These cells are lipoid in character; they can be colorless or can be stained yellowish, and they have light vesicular nuclei [p. 47].

This description indicates clearly that Leydig recognized the specific morphology of these cells; their endocrine nature and ultrastructure have only recently been fully understood.

Leydig is also known for the discovery of the gland of Leydig (1892), a portion of the mesonephros in vertebrates, of which the secretions are thought to stimulate the movement of spermatozoa; and for describing large vesicular cells that occur in the connective tissue and in the walls of blood vessels in crustaceans (1883). Four different types of the latter have been determined.

Leydig became professor of comparative anatomy at the University of Bonn in 1875. He was made emeritus in 1887, and retired to the town of his birth. He had married Katharina Jaeger, the daughter of a professor of surgery at Erlangen, who survived him; they had no children. During his lifetime Leydig was granted many honors, including personal ennoblement, and an honorary doctorate of science from the University of Bologna. He was a member of a number of medical and scientific societies, among them the Royal Society of London, the Imperial Academy of Science of St. Petersburg, and the New York Academy of Sciences.

BIBLIOGRAPHY

I. ORIGINAL WORKS. Leydig's most important writings include "Die Dotterfurchung nach ihrem Vorkommen in der Tierwelt und nach ihrer Bedeutung," in *Isis. Encyclopädische Zeitschrift, vorzüglich für Naturgeschichte, vergleichende Anatomie und Physiologie von [Lorenz] Oken*, pt. 3 (1848), cols. 161–193; "Zur Anatomie der männlichen Geschlechtsorgane und Analdrüsen der Säugetiere," in *Zeitschrift für wissenschaftliche Zoologie*, **2** (1850), 1–57; "Über Flimmerbewegung in den Uterindrüsen des

Schweines," in *Archiv für Anatomie, Physiologie und wissenschaftliche Medicin* (1852), 375–378; *Beiträge zur mikroskopischen Anatomie und Entwicklungsgeschichte der Rochen und Haie* (Leipzig, 1852); "Zum feinen Aufbau der Arthropoden," in *Archiv für Anatomie, Physiologie und wissenschaftliche Medicin* (1855), 376–480; "Über Tastkörperchen und Muskelstruktur," *ibid.* (1856), 150–159; *Lehrbuch der Histologie des Menschen und der Tiere* (Frankfurt, 1857); "Über das Nervensystem der Anneliden," in *Archiv für Anatomie und Physiologie* (1862), 90–124; "Neue Beiträge zur anatomischen Kenntnis der Hautdecke und Hautsinnesorgane der Fische," in *Festschrift zur Feier der 100jährigen Bestehens der Naturforschenden Gesellschaft zu Halle* (Halle, 1879), 129–186; *Zelle und Gewebe. Neue Beiträge zur Histologie des Tierkörpers* (Frankfurt, 1885); "Die riesigen Nervenröhren im Bauchmark der Ringelwürmer," in *Zoologischer Anzeiger*, **9** (1886), 591–597; "Das Parietalorgan der Wirbeltiere. Bemerkungen," *ibid.*, **10** (1887), 534–539; "Nervenkörperchen in der Haut der Fische," *ibid.*, **11** (1888), 40–44; "Das Parietalorgan der Reptilien und Amphibien kein Sinnesorgan," in *Biologisches Zentralblatt*, **8**, no. 23 (1889), 707–718; "Besteht eine Beziehung zwischen Hautsinnesorganen und Haaren?," *ibid.*, **13**, nos. 11–12 (1893), 359–375; "Zur Kenntnis der Zirbel- und Parietalorgane. Forgesetze Studien," in *Abhandlungen hrsg. von der Senckenbergischen naturforschenden Gesellschaft*, pt. 3 (1896), 217–278; "Der reizleitende Theil des Nervengewebes," in *Archiv für Anatomie und Physiologie*, Anatomische Abt. (1897), 431–464; "Zirbel und Jacobson'sche Organe einiger Reptilien," in *Archiv für mikroskopische Anatomie und Entwicklungsmechanik*, **50** (1897), 385–418; and "Bemerkung zu den 'Leuchtorganen' der Selachier," in *Anatomischer Anzeiger*, **22**, nos. 14–15 (1902), 297–301.

II. SECONDARY LITERATURE. Obituary notices are O. Boettger, in *Zoologischer Beobachter*, **50**, no. 1 (1909), 31; R. von Hanstein, in *Naturwissenschaftliche Rundschau*, **23**, no. 27 (1908), 347–351; M. Nussbaum, in *Anatomischer Anzeiger*, **32**, nos. 19–20 (1908), 503–506; and in *Kölnische Zeitung*, no. 520 (14 May 1908); O. Schultze, in *Münchener medizinische Wochenschrift*, **55**, no. 18 (1908), 972–973; O. Taschenberg, in *Leopoldina*, pt. 45 (1909), 82–88; and O. Zacharias, in *Archiv für Hydrobiologie*, **4**, pt. 1 (1908), 77–82.

P. GLEES

L'HÉRITIER DE BRUTELLE, CHARLES LOUIS

(*b.* Paris, France, 15 June 1746; *d.* Paris, 16 August 1800), *botany.*

L'Héritier was the son of a relatively well-to-do Roman Catholic family belonging to the court circles in Paris. Few details are known of his youth and upbringing. In 1772 he was appointed to the fairly high position of superintendent of the waters and forests of the Paris region, a sinecure which he took seriously. The agronomic duties connected with this position awakened an interest in botany that he developed by independent study and by seeking contact with the botanists of the Jardin du Roi. In 1775 he was appointed counselor at the Cour des Aides in Paris, a position that made him a member of high society. He was a friend of Malesherbes and the group around the *Encyclopédie*.

In 1785 L'Héritier started his botanical career with the publication of the sumptuous *Stirpes novae*, describing many plants that had recently been introduced into Paris gardens from throughout the world. He corresponded with the leading British naturalist Sir Joseph Banks, and worked at his private herbarium in 1786–1787, in order to learn from the collections made by Joseph Dombey. The right to publish on these South American plants was claimed by the Spanish government, and the French government wished to stop L'Héritier from studying the plants, which he had received from Dombey himself. The trip to England was made in order to be free to continue his botanical work but ultimately resulted in the publication of another folio volume, *Sertum anglicum*, dealing with plants newly introduced in London and Kew rather than with the Dombey material.

In December 1787 L'Héritier returned to Paris, where he resumed publication of the *Stirpes novae* and published monographs on *Cornus* and *Geranium* (in his *Geraniologia*). During the Revolution, L'Héritier lost his official position as well as most of his private fortune. Obliged to work in straitened circumstances, he could no longer publish his botanical works at his own expense. On 16 August 1800 he was murdered near his house; the crime was never solved.

L'Héritier married Thérèse Valère Doré in 1775; she bore him five children. He was a member of the Académie des Sciences and retained his seat after its reorganization. L'Héritier discovered the talents of the great botanical artist Pierre-Joseph Redouté, whom he employed to make drawings for the *Stirpes novae* and for subsequent works.

BIBLIOGRAPHY

I. ORIGINAL WORKS. L'Héritier's major works are *Stirpes novae aut minus cognitae, quae descriptionibus et iconibus illustravit*, 9 fascs. (Paris, 1784–1785 [published 1785–1805]); *Sertum anglicum, seu plantae rariores quae in hortis juxta Londinium . . .*, 4 fascs. (Paris, 1788 [published 1789–1792]; 2nd ed., 1788 [published *ca.* 1805]; facs. repr. of 1st ed., Pittsburgh, 1963, with intros. by W. Blunt, J. S. L. Gilmour *et al.*, and F. A. Stafleu); *Cornus. Specimen botanicum sistens descriptiones et icones specierum Corni minus cognitarum* (Paris, 1788 [published

1789]); "On the Genus of *Calligonum*, Comprehending *Pterococcus* and *Pallasia*," in *Transactions of the Linnean Society of London*, **1** (1791), 177; "On the Genus of *Symplocos*, Comprehending *Hopea, Alstonia*, and *Ciponia*," *ibid*., 174; and *Geraniologia, seu Erodii, Pelargonii, Monsoniae et Grieli historia iconibus illustrata* (Paris, 1787–1788 [published Apr. 1792]), 44 plates—the text, unpublished, is at the Conservatoire Botanique, Geneva.

II. SECONDARY LITERATURE. See J. Britten and B. B. Woodward, "Bibliographical Notes, XXXV,—L'Héritier's Botanical Works," in *Journal of Botany, British and Foreign*, **43** (1905), 267–273, 325–329; and F. A. Stafleu, "L'Héritier de Brutelle: The Man and His Work," in G. H. M. Lawrence, ed., *Charles Louis L'Héritier de Brutelle, Sertum anglicum 1788, Facsimile With Critical Studies and a Translation* (Pittsburgh, 1963), with biography, commentaries, and unpublished sources; and *Taxonomic Literature* (Utrecht, 1967), pp. 266–268, which lists secondary literature.

FRANS A. STAFLEU

L'HOSPITAL (L'HÔPITAL), GUILLAUME-FRANÇOIS-ANTOINE DE (Marquis de Sainte-Mesme, Comte d'Entremont) (*b.* Paris, France, 1661; *d.* Paris, 2 February 1704), *mathematics.*

The son of Anne-Alexandre de L'Hospital and of Elizabeth Gobelin, L'Hospital served for a time as a cavalry officer but resigned from the army because of nearsightedness. From that time onwards he devoted his energies entirely to mathematics. He married Marie-Charlotte de Romilley de La Chesnelaye, who bore him one son and three daughters.

L'Hospital's mathematical talents were recognized when he was still a boy. It is reported that when he was only fifteen years of age he solved, much to the surprise of his elders, a problem on the cycloid which had been put forward by Pascal. Later he contributed solutions to several problems posed by Jean (Johann) Bernoulli, among them the problem of the brachistochrone, which was solved at the same time by three others—Newton, Leibniz, and Jacques (Jakob) Bernoulli. His memory has survived in the name of the rule for finding the limiting value of a fraction whose numerator and denominator tend to zero. However, in his own time, and for several generations after his death, his fame was based on his book *Analyse des infiniment petits pour l'intelligence des lignes courbes* (1st ed., 1696, 2nd ed. 1715). Following the classical custom, the book starts with a set of definitions and axioms. Thus, a *variable* quantity is defined as one that increases or decreases continuously while a *constant* quantity remains the same while others change. The *difference* (differential) is defined as the

infinitely small portion by which a variable quantity increases or decreases continuously. Of the two axioms, the first postulates that quantities which differ only by infinitely small amounts may be substituted for one another, while the second states that a curve may be thought of as a polygonal line with an infinite number of infinitely small sides such that the angle between adjacent lines determines the curvature of the curve. Following the axioms, the basic rules of the differential calculus are given and exemplified. The second chapter applies these rules to the determination of the tangent to a curve in a given point. While many examples are given, the approach is perfectly general, that is, it applies to arbitrary curves or to the relation between two arbitrary curves. The third chapter deals with maximum-minimum problems and includes examples drawn from mechanics and from geography. Next comes a treatment of points of inflection and of cusps. This involves the introduction of higher-order differentials, each supposed infinitely small compared to its predecessor. Later chapters deal with evolutes and with caustics. L'Hospital's rule is given in chapter 9.

The *Analyse des infiniment petits* was the first textbook of the differential calculus. The existence of several commentaries on it—one by Varignon (1725)—attests to its popularity. The question of its intellectual ownership has been much debated. Jean Bernoulli, who is known to have instructed L'Hospital in the calculus about 1691, complained after L'Hospital's death that he (Bernoulli) had not been given enough credit for his contributions. L'Hospital himself, in the introduction to his books, freely acknowledges his indebtedness to Leibniz and to the Bernoulli brothers. On the other hand, he states that he regards the foundations provided by him as his own idea, although they also have been credited by some to Jean Bernoulli. However, these foundations can be found, less explicitly, also in Leibniz, although Leibniz made it clear that he did not accept L'Hospital's Platonistic views on the reality of infinitely small and infinitely large quantities.

At his death L'Hospital left the completed manuscript of a second book, *Traité analytique des sections coniques et de leur usage pour la résolution des équations dans les problèmes tant déterminés qu'indéterminés*. It was published in 1720. L'Hospital had also planned to write a continuation to his *Analyse des infiniment petits* which would have dealt with the integral calculus, but he dropped this project in deference to Leibniz, who had let him know that he had similar intentions.

L'Hospital was a major figure in the early development of the calculus on the continent of Europe. He advanced its cause not only by his scientific works but also by his many contacts, including correspondence with Leibniz, with Jean Bernoulli, and with Huygens. Fontenelle tells us that it was he who introduced Huygens to the new calculus.

According to the testimony of his contemporaries, L'Hospital possessed a very attractive personality, being, among other things, modest and generous, two qualities which were not widespread among the mathematicians of his time.

BIBLIOGRAPHY

L'Hospital's principal works are *Analyse des infiniment petits pour l'intelligence des lignes courbes* (Paris, 1696; 2nd ed., 1715); and the posthumous *Traité analytique des sections coniques et de leur usage pour la résolution des équations dans les problèmes tant déterminés qu'indéterminés* (Paris, 1720).

On his life and work, see the *éloge* by Fontenelle in the *Histoires* of the Paris Academy of Sciences for 1704, p. 125, and in Fontenelle's *Oeuvres diverses*, III (The Hague, 1729); J. E. Montucla, *Histoire des mathématiques*, II (Paris, 1758), 396; O. J. Rebel, *Der Briefwechsel zwischen Johann (I.) Bernoulli und dem Marquis de l'Hospital* (Heidelberg, 1932); and P. Schafheitlin, ed., *Die Differentialrechnung von Johann Bernoulli aus den Jahren 1691–1692*, Ostwalds Klassiker der Exacten Wissenschaften no. 211 (Leipzig, 1924).

ABRAHAM ROBINSON

L'HUILLIER (or **LHUILIER**), **SIMON-ANTOINE-JEAN** (*b.* Geneva, Switzerland, 24 April 1750; *d.* Geneva, 28 March 1840), *mathematics*.

L'Huillier, the fourth child of Laurent L'Huillier and his second wife, Suzanne-Constance Matte, came from a family of jewelers and goldsmiths originally from Mâcon. In 1691 they became citizens of Geneva, where they had found refuge at the time of the revocation of the Edict of Nantes. Attracted to mathematics at an early age, L'Huillier refused a relative's offer to bequeath him a part of his fortune if the young man consented to follow an ecclesiastical career. After brilliant secondary studies he attended the mathematics courses given at the Calvin Academy by Louis Bertrand, a former student of Leonhard Euler. He also followed the physics courses of Georges-Louis Le Sage, his famous relative, who gave him much advice and encouragement. Through Le Sage he obtained a position as tutor in the Rilliet-Plantamour family, with whom he stayed for two years. At Le Sage's prompting, in 1773 he sent to the *Journal encyclopédique* a "Lettre en réponse aux objections élevées contre la gravitation newtonienne."

Le Sage had had as a student and then as a collaborator Christoph Friedrich Pfleiderer, who later taught mathematics at Tübingen. In 1766, on the recommendation of Le Sage, Pfleiderer was named professor of mathematics and physics at the military academy in Warsaw recently founded by King Stanislaus II. He was subsequently appointed to the commission in charge of preparing textbooks for use in Polish schools. In 1775 he sent the commission's plans for a textbook contest to Le Sage, who tried to persuade L'Huillier to submit a proposal for a physics text, but the latter preferred to compete in mathematics. He rapidly drew up an outline, sent it to Warsaw, and won the prize. The king sent his congratulations to the young author, and Prince Adam Czartoryski offered him a post as tutor to his son, also named Adam, at their residence in Puławy.

L'Huillier accepted and spent the best years of his life in Poland, from 1777 to 1788. His pedagogical duties did not prevent him from writing his mathematics course, which he put in finished form with the aid of Pfleiderer, and which was translated into Polish by the Abbé Andrzej Gawroński, the king's reader. L'Huillier had an unusually gifted pupil and proved to be an excellent teacher. He had numerous social obligations arising from his situation (including hunting parties), but he still found time to compose several memoirs and to compete in 1786 in the Berlin Academy's contest on the theory of mathematical infinity. The jury, headed by Lagrange, awarded him the prize.

L'Huillier returned home in 1789 and found his native country in a state of considerable agitation. Fearing revolutionary disturbances, he decided to stay with his friend Pfleiderer in Tübingen, where he remained until 1794. Although offered a professorship of mathematics at the University of Leiden in 1795, L'Huillier entered the competition for the post left vacant in Geneva by his former teacher Louis Bertrand. In 1795 he was appointed to the Geneva Academy (of which he soon became rector) and held the chair of mathematics without interruption until his retirement in 1823. Also in 1795 he married Marie Cartier, by whom he had one daughter and one son.

Whereas the Poles found L'Huillier distinctly puritanical, his fellow citizens of Geneva reproached him for his lack of austerity and his whimsicality, although the latter quality never went beyond putting geometric theorems into verse and writing ballads on the number three and on the square root of minus one. Toward the end of his career Charles-François Sturm was among his students.

L'Huillier was also involved in the political life of Geneva. He was a member of the Legislative

Council, over which he presided in 1796, and a member of the Representative Council from its creation. His scientific achievements earned him membership in the Polish Educational Society, corresponding memberships in the academies of Berlin, Göttingen, and St. Petersburg, and in the Royal Society, and an honorary professorship at the University of Leiden.

L'Huillier's extensive and varied scientific work bore the stamp of an original intellect even in its most elementary components; and while it did not possess the subtlety of Sturm's writings, it surpassed those of Bertrand in its vigor. L'Huillier's excellent textbooks on algebra and geometry were used for many years in Polish schools. His treatise in Latin on problems of maxima and minima greatly impressed the geometer Jacob Steiner half a century later. L'Huillier also considered the problem, widely discussed at the time, of the minimum amount of wax contained in honeycomb cells. While in Poland he sent articles to the Berlin Academy, as well as the prize-winning memoir of 1786: *Exposition élémentaire des principes des calculs supérieurs*. Printed at the Academy's expense, the memoir was later discussed at length by Montucla in his revised *Histoire des mathématiques* and was examined in 1966 by E. S. Shatunova. In this work, which L'Huillier sent to Berlin with the motto "Infinity is the abyss in which our thoughts vanish," he presented a pertinent critique of Fontenelle's conceptions and even of Euler's, and provided new insights into the notion of limit, its interpretation, and its use. Baron J. F. T. Maurice recognized the exemplary rigor of L'Huillier's argumentation, although he regretted, not unjustifiably, that it "was accompanied by long-winded passages that could have been avoided."

In 1796 L'Huillier sent to the Berlin Academy the algebraic solution of the generalized Pappus problem. Euler, Fuss, and Lexell had found a geometric solution in 1780, and Lagrange had discovered an algebraic solution for the case of the triangle in 1776. L'Huillier based his contribution on the method used by Lagrange. More remarkable, however, were the four articles on probabilities, written with Pierre Prévost, that L'Huillier published in the *Mémoires de l'Académie de Berlin* of 1796 and 1797. Commencing with the problem of an urn containing black and white balls that are withdrawn and not replaced, the authors sought to determine the composition of the contents of the urn from the balls drawn. In this type of question concerning the probabilities of causes, they turned to the works of Jakob Bernoulli, De Moivre, Bayes and Laplace, their goal being clearly to find a demonstration of the principle that Laplace stated as follows and that L'Huillier termed the etiological

principle: "If an event can be produced by a number *n* of different causes, the probabilities of the existence of these causes taken from the event are among themselves as the probabilities of the event taken from these causes." The four articles are of considerable interest, and Isaac Todhunter mentions them in his *History of the Mathematical Theory of Probability*.

The two-volume *Éléments raisonnés d'algèbre* that L'Huillier wrote for his Geneva students in 1804 was really a sequel to his texts for Polish schools. The first volume, composed of eight chapters, was concerned solely with first- and second-degree equations. One chapter was devoted to an account of Diophantine analysis. Volume II (chapters 9–22) treated progressions, logarithms, and combinations and went as far as fourth-degree equations. A chapter on continued fractions was based on the works of Lagrange and of Legendre; another concerned the method of indeterminate coefficients. Questions of calculus were discussed in an appendix. The main value of these two volumes lay in the author's clear exposition and judicious selection of exercises, for some of which he furnished solutions.

L'Huillier's last major work appeared in 1809 in Paris and Geneva. Dedicated to his former pupil Adam Czartoryski, who was then minister of public education in Russia, it dealt with geometric loci in the plane (straight line and circle) and in space (sphere). Between 1810 and 1813 L'Huillier was an editor of the *Annales de mathématiques pures et appliquées* and wrote seven articles on plane and spherical geometry and the construction of polyhedrons.

BIBLIOGRAPHY

I. ORIGINAL WORKS. L'Huillier's writings include *Éléments d'arithmétique et de géométrie* ... (Warsaw, 1778), partly translated by Gawroński as *Geometrya dla szkoł narodowych* (Warsaw, 1780) and *Algiebra dla szkoł narodowych* (Warsaw, 1782); "Mémoire sur le minimum de cire des alvéoles des abeilles, et en particulier un minimum minimorum relatif à cette matière," in *Mémoires de l'Académie Royale des sciences et belles-lettres de Berlin* (1781), 277–300; *De relatione mutua capacitatis et terminorum figurarum seu de maximis et minimis* (Warsaw, 1782); "Théorème sur les solides plano-superficiels," in *Mémoires de l'Académie Royale des sciences et belles-lettres de Berlin* (1786–1787), 423–432; *Exposition élémentaire des principes des calculs supérieures*, ... (Berlin, 1787); "Sur la décomposition en facteurs de la somme et de la différence de deux puissances à exposants quelconques de la base des logarithmes hyperboliques ...," in *Mémoires de l'Académie Royale des sciences et belles-lettres de Berlin* (1788–1789), 326–368; *Polygonométrie et abrégé d'isopérimétrie élémentaire* (Geneva, 1789); *Examen du mode* d'élection proposé à la Convention nationale de France et adopté à Genève (Geneva, 1794); and *Principiorum calculi differentialis et integralis expositio elementaris* (Tübingen, 1795).

See also "Solution algébrique du problème suivant: A un cercle donné, inscrire un polygone dont les côtés passent par des points donnés," in *Mémoires de l'Académie Royale des sciences et belles-lettres de Berlin* (1796), 94–116; "Sur les probabilités," *ibid.*, Cl. de math., 117–142, written with Pierre Prévost; "Mémoire sur l'art d'estimer les probabilités des causes par les effets," *ibid.*, Cl. de phil. spéc., 3–24, written with Pierre Prévost; "Remarques sur l'utilité et l'étendue du principe par lequel on estime la probabilité des causes," *ibid.*, 25–41, written with Pierre Prévost; "Mémoire sur l'application du calcul des probabilités à la valeur du témoignage," *ibid.* (1797), Cl. de phil. spéc., 120–152, written with Pierre Prévost; *Précis d'arithmétique par demandes et réponses à l'usage des écoles primaires* (Geneva, 1797); *Éléments raisonnés d'algèbre publiés à l'usage des étudiants en philosophie*, 2 vols. (Geneva, 1804); *Éléments d'analyse géométrique et d'analyse algébrique* (Geneva–Paris, 1809); and "Analogies entre les triangles, rectangles, rectilignes et sphériques," in *Annales de mathématiques pures et appliquées*, **1** (1810–1811), 197–201.

II. Secondary Literature. The first articles on L'Huillier, which appeared during his lifetime, were Jean Sénebier, *Histoire littéraire de Genève*, III (Geneva, 1786), 216–217; and J.-M. Quérard, *France littéraire*, V (Paris, 1833), 295. Shortly after his death there appeared Auguste de La Rive, *Discours sur l'instruction publique* (Geneva, 1840); and "Discours du prof. de Candolle à la séance publique de la Société des arts du 13 août 1840," in *Procès-verbaux des séances annuelles de la Société pour l'avancement des arts*, **4** (1840), 10–15. Brief articles are in Haag, *France protestante*, VII (Paris, 1857), 85; and A. de Montet, *Dictionnaire biographique des Genevois et des Vaudois*, II (Lausanne, 1878), 66–68.

The best account of L'Huillier's life and work is Rudolf Wolf, *Biographien zur Kulturgeschichte der Schweiz*, I (Zurich, 1858), 401–422. See also L. Isely, *Histoire des sciences mathématiques dans la Suisse française* (Neuchâtel, 1901), pp. 160–167.

More recent publications are Samuel Dickstein, "Przyczynek do biografji Szymona Lhuiliera (1750–1840)," in *Kongres matematyków krajów słowiańskich. sprawozdanie* (Warsaw, 1930), pp. 111–118; Émile L'Huillier, *Notice généalogique sur la famille L'Huillier de Genève* (Geneva, 1957); Emanuel Rostworowski, "La Suisse et la Pologne au XVIIIe siècle," in *Échanges entre la Pologne et la Suisse du XIVe au XIXe siècle* (Geneva, 1965), pp. 182–185; and E. S. Shatunova, "Teoria grani Simona Luilera" ("Simon L'Huillier's Theory of Limits"), in *Istoriko-matematicheskie issledovaniya*, **17** (1966), 325–331.

A. P. Youschkevitch discusses L'Huillier's 1786 prize-winning memoir in an essay, "The Mathematical Theory of the Infinite," in Charles C. Gillispie, *Lazare Carnot, Savant* (Princeton, 1971), 156–158.

Pierre Speziali

LHWYD, EDWARD (*b.* Cardiganshire, Wales, 1660; *d.* Oxford, England, 30 June 1709), *paleontology, botany, philology.*

Lhwyd (he used this spelling for his signature; but his name was also variously rendered Lhuyd, Llwyd, Lloyd, and Luidius) was the natural son of Edward Lloyd of Llanforda, near Oswestry, and of Bridget Pryse of Gogerddan, Cardiganshire. In 1682 he entered Jesus College, Oxford, where he studied for five years. In order to increase his limited means, he soon became assistant to Robert Plot, professor of chemistry and first keeper of the Ashmolean Museum. This museum, opened in 1683, was founded on the collections of John Tradescant father and son, augmented by the donor, Elias Ashmole. It was through his connection with the museum and with Plot, at that time secretary of the Royal Society, that Lhwyd was able to establish important scientific contacts.

During visits to north Wales, Lhwyd collected plants around the hill mass of Snowdon. He was the first to record, in Edmund Gibson's edition of *Camden's Britannia* (1695), that the mountains of Britain have a distinctive alpine flora and fauna. Lhwyd compiled a list of plants from Snowdon, which was published by John Ray in his *Synopsis methodica Stirpium Britannicarum* (1690), and Ray referred to these records as "the greatest adornment" of his book.

Lhwyd also assisted Martin Lister with lists of Oxfordshire species of mollusks and fossils, and some of his specimens were used in Lister's *Historiae sive synopsis methodice Conchyliorum* (1685–1692). By the time he succeeded Plot as keeper of the Ashmolean Museum in 1691, Lhwyd's interest in formed stones (fossils) had superseded his botanical interests. In 1686 he put before the Oxford Philosophical Society a new catalog of the shells in the Ashmolean Museum; and during the next few years he continued to add to it, with a view to publication. The work eventually appeared in 1699 in a limited edition of only 120 copies. The cost was subscribed by some of his patrons and friends, including Isaac Newton, Hans Sloane, and Martin Lister. Written in Latin and entitled *Lithophylacii Britannici ichnographia*, it consisted of a catalog of 1,766 localized items arranged systematically and was the first illustrated catalog of a public collection of fossils to be published in England.

As an appendix to his list Lhwyd printed six letters to friends, also in Latin, dealing with geological subjects. The most important of these was to John Ray on the problem of the origin of "marine bodies and mineral leaves." Although Lhwyd's theory was completely erroneous, his arguments illustrate the flexibility of thought which existed on this subject during the late seventeenth century. For Lhwyd, who had viewed the fossil content of the rocks in depth in the sea cliffs of south Wales and in limestone caves, there were obvious difficulties in accepting the generally held belief that all fossils had been laid down at the time of the universal deluge; and in his letter he set out several cogent arguments against the idea of a single inundation.

Lhwyd hoped that the considerable depth at which fossils are found could be explained by the hypothesis he put forward. He suggested a sequence in which mists and vapors over the sea were impregnated with the "seed" of marine animals. These were raised and carried for considerable distances before they descended over the land in rain and fog. The "invisible animalcula" then penetrated deep into the earth and there germinated; and in this way complete replicas of sea organisms, or sometimes only parts of individuals, were reproduced in stone. Lhwyd also suggested that fossil plants, known to him only as resembling leaves of ferns and mosses which have minute "seed," were formed in the same manner. He claimed that this theory explained a number of features about fossils in a satisfactory manner—the presence in England of nautiluses and exotic shells which were no longer found in neighboring seas; the absence of birds and viviparous animals not found by Lhwyd as fossils; the varying and often quite large size of the forms, not usual in present oceans; and the variation in preservation from perfect replica to vague representation, which was thought to indicate degeneration with time.

It does not seem that Lhwyd made any further effort to defend or propound his theory, and he assured Ray in his original letter that "They who have no other aim than the search of Truth, are no ways concerned for the honour of their opinions: and for my part I have always been led thereunto by your example, so much the less an admirer of hypotheses, as I have been a lover of Natural History."

Ray's later letters to Lhwyd reiterated his own opinion that fossils were remains of once-living organisms and that the strata in which they are found were once sediments of land floods or sea inundations. He did, however, generously allow a degree of possibility of his friend's theory; and certainly the republication of Lhwyd's letter, in English, in the third (posthumous) edition of Ray's *Miscellaneous Discourses* (1713) served to bring it to the notice of a much wider readership.

In 1695 Lhwyd contributed notes on the southern counties of Wales to *Camden's Britannia*, and out of this there arose an invitation to undertake a work on the natural history of Wales. Eventually it was proposed to include all the Celtic countries and to cover natural history, geology, history, archaeology, and philology. In May 1697, Lhwyd began a great tour which took him through Wales, Ireland, part of Scotland, Cornwall, and across into Brittany. He collected or transcribed many Welsh and Gaelic manuscripts; and when he returned to Oxford in 1701, he intended to publish his researches in two volumes, the first on linguistic studies, the second on archaeology and natural history. The first volume of *Archaeologia Britannica* appeared in 1707 and contained the first comparative study of the Celtic languages and an Irish Gaelic dictionary. Thus, Lhwyd can be considered the founder of comparative Celtic philology, but owing to his early death the remaining branches of his researches were not published.

BIBLIOGRAPHY

I. ORIGINAL WORKS. In 1945 R. T. Gunther published *Life and Letters of Edward Lhwyd* as vol. XIV of his Early Science in Oxford series and included those letters preserved in the Martin Lister and John Aubrey collections at the Bodleian Library, Oxford, in addition to others previously published. Correspondence addressed to Lhwyd is also in the Bodleian.

Lhwyd's MS collections were originally very extensive; and at his death they were offered for purchase to the University of Oxford and to Jesus College, but the offers were not accepted. They were then sold to Sir Thomas Sebright of Beechwood, Hertfordshire. The Irish portion of the Celtic MSS was presented to Trinity College, Dublin, by Sir John Sebright in 1786. The remainder was sold at Sotheby's, London, in 1807—see *Gentleman's Magazine*, **77** (1807), 419—but it is believed that most of these were destroyed shortly afterward in a fire at a bookbinder's workshop.

Besides *Lithophylacii Britannici ichnographia* (London, 1699) and the first volume of *Archaeologia Britannica* (Oxford, 1707), Lhwyd made numerous contributions to the *Philosophical Transactions of the Royal Society*.

II. SECONDARY LITERATURE. A memoir of Lhwyd was included in N. Owen's *British Remains* (London, 1777). R. T. Gunther's book, cited above, is a comprehensive work respecting Lhwyd's correspondence and fossil collections. J. L. Campbell and D. Thomson, *Edward Lhuyd in the Scottish Highlands* (Oxford, 1963), is devoted to his Gaelic studies.

M. E. Jahn has written on the editions of Lhwyd's catalogue, including the pirated Leipzig edition, in *Journal of the Society for the Bibliography of Natural History*, **6**, pt. 2 (1972), 86–97; other notes by Jahn on Lhwyd are in **4**, pt. 5 (1966), 244–248, **6**, pt. 1 (1971), 61–62.

J. M. EDMONDS

LIBAVIUS (or **LIBAU**), **ANDREAS** (*b.* Halle, Saxony, *ca.* 1560; *d.* Coburg, 25 July 1616), *chemistry, medicine, logic.*

Libavius was the son of a poor linen weaver, Johann Libau, who, in search of work, went from Harz to Halle, where he settled. Libavius attended the Gymnasium in Halle during the rectorship of Johannes Rivius the Younger. In 1578 he entered the University of Wittenberg and in 1579 moved to the University of Jena, where in 1581 he received the Ph.D. and the title of poet laureate. In the same year he became a teacher at Ilmenau. In 1586 he was appointed "Stadt- und Raths-Schulen Rector" in Coburg.

At the beginning of 1588 Libavius enrolled in the University of Basel, where he received the M.D. after presenting a thesis entitled *Theses de summo et generali in medendo scopo.* The Medical Faculty at Basel was still strongly influenced by Thomas Erastus, who had died not long before (1583). He was an opponent of Paracelsus, whose position Libavius represented to the end of his life. Libavius' bond with the University of Basel was strong, however; among his friends were the professors Johannes Stupanus, Felix Platter, Gaspard Bauhin, and Jacob Zwinger.

In 1588 Libavius became professor of history and poetry at the University of Jena. Three years later he moved to Rothenburg, where he became municipal physician. From 1592 he was also inspector of schools. Endless quarrels with the rector of the town school, Elias Ehinger, led Libavius to return to Coburg on 21 February 1607; there he was named rector of the newly founded Gymnasium Casimirianum Academicum. From its very beginning the school was regarded as a university by its founder, Duke John Casimir of Coburg; but because it represented orthodox Lutheranism, it failed to receive the necessary imperial charter from Rudolf II. At the opening Libavius delivered the oration *Declamatio de discendi modis.*

There is little information about Libavius' private life, although it is known that he had two sons, Michael and Andreas; the latter was a physician who practiced for a time with Martin Ruhland the Younger in Prague and later was a physician in Moravia, and then a teacher in Leszno, Poland. Libavius also had two daughters. One of them, Susanna, was the wife of the physician Pancratius Gallus; the second, whose name is not known, was the wife of Philip Walther Seidenbecker, professor at the Gymnasium in Coburg.

Some light is thrown on Libavius' life by his correspondence (not yet published) with Leonhard Dolde, a medical doctor in Nuremberg (142 letters from 1600–1611 are extant), and the published letters to Sigismund Schnitzer of Bamberg. As can be seen from these letters, although Libavius traveled very little, he maintained contacts with many scientists and read a great deal. He paid little attention to medical practice.

Libavius' activities were many-sided, and his teaching is noteworthy. There are several printed works in various fields—disputations and exhibit-day lectures—which on the title page bear the note "Sub praeside A. Libavii." Between 1599 and 1601 Libavius published four volumes of *Singularium,* probably his lectures in natural science. Both the *Singularium* and his *Schulordnung* have considerable interest for the history of education.

An orthodox Lutheran, Libavius opposed the Catholics, especially the Jesuits (for instance, in *Gretserus triumphatus* [1604]). Toward the end of his life he also became an opponent of Calvinism. He wrote his theological treatises under the anagram Basilius de Varna. As a poet he wrote *Poemata epica* (1602). As a philosopher and logician he was known as the author of *Quaestionum physicarum* (1591), *Dialectica* (1593), *Exercitiorum logicorum liber* (1595), *Dialogus logicus* (1595), and *Tetraemerum* (1596). From the contents of his books it appears that he was a follower of Aristotle and opposed Petrus Ramus and —especially—his two British disciples, William Temple, of Cambridge, and James Martin, of Oxford. His correspondence with Dolde shows that Libavius was also interested in medicine, pharmacology, botany, mineralogy, zoology, and, above all, chemistry.

A man of exceptional industry and perhaps overweening self-confidence, Libavius underestimated others; consequently he fell easily into conflicts and lost friends. His voluminous works brought him recognition but also often attracted criticism. Joseph Duchesne (Quercetanus), in *Ad veritatem hermeticae medicinae* (1605), wrote of him: "Andreas Libavius Hallensis Sax. medicus, doctor celeberrimus rerumque naturalium perscrutator fidissimus et diligentissimus, verae Chymiae defensor acerrimus, cuius doctissima scripta . . . ." In spite of this Libavius quarreled with Quercetanus a few years later. He wasted the greater part of his life on fruitless polemics, which earned him many enemies.

In 1591 Georgius an und von Wald (Amwald), a physician in Augsburg, wrote an account of the "universal medicine" he had discovered, *Kurzer Bericht . . . wie das Panacea am Waldiana . . . anzuwenden sei.* The book is an interesting example of the printed advertising of the time; half of it consists of testimonial letters from princes, counts, doctors, and other eminent men, while Rudolf II's imperial imprimatur emphasized its significance. Libavius, however, claimed that Amwald's drug contained not gold but mercury and presented harsh criticism of Amwald, his panacea, and his book in four publications: *Neoparacelsica* (1594), *Tractatus duo physici* (1595), *Gegenbericht von der Panacea Amwaldina* (1596), and *Panacea Amwaldina victa* (1596). The import of these works was that Amwald's medicine was quackery and his methods of healing worthless. At the same time Libavius took the opportunity to criticize the works and activities of the Paracelsian physicians Johann Graman of Erfurt, to whom he also devoted a separate critique, *Antigramania* (1595), and Joseph Michelius of Lucca. It is possible that these works all followed from Libavius' ire at not being invited to the court of Rudolf II, a well-known Maecenas of alchemy.

In 1600 Libavius issued *Variarum controversarium libri duo*, which was, as it were, a summing up of all the previous polemics. In 1607 he stated his opposition to Nicolas Guibert, a French physician who denied the possibility of the transmutation of metals, in a treatise in which he declared that the transmutation of base metals into gold was possible and that the secret of the philosophers' stone was known to many alchemists.

Libavius was also involved in the conflict between, on one side, the French Calvinist-Paracelsists Joseph Duchesne and Israel Harvet—whom he supported—and, on the other, the Galenist Catholic professor of medicine of the University of Paris, Jean Riolan. To an aggressive pamphlet by Riolan Libavius replied with the 926-page *Alchymia triumphans* (1607), demonstrating point by point the ignorance of his adversary.

Petrus Palmarius also became involved in the polemic and was answered by Libavius in *Syntagma arcanorum* (1613). This whole polemic, which took on an international character, was a battle of Paracelsists, anti-Paracelsists, Galenists, and Hermetics; in a word, everyone against everyone. Each accused the other of using ineffectual medicines, of not understanding the meaning of the words used by Paracelsus, Galen, or even the mythical Hermes. Entering the fray, the Medical Faculty of the University of Paris formally condemned Paracelsian chemical remedies.

Until 1607 Libavius was on good terms with Oswald Crollius, Théodore Turquet de Mayerne, Johannes Hartmann, Bernard Penotus, and Quercetanus, who were Calvinist-Hermetics. He visited Hartmann in Marburg and corresponded with Turquet de Mayerne and Quercetanus; the latter made him a present of his new publication *Pharmacopea* (1607). Some time in the period from 1608 to 1610 his friendship with these men turned to hatred, but the cause is difficult to state. One might suppose that it was caused either by Libavius' increasing religious orthodoxy or by professional disappointment. Libavius had maintained friendly contacts with Landgrave Maurice of Hesse, corresponded with him, and dedicated the *Commentationum metallicorum libri* to him. He therefore counted on obtaining a position at the court of Maurice, known for his liking for alchemy, at the University of Marburg, or at the Collegium Adelphicum Mauricianum in Kassel. But when a "chair of chymiatry" was founded in 1609, Hartmann was named professor.

Libavius gave vent to his bitterness in a letter to Leonard Dolde of 21 December 1609, in which he wrote that the Marburg school (the chair held by Hartmann) is a "pugnarum mare," a sea of impostures. He manifested his open enmity to the Hermetics in *Syntagmatis arcanorum chymicorum* (1613) and *Examen philosophiae novae* (1615). Of his former friend Hartmann he wrote: "Your philosophy is nothing but pure dung, sown with nonsense, impostures, the obscurest puzzles and allegories."

Libavius' last polemic is contained in two pamphlets against the Rosicrucians: *Analysis confessionis Fraternitatis de Rosae Cruce* (1615) and *Wohlmeinendes Bedencken von der Fama und Confessio der Brüderschaft des Rosen Creuzes* (1616). He hated things to be unclear and unintelligible and was greatly irritated by the anonymous fellowship of the Rosicrucians, which was much discussed throughout Europe at this time.

Libavius' main value to the history of science resides in his extraordinarily voluminous alchemical works, which represent a compendium of the chemical knowledge of his times. His first work was *Rerum chemicarum epistolica forma . . . liber* (two volumes in 1595 and the third in 1599), chemical lectures in the form of letters addressed to well-known physicians, including J. Stupanus, F. Platter, M. Ruland, and J. Camerarius. These lectures contain a definition of chemistry—"Chimia est a mineralium elaboratio"—a clarification of several obscure alchemical terms and phrases, a critique of Paracelsus, notes and considerations on the philosophers' stone, and chemical processes and preparations.

Libavius' chief work was *Alchemia*, which, together with the separately published *Commentationum metallicorum libri* (1597), appeared in a shortened form in German as *Alchymistische Practic* (1603) and in Latin as *Praxis alchymiae* (1604)—and, significantly enlarged, as *Alchymia* (1606). This last edition, with commentary, is considered the greatest and most beautiful (because of the numerous illustrations) of all books on chemistry in the seventeenth century. It is a folio edition with more than 200 designs and pictures of various sorts of chemical glassware, vessels, apparatuses, and furnaces, as well as architectural plans for the building of a chemical laboratory, "domus chymici."

In one sense, the *Alchemia* was completed by *Syntagma selectorum* (1611), *Syntagma arcanorum tomus secundus* (1613), and *Appendix philosophiae novae* (1615). These works, however, are devoted mainly to polemics. Although the *Alchymia* and its "continuation" comprise more than 2,000 folio pages, Libavius did not consider this to be everything that could be written on the subject and explained himself by saying: "Uni homini impossibile est chymiam condere et absolvere."

The *Alchymia* is unusually clear and highly systematic. The same cannot be said of the commentaries and supplements, especially if we consider Libavius' deliberations on the philosophers' stone, its contents, and the transmutation of metals. Libavius scrupulously cites the more than 200 authors whose works he used. He divided alchemy into two parts: "encheria" and "chymia." Encheria was the knowledge of chemical procedure and included furnaces, ovens, and vessels. Chymia meant the knowledge of how to prepare substances. Independent of these are two further divisions of alchemy: "ars probandi," the analysis of minerals, metals, and mineral waters, and "theoretical alchemy," knowledge concerning the philosophers' stone. Ars probandi (also ars probatoria), or assaying, was divided into "scevasia" and "ergastia." Scevasia was a kind of encheria: the technique of preparing crucibles, fluxes, and acids, the use of balances and weights, and the knowledge of alchemical symbols (Libavius gave examples of alchemical ciphers). Ergastia (or doecimasia) included assaying techniques. Libavius devoted a great deal of space to the analysis of mineral waters, "judicio aquarum mineralium."

In all practical recipes Libavius' style is extremely clear, in marked contrast to the bombastic verbosity of Paracelsus. It becomes obscure in the sections and fragments dealing with the philosophers' stone or transmutation of metals, in which he stated that these secrets were possessed by, to name a few, Pico della Mirandola, Giambattista della Porta, Edward Kelley, Alexander Seton, and Michael Seindivogius (Sendivogius).

Libavius tried to penetrate and understand works on the philosophers' stone, and commented broadly in his own way. He declared, for example, that the mysterious alchemical substance called "azoth" was really what he obtained and called "liquor [or spiritus] sublimati" (stannic chloride). The name "spiritus fumans Libavii" did not appear until the eighteenth century. Another secret alchemical substance, "lac virginis" (maiden's milk), was, according to Libavius, the product of the reaction of a solution of litharge in vinegar and salt brine or a solution of alum (lead chloride or sulfate).

This sort of interpretation caused Libavius to be criticized by many alchemists: J. Tancke, P. Palmarius, H. Scheunemann, and H. Khunrath declared that Libavius knew nothing of alchemy. It must be admitted that he indeed did not understand the chief ideas of the Hermetics, such as that of the existence in the air of an invisible life-giving substance. Nevertheless, Libavius can be ranked as a first-rate chemist on the basis of those parts of his book which can be considered truly chemical.

Alchemy, according to Libavius, was also—apart from the previous definitions of it—the art of extracting perfect magistracies and pure essences valuable in medicine. The term *magisterium* (magistracy) has various meanings. Sometimes it is a chemical species extracted from a given mixture, while at others it means the procedure, mystery, or secret of the nature or composition of substances.

Libavius was an exponent of the iatrochemical trend in medicine, and consequently the application of chemicals is stressed in his writings. The first part of *Syntagmatis*, for instance, is entitled "Alchymia pharmaceutica" and contains recipes for such substances as "tabulae perlatae," "elixir catharicum," and "balsamus sulphuris." He thought that drugs could be prepared in two ways: pharmaceutically, by gently infusing or cooking, and alchemically, by ennobling substances through the nature of fire.

Libavius had in his home (at both Rothenburg and Coburg) a chemical laboratory in which, either alone or with assistants, he carried on chemical experiments. It is difficult, however, to determine which of the compounds of which he wrote he obtained himself and which he merely tested from formulas he had been given.

He gave many recipes or remedies popular at that time, including "thurpethum minerale," the basic sulfate of mercury; "hepar sulphuris," potassium sulfide or polysulfide; "aurum potabile," potable gold (perhaps a colloidal gold solution); some antimony preparations which had purgative, emetic, or sudorific effects; and "sal prunellae mineralis," the contemporary fever remedy. Libavius' "butyra" (butters) were substances with the consistency of butter: butyrum antimonii ($SbCl_3$), butyrum arsenici (K_3AsO_4).

Libavius repeated Cesalpino's view that lead increases its weight while being calcined, this being caused by condensation of the smoke. He believed that iron turns into copper if immersed in vitriol water, although this was denied by Ercker, from whom Libavius had taken a great deal. Libavius also described the methods of distilling mineral acids and alcohol and gave a recipe for obtaining "quinta essentia Saturni" (acetone) by dry distillation of "saccharum Saturni" (lead acetate). Refluxing spirit of wine with oil of vitriol he obtained "oleum dulce" (ether).

Libavius can be regarded as one of the founders of chemical analysis, even though he took almost all his information from the books of Agricola, Ercker, and M. Fachs. He paid special attention to the analysis of mineral waters, investigating those in the environs of Rothenburg (*Singularium*, 1601) and Coburg (*Tractatus medicus physicus . . . und Historia Casimirianischen Sawer Brunnen*, 1610).

He gave quantitative methods of determining gold and silver in alloys and the analytical reactions of iron in water with an infusion of bile, a darkening of the blue of copper vitriol solution with the addition of "spiritus urinae" (ammonia). He was aware that water can yield a volatile acid (carbon dioxide). He also knew that a solution of lead, silver, or copper salts darkens when it comes in contact with sulfur vapors (H_2S) and that a solution of nitrate of mercury in nitric acid dyes the skin red (Millon's reaction).

Although Libavius had no pupils of his own, his books were used by many adepts of chemistry throughout most of the seventeenth century.

BIBLIOGRAPHY

I. Original Works. Libavius' most important books are cited in the text with shortened titles.

Libavius gives a list of his treatises in *Syntagmatis arcanorum chymicorum tomus secundus* (Frankfurt, 1613), pp. ix, x, where he writes that he would like to publish his correspondence with his friends in 3 vols. From this collection of Libavius' letters, those addressed to Sigismund Schnitzer were edited by Johann Hornung as *Cista medica* (Nuremberg, 1626).

A large collection of Libavius' letters to Wald, J. Camerarius the Younger, and especially to L. Dolde is in the Universitätsbibliothek, Erlangen, MS 1284. Letters addressed to Landgrave Maurice of Hesse are in Marbachsche und Landesbibliothek in Kassel, MS fol. 19, and in Universitätsbibliothek, Basel, e.g., "Jacob Zwingers Korrespondenz."

The fullest—but not complete—bibliography of Libavius' works is in E. Pietsch, A. Kotowski, and F. Rex, *Die Alchemie des Andreas Libavius* (Weinheim, 1964). It erroneously states, however, that *Syntagmatis selectorum . . . tomus primus* (no. 42) appeared in 1615, instead

of 1611. An additional imperfection of this bibliography is that it does not give the sizes of Libavius' books. From 1606 almost all were printed in folio, while the earlier ones were in quarto or octavo. Folio books were rather rare in those times, so the fact that Libavius' works were printed in folio indicates how well his books sold.

The Pietsch-Kotowski-Rex *Die Alchemie des Andreas Libavius* is a very good trans. of the *Alchemia* (1597) into modern German. A kind of supplement is formed by the "Bildteil," 197 designs of chemical vessels, ovens, and instruments taken from the *Commentatorium alchymiae* (1606). The editorial commentary on the whole is good.

II. Secondary Literature. See the following, listed chronologically: G. Ludwig, *Ehre des Hoch-Fürstlichen Casimiriani Academici in Coburg*, I (Coburg, 1725), 72, 77, 84, 139–159; II (Coburg, 1729), 244–256; J. F. Gmelin, *Geschichte der Chemie*, I (Göttingen, 1797), 345–351; H. Kopp, *Beiträge zur Geschichte der Chemie*, III (Brunswick, 1875), 145–150; J. Ferguson, *Bibliotheca chemica*, II (Glasgow, 1906), 31–34; J. Ottmann, "Erinnerung an Libavius in Rothenburg ob der Tauber," in *Verhandlungen Gesellschaft der Naturforscher*, **65** (1894), 79–84; C. Beck, *Festschrift zur Feier des dreihundertjährigen Bestehens des Gymnasium Casimirianum in Coburg 1605–1905* (Coburg, n.d.), pp. 76–88; A. Schnizlein, "Andreas Libavius, der Stadt Rothenburg Physicus von 1591–1607 und gekrönter Poet," in *Die Linde, Beilage zum fränkischen Anzeiger 22. Juni 1912* (Rothenburg, 1912), pp. 21–24; and "Andreas Libavius und seine Tätigkeit am Gymnasium zu Rothenburg," in *Beilage zum Jahresbericht des Kgl. Progymnasiums Rothenburg ob der Tauber für das Schuljahr 1913/14* (Rothenburg, 1914); E. Darmstaedter, in G. Bugge, *Das Buch der grossen Chemiker*, I (Weinheim, 1955), 107–124; L. Thorndike, "Libavius and Chemical Controversy," in his *History of Magic and Experimental Science*, VI (New York, 1951), 238–253; R. P. Multhauf, "Libavius and Beguin," in E. Farber, ed., *Great Chemists* (New York–London, 1961), pp. 65–79; J. R. Partington, *History of Chemistry*, II (London, 1961), 244–270; and E. Pietsch and A. Kotowski, *Die Alchemie des Andreas Libavius, ein Lehrbuch der Chemie aus dem Jahre 1597* (Weinheim, 1964), plus supp. with illustrations and F. Rex, "Kommentarteil," pp. 77–136.

Włodzimierz Hubicki

LICEAGA, EDUARDO (*b.* Guanajuato, Mexico, 13 October 1839; *d.* Mexico City, Mexico, 14 January 1920), *medicine, public health.*

The son of a physician, Liceaga received his primary education at Guanajuato. After attending college in Mexico City and Guanajuato, he entered the School of Medicine in Mexico City, where he received the M.D. in 1866. After graduation he taught physics and natural history at the College of San Ildefonso. In 1868 he joined the staff of the School of Medicine as associate professor of surgery and became professor the following year. Appointed dean in 1902, he reformed the curriculum and resigned in 1911. Liceaga served on the staff of the San Andrés and maternity hospitals in addition to conducting a private practice. A member of the National Academy of Medicine, he was its president in 1878–1879 and 1906–1907.

Liceaga is better known as a hygienist and is considered the father of modern public health in Mexico. His interest was awakened by Chandler, chairman of the New York State Board of Health, while on a visit to the United States in 1883. As chairman of the Council of Public Health, which post he held until his resignation in 1914, Liceaga helped to organize public health work throughout Mexico. In 1891 he drafted the first sanitary code. Read at a meeting of the American Public Health Association, it was characterized by Baker as more advanced than any in the United States. Under Liceaga's influence the code was amended in 1894 and a new version enacted in 1902.

In 1887–1888 Liceaga visited Europe, inspecting public health works—mostly water supply, sewage, and fumigation facilities—in Paris, Vienna, Brussels, and Berlin. At Vienna he attended the International Congress of Hygiene and Demography; and in Paris he obtained rabies virus from the Pasteur Institute through Roux, which enabled him to administer the first human vaccination in Mexico in 1888.

Liceaga's successful campaigns against plague, yellow fever, and malaria and his efforts to arouse public interest in the fight against tuberculosis brought him international recognition. He organized the first and second Mexican Medical Congresses (1876, 1878) and was president of both. At the 1883 National Congress of Hygiene he presented a full program for public health legislation and administration. At the first Pan-American Sanitary Conference (Washington, 1902) he was influential in establishing the Pan-American Sanitary Bureau. Liceaga was president of the third convention, held in Mexico City in 1907. He also was president of the American Public Health Association in 1895.

In 1941 the Mexican government created the Eduardo Liceaga Medal (three classes) as the highest national distinction awarded in the field of public health.

BIBLIOGRAPHY

I. ORIGINAL WORKS. Liceaga's autobiography is *Mis recuerdos de otros tiempos* (Mexico City, 1949). His articles include "Defensa de los puertos y ciudades fronterizas de México contra la epidemia de cólera que invadió Europa,"

in *Documentos e informes de la 20a. reunión de la Asociación americana de salud pública* (Mexico City, 1894), 257–266; "El combate contra la tuberculosis," in *Gaceta médica de México*, 3rd ser., **2** (1907), 117–147; and "El combate contra la fiebre amarilla y la malaria en la República mexicana," in *Memorias IV Congreso médico nacional mexicano* (Mexico City, 1910), pp. 579–587.

II. SECONDARY LITERATURE. See A. Pruneda, "El Dr. Liceaga miembro de la Academia nacional de Medicina," in *Gaceta médica de México*, **70** (1940), 68, 74; B. Bandera, "El Dr. E. Liceaga, profesor y director de la Escuela nacional de Medicina," *ibid.*, 74–78; and M. E. Bustamante, "El doctor Liceaga higienista," *ibid.*, 79–91.

ENRIQUE BELTRÁN

LI CHIH, also called **LI YEH** (*b.* Ta-hsing [now Peking], China, 1192; *d.* Hopeh province, China, 1279), *mathematics.*

Li Chih (literary name, Jen-ch'ing; appellation, Ching-chai) has been described by George Sarton as one of the greatest mathematicians of his time and of his race. His father, Li Yü, served as an attaché under a Jurchen officer called by the Chinese name Hu Sha-hu. Li Yü later sent his family back to his home in Luan-ch'eng, Hopeh province. Li Chih went alone to the Yüan-shih district in the same province for his education.

In 1230 Li Chih went to Loyang to take the civil service examination; after he passed, he was appointed registrar in the district of Kao-ling, Shensi province. Before he reported for duty, however, he was made governor of Chün-chou (now Yü-hsien), Honan province. In 1232 the Mongols captured the city of Chün-chou, and Li Chih was forced to seek refuge in Shansi province. The kingdom of the Jurchen fell into the hands of the Mongols in 1234. From that time on, Li Chih devoted himself to serious study, frequently living in poverty. It was during this period that he wrote his most important mathematical work, the *Ts'e-yüan hai-ching* ("Sea Mirror of the Circle Measurements").

About 1251 Li Chih, finding himself in an improved financial position, returned to the Yüan-shih district of Hopeh province and settled near Feng-lung, a mountain in that district. Although he continued to lead the life of a scholarly recluse, he counted Chang Te-hui and Yuan Yü among his friends; the three of them became popularly known as "the Three Friends of [Feng-]Lung Mountain." In 1257 Kublai Khan sent for Li Chih and asked him about the government of the state, the selection and deployment of scholars for civil service, and the reasons for earthquakes. Li Chih completed another mathematical text, the

I-ku yen-tuan ("New Steps in Computation") in 1259. Kublai Khan ascended the throne in 1260 and the following year offered Li Chih a government post, which was politely declined with the plea of ill health and old age. In 1264 the Mongolian emperor set up the Han-lin Academy for the purpose of writing the official histories of the kingdoms of Liao and Jurchen, and the following year Li Chih was obliged to join it. After a few months he submitted his resignation, again pleading infirmity and old age. He returned to his home near Feng-lung, and many pupils came to study under him.

Li Chih changed his name to Li Yeh at some point in his life because he wished to avoid having the same name as the third T'ang emperor, whose dynastic title was T'ang Kao-tsung (650–683). This circumstance has given rise to some confusion as to whether Li Yeh was a misprint for Li Chih.

Besides the *Ts'e-yüan hai-ching* and the *I-ku yen-tuan*, Li Chih wrote several other works, including the *Fan shuo*, the *Ching-chai ku-chin chu*, the *Wen chi*, and the *Pi-shu ts'ung-hsiao*. Before his death Li Chih told his son, Li K'e-hsiu, to burn all his books except the *Ts'e-yüan hai-ching*, because he felt that it alone would be of use to future generations. We do not know to what extent his wishes were carried out; but the *I-ku yen-tuan* survived the fire, and the *Ching-chai ku-chin chu* has also come down to us. His other works are now lost, although some passages from the *Fan shuo* are quoted in the *Ching-chai ku-chin chu*. Only the *Ts'e-yüan hai-ching* and the *I-ku yen-tuan* will be further described here, since the other extant work has neither mathematical nor scientific interest.

Originally called the *Ts'e-yüan hai-ching hsi-ts'ao* and completed in 1248, the *Ts'e-yüan hai-ching* was not published until some thirty years later, at about the same time as the *I-ku yen-tuan*. From a preface written by Wang Te-yüan, it appears that there was a second edition in 1287. In the late eighteenth century the *Ts'e-yüan hai-ching* was included in the imperial encyclopedia, the *Ssu-k'u ch'üan-shu*. It came from a copy preserved in the private library of Li Huang (*d.* 1811). A handwritten copy of the book was made by Juan Yuan (1764–1849) from the version in the *Ssu-k'u ch'üan-shu*. Later Ting Chieh presented a handwritten fourteenth-century copy of the *Ts'e-yüan hai-ching hsi-ts'ao* with the seal of Sung Lien (1310–1381) to Juan Yuan. This is probably the copy that is now preserved in the Peking Library. At the request of Juan Yuan, the Ch'ing mathematician Li Jui (1768–1817) collated the two versions in 1797. This has become the most widely circulated edition of the *Ts'e-yüan hai-ching* that exists today. In 1798 Li

Jui's version was incorporated in the *Chih-pu-tsu-chai ts'ung-shu* collection, and in 1875 in the *Pai-fu-t'ang suan-hsüeh ts'ung-shu* collection. The modern reproduction in the *Ts'ung-shu chi-ch'eng* series is based on the version in the *Chih-pu-tsu-chai ts'ung-shu* collection.

The *Ts'e-yüan hai-ching* was studied by many eighteenth- and nineteenth-century Chinese mathematicians, such as K'ung Kuang-shen (1752–1786) and Li Shan-lan (1811–1882). A detailed analysis of the work was made by Li Yen (1892–1963), but it has not yet been translated.

The *I-ku yen-tuan* was completed in 1259 and was published in 1282. It has been regarded as a later version of a previous mathematical text, the *I-ku-chi*, which is no longer extant. The *I-ku yen-tuan* is incorporated in both the *Chih-pu-tsu-chai ts'ung-shu* and the *Pai-fu-t'ang suan-hsüeh ts'ung-shu* collections. The modern reproduction of the *I-ku yen-tuan* in the *Ts'ung-shu chi-ch'eng* series is based on the version in the *Chih-pu-tsu-chai ts'ung-shu* collection. It has been translated into French by L. van Hée.

Li Chih introduced an algebraic process called the *t'ien yüan shu* ("method of the celestial elements" or "coefficient array method") for setting up equations to any degree. The *t'ien yüan shu* occupied a very important position in the history of mathematics in both China and Japan. From the early fourteenth century until algebra was brought to China from the West by the Jesuits, no one in China seemed to understand this method. Algebra enabled Chinese mathematicians of the eighteenth century, especially Mei Ku-ch'eng, to recognize the algebra of the *t'ien yüan shu* and the *ssu yüan shu* of Chu Shih-chieh despite their unfamiliar notation. Knowing that algebra originally entered Europe from the East, some enthusiastic Chinese scholars of that time went so far as to claim that the *t'ien yüan shu* had gone from China to the West and there became known as algebra. The *t'ien yüan shu* also exerted a profound influence in Japan, where it became known as the *tengenjutsu*. The seventeenth-century Japanese mathematician Seki Takakazu (also known as Seki Kōwa), for example, developed from the algebra of Li Chih and Chu Shih-chieh a formula for infinite expansion, which is now arrived at by means of the infinitesimal calculus.

Li Chih did not claim to be the originator of the *t'ien yüan shu*. From his *Ching-chai ku-chin chu* it appears that he had copied the method from a certain mathematician in Taiyuan (in modern Shansi) named P'eng Che (literary name, Yen-ts'ai), of whom we know little. Chu Shih-chieh wrote in the early fourteenth century that one of Li Chih's friends, the

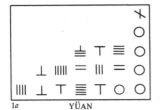

YÜAN

FIGURE 1a

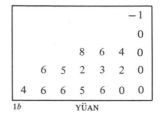

YÜAN

FIGURE 1b

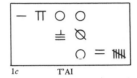

T'AI

FIGURE 1c

T'AI

FIGURE 1d

famous poet Yuan Hao-wen, was also versed in the method of the celestial element. In the *t'ien yüan shu* method the absolute term is denoted by the character *t'ai* and the unknown by *yüan*, or element. An equation is arranged in a vertical column in which the term containing the unknown is set above the absolute term, the square of the unknown above the unknown, then the cube, and so on in increasing powers. Reciprocals or negative powers can also be placed in descending order after the absolute term. Thus the equation

$$- x^2 + 8640 + 652320x^{-1} + 4665600x^{-2} = 0$$

is represented on the countingboard as in Figure 1a, with its equivalent in Arabic numerals shown in Figure 1b. It is sufficient to indicate one position of the unknown and one of the absolute term by writing the words *yüan* and *t'ai*. It is curious that Li Chih reversed the process of expressing algebraic equations in his *I-ku yen-tuan* by writing the unknown below the absolute, the square below the unknown, and so on. For example, the equation $1700 - 80x - 0.25x^2 = 0$ is shown in Figure 1c and in Arabic numerals in Figure 1d. Li Chih's method was followed by later Chinese mathematicians.

Li Chih indicated negative quantities by drawing an oblique line over the final digit of the number concerned. He also used the zero symbol as his contemporary Ch'in Chiu-shao did, although there is no evidence that the two ever met or even heard of each other. It is likely that the zero symbol was used earlier in China, and it has even been suggested by Yen Tun-chieh that although the dot (*bindu*) was introduced from India in the eighth century and the circle for zero appeared in a magic square brought from the area of Islamic culture in the thirteenth century, the circle was nevertheless evolved independently in

China from the square denoting zero sometime during the twelfth century.

Li Chih made use of numerical equations up to the sixth degree. He did not describe the procedure of solving such equations, which omission indicates that the method must have been well known in China during his time. This method must be similar to that rediscovered independently by Ruffini and Horner in the early nineteenth century, as described by Ch'in Chiu-shao. Li Chih stabilized the terminology used in connection with equations of higher degrees in the form

$$+ax^6 + bx^5 + cx^4 + dx^3 + ex^2 + fx + g = 0.$$

The absolute term g is called by the general term *shih*, or by the more specific terms *p'ing shih, fang shih, erh ch'eng fang shih, san ch'eng fang shih, shih ch'eng fang shih,* and *wu ch'eng fang shih* for linear equations, quadratic equations, cubic equations, quartic equations, and equations of the fifth and sixth degrees, respectively. The coefficient of the highest power of x (in this case, a) in the equation is called *yü, yü fa,* or *ch'ang fa*. The coefficient of the lowest power of x (in this case, f) is called *ts'ung* or *ts'ung fang*. All coefficients between the lowest and the highest powers are described by the word *lien*. For a cubic equation the coefficient of x^2 is known by the term *lien*. For a quartic equation the coefficient of x^2 is called *ti i lien*, that is, the first *lien*, and the coefficient of x^3 is *ti erh lien*, that is, the second *lien*. Hence, in the sixth-degree equation above we have e, *ti i lien* (first *lien*); d, *ti erh lien* (second *lien*); c, *ti san lien* (third *lien*); and b, *ti shih lien* (fourth *lien*).

All the above, except in the case of the absolute term, apply only to positive numbers. To denote negative numbers, Li Chih added either the word *i* or the word *hsü* before the terms applying to coefficients of the highest and lowest powers of x and before the word *lien*. He did not use different terms to distinguish between positive and negative absolute terms and, unlike Ch'in Chiu-shao, he did not make it a rule that the absolute term must be negative.

It is interesting to see how Li Chih handled the remainder in extracting a square root. An example is encountered in the equation

$$-22.5x^2 - 648x + 23002 = 0,$$

which occurred in the fortieth problem of his *I-ku yen-tuan*. He put $y = nx$, where $n = 22.5$, and transformed the equation into

$$-y^2 - 648y + 517545 = 0.$$

From the above, $y = 465$, and hence $x = 20^2/_3$. The same method was also used by Ch'in Chiu-shao.

The *Ts'e-yüan hai-ching* includes 170 problems dealing with various situations based on a circle inscribed in or circumscribing a right triangle. The same question is asked in all these problems and the same answer obtained. The book begins with a diagram showing a circle inscribed in a right triangle, *ABC* (Fig. 2). The square *CDEF* circumscribing the

circle lies along the base and height of $\triangle ABC$ and intersects the hypotenuse *AB* at *G* and *H*, from which perpendiculars *GJ* and *HK* are dropped on *BC* and *AC*, respectively. *GJ* and *HK* intersect at *L*. Through *O*, the center of the circle, *MNPOQ* is drawn parallel to *AC*, meeting *AB* at *M* and *BC* at *Q* and cutting *ED* at *N* and *HK* at *P*. Also through *O* is drawn *RSTOU*, parallel to *BC*, meeting *AB* at *R* and *AC* at *U* and cutting *EF* at *S* and *GJ* at *T*. Finally, *MV* is drawn parallel to *BC*, meeting *AC* at *V*, and *RW* is drawn parallel to *AC*, meeting *BC* at *W*.

Special terms are then given for the three sides of each of the fifteen triangles in the diagram. These are followed by a list of relationships between the sides of some of these triangles and the circle. For example: the sides of $\triangle ABC$ and the diameter of the inscribed circle have the relationship $D = 2ab/(a + b + c)$; the sides of $\triangle ARU$ and the diameter of a circle with its center at one of the sides and touching the other two sides have the relationship $D = 2ar/(r + u)$; and the sides of $\triangle AGD$ and the diameter of an escribed circle touching the side *ED* and the sides *AG* and *AD* produced have the relationship $D = 2ag/(g + d - a)$. Similarly, for $\triangle MBQ$, $D = 2mb/(m + q)$; for $\triangle HBF$, $D = shb/(h + f - b)$; for $\triangle MRO$; $D = 2mr/o$; for $\triangle GHE$, $D = 2hg/(h + g - e)$; for $\triangle MGN$, $D = 2mg/(n - m)$; and for $\triangle HRS$, $D = 2hr/(s - r)$.

All the above are given in chapter 1 of the book. In the subsequent chapters Li Chih showed how these results can be applied to various cases. For example, the second problem in chapter 2 says:

> Two persons, *A* and *B*, start from the western gate [of a circular city wall]. *B* [first] walks a distance of 256 *pu* eastward. Then *A* walks a distance of 480 *pu* south before he can see *B*. Find [the diameter of the wall] as before.

The equation for $\triangle MBQ$ was then applied directly to give the diameter of the circular city wall.

Li Chih showed how to solve a similar problem by the use of a cubic equation. The fourth problem in chapter 3 says:

> *A* leaves the western gate [of a circular city wall] and walks south for 480 *pu*. *B* leaves the eastern gate and walks straight ahead a distance of 16 *pu*, when he just begins to see *A*. Find [the diameter of the city wall] as before.

Here Li Chih found x, the diameter of the city wall, by solving the cubic equation

$$x^3 + cx^2 - 4cb^2 = 0,$$

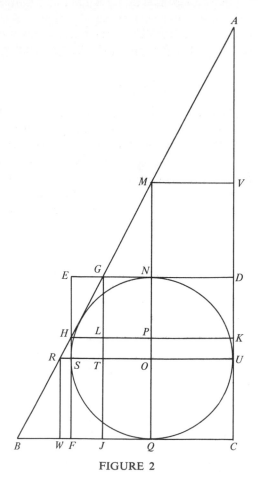

FIGURE 2

where $c = 16$ *pu* and $b = 480$ *pu*. This obviously came from the quartic equation

$$x^4 + 2cx^3 + c^2x^2 - 4cb^2x - 4c^2b^2 = 0,$$

which can be derived directly from the equation for $\triangle MBQ$. In doing this Li Chih had discarded the factor $(x + c)$, knowing that the answer $x = -c$ was inadmissible. It is interesting to compare this with the tenth-degree equation used by Ch'in Chiu-shao for the same purpose.

All the 170 problems in the *Ts'e-yüan hai-ching* have been studied by Li Yen. To illustrate Li Chih's method of solving these problems, we shall follow step by step the working of problem 18 in chapter 11, which says:

> 135 *pu* directly out of the southern gate [of a circular city wall] is a tree. If one walks 15 *pu* out of the northern city gate and then turns east for a distance of 208 *pu*, the tree becomes visible. Find [the diameter of the city wall] as before. [The answer says 240 *pu* as before.]

Using modern conventions but following the traditional Chinese method of indicating the cardinal points in such a way that south is at the top, north at the bottom, east to the left, and west to the right, the problem is as illustrated in Figure 3.

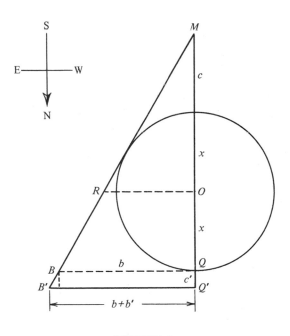

FIGURE 3

First, the method is given:

> Take the product of the distance to the east and that to the south [that is, $c(b + b')$], square it, and make it the *shih* [that is, $c^2(b + b')^2$ is taken as the absolute term]. Square the distance to the east, multiply it by

the distance to the south, and double it to form the *ts'ung* [that is, the coefficient of x, the radius, is $2c(b + b')^2$]. Put aside the square of the distance to the east [that is, $(b + b')^2$]; add together the distance to the south and north, subtract the sum from the distance to the east, square the result, and subtract this from the distance to the east [that is, $(b + b')^2 - \{(b + b') - (c + c')\}^2$]; put aside this value. Again add together the distances to the south and north, multiply the sum first by the distance to the east and then by 2 [that is, $2(b + b')(c + c')$]; subtracting from this the amount just set aside gives the *tai i i lien* [that is, the coefficient of x^2 is $-2\{(b + b')(c + c')\} - [(b + b')^2 - \{(b + b') - (c + c')\}^2]]$. Multiply the distance to the east by 4 and put this aside [that is, $4(b + b')$]; add the distances to the south and north, subtract the sum from the eastward distance and multiply by 4 [that is, $4\{(b + b') + (c + c')\}$]; subtracting this result from the amount put aside gives the *tai erh i lien* [that is, the coefficient of x^3 is $-4(b + b') - 4\{(b + b') + (c + c')\}$]. Take 4 times the *hsü yü* [that is, $-4x^4$]. Solving the quartic equation gives the radius.

The procedure is as follows:

Set up one celestial element to represent the radius. (This is the *kao kou.*) Adding to this the distance to the south gives Figure 4a (below), which represents the

FIGURE 4a

kao hsien (that is, the vertical side MO in MRO in Figure 3 is $x + 135$). Put down the value for the *ta kou* (base of $MB'Q'$) of 208 and multiply it by the *kao hsien* $(x + 135)$; the result is $208x + 28080$ (Figure 4b).

FIGURE 4b

Dividing this by the *kao kou* gives $208 + 28080x^{-1}$ (Figure 4c).

FIGURE 4c

This is the *ta hsien* (the hypotenuse MB' of $\triangle MB'Q'$), and squaring this yields $43264 + 11681280x^{-1} + 788486400x^{-2}$ (Figure 4*d*).

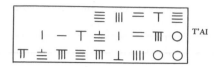

FIGURE 4*d*

The above is temporarily set aside. Take 2 as the celestial element and add this to the sum of the distances to the south and north, giving $2x + 150$ (Figure 4*e*),

FIGURE 4*e*

or the *ta ku* (the vertical side MQ' of $\triangle MB'Q'$). Subtracting from this the value of the *ta kou*, 208, $2x - 58$ is obtained (Figure 4*f*).

FIGURE 4*f*

This is known as the *chiao*. Squaring it gives the *chiao mi*, $4x^2 - 232x + 3364$, shown in Figure 4*g*.

FIGURE 4*g*

Subtracting the *chiao mi* from the quantity set aside (Figure 4*d*) yields $-4x^2 + 232x + 39900 + 11681280x^{-1} + 788486400x^{-2}$ (Figure 4*h*).

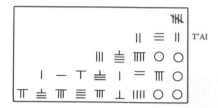

FIGURE 4*h*

This value, known as *erh-chih-chi*, is set aside at the lefthand side of the countingboard. Next multiply the *ta ku* (MQ') by the *ta kou* ($B'Q'$), which yields $416x + 31200$ (Figure 4*i*).

FIGURE 4*i*

This is the *chih chi*, which, when doubled, gives $832x + 62400$ (Figure 4*j*).

FIGURE 4*j*

This value is the same as that set aside at the left (that is, the value represented by Figure 4*h*). Equating the two values, one obtains $-4x^4 - 600x^3 - 22500x^2 + 11681280x + 788486400 = 0$ (Figure 4*k*).

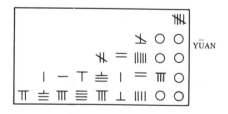

FIGURE 4*k*

Note that the position of the celestial element is no longer indicated here.

Solving this as a quartic equation, one obtains 120 *pu*, the radius of the circular city wall, which corresponds with the required answer.

Although written much later than the *Ts'e-yüan*

hai-ching, the *I-ku yen-tuan* is considerably simpler in its contents. It is thought that Li Chih took this opportunity to explain the *t'ien yüan shu* method in a less complicated manner after finding his first book too difficult for people to understand. This second mathematical treatise has also been regarded as a later version of another work, *I-ku chi*, published between 1078 and 1224 and no longer extant. According to a preface in Chu Shih-chieh's *Ssu-yüan yu-chien*, the *I-ku chi* was written by a certain Chiang Chou of P'ing-yang. Out of a total of sixty-four problems in the *I-ku yen-tuan*, twenty-one are referred to as the "old method" (*chiu shu*), which presumably means the *I-ku chi*. Sixteen of these twenty-one problems deal with the quadratic equation

$$ax^2 + bx - c = 0,$$

where $a > 0$ or $a < 0$, $b > 0$ and $c > 0$. When $c > 0$ and $b > 0$, they are called by the terms *shih* and *ts'ung*, respectively. When $a > 0$, it is known as *lien* instead of the more general term *yü*, and when $a < 0$, it is also known as *lien*, but is followed by the words *chien ts'ung*.

Divided into three chapters, the *I-ku yen-tuan* deals with the combination of a circle and a square or, in a few cases, a circle and a rectangle. A full translation of the first problem in chapter 1 is given below:

A square farm with a circular pool of water in the center has an area 13 *mou* and 7 1/2 tenths of a *mou* [that is, 13.75 *mou*]. The pool is 20 *pu* from the edge [1 *mou* = 240 square *pu*]. Find the side of the square and the diameter of the pool.

Answer: Side of square = 60 *pu*, diameter of pool = 20 *pu*.

Method: Put down one [counting rod] as the celestial element to represent the diameter of the pool. By adding twice the distance from the edge of the pool to the side of the farm, the side of the square farm is given by $x + 40$ [Figure 5a].

FIGURE 5a

The square of the side gives the area of the farm and the circular pool. That is, the total area is given by $x^2 + 80x + 1600$ [Figure 5b].

Again, put down one [counting rod] as the celestial element to denote the diameter of the pool. Squaring the diameter, and multiplying the result by 3 [the ancient approximate value of π], then dividing the

FIGURE 5b

result by 4, yields the area of the pool: $0.75x^2$ [Figure 5c].

FIGURE 5c

Subtracting the area of the pool from the total area gives $0.25x^2 + 80x + 1600$ [Figure 5d].

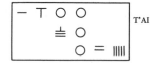

FIGURE 5d

The given area is 3,300 [square] *pu*. Equating this with the above yields $-0.25x^2 - 80x + 1700 = 0$ [Figure 5e].

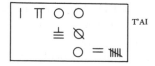

FIGURE 5e

Applying the method of solving quadratic equations shows the diameter of the pool to be 20 *pu*. If the distance from the side of the square to the edge of the pool is doubled and added to the diameter of the pool, the side of the farm is found to be 60 *pu*.

The first ten problems in the *I-ku yen-tuan* deal with a circle in the center of a square, each with different given parameters; the next ten problems are concerned with a square inside a circle. Problems 21 and 22, the last two problems in chapter 1, are concerned only with squares. In chapter 2, problems 23–29, we have the combination of a square with a circumscribed circle, while problem 30 gives the combination of two circles. Problem 31 concerns a rectangle with a circle in the center, and problems 32–37 give a circle with a rectangle at its center. In problem 38 two rectangles are given. Problems 39–42 treat various cases of a circle inside a rectangle. Problem 43, the first in chapter 3, deals with the three different values of π: the ancient value $\pi = 3$, the "close" value $\pi = 22/7$, and Liu Hui's value $\pi = 3.14$. Problem 44 is concerned with a trapezium, problem 45 with a square inside another square, problem 46 with a circle set outside but along the extended diagonal of a square, problem 47 with a square within a rectangle, and problem 48 with a rectangle within a square. In problems 49–52 a square is placed in the center of a larger square so that the diagonal of one is perpendicular to two sides of the other. In problems 53 and 54 the central square is replaced by a rectangle. Problems 55 and 56 are concerned with the annulus, and problems 57 and 58 with a rectangle inside a circle. In problem 59 a square encloses a circle, which in turn encloses another square at the center; and in problem 60 a circle encloses a square, which in turn encloses a circle at the center. Problem 62 concerns a square placed diagonally at a corner of another square. Problem 63 concerns a circle and two squares with another circle enclosed in one of them. The last problem, 64, has an annulus enclosed by a larger square.

Li Chih and Ch'in Chiu-shao were contemporaries, but they never mentioned each other in their writings. Li Chih lived in the north and Ch'in Chiu-shao in the south during the time when China was ruled in the south by the Sung dynasty and in the north first by the Jurchen Tartars and later by the Mongols. It is very likely that the two never even heard of each other. The terminology they used for equations of higher degree is similar but not identical. They also employed the so-called celestial element in different ways. Li Chih used it to denote the unknown quantity; but to Ch'in Chiu-shao the celestial element was a known number, and he never used the term in connection with his numerical equations. Ch'in Chiu-shao went into great detail in explaining the process of root extraction of numerical equations, but he did not describe how such equations were constructed by algebraic considerations from the given data in the problems. On the contrary, Li Chih concentrated on the method of setting out such equations algebraically without explaining the process of solving them. Thus Li Chih was indeed, as George Sarton says, essentially an algebraist.

BIBLIOGRAPHY

Works that may be consulted for further information on Li Chih and his writings are Ch'ien Pao-tsung, *Chung-kuo suan hsüeh-shih* ["History of Chinese Mathematics"] (Peking, 1932), pp. 116–124; Ch'ien Pao-tsung *et al.*, *Sung Yuan shu-hsüeh-shih lun-wen-chi* ["Collection of Essays on Chinese Mathematics in the Periods of Sung and Yuan"] (Peking, 1966), pp. 104–148; L. van Heé, "Li Yeh, mathématicien chinois du XIIIe siècle," in *T'oung Pao*, **14** (1913), pp. 537–568; Juan Yuan, *Ch'ou-jen chuan* ["Biographies of Mathematicians and Astronomers"] (Shanghai, 1935); Li Yen, *Chung-kuo shu-hsüeh ta-kang* ["Outline of Chinese Mathematics"], I (Shanghai, 1931), pp. 141–156; *Chung-kuo suan-hsüeh-shih* ["History of Chinese Mathematics"] (Shanghai, 1937), pp. 99–100; and "Chung-suan-shih lun-ts'ung," in *Gesammelte Abhandlungen über die Geschichte der chinesischen Mathematik*, **4**, no. 1 (1947), 15–251; Li Yen and Tu Shih-jan, *Chung-kuo ku-tai shu-hsüeh chien-shih* ["Concise History of Ancient Chinese Mathematics"], II (Peking, 1964), pp. 145, 147; Yoshio Mikami, *The Development of Mathematics in China and Japan* (Leipzig, 1913), pp. 79–84; Joseph Needham, *Science and Civilisation in China*, III (Cambridge, 1959), esp. pp. 40–41; George Sarton, *Introduction to the History of Science*, 3 vols. (Baltimore, 1927–1947), esp. vol. 2, pp. 627–628; Sung Lien *et al.*, *Yuan shih* ["Official History of the Yuan Dynasty"] (*ca.* 1370), ch. 160; and Alexander Wylie, *Notes on Chinese Literature* (Shanghai, 1902), p. 116.

Ho Peng-Yoke

LICHTENBERG, GEORG CHRISTOPH (*b.* Oberramstadt, near Darmstadt, Germany, 1 July 1742; *d.* Göttingen, Germany, 24 February 1799), *physics.*

Lichtenberg was the seventeenth child—the fifth to survive—of a Protestant pastor. From his father he received his early schooling, including mathematics and natural science, for which subjects he developed an early predilection. A permanent spinal deformity in his childhood perhaps enhanced his propensity for scholarly work. Upon graduation from the secondary school at Darmstadt, Lichtenberg was accorded the patronage of his sovereign, Ludwig VIII, the duke of Hesse-Darmstadt, and he continued his studies at the University of Göttingen.

At the university Lichtenberg studied a wide range of subjects, particularly literature under Christian Gottlob Heyne, history under Johann Christoph Gatterer, and natural sciences under the witty Abraham Gotthelf Kästner. He studied avidly and with such thoroughness that he frequently found himself digressing into cognate fields. As he himself put it: ". . . I have covered the path which leads toward science like a dog accompanying his master on a walk . . .. I have covered it over and over again in all directions . . ." As a result he became the leading German expert in a number of scientific fields, including geodesy, geophysics, meteorology, astronomy, chemistry, statistics, and geometry, in addition to his foremost field and prime interest—experimental physics. To all these areas he contributed respectably for his time, gaining the admiration and friendship of such contemporaries as Volta, F. W. Herschel, Kant, Goethe, Humboldt, and George III of England, with whom he became well acquainted during one of his visits to that country. Lichtenberg was appointed *professor extraordinarius* at the University of Göttingen in 1769 and was made *professor ordinarius* in 1775. He was given the title of royal British privy councillor in 1788 and in 1793 was elected to membership in the Royal Society (London) and in 1795 to membership in the Petersburg Academy of Sciences.

In geodesy Lichtenberg carried out a precise determination of the geodetic coordinates of Hannover, Stade, and Osnabrück. These measurements were performed at the request of George III (who, besides being the king of England, was also elector of Hannover) for purposes of military cartography, and also to help verify the concept advanced by Christiaan Huygens and Isaac Newton that the earth is an oblate spheroid.

Lichtenberg was particularly interested in volcanology. Among his writings on the subject is a calculation of the volume of lava ejected from Vesuvius during its eruption of 1784.

Also concerned with meteorology, Lichtenberg in 1780 was the first to erect in Germany a correct version of Benjamin Franklin's lightning rod. (A year earlier a lightning rod had been installed at Hamburg by the physician J. A. H. Reimarus, but without the essential connection between rod and ground.) In 1796 Lichtenberg wrote a brilliant monograph in defense of Jean André Deluc's theory of rain formation.

Along with Joseph Priestley and Carl Wilhelm Scheele, Lichtenberg was one of the last notable holdouts against the "French and new chemistry" of Lavoisier. Convinced in the end that Lavoisier was right, Lichtenberg capitulated by admitting that the new chemistry was a "magnificent structure." A fusible metal of 50 percent bismuth, 30 percent lead, and 20 percent tin, having a melting point of 91.6° C., is known as Lichtenberg's alloy.

In mathematics Lichtenberg attempted to clear up the controversy between Daniel Bernoulli and d'Alembert regarding the probabilities in the "St. Petersburg problem."[1] He sided with the former but admitted that an element of paradox remained in the solution. It was not until 1928 that an acceptable

resolution of this paradox was suggested by Thornton C. Fry. This resolution was formalized in 1945 by William Feller, who cleared up the question of what constitutes a "fair" game and showed the Petersburg game to be "fair" in the classical sense.

Lichtenberg edited and published works of the great German astronomer Johann Tobias Mayer, the founder of the astronomical observatory of Göttingen. He also prepared for engraving and published Mayer's detailed map of the moon, which was highly appreciated by contemporary astronomers. In 1795 he published a biography of Copernicus. Himself an active observer, Lichtenberg sighted and described a comet, studied the fall of meteorites, and observed the transit of Venus on 19 June 1769. In 1807 the astronomer Johann Hieronymus Schröter gave to a feature on the moon the "unforgettable name of the great naturalist Lichtenberg." Later the selenographer J. H. Mädler reassigned the name of Lichtenberg to a much more prominent feature—a first-order ring plain north of the Ocean of Storms ($-67°$ $5'3''$ long., $+31°$ $25'20''$ lat.).[2]

Yet it was in physics that Lichtenberg produced his greatest scientific achievements. First and foremost he was a teacher. The first German university chair of experimental physics was established for him. As professor at the University of Göttingen, he was enormously popular with students, and his lecture-demonstrations attracted an extremely large number of auditors. Along with the scrupulous presentation of facts, Lichtenberg offered his students a view of physics which would not be out of tune with the attitudes of the twentieth century. He combined bold imagining with radical scientific skepticism and left a legacy of maxims, many of which are as valid today as they were in his time. He wrote: "Almost everything in physics must be investigated anew, even the best-known things, because it is precisely here that one least suspects something new or incorrect." Accordingly, he was among the first to question the validity of the postulates of Euclidean geometry, in particular the postulate that only one straight line can pass through two points. He questioned the usefulness of the concept of ether because of the absence of any measurable effects that could be attributed to it. At the same time he recognized the importance of "experimenting with ideas," provided they are based on fact and the resulting theory is verifiable experimentally. He was contemptuous of dogmatists and scornful of those who confuse "facts" and "dreams."

Lichtenberg saw as the purpose of his teaching the "coherent exposition of physical relationships as preparation for a *future* science of nature." He used hypotheses very much as we use "models" in physics of the twentieth century. He wrote, "I see such hypotheses in physics as nothing else but convenient *pictures* that facilitate the conception of the whole." The interconnectedness of things, the wholeness of nature, was a postulate that guided all his work. In his quest for the "conception of the whole" Lichtenberg expressed some ideas which must have sounded rather farfetched to his contemporaries. For example, commenting on the controversy concerning the Huygens-Euler undulatory theory and the Newton-Kant corpuscular theory of light, Lichtenberg wrote, "Wouldn't one perhaps accomplish most by unifying the two theories . . . considering the limitation of our knowledge; both deserve respect, and both may indeed be right."[3] In addition to his penetrating philosophical insight, Lichtenberg displayed an experimental skill and thoroughness of the highest order. Guided by the precept that "repeating an experiment with larger apparatus is tantamount to looking at the phenomenon through a microscope," Lichtenberg constructed a gigantic electrophorus and, while experimenting with it, discovered in 1777 the basic process of xerographic copying. In the words of Chester F. Carlson, the inventor of modern xerography, "Georg Christoph Lichtenberg, professor of physics at Göttingen University and an avid electrical experimenter, discovered the first electrostatic recording process, by which he produced the so-called 'Lichtenberg figures' which still bear his name."

Lichtenberg must be considered the most significant early observer of the subconscious. Concepts of repression, compensation, subconscious motivation, and sublimation are all in his writings. Lichtenberg is quoted over a dozen times by Sigmund Freud. In particular, Lichtenberg examined the interrelation between moods and facial expressions and gestures. The term "pathognomy"—which he coined to describe outward signs of emotion—is still used in psychology of expression. At the same time Lichtenberg combated the mystical aspects of Johann Kaspar Lavater's "physiognomic theory"—fashionable in those times—which maintained that anatomical structure was the outward expression of the soul.[4]

Lichtenberg's insight into human nature, coupled with an elegant and lucid style, made him a leading literary figure and earned him a secure place in German literature. His aphorisms and his commentaries on the engravings of Hogarth are unsurpassed. This facet of Lichtenberg is even more impressive than his scientific work. It is for his role as a "heretic" and an "antifaust," who in his superb satiric and aphoristic writings stood out strongly against "metaphysical and romantic excesses," that Lichtenberg is known best.

NOTES

1. A player pays the "bank" an *entrance fee* of X dollars. A coin is then tossed until heads shows up, say at the *n*-th toss. The player is now paid by the bank the amount of 2^n dollars. *Example:* Suppose the entrance fee is 7 dollars. If heads shows up at the first toss ($n = 1$) the player gets 2 dollars, losing 5 dollars. If heads shows up at $n = 2$, the player gets $2^2 = 4$ dollars, losing 3 dollars. If heads shows up at $n = 3$, the player gets $2^3 = 8$ dollars, winning 1 dollar. If heads does not show up until the 8th toss, the player gets $2^8 = 256$ dollars, winning 249 dollars. The problem is to determine what the "fair" *entrance fee* should be. Classical theory of probability gives

$$X = \sum_{n=1}^{\infty} 2^n \left(\frac{1}{2}\right)^n = \infty$$

which is not only paradoxical but absurd as well.
2. The selenographic longitudes are measured in the plane of the moon's equator *positive* toward the *west* in the sky and negative toward the east in the sky. The reference axis (0° longitude) is the radius of the moon passing through the mean center of moon's visible disk. The latitudes are measured from the moon's equator *positive* toward the *north* in the sky and negative toward the south.
3. It may be of interest to compare this statement to one made by Niels Bohr in 1928 in a similar context: "However contrasting such phenomena may at first appear, it must be realized that they are complementary, in the sense that taken together they exhaust all information about the atomic object which can be expressed in common language without ambiguity."
4. The differences between Lavater's "physiognomic theory" and Lichtenberg's "pathognomy" were best summarized by Franz H. Mautner (in his *Lichtenberg—Geschichte seines Geistes*, Berlin, 1968, p. 188): "Lavater was concerned primarily about revelation, Lichtenberg about learning; Lavater about principle, Lichtenberg about practical applicability; Lavater about religion, Lichtenberg about science; Lavater mainly about symbolism, Lichtenberg about scientific phenomenologic research."

BIBLIOGRAPHY

I. Original Works. Collections of Lichtenberg's writings are *Georg Christoph Lichtenbergs vermischte Schriften*, Ludwig Christian Lichtenberg and Friedrich Kries, eds., 9 vols. (Göttingen, 1800–1806); and *Georg Christoph Lichtenberg, Schriften und Briefe*, Wolfgang Promies, ed., 4 vols. (Munich, 1967–1972). A third collection, *Lichtenberg: Schriften*, Franz H. Mautner, ed., is to be published.

Other writings and letters by Lichtenberg are listed in the following, along with rich biographical and secondary bibliographical material (presented chronologically): F. Lauchert, *G. Chr. Lichtenbergs schriftstellerische Tätigkeit in chronologischer Übersicht dargestellt* (Göttingen, 1893); Albert Schneider, *G. C. Lichtenberg, précurseur du romantisme* (Nancy, 1954); J. P. Stern, *Lichtenberg: A Doctrine of Scattered Occasions* (Bloomington, Ind., 1959); W. Promies, *Georg Christoph Lichtenberg in Selbstzeugnissen und Bilddokumenten*, Rowohlt Monographien no. 90 (Reinbek bei Hamburg, 1964); Franz H. Mautner, *Lichtenberg: Geschichte seines Geistes* (Berlin, 1968); and Anacleto

Verrecchia, *Georg Christoph Lichtenberg: L'eretico dello spirito tedesco* (Florence, 1969).

Lichtenberg's anonymous contributions to *Göttingische Anzeigen von gelehrten Sachen* are identified by Karl S. Guthke in *Libri*, **12** (1963), 331–340.

II. SECONDARY LITERATURE. "Lichtenberg figures" are discussed in the following and in references therein (listed chronologically): Karl Przibram, "Die elektrischen Figuren," in *Handbuch der Physik*, **14** (1927), 391–404; C. E. Magnusson, "Lichtenberg Figures," in *Journal of the American Institute of Electrical Engineers*, **47** (1928), 828–835; F. H. Merrill and A. von Hippel, "The Atomphysical Interpretation of Lichtenberg Figures and Their Application to the Study of Gas Discharge Phenomena," in *Journal of Applied Physics*, **10** (1939), 873–887; A. Morris Thomas, "Heat Developed and Powder Lichtenberg Figures and the Ionization of Dielectric Surfaces Produced by Electrical Impulses," in *British Journal of Applied Physics*, **2** (1951), 98–109; J. M. Meek and J. D. Craggs, *Electrical Breakdown of Gases* (Oxford, 1953), 215–222; and Chester F. Carlson, "History of Electrostatic Recording," in John H. Dessauer and Harold E. Clark, eds., *Xerography and Related Processes* (London–New York, 1965), 15–49.

Lichtenberg's other scientific activity is discussed in the following and in references therein (listed chronologically): Herbert Pupke, "Georg Christoph Lichtenberg als Naturforscher," in *Naturwissenschaften*, **30** (1942), 745–750; P. Hahn, "Lichtenberg und die Experimentalphysik," in *Zeitschrift für physikalischen und chemischen Unterricht*, **56** (1943), 8–15; F. H. Mautner and F. Miller, "Remarks on G. C. Lichtenberg, Humanist-Scientist,'" in *Isis*, **43** (1952), 223–232; D. B. Herrmann, "Georg Christoph Lichtenberg und die Mondkarte von Tobias Mayer," in *Mitteilungen der Archenhold-Sternwarte Berlin-Treptow*, no. 72 (1965), 2–6; D. B. Herrmann, "Georg Christoph Lichtenberg als Herausgeber von Erxlebens Werk 'Anfangsgründe der Naturlehre,'" in *NTM, Schriftenreihe für Geschichte der Naturwissenschaften, Technik und Medizin*, **6**, no. 1 (1970), 68–81, and **6**, no. 2 (1970), 1–12; and Eric G. Forbes, "Georg Christoph Lichtenberg and the *Opera Inedita* of Tobias Mayer," in *Annals of Science*, **28** (1972), 31–42.

For a discussion of the "Petersburg game," see Thornton C. Fry, *Probability and Its Engineering Uses* (New York, 1928), 197, and W. Feller, "Note on the Law of Large Numbers and 'Fair' Games," in *Annals of Mathematical Statistics*, **16** (1945), 301–304; and his *An Introduction to Probability Theory and Its Applications*, 2nd ed. (New York, 1957), 233–237.

Breakdowns of references on Lichtenberg according to his areas of activity (science, philosophy, literature, and so on) are in the bibliographical sections of the books by J. P. Stern and A. Verrecchia (see above).

A definitive bibliography is *Lichtenberg-Bibliographie*, prepared by Rudolf Jung, in the series Repertoria Heidelbergensia, II (Heidelberg, 1972).

OLEXA MYRON BILANIUK

LIE, MARIUS SOPHUS (*b.* Nordfjordeide, Norway, 17 December 1842; *d.* Christiania [now Oslo], Norway, 18 February 1899), *mathematics.*

Sophus Lie, as he is known, was the sixth and youngest child of a Lutheran pastor, Johann Herman Lie. He first attended school in Moss (Kristianiafjord), then, from 1857 to 1859, Nissen's Private Latin School in Christiania. He studied at Christiania University from 1859 to 1865, mainly mathematics and sciences. Although mathematics was taught by such people as Bjerknes and Sylow, Lie was not much impressed. After his examination in 1865, he gave private lessons, became slightly interested in astronomy, and tried to learn mechanics; but he could not decide what to do. The situation changed when, in 1868, he hit upon Poncelet's and Plücker's writings. Later, he called himself a student of Plücker's, although he had never met him. Plücker's momentous idea to create new geometries by choosing figures other than points—in fact straight lines—as elements of space pervaded all of Lie's work.

Lie's first published paper brought him a scholarship for study abroad. He spent the winter of 1869–1870 in Berlin, where he met Felix Klein, whose interest in geometry also had been influenced by Plücker's work. This acquaintance developed into a friendship that, although seriously troubled in later years, proved crucial for the scientific progress of both men. Lie and Klein had quite different characters as humans and mathematicians: the algebraist Klein was fascinated by the peculiarities of charming problems; the analyst Lie, parting from special cases, sought to understand a problem in its appropriate generalization.

Lie and Klein spent the summer of 1870 in Paris, where they became acquainted with Darboux and Camille Jordan. Here Lie, influenced by the ideas of the French "anallagmatic" school, discovered his famous contact transformation, which maps straight lines into spheres and principal tangent curves into curvature lines. He also became familiar with Monge's theory of differential equations. At the outbreak of the Franco-Prussian war in July, Klein left Paris; Lie, as a Norwegian, stayed. In August he decided to hike to Italy but was arrested near Fontainebleau as a spy. After a month in prison, he was freed through Darboux's intervention. Just before the Germans blockaded Paris, he escaped to Italy. From there he returned to Germany, where he again met Klein.

In 1871 Lie was awarded a scholarship to Christiania University. He also taught at Nissen's Private Latin School. In July 1872 he received his Ph.D. During this period he developed the integration theory of partial differential equations now found in many textbooks, although rarely under his name.

Lie's results were found at the same time by Adolph Mayer, with whom he conducted a lively correspondence. Lie's letters are a valuable source of knowledge about his development.

In 1872 a chair in mathematics was created for him at Christiania University. In 1873 Lie turned from the invariants of contact transformations to the principles of the theory of transformation groups. Together with Sylow he assumed the editorship of Niels Abel's works. In 1874 Lie married Anna Birch, who bore him two sons and a daughter.

His main interest turned to transformation groups, his most celebrated creation, although in 1876 he returned to differential geometry. In the same year he joined G. O. Sars and Worm Müller in founding the *Archiv för mathematik og naturvidenskab*. In 1882 the work of Halphen and Laguerre on differential invariants led Lie to resume his investigations on transformation groups.

Lie was quite isolated in Christiania. He had no students interested in his research. Abroad, except for Klein, Mayer, and somewhat later Picard, nobody paid attention to his work. In 1884 Klein and Mayer induced F. Engel, who had just received his Ph.D., to visit Lie in order to learn about transformation groups and to help him write a comprehensive book on the subject. Engel stayed nine months with Lie. Thanks to his activity the work was accomplished, its three parts being published between 1888 and 1893, whereas Lie's other great projects were never completed. F. Hausdorff, whom Lie had chosen to assist him in preparing a work on contact transformations and partial differential equations, got interested in quite different subjects.

This happened after 1886 when Lie had succeeded Klein at Leipzig, where, indeed, he found students, among whom was G. Scheffers. With him Lie published textbooks on transformation groups and on differential equations, and a fragmentary geometry of contact transformations. In the last years of his life Lie turned to foundations of geometry, which at that time meant the Helmholtz space problem.

In 1889 Lie, who was described as an open-hearted man of gigantic stature and excellent physical health, was struck by what was then called neurasthenia. Treatment in a mental hospital led to his recovery, and in 1890 he could resume his work. His character, however, had changed greatly. He became increasingly sensitive, irascible, suspicious, and misanthropic, despite the many tokens of recognition that were heaped upon him.

Meanwhile, his Norwegian friends sought to lure him back to Norway. Another special chair in mathematics was created for him at Christiania University, and in September 1898 he moved there.

He died of pernicious anemia the following February. His papers have been edited, with excellent annotations, by F. Engel and P. Heegaard.

Lie's first papers dealt with very special subjects in geometry, more precisely, in differential geometry. In comparison with his later performances, they seem like classroom exercises; but they are actually the seeds from which his great theories grew. Change of the space element and related mappings, the lines of a complex considered as solutions of a differential equation, special contact transformations, and trajectories of special groups prepared his theory of partial differential equations, contact transformations, and transformation groups. He often returned to this less sophisticated differential geometry. His best-known discoveries of this kind during his later years concern minimal surfaces.

The crucial idea that emerged from his preliminary investigations was a new choice of space element, the contact element: an incidence pair of point and line or, in n dimensions, of point and hyperplane. The manifold of these elements was now studied, not algebraically, as Klein would have done—and actually did—but analytically or, rather, from the standpoint of differential geometry. The procedure of describing a line complex by a partial differential equation was inverted: solving the first-order partial differential equation

$$F\left(x, x_1, \cdots, x_{n-1}, \frac{\partial x}{\partial x_1}, \cdots, \frac{\partial x}{\partial x_{n-1}}\right) = 0$$

means fibering the manifold $F(x, x_1, \cdots, x_{n-1}, p_1, \cdots, p_{n-1}) = 0$ of $(2n-1)$-space by n-submanifolds on which the Pfaffian equation $dx = p_1 dx + \cdots + p_{n-1} dx_{n-1}$ prevails. This Pfaffian equation was interpreted geometrically: it means the incidence of the contact elements $\ulcorner x, x_1, \cdots, x_{n-1}, p_1, \cdots, p_{n-1}\urcorner$ and $\ulcorner x + dx, x_1 + dx_1, \cdots, x_{n-1} + dx_{n-1}, p_1 + dp_1, \cdots, p_{n-1} + dp_{n-1}\urcorner$. This incidence notion was so strongly suggested by the geometry of complexes (or, as one would say today, by symplectic geometry) that Lie never bothered to state it explicitly. Indeed, if it is viewed in the related $2n$-vector space instead of $(2n+1)$-projective space, incidence means what is called conjugateness with respect to a skew form. It was one of Lie's idiosyncrasies that he never made this skew form explicit, even after Frobenius had introduced it in 1877; obviously Lie did not like it because he had missed it. It is another drawback that Lie adhered mainly to projective formulations in $(2n-1)$-space, which led to clumsy formulas as soon as things had to be presented analytically; homogeneous formulations in $2n$-space are more elegant and make the ideas much clearer, so they will be used in the sequel such that the partial differential equation is written as $F(x_1, \cdots, x_n, p_1, \cdots p_n) = 0$, with $p_1 dx_1 + \cdots + p_n dx_n$ as the total differential of the nonexplicit unknown variable. Then the skew form (the Frobenius covariant) has the shape $\sum(\delta p_i dx_i - dp_i \delta x_i)$.

A manifold $z = f(x_1, \cdots, x_n)$ in $(n + 1)$-space, if viewed in the $2n$-space of contact elements, makes $\sum p_i dx_i$ a complete differential, or, in geometrical terms, neighboring contact elements in this manifold are incident. But there are more such n-dimensional *Elementvereine*: a k-dimensional manifold in $(n + 1)$-space with all its n-dimensional tangent spaces shares this property. It was an important step to deal with all these *Elementvereine* on the same footing, for it led to an illuminating extension of the differential equation problem and to contact transformations. Finding a complete solution of the differential equation now amounted to fibering the manifold $F = 0$ by n-dimensional *Elementvereine*. In geometrical terms the Lagrange-Monge-Pfaff-Cauchy theory (which is often falsely ascribed to Hamilton and Jacobi) was refashioned: to every point of $F = 0$ the skew form assigns one tangential direction that is conjugate to the whole $(2n - 1)$-dimensional tangential plane. Integrating this field of directions, or otherwise solving the system of ordinary differential equations

$$\frac{dx_i}{dt} = \frac{\partial F}{\partial p_i}, \frac{dp_i}{dt} = -\frac{\partial F}{\partial x_i},$$

one obtains a fibering of $F = 0$ into curves, the "characteristic strips," closely connected to the Monge curves (touching the Monge cones). Thus it became geometrically clear why every complete solution also had to be fibered by characteristic strips.

Here the notion of contact transformation came in. First suggested by special instances, it was conceived of as a mapping that conserves the incidence of neighboring contact elements. Analytically, this meant invariance of $\sum p_i dx_i$ up to a total differential. The characteristic strips appeared as the trajectories of such a contact transformation:

$$(F, \cdot) = \sum \left(\frac{\partial F}{\partial p_i} \frac{\partial}{\partial x_i} - \frac{\partial F}{\partial x_i} \frac{\partial}{\partial p_i} \right).$$

Thus characteristic strips must be incident everywhere as soon as they are so in one point. This led to a geometric reinterpretation of Cauchy's construction of one solution of the partial differential equation. From one $(n - 1)$-dimensional *Elementverein* on $F = 0$, which is easily found, one had to issue all characteristic strips. But even a complete solution was obtained in this way: by cross-secting the system of characteristics, the figure was lowered by two dimen-

sions in order to apply induction. Solving the partial differential equation was now brought back to integrating systems of ordinary equations of, subsequently, $2, 4, \cdots, 2n$ variables. In comparison with older methods, this was an enormous reduction of the integration job, which at the same time was performed analytically by Adolph Mayer.

With the Poisson brackets $(F, \cdot)$ viewed as contact transformations, Jacobi's integration theory of systems

$$F_j(x_1, \cdots, x_n, p_1, \cdots p_n) = 0$$

was reinterpreted and simplified. Indeed, $(F, \cdot F_j)$ is nothing but the commutator of the related contact transformations. The notion of transformation group, although not yet explicitly formulated, was already active in Lie's unconscious. The integrability condition $(F_i, F_j) = \sum \rho_{ij}^k F_k$ (where the ρ_{ij}^k are functions) was indeed closely connected to group theory ideas, and it is not surprising that Lie called such a system a group. The theory of these "function groups," which was thoroughly developed for use in partial differential equations and contact transformations, was the last stepping-stone to the theory of transformation groups, which was later applied in differential equations.

Lie's integration theory was the result of marvelous geometric intuitions. The preceding short account is the most direct way to present it. The usual way is a rigmarole of formulas, even in the comparatively excellent book of Engel and Faber. Whereas transformation groups have become famous as Lie groups, his integration theory is not as well known as it deserves to be. To a certain extent this is Lie's own fault. The nineteenth-century mathematical public often could not understand lucid abstract ideas if they were not expressed in the analytic language of that time, even if this language would not help to make things clearer. So Lie, a poor analyst in comparison with his ablest contemporaries, had to adapt and express in a host of formulas, ideas which would have been said better without them. It was Lie's misfortune that by yielding to this urge, he rendered his theories obscure to the geometricians and failed to convince the analysts.

About 1870 group theory became fashionable. In 1870 C. Jordan published his *Traité des substitutions*, and two years later Klein presented his *Erlanger Programm*. Obviously Klein and Lie must have discussed group theory early. Nevertheless, to name a certain set of (smooth) mappings of (part of) n space, depending on r parameters, a group was still a new way of speaking. Klein, with his background in the theory of invariants, of course thought of very special groups, as his *Erlanger Programm* and later works prove.

Lie, however, soon turned to transformation groups in general—finite continuous groups, as he christened them ("finite" because of the finite number of parameters, and "continuous" because at that time this included differentiability of any order wanted). Today they are called Lie groups. In the mid-1870's this theory was completed, although its publication would take many years.

Taking derivatives (velocity fields) at identity in all directions creates the infinitesimal transformations of the group, which together form the infinitesimal group. The first fundamental theorem, providing a necessary and sufficient condition, tells how the derivatives at any parameter point $a_1, \cdots, a_r$ are linearly combined from those at identity. The second fundamental theorem says that the infinitesimal transformations will and should form what is today called a Lie algebra,

$$[X_i, X_j] = X_i X_j - X_j X_i = \sum_k c_{ij}^k X_k,$$

with some structure constants c_{ij}^k. Antisymmetry and Jacobi associativity yield the relations

$$c_{ij}^k + c_{ji}^k = 0,$$

$$\sum_k (c_{ij}^k c_{kl}^m + c_{jl}^k c_{ki}^m + c_{li}^k c_{kj}^m) = 0$$

between the structure constants. It cost Lie some trouble to prove that these relations were also sufficient.

From these fundamental theorems the theory was developed extensively. The underlying abstract group, called the parameter group, showed up. Differential invariants were investigated, and automorphism groups of differential equations were used as tools of solution. Groups in a plane and in 3-space were classified. "Infinite continuous" groups were also considered, with no remarkable success, then and afterward. Lie dreamed of a Galois theory of differential equations but did not really succeed, since he could not explain what kind of *ausführbare* operations should correspond to the rational ones of Galois theory and what solving meant in the case of a differential equation with no nontrivial automorphisms. Nevertheless, it was an inexhaustible and promising subject.

Gradually, quite a few mathematicians became interested in the subject. First, of course, was Lie's student Engel. F. Schur then gave another proof of the third fundamental theorem (1889–1890), which led to interesting new views; L. Maurer refashioned the proofs of all fundamental theorems (1888–1891); and Picard and Vessiot developed Galois theories of differential equations (1883, 1891). The most astonishing fact about Lie groups, that their abstract structure was determined by the purely algebraic phenomenon of their structure constants, led to the most important investigations. First were those of Wilhelm Killing, who tried to classify the simple Lie groups. This was a tedious job, and he erred more than once. This made Lie furious, and according to oral tradition he is said to have warned one of his students who was leaving: "Farewell, and if ever you meet that s.o.b., kill him." Although belittled by Lie and some of his followers, Killing's work was excellent. It was revised by Cartan, who after staying with Lie wrote his famous thesis (1894). For many years Cartan—gifted with Lie's geometric intuition and, although trained in the French tradition, as incapable as Lie of explaining things clearly—was the greatest, if not the only, really important mathematician who continued Lie's tradition in all his fields. But Cartan was isolated. Weyl's papers of 1922–1923 marked the revival of Lie groups. In the 1930's Lie's local approach gave way to a global one. The elimination of differentiability conditions in Lie groups took place between the 1920's and 1950's. Chevalley's development of algebraic groups was a momentous generalization of Lie groups in the 1950's. Lie algebras, replacing ordinary associativity by Jacobi associativity, became popular among algebraists from the 1940's. Lie groups now play an increasingly important part in quantum physics. The joining of topology to algebra on the most primitive level, as Lie did, has shown its creative power in this century.

In 1868 Hermann von Helmholtz formulated his space problem, an attempt to replace Euclid's foundations of geometry with group-theoretic ones, although in fact groups were never explicitly mentioned in that paper. In 1890 Lie showed that Helmholtz's formulations were unsatisfactory and that his solution was defective. His work on this subject, now called the Helmholtz-Lie space problem, is one of the most beautiful applications of Lie groups. In the 1950's and 1960's it was reconsidered in a topological setting.

BIBLIOGRAPHY

I. ORIGINAL WORKS. Lie's collected papers were published as *Gesammelte Abhandlungen*, F. Engel and P. Heegaard, eds., 6 vols. in 11 pts. (Leipzig–Oslo, 1922–1937). His writings include *Theorie der Transformationsgruppen*, 3 vols. (Leipzig, 1888–1893), on which Engel collaborated; *Vorlesungen über Differentialgleichungen mit bekannten infinitesimalen Transformationen* (Leipzig, 1891), written with G. Scheffers; *Vorlesungen über continuierliche Grup-*

pen mit geometrischen und anderen Anwendungen (Leipzig, 1893), written with G. Scheffers; and *Geometrie der Berührungstransformationen* (Leipzig, 1896), written with G. Scheffers.

II. SECONDARY LITERATURE. Works on Lie or his work are F. Engel, "Sophus Lie," in *Jahresbericht der Deutschen Matematiker-Vereinigung*, **8** (1900), 30–46; and M. Noether, "Sophus Lie," in *Mathematische Annalen*, **53** (1900), 1–41.

HANS FREUDENTHAL

LIEBER, THOMAS. See **Erastus, Thomas.**

LIEBERKÜHN, JOHANNES NATHANAEL (*b.* Berlin, Germany, 5 September 1711; *d.* Berlin, 7 December 1756), *anatomy.*

One of the most skillful German anatomists of the early eighteenth century, Lieberkühn was the son of Johannes Christianus Lieberkühn, a goldsmith. His father insisted that Johannes and his brother plan for careers in theology; thus prior to attending the academy at Jena, the boy was sent to the Halle Magdeburg Gymnasium.

At Jena, Lieberkühn studied mathematics, mechanics, and natural philosophy, coming under the influence of the physician-iatromathematician G. E. Hamberger (1697–1755). His interest in medicine was sharpened by this experience and he went on to study chemistry, anatomy, and physiology with Hermann Friedrich Teichmeyer (1685–1744) and Johann Adolph Wedel (1675–1747). Lieberkühn left Jena in 1733 and joined his brother at Rostock as a candidate to become a preacher. Here he delivered only a few sermons, choosing instead to continue studies of what most interested him. Johann Gustav Reinbech (1683–1741), the noted Protestant theologian, recognized Lieberkühn's aptitude for scientific studies and introduced him to the Prussian king, Frederick William I. After interviewing Lieberkühn, the king released him from the career set by his father, who had died in the meantime, so that he could devote full time to science and medicine.

Even before Lieberkühn returned to Jena in 1735, the Berlin Academy of Sciences enrolled him as a fellow as a result of his earlier work at Jena. Subsequent to his second period at Jena, Lieberkühn traveled and studied in other centers, including the Imperial Natural Sciences Academy in Erfurt, where its president, A. E. Buchner, made him a fellow.

He pursued further medical study, especially of anatomy and chemistry, at Leiden under Boerhaave,

B. S. Albinus, J. D. Gaub, and Swieten. Lieberkühn's Leiden tutelage culminated in the award of a medical degree in 1739. His dissertation, *De valvula coli et usu processus vermicularis*, was commended by Boerhaave and Swieten. Another dissertation written at this time, "De plumbi indole," was not published and apparently is no longer extant.

Lieberkühn's fascination with anatomical structures and their mechanisms expressed itself in his *De fabrica et actione villorum intestinorum tenuium hominis* (1745). Here, for the first time, were described, in greatest detail, the structure and function of the numerous glands attached to the villi, appropriately called Lieberkühnian glands, as well as the structure and function of the villi found in the intestines.

All of these were made comprehensible by the meticulous and skillful injections of a mixture of wax, turpentine, and colophony or dark resin.

To explain the flow of fluids into these intestinal components Lieberkühn constructed a model. By means of an open curved brass tube, cone-shaped at both ends, with two outlet tubes placed toward the narrow center, each of which drained into a separate vessel, he demonstrated the flow of chyle from the arterioles to the villi and the ascent of the lymph from the villi into the small veins. He used tinted water to show the flow of lymph from the villus into the veins and plain water to emulate the flow of chyle to the villus. As a result of his excellent demonstrations of the intestinal contents of an experimental animal before the members of the Royal Society of London, Lieberkühn was made a fellow in 1740.

In the tradition of Hamberger, his first medical teacher at Jena, Lieberkühn explored the circulatory vessels, devising special microscopes to view in greater detail the intricacies of fluid motion within the living animal. One of these was the anatomical microscope used for viewing the circulation in frogs. The specimen was attached to the body of the microscope, which consisted of two thin silver plates between which was placed a small lens and around which were arranged hooks to hold and manipulate the animal. The part of the animal to be observed was fixed over the lens.

En route to Leiden, Lieberkühn had visited Amsterdam, where he saw a solar microscope similar to the one Fahrenheit made in 1736. Another microscope, for the invention of which Lieberkühn has been given credit, to be used in illuminating opaque objects, was based on the principle of Fahrenheit's solar microscope. It consisted of a small, concave, highly polished silver speculum, later termed a Lieberkühn, that provided intense reflection of the sun's rays directly upon the object. Although Descartes had shown a solar microscope in his *Dioptrique* as early as 1637, it was probably due to Lieberkühn's revival of interest in it that the speculum arrangement on this microscope received his name. Lieberkühn's solar microscope is illustrated in William Carpenter's *The Microscope and Its Revelations* (7th ed. [Philadelphia, 1891], p. 138). The noted English microscope maker John Cuff (*ca.* 1708–1772) later adapted Lieberkühn's model by adding a mirror to it which provided better control by reflecting the sun's rays to the speculum and then to the object.

After settling in Berlin in 1740, Lieberkühn practiced medicine until his death at the age of 45. His most significant contribution during these last sixteen years of his life grew out of his desire to expose and preserve the vascular tissues of various animals. He assembled a collection of over 400 items which consisted of three main types of anatomical preparations: those preserved in a transparent liquid; dry specimens injected and hardened; and injected preparations of minute pieces of tissue (especially lung) to be viewed under the microscope. After his death this collection was advertised by a Paris dealer named Mettra and eventually was broken up and sold to several museums, as were other instruments he had constructed, including pneumatic pumps, pyrometers, and air guns.

Lieberkühn was survived by his wife, the former Catherine Dorothy Neveling, and a son and a daughter.

Lieberkühn combined a gift for observation with technical facility, enabling him to perfect the instruments and injections required to explore the most minute vascular structure of both living and preserved organisms.

BIBLIOGRAPHY

I. ORIGINAL WORKS. A collected ed. of Lieberkühn's works appeared under the title *Dissertationes quatuor, omnia nunc primum in unum collecta . . .*, John Sheldon, ed. (London, 1782). This ed. contains *Memoria* extracted from the Berlin Academy *Memoirs* (1758), "Sur les moyens propres à découvrir la construction des viscères," which appeared originally in the *Memoirs* of 1748, and "Description d'un microscope anatomique," which appeared originally in the *Memoirs* of 1745. Other writings are *De fabrica et actione villorum intestinorum tenuium hominis* (Leiden, 1739); and *De valvula coli et usu processus vermicularis*, his dissertation for the medical degree (Leiden, 1745).

II. SECONDARY LITERATURE. The best sources for an account of Lieberkühn's life are the *Memoria* published in the Sheldon ed. and the *éloge* by Formey published in the Berlin Academy *Memoirs* in 1756. The most explicit description of his anatomical preparations appears in *L'année littéraire* (1764), 136–140.

AUDREY B. DAVIS

LIEBERMANN, CARL THEODORE (*b.* Berlin, Germany, 23 February 1842; *d.* Berlin, 28 December 1914), *chemistry.*

Liebermann was the son of Benjamin Liebermann, a cotton manufacturer. As a child he attended a private boys' school and then the Gray Cloister Gymnasium, from which he graduated in 1859. His father wanted him to work in his factory and eventually assume its direction, but Liebermann preferred to continue his studies at the university. Since he chose to study chemistry—which might have been useful in the cotton industry—his father encouraged him. In 1861 he went to Heidelberg to study spectral analysis with Bunsen. The following year he returned to Berlin. Although laboratory space was scarce, he found a place with F. Sonnenschein. In 1863 he moved to Baeyer's laboratory and two years later completed a paper on propargyl ether.

Liebermann then joined the firm of Koechlin, Baumgarten and Co. as a chemist. Here he learned about the dye industry while also discovering that his real interest lay in pure rather than applied science. After spending several months in the family factory to satisfy his father, he returned to Baeyer's laboratory in 1867. After Graebe's departure from the laboratory, Liebermann became Baeyer's assistant. He soon formed a close personal relationship with Baeyer and qualified himself to teach at the technical school in Berlin. In 1870 he also became a privatdocent at the University of Berlin. When Baeyer left Berlin in 1873, Liebermann became professor ordinarius at the Gewerbeakademie. He remained at the academy, which later became the Charlottenburg Technical High School, for the rest of his career. During this time he directed the research of dozens of students.

In 1868 Liebermann became a member of the Deutsche Chemische Gesellschaft. After 1870 he continually held a position of leadership in the society and was president twice. He helped to found the Hofmann Haus and to promote an association of laboratory students. He was a member of the scientific academies of Uppsala, Christiania, and Göttingen, the Manchester Literary and Philosophical Society, and the Chemical Society of London. In 1906 he received the Perkin Medal. He married Tony Reichenheim in 1869 and they had one daughter, Else.

Liebermann produced more than 350 scientific papers and directed the work of many students. Most of his work was in the area of aromatic organic chemistry. He became interested in this area as a student when he synthesized alizarin with Graebe. They used Baeyer's zinc dust method to show that alizarin is derived from anthracene; they also showed that purpurin, a second colored substance of madder, was trihydroxyanthraquinone.

With this introduction to anthracene compounds, Liebermann prepared halogen derivatives and investigated the hydrogen addition products. He studied the monocarbonic acids of anthracene and prepared phenol derivatives. As early as 1868 Graebe and Liebermann had suggested that anthracene was a ring structure. Heinrich Limpricht's synthesis made both

and

possible formulas; Liebermann felt through his work on the placement of oxygen in alizarin that the latter formula was the most probable. Liebermann's formula proved to be correct when W. A. van Dorp in 1872 produced anthracene from benzyl toluol in Liebermann's laboratory. While studying the hydroxyl isomers of anthraquinones, Liebermann found a way of exchanging the hydroxyl with an amide and eliminating the latter through a diazo reaction.

Liebermann then turned to the methyl homologs of anthraquinones; he investigated chrysophanic acid found in rhubarb and showed it to be methyldihydroxyanthraquinone. He proposed that the hydroxyanthraquinones were part of a reduction series of anthracene. Between 1876 and 1881 he was able to produce most of the compounds for which he had proposed structural formulas. In his work on reduction series of anthracene, Liebermann also became interested in oxyanthraquinones. One of these compounds, Goa powder or chrysarobin, was of pharmacological interest. Later researchers extended his work on the relationship between hydroxyl placement and therapeutic effectiveness.

Liebermann also undertook an extensive study of naphthalene compounds. He wanted to understand the basis for the location of substitution derivatives of naphthalene and to produce a whole series of β-naphthalene derivatives. He was successful, for he produced β-naphthylamine from α-naphthylamine with Scheidung. He also found retene, chrysene, and picene, and soon began to study other highly colored condensed aromatics.

Liebermann also studied the dye cochineal, or carminic acid. Paul Schützenberger and Warren de la Rue had both investigated this substance and each had assigned to it a different formula. Liebermann and van Dorp finally showed that it contains ruficoccin and ruficarmin, derivatives of anthracene and

α-naphthaquinone. Other natural and artificial dyes on which Liebermann worked include β-rosaniline, hematoxylin, and xanthorhamnin. He was interested in spectrographic work which might relate color production in plants to molecular constitution.

Liebermann and his students investigated the alkaloids of coca. They devised technical methods for the production of cocaine and related compounds and studied the isomeric cinnamic acids.

Since his work on alizarin in 1868, Liebermann had tried to relate the structure of a compound with its color and its usefulness as a dye. Colors were generally produced by reduction. He felt that the color must therefore be due to unsaturated valences or an inner storage capacity in a molecule which exceeded the minimum force necessary to hold the molecule together. Compounds must have a specific composition to be mordants. In alizarin he found that the placement of the two hydroxyl groups influenced the color. Further study on the significance of the ortho position was done by Alfred Werner with organometallic compounds.

BIBLIOGRAPHY

I. ORIGINAL WORKS. Works by Liebermann include "Ueber Alizarin und Anthracene," in *Berichte der Deutschen chemischen Gesellschaft*, **1** (1868), 49–51, written with K. Graebe; "Ueber den Zusammenhang zwischen Molecularconstitution und Farbe bei organischen Verbindungen," *ibid.*, **1** (1868), 106–108, written with Graebe; "Ueber kunstliche Bildung von Alizarin," *ibid.*, **2** (1869), 332–334, written with Graebe; "Ueber die isomeren α- und β-Derivate des Naphtalins," *ibid.*, **6** (1873), 945–951, written with A. Dittler; "Zur Kenntniss des Cochenillefarbestoffs," *ibid.*, **4** (1871), 655–658, written with W. A. van Dorp; and "Reduktionsversuche am Anthrachinon," *ibid.*, **13** (1880), 1596–1603.

II. SECONDARY LITERATURE. For information on Liebermann's life, see James Partington, *A History of Chemistry*, IV (New York, 1961), 790; and O. Wallach and P. Jacobsen, "C. Liebermann," in *Berichte der Deutschen chemischen Gesellschaft*, **51**, pt. 2 (1918), 1135–1204.

RUTH GIENAPP RINARD

LIEBIG, JUSTUS VON (*b.* Darmstadt, Germany, 12 May 1803; *d.* Munich, Germany, 18 April 1873), *chemistry.*

Justus Liebig was the second of the nine children of Johann Georg and Maria Karoline Moserin Liebig. He taught chemistry at the University of Giessen from 1825 until 1851, and for the remainder of his life at the University of Munich. In 1826 he married Henriette Moldenhauer, who survived him. There were five children: Georg, Hermann, Agnes, Johanna, and Marie. In 1845 he was made a baron. Liebig achieved prominence in general analytical, organic, agricultural, and physiological chemistry. He wrote many books and articles popularizing chemistry, and sought to turn the results of his research to social use by marketing such products as a meat extract and artificial milk. He played a leading role in the formation of scientific laboratories and agricultural experiment stations. His scientific reputation, however, rests mainly on his role in the development of organic chemistry between 1829 and 1839.

As a child Liebig learned to perform chemical operations in the small laboratory his father maintained to supply a family drug and painting materials business. He reproduced many of the experiments described in the chemical books available in the town library. After watching an itinerant trader make the explosive silver fulminate, Liebig produced the same compound. He was much less interested in ordinary school subjects. Recognizing his preferences, his father apprenticed him to an apothecary. Within a year, however, he returned home to continue his experiments. In 1820 he went to the University of Bonn to study chemistry under Wilhelm Gottlob Kastner. He followed Kastner to Erlangen, where he received the doctorate in 1822. Liebig found Kastner unskilled in analyses and unable to provide comprehensive chemical instruction, and he continued his own investigation of fulminate of mercury. Liebig soon realized he would have to go abroad to complete his education, and he obtained from Grand Duke Louis I of Hesse a grant to study in Paris, where he remained from 1822 until early 1824.

Liebig attended the lectures of Gay-Lussac, Thenard, and Dulong, where he encountered a rigorous, quantitative, experimental chemistry unlike anything he had found in Germany and learned for the first time some of the general principles connecting his knowledge of particular compounds and processes. Continuing his own investigations of the fulminates, he submitted a memoir on the subject to the Académie des Sciences in December 1823. He argued that silver and mercury fulminate were salts of a peculiar acid which could not be separated from the metals except by combining with other metals, with which it formed a number of new salts. Among those impressed by his paper was Humboldt, who arranged for Liebig to work with Gay-Lussac. For Liebig this opportunity was the most important of his life, for with Gay-Lussac he not only mastered methods of analysis, but learned to pursue investigations systematically.

Their collaboration soon resulted in another memoir on the fulminates, a paper making apparent that Liebig had learned from Gay-Lussac to pay stricter attention to precise determinations of the quantitative elementary composition of substances. Among their new experiments was a combustion analysis of the percentages of carbon, hydrogen, and oxygen in the fulminates. Although Liebig had produced silver fulminate entirely from inorganic reagents, he and Gay-Lussac applied to it a modification of the method for organic substances that Gay-Lussac had helped to develop. Thus, although working in inorganic chemistry, Liebig was introduced to the general problem of organic analysis to which he afterward made major contributions.

Laboratory at Giessen. Humboldt once again gave timely aid by recommending to Louis I of Hesse that he provide Liebig with an academic position, and in 1824 Liebig was appointed extraordinary professor at the University of Giessen. He returned to Germany determined to make opportunities similar to that afforded him by his work with Gay-Lussac available to a larger number of students. Together with a mineralogist and a mathematician, he proposed that a pharmaceutical training institute be established. Their proposal was turned down, but they were permitted to set up the institution by themselves in a recently evacuated military barracks. By 1827 chemistry dominated the instruction, and the twenty places in the laboratory were soon filled.

Liebig's first laboratory consisted of one unventilated room, containing a large coal oven in the center and benches around the walls. Liebig had to buy most of the supplies and pay his assistant from his own modest salary. Nevertheless this laboratory saw the beginning of a whole new mode of training scientists. It was the first institution deliberately designed to enable a number of students to progress systematically from elementary operations to independent research under the guidance of an established scientist. A carefully planned program of exercises led the students from one stage to the next. Liebig's success derived in part from his own analytical skill and his magnetic qualities as a teacher, but in part also from the state of knowledge in chemistry. The science had attained to general principles which were technically demanding and which invited application to a nearly limitless number of particular cases. For the first time it offered great scope for clearly delimited research projects under the leadership of one man in command of the field. Even as he trained others, he was able to extend his own investigations far beyond what he could perform with his own hands. If other chemists wished to compete with him, they had little choice but to imitate his approach, and the example soon spread to other experimental sciences.

Students began by learning a system of qualitative analysis, that is, an orderly way to separate and identify the acids and bases present in a solid or solution of unknown composition. To develop this system Liebig drew upon a great knowledge of the chemical properties of the acids, alkalies, alkaline earths, metals, and salts in order to standardize a sequence of operations by which the presence of any of these substances in combination with any others in a given material could most effectively be determined. The procedure began with application of general reagents which separated the components of a solution into groups that could then be further separated and distinguished by more specific reactions. Liebig believed that mastery of these reactions was the first requirement for a chemist. In developing his analytical system he drew on the traditions of distinguished analysts both before and after Lavoisier. He later turned over the elementary teaching of this system to assistants, while he gave his attention to advanced students. Two of his assistants, Fresenius and Will, published textbooks outlining the methods which in modified form have been used by students ever since.

During his first five years in Giessen, Liebig carried out many investigations concerning methods for preparing known inorganic substances. When Wöhler published an analysis of silver cyanate giving the same composition that he and Gay-Lussac had found for silver fulminate, Liebig confirmed the unusual result. He drew from it the important new idea that two chemical compounds with entirely different properties could have the same elementary compositions, differing only in the manner in which the elements were joined. In 1829 he completed an extensive study of the decomposition of a variety of chemical combinations by means of chlorine. Among the compounds with which he reacted the gas was silver cyanide. He was attempting to convert the cyanic acid which Wöhler had previously investigated into a similar acid which Georges Serullas had produced from cyanogen chloride, but which seemed to contain more oxygen. Learning that Wöhler was pursuing a similar investigation, Liebig wrote to him, and they collaborated to settle the question of the relation between the two acids. After encountering a series of difficulties, Liebig found that Serullas's analysis of his cyanic acid was incorrect, that its percentage composition was the same as that of Wöhler's acid. Wöhler inferred that the two compounds were isomers, according to Berzelius' recent definition of that term, and renamed them, respectively, cyanuric acid and cyanic acid. Liebig and Wöhler continued the cooperation begun in this study,

became close friends, and made several important investigations in common.

Liebig also utilized chlorine in an effort to determine the composition of uric acid. The reaction produced cyanic acid, ammonia, and oxalic acid. Probably hoping to emulate Wöhler's synthesis of urea, Liebig tried unsuccessfully to compose uric acid from oxalic acid, potassium cyanate, and ammonia. Despite the indecisive result, his interest in uric acid carried him from inorganic into organic chemistry. He thought he might find a clue to the composition of the acid in an earlier discovery by Fourcroy and Vauquelin that horse urine yields benzoic acid. Liebig soon ascertained that the acid in the urine was distinct from benzoic acid but yielded the latter on distillation. He named the new compound hippuric acid.

Liebig's study of hippuric acid confronted him with some general difficulties in the elementary analysis of organic compounds. The customary combustion analysis, he found, gave unreliable results for nitrogen, because of the very small proportion of that element in the acid. He was able to reduce the error by using a method that he and Gay-Lussac had devised earlier for burning the compound in a vacuum. To determine the hydrogen content more accurately, he measured it in a separate analysis. This method enabled him to burn a larger amount of the compound than he could use in measuring the carbon, for the necessity to handle the carbonic acid gas that the latter element produced limited the quantity of the compound that could be analyzed. Liebig applied the same procedures to other organic acids, and entered the discussions arising then over the general question of the best method for elementary analysis. The procedures worked out by Gay-Lussac, Thenard, and Berzelius between 1810 and 1820 had become the customary method, but chemists were still seeking to improve on it. In 1830 Liebig wrote a critique of several recent efforts, arguing that the techniques he himself had worked out for hippuric acid best solved the crucial problems.

When Liebig turned to the analysis of alkaloids, he met further obstacles. He was attracted to these distinctive plant substances because an investigation of ten of them by Pelletier and Dumas had given the paradoxical result that the nitrogen in the various compounds, the supposed source of their alkaline properties, was not proportional to the quantities of acid with which each could combine. Liebig set out to improve the measurement of nitrogen, but he soon found that carbon also posed special difficulties. Because of the unusually large molecular weights of the alkaloids, errors of the order of 1 percent in the determination of carbon could lead to incorrect empirical formulas. The solution, he thought, would be to make it possible to analyze larger amounts of the organic compound, just as he had done earlier for hydrogen. In order to achieve this, Liebig made a crucial technical innovation. In his apparatus the combustion gases passed through a tube containing calcium chloride, which absorbed the water vapor. Then they entered a tube bent into a triangle, with five bulbs blown into it. A caustic potash solution in this tube completely absorbed the carbonic acid. He could then simply weigh the increase in the weight of the tube and dispense with the collection of gases pneumatically for non-nitrogenous compounds. He could now analyze in one operation ten times the amount of organic compound as by the older methods. In addition he made a number of small refinements, resulting in a much simplified, reliable procedure that soon became standard. He could, however, find no such satisfactory solution for the problem of nitrogen. He was able to improve the results Dumas and Pelletier had published for the nitrogen in the alkaloids, but he did this mostly by sheer persistence, repeating his analyses many times. The corrections he made partially resolved the theoretical problem with which he had begun, for he showed that within one class of the plant bases the nitrogen was strictly proportional to the quantities of sulfuric acid which would combine with them.

Although Liebig's new method for non-nitrogenous compounds did not immediately produce results strikingly better than had previously been attained, the simplifications he introduced eliminated much of the tedium and extraordinary skill formerly demanded. Not only could he analyze many more compounds in far shorter time than his predecessors, but he could entrust analyses to his students. Because he had many students, his laboratory began turning out hundreds of analyses annually. Liebig could now determine the elementary compositions not only of the most important organic compounds, but of all of the products of the reactions encountered in most of his investigations. His combustion apparatus became a symbol of the new era of organic chemistry that he helped to establish.

Liebig's organic research soon involved him in a question which was growing increasingly important as a consequence of the ability to depict the numbers of atoms of each element in more and more organic compounds. How are these atoms ordered in the molecules? The discoveries of different compounds with the same elementary proportions added urgency to the problem. In 1830 Berzelius showed that tartaric acid and racemic acid have identical compositions but distinguishable properties. On the basis of this and several previously reported examples, he predicted that such situations were commonplace, and named the compounds so related isomeric bodies. Liebig and Wöhler from their experiences with fulminic acid and cyanic acid were well prepared to appreciate the importance of isomerism. Impressed with Berzelius' investigation, they treated the results of their work on cyanic acid and cyanuric acid similarly and inferred that these compounds could be explained only "by a different arrangement of their molecules."

Dumas had already proposed one way to approach the problem of the ordering of atoms in compounds. An investigation of ethers (esters) in 1827 and 1828 had led him and Polydore Boullay to believe that olefiant gas, which they called *hydrogène bicarboné*, C_2H_2, acted as a base and combined with water, an acid, or both to form the various ethers and alcohol. [*Note:* Each chemist's original names and formulas are used here because the substitution of modern equivalents would be misleading. Dumas and most French chemists at this time adopted the atomic weight for carbon proposed by Gay-Lussac. Liebig followed Berzelius in taking a weight for carbon double Gay-Lussac's value. Consequently Dumas's formulas depict twice as many carbon atoms as those of Berzelius and Liebig. Berzelius' barred symbols indicating double atoms, dots for oxygen atoms, and variant symbols for elements such as chlorine and nitrogen have not been used.]

Dumas and Boullay represented a series of ethers as a sequence of compounds containing ammonia in place of olefiant gas. Their discussion implied that the elementary particles in organic molecules form persistent subgroups exchanged as units in reactions, just as ammonia is; and they assumed in their formulas that the groupings were in accordance with the electrochemical theory of Berzelius. Their theory attracted a great deal of attention, but Liebig and Wöhler dismissed it as an ingenious idea with no empirical foundation. They considered their own finding, i.e., that the same elements are combined in different ways to form cyanic acid and cyanuric acid, to be a sufficient refutation of Dumas's view. But Dumas for his part could see the same phenomena as additional support for his theory.

Despite his skepticism about Dumas's attempts to define groups of atoms which function as units in organic compounds, Liebig soon began to apply similar reasoning to other substances. In 1831 he analyzed camphor and camphoric acid. He depicted the composition of camphor as $6(2C + 3H) + O$, and that of camphoric acid as $5(2C + 3H) + 5O$, and he suggested that the unit $2C + 3H$ "acts as an elementary body." He admitted that his opinion could only be regarded as a hypothesis. A year later he and Wöhler were able to provide a far more impressive illustration of their case for a unit appearing in a series of compounds.

In 1830 Pierre Robiquet and Antoine Boutron-Charland had converted the oil of bitter almonds to benzoic acid by oxidation. They had also formed from the oil a neutral compound which decomposed to benzoic acid and another crystalline substance which formed the same acid. They named the crystalline material amygdalin, and inferred that the oil was a "benzoic radical." During the summer of 1832, Liebig and Wöhler repeated and extended the experiments of the French pharmacists. They were able to show that the conversion of oil of bitter almonds to benzoic acid can be represented as the replacement of two atoms of hydrogen by one of oxygen. They also produced a series of related compounds containing bromine, iodine, sulfur, and cyanide. From their elementary analyses they deduced that a "benzoyl radical," $C^{14}H^{10}O^2$, persisted unchanged through all of these reactions. Although unable to isolate the radical, they presented persuasive evidence that it actually existed. When Berzelius saw their result, he praised it as the most important step yet made in plant chemistry.

Liebig had several times undertaken studies of the action of chlorine on alcohol and on ether, but so many compounds had formed that he had given up the investigations. Late in 1831 he had more success. He devised a new method to decompose the alcohol, passing the chlorine gas through it and periodically driving off the hydrochloric acid that formed by heating the solution. This process left behind a new compound which he named chloral and which he wrote $C^9Cl^{12}O^4$. He discovered that chloral decomposed with alkalies to yield another compound containing only carbon and chlorine C^2Cl^5. He emphasized that these compositions satisfied not only the elementary analyses but the relationship of chloral to its decomposition products.

The hydrocarbon radical which Dumas and Boullay had defined in 1828 continued to be influential. The boldness of their generalization combined with the uncertainty of their evidence invited others to challenge their views, in part because their theory involved an explanation of one of the most important reactions in organic chemistry—the conversion of alcohol to ether by the action of sulfuric acid. The reaction was unusually complex because, depending on the conditions, a number of other products also formed. By 1827 chemists had become particularly interested in a compound known as "sulfovinic acid," which

appeared to accompany the formation of ether. The acid contained sulfur and a substance composed of carbon and hydrogen. Dumas and Boullay believed that the sulfur was in the form of sulfurous acid, and that the other substance was "oil of wine," another product of the etherification reaction that they had discovered and given the formula C^4H^3. Henry Hennell determined, however, that the hydrocarbon contained equal portions of carbon and hydrogen, and that therefore it was probably Dumas's and Boullay's *hydrogène bicarboné*. Unlike Dumas and Boullay, Hennell considered sulfovinic acid an essential intermediary in etherification, supporting his position with several elegant and persuasive experiments. Georges Serullas also analyzed the compounds associated with etherification, and concluded that the hydrocarbon in sulfovinic acid was *hydrogène bicarboné*, but combined with water to form ether. The conflict of opinions drew Liebig and Wöhler to study the acid in 1831.

The Ether Question. Liebig and Wöhler were able to show easily that Dumas's and Boullay's formula, C^4H^3, was based on incorrect elementary proportions. It was more difficult to decide whether the olefiant gas in sulfovinic acid was combined with water, in the form of ether, or directly joined with anhydrous sulfuric acid. Since they could not isolate the acid itself, they tried to deduce its composition indirectly by analyzing barium sulfovinate. Their results fitted either the interpretation that sulfovinic acid contains anhydrous sulfuric acid combined with alcohol or, as they thought more probable, hydrated sulfuric acid combined with ether. Either view, they thought, lent itself to a satisfactory explanation of the intermediary action of sulfovinic acid in the formation of ether.

Even though Serullas, Hennell, and Liebig and Wöhler had overturned certain of Dumas's and Boullay's conclusions, they had not undermined the general theory that alcohol, ethers, and related compounds were combinations of the same hydrocarbon base. The critics envisioned these compounds in the same way, and even strengthened the theory by making sulfovinic acid and oil of wine fit within the scheme more convincingly than its authors had done. Berzelius was not persuaded that the compounds were necessarily constituted in this way, but he acknowledged that such a representation placed so many phenomena in a simple and convenient order that the idea was worth attention. He believed, however, that the radical was not olefiant gas itself, but a multiple of it, which he named etherin.

New research soon forced further reassessments of the olefiant gas radical. In 1833 Gustav Magnus published the results of an investigation of sulfovinic acid, in which he claimed that the formula contained one molecule of water more than Liebig and Wöhler had assigned it. From arguments based on analogy and on the conditions under which sulfovinic acid was formed, Magnus inferred that two of the three atoms of water were attached to the hydrocarbon in the compound, forming alcohol with it. By reacting anhydrous sulfuric acid with absolute alcohol, he obtained a new acid containing only one molecule of water; he named it ethionic acid. In this acid, he asserted, anhydrous sulfuric acid is combined with ether in place of the alcohol in sulfovinic acid. Magnus depicted both alcohol and ether as compounds of the etherin radical, but he disputed Dumas and Boullay's view that the radical acts as a base analogous to ammonia. Meanwhile Pelouze was studying an acid similar to sulfovinic acid, but formed by the action on alcohol of phosphoric acid instead of sulfuric acid. Phosphovinic acid was more stable, so that Pelouze was able to dry and analyze it directly. The compound yielded carbon and hydrogen in the proportions necessary to form alcohol, from which finding Pelouze concluded that it was constituted from that substance combined with phosphoric acid. He too challenged the theory that the etherin radical plays the part of a base in such compounds. Liebig examined a sample of Pelouze's barium phosphovinate and saw that the substance absorbed water so rapidly that Pelouze's combustion analyses had shown an excess of hydrogen and carbon over the true composition of the dry salt. Liebig therefore analyzed the crystalline salt and subtracted from the measured carbon and hydrogen the elements of the water of crystallization. The results, he concluded, fitted the view that the salt was composed of phosphoric acid and ether.

The new studies of phosphovinic, sulfovinic, and ethionic acid induced Berzelius to change his views concerning the first-order compound radicals in organic chemistry. None of these acids could contain etherin and water, he thought, because the water ought then to be removable, like the water of crystallization in the corresponding salts of ordinary bases. Furthermore, if ether consisted of etherin plus one atom of water, and alcohol of etherin and two atoms of water, then sulfovinic acid ought to be convertible to ethionic acid by driving off some of the water. Neither did that occur, however, and therefore Berzelius asserted that alcohol and ether could not be hydrates of the same radical. Discarding the etherin radical, Berzelius proposed that alcohol and ether were oxides of different radicals composed of carbon and hydrogen. Ether he considered to be $C^4H^{10} + O$ and alcohol to be $C^2H^6 + O$. The compounds were, he thought, equivalent to the oxides of inorganic chemistry.

When Berzelius expressed these views to Liebig in a letter (May 1833), Liebig wrote back enthusiastically that they were the only satisfactory explanation of all the phenomena. He had, he said, been thinking along similar lines himself. Several months later he wrote an article for a chemical dictionary in which he took up the principal evidence for Dumas and Boullay's theory, and systematically refuted it. The first argument was that olefiant gas was supposed to combine directly with sulfuric acid to produce sulfovinic acid. Using olefiant gas specially purified of the ether and alcohol vapor which he believed usually to be mixed with it, Liebig found that the reaction no longer took place; he therefore asserted that it was not the olefiant gas but the ether ordinarily accompanying it that actually combined with sulfuric acid. The second case was a compound Zeise had recently produced by reacting alcohol with platinum chloride. Zeise had concluded that the resulting salt contained carbon and hydrogen in the proportions for olefiant gas, and no oxygen. According to Liebig, however, Zeise's own data fit better with a formula including oxygen, joined with carbon and hydrogen to form ether rather than olefiant gas. The most difficult evidence to counter involved a compound which Dumas and Boullay had produced by reacting dry ammonia with oxalic ether. From the fact that the resulting salt, which they named ammonium oxalovinate, yielded carbonic acid and nitrogen in the ratio of 8:1; and from some indirect considerations, they inferred that it was composed of oxalic acid, ammonia, and the radical *hydrogène bicarboné*. On repeating the reaction, Liebig found that the product he obtained was oxamide, with a ratio of carbonic acid to nitrogen of only 2:1. This outcome seemed to him to eliminate the last foundation of the etherin theory, for that radical could not be assigned to the composition of oxamide. Liebig believed that in eliminating Dumas and Boullay's theory he had firmly established that of Berzelius. He had no doubt that the radical of ether, C^4H^{10}, would soon be isolated, even though he failed in his first attempt.

Although Liebig supported Berzelius' conception of the ether radical, he could not accept the latter's opinion that alcohol was the oxide of a different radical. Some of the reactions of sulfovinic acid and phosphovinic acid, as well as the conversions of alcohol to compound ethers, involved principally the removal of water—so he argued—and were best explained by assuming that alcohol is the hydrate of ether. By thus rejecting one aspect of Berzelius' theory, Liebig attained much greater generality for Berzelius' ether radical. Giving it the name ethyl, and the symbol E, Liebig presented rational formulas based on it for over twenty compounds. Among them were the following, compared here with their interpretation according to the etherin theory:

	Ethyl Radical	Etherin Radical
Radical	$E = C^4H^{10}$	C^4H^8
Ether	$E+O$	$C^4H^8+H^2O$
Alcohol	$EO+H^2O$	$C^4H^8+2H^2O$
Hydrochloric ether (ester)	$E+Cl^2$	C^4H^8+2HCl
Sulfovinic acid	$(EO+H^2O)+2SO^3$	$C^4H^8+2SO^3+2H^2O$

Controversy With Dumas. Dumas strongly defended his own theory during the following years. He maintained his position that under the circumstances in which he had carried out the reaction of ammonia with oxalic acid, he did obtain ammonium oxalovinate, and he supported his view of its constitution with a fuller analysis of its elementary composition. Searching for a situation in which he could test the consequences derived from his theory, he noted that, according to his view, alcohol contains hydrogen in two states. Four volumes of hydrogen are combined with oxygen in water, and eight volumes with carbon in the hydrocarbon radical. It ought, therefore, to be possible to distinguish these two states in the reactions of the compound ethers. He found a verification of this prediction in the formation of chloral, the compound recently isolated by Liebig. Reexamining the reactions and products Liebig had investigated, Dumas detected a small amount of hydrogen, which Liebig had missed, both in chloral and in the decomposition product Liebig had described. Dumas renamed the latter chloroform. He gave the two compounds, respectively, the formulas $C^8H^2Cl^6O^2$ and C^2HCl^3. Stressing that in the reaction producing chloral from alcohol, ten volumes of hydrogen were replaced by only six of chlorine, Dumas explained the anomaly in terms of his view of the composition of alcohol, and of two substitution rules that he postulated. He then showed that similar rules could account for the conversion of alcohol to acetic acid. Later in the same year, Dumas and Eugene Peligot discovered a new compound "isomorphic" with alcohol, and a series of compounds analogous to those formed by alcohol. They interpreted these in terms of a new hypothetical radical, methylene, C^4H^4, corresponding to the *hydrogène bicarboné* radical. These investigations won Liebig's grudging admiration, in spite of his continuing dissatisfaction with Dumas's theoretical deductions.

In 1835 Liebig began deliberately to seek reactions which might contradict Dumas's ether theory. One such opportunity arose when he repeated some of the experiments of Magnus which had corrected his own work with Wöhler on sulfovinic acid. From the com-

position and reactions of Magnus' ethionic acid, Liebig inferred that during the formation of that compound one atom of oxygen from the sulfuric acid in the process must combine with two atoms of hydrogen from the ether to form water. Liebig considered that reaction to be proof that ether is not a hydrate of olefiant gas, for the water would not form at the expense of the elements of the ether and sulfuric acid if it were already present in the ether.

Shortly afterward Liebig discovered an important new compound which he thought revealed another fatal flaw in Dumas's theory. Since 1831, when Döbereiner had sent him an "ether-like" fluid obtained from the oxidation of alcohol, Liebig had tried several times to identify the resultant compounds. Döbereiner maintained that the fluid contained an "oxygen ether." In 1833 Liebig found two distinct compounds present. One of them, Döbereiner's oxygen ether, he examined more thoroughly and renamed acetal. Early in 1835 he was able to isolate the other substance. It turned out to be an unknown and extraordinarily volatile compound, which he called aldehyde. By analyzing aldehyde and its ammonium salt, he determined its composition to be $C_4H_8O_2$, and concluded that it is formed from alcohol by the loss of four hydrogen atoms. In keeping with his view of alcohol as the hydrate of ether, $C_4H_{10}O + H_2O$, he postulated that aldehyde is $C_4H_6O + H_2O$, and described it as the hydrate of C_4H_6O, an unknown oxide of a hypothetical hydrocarbon, C_4H_6. Liebig pointed out that if Dumas's view of the composition of alcohol as $C_4H_8 + H_4O_2$ was accepted, then aldehyde might be considered an oxide containing the same hydrocarbon radical, or $C_4H_8 + 2O$. This interpretation required fewer new hypothetical compounds. Liebig argued, however, that it would be impossible in these terms to account for the conversion of alcohol to aldehyde. It would have to be assumed either that the hydrogen in the water of the alcohol is oxidized, or that the alcohol gives up all its water at the same time that two atoms of oxygen are added to its radical. He regarded both possibilities as absurd.

At the same time Liebig drew a refutation of another feature of Dumas's theory from work done under his direction by Regnault. Dumas had listed the "oil of the Dutch chemists" first among the binary combinations of the *hydrogène bicarboné* radical. It was a substance obtained by reacting olefiant gas with chlorine, which he represented as C^8H^8, Cl^4. Regnault produced from the oil a new ether-like substance of composition $C_4H_6Cl_2$ (in Liebig's notation). Regnault concluded that in the reaction half of the chlorine of the Dutch oil was separated, together with enough of the hydrogen to form hydrochloric acid. It followed, he asserted, that the chlorine in the Dutch oil was combined in two different ways, so that Dumas's view of the compound as a simple combination of chlorine and olefiant gas could not be correct. Liebig triumphantly concluded that the "first limb" of Dumas's ether theory had been proven completely false.

In the fall of 1836 Liebig appended a lengthy footnote attacking Dumas's ether theory to a joint memoir reporting investigations he had made with Pelouze. First he countered the idea that olefiant gas is the basis of the composition of ether by rejecting supporting arguments that Dumas had derived from the reactions of analogous compounds. Then he enumerated ways in which the behavior of ether differed from that of hydrates and resembled that of oxides. Finally, he tried to prove that Dumas's rules of substitution, applied to his own formulas for ether and alcohol, failed to give results in accord with the reactions these compounds undergo, and that Dumas had used the rules inconsistently. He showed in detail how the conversion of alcohol to acetic acid, either directly or through the intermediary of aldehyde, and the formation of chloral, led to contradictions if Dumas's formulas and rules were applied strictly. Liebig believed that his note thoroughly destroyed the credibility of Dumas's ether theory and his rules of substitution.

As he confronted Dumas's theory, Liebig had presumed that he and Berzelius stood united in support of a shared ether theory, for he still regarded his view of alcohol as the hydrate of ether to be only an improvement on Berzelius' original theory. It was therefore very disappointing to find on reading Berzelius' *Jahresbericht* for 1836 that he was depicted as disputing Berzelius' own theory of the composition of ether and alcohol. Berzelius discounted Liebig's arguments and maintained his previous opinion that alcohol was too unlike ether to be merely a hydrate of it. In February 1837 Liebig wrote Berzelius to try to overcome his objections; he was anxious, he said, to reach an agreement, lest their division encourage the opponents of "the new ether theory." Later in the year Liebig found a new occasion to strike a blow at this opposition and simultaneously to try to dispel Berzelius' reservations. Recently Zeise had defended his earlier conclusion that the double salt formed by alcohol and platinum chloride was a combination of the etherin radical. Liebig asserted that even though Zeise's new analyses appeared more accurate than the older ones, the fit between observation and theory was fortuitous; his formula was based on elementary analyses alone, unsupported by relationships between the compound and its decomposition products. Zeise was, according to Liebig, basing his interpretation

mostly on a prior and misguided allegiance to the etherin theory. Reactions which could remove the oxygen and hydrogen of the water of hydration of alcohol demonstrated that that hydrogen was in a different state from the rest of the hydrogen in the compound. There were no grounds at all, however, for distinguishing any of the hydrogen atoms in ether from the others, so that ether must be a simple oxide of the hydrocarbon, rather than a hydrate. Finally Liebig tried to counter various objections that defenders of the etherin theory had raised against treating ether as an oxide.

Liebig's adamant defense of his ether theory and his relentless opposition to that of Dumas seems hard to reconcile with the attitude that both he and Dumas professed, that all of their theories were necessarily provisional. In principle both recognized that no theory yet available was general enough to encompass all the relevant data. They believed that they must formulate broad theories even though these might prove wrong, in order to organize a burgeoning mass of analytical results. Like Dumas and Berzelius, Liebig repeatedly said that debates over divergent theories were beneficial because the defenders of each were led to discover and analyze new compounds while searching for support for their views. In this judgment they were correct, for almost every investigation conducted to advance a particular theoretical goal revealed compounds and reactions which helped expand the foundations of chemistry. The stubbornness with which Liebig sought to advance his theory and to discredit that of his rival probably owed less to the issues than to the personalities.

As Dumas's influence grew after 1832, Liebig began to perceive him as the leader of the French school of organic chemistry, a school which he thought stood in opposition to himself and Berzelius. He believed that Dumas was using his dominant position to impose his views on the other chemists in Paris. As an influential independent voice, Liebig felt he had a duty to oppose these tendencies and to rescue French chemistry from the "false route" on which Dumas was directing it. Liebig was also resentful because he thought that the younger French chemists still acted as though no important investigations were going on outside Paris. In seeking to overthrow Dumas's ether theory Liebig was in part trying to make the French acknowledge him and his followers as a leading force in organic chemistry. Besides these calculated reasons for treating his scientific differences with Dumas as political struggles, there were strong emotional elements moving Liebig. Since 1830 he and Dumas had opposed each other repeatedly on both theoretical and experimental questions, and during the course of their published debates each had allowed himself to inter-ject into his arguments personal criticisms which wounded the pride of the other. Liebig was particularly prone to give free rein to the expression of heated reproaches which caused the disputes to take on a harshness out of proportion to the depth of their intellectual differences. Their scientific differences were not fundamental, and in 1837 it appeared possible that the two men might be able to reconcile them.

Since 1831 Pelouze had been Liebig's closest friend and colleague in Paris. They corresponded frequently, exchanging scientific news and research ideas. In 1836 Pelouze spent the summer in Giessen working with Liebig. When Liebig attached his attack on Dumas's ether theory to the joint memoir reporting these investigations, he was intentionally linking Pelouze with himself as the representative of his school in Paris, hoping that Pelouze could act as a counter-balance to Dumas's position there. No sooner had he done this, however, than it appeared that the alliance might have been constructed at Pelouze's expense; Pelouze had become a candidate for the Academy of Sciences, where Dumas had much influence. Liebig reflected that if he could reach a reconciliation with Dumas, Pelouze would have a better chance. Accord-ingly he wrote Dumas in May 1837, explaining away as best he could his motives for combating Dumas's theory and offering to put their quarrels behind them so that they could cooperate in the future. Dumas seemed pleased at the prospect of ending the hostilities, which he acknowledged had been a burden, and accepted Liebig's suggestion that they publish together. Liebig visited Dumas in October on his return from a trip to England; and the meeting went so well that Liebig left Paris feeling that all of the points in dispute had been settled and that he had converted Dumas to his ether theory. Dumas com-posed a note "Sur l'état actuel de la chimie organique," which he presented in both their names to the Academy. The note suggests that Dumas had not necessarily accepted Liebig's views, for their common beliefs were stated in propositions so general as to skirt the points of contention. He proclaimed their faith that the laws of combination and reactions in organic chemistry were the same as those of inorganic chemistry, but that the role played in the latter by elements was represented in the former by radicals. Further, the characterization of these radicals had been the constant task of both men for ten years, and they regretted that they had debated their differences of opinion so heatedly. They announced their new alliance and appealed to all chemists to join their effort to classify all organic compounds according to the radicals they contained. This "manifesto," as it

was soon called, was most unfortunate. Instead of resolving Dumas's and Liebig's disagreements, it suppressed them. Moreover it publicly committed them to a doctrine which both were already coming to doubt. Liebig had publicly and privately questioned whether fixed radicals really exist. Instead of uniting other chemists, the document divided them. Older chemists got the impression that Dumas and Liebig claimed to have originated organic chemistry and were dismissing the contributions of their predeces-sors. Younger chemists saw the program as an attempt by the two to set themselves up as privileged directors of the work of everyone else. Sensing the hostile reactions, Liebig sought to dissociate himself from the note and prevented its publication in German.

In 1837 Liebig regarded the defense of his ether theory as one of his principal tasks, and by the end of that year he was confident that he had eliminated all opposition to it. Yet two years later he acknowledged that the opposing views were basically the same. He now represented the compounds involved in the earlier debates as combinations of an acetyl radical, $Ac = C_4H_6$, and claimed that this system satisfied the aims of both of the earlier theories. This sudden switch in his attitude resulted from a complex blend of scientific and personal developments.

The origins of the acetyl radical were in Liebig's 1835 paper on aldehyde, which he had described as a combination of the hypothetical hydrocarbon C_4H_6. Shortly afterward Regnault produced two new com-pounds by reacting alcohol with bromine and iodine; he assigned to them the formulas C_4H_6Br and C_4H_6I. He thought these compounds and the Dutch oil, C_4H_6Cl, could best be regarded as combinations of the hypothetical radical C_4H_6, which he named aldehyden because he considered it the same as the radical which Liebig had discovered in aldehyde. Berzelius renamed Regnault's aldehyden "acetyl." From measurements of gas densities Berzelius con-firmed the application of Regnault's formulas to acetic acid and aldehyde, and by 1838 he wrote in his *Jahres-bericht* that there was a firm basis for the acetyl theory.

In his new system of 1839 Liebig extended the acetyl combinations to include the compounds formerly interpreted by the etherin or ethyl theories. Thus, if acetyl, C_4H_6, $= Ac$;

then
$$AcH_2 = \text{olefiant gas;}$$
$$AcH_4 = \text{ethyl;}$$
$$AcH_4O = \text{ether;}$$
and
$$AcH_4O + H_2O = \text{alcohol.}$$

Liebig added a long list of related compounds. Neither etherin nor ethyl appeared any longer as fundamental radicals, but as combinations of acetyl with hydrogen. The formulas were compatible both with his own view that ether is an organic oxide and with the view of Dumas and Boullay that the compounds of ether resemble those of ammonia. The man who had recently contrasted the emptiness of the etherin theory with the soundness of his own, now stated that from his new standpoint "both . . . theories have the same foundation." He could now compromise on the issue partly because he could appreciate more fully than before that the composition of ether had been less important for itself than as a testing ground for general principles of organic composition. He had already been to some degree aware of that. He had written in 1837 that the question of the constitution of ether embraced the general question of whether organic materials which contain oxygen were oxides of a complex radical or combinations of a radical with a compound body. He believed, therefore, that in settling the problem of ether he would orient all future investigations in organic chemistry. By 1839 he had recognized that so much could not depend on one case. The existence of organic oxides was so well established in other situations that he no longer needed to defend that concept by insisting that ether was the oxide of the ethyl radical. Liebig was also more flexible because he had become far less confident that there was any satisfactory single way to envision organic composition. He was readier to accommodate his views with those of Dumas because he was coming to see that Dumas's theoretical flexibility was more viable than the fixed principles that Berzelius maintained. Within this period the man whom Liebig had regarded since 1830 as his mentor came to appear to him as an increasingly rigid voice of the past. These shifts in Liebig's attitude grew largely out of the problem of organic acids.

The Problem of Acidity. By 1830 the unifying conception derived from Lavoisier's oxygen theory of acids was no longer intact. The discovery that muriatic and other acids contained no oxygen had led to the division of acids into two categories, oxacids and hydracids. When a hydracid reacted with an inorganic base it was thought not to combine directly but to decompose the base. The hydrogen formed water with its oxygen, while the metal of the base replaced the hydrogen of the acid. Oxacids were thought to be combined with a quantity of water which, unlike the water of crystallization, could not be removed by drying. These hydrated acids combined directly with bases, which displaced the combined water. According to Berzelius, a given acid, when reacted with different bases, always combined with quantities of the base containing the same amount of oxygen. If the resulting salt were neutral, the acidic oxide had the same number of atoms of oxygen as did the basic oxide. A few oxacids could be obtained both in the hydrous and anhydrous states, but in most cases the anhydrous acid was hypothetical. Its composition was inferred by subtracting the quantity of water separated during the formation of a neutral salt from the formula determined by analyzing the free hydrated acid. In this system the organic acids formed the class of oxacids of compound radicals. For the case of acetic acid these considerations led to the formulas $C_4H_6O_3$ for the theoretical anhydrous acid; $C_4H_6O_3 + H_2O$ for the aqueous acid; and $C_4H_6O_3 + BaO$ for the barium salt.

Most of the organic acids fitted very well into this scheme, but two anomalies developed. Oxalic acid contained so little hydrogen that the subtraction of a molecule of water from its formula left the anhydrous acid with no hydrogen at all. This peculiarity caused Dulong to propose in 1816 that oxalic acid was a hydracid, $H_2 + C_4O_4$. The second difficulty concerned citric acid. From the analysis of its lead salt Berzelius had given the anhydrous acid the formula $C_4H_4O_4$. During the summer of 1832 Jules Gay-Lussac, who was studying chemistry in Liebig's laboratory, performed an analysis of copper citrate, the results of which seemed to fit the formula for the hydrate of the acid rather than the anhydrous acid. Consequently Liebig asked Berzelius to reexamine his earlier analyses. A few months later Berzelius reported back that his new results were quite puzzling. The proportions of acid and base in the lead salt varied according to the acidity or alkalinity of the solution in which it formed, a phenomenon which he ascribed vaguely to the propensity of the acid to form acidic and basic salts. The sodium salt formed only a single combination of fixed proportions, but the amount of removable water of crystallization was equivalent to 2 1/3 atoms. The dry salt could be represented as $NaC_4H_4O_4 + H_2O$, but when heated further it lost one-third of an atom more than the formula indicated it contained. Berzelius could not give a satisfactory explanation for these results. It occurred to Liebig that the contradictions might be resolved if citric acid were considered to be $C_6H_6O_6$ or $C_3H_3O_3$. He suggested for the sodium salt the formula

$$2(C_6H_6O_6) + 3NaO + 11H_2O \text{ (or } 12H_2O\text{),}$$

which he thought accounted fairly closely for the amount of water lost in drying the salt. Berzelius objected, however, that the error would still be too large, and that it was contrary to experience for a neutral salt to have more atoms of base than of acid. Both men agreed that the problem could not be solved until organic chemistry had progressed further.

During the same years the number of organic acids under investigation began to grow rapidly. Some were isolated from natural materials; others, known as "pyrogenic" acids, were produced by heating the natural acids. In 1832 Liebig interpreted the conversion of meconic acid to "metameconic acid" as the removal of one atom of carbonic acid from each atom of meconic acid, leaving one-half atom of metameconic acid. Soon afterward Pelouze learned to produce simple controlled decompositions systematically, by distilling various acids at moderate, constant temperatures. In this way he found a sublimate of lactic acid which contained two equivalents of water less than the ordinary lactic acid. He converted tannic acid to gallic acid, interpreting the reaction as the loss of one equivalent each of carbonic acid and water. He treated similarly the conversion of malic acid to fumaric acid, and tartaric acid to pyrotartaric acid. Liebig followed these investigations with close interest and judged Pelouze's new approach to be one of the most important discoveries in organic chemistry.

Following the prevalent opinion of the time, Pelouze assumed that the pyrogenic acids were oxacids. Liebig, however, already considered the division between oxacids and hydracids to be unnatural. He and Wöhler had thought for a while of interpreting benzoic acid as a hydracid in 1832. A year later he speculated briefly that tartaric acid and malic acid might be hydracids. Early in 1836 he still seemed uncertain of his position on acids, but by the end of that year he was trying to persuade Berzelius that several organic acids were hydracids. He also asserted that there are organic acids that neutralize one, two, and three atoms of base. This break with Berzelius' general conception of salts was inspired by Thomas Graham's recent discovery that there are three types of phosphoric acid containing respectively three atoms, two atoms, and one atom of water replaceable by bases. Liebig believed that a number of organic acids are analogous to phosphoric acid. According to Berzelius, potassium cyanurate is $C_3N_3H_3O_3 + KO$. Liebig contended, however, that the so-called neutral potassium salt is $C_6N_6H_2O_4 + 2KO$, whereas the so-called acid salt is $C_6N_6H_4O_5 + KO$. He discovered a new silver salt which he depicted as $C_6N_6O_3 + 3AgO$. Thus in the second case one atom of base replaced one atom of water; in the first, two atoms replaced two of water; and in the third, three atoms replaced three of water. With meconic acid he obtained a silver salt containing two atoms of silver oxide and another containing three of silver oxide with no water. The same principles could explain the anomalies in the composition of citric acid.

A new analysis of silver citrate gave Liebig slightly more silver and less water than Berzelius had found, enabling Liebig to substitute for Berzelius' formula, $C_4H_4O_4 + AgO$, one that required three atoms of silver. Liebig wrote it $C_{12}H_{10}O_{11} + 3AgO$. Tripling the formula eliminated the fractional atoms Berzelius had encountered and favored the interpretation that citric acid, too, can neutralize three atoms of base. Liebig also argued that tartar emetic has four atoms of replaceable water. From Liebig's first letter, Berzelius thought that the replacement of water in these reactions represented the ordinary removal of water from acids and salts by heating. In a second letter Liebig emphasized that he had dried silver citrate and the salts of cyanuric acid at room temperature. His results, therefore, must directly involve the constitution of the acids themselves.

Liebig especially wanted to clarify that point because it was one of the reasons that he did not think his results could be interpreted by an adaptation of the oxacid theory to the idea of multiple bases. He was now convinced that alkali and metallic bases did not simply replace water already present in the acid, but that the oxygen of the bases combined with hydrogen to form the water. His other reason was that silver oxide, a weak base, could displace all the water, whereas potash, a strong base, could displace only part of it. This was anomalous under the old theory, but predictable in terms of hydracids. Silver is easily reducible and would therefore more readily give up its oxygen to the hydrogen. Consequently cyanuric acid was not $3Cy_2O + 3Ag$, but $C_6N_6O_6 + 6H$. He thought that potassium sulfate might similarly be regarded as $K + SO_4$ rather than $KO + SO_3$. Sulfates would then be exactly analogous to chlorides, and all compounds would fit into a simple, harmonious system.

Liebig returned to these ideas nine months later, as he set out on the reformulation of organic chemistry that he and Dumas had decided upon during their meeting. On 16 November 1837 he sent Dumas a letter proposing that they begin their collaboration by extending to the rest of the organic acids the consequences of his hypothesis that all acids are hydracids. Dumas hesitated and cautioned Liebig to be prudent about proposing theories. Although annoyed by this reaction, Liebig wrote again, explaining his ideas more fully, and succeeded in overcoming Dumas's reservations. In December Dumas presented a short note, "Sur la constitution de quelques acides," to the Academy summarizing the views on organic acids upon which they agreed. The contents came mostly from Liebig's two letters. The note summarized the arguments for considering citric acid, meconic acid, and cyanuric acid as tribasic, and stressed that by tripling the formula for citric acid the authors had resolved the dilemma that Berzelius' research had posed. They asserted that the phenomena could be envisioned in a simpler, more direct manner, if these acids were regarded as hydracids. Using tartaric acid as an example, they showed that in the old system complicated double formulas were necessary to represent salts such as cream of tartar. But if tartaric acid were a hydracid, $C_8H_4O_{12}$, H_8 then all of its compounds would appear as ordinary substitutions of different amounts of metal for equivalent amounts of the hydrogen. Thus:

$$C_8H_4O_{12} \begin{Bmatrix} K_2 \\ H_4 \end{Bmatrix} \text{ neutral potassium tartrate}$$

$$C_8H_4O_{12} \begin{Bmatrix} K \\ H_6 \end{Bmatrix} \text{ cream of tartar.}$$

The anhydrous acid assumed in the old theory would not exist. Relying entirely on the advantage of simplicity in representation as justification, and presenting only a few of the examples Liebig had worked out, the note did not reveal the full scope of his argument.

Even as he exchanged letters with Dumas concerning how they would proceed in their new venture, Liebig was becoming increasingly anxious about Berzelius' reaction to his acid theories. He wrote Berzelius repeatedly, expanding and developing his earlier arguments, and pleading for considerate, forbearing criticism. Berzelius tactfully referred to the analyses underlying Liebig's ideas as "highly interesting discoveries," but could not accept the explanation that the acids were hydracids. By February 1838 Liebig's hope that he could win Berzelius over was waning, and the rapprochement with Dumas had proved to be only temporary. When Pelouze read Dumas and Liebig's note on acids in the *Comptes rendus de l'Académie des sciences*, he saw that Dumas had referred to the fact that many citrates in addition to those investigated by Berzelius lose one-third of an atom of water. Pelouze was convinced that Dumas had appropriated without acknowledgment his own research on citrates, work which he had mentioned to Dumas in the fall of 1837. Pelouze therefore wrote Liebig expressing his displeasure. At first Liebig did not consider the problem serious, but during the exchange of letters and the events that followed he once again became suspicious of Dumas's motives. Moreover, Liebig had moved ahead with his research on the organic acids while, as far as he could see, Dumas had done no significant work on the problem. He persuaded himself, therefore, that Dumas was only seeking to share in the credit.

By mid-February, Liebig was nearly ready to publish his own results; he wrote Dumas that he had decided to give up their collaboration and that he would continue independently.

Liebig's massive article on organic acids, "Über die Constitution der organischen Säuren," appeared in April 1838. The first part contained his analyses of the acids and their salts and the remainder treated three related theoretical questions. Liebig gave detailed arguments for considering that some organic acids neutralize more than one base and that all acids are hydrogen acids. In addition he tried to account for the molecular rearrangements involved in the conversion of some of the organic acids to their related pyrogenic acids. In part he was extending the approach of Pelouze, but he was attempting also to explain in terms of changes in composition the decrease in the number of atoms of base which the resulting acids could neutralize.

The interpretive portion began with a discussion of phosphoric acid based on Graham's work. After reviewing the three series of phosphoric acid salts, Liebig proposed various ways in which the isomeric changes in the acid might be envisioned to account for the differences in the number of bases with which the three forms could combine. He also pointed out that the property of the acid of combining with more than one base revealed the uncertainty underlying the customary conception of neutrality. He suggested that the property that most clearly distinguished acids like phosphoric from the majority of acids was the ability to form true double salts such as sodium–potassium phosphate; for this capacity was the same as that of combining with more than one atom of a single base.

Liebig next applied the principles he had drawn from the example of phosphoric acid to the organic acids which embodied similar combining properties. From this viewpoint he depicted the constitution of cyanuric, meconic, citric, tartaric, mucic, malic, gallic, and aspartic acids, their salts, and their pyrogenic products. The case of meconic acid will illustrate his approach:

$$C_{14}H_2O_{11} + 3H_2O \quad \text{dried acid}$$

$$C_{14}H_2O_{11} + 3AgO \quad \text{silver salt}$$

$$C_{14}H_2O_{11} + \begin{Bmatrix} H_2O \\ 2AgO \end{Bmatrix} \text{ silver salt}$$

$$C_{14}H_2O_{11} + \begin{Bmatrix} 2H_2O \\ KO \end{Bmatrix} \text{ so-called acid potassium salt}$$

$$C_{14}H_2O_{11} + \begin{Bmatrix} H_2O \\ 2KO \end{Bmatrix} \text{ so-called neutral potassium salt}$$

Liebig showed that the pyrogenic acids related to meconic, citric, tartaric, and gallic acids usually neutralized only one or two atoms of base. For example, heat and concentrated acid transformed meconic acid into comenic acid, which could combine with two bases. The constitution of comenic acid he considered to be

$$C_{12}H_4O_8 + 2H_2O \text{ crystalline acid}$$

$$C_{12}H_4O_8 + \left.\begin{array}{l} H_2O \\ KO \end{array}\right\} \text{ so-called potassium salt, etc.}$$

In the formation of comenic acid two atoms of carbonic acid were removed. That did not account, however, for the loss of one-third of the saturation capacity, a change caused, according to Liebig, by the incorporation of one atom of the previously separable water into the acid radical itself, where it could no longer be exchanged for another base. The further conversion of comenic acid to pyromeconic acid involved the separation of another atom of carbonic acid and the transfer of another atom of water to the radical. The resulting constitution, $C_{10}H_6O_5 + H_2O$, accorded with the capacity of the acid to neutralize only one atom of base. Liebig described in a similar manner the conversions of other acids to their pyrogenic products, although some of the changes were more complex, and in some cases unsolved difficulties prevented him from accounting fully for the reactions.

In the last section of his article, Liebig noted that he had built the preceding interpretations on current conceptions of acids and bases. For certain of the phenomena, however, he could find no explanation in that system. Besides the previously mentioned paradox that silver oxide displaced more water than did potash, there was another question. Why, if the saturation capacity of an acid depends on water it contains, do those acids which lose part of their saturation capacity in the modifications that displace some of the water not regain both when they are placed again in water? Such situations suggested that it might be profitable to consider generalizing the view that some acids are hydracids. He ascribed the strangeness of resulting formulas such as $SO_4 + K$ mostly to habit, and argued that the hydrogen theory was as valid a way as the conventional theory to envision acids containing oxygen. The close similarity of various reactions of bases with the halogen acids and with oxygen acids such as sulfuric made it unlikely that water was formed in the first type and merely separated in the second. The hydrogen theory led to some deeper insights into the nature of compounds, which the oxygen theory could not provide.

A comparison of the acids formed by the various oxidation states of chlorine showed that their saturation capacities depended only on the amount of hydrogen present, not on the composition of the radicals. Liebig thought he could apply the same principle to numerous organic acids; various complicated combinations of elements could be added to their radicals without changing their saturation capacity. After completing a few more general arguments, Liebig sketched only briefly with a single example what the constitution of organic acids would be like in the framework of the hydrogen theory.

$$C_{12}H_4O_{10} + H_4 = \text{meconic acid}$$

$$C_{10}H_6O_6 + H_2 = \text{pyromeconic (comenic) acid}$$

Liebig carefully presented his theory as a hypothesis which might not necessarily express the true constitution of the compounds. He maintained only that it had guided him in his investigations, that it brought certain relations into a simple and general form, closing gaps that the prevailing theory could not close, and that he was deeply persuaded that the theory would lead chemists to important discoveries.

The paper on organic acids was one of Liebig's finest achievements, reflecting the best of the attributes that had marked his previous work. He based his position on precise analyses of numerous compounds. Some concerned substances he had discovered, but many were refinements of analyses done by others. He had not originated the theories he defended, but had greatly extended approaches drawn from Davy, Graham, Pelouze, and others. Through his extensive knowledge of compounds and reactions, he was able to amass impressive evidence for his inferences. He displayed a realistic sense of the value and limits of theoretical conceptions. He utilized flexibly such currently accepted foundations of reasoning as the radical theory. He was able to weld these elements into a comprehensive, unifying whole. He took a major step in one of the most important revisions in general chemical theory since the acceptance of Lavoisier's system of chemistry: a revision completed a few years later in the more universal statement of the hydrogen theory of acids by Liebig's former student, Gerhardt.

For Liebig his investigation of the organic acids only continued to be a source of personal turmoil. In part this was inevitable, for the new system he was building entailed the disruption of that which had guided Berzelius for many years and which had been the foundation for their scientific partnership. Recognizing the seriousness of the breach between them, both men made strenuous efforts to repair it. Liebig tried again and again to overcome Berzelius' disapproval of his new ideas. Diplomatically he portrayed them as generalizations of interpretations Berzelius himself had given in specific cases, and he appealed to Berzelius to join him in exploring the consequences of his theory. Berzelius studied Liebig's views with care, but he could not subscribe to them. Within the framework in which he viewed organic composition, Liebig's formulas were incomprehensible. Both men acknowledged that no single theory was exclusively true, which was a step toward reconciling their intellectual differences, but at the same time non-rational factors were making harmony difficult. Liebig had recently published the *Anleitung zur Analyse organischer Körper*, in which he had included several criticisms of details of Berzelius' methods. Berzelius was hurt by what seemed to him an abrupt dismissal of his earlier contributions, and began to feel that Liebig was trying to enhance his own reputation at the expense of his colleagues. Liebig expressed regrets at his thoughtlessness, and the two men appeared reconciled; but they were estranged again by Pelouze's quarrel with Dumas.

In January 1838 Dumas had assured Pelouze that his claims concerning the citrates would be given full credit in an article that he and Liebig would publish as soon as Berzelius had confirmed Liebig's analysis of silver citrate. By March, Pelouze felt that he could wait no longer, and he wrote Berzelius to find out if Berzelius actually intended to do the analyses in question. If not, Pelouze said, he planned to present his own case at the Academy of Sciences. In his letter Pelouze described Dumas's conduct in very harsh terms. Berzelius, who had long distrusted Dumas, wrote a letter to the Academy in which he not only supported Pelouze's assertion that the explanation given in the joint note of Dumas and Liebig of the loss of water in citrates was the same as that which Pelouze had written him, but attacked Dumas's theory of substitutions and the joint theory of organic acids as well. After Pelouze read this letter at the Academy, he and Dumas engaged in an acrimonious debate over what had actually happened. Liebig was soon drawn into the fracas. Pelouze and Dumas both sought to enlist Liebig's support, each writing to persuade him that honor and self-interest required Liebig to join him in defense against the accusations of the other. For a time Liebig sided with Dumas and unsuccessfully attempted to persuade Pelouze to drop the affair. Berzelius' open attack on his theory of organic acids greatly angered Liebig; and, in a letter to Dumas, he was led in turn to criticize Berzelius' acid theory. He authorized Dumas to read the scientific portions of the letter at the Academy.

As the dispute continued, however, Liebig's old suspicions about Dumas reasserted themselves. On the basis of a partial knowledge of what was happening in Paris, reflected especially in an inaccurate report in the daily press, Liebig decided that Dumas had violated his confidence and was manipulating him for personal advantage. By June 1838 he had made a "total break" with Dumas and thought of him as an "implacable" enemy. With Berzelius, however, he tried hard to repair the damage the events of the preceding weeks had done to their relationship. Patiently the two men renewed their efforts to reconcile their views about organic acids. Yet they were inexorably drifting apart, and Liebig was beginning to see Berzelius as a spent force in chemistry. Despite the personal enmity between Liebig and Dumas, they were coming to share a general conviction that organic chemistry was so much more complex than inorganic that new rules were required for it, and that whatever promised to simplify and order some of the phenomena deserved consideration. Like it or not, during the next two years Liebig was drawn toward an intellectual alliance with his most formidable rival directed against his most revered friend.

During the years that Liebig was preoccupied with the ether theory and with organic acids, he also carried out two important investigations with Wöhler. In October 1836 Wöhler wrote that he had discovered a way to transform amygdalin to oil of bitter almonds and hydrocyanic acid, by distilling it with manganese and sulfuric acid, and he invited Liebig to join in pursuing the topic. Two days later he made a more remarkable discovery. It had occurred to him that perhaps the transformation of amygdalin could be effected by the albumin in the almonds, in a manner similar to the action of yeast on sugar. He was able to confirm his expectation, for either crushed almonds or an aqueous emulsion derived from them produced the reaction. Wöhler suspected that the decomposition was an example of what Berzelius had recently defined as catalysis. Liebig and Wöhler then divided up the detailed examination of the properties and composition of amygdalin. They precipitated from the emulsion of almonds a substance which when redissolved retained its action. They named the active substance "emulsin." Its effectiveness in very small quantities confirmed that it acted like yeast. Liebig wrote up the memoir "Über die Bildung der Bittermandelöls," which they published in 1837, but the critical ideas and experiments came from Wöhler. Their characterization of emulsin, following that of diastase by Payen and Persoz, and of pepsin by Theodor Schwann, helped to generalize the conception of specific fermenting actions, which became a central theme in organic and physiological chemistry during the next decade.

Wöhler also provided the initial impulse for their other major joint investigation. In June 1837 he wrote Liebig that he had found a way to identify the constituents of uric acid by decomposing it in water with lead peroxide as the oxidizing agent. The products formed were urea, carbonic acid, and a colorless crystalline substance. Invited by Wöhler to take up the investigation with him, Liebig immediately determined the elementary composition of the new substance and identified it with allantoin, a compound long known to be present in the allantoic fluid of calves. The composition of uric acid was $C_5N_4H_4O_3$ and that of allantoin $C_4N_4H_6O_3$. Both men then started to examine other means of oxidizing uric acid. When Liebig attended the meeting of the British Association for the Advancement of Science later in the summer, he presented a preliminary report on the new work. He depicted the reaction which formed allantoin as:

$$C_{10}N_4H_4O_6 + Pb_2O_4$$

1 atom	2 atoms
uric acid	peroxide
	of lead

$$= \underbrace{CO + O_2 + 2PbO}_{\text{oxalate of lead}} + \underbrace{4Cy + 3H_2O}_{\text{allantoin}} + \underbrace{Ur.}_{\substack{\text{1 atom} \\ \text{urea}}}$$

On the basis of the reaction and the conventional assumption that a compound containing four elements must be formed by a union of binary compounds, Liebig interpreted uric acid as a compound of urea with a peculiar unknown acid, the latter containing the radical of oxalic acid combined with cyanogen. He represented this formulation as $4(CO + Cy) + $ urea. Wöhler came to Giessen at Christmas so that he and Liebig could complete the project together; but they found such an astonishing number of new compounds that they were unable to finish. Liebig continued the experiments through the spring, and the results were finally ready for publication in June 1838.

The paper, "Über die Natur der Harnsäure," described the conversion of uric acid into allantoin and then the products of its decomposition by nitric acid. In dilute nitric acid and ammonia, uric acid produced ammonium oxalurate, $C_6N_4H_8O_8$. In more concentrated cold nitric acid it yielded crystals of a water-soluble substance which they named alloxan and gave the formula $C_8N_4H_8O_{10}$. If an excess of ammonia were present the reaction produced instead the ammonium salt of purpuric acid, a remarkable

compound identified earlier by William Prout. Liebig and Wöhler renamed it murexid and considered its composition to be $C_{12}N_{10}H_{12}O_8$. Under other circumstances uric acid produced a substance they named alloxantin, the composition of which, $C_8N_4H_{10}O_{10}$, was closely related to that of alloxan. Alloxan could readily be converted to alloxantin by reducing agents, and back again with oxidizing agents. The diverse products of the direct decomposition of uric acid gave rise in turn to numerous other products. Among those that Liebig and Wöhler discovered and named were thionuric acid, uramil, uramilic acid, dialuric acid, alloxic acid, mesoxalic acid, and mycomelinic acid.

The complexity of the reactions made it difficult for Liebig and Wöhler to draw unequivocal conclusions concerning the rational constitution of the compounds involved. They elaborated essentially the same interpretation of the relation between uric acid and allantoin that Liebig had summarized the previous summer. They considered, as an admittedly provisional and "prejudiced" view, that urea preexisted in uric acid. Assuming this to be so, they subtracted the formula for urea from that for uric acid and derived a hypothetical body, $C_8N_4O_4$, which they named uril. They then proposed interpretations of reactions such as the conversion of uric acid to alloxan based on the supposed separation of uric acid into urea and uril. In general they recognized that the diversity of decomposition reactions made it impossible to deduce from the products that the same ones preexisted in the original compounds. Often two or more explanations of a reaction seemed equally conformable to the result. The most general conclusion they reached was that uric acid demonstrated that organic compounds undergo "innumerable metamorphoses," a characteristic setting them quite apart from inorganic compounds.

Further research on the decomposition products of uric acid occupied Liebig's laboratory during 1839, although he began to spend more of his time writing textbooks. He was now supreme in his field, and at the age of thirty-six at the peak of his experimental productivity. His grasp of theoretical issues was firmer yet more flexible than ever before, and he headed the largest scientific laboratory and school in the world. By August of that year additions to his laboratory and improved financial support enabled him to expand his training and research programs. Yet within a year Liebig had nearly given up those experimental areas in which he excelled and was devoting his energy to applications of chemistry in agriculture and physiology. To some extent his switch was a response to new opportunities; but it reflected also a weariness with the work he had been doing, and especially with the disputes which pervaded organic chemistry. In 1839 and 1840 the debates over Dumas's substitution theory reached a climax, as Dumas responded to new objections by Berzelius. Liebig supported the basic conception of substitution, and dissociated himself from Berzelius' alternative explanations of the reactions Dumas had used to support his theories. Early in 1840, however, Pelouze joined the opposition to Dumas and urged Liebig also to join in refuting the substitution theory. As he saw himself in danger of being pulled into further arguments dominated by personalities more than by issues, Liebig began to feel an aversion toward the activities of chemistry. He therefore turned to new subjects, in part to escape the impasse he had reached in his old field.

If Liebig's significance were to be judged in terms of his lasting tangible contributions to organic chemistry, the emphasis would have to be on the methods he devised or refined, and the many compounds and reactions he discovered or described. Few of his theories were highly original, and none of them definitive. Yet a summation of Liebig's achievements in terms of discoveries and general theories is bound to underrate his stature, for that is measurable more by the way in which he participated in a crucial stage in the development of chemistry. The manner in which he did organic chemistry was as important as the tabulation of his results. Through the reliability of his analyses, the thoroughness of his examination of all the products and reactions related to any particular problem, the quality of his reasoning, and the soundness of his judgment about most theoretical issues, Liebig helped his contemporaries and successors to see more clearly how the science ought to be pursued. Similarly, his new way of training chemists was as important as the many excellent chemists he himself taught. He helped to set standards in another way in his role as the critical editor of the *Annalen der Pharmacie und Chemie*, a journal he turned into the preeminent publication in chemistry. Liebig did as much as any one person to bring about the era of large-scale research, in which the ability to organize men became as critical as the ability to conceive and carry out experiments. Between 1830 and 1840 he was at the very center of the rapidly growing field of chemistry and he gave it an impetus that was felt long after he had ceased actively to participate in it.

Agricultural Chemistry. Liebig moved into his new areas of interest at his usual pace. Within four months after he began systematically studying the relation of organic chemistry to agriculture and physiology, he had produced the first version of one of the most important books in the history of scientific agriculture. In a letter to Berzelius in April 1840, he wrote that he had derived his general arguments from several surprising discoveries. First, from analyses of straw, hay, and fruits, he reached the "very remarkable result" that a given area of land, whether cultivated field or forest, produces each year the same total quantity of carbon in the composition of whatever plants grow on it. That inference became the starting point for his argument that the carbon must derive from the atmosphere rather than from humus in the soil. The problem of the source of nitrogen had "long occupied" him, he said, but after he found ammonia in the sap of every plant he investigated he became persuaded that the nitrogen must come from ammonia dissolved in rainwater, and he found that all of it contained determinate amounts of ammonia. Next Liebig examined the alkalies and alkaline earths in plants. Because they were always present, he presumed that they were essential, and set out to explain why they nevertheless varied according to the soil in which the plants grew. He surmised that the total equivalent quantity of base must be constant for a given species of plant, but that one type of base might substitute for another. He verified this prediction by reference to analyses that other chemists had made of the ashes of evergreens. Pine trees grown in one locality contained magnesia, while those grown in another place did not, but the total oxygen content (and thus by current acid-base theory the saturation capacity) of the potash, lime, and magnesia was in both cases the same. Fir trees grown in different regions also yielded different proportions of the specific alkalies, but the same total, a total which differed from that of the spruce ashes. Liebig thought these uniformities could not be accidental, and he explained them by postulating that the bases served to neutralize the organic and inorganic acids which were characteristic, essential constituents of each type of plant. Liebig drew a last key observation from the sad experience of a farmer near Göttingen who had grown absinthe in his fields to use as a source of potash; he found afterward that he could not raise ordinary crops in the field because the potash of the soil was exhausted. From all these considerations Liebig concluded that the true purpose of a fertilizer is to supply ammonia and such salts as potassium silicate, calcium phosphate, and magnesium phosphate to plants. He wrote Berzelius that a large number of practical applications for farmers could be developed from his results, and he would describe them in a forthcoming book.

Liebig's letter implied that he had derived his views on agricultural chemistry chiefly from investigations he had carried out himself. No doubt he felt he had, and the observations and calculations he made may well have been decisive in shaping his opinions. Yet in the short time he had devoted to the subject he could not have mastered the whole field of investigation, and the full treatment he published shortly afterward shows that he drew most of his arguments from the work of others and from strongly deductive reasoning. He had ably and impressively reviewed an area of activity that was new to him but that had been pursued with varying intensity for several decades. He joined the scattered conclusions of his predecessors into the most comprehensive picture of the problems of plant nutrition that had ever been presented, using his own findings at certain crucial points to decide between alternative theories.

Liebig's *Die organische Chemie in ihre Anwendung auf Agricultur und Physiologie* (Brunswick, 1840; English trans., *Organic Chemistry in Its Applications to Agriculture and Physiology* [London, 1840]) begins with a discussion of the role of carbon in plant nutrition. He refuted the widely held theory that humus, the product of the decay of plant matter, formed the main nutrient substance for plant growth and supported the view that the source of the carbon assimilated into plant substances is the atmosphere. The stability of the carbonic acid content of the air, despite the continual exhalation of that compound by animals, required that something else must be continually removing it from the atmosphere. Even though the percentage of carbonic acid in the air was very small, the atmosphere contained an ample amount to supply all of the plant material on the surface of the earth. The most important plant function, Liebig asserted, was to separate the carbon and oxygen of carbonic acid, releasing the oxygen and assimilating the carbon into compounds such as sugar, starch, and gum. In a later section he admitted uncertainty as to whether carbon was separated and joined with the elements of water to produce these compounds, or whether the plant in fact separated the oxygen from the water and combined its hydrogen with carbonic acid. He favored the latter alternative, because it was evident that in the formation of waxes, oils, and resins, the hydrogen in excess of the proportions of water must come from the decomposition of water.

Liebig denied the view that the consumption of oxygen and the exhalation of carbonic acid by plants at night constituted a "true respiration." That transformation was, he thought, a purely chemical decomposition. He believed that the starch, sugar, and gum formed by the primary nutritive process were transported throughout the plant and converted by numerous further metamorphoses into the special constituents of such parts as the flowers and fruit. Liebig's general picture of plant physiology was not original; he had obtained most of it from the earlier investigations of Priestley, Sénebier, Ingen-Housz, and Saussure. Through his knowledge of recent developments in organic chemistry, however, Liebig was able to give many more examples of chemical processes of the kind that might occur in plants. From the elementary compositions of various plant compounds he could calculate the amounts of carbonic acid and water consumed, and of oxygen released, in the formation of a given quantity of each compound. Although he had not investigated directly the chemical processes in plants, he could depict impressively the types of metamorphoses which he supposed took place by likening them to the metamorphoses he had produced in the laboratory. The creation in the laboratory of such important organic compounds as formic acid, oxalic acid, and urea enabled him to predict that vegetative processes would be explained through chemistry. One of his main purposes was to persuade botanists and physiologists that they must pay more attention to chemistry if they were to make further progress.

This glimpse of a chemical understanding of the internal processes of vegetables was, however, not what gave Liebig's book its most forceful impact. Whatever explanations he gave of the necessity for certain nutrient materials in terms of their role in plant growth, his views on the external sources of the substances he deemed essential were what aroused immediate interest, for these conclusions directly impinged on agricultural practices. The source of hydrogen was no problem, since all agreed that it was water. Nitrogen was a more pressing question. To support his claim that plants are supplied with nitrogen by means of ammonia washed out of the atmosphere, Liebig had to dispose of the fact that the ammonia in the air is so small in amount as to be undetectable, whereas nitrogen gas constitutes about 80 percent of the atmosphere. His confirmation that ammonia exists in rainwater provided him with an important supporting argument, but his conviction was based on his general chemical experience. Atmospheric nitrogen is one of the least reactive of substances, whereas ammonia enters readily into many organic compounds, a large number of which Liebig had investigated. Therefore he considered it most probable that ammonia is also the medium through which nitrogen is introduced into the constitution of plants. His reasoning was typical of the approach which Liebig and other organic chemists brought to the discussion of physiological questions; that is, they expected to predict the behavior of the substances within living organisms from their knowledge of chemical properties of elements and compounds in laboratory reactions. The separation of carbon from oxygen by plants was the one great and mysterious exception to this rule: "a force and capacity for assimilation which we cannot match with an ordinary chemical action, even the most powerful."

Turning to the inorganic constituents of plants, Liebig elaborated his view that plants need alkalies and alkaline earths to neutralize their essential acids. Analyses of ash contents, he contended, form the basis for determining the requirements of different plants for bases. Because these contents differ from one plant to another, some plants can flourish in soils that will scarcely support others. After finishing his discussion of plant nutrients, Liebig drew the appropriate lessons for agriculture. Cultivation of the same crop year after year gradually diminishes the fertility of the soil as the inorganic constituents essential to the growth of that crop are depleted. Rotation of crops can extend the resources of a given field because one plant can utilize those particular bases that the other did not require, but eventually the soil will become totally infertile unless these elements are returned to it. Allowing land to lie fallow slowly restores its fertility because the weathering of minerals gradually restores the acids and bases. A rational agriculture, however, would sustain fertility more effectively by supplying artificially the necessary elements. Liebig defined fertilizer as the means for adding to the soil the nutritional requirements of crops not supplied naturally from the atmosphere. The composition of a good fertilizer therefore varied according to the ash content of each specific crop. Fertilizers should ordinarily be composed of bases such as lime, potash, and magnesia, but since all plants contain phosphoric acid that compound should be included also. Liebig considered the best source of phosphoric acid to be pulverized animal bones. The bones should be dissolved in sulfuric acid and the phosphoric acid would thus be freed to combine with the bases in the soil. The best available sources of the other inorganic salts were plant ashes and human and animal excrement. But Liebig looked forward to the day when chemical industries would be able to produce salts to make up specific fertilizers for each crop.

Liebig was then rather ambivalent about the need for nitrogen in fertilizers. The ammonia derived from rainwater was sufficient, he argued, for natural plant growth, but plants could convert added ammonia into greater yields of nitrogenous organic compounds, and therefore increase the supply of the important nitrogenous constituents of human and animal diets. Gypsum, calcium chloride, and sulfuric acid were effective in increasing growth because they transferred ammonia from ammonium carbonate to less volatile salts so that the ammonia remained in the soil until absorbed by plants.

Liebig's book excited an unexpectedly intense interest among practical agriculturalists, especially in England, where his former student, Lyon Playfair, acted as translator and propagandist. Playfair arranged for large-scale tests of Liebig's ideas on several farms. In America some of his ideas also aroused a lively response. Liebig thus became more deeply involved in the application of his general ideas to actual farming practices. The changing titles that he gave his book symbolized his shifting conception of the scope of the topic with which he was dealing. The work appeared first in French (April 1840) as volume one of a *Traité de chimie organique*, with the explanation that Liebig was publishing it separately because the material lay outside of chemistry proper. The German edition, four months later, reflected that situation directly in its title. In later editions the adjective "organic" disappeared.

Although he had taken up the subject as an application of organic chemistry, which he regarded as the chemistry of materials of biological origin, the problem had proved to have different boundaries; the analysis of inorganic compounds had in fact become dominant. The main additions Liebig made in the second edition were efforts to specify more concretely the types of fertilizers that would be suitable for particular crops in given localities. Thus he discussed the mineral constituents characterizing the major crops in England as a guide to the selection of inorganic fertilizers. Anticipating the substitution of artificial for natural fertilizers, he suggested a method for converting the ammoniacal liquid left over from industrial production of coal gas into a purified ammonium sulfate. Stressing that knowledge of the composition of soils was the basis for the whole system of rational agriculture, he appended a long list of soil analyses carried out earlier by Kurt Sprengel. In the third edition (1843), Liebig revised his previous opinion that agriculturists should supplement the natural supply of nitrogen by adding or fixing ammonium salts. The addition of nitrogenous fertilizers alone, he said, could not augment the fertility of a field, for its productivity increased or decreased in direct proportion to the mineral nutrients provided in its fertilizer. In keeping with his greater emphasis on the mineral requirements of plants, he added analyses performed in his laboratory of the ash contents of various crops.

In 1845 Liebig took another step toward the practical implementation of his theories; he devised instructions for making artificial fertilizers formulated entirely of mineral salts that were combined in proportions corresponding to the ash contents of various crops. Muspratt and Co. of Liverpool put them into production. The venture proved a severe setback for Liebig's views, for nowhere did the fertilizers cause increased yields sufficient to cover costs. Surprised and dismayed, Liebig purchased a plot of sterile grazing land outside Giessen and began to investigate why his fertilizer was ineffective. Between 1845 and 1849 he managed to convert the plot into a fertile field, but he remained puzzled by the slowness of the action of the fertilizer. Not until over a decade later did he identify the cause of the difficulty. In order to prevent the potash from being washed out of the soil, he had fused it with calcium carbonate into a highly insoluble combination, and its insolubility had prevented the plant roots from absorbing the alkali. By this time he realized that he need not have worried about soluble salts being removed by rainwater, because the topsoil itself absorbed and held them. Meanwhile the error had threatened to discredit the general principles he had espoused.

At Rothamsted, in England, Lawes and Gilbert tested one of Liebig's fertilizers on wheat and found no noticeable increase in production, whereas ammonium salts added annually brought about significant improvements year after year in the harvests. Lawes and Gilbert regarded these results as a refutation of Liebig's entire "mineral theory," and other agriculturists came to regard it as a hastily conceived mistake. The success with guano, a substance rich in ammonia, seemed further to contradict Liebig's views. Liebig defended himself ably, however, in a series of polemic tracts published during the 1850's. Lawes and Gilbert's experiments were not decisive, he argued, because they had conducted their investigation under conditions which precluded a fair test of his fertilizer. From their description of the fields they had used, Liebig inferred that the soil already contained such ample quantities of the essential minerals that the provision of more thorough fertilizers could not significantly affect its productivity. Furthermore, he asserted that the English experimenters had misrepresented him, for he had not claimed that agricultural yields are dependent solely on the addition of mineral constituents to the soil, nor that it is never useful to add ammonia. He had only stated that in most cases it is superfluous to supplement the natural supply of ammonia and that fertilizers cannot be evaluated by their nitrogen contents. The current fashion for fertilizing with nitrogenous salts, he believed, would simply cause the mineral stores of the soil to be more rapidly exploited by quicker plant growth; if not supplemented by proportionate quantities of mineral fertilizers that practice would only deplete the soil sooner. Farmers, he contended, must think beyond the objective of obtaining the largest possible crop in a given year. In order to protect their capital, they must preserve the productivity of their land for future years by restoring to it all that their harvests removed. Nitrogen is replenished from the atmosphere but minerals come from the soil alone, and therefore it was the minerals with which they must be chiefly concerned.

While defending his theories, Liebig also clarified them. The discrepant effects of fertilizers in different situations led him to perceive that the addition of any one constituent to a field has value only in relation to the availability of the other required constituents of a given crop. If one is lacking, even though all others are in excess, plants will still not thrive. The addition of a single constituent will increase the crop only if a particular soil can deliver the other necessary constituents in greater quantities as well. Depending on the circumstances, therefore, any of the essential minerals might become the controlling factor. This generalization became known as Liebig's "Law of the Minimum."

In 1862 Liebig completed an expanded seventh edition of his *Chemistry in Its Applications to Agriculture and Physiology;* the sixth edition had appeared in 1847. The new book was the most comprehensive statement of his views, backed with the most extensive analytical and field data, and it was also his last major scientific endeavor. His theories remained controversial and vulnerable. Some of the issues dividing him from his critics could not be settled at the time, for the question of the source of nitrogen depended on phenomena they did not yet understand. Liebig's role in agricultural chemistry was far different from his earlier role in organic chemistry. In both areas he displayed an acute perception of central issues and was a powerful advocate for his own opinions; but in organic chemistry he had also been the most distinguished experimentalist of his time. He could support his theoretical positions with analyses he knew to be more reliable than those of most of the chemists who disagreed. In agricultural chemistry he did carry out important analyses of plant composition and tested fertilizers on a small scale, but he was aware that for the large-scale investigations which would decide the key questions he was dependent on other people. He could act only as catalyst and critic, providing the chemical principles and the theory which he claimed would lead agriculturists to achieve significant investigations. When these agriculturists reached conclusions which appeared to contradict his views, he could not improve on their experiments, but only complain that they had failed to follow his reasoning. He could not direct the emergence of a new science from the inside, as he had done in organic chemistry, but only draw on the influence he had attained through his earlier leadership to induce others to follow the program he had laid out.

In agricultural chemistry, Liebig also indulged in bolder speculative conclusions than he had done in his previous investigations. In organic chemistry his deep knowledge of the properties and reactions of compounds had helped to control his theoretical bent. He acquired his knowledge of agriculture more hastily and largely at secondhand, and his reasoning from chemical principles was less checked by anticipations of complicating physiological or physiographical factors. From the rebuffs of his initial views, he learned to be a good deal more cautious. Yet he justly claimed that even though he had made mistakes, even though there were in the first edition of his book the most extraordinary inconsistencies and the greatest disorder, its appearance had completely changed the nature of the problem of scientific agriculture. Before 1840 it was generally believed that both plant and animal life were dependent on the circulation of an organic, previously living material. Now, whatever opinion individuals held on specific points, they agreed that the nutrient substances of plants were inorganic. That change had transformed the objectives of agriculture, for under the older conception the potential production of foodstuffs would seem to have a fixed limit, whereas in the new view an unbounded increase in organic life appeared possible.

Liebig's students and followers provided much of the means for the rigorous scientific study of agriculture that he envisioned, as they began to set up experiment stations in Europe and the United States. In that way they gradually removed the questions involved from the control of the scientifically unsophisticated farmers who had caused Liebig so much trouble. His abrupt change of subjects in 1840 thus marked a crucial step in the emergence of modern scientific agriculture.

Physiology. After finishing his first treatise on agricultural chemistry in 1840, Liebig entered with equal intensity into the study of animal chemistry. He brought to this topic the same confidence that his knowledge of the chemical properties of organic compounds would enable him to infer the transformations occurring within living organisms; the application of quantitative chemical methods would solve the problems that physiologists had failed to solve. He had already become interested in nutrition in 1838 when G. J. Mulder found that the elementary compositions of plant albumin, animal fibrin, casein, and albumin were identical. During the next three years Liebig's students verified and extended Mulder's results. From that basis Liebig concluded that animals receive the chief constituents of their blood already formed in their nutrients. He developed the idea that the nitrogenous plant substances were assimilated in the blood and organized tissues of animals, while starch, sugar, and other nonnitrogenous compounds were consumed in respiration. During 1841 and 1842 Liebig expressed his physiological ideas in three articles, then elaborated them more extensively in his book *Die Thierchemie oder die organische Chemie in ihrer Anwendung auf Physiologie und Pathologie* (Brunswick, 1842; English trans., *Animal Chemistry or Organic Chemistry in Its Applications to Physiology and Pathology* [London, 1842]). He maintained that animal heat is produced solely by the oxidation to carbon dioxide and water of the carbon and hydrogen of the nutrient compounds. The idea dated from Lavoisier's experiments on combustion and respiration, but during the intervening years some physiologists had proposed other views, and the most thorough experimental investigations undertaken had cast some doubt on it. Liebig had no new evidence to prove Lavoisier correct, but from his understanding of chemical reactions it seemed to him that there was no other possibility. Liebig broadened the combustion theory by perceiving that the respiratory oxidations were net reactions, encompassing the cumulative results of all of the transformations that nutrients may undergo while in the body. He also examined the mutual proportionalities between the internal nutritive metamorphoses within an animal, its respiratory exchanges, intake of food, excretions, and production of heat or work.

Beyond establishing such general principles, Liebig attempted to deduce the actual chemical transformations which the three classes of nutrients undergo within the body; and in order to depict these more concretely, he constructed hypothetical chemical equations similar in form to those he and his colleagues had been using to interpret the reactions of organic compounds in their laboratories.

Liebig's *Animal Chemistry* aroused sharply divergent reactions. Some accepted it uncritically as a revelation of the true inner workings of animals and humans. Others were so antagonized by its speculative excesses that they refused to credit the important insights it contained. Even those who reacted against it, however, began to view the chemical phenomena of life differently than they had before, for Liebig had provided one of the first comprehensive pictures of the overall meaning of the ceaseless chemical exchanges which form an integral part of the vital processes. A few men adopted it as a guide for further investigation, and Bischoff and Voit based the field of energy metabolism on Liebig's ideas. As with his agricultural chemistry, Liebig's physiological writings provided an impetus which outlasted the refutation of some of his specific theories.

By transferring his investigations into agriculture and animal chemistry, Liebig had hoped to avoid further disputes with his old rival Dumas, but to his dismay Dumas's interests were moving in the same direction. In August 1841 Dumas published a lecture which expressed nutritional ideas similar in general outline to those Liebig had already presented in his agricultural chemistry, and also to those on animal chemistry which he had begun to teach in Giessen. Liebig now accused Dumas of plagiarism, a charge that could only exacerbate the earlier bitterness between them. Over the following years Liebig engaged Dumas and his associates Boussingault and Payen in a debate over the most prominent difference between their respective physiological views. Liebig had asserted that animals can convert dietary starch into fats, whereas the French chemists insisted that the source of all animal constituents, including fats, is in plant nutrients. The French chemists carried out extensive feeding experiments on bees, geese, hogs, and cattle, which were expected to demonstrate the sufficiency of dietary fat, but which instead proved Liebig to be correct. The outcome enhanced the prestige of Liebig's physiological views.

Industrial Chemistry. Liebig did not directly involve himself in industrial chemistry as he did in agricultural chemistry, but his indirect influence was nearly as great. Many of his students founded or worked in the new large-scale chemical factories, and a number of the analytical methods he developed for research purposes found important industrial applications. Most decisive, however, was his effect on the dye industry. In 1843 Ernest Sell, a former student who had recently set up a plant to distill coal tar, sent Liebig a sample of a light oil which he had produced. Liebig asked one of his assistants, August Wilhelm Hofmann, to analyze the oil. Hofmann separated two organic bases, one of which, afterward named aniline, reacted with concentrated nitric acid to give a deep blue fluid that became yellow and then deep scarlet when heated. Liebig, who had already been interested in colored organic compounds as potential sources of dyes,

predicted that aniline would have important effects on the dye industry. At first, Hofmann was more interested in using the new substance to help solve a theoretical question previously raised by Liebig: organic bases contain a hypothetical compound, amid (NH_2), combined with an organic radical, so that the radical substituted for one of the hydrogens of ammonia. Hofmann, who had found by the usual elementary analyses that aniline has the formula $C_{12}H_7N$, interpreted its composition in the light of Liebig's view, as

$$\left.\begin{array}{c} H \\ H \\ C_{12}H_5 \end{array}\right\} N.$$

Hofmann then began to try to substitute other organic radicals for the remaining hydrogen atoms. He followed this general approach over the next two decades, and it eventually yielded many of the compounds which formed the basis for the synthetic dye industry that burgeoned after 1860. Thus Liebig provided the institutional, analytical, and conceptual framework within which Hofmann began the study that helped give birth to the first industry based entirely on the application of the results of systematic scientific research.

In 1839 Liebig advanced the theory that fermentation is caused by the decomposition of a nitrogenous material, the reaction of which evokes a similar decomposition in another compound such as sugar. Although formulated mainly because of his dissatisfaction with Berzelius' definition of catalysis, which in Liebig's view provided no explanation for the phenomena it designated, the theory placed Liebig in the middle of the debate over whether fermentation is a vital or a purely chemical process. Ultimately his position drew him into a famous controversy with Pasteur, who defended with great resourcefulness the belief that living microorganisms are essential for fermentation.

In 1852 Liebig left Giessen for Munich. His old laboratory had continued to attract students from all over Europe, and increasingly from the United States, but he himself had grown weary of the unremitting burdens of his teaching. In Munich he had an institute built to his specifications, with better research facilities than in Giessen and a large lecture hall. He no longer carried on a formal program of instruction, but allowed only a few selected assistants and students to work in his laboratory. He himself continued to do some experiments, mostly following up certain aspects of his earlier research; but he devoted most of his time to writing, especially in support of his agricultural ideas. In the livelier milieu of Munich he also became more involved in society than he had been. He instituted a popular series of evening talks on scientific topics of broad interest. Although he remained quite active until his last illnesses, it was for Liebig a more quiet time than those twenty-eight hectic years when he was one of the most formidable figures of a formidable scientific age.

BIBLIOGRAPHY

The articles by Liebig and his contemporaries on which this text is based are mostly found in Poggendorff's *Annalen der Physik und Chemie*, Liebig's *Annalen der Pharmacie*, and the *Annales de Chimie et de Physique*. Indispensable sources are *Berzelius und Liebig Ihre Briefe von 1831–1845*, Justus Carrière, ed. (Munich, 1893; repr. Wiesbaden, 1967); and *Aus Justus Liebig's und Friedrich Wöhler's Briefwechsel in der Jahren 1829–1873*, A. W. Hofmann, ed. (Brunswick, 1888). The correspondence of Berzelius and Pelouze in *Jac. Berzelius Brev*, H. G. Söderbaum, ed. (Uppsala, 1941), supp. 2, contains useful references to Liebig.

Convenient descriptions of the analytical methods used in Liebig's laboratory are Justus Liebig, *Instructions for the Chemical Analysis of Organic Bodies*, William Gregory, tr. (Glasgow, 1839), and Henry Will, *Outlines of the Course of Qualitative Analysis Followed in the Giessen Laboratory* (London, 1841).

Carlo Paoloni, *Justus von Liebig. Eine Bibliographie sämtlicher Veröffentlichungen* (Heidelberg: Carl Winter, 1968), contains a full bibliography of Liebig's articles and books and published collections of letters, and a list of secondary literature concerning Liebig.

The most important collections of MSS of Liebig are in the Bibliothek der Liebig-Museum-Gesellschaft and the Universitätsarchiv of the Justus Liebig Universität in Giessen, which contain especially documents concerning Liebig's laboratory; and the Bayerische Staatsbibliothek in Munich, which has an extensive collection of correspondence.

The discussions in the present article based on unpublished letters between Liebig, Pelouze, and Dumas are derived from the following sources: the letters from Liebig to Pelouze and to Dumas are preserved in the Dumas dossier at the Archives of the Académie des Sciences in Paris; letters to Liebig from Pelouze and from Dumas are in the Bayerische Staatsbibliothek. I am grateful to these two institutions for making available to me microfilms of these documents.

Liebig's laboratory in Giessen is preserved as a museum in the state in which it existed after the additions of 1839.

The most extensive biography of Liebig is Jakob Volhard, *Justus Von Liebig* (Leipzig, 1909). A. W. Hofmann, *The Life-Work of Liebig*, Faraday lecture for 1875 (London, 1876), gives a laudatory but valuable discussion of Liebig's personality and contributions to organic chemistry. Many of the chemical investigations discussed above are summarized in J. R. Partington, *A History of Chemistry*, IV (London, 1964). For Liebig's agricultural chemistry, see F. R. Moulton, ed., *Liebig and After Liebig: a Century of Progress in Agricultural Chemistry*, Publications of the American Association for the Advancement of Science, no. 16 (Washington, 1942); and Margaret W. Rossiter, *Justus Liebig and the Americans: a Study in the Transit of Science, 1840–1880* (unpub. diss., Yale Univ., 1971).

For Liebig's animal chemistry, see F. L. Holmes, "Introduction," to Justus Liebig, *Animal Chemistry* (New York, 1964); and *Claude Bernard and Animal Chemistry* (Cambridge, Mass., 1974); and Timothy O. Lipman, "Vitalism and Reductionism in Liebig's Physiological Thought," in *Isis*, **58** (1967), 167–185.

Liebig's role in the controversies over fermentation is treated in Joseph S. Fruton, *Molecules and Life* (New York, 1972). Liebig's laboratory at Giessen is discussed most recently in J. B. Morrell, "The Chemist Breeders: the Research Schools of Liebig and Thomas Thomson," in *Ambix*, **19** (1972), 1–47. For Liebig's influence on the dye industry, see John J. Beer, *The Emergence of the German Dye Industry* (Urbana, Ill., 1959).

F. L. Holmes

LIESGANIG, JOSEPH XAVER (*b*. Graz, Austria, 13 February 1719; *d*. Lemberg, Galicia [now Lvov, U.S.S.R.], 4 March 1799), *astronomy, geodesy*.

Liesganig was the son of Wolfgang Lisganig, *Hofmeister* of Graz, and his wife Rosalie. He entered the Society of Jesus in 1734 and received his education at the Jesuit College in Vienna. From 1742 to 1751 he served the order in various academic and ecclesiastical posts (having been ordained in 1749) in Austria, Hungary, and Slovakia; in 1752 he returned to the Vienna Jesuit College as *professor matheseos*. At the same time he was attached to the Jesuit astronomical observatory (of which he was appointed prefect in 1756, a position he held until the order was suppressed in 1773) and professor of mathematics at the University of Vienna. He was made dean of the university's philosophical faculty in 1771.

Liesganig's scientific career may be said to have begun with his prefecture of the observatory. In 1757, at the suggestion of Bošković, Liesganig constructed with Joseph Ramspoeck a ten-foot zenith sector that indicated tangents instead of angles. He also designed a quadrant (built by Ramspoeck) with a radius of two and one-half feet; it was provided with micrometer screws for accuracy in reading. Another of Liesganig's instruments consisted of a Graham clock fitted with a gridiron compensation pendulum.

In 1758 Liesganig had used his zenith sector to determine the latitude of Vienna to be 48° 12′ 34.5″.

In 1760 Maria Theresia, at Bošković's urging, commissioned Liesganig to survey the environs of the city. Liesganig for this purpose obtained from Canivet a copy of the Paris toise, on which he calibrated the Vienna fathom. During the following years, Liesganig established a series of bases near Wiener Neustadt and in the Marchfeld region; he incorporated these into a triangulation system with the azimuth of Mt. Leopold, near Vienna, and calculated the geographic latitudes of Warasdin, Brünn (Brno), and Graz. (A later survey, made in 1803, confirmed the exactness of Liesganig's measurements of the Graz–Vienna–Brünn triangle, but found other errors in his survey which were attributed to defects in his azimuth zenith.) He also carried out experiments with a seconds pendulum (1765) to determine the length of the Vienna fathom, and made computations with a sphere in which the reduction to sea level represented 2.3 fathoms per degree of meridian.

In 1769 Liesganig undertook a survey in Hungary between Szeged and Peterwardein (now Petrovaradin, Yugoslavia). For this purpose he constructed bases near Kistelek and Csuróg and linked them, by a chain of twenty-six triangles, to the meridian of Budapest. In connection with this project Liesganig wrote a manual on map-making methods, preserved in manuscript in the Vienna war archives.

From 1772 until 1774 Licsganig was engaged in a trigonometric survey of East Galicia and Lodomeria (now Vladimir-Volynsky, Ukrainian S.S.R.), which had just become a part of that province. He made use of five brass quadrants that had been built to his specifications by Ramspoeck and the Viennese clockmaker Schreibelmayer; each was equipped with a movable telescope having a cross-hair micrometer at the focal point and a fixed telescope having a micrometer at the focal point of a microscope. (These instruments could also be used as spirit levels.) During the same period Liesganig observed solar azimuths in Lemberg, near Cracow, and in Rzeszów, reducing all the measurements to the meridian and clock of the Lemberg observatory. At the same time he held the position of Imperial and Royal Building Inspector in that city and from 1775 was professor of mechanics at the Collegium Nobilium there, as well as provincial director of military engineering and navigation.

Liesganig made six circular maps from his data of the Lemberg area, although these lacked place names and topographical information. In 1784 he reviewed the cadastral survey of the area of Gutenbrunn, in Lower Austria; the following year he took over the direction of the cadastral survey of Galicia and prepared for it a manual that was translated into Polish, Czech, Slovene, and Italian. In this work he recommended that measurements be made in local linear units to permit their comparison to the Vienna fathom.

BIBLIOGRAPHY

I. ORIGINAL WORKS. Liesganig's writings include *Tabulae memoriales praecipue arithmeticae tum numericae tum literalis cum tabulis tribus figurarum* (Vienna, 1746); *Prolusio ad auditores matheseos* (Vienna, 1753); *Tabulae memoriales praecipue arithmeticae tum numericae tum literalis, geometriae, etiam curvarum et trigonometriae, atque utriusque architecturae elementa complexae* (Vienna, 1754); "A Short Account of the Measurement of Three Degrees of Latitude Under the Meridian of Vienna," in *Philosophical Transactions of the Royal Society*, **58** (1767), 15–16; and *Dimensio graduum meridiani Viennensis et Hungarici, Augustorum jussu et auspiciis suscepta* (Vienna, 1770).

II. SECONDARY LITERATURE. For early biographical literature, see Constant von Wurzbach, *Biographisches Lexikon des Kaiserthums Österreich*, XV (Vienna, 1866), 179–180. Important details are in Franz Freiherr von Zach, "Über die Sternwarte von Lemberg," in *Monatliche Correspondenz zur Beförderung der Erd- und Himmelskunde*, **4** (1801), 547–550.

See also "Zusätze des Herausgebers: Über die Lemberger Sternwarte, über die trigonometrische Aufnahme von Galizien und Lodomerien und die darauf gegründete Karte dieser Länder, und über die geographische Bestimmung von Lemberg," *ibid.*, 550–558; "Nachschrift des Herausgebers zu D. Seetzen's Reise-Nachrichten," *ibid.*, **7** (1803), 24–36; "Geographische Bestimmung einiger Orte in Ungarn, aus Liesganig's Ungarischer Gradmessung, nebst einem Verzeichniss aller in Ungarn astronomisch und trigonometrisch bestimmten Orte," *ibid.*, 37–48 (including commentary on 50–52 attributed in most biographies to Liesganig); "Beweis, dass die Oesterreichische Gradmessung des Jesuiten Liesganig sehr fehlerhaft, und zur Bestimmung der Gestalt der Erde ganz untauglich war," *ibid.*, **8** (1803), 507–527, and **9** (1804), 32–38, 120–130.

More recent treatments of Liesganig are Günther, in *Allgemeine deutsche Biographie*, XVIII (Leipzig, 1883), 637; A. Westphal, "Basisapparate und Basismessungen," in *Zeitschrift für Instrumentenkunde*, **5** (1885), 257–274, 333–345, 373–385, 420–432 (esp. 342–345, 374); Ernst Nischer, *Österreichische Kartographen. Ihr Leben und Wirken* (Vienna, 1925), esp. pp. 76–80; Richard Krauland, "Legales und internationales Meter in Österreich," in *Österreichische Zeitschrift für Vermessungswesen*, **37** (1949), 30–42; K. Lego, "Abbé Joseph Liesganig zur 150. Wiederkehr seines Todestages," *ibid.*, 59–62; Paula Embacher, "Die Liesganig'sche Gradmessung," *ibid.*, **39** (1951), 17–22, 51–55; and Herwig Ebner, "Joseph Liesganig. Ein Beitrag zu seiner Biographie," in *Blätter für Heimatkunde*, **36** (1962), 129–131.

WALTHER FISCHER

LIEUTAUD, JOSEPH (*b*. Aix-en-Provence, France, 21 June 1703; *d*. Versailles, France, 6 December 1780), *anatomy, medicine.*

Lieutaud was raised by his uncle, the physician and botanist Pierre-Joseph Garidel. He received a degree in medicine at Aix and a later, honorary one from Paris in 1752. Lieutaud moved to Paris and, with the help of Sénac, chief physician to Louis XV, began a career as a royal physician. He held successive appointments as physician to the royal children (in 1755), chief physician to Monsieur and to the Comte d'Artois, and finally chief physician to Louis XV. An essentially modest man, Lieutaud then asked J. M. F. de Lassone to assume his duties at court so that he might devote his time to his own research. By so doing he further stimulated the professional activity of the other court physicians, as well as that of the doctors of the Versailles infirmary, of which he was more or less the director.

Lieutaud's lifework was strongly oriented toward practical medicine, a notion that was then being defined. Practical medicine as such rejected all theoretical systems and speculative etiologies; in the schools it sought to replace Latin with the vernacular to benefit physicians who should "read little, see a great deal, and do a great deal," as Fourcroy later put it. Such medicine was to be concerned with facts, not opinions, and to be learned at the bedside and in the autopsy room. While it might be illuminated by the "preliminary sciences"—that is, by "most of mathematics, experimental physics, chemistry, anatomy, natural history, etc."—erudition alone was insufficient to the discipline. Lieutaud, as one of the leaders of the new school, "reproached those whom he saw occupied solely with accumulating books" (although he himself possessed a splendid library, in part inherited from his uncle).

For these reasons Lieutaud devoted a great deal of attention to postmortem observations. From 1750 on, he examined more than 1,200 cadavers at the Versailles infirmary, as well as attending the autopsies of the son of the dauphin (1761), the dauphin (1765), and the dauphine (1765). He used postmortem materials to study both normal anatomy and pathology; he further undertook to determine the correlation between the symptoms recorded during the life of a patient and the physical lesions found after his death. Lieutaud thus established a method based upon complete and precise observation of the patient which was carried on by his students, including Pierre Edouard Brunyer, his successor at the infirmary. He may thus be considered one of the French pioneers in the pathological anatomy and anatomico-clinical concept of disease that gradually replaced the various medical systems of the eighteenth century.

Lieutaud's clinical practice included the inoculation of his patients against smallpox, using Sutton's method. Lassone reported to the Académie des Sciences the successful results of a series of inoculations that Lieutaud performed on 18 June 1774 at the Château of Marly; this communication contributed greatly toward modifying the generally conservative French attitude toward inoculation. Lieutaud himself reported to the Academy on a number of subjects, including the pathology of the gall bladder; empyema of the frontal sinus; hydrocephalus; osteoma of the cerebellum; pathological anatomy of the spleen, heart, and stomach; hydatids of the thyroid; laryngeal polyps; and the correlation between stomach contraction and splenic hypertrophy (or, conversely, between stomach distension and splenic hypotrophy). This last finding was accepted by Haller and Soemmerring, but criticized severely by Bichat.

Like his clinical work, Lieutaud's writings were directed toward practical medicine. His *Essais anatomiques* of 1742 was widely read for thirty years, and was given a scholarly second edition, as *Anatomie historique et pratique*, by A. Portal in 1776–1777. Although Lieutaud's intent was to place basic practical knowledge of both normal and pathological anatomy (which he considered to be two branches of the same field) at the disposal of the practitioner, his book and the techniques presented in it surpassed this aim. The first part of the book is devoted to descriptive anatomy, while the second gives precise instructions for dissecting both mature and fetal human bodies, ending with a "recapitulation" that is actually an essay on topographical anatomy in which Lieutaud demonstrates the disposition of the organs in one system after another. (It is typical of Lieutaud's thoroughness that in the second section he devoted a full seven pages to the technique for dissecting the middle and inner ear.)

In *Précis de la médecine pratique* of 1759, Lieutaud offered a classification of diseases as being those of the general population or those affecting men, women, or children, respectively. He set out the symptomatology of each disease and discussed the therapy for it; although he treated surgical therapy only in broad outline, his prescriptions of medical treatments are fully detailed. The book includes a number of case histories drawn from Lieutaud's own observations and from the literature.

Précis de la matière médicale (1766) is a catalog, with an index in both French and Latin, in which Lieutaud classified drugs by their pharmaceutical complexity and gave directions for their compounding and their therapeutic indications. In it he recommended the use of simple, "domestic" (or "Galenic") medicines, of which the effects are well known, and denounced the polypharmacy of the Arabs and the pyrotechnical remedies that had been fashionable in the preceding century. Lieutaud's standards for inclusion in his materia medica were, indeed, so strict that he here presented "only a twentieth part" of the contents of other contemporary manuals.

Lieutaud's work earned him admission to the Académie des Sciences as a corresponding member in 1731; in 1751 he became adjunct anatomist and, in 1759, associate anatomist. He was also a member of the Royal Society. He remained a grateful friend of the Paris Faculty of Medicine, and did not hesitate to support it against its opponents—as when on 22 December 1777 he arranged to present at court Sigault, who had, against the unanimous advice of the Académie Royale de Chirurgie, just performed a symphysiotomy on a woman named Souchot. Although he actively opposed the founding of the Société Royale de Médecine, which was nonetheless accomplished by Lassone and Vicq d'Azyr in 1778, he later accepted its presidency.

Lieutaud died five days after contracting pneumonia; faithful to his principles, he refused all remedies. He was by royal favor buried in the Ancienne Église near Notre-Dame de Versailles. He had previously sold his library to the Comte de Provence, who had allowed him to continue to use it; at the death of the Comte de Provence Lieutaud's books were taken to Versailles, where they now constitute the bulk of the medical collection of the municipal library. His name is perpetuated in the medical literature in Lieutaud's sinus, Lieutaud's uvula, and, especially, Lieutaud's body—the triangular area, limited by the interureteric fold and by the uvula of the bladder, that he isolated and described.

BIBLIOGRAPHY

I. ORIGINAL WORKS. Lieutaud's communications to the Académie des Sciences, all published in *Histoire de l'Académie royale des sciences*, include "Observations sur la vésicule du fiel, sur une quantité très considérable de pus dans les sinus frontaux, sur deux livres au moins de sérosité très claire, trouvées dans les ventricules du cerveau," in *Histoire . . . année 1735* (1738), 16–22; "Observation sur un corps osseux . . . trouvé dans le cervelet d'un jeune homme de 18 ans . . .," in *Histoire . . . année 1737* (1740), 51; "Observation sur la grosseur naturelle de la rate," in *Histoire . . . année 1738* (1740), 39; "Sur une maladie rare de l'estomac, sur le vomissement et sur l'usage de la rate, sur un écu de six livres avalé, sur une maladie singu-

lière . . .," in *Histoire . . . année 1752* (1756), 45–49, 71–75; "Relation d'une maladie rare de l'estomac avec quelques observations concernant le méchanisme du vomissement et l'usage de la rate," *ibid.*, 223–232; "Observations anatomiques sur le coeur," *ibid.*, 244–265, 308–322; "Observations anatomiques sur la structure de la vessie," in *Histoire . . . année 1753* (1757), 1–26; "Observations anatomiques sur le coeur. Troisième mémoire contenant la description particulière des oreillettes du trou oval et du canal artériel," in *Histoire . . . année 1754* (1759), 369–381; and "Observations sur les suites d'une suppression et sur les hydatides formées dans la glande thyroïde, sur un polype en forme de grappe, situé immédiatement au dessous du larynx," *ibid.*, 70–74.

Lieutaud's books, most of which were published in several editions, are *Essais anatomiques contenant l'histoire exacte de toutes les parties qui composent le corps de l'homme avec la manière de disséquer* (Paris, 1742); 2nd ed. by A. Portal, as *Anatomie historique et pratique. Nouvelle edit. augmentée de diverses remarques historiques et critiques et de nouvelles planches*, 2 vols. (Paris, 1776–1777); *Elementa physiologiae, juxta solertiora, novissimaque physicorum experimenta et accuratiores anatomicorum observationes concinnata* (Amsterdam, 1749); *Précis de la médecine pratique, contenant l'histoire des maladies et de la manière de les traiter avec des observations et remarques critiques sur les points les plus intéressants* (Paris, 1759); *Synopsis universae praxeos medicae in binas partes divisa* (Amsterdam, 1765); English trans. by E. A. Atlee as *Synopsis of the Universal Practice of Medicine. Exhibiting a Concise View of all Diseases, Both Internal and External; Illustrated With Complete Commentaries* (Philadelphia, 1816); *Précis de la matière médicale, contenant les connaissances les plus utiles sur l'histoire, la nature, les vertus et les doses des médicaments, tant simples qu'officinaux, usités dans la pratique actuelle de la médecine avec un grand nombre de formules éprouvées* (Paris, 1766); and A. Portal, ed., *Historia anatomica medica, sistens numerosissima cadaverum humanorum extispicia, quibus in apricum venit generina morborum sedes, horumque reserantur causae, vel patent effectus. Recensuit suas observationes numero plures adjecit* (Paris, 1767).

II. SECONDARY LITERATURE. On Lieutaud and his work see the article under his name in *Biographie universelle ancienne et moderne*, XXIV (Paris, 1819), 470–471; that by A.-L. Bayle and A.-J. Thillaye, in their *Biographie médicale*, II (Paris, 1855), 321–322; and A. Chéreau, in *Dictionnaire encyclopédique des sciences médicales Dechambre*, 2nd scr., II (Paris, 1876), 555–556.

See also M. Bariéty, "Lieutaud et la méthode anatomoclinique," in *Mémoires de la Société française d'histoire de la médecine*, 3 (1947), 13–16; P. Brassart, "Contribution à l'étude du monde médical versaillais sous le règne de Louis XVI et pendant la Révolution," medical thesis, University of Rennes (1965); P. Delaunay, "Le monde Médical parisien au XVIIIème siècle," medical thesis, University of Paris (1906), 443–453; and C. Fiessinger, "La thérapeutique de Joseph Lieutaud," in his *Thérapeutique des vieux maîtres* (Paris, 1897), 250–256.

Éloges are that published anonymously in *Histoire de la Société royale de médecine . . . année 1779* (1782), 94–117; and Á. de Condorcet, in *Mémoires de l'Académie royale des sciences . . . année 1780* (1784), 46–59.

PIERRE HUARD
MARIE JOSÉ IMBAULT-HUART

LIGNIER, ÉLIE ANTOINE OCTAVE (*b.* Pougy, Aube, France, 25 February 1855; *d.* Paris, France, 19 March 1916), *botany.*

His father, who was probably a farmer, is described on Octave's birth certificate as a landowner. Nothing is known of the botanist's primary and secondary schooling. He obtained his bachelor of arts degree in Paris in 1873, and a baccalaureate in science at Lille in 1880.

As teaching assistant in the Faculté des Sciences at Lille, he worked under the direction of the paleobotanist Charles Eugène Bertrand and helped to organize the Botanical Teaching and Research Laboratory. He subsequently helped to reorganize the Botanical Gardens, which had been moved from Lille to La Louvière. At the same time, he was working toward his licentiate, which he was awarded in 1882, having studied under the geologist Gosselet and the zoologist Giard, as well as Bertrand. In 1887 he received his doctorate in natural sciences from the University of Paris. In the same year he was appointed assistant lecturer in the Faculté des Sciences at Caen, where in 1889 he was made full professor.

When he first arrived in Caen, the town had only a few collections of dried plants, a Municipal School of Botany, some greenhouses, and a park. Lignier had to compile a catalog, which he published with B. Le Bey, and later with M. Lortet. Through sheer persistence he succeeded in having a botanical institute built. His teaching covered all aspects of botany, including paleobotany. He published some 110 writings of his own and coauthored others. His work encompassed both existing and fossil plants.

His anatomical research was directed particularly at the floral organs, seeds, and fruit of the Myrtaceae, Oenothera, Cruciferae, and Fumariaceae, and at the vascular bundles of the stems and leaves of many families, but only part of his research was ever published. He regarded the Gnetales as angiosperms.

He published some remarkable studies of the Bennettitales of Normandy. He was wrong, though, in believing the *Bennettites morierei* to be parthenogenetic, which he inferred from the closed micropyles that he had found in them, and he assumed that the loss of sexual reproduction was responsible for the disappearance of progeny.

He was also interested in paleozoic materials, specifically the *Radiculites reticulatus*, which he first placed in the Taxodiaceae and then assigned to the *Poroxylon*, close to the *Cordaites*. Finally, he described for the first time with rare precision fossil woods that came from Normandy.

But what attracted the attention of the world's leading paleobotanists were Lignier's theories on evolution and proposed classifications. Among his theories were the cauloid concept, involving an undifferentiated fundamental element with dichotomous ramification, which underlies the theory of the present telome, and the meriphyte concept, which attributes such great importance to the fibrovascular system of the leaf in phanerogams.

He contributed greatly to our understanding of the group of Articuleae, a name which he invented to cover various genera. He became interested also in the *Stauropteris* because of their relevance to theory.

Concerning the hypotheses advanced by E. A. N. Arber and J. Parkin on the Euanthostrobiles and the Proanthostrobiles to explain the origin of the angiosperms, Lignier was generally inclined to go along with them, although he did suggest some modifications. He disagreed in particular with the conclusions about the Bennettitales. Notwithstanding G. R. Wieland's opinion, he regarded their fruiting as an inflorescence and not as a flower or part of a flower.

BIBLIOGRAPHY

I. ORIGINAL WORKS. For a listing of Lignier's writings, see *Titres et travaux scientifiques de M. Octave Lignier* (Laval, 1914).

II. SECONDARY LITERATURE. For further information on Lignier's work, see L. Emberger, *Les plantes fossiles dans leurs rapports avec les végétaux vivants* (Paris, 1968). pp. 157–158, 382, 651; C. Houard, and M. Lortet, "Rapport annuel pour 1916 sur l'Institut botanique et les collections botaniques de Caen," in *Bulletin de la Société linnéenne de Normandie*, 6th ser., **9** (1919), 237; E. C. Jeffrey, "Octave Lignier," in the *Botanical Gazette*, **62** (1916), 507–508; D. H. Scott, *Studies in Fossil Botany*, I (London, 1920), 334–337, 413 ff.; II (1923), *passim;* and A. C. Seward, *Fossil Plants* (Cambridge, 2, 1910; 3, 1917; 4, 1919).

F. STOCKMANS

LILLIE, FRANK RATTRAY (*b.* Toronto, Canada, 27 June 1870; *d.* Chicago, Illinois, 5 November 1947), *embryology, zoology.*

Lillie's father, George Waddell Lillie, accountant and partner in a wholesale drug company, was a man of exceedingly upright character, but without special intellectual interests. His mother, the former Emily Ann Rattray, was the daughter of a Scottish tobacco merchant who later became a Congregational minister and amateur astrologer.

An indifferent student at a boys' grammar school, in high school Lillie was most interested in extracurricular scientific activities. High school was a time of emotional stress and religious doubts, but he was converted to the Church of England and decided to make religion his lifework. During his last year in high school he met Alexander J. Hunter, who taught him to collect, identify, and arrange insects and fossils. Both entered the University of Toronto expecting to study for the ministry. They majored in natural sciences, believing that science posed a threat to religion. During their last two years they worked with minimum guidance and literally lived in the laboratory except when discussing science and evolutionary theory, or conducting their collecting expeditions. Lillie was increasingly disillusioned by many churchmen. A. B. Macallum showed him how he could devote his life to science, a choice Lillie made during his senior year, and also transmitted to him his physiological point of view. R. Ramsey Wright imbued Lillie with his lifelong interest in embryology and recommended him, upon his graduation with honors, to work as a fellow with C. O. Whitman at the Marine Biological Laboratory at Woods Hole, Massachusetts, and afterward (1891–1892) at Clark University.

In 1891, when Lillie arrived at Woods Hole, E. B. Wilson, E. G. Conklin, A. B. Mead, and L. Treadwell were conducting cell-lineage studies in an attempt to determine the exact contribution of each blastomere to the formation of larval organs. Local ponds contained abundant supplies of freshwater clams bearing eggs and embryos in their gills; Whitman suggested that Lillie study the cell lineage of these lamellibranchs for his doctoral dissertation. In 1892 Whitman, accompanied by Lillie and his other students, moved to the newly established University of Chicago as chairman of the zoology department.

During 1892–1893 Lillie was a fellow in morphology at Chicago and the following year a reader in embryology. He received his doctorate in zoology *summa cum laude* in 1894 with an outstanding thesis which received wide praise and established him as a young investigator of great promise. From 1894 to 1899 he was instructor in zoology at the University of Michigan and from 1899 to 1900 professor of biology at Vassar College; he then returned to the University of Chicago as assistant professor of embryology. He became associate professor in 1902, professor in 1906, chair-

man of the department of zoology in 1910, Andrew MacLeish distinguished service professor of embryology and dean of the newly established division of biological sciences in 1931, and emeritus professor in 1935.

In 1895 Lillie married Frances Crane, who in the summer of 1894 had been a student in his embryology course at Woods Hole. They had five daughters and one son and adopted three sons. Their Chicago and Woods Hole homes offered warmth and hospitality to a wide circle of friends, although life with Mrs. Lillie was anything but peaceful because of her extensive social work and marked changes in religious preference. The Lillies gave the Whitman Laboratory of Experimental Zoology to the University of Chicago at a time when that institution would permit solicitation of funds only for its new medical school.

Until 1916 Lillie taught an embryology course for medical students and until 1924 another for advanced undergraduate and beginning graduate students. His undergraduate teaching resulted in publication of a useful laboratory manual (1906), twice revised under slightly different titles (1919, 1923). More important, it resulted in publication of his classic book on chick embryology (1908), revised by Lillie (1919) and later by H. L. Hamilton (1952), one of Lillie's "scientific grandchildren." This textbook has been used by students throughout the world and remains one of the best accounts of bird development.

Lillie offered graduate seminars on the physiology of development, problems of fertilization, and the biology of sex. His approach to research training was rigorous. He suggested a problem, usually related to his own current investigations, briefly discussed possible approaches, let the student know that conscientious application and results were expected, then left him largely to his own resources until he was prepared to discuss his results and present a preliminary interpretation of their meaning.

Upon Lillie's return to Chicago (1900) the operation of the department of zoology devolved increasingly on him as Whitman became progressively more engrossed in his own research. In 1910 Lillie was named second chairman of the department. Although adhering to Whitman's emphasis upon original research and graduate student training as the primary mission of the department, Lillie's administration differed from Whitman's in two ways: the department functioned more democratically, and the scope and importance of the undergraduate program in zoology were greatly strengthened, with all members of the department teaching courses specifically for undergraduates.

Lillie resigned his chairmanship in 1931 to become dean of the newly established division of biological sciences, which included not only the usual biological science departments but also the departments of psychology, home economics, physical culture, and preclinical and clinical medicine. He was faced with amalgamating established preclinical departments with newly established clinical ones at a time when there was much disagreement about the advisability of attempting to operate both Rush Medical College and the university's new medical school and about the basic organization and management of the latter. By the time of his retirement four years later he had succeeded.

Lillie is most widely known for his vital roles in development of the Marine Biological Laboratory, one of the strongest influences on the rapid development of the broad field of biology in America. He first arrived at the laboratory at the beginning of its fourth summer session. There was only one small building and no equipment besides a steam launch and a few skiffs. Accommodations existed for only a few investigators. There was no endowment; each summer ended with a deficit, covered initially by members of the board of trustees. Lillie returned to Woods Hole every summer thereafter for fifty-five years and during his lifetime became the leader in every aspect of the growth and development of the laboratory.

Lillie was assistant in the embryology course at Woods Hole when Whitman started it in 1893; he became course director the following year. At the same time operation of the entire laboratory began to devolve increasingly on Lillie, while the board of trustees resisted expansion and became increasingly reluctant to meet annual deficits. In 1900 Lillie was named assistant director. He immediately interested Charles R. Crane, his wife's favorite brother, in the operation and support of the laboratory and firmly backed Whitman in convincing the corporation and board of trustees to reverse their decision to transfer the laboratory to the Carnegie Institution of Washington as its permanent marine laboratory. Lillie was named director of the laboratory in 1910, and held that position until 1926. During this period, coinciding closely with the period in which Crane served as president of the board of trustees (1904–1924) and contributed much to the support of the laboratory, Lillie and Crane convinced financiers and foundations that the laboratory deserved their strong support. Consequently, Woods Hole became a great institution for marine biology. Lillie served as president of the corporation and board of trustees from 1925 to 1942 and then as president emeritus.

In 1915, a year before the National Research Council was established, Lillie was elected to the National Academy of Sciences. In 1919, as representative of the American Society of Zoologists to the Division of Biology and Agriculture of the National Research Council, he was made a member of the executive committee and immediately received their unqualified support in his efforts to obtain increased financial support for the marine biological laboratory. He was vice-chairman and chairman of the division in 1921 and 1922, respectively. He was further active in the establishment, in 1922, of the Union of Biological Sciences, which assumed full responsibility for publication of *Biological Abstracts* and became chairman of the board administering the newly established National Research Council fellowships in the biological sciences (1923), later serving on the natural sciences fellowship board when the separate programs in physical and biological sciences were combined. He served effectively on the Division of Medical Sciences of the National Research Council Committee for Research in Problems of Sex, established in 1921 to administer grants and offer advice to investigators in this area, and wrote the first chapter of the 1932 and 1939 editions of *Sex and Internal Secretions.*

The year he became emeritus professor, Lillie was unanimously elected president of the National Academy of Sciences (1935–1939) and chairman of the National Research Council (1935–1936), the first man to hold these two key positions simultaneously. He was given this extraordinary joint responsibility in an attempt to eliminate serious controversies concerning the activities rightfully belonging to each of these two organizations. He did so with such dispatch that the task was accomplished in one year. He simultaneously strengthened relations of the Academy and Council with agencies of the federal government.

For some years Lillie had discussed with Wickliffe Rose, president of the General Education Board—and the latter with John C. Merriam, president of the Carnegie Institution of Washington, and Vernon Kellogg, chairman of the National Research Council—the need for an oceanographic institution on the East Coast. In large part the result of his labors, the Woods Hole Oceanographic Institution was formally incorporated on 6 January 1930. Financing was so well organized in advance that the building was occupied 15 June 1931 and its research ship, *Atlantis,* was available 31 August 1931. Lillie was president of the Oceanographic Institution from 1930 to 1939 and in 1940 received the Agassiz Medal of the National Academy in recognition of his efforts.

Lillie's research contributions were as remarkable as his administrative accomplishments. His chronological bibliography (Willier, 1957) contains 109 titles, sixty-six of which are original works dealing with varied but always fundamental problems of development; some were published ten years after his retirement. He only rarely published research papers with his students, although after his retirement he did publish jointly with his research associates, Mary Juhn and Hsi Wang.

Lillie's research was masterfully planned and executed. His work invariably opened up new areas of research. He was adept at creative interpretation and constantly strove to tie details together by broad interpretive concepts because he firmly believed that sound speculation was the only true stimulus for future research, whether or not it survived additional probing. That he never gave up active participation in research is exemplified by his service as managing editor or member of the editorial boards of several journals in biology and experimental zoology.

Beginning with his doctoral dissertation (1895), a superb descriptive study on cell lineage of the freshwater mussel *Unio*, Lillie's early work (1892–1909) dealt primarily with problems of mechanisms of cleavage and of early development of eggs of invertebrates, notably those of *Unio* and of the marine annelid *Chaetopterus*. His emphasis was on how the special features of cleavage in each species were adapted to the needs of the future larva, rather than on the common features of cleavage even in different phyla, which were emphasized by many others. His studies on eggs with rigid mosaic cleavage (with developmental fates of cleavage cells already determined in early cleavage stages) led him to explore in detail the cytology of such eggs in an attempt to find some material basis for cleavage patterns, polarity, bilateral symmetry, and so on. His light microscope studies on the organization of egg protoplasm in normal and centrifuged eggs and on the extent to which differentiation without cleavage is possible in activated *Chaetopterus* eggs led to the conclusion that the control of early development must reside in the architecture of the ground substance of the egg, that is, on its physical and chemical properties. Thus, along with E. B. Wilson, he focused attention on the necessity for studying the ultramicroscopic organization of the egg; but even with modern ultrastructural techniques there is still a long way to go in understanding the basic nature of egg organization, established in the mother's ovary and important in control of early development.

During this period Lillie deviated briefly from his major line of investigation. One paper concerned regeneration in the protozoan *Stentor*; two others, regeneration and regulation in planarians; one, the effect of temperature on animal development. Of greater import was the appearance of two papers in 1903 and two in 1904 involving operations on living chick embryos *in ovo*. The first two described and analyzed experimentally the formation of the amnion (which fills with amniotic fluid, thus enclosing the embryo in its own miniature aquarium). By the use of heated needles or electrocautery he produced anamniote embryos which could develop normally for five to six days, and by localized destruction of specific sectors of the amniotic folds he could demonstrate convincingly certain causal relationships between them and the role of their progressive fusion in elevating amniotic folds at adjacent levels.

The second two papers primarily demonstrated the inability of parts of the embryo posterior to the vitelline arteries to regenerate following cauterization of the areas or rudiments that should have formed them; they further showed the inability of the right wing bud to regenerate following its extirpation. Although his own experimental analysis of chick embryo development was limited to these four publications, Lillie was convinced that chick embryos were suitable material for almost any type of experimental analysis of embryological problems.

From 1910 to 1921 Lillie's research centered primarily on the morphology and physiology of fertilization in the annelid *Nereis* and the sea urchins *Arbacia* and *Strongylocentrotus*, resulting in the publication of eighteen papers, one book (1919), and a chapter in a book (1924). Lillie hypothesized the existence of specific combining groups in sperm and in eggs and developed a far-reaching, comprehensive "fertilizin theory" of the role of union (linkage) of such combining groups in fertilization phenomena, including activation of the egg by sperm or parthenogenetic agents, species-specificity of fertilization, prevention of polyspermy, inhibition of fertilization by what he believed to be a blood inhibitor from adult sea urchins, and so on; these results are summarized schematically in ". . . The Mechanism of Fertilization in *Arbacia*" (1914, fig. 1, p. 579). Lillie was the first to visualize the linkage of his hypothetical specific combining groups in lock-and-key fashion, analogous with hypothetical antigen-antibody or immunological reactions. He thus applied entirely new ideas to the physiology of fertilization. Although many aspects of his basic theory have had to be modified in the light of increased knowledge and understanding of the molecules and combining groups involved, many investigators still believe that interactions between specific combining groups in antifertilizin molecules on the sperm surface and specific combining groups in the fertilizin molecules of the egg cortex play essential roles in the fertilization process (see Metz, 1957, 1967, for the continuing impact of Lillie's ideas in this research area).

Lillie's first publication concerning sexual differentiation appeared in 1907. His interest in this research area soared in 1914, when the manager of his large Buffalo Creek farm, where he kept a herd of purebred cattle in which the birth of freemartins occurred, sent him a pair of calf fetuses still within their fetal membranes. H. H. Newman, because of his interest in twins, was first offered this material for study but he was too heavily committed to other tasks to examine it. Therefore Lillie tackled it and immediately became intensely interested in analyzing the factors responsible for development of the freemartin, which, largely on the basis of his work, was subsequently defined as a sterile genetic female born twin to a normal genetic male. The cooperative foreman of the Swift and Company abattoir at the nearby Union Stockyards agreed to notify Lillie whenever he found a pregnant uterus (preferably with both ovaries attached) containing twins as young as possible.

By 24 February 1916 Lillie had carefully analyzed forty-one cases of bovine twins and announced his theory of the freemartin. His full analysis, based on fifty-five pairs of fetal twins, was published the following year (1917). This work is usually considered his most significant and enduring contribution to research (see Burns, 1961, for an authoritative review and impact of this theory), although Lillie's explanation of causal relationships in freemartin development has been criticized by Short (1970).

Briefly, Lillie's findings were as follows:

1. Cattle twins are two-egg or nonidentical twins (each ovary contains an ovulation site or corpus luteum).

2. The outermost extraembryonic membrane of bovine fetuses, the chorion, is greatly elongated and, in the case of twin fetuses, the two chorions (and their contained allantoic or umbilical blood vessels, especially the arteries) usually fuse at an early stage, so that blood is freely exchanged between the twin fetuses.

3. Differentiation of the gonads of genetic males into testes occurs early in fetal life, as does the differentiation of the interstitial cells of the testes, known to secrete male hormone in adult males.

4. Under such circumstances the gonads of the genetic female twin differentiate as ovotestes or as rudimentary testes, which are usually sterile.

5. The mesonephric or Wolffian ducts, and some of the mesonephric tubules, of the genetic female twin persist and develop into typical male vasa deferentia and vasa efferentia (instead of degenerating, as they would in genetic females).

6. The Müllerian ducts of the genetic female twin usually degenerate (as they normally do in genetic males) instead of forming oviducts, uterus, and possibly the vagina (as they normally do in genetic females).

7. The degree of masculinization of the gonads and reproductive ducts in the genetic female twin is greater the earlier and the more complete the fusion of the extraembryonic blood vessels of the twin fetuses.

8. The development of the genetic male reproductive system is always normal under such circumstances.

9. In those rare instances when the extraembryonic blood vessels of the heterosexual twins fail to fuse during fetal life, the reproductive systems of both members of the heterosexual twin pair develop normally.

Lillie concluded that male hormone produced by the fetal testes of the genetic male twin enters the genetic female twin via the fused extraembryonic circulations and in the genetic female inhibits development of gonads into ovaries, stimulates development of mesonephric ducts and tubules into male-type sperm passageways, and inhibits development of Müllerian ducts into components of the female reproductive system. An almost identical theory was proposed independently by two Austrian investigators in an obscure publication (see in *Science*, 1919).

This theory to account for development of the freemartin condition led directly to the concept that fetal sex hormones play a comparable role in normal sex differentiation in mammals and other vertebrates, once gene control of sex differentiation causes the gonads to develop into testes or ovaries. Thus in the normal sex differentiation of mammals the duct system develops in the male direction in genetic males because of the presence of fetal testes producing male hormone during fetal life, whereas the duct system develops in the female direction in genetic females because of the absence of fetal testes producing male hormone during fetal life. Thus fetal castration of genetic male and genetic female mammals, such as rabbits, should result in development of typical female-type reproductive systems regardless of genetic sex. This result has been amply demonstrated (see Jost, 1954, 1961, 1971).

Lillie's freemartin research introduced biologists to the problem of the nature, origin, and action of sex hormones at a time when almost nothing was known about them. It stimulated attempts to duplicate the circumstances producing freemartins in cattle by parabiosis of amphibian larvae of opposite genetic sex, or by grafting gonads of donor chick embryos of one genetic sex onto the choriallantoic membrane or into the coelom of host chick embryos of the opposite sex. The freemartin research led Lillie directly into collaborative work with members of the department of biochemistry that resulted in the isolation, chemical analysis, and synthesis of sex hormones.

The first known androgens were isolated in the laboratory of F. C. Koch at the University of Chicago with Lillie as colleague. These pure chemical substances were then available for injection into experimental animals to determine to what extent development of the reproductive systems of the injected animals could be modified. This work opened up for investigation the field of the biology of sex, the physiology of sex hormones and, more recently, the role of sex hormones in animal behavior. It also opened up for investigation the role in sex hormone production of gonadotrophic hormones from the anterior pituitary gland and, later, of specific gonadotrophin-releasing factors from special neurosecretory cells of the hypothalamus, the nature of feedback mechanisms, and so on.

After his retirement Lillie turned to a series of investigations on the physiology of development of regenerating feathers, which, in certain breeds of fowl, such as the Brown Leghorn, are especially sensitive to estrogen, thyroxin, and similar hormones. In a series of papers published between 1932 and 1947, mostly in collaboration with Mary Juhn and Hsi Wang, Lillie added much to our understanding of the highly complex development of a regenerating feather, whose definitive structure, according to Cohen, is "... the sum of the debris of some 1.5×10^7 to 5×10^9 cells, exactly organized and engineered to the utmost precision" (1965, p. 9). The regenerating feather forms from the feather papilla or feather germ, a morphogenetic system in miniature.

Lillie and his co-workers studied the role of induction and of the processes of twinning in feather development, attempting especially to reveal some of the factors responsible for the consistent morphogenetic and color reactions of parts of the individual feather papilla, and of feather papillae in different feather tracts, to different concentrations of hormones. Although Cohen is sharply critical of some of Lillie's general interpretations about mechanisms of feather development and reaction to hormones, his criticisms are relatively minor when viewed against Lillie's overall contributions to our understanding of development of the regenerating feather, examination of whose definitive structure is, according to Cohen, "a humbling process."

Lillie received the Sc.D. from the University of Toronto (1920), Yale University (1932), and Harvard University (1938), and the LL.D. from Johns Hopkins University (1942). He was a member of several learned societies, both American and foreign.

BIBLIOGRAPHY

I. ORIGINAL WORKS. Lillie's writings include "The Embryology of the *Unionidae*. A Study in Cell-Lineage," in *Journal of Morphology*, **10** (1895), 1–100; "Experimental Studies on the Development of the Organs in the Embryo of the Fowl *(Gallus domesticus)*," in *Biological Bulletin, Marine Biological Laboratory, Woods Hole, Mass.*, **5** (1903), 92–124; "Experimental Studies on the Development of Organs in the Embryo of the Fowl *(Gallus domesticus)*. II. The Development of Defective Embryos, and the Power of Regeneration," *ibid.*, **7** (1904), 33–54; *Laboratory Outlines for the Study of the Embryology of the Chick and the Pig* (Chicago, 1906), 2nd ed., rev., *A Laboratory Outline and Manual for the Study of Embryology* (Chicago, 1919), written with C. R. Moore, 3rd ed., rev., *A Laboratory Outline of Embryology With Special Reference to the Chick and the Pig* (Chicago, 1923), written with C. R. Moore; "The Biological Significance of Sexual Differentiation—A Zoological Point of View," in *Science*, **25** (1907), 372–376; *Development of the Chick. An Introduction to Embryology* (New York, 1908, 2nd ed., New York, 1919); 3rd ed., rev., *Lillie's Development of the Chick* (New York, 1952), by H. L. Hamilton; "Studies of Fertilization. VI. The Mechanism of Fertilization in *Arbacia*," in *Journal of Experimental Zoology*, **16** (1914), 523–590; "The Theory of the Freemartin," in *Science*, **43** (1916), 611–613; "The Free-Martin; a Study of the Action of Sex Hormones in the Foetal Life of Cattle," in *Journal of Experimental Zoology*, **23** (1917), 371–452; *Problems of Fertilization* (Chicago, 1919); "Tandler and Keller on the Freemartin," in *Science*, **50** (1919), 183–184; "Fertilization," in E. V. Cowdry, ed., *General Cytology* (Chicago, 1924), pp. 449–536, written with E. E. Just; "General Biological Introduction," in E. Allen, ed., *Sex and Internal Secretions* (Baltimore, 1932), pp. 1–11, also in E. Allen, C. H. Danforth, and E. A. Doisy, eds., *Sex and Internal Secretions*, 2nd ed. (Baltimore, 1939), pp. 3–14; "The Builders of the Marine Biological Laboratory," in *Collecting Net*, **13** (1938), 107–108; and *The Woods Hole Marine Biological Laboratory* (Chicago, 1944).

An undated 33-p. MS entitled "My Early Life" provides much information on his ancestry, youth, and early education. It is filed with the F. R. Lillie reprint collection at the Marine Biological Laboratory.

II. SECONDARY LITERATURE. See "Appreciations of Professor Frank R. Lillie on the Occasion of his Sixtieth Birthday," in *Collecting Net*, **5** (anniversary supp., 28 June 1930), 1–12; Mary Prentice Lillie Barrows, *Moon out of the Well. Reminiscences* (1970), copy filed with F. R. Lillie reprints at the Marine Biological Laboratory; and *Frances Crane Lillie (1869–1958). A Memoir* (1970), copy provided through the courtesy of B. H. Willier; R. K. Burns, "Role of Hormones in the Differentiation of Sex," in W. C. Young, ed., *Sex and Internal Secretions*, 3rd ed. (Baltimore, 1961), pp. 76–158; J. Cohen, "Feathers and Patterns," in M. Abercrombie and J. Brachet, eds., *Advances in Morphogenesis* (New York, 1966), V, 1–38; E. G. Conklin, "Science and Scientists at the M. B. L.

Fifty Years Ago," in *Collecting Net*, **13** (1938), 101–106; and "The Contributions of Dr. Frank R. Lillie to Oceanography," in *Collecting Net*, **15** (1940), 30–31 (on the occasion of the presentation of the Agassiz Medal for Oceanography by the National Academy of Sciences); G. Fankhauser, "Memories of Great Embryologists," in *American Scientist*, **60** (1972), 46–55; and R. J. Harrison, "Frank Rattray Lillie (1870–1947)," in *Yearbook. American Philosophical Society* (1947), pp. 264–270.

See also A. Jost, "Hormonal Factors in the Development of the Fetus," in *Cold Spring Harbor Symposia on Quantitative Biology*, XIX, *The Mammalian Fetus: Physiological Aspects of Development* (Cold Spring Harbor, N.Y., 1954), 167–181; "The Role of Fetal Hormones in Prenatal Development," in *Harvey Lectures*, **55** (1961), 201–226; and "Hormones in Development: Past and Prospects," in M. Hamburgh and E. J. W. Barrington, eds., *Hormones in Development* (New York, 1971), pp. 1–18; C. B. Metz, "Specific Egg and Sperm Substances and Activation of the Egg," in A. Tyler, R. C. von Borstel, and C. B. Metz, eds., *The Beginnings of Embryonic Development* (Washington, D.C., 1957), pp. 22–69; and "Gamete Surface Components and Their Role in Fertilization," in C. B. Metz and A. Monroy, eds., *Fertilization: Comparative Morphology, Biochemistry and Immunology*, I (New York, 1967), 163–236; C. R. Moore, "Frank Rattray Lillie 1870–1947," in *Science*, **107** (1948), 33–35; and "Frank Rattray Lillie. 1870–1947," in *Anatomical Record*, **101** (1948), 1–4; H. H. Newman, "History of the Department of Zoology in the University of Chicago," in *Bios*, **19** (1948), 215–239; A. N. Richards, "Dr. Frank R. Lillie," a typewritten memorial read at a dinner of the National Academy of Sciences, November, 1947, two weeks after Lillie's death (filed with the F. R. Lillie reprint collection at the Marine Biological Laboratory); R. V. Short, "The Bovine Freemartin: A New Look at an Old Problem," in *Philosophical Transactions of the Royal Society*, **B259** (1970), 141–147; B. H. Willier, "Frank Rattray Lillie," in *Anatomical Record*, **100** (1948), 407–410; and "Frank Rattray Lillie 1870–1947," in *Biographical Memoirs. National Academy of Sciences*, **30** (1957), 179–236; B. H. Willier, R. J. Harrison, H. B. Bigelow, and E. G. Conklin, "Addresses at the Lillie Memorial Meeting Woods Hole, August 11, 1948," in *Biological Bulletin. Marine Biological Laboratory, Woods Hole, Mass.*, **95** (1948), 151–162; B. H. Willier, "The Work and Accomplishments of Frank R. Lillie at Chicago," pp. 151–153; R. G. Harrison, "Dr. Lillie's Relations With the National Academy of Sciences and the National Research Council," pp. 154–157; H. B. Bigelow, "Dr. Lillie and the Founding of the Woods Hole Oceanographic Institution," pp. 157–158; and E. G. Conklin, "Frank R. Lillie and the Marine Biological Laboratory," pp. 158–162; and W. C. Young, ed., *Sex and Internal Secretions*, 3rd ed., 2 vols. (Baltimore, 1961).

RAY L. WATTERSON

LINACRE, THOMAS (*b*. Canterbury, England, 1460[?]; *d*. London, England, 1524), *medicine*.

Linacre received his early education at the school of Christ Church Monastery, Canterbury, under the direction of William de Selling, later prior. It appears at the age of twenty Linacre went to Oxford, where he learned some Greek and in 1484 was elected fellow of All Souls College. About 1487 he accompanied Selling to Italy. He studied Greek with Demetrius Chalcondylas in Florence, met Hermolaus Barbarus in Rome, became acquainted with the printer Aldus Manutius (and was involved in the editing of the Aldine edition of the Greek *Opera omnia* of Aristotle [1495–1498]) in Venice, and graduated M.D. from Padua in 1496. He then engaged in further study with the humanist-physician Nicolò Leoniceno in Vicenza and returned to England by way of Geneva, Paris, and Calais.

Back at Oxford, Linacre was incorporated M.D. in consequence of his Paduan degree. He is said to have given some public lectures on medicine and seems also to have taught Greek privately, one of his students being Sir Thomas More. During this period he also made a Latin translation of Proclus' *De sphaera*, which was published by Aldus in a collection of ancient Greek astronomical works (1499). About 1501 Linacre became tutor to Prince Arthur (who died in the following year) and in 1509 was chosen as one of the physicians to Henry VIII at a salary of £50 a year. From this time onward he lived chiefly in London, where his patients and friends included Cardinal Wolsey, Archbishop Warham, Bishop Fox, and such eminent scholars as Colet, More, Erasmus, and William Lily.

At about the same time Linacre, in search of greater leisure, took holy orders. His highly placed friends found him a succession of ecclesiastical livings, which he either sold or deputized; he was thus enabled to devote most of his efforts to scholarship (although he remained physician to the king, in which post his duties were nominal). Linacre was especially concerned in translating Galen's writings into Latin, beginning with the treatise of hygiene, *De sanitate tuenda*. Since there was then no printer in England sufficiently able or willing to assume the financial risk of producing this work for the English market, the tract, dedicated to Henry VIII, was published in Paris in 1517. Linacre's second translation, Galen's *Methodus medendi*, was also published in Paris (1519). It, too, was dedicated to the English king.

Linacre's next translation of Galen, *De temperamentis*, was, however, published in England, from the press of John Siberch in Cambridge (1521). In 1522, Linacre saw two Galenic translations by his former teacher, Nicolò Leoniceno, through the press of Richard Pynson in London; Pynson also published Linacre's own subsequent translations, *De usu pulsuum* (1522), *De facultatibus naturalibus* (1523), and *De symptomatis differentiis* (1524).

Linacre was a medical humanist as well as one of the finest Greek scholars of his day; his major effort, therefore, was directed toward bringing to English physicians a series of classical medical texts that he considered essential and that were, in fact, superior to other medical writings published in England at that time. In addition to the works that he brought to publication, he is known to have translated yet others, but with the one exception, a brief extract from Paul of Aegina, these were either lost or destroyed after his death. His very considerable Continental reputation, especially in Greek medical scholarship, was clearly recognized by Erasmus: "Medicine has begun to make herself heard in Italy through the voice of Nicolaus Leonicenus . . . and among the French by Guillaume Cop of Basel; while among the English, owing to the studies of Thomas Linacre, Galen has begun to be so eloquent and informative that even in his own tongue he may seem to be less so." Such commendation remained unheeded in England, however, and Linacre's translations were not republished there, although there were approximately forty Continental reprintings of them between 1524 and 1550.

Linacre himself may have come to realize that more than the Greek medical classics were necessary to improve the state of English medicine. Just prior to his death he arranged that funds from his considerable estate should be used to establish the Linacre lectures at Oxford and Cambridge. Although he did not specifically declare that the lectures must be devoted to medical subjects, there nonetheless seems little doubt that such was his intention. He may have hoped that the oral presentation of classical medicine would prove attractive to physicians and medical students who might resist the printed word. He did not live to see the misuse of this endowment. The lectures failed through the conservatism and lethargy of the universities, and whatever potential they might have had for revitalizing the medical curriculum or promoting a more advanced medicine in England was unrealized.

Linacre was nevertheless responsible for an important contribution to English medicine in his work toward founding the College of Physicians of London. Through his influence the College was granted, from its foundation in 1518, the power to license physicians in London and for seven miles surrounding. The right to practice medicine had previously been conferred only upon medical graduates of Oxford or Cambridge or to such men as were licensed by bishops (or in London by the bishop or by the dean of St. Paul's). The more stringent professional license enhanced the prestige of the relatively small group who met the College's standards. This result, desirable from the physicians' standpoint, was recognized and envied by those practicing outside the area of the College's supervision, where licensing remained beyond the control of the medical profession.

Linacre's sense of the dignity of medicine was paramount. As the College served to promote that dignity, so it also maintained it. Although the medical profession in Continental cities was able to rally around the faculty of medicine of a university, this was not possible in England, since the universities were in relatively small and inaccessible towns. For this reason the College of Physicians of London became the focus of physicians in London and, to some degree, elsewhere. The College, which Linacre directed until his death, established the character of English medicine for centuries to follow. It thus represents his most enduring work.

Apparently it was of the complications of a calculary disorder that Linacre died.

BIBLIOGRAPHY

I. ORIGINAL WORKS. The original editions of Linacre's translations of Galen are very rare, but one of them, *De temperamentis*, was published in facsimile with a biographical introduction by J. F. Payne (Cambridge, 1881).

II. SECONDARY LITERATURE. On Linacre's life and work see Josephine W. Bennett, "John Morer's Will: Thomas Linacre and Prior Sellying's Greek Teaching," in *Studies in the Renaissance*, **15** (New York, 1968), 70–91; George Clark, *A History of the Royal College of Physicians of London*, I (Oxford, 1964), 37; John Noble Johnson, *The Life of Thomas Linacre, Doctor of Medicine*, Robert Graves, ed. (London, 1835); C. D. O'Malley, *English Medical Humanists. Thomas Linacre and John Caius* (Lawrence, Kans., 1965); and William Osler, *Thomas Linacre* (Cambridge, 1908).

C. D. O'MALLEY

LIND, JAMES (*b.* Edinburgh, Scotland, 4 October 1716; *d.* Gosport, Hampshire, England, 13 July 1794), *medicine.*

The discoverer of citrus fruit as a cure for scurvy, Lind was the son of Margaret Smelum (alternately spelled Smellum or Smellome) and James Lind, a substantial Edinburgh merchant. (Many early biographical sketches confuse him with his cousin, also named James Lind, a physician to the household of George III.) After attending grammar school in Edinburgh, in December 1731 he was apprenticed to George Langlands, an Edinburgh physician; and in 1739 he entered the British navy as a surgeon's mate. He was promoted to surgeon in 1747. Most of his naval service was aboard ships patrolling the English Channel during the War of Austrian Succession (1740–1748), and his longest cruise was on the fourth-rated ship H.M.S. *Salisbury* (August–October 1746) in the English Channel. It was on a somewhat shorter cruise on this ship in 1747 that he carried out his classic experiments on scurvy.

Lind left the navy in 1748 and obtained his M.D. from the University of Edinburgh in the same year. His doctoral thesis on venereal lesions, *De morbis venereis localibus*, gives evidence of having been written in haste and is a trivial work but was sufficient to win him a license to practice in Edinburgh. In 1750 Lind became a fellow of the Royal College of Physicians of Edinburgh and served as treasurer from December 1756 to 1758, when he was appointed first chief physician to the new Royal Naval Hospital at Haslar. Lind was also a member of the Philosophical and Medical Society of Edinburgh and an original fellow of the Royal Society of Edinburgh. In 1753 he published *A Treatise of the Scurvy*, which created little stir in Edinburgh but apparently attracted the attention of Lord Anson, then first Lord of the Admiralty, to whom it was dedicated. It is believed that Anson was later influential in securing Lind's appointment to the Royal Naval Hospital.

This post gave Lind additional opportunity for study. In the first two years of his administration the hospital received 5,734 admissions, of which 1,146 were cases of scurvy. The last edition of his *Treatise* includes additions derived, said the author, from four large notebooks of case histories and observations made at Haslar. Lind served as chief physician until 1783, when he was succeeded by his son John, who had been his assistant. On his retirement his portrait, now lost, was painted by Sir George Chalmers; a print of an engraving made from the picture is extant. Lind was buried in St. Mary's Church, Gosport. The church register mentions his wife, Isobel (Isabel) Dickic, whom Lind must have married while practicing in Edinburgh.

Lind's *An Essay on the Most Effectual Means of Preserving the Health of Seamen in the Royal Navy* (1757) throws much light on the living conditions and the diet of seamen. In *Two Papers on Fevers and Infections* (1763), which contains most of what is known of the medical history of the Seven Years War, Lind emphasized that the "number of seamen in time of war who died by shipwreck, capture, famine, fire

or sword" was only a small proportion compared to those who died by "ship diseases and the usual maladies of intemperate climates." (During the Seven Years War 133,708 men were lost to the navy by disease or desertion; 1,512 were killed in action.) Lind's last major work, *An Essay on Diseases Incidental to Europeans in Hot Climates* (1768), was written primarily for the use of travelers and emigrants to tropical colonies and remained the standard work on tropical medicine in English for half a century.

Although Lind is now recognized as the greatest of naval doctors and as the "father of nautical medicine," in his own day he was not elected a fellow of the Royal Society. He has also come to be regarded as one of the first modern clinical investigators and clearly was one of the first to have complete faith in the validity of his own observations and the logic of his conclusions. Lind's scurvy cure was not officially introduced into the diet of the Royal Navy until after his death, and this delayed recognition has aroused considerable historical interest. Herbert Spencer, in his *Study of Sociology*, cited the navy's neglect of Lind's findings as the most flagrant example of administrative apathy on record. More recent investigators such as Sir Humphrey Rolleston and A. P. Meiklejohn regarded it as yet another example of the prejudice which greets many innovators.

Lind's basic experiments were carried out in May 1747 while he was serving as surgeon aboard the *Salisbury*. Lind selected twelve scurvy patients with the most similar cases. He divided them into six groups of two, and although all received the same basic diet, he added different supplements to each one. Two he gave a quart of cider a day; two others, twenty-five drops of elixir vitrio three times a day; two were given spoonfuls of vinegar; two were treated with seawater; two, with an electuary of garlic, mustard seed, horseradish, and other ingredients; and two were given two oranges and a lemon every day. Lind observed the most sudden and visible improvement in those fed citrus fruit: one was pronounced fit for duty after six days, and the other was reported to have made the best recovery of all. Lind held that cider had the next best effect (although only small improvements were noticeable) and that the other treatments were useless. The question is why Lind's remedy was not quickly adopted. Meiklejohn held that it was because Lind was confronted with tenaciously held current medical practices and concepts about scurvy; Christopher Lloyd has given a somewhat more complex explanation.

Lloyd pointed out that while the voyages of Captain James Cook between 1768 and 1780 are assumed to have demonstrated the effectiveness of citrus fruits in preventing scurvy, this is not exactly the case. Cook himself emphasized that the absence of scurvy on his voyages was due to a diet of sauerkraut, soup, and malt. On his second voyage Cook also insisted on obtaining fresh water and vegetables at every opportunity, and while they undoubtedly served to prevent scurvy, no genuine experiments were made to determine their therapeutic effectiveness. Cook's surgeons in their report attributed the absence of scurvy to the inclusion of malt, and this idea dominated naval thinking for a time.

The outbreak of the American revolution forced the British navy to reexamine this supposition, since in 1780, despite the inclusion of malt, one-seventh of the fleet, some 2,400 cases, were landed for treatment of scurvy. The high cost of Mediterranean lemons was also a major factor in the delay of their use by the navy. By the last decade of the eighteenth century the navy had finally adopted citrus fruits as a remedy. By 1796 it was generally accepted that scurvy could be prevented by fresh vegetables and cured effectively by lemons or their juice, preserved effectively by boiling; and since that time scurvy has played little part in medical history. (One of the seamen's demands during the mutiny of 1797 was a ration of lemon juice.) Limes replaced lemons in the British navy in the mid-nineteenth century because the West Indian lime was cheaper and easier to obtain than the Mediterranean lemon. However, there were still serious outbreaks of scurvy on several Arctic expeditions, and it was not until 1917 that preserved lime juice was discovered to have only one-third the antiscorbutic value of lemon. Unfortunately the same dosages had usually been followed.

Second only to his treatise on scurvy in importance to naval medicine was his general effort to improve the health of seamen. In his book on the subject, Lind included recommendations for the practice of shipboard hygiene, comments upon diseases in northern latitudes (especially scurvy), advice on the prevention of tropical fevers, and a means for procuring a wholesome water supply at sea. Others had suggested ways for distilling seawater, but Lind's method did not require the addition of chemicals as did those of his predecessors or even of his contemporaries. Lind's importance in medical history lies in his willingness to experiment and to break with past medical tradition when it conflicted with his own observations. Although his ideas were very much of his own time, he modified them where necessary. Lind's younger contemporaries and ardent supporters, Thomas Trotter and Sir Gilbert Blane, helped carry on his tradition; and the triumvirate is now regarded as responsible for the founding of the modern naval health service.

BIBLIOGRAPHY

I. ORIGINAL WORKS. *A Treatise of the Scurvy* (Edinburgh, 1753) went through three eds.; the second ed. (London, 1757) is little more than a reprint, but the third edition, retitled *A Treatise on the Scurvy* (London, 1772)—the title most often cited—contains some additions based on Lind's observations at Haslar and an updated bibliography. The French trans., *Traité du scorbut*, 2 vols. (Paris, 1756; repr. 1783), was published with a treatise on the same subject by Boerhaave. An Italian ed. was published at Venice in 1766, and a German ed. at Leipzig in 1775. The first ed. was reprinted as *Lind's Treatise on Scurvy* (Edinburgh, 1953) with additional notes and comments by C. P. Stewart, D. Guthrie, and others as part of observances commemorating the bicentenary of its original publication.

An Essay on the Most Effectual Means of Preserving the Health of Seamen in the Royal Navy (London, 1757) was reprinted in 1762; the third ed. (1779) includes *Two Papers on Fevers and Infections*, originally read before the Philosophical and Medical Society of Edinburgh and first published separately in 1763 in London. The *Essay* was translated into Dutch (Middleburgh, 1760) and was probably also published in French and German. *Two Papers on Fevers and Infections* was translated into French (Lausanne, 1798). Most of the *Essay* as well as the papers on fevers and infections were reprinted by the Navy Records Society as *The Health of Seamen*, C. Lloyd, ed. (London, 1965). *An Essay on Diseases Incidental to Europeans in Hot Climates, With the Method of Preventing Their Fatal Consequences* (London, 1768; 6th ed., 1808; Philadelphia, 1811), Lind's most popular work during his lifetime, was translated into German (Leipzig, 1773), Dutch (Amsterdam, 1781), and French (Paris, 1785).

Two letters addressed to Sir Alexander Dick in Lind's handwriting are extant, one resigning his office of treasurer of the Royal College, and a second describing his new place of work, Haslar Hospital; for text of both and photograph of one, see *Lind's Treatise on Scurvy* (1953), pp. 390–391.

II. SECONDARY LITERATURE. L. H. Roddis, *James Lind* (New York, 1950), is a rather naïve biography, valuable primarily for the author's attempt to locate all eds. of Lind's works. Much biographical information was gathered in Sir H. D. Rolleston, "James Lind, Pioneer of Naval Hygiene," in *Journal of the Royal Naval Medical Service*, **1** (1915), 181–190. For explanations of the delay in adopting Lind's cure see A. P. Meiklejohn, "The Curious Obscurity of Dr. James Lind," in *Journal of the History of Medicine and Allied Sciences*, **9** (1954), 304–310; and esp. C. Lloyd, "The Introduction of Lemon Juice as a Cure for Scurvy," in *Bulletin of the History of Medicine*, **35** (1961), 123–132. See also E. A. Hudson and A. Herbert, "James Lind: His Contribution to Shipboard Sanitation," in *Journal of the History of Medicine*, **11** (1956), 1–12; C. Lloyd and J. L. S. Coulter, *Medicine and the Navy*, III (Edinburgh, 1957); and the various articles on Lind, naval medicine, and scurvy in *Lind's Treatise on Scurvy*, cited above.

VERN L. BULLOUGH

LINDBLAD, BERTIL (*b*. Örebro, Sweden, 26 November 1895; *d*. Stockholm, Sweden, 25 June 1965), *astronomy*.

Lindblad's father, Lieutenant Colonel Birger Lindblad, was from Askersund, where four generations of his family had been merchants and active members of the magistrates court. Bertil Lindblad's paternal grandmother, Jenny Hybbinette, belonged to a distinguished Walloon family that migrated to Sweden around 1630 to work in the iron industry. His mother, Sara Gabriella Waldenström, belonged to an intellectual Swedish family whose members for several generations had distinguished themselves in theology and medicine.

Lindblad graduated in 1914 from the Karolinska Läroverket in Örebro. That same year he began studies in mathematics, physics, and astronomy at Uppsala University. Östen Bergstrand, director of the Uppsala observatory, soon realized that Lindblad was an unusually gifted student. Lindblad became interested in the study of the colors of stars, and he was encouraged in his early research not only by Bergstrand himself but also by Hugo von Zeipel, associate professor of astronomy.

In 1920 Lindblad defended his doctoral thesis, an important contribution to the theory of radiative transfer in the solar atmosphere with special application to the phenomenon of solar limb darkening. In the same paper he presented a first approach to the problem of determining absolute magnitudes of stars by combining two color indices from different parts of the spectrum. During a research period (1920–1922) at the Lick and Mount Wilson observatories, Lindblad was able to establish new, important spectroscopic criteria of stellar luminosity in addition to those which had been found somewhat earlier by Kohlschütter and Adams. He thus found that absorption bands of the cyanogen molecule CN are considerably stronger in the spectra of giants than in the spectra of dwarfs for stars with the same temperature as the sun or with a somewhat lower temperature. Compared with Kohlschütter's and Adams' criteria, the new criteria had the great advantage of being visible also in spectra for very low dispersion. Thus, faint stars could also be studied with this new spectroscopic method, and it soon became a most efficient tool in stellar research.

Upon his return to Uppsala in 1922 Lindblad continued his work with one of the observatory astrographs which had been especially equipped with an objective prism giving short dispersion spectra. He also included other principal spectrum lines and bands in his analysis and was able to use this astrograph for a first survey of faint stars in selected regions of the sky. In order to improve the calibration of his luminosity criteria he selected regions where the proper motions were known down to the limiting magnitude. In this way he improved considerably the basis of stellar statistics, and derived more accurately the density distribution of stars and the state of motion. This work gave a great stimulus to Swedish astronomy, and many young astronomers joined in the development of this field of research, which remains a major program at the observatories of Uppsala, Stockholm, and Lund.

Lindblad married Dagmar Bolin in 1924. The couple had four children.

In 1927 Lindblad was appointed director of the Stockholm observatory and was thus in charge of building the new observatory in Saltsjöbaden. The instruments for the new institution were selected to allow further applications of the spectroscopic criteria of stellar luminosity.

During his last years in Uppsala, Lindblad became increasingly interested in stellar dynamics and he introduced new concepts which could explain the asymmetric drift of high velocity stars. He advanced the fundamental idea that the galactic system is rotating around a distant center. In his detailed discussion he introduced a model of the galactic system consisting of a number of subsystems of different speeds of rotation and with different degrees of flatness and velocity dispersion.

Lindblad's ideas were soon confirmed by J. H. Oort with his discovery of the differential rotation. Following that discovery, Lindblad became increasingly engaged in stellar dynamics and soon became a leading authority. He devoted much time to the difficult problem of explaining the spiral structure of rotating stellar systems assuming gravitational forces only. His first results indicated that spiral arms probably open up in their motion, but important numerical calculations made on his suggestion by his son Per Olof Lindblad (appointed director of the Stockholm observatory in 1967) have shown that trailing arms probably are the most frequent ones. This led Lindblad to a further development of his theory. He now introduced the concepts "dispersion orbits" and "density waves," which were followed up with considerable success by C. C. Lin. Lindblad also found ways of explaining how spiral features may be preserved.

Despite his many official duties, Lindblad continued his scientific research; and even in his later years he found time to do observational work on eclipses and photometric studies of nebulae.

Lindblad was very active internationally; he was president of the International Astronomical Union from 1948 to 1952, when he became President of the International Council of Scientific Unions. A few months before his death, he was elected president of the council of the European Southern Observatory.

While director of the Stockholm observatory, Lindblad was also professor of astronomy at Stockholm University. He was elected to the Royal Swedish Academy of Sciences in 1928 and served as president in 1938 and 1960 and as vice-president for many years. He served as chairman of the Swedish Natural Science Research Council from 1951. Lindblad was honored with the Gold Medal of the Royal Astronomical Society in 1948, and he was a foreign member of academies in Denmark, Finland, Belgium, Portugal, Italy, France, Germany, Poland, and the United States. At his death he was chairman of the Nobel Foundation.

BIBLIOGRAPHY

A comprehensive list of publications (about 100) has been given by J. H. Oort in his obituary notice printed in *Quarterly Journal of the Royal Astronomical Society*, **7** (1966).

YNGVE ÖHMAN

LINDE, CARL VON (*b*. Berndorf, Germany, 11 June 1842; *d*. Munich, Germany, 16 November 1934), *engineering, cryogenics.*

Linde was the third of nine children of Friedrich Linde and his wife Franziska Linde, the daughter of a businessman from Neuwied. In Kempten, where his father, a minister, had been transferred, the young Linde pursued classical studies at the Gymnasium. To his literary and cultural interests he soon added a great enthusiasm for technical matters which led him to study machine construction. Thus from 1861 to 1864 he attended the famous Eidgenössische Polytechnikum in Zurich, where he studied science and engineering with Clausius, Zeuner, and F. Reuleaux, as well as aesthetics with F. T. Vischer and art history with W. Lübke. From 1864 to 1866 Linde received practical training in the workshop and drafting studios of, among others, the locomotive and machine factory of A. Borsig in Tegel, near Berlin. In 1866 he became the head of the technical department of the newly founded Krauss and Company, locomotive manufacturers in Munich. There he was able to implement a series of his own ideas, including those on braking arrangements.

On the founding of the Munich Polytechnische Schule (later the Technische Hochschule) in 1868,

Linde became extraordinary professor, and in 1872, full professor of theoretical engineering. Here, in 1875, he established an engineering laboratory, the first of its kind in Germany. He lectured on a number of subjects—motors in general; the theory of steam engines, crank motion, and water wheels; turbines; hot-air engines; locomotives; and steamships—and carried out practical laboratory projects. Among his colleagues at the Polytechnische Schule he was especially close to Felix Klein, who taught mathematics there from 1875 to 1880.

In 1870 Linde started to investigate refrigeration. His research on heat theory led, from 1873 to 1877, to the development of the first successful compressed-ammonia refrigerator. Refrigerators existed before Linde's, but his was especially reliable, economical, efficient. He stressed that refrigerators should be useful not only for the making of ice, but also for the direct cooling of liquids. For these reasons breweries were particularly interested in his device.

Linde left his teaching position in 1879 and founded the Gesellschaft für Linde's Eismaschinen in Wiesbaden to develop his process industrially. Because of the many applications of artificial cooling the undertaking was an international success. In order to explore the subject of low temperatures at a research station (founded in 1888) and to teach again on a reduced schedule, Linde retired from the management of the business in 1891; at that time twelve hundred refrigerators of his construction were already in operation.

In 1895 Linde succeeded in liquefying air with the help of the Joule-Thomson effect and by the application of the counterflow principle, and the foundations were thereby laid for the maintenance of low temperatures. In London Hampson arrived at a similar process shortly after Linde (1896). Linde also successfully developed devices for obtaining pure oxygen by means of rectification (1902), for the production of pure nitrogen through the use of the nitrogen cycle process (1903), and for producing hydrogen from water gas by means of partial condensation of carbon monoxide (1909). The production of pure oxygen was of great importance for oxyacetylene torches used in metalworking, as was that of pure nitrogen for the large-scale production of calcium nitrate, ammonia, and saltpeter. Linde founded a group of enterprises in Europe and overseas to utilize his processes.

In the second phase of his teaching, beginning in Munich in 1891, Linde dealt primarily with the theory of refrigeration machines. It was at his instigation that the first laboratory for applied physics in Germany was founded at the Munich Technische Hochschule in 1902. Linde was also active on numerous scientific and technical committees. He was a member of the Bavarian Academy of Sciences and a corresponding member of the Vienna Academy. In addition, he belonged to the board of trustees of the Physikalisch-Technische Reichsanstalt and to boards of directors of the Verein Deutsche Ingenieure and of the Deutsches Museum.

In 1866 Linde married Helene Grimm; they had six children. In 1897 he was made a nobleman. The exceedingly fortunate combination of scientific, technical, and entrepreneurial abilities met and were developed in this simple man of strong moral character and an uncommon capacity for work.

BIBLIOGRAPHY

I. ORIGINAL WORKS. Linde's manuscript material is in the Archiv des Polytechnischen Vereins in Bayern (now in the MS collection of the library of the Deutsches Museum in Munich) and at his company, Linde A. G. in Wiesbaden.

Linde's important published works are: *Über einige Methoden zum Bremsen der Lokomotiven und Eisenbahnzüge* (Munich, 1868); "Wärmeentziehung bei niedrigen Temperaturen durch mechanische Mittel," in *Bayerisches Industrie- und Gewerbeblatt*, **2** (1870), 205; "Eine neue Eis- und Kühlmaschine," *ibid.*, **3** (1871), 264; "Theorie der Kälteerzeugungsmaschinen," in *Verhandlungen des Vereins zur Beförderung des Gewerbefleisses*, **54** (1875), 357 and **55** (1876), 185; "The Refrigerating Machine of Today," in *Transactions of the American Society of Mechanical Engineers*, **14** (1893), 1414; and "Refrigerating Apparatus," in *Journal of the Society of Arts*, **42** (1894), 322.

Also see his "Erzielung niedrigster Temperaturen," in *Annalen der Physik und Chemie*, n.s. **57** (1896), 328; "Process and Apparatus for Attaining Lowest Temperatures," in *Engineer* (London), **82** (1896), 485; "Kälteerzeugungsmaschine," in *Luegers Lexicon der gesamten Technik*, V (Stuttgart, 1897), 353; "Über die Veränderlichkeit der specifischen Wärme der Gase," in *Sitzungsberichte der Bayerischen Akademie der Wissenschaften zu München*, **27** (1897), 485; "Die Entwicklung der Kältetechnik," in *Festschrift 71. Versammlung der Gesellschaft Deutscher Naturforscher und Ärzte* (Munich, 1899), 189. Among Linde's later works are: "Zur Geschichte der Maschinen für die Herstellung flüssiger Luft," in *Berichte der Deutschen Chemischen Gesellschaft*, **32**, no. 1 (1899), 925; "Über Vorgänge bei Verbrennung in flüssiger Luft," in *Sitzungsberichte der Bayerischen Akademie der Wissenschaften zu München*, **29** (1899), 65; "Sauerstoffgewinnung mittels fraktionierter Verdampfung flüssiger Luft," in *Zeitschrift des Vereins Deutscher Ingenieure*, **46** (1902), 1173; "Die Schätze der Atmosphäre," in *Deutsches Museum. Vorträge und Berichte*, no. 1 (1908); and "Physik und Technik auf dem Wege zum absoluten Nullpunkt," in *Festrede in der Bayerischen Akademie der Wissenschaften* (Munich, 1912); and *Aus mein Leben und von meiner Arbeit* (Munich, 1916).

II. SECONDARY LITERATURE. Works about Linde are (in chronological order) *50 Jahre Kältetechnik, 1879–1929. Geschichte der Gesellschaft für Linde's Eismaschinen A.G., Wiesbaden* (Wiesbaden, 1929); "Carl von Linde zum 90 Geburtstag," in *Abhandlungen und Berichte des Deutschen Museums*, **4** (1932), 55; R. Plank, "Carl von Linde und sein Werk," in *Zeitschrift für die gesamte Kälte-Industrie*, **42** (1935), 162; H. Mache, "Carl von Linde," in *Almanach der Akademie der Wissenschaften in Wien*, **85** (1936), 272. W. Meissner, "Carl von Lindes wissenschaftliche Leistungen," in *Zeitschrift für die gesamte Kälte-Industrie*, **49** (1942), 101; R. Plank, "Geschichte der Kälteerzeugung," in *Handbuch der Kältetechnik*, **1** (1954), 1; *75 Jahre Linde* (Munich, 1954); and *Technische Hochschule München, 1868–1968* (Munich, 1968), 102.

FRIEDRICH KLEMM

LINDELÖF, ERNST LEONHARD (*b*. Helsingfors, Sweden [now Helsinki, Finland], 7 March 1870; *d*. Helsinki, 4 June 1946), *mathematics.*

Lindelöf was the son of the mathematician Leonard Lorenz Lindelöf, who was a professor in Helsingfors from 1857 to 1874. He studied in Helsingfors from 1887 to 1900, and spent the year 1891 in Stockholm, 1893 and 1894 in Paris, and 1901 in Göttingen. He passed his university examination in 1895 in Helsingfors and then gave courses in mathematics as a docent. In 1902 he became assistant professor and in 1903 full professor of mathematics. From 1907 he belonged to the editorial board of the *Acta Mathematica*, and he was a member of many learned academies and societies. He received honorary doctoral degrees from the Universities of Uppsala, Oslo, and Stockholm, and he was also named honorary professor by the University of Helsinki. He retired in 1938.

At the beginning of his career Lindelöf published a remarkable work on the theory of differential equations, in which he investigated the existence of solutions ("Sur l'intégration de l'équation differentielle de Kummer," in *Acta Societatis Scientiae Fennicae*, 19 [1890], 1). He soon turned his attention to function theory, and in this area solved some fundamental problems in the theory of analytic functions. His primary field of interest, however, was in entire functions. He considered the mutual dependency between the growth of the function and the coefficients of the Taylor expansion. He also treated the behavior of analytic functions in the neighborhood of a singular point. The investigations concern questions which arise from Picard's problem. Together with Phragmén he developed a general principle that he applied to function theory. His works are characterized by clarity and purity of method as well as elegance of form.

Lindelöf's investigations of analytic continuation with the help of summation formulas had far-reaching results, which are set down in his excellent book *Le calcul des résidus*. In it he examines the role which residue theory (Cauchy) plays in function theory as a means of access to modern analysis. In this endeavor he applies the results of Mittag-Leffler. Moreover, he considers series analogous to the Fourier summation formulas and applications to the gamma function and the Riemann function. In addition, new results concerning the Stirling series and analytic continuation are presented. The book concludes with an asymptotic investigation of series defined by Taylor's formula. The method of successive correction and the examination of this procedure following the studies of Picard and Schwarz is characteristic of Lindelöf's work. His last works dealt with conformal mapping.

Lindelöf early abandoned creative scientific research and devoted himself enthusiastically to his duties as a professor; he was always available to researchers and colleagues. He laid the foundations for the study of the history of mathematics in Finland and trained many students. In an interesting festschrift published in honor of Lindelöf's sixtieth birthday fourteen authors presented papers on function theory, diophantine equations, correlation theory, and number theory.

Lindelöf devoted his last years mainly to publishing textbooks which were noted for their lucidity and comprehensible style. Of his publications, eight deal with the theory of differential equations, twenty-three with function theory, four with the theory of error in harmonic analysis, and five with other fields.

BIBLIOGRAPHY

A listing of Lindelöf's mathematical works may be found in P. J. Myrberg, "Ernst Lindelöf in memoriam," in *Acta Mathematica*, **79** (Uppsala, 1947), i–iv. Lindelöf's major textbooks are *Le calcul des résidus et ses applications à la théorie des fonctions* (Paris, 1905; New York, 1947); *Inldening til högre Analysen* (Stockholm, 1912), translated into Finnish as *Johdatus korkeampaan analysiin* (Helsinki, 1917, new ed., 1956), and German as *Einführung in die höhere Analysis* (Berlin, 1934); *Differentiaali- ja integraali-laska ja sen sovellutukset* ("Differential and Integral Calculus and their Application"), 4 vols. (Helsinki, 1920–1946); and *Johdatus funktioteoriaan* ("Introduction to Function Theory"; Helsinki, 1936).

The festschrift, *Commentationes in honorem Ernesti Leonardi Lindelöf. Die VII Mensis Martii A MCMXXX Sexagenarii*, edited by his students, is in *Suomalaisen tiedeakatemiam toimituksia*, ser. A, **32** (Helsinki, 1929).

HERBERT OETTEL

LINDEMANN, CARL LOUIS FERDINAND (*b.* Hannover, Germany, 12 April 1852; *d.* Munich, Germany, 6 March 1939), *mathematics*.

Lindemann studied in Göttingen, Erlangen, and Munich from 1870 to 1873. He was particularly influenced by Clebsch, who pioneered in invariant theory. Lindemann received the doctorate from Erlangen in 1873, under the direction of F. Klein. His dissertation dealt with infinitely small movements of rigid bodies under general projective mensuration. He then undertook a year-long academic journey to Oxford, Cambridge, London, and Paris, where he met Chasles, J. Bertrand, C. Jordan, and Hermite. In 1877 Lindemann qualified as lecturer at Würzburg. In the same year he became assistant professor at the University of Freiburg. He became full professor in 1879. In 1883 he accepted an appointment at Königsberg and finally, ten years later, one at Munich, where he was for many years also active on the administrative board of the university. He was elected an associate member of the Bavarian Academy of Sciences in 1894, and a full member in 1895.

Lindemann was one of the founders of the modern German educational system. He emphasized the development of the seminar and in his lectures communicated the latest research results. He also supervised more than sixty doctoral students, including David Hilbert. In the years before World War I, he represented the Bavarian Academy in the meetings of the International Association of Academies of Sciences and Learned Societies.

Lindemann wrote papers on numerous branches of mathematics and on theoretical mechanics and spectrum theory. In addition, he edited and revised Clebsch's geometry lectures following the latter's untimely death (as *Vorlesungen über Geometrie* [Leipzig, 1876–1877]).

Lindemann's most outstanding original research is his 1882 work on the transcendence of π. This work definitively settled the ancient problem of the quadrature of the circle; it also redefined and reanimated fundamental questions in the mathematics of its own time.

In the nineteenth century mathematicians had realized that not every real number was necessarily the root of an algebraic equation and that therefore non-algebraic, so-called transcendental, numbers must exist. Liouville stated certain transcendental numbers, and in 1873 Hermite succeeded in demonstrating the transcendence of the base e of the natural logarithms. It was at this point that Lindemann turned his attention to the subject.

The demonstration of the transcendence of π is based on the proof of the theorem that, except for trivial cases, every expression of the form $\sum_{i=1}^{n} A_i e^{a_i}$, where A_i and a_i are algebraic numbers, must always be different from zero. Since the imaginary unity i, as the root of the equation $x^2 + 1 = 0$, is algebraic, and since $e^{\pi i} + e^0 = 0$, then πi and therefore also π cannot be algebraic. So much the less then is π a root, representable by a radical, of an algebraic equation; hence the quadrature of the circle is impossible, inasmuch as π cannot be constructed with ruler and compass.

Lindemann also composed works in the history of mathematics, including a "Geschichte der Polyder und der Zahlzeichen" (in *Sitzungsberichte der mathematisch-physikalischen Klasse der Bayrischen Akademie der Wissenschaften* [1896]). He and his wife collaborated in translating and revising some of the works of Poincaré. Their edition of his *La science et l'hypothèse* (as *Wissenschaft und Hypothese* [Leipzig, 1904]) contributed greatly to the dissemination of Poincaré's ideas in Germany.

BIBLIOGRAPHY

I. ORIGINAL WORKS. In addition to the works cited in the text, see especially "Über die Ludolphsche Zahl," in *Sitzungsberichte der Preussischen Akademie der Wissenschaften zu Berlin*, math.-phys. Klasse, **22** (1882); and "Über die Zahl π," in *Mathematische Annalen*, **25** (1882).

II. SECONDARY LITERATURE. See "Druckschriften-Verzeichnis von F. Lindemann," in *Almanach der Königlich Bayrischen Akademie der Wissenschaften zum 150. Stiftungsfest* (Munich, 1909), 303–306; "F. von Lindemanns 70. Geburtstag," in *Jahresberichte der Mathematikervereinigung*, **31** (1922), 24–30; and C. Carathéodory, "Nekrolog auf Ferdinand von Lindemann," in *Sitzungsberichte der mathematisch-naturwissenschaftlichen Abteilung der Bayrischen Akademie der Wissenschaften zu München*, no. 1 (1940), 61–63.

H. WUSSING

LINDEMANN, FREDERICK ALEXANDER, later **Lord Cherwell** (*b*. Baden-Baden, Germany, 5 April 1886; *d*. Oxford, England, 3 July 1957), *physics*.

Lord Cherwell's father was A. F. Lindemann, a wealthy Alsatian engineer who became a British subject after the Franco-Prussian War; his mother, Olga Noble, was American and of Scottish descent. He was educated in Scotland and Germany, and took his Ph.D. with Nernst in 1910. Together they formulated the Nernst-Lindemann theory of specific heats, and at the same time Lindemann derived his formula relating the melting point of a crystal to the amplitude of vibration of its atoms.

He returned to Britain in August 1914 and joined the Royal Aircraft Establishment to work on problems of flight. Aircraft at that time were prone to spin uncontrollably, often crashing fatally. Lindemann worked out the relevant theory, showed how to recover an aircraft from a spin, and made the first tests of the theory himself. Despite defective eyesight, he had already learned to fly.

In 1919, backed by his friend Henry Tizard, whom he had met in Nernst's laboratory, Lindemann was appointed Dr. Lee's professor of experimental philosophy at Oxford and head of the Clarendon Laboratory. The laboratory was then moribund, for almost no research had been done during its fifty years of existence. Lindemann started the long fight to build it up, often against the prejudice of the classical tradition at Oxford; and in 1933 he strengthened it by giving hospitality to Jewish emigrés from Germany, led by Franz Simon.

During this period he had become the friend of Winston Churchill, and from 1932 the two fought to awaken Britain to the German threat and to the need—and hope—for effective air defense. Here, unhappily, he quarreled with Tizard, who had returned to this field. Ostensibly the quarrel was over priorities, but there was a deeper conflict of personalities, and from 1933 to 1939 Lindemann was in eclipse.

The return of Churchill to the Admiralty brought Lindemann forward as his scientific adviser, a relationship maintained after Churchill became prime minister in 1940. Lindemann advised him over the entire fields of science and economics. Although the two men were apparently very different (Lindemann was aloof, a vegetarian, and a total abstainer), each respected the complementary qualities in the other and they had essentials in common—courage, humor, and a love of language. And while Churchill had excelled at polo, Lindemann was outstanding at tennis; he had won the European championship in Germany in 1914 and later competed at Wimbledon.

Lindemann's wartime advice was sometimes controversial, but the fact that it was sought and accepted signified a changed attitude in the British government. For the first time since the brilliant exception of Lyon Playfair in the nineteenth century, a scientist had a direct voice in national affairs. This change was effected mutually by Churchill and Cherwell, who had been ennobled in 1941 and appointed paymaster general in 1942.

Cherwell returned to Oxford in 1945 but was again with Churchill as paymaster general from 1951 to 1953 and accompanied him to summit meetings. He was primarily responsible for establishing the Atomic

Energy Authority, and when this was assured he returned to Oxford. He retired from his chair in 1956 but continued to influence Churchill's thought, especially regarding technology. The two wanted to establish in England an institution similar to MIT; but tradition proved too strong and a compromise was reached in founding a new college at Cambridge, Churchill College, intended especially to promote technology.

Lindemann's wide interests in physics were reflected in the Lindemann electrometer (in which he perceived the advantages of reducing instrument size), Lindemann glass for transmitting X rays, the Dobson-Lindemann theory of the upper atmosphere, indeterminacy, chemical kinetics, and, with Aston in 1919, the separation of isotopes. While serving as paymaster general during World War II, he proved the prime-number theorem by a new argument. The task of building up the Clarendon Laboratory in a difficult environment took effort that would otherwise have earned him a greater place in personal research; but his ideas illuminated many fields of physics at the pioneering stage. Beyond this, his achievements lie in the success of the laboratory and in the help that he gave Churchill.

BIBLIOGRAPHY

See *The Physical Significance of the Quantum Theory* (London, 1931).

For information on Lindemann's work, see Lord Birkenhead, *The Prof in Two Worlds* (London, 1961); R. F. Harrod, *The Prof* (London, 1959); and G. P. Thomson, "Frederick Alexander Lindemann, Viscount Cherwell 1886–1957," in *Biographical Memoirs of Fellows of the Royal Society*, **4** (1958), 45.

Both Birkenhead and Thomson give complete bibliographies.

R. V. JONES

LINDENAU, BERNHARD AUGUST VON (*b.* Altenburg, Germany, 11 June 1779; *d.* Altenburg, 21 May 1854), *astronomy.*

Lindenau was the son of Johann August Lindenau, a regional administrator *(Landschaftsdirektor).* He began the study of law and mathematics at Leipzig in 1793; and beginning in 1801 he worked at the astronomical observatory directed by F. X. von Zach located at Seeberg, near Gotha. For this purpose he procured a leave of absence from government service. Following Zach's departure (1804) Lindenau became temporary, and in 1808 official, director of the Gotha observatory. There he also was editor of the important technical journal *Monatliche Correspondenz zur Beförderung der Erd- und Himmelskunde.* In 1816, after a temporary absence required by the "War of Liberation" against Napoleon, Lindenau founded, with J. G. F. von Bohnenberger, the *Zeitschrift für Astronomie und verwandte Wissenschaften.* In 1818 he was forced to return to the civil service. His successor at Gotha was J. F. Encke.

Lindenau rapidly advanced from vice-president of the Altenburg board of finance to chief minister of Saxe-Gotha-Altenburg (1820). Later he became minister of the interior of Saxony. In 1848 he was elected to the Frankfurt Parliament. His political activity was comparable with the reforming efforts of Baron Karl vom und zum Stein in Prussia.

An art collector, during his lifetime he established a museum in Altenburg, today known as the Staatliche Lindenau-Museum, which contains one of the most important collections of early Italian panel painting.

Aside from his editorial activity (and considerable assistance in the publication of Bessel's *Fundamenta astronomiae*), Lindenau's importance for astronomy lies mainly in the tables of planets he produced for the calculation of the ephemerides of Mercury, Venus, and Mars. He also published improved values for the constants of aberration and nutation, as well as papers on the history of astronomy. Regrettably, however, astronomy represented only an episode in his life.

BIBLIOGRAPHY

I. ORIGINAL WORKS. Many of Lindenau's publications are listed in J. G. Galle, ed., *Register zu von Zach's Monatlicher Correspondenz zur Beförderung der Erd- und Himmelskunde* (Gotha, 1850), pp. 104–105. Among his writings are *Tabulae Veneris novae et correctae ex theoria gravitatis cl. de Laplace et ex observationibus recentissimis in specula astronomica Seebergensi habitis erutae* (Gotha, 1810); *Tabulae Martis novae et correctae ex theoria gravitatis cl. De la Place et ex observationibus recentissimis erutae* (Eisenberg, 1811); *Investigatio nova orbitae a Mercurio circa solem descriptae cum tabulis planetae* (Gotha, 1813); and "Beitrag zur Geschichte der Neptuns-Entdeckung," in *Ergänzungsheft zu "Astronomische Nachrichten"* (Altona, 1849), pp. 1–32.

II. SECONDARY LITERATURE. Biographies are P. von Ebart, *Bernhard August v. Lindenau* (Gotha, 1896); F. Volger, *Bernhard von Lindenau* (Altenburg, n.d.); and Pasch, "Lindenau," in *Allgemeine Deutsche Biographie*, XVIII (Leipzig, 1883), 681–686. On his political activity, see G. Schmidt, *Die Staatsreform in Sachsen in der ersten Hälfte des 19. Jahrhunderts* (Weimar, 1966), especially pp. 110 ff. Lindenau as an art collector is discussed in H. C. von der Gabelentz and H. Scherf, *Das Staatliche Lindenau-Museum, seine Geschichte, seine Sammlungen* (Altenburg, 1967).

On Lindenau's scientific work, see W. Gresky, "Aus Bernhard v. Lindenaus Briefen an C. F. Gauss," in *Mitteilungen der Gauss-Gesellschaft*, no. 5 (1968), 12–46; D. B. Herrmann, "Lindenaus Abschied von der Astronomie," in *Die Sterne*, **42** (1966), 66–72; and "Bernhard August von Lindenau und die Herausgabe der *Fundamenta astronomiae* von F. W. Bessel," in *Vorträge und Schriften der Archenhold-Sternwarte Berlin-Treptow*, no. 20 (1968); and F. Lessig, "Der Astronom Bernhard von Lindenau," in *Abhandlungen des Naturkundlichen Museums "Mauritianum" Altenburg*, **2** (1960), 29–34.

DIETER B. HERRMANN

LINDGREN, WALDEMAR (*b.* Kalmar, Sweden, 14 February 1860; *d.* Brookline, Massachusetts, 3 November 1939), *geology.*

The leading contributor in his generation to the science of ore deposition, Lindgren stressed the dominance of igneous processes in ore formation, developed a still-useful classification of the metasomatic processes in fissure veins, and was one of the first to identify contact-metamorphic ore bodies in North America. He pioneered in the application of the petrographic microscope to the study of ores and their constituent minerals. The unified study of the geology and ore deposits of extensive regions, which he inaugurated, led to important ideas concerning metallogenetic epochs and laid the foundations for modern concepts of metallogenetic provinces.

The son of Johan Magnus Lindgren, a judge of a provincial court, and Emma Bergman Lindgren, whose ancestors had been important in the history of Sweden for more than three centuries, Waldemar Lindgren displayed a keen interest in mines and minerals when he was young. Encouraged by his parents, he entered the Royal Mining Academy at Freiberg, Saxony, at the age of eighteen. Graduating in 1882 with the degree of mining engineer, he remained there for postgraduate studies in metallurgy and chemistry until, in June 1883, he sailed for America with the hope of participating in the mining and geological activity then flourishing in the western United States. Letters from professors at Freiberg introduced him to Raphael Pumpelly and George F. Becker, and in November 1884 he began an association with the U.S. Geological Survey that continued for thirty-one years.

At first Lindgren was assigned to fieldwork that took him from one western mining district to another; then, in 1905, he became head of the section in the Division of Mineral Resources devoted to the non-ferrous metals, and in 1908 he was made chief of the Division of Metalliferous Geology. Appointed chief geologist of the Survey in 1911, he resigned from that post in 1912 to become William Barton Rogers professor of geology and head of the department of geology at the Massachusetts Institute of Technology. There he served with great distinction, well past the normal retirement age of seventy, until he became professor emeritus in 1933.

A founder of *Economic Geology* in 1905, Lindgren continued as an associate editor of that journal for the rest of his life. While he was chairman of the Division of Geology and Geography of the National Research Council in 1927 and 1928, he established the *Annotated Bibliography of Economic Geology* and subsequently supervised the abstracting of an enormous volume of current literature, foreign as well as American. He also found time to serve as consulting geologist for mining companies in Canada, Mexico, Chile, Bolivia, and Australia. In 1886 he married Ottolina Allstrim of Goteborg, Sweden, who was his inseparable companion until her death in 1929. They had no children.

Lindgren was a member, fellow, or corresponding member of many scientific societies in the United States, Canada, Sweden, Belgium, England, and the Soviet Union. He was president of the Mining and Metallurgical Society of America in 1920, of the Society of Economic Geologists in 1922, and of the Geological Society of America in 1924. The latter society awarded him its Penrose Medal in 1933, and the Geological Society of London bestowed its Wollaston Medal upon him in 1937. The American Institute of Mining and Metallurgical Engineers made Lindgren an honorary life member in 1931, and in 1933 he was honorary chairman of the Sixteenth International Geological Congress.

BIBLIOGRAPHY

I. ORIGINAL WORKS. A "classified list" of Lindgren's scientific writings prior to 1933 (228 titles) accompanies the biographical sketch by L. C. Graton (see below). Many of these writings are in the geologic atlases, annual reports, professional papers, and bulletins of the U.S. Geological Survey; others are contributions to technical journals. To Graton's bibliography should be added 12 titles published in 1933–1938. Among the latter, two are of prime importance: "Differentiation and Ore Deposition, Cordilleran Region of the United States," in *Ore Deposits of the Western States* (New York, 1933), pp. 152–180; and "Succession of Minerals and Temperature of Formation in Ore Deposits of Magmatic Affiliations," in *Technical Publications, American Institute of Mining and Metallurgical Engineers*, no. 713, also in *Transactions of the American Institute of Mining and Metallurgical Engineers*, **126** (1937), 356–376. Notable also is Lindgren's *Mineral Deposits*

(New York, 1913), with rev. and enl. eds. in 1919, 1928, and 1933, which was the standard textbook in economic geology for at least a third of a century.

A considerable file of Lindgren's personal records, correspondence, and memorabilia is in the archives of the Massachusetts Institute of Technology, where the library of the department of earth and planetary sciences is named for him.

II. SECONDARY LITERATURE. The most inclusive and perceptive article about Lindgren is L. C. Graton's "Life and Scientific Works of Waldemar Lindgren," in *Ore Deposits of the Western States*, *Lindgren Volume* (New York, 1933), pp. xiii–xxxii. Among the several obituaries published soon after his death are those by Hans Schneiderholm in *Zentralblatt für Mineralogie*, Abt. A, no. 3 (1940), 65–69; and M. J. Buerger, in *American Mineralogist*, **25** (1940), 184–188.

KIRTLEY F. MATHER

LINDLEY, JOHN (*b.* Catton, near Norwich, England, 5 February 1799; *d.* Turnham Green, Middlesex, England, 1 November 1865), *botany, horticulture.*

A man endowed with an extraordinary capacity for work and a restless, aggressive, untiring intellect, who attained distinction in all his varied activities, Lindley was among the most industrious, many-sided and productive of the nineteenth-century botanists. As administrator, professor, horticulturist, taxonomist, editor, journalist, author, and botanical artist he used to the full his time, his abundant energy, and his remarkable talents, with lasting beneficial results in many fields of botany and horticulture. His major botanical contribution was to the study of orchids.

His father, George Lindley, a skilled but financially unsuccessful nurseryman, could not afford to buy his son an officer's commission in the army or a university education but gave him a good schooling in Norwich to the age of sixteen. Young Lindley then went to Belgium as a British seedsman's representative. He early displayed his remarkable powers of sustained work by translating into English at one sitting L. C. M. Richard's *Démonstrations botaniques, ou Analyse du Fruit* (1808), published in 1819 as *Observations on the Structure of Seeds and Fruits*. In 1818 or 1819 he entered the employment of Sir Joseph Banks as an assistant in the latter's rich library and herbarium, working there for eighteen months with Robert Brown. Banks died in 1820. The Horticultural Society of London had commissioned Lindley in that year to draw some single roses, and in 1822 he entered its service as assistant secretary of its newly established Chiswick garden, thus beginning an association of

forty-three years. His early publications, for which Banks's library and herbarium provided facilities then unrivaled, included *Rasarum monographia* (1820), *Digitalium monographia* (1821), *Collectanea botanica* (1821–1825) and a survey of the Rosaceae subfamily Pomoideae (Pomaceae), published in *Transactions of the Linnean Society of London* (**13** [1821], 88–106), in which he established the genera *Chaenomeles*, *Osteomeles*, *Eriobotrya*, *Photinia*, *Chamaemeles*, and *Raphiolepis*, all still accepted. Together with contributions to the *Botanical Register* (beginning with volume 5, plate 385, August 1819), they quickly won him an international reputation.

These youthful publications displayed remarkable taxonomic judgment, detailed observation, and precision of language in both English and Latin. In 1828, despite his lack of a university education, Lindley was elected Fellow of the Royal Society of London and appointed professor of botany in the newly founded University of London, giving his inaugural lecture in April 1829. He did not, however, relinquish his employment by the Horticultural Society, of which he became general assistant secretary in 1827 and secretary in 1858; indeed, he carried a heavy load of responsibility and made important innovations during the society's troubled years. Late in 1832 the University of Munich, at the instigation of Martius, enterprisingly conferred an honorary Ph.D. upon Lindley. In 1838 he prepared the report on the management of the royal gardens at Kew which led ultimately to the foundation of the Royal Botanic Gardens, Kew, as a national botanical institution.

Time-consuming though his official duties and public activities certainly were, Lindley nevertheless managed to prepare the specific characters for the 16,712 species of flowering plants and cryptogams included in John Loudon's *Encyclopaedia of Plants* (1829) and to produce a series of well-documented, clearly written, authoritative educational publications, including *An Introduction to Botany* (1832; 2nd ed., 1835; 3rd ed., 1839; 4th ed., 1848), of permanent value for its botanical vocabulary (reprinted in W. T. Stearn, *Botanical Latin* [1966], pp. 314–353, and elsewhere), *Flora medica* (1838), *School Botany* (1839; 12th ed., 1862), and *The Theory of Horticulture* (1840; 2nd ed., entitled *The Theory and Practice of Horticulture*, 1855), which Lindley himself considered his best book. He also managed to engage in research, notably in paleobotany, to which Lindley and Hutton's *Fossil Flora of Great Britain* (3 vols., 1831–1837) bears witness, and in orchidology. During Lindley's lifetime European penetration into the moist tropics abounding with Orchidaceae, the employment of professional plant collectors by European nurseries, swifter transport by sea, improved methods of green-house construction and management, and the social prestige associated with orchid-growing by the aristocracy and gentry of Britain, who spent vast sums on this, led to the introduction and successful cultivation of orchids in unprecedented quantity and diversity. They became Lindley's major botanical specialty, and he became the leading authority on their classification. Ultimately he established more than 120 genera of Orchidaceae, among them *Cattleya*, *Cirrhopetalum*, *Coelogyne*, *Laelia*, *Lycaste*, and *Sophronitis*; described many hundreds of new species; and produced three major works: *Genera and Species of Orchidaceous Plants* (1830–1840), *Sertum orchidaceum* (1838), and *Folia orchidacea* (1852–1855), as well as many articles in periodicals.

As a young man Lindley campaigned vigorously against the artificial "sexual system" of classification of plants introduced by Linnaeus and in favor of a more natural system, as propounded by A. L. de Jussieu and A. P. de Candolle and improved in detail by Robert Brown. On his appointment as a professor, he immediately prepared for the use of students *A Synopsis of the British Flora, Arranged According to the Natural Orders* (1829; 2nd ed., 1835; 3rd ed., 1841), the second account of British plants thus classified. In 1830 he published *Introduction to the Natural System of Botany*, which was the first work in English to give descriptions of the families (then called "natural orders") on a worldwide basis; it embodied detailed, firsthand observations of their representatives in the garden and herbarium. Uninfluenced by theories of evolution, and hence without thought of phylogeny, Lindley regarded the characters of plants as "the living Hieroglyphics of the Almighty which the skill of man is permitted to interpret. The key to their meaning lies enveloped in the folds of the Natural System." This he continuously sought to unfold, with but partial success. He took the view that "the investigation of structure and vegetable physiology are the foundation of all sound principles of classification," that within the vegetable kingdom "no sections are capable of being positively defined, except as depend upon physiological peculiarities," and that "physiological characters are of greater importance in regulating the natural classification than structural."

This emphasis led Lindley astray and resulted in major classifications which he himself never found wholly satisfactory, since he changed them from work to work, and which other botanists accepted only in part. Because, however, he also believed "that the affinities of plants may be determined by a consideration of all the points of resemblance between their various parts, properties and qualities; and that thence an arrangement may be deduced in which these species will be placed next each other which have the highest degree of relationship," he gave attention to a much wider range of characters than did many of his contemporaries. Such information, derived from Lindley's profound and extensive observation of plants and a thorough study of available literature, made his *Introduction to the Natural System* (374 pages, 1830) and its enlarged successors, *A Natural System of Botany* (526 pages, 1836) and *The Vegetable Kingdom* (908 pages, with more than 500 illustrations, 1846; 3rd ed., 1853), reference works long unrivaled for matters of detail. In the 1836 work Lindley introduced a nomenclatural reform by proposing that divisions of the same hierarchical standing should have names formed in the same distinctive way, with terminations indicative of these divisions. Thus he consistently used the termination "-aceae" for names of natural orders (now called "families"), replacing, for example, "Umbelliferae" by "Apiaceae" (from *apium*, celery) and "Leguminosae" by "Fabaceae" (from *faba*, broad bean), and the termination "-ales" for alliances (now called "orders"); this became the internationally followed procedure.

In his youth Lindley gallantly but unwisely assumed responsibility for his father's heavy debts, and their redemption burdened him for many years. Hence, driven partly by financial necessity, he took on ever more tasks and duties without relinquishing those he already had. In 1826, for example, he became *de facto* editor of *Botanical Register*; in 1836, superintendent of the Chelsea Physic Garden; in 1841, horticultural editor of *Gardeners' Chronicle*. Between 1833 and 1840 he completed Sibthorp and Smith's magnificent *Flora Graeca* (see *Taxon*, **16** [1967], 168–178); he also wrote innumerable botanical articles in the *Penny Cyclopaedia*. For the London exhibition of 1862 he took charge of the Colonial Department, but the load of manifold onerous activities had now become too great even for a man of his sturdy constitution and stubborn, determined mind. In 1862 his health declined, and Lindley had reluctantly to give up posts he had so honorably and industriously held over many years. In 1865 he died, within a few months of his lifelong friends William Jackson Hooker and Joseph Paxton. His orchid herbarium was acquired by the Royal Botanic Gardens, Kew; his general herbarium by the department of botany, University of Cambridge. His private library, very rich in botanical tracts and pamphlets, became the foundation of the Lindley Library of the Royal Horticultural Society of London, of which he had been so long an efficient servant.

BIBLIOGRAPHY

I. ORIGINAL WORKS. Lindley's books are listed in the text. There is a more detailed list in the Royal Horticultural Society, *The Lindley Library Catalogue* (London, 1927), pp. 256–257. His contributions to periodicals other than the numerous articles in the *Botanical Register* and the *Gardeners' Chronicle* are listed in the Royal Society of London, *Catalogue of Scientific Papers 1800–1863*, IV, 31–32. An unpublished "Bibliography of the Published Works of John Lindley," compiled by J. M. Allford in 1953, lists 236 publications (including eds.) by Lindley. His first publication, "a most ingenious and elaborate description by Mr Lindley, junior" of *Maranta zebrina*, appeared in *Botanical Register*, **5**, pl. 385 (Aug. 1819) and was followed by the text to pls. 397, 404, 419, 420, 425, 430, 431 (1819–1820). He was officially editor of the *Botanical Register* from vol. **16** (1829) to vol. **33** (1847) but contributed most of the articles from vol. **11** (1825) on. Many letters to and from Lindley are at the Royal Botanic Gardens, Kew.

II. SECONDARY LITERATURE. The major sources of biographical information are the obituary in *Gardeners' Chronicle* (1865), 1058–1059, 1082–1083; W. Gardener, "John Lindley," *ibid.*, **158** (1965), 386, 406, 409, 430, 434, 451, 457, 481, 502, 507, 526; and F. Keeble, "John Lindley," in F. W. Oliver, ed., *Makers of British Botany* (London, 1912), 164–177. J. R. Green, *A History of Botany in the United Kingdom* (London, 1914), pp. 336–353, gives a fair assessment of Lindley's scientific work. H. R. Fletcher, *The Story of the Royal Horticultural Society 1804–1968* (London, 1969), contains many references to Lindley in connection with the Society's affairs. Lindley's part in the 1838 committee of inquiry into the management of the Royal Gardens at Kew is summarized by W. T. Stearn, "The Self-Taught Botanists Who Saved the Kew Botanic Garden," in *Taxon*, **14** (Dec. 1965), 293–298.

WILLIAM T. STEARN

LINK, HEINRICH FRIEDRICH (*b.* Hildesheim, Germany, 2 February 1767; *d.* Berlin, Germany, 1 January 1851), *zoology, botany, chemistry, geology, physics.*

Link studied medicine and natural sciences at the University of Göttingen, from which he received the M.D. in 1789 with a dissertation entitled *Florae Göttingensis specimen, sistens vegetabilia saxo calcareo propria* (published in Usteri's *Delectus opusculorum botanicorum*, I [1790], 299–336). In 1792 he was appointed full professor of zoology, botany, and chemistry at the University of Rostock; in 1811, of chemistry and botany at the University of Breslau; and in 1815, of botany at the University of Berlin. In Berlin he was also director of the university's botanic garden.

Link published a great many articles on topics in botany, zoology, geology, and chemistry. His primary interest was in chemistry and physics, and he conducted experiments on adhesion, solution, crystallization, and double salts and acid salts. In his dissertation Link declared himself an adherent of Lavoisier's oxidation theory; he published a critical discussion on phlogiston, "Bemerkungen über das Phlogiston" (1790), as well as papers on the general concept of chemical affinity (1791) and Berthollet's theory of chemical equilibrium (1807). In 1814 Link published an article on the action of sulfuric acid on vegetable material, and in 1815 one on chemical reactions of solids produced by trituration. In 1806 he wrote a textbook on antiphlogistic chemistry: *Die Grundwahrheiten der neuern Chemie.*

Link also published on botany and geology. In 1797–1799 he traveled with Count J. C. von Hoffmannsegg through Portugal, where he studied the flora as well as the geology, agriculture, and industry. In his *Versuch einer Anleitung zur geologischen Kenntniss der Mineralien* (1790), Link declared himself an adherent of neither the neptunist nor the plutonic geological school; rather, he defended the general view that inorganic nature can produce the same materials by different means. In botany, Link published on morphology, classification, anatomy, and physiology of plants; and in zoology, a work on mollusks (1806) which was used by Lamarck. His last zoological publication (1830) dealt with zoophytes.

Link was always deeply interested in the philosophical foundations of the natural sciences. Throughout his life he followed critically the various philosophical currents in Germany. His philosophical thought formed no complete system, and he sought a position intermediate between the prevailing more or less speculative philosophies. In particular, Link was strongly influenced by Kant's dynamical theories of matter; the influence of Schelling's more speculative dynamical concepts was much less, and that of Hegel was negligible. Like the majority of the scientists of his day, Link was greatly interested in the idea of unity in all natural sciences, but he rejected emphatically the speculative *Naturphilosophie* of Schelling and his adherents.

In his first philosophical work, *Ueber Naturphilosophie* (1806), Link started from the concept that it is absolutely necessary for both physicists and chemists to study philosophy. He declared himself against a speculative natural-philosophical mode of thought but praised the dynamical theory of matter given by Kant, although he mentioned many objections against it. It remained the primary task of the natural scientist constantly to examine all natural phenomena. This critical and—to the then-ruling philosophical systems—negative attitude was undoubtedly the reason why Link's views met with great approval among the opponents of *Naturphilosophie* but, on the other hand, could not convince its adherents. The same is true of Link's other philosophical publications, of which *Propyläen der Naturkunde* (1836–1839) is the most important.

From his first publications, Link was averse to an atomic theory of matter. In 1798 he already accepted the infinite divisibility of matter. Like many of his contemporaries, however, in practice Link worked with little particles from which matter could be built up, since he found it possible to explain more phenomena in this way than with the dynamical construction. Link was also very interested in the problem of the nature *(Wesen)* of the liquid and solid states. He took the liquid state as the original form of matter and tried to derive the solid state from it. Many mineralogists, most notably J. J. Bernhardi and J. J. Prechtl, accepted Link's theory as a starting point for a theory of crystallization. Link applied his ideas to the explanation of such phenomena as solution, formation of crystals, chemical reactions, flexibility, and elasticity.

BIBLIOGRAPHY

Link's most important philosophical works are *Ueber Naturphilosophie* (Leipzig–Rostock, 1806); *Ideen zu einer philosophischen Naturkunde* (Breslau, 1814); and *Propyläen der Naturkunde*, 2 vols. (Berlin, 1836–1839).

Among his other publications are *Versuch einer Anleitung zur geologischen Kenntniss der Mineralien* (Göttingen, 1790); *Beyträge zur Physik und Chemie*, 3 vols. (Rostock, 1795–1797); *Beyträge zur Naturgeschichte*, 2 vols. (Rostock–Leipzig, 1797–1801); *Grundriss der Physik* (Hamburg, 1798); *Die Grundwahrheiten der neuern Chemie, nach Fourcroy's Philosophie chimique herausgegeben, mit vielen Zusätzen* (Leipzig–Rostock, 1806); *Grundlehren der Anatomie und Physiologie der Pflanzen* (Göttingen, 1807); *Flore portugaise ou Description de toutes les plantes, qui croissent naturellement en Portugal*, 2 vols. (Berlin, 1809–1820), written with J. C. von Hoffmannsegg; *Elementa philosophiae botanicae* (Berlin, 1824); *Handbuch der physikalischen Erdbeschreibung*, 2 vols. (Berlin, 1826–1830); and *Ueber die Bildung der festen Körper* (Berlin, 1841).

On Link, see C. F. P. von Martius, *Denkrede auf Heinrich Friedrich Link* (Munich, 1851).

H. A. M. SNELDERS

LINNAEUS (or **VON LINNÉ**), **CARL** (*b*. Södra Råshult, Småland, Sweden, 23 May 1707; *d*. Uppsala, Sweden, 10 January 1778), *botany, zoology, geology, medicine.*

During his lifetime, Linnaeus exerted an influence in his fields—botany and natural history—that has had few parallels in the history of science. Driven by indomitable ambition and aided by an incredible capacity for work, he accomplished the tremendous task that he had set for himself in his youth: the establishment of new systems for the three kingdoms of nature to facilitate the description of all known animals, plants, and minerals.

His father, Nils Linnaeus, a country parson in the south Swedish province of Småland, settled in 1709 in Stenbrohult, where Linnaeus grew up. The father was a great lover of flowers and laid out a beautiful garden in the parsonage grounds. He also introduced his son to the mysteries of botany. In 1716 Linnaeus entered the Latin School in the nearby cathedral city of Växjö, and from that time natural history remained his favorite study. An average boy, he was set apart only by his delight in botanizing and learning about plants.

Of great importance for Linnaeus' future development was an outstanding teacher during his last years at Växjö, Johan Rothman, who encouraged his aptitude for botany and taught him Tournefort's system. In 1727 he entered the University of Lund to study medicine. Medical instruction was poor there, but during his stay Linnaeus undertook extensive botanical excursions in the surrounding area and met Kilian Stobaeus, one of the many patrons who helped him in his youth. A medical doctor and a learned polymath, Stobaeus placed his rich library and his collection of natural specimens at Linnaeus' disposition.

In the fall of 1728 Linnaeus went on to the University of Uppsala, lured by its greater reputation. On the whole he must have been disappointed, for the medical faculty was not much better than at Lund. Although he came to rely mostly on his own, independently acquired abilities as a botanist and natural historian, the atmosphere of Uppsala was in many ways useful. The botanical garden, although somewhat neglected, contained rare foreign plants, and he found influential promoters: the elderly professor of medicine Olof Rudbeck the younger, formerly an outstanding botanist and zoologist, and the learned Olof Celsius, with whom Linnaeus studied the flora of the surrounding region.

Around 1730 Linnaeus matured as a researcher and began delineating the fundamental features of his botanical reform. In a series of manuscripts, unpublished at the time, he noted the results of his observations and thoughts. He had already found the tool with which to construct a new system of plant taxonomy—the new theory of plant sexuality. At this time Linnaeus' sexual system first appeared, still incomplete, in a manuscript version of his *Hortus uplandicus* (1730).

Linnaeus barely supported himself during this period by substituting for Rudbeck in conducting demonstrations at the botanical garden and by giving private lessons. In the spring of 1732, sponsored by the Uppsala Society of Science, he made a trip to Lapland that lasted until the fall. His account of the journey (first published in English translation in 1811) gives vivid evidence of his joy in the unfamiliar world of the Scandinavian mountains, in which he studied the unknown alpine flora and Lapp customs. Two years later (1734) he undertook another, more modest study trip in the Dalarna region of central Sweden. He constantly revised his manuscripts and widened his teaching activities with courses in mineralogy and assaying. In the spring of 1735 Linnaeus left Sweden—with a Lapp costume, a troll-drum, and unpublished manuscripts in his luggage—to obtain the M.D. in Holland. At the University of Harderwijk he defended a thesis on the causes of ague, received his degree, and went on to Leiden.

Linnaeus' sojourn in Holland lasted until 1738. It was a period of uninterrupted success in approaching his goal of being acknowledged as Europe's outstanding botanist. Learned and wealthy patrons continued to help him: Boerhaave, J. F. Gronovius in Leiden, and the botanist Jan Burman in Amsterdam fostered Linnaeus' plans and helped to see his works through to publication. During a short visit to England in 1736 he met Sir Hans Sloane and J. J. Dillenius. Most of the time he stayed with George Clifford, a wealthy merchant who established an incomparable botanical garden at the Hartekamp, near Haarlem; as its superintendent Linnaeus could concentrate on his botanical work.

Linnaeus' literary production during his three years in Holland is astonishing. Most of the works had been nearly finished in Sweden; but others, such as *Hortus Cliffortianus* (1737), a beautiful folio on the plants in Clifford's garden and greenhouse, were newly composed. Linnaeus' key work, and the first to be published in Holland, was *Systema naturae* (1735). On seven folio leaves he presented in a schematic arrangement his new system for the animal, plant, and mineral kingdoms; the plants were arranged according to the sexual system that this work first made known to the scientific world. In the small *Fundamenta botanica* (1736) Linnaeus put forward with dictatorial authority his theory for systematic botany, and in *Bibliotheca botanica* he listed the botanical literature in systematic fashion. Other works of this period are *Flora lapponica* (1737), in which he described his botanical collections from the Lapland journey; *Critica botanica* (1737), with rules for botanical nomenclature; *Classes plantarum* (1738), in which he reviewed the various plant systems going back to Cesalpino; and *Genera plantarum* (1737), which, next to *Systema naturae*, is his outstanding early work and contains short descriptions of all 935 plant genera known at the time.

Linnaeus then set out for Sweden via Paris, where he visited the brothers Jussieu, and by June 1738 he was back in his native country. His foreign triumphs had not gone unnoticed; but no academic position awaited him, and he was obliged to become a practicing physician in Stockholm. He married Sara Elisabeth Moraea, the daughter of a wealthy city physician. In 1739 he was appointed physician to the admiralty and was one of the moving powers in the founding of the Swedish Academy of Science in Stockholm, of which he became the first president and eventually the most outstanding member.

A new phase of Linnaeus' life began in the spring of 1741. After a rather scandalous fight for tenure he was appointed professor of practical medicine at the University of Uppsala; in 1742, through a sort of job exchange, he took over the more suitable chair of botany, dietetics, and materia medica. For the rest of his life Linnaeus remained in Uppsala as professor of medicine, while his fame as premier botanist spread throughout the world.

One of his first tasks was to renovate the university's neglected botanical garden, founded in 1655 by Rudbeck the elder. Remodeled in French style with formal parterres and an ornamental orangery, it was filled over the years with innumerable plants from Europe and distant parts of the world. Linnaeus spent the rest of his life in the professorial residence in a corner of the garden.

As a teacher and supervisor Linnaeus was incomparable. Students flocked to his lectures, which were characterized by humor and the presentation of unusual ideas, and which included the whole of botany and natural history. He liked dealing with what he called "the natural diet," that is, man's way of living under the pressure of civilization. In private seminars he gave deeper insights into his botanical thought. His botanical excursions held near Uppsala were immensely popular; these *herbationes* were organized according to a fixed ritual: on the return home the participants marched in closed formation to the music of French horns and drums.

Linnaeus took an unselfish and devoted interest in his more mature students, supporting and encouraging them. He persuaded an imposing number of them to obtain the doctorate, but he usually wrote their theses himself (collected under the title *Amoenitates academicae*, I–VII [1749–1769]; VIII–X [1785–1790]).

From 1759 Linnaeus was assisted by his son Carl von Linné the younger, who had been appointed botanical demonstrator and who succeeded his father. Linnaeus occasionally worked for the royal court: he described the valuable natural history collections at Ulriksdal and at the castle of Drottningholm, and charmed the discerning queen, Lovisa Ulrika, by his unaffected manner. On the whole he had an unerring instinct for profitable social connections; he counted among his friends and admirers the country's outstanding cultural leaders, including the president of the chancellery, Carl Gustaf Tessin.

Linnaeus was in contact with the world's botanists and collectors of natural history specimens. He corresponded with them and received seeds for his garden and plants for his herbarium, which became very extensive. He became a member of innumerable foreign scientific societies (he was one of the eight foreign members of the Paris Academy in 1762) and received distinctions and honors in Sweden; in 1747 he was appointed court physician and in 1762 he was elevated to the nobility as von Linné. In later years he traveled every summer to Hammarby, his small estate outside Uppsala; there, free from academic chores, he devoted himself to botany or taught selected students.

Linnaeus' research work during his mature years began with trips to various Swedish provinces. By order of the parliament, which wanted an inventory of all the natural resources of the country, during three summers in the 1740's Linnaeus traveled through selected areas to describe them and to search for dyestuffs, minerals, clay, and other economically useful substances. His reports of these expeditions were published as *Ölandska och gothländska resa* (1745), *Västgöta resa* (1747), and *Skånska resa* (1751), all written in Swedish. Nothing escaped his attention on his travels on horseback—plants and insects, runic stones and other ancient remnants, farmers working in the fields and meadows, the changes in the weather. His prose style was simple and strong, sometimes rising to lyrical outbursts or spiced with effective similes.

But Linnaeus' main mission was to complete his reform of botany. In the work produced during his stay in Holland he had established the principles, maintained more or less unchanged for the rest of his life, but they still had to be developed and put into practice. In 1751 he published *Philosophia botanica*, his most influential work but actually only an expanded version of *Fundamenta botanica*. In it Linnaeus dealt with the theory of botany, the laws and rules that the botanist must follow in order to describe and name the plants correctly and to combine them into higher systematic categories. At the same time he struggled with the enormous undertaking of cataloging all of the world's plant and animal species and giving each its correct place in the system.

Linnaeus started modestly with his native land: *Flora suecica*, containing 1,140 species, appeared in 1745 and *Fauna suecica* followed a year later. The remaining inventory of the world's flora was arduous; surrounded by herbarium sheets and folios, Linnaeus occasionally felt unable to continue. Yet before long he completed the monumental *Species plantarum* (1753), the work he valued the most. In its two volumes he described in brief Latin diagnoses about 8,000 plant species from throughout the world. He also continued to update his *Systema naturae*, which, as the bible of natural history, was to present the current state of knowledge and which he periodically expanded and revised. The definitive tenth edition (1758–1759), which included only animal and plant species, was a two-volume work of 1,384 pages.

Linnaeus had to pay the price his ambitions demanded. After suffering a fit of apoplexy in the spring of 1774 that forced him to retire from teaching, his mind became increasingly clouded; another stroke followed in the fall of 1776, and he died early in 1778.

A born taxonomist and systematist, Linnaeus had a deep-rooted, almost compulsive need for clarity and order; everything that passed through his hands he cataloged and sorted into groups and subgroups. This characteristic typifies all of his writings, including his private correspondence. His view of the universe as a gigantic nature collection that God had given him to describe and to fit into a framework was applied first to his reform of botany. There was at that time an urgent need for a simple and easy-to-grasp system for the plant kingdom. A stream of previously unknown plants was reaching Europe, and botanists felt chaos threatening. Since the time of Cesalpino many botanists had tried to create a useful system; and toward the eighteenth century some of these systems had begun to win considerable support, especially those of John Ray and Tournefort, based upon the appearance of the corolla. But none was sufficiently practical, and the various systems were reciprocally competitive, thus increasing the confusion. Only Linnaeus' system, based on sexuality, had the requisite of being generally adoptable.

Around 1720 the sexuality of plants was still being disputed by many botanists. Linnaeus had already learned about it from his teacher Rothman at the Växjö Gymnasium, following the publication of Sébastien Vaillant's *Sermo de structura florum* (1717). As a student at Uppsala he had pursued the subject through his own investigations and soon was convinced of its truth. In the small *Praeludia sponsaliorum plantarum* (1730), written in Swedish, he announced that the stamens and pistils were the sexual organs of plants. At the same time he began to investigate whether the stamens and pistils could be used to construct a new botanical system. After a short period of doubt he was sure that they could, and in *Systema naturae* he presented the sexual system in its definitive form. The various plants are grouped into twenty-four classes according to the number of stamens and their relative order; each class is then divided into certain orders, mostly according to the number of pistils. The practical applicability of the sexual system made botany an easy and pleasant science; after one look at the organs of fertilization, any plant could quickly be placed in the proper class and order. To be sure, the system was attacked: in Germany by J. G. Siegesbeck and Heister, in Switzerland by Haller, and in France, where Tournefort's system had long been generally accepted. But acceptance of the sexual system could not be halted; it gained footing almost everywhere, especially in England, beginning in the 1760's.

Linnaeus was aware that the sexual system was an artificial structure. It was founded with rigid consistency upon a single principle of division and therefore represented the natural affinities only partially. Linnaeus tried throughout his life to replace the sexual system with a *methodus naturalis*, a botanical system that would express the "natural" relations. In *Classes plantarum* (1738) he described sixty-five plant orders that he considered natural, and he returned to the problem in private lectures toward the end of his life—but he never succeeded in solving it. A natural plant system presented theoretical difficulties that he was unable to overcome; in practice he seems to have depended on an intuitive knowledge of the general similarity (facies) of plants. Therefore Linnaeus and his pupils continued to use the sexual system, and it remained for the French (Adanson, A. L. de Jussieu) to lay the foundation of a natural botanical system in the modern sense of the word.

Linnaeus' other achievements as the reorganizer of botany were as fundamental as the sexual system. He made a deep study of the principles of taxonomy and with masterly clarity worked out fixed rules for the differentiation of the lowest systematic categories—genera and species—both of which were, according to him, "natural." Although Tournefort had already delineated the genus with great precision, it remained for Linnaeus, inspired by Ray, to be the first to work with species as a clearly defined concept. The species were the basic units of botany, and for a long time he considered them to be fixed and unchangeable:

"We can count as many species now as were created at the beginning." He united closely related species in genera according to the appearance of their sexual organs.

Linnaeus dictated with inexorable logic in *Philosophia botanica* how botanists should proceed in practice. Every species had to be differentiated from all other species within the genus through a Latin *differentia specifica*, that is, a short diagnosis (twelve words at most) including the characteristic scientific name or *nomen specificum*. Furthermore, there had to be a longer, complete description of the whole plant. Linnaeus himself laid down the morphological terms that every taxonomist should use for each part of the plant, in order to avoid confusion.

Latin species names notwithstanding, the precision ordered by Linnaeus was nevertheless found to be unmanageable, and he therefore took a decisive step—the introduction of binomial nomenclature. Heralded in his bibliographical writings, it is effectively used for the first time in his dissertation on the plants eaten by animals, "Pan suecicus" (1749), and was subsequently applied in *Species plantarum* (1753). The binomial nomenclature implied that every plant species would be provided with only two names: one for the genus and one for the species. Linnaeus was delighted by the idea; it "was like putting the clapper in the bell." Yet at the beginning he did not realize its full import. He considered the new species names only as handy labels, calling them "trivial names"; they could never replace the scientific "specific" names. Only gradually did he understand the practical advantages offered by the new nomenclature, and he then decreed that the "trivial name" should be unchangeable. Since then his own *Species plantarum* has been the solid basis for botanical nomenclature.

Linnaeus' botanical ideas changed over the years on an important point: he was forced to relinquish confidence in the constancy of the number of species. In *Peloria* (1744) he described a monstrous form of *Linaria vulgaris* that he wrongly interpreted as a hybrid between *Linaria* and a completely different plant. He thereafter held that new plant species could develop through hybridization (see *Plantae hybridae* [1751]) and reached the daring conclusion that within every genus only one species had originally been created, and that new species had developed in time through hybridization of the mother species with species of other genera. This concept was based upon a peculiar theory, traceable to Cesalpino, concerning the "marrow" and the "bark": Every organism was supposed to consist of a marrow substance (medulla), which was inherited from the mother, and a bark substance (cortex), inherited from the father.

All species within the same genera had a common marrow covered by bark substances deriving from different fathers. Around 1760 Linnaeus took the full step and asserted that for every natural plant order only one species had been created at the beginning; the various genera and species came into existence through cross-fertilization at different levels. The theory, although interesting as an attempt to approach a genetic kinship concept, has nothing to do with a theory of evolution in the modern, Darwinian sense of the word.|

As a botanist Linnaeus was monumentally one-sided. To order the plants in a system *(divisio)* and to name them *(denominatio)* was for him the real task of botany. He scorned anatomy and physiology and had little understanding of the then developing experimental biological investigations. To be sure, many acute observations in various areas of botany can be found in his works, especially in his academic dissertations. They deal in large part with ecology. Linnaeus investigated the dormancy of plants and the pollination process, undertaking some simple experiments in connection with the latter. With a sharp eye he distinguished different climatic and phytogeographical regions and dealt successfully with problems of dispersion (wind dissemination of seeds and fruits, and so on).

Worked out in *Oeconomia naturae* (1749) and *Politia naturae* (1760), Linnaeus' views on the harmony or order in nature are of great interest. Here his perspective broadens; he sees organic nature as an eternal cyclic course of life and death in which every plant and animal species fulfills its destined task in the service of the whole. The domination of the insects prevents the plants from filling the world; the birds contain the insects within fixed limits. Intense competition prevails in nature, but precisely because of it a delicate balance is maintained that permits the work of creation to function. Both Erasmus and Charles Darwin later profitably adopted some of Linnaeus' views on the hidden struggle in nature.

Linnaeus' real mastery, in botanical systematics, was more problematic than generally realized. He was an empiricist and a brilliant observer whom nothing escaped. As an exact depicter of natural phenomena he scarcely had an equal. His herbarium comprised dried plants from all parts of the world, and he himself scrutinized more plant species than any of his predecessors. But he was ultimately forced by his special talents to abandon empiricism and instead stamped his work as taxonomist and systematist with a dogmatic and philosophical spirit. Order was paramount, and therefore he resorted to an artificial structure in his effort to place nature's swarming multitudes in a simple, clear scheme. He violated nature, as in the sexual system he devised. Linnaeus' scientific method implied that with the aid of certain rules, once and for all determined by himself, the three kingdoms of nature would be organized. He considered the *Philosophia botanica* to be a statute book spelling out the terminology and concepts to be used by botanists. Logic and definitions of concepts were the true tools of botany.

The fixed basis of Linnaeus' system was derived from Aristotelian logic, and as a taxonomist he strictly applied its procedure *per genus et differentiam.* Significantly, he gratefully acknowledged his dependence on the neo-Aristotelian Andrea Cesalpino. As pointed out by Julius Sachs (1875), Linnaeus' reformation of botany undoubtedly carried a Scholastic stamp, the problems that he wanted to solve with his systematic work being of a logical nature. The Scholastic feature is also noticeable in his conviction that the sexual organs are the real "essences" of plants and therefore must be made the basis for the classification system. He preferred to give his writing a Scholastic form and argued *pro* and *contra* like a medieval doctor. All of his work shows a tension between empirical and logical demands, and in situations of conflict the latter almost always wins.

| Linnaeus' classification of the animal and mineral kingdoms does not display the same rigorous consistency as his plant system. Presented and revised in the various editions of *Systema naturae,* his animal system was of considerable influence. It is somewhat forced and artificial; but Linnaeus, who here had Ray as principal forerunner, nevertheless sought a natural arrangement and often succeeded brilliantly. He did not use, as in botany, a single, universally valid basis for division but tried to divide the six animal classes he had distinguished by means of a specific organ: mammals according to teeth, birds according to bills, fishes according to fins, and insects according to wings. Added to these are the reptiles (Amphibia) and the "worms" (Vermes), the large group of animals without backbone. In the first edition of *Systema* Linnaeus described 549 animal forms; the last edition included 5,897 species.

In details he was rather unfortunate as a zoological taxonomist, particularly with the "worms" (Vermes), which he arranged elaborately according to misleading exterior features. He united pigs, armadillos, and moles in the same mammalian order and considered the rhinoceros to be a rodent. But as a whole Linnaeus' animal system signified a considerable advance. He unhesitatingly united man with the apes and was the first to recognize whales as mammals (1758). Linnaeus was at his best in entomology, which from his youth had been his favorite field apart from botany; the insect orders he recognized are essentially still valid. In the important tenth edition of *Systema* (1758–1759), he used the "trivial name" consistently in the animal kingdom. As a result it became the standard text for all zoological nomenclature.

Linnaeus' system of the mineral kingdom had little influence but was not without its interesting features. Although he attached great importance to crystal structure for classification and thus was one of the pioneers in crystallography (*De crystallorum generatione*[1747]), he had no feeling for the chemical composition of minerals and consequently stood outside of the fruitful contemporary trends in mineral systematics. More important were his contributions to paleontology and historical geology: he described many fossils, including trilobites (entomolithus), which he correctly placed among the arthropods. In his odd speech on "The Growth of the Earth" ("Oratio de telluris habitabilis incremento" [1743]) and in later works Linnaeus gave his conception of the development of the planet. Inspired by the Christian doctrine of paradise and the old concept of the golden age, he imagined paradise as an island on the equator, from which animals and plants, with the decrease of the water, spread out over the earth. In the 1740's he contributed observations in the field to the lively debates in Sweden about "water reduction," i.e., the uplift of the Swedish plateau in postglacial time. He believed that the sedimentary strata had been deposited over enormous time periods but, mindful of ecclesiastical orthodoxy, he was wary of expressing his heretical views on the age of the world and the length of the geological epochs.

As a university teacher Linnaeus worked within the medical faculty and published many medical works of varying value. His passion for order and classification extended to his medical work, and through his *Genera morborum* (1763) he figures with François Boissier de Sauvages as the founder of systematic nosology. To a great extent inspired by Sauvages, with whom he maintained a lively correspondence, Linnaeus methodically grouped diseases into classes, orders, and genera according to their symptoms. His theory, explained in *Exanthemata viva* (1757), which holds that certain diseases are caused by invisible living organisms *(acari)*, is interesting but not original; he cites A. Q. Bachmann (Rivinus) as precursor. Linnaeus applied his botanical knowledge in the three-volume *Materia medica* (1749–1763) and sought medical profundity in the peculiar *Clavis medicinae* (1766). Filled with number mysticism and based upon speculations about "marrow" and "bark," *Clavis medicinae* is almost incomprehensible in its

classification of diseases according to complaints deriving from maternal marrow or paternal bark substance.

Linnaeus had a tendency toward unrestrained, impulsive speculation; for him, vague fancies often became eternal truths that needed no close examination. Similarly, he sometimes put blind faith in fables and folk tales; during his entire life he remained convinced that swallows slept on the bottom of lakes during the winter. He was also rather old-fashioned and simplistic in his general theory of nature, which had a strong Stoic-Aristotelian basis. The peculiar theological remarks that Linnaeus later in life collected under the title *Nemesis divina* (first published in 1848) also belong in this category. They deal, in melancholic fatalism, with divine retribution as the law ruling human existence.

Linnaeus attained worldwide influence not only through his writings but also through his students. A great many foreign students came to him in Uppsala to learn the foundations of systematic natural science. They included the Scandinavians Peter Ascanius and J. C. Fabricius, the entomologist; the Germans Johann Beckmann, Paul D. Giseke, J. C. D. Schreber; the Russian Barons Demidoff; and the American Adam Kuhn, who became professor in Philadelphia. All of them helped to spread the Linnaean doctrine in their own countries.

The world was Linnaeus' sphere of activity also in another sense. He sent many of his students abroad, rejoicing in the plants and other natural specimens that he received from them but grieving bitterly when they died of disease or hardship. Peter Kalm traveled in North America and Fredrik Hasselquist in Egypt, Syria, and Palestine; Peter Osbeck and others sailed on East Indian merchant ships to China. Peter Forsskål went to Arabia as a member of a Danish-German expedition, while Pehr Loefling, Linnaeus' favorite pupil, died in Venezuela. Daniel Solander sailed with Joseph Banks on Captain Cook's first global circumnavigation, and later Anders Sparrman sailed under Cook's command across the Pacific. The most industrious of all Linnaean travelers, Karl Peter Thunberg, managed after many trips to gain entry into Japan. Linnaeus not only received botanical specimens from his pupils but also, on occasion, published posthumously their travel descriptions, such as Hasselquist's *Iter Palaestinum* (1757) and Loefling's *Iter Hispanicum* (1758).

Linnaeus was a complicated man. His enormous scientific production was supported by a self-esteem almost without parallel. He considered his published works to be unblemished masterpieces; no one had ever been a greater botanist or zoologist. Unable to accept criticism, he sulked like a child when he encountered it. He persecuted those, like Buffon, who did not accept him. Linnaeus looked upon himself as a prophet called by God to promulgate the only true dogma; botanists who did not follow the rules and regulations in *Philosophia botanica* clearly were "heretics." Of unstable temperament and essentially naïve, he vacillated between overweening pride and brooding despair. His peculiarities often made him difficult; many were repelled by his egocentric behavior, and over the years he became increasingly isolated.

Yet Linnaeus also could radiate an overpowering charm, and almost all of his students loved him. In a sunny mood, as one sees him in his letters and other relaxed moments, he was irresistible. In playful moods he interpreted nature in the light of classical mythology or personified it. His view of nature was deeply religious; central to all his work was God's omnipotence. He never deviated from the devout physico-theology that was widespread in the eighteenth century, but he stamped it with his peculiar sense of mystery and wonder. "I saw," he wrote in the introduction to the later editions of *Systema naturae*, "the infinite, all-knowing and all-powerful God from behind as He went away and I grew dizzy. I followed His footsteps over nature's fields and saw everywhere an eternal wisdom and power, an inscrutable perfection."

BIBLIOGRAPHY

I. ORIGINAL WORKS. Linnaeus' library, herbarium, archives, and MSS were left to his only son, Carl von Linné the younger, who succeeded his father as professor of botany. After the son's death in 1783, the collections were sold for 900 guineas to the young English physician James Edward Smith, who in 1788 founded the Linnean Society of London. Since then the Linnean Society has been the keeper of all Linnaeus' collections. Swedish libraries have only a few of the more important MSS, such as *Praeludia sponsaliorum plantarum* and *Nemesis divina*, both in the library of Uppsala University.

Two complete modern bibliographies are J. M. Hulth, *Bibliographia Linnaeana*, I, pt. 1 (Uppsala, 1907); and B. H. Soulsby, *A Catalogue of the Works of Linnaeus* (London, 1933), which includes works about Linnaeus. Two modern facsimile eds. are *Genera plantarum*, which is Historiae Naturalis Classica, III (Weinheim, 1960); and *Species plantarum*, 2 vols. (London, 1957–1959), both with important intros. by W. T. Stearn.

Praelectiones in ordines naturales plantarum was published by P. D. Giseke (Hamburg, 1792). Collections of letters from Linnaeus or to him include D. H. Stöver, ed., *Collectio epistolarum quas ... scripsit Carolus a Linné* (Hamburg, 1792); J. E. Smith, ed., *A Selection of the*

Correspondence of Linnaeus and Other Naturalists, 2 vols. (London, 1821); C. N. J. Schreiber, ed., *Epistolae ad Nicolaum Josephum Jacquin* (Vienna, 1841); and *Lettres inédites de Linné à Boissier de la Croix de Sauvages* (Alais [Alès], 1860). Publication of the whole of Linnaeus' correspondence was never completed: T. M. Fries, J. M. Hulth, and A. H. Uggla, eds., *Bref och skrifvelser af och till Carl von Linné*, 10 vols. (I, 8 vols.; II, 2 vols.) (Stockholm–Uppsala, 1907–1943). E. Ährling, *Carl von Linnés brefvexling* (Stockholm, 1885), contains a complete list of the letters to Linnaeus in the Linnean Society.

A critical ed. of Linnaeus' five preserved autobiographies is in E. Malmeström and A. H. Uggla, *Vita Caroli Linnaei* (Stockholm, 1957).

Works from Linnaeus' youth, including those on the Lapland and Dalarna trips, are in E. Ährling, *Carl von Linnés ungdomsskrifter*, 2 vols. (Stockholm, 1888–1889). The Lapland voyage, *Iter lapponicum*, was translated by J. E. Smith as *Lachesis lapponica or a Tour in Lappland*, 2 vols. (London, 1811); a critical ed. is in T. M. Fries, ed., *Skrifter af Carl von Linné*, V (Uppsala, 1913). There is also A. H. Uggla, ed., *Dalaresa* (with *Iter ad exteros* and *Iter ad fodinas*) (Stockholm, 1953), with commentary.

See also A. H. Uggla, ed., *Diaeta naturalis 1733* (Uppsala, 1958); A. O. Lindfors, ed., "Linnés dietetik," in *Uppsala universitets årsskrift* (1907); Einar Lönnberg, ed., *Föreläsningar öfver djurriket* (Uppsala, 1913); E. Malmeström and T. Fredbärj, eds., *Nemesis divina* (Stockholm, 1968), the first complete ed.

II. SECONDARY LITERATURE. The literature on Linnaeus is very comprehensive; a survey is given in Sten Lindroth, "Two Centuries of Linnaean Studies," in *Bibliography and Natural History* (Lawrence, Kans., 1966), pp. 27–45.

The first biographies appeared in the eighteenth century: Richard Pulteney, *A General View of the Writings of Linnaeus* (London, 1781); and D. H. Stöver, *Leben des Ritters Carl von Linné*, 2 vols. (Hamburg, 1792), also translated into English (London, 1794). Another older biography is J. F. X. Gistel, *Carolus Linnaeus. Ein Lebensbild* (Frankfurt, 1873). T. M. Fries, *Linné*, 2 vols. (Stockholm, 1903), translated into English in an abridged version by Benjamin Daydon Jackson as *Linnaeus: The Story of His Life* (London, 1923), is the indispensable modern biography for all Linnaean research. Among later, shorter popular biographies are Knut Hagberg, *Carl Linnaeus* (Stockholm, 1939; rev. ed., 1957), also translated into English (London, 1952); Norah Gourlie, *The Prince of Botanists: Carl Linnaeus* (London, 1953); Elis Malmeström, *Carl von Linné* (Stockholm, 1964); Heinz Goerke, *Carl von Linné*, which is Grosse Naturforscher no. 31 (Stuttgart, 1966); and Wilfrid Blunt, *The Compleat Naturalist. A Life of Linnaeus* (London, 1971). For Linnaean iconography, see Tycho Tullberg, *Linnéporträtt* (Uppsala, 1907).

A. J. Boerman has dealt with *Carolus Linnaeus als middelaar tussen Nederland en Zweden* (Utrecht, 1953). Articles on Linnaeus' life and work are being published in *Svenska Linnésällskapets årsskrift* (Uppsala, 1918–   ). *Carl von Linné's Bedeutung als Naturforscher und Arzt* (Jena, 1909), published by the Swedish Academy of Science in a collection of papers, reviews Linnaeus' scientific achievements. Nils von Hofsten deals with Linnaeus' conception of nature in *Kungliga Vetenskaps-societetens årsbok 1957* (Uppsala, 1958), pp. 65–105. An attempt to evaluate Linnaeus in terms of the history of ideas and psychology is Sten Lindroth, "Linné–legend och verklighet," in *Lychnos* (1965–1966), pp. 56–122.

Valuable insights on Linnaeus as a botanist are in Julius Sachs, *Geschichte der Botanik* (Munich, 1875). The best modern summary of Linnaeus' botanical ideas is Gunnar Eriksson, *Botanikens historia i Sverige intill år 1800*, which is Lychnos-Bibliotek, XVII, 3 (Uppsala, 1969). His taxonomic and systematic principles are investigated in J. Ramsbottom, "Linnaeus and the Species Concept," in *Proceedings of the Linnean Society of London*, **150** (1938), 192–219; H. K. Svenson, "On the Descriptive Method of Linnaeus," in *Rhodora*, **47** (1945), 273–302, 363–388; C. E. B. Bremekamp, "Linné's Views on the Hierarchy of the Taxonomic Groups," in *Acta botanica neerlandica*, **2** (1953), 242–253; A. J. Cain, "Logic and Memory in Linnaeus's System of Taxonomy," in *Proceedings of the Linnean Society of London*, **169** (1958), 144–163; W. T. Stearn, *Three Prefaces on Linnaeus and Robert Brown* (Weinheim, 1962); and James L. Larson, *Reason and Experience. The Representation of Natural Order in the Work of Carl von Linné* (Berkeley, 1971).

On the binomial nomenclature, see W. T. Stearn, "The Background of Linnaeus's Contributions to the Nomenclature and Methods of Systematic Biology," in *Systematic Zoology*, **8**, no. 1 (1959), 4–22; and John L. Heller, "The Early History of Binomial Nomenclature," in *Huntia*, **1** (1964), 33–70. Linnaeus' relations to other botanists are discussed in Heinz Goerke, "Die Beziehungen Hallers zu Linné," in *Sudhoffs Archiv für Geschichte der Medizin und der Naturwissenschaften*, **38** (1954), 367–377; and Hans Krook, "Lorenz Heister och Linné," in *Svenska Linné-sällskapets årsskrift*, **31** (1948), 57–72.

On Linnaeus' zoological system, see Nils von Hofsten, "Linnés djursystem," in *Svenska Linnésällskapets årsskrift*, **42** (1959), 9–43; and "A System of 'Double Entries' in the Zoological Classification of Linnaeus," in *Zoologiska bidrag från Uppsala*, **35** (1963), 603–631. In addition there is Thomas Bendyshe, "On the Anthropology of Linnaeus," in *Memoirs Read Before the Anthropological Society of London*, **1** (1863–1864), 421–458. On Darwin and Linnaeus, see Robert C. Stauffer, "Ecology in the Long Manuscript Version of Darwin's *Origin of Species* and Linnaeus," in *Proceedings of the American Philosophical Society*, **104** (1960), 235–241. Linnaeus' geological thought is examined in Tore Frängsmyr, *Geologi och skapelsetro. Föreställningar om jordens historia från Hiärne till Bergman*, which is Lychnos-Bibliotek, XXVI (Uppsala, 1969), ch. 4; and his nosological system in Fredrik Berg, "Linné et Sauvages: Les rapports entre leurs systèmes nosologiques," in *Lychnos* (1956), pp. 31–54; and *Linnés Systema morborum* (Uppsala, 1957).

Elis Malmeström considers Linnaeus as theological thinker in *Carl von Linnés religiösa åskådning* (Stockholm, 1926); and "Die religiöse Entwicklung und die Weltan-

schauung Carl von Linnés," in *Zeitschrift für systematische Theologie*, **19** (1942), 31–58. See also Elof Ehnmark, "Linnaeus and the Problem of Immortality," in *Kungliga Humanistiska vetenskapssamfundet i Lund, Årsberättelse* (1951–1952), pp. 63–93. Linnaeus' view of man is analyzed in K. R. V. Wikman, *Lachesis and Nemesis*, which is Scripta Instituti Donneriani Aboensis, no. 6 (Stockholm, 1970).

For the spread of Linnaean botany, see Frans A. Stafleu, *Linnaeus and the Linnaeans. The Spreading of Their Ideas in Systematic Botany (1735–1789)* (Utrecht, 1971).

STEN LINDROTH

LIOUVILLE, JOSEPH (*b.* St.-Omer, Pas-de-Calais, France, 24 March 1809; *d.* Paris, France, 8 September 1882), *mathematics*.

Liouville is most famous for having founded and directed for almost forty years one of the major mathematical journals of the nineteenth century, the *Journal de Liouville*. He also made important contributions in pure and applied mathematics and exerted a fruitful influence on French mathematics through his teaching.

The few articles devoted to Liouville contain little biographical data. Thus the principal stages of his life and career must be reconstructed on the basis of original documentation. There is no exhaustive list of Liouville's works, which are dispersed in some 400 publications—the most nearly complete is that in the Royal Society's *Catalogue of Scientific Papers*. His work as a whole has been treated in only two original studies of limited scope, those of G. Chrystal and G. Loria. On the other hand, certain of Liouville's works have been analyzed in greater detail, such as those on geometry. In view of the limited space available, this study cannot hope to provide a thorough account of Liouville's work but will attempt instead to present its major themes.

Life. Liouville was the second son of Claude-Joseph Liouville (1772–1852), an army captain, and Thérèse Balland, both originally from Lorraine. Liouville studied in Commercy and then in Toul. In 1831 he married a maternal cousin, Marie-Louise Balland (1812–1880); they had three daughters and one son. Liouville lived a calm and studious life, enlivened by an annual vacation at the family house in Toul. His scientific career was disturbed only by a brief venture into politics, during the Revolution of 1848. Already known for his democratic convictions, he was elected on 23 April 1848 to the Constituent Assembly as one of the representatives from the department of the Meurthe. He voted with the moderate democratic party. His defeat in the elections for the Legislative

Assembly in May 1849 marked the end of his political ambitions.

Admitted to the École Polytechnique in November 1825, Liouville transferred in November 1827 to the École des Ponts et Chaussées, where, while preparing for a career in engineering, he began original research in mathematics and mathematical physics. Between June 1828 and November 1830 he presented before the Académie des Sciences seven memoirs, two of which dealt with the theory of electricity, three with the analytic theory of heat, and two with mathematical analysis. Although Academy reporters expressed certain reservations, these first works were on the whole very favorably received; and their partial publication in the *Annales de chimie et de physique*, in Gergonne's *Annales*,[1] and in Férussac's *Bulletin* gained their author a certain reputation. In order to secure as much freedom as possible to pursue his research, Liouville soon thought of changing professions. In 1830, upon graduating from the École des Ponts et Chaussées, he refused the position of engineer that he was offered, hoping that his reputation would permit him to obtain a teaching post fairly soon.

In November 1831 Liouville was selected by the Council on Instruction of the École Polytechnique to replace P. Binet as *répétiteur* in L. Mathieu's course in analysis and mechanics. This was the beginning of a brilliant career of some fifty years, in the course of which Liouville taught pure and applied mathematics in the leading Paris institutions of higher education.

In 1838 Liouville succeeded Mathieu as holder of one of the two chairs of analysis and mechanics at the École Polytechnique, a position that he resigned in 1851, immediately after his election to the Collège de France. From 1833 to 1838 Liouville also taught mathematics and mechanics, but at a more elementary level, at the recently founded École Centrale des Arts et Manufactures. In March 1837 he was chosen to teach mathematical physics at the Collège de France as *suppléant* for J. B. Biot. He resigned in March 1843 to protest the election of Count Libri-Carrucci to the chair of mathematics at that institution.

Liouville did not return to the Collège de France until the beginning of 1851, when he succeeded Libri-Carrucci, who had left France.[2] This chair had no fixed program, and so for the first time Liouville could present his own research and discuss current topics. He took advantage of this to present unpublished works, some of which were developed by his students before he himself published them.[3] Appreciating the interest and flexibility of such teaching, he remained in the post until 1879, when he arranged for O. Bonnet to take over his duties.

Liouville also wished to teach on the university level. Toward this end he had earned his doctorate with a dissertation on certain developments in Fourier series and their applications in mathematical physics (1836). He was therefore eligible for election, in 1857, to the chair of rational mechanics at the Paris Faculty of Sciences, a position vacant since the death of Charles Sturm. In 1874, he stopped teaching there and arranged for his replacement by Darboux.

Parallel with this very full academic career, Liouville was elected a member of the astronomy section of the Académie des Sciences in June 1839, succeeding M. Lefrançois de Lalande; and in 1840 he succeeded Poisson as a member of the Bureau des Longitudes. From this time on, he participated regularly in the work of these two groups. For forty years he also passionately devoted himself to another particularly burdensome task, heading an important mathematical journal. The almost simultaneous demise, in 1831, of the only French mathematical review, Gergonne's *Annales de mathématiques pures et appliquées*, together with one of the principal science reviews, Férussac's *Bulletin des sciences mathématiques, astronomiques, physiques et chimiques*, deprived French-language mathematicians of two of their favorite forums. Liouville understood that the vigor of French mathematical writings demanded the creation of new organs of communication. Despite his youth and inexperience in the problems of editing and publishing, he launched the *Journal de mathématiques pures et appliquées* in January 1836. He published the first thirty-nine volumes (the twenty of the first series [1836–1855] and the nineteen of the second series [1856–1874]), each volume in twelve fascicles of thirty-two to forty pages. Finally, at the end of 1874, he entrusted the editorship to H. Résal.

Open to all branches of pure and applied mathematics, the publication was extremely successful and was soon called the *Journal de Liouville*. Its first volume contained articles by Ampère, Chasles, Coriolis, Jacobi, Lamé, V.-A. Lebesgue, Libri-Carrucci, Plücker, Sturm, and Liouville himself. Although not all the tables of contents are as brilliant as that of the first, the thirty-nine volumes published by Liouville record an important part of the mathematical activity of the forty years of the mid-nineteenth century. In fact, Liouville secured regular contributions from a majority of the great mathematicians of the era and maintained particularly warm and fruitful relations with Jacobi, Dirichlet, Lamé, Coriolis, and Sturm. At the same time he sought to guide and smooth the way for the first works of young authors, notably Le Verrier, Bonnet, J. A. Serret, J. Bertrand, Hermite, and Bour. But his outstanding qualities as an editor are most clearly displayed in his exemplary effort to assimilate as perfectly as possible the work of Galois. He imposed this task on himself in order to establish in an irreproachable fashion the texts he published in volume 11 of the *Journal de mathématiques*.

During the first thirty years of his career Liouville, while maintaining a very special interest in mathematical analysis, also did research in mathematical physics, algebra, number theory, and geometry. Starting in 1857, however, he considerably altered the orientation of his studies, concentrating more and more on particular problems of number theory. Departing in this way from the most fruitful paths of mathematical research, Liouville saw his influence decline rapidly. Yet it was the abandonment of the editorship of his *Journal* in 1874 that signaled the real end of his activity. His publications, which had been appearing with decreasing frequency since 1867, stopped altogether at this time. Simultaneously he gave up his courses at the Sorbonne, where his *suppléants* were Darboux and then Tisserand. He still attended the sessions of the Académie des Sciences and of the Bureau des Longitudes and still lectured at the Collège de France; but he no longer really participated in French mathematical life.

Mathematical Works. Liouville published thirty-nine volumes of the *Journal de mathématiques*, republished a work by Monge, and published a treatise by Navier; but he never composed a general work of his own. He did write nearly 400 memoirs, articles, and notes on a great many aspects of pure and applied mathematics. Despite its great diversity, this literary output is marked by a limited number of major themes, the majority of which were evident in his first publications. Liouville also published numerous articles correcting, completing, or extending the results of others, especially of articles that had appeared in the *Journal de mathématiques*. Other articles by him were summaries of or extracts from courses he gave at the Collège de France.

The divisions used below tend to obscure one of the main characteristics of Liouville's works, their interdisciplinary nature. Yet they are indispensable in the presentation of such a diverse body of work. References generally will be limited to the year of publication; given that information, further details can rapidly be found by consulting the *Catalogue of Scientific Papers*.

Mathematical Analysis. It was in mathematical analysis that Liouville published the greatest number and the most varied of his works. Composed mainly from 1832 to 1857, they number about one hundred. It is thus possible to mention only the most important

and most original of these contributions, including some that were virtually ignored by contemporaries. To grasp their significance fully, it must be noted that these apparently disordered investigations were actually guided—for lack of an overall plan—by a few governing ideas. It is also important to view each of them in the context of the studies carried out at the same time by Gauss, Jacobi, Cauchy, and Sturm. It should be remembered that in his courses at the Collège de France, Liouville treated important questions that do not appear among his writings and that he inspired many disciples.

Certain of Liouville's earliest investigations in mathematical analysis should be viewed as a continuation of the then most recent works of Abel and Jacobi. The most important are concerned with attempts to classify all algebraic functions and the simplest types of transcendental functions, with the theory of elliptic functions, and with certain types of integrals that can be expressed by an algebraic function.

Following the demonstration by Abel and Galois of the impossibility of algebraically solving general equations higher than the fourth degree, Liouville devoted several memoirs to determining the nature of the roots of algebraic equations of higher degree and of transcendental equations. One of the results he obtained was that according to which the number e cannot be the root of any second- or fourth-degree equation (1840). In 1844 he discovered a specific characteristic of the expansion as a continued fraction of every algebraic number, and showed that there are continued fractions that do not possess this characteristic. This discovery ("Liouville's transcendental numbers") is set forth in a memoir entitled "Sur des classes très-étendues de nombres dont la valeur n'est ni algébrique, ni même réductible à des irrationnelles algébriques" (*Journal de mathématiques*, **16** [1851], 133–142). It was not until 1873 that G. Cantor demonstrated the existence of much more general transcendental numbers.

In 1844 Liouville took up the study of all the functions possessing—like the elliptic functions—the property of admitting two periods. He set forth his theory to Joachimsthal and Borchardt (1847) before presenting it at the Collège de France (1850–1851). Thus, although he published little on the subject, the theory itself rapidly became widely known through the publications of Borchardt and the *Théorie des fonctions doublement périodiques* (1859) of Briot and Bouquet. Liouville made important contributions to the theory of Eulerian functions. He also sought to develop the theory of differential equations and of partial differential equations. In addition to numerous memoirs treating particular types of differential equations, such as Riccati's equation, and various technical questions, Liouville also worked on general problems, such as the demonstration (1840) of the impossibility, in general, of reducing the solution of differential equations either to a finite sequence of algebraic operations and indefinite integrations or—independently of Cauchy—to a particular aspect of the method of successive approximations (1837–1838). His contributions in the theory of partial differential equations were also of considerable value, even though a large portion of his "discoveries" had been anticipated by Jacobi. Much of his research in this area was closely linked with rational mechanics, celestial mechanics, and mathematical physics.

Pursuing the pioneer investigations of Leibniz, Johann Bernoulli, and Euler, Liouville devoted a part of his early work (1832–1836) to an attempt to enlarge as far as possible the notions of the differential and the integral, and in particular to establish the theory of derivatives of arbitrary index. Assuming a function $f(x)$ to be representable as a series of exponentials

$$f(x) = \sum_{n=0}^{n=+\infty} (c_n e^{a_n x}),$$

he defined its derivative of order s (s being an arbitrary number, rational or irrational, or even complex) by the series

$$D_s f(x) = \sum_{n=0}^{n=+\infty} c_n a_n^s \, e^{a_n x}.$$

This definition does in fact extend the ordinary differential calculus of integral indexes, but its generality is limited: not every function admits an expansion of the type proposed; and the convergence and uniqueness of the expansion are not guaranteed for all values of s. Despite its weaknesses and deficiencies, Liouville's endeavor, one of the many efforts that led to the establishment of functional calculus, shows his great virtuosity in handling the analysis of his time.

Liouville and Sturm published an important series of memoirs in the first two volumes of the *Journal de mathématiques* (1836–1837). Bourbaki (*Éléments d'histoire des mathématiques*, 2nd ed., pp. 260–262) shows that these investigations, which extended the numerous earlier works devoted to the equation of vibrating strings, permitted the elaboration of a general theory of oscillations for the case of one variable. He also shows that they are linked to the beginning of the theory of linear integral equations that contributed to the advent of modern ideas concerning functional analysis.

This constitutes only a broad outline of Liouville's chief contributions to analysis. The principal works mentioned below in connection with mathematical physics should for the most part be considered direct applications—or even important elements—of Liouville's analytical investigations.

Mathematical Physics. Under the influence of Ampère and of Navier, whose courses he had followed at the Collège de France and at the École des Ponts et Chaussées from 1828 to 1830, Liouville directed his first investigations to two areas of mathematical physics of current interest: the theory of electrodynamics and the theory of heat. After these first studies he never returned to the former topic. On the other hand he later (1836–1838, 1846–1848) devoted several memoirs to the theory of heat, but only for the purpose of employing new analytic methods, such as elliptic functions. Similarly, it was to demonstrate the power of analysis that he considered certain aspects of the theory of sound (1836, 1838) and the distribution of electricity on the surface of conductors (1846, 1857).

Celestial Mechanics. Liouville came in contact with celestial mechanics in 1834, through a hydrodynamical problem: finding the surface of equilibrium of a homogeneous fluid mass in rotation about an axis. He showed that with Laplace's formulas one can demonstrate Jacobi's theorem concerning the existence among these equilibrium figures of an ellipsoidal surface with unequal axes. Between 1839 and 1855 Liouville returned to this topic on several occasions, confirming the efficacy of the Laplacian methods while verifying the great power of the new procedures. From 1836 to 1842 he wrote a series of memoirs on classical celestial mechanics (perturbations, secular variations, the use of elliptic functions). Subsequently, although he was active in the Bureau des Longitudes, he devoted only a few notes to the problem of attraction (1845) and to particular cases of the three-body problem (1842, 1846).

Rational Mechanics. Rational mechanics held Liouville's interest for only two short periods. From 1846 to 1849, influenced by the work of Hamilton and Jacobi, he sought to erect a theory of point dynamics. He did not return to related subjects until 1855 and 1856, when he published, respectively, two studies of the differential equations of dynamics and an important note on the use of the principle of least action.

Algebra. Although Liouville wrote only a few memoirs dealing with algebraic questions, his contributions in this field merit discussion in some detail.

In 1836, with his friend Sturm, Liouville demonstrated Cauchy's theorem concerning the number of complex roots of an algebraic equation that are situated in the interior of a given contour, and in 1840 he gave an elegant demonstration of the fundamental theorem of algebra. From 1841 to 1847 he took up, on new bases, the problem of the elimination of an unknown from two equations in two unknowns, and applied the principles brought to light in this case to the demonstration of various properties of infinitesimal geometry. In 1846 he presented a new method for decomposing rational functions, and in 1863 he generalized Rolle's theorem to the imaginary roots of equations.

Liouville's most significant contribution by far, however, was concerned with the theory of algebraic equations and group theory. He published very little on these questions, but from 1843 to 1846 he conducted a thorough study of Galois's manuscripts in order to prepare for publication, in the October and November 1846 issues of his *Journal de mathématiques*, the bulk of the work of the young mathematician who tragically had died in 1832. Liouville's brief "Avertissement" (pp. 381–384) paid fitting homage to the value of Galois's work, but the second part of the *Oeuvres*, announced for the following volume of the *Journal*, was not published until 1908 by J. Tannery. According to J. Bertrand, Liouville invited a few friends, including J. A. Serret, to attend a series of lectures on Galois's work.[4] Although he did not publish the text of these lectures, Liouville nevertheless contributed in large measure to making known a body of work whose extraordinary innovations were to become more and more influential. He thus participated, indirectly, in the elaboration of modern algebra and of group theory.

Geometry. Liouville's work in geometry, the subject of an excellent analysis by Chasles (*Rapport sur les progrès de la géométrie* [Paris, 1870], pp. 127–130), consists of about twenty works written over the period from 1832 to 1854. The majority of them are applications or extensions of other investigations and are more analytic than geometric in their inspiration.

In 1832 Liouville showed that his "calculus of differentials of arbitrary index" could facilitate the study of certain questions of mechanics and geometry. In 1841 and 1844 he demonstrated and extended, by employing elimination theory, numerous metric properties of curves and surfaces that were established geometrically by Chasles. In 1844 Liouville published a new method for determining the geodesic lines of an arbitrary ellipsoid, a problem that Jacobi had just reduced to one involving elliptic transcendentals. In 1846 he proposed a direct demonstration of the so-called Joachimsthal equation and generalized the study of polygons of maximal or minimal perimeter

inscribed in or circumscribed about a plane or spherical conic section to geodesic polygons traced on an ellipsoid. Finally, in 1847, prompted by a note of W. Thomson concerning the distribution of electricity on two conducting bodies, Liouville undertook an analytic study of inversive geometry in space, which he called "transformation by reciprocal vector rays." He showed that the inversion is the only conformal nonlinear spatial transformation and pointed out its applications to many questions of geometry and mathematical physics.

When Liouville published the fifth edition of Monge's *Application de l'analyse à la géométrie* (1850), he added to it Gauss's famous memoir *Disquisitiones generales circa superficies curvas*. He also appended to it seven important related notes of his own; these dealt with the theory of space curves, the introduction of the notions of relative curvature and geodesic curvature of curves situated on a surface, the integration of the equation of geodesic lines, the notion of total curvature, the study of the deformations of a surface of constant curvature, a particular type of representation of one surface on another, and the theory of vibrating strings.

Liouville returned to certain aspects of the general theory of surfaces in later works and in his lectures at the Collège de France—for instance, the determination of the surface the development of which is composed of two confocal quadrics (1851). Although they treat rather disparate topics, these works on infinitesimal geometry exerted a salutary influence on research in this field, confirming the fruitfulness of the analytic methods of Gauss's school.

Number Theory. Liouville entered the new field of number theory in 1840 with a demonstration that the impossibility of the equation $x^n + y^n = z^n$ entails that of the equation $x^{2n} + y^{2n} = z^{2n}$. He returned to this field only occasionally in the following years, publishing a comparison of two particular quadratic forms (1845) and a new demonstration of the law of quadratic reciprocity (1847). In 1856, however, he began an impressive and astonishing series of works in this area, abandoning—except for some brief notes on analysis—the important investigations he was carrying out in other branches of mathematics. At first he took an interest in quite varied questions, including the sum of the divisors of an integer; the impossibility, for integers, of the equation $(p - 1)! + 1 = p^m$, p being a prime number greater than 5; and the number $\varphi(n)$ of integers less than n that are prime to n. From 1858 to 1865, in eighteen successive notes published in the *Journal de mathématiques* under the general title "Sur quelques formules générales qui peuvent être utiles dans la théorie des nombres," Liouville stated without demonstration a series of theorems—a list is given in volume II of L. E. Dickson, *History of the Theory of Numbers*—that constitute the foundations of "analytic" number theory.

But from 1859 to 1866 Liouville devoted the bulk of his publications—nearly 200 short notes in the *Journal de mathématiques*—to a monotonous series of particular problems in number theory. These problems are reducible to two principal types: the exposition of certain properties of prime numbers of a particular form and their products (properties equivalent to the existence of integral solutions of equations having the form $ax + by = c$, the numbers a, b, c being of a given form); and the determination of different representations of an arbitrary integer by a quadratic form of the type $ax^2 + by^2 + cz^2 + dt^2$, where a, b, c, and d are given constants.

L. E. Dickson mentions the examples Liouville studied in this series and the demonstrations that were published later: Liouville's notes contain only statements and numerical proofs. One may well be astonished at his singular behavior in abandoning his other research in order to amass, without any real demonstration, detailed results concerning two specialized topics in number theory. He never explained this in his writings. Hence one may wonder, as did G. Loria, whether he may have justified his apparently mysterious choice of examples in the course of his lectures at the Collège de France. Bôcher, more severe, simply considers these last publications to be mediocre.

Four hundred memoirs, published mainly in the *Journal de mathématiques* and the *Comptes rendus hebdomadaires des séances de l'Académie des sciences*, and 340 manuscript notebooks[5] in the Bibliothèque de l'Institut de France, Paris—this is the mass of documents that must be carefully analyzed in order to provide an exhaustive description of Liouville's work. To complete this account, it would also be necessary to trace more exactly his activity as head of the *Journal de mathématiques*, to assemble the greatest amount of data possible on the courses he taught, above all at the Collège de France, and to ascertain his role in the training of his students and in their publications.

NOTES

1. This, Liouville's second publication—he was then twenty-one—appeared in *Annales de mathématiques pures et appliquées* (**21**, nos. 5 and 6 [Nov. and Dec. 1830]). The second of these issues also contains two short notes by Evariste Galois, whose work Liouville published in *Journal de mathématiques pures et appliquées*, **11** (1846). But this circumstance obviously is not sufficient to prove that the two knew each other. A note by Gergonne, following Liouville's memoir, severely criticizes its style and presentation. The editor of the *Annales* denied all hope of a future for the young man who, five years later, succeeded him by creating the *Journal de mathématiques*. See also Liouville's "Note sur l'électro-dynamique," in *Bulletin des sciences mathématiques* . . ., **15** (Jan. 1831), 29–31, which is omitted from all bibliographies.

2. In 1843 the election for the chair of mathematics left vacant by the death of S. F. Lacroix saw three opposing candidates, all members of the Académie des Sciences: Cauchy, Liouville, and Libri-Carrucci. At the time Liouville was engaged in a violent controversy with Libri-Carrucci, whose abilities he publicly disputed. He therefore resigned as soon as he learned that the Council of the Collège de France was recommending that the Assembly vote for Libri-Carrucci. In 1850, when this chair became vacant, following Libri-Carrucci's dismissal, Cauchy and Liouville again were candidates. The particular circumstances of the votes that resulted in Liouville's finally being chosen (18 Jan. 1851) gave rise to vigorous protests by Cauchy.

3. Thus the works on doubly periodic functions that Liouville had presented privately (1847) or in public lectures (1851) were used by Borchardt and Joachimsthal and also by Briot and Bouquet. Similarly, Lebesgue published in his *Exercices d'analyse numérique* (1859) Liouville's demonstration, unpublished until then, of Waring's theorem for the case of biquadratic numbers.

4. J. Bertrand (*Éloges académiques*, II [Paris, 1902], 342–343) wrote that it was out of deference to Liouville, who had taught him Galois's discoveries, that J. A. Serret mentioned these discoveries in neither the first (1849) nor the second edition (1859) of his *Cours d'algèbre supérieure*, but only in the third (1866).

5. A rapid examination of some of these notebooks shows that they consist mainly of outlines and final drafts of the published works, but the whole collection would have to be gone over very thoroughly before a definitive evaluation could be made.

BIBLIOGRAPHY

I. ORIGINAL WORKS. Liouville published only two of his works in book form: his thesis, *Sur le développement des fonctions ou parties de fonctions en séries de sinus et de cosinus, dont on fait usage dans un grand nombre de questions de mécanique et de physique* . . . (Paris, 1836); and a summary of a course he gave at the École Centrale des Arts et Manufactures in 1837–1838, *Résumé des leçons de trigonométrie. Notes pour le cours de statique* (Paris, n.d.). He edited and annotated Gaspard Monge, *Application de l'analyse à la géométrie*, 5th ed. (Paris, 1850); and H. Navier, *Résumé des leçons d'analyse données à l'École polytechnique* . . ., 2 vols. (Paris, 1856).

Liouville published the first 39 vols. of the *Journal de mathématiques pures et appliquées*: 1st scr., **1–20** (1836–1855); 2nd ser., **1–19** (1856–1874). He also wrote approximately 400 papers, of which the majority are cited in the Royal Society's *Catalogue of Scientific Papers*, IV (1870), 39–49 (nos. 1–309 for the period 1829–1863, plus three articles written in collaboration with Sturm); VIII (1879), 239–241 (nos. 310–377 for the period 1864–1873); X (1894), 606 (nos. 378–380 for the period 1874–1880). See also Poggendorff, I, cols. 1471–1475 and III, p. 818.

The list of Liouville's contributions to the *Journal de mathématiques* is given in the tables of contents inserted at the end of vol. **20**, 1st ser. (1855), and at the end of vol. **19**, 2nd ser. (1874). (The articles in the *Journal de mathématiques* signed "Besge" are attributed to Liouville by H. Brocard, in *Intermédiaire des mathématiciens*, **9** [1902], 216.) The memoirs and notes that Liouville presented to the Académie des Sciences are cited from 1829 to July 1835 in the corresponding vols. of the *Procès-verbaux des séances de l'Académie des sciences* (see index) and after July 1835 in the vols. of *Tables des Comptes rendus hebdomadaires de l'Académie des sciences*, published every 15 years.

J. Tannery edited the *Correspondance entre Lejeune-Dirichlet et Liouville* (Paris, 1910), a collection of articles published in the *Bulletin des sciences mathématiques*, 2nd ser., **32** (1908), pt. 1, 47–62, 88–95; and **33** (1908–1909), pt. 1, 47–64.

Liouville's MSS are in the Bibliothèque de l'Institut de France, Paris. They consist of 340 notebooks and cartons of various materials, MS 3615–3640. See also the papers of Evariste Galois, MS 2108, folios 252–285.

II. SECONDARY LITERATURE. Liouville's biography is sketched in the following articles (listed chronologically): Jacob, in F. Hoefer, ed., *Nouvelle biographie générale*, XXXI (Paris, 1872), 316–318; G. Vapereau, *Dictionnaire universel des contemporains*, 5th ed. (Paris, 1880), 1171–1172; H. Faye and E. Laboulaye, in *Comptes rendus hebdomadaires des séances de l'Académie des sciences*, **95** (1882), 467–471, a speech given at his funeral; David, in *Mémoires de l'Académie des sciences, inscriptions et belles-lettres de Toulouse*, 8th ser., **5** (1883), 257–258; A. Robert and G. Cougny, *Dictionnaire des parlementaires français*, II (Paris, 1890), 165; H. Laurent, in *Livre du centenaire de l'École polytechnique*, I (Paris, 1895), 130–133; and L. Sagnet, in *La grande encyclopédie*, XXII (Paris, 1896), 305; and *Intermédiaire des mathématiciens*, **9** (1902), 215–217; **13** (1906), 13–15; **14** (1907), 59–61.

The principal studies dealing with Liouville's work as a whole are G. Chrystal, "Joseph Liouville," in *Proceedings of the Royal Society of Edinburgh*, **14** (1888), 2nd pagination, 83–91; and G. Loria, "Le mathématicien J. Liouville et ses oeuvres," in *Archeion*, **18** (1936), 117–139, translated into English as "J. Liouville and His Work," in *Scripta mathematica*, **4** (1936), 147–154 (with portrait), 257–263, 301–306.

Interesting details and comments concerning various aspects of Liouville's work are in J. Bertrand, *Rapport sur les progrès les plus récents de l'analyse mathématique* (Paris, 1867), pp. 2–5, 32; M. Chasles, *Rapport sur les progrès de la géométrie* (Paris, 1870), 127–140; N. Saltykow, "Sur le rapport des travaux de S. Lie à ceux de Liouville," in *Comptes rendus hebdomadaires des séances de l'Académie des sciences*, **137** (1903), 403–405; M. Bôcher, "Mathématiques et mathématiciens français," in *Revue internationale de l'enseignement*, **67** (1914), 30–31; F. Cajori, *History of Mathematics*, rev. ed. (New York, 1919), see index; L. E. Dickson, *History of the Theory of Numbers*, 3 vols. (Washington, D.C., 1919–1923), see index; and N. Bourbaki, *Éléments d'histoire des mathématiques*, 2nd ed. (Paris, 1964), 260–262.

RENÉ TATON

LIPPMANN, GABRIEL JONAS (*b.* Hollerich, Luxembourg, 16 August 1845; *d.* at sea 12 July 1921), *physics, instrumental astronomy.*

Lippmann's parents were French and settled in Paris while he was still a boy. There he attended first the Lycée Napoléon and later the École Normale Supérieure. In the early stages of his career he collaborated with Bertin in the publication of *Annales de chimie et de physique* by abstracting German papers. This work led him to develop an interest in contemporary research in electricity. While on a scientific mission to Germany he was shown by Wilhelm Kühne, professor of physiology at Heidelberg, an experiment in which a drop of mercury, covered by dilute sulfuric acid, contracts on being touched with an iron wire and regains its original shape when the wire is removed. Lippmann realized that there was a connection between electrical polarization and surface tension and obtained permission to conduct a systematic investigation of this phenomenon in Kirchhoff's laboratory.

These experiments resulted in the development of the capillary electrometer, a device sensitive to changes in potential of the order of 1/1,000 of a volt. The instrument consists essentially of a capillary tube, which is inclined at a few degrees from the horizontal, containing an interface between mercury and dilute acid. If the potential difference between the two liquids is varied, the effective surface tension at the meniscus is altered and, as a result, the meniscus moves along the capillary tube. Although the device could be calibrated, it was more usually employed in potentiometer and bridge measurements as a null instrument. It possessed the advantage, significant at the time, of being independent of magnetic and electric fields. Lippmann's researches on electrocapillarity received recognition in the form of a doctorate awarded by the Sorbonne in 1875. In a paper published in 1876, Lippmann investigated the application of thermodynamic principles to electrical systems.

In 1883 Lippmann was appointed professor of mathematical physics at the Faculty of Sciences in Paris. In 1886 he succeeded Jules Jamin as professor of experimental physics and later became director of the research laboratory, which was subsequently transferred to the Sorbonne. He retained this position until his death.

Lippmann made numerous contributions to instrumental design, particularly in connection with astronomy and seismology. His most notable contribution was the invention of the coelostat. In this instrument the light from a portion of the sky is reflected by a mirror which rotates around an axis parallel to its plane once every forty-eight sidereal hours. This axis is arranged parallel to the axis of the earth. The light from the mirror enters a telescope fixed to the earth. The arrangement ensures that a region of the sky, and not merely one particular star, may be photographed without apparent movement. In this respect it represented an improvement on the siderostat. Lippmann later put forward a suggestion for the accurate adjustment of a telescope directed at its zenith by reflecting light from a pool of mercury.

Lippmann also devised a number of improvements on observational technique by the introduction of photographic or electrical methods of measurement. These include a method for the measurement of the difference in longitude between two observatories by means of radio waves and photography and an improvement on the method of coincidences for measuring the difference between the periods of two pendulums. The pendulum measurements involve the use of a high-speed flash photograph to determine the change in phase over a short interval of time. Lippmann later investigated the problem of maintaining a pendulum in continuous oscillation. He showed that the period will be unaffected if the maintaining impulse is applied at the instant the pendulum swings through the point of zero displacement. The necessary impulse could, he suggested, be obtained by alternately charging and discharging a capacitor through coils mounted on either side of the pendulum. This arrangement ensures that the impulse is of short duration and is independent of wear on the pendulum contacts.

Lippmann's contributions to seismology include a suggestion for the use of telegraph signals to give early warning of earth tremors and for the measurement of their velocity of propagation. He also proposed a new form of seismograph intended to give directly the acceleration of the earth's movement.

In 1908 Lippmann was awarded the Nobel Prize in physics "for his method, based on the interference phenomenon, for reproducing colours photographically." In the same year he was elected a fellow of the Royal Society of London. In Lippmann's color process the sensitive emulsion, which is relatively thick, is backed by a reflecting surface of mercury. As a result the incident light is reflected back toward the source, and the incident and reflected beams combine to produce stationary waves. After development the film is found to contain reflecting planes of silver separated by distances of half a wavelength. When the film is viewed by reflected light, the color corresponding to the original beam is strongly reinforced by reflection from successive planes.

BIBLIOGRAPHY

I. ORIGINAL WORKS. Lippmann's writings are "Relation entre les phénomènes électriques et capillaires," in Comptes rendus ... de l'Académie des sciences, 76 (1873), 1407; "Sur une propriété d'une surface d'eau électrisée," ibid., 81 (1875), 280—see also ibid., 85 (1877), 142; "Extension du principe de Carnot à la théorie des phénomènes électriques," ibid., 82 (1876), 1425; "Photographies colorées du spectre, sur albumine et sur gélatine bichromatées," ibid., 115 (1892), 575; "Sur la théorie de la photographie des couleurs simples et composées par la méthode interférentielle," ibid., 118 (1894), 92; "Sur un coelostat," ibid., 120 (1895), 1015; "Sur l'entretien du mouvement du pendule sans perturbations," ibid., 122 (1896), 104; "Méthodes pour comparer, à l'aide de l'étincelle électrique, les durées d'oscillation de deux pendules réglés sensiblement à la même période," ibid., 124 (1897), 125; "Sur l'emploi d'un fil télégraphique pour l'inscription des tremblements de terre et la mesure de leur vitesse de propagation," ibid., 136 (1903), 203; "Appareil pour enregistrer l'accélération absolue des mouvements séismiques," ibid., 148 (1909), 138; "Sur une méthode photographique direct pour la détermination des différences des longitudes," ibid., 158 (1914), 909; and "Méthode pour le réglage d'une lunette en collimation," ibid., 88.

II. SECONDARY LITERATURE. Obituary notices are in Annales de physique, 16 (1921), 156; and Proceedings of the Royal Society, ser. A, 101 (1922). See also H. H. Turner, "Some Notes on the Use and Adjustment of the Coelostat," in Monthly Notices of the Royal Astronomical Society, 56 (1896), 408.

I. B. HOPLEY

LIPSCHITZ, RUDOLF OTTO SIGISMUND (b. near Königsberg, Germany [now Kaliningrad, R.S.F.S.R.], 14 May 1832; d. Bonn, Germany, 7 October 1903), *mathematics.*

Lipschitz was born on his father's estate, Bönkein. At the age of fifteen he began the study of mathematics at the University of Königsberg, where Franz Neumann was teaching. He then went to Dirichlet in Berlin, and he always considered himself Dirichlet's student. After interrupting his studies for a year because of illness, he received his doctorate from the University of Berlin on 9 August 1853. After a period of training and teaching at the Gymnasiums in Königsberg and Elbing, Lipschitz became a *Privatdozent* in mathematics at the University of Berlin in 1857. In the same year he married Ida Pascha, the daughter of a neighboring landowner. In 1862 he became an associate professor at Breslau, and in 1864 a full professor at Bonn, where he was examiner for the dissertation of nineteen-year-old Felix Klein in 1868. He rejected an offer to succeed Clebsch at

Göttingen in 1873. Lipschitz was a corresponding member of the academies of Paris, Berlin, Göttingen, and Rome. He loved music, especially classical music.

Lipschitz distinguished himself through the unusual breadth of his research. He carried out many important and fruitful investigations in number theory, in the theory of Bessel functions and of Fourier series, in ordinary and partial differential equations, and in analytical mechanics and potential theory. Of special note are his extensive investigations concerning n-dimensional differential forms and the related questions of the calculus of variations, geometry, and mechanics. This work—in which he drew upon the developments that Riemann had presented in his famous lecture on the basic hypotheses underlying geometry—contributed to the creation of a new branch of mathematics.

Lipschitz was also very interested in the fundamental questions of mathematical research and of mathematical instruction in the universities. He gathered together his studies on these topics in the two-volume *Grundlagen der Analysis*. Until then a work of this kind had never appeared in German, although such books existed in French. The work begins with the theory of the rational integers and goes on to differential equations and function theory. The foundation of mathematics is also considered in terms of its applications.

In basic analysis Lipschitz furnished a condition, named for him, which is today as important for proofs of existence and uniqueness as for approximation theory and constructive function theory: If f is a function defined in the interval $\langle a, b \rangle$, then f may be said to satisfy a Lipschitz condition with the exponent α and the coefficient M if for any two values x, y in $\langle a, b \rangle$, the condition

$$|f(y) - f(x)| \leqslant M\,|\,y - x\,|^{\alpha}, \qquad \alpha > 0,$$

is satisfied.

In his algebraic number theory investigations of sums of arbitrarily many squares, Lipschitz obtained certain symbolic expressions from real transformations and derived computational rules for them. In this manner he obtained a hypercomplex system that is today termed a Lipschitz algebra. In the case of sums of two squares, his symbolic expressions go over into the numbers of the Gaussian number field; and in that of three squares, into the Hamiltonian quaternions. Related studies were carried out by H. Grassmann.

Lipschitz's most important achievements are contained in his investigations of forms on n differentials which he published, starting in 1869, in numerous articles, especially in the *Journal für die reine und angewandte Mathematik*. In this area he was one of the direct followers of Riemann, who in his lecture of 1854, before the Göttingen philosophical faculty, had formulated the principal problems of differential geometry in higher-dimension manifolds and had begun the study of the possible metric structures of an n-dimensional manifold. This lecture, which was not exclusively for mathematicians and which presented only the basic ideas, was published in 1868, following Riemann's death. A year later Lipschitz published his first work on this subject. With E. B. Christoffel, he was one of the first to employ cogredient differentiation; and in the process he created an easily used computational method. He showed that the vanishing of a certain expression is a necessary and sufficient condition for a Riemannian manifold to be Euclidean. The expression in question is a fourth-degree curvature quantity. Riemann knew this and had argued it in a work submitted in 1861 to a competition held by the French Academy of Sciences. Riemann did not win the prize, however; and the essay was not published until 1876, when it appeared in his collected works.

Lipschitz was especially successful in his investigations of the properties of Riemannian submanifolds V_m of dimension m in a Riemannian manifold V_n of dimension n. He showed flexure invariants for V_m in V_n, proved theorems concerning curvature, and investigated minimal submanifolds V_m in V_n. He was also responsible for the chief theorem concerning the mean curvature vector that yields the condition for a minimal submanifold: A submanifold V_m of V_n is a minimal submanifold if and only if the mean curvature vector vanishes at every point. Thus a manifold V_m is said to be a minimal manifold in V_n if, the boundary being fixed, the variation of the content of each subset bounded by a closed V_{m-1} vanishes. The definition of the mean curvature vector of a submanifold V_m is based on the fundamental concept of the curvature vector of a nonisotropic curve in V_m. This vector can be described with the help of Christoffel's three index symbols. Its length is the first curvature of the curve and vanishes for geodesics in V_m.

Lipschitz's investigations were continued by G. Ricci. The latter's absolute differential calculus was employed, beginning in 1913, by Einstein, who in turn stimulated interest and further research in the differential geometry of higher-dimension manifolds.

BIBLIOGRAPHY

Lipschitz's books are *Grundlagen der Analysis*, 2 vols. (Bonn, 1877–1880); and *Untersuchungen über die Summen von Quadraten* (Bonn, 1886). He also published in many German and foreign journals, especially the *Journal für die reine und angewandte Mathematik* (from 1869). There is a bibliography in Poggendorff, IV, 897.

A biographical article is H. Kortum, "Rudolf Lipschitz," in *Jahresberichte der Deutschen Matematiker-Vereinigung*, **15** (1906), 56–59.

BRUNO SCHOENEBERG

LISBOA, JOÃO DE (*b.* Portugal; *d.* Indian Ocean, before 1526), *navigation.*

It has been claimed that Lisboa, a Portuguese pilot, accompanied Vasco da Gama on the voyage on which the route to the Indies was discovered (1497–1499). While this claim is probably false, there are documents proving that he navigated the coast of Brazil (at an unknown date), that he participated in an expedition to the fortress of Azamor in northern Africa (1513), and that he sailed to the Indies at least three times: in 1506, as pilot of the fleet led by Tristão da Cunha; in 1518, in the squadron of Diogo Lopes de Sequeira; and in the squadron commanded by Filipe de Castro in 1525. The last fleet had a difficult crossing from Madagascar to the Curia-Muria Isles; and it is likely that Lisboa, then advanced in age, did not survive this arduous passage.

In the course of his first documented visit to the Indies, Lisboa and the pilot Pêro Anes carried out observations to determine the magnetic declination with the aid of the constellations Ursa Minor and the Southern Cross. The method is set forth in the *Tratado da agulha de marear*, a small book written by Lisboa in 1514. It contains the first description of the nautical "dip" compass and the first presentation of a method for measuring the magnetic declination. Present knowledge of the text derives from copies that are incomplete and faulty but numerous enough to allow one, through comparison, to determine its complete and correct form. The treatise consists of an introduction and ten chapters. The first three are concerned with the construction of the compass, the following three with the observation of the magnetic declination with the aid of stars, and the seventh with the method of magnetizing the needle. In the last three chapters Lisboa presents a theory without any experimental support; he assumes that the declination of the compass undergoes variations proportional to the longitude and is convinced that this "law" can enable sailors to determine this coordinate.

BIBLIOGRAPHY

Portions of João de Lisboa's treatise can be found in the following MSS:

"Livro de marinharia," attributed to Lisboa himself (but completed about 1550, well after his death), in the National Library, Lisbon. The text was published by Brito Rebelo (Lisbon, 1903).

"Livro de marinharia" by Bernardo Fernandes, in the Vatican Library, Codex Borg. lat. 153. An ed. was published by Fontoura da Costa (Lisbon, 1940).

"Livro de marinharia" by André Pires in the Bibliothèque Nationale, Paris, MS portugais, 40. Published by L. de Albuquerque (Coimbra, 1963).

"Livro de marinharia" by Gaspar Moreira, in the Bibliothèque Nationale, Paris, still unpublished.

"Rotero de navigación," written in Portuguese despite the title, in the library of the Academia Real de la Historia, Madrid, Cortes 30-2165. This compilation is anonymous and is unpublished.

LUÍS DE ALBUQUERQUE

LI SHIH-CHEN[1] (*tzu* Tung-pi,[2] *hao* P'in-hu[3]) (*b.* Wa-hsiao-pa,[4] near Chichow [now Hupeh province], China, 1518; *d.* autumn 1593), *pharmacology.*

Li Shih-chen was the son of Li Yen-wen,[5] the educated and comparatively successful offspring of several generations of medical practitioners who, as was common in China, also practiced pharmacy. The father was at one time a medical officer of lower rank in the Imperial Medical Academy and, at another time, a client in the house of the philosopher and administrator Ku Wen.[6] He wrote five treatises, no longer extant, on diagnosis, smallpox, sphygmology, ginseng, and the *Artemisia* of Hupeh.

Li Shih-chen was bright and inquisitive about nature in his youth. His father encouraged him to prepare for the civil service examinations. At fourteen he passed the preliminary examinations but, despite three attempts, was unable to advance further. Thus ineligible for a bureaucratic career, he obtained his father's permission to devote himself to medicine. His education was, typically, not institutional but combined clinical experience in his father's practice and study of the literature of theoretical medicine, therapeutics, and materia medica. Li's skill as a physician won him considerable renown in his lifetime and even official posts in medical administration—which provided him access to rare drugs and books—for two short periods. He wrote at least twelve books, which, in addition to medical works, include a treatise on the rules of prosody and a collection of poetry and short prose writings. Reports also mention writings of unknown scope, size, and title on astrology, geomancy, and divination.

Li's greatest work, known to every educated Chinese even today as the culmination of the pharmacognostic tradition, is the *Pen-ts'ao kang mu* ("Systematic Pharmacopoeia"). At about the age of thirty Li assumed the enormous task of producing a comprehensive and up-to-date encyclopedia of pharmaceutical natural history, taking into account the need for correcting the many mistakes of identification, classification, and evaluation in the previously standard Sung dynasty series of pharmacognostic treatises, which begins with T'ang Shen-wei's *Ching shih cheng lei pei chi pen-ts'ao* ("Pharmacopoeia for Every Emergency, With Classifications Verified From the Classics and Histories," drafted in 1082–1083) and reaches its apogee in Chang Ts'un-hui's *Ch'ung hsiu Cheng-ho ching shih cheng lei pei yung pen-ts'ao* ("Revised Pharmacopoeia of the Cheng-ho Reign Period for Every Use . . .," 1249), which incorporates part of the brilliant collection of critical notes of K'ou Tsung-shih, *Pen-ts'ao yen i* ("Dilatations Upon the Pharmacopoeias," 1116). By Li's time many new substances, some of them imported, had been introduced into therapeutic use. Lacking the imperial patronage usual for works of this magnitude, Li over a span of thirty years incorporated in three successive drafts the contributions of over 800 books; and, from 1556, traveled widely in major drug-producing provinces (Honan, Kiangsu, Anhwei), collecting specimens and studying the natural occurrences of minerals, plants, and animals. After completion of the final draft in 1587 he visited Nanking to arrange for publication. When, in 1590, an agreement with a printer was concluded, Li's eminent literary friend Wang Shih-chen[7] wrote a preface in which he praised Li for his lucidity as "a scholar unique south of the Great Bear." The first printed edition (the so-called Chin-ling xylograph) did not appear until 1596, after Li's death.

That the *Pen-ts'ao kang mu* is far more than a pharmacopoeia is immediately evident from its introduction. There Li affirms his intention of discussing everything that has been recorded about the simples under discussion, whether strictly concerned with medical practice or not; thus the book became a comprehensive treatise on mineralogy, metallurgy, botany, and zoology. His critical approach to the factual record led him to cite previous accounts with clear ascription and in chronological order. In both of these respects he follows well-established precedent. The catholicity of Li's book goes back to the beginning of the pharmacognostic tradition in China, and his citations of early literature follow the lead of T'ang Shen-wei. Neither author is extremely accurate in quoting, and critical historians of science do not rely upon them for citations from early works.

The articles on drugs in the body of the book are arranged in a taxonomic order based on that of T'ang Shen-wei but somewhat more systematic. This classification is far from rigorous; the rubrics indifferently reflect habitat, physical characteristics, and use. Nevertheless it is more detailed, and based less on purely verbal criteria, than any which preceded it. As in modern practice, the earliest name given in the literature to any drug is made the basis for classification; and varieties are subgrouped into families, which correspond in a very rough way to the Linnaean genera. The *t'ung*[8] trees, for instance, are characterized by specific differences, and names which correspond to varieties are meticulously distinguished from mere synonyms. Location of a particular item depends both upon its morphology (a *yin* feature, because static) and its qualitatively defined energy (a *yang* feature, because dynamic). In principle the latter is defined largely in terms of physiological action, according to a conceptual scheme closer to that of Renaissance medicine than to that of modern pharmacodynamics.

Li's most obvious modification of T'ang Shen-wei's taxonomy, as this outline of the *Pen-ts'ao kang mu*'s rubrics shows, is rearrangement according to a hierarchy of being from the inorganic world to man (compare Aristotle's *scala naturae*):

1. The substances corresponding to the Five Phases (*wu hsing*,[9] sometimes misleadingly translated "five elements"). The Five Phases, which in every field of traditional science were used analytically to represent divisions of generalized dynamic processes (or, to a lesser extent, of static configurations), were named for wood, fire, earth, metal, and water. Although in this section Li gives special consideration to the namesakes of the Phases, every medical substance was understood to correspond to one of the five as part of the definition of its specific energy. Actually only four of the five substances are represented here; wood, which never needed so abstract a rationale for inclusion in the materia medica, is treated separately in section 8.

Natural varieties of water, both celestial and terrestrial

Natural varieties of fire

Natural varieties of earth (including clay, ink, and ash)

Natural varieties of metal (including ores and corrosion products)

2. Jades (including coral and quartzes)

3. Inorganic substances

Minerals

Salt and salt derivatives

4. Herbs
   Mountain herbs
   Aromatic herbs
   Moist herbs
   Toxic herbs
   Creeping herbs
   Aquatic herbs
   Herbs of stony habitat
   Mosses
5. Grains
   Hemp, wheat, rice
   Millet
   Legumes
   Fermented grains
6. Vegetables
   Aromatic vegetables
   Soft and slippery vegetables
   Ground vegetables (gourds, eggplant, and such)
   Aquatic vegetables
   Fungi
7. Fruit
   Classic edible fruits
   Mountain fruits
   Fruits of foreign origin
   Spices
   Ground fruits (melons, grapes, sugarcane, and such)
   Aquatic fruits
8. Arboreal drugs
   Aromatic woods
   Woods from trees
   Woods from shrubs
   Parasitic plants (including amber)
   Canes (including bamboo)
   Miscellaneous woods
9. Furnishings and implements
   Cloth and clothing
   Articles of use (from paper to privy buckets)
10. Insects and insect products
    Oviparous insects
    Insects engendered by transformation
    Insects born of moisture (including frogs)
11. Scaly creatures and their products
    Dragons
    Snakes
    Fish
    Fish without scales (including eels)
12. Creatures with shells
    Turtles and tortoises
    Oysters and clams
13. Birds
    Aquatic birds
    Plains birds

   Forest birds
   Mountain birds
14. Animals
    Domestic animals
    Wild animals
    Rodents
    Parasites and prodigious beasts (including apes)
15. Man (including hair, meat, bone, and assorted secretions and excrements)

In addition to this basic taxonomic arrangement, Li incorporated in his preliminary chapters a second classification according to diseases cured. This had been done often by earlier writers, but Li's carefully appended notes on the physiological functions of each drug with respect to each disease (phrased in the abstract terminology of rational medicine) were his own innovation. There is elsewhere in his treatise a more condensed classification according to the theoretical variables of physiological action, without reference to specific disease, probably generalized from a much more partial schema of Ch'en Ts'ang-ch'i[10] (early eighth century). Finally, Li noted in each major entry, for drugs which had appeared in the first classic of materia medica, the *Shen-nung pen-ts'ao* ("Canonic Pharmacopoeia," attributed to the legendary emperor Shen-nung, probably first century), where the substance belonged in the tripartite order of that book—whether it was assigned to the lower class, which merely cured disease; the middle class, which maintained health; or the higher class, which conferred immortality. These rubrics were still functional as secondary divisions in the *Pen-ts'ao p'in hui ching yao* ("Classified Essential Pharmacopoeia"), compiled for use in the imperial palace less than a century earlier, but apparently had only antiquarian interest for Li Shih-chen.

The internal arrangement of the articles is also a step forward in terms of system. The general name of the substance is followed by an etymologic explanation of variant names (*shih ming*[11]); corrections of errors in earlier pharmacopoeias (*cheng wu*[12]); a pastiche of quotations, with Li's own comments added, about the habitat, varieties, and qualities of the substance, with tests for the genuine article (*chi chieh*[13]); instructions for processing and storing the drug (*hsiu chih*[14]); a specification of the physiological activity of the drug and of diseases cured (*chu chih*[15]); a statement of essential energetic qualities in terms of sapidity (correlated with the Five Phases), warming or cooling activity, and toxicity (*ch'i wei*[16]); quotations which account for these qualities theoretically (*fa ming*[17]); and a number of prescriptions in which the drug is employed (*fu fang*[18]).

FIGURE 1

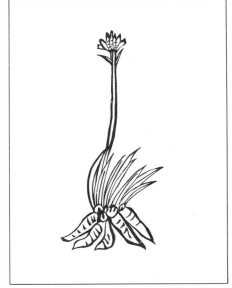

FIGURE 2

FIGURE 3

FIGURE 4

Some representative illustrations from various editions and a predecessor of *Pen-ts'ao kang mu*. The root most commonly sold by Chinese druggists as *she kan* is that of *Belamcanda chinensis*, the blackberry lily or leopard flower; but some classical authorities on materia medica, among them Li Shih-chen, tended to confuse this plant with various Iris species, especially *Iris tectorum maxim*. The latter, ordinarily called *yuan wei*, is still found on the market in Szechuan province as *she kan*.

FIGURE 1.   Reproduced from the 1929 Wuchang reproduction of the 1302 edition of the *Ta-kuan pen-ts'ao* (see Bibliography II, item 5).

FIGURE 2.   From the first printed edition of *Pen-ts'ao kang mu* (1596).

FIGURE 3.   From the 1640 edition of *Pen-ts'ao kang mu* as reproduced in 1712 by the Edo Karahonya Seibei, Tokyo. The branching of the blossoms unambiguously suggests the blackberry lily, although in other respects the limning is defective.

FIGURE 4.   From the 1885 Anui edition and a good likeness of an iris. Because this illustration was copied from *Chih wu ming shih t'u k'ao*, a compilation oriented toward botanical philology rather than medical therapy, it is uninformative about the appearance of the root, the part used in medicine.

One finds in the *Pen-ts'ao p'in hui ching yao* an even more systematic scheme of presentation, but this book had no important influence in Chinese medicine. Li never saw this manuscript; and it was not printed until 1936. Its framework, while clearly superior for concise presentation of factual information, did not provide for the depth of critical discussion unique to Li's treatise.

The systematic order used in this imperial pharmacopoeia of 1505 is set out here as a summary of the most fully elaborated parameters of Chinese pharmacognosy.

1. Name of substance
2. Specification of toxicity (an indication of potency)
3. Curative properties (a concise description quoted from or patterned after that of earlier compendiums)
4. Variant names (*ming*[19])
5. Description of plant (for botanicals) (*miao*[20])
6. Habitat (*ti*[21])
7. Times of growth and gathering (*shih*[22])
8. Processing and storage procedures (*shou*[23])
9. Part (or physical state in which) used (*yung*[24])
10. Physical characteristics of part, form, or type used (generally comparative) (*chih*[25])
11. Color (five possibilities, corresponding to the five phases) (*se*[26])
12. Sapidity (five possibilities) (*wei*[27])
13. Nature (nine possibilities) (*hsing*[28])
14. Strength of configurational energy (*ch'i*), *yin-yang* activity (*ch'i*[29])
15. Odor (five possibilities) (*hsiu*[30])
16. Physiological action (*chu*[31])
17. Circulation subsystems affected (*hsing*[32])
18. Ancillary action of other drugs (*chu*[33])
19. Antagonistic substances (*fan*[34])
20. Preparation for ingestion (that is, prescriptions) (*chih*[35])
21. Specific diseases cured (*chih*[36])
22. Use in combination with other drugs to cure specific diseases (*ho chih*[37])
23. Conditions in which administration is prohibited, limits on dosage (*chin*[38])
24. Substitutes for the drug in question, or its use as a substitute for other drugs (*tai*[39])
25. Dietary prohibitions when the drug is taken (*chi*[40])
26. Poisons neutralized (*chieh*[41])
27. Adulterants (*yen*[42])

The fifty-two chapters of *Pen-ts'ao kang mu* contain 1,892 entries, of which 275 are mineral and 444 animal. (Another 921 substances were added two centuries later in the supplement, *Pen-ts'ao kang mu shih-i.*) Li himself introduced 374 substances into the literature and credited thirty-nine more, not previously recorded, to doctors of the preceding four centuries. Of the 11,096 prescriptions included, 8,161 were recorded or created by Li.

The more than 1,100 illustrations in the first edition (see Figure 2) are not, in general, up to the level of those in the Sung series of pharmacopoeias which began five centuries earlier. Lu Gwei-djen has compared Li's illustrations, on the whole, to those in late fifteenth-century European herbals (such as Arnald of Villanova), and those of the Sung compilations to those of the sixteenth-century Occident (such as Fuchs); but in many cases Li's leave little to be desired in terms of accuracy of identification. There were two major revisions of the illustrations, one for the printing of 1640 (Figure 3) and the other for the Anhwei edition of 1885 (Figure 4). The latter, from which the pictures in most modern reprints are descended, borrows considerably from Wu Ch'i-chün's[43] fastidiously illustrated botanical compendium *Chih wu ming shih t'u k'ao*[44] ("Illustrated Investigations of the Names and Identities of Plants," 1848). Thus, in addition to an overall increase in delicacy there are many improvements in precision.

Although it is impossible to specify the first European influence of the *Pen-ts'ao kang mu*, we know that a copy was taken by Portuguese or Dutch traders to Japan, where about 1607 it came into the possession of the shogun Ieyasu and his scholarly secretary Hayashi Dōshun. The first of many Japanese editions appeared in 1637. In 1783 there was an immensely influential Japanese translation, amply annotated, by the great naturalist Ono Ranzan.

Europeans first learned of China's botanical riches in the Polish Jesuit Michael Boym's *Flora sinensis* (Vienna, 1656), which describes twenty-two plants in detail. About forty years later the physician G. E. Rumpf, deputy governor of Amboina, sent to Holland a copy of the first edition of *Pen-ts'ao kang mu*, which subsequently was long preserved in Germany. In 1735 J. B. du Halde cited *Pen-ts'ao kang mu* extensively as part of the general account of China in his *Description géographique, historique ... de l'empire de la Chine et de la Tartarie chinoise*. The extracts from earlier pharmacopoeias, abridged from the introduction to *Pen-ts'ao kang mu*, made it clear to European readers that Li's compilation belonged to a long and cumulative tradition. Du Halde also provided French renderings of the table of contents, Li's systematic account of the principles and types of prescriptions, and about fifteen articles on simples of special interest, including ginseng, tea, musk, and rhubarb.

Because du Halde was soon translated into English (1736, 1741), we can be reasonably confident that Li's method of classification, reflected in his table of contents, was known to the great seventeenth-century taxonomists and to Linnaeus. Linnaeus also knew indirectly of the work on Chinese plants grown in the Philippines carried out by the Jesuit Georg Josef Kamel, after whom he named the genus *Camellia*.

Considering the greater lapse of time, it is not surprising that Li Shih-chen's influence on Charles Darwin is much more easily documented. In *Variation of Animals and Plants Under Domestication* (London, 1868; I, 247), Darwin notes that seven breeds of fowls "including what we should now call jumpers or creepers, and likewise fowls with black feathers, bones and flesh" are described in a "Chinese Encyclopaedia published in 1596." In his account of goldfish he cites "an old Chinese work" to the effect that "fish with vermilion scales were first raised in confinement during the Sung dynasty (which commenced in A.D. 960) and now they are cultivated in families everywhere for the sake of ornament"—a literal rendition from *Pen-ts'ao kang mu*, chüan 44. The sinologist W. F. Mayers was led by Darwin's book to make a study published in China as "Gold Fish Cultivation" (*Notes and Queries on China and Japan*, 2 [1868], 123–124). Mayers in turn was quoted in Darwin's account of the secondary sexual characteristics of fishes in *The Descent of Man* (London, 1881; p. 343). Thus was Li Shih-chen's work woven into the fabric of modern science.

BIBLIOGRAPHY

I. Lɪ Sʜɪʜ-cʜᴇɴ. The major documents for the life of Li Shih-chen are the many pertinent remarks in *Pen-ts'ao kang mu* and the document (*su*[45]) composed by his son Li Chien-yuan[46] to accompany the presentation of the book to the government. The latter is printed as part of the front matter of most editions of *Pen-ts'ao kang mu*. The "official" life in *Ming shih*[47] ("Standard History of the Ming Period"), Po-na ed., ch. 299, pp. 19*b*–20*a*, is derived from the latter. Other early biographical sketches, such as that in Ku Ching-hsing's[48] collected works, *Pai mao t'ang chi*[49], ch. 38; and that found in the collected prose of the great historiographer Chang Hsueh-ch'eng,[50] *Chang shih i shu*,[51] Chia yeh t'ang ed. (1922), ch. 25, pp. 44*a*–47*a*, are considerably less reliable.

The most notable modern studies of Li Shih-chen and his work are Chang Hui-chien,[52] *Li Shih-chen* (Shanghai, 1954), a severely positivistic popular account, also published in English (Peking, 1956); Lu Gwei-djen, "China's Greatest Naturalist, a Brief Biography of Li Shih-chen," in *Physis*, 8, no. 4 (1966), 383–392, the most authoritative to date; Alfred Mosig and Gottfried Schramm, *Der Arz-*

neipflanzen- und Drogenschatz Chinas und die Bedeutung des Pen-ts'ao Kang-mu als Standardwerk der chinesischen Materia Medica, supp. to *Pharmazie*, no. 4 (1955), a rather slovenly jaunt through traditional pharmacology; Ts'ai Ching-feng,[53] "Shih lun Li Shih-chen chi ch'i tsai k'o-hsueh shang ti ch'eng-chiu"[54] ("An Essay on Li Shih-chen and His Scientific Achievements"), in *K'o-hsueh-shih chi-k'an*, 7 (1964), 63–80; Watanabe Kōzō,[55] "Ri Ji-chin no Honzo komoku to sono hampon"[56] ("Li Shih-chen's *Pen-ts'ao kang mu* and Its Editions"), in *Tōyōshi kenkyū*, 12, no. 4 (1953), 333–357, which details Japanese as well as Chinese printed eds.; and the important series of evaluative essays by Japanese specialists which constitutes pp. 147–325 of Yabuuchi Kiyoshi[57] and Yoshida Mitsukuni,[58] eds., *Min-Shin jidai no kagaku gijutsu shi*[59] ("History of Science and Technology in the Ming and Ch'ing Periods"; Kyoto, 1970).

To this day there has not been a complete translation into a Western language of even one article of *Pen-ts'ao kang mu*. A great deal of material on botanicals has been summarized in E. V. Bretschneider, *Botanicon sinicum. Notes on Chinese Botany From Native and Western Sources*, 16 (1881), 25 (1893), and 29 (1895) of the *Journal of the North China Branch of the Royal Asiatic Society;* reprinted at London (1882–1895) and Tokyo (1937). An index to other treatises on Chinese simples is Bernard E. Read, *Chinese Medicinal Plants From the Pen Ts'ao Kang Mu . . . 1596*, 3rd ed. (Peking, 1936). On animal drugs see B. E. Read, *Chinese Materia Medica* (Peking, 1931–1941); for a detailed list of fascicles see J. Needham *et al., Science and Civilisation in China* (Cambridge, 1959), III, 784–785. B. E. Read and C. Pak, *A Compendium of Minerals and Stones Used in Chinese Medicine From the Pen Ts'ao Kang Mu . . . [of] Li Shih-Chen . . . 1597 A.D.* (2nd ed., Peking, 1936), is not a translation but a raw juxtaposition of data from heterogeneous sources. Its historical usefulness is therefore somewhat limited, although its general accuracy is high. For complete and literal translations of all prescriptions given in *Pen-ts'ao kang mu* for a number of medicinal substances see William C. Cooper and N. Sivin, "Man as a Medicine. Pharmacological and Ritual Aspects of Traditional Therapy Using Drugs Derived From the Human Body," in S. Nakayama and N. Sivin, eds., *Chinese Science;* M.I.T. East Asian Science Series, I (Cambridge, Mass., 1972).

II. Lᴀɴᴅᴍᴀʀᴋs ᴏғ ᴛʜᴇ Pʜᴀʀᴍᴀᴄᴏɢɴᴏsᴛɪᴄ ᴛʀᴀᴅɪᴛɪᴏɴ. This list of basic works is provided for the reader not only because of their pertinence to the development of materia medica but also because they are essential to the historical study of botany, zoology, mineralogy, and natural history in China. The selection encompasses only a few of the many works belonging to what might be called the main line of development of the pharmacognostic tradition, as well as examples of intrinsically important but less influential or more specialized books on materia medica. The "main line" is defined most objectively as the series of pharmacopoeias spanning the millennium and a half from *Shen nung pen-ts'ao* to *Pen-ts'ao kang mu*, each of which largely incorporates, amplifies, and improves upon its predecessors. This succession has been sketched by Okanishi Tameto[66] in his preface to *Hsin hsiu pen-ts'ao;* and a much fuller flow chart is provided by Kimura Kōichi[81] in his explanatory essay appended to the reprint cited under *Ching shih cheng lei pei chi pen-ts'ao.* Other bibliographical sources are noted in part III.

1. *Shen nung pen-ts'ao ching*[60] ("Canonic Pharmacopoeia of the Emperor Shen-nung"; the last word of the title is often omitted in citations).

Anonymous and almost certainly compiled in the first or second century, this work covers 365 medicinal substances in tripartite arrangement (as noted above). It is no longer extant but is quoted fully in later pharmacopoeias because of its canonical status. Of the seven published reconstructions, that by Sung Hsing-yen and Sun P'ing-i[61] (*ca.* 1800, many reliable editions) is superior, although far from thorough in its use of sources.

2. *Pen-ts'ao ching chi chu*[62] ("Canonic Pharmacopoeia [of Shen-nung] With Collected Commentaries").

An annotated version of *Shen nung pen-ts'ao ching* compiled by the physician and Taoist magus T'ao Hung-ching, probably shortly after 500. The number of medically active substances was doubled; and detailed descriptions of drugs and notes on their gathering, preparation, and use were added. A copy of a MS of the preface dated 718 was published under the title *Pen-ts'ao ching chi chu ts'an chüan*[63] in the Chi shih an collection *(Chi shih an ts'ung-shu*[64]*)* of 1917 and was reprinted at Peking in 1955. The 1849–1852 Mori manuscript reconstruction of the complete text has been supplemented and reproduced by Okanishi Tameto[65] (Osaka, 1972).

3. *Hsin hsiu pen-ts'ao*[66] ("New Pharmacopoeia").

Compiled under imperial sponsorship by Su Ching and others, and completed in 659. Compared with the previous item, on which it was based, the number of substances included in this book was not much increased. Coverage was revised to take into account the wider resources of a reunited China, and illustrations were provided. Classification was by mineral, vegetable, or animal origin, in only seven categories (and one more containing drugs no longer in use), with the threefold system of the earlier pharmacopoeias retained for subdivisions.

Slightly over half of the text is preserved in four fragments, which have been used in the preparation of a definitive reconstruction of the whole text with variorum notes by Okanishi Tameto, *Ch'ung chi hsin hsiu pen-ts'ao*[67] (Ch'ing-t'an, Taiwan, 1964).

4. *Shih liao pen-ts'ao*[68] ("Dietary Pharmacopoeia").

Compiled by Meng Shen,[69] probably shortly after 700, and expanded by Chang Ting (between 720 and 740[?]) to include 227 substances of value in dietary hygiene for both health and illness. According to Nakao Manzō,[70] Chang changed the title from *Pu yang fang*[71] ("Restorative and Tonic Prescriptions"); see "Tonkō sekishitsu hakken Shokuryō honzō zankan kō"[72] ("Study of a Fragment of the *Shih liao pen-ts'ao* Discovered in a Tun-huang Grotto"), in *Shanhai shizen kagaku kenkyūsho ihō* (Shanghai), **1**, no. 3 (Feb. 1930), 9–18. *Shih liao pen-ts'ao* is perhaps the most important and most often cited book in the tradition

of dietary regulation and therapy, which goes back to the beginnings of pharmacology in China.

The manuscript fragment just mentioned was found in northwest China in 1907; written in 933, it comprises about a tenth of the original book. Nakao published it as "Shokuryō honzō no kōsatsu"[73] ("A Study of the *Shih liao pen-ts'ao*"), *ibid.*, pp. 79–216, repr. as *Tun-huang shih shih ku pen-ts'ao ts'an chüan*[74] ("Fragment of an Ancient Pharmacopoeia From a Tun-huang Grotto"; Shanghai, 1937; repr. Taipei, 1970).

5. *Ching shih cheng lei pei chi pen-ts'ao*[75] ("Pharmacopoeia for Every Emergency, With Classifications Verified From the Classics and Histories").

Compiled by T'ang Shen-wei,[76] this work was drafted in 1082–1083 and, after conflation with the *Ch'ung kuang pu-chu pen-ts'ao*[77] ("Reamplified Pharmacopoeia With Added Commentary"; 1092) of Ch'en Ch'eng[78] was printed in 1108 under the title *Ching shih cheng lei Ta-kuan pen-ts'ao*[79] (usually abbreviated as *Ta-kuan pen-ts'ao;* Ta-kuan is the name of the reign period in which it was published). This book contains more than twice as many substances (*ca.* 1,750) as *Hsin hsiu pen-ts'ao.* The principle of classification was unchanged, but the number of rubrics was slightly increased. The series which this book begins comprises more than forty printed revisions and recensions in China, Japan, and Korea. See Watanabe Kōzō, "Tō Shimbi no Keishi shōrui bikkyū honzō to sono hampon"[80] ("On the Series Descended From T'ang Shen-wei's *Ching shih cheng lei pei chi pen-ts'ao*, and Its Editions"), in *Tōhō gakuhō* (Kyoto), **21** (1952), 160–206.

The earliest extant printed edition of the *Ta-kuan pen-ts'ao* is that of 1195, which had been further augmented by appending the *Pen-ts'ao yen i.* The recent reduced reprint with an index and a valuable historical introduction, *Ching shih cheng lei Ta-kuan pen-ts'ao*, Kimura Kōichi and Yoshizaki Masao,[81] eds. (Tokyo, 1970), is based on a 1904 repro. of the ed. of 1215.

6. *Pen-ts'ao yen i*[82] ("Dilatations Upon the Pharmacopoeias").

A collection of critical notes on 472 medical substances by K'ou Tsung-shih, printed in 1119. The original title was apparently *Pen-ts'ao kuang i,*[83] but the necessity to avoid a taboo on use of the personal name of Emperor Ning-tsung (1195–1201) led to the minor change in wording. This work, which made influential contributions to pharmacological theory, takes *Hsin hsiu pen-ts'ao* as its point of departure. K'ou, a minor medical official, did not have access to *Ching shih cheng lei pei chi pen-ts'ao* or its early successors. Submission of his work to the central government led to his promotion but not to imperial sponsorship of the book's publication.

The earliest surviving version was printed in 1195. A critical text based on surviving editions and citations was published at Peking in 1937 (repr. 1957).

7. *Ch'ung hsiu Cheng-ho ching shih cheng lei pei yung pen-ts'ao*[84] ("Revised Pharmacopoeia of the Cheng-ho Reign Period for Every Use, With Classifications Verified From the Classics and Histories").

This is a revision by Chang Ts'un-hui,[85] printed in 1249,

of the *Cheng-ho hsin hsiu ching shih cheng lei pei yung pen-ts'ao* ("Pharmacopoeia of the Cheng-ho Reign Period . . ."), which had been published under imperial auspices by Ts'ao Hsiao-chung[86] and others in 1116. Aside from minor discrepancies in content from *Ching shih cheng lei pei chi pen-ts'ao* (the net increase is only two substances), the major difference is that in this book the contents of *Pen-ts'ao yen i* are distributed among the articles to which they are related.

The exceptional usefulness of this member of the *Cheng lei pen-ts'ao* series results largely from the existence of the printed edition of 1249, which has been photographically reproduced in a widely distributed edition (Peking, 1957). The earlier edition in the Ssu pu ts'ung k'an collection (Shanghai, 1929), represented as based on the 1249 ed., is actually a reprint of the version of 1468.

8. *Chiu huang pen-ts'ao* ("Famine Relief Pharmacopoeia").

By Chu Hsiao,[87] fifth son of the Ming Emperor T'ai-tsu, preface dated 1406. Includes 440 substances which could be used to sustain life in time of famine, with illustrations and systematic notes on habitat, preparation, and ingestion. For a detailed description and historical appreciation see Lu Gwei-djen and Joseph Needham, "The Esculentist Movement in Mediaeval Chinese Botany; Studies on Wild (Emergency) Food Plants," in *Archives internationales d'histoire des sciences*, **21** (1968), 226–248; and Amano Motonosuke,[88] "Mindai ni okeru kyūkō sakumotsu chojutsu kō,"[89] ("A Study of the Writing of Works on Famine Relief in the Ming Period"), in *Tōyō gakuhō*, **47**, no. 1 (1964), 32–59.

The oldest extant printed edition is the xylograph 2nd ed. of 1525 (facs. repr., Shanghai, 1959). The most accessible edition is *Nung cheng ch'üan shu*[90] ("Complete Writings on Agricultural Administration"; completed 1628; repr. Peking, 1956), chüan 46–59. Later separate versions of *Chiu huang pen-ts'ao* (1837, 1856; Japan, 1718) are extracts from this agricultural handbook.

9. *Pen-ts'ao p'in hui ching yao*[91] ("Classified Essential Pharmacopoeia").

Compiled by a board including Liu Wen-t'ai[92] and others in 1505 but not printed until 1936, probably because of the death of its patron, Emperor Hsiao-tsung, soon after its completion. Since the MS was kept in the imperial palace, its historic influence was negligible. This is a work of great sophistication, on the scale of *Pen-ts'ao kang mu*, but based more narrowly on written sources.

The whereabouts of the MS are now unknown. While still in the palace library, it was published in a typeset edition under the title *Tien pan*[93] *pen-ts'ao p'in hui ching yao* (Shanghai, 1937). This included a supplement of 1701 (which incorporated material from *Pen-ts'ao kang mu*) but did not reproduce the fine color illustrations of the MS. On the illustrations see Giuliani Bertuccioli, "A Note on Two Ming Manuscripts of the Pên-Ts'ao P'in-Hui Ching-Yao," in *Journal of Oriental Studies*, **3** (1956), 63–68.

10. *Pen-ts'ao kang mu*[94] ("Systematic Pharmacopoeia").
Of the many available editions, the most convenient for scholarly use is the 2-vol. reprint (Peking, 1957) of the Anhwei recension of 1885. It adds not only variorum notes but also indexes of drug names and synonyms. The *Pen-ts'ao kang mu* and Chao Hsueh-min's[95] useful supplement, *Pen-ts'ao kang mu shih i*[96] ("Gleanings for the *Pen-ts'ao kang mu*"; compiled and revised between 1760 and 1803 or later, first printed 1871), are available in a punctuated typeset edition with index according to the four-corner system (Shanghai, 1954–1955).

III. IMPORTANT REFERENCE TOOLS FOR THE HISTORY OF PHARMACOGNOSY. The standard descriptive guide to the extant pharmacopoeias of China and to Japanese pharmacopoeias in the Chinese tradition is Lung Po-chien,[97] *Hsien ts'un pen-ts'ao shu lu*[98] ("Bibliography of Extant Pharmacopoeias"; Peking, 1957). An invaluable pastiche of bibliographical data, prefaces and colophons, critical discussions, and analytic information is provided for the entire Chinese medical literature, extant or lost, up to the late thirteenth century in Okanishi Tameto, *Sung i-ch'ien i chi k'ao*[99] ("Studies of Medical Books Through the Sung Period"; Peking, 1958), which devotes nearly 200 pages to the classics of pharmacognosy. Less detailed information of a similar kind is provided for later works as well in Tamba Mototane[100] (*nom de plume* of Taki Gen'in[101]), *Chung-kuo i chi k'ao*[102] ("Studies of Chinese Medical Books"; Peking, 1956). Liou Ho and Claudius Roux, *Aperçu bibliographique sur les anciens traités chinois de botanique, d'agriculture, de sériciculture et de fungiculture* (Lyons, 1927), reflects very limited study.

There is no reliable general historical study of Chinese materia medica in any Western language. Pierre Huard and Ming Wong, "Évolution de la matière médicale chinoise," in *Janus*, **47** (1958), reviews the main pharmacopoeias, but because of carelessness and excessive reliance on uncritical modern Chinese secondary sources this article must be used with caution. The historical data in vol. I of Bretschneider's book (cited above), because less ambitious, is perhaps more useful. Needham *et al.*, *Science and Civilisation in China*, VI, can be expected to fill this gap.

In Chinese there is as yet nothing on medicine in general to replace Ch'en Pang-hsien,[103] *Chung-kuo i-hsueh shih*[104] ("History of Chinese Medicine"; Shanghai, 1920), almost completely bibliographical in approach; and there is no monograph on the history of materia medica. In Japanese the survey of Liao Wen-jen,[105] *Shina chūsei igaku shi*[106] ("History of Medieval Chinese Medicine"; Kyoto, 1932), is similar in style and value to that of Ch'en; and scholarship on Chinese pharmacognosy is scattered through a great many articles on special subjects. Among the most informative of these is Okanishi, "Chūgoku honzō no dentō to Kin-Gen no honzō,"[107] ("The Chinese Pharmacognostic Tradition and the Pharmacopoeias of the Chin and Yuan Periods"), in Yabuuchi, ed., *Sō-Gen jidai no kagaku gijutsushi*[108] ("History of Science and Technology in the Sung and Yuan Periods"; Kyoto, 1967), pp. 171–210.

The major guides to the secondary literature of Chinese medicine, and thus of materia medica, are Chi Hung and

Wu Kuan kuo,[109] *Chung wen i hsueh wen-hsien fen-lei so-yin*[110] ("Classified Index of Medical Contributions in Chinese"; Peking, 1958), esp. pp. 8–14 on history; A. R. Ghani, *Chinese Medicine and Indigenous Medicinal Plants*, Pansdoc Bibliography no. 396 (Karachi, 1965), a random collection of citations; and Medical History Research Subcommittee, Shanghai Municipal Research Committee on Chinese Materia Medica, ed., *Chung-wen i-shih lun-wen so-yin*[111] ("Index to Articles in Chinese on the History of Medicine"), 3 vols. (Shanghai, 1957–1958).

This article is, with some additions and omissions and a new bibliography, adapted with permission from the study of Lu Gwei-djen noted above. The aid of Miyasita Saburō, librarian for Takeda Chemical Industries, Osaka, Japan, especially in procuring the illustrations, is gratefully acknowledged.

N. SIVIN

NOTES

1. 李時珍	32. 行	科學技術史	84. 重修政和新修
2. 東壁	33. 助	60. 神農本草經	經史證類備用
3. 瀕湖	34. 反	61. 孫星衍，孫馮翼	本草
4. 瓦硝罍	35. 製	62. 本草經集注	85. 張存惠
5. 李言聞	36. 治	63. 殘卷	86. 曹孝忠
6. 顧問	37. 合治	64. 吉石盦叢書	87. 朱櫹
7. 王世貞	38. 禁	65. 岡西爲人	88. 天野元之助
8. 桐	39. 代	66. 新修本草	89. 明代における救荒作物著述考
9. 五行	40. 忌	67. 重輯新脩本草	90. 農政全書
10. 陳藏器	41. 解	68. 食療本草	91. 本草品彙精要
11. 釋名	42. 贗	69. 孟詵	92. 劉文泰
12. 正誤	43. 吳其濬	70. 中尾万三	93. 殿板
13. 集解	44. 植物名實圖考	71. 補養方	94. 本草綱目
14. 脩治	45. 疏	72. 敦煌石室發	95. 趙學敏
15. 主治	46. 李建元	見食療木草	96. 拾遺
16. 氣味	47. 明史	殘卷考	97. 龍伯堅
17. 發明	48. 顧景星	73. 食療本草の考祭	98. 現存本草書録
18. 附方	49. 白茅堂集	74. 敦煌石室古	99. 宋以前醫籍考
19. 名	50. 章學誠	本草殘卷	100. 丹波元胤
20. 苗	51. 章氏遺書	75. 經史證類備急本草	101. 多紀元胤
21. 地	52. 張慧劍	76. 唐愼徵	102. 中國醫籍考
22. 時	53. 蔡景峯	77. 重廣補注本草	103. 陳邦賢
23. 收	54. 試論李時珍	78. 陳承	104. 中國醫學史
24. 用	及其在科學	79. 經史證類大觀	105. 廖溫仁
25. 質	上的成就	本草	106. 支那中世醫學史
26. 色	55. 渡邊幸三	80. 唐愼徵の經史證	107. 中国本草の伝統と金元の本草
27. 味	56. 李時珍の本草綱目	類備急本草の系統とその版本	108. 宋元時代の科學技術史
28. 性	とその版本	81. 木村康一，	109. 吉鴻，吳覌國
29. 氣	57. 藪內淸	吉崎正雄	110. 中文醫學文献分類索引
30. 臭	58. 吉田光邦	82. 本草衍義	111. 中文醫史論文索引
31. 主	59. 明淸時代の	83. 廣義	

LISSAJOUS, JULES ANTOINE (*b.* Versailles France, 4 March 1822; *d.* Plombières, France 24 June 1880), *physics.*

Lissajous developed an optical method for studying vibration and was generally interested in the physics of wave motion. "Lissajous figures" are the curves in the xy plane generated by the functions $y = a \sin(w_1 t + q_1)$ and $x = b \sin(w_2 t + q_2)$, where w_1 and w_2 are small integers. The curves are today easily produced on an oscilloscope screen; but Lissajous obtained them in the context of acoustics, from the superposition of the vibrations of tuning forks. He entered the École Normale Supérieure in 1841 and received the *agrégé* in 1847. He then became professor of physics at the Lycée Saint-Louis. In 1850 he presented his thesis, *Sur la position des noeuds dans les lames qui vibrent transversalement,* to the Faculty of Sciences. In 1874 he became rector of the academy of Chambéry and, in the following year, of the academy of Besançon. Lissajous was a candidate for the physics section of the Paris Academy in 1873 but was only elected corresponding member in 1879. In 1873 he received the Lacaze Prize, primarily for his work on the optical observation of vibration.

Like some other physicists of the time, Lissajous was interested in demonstrations of vibration that did not depend on the sense of hearing. Most of his experiments involved visual manifestations of vibrations: in the thesis on vibrating bars he used Chladni's sand-pattern method to determine nodal positions; he studied the waves produced by tuning forks in contact with water; and he did experiments on the popular phenomenon of "singing flames." Lissajous's most important research, first described in 1855, was the invention of a way to study acoustic vibrations by reflecting a light beam from the vibrating object onto a screen. He introduced his discussion of this topic with the assertion that, although sound vibrations are too rapid for direct observation, he could provide a visual demonstration of the wave form and obtain precise tuning without using the ear. (Lissajous was concerned with the problem of tuning—in 1855 he strongly recommended defining a standard frequency for the tuning of musical instruments.) He wrote that he thought of projecting the motion of vibration by reflecting light because he wanted to avoid the mechanical linkage present in some graphic devices (such as Duhamel's). He claimed that the use of rapidly rotating mirrors in some contemporary experiments (such as that of his friend Léon Foucault, on the velocity of light) had influenced his thinking.

Lissajous produced two kinds of luminous curves. In the first kind, light is reflected from a tuning fork (to which a small mirror is attached), and then from a large mirror that is rotated rapidly. When viewed on a screen, the beam shows the trigonometric form of the displacements, because the vibrations have been "spread out." The second kind of curve, named the "Lissajous figure," is more useful. The light beam is successively reflected from mirrors on two forks that are vibrating about mutually perpendicular axes. Persistence of vision causes various curves, whose shapes depend on the relative frequency, phase, and amplitude of the forks' vibrations, to be seen on the screen. For example, forks vibrating with the same amplitude and frequency produce ellipses the parameters of which depend on the phase difference between them.

Lissajous was interested in using his superposition curves to measure vibration parameters and to analyze more complicated acoustical problems. If one of the forks is a standard, the form of the curve enables an estimate of the parameters of the other. As Lissajous said, they enable one to study beats (the ellipses rotate as the phase difference changes). "Lissajous figures" have been, and still are, important in this respect. For further use in research Lissajous invented the "phonoptomètre," a vibrating microscope in which a tuning fork is attached to the objective lens. The vibrations of the object being observed combine with those of the lens and can therefore be analyzed in terms of the Lissajous figures produced. Helmholtz used this instrument in his investigations of string vibration (Helmholtz, *On the Sensations of Tone*, Dover reprint, p. 80).

Lissajous's optical method of observing vibration and the vibrating microscope were shown at the Paris exhibition of 1867 (they are described in *Reports of the United States Commissioners to the Paris Universal Exposition 1867* [Washington, D.C., 1870], III, 507–509). The French physicists awarded the Lacaze Prize to Lissajous for his "beautiful experiments," and both Rayleigh and Tyndall discussed his work in their treatises on sound. Scientists were enthusiastic about the work because there were still not many ways of demonstrating and measuring the parameters of vibration. Lissajous's optical experiments are simple, but the reasoning behind them depends on the principle of superposition; it is probably for this reason that they were done only in the middle of the nineteenth century.

BIBLIOGRAPHY

Lissajous's most important papers are "Note sur un moyen nouveau de mettre en évidence le mouvement vibratoire des corps," in *Comptes rendus hebdomadaires des séances de l'Académie des sciences*, **41** (1855), 93–95; "Note sur une méthode nouvelle applicable à l'étude des mouvements vibratoires," *ibid.*, 814–817; "Mémoire sur l'étude optique des mouvements vibratoires," in *Annales de chimie*, 3rd ser., **51** (1857), 147–231 (this is the most substantial article on the optical method); "Sur l'interférence des ondes liquides," in *Comptes rendus hebdomadaires des séances de l'Académie des sciences*, **58** (1868), 1187; "Sur le phonoptomètre, instrument propre à l'étude optique des mouvements périodiques ou continus," *ibid.*, **76** (1873), 878–880; and "Notice historique sur la vie et les travaux de Léon Foucault," in J. B. L. Foucault, *Recueil des travaux scientifiques*, II (Paris, 1878). For other papers by Lissajous, see the Royal Society's *Catalogue of Scientific Papers*, IV, 52; VIII, 244.

On Lissajous's work, see "Prix Lacaze, physique," in *Comptes rendus hebdomadaires des séances de l'Académie des sciences*, **79** (1874), 1607–1610.

SIGALIA DOSTROVSKY

LISTER, JOSEPH (*b.* Upton, Essex, England, 5 April 1827; *d.* Walmer, Deal, Kent, England, 10 February 1912), *surgery*.

The antiseptic doctrines and practices developed by Joseph Lister in the mid-Victorian era transformed the ancient craft of surgery into an enlightened art governed by scientific disciplines. His methodical, conscientious determination to reduce the appalling mortality rates resulting from traumatic and postoperative sepsis in the surgical wards of hospitals, allied with extraordinary probity and charm of character, captured the devotion of adherents in many countries and eventually silenced opponents. During his lifetime surgery expanded tremendously in resources and scope; the terrified despair of prospective victims gave place to faith and confidence that injury could be remedied and suppuration averted; and Lister himself became widely acknowledged as one of mankind's greatest benefactors.

Lister was the fourth child and second son of Quaker parents, Joseph Jackson Lister and the former Isabella Harris, who had four sons and three daughters. Several generations of the Lister family had lived in Yorkshire when Joseph Lister, the illustrious surgeon's great-grandfather (whose parents had joined the Society of Friends), went to London about 1720 and set up as a tobacconist. His youngest son, John, acquired a vintnery from Stephen Jackson, his father-in-law. John's only son, Joseph Jackson, left school at fourteen to become apprenticed to the prospering wine business. In his early thirties he married a schoolteacher about ten years his junior, daughter of the headmistress of Ackworth Quaker School. In 1826 he purchased Upton House, a mansion set on seventy acres about five miles east of London. Here Joseph Lister was born. The estate remained the family home until his father's death in 1869.

Lister's pensive, handsome mother was an unfailing source of affection, guidance, and instruction to the young boy. His remarkable father had artistic talent and, despite meager schooling, became a good Latin scholar and achieved distinction in mathematics, particularly in application to optics. Joseph Jackson Lister's work led to production of the achromatic microscope objective and to his election to fellowship in the Royal Society of London in 1832. The close-knit household was happy and lively, enjoying occasional fun. Amusements were restrained, however, and relaxations purposeful; and the high-mindedness of parents and neighboring Friends was reflected by scientists who occasionally visited Upton House for group discussions. Lister was introduced by his father to microscopy and to pursuits in natural history that gave him lifelong pleasure. As a child he macerated bones, dissected animals and articulated their skeletons, and announced his intention to become a surgeon. A close sympathy developed between father and son, the latter habitually writing home about his affairs and appreciating the shrewd paternal comments and counsel.

Lister attended two private schools, the first at Hitchin, where he was ahead of his year, especially in classics. At about thirteen he went to the Quaker school of Grove House, Tottenham, which emphasized mathematics, natural science, modern languages, and the writing of formal essays on various topics. (Lister's subjects included chemistry, human osteology, and laughing gas.) He left school at seventeen with a well-rounded education that included considerable familiarity with the classics, some facility in French and German, and a punctiliousness in speech and writing that became his hallmark.

In 1844 Lister entered the nonsectarian University College, London. It presented no obstacles to registration on religious grounds; possessed a modern hospital and a distinguished medical faculty; and was dedicated to sober study. In three years he received his B.A. degree; but soon after he began to study medicine, he contracted smallpox. Premature return to work brought on nervous depression, necessitating a long holiday in 1848. He resumed his studies in London that autumn. In those days students interspersed their classes in botany, physics, and chemistry (subsequently termed "premedical" courses) with physiology and anatomy ("preclinical" courses), and with ward visits, as the opportunity offered. Lister's painstaking system of learning and his retentive memory allowed him to profit from this system. He always showed talent for integrating and applying knowledge acquired from manifold sources.

In his first years as a medical student, Lister worked very seriously under austere living conditions. A more cheerful and wholesome life supervened when he became a hospital resident and met at close quarters intelligent young men of diverse backgrounds, some destined for prominent careers. Participating in the debating society and the hospital medical society, he attacked the homeopaths and read papers (never published) on hospital gangrene and on the use of the microscope in medicine. After being house physician to the cardiologist W. H. Walshe, he was house surgeon for nine months in 1851 to J. (later Sir John) Erichsen. Awarded many examination honors, in 1852 he received the M.B. degree of the University of London and the fellowship of the Royal College of Surgeons.

In his final years at University College, Lister was influenced particularly by two professors: the ophthalmic surgeon Wharton Jones—well-known for researches on inflammation—and the eminent physiologist William Sharpey. Under their guidance and example, and with his father's practical encouragement, he launched some histological investigations. These studies, conducted before modern methods of section cutting and tissue staining were available, evoked the technical enterprise and tenacity that marked Lister's subsequent microbiological researches and antiseptic practices. The first published report,

"Observations on the Contractile Tissue of the Iris" (1853), confirmed R. A. von Kölliker's claim that the iris comprises involuntary muscle and demonstrated that pupillary size is controlled by two distinct muscles. Another report soon appeared, "Observations on the Muscular Tissue of the Skin" (1853), dealing mainly with involuntary muscles of the scalp. Both papers, illustrated by delicate camera lucida drawings, attracted favorable attention at home and abroad. Lister's first experimental inquiry, begun shortly afterward (but unreported for four years), concerned the flow and absorption of chyle in the mesenteric lacteals of mice given indigo in their feed.

Although these microscopic excursions fascinated Lister, his interest in surgery wavered only briefly. He had been present at University College Hospital in December 1846, when Robert Liston performed the first major operation under ether anesthesia in Britain. Several years elapsed before the availability of anesthetics persuaded surgeons to broaden the scope and reduce the haste of their procedures—thus increasing the mortality from postoperative sepsis. Prolonged suffering and death often followed treatment of a minor disability. A conscientious surgeon-to-be might well be appalled at the unpredictable prospect for his patients, and saddened by the grim mortality associated with his calling. But Lister was undaunted; after nine years of studies at University College he was now twenty-six, and it was time to establish himself. Sharpey advised that after spending a month with James Syme, professor of clinical surgery at the University of Edinburgh—perhaps the most original and thoughtful surgeon of his day—Lister should broaden his experience by visiting famous Continental medical centers.

In September 1853 Lister was warmly received at Edinburgh by the brilliant, opinionated Syme, who entrusted him with so much responsibility at the infirmary that before long Lister decided to stay the winter. Syme appointed him supernumerary house surgeon and made him welcome in his household. Early in 1854 Lister became his resident house surgeon, a post that brought special privileges: twelve dressers to supervise, a wide choice of hospital patients to operate upon, and opportunities of assisting in his chief's private practice. The close relationship between the two men was enhanced when Lister became engaged in July 1855 to Syme's eldest daughter, Agnes. He resigned his membership in the Society of Friends (but continued to use the Quaker form of address to his parents and siblings) and later joined the Scottish Episcopal Church. The marriage took place in April 1856 and, although childless, was very happy. For nearly forty years his wife proved a devoted companion, an understanding helpmate, and a patient and competent amanuensis.

Late in 1854, an assistant surgeoncy at the Royal Infirmary fell vacant, and Lister was urged to apply for it. The duties of the appointment included giving a course on the principles and practice of surgery, which he painstakingly prepared and began to give in the autumn of 1855, although he was not elected to the post until a year later, shortly after returning with his wife from a prolonged wedding tour. (At such renowned medical centers as Pavia, Padua, Vienna, Prague, Würzburg, Leipzig, and Berlin he had met many well-known figures, particularly in the field of ophthalmic surgery, to which he was then attracted.) The new appointee zestfully undertook a second lecture course, on surgical pathology and operative surgery. He also conducted "public" operations at the Royal Infirmary—sometimes applauded by students—and extended his microscopic researches.

After presenting a paper entitled "On the Minute Structure of Involuntary Muscular Fibre" to the Royal Society of Edinburgh, Lister intensified his inquiries into inflammation, launched the previous year following "a most glorious night" at the microscope. He read three reports to the Royal Society of London in June 1857; they were published in its *Philosophical Transactions* (1858), the most important being "On the Early Stages of Inflammation." This records the earliest vascular and tissue changes induced in the frog's web by such irritants as hot water and mustard. He concluded and thereafter taught that "the primary lesion in inflammatory congestion" is a "suspension of function or temporary abolition of vital energy," characterized by "adhesiveness" of the blood corpuscles. Led thence to investigate blood coagulation, he summarized current knowledge of this phenomenon in his Croonian lecture of 1863.

Lister's reputation as an original and thorough investigator brought him election to fellowship of the Royal Society in 1860, when he was only thirty-three years old. His scrupulous concern to verify conclusions and give full weight to conflicting evidence is revealed in letters he wrote in 1857–1858 to William Sharpey. Lister's genuine modesty and obvious integrity, and a capacity to inspire students with enthusiasm and respect for their calling, made him a natural candidate for the regius professorship of surgery at the University of Glasgow, which became vacant late in 1859. Syme persuaded him to apply and canvass for the post, and his appointment was confirmed early in 1860. Nearly seven formative years at Edinburgh thus closed with regretful congratulations from students and a testimonial dinner from colleagues.

Lister was broadly trained, well reputed, courageous and conciliatory, and in the prime of physical and mental vigor. Glasgow's medical school was prosperous, with a talented and congenial faculty. Lister was initially handicapped, however, by lack of a hospital appointment, for the professorial chair did not automatically involve the surgeoncy at the Royal Infirmary. Nevertheless, he assumed heavy teaching and administrative duties, including the preparation of a daily lecture in systematic surgery for a class of 182 enthusiastic students. Characteristically, he renovated the students' desks and redecorated the lecture theater at his own expense. He set up a meticulously detailed and troublesome system of marking each question in his written and oral examinations; became actively interested in arrangements for removal of the university to a new locality; and served as secretary of the medical faculty. Lister also wrote lengthy and valuable chapters on amputations and anesthetics for T. Holmes's comprehensive *System of Surgery* (1860–1864), to which he was sole contributor from outside London. These undertakings left little time for the demands of private practice.

Lister worked even harder when elected in 1861 to take charge of the surgical wards at the Royal Infirmary. He explored the greater opportunities, more conservative procedures, and lessened shock offered by the advent of anesthesia. (He favored chloroform, discovered in 1847 by Sir James Y. Simpson, an eminent gynecologist at Edinburgh—who later attacked the antiseptic system.) During this period Lister invented several ingenious instruments, including a needle for silver-wire sutures, a hook for extracting small objects from the ear, a slender-bladed sinus forceps, and a screw tourniquet for compressing the abdominal aorta. Later he devised many kinds of dressings, ligatures, and drains for wounds. He was a cautious operator, deliberate and thorough rather than spectacular, but alert and resolute in an emergency. Broad-shouldered and of powerful physique, with very strong hands, Lister was yet extremely gentle; and the most delicate manipulations, such as removal of a cataract or a urethral stone, were performed unfalteringly. His innovations—such as radical mastectomy for breast cancer, the wiring of fractured patellae and pegging of un-united fractures, and the revival of supra-pubic cystotomy—were a consequence of greater surgical boldness following the introduction of antiseptic techniques. Improved methods of amputating through the thigh or at the hip dated from the pre-antiseptic era, however, as did Lister's practice of rendering the site of operation bloodless by elevating the involved limb before applying the tourniquet.

The manifold commitments and heavy routine were incompatible with Lister's research aspirations. Moreover, tenure of his hospital appointment was limited to ten years. Hence, when the chair of systematic surgery at Edinburgh became vacant in 1864, he was persuaded to apply for it. His disappointment when James Spence was chosen became mingled with grief at the almost simultaneous death of his mother; but he involved himself in helping to select a site for Glasgow's new College Hospital (the future Western Infirmary) and in preparing a pioneer paper, "Excision of the Wrist for Caries" (1865). This describes how, out of fifteen cases of tuberculosis of the wrist joint, at least ten hands were spared from amputation and rendered functional.

Lister was dismayed that surgical progress should be blocked by the threat of erysipelas, septicemia, pyemia, or hospital gangrene. Admittance to the New Surgical Hospital portion of the Royal Infirmary meant courting unpredictable catastrophe. The mortality from amputations, as in many other well-known hospitals, was around 40 percent. Abdominal surgery was seldom contemplated and was limited to ovariotomy, and the thoracic and cranial cavities were practically sacrosanct. Lister's wards never assumed the frightful conditions that necessitated closure of other parts of the building—probably because he was unusually fastidious, demanded strict attention to rules of cleanliness, ensured good air circulation, and refused to tolerate overcrowding. Yet the sufferings of his patients were so heartrending that it sometimes seemed "a questionable privilege to be connected with the institution."

In the early 1860's Lister began declaring wound suppuration a form of decomposition. The prevailing medical doctrine about the cause of putrefaction derived from Liebig's dictum (1839) that organic substances in the moist state and in the presence of oxygen undergo a peculiar form of combustion. Liebig rode roughshod over the observations in 1837 of the physicist Charles Cagniard de la Tour and the physiologist Theodor Schwann that fermentative phenomena resulted from the multiplication of yeast cells. A subsequent generation of misguided surgeons had treated wounds systematically on the supposition that they should be shielded from the effects of atmospheric oxygen. One system encouraged scab formation through application of powders, caustics, or fragrant balsams. Every surgeon had his favorite dressing, dry or wet. The alternative system entailed mechanical occlusion of the wound with agents such as collodion, adhesive plaster, and goldbeater's skin.

Lister realized that oxygen could not be excluded from wounds, and he soon doubted its responsibility for provoking suppuration. His 1865 paper referred to the oral administration of potassium sulfite to a patient who developed fatal pyemia, "with the view of counteracting the poisonous effect of any septic matter already introduced into the circulation." Further, when two persistent sores became gangrenous in a patient whose wrist he had successfully excised, the process was "checked by the application of carbolic acid. . . ."

Thomas Anderson, professor of chemistry at Glasgow University, drew Lister's attention in 1865 to the work and writings of Louis Pasteur. In several notable reports, especially "Mémoire sur les corpuscules organisés qui existent dans l'atmosphère. Examen de la doctrine des générations spontanées" (1861) and "Recherches sur la putréfaction" (1864), Pasteur had claimed that putrefaction was a fermentative process caused by living microorganisms carried on dust particles and transported by the air; that the air could be freed of these agents by filtration, heat, and other means; that certain body fluids, such as blood and urine, would keep indefinitely without decomposing if collected and stored under sterile conditions; and that spontaneous generation was a myth. These claims revealed startlingly to Lister the causes of wound sepsis and provided the key to banishment of hospital diseases. He always gladly acknowledged his indebtedness to Pasteur, as in the 1867 address "On the Antiseptic Principle in the Practice of Surgery" to the British Medical Association:

> When it had been shown by the researches of Pasteur that the septic property of the atmosphere depended not on the oxygen or any gaseous constituent, but on minute organisms suspended in it, which owed their energy to their vitality, it occurred to me that decomposition in the injured part might be avoided without excluding the air, by applying as a dressing some material capable of destroying the life of the floating particles.

In 1864 Lister learned that carbolic acid treatment of the sewage at Carlisle had rendered neighboring irrigated lands odorless and had destroyed entozoa that infected cattle grazing there. Procuring a sample of crude "German creosote" from his colleague Anderson, he used it (unsuccessfully) in March 1865 in the treatment of a compound fracture of the leg. The impure material, immiscible with water, was superseded by the less irritating crystalline carbolic acid—newly manufactured at Manchester by F. C. Calvert. This was soluble up to 5 percent in water but dissolved readily in such organic fluids as olive oil or linseed oil. Between August 1865 and April 1867, by

means of these agents, Lister obtained results exceeding all expectations: of eleven cases of compound fractures of limbs, nine recovered. The main features of his antiseptic treatment were thorough cleansing of the wound with carbolic acid and its protection from airborne germs by a dressing soaked in the acid. The site was covered with a molded sheet of tin to diminish evaporation, around which absorbent material was packed to collect discharge. The dressings were changed daily and the tenacious crust of carbolized blood at the site of injury retouched with the acid.

Lister adapted his principle and technique to drainage of indolent abscesses (including a large psoas abscess), associated with tuberculous bones or joints. Until opened, such lesions generally contained no "septic organisms," so it was unnecessary to introduce antiseptic into them. To protect against environmental living particles during and after surgical intervention, however, the overlying skin was dressed with rag soaked in a 1 : 4 solution of crystalline carbolic acid in boiled linseed oil. Under this "antiseptic curtain" the abscess was incised and its contents evacuated. To prevent persistent discharge from such abscesses becoming contaminated, Lister prepared an antiseptic putty by mixing ordinary whiting with carbolic acid solution in linseed oil. This was spread thickly upon tinfoil and secured over the site with adhesive plaster.

Lister described these remarkable advances in a classic series of reports in *The Lancet*, "On a New Method of Treating Compound Fracture, Abscess, etc., With Observations on the Conditions of Suppuration" (1867), which included two novel observations on the healing capacities of tissues rendered uninfected by antiseptic treatment. First, a carbolized blood clot, left undisturbed, became organized into living tissue by ingrowth of cells and blood vessels from surrounding parts. Second, in an aseptic wound, portions of dead bone were absorbed by adjacent granulation tissue. Encouraged by these results, Lister began to apply the antiseptic principle to surgical wounds toward the end of 1866. In August 1867, at the Dublin meeting of the British Medical Association, he announced that during the last nine months his wards—previously "amongst the unhealthiest in the whole surgical division of the Glasgow Royal Infirmary"—had been entirely free from hospital sepsis.

Lister's accomplishments were viewed by his university colleagues with sympathetic interest and by his assistants with unfeigned admiration; but many fellow surgeons, unaccustomed to weighing scientific evidence and prone to polemics (in which Lister never engaged), were indifferent, skeptical, or even hostile. For example, the chief of an adjacent surgical ward at the Royal Infirmary evinced no interest whatever in Lister's patients or methods. Others found his system too exactingly detailed or, overlooking crucial points of technique, performed ambitious operations with disastrous results. His detractors deplored the frequent changes in technique and questioned the significance of such unsettled rituals. They did not realize that every modification followed exhaustive tests, often conducted far into the night in Lister's home laboratory. His "protective" oiled-silk dressing, which allowed secretions to escape while sparing skin and tissues from carbolic acid irritation, took great time and trouble to develop. For three decades Lister sought improvements in the catgut ligature—a quest that began in 1868 at Upton, where he ligated a calf's carotid artery during the last Christmas holidays before his father died. The animal was killed one month later and the catgut absorption process examined microscopically.

Some misunderstandings arose because Lister chose compound fractures for preliminary trials of his antiseptic method, in view of their frequency in heavily industrialized Glasgow and of the extremely high mortality rate resulting from them. To his distress, carbolic acid often was looked upon as a specific nostrum against sepsis, rather than as a potent protective barrier behind which injured parts could exercise their natural recovery powers. He was blamed both when the agent failed through tardy or inadequate usage and when its careless or excessive application caused tissue devitalization or carbolic acid poisoning.

Although he disdained recrimination, Lister felt obliged to refute the allegation of a formidable opponent, Sir James Simpson, that he had plagiarized the work of French and German surgeons, especially of Jules Lemaire, a pharmaceutical chemist of Paris, whose book *De l'acide phénique* (1863) described the medical and surgical uses of carbolic acid. Simpson's bitter attack began with a letter signed "Chirurgicus," published in the *Edinburgh Daily Review* of 23 September 1867. This was reproduced unworthily in *The Lancet*, which a few weeks later published an article by Simpson, "Carbolic Acid and Its Compounds in Surgery," insinuating that Lister was culpably ignorant of medical literature and had merely transplanted an established Continental system of treatment. The latter had never heard of Lemaire but with some difficulty located a copy of his book. In a letter to *The Lancet*, Lister disavowed ever having claimed the first usage of carbolic acid in surgery and dismissed Lemaire's work by stating: "The principles and practice which he mentions are such as suffi-

ciently to explain the insignificance of the results."

Simpson was Syme's rival for leadership of the Edinburgh medical profession; but he resented the antiseptic doctrine chiefly because it could render superfluous his proposal to replace existing large hospitals with small disposable units—in order to combat "hospitalism" or hospital sepsis—as well as his "acupressure" method of arresting hemorrhage, which would remove a common cause of postoperative infection by dispensing with ligatures. According to Lister, efficient antisepsis permitted ligatures to be cut short and left within wounds, instead of dangling purulently outside.

Favorable reports in medical journals now began to counterbalance the opposition. Visitors, including emissaries from European professors, although sometimes shocked by Lister's surgical temerity, were impressed by the results. Students, house surgeons, and assistants, such as Hector Cameron, were his most enthusiastic disciples and increasingly promoted the doctrine. In April 1868, in a well-received review of the antiseptic system for the Medico-Chirurgical Society of Glasgow, illustrated by clinical cases, Lister advocated the transient germicidal potency of the 5 percent aqueous solution of carbolic acid for initially cleansing a wound; the bland, more retentive oily preparation was reserved for external dressing. On this occasion he presented his first modified Pasteurian demonstration of the airborne nature of putrefactive germs. Several months previously he had boiled for five minutes three bent-necked flasks containing fresh urine and a similar flask with attenuated and shortened vertical neck. In the former flasks the urine remained unaltered, but in the other decomposition had occurred and microorganisms abounded. This classic demonstration was used repeatedly to illustrate that putrefaction was not due to atmospheric gases alone but to mechanically arrestive, viable particles floating in the air. (Lister wrote subsequently to his father, describing attempts to exclude airborne germs by sheathing amputation stumps in thin rubber.) Meanwhile, his Royal Infirmary colleagues remained aloof, supported by a management that attributed the lower surgical mortality to improvements in hygiene, diet, and nursing.

In 1866 Lister unsuccessfully applied for the chair of surgery at his alma mater, University College, London. Three years later he submitted his candidacy as successor to Syme (who had suffered a severe stroke), and in August 1869 was elected professor of clinical surgery at Edinburgh. Within a month his father developed a fatal illness. Syme died the following summer, a few weeks after Simpson.

Although Lister left Glasgow amid expressions of regret, shortly after his arrival in Edinburgh a discordant note was struck by publication of his article "On the Effects of the Antiseptic System of Treatment Upon the Salubrity of a Surgical Hospital" (1869). He contended that the prevailing deplorable conditions at the Glasgow Royal Infirmary, aggravated on the ground floor by adjacent pit burials of victims of the 1849 cholera epidemic, should be contrasted with the healthy conditions brought about in his men's accident ward on that floor by antiseptic treatment. On this and other occasions when Lister's ingenuous candor and reforming zeal bruised the sensitivities of others, he was apologetic and sought to make amends without sacrifice of principle or dilution of precept.

The next eight years in Edinburgh were the happiest of his life. He was summoned and warmly welcomed by faculty and students as the exponent of a liberating new doctrine; both his wisest counselor and fiercest opponent had died; and he had assured respect and independence. Comparatively wealthy since his father's death, he bought a costly house in the finest square and eventually built up an extensive practice. Less onerous university duties allowed Lister to devote himself to perfecting and propagating his antiseptic system. This demanded unstinting personal attention to patients of every class, besides greatly expanded laboratory researches. Most of his important work on pure and applied bacteriology was done during these Edinburgh years.

In his introductory lecture Lister reviewed the researches of Pasteur and his precursors on atmospheric germs, emphasizing their role in putrefaction without mentioning antiseptic surgery. He thus challenged the claims of the professor of medicine at Edinburgh, John Hughes Bennett, a microscopist who (like Sir James Simpson) ridiculed microbes as "mythical fungi." Lister's belief in atmospheric bacteria as the principal source of wound contamination, reinforced by John Tyndall's essay "On Dust and Disease," led him in 1871 to recommend carbolic spray as a means of pervading the vicinity of surgical wounds with antiseptic. During the next decade various types of atomizers were added to the operating room paraphernalia. Hand sprays evolved into foot sprays, both types requiring relays of perspiring assistants. The "donkey engine," a long-handled model mounted on a tripod, was easier to manipulate but very cumbersome. Eventually, a portable "steam spray" was manufactured in large numbers. These devices kept the patient, surgeon, and assistants in intimate contact with droplets of 1:40 aqueous solution of carbolic acid, which were inevitably inhaled, sometimes with toxic effects, although

Lister denied that any of his patients suffered carbolic acid poisoning. His own skin was delicate, yet it tolerated the acid well. The operator's hand went white and numb, however, and the ultrasensitive found the regimen impossible. Although Lister never tested the spray's action experimentally, from the first he regarded it as a necessary evil. Eventually growing skeptical, he abandoned it in 1887.

Lister's time and ingenuity were now devoted mainly to the improvement of wound dressings and to various bacteriological researches. Because carbolic acid was evidently an irritant, liable to interfere with tissue healing, he developed an impermeable "protective" of oiled silk covered with copal varnish for direct application to the wound. This was covered by an antiseptic plaster of four parts shellac and one part carbolic acid. He summarized the underlying principle thus in 1870: "An antiseptic to exclude putrefaction, with a protective to exclude the antiseptic, will by their joint action keep the wound from abnormal stimulus." Soon afterwards he replaced the nonabsorbent lac plaster with carbolized, absorbent muslin gauze, which remained in vogue for many years. Besides the spray and dressings, in 1871 Lister introduced into British practice the rubber drainage tube, invented by P. M. E. Chaussaignac in France twelve years before. Shortly after becoming surgeon in ordinary in Scotland to Queen Victoria, he treated her at Balmoral for an axillary abscess, obtaining good results after inserting a small drainage tube into the incision.

The elaborate safeguards for wounds, devised on the supposition that "after being exposed even for a second to the influence of septic air, putrefaction would be pretty certain to occur," contrasted with Lister's simple personal precautions in the operating room. Removing his coat and rolling up his sleeves, he pinned a large towel (clean but unsterilized) over his waistcoat and trousers. He wore neither gown, nor mask, nor gloves. Two strengths of carbolic acid solution, 1:20 and 1:40, were kept in trays and basins, the stronger being used for preliminary hand washing, for cleansing the patient's skin at the operative site, and for immersing instruments. The weaker lotion, held in saturated sponges, served for frequent hand-dipping during the operation.

Many of Lister's microbiological studies, recorded on more than 400 foolscap sheets closely written by his wife or himself, were tests of his antiseptic system and methods, not intended for publication. Besides his 1868 address at Glasgow and the inaugural lecture "On the Causation of Putrefaction and Fermentation" (1869), his *Collected Papers* include six reports under the heading "Bacteriology," two dating from this

Edinburgh period. His lengthy address to the Royal Society of London in 1873, on the germ theory of putrefaction and other fermentative changes, was largely provoked by John Burdon-Sanderson's report "On the Origin and Distribution of Microzymes (Bacteria) in Water . . ." (1871), which claimed that bacteria are conveyed by water but not by air, and are killed by simple drying at 100° F. These contentions, if true, would have nullified Lister's efforts to provide an "antiseptic atmosphere" in surgical practice. In unboiled human urine taken with antiseptic precautions—a better medium than Pasteur's 10 percent sucrose and yeast ash solution employed by Burdon-Sanderson—bacteria grew when drops of tap water were added and also after this medium had been exposed for some hours to room air. The resulting aerial flora included a yeast and a filamentous fungus. Lister mistakenly concluded that the latter could develop into either the yeast or the bacteria.

He renewed this pleomorphist interpretation when subsequently reporting the behavior of two bacterial species and a filamentous fungus that developed in an exposed milk sample. One of the bacterial species soured and curdled milk. Early in 1874 Lister sent his article to Pasteur, who had noted this phenomenon in 1857. The resulting correspondence initiated a lifelong mutual admiration. Pasteur's delicately suggested explanation of these findings was duly acknowledged: "Next to the promulgation of new truth, the best thing, I conceive, that a man can do, is the recantation of a published error."

Some false starts notwithstanding, Lister made several fruitful contributions to bacteriology. He noted morphological and fermentative variations undergone by microorganisms in different nutrient media, and he observed that bacterial metabolites of a proteinaceous fluid could be odorless, or devoid of putrefactive smell. He devised novel apparatus—lidded glassware, a sterilizable syringe-pipette, and the "hot box," a pioneer autoclave providing diffuse dry heat of 300° F. By confirming, extending, and unequivocally sponsoring Pasteur's fundamental contentions, he induced many British colleagues to reappraise the germ theory or to launch fresh inquiries.

Meanwhile, antiseptic surgery gained more adherents abroad than at home. In England its chief proponents were younger surgeons at hospitals in large provincial cities, such as Liverpool, Birmingham, and Manchester. In Scotland, Listerian techniques yielded highly successful results at Glasgow Royal Infirmary in the mid-1870's, when Hector Cameron and William Macewen became surgeons there. Alexander Ogston of Aberdeen, who later discovered the pyogenic staphylococcus, was a staunch supporter. At Edinburgh the chief sympathizer among the senior staff was Thomas Keith, who with T. Spencer Wells of London had achieved a remarkably low mortality rate in ovariotomy, mainly through scrupulous attention to surgical cleanliness. After he adopted antiseptic techniques, Keith's results improved. In London, with few exceptions, apathy had given place to opposition. This trend, encouraged by the influential *The Lancet*, stemmed from various factors, including plain prejudice, misconceptions about details of the antiseptic ritual, Florence Nightingale's campaign to improve hospital hygiene, and H. Charlton Bastian's revival of the spontaneous-generation obsession.

In Germany, Karl Thiersch of Leipzig successfully adopted Lister's system as early as 1867. A simplified form of antiseptic treatment for battle wounds in the Franco-Prussian War gave disappointing results; but Richard von Volkmann became a doughty devotee after 1872, when his hospital at Halle, overcrowded with wounded soldiers and so dreadfully infected that its closure was imminent, obtained astonishing benefits from Listerian techniques. Other prominent supporters included J. von Nussbaum of Munich, A. Bardeleben and A. W. Schultze of Berlin, and Friedrich von Esmarch of Kiel. The particularly strong support for Lister's methods in Germany was attributed by some British surgeons to that country's less advanced state of sanitary science.

Among the earliest foreign visitors to become enthusiastic disciples were M. H. Saxtorph of Copenhagen and J. Lucas-Championnière of Paris (author of the first manual of antiseptic surgery). Other European adherents included Theodor Kocher in Bern and J. W. R. Tilanus in Amsterdam. Enrico Bottini's use of carbolic acid as a surgical antiseptic at Novara, Italy, reported in "Dell'acido fenico nella chirurgia pratica e nella tassidermia" (1866), was unknown to Lister and was generally ignored.

The reality of Lister's fame abroad became obvious in 1875, during a much feted European tour with his wife, his brother Arthur, and other relatives. *The Lancet* termed his progress through the university towns of Germany "a triumphal march." In America antiseptic surgery made slow progress until Lister personally expounded his doctrine, as president of the Surgical Section, to the 1876 International Medical Congress at Philadelphia. Again accompanied by his wife and brother, he paid pre-Congress visits to Montreal and Toronto, subsequently crossed the United States to San Francisco, and met enthusiastic receptions in Boston and New York.

Meanwhile, Lister campaigned against the antivivisectionists, whose allegations caused the appointment of a royal commission in 1875. To the queen's plea that he should condemn vivisection, he responded by declaring "legislation on this subject is wholly uncalled for." He deplored the inconsistency of those who approve fox-hunting but brand as cruel the animal experimenter who takes "every care to render the pain as slight as is compatible with the high object in view"; and he reaffirmed his stand in evidence before the commission. Appointed to the General Medical Council in 1876, Lister was designated chairman of its committee to report on the Cruelty to Animals Bill before Parliament. The final act contained relaxations for which Lister was largely responsible.

Between 1870 and 1876 Lister published ten papers on antiseptic surgery, including a major address to the British Medical Association at Plymouth in 1871, and presented masterful demonstrations before that organization at Edinburgh in 1875. Notwithstanding these evangelistic efforts and successful European and North American missions, the persistent hostility of many London surgeons represented a challenge to Lister (himself a Londoner) to carry his gospel to the metropolis. The opportunity came early in 1877, when he was approached as possible successor to Sir William Fergusson, titular professor of surgery at King's College, who had died. His students, hearing rumors, presented a complimentary memorial with 700 signatures, begging him to remain. An impromptu response, in which Lister incautiously called the London system of teaching clinical surgery "a mere sham" that largely neglected "magnificent opportunities of demonstrative teaching" appeared the next day in the Edinburgh and London newspapers. When castigated by The Lancet, Lister temperately explained that his words were not intended as a personal affront. Negotiations were resumed, and in June he was elected to a newly created chair of clinical surgery.

Lister's brilliant interlude in Edinburgh ended in his fiftieth year, without fuss or fanfare. In London he settled in Park Crescent, near Regent's Park and the Botanical Gardens, where he liked to roam and meditate. A nursing home for private patients was also close. Among the four-man team accompanying him were Watson Cheyne and John Stewart of Halifax, Nova Scotia, who as house surgeons disconsolately faced two dozen empty beds at King's College Hospital instead of six wards and up to seventy patients at Edinburgh. The nursing sisters of St. John were uncooperative because the Listerian regimen conflicted with their time-honored routine. Eager lecture audiences of more than 400 auditors had dwindled to fewer than twenty listless students who feared examination penalties for airing antiseptic doctrines.

Without complaining, Lister overcame student apathy, nursing obstructiveness, and much professional opposition. James Spence, his former Edinburgh rival, and Robert Lawson Tait, the Birmingham gynecologist, remained antagonistic; but the latter's truculence was largely neutralized by support from another expert ovariotomist, Spencer Wells. During a debate on antiseptic surgery at St. Thomas' Hospital in December 1879, Lister fulfilled William Savory's demands, echoed in The Lancet, for statistical data justifying his claims. Thereafter the few loyal but inarticulate followers of "Listerism" in London, backed by the British Medical Journal, were reinforced by the outspoken advocacy of such leading surgeons as William MacCormac, Jonathan Hutchinson, John Wood, and (a late convert) Sir James Paget.

Lister's complete sincerity, pertinacious but conciliatory approach, and dramatic surgical achievements—such as the successful wiring of a broken kneecap—largely account for this transformation. Advances in bacteriology also strengthened the antiseptic doctrine. His introductory address at King's College, "The Nature of Fermentation," inferentially clinched the microbic etiology of putrefaction by linking the lactic acid fermentation of milk to growth of a specific bacillus, which he termed Bacterium lactis. With small inocula of this microorganism, prepared in pure culture by a novel dilution method, he curdled boiled milk at will. An expanded lecture-demonstration on the lactic fermentation before the Pathological Society of London late in 1877 was his last major contribution to bacteriological research. For many years thereafter Lister maintained his laboratory for testing antiseptics, read the foreign literature punctiliously, and occasionally reviewed developments in microbiology; but he found restrictions on animal experiments a handicap and left the field to specialists.

His prestige at home was further enhanced by his celebrity abroad. Lister visited Paris in 1878 as president of the jury on medical matters at the Universal Exhibition, lectured (in French) at the Academy of Medicine, and met Pasteur. At the 1879 International Medical Congress in Amsterdam, he was acclaimed with unprecedented enthusiasm. He received honorary doctorates from Oxford and Cambridge in 1880. The queen appointed him surgeon-in-ordinary in 1878 and conferred a baronetcy on him in 1883. Among the earliest foreign honors awarded him were the Boudet Prize (1881), for his application of Pasteur's researches to the healing art, and the Prussian Ordre pour le Mérite (1885).

Robert Koch's discoveries on the etiology of anthrax and wound infections (1876–1878) evoked Lister's admiration. Correspondence ensued, and the *Wund-infectionskrankheiten* monograph was translated into English by Cheyne in 1880. Lister summarized this work, and Pasteur's early experiments on immunity against fowl cholera, in masterly addresses on the relation of microorganisms to disease and inflammation, given at Cambridge and at the 1881 International Medical Congress in London. The Surgical Section of the Congress sponsored a symposium on the treatment of wounds, in which Lister stressed the defensive powers of the blood and tissues and spoke diffidently about the carbolic spray, lately declared superfluous in an article by P. Bruns of Tübingen, arrestingly titled "Fort mit dem Spray!" Both Pasteur and Koch attended the congress and at Lister's instigation met at King's College, where the latter demonstrated his gelatin medium for cultivating and isolating pure cultures.

Koch's initial report on disinfection (1881) revealed that the antiseptic supremacy of carbolic acid was overestimated, at least as regards anthrax spores, on which mercuric chloride had far greater "disinfectant" (bactericidal) and "antiseptic" (bacteriostatic) actions. In 1884 Lister adopted external dressings impregnated with mercuric chloride; but these proved too irritating, and after five years of laboratory tests and manufacturing problems he recommended that the outer gauze dressing should contain the double cyanide of mercury and zinc. The frequent modifications in Listerian technique were now approved by *The Lancet*, as evidence that the paramount issue was the principle of antisepsis, rather than the peculiar virtues of any given antiseptic. Lister kept faith in his favorites, however; an address in 1893, "The Antiseptic Management of Wounds," extolled the manifold virtues of 1:20 carbolic acid.

Developments in some German hospitals and clinics took another direction. Further studies from Koch's laboratory, evaluating the bactericidal power of dry heat and the greater efficiency of steam sterilization for inert objects, coincided with increased awareness (anticipated earlier by Lister) that chemical antiseptics are liable to damage natural healing mechanisms, notably the phagocytic phenomenon first described in 1883 by Elie Metchnikoff. Berlin's leading surgeon, Ernst von Bergmann, and his assistant Curt Schimmelbusch became apostles of "aseptic" surgery. They proclaimed great respect for Lister, although the ritualistic details and expensive paraphernalia published by Schimmelbusch in a text on aseptic surgery (1892) tended to disparage Listerism as outmoded.

To satisfy himself that the full-fledged aseptic tenets were feasible, Lister removed a tumor success-fully "without contact of any antiseptic material with the wound." He deplored the pretense that aseptic surgery completely obviates antiseptics and contended that its techniques, to achieve results comparable with his own, entailed greater care and trouble, as well as compelling hospitalization. He considered the terms "antisepsis" and "asepsis" to be interchangeable and kept aloof from extremist viewpoints, but he unwaveringly upheld the basic doctrine common to both systems. On details of antiseptic technique he was more pliable. The spray was renounced when he realized that the great majority of atmospheric microbes were neither pathogenic nor eliminated by carbolic acid droplets. In his address to the 1890 International Medical Congress in Berlin, "The Present Position of Antiseptic Surgery," he commented: "As regards the spray, I feel ashamed that I should ever have recommended it. . . ." The tributes paid him at this congress nevertheless proved "almost overpowering." Next year, at the International Congress of Hygiene in London, Lister presided over the exceptionally well-attended Bacteriology Section; and a galaxy of delegates dined at Park Crescent. In 1892 he reached retirement age and relinquished the King's College chair, but agreed to retain charge of his wards for another year. That December he represented the Royal Societies of London and Edinburgh at the Sorbonne ceremonies commemorating Pasteur's jubilee. The artist J. A. Rixens captured the memorable scene as Lister stepped forward to embrace Pasteur after completing his eulogy.

Lister and his wife took frequent holidays in the British Isles and on the Continent. They enjoyed collecting flowers and studying wildlife, and kept diaries about these interludes. In the spring of 1893, at Rapallo, Lady Lister contracted pneumonia and died four days later, leaving her husband bereft of all intimate daily companionship and overwhelmed by sudden grief. He fulfilled the commitment to King's College Hospital; but his private practice almost vanished, his laboratory experiments languished, and he generally avoided social gatherings. Lucy Syme, a sister-in-law who had often stayed with them, lightened the solitude by keeping house for him. Although Lister never ceased to mourn his wife, personal sadness was not allowed to interfere with public duty. In the following decade he filled many highly responsible offices with appropriate dignity and learning.

Elected foreign secretary of the Royal Society late in 1893, Lister became president two years later. His wide reading, logical exposition, and acute grasp of public health issues were apparent in five annual presidential addresses, which dealt mainly with developments in medical and veterinary sciences, particularly in microbiology. In 1896 Lister's presidential address to the British Association, "The Interdependence of Science and the Healing Art," included his first public explanation of Pasteur's scientific influence upon his surgical practices, and also his last major allusion to antisepsis.

Lister's concern for public health found expression in his persistent efforts to secure establishment of a British Institute of Preventive Medicine. Despite irrational opposition and studied indifference, it was incorporated in 1891 with Lister as chairman; and by 1895 it was producing diphtheria antitoxin under Armand Ruffer's direction. In 1897, the centenary of the discovery of vaccination, Jenner's name was attached to the Institute. Since this caused conflict with a vaccine lymph manufacturer, in 1903 it was finally named after Lister, who was its governing board's first chairman and president for several years.

He was raised to the peerage in 1897, assuming the title Baron Lister of Lyme Regis, a small Dorsetshire town where he and his brothers had purchased a seaside house many years before. That autumn Lister attended the annual meetings of the British Association in Toronto and the British Medical Association in Montreal, afterward traveling across Canada by special railroad car with his brother and nieces. His final journey abroad was a voyage to South Africa in the winter of 1901–1902; but he continued to visit Lyme Regis, Buxton, and other health resorts in Britain, hoping to relieve his increasing rheumatic afflictions. Now a greatly venerated figure, he emerged from retirement only on such special occasions as that of his last great public address, the third Huxley lecture (1900)—a sweeping retrospect of his early physiological and pathological researches—or for his resourceful chairmanship of the session of the Second Tuberculosis Congress in London (1901), when Koch asserted that bovine tuberculosis was a negligible hazard to human health. Disappointed at Koch's premature disclosure of tuberculin ten years before, Lister unhesitatingly revealed flaws in his present argument.

In 1903, at Buxton, Lister apparently suffered a slight stroke, which hampered walking and mental effort; but he recovered sufficiently to deal with matters of personal import. For example, in 1906 he refuted the allegation that his antiseptic system was derived from the work of I. P. Semmelweis; and in 1907 he actively cooperated with friends in editing his *Collected Papers* to memorialize his eightieth birthday. This anniversary was celebrated in many countries and

Lister received innumerable congratulatory messages. His last public appearance was at the Guildhall a few weeks later, to receive the freedom of the City of London.

Lister and his sister-in-law moved in 1908 to the small town of Walmer, on the Kentish coast. The bracing air, however, failed to renew his strength; his sight and hearing became impaired; and he fell into a gradual, prolonged decline. The end came almost imperceptibly. A widespread desire that Lister should be buried in Westminster Abbey was overridden by his own wish to be interred beside his wife in West Hampstead Cemetery. An impressive funeral service was nonetheless held in the Abbey, where a medallion by Sir Thomas Brock, one of the finest of Lister's many portraits and busts, commemorates his fame.

During later years Lister's multiplying tributes included the freedom of Edinburgh, Glasgow, and London; honorary doctorates from many British and foreign universities; corresponding or honorary membership in some sixty scientific and medical societies in various countries; and the Copley and several other medals. He became sergeant-surgeon to Queen Victoria in 1900 and, at his accession, to King Edward VII, who appointed Lister to the newly instituted Order of Merit and also to the Privy Council.

In analyzing Lister's personality, his chief biographer, Sir Rickman Godlee, was restrained by his uncle's expressed desire for a simple record of his contributions to science and surgery. His faults were trivial and easily explained. He was unpunctual; he often greatly exceeded the allotted time in addresses and discussions; and he embarrassed patients and professional colleagues by refusing to specify his fees. He epitomized himself in a letter to his father soon after first arriving in Edinburgh: "I am by disposition very averse to quarrelling and contending with others," he wrote, "but at the same time I do love honesty and independence." The rare nobility of his character inspired one of his ward patients, the poet W. E. Henley, to express his admiration in the sonnet "The Chief," which compared him to Hercules, "Battling with custom, prejudice, disease...." A fellow surgeon, Sir Frederick Treves, provided a fitting epitaph for his accomplishments:

> Lister created anew the ancient art of healing; he made a reality of the hope which had for all time sustained the surgeon's endeavours; he removed the impenetrable cloud which had stood for centuries between great principles and successful practice, and he rendered possible a treatment which had hitherto been but the vision of the dreamer.

BIBLIOGRAPHY

I. ORIGINAL WORKS. The only ed. of Lister's works is *The Collected Papers of Joseph, Baron Lister*, 2 vols. (Oxford, 1909). This was prepared by a committee consisting of Hector C. Cameron, W. Watson Cheyne, R. J. Godlee, C. J. Martin, and D. Williams, in response to the widely expressed desire, on Lister's eightieth birthday, for some appropriate memorial of "a life so rich in benefits to mankind." The committee was advised by Lister on the selection of papers and addresses—about half of all his publications—which he himself thought possessed permanent interest and importance. Vol. I contains 16 contributions to physiology (pt. 1), and 9 to pathology and bacteriology (pt. 2). In vol. II are 26 publications on the antiseptic system (pt. 3), and 6 on surgery (pt. 4), while pt. 5 comprises 4 addresses and communications on miscellaneous topics, including an obituary tribute to his father.

Lister's publications were incompletely compiled by C. W. W. Judd in his prize essay on the life and work of Lister (see below); by J. Chiene in the Lister no. of the *British Medical Journal* (1902), **2**, 1853–1854; and by C. N. B. Camac in *Epoch-Making Contributions to Medicine, Surgery and the Allied Sciences* (London, 1909), appended to a repr. of "On the Antiseptic Principle in the Practice of Surgery," pp. 9–22. A more extensive bibliography, supplemented by biographical articles, precedes (pp. 9–27) the repr. of three of Lister's papers on antisepsis in *Medical Classics*, **2** (1937–1938), 28–101. The *Souvenir Handbook of the Lister Centenary Exhibition at the Wellcome Historical Medical Museum* (London, 1927), pp. 155–166, offers the most complete record of his published work, numbering more than 120 items. None of these sources is free from errors.

Reports on researches in physiology and pathology include "Observations on the Contractile Tissue of the Iris," in *Quarterly Journal of Microscopical Science*, **1** (1853), 8–17; "Observations on the Muscular Tissue of the Skin," *ibid.*, 262–268; "On the Flow of Lacteal Fluid in the Mesentery of the Mouse," in *Report of the 27th Meeting of the British Association for the Advancement of Science* (Dublin, 1857), 114; "On the Minute Structure of Involuntary Muscle Fibres," in *Transactions of the Royal Society of Edinburgh*, **21** (1857), 549–557; "On the Early Stages of Inflammation," in *Proceedings of the Royal Society*, **8** (1857), 581–587; "An Enquiry Regarding the Parts of the Nervous System Which Regulate the Contractions of the Arteries," in *Philosophical Transactions of the Royal Society*, **148** (1858), 607–625; "On the Cutaneous Pigmentary System in the Frog," *ibid.*, 627–643; "Spontaneous Gangrene From Arteritis and the Causes of Coagulation of the Blood in Diseases of the Blood-Vessels," in *Edinburgh Medical Journal*, **3** (1858), 893–907; "Preliminary Account of an Enquiry Into the Functions of the Visceral Nerves, With Special Reference to the So-Called 'Inhibitory System,'" in *Proceedings of the Royal Society*, **9** (1859), 367–380; "Some Observations on the Structure of Nerve-Fibres," in *Quarterly Journal of*

Microscopical Science, **8** (1860), 29–32, written with W. Turner but with "Supplementary Observations" by Lister, 32–34; "Notice of Further Researches on the Coagulation of the Blood," in *Edinburgh Medical Journal*, **5** (1860), 536–540; "Coagulation of the Blood," in *Proceedings of the Royal Society*, **12** (1863), 580–611, the Croonian lecture; and "Address on the Value of Pathological Research," in *British Medical Journal* (1897), **1**, 317–319.

Lister's earlier papers on the antiseptic treatment in surgery include "On a New Method of Treating Compound Fracture, Abscess, etc., With Observations on the Conditions of Suppuration," in *Lancet* (1867), **1**, 326–329, 357–359, 387–389, 507–509, and **2**, 95–96; "On the Antiseptic Principle in the Practice of Surgery," *ibid.*, 353–356; "On the Antiseptic Treatment in Surgery," in *British Medical Journal* (1868), **2**, 53–56, 101–102, 461–463, 515–517, and (1869), **1**, 301–304—these three reports are repr. in German in Karl Sudhoff's Klassiker der Medizin, no. 17 (Leipzig, 1912); "Observations on Ligature of Arteries on the Antiseptic System," in *Lancet* (1869), **1**, 451–455; "On the Effects of the Antiseptic System Upon the General Salubrity of a Surgical Hospital," *ibid.* (1870), **1**, 4–6, 40–42; "The Glasgow Infirmary and the Antiseptic Treatment," *ibid.*, 210–211, letter to the editor; "Remarks on a Case of Compound Dislocation of the Ankle, With Other Injuries, Illustrating the Antiseptic System of Treatment," *ibid.*, 404–406, 440–443, 512–513; "Further Evidence Regarding the Effects of the Antiseptic Treatment Upon the Salubrity of a Surgical Hospital," *ibid.*, **2**, 287–289; "A Method of Antiseptic Treatment Applicable to Wounded Soldiers in the Present War," in *British Medical Journal* (1870), **2**, 243–244; "On Recent Improvements in the Details of Antiseptic Surgery," in *Lancet* (1875), **1**, 365–367, 401–402, 434–436, 468–470, 603–605, 717–719, 787–789; and "Clinical Lecture Illustrating Antiseptic Surgery," *ibid.* (1879), **2**, 901–905.

Lister's chief publications on pure and applied bacteriology are "Introductory Lecture" (delivered at the University of Edinburgh, 8 Nov. 1869), in *British Medical Journal* (1869), **2**, 601–604; "The Address in Surgery" (at the 39th annual meeting of the British Medical Association, Plymouth), *ibid.* (1871), **2**, 225–233; "A Further Contribution to the Natural History of Bacteria and the Germ Theory of Fermentative Changes," in *Quarterly Journal of Microscopical Science*, n.s. **13** (1873), 380–408; "A Contribution to the Germ Theory of Putrefaction and Other Fermentative Changes, and to the Natural History of Torulae and Bacteria," in *Transactions of the Royal Society of Edinburgh*, **27** (1875), 313–344; "On the Nature of Fermentation," in *Quarterly Journal of Microscopical Science*, n.s. **18** (1878), 177–194; "On the Lactic Fermentation, and Its Bearings on Pathology," in *Transactions of the Pathological Society of London*, **29** (1878), 425–467; "On the Relation of Microorganisms to Disease," in *Quarterly Journal of Microscopical Science*, n.s. **21** (1881), 330–342; "On the Relations of Minute Organisms to Unhealthy Processes Arising in Wounds, and to Inflammation in General," in *Transactions of the 7th International*

Medical Congress, I (London, 1881), 1311–1319; and "The Causes of Failure in Obtaining Primary Union in Operation Wounds, and on the Methods of Treatment Best Calculated to Secure It" (discussion), *ibid.*, II, 369–383. (Many of the reports in this and the preceding paragraph appeared in French in G. Borginon, trans., *Oeuvres réunies de chirurgie antiseptique et théorie des germes* [Paris, 1882].

Reports of progress in antiseptic techniques include "Corrosive Sublimate as a Surgical Dressing," in *Lancet* (1884), **2**, 723–728; "A New Antiseptic Dressing," *ibid.* (1889), **2**, 943–947; "On Two Cases of Long-Standing Dislocation of Both Shoulders Treated by Operation; With Further Observations on the Cyanide of Zinc and Mercury," *ibid.* (1890), **1**, 1–4; "An Address on the Present Position of Antiseptic Surgery," in *British Medical Journal* (1890), **2**, 377–379; "An Address on the Antiseptic Management of Wounds," *ibid.* (1893), **1**, 161–162, 277–278, 337–339; "On Early Researches Leading up to the Antiseptic System of Surgery," in *Lancet* (1900), **2**, 985–993, the Huxley lecture; "Note on the Preparation of Catgut for Surgical Purposes," *ibid.* (1908), **1**, 148–149; and "Remarks on Some Points in the History of Antiseptic Surgery," *ibid.*, 1815–1816.

Important and characteristic writings on surgery are "Report of Some Cases of Articular Disease Occurring in Mr. Syme's Practice, Illustrating the Advantages of the Actual Cautery," in *Monthly Journal of Medical Science*, **19** (1854), 134–137; "On Excision of the Wrist for Caries," in *Lancet* (1865), **1**, 308–312, 335–338, 362–364; "Clinical Lecture on a Case of Excision of the Knee-Joint, and on Horsehair as a Drain for Wounds; With Remarks on the Teaching of Clinical Surgery" (delivered at King's College Hospital, 10 Dec. 1877), in *Lancet* (1878), **1**, 5–9; "A Case of Multiple Papillomatous Growths in the Larynx, Extirpated by Complete Laryngotomy; Removal of the Whole Length of Both True and False Vocal Cords; Preservation of the Voice; Co-existence of Thoracic Aneurism," in *Transactions of the Clinical Society of London*, **11** (1878), 104–113, written with J. B. Yeo; "An Address on the Treatment of Fracture of the Patella," in *British Medical Journal* (1883), **2**, 855–860; "Amputation," in Holmes's *System of Surgery*, 3rd ed., III (London, 1883); "Anaesthetics" (pt. 1 written in 1861, pt. 2 in 1870, pt. 3 in 1882), *ibid.*; "Remarks on the Treatment of Fractures of the Patella of Long Standing," in *British Medical Journal* (1908), **1**, 849–850.

Miscellaneous writings of lasting interest include "Obituary Notice of the Late Joseph Jackson Lister, F.R.S., With Special Reference to His Labours in the Improvement of the Achromatic Microscope," in *Monthly Microscopical Journal*, **3** (1870), 134–143; "On the Coagulation of the Blood in Its Practical Aspects," in *British Medical Journal* (1891), **1**, 1057–1060; "On the Relations of Clinical Medicine to Modern Scientific Development," *ibid.* (1896), **2**, 733–741; "Presidential Address Before the British Association for Advancement of Science," in *Science*, n.s. **4** (1896), 409–429; "Presidential Address at the Anniversary Meeting of the Royal Society," in *Year-Book of the Royal Society* (London, 1900), 144–156; "On Recent

Researches With Regard to the Parasitology of Malaria," in *British Medical Journal* (1900), **2**, 1625–1627; and the intro. to Stephen Paget's *Experiments on Animals* (London, 1900), pp. xi–xii.

Many of Lister's papers were published also in pamphlet form, or in more than one journal. Some appeared in foreign medical periodicals, trans. into German, French, or Italian. Handwritten letters from him are heirlooms in many families and are treasured by numerous institutions. Interesting small collections of his letters are in the Royal Faculty of Physicians and Surgeons, Glasgow, and the Osler Library, McGill University, Montreal. The former includes 14 unpub. letters (1897–1906) to Peter Paterson (later professor of surgery, Glasgow Royal Infirmary) about induced immunity to tuberculosis in experimental animals. Of the Osler Library letters, written to A. E. Malloch of Hamilton, Ontario, a former house surgeon at Glasgow Royal Infirmary, the earliest, dated 10 Sept. 1868, gives detailed instructions on treatment of a ward case and is reproduced in Godlee's biography of Lister. The others, written during his last decade of life, thank Malloch for Canadian apples sent each Christmas to his former chief. Lister's letters (1857–1864) to W. Sharpey, professor of physiology at University College, mostly concerning researches on inflammation, were published by C. R. Rudolf, "Eight Letters of Joseph (Lord) Lister to William Sharpey," in *British Journal of Surgery*, **20** (1932), 145–164, 459–466.

Memorabilia of Lister are in many institutions, especially Edinburgh and Glasgow universities, and King's College Hospital, London. The richest collections are at the Wellcome Institute of the History of Medicine, comprising some of his holiday diaries, manuscript notes on clinical surgery, and a volume of about 100 autograph letters; and at the Royal College of Surgeons of England, where the Lister Cabinet contains his "Common Place Book" (3 vols.), case notes, and other MSS, along with surgical instruments.

II. SECONDARY LITERATURE. Tributes to Lister's work during his lifetime include the editorials "Professor Lister in Germany," in *Lancet* (1875), **1**, 868; "The Surgical Use of Carbolic Acid," *ibid.*, **2**, 234–235; and "Lord Lister and the Antiseptic Method," *ibid.* (1909), **1**, 1617–1620; J. Finlayson, "Lord Lister and the Development of Antiseptic Surgery," in *Janus*, **5** (1900), 1–5, 57–63; L. L. Hill, "Some Personal Reminiscences of Lord Lister," in *Medical Record*, **80** (1911), 327–329; C. C. W. Judd, "The Life and Work of Lister," in *Bulletin of the Johns Hopkins Hospital*, **21** (1910), 293–304, the Lister Prize essay; W. W. Keen, "Lister on the Use of Animals in Research," in *Journal of the American Medical Association*, **68** (1917), 53; H. Tillmanns, "Sir Joseph Lister," in *Nature*, **54** (1896), 1–3, followed by an editorial on Lister, pp. 3–5; and Frederick Treves, "The Progress of Surgery," in *Practitioner*, **58** (1897), 619–630.

The Lister jubilee no. of the *British Medical Journal* (1902), **2**, 1817–1861, commemorates the fiftieth anniversary of his entering the medical profession. Among the more noteworthy contributions are T. Annandale, "Early

Days in Edinburgh," pp. 1842–1843; O. Bloch, "On the Antiseptic Treatment of Wounds," pp. 1825–1828; Hector C. Cameron, "Lord Lister and the Evolution of Modern Surgery. Glasgow, 1861–1869," pp. 1844–1848; W. W. Cheyne, "Listerism and the Development of Operative Surgery," pp. 1851–1852; J. Chiene, "Edinburgh Royal Infirmary, 1869–1877," pp. 1848–1851; the editorial "The Listerian System," pp. 1854–1861; J. Lucas-Championnière, "An Essay on Scientific Surgery. The Antiseptic Method of Lister in the Present and in the Future," pp. 1819–1821; and A. Ogston, "The Influence of Lister Upon Military Surgery," pp. 1837–1838.

Obituaries include W. Watson Cheyne, "Lord Lister, 1827–1912," in *Proceedings of the Royal Society*, **86B** (1912–1913), i–xxi; J. Stewart, "Lord Lister," in *Canadian Journal of Medicine and Surgery*, **31** (1912), 323–330; Frederick Treves, "Lister," in *London Hospital Gazette*, **15** (1911–1912), 171–172; and also (unsigned) "Death of Lord Lister," in *Boston Medical and Surgical Journal*, **166** (1912), 301–302; "Lord Lister," in *British Medical Journal* (1912), **1**, 397–402; "Lister," in *Glasgow Medical Journal*, **77** (1912), 190–196; and "Lord Lister, O.M.," in *Lancet* (1912), **1**, 465–472. Accounts of the obsequies are "Funeral of Lord Lister," in *British Medical Journal* (1912), **1**, 440–446, followed by the editorial "The Maker of Modern Surgery," pp. 447–448; and William Osler, "The Funeral of Lord Lister," in *Canadian Medical Association Journal*, **2** (1912), 343–344.

Among foreign-language obituaries are H. Coenen, "Joseph Lister † 1827–1912," in *Zeitschrift für Ärtzliche Fortbildung*, **9** (1912), 161–164; P. Daser, "Lord Lister," in *Münchener medizinische Wochenschrift*, **59** (1912), 480–481; A. Fraenkel, "Gedenkrede auf Lord Josef Lister," in *Wiener klinische Wochenschrift*, **25** (1912), 381–386; O. Lanz, "Joseph Lister †," in *Nederlandsch Tijdschrift voor Geneeskunde* (1912), **1**, 425–428; J. Lucas-Championnière, "Mort de Lord Lister," in *Journal de médecine et chirurgie pratique*, **83** (1912), 129–135; and F. Trendelenburg, "Zur Erinnerung an Joseph Lister," in *Deutsche medizinische Wochenschrift*, **38** (1912), 713–716.

Reminiscences and posthumous tributes include those of Hector C. Cameron, *Lord Lister, 1827–1912. An Oration Delivered in the University of Chicago on Commemoration Day, 23rd June, 1914* (Glasgow, 1914); W. Watson Cheyne, "Lister, the Investigator and Surgeon," in *British Medical Journal* (1925), **1**, 923–926; A. E. Malloch, "Personal Reminiscences of Lister," in *Canadian Medical Association Journal*, **2** (1912), 502–506; J. Stewart, "First Listerian Oration," *ibid.*, **14** (1924), 1011–1040; and St. Clair Thomson, "A House-Surgeon's Memories of Joseph Lister (Born April 5, 1827. Died February 10, 1912)," in *Annals of Medical History*, **2** (1919), 93–108.

The centenary of Lister's birth occasioned many biographical articles in medical and scientific journals, including A. P. C. Ashhurst, "Centenary of Lister: Tale of Sepsis and Antisepsis," in *Annals of Medical History*, **9** (1927), 205–221; John Bland-Sutton, "The Conquest of Sepsis," in *Lancet* (1927), **1**, 781; W. Bulloch, "Lord Lister as a Pathologist and Bacteriologist," *ibid.*, 744–746;

D. Cheever, "Lister: 1827–1927," in *Boston Medical and Surgical Journal*, **196** (1927), 984–993; E. L. Gilcreest, "Lord Lister and the Renaissance of Surgery," in *Surgical Clinics of North America*, **7** (1927), 1117–1123; W. W. Keen, "Some Personal Recollections of Lord Lister," in *Surgery, Gynecology and Obstetrics*, **45** (1927), 861–864; C. J. Martin, "Lister's Contribution to Preventive Medicine," in *Nature*, **119** (1927), 529–531; C. F. Painter, "Sir Joseph Lister. An Historical Sketch," in *Boston Medical and Surgical Journal*, **196** (1927), 1093–1096; Charles S. Sherrington, "Lister's Contributions to Physiology," in *Lancet* (1927), **1**, 743–744; and "Listerian Oration, 1927," in *Canadian Medical Association Journal*, **17** (1927), 1255–1263; J. Tait, "Lister as Physiologist," in *Science*, **66** (1927), 267–272; C. J. S. Thompson, "Surgical Instruments Designed by Lord Lister," in *Boston Medical and Surgical Journal*, **196** (1927), 946–951; and A. Young, "Lord Lister's Life and Work," in *Janus*, **31** (1927), 318–335. Among articles in foreign journals commemorating Lister's centenary are J. P. zum Busch, "Zur Erinnerung an Joseph Lister," in *Deutsche medizinische Wochenschrift*, **53** (1927), 583–585; A. Eiselberg, "Zu Josef Lister's 100. Geburtstage," in *Wiener klinische Wochenschrift*, **40** (1927), 461–465; B. F., "Le centenaire de Lister," in *Presse médicale*, **35** (1927), 523–524; and M. von Gruber, "Lord Lister und Deutschland," in *Münchener medizinische Wochenschrift*, **74** (1927), 592–593.

Other biographical accounts and articles on miscellaneous aspects of Lister's life and work, mostly published after 1927, include: E. Archibald, "The Mind and Character of Lister," in *Canadian Medical Association Journal*, **35** (1936), 475–490, fifth Listerian oration; C. Ballance, "Lister and His Time," in *Lancet* (1933), **1**, 815–816; H. C. Cameron, "Lord Lister and the Catgut Ligature," in *British Medical Journal* (1912), **1**, 579 (correspondence); Johnson and Johnson, *Lister and the Ligature. A Landmark in the History of Modern Surgery* (New Brunswick, N. J., 1925); C. Martin, "Lister's Early Bacteriological Researches and Origin of His Antiseptic System," in *Medical Journal of Australia* (1931), **2**, 437–444, the Listerian oration; Lord Moynihan, "Lister—the Idealist," in *Canadian Medical Association Journal*, **23** (1930), 479–488, the third Listerian oration; R. Muir, "The Fourth Listerian Oration," *ibid.*, **29** (1933), 349–360; J. Riera, "The Dissemination of Lister's Teaching in Spain," in *Medical History*, **13** (1969), 123–153; I. M. Thompson, "Lister's Early Scientific Background," in *Manitoba Medical Review*, **20** (1940), 95–100; I. Veith, "Lord Lister and the Antivivisectionists," in *Modern Medicine of Canada*, **16** (1961), 43–57; and A. O. Whipple, "A Consideration of Recent Advances in Medical Science in the Light of Lord Lister's Studies," in *Canadian Medical Association Journal*, **41** (1939), 323–331, the sixth Listerian oration.

Writings that provide background and perspective to Listerian doctrines and methods are J. P. Arcieri, "Enrico Bottini and Joseph Lister in the Method of Antisepsis. Pioneers of Antiseptic Era," in *Alcmaeon*, **1** (1939), 2–13, repr. by Istituto di Storia della Medicina dell'Università di Roma (Rome, 1967); E. Bottini, "Dell'acido fenico nella chirurgia pratica e nella tassidermica," in *Annali universali di medicina*, **198** (1866), 585–636; A. K. Bowman, *The Life and Teaching of Sir William Macewen* (London, 1942); J. Burdon-Sanderson, "The Origin and Distribution of Microzymes (Bacteria) in Water, and the Circumstances Which Determine Their Existence in the Tissues and Liquids of the Living Body," in *Quarterly Journal of Microscopical Science*, n.s. **11** (1871), 323–352; W. W. Cheyne, *Antiseptic Surgery* (London, 1882); D. J. Ferguson, "Paréian and Listerian Slants on Infections in Wounds," in *Perspectives in Biology and Medicine*, **14** (1970), 63–68; S. Gamgee, "The Present State of Surgery in Paris," in *Lancet* (1867), **2**, 392–393, 483–484; T. W. Jones, *Report on the State of the Blood and the Blood Vessels in Inflammation* (London, 1891); T. Keith, "Fifty-one Cases of Ovariotomy," in *Lancet* (1867), **2**, 290–291; and "Second Series of Fifty Cases of Ovariotomy . . .," *ibid.* (1870), **2**, 249–251; J. Lemaire, *De l'acide phénique* (Paris, 1863); J. Lucas-Championnière, *Chirurgie antiseptique* (Paris, 1876), of which the 2nd ed., trans. by F. H. Gerrish, appeared as *Antiseptic Surgery. The Principles, Modes of Application and Results of the Lister Dressing* (Portland, Me., 1881); W. MacCormac, *Antiseptic Surgery* (London, 1880); V. Manninger, *Der Entwicklungsgang der Antiseptik und Aseptik* (Breslau, 1904); L. Munster, "Ein vergessener Vorkämpfer der Parasitenlehre: Agostino Bassi aus Lodi . . .," in *Janus*, **37** (1933), 221–246; J. N. Ritter von Nussbaum, *Leitfaden zur antiseptischen Wundbehandlung insbesondere zur Lister'schen Methode* (Stuttgart, 1881); L. Pasteur, "Recherches sur la putréfaction," in *Comptes rendus hebdomadaires des séances de l'Académie des sciences*, **56** (1863), 1189–1194; and related papers in *Oeuvres de Pasteur*, II (Paris, 1922); A. Sabatier, *Des méthodes antiseptiques chez les anciens et chez les modernes* (Paris, 1883); C. Schimmelbusch, *Anleitung zur aseptischen Wundbehandlung* (Berlin, 1892), trans. by F. J. Thornbury as *A Guide to the Aseptic Treatment of Wounds* (New York, 1895); T. Spencer Wells, "Some Causes of Excessive Mortality After Surgical Operations," in *British Medical Journal* (1864), **2**, 384–388; J. Tyndall, "On Dust and Disease," in *Fragments of Science* (London, 1871); and *Essays on the Floating-Matter of the Air, in Relation to Putrefaction and Infection* (London, 1881); and B. A. G. Veraart, "Semmelweis and Lister," in *Nederlandsch Tijdschrift voor Geneeskunde*, **74** (1930), 1762–1775.

Skeptical or critical articles include those of P. Bruns, "Fort mit dem Spray!," in *Berliner klinische Wochenschrift*, **17** (1180), 609–611; the editorials "Antiseptic Surgery," in *Lancet* (1875), **2**, 565–566, 597–598; and "The Debate on Antiseptic Surgery," *ibid.*, 744–747; J. Y. Simpson, "Carbolic Acid and Its Compounds in Surgery," *ibid.*, 546–549; the editorial "Professor Lister," *ibid.* (1877), **1**, 361; and letters to the editor by T. Bryant, "Professor Lister and Clinical Surgery in the London Hospitals," *ibid.* (1877), **1**, 367–368; W. A. Leslie, *ibid.*, 368; and T. Smith, *ibid.*, with Lister's reply appearing as "Clinical Surgery in London and Edinburgh," *ibid.*, 475–477.

Biographies of Lister are J. R. Bradford, in *Dictionary of National Biography* (1912–1921 supp.), pp. 339–343;

Hector C. Cameron, *Joseph Lister the Friend of Man* (London, 1949); W. Watson Cheyne, *Lister and His Achievement* (London, 1925); J. D. Cromie, *History of Scottish Medicine* (London, 1932), II, 597–600, 635–639, 669–671; Cuthbert Dukes, *Lord Lister* (London, 1924); Rickman J. Godlee, *Lord Lister* (London, 1917); D. Guthrie, *Lord Lister, His Life and Doctrine* (Edinburgh, 1949); J. R. Leeson, *Lister as I Knew Him* (New York, 1927); A. E. Maylard, J. A. Morris, and L. W. G. Malcolm, *Lister and the Lister Ward* (Glasgow, 1927); J. G. Mumford, *Surgical Memoirs* (New York, 1908), pp. 100–113; J. Pagel and W. Haberling, "Lister, Lord Joseph," in *Biographisches Lexikon der hervorragender Aerzte*, III (Berlin–Vienna, 1929–1935), 803–805; H. Sigerist, "Joseph Lister (1827–1912)," in *Grosse Ärzte* (Munich, 1932), pp. 277–280; St. Clair Thomson, "Joseph Lister (1827–1912), the Founder of Modern Surgery," in D'Arcy Power, ed., *British Masters of Medicine* (London, 1936), ch. XVII, pp. 137–147; R. Truax, *Joseph Lister, Father of Modern Surgery* (London, 1947); A. L. Turner, ed., *Joseph, Baron Lister, Centenary Volume 1827–1927* (Edinburgh–London, 1927); Kenneth Walker, *Joseph Lister* (London, 1956); M. E. M. Walker, "Lord Lister, O.M., F.R.S., 1st Baron of Lyme Regis, 1827–1912," in *Pioneers of Public Health* (Edinburgh, 1930), pp. 154–165; and G. T. Wrench, *Lord Lister, His Life and Work* (London, 1913).

Claude E. Dolman

LISTER, JOSEPH JACKSON (*b.* London, England, 11 January 1786; *d.* West Ham, Essex, England, 24 October 1869), *optics.*

Lord Lister (1827–1912) has taken most of the glory of the family name, but the contribution to the perfection of the objective lens systems of the microscope by his father, Joseph Jackson Lister, marks a spectacular turning point in the development of that important and ubiquitous instrument. At the time of the elder Lister's death, at the age of eighty-three, he was described as "the pillar and source of all the microscopy of the age."

Lister was the third child and only son of John Lister and the former Mary Jackson, Quakers who were wine merchants in the City of London. At the age of fourteen he joined his father in the firm, later becoming a partner. In the summer of 1818 he married Isabella Harris; they lived above the business at 5 Tokenhouse Yard until 1822, moving then to Stoke Newington and shortly after to Upton House, West Ham. It was here that Lister occupied himself with his microscopy and optical experiments. When the Listers vacated Tokenhouse Yard, their place as resident partner was taken by Richard Low Beck, the son of Lister's sister Elizabeth. Beck had just married

Rachel Lucas; and two of their many children, Richard and Joseph, formed the optical instrument-making firm still known as R. & J. Beck Ltd.

Although Lister's approach to his investigations was that of an amateur, the standard of his work was to the highest degree professional. His interest in optics originated in his boyhood; of his schoolmates only he owned a telescope. Nevertheless, he did not become an innovator until his thirty-eighth year. Among the papers he left to his son is one that gives a brief survey of his involvement with the microscope from 1824 to 1843:

> I had been from early life fond of the compound microscope, but had not thought of improving its object-glass till about the year 1824, when I saw at W. Tulley's an achromatic combination made by him at Dr. Goring's suggestion, of two convex lenses of plate glass, with a concave of flint glass between them, on the plan of the telescopic objective. They were thick and clumsy. I showed him this by a tracing with a camera lucida, which I had attached to my microscope, and the suggestions resulted in "Tulley's 9/10", which became *the* microscopic object-glass of the time. But the subject continued to engage my thoughts, and resulted in the paper "On the Improvement of Compound Microscopes" read before the Royal Society, Jan. 21st, 1830, announcing the discovery of the existence of two aplanatic foci in a double achromatic object-glass [Joseph Lister, "Obituary...," p. 141].

In this paper Lister reported that an achromatic combination of a negative flint-glass lens with a positive crown-glass lens has two aplanatic focal points. For all points between these foci the spherical aberration is overcorrected; for points outside, it is undercorrected. If, then, a doublet objective is formed that is composed of two sets of achromatic lens combinations, spherical aberration is avoided if the object is at the shorter aplanatic focus of the first lens pair, which then passes the rays on to the longer aplanatic focus of the second element. This design removed, for the first time, the fuzziness of the image caused by both chromatic and spherical aberrations and, in addition, nullified coma. The new principle elevated the making of microscope objectives from the traditional trial-and-error procedure of Tulley, Chevalier, and Amici to a scientific one, and it continues as the basis for the design of low-power objectives. As a result of this paper Lister was elected a fellow of the Royal Society on 2 February 1832.

Having established a principle, Lister naturally wished to continue experimenting; but he found that Tulley was too busy to make lenses for him. In November 1830, therefore, Lister began the grinding and polishing of lenses in his own home. The result was, he said in a letter to Sir John Herschel, beyond his expectations: "... without having ever before cut brass or ground more than a single surface of a piece of glass, I managed to make the tools and to manufacture a combination of three double object-glasses, without spoiling a lens or altering a curve, which fulfilled all the conditions I proposed for a pencil of 36 degrees" (*ibid.*, p. 140). Some of Lister's optical lathe chucks, polishing sticks, and experimental lenses are extant.

The optical instrument-makers in London did not immediately adopt Lister's ideas in designing their objectives; but in 1837 he gave details for the construction of an objective of 1/8-inch focal length to Andrew Ross, one of the foremost optical instrument-makers of the time. In 1840 Lister instructed James Smith in the techniques for constructing 1/4-inch objectives, which were for a long time known as "Smith's quarters" among microscopists. Such new objectives, commercially available in quantity for the first time, turned the microscope into a serious scientific instrument; and it continued to develop very rapidly until the 1880's, when the limit of resolution of the light microscope was reached. Richard Beck, the grandnephew of Lister, was apprenticed to James Smith and joined him in partnership in 1847. When Smith retired, Joseph Beck joined his brother; and the firm traded as R. & J. Beck, with their factory in Holloway appropriately known as the Lister Works.

When first working with Tulley's improved objective, Lister realized that the mounting of the compound body tube of his microscope was not sufficiently stable for the increased magnification that could now be used. He therefore designed a completely new form of stand, which was fabricated by James Smith in 1826. Throughout his life Lister maintained his interest in microscopical observations. He published a paper in 1827 with Thomas Hodgkin on red blood cells, giving their true form and the most accurate measurement of their diameter that had yet been achieved. His patient work on zoophytes and ascidians was read to the Royal Society in 1834. His research into the resolving power of the human eye and of the microscope, which anticipated some of the findings of Abbe and Helmholtz, was not published during his life, even though it was prepared for press. The manuscript was found among his son's papers and was published by the Royal Microscopical Society in 1913.

Lister died at Upton House in 1869, having received few honors. That he was responsible for changing the microscope from a toy to a vital scientific instrument can be fully appreciated only in historical perspective.

BIBLIOGRAPHY

I. ORIGINAL WORKS. Lister's writings include "Notice of Some Microscopic Observations of the Blood and Animal Tissues," in *Philosophical Magazine*, n.s. **2** (1827), 130–138, written with T. Hodgkin; "On the Improvement of Achromatic Compound Microscopes," in *Philosophical Transactions of the Royal Society*, **120** (1830), 187–200; "Some Observations on the Structure and Functions of Tubular and Cellular Polypi, and of Ascidiae," *ibid.*, **124** (1834), 365–388; and "On the Limit to Defining-power, in Vision With the Unassisted Eye, the Telescope, and the Microscope" (dated 1842–1843), in *Journal of the Royal Microscopical Society*, **33** (1913), 34–35. Uncataloged MS material is in the possession of the Royal Microscopical Society, as are some tools and experimental lenses. Four of Lister's microscopes, including the first made to his design by James Smith, are in the possession of the Well-come Institute of the History of Medicine, London.

II. SECONDARY LITERATURE. See William Beck, *Family Fragments Respecting the Ancestry, Acquaintance and Marriage of Richard Low Beck and Rachel Lucas* (Gloucester, 1897); A. E. Conrady, "The Unpublished Papers of J. J. Lister," in *Journal of the Royal Microscopical Society*, **33** (1913), 27–33; "Obituary Notice of the Late Joseph Jackson Lister, F.R.S., Z.S., With Special Reference to His Labours in the Improvement of the Achromatic Microscope . . .," in *Monthly Microscopical Journal*, **3** (1870), 134–143; *Lister Centenary Exhibition at the Wellcome Historical Medical Museum. Handbook. 1927*, 133 f., 138; G. L'E. Turner, "The Microscope as a Technical Frontier in Science," in *Historical Aspects of Microscopy*, S. Bradbury and G. L'E. Turner, eds. (Cambridge, 1967), pp. 175–199; and "The Rise and Fall of the Jewel Microscope 1824–1837," in *Microscopy*, **31** (1968), 85–94.

G. L'E. TURNER

LISTER, MARTIN (christened Radclive, Buckinghamshire, England, 11 April 1639; *d.* Epsom, England, 2 February 1712), *zoology, geology.*

Born into a landed family with estates in the North and Midlands, Lister was educated at St. John's College, Cambridge (B.A. 1658, M.A. 1662), becoming a fellow, at the Restoration, by royal mandate; his uncle, Sir Matthew Lister, had been physician to the new king's mother. He studied medicine at Montpellier from 1663 to 1666 but did not graduate. He resigned his fellowship in 1669 and began to practice medicine in York, where, in comparative isolation, he carried out and published pioneer studies in several fields of invertebrate zoology.

Lister's work on mollusks was at first confined to natural history and taxonomy. The latter, although conventionally artificial, attempted to be comprehensive; his spider classification was, for its date,

masterly, and agrees remarkably well with a modern system. Based *ex moribus et vita* and on a wide range of characteristics, it includes, for example, exemplary descriptions of the eye arrangement in each group. He was aware of intraspecific variation and came close to a biological definition of the species. Lister's systematic attention to field observation is noteworthy; some of his notes on courtship behavior and on the early stages of some species have never been repeated. This work was not appreciated fully at the time, even by other zoologists; and Thomas Shadwell clearly had Lister in mind when he created Sir Nicholas Gimcrack.

This early enthusiasm is also seen in Lister's work on the life histories of several parasites—gall wasps, ichneumons, gut worms, and horsehair worms—which had been used by others as evidence of spontaneous generation. Lister was very close to giving a complete account of the life histories of these animals, but his enthusiasm declined about 1676. It revived in the early 1680's, but in a different direction. In 1684, after receiving an Oxford M.D.—largely because of his donations to the Ashmolean Museum—he moved to London. A fellow of the Royal Society since 1671, he now regularly attended its meetings and was vice-president from January 1685. Two years later, however, he was involved in some personal controversy at the Society and ceased attending. He became a fellow of the College of Physicians in 1687.

Lister's work was now concentrated on mollusk anatomy and taxonomy. His best-known work, the *Historia . . . conchyliorum* of 1685–1692, consists entirely of engravings by his wife and daughter, with no real text or even titles. Because of the popularity of conchology, the work became well-known; but the three illustrated anatomical supplements were of greater scientific value. These were the first attempt to cover the morphology of a whole invertebrate group in detail. Each contained detailed descriptions of a small number of types, with briefer notes on the structure of a number of other species. Although not of Swammerdam's standard, Lister's dissections were reasonably competent. Not surprisingly, he had difficulty with the complex mollusk reproductive system, and he suffered from the contemporary tendency to overanalogize; thus, he assumed that the "gill" of a snail must receive blood directly from the heart, as in the fish, and thus believed the blood to circulate in what is in fact the wrong direction. On the other hand, he used sound comparative methods to show the true nature of the mollusk "liver."

His concern with mollusk classification brought Lister into the controversy on the nature of fossils. Many ideas on the origin of these "shell stones" had been suggested, ranging from the supernatural theories of Paracelsus to those of writers such as Palissy and Leonardo da Vinci, who accepted their animal origin. The problem could not become of fundamental importance, however, until the second half of the seventeenth century, when the rejection of the idea of spontaneous generation caused a clear distinction to be made between the living and the nonliving. The controversy was centered in England, where the interest in natural theology made important any evidence for the Noachian flood and the interest in natural history encouraged the collection of fossils and the gathering of reliable information on them. In the period 1660–1690 an animal origin was generally accepted in England for formed stones; but those natural philosophers accepting this idea, such as Robert Hooke and John Ray, were not themselves collectors and systematizers of fossils. The men with greatest firsthand knowledge of the subject—Martin Lister, Edward Lhwyd, Robert Plot, John Beaumont, and William Coles—found the difficulties of explaining the distribution of fossils too great for them to accept their dispersal by a universal flood; and, having a nonevolutionary outlook, they were convinced by the differences in detail between extant and fossil shells that there could be no direct link between them. It is likely that Lister's criticism of his ideas encouraged Hooke's suggestions on the mutability of these specific characteristics. Lister was in fact the center of this group of collectors, and his arguments were worked out in most detail. He noticed that the distribution of fossil shells is correlated with the distribution of rocks, and he believed that this was an argument for their geological origin. In tracing the distribution of one particular fossil through a certain rock formation across half of England, he came close to a stratigraphical use for these formed stones (being interested in the classification and distribution of rock types, Lister in 1684 made the first suggestions for the compilation of geological maps). He explained the growth of fossils in rock as a complex crystallization from lapidifying juices found naturally in the earth. Living mollusks were also able to secrete such juices, from which, by a nonvital process, their shells crystallized; in fact he tried to grow such shells from the body juices of mollusks.

Lister's energies were, from the middle 1690's, concerned mainly with the College of Physicians, of which he was censor in 1694. In 1698 he accompanied Lord Portland as paid physician on his embassy to Paris; his account of the city, satirized at the time for its attention to detail, is now a valuable source book. In 1702 he was appointed one of Queen Anne's physicians, apparently largely through the influence of his niece, Sarah Churchill. This influence, and his philosophical activities, appear to have helped to make Lister unpopular among his fellow physicians. He was, however, a difficult man in any case; and the only close friends he ever had appear to have been John Ray in the 1670's and Edward Lhwyd in the 1690's.

After 1700 Lister almost ceased scientific activity, although he did publish some medical works. His attempt at a comprehensive physiology, *Dissertatio de humoribus* (1709), is extremely speculative, containing little observation or experiment. It was old-fashioned in its reliance on humors, and Lister was unsympathetic to the mathematical physiologists of his day—Keill, Friend, and Pitcairne. The book completes the course of Lister's work, from the diligent and original fieldworker of 1670, through the laboratory anatomist and systematist of 1690, to the armchair philosopher of 1709. The superficiality of much of Lister's thought, largely concealed by his early enthusiasm, was now obvious.

BIBLIOGRAPHY

I. ORIGINAL WORKS. *Historiae animalium Angliae tres tractatus* (London, 1678), despite the title, has four sections, covering spiders, land snails, freshwater and saltwater mollusks, and fossil shells; the latter has a separate preface and all have individual title pages. An appendix to this work was issued in 1685, bound in with the Latin ed. by Goedart. A German trans. of the spider section by J. A. E. Goeze was published as *Naturgeschichte der Spinnen* (Quendlingburg–Blankenburg, 1778).

De fontibus medicatis Angliae, exercitatio nova et prior (York, 1682) is an account of medical mineral waters and includes an outline of Lister's physiological system. Rev. and enl. eds. were published as *De thermis et fontibus medicatis Angliae* (London, 1684); and *Exercitationes et descriptiones thermarum et fontium medicatorum Angliae* (London, 1685; 1689).

Johannes Geodartius of Insects. Done Into English and Methodized. With the Addition of Notes (York, 1682) has Lister's notes as a substantial part of the whole and new plates by F. Place. A Latin version was published by the Royal Society as *J. Goedartius de insectis in methodum redactum* (London, 1685).

Letters and Divers Other Mixt Discourses in Natural Philosophy (York, 1683) is a collection of papers, almost all of which had been published in the *Philosophical Transactions of the Royal Society*.

Historia sive synopsis methodica conchyliorum (London, 1685–1692; 2nd ed., London, 1692–1697) is bibliographically extremely complex. It was published in parts, and few copies appear to be identical. A number of bound sets of samples of the earlier sheets, issued with the title *De cochleis*, about 1685, survive; it is debatable whether they should be looked upon as a separate work. See G. L. Wilkins, *Journal of the Society for the Bibliography of Natural History*, **3**, no. 4 (1957), 196–205. A 3rd ed., edited by G. Huddesford, was published at Oxford in 1770; and a 4th ed., L. W. Dillwyn, ed., at Oxford in 1823, with a correlation of Lister's arrangement with the Linnaean system. This last ed. bears the words *editio tertia.*

Exercitatio anatomica in qua de cochleis maxime terrestribus et limacibus agitur (London, 1694).

Exercitatio anatomica altera de buccinis fluviatilibus et marinis (London, 1695) was issued bound with *Exercitatio medicinalis de variolis.* Some copies of pt. I were issued separately as *Dissertatio anatomica altera . . .* (London, 1695), and pt. II was issued as *Disquisitio medicinalis de variolis* (London, 1696).

Conchyliorum bivalvium utriusque aquae exercitatio anatomica tertia huic accedit dissertatio medicinalis de calculo humano (London, 1696), with the two *Exercitatio anatomica,* was intended as an anatomical supplement to the *Historia conchyliorum.*

Sex exercitationes medicinales de quibusdam morbis chronicis . . . (London, 1694; a rev. and enl. ed. published as *Octo exercitationes medicinales,* 1697).

A Journey to Paris in the Year 1698 (London, 1699) had 2 further eds. in the same year. Repr. in Pinkerton's *General Collection of the Best and Most Interesting Voyages and Travels . . .* (London, 1809); and there is a rev. ed. by George Henning, *An Account of Paris at the Close of the Seventeenth Century . . .* (London, 1823). Henning's ed. was trans. into French as *Voyage de Lister à Paris . . .* (Paris, 1873), and there is a facs. repr. of the 3rd ed. with notes by R. P. Stearns (Urbana, Ill., 1967).

Other works are *S. sanctorii de statica medicina . . . cum commentario* (London, 1701; new ed., 1728); *Commentariolus in Hippocratem* (London, 1702), repub. as part of *Hippocratis aphorismi cum commentariolo* (London, 1703); *De opsoniis et condimentis sive arte coquininaria* (London, 1705; 2nd ed., 1709), Lister's ed. of Apicius Caelius' work; and *Dissertatio de humoribus in qua veterum ac recentiorum medicorum ac philosophorum opiniones et sententiae examinantur* (London, 1709; new ed., Amsterdam, 1711)—"As full and compleat a system of the animal oeconomie . . . as I could contrive."

Lister's *De scarabaeis Britannicus* was printed as part of John Ray's publication of Francis Willughby's *Historia insectorum* (London, 1710).

Lister was a frequent contributor to the *Philosophical Transactions of the Royal Society,* submitting papers on insects, spiders, parasites, mollusks, birds, plants, physiology (particularly on the lymphatics), medicine, geology, meteorology and archaeology. There are in all 51 papers by Lister, from vol. **4** (1669) to vol. **22** (1701). In addition, 31 letters sent to Lister were passed on by him for publication in the *Transactions* in the same period.

The Lister MSS at the Bodleian Library, Oxford, form a set of 40 vols. of mixed letters and papers. The letters, although from a large number of correspondents, are incomplete—containing, for example, not a single letter from John Ray. In general, they are of slight scientific interest. The other papers include drafts of parts of his published works; sketches for unfinished geological works; papers on fossils, geology, and barnacles; diaries and account books; and so on. Letters to or from Lister can be found in MSS Ashmole 1816, 1829, and 1830 (particularly concerning Lhwyd) and in MSS Smith 51 and 52 (Thomas Smith, the Cotton librarian, was arranging Lister's papers but died with the work incomplete). There are a few letters in the British Museum, MSS Sloane and Stowe. The correspondence between Lister and Ray has been published in E. R. Lankester, ed., *The Correspondence of John Ray* (London, 1848); and R. T. Gunther, ed., *The Further Correspondence of John Ray* (London, 1928). Letters to and from Robert Plot and Edward Lhwyd have been published by Gunther in *Early Science in Oxford,* vols. XII and XIV (Oxford, 1939 and 1945).

II. SECONDARY LITERATURE. There is no full-length study of Lister's life or works. Of several articles in English local journals, the only one which can be recommended is Davies, in *Yorkshire Archaeological Journal,* **2** (1873), 297–320. The eds. of *A Journey to Paris* by Henning and Stearns (see above) both contain a biographical introduction. The author of this article has a thesis on Lister in progress at the University of Leeds.

JEFFREY CARR

LITKE, FYODOR PETROVICH (*b.* St. Petersburg, Russia, 17 September 1797; *d.* St. Petersburg, 8 October 1882), *earth sciences, geography.*

Litke's parents died when he was young. He was poor during his childhood and thus could not obtain advanced education. In 1812, however, he was accepted as a sailor in the Baltic fleet; and his resourcefulness and boldness led to his rapid promotion. Litke's participation in the round-the-world voyage (1817–1819) of the sloop *Kamchatka,* commanded by the well-known geographer and traveler V. M. Golovnin, decisively determined his future. Soon after his return from this voyage Litke, on the recommendation of Golovnin, was appointed commander of an expedition to survey the shores of Novaya Zemlya. In 1821–1824 the expedition made four attempts to circumnavigate Novaya Zemlya from the north. Although exceptionally heavy ice prevented it from succeeding, the expedition contributed much to science. Important mistakes on maps in the position of the western coast of Novaya Zemlya, Matochkin Shar, Proliv, Strait, Kanin Nos, the eastern coast of the mouth of the White Sea, and the Murmansk coast of the Barents Sea were corrected; a number of bays of the Barents Sea were investigated with the aim of determining the possibility of using them for anchorage; and extensive areas of the Barents Sea were studied, including its northern part, between Spitsbergen and Novaya Zemlya.

In 1826–1829 Litke commanded the sloop *Senyavin*, on a round-the-world voyage designed to survey the little-known islands of the central Pacific and the coast of the Bering Sea.

In the Bering Sea, Litke made astronomical determinations of the most important points of the coast of Kamchatka north from the Avachinskaya gulf; he measured the height of many hills; he described in detail the hitherto unknown Karaginskiy Pribilof Ostrova, and Matveyev Islands and also the Chukchi coast from East Cape almost to the mouth of the Anadyr River. In the central Pacific he made a detailed investigation of the Carolines, discovering twelve previously unknown islands, describing the entire archipelago in detail, and placing it on the map. The expedition gathered materials on the botany, zoology, ethnography, geophysics, and oceanography of the regions explored.

After the voyage of the *Senyavin*, Litke became well known and was considered to be one of the most famous travelers of the first half of the nineteenth century. Soon afterward Litke became involved in organizing the Russian Geographical Society and was elected its president at the first meeting, in 1845.

Led by Litke, the Russian Geographical Society conducted a number of important expeditions to the outlying areas of the country and beyond its borders. In 1873, citing his advanced years, he asked to be relieved of the presidency; the society agreed, and in recognition of his exceptional services it established a gold medal in his name to honor especially distinguished geographical discoveries and research.

From 1864 to 1881 Litke was president of the St. Petersburg Academy of Sciences, retiring only a few months before his death. As president he did much to make the Academy flourish, helping various scientific institutions and societies to develop rapidly. In particular, through his efforts the Pulkovo observatory, the main physical observatory, and the Pavlov magnetic-meteorological observatory substantially broadened their activities.

Litke was an honorary member of the Naval Academy, of Kharkov and Dorpat universities, and of the geographical societies of London and Antwerp, as well as a corresponding member of the Paris Academy of Sciences.

BIBLIOGRAPHY

I. ORIGINAL WORKS. Litke's most important published writings are *Chetyrekhkratnoe puteshestvie v Severny Ledovity okean na voennom brige "Novaya Zemlya," v 1821–1824 godakh* ("Four Journeys to the Northern Arctic Ocean on the Military Brig *Novaya Zemlya*, in 1821–1824"; St. Petersburg, 1828; 2nd ed., Moscow, 1948); and *Puteshestvie vokrug sveta na voennom shlyupe "Senyavin" v 1826–1829 godakh* ("A Trip Around the World in the Military Sloop *Senyavin* in 1826–1829"), 3 vols. (St. Petersburg, 1834–1836; 2nd ed., Moscow, 1948).

II. SECONDARY LITERATURE. The most important publications on Litke are the following, listed chronologically: O. V. Struve, *Ob uchenykh zaslugakh grafa F. P. Litke* ("On the Scientific Contributions of Count F. P. Litke"; St. Petersburg, 1883); V. P. Bezobrazov, "Graf Fyodor Petrovich Litke," in *Zapisok Akademii nauk*, **57** (1888), app. 2; F. Wrangel, "Graf Fyodor Petrovich Litke," in *Izvestiya Russkogo Geograficheskogo obshchestva,* **33** (1897), 326–347; and A. D. Dobrovolsky, *Plavania F. P. Litke* ("Voyages of F. P. Litke"; Moscow, 1948).

For further reference, see B. P. Orlov, *Fyodor Petrovich Litke . . . (k 150-letiyu so dnya rozhdenia)* ("Fyodor Petrovich Litke . . . [for the 150th Anniversary of His Birth]"; Moscow, 1948); M. Marich, *Zhizn i plavania flota kapitan-leytenanta Fyodora Petrovicha Litke* ("Life and Voyages of the Fleet of Captain-Lieutenant Fyodor Petrovich Litke"; Moscow–Leningrad, 1949); A. E. Antonov, *F. P. Litke* (Moscow, 1955); and N. N. Zubov, *Fyodor Petrovich Litke*, in the series Otechestvennye Fiziko-Geografy i Puteshestvenniki ("Native Physical Geographers and Travelers"; Moscow, 1959).

A. F. PLAKHOTNIK

LIU HUI (*fl.* China, *ca.* A.D. 250), *mathematics.*

Nothing is known about the life of Liu Hui, except that he flourished in the kingdom of Wei toward the end of the Three Kingdoms period (A.D. 221–265). His mathematical writings, on the other hand, are well known; his commentary on the *Chiu-chang suan-shu* ("Nine Chapters on the Mathematical Art") has exerted a profound influence on Chinese mathematics for well over 1,000 years. He wrote another important, but much shorter, work: the *Hai-tao suan-ching* ("Sea Island Mathematical Manual").

Some scholars believe that the *Chiu-chang suan-shu*, also called the *Chiu-chang suan-ching* ("Mathematical Manual in Nine Chapters"), was already in existence in China during the third century B.C. Ch'ien Pao-tsung, in his *Chung-kuo suan-hsüeh-shih*, and Chang Yin-lin (*Yenching Hsüeh Pao*, **2** [1927], 301) have noted that the titles of certain officials mentioned in the problems date from Ch'in and earlier (third and early second centuries B.C.). There are also references which must indicate a taxation system of 203 B.C. According to Liu Hui's preface, the book was burned during the time of Emperor Ch'in Shih-huang (221–209 B.C.); but remnants of it were later recovered and put in order. In the following two centuries, commentaries on this book were written by Chang Ts'ang (*fl.* 165–142 B.C.) and Keng Shou-ch'ang (*fl.* 75–49 B.C.). In a study by Ch'ien Pao-tsung (1963) it is suggested, from internal textual evidence, that the *Chiu-chang suan-shu* was written between 50 B.C. and A.D. 100 and that it is doubtful whether Chang Ts'ang and Keng Shou-ch'ang had anything to do with the book. Yet Li Yen and Tu Shih-jan, both colleagues of Ch'ien Pao-tsung, still believed Liu Hui's preface when they wrote about the *Chiu-chang suan-shu* in the same year.

During the seventh century both the *Chiu-chang suan-shu* and the *Hai-tao suan-ching* (A.D. 263) were included in *Suan-ching shih-shu* ("Ten Mathematical Manuals," A.D. 656), to which the T'ang mathematician and astronomer Li Shun-feng (602–670) added his annotations and commentaries. These works then became standard texts for students of mathematics; official regulations prescribed that three years be devoted to the works of Liu Hui. Liu Hui's works also found their way to Japan with these ten mathematical manuals. When schools were established in Japan in 702 and mathematics was taught, both the *Chiu-chang suan-shu* and the *Hai-tao suan-ching* were among the prescribed texts.

According to Ch'eng Ta-wei's mathematical treatise, the *Suan-fa t'ung-tsung* ("Systematic Treatise on Arithmetic"; 1592), both the *Chiu-chang suan-shu* and the *Hai-tao suan-ching* were first printed officially in 1084. There was another printed version of them by Pao Huan-chih in 1213. In the early fifteenth century they were included, although considerably rearranged, in the vast Ming encyclopedia, the *Yung-lo ta-tien* (1403–1407). In the second part of the eighteenth century Tai Chen (1724–1777) reconstructed these two texts after having extracted them piecemeal from the *Yung-lo ta-tien*. They were subsequently included by K'ung Chi-han (1739–1787) in his *Wei-po-hsieh ts'ung-shu* (1773). Three years later Ch'ü Tseng-fa printed them separately with a preface by Tai Chen.

Other reproductions based on Tai Chen's reconstruction in the *Wei-po-hsieh ts'ung-shu* are found in the *Suan-ching shih-shu* ("Ten Mathematical Manuals") of Mei Ch'i-chao (1862) and in the *Wan-yu-wen-k'u* (1929–1933) and *Ssu-pu ts'ung-k'an* series (1920–1922; both of the Commercial Press, Shanghai). Two nineteenth-century scholars, Chung Hsiang and Li Huang, discovered that certain passages in the text had been rendered incomprehensible by Tai Chen's attempt to improve on the original text of the *Chiu-chang suan-shu*. A fragment of the early thirteenth-century edition of the *Chiu-chang suan-shu*, consisting

of only five chapters, was found during the seventeenth century in Nanking, in the private library of Huang Yü-chi (1629–1691). This copy was seen by the famous Ch'ing scholar Mei Wen-ting (1633–1721) in 1678, and it later came into the possession of K'ung Chi-han (1739–1784) and then Chang Tun-jen (1754–1834); finally it was acquired by the Shanghai Library, where it is now kept. In 1684, Mao I (1640–after 1710) made a handwritten copy of the original text found in the library of Huang Yü-chi. This copy was later acquired by the emperor during the Ch'ien-lung reign (1736–1795). In 1932 it was reproduced in the *T'ien-lu-lin-lang ts'ung-shu* series.

In 1261 Yang Hui wrote the *Hsiang-chieh chiu-chang suan-fa* ("Detailed Analysis of the Mathematical Rules in the Nine Chapters") to elucidate the problems in the *Chiu-chang suan-shu*. Ch'ien Pao-tsung in 1963 collated the text of the *Chiu-chang suan-shu* from Tai Chen's version, the fragments of the late Sung edition as reproduced in the *T'ien-lu-lin-lang ts'ung-shu* series, and Yang Hui's *Hsiang-chieh chiu-chang suan-fa*.

As for the *Hai-tao suan-ching*, only the reconstructed version by Tai Chen remains. It was reproduced in the *Wu-ying-tien* palace edition (before 1794), the "Ten Mathematical Manuals" in K'ung Chi-han's *Wei-po-hsieh ts'ung-shu*, and the appendix to Chü Tseng-fa's *Chiu-chang suan-shu*.

The *Chiu-chang suan-shu* was intended as a practical handbook, a kind of aide-mémoire for architects, engineers, officials, and tradesmen. This is the reason for the presence of so many problems on building canals and dikes, city walls, taxation, barter, public services, etc. It consists of nine chapters, with a total of 246 problems. The chapters may be outlined as follows:

(1) *Fang-t'ien* ("Land Surveying") contains the rules for finding the areas of triangles, trapezoids, rectangles, circles, sectors of circles, and annuli. It gives rules for addition, subtraction, multiplication, and division of fractions. There is an interesting but inaccurate formula for the area of the segment of a circle, where the chord c and the sagitta s are known, in the form $s(c + s)/2$. This expression later appeared during the ninth century in Mahāvīra's *Gaṇitasāra-sangraha*.

Of special interest is the value of the ratio of the circumference of a circle to its diameter that Liu Hui used. The ancient value of π used in China was 3, but since the first century Chinese mathematicians had been searching for a more accurate value. Liu Hsin (*d.* A.D. 23) used 3.1547, while Chang Heng (78–139) gave $\sqrt{10}$ and 92/29. Wang Fan (219–257) found 142/45, and then Liu Hui gave 3.14. The most important names in this connection are, however, those of Tsu Ch'ung-chih (430–501), a brilliant mathematician, astronomer, and engineer of the Liu Sung and Ch'i dynasties, and his son, Tsu Cheng-chih. Tsu Ch'ung-chih gave two values for π, first an "inaccurate" one (*yo lü*), equal to 22/7, given earlier by Archimedes, and then a "more accurate" one (*mi lu*), 355/113 (3.1415929). He even looked for further approximations and found that π lies between 3.1415926 and 3.1415927. His method was probably described in the *Chui Shu*, which he and his son wrote but is now lost. Tsu Ch'ung-chih's value of 355/113 for π disappeared for many centuries in China until it was again taken up by Chao Yu-ch'in (*fl. ca.* 1300). Liu Hui obtained the accurate value 3.14 by taking the ratio of the perimeter of a regular polygon of ninety-six sides to the diameter of a circle enclosing this polygon. Let us begin with a regular hexagon of side L_6. The ratio of the perimeter of the hexagon to the diameter of the circle enclosing it is 3. If we change the hexagon to a regular polygon of twelve sides, as shown in Figure 1—noting that $L_6 = r$, the radius of the circumscribed circle—then the side of the twelve-sided polygon is given by

$$L_{12} = \sqrt{2r\left[r - \sqrt{r^2 - \left(\frac{L_6}{2}\right)^2}\right]}.$$

Hence, if L_n is known, then L_{2n} can be found from the expression

$$L_{2n} = \sqrt{2r\left[r - \sqrt{r^2 - \left(\frac{L_n}{2}\right)^2}\right]}.$$

Taking $r = 1$, the following values can be found: $L_6 = 1$; $L_{12} = 0.517638$; $L_{24} = 0.261052$; $L_{48} = 0.130806$; $L_{96} = 0.065438$.

The perimeter of a regular polygon of $n = 96$ and $r = 1$ is $96 \times 0.065438 = 6.282048$. Hence $\pi = 6.282048/2 = 3.141024$, or approximately 3.14. Liu Hui also used a polygon of 3,072 sides and obtained his best value, 3.14159.

(2) *Su-mi* ("Millet and Rice") deals with percentages and proportions. Indeterminate equations are avoided in the last nine problems in this chapter by the use of proportions.

(3) *Ts'ui-fen* ("Distribution by Progression") concerns distribution of properties among partners according to given rates. It also includes problems in taxation of goods of different qualities, and others in arithmetical and geometrical progressions, all solved by use of proportions.

(4) *Shao-kuang* ("Diminishing Breadth") involves finding the sides of a rectangle when the area and one of the sides are given, the circumference of a circle

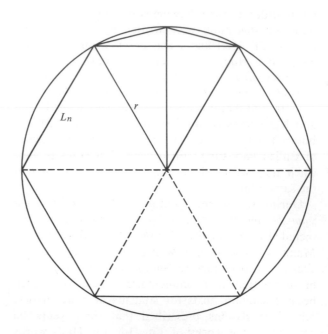

FIGURE 1

when its area is known, the side of a cube given its volume, and the diameter of a sphere of known volume. The use of the least common multiple in fractions is shown. It is interesting that unit fractions are used, for example, in problem 11 in this chapter. The given width of a rectangular form is expressed as

$$1 + 1/2 + 1/3 + 1/4 + 1/5 + 1/6 + 1/7 + 1/8$$
$$+ 1/9 + 1/10 + 1/11 + 1/12.$$

The problems in this chapter also lead to the extraction of square roots and cube roots; problem 13, for example, involves finding the square root of 25,281. According to the method given in the *Chiu-chang suan-shu*, this number, known as the *shih* (dividend), is first placed in the second row from the top of the counting board. Next, one counting rod, called the preliminary *chieh-suan*, is put on the bottom row of the counting board in the farthest right-hand digit column. This rod is moved to the left, two places at a time, as far as it can go without overshooting the farthest left digit of the number in the *shih* row. With its new place value this rod is called the *chieh-suan*. It is shown in Figure 2a.

		fang	1
2 5 2 8 1		*shih*	1 5 2 8 1
		fa	1 0 0 0 0
1		*chieh-suan*	1

FIGURE 2a   FIGURE 2b

The first figure of the root is found to lie between 100 and 200. Then 1 is taken as the first figure of the root and is placed on the top row in the hundreds column. The top row is called *fang*. The *chieh-suan* is multiplied by the first figure of the root. The product, called *fa*, is placed in the third row. The *shih* (25,281) less the *fa* (10,000) leaves the "first remainder" (15,281), which is written on the second row, as shown in Figure 2b. After the division has been made, the *fa* is doubled to form the *ting-fa*. This is moved one digit to the right, while the *chieh-suan* is shifted two digits to the right, as shown in Figure 2c.

1	*fang*	
1 5 2 8 1	1st / 2nd re.	2 7 8 1
2 0 0 0	*ting-fa*	2 5 0 0
1	*chieh-suan*	1

FIGURE 2c   FIGURE 2d

The second figure, selected by trial and error, is found to lie between 5 and 6. The tens' digit is therefore taken to be 5 and will be placed in its appropriate position on the top row in Figure 2e. The *chieh-suan* (which is now 100) is multiplied by this second figure and the product is added to the *ting-fa*, which becomes 2,500. The *ting-fa* multiplied by 5 is subtracted from the first remainder, which gives a remainder of 2,781 $(15,281 - 2,500 \times 5 = 2,781)$, as shown in Figure 2d. The *ting-fa* is next shifted one digit to the right and the *chieh-suan* two places (see Figure 2e). The third figure, again selected by trial and error, is found to be 9. This unit digit is placed in its appropriate position on the top row. The *chieh-suan*, which is now 1, is multiplied by this third figure and the product is added to the *ting-fa*, which becomes 259. The second remainder is divided by the *ting-fa*, which leaves a remainder of zero $(2,781 \div 259 = 9 + 0)$. Hence the answer is 159 (see Figure 2f).

1 5	*fang*	1 5 9
2 7 8 1	2nd / last re.	0
2 5 0	*ting-fa*	2 5 9
1	*chieh-suan*	1

FIGURE 2e   FIGURE 2f

(5) *Shang-kung* ("Consultations on Engineering Works") gives the volumes of such solid figures as the prism, the pyramid, the tetrahedron, the wedge, the cylinder, the cone, and the frustum of a cone:

(*a*) Volume of square prism = square of side of base times height.

(*b*) Volume of cylinder = 1/12 square of circumference of circle times height (where π is taken to be approximately 3).

(*c*) Volume of truncated square pyramid = 1/3 the height times the sum of the squares of the sides of the upper and lower squares and the product of the sides of the upper and lower squares.

(*d*) Volume of square pyramid = 1/3 the height times the square of the side of the base.

(*e*) Volume of frustum of a circular cone = 1/36 the height times the sum of the squares of the circumferences of the upper and lower circular faces and the product of these two circumferences (where π is taken to be approximately 3).

(*f*) Volume of circular cone = 1/36 the height times the square of the circumference of the base (where π is taken to be approximately 3).

(*g*) Volume of a right triangular prism = 1/2 the product of the width, the length, and the height.

(*h*) Volume of a rectangular pyramid = 1/3 the product of the width and length of the base and the height.

(*i*) Volume of tetrahedron with two opposite edges perpendicular to each other = 1/6 the product of the two perpendicular opposite edges and the perpendicular common to these two edges.

(6) *Chün-shu* ("Impartial Taxation") concerns problems of pursuit and alligation, especially in connection with the time required for taxpayers to get their grain contributions from their native towns to the capital. It also deals with problems of ratios in connection with the allocation of tax burdens according to the population. Problem 12 in this chapter says:

> A good runner can go 100 paces while a bad runner goes 60 paces. The bad runner has gone a distance of 100 paces before the good runner starts pursuing him. In how many paces will the good runner catch up? [Answer: 250 paces.]

(7) *Ying pu-tsu* or *ying-nü* ("Excess and Deficiency"). *Ying*, referring to the full moon, and *pu-tsu* or *nü* to the new moon, mean "too much" and "too little," respectively. This section deals with a Chinese algebraic invention used mainly for solving problems of the type $ax + b = 0$ in a rather roundabout manner. The method came to be known in Europe as the rule of false position. In this method two guesses, x_1 and x_2, are made, giving rise to values c_1 and c_2, respectively, either greater or less than 0. From these we have the following equations:

(1) $$ax_1 + b = c_1$$
(2) $$ax_2 + b = c_2.$$

Multiplying (1) by x_2 and (2) by x_1, we have

(1') $$ax_1x_2 + bx_2 = c_1x_2$$
(2') $$ax_1x_2 + bx_1 = c_2x_1$$
(3) $$\therefore b(x_2 - x_1) = c_1x_2 - c_2x_1.$$

From (1) and (2),

(4) $$a(x_2 - x_1) = c_2 - c_1$$

$$\therefore \frac{b}{a} = \frac{c_1x_2 - c_2x_1}{c_2 - c_1}.$$

Hence

(5) $$x = -\frac{b}{a} = \frac{c_1x_2 - c_2x_1}{c_1 - c_2}.$$

Problem 1 in this chapter says:

> In a situation where certain things are purchased jointly, if each person pays 8 [units of money], the surplus is 3 [units], and if each person pays 7, the deficiency is 4. Find the number of persons and the price of the things brought. [Answer: 7 persons and 53 units of money.]

According to the method of excess and deficiency, the rates (that is, the "guesses" 8 and 7) are first set on the counting board with the excess (3) and deficiency (−4) placed below them. The rates are then cross multiplied by the excess and deficiency, and the products are added to form the dividend. Then the excess and deficiency are added together to form the divisor. The quotient gives the correct amount of money payable by each person. To get the number of persons, add the excess and deficiency and divide the sum by the difference between the two rates. In other words, x and a are obtained using equations (5) and (4) above.

Sometimes a straightforward problem may be transformed into one involving the use of the rule of false position. Problem 18 in the same chapter says:

> There are 9 [equal] pieces of gold and 11 [equal] pieces of silver. The two lots weigh the same. One piece is taken from each lot and put in the other. The lot containing mainly gold is now found to weigh less than the lot containing mainly silver by 13 ounces. Find the weight of each piece of gold and silver.

Here two guesses are made for the weight of gold. The method says that if each piece of gold weighs 3 pounds, then each piece of silver would weigh 2 5/11 pounds, giving a deficiency of 49/11 ounces; and if each piece of gold weighs 2 pounds, then each piece of silver would weigh 1 7/11 pounds, giving an excess of 15/11 ounces. Following this, the rule of false position is applied.

(8) *Fang-ch'eng* ("Calculation by Tabulation") is concerned with simultaneous linear equations, using both positive and negative numbers. Problem 18 in this chapter involves five unknowns but gives only four equations, thus heralding the indeterminate equation. The process of solving simultaneous linear equations given here is the same as the modern procedure for solving the simultaneous system

$$a_1x + b_1y + c_1z = d_1$$
$$a_2x + b_2y + c_2z = d_2$$
$$a_3x + b_3y + c_3z = d_3,$$

except that the coefficients and constants are arranged in vertical columns instead of being written horizontally:

a_1	a_2	a_3
b_1	b_2	b_3
c_1	c_2	c_3
d_1	d_2	$d_3.$

In this chapter Liu Hui also explains the algebraic addition and subtraction of positive and negative numbers. (Liu Hui denoted positive numbers and negative numbers by red and black calculating rods, respectively.)

(9) *Kou-ku* ("Right Angles") deals with the application of the Pythagorean theorem. Some of its problems are as follows:

> A cylindrical piece of wood with a cross-section diameter of 2 feet, 5 inches, is to be cut into a piece of plank 7 inches thick. What is the width? [problem 4]
> There is a tree 20 feet high and 3 feet in circumference. A creeper winds round the tree seven times and just reaches the top. Find the length of the vine. [problem 5]
> There is a pond 7 feet square with a reed growing at the center and measuring 1 foot above the water. The reed just reaches the bank at the water level when drawn toward it. Find the depth of the water and the length of the reed. [problem 6]
> There is a bamboo 10 feet high. When bent, the upper end touches the ground 3 feet away from the stem. Find the height of the break. [problem 13]

It is interesting that a problem similar to 13 appeared in Brahmagupta's work in the seventh century.

Problem 20 has aroused even greater interest:

> There is a square town of unknown dimension. A gate is at the middle of each side. Twenty paces out of the north gate is a tree. If one walks 14 paces from the south gate, turns west, and takes 1,775 paces, the tree will just come into view. Find the length of the side of the town.

The book indicates that the answer can be obtained by evolving the root of the quadratic equation

$$x^2 + (14 + 20)x = 2(1775 \times 20).$$

The method of solving this equation is not described. Mikami suggests that it is highly probable that the root extraction was carried out with an additional term in the first-degree coefficient in the unknown and that this additional term was called *tsung*, but in his literal translation of some parts of the text concerning root extractions he does not notice that the successive steps correspond closely to those in Horner's method. Ch'ien Pao-tsung and Li Yen have both tried to compare the method described in the *Chiu-chang suan-shu* with that of Horner, but they have not clarified the textual obscurities. Wang Ling and Needham say that it is possible to show that if the text of the *Chiu-chang suan-shu* is very carefully followed, the essentials of the methods used by the Chinese for solving numerical equations of the second and higher degrees, similar to that developed by Horner in 1819, are present in a work that may be dated in the first century B.C.

The *Hai-tao suan-ching*, originally known by the name *Ch'ung ch'a* ("Method of Double Differences"), was appended to the *Chiu-chang suan-shu* as its tenth chapter. It was separated from the main text during the seventh century, when the "Ten Mathematical Manuals" were chosen, and was given the title *Hai-tao suan-ching*. According to Mikami, the term *ch'ung ch'a* was intended to mean double, or repeated, application of proportions of the sides of right triangles. The name *Hai-tao* probably came from the first problem of the book, which deals with an island in the sea. Consisting of only nine problems, the book is equivalent to less than one chapter of the *Chiu-chang suan-shu*.

In its preface Liu Hui describes the classical Chinese method of determining the distance from the sun to the flat earth by means of double triangulation. According to this method, two vertical poles eight feet high were erected at the same level along the same meridian, one at the ancient Chou capital of Yan-ch'eng and the other 10,000 *li* (1 *li* = 1,800 feet) to the north. The lengths of the shadows cast by the sun at midday of the summer solstice were measured, and from these the distance of sun could be derived. Liu Hui then shows how the same method can be applied to more everyday examples. Problem 1 says:

> A sea island is viewed from a distance. Two poles, each 30 feet high, are erected on the same level 1,000 *pu* [1 *pu* = 6 ft.] apart so that the pole at the rear is in a straight line with the island and the other pole. If one moves 123 *pu* back from the nearer pole, the top of the

island is just visible through the end of the pole if he views it from ground level. Should he move back 127 *pu* from the other pole, the top of the island is just visible through the end of the pole if viewed from ground level. Find the elevation of the island and its distance from the [nearer] pole. [Answer: The elevation of the island is 4 *li*, 55 *pu*. The distance to the [nearer] pole is 102 *li*, 150 *pu* (300 *pu* = 1 *li*).]

The rule for solving this problem is given as follows:

> Multiply the height of the pole by the distance between the poles and divide the product by the difference between the distances that one has to walk back from the poles in order to view the highest point on the island. Adding the height of the pole to the quotient gives the elevation of the island. To find the distance from the nearer pole to the island, multiply the distance walked back from that pole by the distance between the poles. Dividing the product by the difference between the distances that one has to walk back from the poles gives that distance.

Problem 7 is of special interest:

> A person is looking into an abyss with a piece of white rock at the bottom. From the shore a crossbar is turned to lie on the side that is normally upright [so that its base is vertical]. If the base is 3 feet and one looks at the surface of the water [directly above the rock] from the tip of the base, the line of sight meets the height of the crossbar at a distance of 4 feet, 5 inches; and when one looks at the rock, the line of sight meets the height of the crossbar at a distance of 2 feet, 4 inches. A similar crossbar is set up 4 feet above the first. If one looks from the tip of the base, the line of sight to the water surface [directly above the rock] would meet the height of the crossbar at a distance of 4 feet; and if one looks at the rock, it will be 2 feet, 2 inches. Find the depth of the water.

In Figure 3, if P is the water surface above the white rock, R, and BC and FG are the two crossbars, then $BC = FG = 3$ feet; $GC = 4$ feet; $AC = 4$ feet, 5 inches; $DC = 2$ feet, 4 inches; $EG = 4$ feet; and $HG = 2$ feet, 2 inches. The depth of the water, PR, is sought. To obtain the answer, Liu Hui gives the following rule:

$$PR = GC \, \frac{EG(DC - HG) - HG(AC - EG)}{(DC - HG)(AC - EG)}.$$

Liu Hui has not taken into account here the refractive index of water. The rule given is an extension of that used in solving problem 4, which uses the same method for determining the depth of a valley:

> A person is looking at a deep valley. From the edge of the valley a crossbar is turned to lie on the side that is normally upright [so that its base is vertical]. The base

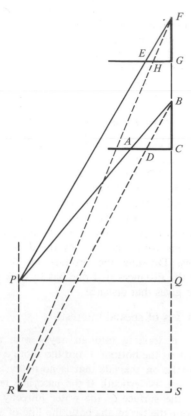

FIGURE 3

Hence,

$$CQ = \frac{GC \cdot EG}{AC - EG} - CB.$$

In problem 7 one can also obtain the distance from the bank to the bottom of the abyss (*CS* in Figure 3) from the expression

$$CS = \frac{GC \cdot HG}{(DC - HG)} - CB.$$

PR is derived from the difference between *CS* and *CQ*.

As for the other problems, problem 2 concerns finding the height of a tree on a hill; problem 3 deals with the size of a distant walled city; problem 5 shows how to measure the height of a tower on a plain as seen from a hill; problem 6 gives a method for finding the width of a gulf seen from a distance on land; problem 8 is a case of finding the width of a river seen from a hill; and problem 9 seeks the size of a city seen from a mountain.

BIBLIOGRAPHY

A modern ed. of the *Chiu-chang suan-shu* is vol. 1121 in the *Ts'ung-Shu Chi-Chêng* series (Shanghai, 1936).

Works dealing with Liu Hui and his writings are Ch'ien Pao-tsung, *Suan-ching shih-shu* ("Ten Mathematical Manuals"), 2 vols. (Peking, 1963), 83–272; and *Chung-kuo suan-hsüeh-shih* ("History of Chinese Mathematics") (Peking, 1964), 61–75; L. van Hée, "Le Hai Tao Suan Ching de Lieou," in *T'oung Pao*, **20** (1921), 51–60; Hsü Shun-fang, *Chung-suan-chia te tai-shu-hsüeh yen-chiu* ("A Study of Algebra by Chinese Mathematicians") (Peking, 1955), 1–8; Li Yen, *Chung-kuo shu-Hsüeh ta-kang* ("Outline of Chinese Mathematics"), I (Shanghai, 1931); and *Chung-kuo suan-hsüeh-shih* ("History of Chinese Mathematics") (Shanghai, 1937; rev. ed., 1955), 16, 19, 21; Li Yen and Tu Shih-jan, *Chung-kuo ku-tai shu-hsüeh chien-shih* ("Brief History of Ancient Chinese Mathematics"), I (Peking, 1963), 45–77; Yoshio Mikami, *The Development of Mathematics in China and Japan* (New York, 1913); Joseph Needham, *Science and Civilisation in China*, III (Cambridge, 1959), 24–27; George Sarton, *Introduction to the History of Science*, 3 vols. (Baltimore, 1927–1947), esp. I, 338; Wang Ling, "The Chiu Chang Suan Shu and the History of Chinese Mathematics During the Han Dynasty," a doctoral diss. (Cambridge Univ., 1956); Wang Ling and Joseph Needham, "Horner's Method in Chinese Mathematics; Its Origins in the Root-Extraction Procedure of the Han Dynasty," in *T'oung Pao*, **43** (1955), 345–401; and Alexander Wylie, *Chinese Researches* (Shanghai, 1897; repr. Peking, 1936, and Taipei, 1966), 170–174.

Some important special studies on the *Chiu-chang suan-shu* are E. I. Berezkina, "Drevnekitaysky traktat matematika v devyati knigach" ("The Ancient Chinese Mathematical Treatise in Nine Books"), in *Istoriko-matematicheskie issledovaniya*, **10** (1957), 423–584, a Russian trans. of the

is 6 feet long. If one looks at the bottom of the valley from the edge of the base, the line of sight meets the vertical side at a distance of 9 feet, 1 inch. Another crossbar is set 30 feet directly above the first. If the bottom of the valley is observed from the edge of the base, the line of sight will meet the vertical side at a distance of 8 feet, 5 inches. Find the depth of the valley.

If we refer again to Figure 3, ignoring the broken lines, we have $CB = GF = 6$ feet; $CG = 30$ feet; $AC = 9$ feet, 1 inch; $EG = 8$ feet, 5 inches; and CQ is the depth. From similar triangles ABC and PBQ,

$$QB \cdot AC = PQ \cdot CB;$$

and from similar triangles EFG and PFQ,

$$QF \cdot EG = PQ \cdot GF.$$

Since $CB = GF$, and $QF = QB + BF$,

$$QB \cdot AC = (QB + BF)\,EG,$$

$$QB(AC - EG) = BF \cdot EG = GC \cdot EG,$$

that is,

$$(CQ + CB)(AC - EG) = GC \cdot EG.$$

Chiu-chang suan-shu; Kurt Vogel, *Neun Bücher arithmetischer Technik* (Brunswick, 1968), a German trans. and study of the work; and A. P. Youschkevitsch, *Geschichte der Mathematik im Mittelalter* (Leipzig, 1964), 1–88 ("Die Mathematik in China"), translated from the Russian.

Access to old biographical notes and bibliographical citations concerning mathematical works are Hu Yü-chin, *Ssu-K'u-T'i-Yao Pu-Chêng* ("Supplements to the *Ssu-K'u-T'i-yao*"), 2 vols. (Taipei, 1964–1967); and Ting Fu-pao and Chou Yün-ch'ing, *Ssu-Pu-Tsung-Lu Suan-Fa-Pien* ("Bibliography of Mathematical Books to Supplement the *Ssu-K'u-Ch'uan-Shu* Encyclopedia"; Shanghai, 1956).

More information on the *Suan-Ching Shi-Shu* can be found in Needham, *Science and Civilisation in China*, III, 18; and in A. Hummel, *Eminent Chinese of the Ch'ing Period* (Washington, 1943), p. 697.

The two extant volumes of the *Yung-Lo Ta-Tien* encyclopedia have been reproduced photographically (Peking, 1960); they show that the arrangement was according to mathematical procedures and not by authors.

HO PENG-YOKE

LIVINGSTON, BURTON EDWARD (*b.* Grand Rapids, Michigan, 9 February 1875; *d.* Baltimore, Maryland, 8 February 1948), *plant physiology, physiological ecology.*

The son of Benjamin and Keziah Livingston, Burton was raised in a home and environment that gave him early contact with and love of flora and natural history. Since his father was a contractor in the street paving and sewer construction business, he became familiar with tools and machinery. Moreover, a large home library and access to simple microscopes gave him considerable familiarity with science before he entered school. In high school Livingston became proficient in languages and began a herbarium. Upon graduation he worked in a Short Hills, New Jersey, nursery and then entered the University of Michigan in 1894, receiving ten hours of advanced credit in botany. He was awarded the B.S. degree in 1898 and received the Ph.D. from the University of Chicago in 1901. From 1899 to 1904 he was assistant in plant physiology at Chicago, then became a soil expert for the U.S. Bureau of Soils, Department of Agriculture, from 1905 to 1906. He was a staff member of the department of botanical research at the desert laboratory of the Carnegie Institution of Washington at Tucson, Arizona, from 1906 to 1909; professor of plant physiology at Johns Hopkins University from 1909 to 1940; and director of the laboratory of plant physiology at Johns Hopkins from 1913 to 1940. His marriage to Grace Johnson in 1905 ended in divorce in 1918; he married Marguerite Anna Brennan MacPhilips in 1921. He had no children.

Livingston's early interests and training prepared him for a research career in plant physiology at a time when that science was not given academic standing at most American universities. It was mainly through his efforts at Johns Hopkins that plant physiology was gradually given full standing elsewhere. His interests were broad but centered mainly on the water relations of plants. He studied soil moisture and the evaporative power of the environment, with special emphasis on the effects of light, temperature, wind, and other factors on foliar transpiring power. His careful compilations of data on the daily course of transpiration, the seasonal soil moisture conditions, the water-supplying power of soils in relation to wilting, and the oxygen-supplying ability of soils in relation to seed germination contributed immensely to the foundations of modern physiological plant ecology.

Livingston invented the porous cup atmometer, an instrument for measuring the evaporating capacity of air; the auto-irrigator, for automatic control of soil moisture of potted plants; water-absorbing points for measuring the water-supplying power of soil; and rotating tables for assuring equal exposure of plant cultures to environmental conditions. These inventions or modifications of them are still in use.

Livingston's laboratory became a mecca for plant physiologists, and more than 300 papers were published with his students and colleagues. His book *The Role of Diffusion and Osmotic Pressure in Plants* (1903) is still an authoritative summary of the early work. In 1921 he published with Forrest Shreve *The Vegetation of the United States as Determined by Climatic Conditions.* His translation, with extensive editorial comment, of V. I. Palladin's *Plant Physiology* in 1918 gave the work the impetus it needed to become the standard American textbook in plant physiology for many years. It ran to three editions, the last appearing in 1926.

BIBLIOGRAPHY

See D. T. MacDougal, "Burton Edward Livingston (1875–1948)," in *Yearbook. American Philosophical Society*, **12** (1948), 278–280; and an article on Livingston in *National Cyclopedia of American Biography*, **36** (1950), 334; and C. A. Shull, "Burton Edward Livingston (1875–1948)," in *Science*, **107** (1948), 558–560; and "Burton Edward Livingston (1875–1948)," in *Plant Physiology*, **23** (1948), iii–vii.

A. D. KRIKORIAN

LI YEH. See **Li Chih.**

LLOYD, HUMPHREY (*b*. Dublin, Ireland, 16 April 1800; *d*. Dublin, 17 January 1881), *physics*.

An active member of the Church of Ireland and provost of Trinity College, Dublin, Lloyd was known among physicists as an expert in optics and a leader in the British program to map the earth's magnetic field. His career closely paralleled that of his father, the Reverend Bartholomew Lloyd, who was professor of mathematics, natural philosophy, Greek, and divinity at Trinity College, as well as provost of the college, and president of the Royal Irish Academy. Humphrey displayed his abilities while young, placing first on the entrance examination for Trinity and, upon his graduation in 1819, receiving a gold medal for excellence in science. He became a member of the faculty and rose through the ranks: junior fellow (1824), professor of natural and experimental science (1831), senior fellow (1843), vice provost (1862), and provost (1867). During this period he received his Master of Arts and Doctor of Divinity. He was president of the Royal Irish Academy from 1846 to 1851, and a member of the Royal Societies of London and Edinburgh and of the British Association for the Advancement of Science. At the age of forty he married Dorothea Bulwer, the daughter of a clergyman.

Lloyd's first important original research was in optics. In 1832 W. R. Hamilton deduced from Fresnel's equations for double refraction in a biaxial crystal the consequence that under certain conditions a ray of light within the crystal would split into an infinite number of rays forming a conic surface. Hamilton asked Lloyd to investigate this "conical refraction" experimentally, and Lloyd succeeded in giving a demonstration of the phenomenon and finding the direction of polarization of the rays making up the luminous cone. This achievement gave new support to the wave theory of light and established Lloyd's reputation as an expert in optics.

In 1834, while examining Fresnel's classic experiment in which an interference pattern is produced by light from a single source reflected by two mirrors, Lloyd discovered that a similar effect could be produced by using a single reflecting surface. Arranging a light source, mirror, and screen as shown in Figure 1, he caused reflected light to interfere with direct light from the source in a limited area on the screen. The location of the bands of this pattern could be deduced by imagining they were caused by a second source of light, located at the mirror image of the first and producing an interference pattern. This treatment enabled Lloyd to establish two important properties of reflection: first, that the intensity of light reflected at a 90° incidence is equal to that of direct light (as Fresnel had predicted), and second, that a half-wavelength phase acceleration takes place upon reflection by a higher-density medium.

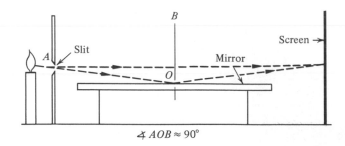

$\sphericalangle\,AOB \approx 90°$

FIGURE 1

Lloyd's other contributions to optics include a report to the British Association on the state of the subject in 1833, two textbooks expounding the wave theory, and a study of reflection and refraction by thin plates. The bulk of his remaining scientific work was devoted to terrestrial magnetism.

In 1831–1832 the British Association proposed that a series of observations of the intensity of the earth's magnetic field be made in various parts of the kingdom. It appointed a committee to coordinate this activity and Lloyd was made a member. Shortly thereafter he undertook a series of magnetic observations in Ireland with Sir Edward Sabine. During the course of this project Lloyd made measurements in twenty-four areas of his native land and invented a new technique for the simultaneous determination of magnetic inclination and intensity.

By 1838 the discovery of temporal variations in the earth's magnetic field created the need for a set of permanent observatories capable of making simultaneous measurements in different parts of the world. The British Association, with government financial support, undertook the construction of these stations and assigned Lloyd the important job of drawing up instructions for the observers and teaching the officers in charge the use of the instruments. Lloyd's own observatory at Trinity College, which had been constructed under his supervision in 1837, served as a model for the other stations and received the results of their observations.

Lloyd's contributions to the understanding of terrestrial magnetism did not end with his role in setting up the British magnetic survey. He remained active in the field throughout his life and succeeded in demonstrating the existence of currents of electricity in the earth's crust and in calculating their effect on the daily variation in the magnetic field.

BIBLIOGRAPHY

I. ORIGINAL WORKS. Lloyd's articles include "On the Phenomena Presented by Light in Its Passage Along the Axes of Biaxial Crystals," in *Philosophical Magazine*, **2** (1833), 112–120, 207–210; "Report on the Progress and Present State of Physical Optics," in *British Association Reports* (1834), 295–413; "An Attempt to Facilitate Observations of Terrestrial Magnetism," in *Transactions of the Royal Irish Academy*, **17** (1837), 159–170; "Further Developments of a Method . . .," *ibid.*, 449–460; "On a New Case of Interference of the Rays of Light," *ibid.*, 171–178; "On the Light Reflected and Transmitted by Thin Plates," *ibid.*, **24**, pt. 1 (1860), 3–15; and "On Earth-Currents, and Their Connexion With the Phenomena of Terrestrial Magnetism," in *Philosophical Magazine*, **22** (1861), 437–442. His most important scientific papers are reprinted in his *Miscellaneous Papers Connected With Physical Science* (London, 1877), and his other published works are listed in *Dictionary of National Biography*, XI, p. 1304. His textbooks are *The Elements of Optics* (Dublin, 1849) and *Elementary Treatise on the Wave Theory of Light* (Dublin, 1857).

II. SECONDARY LITERATURE. The best biographical material on Lloyd is in the *Proceedings of the Royal Society*, **31** (1881), 23. A bibliography of his scientific papers is in Royal Society, *Catalogue of Scientific Papers*, IV, 62–63.

EUGENE FRANKEL

LLOYD, JOHN URI (*b.* West Bloomfield, New York, 19 April 1849; *d.* Van Nuys, California, 9 April 1936), *pharmacy, chemistry.*

Lloyd was the son of Nelson Lloyd, a civil engineer and schoolteacher, and the former Sophia Webster. When the boy was four, the family moved to Kentucky, where his parents taught school in their home. Most of his early education was obtained at home, and in 1863 he was apprenticed to a pharmacist in Cincinnati. After serving for several years as an apprentice and drug clerk, Lloyd was approached by the eclectic physician John King with an offer to join the pharmaceutical firm of H. M. Merrell of Cincinnati as a chemist. In 1871 he joined this firm, which specialized in eclectic remedies; and eventually he and two brothers gained control of the company, which became known as Lloyd Brothers. Although he did not possess a college education, Lloyd served as a professor of chemistry at the Cincinnati College of Pharmacy from 1883 to 1887 and at the Eclectic Medical Institute from 1878 to 1907.

Lloyd was a man of small physical stature and was possessed of a lively and versatile mind. He was a prolific writer whose publications included scientific articles, historical works, and novels. He and his brothers also created the Lloyd Library in Cincinnati, which contains significant collections in pharmacy, botany, medicine, natural history, and allied fields. Among the honors he received in his lifetime were the Remington Medal of the American Pharmaceutical Association (1920), the Procter International Award of the Philadelphia College of Pharmacy and Science (1934), and several honorary degrees. He was married twice and had three children by his second wife.

His commitment to eclecticism, which stressed the use of botanical drugs, led Lloyd to concentrate his scientific studies on plants. He investigated the medicinal and chemical properties of numerous indigenous plants and marketed tinctures, fluid extracts, and other products derived from these plants. The so-called "specific medicines" of Lloyd Brothers, although intended for eclectic practitioners, also found favor with many other physicians and pharmacists. In the course of this work Lloyd developed and patented several useful techniques, such as his "cold still," which extracted the soluble constituents of plants with a minimum of heat, and Lloyd's reagent, hydrous aluminum silicate, which adsorbed alkaloids from solutions. He also wrote several important pharmaceutical textbooks and reference works, such as *Drugs and Medicines of North America.*

Lloyd was a pioneer in the application of physical chemistry to pharmaceutical techniques. In a series of papers published in 1879–1885, he discussed such physical phenomena as adsorption and capillarity and their relationship to the preparation of fluid extracts. Wolfgang Ostwald, one of the founders of the field of colloid chemistry, later found that these works contained much of interest to those studying colloidal phenomena. He felt that they were significant and original enough to merit republication in his journal, *Kolloidchemische Beihefte*, in 1916.

BIBLIOGRAPHY

I. ORIGINAL WORKS. There does not appear to be a published bibliography of Lloyd's writings, which number in the thousands. His most important scientific books are *The Chemistry of Medicines* (Cincinnati, 1881); *Elixirs . . .* (Cincinnati, 1883); *Drugs and Medicines of North America*, 2 vols. (Cincinnati, 1884–1887), written with his brother C. G. Lloyd; and *Origin and History of All the Pharmacopeial Vegetable Drugs, Chemicals and Preparations.* I. *Vegetable Drugs* (Cincinnati, 1921). His novels largely concern Kentucky life and folklore, the best-known being *Stringtown on the Pike* (Cincinnati, 1901). *Etidorpha* (Cincinnati, 1897), a fantasy involving a trip to the center of the earth, is a curious mixture of scientific and metaphysical speculations.

The six articles selected by Ostwald for republication (see text) were originally published in *Proceedings of the*

American Pharmaceutical Association, **27–33** (1879–1885), under the general title "Precipitates in Fluid Extracts" (except for the first paper, which was entitled "On the Conditions Necessary to Successfully Conduct Percolation"). Lloyd also published related papers on adsorption, on solvents, and on physics in pharmacy in Journal of the American Pharmaceutical Association, especially in the period 1916–1936. Several of these papers bear the name of Wolfgang Ostwald, among others, as a coauthor. For Lloyd's first detailed report of the reagent bearing his name, see "Discovery of the Alkaloidal Affinities of Hydrous Aluminum Silicate," in Journal of the American Pharmaceutical Association, **5** (1916), 381–390, 490–495. For his views on colloids in pharmacy and on the methods of extracting active principles of plants, see "Colloids in Pharmacy," in Jerome Alexander, ed., Colloid Chemistry, II (New York, 1928), 931–934.

Lloyd was a frequent contributor to Eclectic Medical Journal; and numerous essays by him on pharmacy, eclecticism, and other subjects can be found in this publication.

The Lloyd Library in Cincinnati possesses correspondence and other MS materials of Lloyd's. A significant amount of his correspondence and other documents related to him are in the Kremers Reference Files of the University of Wisconsin School of Pharmacy in Madison.

II. SECONDARY LITERATURE. The life and work of John Uri Lloyd have not yet been satisfactorily evaluated in detail. Corinne Miller Simons, John Uri Lloyd, His Life and Works, 1849–1936, With a History of the Lloyd Library (Cincinnati, 1972), provides a significant amount of useful biographical information, but the author herself describes the book in her preface as a "chronicle" intended "merely to preserve and enumerate the authentic facts of his life while they are still fresh in the memories of those who knew him"; she acknowledges that she has left for later generations the task of writing biographies of Lloyd "that may be philosophical, analytical or interpretative of his influence and place in contemporary history." For biographical sketches, see the article by Corinne Miller Simons in Dictionary of American Biography, XXII, supp. 2 (1958), 389–390; Roy Bird Cook, "John Uri Lloyd: Pharmacist, Philosopher, Author, Man," in Journal of the American Pharmaceutical Association, Practical Pharmacy Edition, **10** (1949), 538–544; and George Beal, "Lloyds of Cincinnati," in American Journal of Pharmaceutical Education, **23** (1959), 202–206. Eclectic Medical Journal, **96**, no. 5 (May 1936), is a memorial issue which reprints several biographical articles on Lloyd. National Eclectic Medical Quarterly, **41**, no. 2 (Dec. 1949), also contains several short articles about Lloyd.

On the history of the Lloyd Library, as well as for biographical information on its founders, see Caswell Mayo, The Lloyd Library and Its Makers (Cincinnati, 1928); and Corinne Miller Simons, "John Uri Lloyd and the Lloyd Library," in National Eclectic Medical Quarterly (Mar. 1951), 1–5.

On eclecticism, see Alex Berman, "The Impact of the Nineteenth Century Botanico-Medical Movement on American Pharmacy and Medicine" (Ph.D. dissertation, University of Wisconsin, 1954), pp. 251–316, esp. pp. 307–311. See also Berman's "Wooster Beach and the Early Eclectics," in University of Michigan Medical Bulletin, **24** (1958), 277–286; and "A Striving for Scientific Respectability: Some American Botanics and the Nineteenth-Century Plant Materia Medica," in Bulletin of the History of Medicine, **30** (1956), 7–31. Also of interest in this connection is Harvey Felter, History of the Eclectic Medical Institute, Cincinnati, Ohio, 1845–1902 (Cincinnati, 1902)—see pp. 130–132 for a biographical sketch of Lloyd.

JOHN PARASCANDOLA

LLWYD, EDWARD. See **Lhwyd, Edward.**

LOBACHEVSKY, NIKOLAI IVANOVICH (b. Nizhni Novgorod [now Gorki], Russia, 2 December 1792; d. Kazan, Russia, 24 February 1856), mathematics.

Lobachevsky was the son of Ivan Maksimovich Lobachevsky, a clerk in a land-surveying office, and Praskovia Aleksandrovna Lobachevskaya. In about 1800 the mother moved with her three sons to Kazan, where Lobachevsky and his brothers were soon enrolled in the Gymnasium on public scholarships. In 1807 Lobachevsky entered Kazan University, where he studied under the supervision of Martin Bartels, a friend of Gauss, and, in 1812, received the master's degree in physics and mathematics. In 1814 he became an adjunct in physical and mathematical sciences and began to lecture on various aspects of mathematics and mechanics. He was appointed extraordinary professor in 1814 and professor ordinarius in 1822, the same year in which he began an administrative career as a member of the committee formed to supervise the construction of the new university buildings. He was chairman of that committee in 1825, twice dean of the department of physics and mathematics (in 1820–1821 and 1823–1825), librarian of the university (1825–1835), rector (1827–1846), and assistant trustee for the whole of the Kazan educational district (1846–1855).

In recognition of his work Lobachevsky was in 1837 raised to the hereditary nobility; he designed his own familial device (which is reproduced on his tombstone), depicting Solomon's seal, a bee, an arrow, and a horseshoe, to symbolize wisdom, diligence, alacrity, and happiness, respectively. He had in 1832 made a wealthy marriage, to Lady Varvara Aleksivna Moisieva, but his family of seven children and the cost of technological improvements for his estate left him with little money upon his retirement from the university, although he received a modest pension. A worsening sclerotic condition progressively affected his eyesight, and he was blind in his last years.

Although Lobachevsky wrote his first major work, *Geometriya*, in 1823, it was not published in its original form until 1909. The basic geometrical studies that it embodies, however, led Lobachevsky to his chief discovery—non-Euclidean geometry (now called Lobachevskian geometry)—which he first set out in "Exposition succincte des principes de la géométrie avec une démonstration rigoureuse du théorème des parallèles," and on which he reported to the Kazan department of physics and mathematics at a meeting held on 23 February 1826. His first published work on the subject, "O nachalakh geometrii" ("On the Principles of Geometry"), appeared in the *Kazanski vestnik*, a journal published by the university, in 1829–1830; it comprised the earlier "Exposition."

Some of Lobachevsky's early papers, too, were on such nongeometrical subjects as algebra and the theoretical aspects of infinite series. Thus, in 1834 he published his paper "Algebra ili ischislenie konechnykh" ("Algebra, or Calculus of Finites"), of which most had been composed as early as 1825. The first issue of the *Uchenye zapiski* ("Scientific Memoirs") of Kazan University, founded by Lobachevsky, likewise carried his article "Ob ischezanii trigonometricheskikh strok" ("On the Convergence of Trigonometrical Series"). The chief thrust of his scientific endeavor was, however, geometrical, and his later work was devoted exclusively to his new non-Euclidean geometry.

In 1835 Lobachevsky published a long article, "Voobrazhaemaya geometriya" ("Imaginary Geometry"), in the *Uchenye zapiski*. He also translated it into French for Crelle's *Journal für die reine und angewandte Mathematik*. The following year he published, also in the *Uchenye zapiski*, a continuation of this work, "Primenenie voobrazhaemoi geometrii k nekotorym integralam" ("Application of Imaginary Geometry to Certain Integrals"). The same period, from 1835 to 1838, also saw him concerned with writing *Novye nachala geometrii s polnoi teoriei parallelnykh* ("New Principles of Geometry With a Complete Theory of Parallels"), which incorporated a version of his first work, the still unpublished *Geometriya*. The last two chapters of the book were abbreviated and translated for publication in Crelle's *Journal* in 1842. *Geometrische Untersuchungen zur Theorie der Parallellinien*, which he published in Berlin in 1840, is the best exposition of his new geometry; following its publication, in 1842, Lobachevsky was, on the recommendation of Gauss, elected to the Göttingen Gesellschaft der Wissenschaften.

His last work, *Pangéométrie*, was published in Kazan in 1855–1856.

Lobachevskian Geometry. Lobachevsky's non-Euclidean geometry was the product of some two millennia of criticism of the *Elements*. Geometers had historically been concerned primarily with Euclid's fifth postulate: If a straight line meets two other straight lines so as to make the two interior angles on one side of the former together less than two right angles, then the latter straight lines will meet if produced on that side on which the angles are less than two right angles (it must be noted that Euclid understood lines as finite segments). This postulate is equivalent to the statement that given a line and a point not on it, one can draw through the point one and only one coplanar line not intersecting the given line. Throughout the centuries, mathematicians tried to prove the fifth postulate as a theorem either by assuming implicitly an equivalent statement (as did Posidonius, Ptolemy, Proclus, Thābit ibn Qurra, Ibn al-Haytham, Saccheri, and Legendre) or by directly substituting a more obvious postulate for it (as did al-Khayyāmī, al-Ṭūsī, and Wallis).

In his early lectures on geometry, Lobachevsky himself attempted to prove the fifth postulate; his own geometry is derived from his later insight that a geometry in which all of Euclid's axioms except the fifth postulate hold true is not in itself contradictory. He called such a system "imaginary geometry," proceeding from an analogy with imaginary numbers. If imaginary numbers are the most general numbers for which the laws of arithmetic of real numbers prove justifiable, then imaginary geometry is the most general geometrical system. It was Lobachevsky's merit to refute the uniqueness of Euclid's geometry, and to consider it as a special case of a more general system.

In Lobachevskian geometry, given a line *a* and a point *A* not on it (see Fig. 1), one can draw through *A* more than one coplanar line not intersecting *a*. It

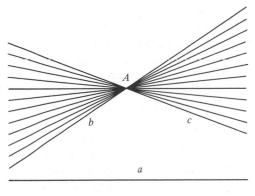

FIGURE 1

follows that one can draw infinitely many such lines which, taken together, constitute an angle of which the vertex is *A*. The two lines, *b* and *c*, bordering that angle are called parallels to *a*, and the lines contained between them are called ultraparallels, or diverging lines; all other lines through *A* intersect *a*. If one measures the distance between two parallel lines on a secant equally inclined to each, then, as Lobachevsky proved, that distance decreases indefinitely, tending to zero, as one moves farther out from *A*. Consequently, when representing Lobachevskian parallels in the Euclidean plane, one often draws them conventionally as asymptotic curves (see Fig. 2). The

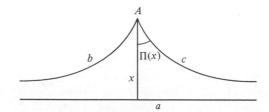

FIGURE 2

angle $\Pi(x)$ between the perpendicular *x* from point *A* to line *a* and a parallel drawn through *A* is a function of *x*. Lobachevsky showed that this function, named after him, can be expressed in elementary terms as

$$\cot \frac{\Pi(x)}{2} = e^x;$$

clearly, $\Pi(0) = \pi/2$, and, for $x > 0$, $\Pi(x) < \pi/2$. Lobachevsky later proved that the distance between two diverging lines, where distance is again measured on a secant equally inclined to each, tends to infinity as one moves farther out from *A*; the distance has a minimum value when the secant is perpendicular to each line, and this perpendicular secant is unique.

A comparison of Euclidean and Lobachevskian geometry yields several immediate and interesting contrasts. In the latter, the sum of the angles of the right triangle of which the vertices are the point *A*, the foot of the perpendicular *x* on *a*, and a point on *a* situated at such a distance from *x* that the hypotenuse of the triangle lies close to a parallel through *A* is evidently less than two right angles. Lobachevsky proved that indeed for all triangles in the Lobachevskian plane the sum of the angles is less than two right angles.

In addition to pencils of intersecting lines and pencils of parallel lines, which are common to both the Euclidean and Lobachevskian planes, the latter also contains pencils of diverging lines, which consist of all perpendiculars to the same line. In both planes,

the circle is the orthogonal trajectory of a pencil of intersecting lines, but the orthogonal trajectories of the other pencils differ in the Lobachevskian plane. That of a pencil of parallel lines (see Fig. 3) is called

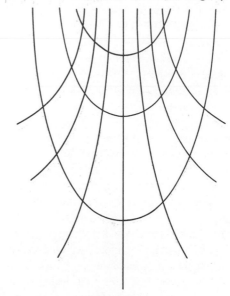

FIGURE 3

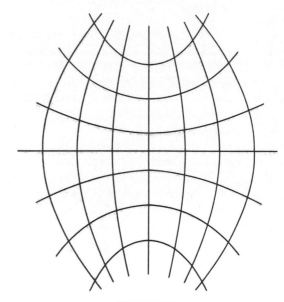

FIGURE 4

a horocycle, or limit circle; as the name implies, it is the curve toward which the circular trajectory of a pencil of intersecting lines tends as the intersection point tends to infinity. The orthogonal trajectory of a pencil of diverging lines (see Fig. 4) is called an equidistant, or hypercycle; it is the locus of points of the Lobachevskian plane that are equally distant from the common perpendicular of the diverging lines in the pencil, and this perpendicular is called the base of the equidistant.

On the basis of these orthogonal trajectories, Lobachevsky also constructed a space geometry. By rotating the circle, the horocycle, and the equidistant about one of the orthogonal lines, he obtained, respectively, a sphere, a horosphere (or limit sphere), and an equidistant surface, the last being the locus of the points of space equally distant from a plane. Although geometry on the sphere does not differ from that of Euclidean space, the geometry on each of the two sheets of the equidistant surface is that of the Lobachevskian plane, the geometry on the horosphere that of the Euclidean plane.

Working from the geometry (and, hence, trigonometry) of the Euclidean plane on horospheres, Lobachevsky derived trigonometric formulas for triangles in the Lobachevskian plane. In modern terms these formulas are:

$$\cosh\frac{a}{q} = \cosh\frac{b}{q}\cosh\frac{c}{q} - \sinh\frac{b}{q}\sinh\frac{c}{q}\cos A,$$

$$\frac{\sinh\dfrac{a}{q}}{\sin A} = \frac{\sinh\dfrac{b}{q}}{\sin B} = \frac{\sinh\dfrac{c}{q}}{\sin C},$$

$$\cos A = -\cos B\cos C + \sin B\sin C\cosh\frac{a}{q}, \quad (1)$$

where q is a certain constant of the Lobachevskian plane.

Comparing these formulas with those of spherical trigonometry on a sphere of radius r, that is,

$$\cos\frac{a}{r} = \cos\frac{b}{r}\cos\frac{c}{r} + \sin\frac{b}{r}\sin\frac{c}{r}\cos A,$$

$$\frac{\sin\dfrac{a}{r}}{\sin A} = \frac{\sin\dfrac{b}{r}}{\sin B} = \frac{\sin\dfrac{c}{r}}{\sin C},$$

$$\cos A = -\cos B\cos C + \sin B\sin C\cos\frac{a}{r}, \quad (2)$$

Lobachevsky discovered that the formulas of trigonometry in the space he defined can be derived from formulas of spherical trigonometry if the sides a, b, c of triangles are regarded as purely imaginary numbers or, put another way, if the radius r of the sphere is considered as purely imaginary. Indeed, (2) is transformed into (1) if it is supposed that $r = qi$ and the correlations $\cos ix = \cosh x$ and $\sin ix = \sinh x$ are employed. In this Lobachevsky saw evidence of the noncontradictory nature of the geometry he had discovered. This idea can be made quite rigorous by introducing imaginary points of Euclidean space, producing the so-called complex Euclidean space; defining in that space the sphere of purely imaginary radius; and considering a set of points on that sphere that have real rectangular coordinates x and y and purely imaginary coordinate z. (Such a set of points

in the complex Euclidean space was first considered in 1908 by H. Minkowski, in connection with Einstein's special principle of relativity; it is now called pseudo-Euclidean space.) The sphere of the imaginary radius in this space thus appears to be a hyperboloid of two sheets, each of which is a model of the Lobachevskian plane, while construction of this model proves it to be noncontradictory in nature.

Lobachevskian geometry is further analogous to spherical geometry. The area of triangle S in Lobachevsky's plane is expressed through its angles (in radian measure) by the formula

$$S = q^2(\pi - A - B - C), \quad (3)$$

whereas the area of spherical triangle S is expressed through its angles (by the same measure) as

$$S = r^2(A + B + C - \pi). \quad (4)$$

Formula (3) is transformed into formula (4) if $r = qi$.

Lines of the Lobachevskian plane are represented on the sphere of imaginary radius of the pseudo-Euclidean space by sections with planes through the center of the sphere. Intersecting lines can then be represented by sections with planes intersecting on a line of purely imaginary length; parallel lines by sections with planes intersecting on lines of zero length (isotropic lines); and diverging lines by sections with planes intersecting on lines of real length. Circles, horocycles, and equidistants of the Lobachevskian plane are represented by sections of the sphere of imaginary radius with planes that do not pass through its center.

If the sides a, b, c of the triangle are very small or the numbers q and r very large, it is necessary to consider only the first members in the series

$$\cosh x = 1 + \frac{x^2}{2} + \frac{x^4}{4!} + \cdots,$$

$$\sinh x = x = \frac{x^3}{3!} + \frac{x^5}{5!} + \cdots,$$

$$\cos x = 1 - \frac{x^2}{2} + \frac{x^4}{4!} - + \cdots,$$

$$\sin x = x - \frac{x^3}{3!} + \frac{x^5}{5!} - + \cdots. \quad (5)$$

If it is assumed for formulas (1) and (2), above, that $\sinh x = x$ and $\cosh x = \cos x = 1$, $\sin x = x$ or $\cosh x = 1 + \dfrac{x^2}{2}$ and $\cos x = 1 - \dfrac{x^2}{2}$, these formulas become

$$a^2 = b^2 + c^2 - 2bc\cos A,$$

$$\frac{a}{\sin A} = \frac{b}{\sin B} = \frac{c}{\sin C},$$

$$A + B + C = \pi, \quad (6)$$

in the Euclidean plane. Euclidean geometry may then be considered as a limiting case of both spherical and Lobachevskian geometry as r and q tend to infinity, or as a particular case for $r = q = \infty$. In analogy to the number $\frac{1}{r^2}$, which represents the curvature of the sphere, the number $-\frac{1}{q^2}$ is called the curvature of the Lobachevskian plane; the constant q is called the radius of curvature of this plane.

Lobachevsky recognized the universal character of his new geometry in naming it "pangeometry." He nevertheless thought it necessary to establish experimentally which geometry—his or Euclid's— actually occurs in the real world. To this end he made a series of calculations of the sums of the angles of triangles of which the vertices are two diametrically opposed points on the orbit of the earth and one of the fixed stars Sirius, Rigel, or 28 Eridani. Having established that the deviation of these sums from π is no greater than might be due to errors in observation, he concluded that the geometry of the real world might be considered as Euclidean, whence he also found "a rigorous proof of the theorem of parallels" as set out in his work of 1826. In explaining his calculations (in "O nachalakh geometrii" ["On the Principles of Geometry"]), Lobachevsky noted that it is possible to find experimentally the deviation from π of the sum of the angles of cosmic triangles of great size; in a later work (*Novye nachala geometrii s polnoi teoriei parallelnykh* ["New Principles of Geometry With a Complete Theory of Parallels"]) he moved to the opposite scale and suggested that his geometry might find application in the "intimate sphere of molecular attractions."

In his earlier papers Lobachevsky had defined imaginary geometry on an a priori basis, beginning with the supposition that Euclid's fifth postulate does not hold true and explaining the principle tenets of his new geometry without defining it (although he did describe the results of his experiment to prove his theorem of parallels). In "Voobrazhaemaya geometriya" ("Imaginary Geometry"), however, he built up the new geometry analytically, proceeding from its inherent trigonometrical formulas and considering the derivation of these formulas from spherical trigonometry to guarantee its internal consistency. In the sequel to that paper, "Primenenie voobrazhaemoi geometrii k nekotorym integralam" ("Application of Imaginary Geometry to Certain Integrals"), he applied geometrical considerations in Lobachevskian space to the calculation of known integrals (in order to make sure that their application led to valid results), then to new, previously uncalculated integrals.

In *Novye nachala geometrii s polnoi teoriei par-*

allelnykh ("New Principles of Geometry With a Complete Theory of Parallels"), Lobachevsky, after criticizing various demonstrations of the fifth postulate, went on to develop the idea of a geometry independent of the fifth postulate, an idea presented in his earliest *Geometriya* (of which a considerable portion was encompassed in the later work). The last two chapters of the book—on the solution of triangles, on given measurements, and on probable errors in calculation—were connected with his attempts to establish experimentally what sort of geometry obtains in the real world. Lobachevsky's last two books, *Geometrische Untersuchungen* and *Pangéométrie*, represent summaries of his previous geometrical work. The former dealt with the elements of the new geometry, while the latter applied differential and integral calculus to it.

At the same time as Lobachevsky, other geometers were making similar discoveries. Gauss had arrived at an idea of non-Euclidean geometry in the last years of the eighteenth century and had for several decades continued to study the problems that such an idea presented. He never published his results, however, and these became known only after his death and the publication of his correspondence. Jànos Bolyai, the son of Gauss's university comrade Farkas Bolyai, hit upon Lobachevskian geometry at a slightly later date than Lobachevsky; he explained his discovery in an appendix to his father's work that was published in 1832. (Since Gauss did not publish his work on the subject, and since Bolyai published only at a later date, Lobachevsky clearly holds priority.)

It may be observed that Lobachevsky's works in other areas of mathematics were either directly relevant to his geometry (as his calculations on definite integrals and probable errors of observation) or results of his studies of foundations of mathematics (as his works on the theory of finites and the theory of trigonometric series). His work on these problems again for the most part paralleled that of other European mathematicians. It is, for example, worth noting that in his algebra Lobachevsky suggested a method of separating roots of equations by their repeated squaring, a method coincident with that suggested by Dandelin in 1826 and by Gräffe in 1837. His paper on the convergence of trigonometric series, too, suggested a general definition of function like that proposed by Dirichlet in 1837. (Lobachevsky also gave a rigorous definition of continuity and differentiability, and pointed out the difference between these notions.)

Recognition of Lobachevskian Geometry. Lobachevsky's work was little heralded during his lifetime. M. V. Ostrogradsky, the most famous mathematician of the St. Petersburg Academy, for one, did not understand Lobachevsky's achievement, and published an uncomplimentary review of "O nachalakh geometrii" ("On the Principles of Geometry"); the magazine *Syn otechestva* soon followed his lead, and in 1834 issued a pamphlet ridiculing Lobachevsky's paper. Although Gauss, who had received a copy of the *Geometrische Untersuchungen* from Lobachevsky, spoke to him flatteringly of the book, studied Russian especially to read his works in their original language, and supported his election to the Göttingen Gesellschaft der Wissenschaften, he never publicly commented on Lobachevsky's discovery. His views on the new geometry became clear only after the publication, in 1860–1865, of his correspondence with H. C. Schumacher. Following this, in 1865, the English algebraist Cayley (who had himself paved the way for the theory of projective metrics in 1859 with his "Sixth Memoir Upon Quantics") brought out his "A Note Upon Lobachevsky's Imaginary Geometry," from which it is evident that he also failed to understand Lobachevsky's work.

The cause of Lobachevskian geometry was, however, furthered by Hoüel, one of its earliest proponents, who in 1866 brought out a French translation of *Geometrische Untersuchungen*, with appended extracts from the Gauss-Schumacher correspondence. The following year he also published Bolyai's appendix on non-Euclidean geometry, which was translated into Italian by Battaglini in 1867. Hoüel's own *Notices sur la vie et les travaux de N. I. Lobachevsky* appeared in 1870. In the meantime, Lobachevsky's *Geometrische Untersuchungen* had been translated into Russian by A. V. Letnikov; it was published in 1868 in the newly founded Moscow magazine *Matematichesky sbornik*, together with Letnikov's article "O teorii parallelnykh linii N. I. Lobachevskogo" ("On the Theory of Parallel Lines by N. I. Lobachevsky").

These translations and reviews were soon augmented by extensions of Lobachevskian geometry itself. In 1858 Beltrami published in the *Giornale di matematiche* his "Saggio di interpretazione della geometria non-euclidea," in which he established that the intrinsic geometry of the pseudosphere and other surfaces of constant negative curvature coincides with the geometry of part of the Lobachevskian plane and that an interpretation of the whole Lobachevskian plane can be constructed in the interior of a circle in the Euclidean plane. This interpretation can be derived by projecting a hemisphere of imaginary radius in pseudo-Euclidean space from its center onto a Euclidean plane tangent to this hemisphere. The article was translated into French by Hoüel in 1869 for publication in the *Annales scientifiques de l'École Normale Supérieure*.

In 1870 Weierstrass led a seminar on Lobachevsky's geometry at the University of Berlin; the young Felix Klein was one of the participants. Weierstrass' own contribution to the subject, the so-called Weierstrass coordinates, are essentially rectangular coordinates of a point on a hemisphere of imaginary radius in pseudo-Euclidean space. Klein compared Lobachevskian geometry with Cayley's projective metrics to establish that Lobachevsky's geometry is in fact one of Cayley's geometries, which Cayley himself (although he was acquainted with Lobachevskian geometry) had failed to notice. The Lobachevskian plane can be regarded as the interior domain of a conic section on a projective plane; when this conic section is a circle, representation of the Lobachevskian plane on the projective plane coincides with Beltrami's interpretation. It thus follows that motions of the Lobachevskian plane are represented in Beltrami's interpretation by projective transformations of the plane mapping a circle into itself. Lines of the Lobachevskian plane are represented in Beltrami's interpretation by chords of the circle, while parallel lines are represented by chords intersecting on the circumference, and diverging lines by non-intersecting chords. There are analogous interpretations for three-dimensional and multidimensional Lobachevskian spaces, in which Beltrami's circle or Klein's conic section is replaced by a sphere or oval quadric, e.g., ellipsoid.

Poincaré made two important contributions to Lobachevskian geometry at somewhat later dates. In 1882 he suggested an interpretation of the Lobachevskian plane in terms of a Euclidean semiplane; in this intrepretation, motions of the Lobachevskian plane are represented by inversive transformations, mapping the border of the semiplane into itself, while Lobachevskian lines are mapped by perpendiculars to this border or by semicircles with centers on it. An important property of this interpretation is that angles in the Lobachevskian plane are mapped conformally. Taking as given that inversive transformations on the plane are represented as fractional linear functions of a complex variable, Poincaré used such an interpretation for the theory of automorphic functions.

Poincaré's interpretation is often described in other terms, as when a semiplane is mapped by inversive transformation into the interior of a circle. An interpretation in terms of the circle can also be presented by projecting the hemisphere of imaginary radius in pseudo-Euclidean space from one of its points onto the Euclidean plane perpendicular to the radius through this point. This projection is analogous to stereographic projection, through which the preservation of angles in Poincaré's interpretation is explained. In 1887 Poincaré suggested a second interpretation of the Lobachevskian plane, this one in terms of a two-sheeted hyperboloid coinciding with that on the hemisphere of imaginary radius as already defined.

A further important development of Lobachevsky's geometry came from Riemann, whose address of 1854, *Uber die Hypothesen, welche der Geometrie zu Grundliegen*, was published in 1866. Developing Gauss's idea of intrinsic geometry of a surface, Riemann presented a notion of multidimensional curved space (now called Riemannian space). Riemannian space of constant positive curvature (often called Riemannian elliptic space) is represented by the geometry on a sphere in fourth-dimensional or multidimensional Euclidean space or in the space with a projective metric in which an imaginary quadric plays the part of a conic section (or Klein's quadric). It subsequently, then, became clear that Lobachevskian space (often called hyperbolic space) is the Riemannian space of constant negative curvature. It was with this in mind that Klein, in his memoir of 1871, "Über die sogenannte nicht-euklidische Geometrie," chose to consider all three geometries—Euclidean, elliptic, and hyperbolic—from a single standpoint, whereby groups of motions of all three are subgroups of the group of projective transformations of projective space.

Here the extension of the concept of space, which was introduced by Lobachevsky and Riemann, merges with the concept of group, which was introduced by Galois, a synthesis that Klein developed further in 1872 in *Vergleichende Betrachtungen über neuere geometrische Forschungen* (also known as the *Erlanger Programm*) in which he arrived at a general view of various geometries as theories of invariants of various continuous groups of transformations. A new stage in the development of mathematics thus began, one in which the mathematics of antiquity and the Middle Ages (that is, the mathematics of constant magnitudes) and the mathematics of early modern times (that is, the mathematics of variable magnitudes) were replaced by modern mathematics—the mathematics of many geometries, of many algebras, and of many mathematical systems having no classical analogues. A number of these systems found applications in modern physics—pseudo-Euclidean geometry, one of the projective metrics, figures in the special theory of relativity; Riemannian geometry appears in the general theory of relativity; and group theory is significant to quantum physics.

The presence of specifically Lobachevskian geometry is felt in modern physics in the isomorphism of the group of motions of Lobachevskian space and the Lorentz group. This isomorphism opens the possibility of applying Lobachevskian geometry to the solution of a number of problems of relativist quantum physics. Within the framework of the general theory of relativity, the problem of the geometry of the real world, to which Lobachevsky had devoted so much attention, was solved; the geometry of the real world is that of variable curvature, which is on the average much closer to Lobachevsky's than to Euclid's.

BIBLIOGRAPHY

I. Original Works. Lobachevsky's writings have been brought together in *Polnoe sobranie sochinenii* ("Complete Works"), 5 vols. (Moscow–Leningrad, 1946–1951): vols. I–III, geometrical works; vol. IV, algebraical works; vol. V, works on analysis, the theory of probability, mechanics, and astronomy. His geometrical works were also collected as *Polnoe sobranie sochinenii po geometrii* ("Complete Geometrical Works"), 2 vols. (Kazan, 1883–1886): vol. I, works in Russian; vol. II, works in French and German.

Translations include J. Houël, *Études géométriques sur la théorie des parallèles* (Paris, 1866; 2nd ed., 1900); G. B. Halsted, *Geometrical Researches on the Theory of Parallels*, Neomonic ser. no. 4 (Austin, Tex., 1892; repr. Chicago–London, 1942); and *New Principles of Geometry With Complete Theory of Parallels*, Neomonic ser. no. 5 (Austin, Tex., 1897); F. Engel, *Zwei geometrische Abhandlungen* (Leipzig, 1898); F. Mallieux, *Nouveaux principes de la géométrie avec une théorie complète des parallèles* (Brussels, 1901); and H. Liebmann, *Imaginäre Geometrie und Anwendungen der imaginären Geometrie auf einige Integrale* (Leipzig, 1904).

II. Secondary Literature. Among works on Lobachevsky are the following: A. A. Andronov, "Gde i kogda rodilsya N. I. Lobachevsky?" ("Where and When Was Lobachevsky born?"), in *Istoriko-matematicheskie issledovaniya*, **9** (1956); R. Bonola, *La geometria non-euclidea: Esposizione storico-critico del suo sviluppo* (Bologna, 1906); translated into German as *Die nicht-euklidische Geometrie. Historisch-kritische Darstellung ihrer Entwicklung*, 3rd ed. (Leipzig, 1921); translated into Russian as *Neevklidova geometriya. Kritiko-istoricheskoe issledovanie e razvitiya* (St. Petersburg, 1910); translated into English as *Non-Euclidean Geometry. A Critical and Historical Study of Its Developments* (New York, 1955); J. L. Coolidge, *The Elements of Non-Euclidean Geometry* (Oxford, 1909); H. S. M. Coxeter, *Non-Euclidean Geometry*, 3rd ed. (Toronto, 1957); V. M. Gerasimova, *Ukazatel literatury po geometrii Lobachevskogo i razvitiyu e idei* ("A Guide to Studies on Lobachevskian Geometry and the Development of Its Ideas"; Moscow, 1952); B. V. Gnedenko, "O rabotakh N. I. Lobachevskogo po teorii veroyatnostei" ("On Lobachevsky's Works on the Calculus of Probabilities"), in *Istoriko-matematicheskie issledovaniya*, **2** (1949); N. I. Idelson, "Lobachevskii-astronom" ("Lobachevsky as an Astronomer"), *ibid*.

Also of value are V. F. Kagan, *Lobachevsky*, 2nd ed. (Moscow–Leningrad, 1948); and *Osnovaniya geometrii* ("Foundations of Geometry"), 2 vols. (I, Moscow–Leningrad, 1949; II, Moscow, 1956); E. K. Khilkevich, "Iz istorii rasprostraneniya i razvitiya idei N. I. Lobachevskogo v 60-70-kh godakh XIX stoletiya" ("The History of the Spread and Development of N. I. Lobachevsky's Ideas in the 60th to 70th Years of the Nineteenth Century"), in *Istoriko-matematicheskie issledovaniya*, **2** (1949); F. Klein, *Vorlesungen über nichteuklidische Geometrie*, 3rd ed. (Berlin, 1928), also translated into Russian as *Neevklidova geometriya* (Moscow–Leningrad, 1936); B. L. Laptev, "Teoriya parallelnykh pryamykh v rannikh rabotakh Lobachevskogo" ("Theory of Parallel Lines in Lobachevsky's Early Works"), in *Istoriko-matematicheskie issledovaniya*, **4** (1951); H. Liebmann, *Nicht-euclidische Geometrie*, 3rd ed. (Berlin, 1923); G. L. Luntz, "O rabotakh N. I. Lobachevskogo po matematicheskomu analizu" ("On N. I. Lobachevsky's Work in Mathematical Analysis"), in *Istoriko-matematicheskie issledovaniya*, **2** (1949); M. B. Modzalevsky, *Materialy dlya biografii N. I. Lobachevskogo* ("Materials for N. I. Lobachevsky's Biography"; Moscow–Leningrad, 1948); V. V. Morozov, "Ob algebraicheskikh rukopisyakh N. I. Lobachevskogo" ("On Algebraic Manuscripts of N. I. Lobachevsky"), in *Istoriko-matematicheskie issledovaniya*, **4** (1951); and A. P. Norden, ed., *Ob osnovaniyakh geometrii. Sbornik klassicheskikh rabot po geometrii Lobachevskogo i razvitiyu e idei* ("On Foundations of Geometry. Collection of Classic Works on Lobachevskian Geometry and the Development of Its Ideas"; Moscow, 1956).

See also B. A. Rosenfeld, *Neevklidovy geometrii* (Moscow, 1955); "Interpretacii geometrii Lobachevskogo" ("Interpretations of Lobachevskian Geometry"), in *Istoriko-matematicheskie issledovaniya*, **9** (1956); and *Neevklidovy prostranstva* ("Non-Euclidean Spaces"; Moscow, 1968); D. M. Y. Sommerville, *Bibliography of Non-Euclidean Geometry* (London, 1911); and *The Elements of Non-Euclidean Geometry* (London, 1914); S. A. Yanovskaya, "O mirovozzrenii N. I. Lobachevskogo" ("On N. I. Lobachevsky's Outlook"), in *Istoriko-matematicheskie issledovaniya*, **4** (1951); and A. P. Youschkevitch and I. G. Bashmakova, " 'Algebra ili vychislenie konechnykh' N. I. Lobachevskogo" (" 'Algebra or Calculus of Finites' by N. I. Lobachevsky"), in *Istoriko-matematicheskie issledovaniya*, **2** (1949).

B. A. ROSENFELD

L'OBEL (or **LOBEL**), **MATHIAS DE** (*b*. Lille, France, 1538; *d*. Highgate, near London, England, 3 March 1616), *botany*.

L'Obel's name is ingeniously alluded to in the coat of arms on his books: two poplar trees (in French "aubel" means "abele," or "white poplar") constitute part of the design. Few details of his life are known. He seems to have had a powerful personality—rough, violent, passionate, tireless—worthy of a leader among the sixteenth-century restorers of learning. At the age of sixteen he was already attracted to botany and materia medica. According to Édouard Morren

he undoubtedly practiced medicine, although there is no known evidence that he ever received a medical degree. In 1565 (he was then twenty-seven) he became the favorite student of Guillaume Rondelet, professor at the University of Montpellier. There he met Jacques Uitenhove of Ghent, and a young Provençal, Pierre Pena, who became his friend, his companion in study and in botanizing, and his collaborator.

It is very probable that at their first meeting Rondelet discerned L'Obel's intellectual superiority, for at his death, on 20 July 1566, he bequeathed the latter all his botanical manuscripts. L'Obel then spent three more years in Montpellier, writing a book with Pierre Pena, which appeared in 1570 (or 1571) under the title *Stirpium adversaria nova*. Although one may criticize L'Obel's inelegant, even barbarous, Latin, this work is nevertheless one of the milestones of modern botany. A collection of notes and data on 1,200–1,300 plants that he himself had gathered and observed in the vicinity of Montpellier, in the Cévennes, in the Low Countries, and in England, it also furnished precise information on other subjects, including the making of beer and the cultivation of exotic plants and of chicory.

L'Obel held that the thorough and exact observation of men and things constituted the basis of the two sciences that interested him: medicine and botany. This conviction is clearly evident in his book. Before contemporary botanists he divided the plants into groups according to the form of their leaves (whole, divided, more or less compound). It seems that he had an inkling of natural families and that he attempted to use, if not the terms, at least the concepts of genus and family.

The second edition of *Adversaria* (1576) was published with an appendix including many engravings larger than those in the 1571 edition. *Stirpium observationes*, a sort of complement to the *Adversaria*, was joined to it under the title *Plantarum seu stirpium historia* (1576). In 1581, Christophe Plantin published *Kruydtboeck*, a Flemish translation of the *Stirpium*, and, in a separate volume, the illustrations that L'Obel prefaced with a brief table—"Elenchus plantarum fere congenerum"—which presented the plants according to affinities. Linnaeus subsequently used the table in his *Species plantarum*.

Finding it impossible to work in a country torn by civil war, L'Obel left the Low Countries, where he had been living since 1571, following the assassination of William of Orange in July 1584. He went to England, his wife's native country, where he remained for the rest of his life.

Despite his conceit and unpolished language, which earned him many enemies (he was involved in an unfortunate dispute with Mattioli), L'Obel was one of the great pre-Linnaean botanists. His name was perpetuated by Plumier, who in 1702 dedicated to him the genus *Lobelia*—which Linnaeus later called *Scaevola*, at the same time giving the name "Lobelia" to a genus of aquatic plant.

BIBLIOGRAPHY

I. Original Works. L'Obel's first work was *Stirpium adversaria nova* (London, 1570), written with Pierra Pena; the colophon is dated 1571, and the work may have been printed at Antwerp by Plantin. *Plantarum seu stirpium historia*, 2 vols. (Antwerp, 1576), comprising the 2nd ed. of *Adversaria* together with *Stirpium observationes*, contained 1,486 engravings, most of which are not original. *Kruydtboeck* (Antwerp, 1581), a Flemish trans. of *Stirpium historia*, was followed the same year by *Icones stirpium*, a 2-vol. work printed at Antwerp that included the "Elenchus" and all engravings published to date; a 2nd ed. appeared in 1591. *Balsami, opobalsami, carpobalsami et xylobalsami* (London, 1598) was followed by a new ed. of the *Adversaria* entitled *Dilucidae simplicium medicamentorum explicationes et stirpium adversaria* (London, 1605) that included several new treatises. *Stirpium illustrationes* was published posthumously (London, 1655).

II. Secondary Literature. On L'Obel and his work, see B. C. Dumortier, "Discours sur les services rendus par les belges à la botanique," in *Bulletin. Société r. de botanique de Belgique*, **1** (1862), 16; L. Legré, *La botanique en Provence au XVIe siècle*, I, *Pierre Pena et Mathias de Lobel* (Marseilles, 1899); C. F. A. Morren, "Prologue à la mémoire de L'Obel," in *Belgique horticole*, **2** (1852), v–xviii; C. J. É. Morren, *Mathias de L'Obel. Sa vie et ses oeuvres* (Liége, 1875); and J. É. Planchon, *Rondelet et ses disciples* (Montpellier, 1866).

J. C. Mallet
P. Jovet

LOCKE, JOHN (*b.* Wrington, Somersetshire, England, 29 August 1632; *d.* Oates, Essex, England, 28 October 1704), *philosophy*.

John Locke was the most important British philosopher of the Age of Reason. If the modern Western world has been shaped by scientists, merchants, statesmen, and industrialists, Locke was the first philosopher to expound their view of life, articulate their aspirations, and justify their deeds. No philosopher has exercised a greater influence. Yet it could be said that Locke was not a philosopher at all; he was certainly not a metaphysician in the same sense as his contemporaries Leibniz or Spinoza. Locke offered no all-embracing system to explain the nature of the universe. On the contrary, he tried to show that human understanding is so limited that such comprehensive knowledge is beyond man's reach. Although he did not have the answers to the philosophical problems he formulated, Locke was able to establish the importance of science as an object of philosophical analysis.

Two powerful streams in seventeenth-century thought, the semiskeptical rational theorizing of Descartes and the *ad hoc* scientific experimentation of Bacon and the Royal Society, merged in Locke. Because the streams were so different, their union was imperfect, but his mind was the meeting point that marked a new beginning, not only in theoretical philosophy, but in man's approach to the problems of practical life. Locke, one might almost say, had the first modern mind. Descartes was still in many ways a medieval thinker, with his philosophy bound to theology; and even Gassendi, who anticipated much of Locke, did not free himself completely from its hold. By divorcing philosophy from theology, Locke placed the study of philosophy within the boundaries of man's experience: "Our portion," he wrote, "lies only here in this little spot of earth, where we and all our concernments are shut up."

Yet Locke was not an atheist, and in his capacity as theologian he expounded his own thoughts about God. He quarreled with bishops and with the orthodox of most denominations. He maintained that a Christian need believe no more than the single proposition "that Christ is the Messiah"; but to that minimal creed he clung with the firmest assurance. He had a quiet and steady faith in the immortality of the soul and in the prospect of happiness in the life to come. He had no belief in miracles and no patience with people who had mystical experiences or visions of God. He detested religious enthusiasm, but in an unemotional way he was, like Newton, a deeply religious man.

Locke was born at Wrington, Somersetshire, in western England. His grandfather, Nicholas Locke, was a successful clothier in that county. His father, also named John Locke, was a less prosperous lawyer and clerk to the local magistrates. Baptized by Samuel Crook, a leading Calvinist intellectual, Locke was brought up in an atmosphere of austerity and discipline. He was ten when the Civil War broke out, and his father was mounted as a captain of Parliamentary horse by Alexander Popham, a rich local magistrate-turned-colonel. Apart from demolishing some images in Wells Cathedral, the two officers saw little action, but a grateful Popham became the patron of his captain's eldest son. A few years later, when Westminster School was taken over by the Parliament, Popham found a place for his protégé in what was then the best boarding school in the country.

At Westminster, Locke came under the influence of the Royalist headmaster Richard Busby, whom the Parliamentary governors had imprudently allowed to remain in charge of the school. Locke left Westminster in 1652 to become an undergraduate at Christ Church, Oxford, where he once again came under Puritan influence. Although he did not wholly enjoy the university, he received the M.A. degree and was appointed to a teaching position, lecturing on such subjects as natural law, although he was more interested in medicine.

In the summer of 1666 Locke became friends with Anthony Ashley Cooper, then Lord Ashley and later the first earl of Shaftesbury. Although not yet the leader of a party, Shaftesbury was already the outstanding politician of liberalism and the most forceful champion of religious toleration. In 1667, at the age of thirty-four, Locke went to live at Shaftesbury's house in London. His Oxford career had not been particularly distinguished: he had been a temporary lecturer and a censor at Christ Church; he had become friends with Robert Boyle, one of the founders of the Royal Society, and helped him by collecting scientific data; and he had studied medicine. But he had done no important laboratory work and had failed to get a medical degree. Even so, it was as a domestic physician that Locke entered Shaftesbury's household, and he soon proved himself an able doctor by saving his patron's life (as Shaftesbury believed) when it was threatened by a suppurating cyst of the liver. Convinced that Locke was far too great a genius to be spending his time on medicine alone, Shaftesbury encouraged other pursuits, and under his patronage Locke discovered his own capabilities.

Locke first became a philosopher. At Oxford he had been, like Hobbes before him, bored and dissatisfied with the medieval Aristotelian philosophy that was taught there. Through Descartes, Locke became acquainted with the "new philosophy," and discussions with Shaftesbury and other London friends led him to write, in his fourth year under Shaftesbury's roof, the earliest drafts of his masterpiece, *An Essay Concerning Human Understanding*. In London, Locke also met the physician Thomas Sydenham, who introduced him to the new clinical method that he had learned at Montpellier. Shaftesbury himself introduced Locke to the study of economics and gave him his earliest experience in political administration.

Locke stayed with Shaftesbury intermittently until the latter's death in 1683. In those fifteen years Shaftesbury's Protestant zeal carried him to the point of organizing a rebellion over the Catholic James's legitimate right of succession. But the plot was nipped, and Shaftesbury withdrew to Holland,

where he died a month later. Locke followed the example of Shaftesbury and fled to Holland, remaining in exile until William of Orange invaded England in 1688 and reclaimed the country for Protestantism and liberty. Locke returned to England in 1689 and devoted his remaining fifteen years to scholarship and public service.

While in Holland, Locke had completed *An Essay Concerning Human Understanding* and his first *Letter for Toleration* and may have done some work on his *Civil Government*. The *Letter for Toleration* was published in Locke's original Latin at Gouda in 1689 and an English translation made by the Socinian William Popple—"without my privity" Locke later said—was published in London a few months later. The *Essay* and the *Civil Government* were also brought out by various London booksellers in the winter of 1689–1690. Only the *Essay* bore Locke's name, but its success was so great that he became famous throughout Europe.

In the "Epistle to the Reader," which begins the *Essay*, Locke says that in an age of such "master builders" as Boyle, Sydenham, Huygens, and "the incomparable Mr. Newton" it is, for him, "ambition enough to be employed as an under-labourer in clearing the ground a little and removing some of the rubbish that lies in the way of knowledge." Despite this modest explanation of purpose Locke provided, among other things, the first modern philosophy of science, in which the Cartesian "idea" was a recurrent theme. Locke says that we have ideas in our minds not only when we think but when we see, hear, smell, taste, and feel as well. The core of his epistemology is the notion that the objects of perception are not things but ideas derived in part from things in the external world and dependent, to some extent, on our own minds for their existence. Locke defines an "idea" as the "object of the understanding," whether it is a notion, an entity, or an illusion; perception is for him a "species of understanding."

Locke continues his *Essay* with an attack on the currently established opinion that certain ideas are innate. He claims that they have been considered innate only because people cannot remember first having learned them. Locke believed that we are born in total ignorance and that even our theoretical ideas of identity, quantity, and substance are derived from experience. He says that a child gets ideas of black and white, of sweet and bitter before he gets an idea of abstract principles such as identity or impossibility. "The senses at first let in particular ideas, and furnish the yet empty cabinet...." The mind later abstracts these theoretical ideas and so "comes to be furnished with ideas and language, the materials about which to exercise the discursive faculty." In the child's development "the use of reason becomes daily more visible as these materials that give it employment increase."

Locke had thus to defend the assumption that everything which he calls an idea is derived from sensation, although he admits that an idea may also be produced by reflection—"remembering, considering, reasoning." He classifies ideas as simple (those which the mind receives passively) and complex (those produced by the exercise of the mind's own powers). In the chapters on simple ideas he sets out the main lines of his theory of perception. Most people, if asked what it is that they see, smell, hear, taste, or touch, would answer "things," although they might add "but sometimes illusions, chimeras, mirages, which are not real things." They would probably maintain that there are two elements in an act of perception: the observer and the object. Locke differs from this view in two respects. First, he claims that what we perceive is always an idea, as distinct from a thing; second, that there are not two but three elements in perception: the observer, the idea, and the object that the idea represents.

The reasoning that led Locke to this conclusion is not difficult to appreciate. We look at a penny. We are asked to describe it. It is round, brown, and of modest dimensions. But do we really see just this? We think again and realize that more often than not what we see is elliptical, not circular; in some lights it is golden, in others black; close to the eye it is large, seen from afar it is tiny. The actual penny, we are certain, cannot be both circular and elliptical, both golden all over and black all over. So we may be led to agree that there must be something which is the one and something which is the other, something which changes and something which does not change, the elliptical "penny" we see and the real circular penny, or, in Locke's words, the "idea" in the mind of the observer and the material "body" itself.

Today Locke's theory of perception is defended on the basis of the physicist's description of the structure of the universe and the physiologist's description of the mechanism of perception. To a child a penny is something that looks brown, feels warm, and tastes sharp; to the scientist it is a congeries of electrons and protons. The scientist speaks of certain light waves striking the retina of the observer's eye while waves of other kinds strike different nerve terminals, producing those modifications of the nervous system that are called "seeing," "feeling," or "tasting" a penny. Neither the electrons nor the protons, neither the external waves nor the internal modifications are brown or warm or astringent. The scientist then, in a

certain sense, differentiates what Locke called the secondary qualities—color, taste, sound—which Locke said depended on the observer's mind for their existence. At the same time science seems to accept the objective existence of the qualities that Locke called primary and that he thought belonged to material bodies themselves—impenetrability, extension, figure, mobility, and number. Although the language of primary and secondary qualities was used by earlier theorists, it is Locke's analysis of the distinction which makes it of significance both to science and to common sense. Most people would probably agree that they could imagine an object divested one by one of its qualities of taste, smell, and so forth; but they could not imagine a body divested of impenetrability, shape, size, or position in space. A body without primary qualities would not exist at all.

While there is much to be said for Locke's epistemology, it is not without its faults. If we are aware in our perceptual experience only of ideas (which represent objects) and never of objects themselves, there can be no means of knowing what, if anything, is represented by those ideas. The human predicament, according to Locke's account, is that of a man permanently imprisoned in a sort of diving bell, receiving some signals from without and some from within his apparatus but having no means of knowing which, if any, signals come from outside; hence he has no means of testing their authenticity. Man, therefore, cannot have any definite knowledge whatever of the external world.

In later chapters of the *Essay* Locke places an even heavier emphasis on human ignorance. Our knowledge, he says, "is not only limited to the paucity and imperfections of the ideas we have, and which we employ about it," but is still more circumscribed. Our knowledge of identity and diversity in ideas extends only as far as our ideas themselves; our knowledge of their coexistence extends only a little way, because knowledge of any necessary connection between primary and secondary qualities is unattainable. However, with the area of certainty thus diminished, Locke does not deny the possibility of an assurance which falls short of perfect knowledge. We can have probable knowledge, even though we cannot have certain knowledge. Moreover, unlike most of his successors in empiricist philosophy, Locke admits the existence of substance, which he says is somehow present in all objects even though we do not see or feel it. What we see and feel are the primary and secondary qualities, which are propped up by substance. Beyond that the subject must necessarily remain a mystery:

It seems probable to me that the simple ideas we receive from sensation and reflection are the boundaries of our thoughts; beyond which the mind, whatever efforts it would make, is not able to advance one jot, nor can it make any discoveries, when it would pry into the nature and hidden causes of those ideas.

The tone of the *Essay* is at once moral and pragmatic. Its style is homely rather than elegant, its construction informal and even amateurish. The "pursuit of Truth," Locke says, "is a duty we owe to God . . . and a duty we owe also to ourselves"; here utility is at one with piety. Truth, as Locke defines it, is the "proper riches and furniture of the mind," and he does not claim to have added to that stock, but rather to have shown the conditions under which the mind could acquire truth:

> We have no reason to complain that we do not know the nature of the sun or the stars, that the consideration of light itself leaves us in the dark and a thousand other speculations in nature, since, if we knew them, they would be of no solid advantage, nor help to make our lives the happier, they being but the useless employment of idle or over-curious brains. . . .

Locke's theory of knowledge has obvious implications for a theory of morals. The traditional view in Locke's time was that some sort of moral knowledge was innate in the human person. Locke thought otherwise. What God or Nature had given man was a faculty of reason and a sentiment of self-love. Reason in combination with self-love produced morality and could discern the general principles of ethics, or natural law; and self-love should lead men to obey those principles.

For Locke, Christian ethics was natural ethics. The teaching of the New Testament was a means to an end, happiness in this life and in the life to come. Loving one's neighbor and otherwise obeying the precepts of the Saviour was a way to that end. The reason for doing what Christ said was not simply that He had said it, but that by doing it one promoted one's happiness. There was no need to ask why anyone should desire happiness, because all men were impelled by their natural self-love to desire it.

Wrongdoing was thus for Locke a sign of ignorance. People did not always realize that long-term happiness could usually be bought only at the cost of short-term pleasures. Folly drove them to destroy their own well-being. If people were enlightened, if they used their own powers of reason, they would be good; if they were prudent, reflective, calculating, instead of moved by the transitory winds of impulse and emotion, they would have what they most desired. There is perhaps in this system of morals something rather

naïve and commonplace; but Locke was in many ways a very ordinary thinker, inspired by a prophetic common sense.

BIBLIOGRAPHY

I. ORIGINAL WORKS. See H. O. Christopherson, *A Bibliographical Introduction to the Study of John Locke* (Oslo, 1930). Collected editions and selections of Locke's work are *The Works*, 3 vols. (London, 1714), repr. throughout the eighteenth century; *The Works*, Edmund Law, ed., 4 vols. (London, 1777), the best collected ed.; *The Philosophical Works*, J. A. St. John, ed. (1843); and *Locke on Politics, Religion and Education*, M. Cranston, ed. (1965).

Separate works include *Epistola de tolerantia ad clarissimum virum* . . . (Gouda, 1689), English trans. (London, 1689); *Two Treatises of Government* (London, 1690); P. Laslett, ed. (Cambridge, 1960), a critical ed. with original text, intro., and commentary; *An Essay Concerning Human Understanding* (London, 1690), enl. (1694, 1700); A. C. Fraser, ed., 2 vols. (Oxford, 1894), prepared from a collation of 4 eds. published in Locke's lifetime; John W. Yolton, ed. (London–New York, 1961), the best recent text; see also *An Early Draft of Locke's Essay*, R. I. Aaron and J. Gibbs, eds. (Oxford, 1936), prepared from one of three surviving MSS; *A Second Letter Concerning Toleration* (London, 1690); *Some Considerations of the Consequences of the Lowering of Interest, and Raising the Value of Money* (London, 1692); *A Third Letter For Toleration* (London, 1692)—the letters on toleration have been reprinted together several times, see the eds. by A. Millar (London, 1765) and A. Murray (London, 1870); *Some Thoughts Concerning Education* (London, 1693), enl. (London, 1695); R. H. Quick, ed. (London, 1880); the most useful ed. is in James L. Axtell, ed., *Educational Writings* (Cambridge, 1968); *Locke's Travels in France 1675–1679*, J. Lough, ed. (Cambridge, 1953), Locke's French travel diaries published for the first time; *Essays on the Laws of Nature*, W. von Leyden, ed. (Oxford, 1954), an early Latin text found among the Lovelace papers by the editor, who includes a trans. and an intro. of exceptional interest; and *Two Tracts on Government*, Philip Abrams, ed. (Cambridge, 1965), drawn from early MSS.

For Locke's correspondence, see T. Forster, ed., *Original Letters of John Locke, Algernon Sydney and Lord Shaftesbury* (London, 1830); H. Ollion, ed., *Lettres inédites de John Locke* (The Hague, 1912); and B. Rand, ed., *The Correspondence of John Locke and Edward Clarke* (London, 1927). A definitive ed. of Locke's letters is being prepared by E. S. De Beer.

II. SECONDARY LITERATURE. Some bibliographical and critical studies (in chronological order) are Lord King, *The Life of John Locke With Extracts From His Correspondence, Journals and Commonplace Books*, 2 vols. (London, 1829); H. R. F. Bourne, *The Life of John Locke*, 2 vols. (London, 1876), a substantial Victorian work that has not lost its utility despite later discoveries; J. Gibson, *Locke's Theory of Knowledge* (Cambridge, 1917), a useful guide to the *Essay;* S. Lamprecht, *The Moral and Political Philosophy of John Locke* (London, 1918); A. I. Aaron, *John Locke* (Oxford, 1937), the best-known modern commentary on Locke's philosophy; Willmoore Kendall, *John Locke and the Doctrine of Majority Rule* (New Haven, 1941), which depicts Locke as a forerunner of modern progressive democratic ideas; J. W. Gough, *John Locke's Political Philosophy: Eight Studies* (Oxford, 1952), a well-arranged commentary; M. Cranston, *John Locke: A Biography* (London, 1957), largely based on the earl of Lovelace's inherited collection of Locke's MSS acquired by the Bodleian Library, Oxford, in 1948; R. H. Cox, *Locke on War and Peace* (Oxford, 1961), a distinctive reinterpretation that stresses Locke's affinity with Hobbes; C. B. MacPherson, *The Political Theory of Progressive Individualism* (Oxford, 1962), a critique of Marxian inspiration; Martin Seliger, *The Liberal Politics of John Locke* (London, 1968), a defense of the liberal interpretation of Locke's politics; and John W. Yolton, ed., *John Locke: Problems and Perspectives* (Cambridge, 1969), a series of critical essays by English and American scholars.

MAURICE CRANSTON

LOCKYER, JOSEPH NORMAN (*b.* Rugby, England, 17 May 1836; *d.* Salcombe Regis, England, 16 August 1920), *astrophysics.*

Lockyer came from a middle-class family, derived, it was believed, from early Celtic immigrants from France into England. His father, Joseph Hooley Lockyer, was a surgeon-apothecary with broad scientific interests, and his mother, Anne Norman, was a daughter of Edward Norman, the squire of Cosford, Warwickshire. His formal education, at schools in the English Midlands, tended to concentrate on the classics, but the scientific atmosphere at home, supplemented by travel in Switzerland and France, served to broaden his interests and to produce the type of mind that was later to show a marked versatility. His earliest employment was as a civil servant in the English War Office, which he entered in 1857. He remained there until his striking success as an amateur astronomer led, via a period of temporary service as secretary of the duke of Devonshire's commission on scientific instruction, to a permanent post under the Science and Art Department, which culminated in his appointment as director of the Solar Physics Observatory established at South Kensington. There he remained until, in 1911, the observatory was transferred, much to his disappointment, to Cambridge, whereupon he retired.

In 1858 he married Winifred James, who died in 1879, leaving seven children, and in 1903 he married Thomasine Mary, the younger daughter of S. Woolcott

Browne and widow of Bernhard E. Brodhurst, F.R.C.S., who survived him. After leaving the Solar Physics Observatory he established an observatory near his home in Salcombe Regis, Devonshire, known at first as the Hill Observatory and after his death as the Norman Lockyer Observatory—an institution now attached to the University of Exeter. Lockyer's interests, though very wide, were dominated by his belief in science and its potentialities for the welfare of the human race. Nevertheless, he published, with the collaboration of his daughter Winifred, *Tennyson as a Student and a Poet of Nature*—inspired by his friendship with the poet. He took more than a nominal interest in his membership of the Anglican Church, while on the lighter side he was stimulated to write *The Rules of Golf.* He received numerous honors from scientific bodies throughout the course of a long and exceptionally active life.

The direction of Lockyer's early scientific investigations was determined by the fact that the spectroscope was just beginning to reveal its great possibilities as an almost miraculous means of probing the secrets of nature. It was in 1859 that Kirchhoff and Bunsen laid the foundations of astrophysics by showing how the composition of the heavenly bodies could be determined—a problem not long before selected by Auguste Comte as a type of the permanently insoluble. Lockyer, thrilled by the new prospect thus opened up, obtained a spectroscope, which he attached to his $6\frac{1}{4}$-inch refracting telescope, and began a series of observations which, in 1868, brought him his first major success—the observation, at times other than during a total solar eclipse, of the solar prominences. The dramatic circumstances attending this discovery doubtless added to the attention which it received, but the ingenuity of the method and the importance of its implications would alone have entitled it to full credit.

The observation depended on the possibility of using a dispersion large enough to weaken the spectrum of the diffused sunlight in the atmosphere sufficiently to make visible the bright lines of the prominence spectrum. Lockyer conceived the idea as early as 1866, but, through a series of delays in obtaining a satisfactory instrument, it was not until 20 October 1868 that he was able to observe the prominence spectrum. It happened that on 18 August 1868 a total eclipse of the sun was visible in India, at which the brilliance of the prominence spectrum lines suggested to Jules Janssen, who observed them, the same idea that had occurred long before to Lockyer; and on the following day he successfully applied it. Both Lockyer and Janssen transmitted the news of the discovery to a meeting of the French Academy of Sciences, and by a remarkable coincidence the messages were received within a few minutes of one another. The French government commemorated the event by striking a medal bearing the portraits of the two astronomers.

Following up the observations, Lockyer soon observed a yellow line in the prominence spectrum, and in that of the outer atmosphere of the sun (which he similarly discovered and named the "chromosphere"), which had not been produced in the laboratory. This suggested to him the existence in the sun of an unknown element, which he named helium. In this he ran counter to the general opinion, which was that the line was due to a familiar element under exceptional conditions of excitation; and it was not until 1895 that William Ramsay, by producing the line from terrestrial sources, verified Lockyer's early conclusion. The constitution of the sun remained a leading interest with Lockyer, and he conducted many solar eclipse expeditions with a view to establishing ideas which he had formed from his studies of laboratory spectra.

One of the most conspicuous of such ideas was the "dissociation hypothesis," which much later acquired a special significance through developments in the theory of spectra. Lockyer observed in his experiments that the spectrum of an element varied with the intensity of the stimulus used to produce it. This appeared incompatible with the general view that the spectrum of any element was an invariable characteristic of the atoms (or molecules) of the element itself. It was recognized that the spectra of atoms and of molecules, even of the same element, differed; and Lockyer, following this clue, postulated that a stimulus greater than that necessary to break up the molecule into atoms would break up the atoms themselves and produce subatoms having their own characteristic spectra. The observation that, as he believed, the spectra of different elements contained lines in common led to the hypothesis that the atoms of what were known to the chemist as elements were themselves groupings of smaller constituents, the common lines being due to such constituents obtained by the dissociation of atoms of different elements.

This idea, like many of Lockyer's speculations, met with almost universal opposition, but although, in its original form, it is now believed to be groundless, it is recognized that it contains more than a germ of truth. It is now held that an increase in the energy of stimulus does indeed produce a dissociation of the atoms, and that atoms of different elements are indeed composed of different associations of the same more elementary components; but the apparent coincidences of lines from different elements are found, with the greater accuracy of measurement now possible, to be illusory. Although each element can yield a succession of spectra

(silicon, for instance, to take one of Lockyer's own examples, under continuously increasing stimulus yields spectra known as Si I, Si II, Si III, Si IV), these are all different from any other spectrum that can be produced from anything at all. The data accumulated by Lockyer and, under his direction, by his students and assistants proved of the greatest value when a more tenable explanation became possible.

Another idea of Lockyer's connected with his observations of the sun, to which he devoted much attention and which likewise has not—at least in its original form—been strongly substantiated, was the supposed connection between the sunspot cycle and terrestrial meteorology. The eleven-year cycle of sunspots has been correlated, with greater or less plausibility, with various terrestrial phenomena, but what was peculiar to Lockyer's view of the matter was that he attempted to connect it with his idea of dissociation. He observed that certain lines in the spectra of sunspots varied in width during the course of a cycle, and this to him denoted a change of physical conditions in the sun that manifested itself in parallel effects in the spectra of the spots and in the weather on the earth. These phenomena were thus related not as cause to effect but as effects of the same cause which he postulated as pulsations in the sun. This work came to an abrupt end with the transfer of the Solar Physics Observatory to Cambridge and has not had any significant development.

Perhaps the most far-reaching of Lockyer's ideas was his meteoritic hypothesis, which is one of the most comprehensive schemes of inorganic evolution ever devised and which, though almost none of it now survives, led him to conceptions far in advance of those prevalent in his day. It may be summed up in his own words: "All self-luminous bodies in the celestial spaces are composed either of swarms of meteorites or of masses of meteoritic vapour produced by heat." The idea arose gradually in his mind from a variety of circumstances, but the crucial evidence, as he believed, lay in the examination of the spectra of meteorites under varying conditions. He believed that, by enclosing meteorites in vacuum tubes and subjecting them to gradually increasing degrees of temperature and electrical excitation, he could retrace the course of celestial evolution, and his endeavors for many years were concentrated on the establishment of a parallelism between the various types of meteoritic spectra and the spectra of the several kinds of heavenly body.

Lockyer had the good fortune to witness the very striking meteoric display of 1866, which appears to have left an indelible impression on his mind and predisposed him to give special attention to meteorites when later he began to speculate on the possibility of determining the course of celestial evolution in the light of spectroscopic evidence. Observations of Coggia's comet, which appeared in 1874, produced a further impulse in this direction—a close association between comets and meteors was already known—and he naturally associated the successive changes in the spectrum of the comet with the changes of laboratory spectra that had created in his mind the idea of dissociation. The ultimate result was an all-comprehensive scheme of the following character.

In the beginning space was occupied by a more or less uniform distribution of meteorites which, through their rapid motions and chance collisions, tended to accumulate in groups. These developed in various ways according to the conditions, giving rise to the various types of heavenly body observed. Very large loose groups would constitute nebulae, within which further condensations would occur, destined to become stars. A star, beginning as a meteoritic swarm, would rise in temperature as it condensed, until a stage was reached at which the mass, then completely vaporized, would lose heat by radiation at a rate equal to its generation by condensation; thereafter it would cool down toward its final state as a cold solid body. An exceptionally rapid conglomeration would constitute a nova, or new star, of which Lockyer examined some specimens that appeared during his working life; it would rise rapidly to its maximum temperature, and then decline in the normal stellar manner. Original groupings too small to become nebulae would form comets, while a number of isolated meteors would remain to enter the earth's atmosphere and appear as meteor swarms and occasionally as a meteorite large enough to reach the earth's surface. The final state of the universe would be that of a number of cold, dark bodies moving about aimlessly forever.

The correlation of the various types of celestial spectra with the succession of meteoritic spectra observed in the laboratory was carried out by Lockyer with great ingenuity but, it must be admitted, with insufficient critical power and too great a tendency to special pleading. A band spectrum arising from molecules presents the appearance, under small dispersion, of bright strips, each sharp at one edge and gradually fading out at the other, until, after a short dark gap, the sharp edge of the next appears. Now it is possible to regard this, in spectra so imperfect as those then obtainable from faint celestial sources, in the opposite way—as a dark band with a sharp edge, gradually growing into brightness in the reverse direction and ending abruptly at the beginning of the next dark band. In that case it would be an absorption

instead of an emission spectrum, the substances present revealing themselves by the absorption of light from a strip of continuous radiation produced by a remoter source, and the identification of the substances would accordingly be quite different from that which the assumption of an emission spectrum would yield. Lockyer felt himself free to adopt either explanation, and to allow liberally for errors of measurement, according to the needs of his hypothesis, and it is not surprising that the conclusions he reached failed to convince the more critical of his contemporaries.

One of the most striking features of the hypothesis, however, that aroused some of the strongest opposition, was its implication that a star began as a cold body, rose to a maximum temperature, and then cooled down again, so that the coolest stars observable belonged to two groups, young and old. It was generally held that stars were born hot and cooled continuously throughout their lives, and the succession of stellar spectra was held to support this. According to Lockyer's idea, however, spectra of very young and very old stars, though very similar because their temperatures, the main determining characteristic, were the same, should differ in detail because of the much greater density of the old stars compared with the young. His chief activity in astronomical research during his later years was devoted to the classification of the cooler stars according to criteria which he devised.

It is a striking fact that, before his death, the theory of stellar evolution advanced by Henry Norris Russell and widely accepted, though having no connection with the meteoritic hypothesis, required just such a life history, so far as temperature and density were concerned, as that envisaged by Lockyer; and a really satisfactory criterion was discovered—which Lockyer just missed—for distinguishing young and old (giant and dwarf, as they were called) cool stars from one another. This partial vindication of his ideas gave him great satisfaction in his closing years. The fact that the whole problem now appears much more complex than either Lockyer or Russell could have conceived does not detract from the value of their work as a stimulus to further progress.

Another activity of Lockyer's restless mind was the astronomical interpretation of eastern temples and prehistoric stone circles, of which many examples are to be found in the British Isles. His idea was that these structures were connected with sun and star worship, their orientation being toward the points of rising or setting of conspicuous heavenly bodies. If that were so, a method existed, he conceived, of dating these erections, because our knowledge of the precession of the equinoxes enabled us to determine the precise azimuths of such risings and settings at different epochs, and if a particular temple axis pointed reasonably close to such an azimuth for a particular bright star, it could be assumed that the temple was erected when that star would be on the horizon at the point where the temple axis met it. More cautious archaeologists, while evincing considerable skepticism concerning the fundamental idea, were deterred also by the fact that the erosion of centuries, or even millennia, would have changed the visible horizon too drastically for the method to have much value; but Lockyer exhibited the same fertility of imagination in overcoming such difficulties as he had shown in connection with celestial spectra, and he built up an imposing system of dates associated with a few stars which he regarded as having had special religious significance.

Perhaps the most lasting of Lockyer's achievements was his creation of the scientific journal *Nature*, which, beginning in 1869, he edited for the first fifty years of its existence. *Nature* is now, by common consent, the world's leading general scientific periodical, but for many years it had to struggle to keep alive, and no small credit is due to Lockyer, and the publishers of that time, Messrs. Macmillan, whose faith in its ultimate success led them to persevere in the face of what at the earlier stages must have appeared almost insuperable obstacles. When Lockyer retired from the editorship in 1919 he was succeeded by his former assistant, Sir Richard Gregory, who held the office for the next twenty years.

This was perhaps the most outstanding example of Lockyer's lifelong concern for the recognition of science as a most potent agent in the general progress of civilization. Of his many efforts toward this end it is impossible to omit mention of one which arose from his election as president of the British Association for the Advancement of Science in 1903. His address on "The Influence of Brain Power on History" was intended to stimulate the Association to an extension of its activities from the pursuit of pure science into the realization of another of the objects of its founders —"to obtain a more general attention to the objects of science and a removal of any disadvantages of a public kind which impede its progress." Being unable to carry the council with him to the extent that he desired, he thereupon founded a new body, the British Science Guild, with this as its main object. This organization continued to function until after his death, when the gradual recognition by the British Association that this duty indeed properly lay upon it, led to the Guild relinquishing its activities to the Association.

Lockyer is an outstanding example of the adven- turous rather than the critical scientist. It is easy to find faults in his advocacy of his ideas; it is not so easy to estimate the influence of those ideas on those who were stimulated to oppose them. Just as his specula- tions aroused either enthusiastic support or, more often, violent dissent but never indifference, so did his person: he had devoted friends and implacable enemies. His effect on the course of science is im- possible to assess, but it is undoubtedly greater than the fate of his particular speculations would suggest.

BIBLIOGRAPHY

Lockyer wrote many papers and books on astrophysics. Most of the papers were published in the *Proceedings of the Royal Society* or *Philosophical Transactions of the Royal Society*. His major books are *Contributions to Solar Physics* (London, 1874), containing an account of his early obser- vations of the sun by his new method; *Chemistry of the Sun* (London, 1887), in which the dissociation hypothesis and the evidence for it are presented; *The Meteoritic Hypothesis* (London, 1890); *The Dawn of Astronomy* (London, 1894), explaining the method of dating ancient structures and the results of its application; and *Inorganic Evolution* (London, 1900), which describes the most devel- oped form of the hypothesis and its significance for celes- tial spectroscopy.

The main source of information concerning Lockyer is the biography by his widow and daughter, T. Mary Lockyer and Winifred L. Lockyer: *The Life and Work of Sir Norman Lockyer* (London, 1928). See also A. J. Mea- dows, *Science and Controversy: a Biography of Sir Norman Lockyer* (London, 1972).

HERBERT DINGLE

LODGE, OLIVER JOSEPH (*b.* Penkhull, Stafford- shire, England, 12 June 1851; *d.* Lake, near Salisbury, England, 22 August 1940), *physics.*

Lodge was a member of an uncommonly vigorous and prolific clan. He was the eldest of nine children —eight sons and a daughter— of the merchant Oliver Lodge and grandson of the clergyman and school- master Oliver Lodge, who had twenty-five children; his mother was Grace Heath, likewise descended from educators and clergymen. Lodge and his wife Mary Marshall had twelve children, ten of whom survived them; the youngest son, Raymond, was killed in World War I.

Lodge was educated privately until he was fourteen and then entered the business of his father, who was a supplier of materials used in the pottery industry. His interest in science was periodically sparked by visits to London, where he heard John Tyndall and others lecture at the Royal Institution. He resumed his education at the age of twenty-two at the Royal College of Science and at University College in London, where for a time he served as a demonstrator in physics for George Carey Foster. He received the D.Sc. in 1877 and began publishing papers on electricity, mechanics, and allied topics. In 1881 he became the first professor of physics at the new University College in Liverpool, where he remained for nineteen years. It was during those years that he made his principal contributions, mainly in two areas: theory of the ether and electromagnetic propagation.

The nineteenth-century concept of the ether left numerous questions unresolved, one of which was whether the ether in the vicinity of moving matter moved along with it. The Michelson-Morley experiment of 1887 was thought to have answered the question in the affirmative. But in 1893—by an ingenious experiment involving the interference between two opposing light rays traveling around the space between a pair of rapidly rotating parallel steel disks—Lodge showed that the ether was *not* carried along. The apparent contradiction helped to discredit the theory of the ether and to set the stage for the theory of relativity.

Lodge is also remembered for his experiments on electromagnetic radiation, in which he came close to anticipating Heinrich Hertz's discovery of propagating waves, and for his participation in the beginnings of radiotelegraphy. Lodge's 1887–1888 discovery that oscillations associated with the discharge of a Leyden jar result in waves and standing waves along conducting wires, with measurable wavelengths and other characteristics predicted by Maxwell's theory, was overshadowed by the more spectacular results that Hertz obtained in free space in the same year. Lodge's interest in these phenomena extended to improved methods of detecting electromagnetic waves, in one of which he utilized the observation that electromagnetic irradiation of loosely connected metals makes them stick together. This principle, simultaneously observed and elaborated by others, formed the basis for an early detector of radio waves, a container of loose metal particles subjected to mechanical vibration (so as continually to restore the original conductivity) that he named the coherer.

On 1 June 1894, in a lecture to commemorate the untimely death of Hertz five months earlier, Lodge spoke at the Royal Institution on "The Work of Hertz," stressing the experimental aspects of the work, including the importance of "syntony" (resonant tuning) in obtaining good results. The lecture was published and subsequently incorporated in a book;

it had a widespread influence on the development of radiotelegraphy, inspiring experimenters in Germany, Italy, Russia, and other countries. With an associate, Alexander Muirhead, Lodge formed a syndicate to exploit one of his ideas, the resonant antenna circuit, and obtained some important patents.

In 1900 the University of Birmingham became the first British civic institution to receive a charter as a full-fledged university, and Lodge was appointed its first principal. He held the post until 1919, devoting himself increasingly to administrative work and the leadership of professional societies. He was president of the Physical Society in 1900 and of the British Association for the Advancement of Science in 1913. He received many prizes and honors, including the Rumford Medal of the Royal Society (1898) and the Faraday Medal of the Institution of Electrical Engineers (1932). He was knighted in 1902.

Beginning in 1883, Lodge also became interested in psychic research—telepathy, telekinesis, and communication with the dead—an interest that was intensified after his son's death and his own retirement in 1919. On two occasions he served as president of the Society for Psychical Research. He lived to the age of eighty-nine.

BIBLIOGRAPHY

I. ORIGINAL WORKS. Lodge's Royal Institution lecture was published in *Electrician*, **33** (1894), 153 ff., and reprinted by that journal with addenda as *The Work of Hertz and His Successors* (London, 1894, 1898); the third and fourth eds., retitled *Signalling Through Space Without Wires* (London, 1900, 1908), also contained reprints of several other papers and various correspondence. Among his other books were texts and more popular works, all published in London: *The Ether of Space* (1909), *Talks About Wireless* (1925), *Advancing Science* (1931), and *My Philosophy* (1933), as well as a work on psychical research, *Raymond: Or Life and Death* (1916). He also wrote an autobiography, *Past Years* (London, 1931).

II. SECONDARY LITERATURE. J. A. Hill compiled and annotated *Letters From Sir Oliver Lodge* (London, 1932); and Theodore Besterman assembled *A Bibliography of Sir Oliver Lodge* (London, 1935). There is an entry by Allan Ferguson in the 1931–1940 supp. to *Dictionary of National Biography*, pp. 541–543; and there are obituaries in *Obituary Notices of Fellows of the Royal Society*, **3** (1941), 551–574; *Proceedings of the Physical Society*, **53** (1941), 54–65; and *The Times* (23 Aug. 1940), p. 7. A well-documented chronological account of Lodge's contributions to tuned radiotelegraphy was prepared in support of his petition for extension of his patent by S. P. Thompson, *Notes on Sir Oliver Lodge's Patent for Wireless Telegraphy* (London, 1911).

CHARLES SÜSSKIND

LOEB, JACQUES (*b.* Mayen, Rhine Province, Prussia, 7 April 1859; *d.* Hamilton, Bermuda, 11 February 1924), *physiology, biology.*

The apostle of mechanistic conceptions in biology, Loeb was the elder son of a prosperous Jewish importer. His brother Leo later became professor of pathology at Washington University, St. Louis. His father, an ardent Francophile, encouraged his son to read the classics of eighteenth-century thought. The mature Loeb always sought to harness his empirical researches to the wide-ranging political, social, and philosophical concerns of the *philosophes*. There is no direct evidence that he was influenced by the cognate tradition of the German-speaking medical materialists, led by Jacob Moleschott, Ludwig Büchner, and Carl Vogt, who published their major pronunciamentos in the 1850's. But it would be extraordinary if Loeb had not been acquainted with a celebrated essay by a kindred spirit of the medical materialists—"Die mechanistische Auffassung des Lebens" by Rudolf Virchow.

When he prepared to enter the University of Berlin in 1880, Loeb was not interested in science as a career. Having become intoxicated by reading Schopenhauer and Hartmann, the philosophers of the will, he resolved to become a philosopher in order to discover if freedom of the will existed—preferably to establish that it did not. To his bitter disillusionment, he felt the professors of philosophy at Berlin to be mere "wordmongers," uninterested in resolving the issues they posed and incapable of it.

Rebounding from this disappointment, he turned to science. His quest remained the same—to find a "starting point for an experimental analysis of the will." He thus enrolled at Strasbourg in 1880 to study the localization of function in the brain under Goltz. Loeb presumably conceived of brain surgery upon experimental animals as forcing their wills. He took his M.D. in 1884 with a thesis written under Goltz on blindness induced by injury to the cerebral cortex. Loeb regarded his five years at Strasbourg as totally wasted for his chosen purpose.

Loeb finally found the concatenation of men and impulses that he was looking for at Würzburg in 1886, where he had become assistant to the professor of physiology Adolf Fick, one of the chief pioneers in the application of physics to biology and medicine. The decisive contact of Loeb's career was his intimate friendship with Julius von Sachs, from whom he learned of plant tropisms, obligatory movements elicited by physical stimuli such as light and gravity. The concept was ultimately traceable to T. A. Knight and Candolle but had been greatly amended and enhanced in interest by Sachs's own research. Loeb's task in science suddenly became clear: to establish a concept of tropisms in animals by which they too could be shown to be irresistibly driven by external stimuli and impotent to interpose their wills. He could simultaneously allay his metaphysical anxieties and prosecute a clear-cut program of empirical researches.

Loeb's final period of scientific initiation came in the winter of 1889–1890 at the marine biological station at Naples, where he found himself in an intellectual environment dominated by Wilhelm Roux's *Entwicklungsmechanik*. In this context, he first encountered a group of brilliant young American embryologists and cytologists, including Thomas Hunt Morgan. In 1890 Loeb married an American, Anne Leonard, who had taken a Ph.D. in philology at Zurich; they settled in the United States in 1891. He later wrote that he "could not live in a regime of oppression such as Bismarck had created" and was also disturbed by reading Heinrich von Treitschke, "the court historian of the King of Prussia," on the superiority of the German race. In the United States, Loeb taught successively at Bryn Mawr College, the University of Chicago, and the University of California at Berkeley, and from 1910 until his death at the Rockefeller Institute in New York. He spent his summers at the marine biological laboratories at Pacific Grove, California, or Woods Hole, Massachusetts. Two of his three children, Leonard and Robert, became scientists.

Loeb's publications on animal tropisms began in 1888. Certain caterpillars on emerging in the spring had long been observed to climb to the tips of branches and to feed upon the buds; and this behavior had been attributed to an infallible instinct for self-preservation. Loeb showed, however, that if the only source of light was in the opposite direction from food, the caterpillars would move toward the light and starve to death. The alleged instinct, Loeb maintained, was merely a product of heliotropism: the caterpillars were photochemical machines enslaved to the light. He demonstrated by ingenious experiments that they strove to achieve a frontal fixation upon a light source, with the plane of symmetry bisecting the source of stimulation. Loeb thought that he had found the solution to the problem of will by applying the appropriate tropic stimulus, "forcing, by external agencies, any number of individuals of a given kind of animals to move in a definite direction by means of their locomotor apparatus." He showed that certain organisms, thought to be exempt from tropistic behavior, could be oriented in a single direction by such simple expedients as adding carbonic acid to the medium.

Although some organisms indubitably manifest tropistic behavior, Loeb's conception of animal tropisms as generally applicable soon came under severe attack. The classic refutation was given by the American biologist Herbert Spencer Jennings in his *Behavior of the Lower Organisms* (1906). He showed that some apparently tropistic responses were merely "avoiding reactions," unspecifically elicited by many stimuli and totally unaffected by the direction from which the stimulus was applied. More generally, Jennings invoked the concept, originated by C. Lloyd Morgan and Edward Lee Thorndike, of trial and error reactions to unfamiliar stimuli, leading by chance to rewarded behavior which tended to recur in the future.

Undaunted by such criticism, Loeb saw himself as having suppressed one form of biological mysticism by substituting tropisms for instincts. In the field of development mechanics to which he had been introduced at Naples, he thought that the equivalent achievement would be "the substitution of well-known physico-chemical agencies for the mysterious action of the spermatozoon." To test the hypothesis that salts acted upon the living organism by the combination of their ions with protoplasm, Loeb immersed fertilized sea urchin eggs in salt water the osmotic pressure of which had been raised by the addition of sodium chloride. When replaced in ordinary seawater, they underwent multicellular segmentation. T. H. Morgan then subjected unfertilized eggs to the same process and found that they too could be induced to start segmentation, although without producing any larvae. It was Loeb who first succeeded, in 1899, in raising larvae by this technique —the first notable triumph in achieving artificial parthenogenesis. Although Loeb greatly relished the philosophical implications of artificial parthenogenesis, he also saw it as an addition to the repertory of experimental embryologists.

The third of Loeb's major lines of research, from 1918 until his death in 1924, was summarized in *Proteins and the Theory of Colloidal Behavior* (1922). He demonstrated that proteins are amphoteric electrolytes, capable of reacting chemically either as an acid or as a base, and that many observed properties of proteins and protein solutions are explicable in terms of the creation of a Donnan equilibrium between two solutions separated by a semipermeable membrane. This view seemed to many to be an epoch-making advance in the unification of physiology and physical chemistry. As the Donnan theory postulates the existence of salt solutions, Loeb's concern with these issues was directly linked to his earlier research on artificial parthenogenesis.

Few scientists of Loeb's generation were as well known to the American public. As a materialist in philosophy, a mechanist in science, and a socialist in politics, he offended against the prevalent American orthodoxies. But he was correspondingly idolized by the dissenters and debunkers—including Veblen, Mencken, and Sinclair Lewis—who increasingly set the intellectual tone. Lewis, in his satirical delineation of the Rockefeller Institute in *Arrowsmith* (1925), drew significantly upon Loeb for the only senior scientist consistently exempted from the author's scorn and derision.

Loeb's principal statement of his basic philosophy for a lay audience was his famous address "The Mechanistic Conception of Life," delivered before the First International Congress of Monists in Hamburg in September 1911 and published as the title piece of his most widely read book (1912). In this work Loeb argued that the mechanistic conception had made colossal strides in the first decade of the twentieth century, largely through his own researches: the activation of the egg "completely reduced to a physicochemical explanation"; the instincts of men equated with tropisms; and the field of heredity, traditionally "the stamping ground of the rhetorician and metaphysician," now transformed by Mendelism into "the most exact and rationalistic part of biology." The one great remaining task was to explain the origin of life, but he did not expect this problem to be insurmountable.

The long-term impact of Loeb's work and orientation was substantial. Jennings, his chief critic on tropisms, always affirmed his indebtedness to Loeb as the great pioneer in the objective analysis of behavior, the man who first made the study of behavior a rigorously experimental science. While a graduate student at the University of Chicago, J. B. Watson, the founder of behaviorism in psychology, chose Loeb as his thesis director but was dissuaded by other professors who told him that Loeb was not "safe" for a student to work with. It is a fair inference, however, that Loeb had already instilled in him a latent hostility toward subjective modes of analysis in psychology. Loeb may justly be described as Watson's greatest precursor in exemplifying and proselytizing for this attitude.

BIBLIOGRAPHY

An exhaustive bibliography of Loeb's publications compiled by Nina Kobelt is appended to the standard biographical account, W. J. V. Osterhout, "Jacques Loeb," in *Journal of General Physiology*, **8** (1928), ix–xcii. The other extended account of Loeb is Donald Fleming, "Introduction," in Jacques Loeb, *The Mechanistic Conception of Life*, repr. ed. (Cambridge, Mass., 1964), vii–xli. On Loeb's relationship to Jennings and Watson, see

Donald D. Jensen, "Foreword," in H. S. Jennings, *Behavior of the Lower Organisms*, repr. ed. (Bloomington, Ind., 1962), ix–xvii.

DONALD FLEMING

LOEB, LEO (*b*. Mayen, Germany, 21 September 1869; *d*. St. Louis, Missouri, 28 December 1959), *medicine, pathology, cancer research.*

Loeb's mother, Barbara Isay Loeb, died when he was three; his father, Benedict Loeb, died of tuberculosis when the boy was six. He lived with his maternal grandfather in Trier and at age ten moved to Berlin to live with a maternal aunt and uncle, whose daughter Helene married Albert Schweitzer. Tuberculosis and other ailments interrupted Loeb's schooling and recurred occasionally during his life. After 1889 he attended for short periods the universities of Heidelberg, Berlin, Freiburg (where he studied with August Weismann) and Basel (where he studied with Bunge and Miescher). His disapproval of rising German nationalism and militarism led him to take up medicine at the University of Zurich in 1890–1892. He did his clinical work at the University of Edinburgh and the medical school of London Hospital, occasionally attended lectures at other London medical schools, and returned to Zurich to complete his medical studies in 1895–1897. In his work toward the M.D., which required a thesis, he did skin transplantation experiments on guinea pigs under the direction of the pathologist Hugo Ribbert.

Loeb received the M.D. in 1897, then went to Chicago, where his older brother Jacques was a physiologist at the University. (He had previously visited his brother at Woods Hole, Massachusetts, in 1892 and 1894.) During five years in Chicago, Loeb practiced briefly near the University of Chicago, where he was physician to John Dewey's experimental school and was adjunct professor of pathology at Rush Medical College (later affiliated with the University of Illinois). In a rented room behind a drugstore he did experimental research on the healing of skin wounds of guinea pigs; he extended this research during a brief stay at Johns Hopkins School of Medicine, where he met William Osler, W. S. Thayer, and L. F. Barker (internal medicine); W. S. Halsted (surgery); W. H. Welch and Simon Flexner (pathology); and Mall and Harrison (anatomy). He also did research during summers at the Marine Biological Laboratory at Woods Hole.

Loeb next held a research fellowship under Adami at McGill University in 1902–1903. He was assistant professor of experimental pathology at the University of Pennsylvania in 1904–1910; directed laboratory research at Barnard Skin and Cancer Hospital, St. Louis, 1910–1915; and was professor of comparative pathology at Washington University, St. Louis, in 1915–1924, succeeding Eugene L. Opie as Mallinckrodt professor of pathology and department chairman in 1924–1937. On 3 January 1922, at the age of fifty-three, Loeb married Georgianna Sands, a physician in Port Chester, New York. He became emeritus professor of pathology in 1937 but continued to work as research professor (endowed by the Oscar Johnson Institute) until his final retirement in 1941 at the age of seventy-two.

Loeb continued to do research during summers at the Marine Biological Laboratory until 1950, when he nearly died of tuberculosis. Remaining thereafter in St. Louis, he worked on two books, one on the causes and nature of cancer and the other on the psychical factors of human life; both were unfinished at his death.

Among Loeb's honors were appointments to two endowed professorships; the John Phillips Memorial Prize (1935), awarded annually to an outstanding physician by the American College of Physicians; an annual lectureship in his name, endowed by his students at Washington University; an honorary D.Sc. from Washington University in 1948; and election as a member and officeholder in national and international medical and scientific organizations.

Of his contributions to science, his biographer, Ernest W. Goodpasture, wrote, "Although Loeb did not perfect *in vitro* culture of cells, he conceptually paved the way." Placing Loeb among the pioneers in studying the compatibility reactions of hosts toward transplanted tissues of the same and different species, Goodpasture wrote, "Loeb's histological studies of the fate of transplanted tissue, both normal and tumorous, were probably the first, certainly the most detailed, investigations of this kind."

His chief research writings were on tissue and tumor growth, tissue culture, pathology of circulation, venom of Heloderma, analysis of experimental amoebocyte tissue, internal secretions, and the biological basis of individuality. Philip A. Shaffer cited Loeb as having helped inaugurate the experimental approach to the study of cancer in the United States.

BIBLIOGRAPHY

Loeb's major books, mainly collaborations, are *The Venom of Heloderma*, Carnegie Publication no. 177 (Washington, D.C., 1913); *Edema* (Baltimore, 1924); and *The Biological Basis of Individuality* (Springfield, Ill., 1945). His "Autobiographical Notes" appeared in *Perspectives in Biology and Medicine*, **2**, no. 1 (Autumn 1958), 1–23.

Philip A. Shaffer's "Biographical Notes on Dr. Leo Loeb" precedes a comprehensive (over 400 entries) "Bibliography of Writings of Dr. Leo Loeb From 1896 to 1949," in *Archives of Pathology* (Chicago), **50**, no. 6 (Dec. 1950), 661–675.

See also *New York Times* (Dec. 30, 1959), 21; Ernest W. Goodpasture, "Leo Loeb, September 21, 1869–December 28, 1959," in *Biographical Memoirs, National Academy of Sciences*, **35** (1961), 205–219; and W. Stanley Hartroft, "Leo Loeb, 1869–1959," in *Archives of Pathology* (Chicago), **70**, no. 2 (Aug. 1960), 269–274.

FRANKLIN PARKER

LOEFFLER (LÖFFLER), FRIEDRICH AUGUST JOHANNES (*b.* Frankfurt an der Oder, Germany, 24 June 1852; *d.* Berlin, Germany, 9 April 1915), *microbiology, medicine.*

Loeffler's father, Gottfried Friedrich Franz Loeffler, was a distinguished physician who rose to the rank of *Generalarzt* in the Prussian army. He wrote books on military medicine and from 1867 until his death in 1874 was assistant director of the Friedrich Wilhelm Institut for military doctors in Berlin, where he did much to raise the status of army medical officers. With this advantage the younger Loeffler began his own studies at the French Gymnasium of Berlin and became fluent in French, an important skill for those who were then pursuing microbiology. He attended the medical school of the University of Würzburg before transferring to his father's school just before the Franco-Prussian War. After serving as a hospital assistant in that conflict, he was awarded the medical degree in 1874. Loeffler then became assistant physician at the Charité Hospital in Berlin, where for a year and a half he came in contact with some of the best clinicians of the time. From 1876 to 1879 he served as military surgeon and public health officer in Hannover and Potsdam, and in October 1879 he was assigned to the newly established Kaiserliches Gesundheitsamt in Berlin.

The assignment proved to be the turning point of his career. Nine months later Robert Koch arrived to set up a bacteriological laboratory, which, modest at first, soon became a leading center of research and discovery. Already famous for his work on anthrax, the development of a solid medium for cultivating bacteria, and a monograph on wound infection, Koch chose Loeffler and Georg Gaffky as his assistants. The next four years were to be highly productive for all the members of Koch's group. As Loeffler later recalled:

> The memory of those days, when we still worked in this room, Koch in the center and we about him, when almost daily new wonders in bacteriology arose before our astounded vision, and we, following the brilliant example of our chief, worked from morning to evening and scarcely had regard to our bodily needs—the memory of that time will remain unforgettable to us. Then it was that we learnt what it means to observe and work accurately and with energy to pursue the problem laid before us [in F. Nuttall, "Biographical Notes," 235].

During Loeffler's four years at the imperial health office laboratories he pursued a number of bacteriological problems, including a series of experiments to determine effective means of disinfection. A significant practical result of these studies was the identification of the infectious agent of glanders, a disease seen mainly in horses. With the identification of the bacterium came the practical consequence of prevention. Although several others had described the occurrence of microorganisms in cases of glanders, no positive identification of an etiological agent had been made.

As with most of Loeffler's subsequent bacteriological work, the glanders studies were models of the new experimental methods and criteria as applied to bacteriology by Koch. Loeffler took materials from glanders nodules in the lung and spleen of a horse and cultured them in test tubes containing blood serum. Here the bacteria were successfully grown in succeeding generations and then inoculated into a healthy horse, which began to show typical symptoms of glanders within forty-eight hours. At autopsy Loeffler found fresh nodules which again were productive of bacteria. He now clearly demonstrated them by staining with methylene blue. These bacteria, injected into rabbits, mice, and guinea pigs, produced the signs and symptoms suggestive of glanders. Bacilli cultivated from the small experimental animals, when injected into horses, produced the typical disease of glanders. Thus, in this sequence of experiments Loeffler satisfied the so-called Koch's postulates, in 1882, the year Koch enunciated them: to isolate the organism, to grow it in pure culture, to infect experimental animals with the cultured organism, and then to again isolate the bacteria from the experimental animals.

Loeffler's best-known work is the elucidation of the characteristics of the diphtheria bacillus and its growth in pure culture (1884), which again clearly revealed the imprint of Koch, with whom he was then so closely associated. For the first time bacteriologists could work with single microbial species even though the original specimen taken from the throat of a patient, for instance, might be teeming with myriads of organisms of different species.

Diphtheria, a disease known since antiquity, to the history of which Loeffler also devoted much time, was particularly feared because it produced a false membrane in the throat that could suffocate its victims, especially children. In 1871 Max Oertel, of Munich, showed that the false membrane could be produced in rabbits by swabbing their throats with secretions from human patients. In 1875 Edwin Klebs postulated a fungus as the cause, but at the German Medical Congress of 1883 Klebs presented new information pointing to a specific bacterium that could be seen, after staining, in the throat membranes of diphtheria patients. The task remained to differentiate the several bacteria that were implicated in the disease and to grow in pure culture the one responsible for causing it.

One of the difficulties Loeffler faced in isolating the agent of diphtheria was that the throats of diphtheria patients carried many microorganisms, one of which, the Streptococcus, had already led to much confusion. In a series of twenty-seven cases of fatal throat inflammation, twenty-two had been diagnosed as diphtheria, five as scarlatinal diphtheria. In the latter, Loeffler found that the Streptococcus was the dominant organism. It is now known that scarlet fever is accompanied or preceded by a streptococcal throat infection. In the case of diphtheria, Loeffler reasoned that these chains of cocci played a secondary role.

In the case of typical diphtheria Loeffler observed that the bacteria described by Klebs were easily demonstrated in about half the cases he studied. Loeffler found these bacilli, which stained markedly with methylene blue, in the deeper layers of the false membrane but never in the deeper tissues or other internal organs, although these organs may have been greatly damaged. Loeffler still had to culture both the Klebs bacillus, never grown before, as well as the Streptococcus to prove or disprove either one as the cause of diphtheria. The Streptococci were easily grown on the solid medium of peptone and gelatin devised by Koch. Inoculation into animals produced generalized infections but never a disease resembling human diphtheria.

The bacillus implicated by Klebs—and now strongly suspected by Loeffler as well—as the diphtheria-causing organism was difficult to culture on the usual gelatin plates because it would not grow at the low temperatures required to keep the gelatin solid. The Streptococci, on the other hand, grew well at temperatures below 24° C., needed to keep the medium from liquefying. At this point Loeffler's innovative and experimental skills come out most clearly. He developed a new solid medium using heated blood serum rather than gelatin as the means of solidifying. This medium could now be incubated at 37° C., or body temperature. The Klebs bacilli grew well under these conditions. When they were injected into animals, Loeffler found that the guinea pig developed tissue lesions very similar to those of human diphtheria. Bacilli could be easily recovered from the infection produced at the site of inoculation, but they were never recovered from the damaged internal organs. Loeffler thus postulated that this, too, was similar to human diphtheria, in which the bacteria were confined to the throat membrane. He reasoned that perhaps the bacteria released a poisonous substance that reached other parts of the body through the bloodstream. This supposition was soon proved correct by the work of Émile Roux and Yersin, who did much to reveal the nature of the diphtheria toxin. In practical terms the toxin theory soon bore fruit in the work of Behring and others who developed an effective antitoxin to counter the effects of the soluble poison produced by the bacillus.

One further test carried out by Loeffler in this series of experiments to identify and isolate the agent of diphtheria was an attempt to culture the organisms from healthy children. Much to his surprise he was able to isolate the bacillus from one of the twenty subjects under study. He thereby called attention to the fact that not all people infected by the diphtheria bacillus or the tubercle bacillus had the disease diphtheria or tuberculosis. This concept of a healthy carrier had immense public health significance, especially in the period when medicine was making a headlong rush to ascribe all diseases to bacterial agents and when physicians too often simply equated the presence of a bacillus with a particular disease. The host factors thus had to come under study as well.

With the publication in 1884 of these wide-ranging studies of diphtheria, which in their process revealed not only the identifiable agent but the equally important phenomena of toxin production and the healthy-carrier state, Loeffler may be considered the principal discoverer of the diphtheria bacillus. He thus capped the findings of numerous clinical investigators of diphtheria and those of Klebs, who first observed the bacteria.

In 1884 Loeffler was transferred from the laboratory at the Gesundheitsamt to become director of the hygienic laboratory at the First Garrison Hospital in Berlin, where he continued his bacteriological studies and lectured on sanitation. At this time he discovered the cause of swine erysipelas and of swine plague. In 1886 he was appointed to the Faculty of Hygiene at the University of Berlin, and the following year, with his bacteriological colleagues, R. Leuckart and O. Uhlworm, he founded the *Centralblatt für Bakteriologie und Parasitenkunde* (later the *Zentralblatt für Bakteriologie, Parasitenkunde, Infektionskrank-*

heiten und Hygiene), one of the most influential journals in the field.

In 1888 Loeffler, renowned as a bacteriologist, researcher, and teacher, received calls to chairs in hygiene at the universities of Giessen and Greifswald. He accepted the latter offer and spent twenty-five years as a distinguished professor, serving as rector of the university from 1903 to 1907. In 1905 he was raised to the rank of *Generalarzt* in the army.

Early in his years at Greifswald, Loeffler began work on the problem of mouse typhoid and its bacteriological cause, *Salmonella typhi-murium*. This led to the first attempt to use bacteria for controlling the spread of an unwanted animal population. Pasteur had earlier suggested this be done to reduce the rabbit population in Australia. Having learned of Loeffler's paper describing a new bacteriological method for controlling field mice, in 1892 the Greek government asked him to assist it with control of the rodents that threatened the harvests on the plain of Thessaly. In his laboratory studies Loeffler had shown that *Salmonella typhi-murium* was infectious for mice but not for other farm animals, and he planned to spread the disease among mice by contaminating their food sources. With Rudolf Abel, his assistant at the university, Loeffler journeyed to Greece in April 1892. After determining that the Thessalian vole was as susceptible to the bacteria as his laboratory animals, he began to culture huge quantities of the Salmonella necessary to spread in the fields. The dispersed bacteria killed many field mice, but there was some debate as to the real, practical effectiveness of Loeffler's efforts at biological control. The subsequent realization that the bacteria may not be innocuous to man precluded further study.

In 1897 Loeffler became chairman of a German commission to investigate foot-and-mouth disease of cattle. The following year, working with his assistant, Paul Frosch, Loeffler made yet another fundamental discovery. The first real proof of the existence of a pathogenic organism so small that it was invisible under the microscope came from the work of Dmitry Ivanowsky, who in 1892 demonstrated its activity in tobacco mosaic. The first knowledge that these agents, known as filterable viruses because they passed through porcelain filters that stopped the larger bacteria, were also capable of causing disease in animals resulted from the work of Loeffler and Frosch (1898). They discovered that aphthous fever (foot-and-mouth disease) in cattle was caused by such a virus.

Lymph from infected animals, diluted and filtered so as to be entirely free of bacteria, produced the typical disease after injection into test animals. The question now was whether the lymph contained an effective toxin or a previously undiscovered agent. Loeffler and Frosch believed the latter possibility, that the activity of the lymph in causing further disease was due to an organism that could multiply yet was invisible with existing microscopes. Shortly after their work became known, William H. Welch in Baltimore called it to the attention of Walter Reed, who soon elucidated the viral nature of yellow fever and its transmission by mosquitoes.

Through his discoveries of several microorganisms as well as through his teaching and methods of work, Loeffler contributed greatly to the so-called golden age of bacteriology. Besides his improved culture media, bacteriological technique is also indebted to him for the popularization of the alkaline methylene blue stain as well as a specific stain for cilia and flagella. He introduced the standard medium for cultivation of the typhoid bacillus and improved the methods of isolating and differentiating the numerous fecal bacteria. He is also known for work on disinfection, hygiene of milk and water, and sewage disposal.

In 1913 Loeffler was recalled to Berlin to succeed Gaffky as director of the Institut für Infektionskrankheiten. He was active at the beginning of World War I in planning hygiene programs for the army. His health began to fail in December 1914, and despite surgical intervention he died on 9 April 1915. He was buried in Greifswald.

BIBLIOGRAPHY

I. ORIGINAL WORKS. Loeffler's memoir on the diphtheria bacillus is "Untersuchungen über die Bedeutung der Mikroorganismen für die Entstehung der Diphtherie," in *Mittheilungen aus dem kaiserlichen Gesundheitsamt*, **2** (1884), 421–499; see also "Berichte der Kommission zur Erforschung des Maul und Kanlenseuche," in *Centralblatt für Bakteriologie und Parasitenkunde*, **23**, Abt. 1 (1898), 371–391, written with Paul Frosch. His many other medical and bacteriological papers appeared mainly in the *Mittheilungen aus dem K. Gesundheitsamte*, the *Deutsche medizinische Wochenschrift*, and the *Centralblatt für Bakteriologie*. One of the first books dealing with the history of bacteriology was his *Vorlesungen über die geschichtliche Entwicklung der Lehre von den Bacterien* (Leipzig, 1887).

Loeffler's papers available in English trans. are "On the Bacillus of Glanders"; "Investigations as to the Significance of Microorganisms in the Production of Diphtheria in Man"; and "Disinfection by Steam," written with R. Koch and G. Gaffky, in W. Watson Cheyne, ed., *Recent Essays by Various Authors on Bacteria in Relation to Disease* (London, 1886); and "The History of Diphtheria," in G. H. F. Nuttall and G. S. Graham-Smith, eds., *The Bacteriology of Diphtheria* (Cambridge, 1908), pp. 1–52.

II. SECONDARY LITERATURE. The following works (listed chronologically) contain useful biographical data: F. Goldschmidt, "Die Begründer der modernen Diphtheriebehandlung," in *Münchener medizinische Wochenschrift*, **42** (1895), 335–336; and "Professeur Friedrich Loeffler," in *Revue d'hygiène*, **22** (1900), 652–655; G. Gaffky, "Friedrich Loeffler," in *Zentralblatt für Bakteriologie, Parasitenkunde, Infektionskrankheiten und Hygiene*, **76** (1915), 241–245; George H. F. Nuttall, "Biographical Notes Bearing on Koch, Ehrlich, Behring, and Loeffler . . .," in *Parasitology*, **16** (1924), 214–238; Dexter H. Howard, "Friedrich Loeffler and the Thessalian Field Mouse Plague of 1892," in *Journal of the History of Medicine and Allied Sciences*, **18** (1963), 272–281; and H. A. Lechevalier and M. Soltorovsky, *Three Centuries of Microbiology* (New York, 1965), pp. 122–136, 282–286.

GERT H. BRIEGER

LOEWI, OTTO (*b.* Frankfurt am Main, Germany, 3 June 1873; *d.* New York, N.Y., 25 December 1961), *pharmacology, physiology.*

In 1936 Loewi shared with Henry Dale the Nobel Prize in physiology or medicine for work relating to the chemical transmission of nervous impulses. He was the first child and only son of Jakob Loewi, a wealthy wine merchant, and his second wife, Anna Willstädter. At the Frankfurter Städtisches Gymnasium, where Loewi studied from 1882 to 1891, his record was much better in the humanities than in physics and mathematics, and he hoped to pursue a career in the history of art. For pragmatic reasons, however, his family wanted him to study medicine, and in 1891 he matriculated as a medical student at the University of Strasbourg. Loewi found the preclinical studies there uninteresting and preferred during his first two years to attend the lectures of the philosophical faculty. After barely passing his first medical examination (*Physikum*) in 1893, Loewi spent the next two semesters at Munich and then returned to Strasbourg, where Bernhard Naunyn's clinical lectures now attracted his attention. Nevertheless, with little or no preparation in the subject, Loewi chose to write his dissertation on a topic in pharmacology. Under the direction of the renowned teacher and pharmacologist Oswald Schmiedeberg, he worked on the effects of various drugs on the isolated heart of the frog. Although quite typical of the work done in Schmiedeberg's laboratory, this choice of topic adds force to Loewi's own retrospective testimony that his interest in basic science had been aroused in part by reading Walter Holbrook Gaskell's Croonian lecture of 1883 on the isolated heart of the frog.[1]

After graduating M.D. from Strasbourg in 1896,

Loewi took a course in analytical inorganic chemistry from Martin Freund in Frankfurt and then studied physiological chemistry for several months in Franz Hofmeister's laboratory in Strasbourg. In 1897–1898 Loewi served as Carl von Noorden's assistant in internal medicine at the city hospital in Frankfurt. Assigned to wards for advanced tuberculosis and epidemic pneumonia, Loewi was discouraged by the lack of therapy and resultant high mortality for these cases and later claimed that it was because of this experience that he chose basic research over a clinical career.[2] From 1898 to 1904 Loewi was assistant to Hans Horst Meyer at the pharmacological institute of the University of Marburg. His *Habilitationschrift*, which brought him the title of *Privatdozent* in 1900, dealt with nuclein metabolism in man. During 1902–1903 Loewi spent several months in England, which he believed had by then replaced Germany as the world's leading center for physiology.[3] At E. H. Starling's laboratory in London, where he spent most of this time, and during a brief visit at Cambridge, he met and exchanged ideas with the leading English physiologists of the day, including Walter Gaskell, John Newport Langley, Thomas Renton Elliott, and Dale. Despite the brevity of this trip, it clearly exerted an important influence on Loewi's later research interests and achievements.

In 1904 Loewi was appointed assistant professor at Marburg and briefly succeeded Meyer as director of the pharmacological institute there. In 1905 he followed Meyer to the University of Vienna to serve again as his assistant. He was appointed assistant professor at Vienna in 1907 and in 1909 accepted a post as professor and head of pharmacology at the University of Graz. Despite offers from more famous universities, including Vienna, Loewi remained at Graz until his expulsion by the Nazis in 1938. Like other male Jewish citizens of Graz, Loewi and two of his four children were imprisoned in March of that year. He was released two months later and in September was allowed to leave for London, but only after the Gestapo had forced him to transfer his Nobel Prize money from a bank in Stockholm to a bank under Nazi control.[4] Meanwhile the Nazis detained his wife, Guida Goldschmidt (whom he had married in 1908), while seeking to dispossess her of some real estate in Italy. Stripped of all property and means, Loewi managed during the next year or so to secure invitations to work at the Franqui Foundation in Brussels and then at the Nuffield Institute, Oxford. From 1940 until his death he was research professor of pharmacology at the College of Medicine, New York University. In 1941 his wife was at last able to rejoin him, and in 1946 Loewi became a naturalized citizen of the United States. While in his adopted country, he spent his summers at the Marine Biological Laboratory in Woods Hole, Massachusetts, where his remains are buried.

Although the range of Loewi's research interests and studies was vast, his most influential work fell into two broad categories: (1) protein and carbohydrate metabolism; and (2) the autonomic nervous system, especially the cardiac nerves. Other major interests were the pharmacology and physiology of the kidney and the physiogical role of cations. Loewi produced work in all of these areas quite early in his career, and the later fame of his work on the chemical transmission of nerve impulses ought not to obscure his continued interest in other areas.

Loewi's concern with the problems of metabolism emerged while he was still a medical student at Strasbourg. Naunyn was himself a pioneer in the area of metabolism, as were two members of his staff, Adolph Magnus-Levy and Oscar Minkowski, who had just begun his famous experimental studies on the relationship between the pancreas and diabetes mellitus. Loewi later included one of Minkowski's contributions in a list of the five papers that had most inspired his own career.[5] While working in Schmiedeberg's laboratory, Loewi was introduced to Johann Friedrich Miescher's classic papers on the metabolism of the Rhine salmon during its freshwater phase. It was this work to which Loewi later variously referred as his "scientific bible," as jointly responsible (with Gaskell's paper of 1883) for arousing his interest in basic science, and as the chief influence on his choice of physiology in particular as a calling.[6] Another probable influence on Loewi's interest in metabolism was van Noorden, whose own clinical studies focused on pathologic metabolism.

In his earliest publications on metabolism Loewi argued that of the components of urinary secretion, only the uric acid depended on diet. These studies were followed by papers on phlorizin-induced glycosuria and on the question whether fat could be converted into sugar in dogs; Loewi concluded that it could not. His greatest contribution to metabolic studies, dealing with protein synthesis in the animal body, appeared as early as 1902. Since no one had previously been able to maintain nitrogen balance in animals by feeding them with the degradation products of protein in place of the original protein itself, it was supposed that animals were incapable of protein synthesis. By his own account Loewi became interested in the question after reading a paper by the biochemist Friedrich Kutscher, a colleague at Marburg, who in 1899 showed that extended trypsin digestion of a pancreas could yield end products none of which displayed any

longer the chemical reactions characteristic of protein.[7] This result somehow led Loewi to believe that animals might be able to synthesize protein if their diet consisted of the degradation products of a whole organ rather than of an isolated protein, and he immediately undertook a series of nutritional experiments to test his idea. Although the dogs he used found this diet unpalatable at first, Loewi persisted and eventually established that animals were indeed capable of synthesizing proteins from their degradation products, even from the most elementary end products, the amino acids. This work established Loewi's early reputation and greatly influenced later work in nutrition, including perhaps that of Frederick Gowland Hopkins, who met Loewi during his visit to England and who was to win the Nobel Prize in 1929 for his discovery of "accessory food factors," or vitamins.[8]

Between 1902 and 1905, Loewi—in collaboration with Walter Fletcher, Nathaniel Alcock, and Velyian Henderson—produced a series of five papers on the function of the kidney and the action of diuretics. In the classic monograph, *The Secretion of the Urine* (London, 1917), Arthur Cushny made important use of these studies while criticizing Loewi's early attempt (1902) to strike a compromise between the filtration and vital theories of kidney function. Nonetheless, Loewi's ultimate position, as represented in the last paper of this series, seems to conform quite closely to Cushny's own modified filtration theory.

From 1907 to 1918, Loewi published six additional studies on metabolism, chiefly with regard to the function of the pancreas and glucose metabolism in diabetes[9]; and after Frederick Banting and Charles Best discovered insulin in 1921, he undertook with H. F. Haüsler a long series of studies on the mode of action of insulin and its antagonists. By 1929 Loewi was forced to disavow some of the results of his earlier work on insulin and thereby to withdraw support from his earlier hypothesis that insulin promoted the binding of glucose to erythrocytes. In the 1930's Loewi and his co-workers claimed to have discovered a proprioceptive metabolic reflex ("a mechanism through which the central nervous system . . . is informed of the state of the metabolism in individual organs")[10] and pursued some of the issues raised by the work of Bernardo Houssay on the role of the pituitary gland in carbohydrate metabolism.

By his own account, Loewi "imported" from England (and particularly from Gaskell, Langley, and Elliott) his interest in the "vegetative," or autonomic, nervous system.[11] His earliest publications in the field, all of which postdate his visit to England, concern vasomotor action, salivary secretion, and the action of adrenalin, all topics under active investigation at Cambridge during his visit there. Loewi's first really original contribution in this area was his demonstration with Alfred Fröhlich in 1910 that cocaine increases the sensitivity of autonomically innervated organs to adrenalin, a response so specific that it came to be used as a test for the latter drug.[12] In 1912 Loewi published a series of three communications on the action of the vagus nerve on the heart, dealing particularly with the effects on vagal action of various drugs and of variations in the calcium ion concentration of the nutrient saline solution. Between 1913 and 1921 Loewi pursued these interests in a series of three publications on the role in heart action of physiological cations (especially calcium) and in a series of six publications on the physiological relationship between calcium ions and the series of digitalis drugs, especially with respect to their action on the frog's heart. In the latter studies Loewi emphasized that the digitalis series affects the heart as it does chiefly because digitalis sensitizes the heart to calcium, a conclusion with clinical consequences that Loewi sought to specify.

Thus, for several years before 1921 Loewi had been turning increasingly to the physiology and pharmacology of the frog's heart and its nerves. But none of this research led directly to the work for which he won the Nobel Prize. In fact, there is an element of mystery and drama in the way Loewi came to demonstrate experimentally the chemical transmission of nervous impulses. By the time he did so, in 1921, the hypothesis of chemical transmission was nearly twenty years old. Credit for the hypothesis is usually given to Elliott, who published the suggestion in 1904.[13] In 1929, after Loewi's work had become well known, another Cambridge physiologist, Walter Fletcher, recalled that Loewi had independently proposed the chemical transmission hypothesis in 1903, in a private conversation with Fletcher, who was then working in Loewi's laboratory at Marburg.[14] Before this reminder from Fletcher, Loewi had completely forgotten the conversation; but he thereafter attached considerable significance to it, undoubtedly to emphasize the independence of his own work. However, as Dale suggested more than once, it is hard to believe that Loewi's mind had not been at least somewhat prepared for the idea by his meeting with Elliott and in general by his visit to Cambridge, where the meaning of the neuromimetic effects of drugs was then a topic of intense interest and discussion.[15]

In any case, by 1920 no decisive experimental evidence for chemical transmission had yet been found, and the hypothesis had fallen into rather general discredit. Loewi revived it with an elegant experiment which, by his own account, occurred to him in the midst of sleep on two successive nights:

> The night before Easter Sunday of [1921] I awoke, turned on the light, and jotted down a few notes on a tiny slip of thin paper. Then I fell asleep again. It occurred to me at six o'clock in the morning that during the night I had written down something most important, but I was unable to decipher the scrawl. The next night, at three o'clock, the idea returned. It was the design of an experiment to determine whether or not the hypothesis of chemical transmission that I had uttered seventeen years ago was correct. I got up immediately, went to the laboratory, and performed a simple experiment on a frog heart according to the nocturnal design. I have to describe briefly this experiment since its results became the foundation of the theory of the chemical transmission of the nervous impulse.
>
> The hearts of two frogs were isolated, the first with its nerves, the second without. Both hearts were attached to Straub canulas filled with a little Ringer solution. The vagus nerve of the first heart was stimulated for a few minutes. Then the Ringer solution that had been in the first heart during the stimulation of the vagus was transferred to the second heart. [This second heart] slowed and its beats diminished just as if its vagus had been stimulated. Similarly, when the accelerator nerve was stimulated and the Ringer from this period transferred, the second heart speeded up and its beats increased. These results unequivocally proved that the nerves do not influence the heart directly but liberate from their terminals specific chemical substances which, in their turn, cause the well-known modifications of the function of the heart characteristic of the stimulation of its nerves.[16]

So dramatic an account of a scientific achievement naturally arouses skepticism, but Dale has testified that Loewi told him essentially the same story in 1921 and repeated it virtually unchanged several times during the next four decades.[17] Some of the mystery was dispelled when Loewi eventually realized that the method he used to demonstrate chemical transmission for the cardiac nerves was essentially the same method he had used in two slightly earlier studies "also in search of a substance given off from the heart."[18] For Loewi the remarkable nocturnal experimental design then became nothing more than a sudden unconscious association between the old hypothesis and the recent method.[19]

Loewi's classic experiment was described in a four-page article in *Pflügers Archiv* in 1921, the first in a series of fourteen papers on humoral transmission which Loewi and his several collaborators published in the same journal during the next fifteen years. The initial paper is considerably more modest in its claims than the retrospective accounts of Loewi and others might suggest: although it clearly emphasized chemical mediation of nerve impulses as one plausible interpretation of the experimental results, it also raised the alternative possibility that vagomimetic and accelerator-mimetic substances might be products of altered cardiac activity and thus not directly products of nerve stimulation. In the second paper of the series (1922) Loewi rejected the latter interpretation in favor of direct chemical mediation. The next immediate task, pursued in several papers in the series, was to determine the chemical nature of the substances released by stimulation of the vagus and accelerator nerves. The fact that the action of the vagus-transmitting substance *(Vagusstoff)* was abolished by atropine greatly simplified the search for its chemical equivalent; and as early as the second paper Loewi argued that the *Vagusstoff* must be a choline ester. But not until the tenth and eleventh papers (both published in 1926) did Loewi and his collaborator E. Navratil positively identify the *Vagusstoff* with acetylcholine. For some, notably Dale, this identification seemed to be approached with excessive caution in view of what was already known about acetylcholine, much of it as a result of Dale's own work a decade earlier.

But Loewi's caution may well reflect the skepticism that his work aroused in others, particularly Leon Asher, against whose criticisms some of the papers in the series were specifically directed. Nor was all of the criticism misguided: however simple on the surface, Loewi's famous experiment is not always easy to reproduce, and it is said that he often failed in his own attempts to do so.[20] As Loewi pointed out in the third paper of the series (1924), success depended on achieving a combination of several intricate experimental conditions, including a test heart of appropriate responsiveness (which in turn could depend on species differences and the season of the year). Perhaps because of such difficulties, Loewi was invited to demonstrate his experiment before the Twelfth International Congress of Physiology at Stockholm in 1926. Although he apparently accepted the invitation with some reluctance, Loewi executed the demonstration with great success.[21] By 1934 W. B. Cannon could describe the support for Loewi's work as "conclusive,"[22] a judgment confirmed by G. Liljestrand in his presentation speech at the Nobel Prize ceremonies in 1936.[23]

If Loewi proceeded cautiously toward the identification of *Vagusstoff* with acetylcholine, he moved even more cautiously toward an identification of the substance released by stimulation of the accelerator nerve. Even though Elliott had proposed the hypothesis of chemical transmission in the first place

because of the sympathomimetic effects of adrenalin, it was not until 1936 that Loewi positively identified the *Acceleransstoff* or *Sympathicusstoff* with adrenaline (epinephrine). Like many others, Loewi apparently did assume immediately that his results for the cardiac nerves would apply as well to all other peripheral autonomic nerve fibers, and one of the earliest and most important pieces of evidence for this extension was produced in Loewi's laboratory by E. Engelhart.[24] But the suggestion that chemical transmitters were also released by ordinary voluntary motor fibers or across other nonautonomic synaptic junctions aroused in Loewi what Dale characterized as "almost obstinate scepticism."[25] Chiefly because nervous impulses produce their effects so much more rapidly in voluntary and central nervous processes than in autonomic, Loewi doubted that chemical transmission could be involved in the former. In the end, as Loewi himself emphasized, it was Dale and his associates who were mainly responsible for establishing the existence of chemical transmission outside the postganglionic autonomic nervous system.[26]

In a sense, however, Dale's ability to make this bold extension depended in part on Loewi's caution. For in the course of their careful approach toward a definitive identification of *Vagusstoff*, Loewi and Navratil not only found that the effects of *Vagusstoff* faded rapidly because it was speedily metabolized by an enzyme but also that this enzyme could be inhibited (and *Vagusstoff* thereby protected) by the alkaloid physostigmine (eserine). These results, reported in the tenth and eleventh papers of the famous series, were important for several reasons. (1) Since acetylcholine was also speedily metabolized by the same enzyme (a specific cholinesterase) and also selectively protected by eserine, the identity of *Vagusstoff* and acetylcholine was virtually assured. (2) By this work Loewi and Navratil introduced the concept that the pharmacologic action of an alkaloid could be defined in terms of its inhibition of an enzyme, and thus helped to explain why alkaloids could be effective even in minute doses. (3) The ability of eserine to prevent the destruction of acetylcholine made it possible to develop new methods for detecting the transmitter in tissues where its low concentration or rapid destruction had kept it hitherto undetected. It was chiefly by the use of eserinized solutions that Dale and others were able to establish the existence of chemical transmission in warm-blooded vertebrates and in parts of the nervous system where Loewi himself had doubted its presence. (4) The knowledge that a specific cholinesterase was responsible for the destruction of the acetylcholine transmitter made it easier to understand and to determine why the speed and duration of nervous effects might vary in different species and in different parts of the nervous system. Among other things, these differences might be traced to differences in the amount of the cholinesterase normally present in different tissues. Along lines such as these, an explanation can be proposed for the difficulties encountered in the early attempts to reproduce Loewi's original experiment. According to William Van der Kloot, the heart of the Hungarian frogs that Loewi used contains only a small amount of the cholinesterase, so that the acetylcholine released by vagus stimulation persists unusually well in it.[27] In the era before eserinized solutions, those who used other species would naturally have experienced greater difficulty in detecting the vagus transmitter.

With the publication in 1936 of the fourteenth and final paper in the series on humoral transmission, the truly creative phase of Loewi's research career came to an end. Especially after 1938, when the Nazis forced him out of Graz, Loewi's main role was that of critic, reviewer, and guide for those who more actively pursued the new lines of research opened up by the discovery of the chemical transmission of nervous impulses. This discovery in fact inaugurated a conceptual revolution in neurophysiology. Besides offering an entirely new mode of thinking about such phenomena as inhibition and summation, the concept of chemical transmission had clinical implications as well, particularly with regard to certain symptoms of neurological hyperactivity formerly regarded as purely reflex in nature. Loewi himself often reflected on these questions as well as on the implications of chemical transmission for general physiology and biology. For him, the existence of chemical transmission seemed to give further support to the organismic conception of the living body as an adaptive, regulated, delicately coordinated, and peculiarly biological mechanism. In his inclination toward overtly teleological thinking, in his abiding love of music, art, and culture in general, and in his profound moral and humanitarian sensitivity, Loewi maintained to the end a kinship with that young aspiring historian of art who had been deflected by circumstance into a richly creative career in science.

NOTES

1. Loewi, "Prefatory Chapter," p. 2.
2. Loewi, "An Autobiographic Sketch," p. 7.
3. *Ibid.*, p. 10.
4. *Ibid.*, p. 21.
5. Loewi, "Prefatory Chapter," p. 2.
6. *Ibid.*, p. 2; and Loewi, "An Autobiographic Sketch," p. 6.
7. Loewi, "An Autobiographic Sketch," p. 9.
8. See Dale, "Otto Loewi," p. 70.

9. Of the work done during these two decades, Loewi himself chose to emphasize the following: "One of these studies proved that the preference of pancreatectomized dogs for fructose rather than glucose, as had been demonstrated by Minkowski, is not specific for this deficiency but is shared by dogs deprived of their glycogen by other means, e.g., by phosphorus poisoning. It was further shown that the heart, in contrast to the liver, cannot utilize fructose. It was finally discovered that epinephrine injections into rabbits completely depleted by starvation of their liver glycogen brought the glycogen back to almost normal values in spite of continued starvation." See Loewi, "An Autobiographic Sketch," pp. 12–13.
10. *Ibid.*, p. 15.
11. *Ibid.*, p. 13.
12. *Ibid.*, p. 13. Cf. Loewi, "The Ferrier Lecture," p. 300.
13. See T. R. Elliott, "On the Action of Adrenalin," in *Journal of Physiology*, **31** (1904), xx–xxi; and *ibid.*, **32** (1905), 401–467.
14. See Loewi, *From the Workshop of Discoveries*, p. 33; "An Autobiographic Sketch," p. 17; and the sources cited in note 15 below.
15. See H. H. Dale, "T. R. Elliott," in *Biographical Memoirs of Fellows of the Royal Society*, **7** (1961), 64; and "Otto Loewi," pp. 70–73.
16. Loewi, "An Autobiographic Sketch," p. 17. In an obvious oversight, Loewi here places the nocturnal event in 1920 rather than 1921. For a virtually identical version of the story, but with the correct date, see Loewi, *From the Workshop of Discoveries*, pp. 32–33.
17. Dale, "Otto Loewi," pp. 76–77.
18. Loewi, "An Autobiographic Sketch," p. 18. Loewi does not identify the two studies he has in mind, but the likeliest candidates are "Über Spontanerholung des Froschherzens bei unzureichender Kationenspeisung. II. Mitt. Ein Beitrag zur Wirkung der Alkalien aufs Herz," in *Pflügers Archiv für die gesamte Physiologie des Menschen und der Tiere*, **170** (1918), 677–695; and "III. Mitt. Quantitative mikroanalytische Untersuchungen über die Ursache der Calciumabgabe von seiten des Herzens," *ibid.*, **173** (1919), 152–157, written with H. Lieb.
19. Loewi, "An Autobiographic Sketch," p. 18.
20. Letter from William G. Van der Kloot to G. L. Geison, 2 June 1972.
21. Loewi, "An Autobiographic Sketch," p. 19; Dale, "Otto Loewi," pp. 77–78. Incidentally, neither account corroborates a remarkable claim which Loewi made many years later to William Van der Kloot, who was chairman of the pharmacology department at New York University during Loewi's last years there. According to Van der Kloot (see note 20) Loewi told him that during this demonstration in Stockholm he had been "obliged to stand at one end of the room and simply give instructions, so that the possibility of his secreting some chemical under his fingernails and dropping it on the preparation could be eliminated." This claim also appears to conflict with a photograph taken of Loewi at the time of the demonstration (see Holmstedt and Liljestrand, *Readings in Pharmacology*, p. 194).
22. Walter B. Cannon, "The Story of the Development of Our Ideas of Chemical Mediation of Nerve Impulses," in *American Journal of the Medical Sciences*, n.s. **188** (1934), 149.
23. See *Nobel Lectures Including Presentation Speeches and Laureates' Biographies: Physiology or Medicine 1922–1941* (Amsterdam, 1965), pp. 397–401, esp. p. 399.
24. See e.g., Otto Loewi, "Chemical Transmission of Nervous Impulses," in George A. Baitsell, ed., *Science in Progress*, 4th ser. (New Haven, 1945), p. 102.
25. Dale, "Otto Loewi," p. 79.
26. See, e.g., Otto Loewi, "Salute to Henry Hallet Dale," in *British Medical Journal* (1955), **1**, 1356–1357.
27. Van der Kloot to Geison (see note 20).

BIBLIOGRAPHY

I. ORIGINAL WORKS. Lembeck and Giere (see below) give an apparently complete bibliography of more than 170 items by Loewi, arranged both topically and chronologically. In their topical bibliography, a summary is also given of the contents of most of his research papers. Appended to Henry Dale's biographical memoir of Loewi (see below) is a bibliography of 150 items; Dale omits many of the essentially nonscientific papers included by Lembeck and Giere.

The most important of Loewi's papers on metabolism is "Über Eiweisssynthese im Thierkörper," in *Archiv für experimentelle Pathologie und Pharmakologie*, **48** (1902), 303–330. For the early series of five papers on the kidney, see "Untersuchungen zur Physiologie und Pharmakologie der Nierenfunction," *ibid.*, **48** (1902), 410–438; **50** (1903), 326–331; **53** (1905), 15–32, 33–48, 49–55. Loewi abandoned his earlier hypothesis of the mode of action of insulin in "Insulin und Glykämin," in *Klinische Wochenschrift*, **8** (1929), 391–393. On the concept of the proprioceptive metabolic reflex, see "Über den Glykogenstoffwechsel des Muskels und seine nervöse Beeinflussung," in *Pflügers Archiv für die gesamte Physiologie des Menschen und der Tiere*, **233** (1933), 35–56. For Loewi and Frölich's work on cocaine and adrenaline, see "Untersuchungen zur Physiologie und Pharmakologie des autonomen Nervensystems. II. Mitt. Über eine Steigerung der Adrenalinempfindlichkeit durch Cocain," in *Archiv für experimentelle Pathologie und Pharmakologie*, **62** (1910), 159–169.

For Loewi's work on the heart between 1912 and 1921, see "Untersuchungen zur Physiologie und Pharmakologie des Herzvagus," *ibid.*, **70** (1912), 323–343, 343–350, 351–368; "Über Beziehungen zwischen Herzmittel- und physiologischer Kationenwirkung," *ibid.*, **71** (1913), 251–260; **82** (1918), 131–158; **83** (1918), 366–380; *Pflügers Archiv*, **187** (1921), 105–122, 123–131; **188** (1921), 87–97; and "Über die Spontanerholung des Froschherzens bei unzureichender Kationenspeisung," *ibid.*, **157** (1914), 531; **170** (1918), 677–695; and **173** (1919), 152–157. For the celebrated series of fourteen papers on humoral transmission, see "Über homorale Übertragbarkeit der Herznervenwirkung," *ibid.*, **189** (1921), 239–242; **193** (1922), 201–213; **203** (1924), 408–412; **204** (1924), 361–367, 629–640; **206** (1924), 123–134, 135–140; **208** (1925), 694–704; **210** (1925), 550–556; **214** (1926), 678–688, 689–696; **217** (1927), 610–617; **225** (1930), 721–727; **237** (1936), 504–514. See also Otto Loewi, "Kritische Bemerkungen zu L. Ashers Mitteilungen," *ibid.*, **212** (1926), 695–706.

Loewi's more general views on chemical transmission and his role as historian, reviewer, critic, and guide are best revealed in a number of his lectures given between about 1930 and 1945. Of these, the most important and valuable are "The Humoral Transmission of Nervous Impulse," in *Harvey Lectures*, **28** (1934), 218–233; "The Ferrier Lecture on Problems Connected with the Principle of Humoral Transmission of Nervous Impulses," in *Proceedings of the Royal Society*, **118B** (1935), 299–316; "Die chemische Übertragung der Nervwirkung," in *Schweize-*

rische medizinische Wochenschrift, **67** (1937), 850–855; "Die chemische Übertragung der Herznervenwirkung," in *Les Prix Nobel en 1936* (Stockholm, 1936), translated into English in *Nobel Lectures Including Presentation Speeches and Laureates' Biographies: Physiology or Medicine 1922–1941* (Amsterdam, 1965), pp. 416–429; and "The Edward Gamaliel Janeway Lectures: Aspects of the Transmission of Nervous Impulse," in *Journal of the Mount Sinai Hospital*, **12** (1945), 803–816, 851–865. See also the lecture cited in note 24 above.

For useful autobiographical material, see Otto Loewi, "An Autobiographic Sketch," in *Perspectives in Biology and Medicine*, **4** (1960), 1–25, reprinted in Lembeck and Giere, pp. 168–190; "Prefatory Chapter: Reflections on the Study of Physiology," in *Annual Review of Physiology*, **16** (1954), 1–10, reprinted in *The Excitement and Fascination of Science: A Collection of Autobiographical Essays* (Palo Alto, Calif., 1965), pp. 269–278; and *From the Workshop of Discoveries* (Lawrence, Kans., 1953). Lembeck and Giere have also published two posthumous MSS by Loewi, "Meaning of Life" and "The Organism as a Unit" (pp. 191–203 and 204–217, respectively); as well as a dozen brief ceremonial addresses given by Loewi between 1942 and 1952 (pp. 218–241). Several of these sources emphasize Loewi's organismic philosophy and approach; a few relate to the Jewish question and to more general political and humanitarian concerns.

According to Lembeck and Giere, Loewi's MSS and papers are deposited in thirteen file drawers at the Royal Society of London. In the obituary files of the Medical-Historical Library, Yale University, is a letter from Loewi to Harvey Cushing (27 Nov. 1937) in which Loewi seeks aid for a victim of Nazi persecution. Coming just a few months before his own imprisonment by the Nazis, it is both a reminder of the horror of Nazism and a testimony to the solidarity of its victims.

II. SECONDARY LITERATURE. The basic source for Loewi's life and work is Fred Lembeck and Wolfgang Giere, *Otto Loewi: Ein Lebensbild in Dokumenten* (Berlin, 1968). Although not a scientific biography of Loewi, this remarkable book reprints or provides references to almost all the material that a biographer could conceivably use. Besides the reprinted material and bibliographies mentioned above, there is a brief biographical sketch (pp. 2–16), a list of his honors and the professional associations to which he belonged (pp. 19–21), a bibliography of more than fifty sketches and obituaries (pp. 22–24), and a lengthy section containing extensive and impressive documentation of his life (pp. 27–91).

Of the many biographical sketches of Loewi, the most valuable is that by his Nobel colaureate Henry Dale, "Otto Loewi," in *Biographical Memoirs of Fellows of the Royal Society*, **8** (1962), 67–89, with portrait and bibliography. For short biographical sketches, brief attempts to place Loewi's work in historical perspective, and excerpts in English from his writings, see Lloyd G. Stevenson, *Nobel Prize Winners in Medicine and Physiology, 1901–1950* (New York, 1953), pp. 186–195; B. Holmstedt and G. Liljestrand, *Readings in Pharmacology* (New York,

1963), pp. 190–196; and Edwin Clarke and C. D. O'Malley, *The Human Brain and Spinal Cord: A Historical Study Illustrated by Writings from Antiquity to the Twentieth Century* (Berkeley, Calif., 1968), pp. 250–255.

GERALD L. GEISON

LOEWINSON-LESSING. See **Levinson-Lessing, Frants Yulevich.**

LOEWNER, CHARLES (KARL) (*b*. Lany, Bohemia [now Czechoslovakia], 29 May 1893; *d*. Stanford, California, 8 January 1968), *mathematics.*

Loewner was the son of Sigmund and Jana Loewner. He studied mathematics with G. Pick at the German University of Prague and received the Ph.D. in 1917. From 1917 to 1922 he was an assistant at the German Technical University of Prague; from 1922 to 1928, assistant and *Privatdozent* at the University of Berlin; from 1928 to 1930, extraordinary professor at the University of Cologne; and from 1930 to 1939, full professor at Charles University in Prague, which he left when the Nazis occupied Czechoslovakia. From 1939 to 1944 he was lecturer and assistant professor at the University of Louisville, Kentucky; from 1945 to 1946, associate professor, and from 1946 to 1951, full professor at Syracuse University; and from 1951 until his retirement in 1963, full professor at Stanford University.

Loewner was married to Elizabeth Alexander, who died in 1955; they had one daughter. Of short stature, soft-spoken, modest, shy (but exceedingly kind to his acquaintances), he had a large number of research students, even after his retirement. His knowledge of mathematics was broad and profound, and included significant parts of mathematical physics. His originality was remarkable; he chose as his problems far from fashionable topics.

One idea pervades Loewner's work from his Ph.D. thesis: applying Lie theory concepts and methods to semigroups, and applying semigroups to unexpected mathematical situations. This led him in 1923 to a sensational result (4): the first significant contribution to the Bieberbach hypothesis. (A *schlicht* function $f(z) = \sum a_n z^n$ in the unit circle with $a_0 = 0$, $a_1 = 1$, has $|a_n| \leqslant n$—the case $n = 2$ was Bieberbach's and Loewner proved it for $n = 3$; in its totality the problem is still open.) In 1934 Loewner defined nth-order real monotonic functions by the property of staying monotonic if extended to nth-degree symmetric matrices (7) and characterized ∞th-order monotonic

functions as functions which, analytically extended to the upper half-plane, map it into itself. The semigroups of first- and second-order monotonic mappings are infinitesimally generated; this property breaks down for orders greater than 2 (28, 32). The infinitesimally generated closed subsemigroup of monotonic mappings of infinite order is characterized by *schlicht* extensions to the upper half-plane (21). Loewner studied minimal semigroup extensions of Lie groups; for the group of the real projective line there are two: that of monotonic mappings of infinite order, and its inverse (21). In higher dimensions the question becomes significant under a suitable definition of monotony (30). Loewner also studied semigroups in a more geometrical context: deformation theorems for projective and Moebius translations (19), and infinitesimally generated semigroups invariant under the non-Euclidean or Moebius group (19), particularly if finite dimensionality and minimality are requested (22).

Among Loewner's other papers, many of which deal with physics, one should be mentioned explicitly: his non-Archimedean measure in Hilbert space (8), which despite its startling originality (or rather because of it) has drawn little attention outside the circle of those who know Loewner's work.

BIBLIOGRAPHY

Loewner's works are

(1) "Untersuchungen über die Verzerrung bei konformen Abbildungen des Einheitskreises, die durch Funktionen mit nichtverschwindender Ableitung geliefert werden," in *Berichte über die Verhandlungen der Sächsischen Akademie der Wissenschaften zu Leipzig*, Math.-phys. Klasse, **69** (1917), 89–106;

(2) "Über Extremumsätze bei der konformen Abbildung des Äusseren des Einheitskreises," in *Mathematische Zeitschrift*, **3** (1919), 65–77;

(3) "Eine Anwendung des Koebeschen Verzerrungssatzes auf ein Problem der Hydrodynamik," *ibid.*, 78–86, written with P. Frank;

(4) "Untersuchungen über schlichte konforme Abbildungen des Einheitskreises," in *Mathematische Annalen*, **89** (1923), 103–121;

(5) "Bemerkung zu einem Blaschkeschen Konvergenzsatze," in *Jahresbericht der Deutschen Mathematikervereinigung*, **32** (1923), 198–200, written with T. Rado;

(6) Chapters 3 and 16 in P. Frank and R. von Mises, eds., *Die Differential- und Integralgleichungen der Mechanik und Physik* (Brunswick, 1925), ch. 3, 119–192, and ch. 16, 685–737;

(7) "Über monotone Matrixfunktionen," in *Mathematische Zeitschrift*, **38** (1934), 177–216;

(8) "Grundzüge einer Inhaltslehre im Hilbertschen Raume," in *Annals of Mathematics*, **40** (1939), 816–833;

(9) "A Topological Characterization of a Class of Integral Operators," ibid., **49** (1948), 316–332;

(10) "Some Classes of Functions Defined by Difference or Differential Inequalities," in Bulletin of the American Mathematical Society, **56** (1950), 308–319;

(11) A Transformation Theory of the Partial Differential Equations of Gas Dynamics, NACA Technical Report no. 2065 (New York, 1950);

(12) "Generation of Solutions of Systems of Partial Differential Equations by Composition of Infinitesimal Baecklund Transformations," in Journal d'analyse mathématique, **2** (1952–1953), 219–242;

(13) "On Generation of Solutions of the Biharmonic Equation in the Plane by Conformal Mappings," in Pacific Journal of Mathematics, **3** (1953), 417–436;

(14) "Conservation Laws in Compressible Fluid Flow and Associated Mappings," in Journal of Rational Mechanics and Analysis, **2** (1953), 537–561;

(15) "Some Bounds for the Critical Free Stream Mach Number of a Compressible Flow Around an Obstacle," in Studies in Mathematics and Mechanics Presented to Richard von Mises (New York, 1954), 177–183;

(16) "On Some Critical Points of Higher Order," Technical Note no. 2, Air Force Contract AF 18(600)680 (1954);

(17) "On Totally Positive Matrices," in Mathematische Zeitschrift, **63** (1955), 338–340;

(18) "Continuous Groups," mimeographed notes, University of California at Berkeley (1955);

(19) "On Some Transformation Semigroups," in Journal of Rational Mechanics and Analysis, **5** (1956), 791–804;

(20) "Advanced Matrix Theory," mimeographed notes, Stanford University (1957);

(21) "Semigroups of Conformal Mappings," in Seminar on Analytic Functions, Institute for Advanced Study, I (Princeton, N.J., 1957), 278–288;

(22) "On Some Transformation Semigroups Invariant Under Euclidean and non-Euclidean Isometries," in Journal of Mathematics and Mechanics, **8** (1959), 393–409;

(23) "A Theorem on the Partial Order Derived From a Certain Transformation Semigroup," in Mathematische Zeitschrift, **72** (1959), 53–60;

(24) "On the Conformal Capacity in Space," in Journal of Mathematics and Mechanics, **8** (1959), 411–414;

(25) "On Some Compositions of Hadamard Type in Classes of Analytic Functions," in Bulletin of the American Mathematical Society, **65** (1959), 284–286, written with E. Netanyahu;

(26) "A Group Theoretical Characterization of Some Manifold Structures," Technical Report no. 2 (1962);

(27) "On Some Classes of Functions Associated With Exponential Polynomials," in Studies in Mathematical Analysis and Related Topics (Stanford, Calif., 1962), 175–182, written with S. Karlin;

(28) "On Generation of Monotonic Transformations of Higher Order by Infinitesimal Transformations," in Journal d'analyse mathématique, **11** (1963), 189–206;

(29) "On Some Classes of Functions Associated With Systems of Curves or Partial Differential Equations of First Order," in Outlines of the Joint Soviet-American Symposium on Partial Differential Equations (Novosibirsk, 1963);

(30) "On Semigroups in Analysis and Geometry," in Bulletin of the American Mathematical Society, **70** (1964), 1–15;

(31) "Approximation on an Arc by Polynomials With Restricted Zeros," in Proceedings of the Koninklijke Nederlandse Akademie van Wetenschappen, Section A, **67** (1964), 121–128, written with J. Korevaar;

(32) "On Schlicht-monotonic Functions of Higher Order," in Journal of Mathematical Analysis and Applications, **14** (1966), 320–326;

(33) "Some Concepts of Parallelism With Respect to a Given Transformation Group," in Duke Mathematical Journal, **33** (1966), 151–164;

(34) "Determination of the Critical Exponent of the Green's Function," in Contemporary Problems in the Theory of Analytic Functions (Moscow, 1965), pp. 184–187;

(35) "On the Difference Between the Geometric and the Arithmetic Mean of n Quantities," in Advances in Mathematics, **5** (1971), 472–473, written with H. B. Mann; and

(36) Theory of Continuous Groups, with notes by H. Flanders and M. H. Protter (Cambridge, Mass., 1971).

HANS FREUDENTHAL

LOEWY, ALFRED (b. Rawitsch, Germany [now Rawicz, Poznan, Poland], 20 June 1873; d. Freiburg im Breisgau, Germany, 25 January 1935), mathematics.

Loewy studied from 1891 to 1895 at the universities of Breslau, Munich, Berlin, and Göttingen. He earned his Ph.D. in 1894 at Munich; was granted his Habilitation as Privatdozent at Freiburg in 1897; and became extraordinary professor in 1902. Not until 1919 was he appointed a full professor at Freiburg. In 1935 he was forced into retirement because he was a Jew. From about 1920 he was troubled with poor eyesight and he died totally blind.

Loewy published some seventy papers in mathematical periodicals and a few books. He edited German translations of works by Abel, Fourier, and Sturm; and the greater portion of the first part of Pascal's Repertorium was his work. His publications were concerned mainly with linear groups, with the algebraic theory of linear and algebraic differential equations, and with actuarial mathematics.

BIBLIOGRAPHY

I. ORIGINAL WORKS. Loewy's writings include Versicherungsmathematik, Göschen collection, 180 (Leipzig, 1903); Lehrbuch der Algebra (Leipzig, 1915); and Mathematik des Geld- und Zahlungsverkehrs (Leipzig, 1920).

Translations edited by Loewy or to which he contributed are N. H. Abel, *Abhandlung über eine besondere Klasse algebraisch auflösbarer Gleichungen*, Ostwald's Klassiker no. 111 (Leipzig, 1900); J. B. Fourier, *Die Auflösung der bestimmten Gleichungen*, Ostwald's Klassiker no. 127 (Leipzig, 1902); C. Sturm, *Abhandlung über die Auflösung der numerischen Gleichungen*, Ostwald's Klassiker no. 143 (Leipzig, 1904); and E. Pascal, ed., *Repertorium der höheren Mathematik*, P. Epstein and M. E. Timerding, eds., 2nd ed., I (Leipzig, 1910).

II. SECONDARY LITERATURE. See S. Breuer, "Alfred Loewy," in *Versicherungsarchiv*, **6** (1935), 1–5; and A. Fraenkel, "Alfred Loewy," in *Scripta mathematica*, **5** (1938), 17–22, with portrait.

HANS FREUDENTHAL

LOGAN, JAMES (*b*. Lurgan, Ireland, 20 October 1674; *d*. Germantown, Pennsylvania, 31 October 1751), *dissemination of knowledge*.

The most intellectually capable scientist of colonial America, Logan published works in botany and optics. His major contribution, however, lay in his acknowledged competence in science and in the help and advice that he gave to Thomas Godfrey, John Bartram, Benjamin Franklin, and Cadwallader Colden.

Logan was the son of Patrick Logan, a Scotch Quaker schoolmaster who moved in 1690 from Lurgan to Bristol, where he taught school assisted by his son. James Logan learned Latin and Greek as well as a number of other languages, including Arabic and Italian. He taught himself mathematics by mastering William Leybourn's *Cursus mathematicus*, only one work in his boasted first library of 700 volumes, which he later sold in order to invest in the linen trade. Having failed to so establish himself, in 1699 Logan accepted William Penn's invitation to accompany him to Pennsylvania as his secretary.

On his return to England in 1701, Penn left the twenty-seven-year-old Logan in charge of his affairs. For over four decades—as administrator, land agent, and merchant—he represented, not without dispute, the interests of Penn and his heirs. He was first secretary to and then for most of his life a member of the provincial council, mayor of Philadelphia in 1722–1723, chief justice of the Supreme Court of Pennsylvania in 1731–1739, and acting governor of the colony in 1736–1737. He negotiated treaties with the Indians and foresaw a clash with the French on the frontiers. He designed the Conestoga wagon to transport trade goods to Indian country and furs for export back to Philadelphia. He became rich through personal investments in land and an active mercantile trade.

Logan's copy of the *Principia*, which he bought in 1708 while he was in London, was the first known in America. On the same trip Logan saw Newton perform an experiment on the velocity of falling bodies under the dome of St. Paul's. He also made the acquaintance of a number of learned English men, including Flamsteed, and haunted the bookshops of London. Self-taught from books—which he bought in increasing quantities as he grew older and richer—Logan became highly knowledgeable in mathematics, natural history, and astronomy, making observations with his own telescope. Unhappily alone on the frontier of civilization without intellectual peers to converse with, he entered into extensive correspondence with Robert Hunter and William Burnet, successive governors of New York; the Quaker scholar Josiah Martin; Johann Albrecht Fabricius; William Jones, the British mathematician; John Fothergill, the Quaker physician; and Peter Collinson.

On his second trip to England in 1723–1724, Logan procured a set of sheets of Edmond Halley's still unpublished moon tables and added to them an explanation of Halley's method and an account of his own observation of the solar eclipse of 11 May 1724, which he watched at Windsor with members of the Penn family. Many of his astronomical books, some of which he procured from the widow of Johann Jacob Zimmermann, the German scientist and pietist, are full of notes, corrections, and comments, including Flamsteed's suppressed calculations of stars which Logan inserted in his own copy of Hevelius' *Prodromus Astronomiae*.

Thomas Godfrey, a glazier, was introduced to higher mathematics by Logan and became so proficient that he invented an improved mariner's quadrant. In 1732 Logan vigorously defended Godfrey's claim to the invention before the Royal Society against the simultaneous announcement of a similar instrument by John Hadley. His letters on behalf of Godfrey were supplemented by his own communications to the Royal Society, including in 1735 a preliminary essay on the generation of Indian corn, and in 1736 observations on a Hebrew shekel (which he sent as a gift), further notes on his corn experiments, a theory to explain the crooked aspect of lightning, and a hypothesis to account for the huge appearance of the moon on the horizon. He was, however, never made a fellow of the Royal Society.

In 1727 Logan read of the theories of seminal preformation and aerial pollination and began his own experiments with Indian corn. After his initial letter to the Royal Society, he worked to improve his techniques and to make his conclusions more explicit. Although the British scientists took little notice of his work, it was received enthusiastically on the Continent. Linnaeus hailed Logan as one of the heroes of botany, and Johann Friedrich Gronovius saw that the essay was published in full at Leiden in 1739 as *Experimenta et meletemata de plantarum*. Others had noted the sexuality of plants and pollination; Logan, by covering the flowers of corn with linen bags and by cutting off the tassels, demonstrated how the pollen generates kernels, or seeds, by ascending the tassels. Fothergill translated the work into English as *Experiments and Considerations on the Generation of Plants*, and it was published in London in 1747. Logan's work, a pioneer step toward plant hybridization, was referred to throughout the century. Within a year of the publication of Linnaeus' *Systema naturae* in 1735 Logan had acquired a copy. He introduced the "natural" naturalist, John Bartram, to the advances in taxonomy and taught him enough Latin to be able to read Linnaeus. It was through his encouragement and introductions that Bartram became known to botanists abroad.

Logan's scientific virtuosity found other expression. His simplification of Christiaan Huygens' method of finding the refraction of a lens appeared at the end of his *Experimenta* as "Canonum pro inveniendis refractionum." A second work in optics was even bolder. Starting with Huygens and going beyond Newton, he tried to show that the laws of spherical aberration could be more briefly expressed mathematically otherwise than geometrically. His treatise *Demonstrationes de radiorum lucis in superficies sphaericas* was reprinted at Leiden in 1741 with the help of Gronovius, whose colleague Pieter van Musschenbroek read the proofs. Such was Logan's reputation at home that Franklin brought him the accounts of his experiments in electricity to read before he sent them off to England.

Early in 1728 Logan slipped on ice and broke the head of his thighbone; it never healed, and he was lame for the rest his life. In 1730, after moving to his country house, Stenton, in Germantown, he tried with only moderate success to free himself of administrative responsibilities so that he could devote himself to his books. His translation of the pseudo-Cato's *Moral Distichs* was printed by Franklin in 1735, and his more famous version of Cicero's *Cato major*, written in 1733, was issued in 1744, also from Franklin's press. These, as well as his scientific articles, were minor works. During the second half of the 1730's Logan worked in bursts of energy upon a major philosophical treatise, "The Duties of Man Deduced from Nature." The recently rediscovered manuscript contains three completed chapters, one almost complete, and two only begun. In the section

"Of the Exterior Senses" Logan brought to bear his knowledge of mathematics, harmonics, and medicine. The work, although imperfect, is the only surviving nontheological tractate on moral philosophy written in colonial America.

In 1742 Logan decided to bequeath his extensive library for public use and to spend his remaining years increasing it. By a codicil to his will, canceled because of a disagreement with his son-in-law, Isaac Norris, who had been named one of the trustees, he had left his books to be installed in a building at Sixth and Walnut Streets in Philadelphia. After his death his children established the Bibliotheca Loganiana, then consisting of about 2,600 volumes, as a trust in accordance with their father's unfulfilled intentions. In 1792 the trust was transferred to the Library Company of Philadelphia, where the books have remained ever since. The finest library in British America, it is now the only collection of its kind that has been preserved virtually intact. As he wrote for Franklin in 1749, Logan's library contained "A good Collection of Mathematical Pieces, as Newton in all three Editions, Wallis, Huygens, Tacquet, Deschales, &c. in near 100 Vols. in all Sizes." He had in addition all the works of the ancient mathematicians, a large collection of astronomical works, and as good a representation of books on natural history as could be found in the colonies. His impact as a scientist was limited, for, with few exceptions, he read, worked, and experimented for his own intellectual enjoyment.

BIBLIOGRAPHY

I. ORIGINAL WORKS. Logan's writings have been mentioned in the text; he also published a number of political pamphlets and broadsides. His philosophical treatise, "The Duties of Man Deduced From Nature," in the Historical Society of Pennsylvania, is still unpublished. The principal materials on Logan's life are in the extensive Logan Papers in the Historical Society of Pennsylvania, which include MSS of many of his writings, a virtually complete run of letter books and other documents by and about him, but no corpus of letters received.

II. SECONDARY LITERATURE. The only adequate biography of Logan is Frederick B. Tolles, *James Logan and the Culture of Provincial America* (Boston, 1957) but it is too brief. Logan's experiments on Indian corn are treated by Conway Zirkle, *The Beginnings of Plant Hybridization and Sex in Plants* (Philadelphia, 1935). His mathematical knowledge is noted, somewhat inaccurately, by Frederick E. Brasch, "James Logan, a Colonial Mathematical Scholar, and the First Copy of Newton's *Principia* to Arrive in the Colonies," in *Proceedings of the American Philosophical Society*, **86** (1942), 3–12. The best general appraisal of Logan as a scientist is Frederick B. Tolles, "Philadelphia's First Scientist, James Logan," in *Isis*, **47**

(1956), 2–30. The *Catalogus bibliothecae Loganianae* (Philadelphia, 1760) lists his library as it existed at the time of his death. A detailed catalogue of that library, noting his extensive annotations and his correspondence about the books, is being compiled by the author.

EDWIN WOLF II

LOGAN, WILLIAM EDMOND (*b.* Montreal, Canada, 20 April 1798; *d.* Llechryd, Wales, 22 July 1875), *geology.*

Logan's grandfather, James Logan, emigrated from Stirling, Scotland, to Montreal in 1784 and soon developed a prosperous bakery business, which passed upon his retirement to his eldest son, William. The latter married Janet Edmond of Stirling; and their second son, William Edmond, was born in Montreal. Logan's education began at Skakel's Private School in Montreal and continued at the Edinburgh High School (1814–1816) and Edinburgh University (1816–1817), where he studied chemistry, mathematics, and logic. He spent the years 1818–1831 in his uncle Hart's bank in London, becoming its manager upon his uncle's retirement in 1827. Later (1831–1838) he joined the management of a copper-smelting and coal-mining venture near Swansea, Wales, in which his uncle was interested, remaining there until his uncle's death. He soon found that chemistry and geology were essential to the success of the business and embarked upon a geological study of the local Glamorganshire coalfield—ultimately, in 1838, producing a memoir, with maps and sections. Its excellence was recognized by the director of the Geological Survey of Great Britain, Sir Henry De la Beche, who with Logan's permission incorporated it *in toto* in the Survey's report on that region. From that time on, Logan devoted himself exclusively to geology, particularly to the coal formations.

Logan's work on underclays with fossil *Stigmaria* in South Wales coalfields was to weigh heavily on the side of the *in situ* theory of the origin of coal, and, with his papers on the packing of ice in the St. Lawrence River, soon established him as a geologist of note. In 1842 the appointment of a provincial geologist was approved by the Canadian government under Sir Charles Bagot, who set about finding a suitable candidate. Logan obtained "a mass of testimonials," including letters from four of the most influential British geologists of the time: De la Beche, Roderick Murchison, Adam Sedgwick, and William Buckland. As a consequence he was offered, and accepted, the directorship of the newly created Geological Survey

of Canada, a post which he held until 1869. For twenty-seven years he and his assistants traveled in all reachable parts of Canada from the Great Lakes to the Maritime Provinces; they also issued reports of progress, of which "Report on the Geology of Canada" (1863), his *magnum opus*, provided a compilation of twenty years of research. After more than a century, it is still a reservoir of important information.

Logan was fortunate in the choice of his assistants for both fieldwork and office work. Alexander Murray was his first and most important field geologist until he resigned to become director of the Geological Survey of Newfoundland in 1864. T. Sterry Hunt, his chemist, was responsible for hundreds of analyses of minerals, rocks, and ores. Elkanah Billings, his paleontologist, examined all fossils collected by field geologists and provided Logan with information invaluable for the correct identification of the age and the stratigraphic position of rock formations. Others included the geologists James Richardson and Robert Bell and the draftsman Robert Barlow. Later, Edward Hartley, Thomas Macfarlane, Charles Robb, and H. G. Vennor joined the Survey.

A twelve-hour day in the field was the rule for Logan. He was usually alone, carrying all necessary equipment together with the day's collection of specimens; he recorded his progress by means of pacing and compass in regions of which, for the most part, there were no reliable maps. If at the end of a day in the bush his plotting of his traverse showed an error of more than two chains, he was disappointed. In the evenings he wrote up his notes and completed his maps. Logan's notebooks, preserved in Ottawa, are marvels of simplicity, perspicacity, and brevity, here and there embellished by illuminating pen sketches of the country covered. He was equally tireless during the winters, composing his reports of progress, revising those of his assistants, and above all seeking adequate governmental financial support. Thousands of pounds of his own resources were poured into the early ill-supported organization.

Following the publication of the 1863 report one can detect a slight but increasing diminution of Logan's powers, which in 1869 he recognized had reached a point where a younger man was needed to carry the burden of a vigorous and growing organization. As a consequence, in that year he resigned as director and divided his time between an estate he had bought in Wales and exploration, at his own expense, in Canada, designed to settle certain vexatious problems which had been left unsolved at the time of his resignation. While preparing for a summer's fieldwork in the eastern townships of Quebec, he became ill;

461

and following a short illness he died in 1875. He was buried in the churchyard at Llechryd, Wales.

Logan's bibliography is not extensive and consists mostly of progress reports to the government concerning the work of the Survey. Many of these reports, sixteen in all, he wrote in his own hand—some in quadruplicate. The most important, and nearly the last, was his 1863 report, which provided the first complete coverage, according to information then available, of the geology of Canada from the Great Lakes to the Atlantic seaboard. In this remarkable compilation Logan was ably assisted by Sterry Hunt, whose work as chemist provided the foundation on which much of the information concerning the rocks, minerals, and ores of Canada was based. Early articles on underclay, the Glamorganshire coalfield, and ice packing have been mentioned. Others, mostly short notes, recorded his observations on the copper-bearing rocks of Lake Superior, animal tracks in the Potsdam sandstone, the supposed fossil *Eozoön*, subdivision of the Precambrian rocks of Canada, and remarks on the Taconic question, in which he avoided controversy by using the term "Quebec group" for equivalent rocks in Canada. Although he was the first to publish the discovery of *Eozoön*, and exhibited specimens of it during his visits to England, Logan later became noncommittal as the battle was waged between those who saw it as a fossil and those who advocated its metamorphic origin.

Among Logan's achievements was his recognition of an anomalous structural condition in which rocks of the Quebec Group lay structurally above younger (Middle and Late Ordovician) beds of the St. Lawrence Lowland. This he explained by proposing "an overturn anticlinal fold, with a crack and dislocation running along its summit, by which the [Quebec] group is made to overlap the Hudson River [Upper Ordovician] formation." He traced this thrust fault from Alabama to the Canadian border, and thence to the tip of the Gaspé peninsula. Although made up of a multitude of imbricating faults the structure is still referred to as Logan's Line. The earliest use of that term is not known.

Logan was never directly connected with university affairs, although as a result of his regard for Sir John William Dawson he donated $19,000 to found the Logan chair in geology and lesser amounts for Logan medals. Both McGill University in Montreal (1856) and the University of Bishop's College in Lennoxville, Quebec (1855), conferred honorary degrees on him. The excellence of his display of Canadian rocks and minerals at the London exhibition of 1851 led to his election as fellow of the Royal Society; he was

sponsored by the most prominent contemporary British geologist, Sir Roderick Murchison. A similar exhibit at Paris in 1855 earned him the Grand Gold Medal of Honor from the Imperial Commission and an investiture as chevalier of the Legion of Honor in the same year. The following year he was knighted by Queen Victoria and also received the Wollaston Palladium Medal from the Royal Society. He was a fellow of the Geological Society of London (1837) and of the Royal Society of Edinburgh (1861), and a member of the Academy of Natural Sciences of Philadelphia (1846), the American Academy of Arts and Sciences, Boston (1859), and the American Philosophical Society (1860).

BIBLIOGRAPHY

I. Original Works. Logan's complete bibliography is in John M. Nickles, "Geologic Literature of North America 1785–1918," in *Bulletin of the United States Geological Survey*, no. 746, pt. 1 (1923), 671–672. His most important work was "Report on the Geology of Canada," in Geological Survey of Canada, *Report of Progress to 1863* (Ottawa, 1863), a summation of all his previous annual reports. His bibliography also includes a dozen short reports and articles on various topics.

II. Secondary Literature. See Robert Bell, *Sir William E. Logan and the Geological Survey of Canada* (Ottawa, 1877); B. J. Harrington, "Sir William Edmond Logan," in *American Journal of Science and Arts*, 3rd ser., **11** (1876), 81–93; *Canadian Naturalist and Geologist*, **8** (1876), 31–46, with portrait; and Geological Survey of Canada, *Report of Progress* for 1875–1876 (Ottawa, 1877), 8–21; and *Life of Sir William E. Logan, Kt.* (London, 1883), with portrait; J. M. Harrison and E. Hall, "William Edmond Logan," in *Proceedings of the Geological Association of Canada*, **15** (1963), 33–42; G. P. Merrill, *The First One Hundred Years of American Geology* (New Haven, 1924), 237, 411–416, 636; and W. Notman and Fennings Taylor, "Sir William Edmond Logan, LL.D., F.R.S., F.G.S.," in *Portraits of British Americans With Biographical Sketches*, II (Montreal, 1867), 133–145.

T. H. Clark

LOHEST, MARIE JOSEPH MAXIMIN (called **MAX**) (*b.* Liège, Belgium, 8 September 1857; *d.* Liège, 6 December 1926), *geology, mineralogical sciences, paleontology.*

Lohest was the son of Joseph Lohest, doctor of laws and merchant. After completing his secondary studies at the Collège des Jésuites, he enrolled first in the Faculty of Philosophy and Letters, and then in the School of Mines, of the University of Liège. In 1883 he received an honorary engineering diploma from the Technical Faculty. In the following year Gustave Dewalque engaged him as an assistant for a geology course. Having obtained the rank of *agrégé spécial*, he was put in charge of a course on deposits of fuels and phosphates; on 15 June 1893 he was given an optional course in geology instead. In 1897 Lohest succeeded Dewalque and thereby became professor of the general geology course. In his teaching he eliminated inessential detail to concentrate on geological principles and their possible applications. He took part, along with several colleagues from Liège, in the creation of the rank of engineer-geologist in 1900. During World War I he was involved in the organization of the School of Anthropology.

Lohest was elected a corresponding member of the Académie Royale des Sciences de Belgique in 1904 and a full member in 1910. In 1908 he was awarded the decennial prize in mineralogical science. He achieved membership in numerous Belgian and foreign scientific societies; of these his nomination as corresponding member of the Geological Society of London brought him the most pleasure. Lohest was on the board of directors of the Belgian Geological Commission. In 1919 he became a member of the Geological Council and was named to the commission set up to study the waters at Spa.

Like most scientists of the period, Lohest had many interests. Paleontology, especially the study of Paleozoic fishes, was the subject of his first scientific studies. Mere description of fossils was insufficient for him; from his observations he drew conclusions concerning the mode of life of the organisms and the milieu in which they evolved. In 1888 J. S. Newberry, who was visiting Liège, recognized bony plates from the head of a fish of the Dinichtys genus that until then had been reported only in America. Lohest found, in addition, resemblances—of other bones, fins, and dorsal plates—to fishes of the Upper Devonian of Canada.

Lohest also made mineralogical and petrographic studies. In particular he was interested in tourmaline, the conglomerates (pudding stones) of the Gedinnian, and certain anthracites. He investigated the specific conditions under which the deposits occur. Thus, having discovered in 1884, with G. Rocour, phosphate rocks in Hesbaye, he studied them extensively in 1885 and envisaged their possible extent in 1890. He also devoted a note to the age and origin of the plastic clay in the vicinity of Andenne and another to the Tertiary deposits of upper Belgium.

Stratigraphy and tectonics especially attracted Lohest, particularly those of the Paleozoic formations of eastern Belgium and he carried out a detailed survey of the highway and railway cuts in Belgium. His researches on the Dinantian led him to consider the presence of dolomites to be a local phenomenon unsuitable for stratigraphic reference. He found that the gray breccia encountered at various levels of the Visean were of tectonic origin due to fracturing of the limestone during the formation of the synclines. As for the very different red breccia of Waulsort and Landelies, he erroneously associated them with emersion phenomena. This opinion met with lively opposition in 1912 from one of his former students, Victor Brien.

Lohest was also interested in the details of the sedimentation of the Famennian, such as gullying and intraformational conglomerates. The Cambrian of the Stavelot Massif produced a revision in his views; in collaboration with Henri Forir, following the profound modifications that J. Gosselet had made within the stratigraphy of this system, he demonstrated the soundness of earlier surveys done by André Hubert Dumont.

Opposing Gosselet's thesis concerning the paleogeography of the Paleozoic of the Belgian Ardennes, Lohest defended the purely tectonic origin of anticline zones, stating that the partition into basins was simply a result of the Hercynian deformation.

After having been concerned with the relative age of certain faults of the coal-bearing formation, Lohest turned to those affecting both Mesozoic and Cenozoic formations. He sought to find out whether they indicate the disposition of the Paleozoic substratum; in this regard he attempted to apply the concepts of the American geologist Joseph Le Conte and the French geologist Marcel Bertrand. He also played a prominent role in guiding research on the westward extension into Belgium of the Dutch Limburg coalfields.

In the memoir "Les grandes lignes de la géologie des terrains primaires de la Belgique," Lohest showed himself an ardent partisan of actualism—neglecting, however, certain facts accepted by his contemporaries. Although tectonics was his chief interest—he even attempted to demonstrate its principal features experimentally—he devoted several publications to metamorphism in the Ardennes. He originated the term "boudinage," applied to the pinch and swell of quartz seams within sandstone beds. Various explanations have been offered for this phenomenon since it was first observed. In considering the seismic phenomena of the region around Liège (which are, of course, infrequent and of little consequence), Lohest accepted Élie de Beaumont's view that all geological phenomena are due to the contractions of the earth's crust caused by the cooling of the globe, and he defended this position all his life.

"Introduction à. . . la géologie. La vie de l'écorce terrestre," which appeared in 1924, is a condensation of Lohest's ideas in 224 pages. He wrote of recurrences, of the cyclic evolution of inanimate matter, and even of the succession of species toward an ideal of progress and perfection. Lohest became interested in the Quaternary in 1886, when, with Julien Fraipont and Marcel de Puydt, he discovered a characteristic Neanderthal fossil man—one dated, for the first time, by accompanying evidence of a Mousterian industry— in the terrace of Spy Cavern.

Lohest also devoted some of his time to physical geography; and although he never went to the Congo, he understood the importance of this territory for Belgian engineers. In 1897 he published "Notions sommaires de géologie à l'usage de l'explorateur du Congo." In Belgium he made several surveys on a scale of 1:40,000 and was requested to advise on important questions of applied hydrology, notably those concerning preliminary plans for water catchment and for the extension of water distribution.

BIBLIOGRAPHY

I. ORIGINAL WORKS. There is complete bibliography in Fourmarier (see below). The most important works are "Recherches sur les poissons des terrains paléozoiques de Belgique. Poissons des psammites du Condroz, famennien supérieur," in *Annales de la Société géologique de Belgique*, **15** (1888), 112–203; "De l'origine des failles des terrains secondaires et tertiaires et de leur importance dans la détermination de l'allure souterraine des terrains primaires," *ibid.*, **20** (1893), 275–287; "Les grandes lignes de la géologie des terrains primaires de la Belgique," *ibid.*, **31** (1904), 219–232; "Introduction à l'étude de la géologie. La vie de l'écorce terrestre," in *Mémoires de la Société royale des sciences* (Liège), 3rd ser., **21** (1924); "Stratigraphie du massif cambrien de Stavelot," in *Mémoires de la Société géologique de Belgique*, **25** (1900), 71–119, written with H. Forir; "La race humaine de Néanderthal ou de Canstadt, en Belgique. Recherches ethnographiques sur des ossements humains découverts dans les dépôts quaternaires d'une grotte à Spy et détermination de leur âge géologique," in *Bulletin de l'Académie royale des sciences*, 3rd ser., **12** (1886), 741–784, also in *Archives de biologie* (Ghent), **7** (1887), 587–757, written with J. Fraipont; "Exploration de la grotte de Spy. Notice préliminaire," in *Annales de la Société géologique de Belgique*, **13** (1886), 34–39, written with M. de Puydt.

II. SECONDARY LITERATURE. See P. Fourmarier, "Notice sur Max Lohest, membre de l'Académie," in *Annuaire. Académie royale de Belgique*, **119** (1955), 279–386, with portrait and complete bibliography.

F. STOCKMANS

LÖHNEYSS (or **LÖHNEIS** or **LÖHNEYSSEN**), **GEORG ENGELHARDT VON** (*b.* Witzlasreuth, Fichtelgebirge, Germany, 7 March 1552; *d.* Remlingen, near Wolfenbüttel, Germany, 1625[?]), *mining, metallurgy.*

Löhneyss, who came from a noble family, was brought up in Würzburg and Coburg. Before he was twenty, he entered the service of the prince of Ansbach. In 1575 he went to the court of Elector Augustus I of Saxony as equerry. Beginning in 1583 he held the same position under Augustus' son-in-law, Heinrich Julius of Brunswick and Wolfenbüttel, who in 1589 made him director of Brunswick's mines and foundries in the Upper Harz. In 1596 Löhneyss was appointed inspector general of the mines of Zellerfeld, Clausthal, and Andreasberg. He carried out his official duties first in Wolfenbüttel and on the estate at Remlingen; and from 1613 he worked in Zellerfeld. He was inspector general until 1622. During this time he kept many mines and foundries from being shut down.

Löhneyss was highly regarded as a writer by his contemporaries. From 1596, after a quarrel with his publisher, he brought out his works himself in printing shops he established in Remlingen and Zellerfeld. To illustrate his books he hired a woodblock engraver and a copperplate engraver. Along with *Della cavalleria*, both the text and the illustrations of which command respect, and *Aulico-politica oder Hof-, Staats- and Regierungskunst*, one should mention above all his *Bericht vom Bergkwerck*, which appeared in 1617. The intrinsic value of this book, which treats technical as well as economic and administrative aspects of mining and metallurgy, lies solely in the economic sections. Otherwise, *Bericht vom Bergkwerck* contributes nothing new; and even though it has frequently been called an outstanding description of mining and metallurgy, it in no way merits this praise. The technical material is shameless plagiarism: without citing his sources Löhneyss summarizes Agricola's *De re metallica libri XII* (1556) and copies word for word Lazarus Ercker's *Beschreibung allerfürnemisten mineralischen Ertzt und Berckwercksarten* . . . (1574), then combines them with the mining regulations of Brunswick to form a book.

BIBLIOGRAPHY

I. ORIGINAL WORKS. Löhneyss's major works are *Della cavalleria, grundtlicher Bericht von allem was zu der löblichen Reiterei gehörig und einem Cavallier davon zu wissen geburt* (Remlingen, 1609–1610; 2nd ed., 1624; 3rd ed., Nuremberg, 1729); and *Bericht von Bergkwerck, wie man dieselben Bawen und in guten Wolstandt bringen soll, sampt allen darzu gehörigen Arbeiten, Ordnung und rechtlichen Process* (Zellerfeld, 1617); undated new eds. appeared between 1650 and 1670; in 1690 there appeared an ed. entitled *Gründlicher und ausführlicher Bericht von Bergwercken, wie man dieselbigen nützlich und fruchtbarlich bauen, in glückliches Auffnehmen bringen, und in guten Wolstand beständig erhalten.*

II. SECONDARY LITERATURE. See "Georg Engelhard[t] von Löhneyss," in *Allgemeine deutsche Biographie,* XIX (Leipzig, 1884), 133–134; W. Serlo, *Männer des Bergbaus* (Berlin, 1937), 99–100; H. Dickmann, "Das grösste Plagiat im berg- und hüttenmännischen Schrifttum," in *Das Werk* (Düsseldorf), **16** (1936), 572; W. Hommel, "Berghauptmann Löhneysen, ein Plagiator des 17. Jahrhunderts," in *Chemikerzeitung,* **36** (1912), 137–138; and "Über den Berghauptmann Löhneysen," *ibid.,* 562; M. Koch, *Geschichte und Entwicklung des bergmännischen Schrifttums* (Goslar, 1963), 60–62; and "Berghauptmann Georg Engelhardt von Löhneyss, Bergbauschriftsteller und Plagiator," in *Glückauf!,* **100** (1964), 49–50.

M. KOCH

LOHSE, WILHELM OSWALD (*b.* Leipzig, Germany, 13 February 1845; *d.* Potsdam, Germany, 14 May 1915), *astronomy.*

Lohse, the son of a tailor, attended schools in his native town and then, in 1859–1862, took the preliminary courses of the engineering college in Dresden. In the latter year he entered the University of Leipzig to study chemistry, and in 1865 he received the Ph.D. After some years of practical technical activity at Salzmunde, near Halle, and at Leipzig, he was interested in astronomy by Vogel, who at this time became director of the private observatory of the Kammerherr von Bülow at Bothkamp, near Kiel. Vogel engaged Lohse as a collaborator. Both men made spectroscopic observations; Lohse concentrated on solar observation and celestial photography, for which he prepared the plates himself. In 1874 Vogel and Lohse moved to the new astrophysical observatory at Potsdam, where Lohse worked for more than forty years—from 1882 as observer and from 1901 as head observer. Soon after his arrival Lohse installed the chemical and photographic workrooms and laboratories. At the Berlin observatory he observed *Nova Cygni* 1876 spectroscopically. In 1877, continuing his solar observations at Potsdam, Lohse had the necessary instruments constructed. At the same time he observed Jupiter and Mars. A little later he made photographs of stars and star clusters, and in 1899 he began photographing double stars. By comparing photographs made within twenty-five years Lohse tried to derive proper motions of faint stars; and through investigations of metallic spectra

he contributed to the increased accuracy of spectroscopic measurements, using both prisms and a Rowland concave grating.

After the death of Vogel in 1907, Lohse headed the astrophysical observatory for two years, until advanced age and melancholia led him to resign. He was still healthy, however, and worked in his private workshop and in his garden until the end of 1914, when his health began to fail rapidly. At his death in May 1915 Lohse left his wife, two sons, and two daughters.

BIBLIOGRAPHY

Lohse's books include *Meteorologische und astronomische Beobachtungen in Bothkamp 1871–1873,* 3 vols. (Leipzig, 1872–1874); and *Tafel für numerisches Rechnen mit Maschinen* (Leipzig, 1909). The following articles appeared in *Potsdamer astrophysikalische Publikationen:* "Physische Beschaffenheit des Jupiter, Beobachtungen des Mars" (1882), 1–76; "Abbildungen von Sonnenflecken nebst Bemerkungen über astronomische Zeichnungen" (1883), 1–109; "Heliograph" (1889), 1–15; "Beobachtungen des Mars," **8** (1889), 1–40; "Beobachtungen des südlichen Polarflecks des Mars und der Elemente des Mars-Äquators," **11** (1898), 1–25; "Funkenspektren einiger Metalle," **12** (1902), 1–208; "Doppelsterne," **20** (1909), 1–168; and "Physische Beschaffenheit des Jupiter," **21** (1911), 1–11. He also published many short notes in *Astronomische Nachrichten,* vols. **82, 83, 85, 96, 97, 111, 115, 142, 146,** and **165.**

An obituary by P. Kempf is in *Vierteljahrsschrift der Astronomischen Gesellschaft* (1915), 160–169.

H.-CHRIST. FREIESLEBEN

LOKHTIN, VLADIMIR MIKHAYLOVICH (*b.* St. Petersburg, Russia, 1849; *d.* Petrograd, Russia, 1919), *hydrotechnology, hydrology.*

In 1875 Lokhtin graduated from the St. Petersburg Institute of Communications Engineers, after which he participated in surveys of the tributaries of the Kama River. In 1882 he was appointed head of a party to survey on the Dniester River, and after two years he was put in charge of improving navigation conditions on that river. From 1892 to 1899 Lokhtin, as head of the Kazan Communication District, led major research and corrective work on the Volga River near Nizhni Novgorod (now Gorki) and on a number of its shoals. In the early twentieth century he studied economic problems of water transport, and 1904 he participated in the study of the ice conditions of the Neva River. From 1907 he was inspector of macadam roads of Petersburg Province, and from 1915 he was a member of the Committee of State Construction and edited the journal *Vodnye puti i shosseynye dorogi* ("Waterways and Macadam Roads").

Lokhtin was one of the founders of the hydrology of rivers. The development of his theory on the formation of a riverbed may be followed from his work *Reka Chusovaya* ("The Chusovaya River"; 1878) to the monograph *O mekhanizme rechnogo rusla* ("On the Mechanism of a Riverbed"; 1895). In the first of these works Lokhtin, examining the peculiarities of the Chusovaya as a mountain stream, also touched on several general properties of rivers, the character of the changes in their velocities, their slopes, and the movement of high water. He turned his attention to the change in the transverse profile of the surface of the river during rises and falls in its level; on the basis of his observations, he asserted that a rise in level of the river produces a distended or convex profile while a fall in level leads to formation of a depression or concave profile.

Reports given by Lokhtin at the Russian Technical Society, *Sovremennoe polozhenie voprosa o sposobakh uluchshenia rek* ("The Present State of Methods of Improving Rivers"; 1883) and *Sovremennoe sostoyanie voprosa ob izuchenii svoystv rek* ("The Present Condition of the Study of the Properties of Rivers"; 1884), represented a substantial contribution to the development of the theory of riverbed processes. In the former Lokhtin spoke of the incorrectness of the then prevalent idea of the parallel stream movement of water in rivers and advanced the theory of the inner displacement of water within the current, pointing out that such a displacement explains the spiral movement of water, which determines the form of the riverbed. He did not, however, develop the question of the spiral form of movement of a liquid. In this report Lokhtin spoke of the three elements—climatic conditions, the character of the soil, and the topography of the basin—that determine the peculiarities of each river.

Lokhtin developed his original ideas of the processes which take place in riverbeds, particularly the formation of shoals, spits, and islands, in a work published in 1886, "Reka Dnestr, ee sudokhodstvo, svoystva i uluchshenie" ("The River Dniester, Its Navigation, Properties, and Improvement"). He connected the redistribution of slope between the reach and the shoal portions at the times of low and high water and the formation of shoals with three factors: the longitudinal profile of the riverbed (the influence of rocky "strong points"), the arrangement of the river in the plane (the influence of curvature), and the width of the river (influence of local widening).

Referring to the shoal-reach form of the river, Lokhtin wrote that the low-water reaches and shoals are the result of the action of energetic high water—a result so considerable that weak and brief low waters are not strong enough to erase it or modify it. Lokhtin explained the formation of spits, and then of islands, as the result of the filling up of excess widths by sediment at the time of high water.

The fullest expression of Lokhtin's views on riverbed processes occurs in his monograph *O mekhanizme rechnogo rusla* ("On the Mechanism of a Riverbed"; 1895). It should be noted that in their theories other authors of works on the formation of riverbeds did not take into account the essential consideration that the discharge and level of water in rivers is not constant and can change within considerable limits. They made their generalizations fit chiefly the low-water situation. Moreover, a large range of variation in level is characteristic of the Russian rivers of the plains, which are fed primarily by melted snow. (During spring floods the majority of large Russian rivers rise more than three meters: on the Volga the rise reaches ten–thirteen; on the Don, seven–ten; on the Dnieper, six–eight.)

According to Lokhtin, the character of each river is determined by the following elements, each of which is independent of the others: (1) the amount of water, determined by sedimentation in the basin, and the soil conditions of the basin; (2) the slope or steepness, determined by the topography of a local cross section of the river; and (3) the degree of erosion or stability of the river channel, which depends on the properties cut into it by the flow of the bottom layers. Since all these elements can be present in different degrees and in different combinations, studying the character of a given river requires a knowledge of the physical and geographical conditions of the basin. The equipment which Lokhtin had at his disposal did not permit him to discover the inner structure of the current, determined by the turbulence and action of the centrifugal and Coriolis forces; he regarded the current as affected only by the action of gravity and as counterbalancing the resistance arising from the friction of water against the bottom.

Having examined and compiled longitudinal profiles of the free-water surfaces of the Volga, Dniester, and Garonne rivers at high-water and low-water levels, Lokhtin noted that the slope of the water surface at the transition from high water to low water changes at the same places in such a way that in the reaches it becomes less, and at the shoals more, than it was at high water. From this it follows that at low water, as a result of the increase in the longitudinal slope at the shoals—and thus also of the velocity of the current—

the deposits which accumulate at times of high water or flood are eroded and carried to lower-lying reaches, where at low water the slope and velocity of the current decrease. Lokhtin wrote:

> Having in its fall a single force for carrying away the obstructions which constantly enter the river and sensing an inadequacy in this force, in comparison with the resistance of the deposits, the river, so to speak, economizes the force, concentrating it at the place where, considering this, it is at a given time most necessary. At high water the slope is concentrated at the reaches, so that, cleaning them of deposits, it can go over, when the water level falls, to the shoals and begin carrying away the deposits which were temporarily left there at high water because of a lack of strength. Thus both parts of the riverbed, reaches and shoals, are inevitable and necessary in the attraction of deposits and are, in addition, definitely limited and constantly keep their places corresponding to the organically essential local conditions of the riverbed [*O mekhanizme rechnogo rusla*, p. 33].

Lokhtin classified rivers as stable or unstable. He considered a stepped longitudinal profile of the water surface to be characteristic of stable rivers. Between stable and unstable rivers are those of intermediate character. Unstable rivers, according to Lokhtin, are characterized by a uniform slope of the longitudinal profile of the water surface and by continuous movement of bottom sediments along the whole river. For a measure of the stability of the river, Lokhtin proposed the expression

$$k = \frac{d}{\Delta H},$$

representing the ratio of the mean diameter of the section of the bed to the fall of the water surface. Lokhtin concentrated his analysis of riverbed phenomena on the stable river bed. He believed that rivers could be improved through engineering methods based on the degree of stability of the river. (Although several inadequacies are now apparent in Lokhtin's discussions of separate river phenomena, the basic elements of his theory of formation of riverbeds are still significant.)

Lokhtin's research on the formation of ground ice is of considerable interest. He ascertained the presence of ice crystals at all depths of the current, which showed that they are formed in the open portions of the river as a result of the contact of flowing water with frosty air.

BIBLIOGRAPHY

I. Original Works. Lokhtin's writings include *Reka Chusovaya* ("The Chusovaya River"; St. Petersburg, 1878); "Reka Dnestr, ee sudokhodstvo, svoystva i uluchshenie" ("The Dniester River, Its Navigation, Properties, and Improvement"), in *Inzhener* (1886), no. 9–10, 410–441, no. 11–12, 485–546; *Sovremennoe polozhenie voprosa o sposobakh uluchshenia rek* ("The Present State of Methods of Improving Rivers"; St. Petersburg, 1886); *O mekhanizme rechnogo rusla* ("On the Mechanism of a Riverbed"; Kazan, 1895), also translated into French (Paris, 1909); and *Ledyanoy nanos i zimnie zatory na r. Neve* ("Ice Deposits and Winter Ice Blocks on the Neva River"; St. Petersburg, 1906).

II. Secondary Literature. See I. A. Fedoseyev, *Razvitie gidrologii sushi v Rossii* ("Development of the Hydrology of Dry Land in Russia"; Moscow, 1960), pp. 105–106, 168–172; and A. K. Proskuryakov, *V. M. Lokhtin i N. S. Lelyavsky. Osnovateli uchenia o formirovanii rusla* ("V. M. Lokhtin and N. S. Lelyavsky. Founders of the Theory of the Formation of the Riverbed"; Leningrad, 1951).

I. A. Fedoseyev

LOMONOSOV, MIKHAIL VASILIEVICH (*b.* Mishaninskaya, Arkhangelsk province, Russia, 19 November 1711; *d.* St. Petersburg, Russia, 15 April 1765), *chemistry, physics, metallurgy, optics.*

Lomonosov's father, Vasily Dorofeevich, owned several fishing and cargo ships; his mother, Elena Ivanovna Sivkova, was the daughter of a deacon. A gifted child, Lomonosov learned to read and write at an early age, and by the time he was fourteen was studying M. Smotritsky's Slavonic grammar and Magnitsky's arithmetic (which also dealt with other sciences and with technology).

In December 1730 Lomonosov received permission from local authorities to go to Moscow, where he entered the Slavonic, Greek, and Latin Academy the following month. He displayed brilliant linguistic abilities and soon became an accomplished Latinist. In 1734 he went to Kiev to work in the archives of the Religious Academy; he then returned to Moscow. At the beginning of 1736 he was sent, as one of the Moscow Academy's best pupils, to study at the University of St. Petersburg; and in the fall of that year he went to the University of Marburg, where he studied for three years with Christian Wolff. Lomonosov and Wolff respected each other's abilities but held few scientific views in common, although in 1745 Lomonosov did do a translation of Wolff's work on physics into Russian. That book attempted to combine the views of Newton with the ideas of Leibniz and Descartes and to reconcile the continuous ether with atomic theory. From Wolff, however, Lomonosov acquired a schematic style of scientific description that served him throughout his life.

At Marburg, Lomonosov also studied the humanities, on his own initiative. His studies abroad were in general oriented toward mathematics and chemistry (which he studied with Duising), mining, natural history, physics, mechanics, hydraulics, and hydrotechnics. In the summer of 1739 he traveled to Freiburg to study with Johann Henckel, a specialist in mining. Henckel was an Aristotelian and an opponent of the mechanistic interpretation of chemical phenomena that Lomonosov, for his part, always supported. The teacher and his new student differed sharply, and Lomonosov soon departed, having nevertheless acquired in less than a year much knowledge of mineralogy and metallurgy. By the spring of 1740 Lomonosov was traveling extensively in Germany and Holland. Later that year, in Marburg, he married Elizabeth Zilch; their daughter Elena was born in 1749. In 1741 Lomonosov returned with his wife to St. Petersburg, where he spent the rest of his life.

Lomonosov's two chief interests, poetry and science, had already come to the fore in the course of his foreign studies. In 1739 he composed an ode on the Russian capture of the Turkish fortress of Khotin, to which he appended theoretical considerations on the reform of Russian versification. In two student dissertations in physics (1738–1739), "On the Transformation of a Solid Body Into a Liquid" and "On Distinguishing Mixed Bodies That Consist of Chains of Corpuscles," Lomonosov established the basis of his future atomic-kinetic conceptions. "Corpuscles are different," he wrote, "if they are distinguished by mass or by figure, or by both at the same time." In 1756 he recalled, "From the time when I read Boyle I had a fervent desire to study the smallest particles. I reflected on them for eighteen years." While in Marburg he had also developed the idea of applying algebra to theoretical chemistry and physics, a notion that he began to implement on his return to St. Petersburg. A fully mature scientist, he had turned completely from theology and ancient languages to the natural sciences and technology, and to the Russian language and its poetry. His subsequent life and career may be divided into three distinct stages.

Theoretical Physics (1741–1748). At the beginning of 1742 Lomonosov was named adjunct of the St. Petersburg Academy of Sciences in the class of physics, in which post he remained for three and a half years. He was commissioned to compile a catalog of minerals and fossils, which was followed by "First Principles of Mining Science." His first independent scientific work, "Elements of Mathematical Chemistry," is marked by bold hypotheses and speculations. Defending the unity of theory and experiment, he

wrote that "A true chemist must be both a theorist and a practical worker . . . as well as a philosopher." His notion of the difference between a compound, which is composed of corpuscles, and an element, has been said to resemble the laws of definite and multiple proportion later established in chemistry. The hypothetical nature of Lomonosov's approach to the physical sciences was further conditioned by the circumstances of his time: in the mid-eighteenth century experimental data on the quantitative chemical composition of various substances were not sufficient for testing his suppositions. Thus he was obliged to proceed on the basis of hypothesis.

In the period 1741–1743 he outlined the topics of his future research, compiling 276 notes on physics and corpuscular philosophy. They include his observations that

> When it is warm sound is more intense than when it is cold because the corpuscles move faster and strike each other more forcefully. . . . We must not think of many reasons when one is sufficient; thus corpuscular motion suffices to explain heat . . . there is no need to look for other reasons . . . . Nature strongly adheres to her laws and is everywhere the same . . . . The continuous formation and destruction of bodies speaks sufficiently for corpuscular motion.

Other notes have an ethical character and reflect his scientific outlook: "I will not attack for their errors people who have served the republic of science; rather, I will try to use their good thoughts for useful work."

In 1743–1744 he developed an atomic theory in a series of papers: "On the Intangible Physical Particles That Constitute Natural Substances," "On the Adhesion of Corpuscles," "On the Adhesion and Position of Physical Monads," and "On the Intangible Physical Particles That Constitute Natural Substances, in Which Substances the Sufficient Basis for Specific Qualities is Contained." His theory of matter, which was atomistic in principle, was further developed in his "On the Weight of Bodies" (1748), in which he imagined a materialistic monadology to oppose Leibniz' idealistic picture. Lomonosov's monads were corporeal rather than spiritual, having form, weight, and volume; and he employed them to explain the nature of heat and the elasticity of gases.

In 1745 Lomonosov read his paper "Reflections on the Reason for Heat and Cold" to the St. Petersburg Academy. He considered it to be one of his most important works for its argument against phlogiston in particular and against the theory of weightless fluids in general. He explained heat in terms of the velocity of motion (rotation) of material particles.

Cold was a diminution of motion, and with the full cessation of particle motion the greatest degree of cold was achieved. In "Attempt at a Theory of Elasticity of the Air" (1748) Lomonosov considered the nature of heat more fully. Inasmuch as the particles themselves occupy a certain volume of space, he predicted a deviation from Boyle's law in air subjected to very great pressure. In a letter to Euler of 5 July 1748 Lomonosov set down the general law to which these researches had led him: "All changes that we encounter in nature proceed so that . . . however much matter is added to any body, as much is taken away from another . . . since this is the general law of nature, it is also found in the rules of motion."

Continuing Boyle's line of thought, Lomonosov based his theory of heat on the mechanical action of bodies in contact, rather than upon the dynamics of Newtonian forces. (For this reason the external form of the material monad is important.) But Lomonosov employed corpuscular mechanics in chemical explanations more extensively than Boyle had done. Treating chemical compounds as particles in adhesion, he held that "adhesion is eliminated and renewed by means of motion . . . since no change in a body can take place without motion." He attempted to apply these theories to chemical phenomena—although he was limited to speculation—in papers on the action of chemical solvents in general (read in 1745) and on "metallic brilliance."

Lomonosov's work during this first period was not, however, confined to the physical sciences. In 1744 he described a comet that had appeared that year and, until 1748, he kept a record of the phenomena of thunderstorms. He wrote on electrical experiments in 1745—a subject to which he was to return—and in 1746 sought a method for measuring temperature at the bottom of a frozen sea. Returning to his mineralogical studies, he published a memoir on the wave motion of air observed in mines and conducted chemical analyses of salts, ores, and other rocks sent to the St. Petersburg Academy. He also compiled a syllabus of lectures on physics to be delivered in Russian and, in the summer of 1746, gave the first public lecture on that subject ever to be presented in that language.

Meanwhile, Lomonosov continued to combine science with poetry. In 1743 he wrote two major philosophical poems, "Morning Reflection on the Greatness of God" and "Evening Reflection on the Greatness of God on the Occasion of the Great Northern Lights." In the latter he asked, "What is the ray that surges through the clear night? What is the fine flame that strikes the firmament? . . . How is it possible that the frozen vapor of winter engendered fire?" He competed with the poets Tretyakovsky and Sumarokov in translating a Biblical psalm into Russian and composed a brief guide to rhetoric. In an ode on "The Delight of Earthly Kings and Kingdoms" (1747) he glorified science and the peaceful flowering of Russia. Addressing a patriotic challenge to youth, he summoned them "to show that the Russian land can give birth to its own Platos and quick-witted Newtons."

Despite these accomplishments, Lomonosov became embroiled in a number of heated disputes within the Academy. In 1743 he was arrested and imprisoned for eight months as a result of these encounters with Academy bureaucrats, led by Schumacher, whose interests were far removed from science. Nevertheless, in 1745 he was named professor of chemistry at the Academy. In 1747 Schumacher, hoping for an unfavorable review, sent a copy of Lomonosov's works to Euler; but his malice was rewarded by Euler's complete approval of Lomonosov's "Reflections on the Reason for Heat and Cold." The explanations of physical and chemical problems were so sound, Euler stated, that he was fully convinced of the accuracy of Lomonosov's proofs. Euler greeted with equal enthusiasm other works of Lomonosov that were sent to him from the Academy. It was largely through Euler's good opinion that the pioneering nature of Lomonosov's work was first recognized by that body. All the works that Lomonosov presented for publication were included in the first volume of the Academy's *Novye kommentarii* ("New Commentaries"), issued in 1748.

Experimental Chemistry (1748–1757). On assuming his duties as professor of chemistry, Lomonosov began to plan the construction of the first scientific chemical laboratory in Russia, which was opened in October 1748. Its equipment included balances, so that quantitative methods could be introduced into chemistry and the general law of conservation proven experimentally. Although Lomonosov did not completely suspend work in theoretical physics, he began to turn his interest to the experimental chemistry that he was just learning to do. His first chemical work, on the origin and nature of saltpeter (1749), presents the results of laboratory experiments together with theoretical speculation on the nature of mixed bodies (chemical compounds) and of chemical affinity. The latter were based on Lomonosov's kinetic interpretation of heat. In a paper on the usefulness of chemistry read to the Academy in 1751, he spoke of the problems of chemistry and of training chemists, noting that the discipline "requires a highly skilled practical worker and a profound mathematician in the same person." Thus, Lomonosov worked toward elevating chemistry to the level of a genuine theoretical, rather than a purely empirical, science. Pointing to the practical importance of chemistry, he challenged the dogma that useful minerals—especially precious metals in rocks—do not exist in northern countries.

In 1752 Lomonosov implemented his ideas on the training of chemists by drawing up a program of instruction in physical chemistry designed for young students. In an introductory note he wrote, "The study of chemistry has a dual purpose: advancing the natural sciences and improving the general welfare." He later set forth in detail the theoretical and empirical aspects of this science, considering that physical chemistry explains "on the basis of the ideas and experiments of physics what takes place in mixed bodies under chemical operations."

Lomonosov's surviving laboratory notes and journals testify to the number and variety of experiments that he himself performed. In his journal for 1751, for example, he reported on the results of seventy-four reagents and on their mutual interactions with various solvents, on his experiments on the production of glass, on his work with various powders, and on his investigations of a large number of chemical reactions. From 1752 to 1756 he took notes on physical-chemical experiments with salts and liquids and on the freezing (crystallization) of liquids. In 1756, following up Boyle's experiments on the heating of metals in closed containers, he found that when air is not admitted into the vessel, the total weight of the vessel and its contents remains constant—another confirmation of the general law of conservation as it applies to the total weight of chemically reacting substances. "My chemistry," he wrote in the same year, "is physical."

Lomonosov returned to the study of electrical phenomena in 1753, when he resumed experiments on atmospheric electricity. With G. V. Richmann he attempted to discover methods of conducting lightning and wrote "A Word on Atmospheric Phenomena Proceeding From Electrical Force." Richmann was killed while conducting experiments during a thunderstorm, but Lomonosov continued his researches and drew up a syllabus for further study. In 1756 he compiled 127 notes on the theory of light and electricity, presented a mathematical theory of electricity, and read a paper on the origin of light and on a new theory of colors that constitute it to a public meeting of the Academy. His reflections on the relation between mass and weight (1757) led him to the idea that another concept of measurement, perhaps that of weight, should be introduced as an expression of mass.

Lomonosov was also busy with practical projects. Having undertaken research on the production of glass, he turned to the revival of mosaic as an art form. In 1752 he presented a work on this subject to Czarina Elizabeth and introduced into the Duma a proposal to establish mosaic factories in Russia. In the same year he wrote a poem on the usefulness of glass, in which he contrasted glass and objects made of it with man's lust for gold. In 1753 Lomonosov received permission to build factories "for making varicolored glass and beads" and was given an estate near Moscow for this purpose. He built a mosaic workshop, with an attached chemical and optical laboratory, in St. Petersburg in 1756 and between 1761 and 1764 designed a large mosaic mural, *The Battle of Poltava*. Executed after his death, it is now in the Academy of Sciences in Leningrad. In 1754 he demonstrated at the St. Petersburg Academy a model of an "aerodrome machine" that he had invented and sent to I. I. Shuvalov his project for creating a university in Moscow, which was opened at the beginning of 1755.

During this period Lomonosov was especially active in history, philosophy, and literature. He presented a severe criticism of the historian G. Miller's "Norman theory" of the origin of Russia. In 1750 his dramatic tragedy, *Tamira and Selim*, was presented in St. Petersburg, and the following year an edition of his collected poems and prose works was published by the Academy of Sciences. His Russian grammar (1755–1757) was an important reform of the Russian language.

Lomonosov's Wide Practical Interests (1757–1765). At the beginning of 1757 Lomonosov was named member of the academic chancellery and, a year later, head of the geographical department of the St. Petersburg Academy. Occupied in scientific administration, he was less able to devote attention to physics and chemistry. Although his energies were drawn increasingly to practical matters, his surviving chemical and optical notes indicate that he nevertheless continued to do a considerable amount of pure research. In a paper on the hardness and fluidity of bodies (1760) he once again stated the general law of the conservation of matter and motion.

During the late 1750's Lomonosov became interested in exploration and, extending his earlier work on mining and metallurgy, in the exploitation of Russia's natural resources. Between 1757 and 1763 he wrote three works on mining and metallurgy; "Metals and minerals are not found lying on the doorstep," he stated in one of them. "Eyes and hands must search for them." Interested in navigation, especially of the northern seas, in 1759 he invented a number of instruments for astronomy and navigation, including a self-recording compass, and reflected on the precise determination of a ship's route. In 1761 he communicated to the Swedish Academy of Sciences a paper on the origin of icebergs in the northern seas and, two years later, described various voyages in the northern seas and discussed a possible approach to East India through the Siberian Sea. These works contain the first classification of ice and introduced the ideas of fossil ice and the presence of a huge ice drift.

As head of the geography department of the Academy, Lomonosov attempted to serve the general national interest. In addition to his works on exploiting natural resources, in 1761 he wrote Shuvalov a letter "on the propagation and preservation of the Russian people," in which he considered a broad range of social, economic, and political problems.

Lomonosov's works in literature and linguistics during the last period of his life include a foreword on the usefulness of church books, in the first volume of his collected works, published in 1758 by Moscow University. In it he opposed the current tendency to restore Church Slavonic and established the basis for a Russian scientific language in which the literary idiom approached the vernacular. In 1759–1760 he compiled a brief Russian chronicle with genealogy, wrote a memoir on the need for reforming the Academy, and began a heroic poem on Peter the Great. In 1761 all academic institutions in his region were entrusted to his sole management. His ideas for a pictorial map of Russian history were set forth in 1764.

Lomonosov was elected an honorary member of the Swedish Academy of Sciences (1760), the St. Petersburg Academy of Arts (1763), and a member of the Bologna Academy of Sciences (1764). His strong-willed and independent character created continuing difficulties with the czarist government; and in 1763 the czarina, having granted him the rank of state councillor, ordered his retirement. Several days later she herself rescinded the order.

Shortly before his death Lomonosov intended to produce two major generalizing philosophical works that would embody the whole of his atomic-kinetic principles and would illuminate his concept of the unity of nature. The works, to have been entitled "System of All Physics" and "Micrology," survive in outline notes and in theses that include

> Forces are miracles of harmony, a harmonious structure of causes. . . . The harmony and concord of nature. . . . The voice of nature everywhere in tune. . . . Unanimity and assent. . . . The concord of all causes is the most constant law of nature. . . . Everything is linked by a common force and the concord of nature.

The theses also reflect Lomonosov's ethical character, and many are autobiographical. Death prevented him from carrying out this projected work.

Lomonosov's last years were marred by illness. He appeared at the St. Petersburg Academy of Sciences for the last time early in 1765 and died a few months later. He was buried at the Alexander Nevsky Monastery.

Unique in the history of Russian culture and science, Lomonosov had an encyclopedic education. The first great Russian scientist, he united in himself knowledge not only of every basic area of the science of his time but of history, languages, poetry, literary prose, and art. His outlook on natural science and philosophy was frequently presented in verse. He was a distinguished teacher and social reformer, an enlightened humanist who worked to develop his country's productive forces. Pushkin called him Russia's first university. His scientific creativity consisted especially in his theoretical union of two basic concepts—the atomic (recognition of the discrete structure of matter) and the kinetic (recognition that particles of matter are endowed with motion). It was by basing this theory on the most general concept of the law of conservation of matter and motion that Lomonosov demonstrated experimentally the conservation of matter. A number of predictions in physics and chemistry derived from the combination of these three concepts were not verified until many years after his death.

Lomonosov was described as having "a cheerful temperament, [he] spoke tersely and wittily and loved to use pointed remarks in conversation; he was faithful to his country and friends, protected and encouraged novices in the literary arts; his manner was, for the most part, gentle but was passionate and hot-tempered withal."

Lomonosov was long considered to have been primarily a poet and man of letters, and little was known of his scientific works, which remained in manuscript. At the beginning of the twentieth century, B. N. Menshutkin discovered a great quantity of his unpublished material in the archives of the Academy of Sciences. Their publication revealed Lomonosov's importance as a physicist and chemist to the scientists of our time.

BIBLIOGRAPHY

I. ORIGINAL WORKS. Lomonosov's complete works were published by the Soviet Academy of Sciences, under the general editorship of S. I. Vavilov, as *Polnoe sobranie sochineny,* 10 vols. (Moscow-Leningrad, 1950–1959). An earlier, 8-vol. ed. of his collected works, *Sobranie sochineny* (Moscow–Leningrad, 1934–1948), includes his poetry; works on linguistics and literature; articles on the natural sciences, physics, optics, chemistry, astronomy, and metallurgy; and his correspondence.

Important translations of his works (listed in chronological order) are *Physikalisch-chemische Abhandlungen*, Ostwalds Klassiker der Exacten Wissenschaften no. 178 (Leipzig, 1910), with works dating from 1741 to 1752; *Ausgewählte Schriften*, 2 vols. (Berlin, 1961), with works on natural science, history, and linguistics and collected letters; and *Michail Vasilievitch Lomonosov on the Corpuscular Theory*, trans. and with intro. by Henry M. Leicester (Cambridge, Mass., 1970).

II. SECONDARY LITERATURE. It is impossible here to offer more than a brief indication of the vast literature on Lomonosov and various aspects of his career. The following works, therefore, listed chronologically within each subheading, represent only a small portion of existing nineteenth- and twentieth-century sources in Russian and other languages.

Biographies. See V. I. Lamansky, *Lomonosov* (St. Petersburg, 1864); V. I. Pokrovsky, *Mikhail Vasilievich Lomonosov* (Moscow, 1905); M. de Lur-Saluces, *Lomonossoff. Le prodigieux moujik* (Paris, 1933); G. Shtorm, *Lomonosov* (Moscow, 1933); J. D. Bernal, "M. V. Lomonosov," in *Nature*, no. 3688 (1940), 16–17; B. N. Menshutkin, *Zhizneopisanie Mikhaila Vasilievicha Lomonosova* (Moscow–Leningrad, 1947), the app. by L. B. Modzalevsky is a biographical guide to the basic literature on Lomonosov's life and work; and *Russia's Lomonosov, Chemist, Courtier, Physicist, Poet* (Princeton, 1952); A. A. Morosov, *M. W. Lomonosov* (Berlin, 1954); and *Mikhail Vasilievich Lomonosov* (Moscow, 1955), with bibliography, pp. 909–924; S. I. Vavilov, *Mikhail Vasilievich Lomonosov* (Moscow, 1961), a collection of articles and lectures—see esp. "Zakon Lomonosova" ("Lomonosov's Law"); G. S. Vasetsky, *Mirovozzrenie M. V. Lomonosova* (Moscow, 1961), on his world view; G. T. Korovin, *Biblioteka Lomonosova* (Moscow–Leningrad, 1961), with a catalog of Lomonosov's personal library; B. G. Kuznetsov, *Tvorchesky put Lomonosova* ("Lomonosov's Creative Path"; Moscow, 1961); G. E. Pavlova, ed., *Lomonosov v vospominaniakh i kharakteristikakh sovremennikov* ("Lomonosov Recalled and Described by His Contemporaries"; Moscow–Leningrad, 1962); L. Langevin, *Lomonosov, sa vie, son oeuvre* (Paris, 1967); and G. Vasetsky, *Lomonosov's Philosophy* (Moscow, 1968).

Lomonosov and the Academy of Sciences. Recent works include G. A. Knyazev, ed., *Rukopisi Lomonosova v Akademii nauk SSSR* ("Lomonosov's Manuscripts at the Soviet Academy of Sciences"; Moscow–Leningrad, 1937); V. F. Gnucheva, *Geografichesky departament Akademii nauk* ("The Geography Section of the Academy of Sciences"; Moscow–Leningrad, 1946), pp. 66–86, 178–199; M. I. Radovsky, *Lomonosov i Peterburgskaya Akademia nauk* ("Lomonosov and the St. Petersburg Academy of Sciences"; Moscow–Leningrad, 1961); and E. S. Kulebyako, *Lomonosov i uchebnaya deyatelnost Peterburgskoy*

Akademii nauk ("Lomonosov and the Educational Activity of the St. Petersburg Academy of Sciences"; Moscow–Leningrad, 1962).

Lomonosov as Physicist, Chemist, and Astronomer. Useful sources on particular aspects of Lomonosov's career include B. N. Menshutkin, *Trudy Lomonosova po fizike i khimii* ("Lomonosov's Works on Physics and Chemistry"; Moscow–Leningrad, 1936); B. E. Raykov, *Ocherki po istorii geliotsentricheskogo mirovozzrenia v Rossii* ("Sketches in the History of the Heliocentric View in Russia"; Moscow–Leningrad, 1947); P. G. Kulikovsky, *Lomonosov—astronom i astrofizik* ("Lomonosov—Astronomer and Astrophysicist"; Moscow, 1961); N. M. Raskin, *Khimicheskaya laboratoria Lomonosova* ("Lomonosov's Chemistry Laboratory"; Moscow–Leningrad, 1962); and B. M. Kedrov, *Tri aspekta atomistiki*, II, *Uchenie Daltona* ("Three Aspects of Atomic Theory, II, Dalton's Theory"; Moscow, 1969), see pp. 178–200 for Lomonosov's discoveries of the law of conservation of matter, pp. 219–263 on his atomic-kinetic conceptions, and app., pp. 269–274, 290–292.

Other Aspects. On Lomonosov's other scientific and literary activity, see K. S. Aksakov, *Lomonosov v istorii russkoy literatury i russkogo yazyka* ("Lomonosov in the History of Russian Literature and the Russian Language"; Moscow, 1846); V. I. Vernadsky, *O znachenii trudov Lomonosova v mineralogii i geologii* ("The Significance of Lomonosov's Work in Mineralogy and Geology"; Moscow, 1900); A. P. Pavlov, *Znachenie Lomonosova v istorii pochvovedenia* ("Lomonosov's Importance in the History of Soil Science"; Moscow, 1911); P. N. Berkov, *Lomonosov i literaturnaya polemika ego vremeni, 1750–1765* ("Lomonosov and the Literary Polemic of His Time"; Moscow–Leningrad, 1936); V. P. Lystsov, *Lomonosov o sotsialno-ekonomicheskom razvitii Rossii* ("Lomonosov on the Social and Economic Development of Russia"; Voronezh, 1939); M. A. Bezborodov, *Lomonosov i ego rabota po khimii i tekhnologii stekla* ("Lomonosov and His Work in the Chemistry and Technology of Glass"; Moscow–Leningrad, 1948), published on the 200th anniversary of the founding of the first scientific chemical laboratory in Russia; V. A. Perevalov, *Lomonosov i arktika* ("Lomonosov and the Arctic"; Moscow–Leningrad, 1949); S. I. Volfkovich and V. V. Kozlov, *Tekhnicheskaya khimia v tvorchestve Lomonosova* ("Technical Chemistry in Lomonosov's Creative Work"; Moscow, 1961), with bibliography, pp. 75–81; and P. N. Berkov *et al.*, eds., *Literaturnoe tvorchestvo Lomonosova. Issledovania i materialy* ("Lomonosov's Creative Literary Works. Studies and Material"; Moscow–Leningrad, 1962).

Collections. Collected material on Lomonosov's life and activity include *Lomonosovsky sbornik* ("Lomonosov Collection"; St. Petersburg, 1911); N. A. Golubtsova, ed., *Lomonovsky sbornik* (Arkhangelsk, 1911); and A. I. Andreyev, L. B. Modzelevsky, S. I. Vavilov, V. L. Chenakal, *et al.*, eds., *Lomonosov. Sbornik statey i materialov* ("Lomonosov. A Collection of Articles and Materials"), 6 vols. (Moscow–Leningrad, 1940–1965).

B. M. KEDROV

LONDON, FRITZ (*b*. Breslau, Germany [now Wrocław, Poland], 7 March 1900; *d*. Durham, North Carolina, 30 March 1954), *physics, theoretical chemistry*.

Fritz London and his younger brother, Heinz, were the only children of Franz London, *Privatdozent* in mathematics at Breslau and later professor at Bonn, and Luise Hamburger, daughter of a linen manufacturer. The home atmosphere was that of a cultivated and prosperous liberal German-Jewish family, disturbed only by the premature death of Franz London in 1917. London attended high school at Bonn, where he received a classical education, and the universities of Bonn, Frankfurt, and Munich. His first academic interest was philosophy: in 1921 he received a doctorate *summa cum laude* at Munich for a dissertation on the theory of knowledge based on the symbolic methods of Peano, Russell, and Whitehead and their followers. He had done the work without supervision and entered it for the degree at the suggestion of G. Pfänder, to whom he had shown it for criticism. The philosophic bent remains noticeable throughout London's work, which is characterized by a constant search for general principles and thorough exploration of the logical foundations of his chosen subjects. He was never a mere calculator. In 1939 he published jointly with Ernst Bauer a short monograph in French on the theory of measurement in quantum mechanics.

During the three years following publication of his dissertation London wrote two further philosophical papers and spent some time as a high school teacher in various parts of Germany, but in 1925 he returned to Munich to work in theoretical physics under Sommerfeld. He then held in succession appointments at Stuttgart with P. P. Ewald and at Zurich and Berlin with Schrödinger. In 1933 the Nazi persecution forced both London brothers to leave Germany. London spent two years at Oxford and two years in Paris at the Institut Henri Poincaré. In 1939 he was appointed professor of theoretical chemistry (later chemical physics) at Duke University, where he remained until his death. In 1929 he married the artist Edith Caspary. They had two children.

Between 1925 and 1934 London's interests centered on spectroscopy and the new quantum mechanics, chiefly as applied to the chemical bond. His first scientific paper, written jointly with H. Hönl, was on the intensity rules for band spectra. In 1927 he and W. Heitler produced their classic quantum-mechanical treatment of the hydrogen molecule, "the greatest single contribution to the chemist's conception of valence made since G. N. Lewis' suggestion in 1916 that the chemical bond between two atoms consists of a pair of electrons held jointly by the two atoms."[1] Heitler and London set themselves the problem of determining the energy of a quantum mechanical system having two electrons in motion about two charged nuclei (protons). At large distances, with one electron orbiting each nucleus, the system is just a pair of hydrogen atoms; but when the nuclei are brought closer the forces between all four particles must be taken into account. It had long been recognized that two atoms A, B, may combine as a stable molecule with separation d if the interatomic forces vary so as to make the total energy a minimum at that distance. A complete quantum mechanical calculation of the forces requires precise knowledge of the probability function for the distribution of electrons, which is exceedingly complicated, but Heitler and London were able to approximate the solution by means of an analytical technique developed in the theory of sound by Lord Rayleigh. In a vibrating body, such as a bell, the energy associated with the lowest normal mode of vibration is a minimum. Any motion of slightly different form will have higher energy, but since it is near a minimal point, the increase in energy due to first-order deviations in motion is of the second order of small quantities. A rather good estimate of the energy of vibration may therefore be made from quite a crude approximation to the actual motion; and of any two approximate solutions the one yielding lower energy is nearer the truth. Rayleigh's method supplies a guide for guesswork in the study of complex vibrating systems; equivalent ideas apply to the solution of Schrödinger's wave equation in quantum mechanics. The first trial wave function used by Heitler and London for the hydrogen molecule was simply the known expression for one electron orbiting each nucleus, that being the exact solution at large distances where the interactions between the atoms are negligible. In this case the function probability of the two electrons 1, 2 being found in the same volume element of space is (by ordinary statistical theory) the product of their separate probabilities, and hence their joint wave function $\psi_{AB}(1, 2)$ from which the probabilities are determined is

$$\psi_{AB}(1, 2) = \psi_A(1)\,\psi_B(2), \qquad (1)$$

where $\psi_A(1)$ is the wave function for electron 1 orbiting atom A, and $\psi_B(2)$ for electron 2 orbiting atom B. Insertion of (1) into Schrödinger's equation does yield an attractive force between the atoms at large distances and an energy minimum when they are separated by about 0.9 Å, but the calculated binding energy is far from the experimental value.

The next step hinged on a concept put forward in

another connection by Heisenberg about a year earlier. Since in quantum mechanics the two electrons are indistinguishable, they may be supposed to change places without altering the system in any way, and a better approximation to the wave function will be

$$\psi_{AB}(1, 2) = \psi_A(1)\, \psi_B(2) \pm \psi_A(2)\, \psi_B(1). \quad (2)$$

From (2) with the positive sign Heitler and London obtained an expression for the total energy W_M of the molecule having the form

$$W_M = 2W_H + \frac{e^2}{r_{AB}} + \frac{2J + J' + 2K\triangle + K'}{1 + \triangle^2}, \quad (3)$$

where W_H is the ground state energy of an isolated hydrogen atom, e^2/r_{AB} the electrostatic repulsion between the two nuclei, and J, J', K, K', and $\triangle$ are various integrals, of which J can be interpreted as the net attraction between each electron cloud and the nucleus of the other atom, J' the repulsion between the electron clouds, and K and K' are the so-called exchange integrals whose meaning will be discussed below. The energy is substantially reduced, so by Rayleigh's principle the function (2) is indeed a closer approximation than (1) to the real distribution. Figure 1 reproduces the calculated curve, which has a

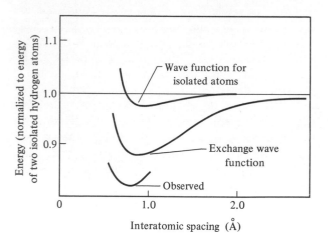

FIGURE 1.   Binding energy for the hydrogen molecule.

pronounced minimum at an interatomic spacing of 0.79 Å and gives a binding energy of 3.14 electron volts, which may be compared with the experimental values 0.74 Å and 4.72 ev. Finally, extending London's earlier interest in the band spectra of molecules Heitler and London determined a vibrational frequency for the molecule from the curvature of the potential near the minimum and obtained a value of 4800 cm⁻¹ as compared with the observed spectral frequency of 4318 cm⁻¹.

Improvements in detail to the Heitler-London solution were soon made by others, chief being corrections for screening of the nuclei by the electron cloud (S. C. Wang), polarization of the charge cloud (N. Rosen), and the addition to equation (2) of terms describing ionic structures (S. Weinbaum). In 1933 H. M. James and A. S. Coolidge gave a laborious investigation introducing the interelectronic distance r_{12} explicitly into the analysis and comparing results for variation functions with five, eleven, and thirteen terms. The calculations converged on values for the binding energy, vibrational frequency, and interatomic spacing extraordinarily close to experiment, and equally good results have since been found for other properties of molecular hydrogen such as its magnetic and electric susceptibilities. All in all, the description of the hydrogen molecule by quantum mechanics achieves a level of success which makes it one of the most compelling pieces of evidence for the theory itself. The remaining major issue is the interpretation of the exchange integrals. Heisenberg had originally illustrated the idea of a quantum mechanical system oscillating between two states by analogy with classical resonance phenomena, for example, the periodic interchange of energy between two tuning forks on a common base. Quantum mechanical resonance, however, differs from its classical analogues by lowering the total energy of the system. Since a reduced energy implies an attraction, contributions to the interaction arising from the use of wave functions like (2) are often spoken of as exchange forces, pictured as the result of a frequent switching of positions of the two electrons in the molecule—a quite unnecessary piece of mystification. All the forces binding the molecule together are electrical in origin: the exchange integral is merely one of a number of contributions to the electromagnetic energy, and there is moreover no intrinsic need to divide the energy in this particular way. Shortly after the Heitler-London paper, another, very different treatment of molecular structures, the molecular-orbital method, was developed by E. U. Condon, F. Hund, R. S. Mulliken and others, which builds up the solution by modifying the wave function for the helium ion rather than those for two hydrogen atoms. It gives results of comparable accuracy without exchange terms, using instead a quite different pair of resonant structures to find the wave function for the ion. A third mode of division appears in James and Coolidge's general variational solution. With these qualifications it must be added that the idea of treating complex molecules as resonating between a number of simple structures, which grew out of the work of Heitler and London and their contemporaries, has been amazingly fruitful. London later used to recall Schrödinger's comment that while he had a high opinion of his equation, expecting it to describe the entire field of chemistry as well as physics was more even than he would have dared.[2]

London continued for several years to work on molecular theory. In 1928 he formulated a description of chemical reactions as activation processes, and in 1930 with R. Eisenschitz he turned his attention to the quantum theory of intermolecular forces. The modern burgeoning of this branch of physics dates effectively from 1875, when van der Waals applied corrections to the ideal gas equation to describe the phenomena of critical points and the condensation of liquids and showed that the additional terms could be attributed to the combination of a long-range attraction and a shorter-range repulsion between molecules. These must, of course, be distinguished from the more powerful chemical forces. Analysis of their effects gradually advanced during the next forty years, and by 1926, largely through the work of J. E. Lennard-Jones on crystal structures and the transport properties of gases, some knowledge had been gained of their magnitude and distance dependence. Meanwhile, P. J. W. Debye and also W. Keesom in 1921 had given elementary calculations of forces due to the electric dipole moments of molecules and had found an attraction varying inversely as the seventh power of the distance. This attraction, however, was far too weak to account for the observed phenomena. Following two false starts by Born and Heisenberg, the corresponding quantum mechanical calculation given in 1927 with numerical errors by Wang was then corrected and extended by Eisenschitz and London in their paper. They found that fluctuation processes cause a dipole-dipole interaction much greater than Debye's, because in effect the orbital motions of the electrons in one molecule create large time-varying fields at the other, and the force is proportional not to the mean but to the mean-square value of the field. Such forces are customarily called dispersion forces because they are determined mainly by the outer electrons, which are also responsible for the dispersion of light. The interaction energy is

$$W = \frac{6e^2 a_o{}^5}{r^6},\tag{4}$$

where e is the electron charge and a_o the Bohr radius of the atom. This was the form finally adopted by Lennard-Jones for the attractive part of his potential: it leads to forces varying inversely as the seventh power of the distance. Eisenschitz and London were able to correlate the forces with molecular polariza-

bilities, and they were later applied to many other matters. More elaborate analyses yielded higher-order corrections. For polar molecules there are additional terms of comparable size, which also obey the inverse-seventh-power law but vary with temperature. A further correction was given in 1946 by H. B. G. Casimir and D. Polder, who discovered that at short distances the retardation of the field introduces phase shifts in the motions of the electrons which make the forces vary more nearly as the inverse eighth power. Effects of this kind are observed in surface phenomena, such as the equilibrium thickness of very thin helium films.

Toward the end of 1932 London completed the manuscript of a book on molecular theory. His agreement for its publication was broken by Springer, the German publisher, after his departure from the country. In England he attempted to arrange a translation, but although several persons offered to help, he was unable to strike a working relationship with any of them. At the time of his death he was planning to rework and translate the material himself. The manuscript is preserved at Duke University Library. London's departure from Germany coincided with a general shift in his scientific interest. Only on one problem in molecular physics, the diamagnetism of the aromatic compounds, did he spend much time thereafter. While studying the benzene ring in 1937 he began to form the ideas about long-range order that became central in his work on superconductivity.[2]

In 1932 London's brother, Heinz, started a Ph.D. thesis on superconductivity in the low-temperature group at Breslau directed by F. E. Simon. Since Kammerlingh Onnes' discovery in 1911 that the electrical resistance of mercury vanishes at very low temperatures, the behavior of superconductors with direct currents had been extensively studied, but nothing was known of the effects of high-frequency alternating currents. Following a suggestion by W. Schottky of Siemens, H. London looked for high-frequency losses in superconductors by attempting to detect the Joule heating caused by currents from a 40 MHz radio source. His search did not lead to anything for several years, but early on he formed some strikingly original ideas about the superconducting state. He decided that a.c. effects, if they exist, probably occur through the existence of two groups of electrons, one subject to losses, the other not. Direct currents then flow only in the superconducting electrons; alternating currents couple inductively to both groups in parallel and so cause dissipation. The same two-fluid model was independently advanced by C. J. Gorter and H. B. G. Casimir in 1934 to account for certain thermodynamic properties of superconductors, and since Heinz London gave the idea only in his thesis, it is commonly associated with their names. He then wrote an acceleration equation for the superconducting electrons,

$$\Lambda\dot{\mathbf{J}} = \mathbf{E}, \qquad (5)$$

where $\mathbf{E}$ is the internal field, $\mathbf{J}$ the current, and Λ a constant equal to m/ne^2, where m and e are the mass and charge of the electrons and n their number density. The constant Λ, known as the London order parameter, is often attributed to Fritz London but is in fact exclusively due to his brother. Combining (5) with Maxwell's electromagnetic equations, H. London then concluded that the currents in any super-conductor are confined to a shallow surface layer characterized by a penetration depth $\lambda = \sqrt{\Lambda/4\pi}$. This idea is evidently analogous in some degree to the well-known a.c. penetration depth derived by Maxwell for alternating currents in normal metals. The quantity λ was the first of a number of characteristic distances important in the theory of superconductivity. Again it was due exclusively to Heinz London. Similar ideas about the acceleration equation and penetration depth were developed independently by R. Becker, G. Heller, and F. Sauter in an interesting paper which also evaluated magnetic effects in a rotating super-conductor.

In 1933 shortly before Heinz London joined his brother at Oxford, W. Meissner and R. Ochsenfeld made a startling discovery. It was well known that currents in superconductors flow in such a way as to shield points inside the material from changes in the external magnetic field. This indeed is an obvious property of any resistanceless medium, fully discussed by Maxwell in 1873 long before the discovery of superconductivity.[3] But a superconductor does more. Whereas a zero resistance medium only counteracts changes in the field, it actually tends to expel the field present in its interior before cooling. The distinction between the two cases is illustrated in Figure 2. The Londons quickly saw its implications and in 1935 published a joint paper on the electrodynamics of superconductors, in which they replaced (5) by a new phenomenological equation connecting the current with the magnetic rather than the electric field,

$$\operatorname{curl} \Lambda\mathbf{J} = -\frac{1}{c}\mathbf{H}. \qquad (6)$$

Formally, (6) is nothing other than the integral of the equation obtained by inserting (5) into Maxwell's equation, $\operatorname{curl} \mathbf{E} = -(1/c)\dot{\mathbf{H}}$, and taking the constant of integration as zero. However, in contrast to many physical processes where constants of integration are

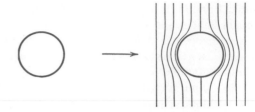

Magnetic field applied to zero resistance medium after cooling in zero field.

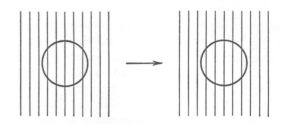

Zero resistance medium cooled in finite field.

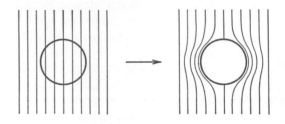

Superconductor cooled in finite field.

FIGURE 2.   The Ochsenfeld-Meissner effect.

trivial, this choice has profound significance: it represents a preferred magnetic state of the super-conductor independent of past history. In the paper the logical relation between the propositions is set forth with Fritz London's philosophical clarity. As the authors observe, equations (5) and (6) stand roughly at the same level of generality; but (6) embraces more in respect to the Meissner effect, yet less in another respect, since it implies not (5) but the weaker condition curl $(\Lambda\mathbf{J} - \mathbf{E}) = 0$ or, after integration,

$$\Lambda\mathbf{J} = \mathbf{E} + \operatorname{grad} \mu, \qquad (7)$$

where μ is an arbitrary scalar quantity. The virtue of the new description is that it covers neither more nor less than the known facts. In the remaining sections the Londons went on to determine boundary conditions, examine the covariant properties of the equations, and give detailed solutions for a sphere and a cylin-drical wire which again showed that the currents are restricted to a penetration layer d of order $c\sqrt{\Lambda/4\pi}$.

London continued to study superconductivity for many years, along with the parallel phenomena of superfluidity in liquid helium which were discovered soon afterward and on which he wrote an important paper in 1938. He expounded his ideas on both subjects in various articles and in the two-volume *Superfluids* (1950–1954). He gradually came to see a deeper meaning to equation (6). In ordinary electrodynamics the canonical momentum of the electron is given by

$$\mathbf{p} = m\mathbf{v} + e\mathbf{A}/c, \tag{8}$$

where $m\mathbf{v}$ is the ordinary momentum and $e\mathbf{A}/c$ is a kind of effective momentum associated with the magnetic field, $\mathbf{A}$ being the vector potential of the field. The electric current is determined by $\mathbf{v}$, but the quantity determining the de Broglie wavelength of the electron is $\mathbf{p}$. Writing $\mathbf{p}_s$ for the average momentum of the superconducting electrons and using Maxwell's relation $\mathbf{B} = \text{curl } \mathbf{A}$ and the definition of Λ, London discovered that (6) is equivalent to

$$\text{curl } \mathbf{p}_s = 0. \tag{9}$$

In the special case of an ideal solid superconductor the solution of (9) is $\mathbf{p}_s = 0$, while for a wire of constant cross section fed at its ends by a current from an external source, $\mathbf{p}_s$ is uniform over the length and breadth of the wire. This last result is of extraordinary interest. It implies that although the superconducting current is concentrated at the surface of the wire, the wave functions of the electrons extend uniformly throughout the material. From this London came to a radically new concept of the nature of the superconducting state. Ordinary substances when cooled to low temperatures lose the kinetic energy of heat and become progressively more ordered in position: they solidify. For particles subject to classical mechanics, that indeed is the only possibility. For quantum mechanical systems, however, the kinetic energy does not quite vanish at the absolute zero; there is a residual zero-point energy because the positions and momenta of the particles are subject to Heisenberg's uncertainty relation $\triangle x \triangle p \sim h$. Hence, London conjectured, there might in some circumstances be an advantage in energy for a collection of particles to condense with respect to momentum rather than position. This would account for the uniformity of $\mathbf{p}_s$ throughout the wire and would imply that the current constitutes a macroscopic quantum state, describable by a single wave function, like a gigantic molecule. A striking corollary is that the magnetic flux through a superconducting ring should be quantized, since there must be an integral number of waves around the ring.[4] This conjectural

condition on the entire current resembles the quantum condition on a single electron in the de Broglie picture of the atom. London's unit of magnetic flux was hc/e or about 4×10^{-7} gauss cm². Some years later the existence of flux quantization was demonstrated independently in Germany and the United States,[5] but the unit was found to be half London's value, a result explained in the microscopic theory of superconductivity by the idea that electrons interact in pairs.

London's concept of long-range order in momentum space transformed the issue of what the theory of superconductivity was about. It no longer had to explain vanishing resistance but, rather, why superconducting electrons acquire order of this particular kind. This opened the way of escape from an embarrassing theorem due to F. Bloch,[6] who had rigorously established that the lowest energy state of a system of electrons isolated from external magnetic fields is one of no current. Now if superconductivity were merely an absence of resistance, fluctuation effects would inevitably disturb the current and cause it to decay. In London's viewpoint no such problem arises, because the current is an excited metastable state, with energy barriers that may (as was later shown) be related to the quantized flux condition.[7] The goal for a microscopic theory of superconductivity is then to find the mechanism for cooperative behavior of the electrons. This was achieved by H. Fröhlich; J. Bardeen, L. N. Cooper, and J. R. Schrieffer; and N. Bogoliubov[8] in the years immediately after London's death. The crucial idea, due to Cooper, is that pairs of electrons moving in opposite directions with opposite spins become briefly paired through interaction with the ionic lattice of the metal. In the general case the London equations apply only in one particular limit, and the currents are better described by more elaborate phenomenological equations given in 1952 by V. L. Ginzburg and L. D. Landau. Many of the clues to the solution came through interpreting experiments on the microwave properties of superconductors, which followed the work of Heinz London.

London's volume of superconductivity contained much else of value on the thermodynamics of superconductors, the intermediate state, and other special topics. One interesting result was that a superconductor spinning with angular velocity $\boldsymbol{\omega}$ should generate a magnetic field $\mathbf{H}_L$ equal to $(2mc/e)\boldsymbol{\omega}$ gauss, where m and e are the mass and charge of the electron. The corresponding calculations for a zero-resistance medium spun from rest had been given by Becker, Heller, and Sauter, but London predicted the field would also spontaneously appear as the spinning body is cooled through its transition temperature, in analogy with Meissner and Ochsenfeld's discovery. The effect was demonstrated experimentally in 1960.[9] An interesting point, which has been little explored, is that H_L appears to depend on the rotation of the superconductor relative to the universe as a whole. There then appears to be some constraint on the underlying quantum condition closely related to that determining rotation in gravitational theory. Besides their theoretical implications, the ideas discussed by London have led to many interesting advances in technology, for example in the application of quantized flux devices to measurement of very low magnetic fields. The authors and their colleagues are planning to use the magnetic moment of a rotating superconductor for readout of a high-precision gyroscope to perform a new test of general relativity in a satellite suggested by L. I. Schiff.

In 1908 Kammerlingh Onnes liquefied helium at a temperature of 4.2° K. During the 1920's evidence began to accumulate that at 2.19° K. the liquid undergoes a peculiar transition, marked by discontinuities in the specific heat and density curves, into another phase which became known as liquid helium II; but not until 1938 were its extraordinary superfluid properties discovered simultaneously by P. Kapitsa and by J. F. Allen and A. D. Misener. The liquid passed through the finest of capillary channels with no measurable resistance. Indications of abnormally high thermal conductivity had previously been found by W. H. and A. P. Keesom. Allen with several colleagues then established that the heat current in the helium II is not linear with temperature and that a pressure gradient proportional to heat input exists in the fluid. The latter effects are often called the fountain pressure, since Allen and J. Jones demonstrated it in an especially striking way by creating a helium fountain. Clearly the mass flow and heat transfer equations of helium II must differ from those of any other fluid; and in addition, the nature of the phase transition—indeed, even the existence of two distinct liquid phases—was puzzling. Thinking over the problem, London was reminded of a strange feature of quantum statistics derived in 1924 by Einstein. In 1923 S. N. Bose had shown that Planck's well-known radiation formula might be derived from the hypothesis of light quanta (photons), by assuming that the photons are subject to a different kind of statistics from classical Maxwell-Boltzmann particles, with the statistical specification based not on the number of particles but on the number of particle states. Bose communicated his result privately to Einstein, who arranged for its publication and then wrote two papers extending the statistics to other quantum gases. One of Einstein's conclusions was

that at low temperatures such a gas would have more particles than the number of available states and would then undergo a peculiar kind of condensation with the surplus molecules concentrated in the lowest possible quantum state. Applying the new statistics to ordinary molecules, Einstein then argued that the condensation would have perceptible effects in gases at low temperatures; the viscosity of helium gas, for example, might be expected to fall off rapidly below 40° K. All this seemed rather farfetched: it was not obvious that the new statistics applied to gases. Indeed, a year later E. Fermi and P. A. M. Dirac showed that electrons obey another, quite different kind of quantum statistics, and in 1927 G. Uhlenbeck claimed that Einstein had mistakenly approximated a sum by an integral and that in the correct calculation no condensation would occur. There things rested until London revived the argument and made the even more radical suggestion that Bose-Einstein condensation might occur in liquids as well as gases and thus might account for the peculiar behavior of liquid helium II.

London's suggestion was controversial and also difficult to develop owing to the unsatisfactory state of the theory of liquids. The next advance was due to L. Tisza. Partly through London's idea and partly through considering the results of experiments with oscillating disks, which unlike those on capillary flow gave a finite viscosity, he suggested that helium II may be conceived of as a mixture of two liquids, superfluid and normal, analogously with the two-fluid model of superconductivity. In 1939 Heinz London made a further important contribution by proving from thermodynamic arguments that the superfluid does not carry entropy. In this form the two-fluid model provided a framework for many experimental discoveries over a number of years. Meanwhile, a different approach to the fundamental theory was advanced by Landau, and the idea of Bose-Einstein condensation was heavily criticized. However, London stuck to his guns. An important test, as he pointed out, was to search for superfluidity in the rare isotope He[3] which, unlike ordinary He[4], contains an odd number of particles and may be expected to obey Fermi-Dirac rather than Bose-Einstein statistics. In fact no superfluidity has been observed in He[3] down to 10^{-2}° K. In volume II of *Superfluids* London gave an approximate treatment of a Bose-Einstein liquid, following E. Guggenheim's smoothed-potential model of the liquid state, and estimated the condensation temperature at roughly 3.13° K. as compared with the experimental value of 2.19° K. He also continued to emphasize the close analogy between superfluidity and superconductivity. Here he was in more difficulty than he cared to admit. Electrons obey Fermi-Dirac statistics, and there seemed to be no grounds for linking superconductivity with Bose-Einstein condensation. With the emergence of the microscopic theory, however, the tables were turned on London's critics: paired electrons do behave as Bose particles, and his interpretation of the condensation extends to superconductivity also.

There is a perspective in London's work that has made many of his ideas become progressively more influential with the passage of time. One of his favorite opinions was that some concept of long-range order would eventually prove important to the understanding of biological systems. Although the suggestion remains in the nascent phase it has already had interesting consequences. W. A. Little has proposed that a particular class of long-chain organic molecules might be expected to have superconductive properties, with transition temperatures around room temperature.[10] Although organic superconductors have not yet been made, the idea has raised many interesting questions of the kind that would have appealed to London.

NOTES

1. L. Pauling and E. B. Wilson, *Introduction to Quantum Mechanics* (New York, 1935), p. 340.
2. Personal recollections of conversations between London and W. M. Fairbank.
3. J. C. Maxwell, *Treatise on Electricity and Magnetism*, II (London, 1873), secs. 654, 655.
4. F. London, in *Physical Review*, **74** (1948), 570, is the earliest statement of flux quantization.
5. B. S. Deaver, Jr. and W. M. Fairbank, in *Physical Review Letters*, **7** (1961), 43; R. Doll and M. Näbauer, *ibid.*, **7** (1961), 51.
6. L. Brillouin, in *Proceedings of the Royal Society*, **75** (1949), 502, crediting theorem to Bloch.
7. N. Byers and C. N. Yang, in *Physical Review Letters*, **7** (1961), 46.
8. H. Fröhlich, in *Physical Review*, **79** (1950), 845; J. Bardeen, L. N. Cooper, and J. R. Schrieffer, *ibid.*, **106** (1957), 162; **108** (1957), 1175; and N. Bogoliubov, in *Zhurnal eksperimentalnoi i teoreticheskoi fisiki*, **34** (1958), 58; translated in *Soviet Physics JETP*, **7** (1958), 41.
9. A. F. Hildebrandt, in *Physical Review Letters*, **12** (1964), 190; A. King, Jr., J. B. Hendricks, and H. E. Rorschach, Jr., in *Proceedings of the Ninth International Conference on Temperature Physics* (New York, 1965), p. 466; M. Bol and W. M. Fairbank, *ibid.*, p. 471.
10. W. A. Little, in *Physical Review*, **134** (1964), 1416.

BIBLIOGRAPHY

I. ORIGINAL WORKS. London's published books are *La théorie de l'observation en mécanique* (Paris, 1939), written with E. Bauer (a copy of this rare work is in Brown University Library); *Superfluids:* Vol. I, *Macroscopic Theory of Superconductivity;* Vol. II, *Macroscopic Theory of*

Superfluid Helium (New York, 1950–1954); 2nd ed., rev., reprinted in the Dover series with additional material by other authors, 2 vols. (New York, 1961–1964), with bibliography of London's scientific papers, by Edith London, I, xv–xviii. A large collection of notebooks and MSS is preserved at the Duke University Library, Durham, N. C., together with two bound vols. containing London's complete published papers. Some MSS of scientific interest remain in Mrs. London's possession.

II. SECONDARY LITERATURE. Personal biographical material by E. London and a sketch of London's scientific work by L. W. Nordheim are in *Superfluids*, 2nd ed., I, v–xviii.

On the chemical bond the monographs by L. Pauling, *Nature of the Chemical Bond*, 3rd ed. (Ithaca, N. Y., 1960); and C. A. Coulson, *Valence* (Oxford, 1960), are useful. On dispersion forces, see S. G. Brush, "Interatomic Forces and Gas Theory From Newton to Lennard-Jones," in *Archives of Rational Mechanics and Analysis*, **39**, no. 1 (1970), 1–29.

On superconductivity, see D. Shoenberg, *Superconductivity* (Cambridge, 1950); J. Bardeen and J. R. Schrieffer, in C. J. Gorter, ed., *Progress in Low Temperature Physics*, III (Amsterdam, 1961), 170–287; and P. de Gennes, *Superconductivity of Metals and Alloys* (New York, 1966). On superfluidity, see K. R. Atkins, *Liquid Helium* (Cambridge, 1958); and J. Wilks, *Properties of Liquid and Solid Helium* (Oxford, 1967).

C. W. F. EVERITT
W. M. FAIRBANK

LONDON, HEINZ (*b.* Bonn, Germany, 7 November 1907; *d.* Oxford, England, 3 August 1970), *physics.*

Like his brother, Fritz London, who exercised close parental influence on him after their father's early death, Heinz received a classical education but was also interested in mathematics and science, especially chemistry. He attended the University of Bonn from 1926 to 1927 and after six months with the W. C. Heraeus chemical company completed undergraduate studies in Berlin and Munich. His graduate work on superconductivity was done at Breslau under F. E. Simon, and his Ph.D., issued early in 1934, was one of the last awarded to a Jew in Nazi Germany. Later in the same year he joined Simon and other members of the Breslau group at Oxford, where they were establishing the first center of low-temperature research in England since the time of James Dewar. Fritz London was already in Oxford, and Heinz lived there with the family for two years. In 1936 he moved to Bristol, where he remained until 1940, when he was for a brief time interned as an alien. After his release he worked with Simon and others on the British atomic bomb project and then spent two years at Birmingham before transferring to Harwell in 1946, where he continued to work until his death. In 1939 he married Gertrude Rosenthal, but the marriage broke up soon afterward. In 1946 he married Lucie Meissner; they had four children.

The origin of London's work on alternating-current losses in superconductors has been described in the preceding entry, along with his early contributions to the theory, culminating in the joint paper with Fritz London on the electrodynamics of the superconducting state. An interesting feature of the theory outlined there is the indeterminate parameter μ in equation (7). Evidently one solution would be $\mu = 0$, in which case the acceleration equation (5) remains valid, although its justification is different from that originally given. A superconductor would then, like any other metal, exhibit surface charges in an electric field. An equally plausible alternative, discussed by the Londons, was to make $\mu = \Lambda c^2 \rho$, where ρ is charge density. This had the advantage of allowing a symmetrical four-dimensional representation of the equations; it implied, however, that the electric field penetrates a superconductor to the same depth as the magnetic field and therefore that the capacity of a condenser with superconducting plates should change appreciably on cooling through its transition from the normal to the superconducting state. In 1935 London tried this experiment at Oxford, showing conclusively that there is no change in capacity and hence that the solution $\mu = 0$ must be accepted. About the same time he published an investigation of the equilibrium between superconducting and normal phases of a metal, based on a thermodynamic analysis of the London equations. He found that the observed transition to the normal state in high magnetic fields depends on the existence of a threshold value for current density in the superconductor. He also discovered that unless a superconductor has a positive surface energy sufficient to counteract the field energy in the penetration layer, it will split into a finely divided mixture of normal and superconducting regions in high fields. Since the superconductivity of most pure metals disappears entirely above the critical field, London concluded that their surface energy is indeed positive. He conjectured however that some hysteresis effects just then observed in superconducting alloys might arise from a negative surface energy. These ideas were later entirely confirmed, and during the 1950's they were elaborated into the distinction between type I and type II superconductors. The special properties of type II superconductors proved of great technical importance in obtaining high field superconducting magnets.

While at Oxford, London continued to search for alternating-current losses in superconductors, but had no success, even though he raised the operating frequency to 150 MHz. After his move to Bristol he took the subject up once more and finally in 1939 succeeded in demonstrating the occurrence of high-frequency losses at 1500 MHz. Figure 1 reproduces the experimental data from London's paper, which shows significant alternating-current dissipation at points well below the ordinary transition temperature. An unexpected by-product was the discovery of the "anomalous skin effect" in normal metals. At low temperatures the resistivity of tin in the normal state, as deduced from Joule heating at 1500 MHz, was several times larger than the measured direct-current resistivity, although at room temperatures the two figures were identical. London tentatively attributed the effect to the electrons' having a mean free path considerably greater than the skin depth, so that relatively few of them contribute to conduction.

London's work on high-frequency losses was terminated by World War II, but the subject was revived in 1946 by several other investigators, using resonant cavity techniques from radar research. A. B. Pippard in particular reached some highly significant results by measuring changes in resonant frequency of cavities above and below the transition temperature. He concluded that the wave functions were indeed coherent over distances greater than the penetration depth but that the coherence length was finite rather than infinite as in the London theory. Pursuing London's idea about the electronic mean free path, he introduced impurities into the material, which acted as scattering centers to reduce both the free path and the coherence length. When this was done the penetration depth increased, the product of the Pippard coherence length l and the penetration depth λ being approximately constant. Other measurements led to the hypothesis of an energy gap in the distribution of conducting particles. These developments provided the basis of ideas for the Bardeen-Cooper-Schrieffer microscopic theory of superconductivity. The Pippard length was then identified with the pairing distance of the electrons.

At Bristol, London also investigated superconductivity of thin metallic films in collaboration with E. T. S. Appleyard, A. D. Misener, and J. R. Bristow. From measurements of critical fields they were able to determine the penetration depth experimentally. Measurements on the magnetic susceptibilities of superconducting particles by D. Shoenberg about the same time gave comparable results. This work on thin films was another example, like the experiments on alternating-current losses, of work begun by London which became a major field of research studied by

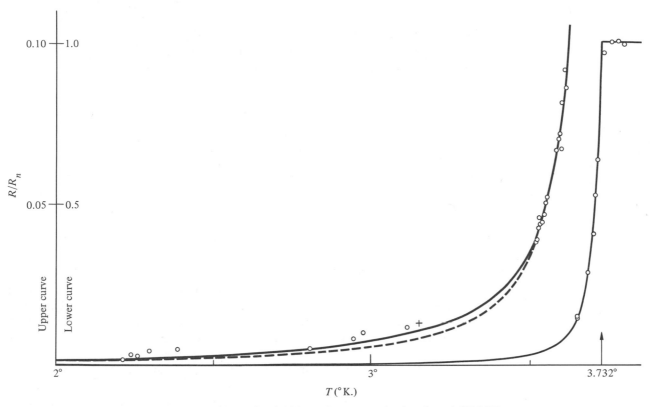

FIGURE 1.   Alternating field losses in superconducting tin at 1,500 MHz.

hundreds of other investigators. A third subject of study from the same period was his work on helium, which included an experiment that helped establish the two-fluid model, and the thermodynamic analysis mentioned in the previous entry, which proved that the superfluid component carries no entropy. A by-product of the analysis was London's prediction of the mechanocaloric or inverse fountain effect, a temperature difference generated by the moving superfluid.

Following the work of Fritz London and Tisza much effort was applied to the theory of liquid helium II. In 1941 Lev Landau formulated the problem in quite a different way, describing the normal fluid in terms of quantized excitations, phonons and rotons, and giving new hydrodynamical equations to describe superfluidity. One of his conclusions was that the superfluid is subject to the condition curl $\mathbf{v}_s = 0$, making it incapable of rotation. Actually the same condition for the superfluid was also strongly advocated by Fritz London in the London-Tisza model, along with the analogous condition on curl $\mathbf{p}_s = 0$ in a superconductor, as evidence that each phenomenon constitutes a macroscopic quantum state. In 1946 Heinz London proposed an experiment to distinguish the behavior of a fluid subject to constraints of this kind from mere absence of viscosity. The idea was to set a cylindrical container of helium I in slow uniform rotation about its axis and then cool the system slowly to a temperature well below the lambda point. If the superfluidity is simply absence of viscosity, the angular momentum of the fluid should be unaffected by the transition; but if the equilibrium state is one of constrained vorticity, the superfluid created by cooling should stop rotating and the container has to rotate more rapidly to conserve the total annular momentum. London then made a further conjecture. In 1941 A. Bijl, J. de Boer, and A. Michels had pointed out that the critical velocity v_c (the maximum velocity for superfluid flow) in a film of helium II seems to obey the condition $v_c \sim h/4\pi md$, where m is the atomic mass of helium and d the film thickness. London suggested that the angular velocity Ω of the helium II might be subject to a similar quantum condition, so that in a container of radius R, rotation stops only if

$$\Omega < h/2\pi mR^2. \tag{1}$$

For a vessel one cm. in diameter the rotational period obtained from (1) is about one day, so the experiment was a difficult one. Experiments at higher speeds tried several times from 1950 onward disclosed no difference between the rotating superfluid and classical rigid-body rotation. Various suggestions about the state of motion were advanced by Fritz London and others; then Lars Onsager and later, independently, Richard Feynman assumed that the circulation around an arbitrary path in the fluid is a multiple of h/m consistent with London's condition (1), but that the rotating fluid as it gains more angular momentum will break up into an array of vortices, each with quantized circulation h/m. Thus by a different path the suggestion of a macroscopic quantum condition entered the theory of helium II as well as the theory of superconductivity; it is re-markable that one suggestion originated with Heinz London and the other with Fritz London. The existence of individual quantized vortices in helium II was first demonstrated experimentally by W. F. Vinen in 1961 through the coupling of vorticity to a vibrating wire;[1] since then they have been observed in several other ways. The rotating-bucket experiment suggested by London was finally performed successfully in 1965.[2] The measurements confirmed that at low angular velocities the superfluid stops rotating and the bucket rotates faster on cooling through the lambda point. Thus the conjecture that curl $v_s = 0$ is an equilibrium state for a superfluid was confirmed. A notable feature was that while quantized vortices of the predicted size were indeed observed, the angular velocity below which rotation ceased was about fifteen times higher than condition (1). The last result is explained by the large amount of energy required to form a single vortex core. It is the equiv-alent for the superfluid of the Ochsenfeld-Meissner effect in a superconductor.

London's work on the atomic bomb project had been on methods of separating uranium 235 by ionic migration and liquid thermal diffusion. At Harwell after the war he continued to work on isotope separa-tion, concentrating on the production of carbon 13 as a stable tracer element for medical research. He developed a method of low-temperature distillation and designed a fractionating column using carbon monoxide for the enrichment of C^{13} and O^{18}. This machine has operated successfully for many years and currently supplies all the C^{13} used in Great Britain and the United States.

During the last fifteen years of his life London worked in collaboration with various colleagues on three main topics, neutron production and neutron-scattering experiments in liquid helium, techniques for producing high field superconducting magnets, and, most important, the He^3-He^4 dilution refrigerator, one of the most ingenious and useful contributions to cryogenic technology in many years. He had suggested

the essential idea of the dilution refrigerator in 1951 at the Oxford Conference on Low-Temperature Physics. He pointed out that since He^3 behaves as a Fermi gas below 1° K., and He^4 as a Bose gas, then if He^3 is allowed to mix with He^4 it will in effect expand. Now in this region He^4, being practically pure super-fluid, has negligible entropy; whereas He^3 has entropy proportional to $n^{-2/3}T$, where n is the atomic con-centration. Dilution to one part in a thousand would therefore cool a bath of helium to 10^{-2}° K., while still retaining appreciable specific heat. In 1951 the idea seemed quite impractical in view of the scarcity of He^3, but in 1955 London revived it in collaboration with E. Mendoza and G. Clarke. They first measured the osmotic pressure of He^3 dissolved in He^4 and attempted adiabatic dilution starting at 0.8° K. but obtained no cooling. After G. K. Walters and W. M. Fairbank had discovered that He^3 and He^4 separate at 0.87° K. into two phases, one concentrated and one dilute, London and Mendoza at first concluded that dilution cooling would be ineffective below about 0.8° K. They later realized that it could be achieved in another way, by exploiting the latent heat of transition from the concentrated to the dilute phase.[3] The essential principle of the dilution refrigerator as conceived by London and Mendoza is illustrated in Figure 2. Refrigeration occurs in the pot A, where the lighter He^3-rich phase floats on top of the dilute

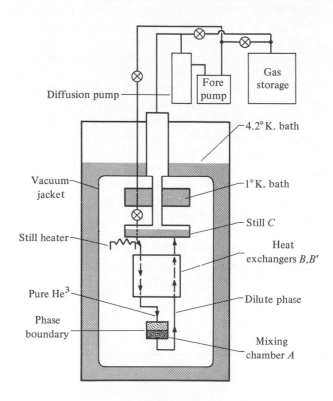

FIGURE 2. The He^3–He^4 dilution refrigerator.

phase and expansion proceeds downward. The diluted mixture is then taken out to a still, C, where the He^3 evaporates and is recycled through heat exchangers B, B'. The effectiveness of the cooling cycle depends on the fortunate coincidence of two special properties of He^3. First, the phase boundary for the mixtures has a shape such that significant proportions of He^3 enter the dilute solution down to the absolute zero. Second, He^3 has a higher vapor pressure than He^4 and is therefore evaporated preferentially in the still. It is customary to use the refrigerator with conventional He^3 cooling as a first stage. After various experiments by Mendoza at Manchester, a working model was built in 1965 by H. E. Hall, P. J. Ford, and K. Thomson.[4] Improved versions with operating temperatures down to 0.005° K. have since been made and marketed in several countries, and the device is now widely used.

The two London brothers form a study of unusual psychological interest. Fritz's influence on Heinz in the critical years after their father's death was strong, yet despite their close professional relationship they are in many ways contrasting figures. Fritz was well-organized, Heinz shockingly untidy. It is customary to think of Fritz as a theoretician and Heinz as an experimentalist, but actually neither fits exactly into ordinary categories. Of Heinz, D. Shoenberg has said: "Though he spent much time on experiments his most valuable contributions have been ideas and inventions. Perhaps he might be described as a cross between a theoretical physicist and an inventor."[5] In their theoretical contributions Fritz's genius consisted in identifying the deep conceptual issues, Heinz's in the vital and far from simple task of bringing experiment into fruitful contact with theory. As an experimentalist he belonged to that not undistinguished class of workers, among whom was J. J. Thomson, whose junior colleagues wisely protect them by various subterfuges from too close contact with apparatus. His clumsiness was a byword. Both brothers brought a remorseless thoroughness to everything they did. Heinz's attitude to physics had also an element of spiritual passion. "For the second law of thermodynamics," he proclaimed vehemently to one colleague, "I would die at the stake."[6]

NOTES

1. W. F. Vinen, "The Detection of Single Quanta of Circulation in Liquid Helium II," in *Proceedings of the Royal Society*, **260** (1961), 218.
2. G. B. Hess and W. M. Fairbank, "Measurement of Angular Momentum in Superfluid Helium," in *Physical Review Letters*, **19** (1967), 216.
3. Many interesting details are given in an unpublished paper
by E. Mendoza, "Early History of the He^3-He^4 Dilutions Refrigerator: Some Personal Impressions."
4. H. E. Hall, P. J. Ford, and K. Thomson, "A Helium-3 Dilutions Refrigerator," in *Cryogenics*, **6** (1966), 80.
5. D. Shoenberg, obituary of H. London, in *Biographical Memoirs of Fellows of the Royal Society*, **17** (1971), 441–461.
6. H. Montgomery, quoted in 5.

BIBLIOGRAPHY

A complete bibliography of London's published papers with an admirable biographical sketch is D. Shoenberg, in *Biographical Memoirs of Fellows of the Royal Society*, **17** (1971), 441–461. His unpublished MSS are in Mrs. London's possession. See also K. Mendelsohn, in *Review of Modern Physics*, **36** (1964), 71.

For further sources on particular areas of low-temperature physics, see the bibliography for Fritz London.

C. W. F. EVERITT
W. M. FAIRBANK

LONGOMONTANUS. See **Severin, Christian.**

LONICERUS (LONITZER), ADAM (*b*. Marburg, Germany, 10 October 1528; *d*. Frankfurt, Germany, 29 May 1586), *botany.*

Lonicerus was the son of Johann Lonitzer, a philologist and professor at Marburg. He received his baccalaureate in 1540 and his master's degree in 1545. In the latter year he began teaching at the Gymnasium in Frankfurt, but he returned to Marburg because of disorders caused by war. He studied medicine there and later in Mainz, where he was a private tutor in the home of a Dr. Osterod. In 1553 Lonicerus became professor of mathematics at Marburg, and in 1554 he received his medical degree. Also in 1554 he married the daughter of the Frankfurt printer Egenolph Magdalena; and following the death of Graff, the municipal physician of Frankfurt, in that year, he was appointed to the post. Lonicerus worked as a proofreader in the printing shop of his father-in-law, who specialized in the revision of old herbals (for example, those of Eucharius Röslin and Dioscorides).

Lonicerus wrote extensively in many fields, including botany, arithmetic, history of medicine, and medicine, particularly public health books such as regulations for controlling the plague (1572) and regulations for midwives (1573). His herbals were so influential that in 1783 at Augsburg—almost 250 years after the first edition—*Adam Lonicers Kräuter-Buch* was still published. In addition, Linnaeus immortalized his name in the genus *Lonicera*.

Lonicerus based the first, Latin edition of his herbal on Röslin's revision of the *Ortus sanitatis* (1551), which contained many illustrations, most of them borrowed from Bock. The popularity of Lonicerus' herbal is shown by the many, steadily enlarged editions he brought out. Although the provision of plant names in German, Latin, Greek, French, Italian, and Spanish lends the herbal a scientific air, the inclusion of fabulous stories betrays its late medieval character. (For example, the formation of bezoars is attributed to the hardening of the tears of stags!) The herbal also lists animal and metallic medicaments and contains one of the earliest descriptions of local flora. In addition, the book distinguishes the deciduous trees from the conifers; the group composed of the yew, the cypress, the juniper, and the savin is contrasted with that containing the spruce and the fir. Lonicerus' son Johann Adam (*b.* 1557) edited his father's writings.

BIBLIOGRAPHY

I. ORIGINAL WORKS. Lonicerus' writings include *Naturalis historiae . . .*, 2 pts.: I, *Naturalis historiae opus novum, in quo tractatur de natura arborum, fructicum, herbarum . . .* (Frankfurt, 1551), II, *Naturalis historiae de plantarum potissimum quae circa Francofurtum nascuntur, descriptione et virtute . . .* (Frankfurt, 1555); *Aphorismoi Hippocratis* (Frankfurt, 1554); *Kreuterbuch, neu zugericht, künstliche Conterfeytunge der Bäume . . . Item von fürnembsten Gethieren der Erden, Vögeln und Fischen; auch von Metallen . . .*, a German version of *Naturalis historiae* (Frankfurt, 1557; later eds. at Frankfurt, 1560–1650; Ulm, 1679–1770; Augsburg, 1783)—this is simply a revision of a work by Cube (municipal physician in Frankfurt 1484–*ca.* 1503), which was first issued by Röslin: only the medicinal plants were described in pt. I, local flora in pt. II; *Botanicon. Plantarum historiae cum earundem ad vivum arteficiose expressis iconibus tomi duo . . .* (Frankfurt, 1565); *Brevis et utilis arithmetices introductio . . .* (Frankfurt, 1570); *Beschreibung der Arzney und fürnehmsten Compositionen* (Frankfurt, 1572); *Hebammenbüchlin, Empfengnuss und Geburt dess Menschen . . .* (Frankfurt, 1582), a revision of Röslin's work; *Omnium corporis humani affectuum explicatio methodica . . .* (Frankfurt, 1594); and *De purgationibus libri III, ex Hippocrate, Galeno Aetio et Mesue depromti . . . foras dati per Teuc. Annaeum Privatum, C. Adami Loniceri . . . filium . . .* (Frankfurt, 1596).

A partial list of his works is in *Catalogue général de la Bibliothèque nationale*, XCIV (Paris, 1930), cols. 925 f.

II. SECONDARY LITERATURE. See A. Arber, *Herbals, Their Origin and Evolution*, 2nd ed. (Cambridge, 1953), 72, 134, 221; A. von Haller, *Bibliotheca botanica*, 2 vols. (Zurich, 1771–1772; repr. Hildesheim, 1969): I, 309 f., II, 451; W. Kallmorgen, *700 Jahre Heilkunde in Frankfurt am Main* (Frankfurt, 1936), 342 (portrait p. 146); Linnaeus, *Bibliotheca botanica* (Amsterdam, 1736), 14, 25; M. Möbius, *Geschichte der Botanik*, 2nd ed. (Stuttgart, 1968), 30,

138; G. A. Pritzel, *Thesaurus literaturae botanicae* (Leipzig, 1872), 195 f.; F. W. E. Roth, "Botaniker Eucharius Rösslin, Theod. Dorsten u. Adam Lonicer (1526–1586)," in *Zentralblatt für Bibliothekswesen*, **19** (1902), 271–286, 338–345; H. Schelenz, *Geschichte der Pharmazie* (Berlin, 1904), 432, 446; and G. Stricker, in *Allgemeine deutsche Biographie*, XIX (1884), 157.

KARIN FIGALA

LONITZER, Adam. See **Lonicerus, Adam.**

LONSDALE, DAME KATHLEEN YARDLEY (*b.* Newbridge, Ireland, 28 January 1903; *d.* London, England, 1 April 1971), *crystallography, chemistry, physics.*

Kathleen Lonsdale was the tenth and youngest child of Harry Frederick Yardley and Jessie Cameron. Her father was postmaster at Newbridge, but the family later moved to England and Kathleen won scholarships which took her to the County High School for girls at Ilford and later to Bedford College for Women, which she entered at the age of sixteen. There she studied mathematics and physics and received a B.Sc. with highest honors at the age of nineteen. She took first place in the University of London list and one of her examiners, W.H. Bragg, was so impressed that he offered her a post in his research team to work on the crystal structure of organic compounds by X-ray analysis. Thus her scientific career began in 1922, first at University College and then at the Royal Institution in London. It continued throughout her life, with only brief interruptions following her marriage to Thomas Lonsdale in 1927, when she moved to Leeds for three years before returning once more to the Royal Institution.

In 1945 she became the first woman to be admitted as a Fellow of the Royal Society. In 1946 she was appointed reader in crystallography at University College, London, and professor of chemistry in 1949. She was appointed Dame Commander of the British Empire in 1956, received the Davy Medal of the Royal Society in 1957 and was its vice-president from 1960–1961. In 1966 she was president of the International Union of Crystallography and president of the British Association from 1967 to 1968. During her long and intensely active scientific career Kathleen Lonsdale raised two daughters and one son, had many outside interests, and traveled widely in most countries of the world. She was a member of the Society of Friends, and worked hard for peace and for prison reforms. But her many and varied interests were always closely integrated with her scientific work.

X-ray crystallography is primarily concerned with deducing the positions of atoms in space from a study of the diffraction patterns obtained when a beam of X rays is passed through a crystal. Kathleen Lonsdale began her work in 1922, ten years after the original discovery of the diffraction effect by Laue. In that time considerable advances in the theory and practice of the method had been made, and the structure of many simple and some quite complex inorganic substances had been deduced. But little was known about the dimensions and exact metrical structure of organic molecules.

As a physicist and mathematician by training, Kathleen Lonsdale's first major contribution to this subject was a profound and systematic study of the theory of space groups, methods for their determination, and the possibilities of molecular symmetry that are involved. This work was published with W. T. Astbury in 1924. To some extent it duplicated the work of Wyckoff and Niggli (of which Astbury and Kathleen Lonsdale were ignorant), but it went further and was much more useful for those whose work was concerned with organic molecular crystals. A later continuation and extension of this work consisted of the structure factor tables published in 1936 in photo-litho-printed form from the handwritten manuscript, and the many volumes of the International Tables for X-Ray Crystallography published from 1952 onwards. These volumes, of which Kathleen Lonsdale was principal editor, are in constant use today and form an essential tool for crystal structure determination.

Kathleen Lonsdale's main task at the Royal Institution was to try to solve the problem of organic crystal structures. Although she confessed that she "knew no organic chemistry and very little of any other kind," she was destined to make one of the most outstanding advances in that subject for many decades. Her work on hexamethylbenzene, published in 1929, and hexachlorobenzene demonstrated for the first time that the benzene ring was hexagonal and planar, and she gave its precise dimensions. Of this result C. K. Ingold wrote, "one paper like this brings more certainty into organic chemistry than generations of activity by us professionals."

Her later work, however, was more concerned with the physics of crystals than with chemistry. She made an intensive study of the magnetic anisotropy of crystals, and by measuring the diamagnetic susceptibilities in and perpendicular to the planes of a number of aromatic molecules, she was able to show that, while the σ electronic orbits were of atomic dimensions,

the π orbits were of molecular dimensions. The far-reaching importance of this result was that it established the reality of the concept of molecular orbitals.

Later she was responsible for the development of divergent-beam X-ray photography of crystals, a technique which gives information about the texture and perfection of the crystal, and can also be used to make precise measurements of lattice constants or wavelength. By this means she was able to measure the C—C distance in individual diamonds to seven significant figures. She had a special interest in the structure of diamonds and made many other important contributions to their study.

Another important field in which she made outstanding contributions was the study of diffuse X-ray reflection by single crystals. She showed that this diffuse scattering is directly related to the elastic constants of the crystal. It is also dependent on the crystal structure and can be used to determine molecular orientation. In general, the thermal motion of atoms and molecules in crystals was one of her special interests.

In her later work she returned again to more chemical interests, as in her study of the solid-state transformation of anthracene to anthraquinone and anthrone, and to medical problems concerned with the mode of action of drugs and the composition of endemic bladder stones.

Kathleen Lonsdale had a profound influence on the development of X-ray crystallography and related fields in chemistry and physics. Very few have made so many important advances in so many different directions.

BIBLIOGRAPHY

Among Lonsdale's more important works are "Tabulated Data for the Examination of the 230 Space-groups by Homogeneous X-Rays," in *Philosophical Transactions of the Royal Society*, **224A** (1924), 221–257, written with W. T. Astbury; "The Structure of the Benzene Ring in $C_6(CH_3)_6$," in *Proceedings of the Royal Society*, **123A** (1929), 494–515; "An X-Ray Analysis of the Structure of Hexachlorobenzene, Using the Fourier Method," *ibid.*, **133A** (1931), 536–552; *Simplified Structure Factor and Electron Density Formulae for the 230 Space Groups of Mathematical Crystallography* (London, 1936), and "Magnetic Anisotropy and Electronic Structure of Aromatic Molecules," in *Proceedings of the Royal Society*, **159A** (1937), 149–161.

With H. Smith, she wrote "An Experimental Study of Diffuse X-Ray Reflection by Single Crystals," *ibid.*, **179A** (1941), 8–50. Also see "Extra Reflections From the Two Types of Diamond," in *Proceedings of the Royal Society*,

179A (1942), 315–320; "X-Ray Study of Crystal Dynamics: An Historical and Critical Survey of Experiment and Theory," in *Proceedings of the Physical Society*, **54** (1942), 314–353; "Divergent Beam X-ray Photography of Crystals," in *Philosophical Transactions of the Royal Society*, **240A** (1947), 219–250; *Crystals and X-rays* (London, 1948); "Geiger Counter Measurements of Bragg and Diffuse Scattering of X-rays by Single Crystals," in *Acta crystallographica*, **1** (1948), 12–20; and "Vibration Amplitudes of Atoms in Cubic Crystals," *ibid.*, **1** (1948), 142–149.

J. M. ROBERTSON

LONSDALE, WILLIAM (*b*. Bath, England, 9 September 1794; *d*. Bristol, England, 11 November 1871), *geology*.

Lonsdale was the younger son of William Lonsdale of Bath. He obtained an army commission in 1812, served in the Peninsular War, and was present at the battle of Waterloo. When peace was restored in 1815, he retired from the army on half-pay and settled near Bath. He never married. Lonsdale's interests inclined toward natural history, and in 1826 he was appointed a curator at the Bath Museum. He was elected to the Geological Society of London in 1829, and soon afterward was appointed curator and librarian to the society. Lonsdale worked hard at cataloging the society's rapidly growing collections; in 1838 his post was redefined, and as assistant secretary and librarian he undertook an increasing administrative and editorial burden. In 1842, poor health forced him to resign, and he retired to southwest England for the rest of his life. In 1846 he was given the society's highest award, the Wollaston Medal, for his work on fossil corals.

Shortly before his election to the Geological Society, Lonsdale contributed an excellent, although conventional, account of the stratigraphy and paleontology of the area around Bath. Once he was in the society's employment, he had little time for writing. His work, however, gave him an unrivaled knowledge of British fossils, which led to his most important contribution to geology.

In the late 1830's the geology of Devonshire became fiercely controversial because of the assertion by Roderick Murchison that the government's official geological surveyor, Henry De la Beche, had misinterpreted the entire sequence of strata and had overlooked the presence of a large area of strata of Coal Measure (that is, late Carboniferous) age. Most geologists agreed, however, that the older strata of Devonshire were pre-Silurian because of their lithological character. In 1837, however, it was asserted instead that the fossils in these rocks indicated a

Mountain Limestone (that is, an early Carboniferous) date. Lonsdale immediately suggested, on the basis of his own studies of the fossil corals, that the strata were neither Carboniferous nor Silurian, but intermediate in age, since some fossil species were known from the Silurian, some from the Carboniferous, and some from neither. This implied that the Devon rocks were the lateral equivalents of the Old Red Sandstone, despite their totally different lithology. This seemed so improbable that Lonsdale's suggestion was virtually forgotten until 1839, when it was adopted by Murchison and Adam Sedgwick and became the basis of their Devonian system. The validity of Lonsdale's hypothesis was then quickly confirmed by the recognition of the same fossil fauna in the expected position in clearer sequences of strata elsewhere in Europe and in North America.

The Devonian controversy involved much more than a technical or local problem. The argument turned on the reliability of fossils for the estimation of the relative geological age of strata in the absence of clear evidence from superposition and in the face of clear contrary evidence from lithology. Even more fundamentally, this methodological argument depended on conceptions of biological history. Lonsdale's hypothesis was based on his perception of the intermediate character of the Devonian corals; it was valid only if the fauna had been transformed in the course of time by the gradual production of new species and extinction of old species and in a roughly synchronous manner over a very wide area, with anomalies in only exceptional circumstances (as, for example, the unusual Old Red Sandstone environment). The vindication of Lonsdale's hypothesis was therefore taken as confirming strongly the validity of correlating strata by means of fossils, even on an intercontinental scale. It was thus highly influential indirectly in the development of stratigraphical geology.

BIBLIOGRAPHY

Lonsdale's principal scientific publications were "On the Oolitic District of Bath," in *Transactions of the Geological Society of London*, 2nd ser., **3**, pt. 2 (1832), 241–276; and "Notes on the Age of the Limestones of South Devonshire," *ibid.*, **5**, pt. 3 (1840), 721–738. The history of the Devonian problem is summarized in M. J. S. Rudwick, "The Devonian System: A Study in Scientific Controversy," in *Actes du XIIe Congrès international d'Histoire des Sciences*, **7** (Paris, 1971), 39–43. Lonsdale's work for the Geological Society is referred to in Horace B. Woodward, *The History of the Geological Society of London* (London, 1907).

M. J. S. RUDWICK

LOOMIS, ELIAS (*b.* Willington, Connecticut, 7 August 1811; *d.* New Haven, Connecticut, 15 August 1889), *meteorology, mathematics, astronomy.*

Loomis graduated from Yale College in 1830, and was a tutor there from 1833 to 1836. He became professor of mathematics and natural philosophy at Western Reserve College, in Hudson, Ohio, in 1836, although he spent the first year of his appointment in further study in Paris. From 1844 to 1860 he was professor at the University of the City of New York. In 1860 he accepted a call to Yale, where he stayed until the end of his life. After the early death of his wife, Loomis led a rather isolated life, centered around his work, his only diversion being the compilation of an extensive genealogy of the Loomis family. He was member of the National Academy of Sciences and of scientific societies in the United States and Europe.

Loomis' interest was divided among several branches of science. Most of his scientific achievements were of a practical, rather than a theoretical, nature. His work, reflecting his conviction that the laws governing natural phenomena can be uncovered only by studying observed data, was carried out with utmost precision, and his research, although not always original, was highly valued because of its great reliability. In his own time, however, Loomis was better known for the publication of a large number of textbooks on mathematics, astronomy, and meteorology than for his scientific investigations.

Loomis made his most important contributions in the field of meteorology. In 1846 he published the first "synoptic" weather map, a new method of data representation that in the following decades exerted a profound influence on the formulation of theories of storms. This method became of fundamental importance in the development of weather prediction. The weather maps presented in Loomis' paper brought clarification to the heated controversy between J. P. Espy and W. C. Redfield concerning the surface wind pattern in storms. Later, Loomis essentially followed Espy in regarding thermal convection, reinforced by the latent heat released during condensation of water vapor, as the chief factor in storm formation. As soon as weather maps began to be published on a daily basis in the United States, in 1871, Loomis embarked on a long series of meticulous statistical investigations of cyclones and anticyclones. His results effectively supported the convection theory of cyclones.

Throughout his life Loomis was strongly interested in geomagnetism. In 1833–1834 he conducted a series of hourly observations of the earth's magnetic field and mapped his results for the United States. In 1860

Loomis prepared the first map of the frequency distribution of auroras and pointed out that the oval belt of most frequent auroras was not centered on the geographic pole but approximately paralleled the lines of equal magnetic dip.

Loomis devoted much of his time to astronomical investigations. These studies dealt mainly with the observation of meteors and the determination of longitude and latitude of various localities. Together with D. Olmsted he rediscovered Halley's comet on its return in 1835 and computed its orbit.

BIBLIOGRAPHY

I. ORIGINAL WORKS. Loomis published a large number of his papers in the *American Journal of Science and Arts*, including his investigations on the aurora borealis (1859–1861) and a series of twenty-three papers entitled "Contributions to Meteorology" (1874–1889). A complete bibliography of Loomis' works is to be found in H. A. Newton, "Biographical Memoir of Elias Loomis," in *Biographical Memoirs. National Academy of Sciences*, **3** (1895), 213–252. Collections of Loomis' papers and correspondence are to be found in the Manuscripts and Archives Department of the Beinecke Rare Book and Manuscript Library at Yale University.

II. SECONDARY LITERATURE. The most complete biographical notice is H. A. Newton, cited above. See also F. Waldo, "Some Remarks on Theoretical Meteorology in the United States, 1855 to 1890," in *Report of the International Meteorological Congress, Chicago*, August 21–24, 1893, edited by O. L. Fassig as *Bulletin. Weather Bureau, United States Department of Agriculture* **2**, pt. 2 (1895), 318–325.

GISELA KUTZBACH

LORENTZ, HENDRIK ANTOON (*b.* Arnhem, Netherlands, 18 July 1853; *d.* Haarlem, Netherlands, 4 February 1928), *theoretical physics.*

Lorentz' father, Gerrit Frederik Lorentz, owned a nursery near Arnhem. His mother, the former Geertruida van Ginkel, died when he was young; and his father married Luberta Hupkes when the boy was nine. Lorentz attended primary and secondary schools in Arnhem and was always the first in his class. From an early age he was drawn to physical science, although he also read widely in Victorian novels and Reformation history. He was unusually quick with foreign languages, inferring grammar and idiom from context. Although he grew up in Protestant circles, he was a freethinker in religious matters; he regularly attended the local French church to improve his French.

By the time Lorentz matriculated at the University of Leiden in 1870, his primary interests were mathematics and physics. He became close friends with the astronomy professor, Frederick Kaiser, and followed his lectures on theoretical astronomy with keen interest. He also attended the lectures of Pieter Leonhard Rijke, the only professor of physics at the time. After a year and a half Lorentz passed his candidate's examination in mathematics and physics and returned to Arnhem to prepare for his doctoral examination and to write his dissertation. He lived at home for seven years, studying on his own and teaching in the evening high school. It was at this time that he bought an edition of Fresnel's collected works, the first reference volume he owned beyond the usual textbooks. He admired Fresnel above any of the early physical authors (as he came to admire Hertz above any of the modern ones), being impressed by his logical clarity and by the sure physical intuition that enabled him to overcome a limited mathematical skill. Following his French master, Lorentz cultivated clarity and physical insight as his own special talents.

Theoretical physics tended to be an isolated activity for the early specialists in the discipline; Lorentz, like his contemporary J. W. Gibbs and like Einstein somewhat later, carried out highly original researches on the central problems of physics while removed from direct contact with other active researchers. Lorentz needed only to make the short trip to Leiden's physics laboratory to borrow Maxwell's works and to keep in touch with the current specialist physics literature. His linguistic fluency was a marked asset in his Arnhem years, enabling him to command a wide range of physical writings in French, German, and English. Trained in Leiden and working in Arnhem, his receptivity to outside influences was not inhibited by any dominant local school of physics. He passed his doctoral examination *summa cum laude* in 1873 and received his doctorate in 1875, at age twenty-one; his dissertation was on physical optics, the subject Fresnel had made his own but which Lorentz treated from the viewpoint of Maxwell, as interpreted by Helmholtz.

Lorentz remained at Arnhem after receiving his doctorate, uncertain whether to follow a career in physics or mathematics. His uncertainty was in part a reflection of the professional condition of physics. Although he did some optical and electromagnetic experiments at Arnhem, he was strongly drawn to the theoretical aspects of physics; at this time, however, theoretical physics was only starting to be organized as an independent discipline within physics; and the prospects for a career in the discipline were problematic. The importance of Lorentz' thesis was early recognized in his own country, as was his academic promise generally; and in 1877 he was offered a chair of mathematics at the University of Utrecht. That same year the University of Leiden offered him its new chair of theoretical physics, which had originally been intended for J. D. van der Waals. Lorentz accepted the appointment, resolving his career uncertainty; he was not yet twenty-five. The Leiden theoretical physics chair was the first of its kind in the Netherlands, and one of the first in Europe. Lorentz holds a major place in the history of physics for his part in shaping the new role of the discipline as well as for his scientific contributions.

In 1881 Lorentz married Aletta Kaiser, a niece of his former astronomy teacher. Their first daughter, Geertruida Luberta, was born in 1885; their second, Johanna Wilhelmina, in 1889. Their first son died in infancy; their second, Rudolf, was born in 1895. Lorentz' elder daughter remembers him as constantly at his writing desk, yet never seeming to be engaged in hard work. He had none of the mannerisms of the eccentric genius nor of the bookish ascetic. He was a disciplined scholar of regular habits and disposition. He was social, with a marked sense of humor and a gift for conversation; he always enjoyed a cigar and glass of wine with friends. To all who knew him, he seemed a man of remarkable inner harmony.

At Leiden, Lorentz developed his most original contribution to theoretical physics, his celebrated electron theory. He announced and articulated the theory in a series of publications beginning in 1892. In his fifteen years at Leiden prior to 1892, Lorentz had not been uncommonly productive by contemporary standards. He had published an average of one paper a year; in addition he had written two widely used textbooks in Dutch, one on the calculus for physical scientists in 1882 and one on elementary physics in 1888. Lorentz' most productive period began in 1892, when he was almost forty. Between 1892 and 1904—the time during which he largely completed his electron theory—he produced an average of three to four research publications a year. For Lorentz, as for others, the electron theory opened up a vast number of new experimental and theoretical directions. Much of the physics community now looked to Leiden for guidance.

Lorentz' influence on theoretical physics was exerted not only through his writings but also through the personal impression he made on young physicists who came to Leiden from all over the world to hear his lectures. His influence was unwitting in the sense that he did not interfere with others and did not inspire a school of the usual kind. He followed the work of students and younger physicists, but he did not try to influence the direction of their interests; his relations with them were in keeping with his basically private nature, at once kindly and aloof. Einstein and other theorists of the younger generation venerated him, making frequent journeys to Leiden to visit him and hear his thoughts on their latest ideas. They prized him for his intellectual daring and mastery, his thorough familiarity with all areas of physics, and his nonmanipulative, natural leadership. Einstein said Lorentz had been the greatest influence in his life.

In 1905 Lorentz considered moving to the University of Munich as professor of theoretical physics. It was only after the University of Leiden relieved him from the chore of delivering introductory lectures by appointing a third professor of physics that he agreed to stay. Lorentz resigned his Leiden chair in 1912, after thirty-five years of lecturing on all aspects of theoretical physics. He moved to Haarlem, where he served as curator of the physical cabinet in Teyler's Stichting, a museum housing science, art, and coin collections, and as secretary of the Hollandsche Maatschappij der Wetenschappen, an organization to promote private patronage for science. The museum contained a laboratory, which was remodeled after that of the Royal Institution of London for Lorentz's use. For the first time Lorentz had his own laboratory, something the University of Leiden had promised him but failed to deliver, to his great disappointment.

For years Lorentz gave popular physics lectures, a task he liked and took seriously; but chiefly he used the greater freedom of his new post to pursue his theoretical researches. He retained a connection with the University of Leiden as an honorary professor, in which capacity he delivered his famous Monday morning lectures on current problems in physics. In the latter part of his career he performed various services for the government. He was keenly interested in education and served on the government board of education from its founding in 1919 until 1926, helping to reform university examinations and to redistribute professorial chairs among the universities; from 1921 he was president of the department of higher education. He also worked on practical applications of physics for the government; in 1920 he took charge of the calculations for the height of the dike closing the Zuider Zee, devoting years to the completion of the problem.

Lorentz lived all his life in a few close-lying Dutch towns—Arnhem, Leiden, Haarlem—yet he was the most cosmopolitan of physicists. For the first twenty years of his career, his cosmopolitanism was of a restricted, literary kind. After that he began to move outside his Leiden study and lecture room to make personal contact with physicists abroad. He did this

at the time his electron theory was securing him a commanding position in physics, which was also the time of a new phase of international awareness of the science. International physics meetings are essentially a twentieth-century phenomenon, although before then physicists of one country sometimes attended physics meetings in another. Lorentz was first drawn out in 1898, when he accepted Boltzmann's invitation to address the physics section of the Düsseldorf meeting of the German Society of Natural Scientists and Physicians. In 1900 he addressed the International Congress of Physics in Paris, a truly worldwide assembly of physicists.

Lorentz' most important international activity in physics was his regular presidency of the Solvay Congresses for physics from their inception in 1911 through 1927, the last meeting before his death. For a quarter-century Lorentz was a kind of institution at these and other international gatherings, where he presided as the willing and acknowledged leader of the physics discipline. Everyone remarked on his unsurpassed knowledge, his great tact, his ability to summarize lucidly the most tangled argument, and above all his matchless linguistic skill. In addition to presiding at congresses, he did a good deal of invited lecturing, further evidence of the increasing internationalism of physics. He spoke on the electron theory and other topics of current physical interest in Berlin in 1904, in Paris in 1905, in New York in 1906, and later in Göttingen, Pasadena, and elsewhere.

After World War I, Lorentz' cosmopolitanism took on a political cast. As president of the physics section of the Royal Netherlands Academy of Sciences and Letters from 1909 to 1921, he used his influence to persuade his countrymen to join the postwar international scientific organizations created by the Allies. He sought to repeal the clauses excluding the Central Powers from the organizations and to restore true internationalism to science. In 1923 he became one of the seven members of the International Commission on Intellectual Cooperation of the League of Nations, succeeding Henri Bergson as its president. Lorentz' efforts to restore internationalism in science made little headway against the powerful nationalisms supporting the scientific boycott and counterboycott of the Central Powers. The continuing divisiveness of science was a source of great unhappiness to him.

In 1902 Lorentz shared the Nobel Prize in physics with his countryman Pieter Zeeman. He also received most of the other honors that ordinarily come to one of his scientific stature: he was awarded the Royal Society's Rumford and Copley medals; he received honorary doctorates from the universities of Paris and

Cambridge; and he was elected a foreign member of the German Physics Society and the Royal Society.

When Lorentz died in 1928, at age seventy-four, he was honored as the greatest cultural figure the Netherlands had produced in recent times. On the day of his funeral the Dutch telegraph and telephone services were suspended for three minutes in tribute. Representatives of the Dutch royalty and government attended his funeral in Haarlem, as did representatives of scientific academies from around the world. Einstein, a leader of the second generation of professional theoretical physicists and representative of the Prussian Academy of Sciences, spoke at the graveside, referring to Lorentz as the "greatest and noblest man of our times."

One of Lorentz' marked characteristics was an uncommon openness to new trains of thought. Again and again Einstein, Erwin Schrödinger, and other theorists sought his opinion, which was at once sympathetic, informed, and critical. Lorentz' openness was rooted partly in temperament and partly in his view of the proper work of the theoretical physicist. In his inaugural lecture at the University of Leiden in 1878, he explained that the object of all physical research was to find simple, basic principles from which all phenomena can be deduced. He warned against placing undue importance on the mental images associated with basic principles or hoping that the principles themselves can be further explained. He believed that we cannot penetrate deeply into the nature of things and that it is therefore unthoughtful to advocate any given approach as the only valid one. Various basic theoretical approaches—such as atoms and distance forces, contiguous action in a material plenum, and vortex-ring atoms—should be explored at the same time by different investigators, for only then could physicists compare approaches and decide which one leads to the simple basic principles. Much of Lorentz' lifework was spent in critically examining others' theories and helping them seek out simple principles, an activity that conformed to his understanding of the critical function of the theoretical physicist. It should be remarked that in his activities as critic and as constructor of physical theories, Lorentz was strongly sympathetic to certain approaches. However, he had an uncommon ability to distinguish between sympathy and critical judgment in his appraisal of theories. This ability—basically a trait of temperament—underlay in large part his seemingly contradictory roles as strongly committed theorist and openminded critic.

Lorentz' most important work was in optical and electromagnetic theory; to follow its bearing on the development of physics, we shall have to look at the state of the fields as he found them in the 1870's. Optical thinking was then dominated by the elastic-solid theory of the luminiferous ether, which had been developed by Fresnel, Cauchy, Neumann, Stokes, and others. The theory had major difficulties. One was the presence of longitudinal as well as transverse waves in elastic solids, whereas in optical phenomena only transverse waves were known. Another was the failure of elastic solids to yield Fresnel's fraction for the light reflected at the interface of two optical media. These and other difficulties resulted in an accumulation of hypotheses. The longitudinal wave could be disregarded if its velocity of propagation were assumed to be infinite. Certain properties of the passage of light through optical media could be explained by assuming different densities for the ether inside and outside of matter; certain others, by assuming different elasticities for the ether inside and outside matter. The state of optical theory in the 1870's was, in a word, unsatisfactory.

The state of electrodynamics in the 1870's was at least as unsatisfactory as that of optics. There was little agreement on the proper theoretical principles for developing electrodynamic theory. The two most successful electrodynamic theories in Germany were those of Weber and Neumann. Both theories had originated in the mid-1840's, and Weber's especially had been extensively developed since then. Encompassing all electric and magnetic phenomena, Weber's theory was based on the hypothesis that an electric current consisted of two fluids of electric particles of opposite signs moving in opposite directions. It was also based on the hypothesis of a central, instantaneous, action-at-a-distance force between pairs of electric particles. The force was analogous to the gravitational attraction between material particles, except that it depended on the relative motion as well as on the separation of the particles and was attractive or repulsive according to the signs of the particles. Weber's motion-dependent force had an unclear relation to the energy principle, and was challenged for this reason. Neumann's theory of induced electric currents was based on the hypothesis of a position- and motion-dependent force between two elements of electric current rather than between pairs of electric particles. Both theories followed Ampère's in referring magnetism to elementary circular electric currents.

Several other electrodynamic theories were subsequently put forward in Germany. Riemann in 1858 and Neumann in 1868 advanced theories modeled after Weber's; they differed in that they postulated a finite velocity of propagation of electric action, introducing retarded potentials for that purpose. Encouraged by the closeness of the values for the speed of light and the ratio of the electromagnetic and electrostatic measures of electricity—a ratio that had units of velocity and that entered all Weber-type force laws—Riemann identified light with the propagation of electric action. Neumann, however, was more impressed by the differences between light and the finitely propagated potential of his theory, rejecting the suggestion that they were the same thing. Clausius introduced another variant of Weber's theory in the mid-1870's, assuming only a single mobile electric fluid and a force between two electric particles that was noncentral and that depended on the absolute, rather than relative, motion of the particles.

A prominent non-German electrodynamic theory was that proposed by the Danish physicist Ludwig Lorenz in 1867. From Kirchhoff's equations—which stemmed from Weberian electrodynamics—for the motion of electricity, Lorenz, with the use of retarded potentials, showed that periodic electric currents behave like the vibrations of light, concluding that light itself consists of electric currents. Another prominent non-German Continental theory was proposed by the Swedish physicist Erik Edlund in 1871. Edlund derived Weber's fundamental law by assuming a single, particulate electric fluid—which he thought was probably the luminiferous ether—and by assuming that electric actions are finitely propagated. Whereas Lorenz broke with action at a distance, Edlund did not; whereas Edlund assumed an electric ether, Lorenz did not. The disagreements multiplied.

The several Continental electrodynamic theories resulted in a maze of incompletely tested hypotheses, and no immediate experimental decision seemed likely. The conflicting hypotheses centered on several issues: the number—whether one or two—of mobile electric fluids; the existence of an electric ether; the identity of light with electric motions; the nature of the forces between electric fluid particles, to which belonged the questions of central or noncentral forces, and of the relative or absolute motion that entered the force laws; and the relation of motion-dependent forces to the principles of dynamics, especially to the energy principle.

Contributing further to the profusion of electrodynamic principles was the very different theoretical tradition that had developed in Britain during the same period. Drawing on Faraday's and William Thomson's work, Maxwell proposed a mathematical theory of electricity and magnetism in papers in the 1850's and 1860's and in his comprehensive *Treatise on Electricity and Magnetism* in 1873. Rejecting action at a distance and the associated particulate electric fluids of Continental electrodynamics, Maxwell based his theory on the concept of an electromagnetic medium.

The essential point of the theory was that the electromagnetic medium supported transverse vibrations that propagated at the speed of light. The theory promised to be fruitful, especially in the prediction it shared with certain Continental theories that light is an electric phenomenon. Maxwell took seriously the optic implications of his theory, investigating a number of optical problems: notably, the pressure exerted by light, the propagation of light in crystals, the relation between electric conductivity and optical opacity of metals, and the magnetic rotation of the plane of polarization of light. He failed, however, to derive the laws of the reflection and refraction of light, the problem that had proved so embarrassing to the elastic-solid optical theories.

For all its promise, Maxwell's theory—in the form, or various forms, in which he left it—was a source of great perplexity for many of its close readers. Ehrenfest recalled that Maxwell's *Treatise* seemed a "kind of intellectual primeval forest, almost impenetrable in its uncleared fecundity." The theory was unclear in precisely those basic features that differentiated it from most Continental theories. Maxwell did not elucidate the nature of electric charge, a concept that had received clear, if not unanimous, interpretations in terms of particulate electric fluids in the action-at-a-distance theories. Indeed, Maxwell refused to commit himself to any position on the nature of electricity. Sometimes he spoke of it as the process of dielectric polarization; in reverse fashion he spoke at other times of polarization as a motion of electricity. He sometimes likened the motion of electricity to that of an incompressible fluid, without intending that the reader should think that electricity is an incompressible fluid. In the *Treatise* he spoke of a "molecule of electricity"; he added, however, that this way of speaking was "out of harmony with the rest of this treatise."

Conceding only that electricity was a physical quantity, Maxwell cautioned against assuming that "it is, or is not, a substance, or that it is, or is not, a form of energy, or that it belongs to any known category of physical quantities." It is small wonder that his Continental interpreters found the task of clarifying the concept of charge to be both essential and difficult. They found Maxwell's concept of the electromagnetic field equally difficult to grasp. Maxwell did not distinguish between the roles of the medium and ordinary matter in electromagnetic processes. The clear distinction in the Continental theories between distance forces—the counterpart of Maxwell's field—and the electricity they arise from and act upon is entirely absent from Maxwell's theory.

The eventual clarification of the conceptual basis of Maxwell's theory was aided immeasurably by a paper that Helmholtz published in 1870. The purpose of his paper was to bring order to electrodynamics by examining the major rival theories for their agreement with dynamical principles and by exposing their differing, testable consequences. To do this he generalized Neumann's electrodynamic potential between two current elements to encompass Maxwell's and Weber's theories; each of the three theories was characterized by a numerical parameter entering the formulas of the general theory. Because of the recent interest in the velocity of propagation of electric actions and because of its great significance for physics, Helmholtz applied his general induction law to the case in which an electrically and magnetically polarizable medium is present. In the spirit of action-at-a-distance theories, he assumed that the electric interaction of bodies depends in part on direct distance forces and in part on the polarization of the medium, which in turn depends on the distance forces and is the source of new distance forces. He showed that the electric displacement in a dielectric obeys the same wave equations as the displacement of ponderable particles in an elastic solid.

Helmholtz thought that the resulting "remarkable analogy" between the motions of electricity and the motions in the luminiferous ether were consequences of the older action-at-a-distance electrodynamics no less than they were of Maxwell's special hypotheses. He concluded that finitely propagated transverse waves of polarization in a dielectric medium were possible without basic changes in the foundations of action-at-a-distance electrodynamics. His general theory also yielded longitudinal waves, which in the special case of Maxwell's theory were propagated with infinite velocity. From his critique of the rival electrodynamic theories, Helmholtz argued that Weber's theory was untenable and that Maxwell's theory, as he had interpreted it, should be taken seriously. Many Continental physicists approached Maxwell's theory through Helmholtz; his action-at-a-distance formulation of the theory rendered it intelligible to physicists nurtured in the Continental tradition, and his favorable judgment assured it serious attention.

Helmholtz recognized that resolution of the difficulties of optical theory might be directly related to resolution of the difficulties of electrodynamics, and this clear recognition was the starting point for Lorentz' optical researches. Lorentz chose his dissertation topic as a result of a footnote in Helmholtz' 1870 paper, which pointed to the superiority of Maxwell's electromagnetic theory of light over the older elastic-

solid theories in yielding the crucial interface conditions required by Fresnel's laws of reflection and refraction.

In 1875 Lorentz submitted to the University of Leiden his doctoral dissertation on electromagnetic optics, "Sur la théorie de la réflexion et de la réfraction de la lumière" (translated from the original Dutch). Although he had studied Maxwell's papers, his starting point was Helmholtz' action-at-a-distance general theory. He was not opposed in principle to Maxwell's contiguous-action point of view, but he felt that Maxwell's theory was incompletely developed and that in its present form it relied on more special and unconfirmed hypotheses than Helmholtz' did. Lorentz' dissertation reveals his characteristic blend of incisive clarity and unifying vision. He opened with a comparative critique of the older wave theories of light and of the new electromagnetic theory of light. He then reproduced Helmholtz' derivation of the wave equation for the propagation of variations in the state of polarization, applying it successively to the reflection and refraction of light by isotropic media, crystal optics, total reflection, and the interaction of light and metals.

The main result of Lorentz' dissertation was his electromagnetic derivation of Fresnel's amplitudes for light reflected at a dielectric interface. He did this without having to make ad hoc assumptions comparable with those of the elastic-solid theory concerning the density and elasticity of the ether. He also showed that in a more natural way than the elastic-solid theories the electromagnetic theory dispensed with embarrassing, unobserved longitudinal vibrations. He concluded that because of its greater simplicity and comprehensiveness, Maxwell's electromagnetic theory of light was to be preferred over the elastic-solid ones. Lorentz closed his dissertation with a prophetic vision of the vast unifying potentiality for physics implicit in the combination of Maxwell's electromagnetic theory of light with the molecular theory of matter, a prospect that proved to be an adumbration of his own future research.

Apart from being the first systematic treatment of electromagnetic optics, one that succeeded where the elastic-solid theories failed most conspicuously, Lorentz' dissertation was significant as a first step toward distinguishing the electromagnetic field from matter and thus clarifying the physical basis of Maxwell's theory. He pointed to Boltzmann's recent experimental investigations of the predicted relation of the specific inductive capacity of gases to their index of refraction as strongly confirming Maxwell's electromagnetic theory of light. He interpreted Boltzmann's results to mean that the ether is the seat of polarizations and that gaseous molecules exert only a small, secondary influence on the specific inductive capacity of the ether pervading the intermolecular spaces; in this sense he viewed the ether as the only proper dielectric.

In a sequel paper in 1878, on the optical theory of matter, Lorentz began the research program he had sketched at the close of his dissertation; and in so doing he further strengthened his distinction between the roles of matter and the ether. He developed there a theory of the dispersion of light by assuming that material molecules contain charged harmonic oscillators and that the ether everywhere—except possibly in the immediate vicinity of the molecules—has the same properties that it does in a vacuum. Lorentz accounted for the dispersion of light in a body in the following way: incident light waves in the ether cause the electric particles in the body to vibrate; the vibrating particles send out secondary waves in the ether which interfere with the incident ones, thus making the velocity of propagation of light through the body depend on frequency. In his 1878 paper Lorentz predicted a relation between the density of a body and its index of refraction, a relation that became known as the Lorentz-Lorenz formula for its independent development by the Danish physicist in 1869.

In the 1880's Lorentz' continuing interest in electromagnetism was reflected in a paper on the force between two current elements regarded from the point of view of Continental electrodynamics, and in another on the Hall effect and the electromagnetic rotation of the plane of polarization of light. His continuing interest in the ether was reflected in a study of the aberration of light in 1886, in which he concluded that Fresnel's view of the luminiferous ether was superior to Stokes's. Unlike Stokes, Fresnel in his theory of aberration assumed that the ether near the earth did not participate in its motion. Lorentz thought that the hypothesis of the complete transparency of matter to the ether was implicit in Fresnel's whole theory.

Lorentz' chief interest in the 1880's was not, however, electromagnetism and optics but the molecular-kinetic theory of heat. The science of thermodynamics had been largely completed by his day, and he did not participate in its construction. But the molecular-kinetic interpretation of thermodynamics was far from complete, and he worked on a number of its problems; for one, he corrected Boltzmann's proof of the *H*-theorem. Lorentz was strongly receptive to the kinetic theory, as he was to the molecular viewpoint in physics in general, the theme he had enlarged on in his inaugural lecture at the University of Leiden.

From the 1890's, the electron theory dominated Lorentz' researches. In constructing a theory of electrons and fields, he brought together a number of insights he had accumulated over several years of varied researches. The particulate concept of electricity that lay at the basis of his electron theory was conditioned by his long familiarity with Continental electrodynamics and its assumption of particulate electric fluids. It was also conditioned by the same molecular orientation in physics that had prompted his intensive work on the molecular-kinetic theory and, before that, on the interaction of light and molecular matter. Equally fundamental to his electron theory was the concept of the stationary ether, which he had reached through his studies of optical aberration. Finally, his pioneering studies of Maxwellian optics in the 1870's prepared the way for the full, explicit separation of the roles of ether and matter in his electron theory.

The immediate occasion for Lorentz to return to the foundations of Maxwell's theory was Hertz's researches in electromagnetism. In the late 1880's, in response to Helmholtz' program for bringing about an empirical decision between the rival electrodynamic theories, Hertz carried out his influential experiments on Maxwellian electric waves. Following his experimental demonstration of electric waves in air, Hertz made theoretical studies in 1890 of the Maxwellian electrodynamics of stationary and moving bodies. Having abandoned the Helmholtzian action-at-a-distance interpretation of Maxwell's theory with which he had begun his experimental researches, Hertz in his theoretical studies accepted Maxwell's contiguous-action interpretation of electromagnetic processes in the ether, together with his denial of particulate electric fluids. Hertz based his study of the electrodynamics of moving bodies on the concept of an ether that was completely dragged by ponderable bodies. Fully realizing that a dragged ether was in conflict with optical facts, he justified its application to narrowly electrodynamic phenomena on the grounds that it was compatible with such phenomena and that it facilitated a systematic presentation of the theory, the sole purpose of his theoretical study. By assuming a dragged ether, Hertz needed only one set of electric and magnetic vectors instead of the two required by an ether that was separable from matter. He also based his study on his version of Maxwell's equations, which he postulated rather than deriving from mechanical models and principles.

Hertz's experimental and theoretical researches generated widespread interest in Maxwell's theory among Continental physicists. Of the major theoretical statements of Maxwellian electrodynamics following Hertz's researches, several advanced a molecular view of electricity together with a stationary ether. Such theories—soon to be called electron theories—were proposed independently in the early 1890's by Lorentz, by Wiechert, and by Larmor. Although the three theories bore large areas of resemblance, they also differed in major respects. Whereas Larmor, for example, viewed electrons as structures in the ether and the ether as the sole physical reality, Lorentz treated electrons and the ether as distinct entities. Of the three theories, Lorentz' gained the greatest authority on the Continent, in part because of its clear, if ultimately unsatisfactory, dualism of electron and field.

In an address to the Dutch Congress of Physics and Medicine in 1891, Lorentz, following Hertz, declared his conversion to contiguous action in electromagnetic processes. Lorentz objected, however, to two features of Hertz's electrodynamics, which prompted his first memoir in 1892 on the electron theory: "La théorie électromagnétique de Maxwell et son application aux corps mouvants." He criticized Hertz's totally dragged ether on well-known optical grounds; and although he admired the clear, succinct mathematical form that Hertz and Heaviside had given to Maxwell's theory, he criticized Hertz's bare postulation of the field equations. Referring to "one of the most beautiful" chapters in Maxwell's *Treatise*, in which Maxwell applied Lagrangian mechanics to elucidate electromagnetism without assuming a detailed mechanism, Lorentz in 1892 continued the mechanical exploration begun by Maxwell. He remarked that "one has always tried to return to mechanical explanations," and properly so, in his opinion. After laying down his own hypotheses concerning the stationary ether and electrons, he applied d'Alembert's principle to derive the field equations and the equations of motion of an electron in the field. Characteristically, Lorentz spelled out at the start the physical suppositions of his theory; it was a constructive effort of exemplary clarity in a science chronically subject to obscurity.

Lorentz incorporated into his electron theory Fresnel's view that the ether penetrates matter (Lorentz held more tenaciously to a stationary ether than even Fresnel, who admitted some dragging), but he rejected Fresnel's further view that the density of the ether varies from substance to substance as well as Neumann's view that the ether differs in elasticity in different substances. For Lorentz the ether had identical properties everywhere, and he was little inclined to speculate about its ultimate nature. He completely separated the ether and ordinary matter; however, since ether and matter were observed to interact, he needed to reestablish their connection. He assumed that their sole connection was provided

by positive and negative electrons, which he regarded as small, ponderable, rigid bodies. He assumed that electrons are contained in all molecules of ordinary matter (Lorentz wrote of "charged particles" in 1892, of "ions" in 1895, and of "electrons" only after 1899; in this article the term "electrons" is used throughout, without suggesting that Lorentz had an unchanging view of the properties of electrons during these years).

In contrast with Maxwell and Hertz, Lorentz provided a clear, simple interpretation of electric charge and current and of their relation to the electromagnetic field. A body carries a charge if it has an excess of one or the other kind of electrons. An electric current in a conductor is a flow of electrons; a dielectric displacement in a nonconductor is a displacement of electrons from their equilibrium positions. The electrons create the electromagnetic field, the seat of which is the ether; the field in turn acts ponderomotively on ordinary matter through the electrons embedded in material molecules.

Because Lorentz completely separated ether and matter, he needed only one pair of directed magnitudes—one electric and one magnetic—to define the field at a point, and this was so whether or not matter was present at the point; in this way he answered Hertz's formal objection to a stationary ether that it required two sets of directed magnitudes to define the field at a point, one for matter and one for ether. Lorentz also answered Hertz's objection that particulate electric fluids belonged to action-at-a-distance, not contiguous-action, electrodynamics. By means of his concepts of a stationary ether and of electrons transparent to it, Lorentz constructed a consistent electrodynamics that at the same time rejected action at a distance and retained particulate electric fluids.

For this reason Lorentz characterized his theory as a fusion of Continental and Maxwellian electrodynamics. He retained the clear understanding of electricity of the theories of Weber and Clausius, and at the same time he accepted the crux of Maxwell's theory: the propagation of electric action at the speed of light. In the electrodynamics of Weber and Clausius, two electric particles act on each other with a force that depends on their separation and their motion at the instant of the action. In Lorentz' theory the force on an electron also depends on the position and motion of other electrons, but at earlier instants, owing to the finite propagation of electric disturbances through the mediating ether.

From his understanding of ether and electricity in 1892, Lorentz explained the interaction of light and matter in a way close to that of his optical theory of the 1870's. Light is turned and retarded in its passage through a body owing to the electrons in the molecules of the body; the incident light sets up vibrations in the electrons, which in turn produce light waves that interfere with the original ones and with one another. With this conception Lorentz in 1892 derived the Fresnel drag coefficient, a measure of the motion that a moving transparent body communicates to light passing through it. The coefficient had been confirmed by Fizeau's 1851 experiment on the motion of light in a moving column of liquid and Michelson and Morley's repetition of it in 1886. Among the physical interpretations that had been given to the coefficient, one was that the moving body partially drags the ether with it. Lorentz demonstrated that the drag coefficient resulted from the interference of light and thus did not imply a true, partial dragging of the ether. This demonstration was the single most impressive achievement of his first memoir on the electron theory, inspiring Max Born to refer to it, rightly, as one of the "most beautiful examples of the might of mathematical analysis in the physical world."

Although in 1892 Lorentz believed that it was important to relate electromagnetic processes to mechanical laws, he had not constructed a wholly mechanistic electrodynamics. In certain respects his ether was inherently a nonmechanical substance. Since his ether occupies the same space as electrons and material molecules, and its properties are unaffected by their coextension, it has no mechanical connection with ordinary matter.

Lorentz' next major exposition of his electron theory was *Versuch einer Theorie der electrischen und optischen Erscheinungen in bewegten Körpern* (1895). He no longer derived the basic equations of his theory from mechanical principles, but simply postulated them. He wrote the equations for the first time in compact vector notation; in electromagnetic units the four equations that describe the electromagnetic field in a vacuum are

$$\operatorname{div} \mathbf{d} = \rho,$$
$$\operatorname{div} \mathbf{H} = 0,$$
$$\operatorname{rot} \mathbf{H} = 4\pi(\rho\mathbf{v} + \dot{\mathbf{d}}),$$
$$-4\pi c^2 \operatorname{rot} \mathbf{d} = \dot{\mathbf{H}},$$

where **d** is the dielectric displacement, **H** the magnetic force, **v** the velocity of the electric charge, ρ the electric charge density, and c the velocity of light. A fifth and final equation describes the electric force of the ether on ponderable matter containing electrons bearing unit charge:

$$\mathbf{E} = 4\pi c^2 \mathbf{d} + \mathbf{v} \times \mathbf{H}.$$

The first four equations embody the content of Maxwell's theory; the fifth equation is Lorentz' own contribution to electrodynamics—known today as the Lorentz force—connecting the continuous field with discrete electricity.

In 1892 Lorentz had briefly discussed the problem of the effects of the earth's motion through the stationary ether; in the *Versuch* he systematically went over the whole problem. Since the ether is not dragged, a moving body such as the earth has an absolute velocity relative to it. The question arises whether or not the earth's absolute velocity is detectable through optical or electromagnetic effects of the accompanying ether "wind." The magnitude of the effects of the wind is measured theoretically by the ratio of the speed of the earth's motion v to the speed of light c. The ratio is small for the earth, but not so small as to be beyond the reach of observation.

The effects of the wind, however, were not observed; and for his theory to be credible Lorentz had to explain why. He showed that, according to the theory, an unexpected compensation of actions eliminates all effects of the ether wind to first-order approximation (neglecting terms involving the very much smaller second and higher powers of v/c). He analyzed the absence of first-order effects of the ether wind in phenomena such as reflection, refraction, and interference with the aid of a formal "theorem of corresponding states." The theorem asserted that to first-order accuracy no experiments using terrestrial light sources could reveal the earth's motion through the ether. By introducing transformations for the field magnitudes, spatial coordinates, and a "local time," Lorentz showed that in first-order approximation the equations describing an electric system in a moving frame were identical with those describing the corresponding electric system in a frame at rest in the ether (for which Lorentz assumed Maxwell's equations to hold exactly).

Lorentz' first-order approximation accounted for nearly all experience with the optics and electrodynamics of moving bodies. Second-order experiments had been performed, however, for which theoretically no compensating actions should occur. The most important second-order experiments were Michelson's interferometer experiment in 1881 and his and Morley's more accurate repetition of it in 1887. Their experiments failed to produce evidence of the second-order ether wind effects expected from Lorentz' theory. The only solution Lorentz could think of was the famous contraction hypothesis that he and Fitzgerald proposed independently at about the same time. Lorentz published an approximate form of his hypothesis in 1892. In 1895 he published an exact form, which stated that the arms of the interferometer contract by a factor of $\sqrt{1 - v^2/c^2}$ in the direction of the earth's motion through the ether. Lorentz regarded the hypothesis as dynamic rather than kinematic, requiring that the molecular forces determining the shape of the interferometer arms are propagated through the ether analogously to electric forces.

In 1899 Lorentz published another important statement of his theory, "Théorie simplifiée des phénomènes électriques et optiques dans des corps en mouvement." It was a response to Alfred Liénard's contention that according to Lorentz' theory, Michelson's experiment should yield a positive effect if the light passes through a liquid or solid instead of air. Lorentz believed that the positive effect was improbable, and he simplified and deepened his theory to support his belief. He now treated his dynamical contraction hypothesis mathematically, as though it were a general coordinate transformation on a par with the local time transformation. Except for an undetermined coefficient, the resulting transformations for the space and time coordinates were equivalent to those he published in his better-known 1904 article: the "Lorentz transformations." In 1899 Lorentz discussed for the first time the extension of his corresponding-states theorem to second-order effects. In connection with this extension he introduced, without thoroughly exploring it, an idea that would soon move to the center of electron theory concerns: the second-order transformations imply that the mass of an electron varies with velocity, and that the mass is different for motions parallel and perpendicular to the direction of translation through the ether. Although he discussed only electrons, his analysis implies that all mass, charged or otherwise, should vary with velocity, an implication that he made explicit in his more comprehensive 1904 paper.

Shortly before 1900 it was empirically established that cathode rays are negatively charged particles and that they are the same regardless of how and from what source they are produced. Since the particulate properties of cathode rays agreed with Lorentz' hypothesis about the nature of electricity, he confidently identified the cathode ray particles with the electrons of his theory. The empirical confirmation of the discrete unit of electricity lent great authority to Lorentz' and others' electron theories. In 1896 Zeeman observed a broadening of the spectral lines when a sodium flame is placed between the poles of a magnet. Lorentz immediately explained the effect on the basis of his electron theory, a result which pointed to his theory as a promising tool for unraveling the complexities of atomic structure.

Lorentz' application of the theory to the Zeeman effect showed that the vibrating electrons in sodium atoms are negative. Moreover, it yielded a value for the ratio of charge to mass of negative electrons which agreed with subsequent estimates by J. J. Thomson, Walther Kaufmann, and others, found by deflecting cathode rays in electric and magnetic fields. The success of Lorentz' analysis of the Zeeman effect further enhanced the standing of his theory. Indeed, at the turn of the century Lorentz' theory could count many solid accomplishments, such as explanations of Fizeau's experiment, of normal and anomalous dispersion, and of Faraday's rotation of light. For both its accomplishments and its promise, Lorentz' electron theory became widely adopted, especially on the Continent around 1900.

In 1904 Lorentz published "Electromagnetic Phenomena in a System Moving With Any Velocity Smaller Than That of Light." He was motivated to make another, nearly final, reformulation of his electron theory by several theoretical and experimental developments. First, Poincaré in 1900 had urged Lorentz not to make ad hoc explanations for each order of null effects, but to adopt instead a single explanation that excluded effects of the earth's motion of all orders. Second, in 1902 Max Abraham had published a rival electron theory based on the hypothesis of a rigid electron. Third, Kaufmann had begun publishing experimental data on the variable mass of moving electrons that seemed to favor Abraham's theory. Finally, new second-order experiments had been performed in 1902–1904 by Lord Rayleigh, D. B. Brace, Frederick Trouton, and H. R. Noble; and Lorentz wanted to discuss their null results in light of his theory. In his 1904 paper Lorentz refined his corresponding-states theorem to hold for all orders of smallness for the case of electromagnetic systems without charges, which meant that no experiment, however accurate, on such systems could reveal the translation of the apparatus through the ether. He also showed that his theory agreed with Kaufmann's data as well as Abraham's theory did. With this paper Lorentz all but solved the problem of the earth's motion through the stationary ether as it was formulated at the time. Poincaré in 1905 showed how to extend Lorentz' corresponding-states theorem to systems that included charges and to make the principle of relativity, as Poincaré understood it, more than approximation within the context of Lorentz' theory.

Lorentz' solution—developed over the years since 1892—entailed a number of radical departures from traditional dynamics; these he spelled out explicitly in 1904. First, the masses of all particles, charged or not, vary with their motion through the ether according to a single law. Second, the mass of an electron is due solely to its self-induction and has no invariant mechanical mass. Third, the dimensions of the electron itself, as well as those of macroscopic bodies, contract in the direction of motion, the physical deformation arising from the motion itself. Fourth, the molecular forces binding an electron and a ponderable particle or binding two ponderable particles are affected by motion in the same way as the electric force. Finally, the speed of light is the theoretical upper limit of the speed of any body relative to the ether; the formulas for the energy and inertia of bodies become infinite at that speed. Thus, to attain a fully satisfactory corresponding-states theorem, Lorentz had to go far beyond the domain of his original electron theory and make assertions about all bodies and all forces, whether electric or not.

The new dynamics of Lorentz' 1904 electron theory was compatible with the leading physical thought of the time. That it was shows how deeply the electron theory—Lorentz' form of it and others'—had changed the foundations of prerelativistic classical physics. To understand the change, we need to look more closely at the place of the electron theory in physics in the years just prior to 1904. In part because of the large and growing number of phenomena encompassed by the electron theory, physicists around the turn of the country extrapolated from it a new physical world view.

Lorentz, Larmor, Wien, Abraham, and others anticipated that mechanics would be replaced by electrodynamics as the fundamental, unifying branch of physics. They believed that mechanical concepts and laws were probably special cases of those of the electron theory. They foresaw a physical universe consisting solely of ether and charged particles, or possibly of ether alone. They were encouraged in their world view anticipations by the mounting experimental evidence for the electromagnetic nature of the electron mass. Lorentz wrote on electromagnetic mass in 1900, urging that experiments be made to determine the exact dependency of the electron mass on velocity. The problem of mass was central not only for its bearing on electron dynamics, but also for its bearing on the question of the electromagnetic foundation of physics and the related question of the connection of the ether and electricity with ordinary matter. Although Lorentz spoke more cautiously than other advocates of the electromagnetic program for physics, he gave it powerful impetus through his own applications of the electron theory. He showed in 1900 that if matter were constituted solely of charged particles, it was possible to give an electron-theoretical interpretation of gravitation as a finitely propagated, etherborne force. In that same year, 1900, he spoke of his belief that the electron theory could be extended to spectroscopy, atomic structure, and chemical forces.

Those physicists seeking an electromagnetic foundation for all of physics recognized the immensity of the reductionist tasks awaiting them. The tasks included the demonstration that all matter is electrical and the further demonstration that molecular and gravitational forces are explicable on wholly electromagnetic grounds. Even within electrodynamic theory itself, however, there were elements of incompleteness, which undermined the classical electromagnetic program for physics. The problem of securing a purely electromagnetic foundation for electrodynamics seemed increasingly unrealizable. The contractile electron at the core of Lorentz' theory presented a major difficulty in this regard.

Following Abraham, Lorentz by 1904 recognized that such an electron contains an energy of deformation that is necessarily nonelectromagnetic. Abraham's theory avoided this nonelectromagnetic dependence, but at the price of postulating a rigid scaffolding for the electron; other electron theorists posed alternative conceptions of the electron's shape, structure, and charge distribution. Another closely related difficulty for the electromagnetic program arose from the need for the electron to be finitely extended in order to avoid infinite self-energy, which in turn required nonelectromagnetic forces or constraints to prevent the finite electron from disintegrating through the electric repulsion of its parts. Yet another formidable difficulty emerged as a result of one of Lorentz' applications of the electron theory. In connection with his electron theory of metals, Lorentz in 1903 derived a formula for the energy distribution in blackbody radiation. He was able to calculate from his theory only the long wavelength limit of the energy spectrum. He recognized that Planck's 1900 quantum theory of blackbody radiation comprehended the entire spectrum; he also recognized that Planck's energy quanta were foreign to the foundations of the electron theory.

In 1908 Lorentz spoke out in favor of Planck's quantum theory as the only theory capable of explaining the complete spectrum of blackbody radiation. He was one of the first to do so and to emphasize the deep antithesis between the quantum hypotheses and those of the electron theory. The discussions of the first Solvay Congress in 1911—which Lorentz chaired—pointed to the conclusion that only through radical reform could the electron theory and the molecular-kinetic theory be made compatible with Planck's theory. Einstein had already long sought a revised electron theory to incorporate light quanta. Bohr's 1913 quantum theory of atoms and molecules was based on an explicit limitation of the validity of the classical electron and mechanical theories in the domain of atomic processes. Lorentz' career was divided roughly in half by the transition from classical to quantum physics. Although he was intensely interested in the new physics, and although he worked with the new quantum axioms and developed their consequences, his heart was never fully in it. He deeply regretted the passing of classical physics.

Einstein's 1905 special relativity paper provided Lorentz' theory with a physical reinterpretation. Reversing Lorentz' logic, Einstein made relativity a principle rather than a problem (Lorentz did not speak of a "principle of relativity" in connection with his own theory until after Einstein's 1905 paper). Likewise, for Einstein the constancy of the velocity of light for all observers was a principle, whereas for Lorentz the constancy was only apparent, a consequence of his theory. From the principles of relativity and the constancy of the velocity of light, Einstein deduced the Lorentz transformations and other results that had first been made known through Lorentz' and others' electron theories. Einstein's and Lorentz' interpretations of the formalisms were, however, very different. For Lorentz, time dilation in moving frames was a mathematical artifice; for Einstein, measures of time intervals were equally legitimate in all uniformly moving frames. For Lorentz the contraction of length was a real effect explicable by molecular forces; for Einstein it was a phenomenon of measurement only.

Einstein argued in 1905 that the ether of the electron theory and the related notions of absolute space and time were superfluous or unsuited for the development of a consistent electrodynamics. Lorentz admired, but never embraced, Einstein's 1905 reinterpretation of the equations of his electron theory. The observable consequences of his and Einstein's interpretations were the same, and he regarded the choice between them as a matter of taste. To the end of his life he believed that the ether was a reality and that absolute space and time were meaningful concepts.

Einstein's special relativity principle began to be widely accepted around 1910. It weakened the goal of a completely electromagnetic physics by questioning the need for an ether. It weakened it even more by questioning inferences from the variation of mass with velocity to the electromagnetic nature of mass. The relativity principle led to the same testable dynamical conclusions as Lorentz' theory, but without relying on the assumptions about electron structure that had been central to electron physics.

The origins of another leading twentieth-century theoretical development, the theory of general relativity, were closely tied to the classical electron theory. Beginning in 1907 and especially from 1911 on,

Einstein sought a gravitational and, subsequently, a unified gravitational and electromagnetic field theory in the context of his general relativity theory. Lorentz was strongly sympathetic to the general relativity theory, making fundamental contributions to it in 1914–1917. Lorentz, and Einstein too, regarded the physical space of general relativity as essentially fulfilling the role of the ether of the older electron theory. A principal objective of Einstein's field theoretical proposals was to relate electrons and material particles to the total field in a more satisfactory way than the earlier electron theories had. Einstein wanted above all to remove the radical dualism of continuous field and discrete particle that had characterized Lorentz' electron theory.

The classical electron theory was related through highly complex conceptual developments to later fundamental theories in physics. The Schrödinger and Dirac equations of the 1920's formed the mathematical bases of electron physics refashioned on nonclassical suppositions. These equations, together with the tradition of earlier electron theory investigations of the self-induction and electromagnetic mass of the electron, formed part of the basis for the development of modern elementary particle theory. Further, problems explored in the context of the electron theory have had a continuous history into the nonclassical period; for instance, the problem of the electron structure of atoms and the electron properties of metals.

Although the classical electron theory did not fulfill the anticipations it stirred at the turn of the century of an electromagnetic world view, it worked a profound change in the thinking of physicists and contributed to new world view perspectives. For Lorentz' immediate followers—those who had struggled to comprehend the obscurities of Maxwell's theory in the aftermath of Hertz's confirmation of electric waves—his electron theory was immensely clarifying. The younger generation of European theoretical physicists who learned much of their electrodynamics from Lorentz—Einstein, Ehrenfest, A. D. Fokker—agreed that Lorentz' great idea was the complete separation of field and matter. Einstein called Lorentz' establishment of the electromagnetic field as an independent reality distinct from ponderable matter an "act of intellectual liberation." The act at the same time determined the outstanding problem for future research, one that is still at the heart of theoretical physics. It is the problem of reestablishing the connection of field and particle in a way that does not contradict experience.

Einstein grasped the need to reject the wave theory of light and to modify the concepts of space and time in part from his analysis of the essential duality of Lorentz' theory: its joint foundation in the continuous electromagnetic field and molecular dynamics. Lorentz and his co-workers in electron theory carried classical physics to its furthest stage of clarity, precision, and unity. In doing so, Lorentz identified the strong limitations of the electron theory, defining the problem areas from which ongoing transformations of the foundations of physics arose. He brought classical physics to a state of development that made the need for reform in its fundamental principles evident and urgent to Einstein and other followers; this is the essential historical significance of Lorentz' work.

BIBLIOGRAPHY

I. ORIGINAL WORKS. Lorentz' dissertation, both in Dutch and in French trans., his 1895 *Versuch*, and most of his important papers are conveniently repub. in *H. A. Lorentz, Collected Papers*, P. Zeeman and A. D. Fokker, eds., 9 vols. (The Hague, 1935–1939). Vols. I–VIII contain technical writings, all in English, French, or German. Vol. IX is a collection of Lorentz' nonmathematical writings, mostly in Dutch; his 1878 inaugural lecture is included in English trans. as well as in the original Dutch. There are both systematic and chronological bibliographies at the end of vol. IX. The bibliographies list all of the eds. and translations of Lorentz' textbooks, all the places of publication of each paper, and all the books, papers, and essays that are not repub. in the *Papers*.

Lorentz' two textbooks are *Leerboeck der differentiaal-en integraalrekening en van de eerste beginselen der analytische meetkunde* (Leiden, 1882) and *Beginselen der Natuurkunde* (Leiden, 1888); both are available in German trans. His lectures were published in Dutch in 1919–1925, in German in 1927–1931, and in English, as *Lectures on Theoretical Physics*, A. D. Fokker *et al.*, eds., 8 vols. (London, 1931). Separate vols. treat radiation, quanta, ether theories and models, thermodynamics, kinetic theory, special relativity, entropy and probability, and Maxwell's theory.

The best introduction to Lorentz' electron theory in English is *Theory of Electrons* (Leipzig, 1909), an expanded version of his 1906 Columbia University lectures. A more mathematical treatment of the electron theory in German is his 1903 encyclopedia article, "Weiterbildung der Maxwellschen Theorie. Elektronentheorie," in *Encyklopädie der mathematischen Wissenschaften*, V, pt. 2 (Leipzig, 1904), 145–280, one of several articles he wrote for the encyclopedia on the electromagnetic theory of light.

Lorentz began an early ed. of his writings but finished only the first vol., *Abhandlungen über theoretische Physik* (Leipzig, 1907). This vol. contains material Zeeman and Fokker did not republish. Other books by Lorentz are *Sichtbare und unsichtbare Bewegungen* (Brunswick, 1902); *Les théories statistiques en thermodynamique* (Leipzig, 1912); *The Einstein Theory of Relativity: A Concise Statement* (New York, 1920); and *Problems of Modern Physics*.

Lectures at the Institute of Technology at Pasadena (Boston, 1927).

Writings on the electron theory by Lorentz in separate English trans. include the discussion of Michelson's interference experiment in his 1895 *Versuch*, in the Dover ed. of *The Principle of Relativity*, edited and translated by W. Perrett and G. B. Jeffery (New York, n.d.), pp. 3–7; and the intro. to his 1895 *Versuch* and his entire 1899 paper, "Simplified Theory of Electrical and Optical Phenomena in Moving Systems," in Kenneth F. Schaffner, *Nineteenth-Century Aether Theories* (Oxford, 1972), pp. 247–254 and 255–273, respectively.

Some Lorentz correspondence has been pub. in *Einstein on Peace*, O. Nathan and H. Norden, eds. (New York, 1960); A. Hermann, "H. A. Lorentz—Praeceptor physicae, sein Briefwechsel mit dem deutschen Nobelpreisträger Johannes Stark," in *Janus*, **53** (1966), 99–114; and *Letters on Wave Mechanics: Schrödinger, Planck, Einstein, Lorentz*, K. Prizbram, ed., translated by M. J. Klein (New York, 1967).

There is a vast amount of unpublished Lorentz material, chiefly letters. The catalog of the Archive for History of Quantum Physics, T. S. Kuhn, *et al.*, *Sources for History of Quantum Physics* (Philadelphia, 1967), lists correspondence between Lorentz and Bohr, Kramers, Schrödinger, and Sommerfeld. Copies of the documents cataloged in *Sources* are deposited in the Niels Bohr Institute, Copenhagen; the library of the University of California, Berkeley; and the American Philosophical Society library, Philadelphia. Subsequent to the publication of *Sources*, the Archive acquired twenty microfilm reels of Lorentz correspondence covering the period 1888–1928. The originals of this correspondence are in the Rijksarchief, The Hague. Other locations of Lorentz papers not included in the Archive are listed in *Sources*.

II. SECONDARY LITERATURE. There is no large-scale study of Lorentz' life and work. His private life is most fully detailed in the memoir by his daughter, G. L. de Haas-Lorentz, in the vol. she edited, *H. A. Lorentz. Impressions of His Life and Work* (Amsterdam, 1957). Other contributors to this volume are Einstein, W. J. de Haas, A. D. Fokker, B. van der Pol, J. T. Thijsse, P. Ehrenfest, and H. B. G. Casimir. Especially valuable are Fokker's essay on Lorentz' scientific work, and Einstein's tribute, "H. A. Lorentz, His Creative Genius and His Personality." Other useful accounts by Lorentz' contemporaries are P. Ehrenfest, "Professor H. A. Lorentz as Researcher 1853–July 18, 1923," in *Paul Ehrenfest: Collected Scientific Papers*, M. J. Klein, ed. (Amsterdam, 1959), pp. 471–477; J. Larmor, "Hendrik Antoon Lorentz," in *Nature*, **111** (1923), 1–6; W. H. Bragg, *et al.*, "Prof. H. A. Lorentz, For. Mem. R. S.," *ibid.*, **121** (1928), 287–291; O. W. Richardson, "Hendrik Antoon Lorentz—1853–1928," in *Proceedings of the Royal Society*, **121A** (1928), xx–xxviii; M. Born, "Antoon Lorentz," in *Nachrichten von der Königlichen Gesellschaft der Wissenschaften zu Göttingen. Geschäftliche Mitteilungen* (1927–1928), 69–73; and M. Planck, "Hendrik Antoon Lorentz," in *Naturwissenschaften*, **16** (1928), 549–555.

The outstanding historical study of Lorentz is T. Hirosige, "Origins of Lorentz' Theory of Electrons and the Concept of the Electromagnetic Field," in *Historical Studies in the Physical Sciences*, **1** (1969), 151–209. Other pertinent writings by Hirosige are "A Consideration Concerning the Origins of the Theory of Relativity," in *Japanese Studies in the History of Science*, no. 4 (1965), 117–123; "Electrodynamics Before the Theory of Relativity, 1890–1905," *ibid.*, no. 5 (1966), 1–49; and "Theory of Relativity and the Ether," *ibid.*, no. 7 (1968), 37–53.

For other useful historical discussions, see Stanley Goldberg, "The Lorentz Theory of Electrons and Einstein's Theory of Relativity," in *American Journal of Physics*, **37** (1969), 982–994; G. Holton, "On the Origins of the Special Theory of Relativity," *ibid.*, **28** (1960), 627–636; R. McCormmach, "H. A. Lorentz and the Electromagnetic View of Nature," in *Isis*, **61** (1970), 459–497; and "Einstein, Lorentz, and the Electron Theory," in *Historical Studies in the Physical Sciences*, **2** (1970), 41–87; and K. F. Schaffner, "The Lorentz Electron Theory and Relativity," in *American Journal of Physics*, **37** (1969), 498–513; and "Interaction of Theory and Experiment in the Development of Lorentz' Contraction Hypothesis," in *Actes du XIIe Congrès internationale de l'histoire des sciences, 1968*, V, 87–90. The standard older discussion is the closing chapter, "Classical Theory in the Age of Lorentz," in E. Whittaker, *History of the Theories of Aether and Electricity. 1: The Classical Theories* (London, 1910).

RUSSELL MCCORMMACH

LORENZ, HANS (*b.* Wilsdruff, Germany, 24 March 1865; *d.* Sistrans, near Innsbruck, Austria, 4 July 1940), *mechanics, mechanical engineering*.

The son of a teacher, Lorenz grew up in Leipzig, then studied (1885–1889) mechanical engineering at the Dresden Polytechnic Institute, where Gustav Zeuner was his principal teacher. His first professional experience (1890–1893) was with the Augsburg firm of L. A. Riedinger, developing a pneumatic power distribution system, and with the Escher-Wyss Company of Zurich, improving refrigeration compressors (1893–1894).

In 1894 Lorenz established himself in Munich as an independent consulting engineer. He founded, and for the first five years edited, the *Zeitschrift für die gesamte Kälteindustrie*, which quickly became the leading international journal of refrigeration technology. In 1894 he received a Ph.D. from the University of Munich—a rare feat then for an engineer—with a dissertation on the thermodynamic limits of energy conversion.

Lorenz' academic career began with brief appointments as extraordinary professor of applied science at Halle (1896) and Göttingen (1900). In Göttingen he was also director of the Institute for Technical Physics, which had recently been established upon recommendation of the mathematician Felix Klein, and which was to become world famous under Lorenz' successor, Ludwig Prandtl. In 1904 Lorenz was appointed to the chair of mechanics at the newly founded Technische Hochschule of Danzig, a position that he held for the rest of his active career. He also served as director of its materials testing laboratory (from 1909) and as rector (1915–1917). After his retirement in 1934, Lorenz lived in Munich and Sistrans.

Whether any of Lorenz' research efforts will be remembered in history is difficult to judge. Without doubt, however, he was an important figure in his own time. He was active in three areas of engineering: practice, teaching, and research. He was sought as a consultant in the burgeoning refrigeration industry, and his professional leadership was recognized in his election to presidencies and honorary memberships of several scientific societies. As an engineering teacher he was a leading proponent of a distinctive style of scientific engineering that flourished in early twentieth-century Germany. It was his belief that a creative engineer combined mathematical and scientific competence of a high order with the ability to translate actual problems into simple, tangible models (and was occasionally willing to sacrifice mathematical rigor for the sake of practical results). For undergraduates, Lorenz was a difficult teacher, but his advanced courses, as many of his former graduate students (prominent among whom are W. Hort, R. Plank, and A. Pröll) have testified, were unforgettable.

Lorenz' original research is characterized by unbounded versatility. His topics derived from his own engineering practice (pneumatic transmission lines, refrigeration), from his work as head of the materials testing laboratory (buckling, plastic deformation), and from ongoing scientific debates (vibrations, gyroscopes, turbomachinery, turbulent flow), to the war effort (ballistics). In his later years he published a considerable amount of work on astrophysics and astronomy.

BIBLIOGRAPHY

I. ORIGINAL WORKS. An almost complete list of Lorenz' scientific papers (approximately 130 items) is given in Poggendorff. His books are *Neuere Kühlmaschinen* (Munich, 1896); *Dynamik der Kurbelgetriebe* (Leipzig, 1901), with O. Schlick; *Lehrbuch der technischen Physik*, 4 vols. (Munich, 1902–1913); *Neue Theorie und Berechnung der Kreiselräder* (Munich, 1906); *Einführung in die Elemente der höheren Mathematik und Mechanik* (Berlin, 1910); *Ballistik* (Munich, 1917); *Technische Anwendungen der Kreiselbewegungen* (Berlin, 1919); *Einführung in die Technik* (Leipzig, 1919); and *Das Verhalten fester Körper im Fliessbereich* (Leipzig, 1922). Lorenz left unpublished MSS of an autobiography, "Praxis, Lehre, und Forschung: Akademische Erinnerungen und Erfahrungen" (*ca.* 1935) and of a book on astronomy (*ca.* 1938).

II. SECONDARY LITERATURE. Biographical writings on Lorenz consist of birthday tributes and obituaries, the most extensive being by Rudolf Plank, "Hans Lorenz zum 70. Geburtstag," in *Zeitschrift für die gesamte Kälteindustrie*, **42** (1935), 42–46. See also G. Cattanco, "Was ich Hans Lorenz verdanke," *ibid.*, **47** (1940), 114; Wilhelm Hort, "Hans Lorenz zum 70. Geburtstag," in *Zeitschrift für technische Physik*, **16** (1935), 93–95; R. Plank, "Hans Lorenz zum 75. Geburtstag," *ibid.*, **47** (1940), 33; and "Hans Lorenz," in *Zeitschrift des Vereins deutscher Ingenieure*, **84** (1940), 638; and A. Pröll, "Zu Geheimrat Lorenz' 70. Geburtstag," in *Zeitschrift für angewandte Mathematik und Mechanik*, **15** (1935), 183–184.

OTTO MAYR

LORENZ, LUDWIG VALENTIN (*b.* Elsinore, Denmark, 18 January 1829; *d.* Copenhagen, Denmark, 9 June 1891), *physics.*

Lorenz, a civil engineer by training, graduated from the Technical University of Denmark in Copenhagen; he taught at the Danish Military Academy and at a teacher's training college in Copenhagen. During the last years of his life he was financially supported by the Carlsberg Foundation to such an extent that he could devote all his time to research.

Lorenz was an eminent physicist, although the content and range of his achievements were not fully recognized by his contemporaries. This lack of recognition was due mainly to his great difficulties in presenting his ideas and mathematical calculations in intelligible form, but it was also due to his publishing some of his important papers only in Danish.

Lorenz' researches in physics, mainly optics and heat and electricity conductivities of metals, were carried out with equal emphasis on theoretical and experimental methods. The basis of his research in optics was the propagation of light waves conceptualized in terms of the theory of elasticity. Finally, however, he was convinced of the incompatibility of the boundary conditions of the theory of elasticity with Fresnel's formulas for reflection and refraction; he then concentrated his efforts on finding a phenomenological description of the propagation of light waves instead of speculating on the nature of light. Independently of the Irish physicist MacCullagh, he

showed in 1863 that the partial differential equation for the light vector $\vec{u}$ should be (in modern notation)

$$- \operatorname{curlcurl} \vec{u} = \frac{1}{a^2} \frac{\partial^2 \vec{u}}{\partial t^2},$$

where the phase velocity a is a constant that is characteristic for the homogeneous optical medium under consideration. He also gave the correct boundary conditions for the light vector when it is passing from one medium to another.

Lorenz then showed that if a is not considered as a constant but as a periodic function of space, his wave equation led to the theory of double refraction; where periods of a are small in comparison with the wavelength. This theory, by use of the same mathematical technique, has again been used recently.

A further remarkable result of Lorenz' optical researches on the basis of his fundamental wave equation was the well-known formula (Lorentz-Lorenz formula) for the refraction constant R, according to which

$$R = \frac{n_\infty^2 - 1}{n_\infty^2 + 2} \, v = \text{constant},$$

where n_∞ is the index of refraction for an infinite wavelength and v is the specific volume. He also showed that for a mixture

$$R = \sum_i \frac{n_i^2 - 1}{n_i^2 + 2} \, v_i,$$

where the index i refers to the components of the mixture. His first paper on the refraction constant, in which he also gave an experimental verification of his formula in the case of water, dates from 1869. In 1870 H. A. Lorentz arrived at the same result, independently of Lorenz.

In 1890, Lorenz published in *Det kongelige danske Videnskabernes Selskab Skrifter* a paper on the diffraction of plane waves by a transparent sphere, again using his fundamental wave equation with the relevant boundary conditions; he thereby anticipated later calculations by Mie and Debye. Unfortunately, this very important paper was published only in Danish, and thus it had no influence on later developments.

This paper contains the first determination of the number of molecules in a given volume of air, based upon the scattering of sunlight in the atmosphere. It is the first fairly accurate estimation of the order of magnitude of Avogadro's number, usually ascribed to Lord Rayleigh, who published it in 1899, nine years after the publication of Lorenz' paper and independently of Lorenz.

Most impressive of all Lorenz' achievements in optics is his electromagnetic theory of light, developed in a relatively unknown paper of 1867, two years after Maxwell's famous paper on the same subject. At that time Lorenz did not know Maxwell's theory, and his own approach was quite different. Lorenz' electromagnetic theory of light can be described briefly as an interpretation of the light vector as the current density vector in a medium obeying Ohm's law. This paper contains the fundamental equations for the vector potential and the scalar potential or —for the first time—the corresponding retarded potentials expressed in terms of the current density vector and the electrical charge density. The concept of retarded potentials had already been introduced in an earlier paper by Lorenz in connection with research on the theory of elasticity. He found that the differential equation for the current density vector was the same as his fundamental wave equation for the light vector, completed with a term which explains the absorption of light in conducting media, and that his theory led to the correct value for the velocity of light.

Lorenz' most important contribution in heat and electricity conductivities of metals was the Lorenz law, according to which the ratio between the conductivities of heat and electricity is proportional to the absolute temperature, where the constant of proportionality is the same for all metals. It had already been shown by R. Franz, who worked with Wiedemann, that this ratio is the same for all metals at the same temperature; and Lorenz then proved, through very accurate measurements of the two conductivities at $0°$ C. and $100°$ C. that this ratio is proportional to the absolute temperature.

It is characteristic of Lorenz' mastery of both theoretical and experimental methods that when, in the determination of the conductivity of heat, he encountered the problem of the cooling of a body by the air through heat convection, he solved the problem by calculations based on Navier's and Stokes's equations of hydrodynamics. It is a very difficult problem in mathematical physics, but he succeeded in solving it by using quite modern methods of similarity. Having finished his calculations, he found them confirmed by experiments.

In the determination of the specific conductivities for electricity, Lorenz used an absolute method of his own invention, which later was applied by himself and others, such as Rayleigh, to fix the international unit of resistance, the ohm.

In an unpublished paper of great interest, Lorenz developed a complete theory of currents in telephone cables, showing that the attenuation of the current along the cable can be reduced by increasing the inductance per unit of length. He therefore proposed the use of cables wound with a covering of soft iron, an idea also proposed by Heaviside, independently of Lorenz, that later was taken up by the Danish electro-technician C. E. Krarup. This improvement is now known as continuous loading.

Lorenz was also deeply interested in problems of pure mathematics, such as the distribution of prime numbers; but here he encountered severe criticism from Danish mathematicians, who did not appreciate the undoubted lightness—if not recklessness—with which he applied the methods of mathematics. It is, however, probable that there also are problems of interest in some of his mathematical works.

Lorenz's contemporaries in the scientific circles of Copenhagen no doubt realized that he was an eminent scientist, and by the standard of his time his work was well supported. But although he was much respected, few understood what he actually did. This lack of deeper understanding, combined with his own tendency to isolation and his rather polemical attitude toward some of his colleagues, made him a somewhat lonely philosopher.

BIBLIOGRAPHY

Lorenz' writings were brought together in *Oeuvres scientifiques de L. Lorenz*, 2 vols., revised and annotated by H. Valentiner (Copenhagen, 1898–1904).

Secondary literature includes Kirstine Meyer, in *Dansk Biografisk Leksikon*, XIII (Copenhagen, 1937), 464–469; and Mogens Pihl, *Der Physiker L. V. Lorenz* (Copenhagen, 1939); and "The Scientific Achievements of L. V. Lorenz," in E. C. Jordan, ed., *Electromagnetic Theory and Antennas*, I (New York, 1963), xxi–xxx.

MOGENS PIHL

LORENZ, RICHARD (*b.* Vienna, Austria, 13 April 1863; *d.* Frankfurt am Main, Germany, 23 June 1929), *physical chemistry*.

Lorenz' father was the historian Ottokar Lorenz; his mother was the daughter of the philosopher and educational reformer Franz Lott. Lorenz studied medicine at the universities of Vienna and Jena, but his main interest was chemistry. He received his doctorate at Jena for work on the valence of boron. After completing his studies he was for a short time an assistant in the physiology institute at the University of Rostock; he left in order to work with Otto Wallach in the chemistry laboratory of the University of Göttingen. Despite this beginning he did not devote his career to organic chemistry, Wallach's principal field of interest. Instead, he took up the study of physical chemistry. Nernst had just been appointed professor at Göttingen, in the first chair ever dedicated to that subject, and in 1892 Lorenz became an assistant and *Privatdozent* under him.

Lorenz then began to explore the field in which he worked for the rest of his life—the electrochemistry of substances in the fused state. In 1896 he was invited to the Technische Hochschule in Zurich to join the newly founded electrochemical laboratory. In Zurich he married Lili Heusler, who bore him two children. Following the death of his wife, Lorenz accepted an offer in 1910 from the Frankfurt Academy to direct its physics and chemistry institute. The academy soon became a university, and Lorenz pursued his work there until his retirement, which occurred shortly before his death. For thirty years he was editor of the *Zeitschrift für anorganische und allgemeine Chemie*.

Lorenz' most important scientific achievement was his demonstration that Faraday's law is completely valid for fused salts. He discovered the cause of earlier results which contradicted it in the formation of the so-called metallic fog, which occurs in the reaction of the precipitated metals with the melt. He then found methods which inhibited this fog formation. With M. Katajama he developed the thermodynamic relations to calculate the electromotive force of galvanic cells consisting of fused salts alone or of the latter joined with metals. By determining the particle sizes in disperse systems, which had been suggested by Einstein, he was able to compute the ion sizes in the fused electrolytes from the mobility and the rate of diffusion.

Lorenz' work contributed to the clarification of many other properties of fused salts, for example internal friction, capillary electricity, and conductivity. In his last years he established that the law of mass action is not valid in highly concentrated fusions. He also developed van der Waals's equation of state taking this fact into account and, with the aid of the concept of thermodynamic potential, developed a law of mass action for condensed systems.

BIBLIOGRAPHY

I. ORIGINAL WORKS. Lorenz wrote about 250 articles; a fairly extensive listing may be found in Poggendorff VI and in the obituary in the *Zeitschrift für Elektrochemie* but there is no complete list. His most important books are *Die Elektrolyse geschmolzener Salze*, 3 vols. (Halle, 1905); *Elektrochemie geschmolzener Salze* (Leipzig, 1909), written with F. Kaufler; *Raumerfüllung und Ionenbeweglichkeit* (Leipzig, 1922); and *Das Gesetz der chemischen Massenwirkung, seine thermodynamische Begründung und Erweiterung* (Leipzig, 1927).

II. SECONDARY LITERATURE. See W. Fraenkel, "Richard Lorenz," in *Zeitschrift für angewandte Chemie und Zentralblatt für technische Chemie*, **42** (1929), 801–802; G. Hevesy, "Richard Lorenz. Erinnerungen aus den Zürcher Jahren," in *Helvetica chimica acta*, **13** (1930), 13–17; and A. Magnus, "Richard Lorenz," in *Berichte der Deutschen chemischen Gesellschaft*, Abt. A, **62** (1929), 88–90; and "Richard Lorenz," in *Zeitschrift für Elektrochemie und angewandte physikalische Chemie*, **35** (1929), 815–822.

F. SZABADVÁRY

LORENZONI, GIUSEPPE (*b*. Rolle di Cisón, Treviso, Italy, 10 July 1843; *d*. Padua, Italy, 7 July 1914), *astronomy, astrophysics, geodesy*.

The son of an elementary school teacher, Lorenzoni received his degree in engineering at the University of Padua in 1863. In the same year, he entered the Padua Observatory as assistant to the director, Giovanni Santini. In 1872 he was appointed professor of astronomy at the University of Padua, where he also held the professorship of geodesy from 1869 to 1885. In 1878 he became the director of the Padua Observatory.

Lorenzoni's first observations and research dealt with astrophysics. He began these studies with spectral analysis applied to the physical study of celestial bodies. As early as 1871, he collaborated with A. Secchi and P. Tacchini in establishing the Società degli Spettroscopisti Italiani and in the publication of its *Memorie*. During the total solar eclipse of 1870, which he observed in Terranova (now Gela), Sicily, he noted many brilliant lines of emission of the prominences, which led him to search for lines of emission besides those commonly visible in the chromosphere in full sunlight. Through this he discovered a new line that proved to be the 4471 A of the diffused series of the neutral helium of which he had measured the wavelength. Later he found that the same line had been independently observed by C. H. Young in the United States. He then published in the *Memorie della Società degli spettroscopisti italiani* important considerations on the spectroscopic visibility of monochromatic images. Among his writings on a variety of subjects published in the *Memorie* is an article dealing with theoretical optics, in which it is possible to foresee the invention of the spectroheliograph (1892) and the interferential filter (1929).

After abandoning spectroscopy, Lorenzoni turned to classical astronomy and the related science of geodesy, which occupied the greater part of his life. A keen observer who used instruments of very modest dimension, Lorenzoni observed several comets and small planets; and using Starke's meridian circle, he continued and completed the stellar catalogs of his predecessors.

His numerous publications on classical astronomy discuss the formulas of precession and of nutation, in which the Euler equations for the rotation of a body around a given point are given by trigonometric and geometric methods.

Lorenzoni also dealt with fundamental formulas of spherical trigonometry used for calculating the parallax in the coordinates of a planet and for determining the angular coordinates by means of astronomical instruments.

In 1878 Lorenzoni was appointed a member of the Commissione Italiana per la Misura del Grado, which was then carrying on intensive geodesic activity. He made important contributions to the commission's work on latitude and azimuth observations in various Italian localities. He also collaborated with Schiaparelli in Milan, with Oppolzer in Vienna, and with other foreign astronomers on telegraphic longitude determinations. His works on classical astronomy are found in the publications of the Commissione Geodetica Italiana.

Realizing the importance of measuring the force of gravity in Italy, especially in collaboration with scientific organizations established in other countries, the commission in 1880 aroused Lorenzoni's interest in this problem. He soon presented a concrete plan of studies and the history of research to determine the length of the simple seconds pendulum. After having participated in a conference at Munich, where the subject was discussed, Lorenzoni was able to begin work in Italy. He had at his disposal a Repsold pendulum that he placed at the base of the Padua Observatory. His patient and accurate measurements and discussions of the problem were presented in a scholarly memoir published by the Accademia dei Lincei in 1888. It is divided into three parts; the first is theoretical; the second deals with the place of observation, instruments, and errors; the third presents the results of observation and reduction.

The value that Lorenzoni computed at Padua (sixty feet above sea level) of the length of the seconds pendulum agreed completely with the value that he had obtained by reducing, for Padua, the values obtained at five other stations. From this he concluded that there were no great anomalies in the gravity at Padua. The site of these experiments was officially named the *Sala di gravità di Giuseppe Lorenzoni* and became the goal of geodetic scholars who use Padua

for gravimetric reference and as a meeting place.

Lorenzoni's fundamental research in gravity and the effect of support flection on the time of pendulum oscillation led to the design and construction of a bipendular support in a vacuum.

BIBLIOGRAPHY

A fairly complete listing of Lorenzoni's papers is in Royal Society *Catalogue of Scientific Papers*, VIII, 260; X, 632; and XVI, 870. The articles cited in the text are "Di un mezzo atto a rendere visibile tutta in una volta una immagine monocromatica completa della cromosfera e delle protuberanze solare al lembo con la costruzione di lenti ipercromatiche," in *Memorie della Società degli spettroscopisti italiani*, **3** (1874), 61–64, on theoretical optics; and "Relazione sulle esperienze istituite ... per determinare la lunghezza del pendolo semplice ...," in *Atti dell'Accademia nazionale dei Lincei. Memorie*, **5** (1888), 41–281.

Obituaries are by A. Abetti, in *Vierteljahrsschrift der Astronomischen Gesellschaft*, **49** (1914), 232–238; A. Antoniazzi, in *Astronomische Nachrichten*, **198** (1914), col. 486; and E. Millosevich, in *Atti dell'Accademia nazionale dei Lincei*, **23**, pt. 2 (1914), 442–446.

GIORGIO ABETTI

LORIA, GINO (*b*. Mantua, Italy, 19 May 1862; *d*. Genoa, Italy, 30 January 1954), *mathematics, history of mathematics.*

After graduating in 1883 from Turin University, where higher geometry was taught by Enrico D'Ovidio, Loria attended a postgraduate course at Pavia University taught by Beltrami, Bertini, and F. Casorati. Loria became D'Ovidio's assistant in November 1884; on 1 November 1886 he was appointed extraordinary professor of higher geometry at Genoa University, becoming full professor in 1891. He held the chair of higher geometry at Genoa for forty-nine years, until he retired in 1935; he also taught the history of mathematics, descriptive geometry, and mathematics education. He wrote a number of treatises on descriptive geometry that were appreciated for their simplicity, elegant constructions, and generality. In them he introduced elements of photogrammetry. He was a member of the Accademia Nazionale dei Lincei and of various other academies.

Loria's geometrical research, at first carried out in cooperation with Corrado Segre, was especially concerned with new applications of algebraic concepts to the geometry of straight lines and spheres, with hyperspatial projective geometry, with algebraic correspondence between fundamental forms, and with Cremona transformations in space. But the field in which Loria's scientific activity was most extensive was the history of mathematics from antiquity down to his own time.

Special mention should be made of *Le scienze esatte nell'antica Grecia* (1914), a reworking of the articles which appeared in the *Memorie della Regia Accademia di scienze, lettere e arti in Modena* in 1893–1902. It constitutes a rich source of information on Greek mathematics. *Storia della geometria descrittiva* (1921) shows Loria's liking for the subject. *Guida allo studio della storia delle matematiche* (last ed., 1946) is methodological in character and places at scholars' disposal the rich source materials and collections on the subject with which he had worked for years. Full bibliographical information is in *Il passato e il presente delle principali teorie geometriche*, updated in the editions of 1897, 1907, and 1931.

Loria devoted two works to special algebraic and transcendental curves which have attracted the attention of mathematicians. The first of these works was published in German in 1902, and only much later (1930–1931) in Italian, with the title *Curve piane speciali algebriche e trascendenti*; the other is *Le curve sghembe speciali algebriche e trascendenti* (1925). As F. Enriques has pointed out, the curves studied by Loria are of special interest because the study of particular cases often leads to general results.

Many of Loria's writings are biographical, notably those on Archimedes, Newton, Cremona, Beltrami, and Tannery. With G. Vassura he edited the largely unpublished writings of Torricelli (E. Torricelli, *Opere*, 4 vols. [Faenza, 1919–1944]). In 1897 Loria recognized, in one of Torricelli's manuscripts, the first known rectification of a curve: the logarithmic spiral.

Some of Loria's works have been collected in the volume *Scritti, conferenze e discorsi sulla storia delle matematiche* (1937); and an overall view of the evolution of mathematical thought, from ancient times to the end of the nineteenth century, is provided in his *Storia delle matematiche* (2nd ed., 1950).

Loria's library, containing many works on the history of mathematics, was left to the University of Genoa.

BIBLIOGRAPHY

I. ORIGINAL WORKS. A list of Loria's works is in the commemorative address delivered by A. Terracini at the Accademia dei Lincei (see below) and includes 386 writings. Some of his more important articles are: "Sur les différentes espèces de complexes du second degré des droites qui coupent harmoniquement deux surfaces du second

ordre," in *Mathematische Annalen*, **23** (1883), 213–235, written with C. Segre; "Sulle corrispondenze proiettive fra due piani e fra due spazi," in *Giornale di matematiche*, **22** (1883), 1–16; "Ricerche intorno alla geometria della sfera e loro applicazione allo studio ed alla classificazione delle superficie di quarto ordine aventi per linea doppia il cerchio immaginario all'infinito," in *Memorie della Reale Accademia delle scienze di Torino*, 2nd ser., **36** (1884), 199–297; "Sulla classificazione delle trasformazioni razionali dello spazio, in particolare sulle trasformazioni di genere uno," in *Rendiconti dell'Istituto lombardo di scienze e lettere*, 2nd ser., **23** (1890), 824–834; "Della varia fortuna d'Euclide in relazione con i problemi dell'insegnamento della geometria elementare," in *Periodico di matematica per l'insegnamento secondario*, **8** (1893), 81–113; "Evangelista Torricelli e la prima rettificazione di una curva," in *Atti dell'Accademia nazionale dei Lincei, Rendiconti*, 5th ser., **6**, no. 2 (1897), 318–323; "Eugenio Beltrami e le sue opere matematiche," in *Bibliotheca mathematica*, 3rd ser., **2** (1901), 392–440; "Commemorazione di L. Cremona," in *Atti della Società ligustica di scienze naturali e geografiche*, **15** (1904), 19; "Necrologio. Paolo Tannery," in *Bollettino di bibliografia e storia delle scienze matematiche pubblicato per cura di Gino Loria*, **8** (1905), 27–30; and "La storia della matematica vista da un veterano," in *Bollettino dell'Unione matematica italiana*, 3rd ser., **5** (1950), 165–170.

His books include *Spezielle algebraische und transscendente ebene Curven* (Leipzig, 1902), trans. by author as *Curve piane speciali algebriche e trascendenti*, 2 vols. (Milan, 1930–1931); *Le scienze esatte nell'antica Grecia* (Milan, 1914); *Newton* (Rome, 1920); *Storia della geometria descrittiva dalle origini sino ai nostri giorni* (Milan, 1921); *Le curve sghembe speciali algebriche e trascendenti*, 2 vols. (Bologna, 1925); *Archimede* (Milan, 1928); *Storia delle matematiche*, 2 vols. (Torino, 1929–1931; 2nd ed., Milan, 1950); *Il passato e il presente delle principali teorie geometriche* (Padua, 1931), an updating of arts. In *Memorie della Reale Accademia delle scienze di Torino*, sers. 2, **38** (1887); *Scritti, conferenze e discorsi sulla storia delle matematiche* (Padua, 1937); and *Guida allo studio della storia delle matematiche* (Milan, 1946).

II. SECONDARY LITERATURE. See A. Terracini, "Gino Loria. Cenni commemorativi," in *Atti dell'Accademia delle scienze di Torino*, **88** (1953–1954), 6–11; and "Commemorazione del socio Gino Loria," in *Atti della Accademia Nazionale dei Lincei, Rendiconti*, 8th ser., Classe di scienze fisiche, matematiche e naturali, **17** (1954), 402–421, with bibliography.

ETTORE CARRUCCIO

LORRY, ANNE CHARLES (*b.* Crosnes, France, 10 October 1726; *d.* Bourbonne-les-Bains, France, 18 September 1783), *medicine.*

The son of a well-known professor of law in Paris, Lorry received an excellent education supervised by

Charles Rollin. Soon after receiving his medical degree (1748), Lorry was presented by the chief royal physician L. G. Le Monnier, to Marshal Noailles. He was thus introduced to Paris high society and became the physician of the Richelieus, of the Fronsacs, of Mlle de Lespinasse, and of Voltaire, all of whom received him warmly but paid him less enthusiastically. He attended the autopsy of the young duke of Burgundy, the dauphin's son, in 1761, and was called in as a consultant on 29 April 1774, during Louis XV's last illness, at the request of the Duc d'Aiguillon, the friend of the Comtesse du Barry. The king (who died on 10 May) spoke to Lorry several times and his baptismal name was, one evening, the password given to the captain of the guards.

Lorry's worldly successes were numerous. He was consequently taken to task by La Mettrie in his *Politique du médecin de Machiavel* (1746) and was a character in a play by Poinsinet. Indeed, according to Paul Delaunay, the elegant Lorry was the darling of the salons and of the ladies. He was extravagant with money and unconcerned about his health; thus he became gouty. A serious stroke, around 1782, caused him to lose the use of his legs; and many of his patients turned to other physicians. He fell into financial difficulties, but obtained a royal pension that enabled him to go to Bourbonne-les-Bains, where he died.

Lorry's worldly concerns did not prevent him from studying with Astruc and Ferrein, nor from doing important scientific work. In 1760 he presented two memoirs to the Académie Royale des Sciences on the then fashionable subject of medullo-cerebral physiology. In the first he studied the normal movements of the encephalon, while in the second he established that compression of the cerebellum produces sleep and that a puncture in the upper part of the spinal cord between the second and third cervical vertebrae is immediately followed by death. It was thus that he placed in the spinal column the seat of the soul—the *sensorium commune*—the location of which had already been discussed by Vieussens, Boerhaave, Astruc, François de La Peyronie, Haller, and Antoine Louis, and later by Soemmerring. This "noeud vital" was later studied by Legallois (1808–1812) and by Flourens (1827); they showed that it was actually a regulatory center of the respiratory system.

In other publications Lorry discussed hygiene, anatomy, physiology, the history of medicine, medical pathology, epidemiology, clinical medicine, and smallpox inoculation, a method he defended in 1763 against Astruc. He is now primarily known, however, for his work in dermatology and mental disease.

Lorry's treatise on dermatology, which he dedicated to his friend E. L. Geoffroy, was the first French monograph devoted to diseases of the skin and, according to L. T. Morton, the first modern work that attempted to classify them according to their physiological, pathological, and etiological similarities. He divided skin diseases into two groups. The first consisted of those he considered to be the external expression of an internal disease; these were the general or *dépuratoires* diseases, which can either invade the entire cutaneous surface or be localized. The second group consists of diseases that originate in the skin itself and do not affect other parts of the body. They can—like those of the first group—cover either small areas or the general surface of the skin. Lorry's book is a source of precise observations, but it is spoiled by an obsolete Galeno-Arabic nomenclature and archaic medical conceptions.

English and French physicians in the eighteenth century were much concerned with depression; the word "suicide" was first used in France in 1737 by Y. Pelicier. In England one spoke of "melancholy" (R. Burton, 1621), of "spleen" (R. Blackmore, 1725), or "English malady" (G. Cheyne, 1733); and in France, of "nostalgie" (J. Hoffer, 1688; La Caze, 1763; Lecat, 1767), "affection vaporeuse" (J. Raulin, 1758; P. Pomme, 1763), or "mélancolie" (C. Andry, 1785). Lorry recognized two types of melancholy, one a consequence of an alteration of the solid parts ("mélancolie nerveuse"), the other originating in the humors ("mélancolie humorale"). The latter could result in hysteria in women and, in men, hypochondria. Lorry stressed spasmodic episodes: torticollis, pyloric spasm with vomiting, pharyngeal spasm with difficulties in swallowing. Although he assigned a physical etiology to melancholy, Lorry sometimes contradicted himself by citing the roles of fear and anguish.

Lorry left the Paris Faculty of Medicine, where he taught surgery (1753), and was one of the founders of the Société Royale de Médecine, of which he became the director and vice-president. It was for his efforts in this capacity that Vicq d'Azyr dedicated to him one of his best memorial addresses.

BIBLIOGRAPHY

I. Original Works. Lorry's writings include *An causa caloris in pulmone aeris actione temperetur?* (Paris, 1746); *Essai sur les aliments, pour servir de commentaire aux livres diététiques d'Hippocrate*, 2 vols. (Paris, 1754–1757), reiss. as *Essai sur l'usage des aliments*, 2 vols. (Paris, 1781), translated into Italian as *Saggio sopra gli alimenti per servire di commentario ai libri dietetici d'Ippocrate*, 2 vols. (Venice, 1787); *De melancholia et morbis melancholicis*, 2 vols. (Paris, 1765); *Tractatus de morbis cutaneis* (Paris, 1777), trans. into German by C. F. Held as *Abhandlung von den Krankheiten der Haut*, 2 vols. (Leipzig, 1779); and *De praecipuis morborum mutationibus et conversionibus tentamen medicum,* J. N. Hallé, ed. (Paris, 1784).

Editions and translations include *Hippocratis aphorismi graece et latine* (Paris, 1759); *Mémoires pour servir à l'histoire de la Faculté de médecine de Montpellier par feu M. Jean Astruc,* revised and published by Lorry (Paris, 1767); J. Barker's *Essai sur la conformité de la médecine ancienne et moderne dans le traitement des maladies aigües,* translated by Schomberg, new ed., revised by Lorry (Paris, 1768); *Sanctorius . . . de medicina statica aphorismi,* comments and notes added by Lorry (Paris, 1770); *Richardi Mead Opera,* translated by Lorry (Paris, 1751); and *Hippocratis aphorismi, Hippocratis et Celsi locis parallelis illustrati,* edited by Lorry (Paris, 1784).

Many writings by Lorry are in the *Mémoires de l'Académie royale des sciences* (1760) and the *Mémoires de la Société royale de médecine* (1776–1779).

II. SECONDARY LITERATURE. See A. Kissmeyer, "Autour d'Anne-Charles Lorry," in *Bulletin de la Société française de dermatologie et de syphiligraphie,* **38** (1931), 1524–1527; E. Bongrand, "Lorry," in *Dictionnaire encyclopédique des sciences médicales de Dechambre,* 2nd ser., III (Paris, 1870), 112–113; P. Delaunay, *Le monde médical parisien au XVIII° siècle* (Paris, 1906), *passim;* R. Desgenettes, "Lorry," in *Biographie médicale,* VI (Paris, 1824), 102–109; "Éloge de Lorry," in *Journal de médecine militaire,* **3** (1784), 379–387; Arne Kissmeyer, *Anne-Charles Lorry et son oeuvre dermatologique* (Paris, 1928); "Lorry," in A. L. J. Bayle and A. G. Thillaye, *Biographie médicale,* II (Paris, 1855), 503–504, with portrait; "Lorry," in *Biographisches Lexicon,* III (Berlin–Vienna, 1962), 843; "Lorry," in Dezeimeris, *Dictionnaire historique de la médecine ancienne et moderne,* III (Paris, 1836), 479–480; "Lorry," in N. F. J. Eloy, *Dictionnaire historique de la médecine* (Mons, 1778), pp. 101–102; Richter, "Geschichte der Dermatologie," in *Handbuch der Haut- und Geschlechtskrankheiten,* **14,** no. 2 (1928), 178a, 180; C. Saucerotte, "Lorry," in *Nouvelle biographie générale,* XXXI (Paris, 1852), 688–690; and F. Vicq d'Azyr, "Éloge de M. Lorry," in *Histoire de la Société royale de médecine années 1782–1783* (Paris, 1787), V, pt. 1, 25–59.

PIERRE HUARD
MARIE JOSÉ IMBAULT-HUART

LOSCHMIDT, JOHANN JOSEPH (*b.* Putschirn, near Carlsbad, Bohemia [now Karlovy Vary, Czechoslovakia], 15 March 1821; *d.* Vienna, Austria, 8 July 1895), *physics, chemistry.*

Loschmidt was the oldest of four children of a poor peasant family. The young Loschmidt showed more aptitude for schoolwork than work in the fields and was enrolled in the parochial school in Schlackenwerth (near Carlsbad) in 1833 with the help of the village priest; in 1837, again with the assistance of the Catholic clergy, he entered Humanistic Gymnasium in Prague. From 1839 he studied classical philology and philosophy at the German University in Prague.

Loschmidt became a lecturer under Franz Exner, who aided the impoverished young man and advised him to concentrate on mathematics. He commissioned Loschmidt to enlarge on Herbart's attempts at a mathematical treatment of psychology and to put it on a more solid basis. However, despite intense efforts, Loschmidt achieved only negative results, primarily because of difficulties encountered in the measurement of the intensities of psychological experiences.

In 1841 Loschmidt joined Exner in Vienna to study the natural sciences, though his favorite field remained the border area between physics and philosophy. Influences of Herbartian philosophy were evident in his thought throughout his life. Loschmidt was unsuccessful in obtaining a teaching post when he graduated in 1843 and he therefore turned to industry. He worked in Anton Schrötter's laboratory until the end of 1846. With his friend Benedikt Margulies, Loschmidt discovered a process for converting sodium nitrate into potassium nitrate, used for manufacturing gunpowder. They could not know, of course, that the same process had been discovered half a century earlier by Thaddäus Haenke, who had actually turned it to practical use in Peru.[1] From then until 1854 Loschmidt tried again and again to establish businesses but the drastic social, political, and financial upheavals of Europe in the mid-nineteenth century made it almost impossible for any businessman to succeed, and in 1854 he went into bankruptcy.

Discouraged by his many failures, Loschmidt decided to return to a career in science. Early in 1856 he passed, with excellent marks, his examinations to qualify as a teacher. In September of that year he obtained a post at a Vienna Realschule, where he taught chemistry, physics, and algebra and used his free time for scientific research. At that time Vienna had become the center of crystallography, and Loschmidt concentrated his studies on the chemistry of crystals.[2] During this period he met J. Stefan, the young director of the Institute of Physics of the University of Vienna, and they became close friends. Stefan soon recognized Loschmidt's talents and offered him the facilities of the institute's laboratory and library, and Loschmidt, who had had enough of practical work, turned to theoretical research.

Various attempts were being made in those days to represent symbolically and graphically molecular formulas in analogy to the efforts at a unified and internally consistent system of atomic weights for the chemical elements. In 1861, at the age of forty, Loschmidt published in Vienna, at his own expense, his first scientific work, *Chemische Studien,* I (there never was a part II). Loschmidt was the first to represent graphically the double and triple bonds of polyvalent atoms by means of connecting lines. He also was probably the first who viewed cane sugar as an "ether-like compound," and he expressed the opinion that ozone consisted of three oxygen atoms. Above all, Loschmidt was the first to envision a ring-shaped chain formula of carbon atoms for benzene, but he expressly rejected the assumption of double bonds, preferring to hold such a decision in abeyance.

In his representation of benzene derivatives, for which he gave 121 graphical formulas, Loschmidt represented the benzene as a hexavalent nucleus by means of a circle, erroneously assuming that the carbon atoms and their valences were unevenly distributed about the circle. This model of the benzene nucleus impeded his understanding of the isomeric relationships in polysubstitution derivatives, whereas the strength of Kekulé's benzene model, by contrast, showed up at just this point. Nevertheless, Loschmidt correctly recognized toluene as methyl benzene, and thus accurately explained the isomerism of cresol with benzyl alcohol. He was the first to state that in alcohols with several OH groups each C atom can bind no more than one OH group.

Loschmidt also assumed that an element could have multiple valences (he used the terms "pollency" and "capacity"). Sulfur, for example, could have a valence of 2, 4, or 6. Thus, Loschmidt arrived at the proper structural formula for sulfuric acid, giving sulfur a valence of 6. According to him, nitrogen had a valence of 3 or 5, carbon always had a valence of 4, oxygen always had a valence of 2, and hydrogen of 1. Exceptions were NO, NO_2, and CO.

Loschmidt's book apparently had little influence on other chemists, except perhaps on Kekulé, who published his textbook *Lehrbuch der organischen Chemie* (Stuttgart) in different volumes between 1859 and 1887, and Crum-Brown, also an organic chemist who was involved with the representation of chemical formulas. Priority disputes and mutual influences among the three men are still open to investigation, but resolving the problem would require the analysis and evaluation of much published and unpublished material. Loschmidt's book remained largely ignored for over fifty years until it was republished in Ostwald's *Klassiker* in 1913,[3] with the subtitle *Constitutions-Formeln der organischen Chemie in graphischer Darstellung*.

Herbart's metaphysical speculations on the antinomies of the real continuum had led him to construct reality out of simple entities, which he considered spherical, and which attract and repel each other by partial penetration. Loschmidt, in *Zur Constitution des Aethers* (Vienna, 1862), extended this Herbartian metaphysics of elementary quanta into the realm of physics in line with Lamé's elasticity and ether theory. He attempted to formulate a mathematical theory for luminiferous ether very similar to that of Lord Kelvin thirty years later. According to Loschmidt, every molecule is surrounded with an envelope of ether, the density of which falls off inversely with distance from the molecule's center. Matter and ether attract each other; the ether particles repel each other. Ether is the carrier of energy exchange in the universe; and the attracting and repelling forces of ether spheres summarized under the term "affinity" are, in a manner of speaking, the souls of the atoms. All natural phenomena were to be derived from the reciprocal action of the atoms by means of their energy spheres. He contrasted the prevalent atomic theory—which ascribed to each atom a sharply limited nucleus of impenetrable matter—with the concept of an energy sphere surrounding the atom, itself perhaps a conglomerate of the smallest ether particles.

Loschmidt's other scientific achievement was the first accurate estimations of the size of air molecules.[4] This linked directly with the speculations of Clausius and Maxwell. Clausius assumed at the outset that all molecules of a gas are at rest and that a mass point moves through them.[5] The probability that this mass point penetrates a layer of thickness x without colliding with the molecules $= a^x$, where a is the probability for thickness 1. Thereby a is a function of the radius ρ of the molecular energy spheres and of the mean distance λ of nearby molecules. With $a = e^{-\alpha}$ (e being the base of the natural logarithms), α has to be determined. For small layer thicknesses δ there results $W_\delta = e^{-\alpha\delta} = 1 - \alpha\delta$. Furthermore, the probability that the point penetrates the layer is equal to the relationship between the superficial area of the layer not covered by the molecular cross sections to the total surface. For a layer of thickness λ the fraction $\pi\rho^2/\lambda^2$ of the total surface is covered with molecular cross sections. For a layer of thickness δ this must be multiplied by δ/λ, that is, $(\pi\rho^2/\lambda^3)\delta$. Thus, the probability that the point penetrates a layer of thickness δ is $W_\delta = 1 - (\pi\rho^2/\lambda^3)\delta$. Equating the two expressions for W_δ, $\alpha = \pi\rho^2/\lambda^3$. For any layer thickness x with this value for α the following formula for the penetration possibility is obtained:

$$W = e^{-\frac{\pi\rho^2}{\lambda^3}x}.$$

Accordingly, out of Z mass points the layer thickness $x + dx$ is penetrated by

$$Z \cdot e^{-\frac{\pi\rho^2}{\lambda^3}(x+dx)} = Z \cdot e^{-\frac{\pi\rho^2}{\lambda^3}x} \cdot \left(1 - \frac{\pi\rho^2}{\lambda^3}\,dx\right).$$

Accordingly, $Z \cdot e^{-(\pi\rho^2/\lambda^3)x} \cdot (\pi\rho^2/\lambda^3)\, dx$ points are retained in layer dx. Multiplication by x gives the total length of path of all these points together. Then, by integration from $x = 0$ to $x = \infty$ and division by Z, the mean free length of path to $l' = \lambda^3/\pi\rho^2$ is obtained for one point. In the case of molecules with radius ρ, instead of mass points, the value of this radius must be doubled—that is, replaced with diameter s. However, if there are no molecules at rest but all molecules move at the same mean speed, this expression must also be multiplied by 0.75, so that

$$l = \frac{3}{4}\, \frac{\lambda^3}{\pi s^2}.$$

The proof is as follows. If, according to Maxwell,[6] v represents the speed of a molecule and $1/\lambda^3 = N$, the number of molecules per volume unit, then the number of collisions per minute for a moving molecule, with the remaining molecules at rest, is:

$$v/l' = v \cdot \pi s^2 N,$$

with $s = 2\rho$. But if the other molecules are also moving, then the v on the right side of the equation must be replaced by the mean speed r of the molecule under consideration relative to the others. In that case, one obtains for the number of collisions per minute of the molecule under consideration: $v/l = r \cdot \pi s^2 N$. Thus

$$v/l : v/l' = v : r, \qquad l' : l = v : r.$$

Now, according to Clausius, the relative speed between one molecule moving at speed v and another at speed u is: $\sqrt{u^2 + v^2 - 2uv \cos\theta}$, if θ is the angle between the directions of movement of the two molecules.[7] Since all angles occur with equal frequency, the number of those molecules whose lines of motion make angles between θ and $\theta + d\theta$ with the line in which the first molecule moves will have the same ratio to the whole number of molecules as the corresponding spherical zone to the total spherical surface—that is, as $2\pi \cdot \sin\theta \cdot d\theta : 4\pi$. Accordingly, the number of these molecules per volume unit is $N \cdot 1/2 \sin\theta \cdot d\theta$. Thus, the mean speed r of the particular molecule relative to the other molecules in motion is

$$r = \frac{1}{2}\int_0^\pi \sqrt{u^2 + v^2 - 2uv \cos\theta} \cdot \sin\theta\, d\theta.$$

On the average, $u = v$; and in this case the pertinent integral is $r = 4v/3$, q.e.d.

Thus $1/l = \frac{4}{3}\pi s^2 N$. As Loschmidt showed, estimates of the relative size of the gas molecules can be obtained from this equation. He initially transformed it to some extent:

$$\frac{1}{N} = \frac{16}{3} \cdot \frac{\pi l s^2}{4}.$$

$1/N$ is that part of the volume unit assigned to one molecule, if the molecules are considered to be evenly distributed. Loschmidt termed it the "molecular gas volume."

Since, according to Avogadro's principle, N is equal for all gases, the same applies to $1/N$. On the right side of the equation, $\pi l s^2/4$ indicates the cylindrical path traveled by the molecule covering the distance l, that is, the "molecular distance volume." Accordingly, the equation states that the latter quantity also is the same for all gases. $\pi s^3/6$ is the volume of a molecule. Its Nfold is that part of the unit of volume which is taken up by the molecules assumed at rest; its ratio to the unit is designated as the condensation coefficient ϵ of the gas. Consequently, the above equation results in $s = 8\epsilon l$. The mean free length of path l for air had already been calculated by Maxwell and O. E. Meyer. The condensation coefficient ϵ can be approximated from increases and decreases in volume due to evaporation and condensation, if the plausible assumption is made that in a liquefied state the action spheres of the molecules almost touch. The regularities indicated by Hermann Kopp also permit an estimation of the condensation coefficient of air from those of condensable gases. With these estimated values for l and ϵ, Loschmidt obtained from the last equation the molecule diameter $s = 8 \times 0.000866 \times 0.000140 = 0.000000970$ mm—that is, the correct size of somewhat less than 10^{-7} cm. He also stressed that this was to be considered only as a rough approximation, although this value certainly was not ten times too large or too small.

The value of 0.000140 mm for l is that given by Meyer. Loschmidt felt that this value was preferable to the older value of 0.000062 given by Maxwell. But had Loschmidt preferred Maxwell's value, he would have obtained for the molecular diameter the more accurate value of $s = 0.0000004295$ mm, that is, approximately 0.5×10^{-7} cm. Thus he could have calculated directly from his first formula a likewise accurate value of $2 \cdot 10^{19}$ molecules per cubic centimeter of gas. But Loschmidt calculated the number of molecules in living organisms, as 13.10^{19}. For the number of gas molecules, in his lecture "Die Weltanschauung der modernen Naturwissenschaft" (1867)[8a], he indicated—generally without basis, although referring to his work of 1865—the figure of 866 billion molecules per cubic millimeter, which is about thirty times too small. He recommends 10^{-18} of a milligram as a suitable unit for atomic weights, which is about 100 or 1,000 times too large. (According to modern measurements, a hydrogen atom weighs 1.67×10^{-24}g.) In conclusion, Loschmidt mentioned the hypothesis that atoms consist of even smaller particles and raised the question of whether his hypothetical ether envelopes could be used to explain the life processes.

Three years after Loschmidt, G. Johnstone Stoney attempted to compute the number of molecules per unit volume on the basis of Clausius' rough estimates. Thereby he obtained a value 100 times too large.[8] In 1870, William Thomson (Lord Kelvin), unaware of Loschmidt's work, published in *Nature* (issue of 31 March, pp. 551 ff.) a fundamental work in which he calculated the sizes of atoms by various methods. Initially he stated that as early as thirty years previously Cauchy had frightened natural scientists with the daring statement that the well-known prism colors indicated that the sphere of molecular action was comparable with the wavelength of light. Eight years previously he himself had published notes on experiments with electrically charged, mutually attractive thin copper and zinc membranes, which enabled him—through a method also outlined there in principle—to estimate a magnitude of $3.3 \cdot 10^{-9}$ cm for atoms.[9] He also obtained from experiments with liquid lamellae a molecular diameter of $\geqslant 5 \cdot 10^{-9}$ cm. From the kinetic theory of gases he calculated, in principle by the same method as Loschmidt, a molecular size not below $2 \cdot 10^{-9}$ cm and, for the number of molecules per cubic centimeter, $\leqslant 6 \cdot 10^{21}$. Thus the values obtained by Thomson were ten times too small for the molecular diameters and 100 times too large for the number of molecules.

Later, Thomson himself acknowledged Loschmidt's priority. In 1890, Lord Rayleigh directed attention to a forgotten work by Thomas Young, printed half a century before Loschmidt's, in the *Supplement* to the fourth edition (1810) of the *Encyclopaedia Britannica*.[10] In it Young had estimated the range of molecular attraction from the surface tension of water, thus obtaining a value between 10^{-10} and $5 \cdot 10^{-10}$ inch for the size of water molecules. Furthermore, from the ratio between water density and steam density he obtained the value 10^{-8} cm for the distance between steam particles. These figures are about 100 times too small.

To date, many methods have been invented for determining these figures. With each method, roughly the same values are obtained: about $0.5 \cdot 10^{-7}$ cm for the molecular diameter. For the distance between molecules the figure was about $3 \cdot 10^{-7}$ cm and, for the number of molecules per cubic centimeter of gas

at 0° C. and 760 mm mercury, $2.7 \cdot 10^{19}$. Thus, one mole of any gas—22.414 liters—contains $6.03 \cdot 10^{23}$ molecules. This figure is called Loschmidt's figure or, sometimes, Avogadro's constant, although Avogadro never performed any pertinent numerical calculations.

In 1868 Loschmidt was appointed to the new position of associate professor of physical chemistry at the University of Vienna, and he received an honorary Ph.D. several months later. He then received modest grants for experimentation and investigated the diffusion of gas in the absence of a porous membrane.[11] This involved the experimental confirmation of certain conformities (diffusion speeds) already theoretically derived by Maxwell from the kinetic gas theory, and a more accurate determination of the mean length of path from diffusion instead of from interior friction, as done previously.

Loschmidt also worked on the electromagnetic wave theory and even attempted to demonstrate experimentally the Kerr and Hall effects, although without success, because of the inadequate equipment. Also, as Hertz did later, he worked on the production of electrical resonances and came close to inventing the dynamo. Jokingly, he proposed the founding of a Viennese journal for unsuccessful experiments.

Loschmidt also continued his theoretical work. In the course of a controversy with Boltzmann, he sought a way to escape the heat death resulting from the kinetic theory ("reverse argument"), although without success.[12] These speculations, however, resulted in Loschmidt's first application of the second law of thermodynamics to the theory of solutions and chemical compounds.[13] Thus he became a forerunner of Horstmann and Gibbs. This also led to a modification of Maxwell's homogeneous-distribution axiom in the case of perceptible gravity effect.

Loschmidt let gases escape into a vacuum in order to observe the effects on their temperature (in accordance with the kinetic theory, the temperature must not change for ideal gases). He also speculated on the manner of propagation of sound in air: "Deduktion der Schallgeschwindigkeit aus der kinetischen Gastheorie."[14] He gave a simpler derivation of the equation of a point system.[15] He attempted to derive the Weber-Ampère law from that of Coulomb, and, in accordance with Kirchhoff, to derive Ohm's law from hydrodynamic flow laws, analogous to Poiseuille's law.[16] Finally, he attempted to calculate, on the basis of Lamé's elasticity theory and his own atomistic concept, the existence of spectral lines from the vibrations of ether spheres surrounding the atoms.[17]

In 1867 Loschmidt was named corresponding member of the Imperial Academy of Sciences in

Vienna, and in 1870 a full member. In 1869 he and Josef Stefan founded the Chemical-Physical Society. Loschmidt became the first director of the Physical-Chemical Laboratory (today the Second Institute of Physics). He was dean of the Philosophical Faculty in 1877–1878 and acting dean in 1878–1879. In 1887 he married his housekeeper; they had a son who died of scarlet fever at the age of ten. Loschmidt retired in 1890 and was decorated with the Order of the Iron Crown, third class. He turned over his institute to his pupil Franz Serafin Exner, the son of his professor. Other important pupils were Gustav Jäger and Ludwig Boltzmann.

NOTES

1. Compare Gicklhorn, in *Sudhoffs Archiv für Geschichte der Medizin und der Naturwissenschaften*, **32** (1939–1940), 337–370; and Donald, in *Annals of Science*, **1** (1936), 29–47.
2. See *Sitzungsberichte der Akademie der Wissenschaften in Wien*, Math.-natwiss. Kl., **51**, Abt. II (1865), and **52**, Abt. II (1866).
3. The problem is treated in detail by the organic chemist and textbook ed. and reviser, R. Anschütz, in *August Kekulé*, 2 vols. (Berlin, 1929), especially pp. 271–306. Also see his "Anmerkungen" in *Ostwalds Klassikern der exakten Wissenschaften* no. 190 (Leipzig, 1913); and *Chemische Studien* in the same ed. for Loschmidt's formulas.
4. "Zur Grosse der Luftmolekule," in *Sitzungsberichte der Akademie der Wissenschaften zu Wien*, Math.-natwiss. Kl., **52**, Abt. II (1866), 395–413.
5. *Philosophical Magazine*, 4th ser., **17** (1859), 81–91.
6. *Ibid.*, **19** (1860), 19–32.
7. *Ibid.*, pp. 434–436.
8. *Ibid.*, **36** (1868), 132–141.
8a. In *Schriften des Vereins zur Verbreitung naturwissenschaftlicher Kenntnisse in Wien*, **8** (1867–1868), 41–106, esp. 53.
9. William Thomson (Lord Kelvin), *Reprint of Papers on Electrostatics and Magnetism* (London, 1972), 400.
10. *Philosophical Magazine*, 5th ser., **30** (1890), 474.
11. "Diffusion von Gasen ohne poröse Scheidewände," in *Sitzungsberichte der Akademie der Wissenschaften in Wien*, Math.-natwiss. Kl., **61**, Abt. II (1870), 367–380; **62**, Abt. II (1870), 468–478.
12. *Sitzungsberichte der Akademie der Wissenschaften in Wien*, Math.-natwiss. Kl., **73**, Abt. II (1876), 128–142, 366–372; **75**, Abt. II (1877), 287–288; **76**, Abt. II (1877), 209–225.
13. *Ibid.*, **59**, Abt. II (1869), 395–418.
14. *Ibid.*, **54**, Abt. II (1866), 646–666.
15. *Ibid.*, **55**, Abt. II (1867), 523–538.
16. *Ibid.*, **58**, Abt. II (1868), 7–14.
17. *Ibid.*, **93**, Abt. II (1886), 434–446.

BIBLIOGRAPHY

Loschmidt's works are cited in the text of the article. A secondary source is Hubert de Martin, "Johann Joseph Loschmidt" (Vienna, 1948), a dissertation in typescript, poorly written but thorough and with a complete bibliography.

WALTER BÖHM

LOSSEN, KARL AUGUST (*b.* Kreuznach, Germany, 5 January 1841; *d.* Berlin, Germany, 24 February 1893), *geology, petrology*.

Lossen was the son of a doctor and his wife Charlotte Mayer. He was educated at the high school and Gymnasium in Kreuznach. He married his cousin Therese Lossen and had two daughters and one son. Lossen began work as a mining engineer in the siderite deposits of the Siegerland in Westphalia and in the coal mines of Saarbrücken. He broadened his studies in geology, mineralogy, and microscopic petrography, which was then just developing, under the guidance of Beyrich, Girard, Rammelsberg, G. Rose, and J. Roth. In 1866, after graduating from the University of Halle, he was introduced by Dechen at the Geological Survey of Prussia, and started working under the direction of Hauchecorne and Beyrich.

Lossen's main work was the mapping and description of the very complicated geology of the Harz Mountains, which were then still rather unknown, but which have since, because of Lossen's work, become one of the classic regions for geological study. He worked there part of every year from 1866 to 1892 and completed a geological map of the area in the scale of 1 : 100,000, and, incidentally, maps of smaller areas in the scale of 1 : 25,000 as by-products. He produced significant papers on the Devonian period, especially the Lower Devonian, and the early Carboniferous period in that region, which had previously been mistaken for Silurian.

Lossen also did essential work in microscopical petrology, and with this, along with geological observations in the field, became one of the first to report the influence of tectonic movements on metamorphism (dynamometamorphism).

By 1866 Lossen could show that gneissic and phyllitic rocks of the Hunsrück Mountains were Lower Devonian sediments. He discovered similar things in the Ostharz, where he also observed transitions between contact metamorphic and dynamometamorphic rocks. For metamorphic tuffs he coined the name "porphyroid."

In 1870 Lossen became a lecturer at the University of Berlin. He was appointed an associate professor in 1882 and full professor of petrology in 1886. While in Berlin, he redefined the old name "Hercynian," which he then used only for the lower part of the Lower Devonian.

Many of Lossen's works concern the magmatic rocks of the Saar-Nahe basin. From these were drawn numerous definitions, in part now completely misused, especially of rocks of the melaphyre-porphyrite-tholeite family.

BIBLIOGRAPHY

A list of Lossen's publications may be found in the obituary by E. Kayser in *Neues Jahrbuch fur Mineralogie, Geologie und Paläontologie,* **2** (1893), App. 1–18.

P. RAMDOHR

LOTKA, ALFRED JAMES (*b.* Lemberg, Austria [now Lvov, Ukrainian S.S.R.], 2 March 1880; *d.* Red Bank, New Jersey, 5 December 1949), *demography, statistics.*

Born of American parents, Lotka received his primary education in France and Germany, took science degrees at the University of Birmingham, England, and subsequently attended graduate courses in physics at Leipzig and Cornell. At various times he worked for the General Chemical Company, the U.S. Patent Office, the National Bureau of Standards, and from 1911 to 1914 was editor of the *Scientific American Supplement.* In 1924, after having spent two years at Johns Hopkins University composing his magnum opus, *Elements of Physical Biology,* he joined the statistical bureau of the Metropolitan Life Insurance Company in New York. There he spent the remainder of his working life (eventually becoming assistant statistician). In 1935 he married Romola Beattie; they had no children. During 1938–1939 he was president of the Population Association of America, and in 1942 he was president of the American Statistical Association.

Lotka's cardinal interests lay in the dynamics of biological populations, and this stemmed from his being struck, as a young physicist, by the similarities between chemical autocatalysis and the proliferation of organisms under specified conditions. He soon developed an "analytical" theory of population that was a function of birthrate, deathrate, and age distribution. His model was more realistic than earlier models; nevertheless he was admirably cautious about its predictive value. He also paid attention to interspecies competition. Building on some mathematical work of Volterra's (in 1926), he formulated a growth law for two competing populations, expressing the process in terms of two interlocking differential equations.

Lotka took a broad culture-conscious view of the quantification of biological change and devoted much thought to the ecologic influence of industrial man. The *Elements of Physical Biology* is an ambitious work, treating the whole biological world from a mathematico-physical standpoint. Later, during his service in the insurance business, he collaborated in writing about life expectancy and allied topics.

BIBLIOGRAPHY

Lotka's most important work, *Elements of Physical Biology* (Baltimore, 1925), was reissued with the title *Elements of Mathematical Biology* (New York, 1956). This ed. carries a full 94-item bibliography of Lotka's scientific and technical papers. With Louis I. Dublin he published three books: *The Money Value of a Man* (New York, 1930); *Length of Life* (New York, 1936); and *Twenty-Five Years of Health Progress* (New York, 1937). The most thorough exposition of his views on population change and evolution is to be found in *Théorie analytique des associations biologiques* (Paris, 1934; 1939), an English trans. of which he was working on at the time of his death. Almost all modern books on population theory mention Lotka's contributions.

NORMAN T. GRIDGEMAN

LOTSY, JAN PAULUS (*b.* Dordrecht, Netherlands, 11 April 1867; *d.* Voorburg, Netherlands, 17 November 1931), *botany.*

Born into a patrician family, Lotsy devoted himself to biological research against the wishes of his father. He studied botany with Beyerinck at the Wageningen Agricultural College and continued his studies at the University of Göttingen, from 1886 to 1890. His doctoral thesis was on German lichens. From 1890 to 1895 he was in the United States as a lecturer at Johns Hopkins University. He showed his versatility in working on the food supply of the adult oyster, the nitrogen assimilation of mustard, a study on the root formation of the swamp cypress, toxic substances of the pear-blight bacteria, the staining of diatoms, the fixing of cells of red algae, the significance of herbaria for botany, and a taxonomical revision of some Euphorbiaceae from Guatemala.

From 1895 to 1900 Lotsy was in Java, where he worked on the localization, physiology, and secretion of quinine in Cinchona species at the Cinchona Experiment Station (for which he received a gold medal). He was later invited by Treub to work in the Botanic Gardens at Buitenzorg (Bogor) and the mountain garden connected with it at Tjibodas. While there, he wrote a basic work on the life history of the genus *Gnetum,* the detailed anatomy and taxonomy of some Balanophoraceae, and sketches of Javanese forest plants. After an attack of malaria he returned to the Netherlands and from 1901 on lived at Leiden.

On his initiative the Association Internationale de Botanistes was founded, for which he edited the journal *Progressus rei botanicae,* which was comparable in scope to the present *Botanical Review.* This association also bought the *Botanisches Centralblatt* (1902), of which Lotsy was also the editorial secretary. In 1904 he was appointed lecturer of plant systematics at Leiden University and in 1906, in addition, director of the Rijksherbarium. He held these posts until 1909, when he entered a new phase. This was a time of great ferment and reform in biological research owing to the rediscovery of Mendel's laws, the publication of De Vries' mutation theory, the recognition of the role of chromosomes, and the close study of haploid and diploid generations in cormophytes. He viewed systematics in a wide sense, and thought that it should be combined with genetics to produce a phylogeny based on evolution. As early as 1903 Lotsy had given a lecture on the implications of the mutation theory, genetics, and hybridization for plant breeding. For teaching he composed in an incredibly short time two major handbooks—lectures on descent theories (1906–1908) and lectures on botanical phylogeny (1907–1911)—which were frequently used for university lectures.

After concluding that knowledge of dicotyledons was insufficient to establish their ancestry, Lotsy switched to a third phase of scientific research, the experimental approach to the mechanism of evolution. At Leiden he wanted a new herbarium with a garden attached for experimental taxonomy. Unfortunately the House of Commons rejected his plan, partly because of the opposition of De Vries, who saw it as a competitive threat. Lotsy and his close friend J. W. C. Goethart then offered to construct the garden from private means, but to no avail. Disgusted by this obstruction he resigned in 1909 from his official functions and with his own funds erected experimental gardens at Haarlem and later at Velp.

About 1912 Lotsy became convinced that species originated and evolved because of hybridization, and the development and advocacy of this theory occupied him for the rest of his life. He defined more precisely the concepts *jordanon*, *linneon*, and *syngameon* to tie systematics to genetics, and thus became a pioneer of modern research. Possibly he and his close collaborator Goethart obtained experimentally allopolyploid new species of *Antirrhinum* and *Scrophularia*. Though the creation of an official center of experimental taxonomy in the Netherlands was frustrated, Lotsy created a forum for genetics with the journal *Genetica* (1919), later adding *Resumptio genetica* and *Bibliographia genetica*. In the years 1920 to 1930 he traveled to North America, New Zealand, South Africa, and Egypt to disseminate his ideas and to test his theories, thus stimulating much research in experimental taxonomy.

Lotsy's writings were prolix and vague. His alter-native hybridization theory and equally untenable ideas found in his writings—*Homo sapiens* as a genus; linneons are homozygous—arose largely as a critical response to De Vries' mutation theory. Although Lotsy was not held in high esteem in the Netherlands, abroad he had many friends—William Bateson, Erwin Baur, Heribert Nilsson, Karl von Goebel, Richard von Wettstein, Leonard Cockayne—who admired him for his many-sided initiatives, energy, and stimulating spirit.

BIBLIOGRAPHY

There are 135 books and papers of Lotsy listed by W. A. Goddijn in his "In Memoriam," in *Genetica*, **13** (1931), i–xx. Lotsy's major works are: *Vorlesungen über Deszendenztheorien*, 2 vols. (Jena, 1906; 1908); *Vorträge über botanische Stammesgeschichte*, 3 vols. (Jena, 1907–1911); *Van den Atlantischen Oceaan naar de Stille Zuidzee in 1922* ('s Gravenhage, 1922); and "Voyages of Exploration to Judge of the Bearing of Hybridisation Upon Evolution. I. South Africa," in *Genetica*, **10** (1928), 1–315, written with W. A. Goddijn. Also important are his shorter works: *De kruisingstheorie, een nieuwe theorie over het ontstaan der soorten* (Leiden, 1914); *Evolution by Means of Hybridisation* ('s Gravenhage, 1916); *Over Oenothera lamarckiana als type van een nieuwe groep van organismen, die der kernchimeren* ('s Gravenhage, 1917); *De wereldbeschouwing van een natuuronderzoeker* ('s Gravenhage, 1917); *Het evolutievraagstuk* ('s Gravenhage, 1921); *Evolution Considered in the Light of Hybridisation* (n.p., 1925); "Versuche über Artbastarde und Betrachtungen über die Möglichkeit einer Evolution trotz Artbeständigkeit," in *Zeitschrift für induktive Abstammungs-Vererbungslehre*, **8** (1912), 325–333; "La théorie de croisement," in *Archives néerlandaises des sciences exactes et naturelles*, ser. IIIB, **2** (1914), 1–61; "Qu'est ce qu'une espèce," in *Archives néerlandaises des sciences exactes et naturelles*, sér. IIIB, **3** (1916), 57–110; "Evolution im Lichte der Bastardierung betrachtet," in *Genetica*, **7** (1925), 365–470; "Kreuzung und Deszendenz," in *Ber. Bot. Ges. Zürich 1924/26* (1926), 16–47; and the Cawthorn Lecture: "A Popular Account of Evolution" (Nelson, New Zealand, 1927), 1–22.

C. G. G. J. VAN STEENIS

LOTZE, HERMANN RUDOLPH (*b.* Bautzen, Germany, 21 May 1817; *d.* Berlin, Germany, 1 July 1881), *theoretical biology*, *metaphysics*.

Lotze was the son of the military doctor Carl Friedrich Lotze and Christiane Caroline Noak of Dresden. He had an older sister and brother, Natalie and Carl Robert. He spent his Gymnasium years in Zittau from 1824 to 1834 and at seventeen graduated first in his class. In the summer semester of 1834 he began to study philosophy and natural science at the University of Leipzig. C. H. Weisse, an idealistic and Hegelian philosopher, made a strong impression at first on Lotze's thinking. A counterbalance was provided by his scientific studies, for example, of physiology under E. H. Weber, of anatomy under A. W. Volkmann, and of physics under Fechner. He completed his philosophical studies with a work in French on Descartes and Leibniz, for which he received his Ph.D. on 1 March 1838. The ideas of Leibniz, moreover, were influential in his own philosophy.

Lotze earned his M.D. on 7 July 1838 with the dissertation *De futuris biologiae principiis philosophicis.* This youthful work contained the essence of his later philosophical system. In it he required that philosophy take careful account of scientific knowledge and reciprocally that physics and the life sciences subject their basic principles to the purifying scrutiny of contemporary philosophical analysis. In particular, he ruled out explanations that resorted to the concept of a life force, although the validity of this principle was then largely unquestioned, and he resolved the mind-body problem by a combination of Leibnizian monadology with the older occasionalism.

After Lotze had practiced medicine in Zittau for about a year (1838–1839), he qualified at Leipzig to lecture in medicine in the fall of 1839 and in philosophy in May 1840. With this combination he hoped to be fully equipped to consider the basic questions of biology, medicine, and anthropology. In that same year (1840) he published a volume of idealistic poems, which were contemplative yet lyrical and dealt with basic religious and aesthetic questions. In the period 1840 to 1844 he lectured on a broad field of subjects— general pathology, anthropology, philosophy of medicine, psychology, logic, and theological medicine —which he attempted to unify in his later works. In 1843 he became an assistant professor of philosophy in Leipzig, and in 1844, at the age of twenty-seven, he obtained, on the recommendation of the anatomist Rudolph Wagner, a full professorship in philosophy in Göttingen, there succeeding the famous Herbart.

In September 1844 Lotze married Ferdinande Hoffmann, a pastor's daughter; they had four sons. In the following decades Lotze devoted all his energies to his extensive scientific work. He maintained friendly relations with Wagner, and especially with members of the Freitagsverein, including the ophthalmologist Carl Ruete, the surgeon Baum, Carl Stumpf, and Karl Ewald Hasse. He remained in Göttingen for thirty-seven years, refusing a call to return to the University of Leipzig in 1859. Finally in April 1881, at the age of sixty-four, he accepted a new offer, this

time for the chair of philosophy at Berlin. A few weeks later, on 1 July 1881, he died in Berlin of pneumonia.

Lotze sought to classify nature, soul, mind, history, and culture in a great unifying concept, and to do so, moreover, with careful consideration of the great advances in the inorganic sciences, biology, and medicine, as well as in psychology. His principal writings appeared in rapid succession beginning in 1841 and reached their high point in his comprehensive three-volume work *Mikrokosmus* (1856–1864). This work is an architectonic one, and forms a kind of keystone joining Herder's *Ideen zur Philosophie der Menschheit* (1784–1791) and Humboldt's *Kosmos.* Here too Lotze displays his intention of explaining the nature of microcosm and macrocosm philosophically through the concepts of soul, mind, and culture, thus creating a philosophic-medical anthropology.

In his *Metaphysik* of 1841 Lotze attempted for the first time, by completely accepting a mechanistic causality in the organic as well as the inorganic world, to inquire into the real meaning and teleology of the cosmos, and therefore into the governing foundation of all phenomena. He concluded that mechanisms (natural laws) are the means by which the immanent goals of the universe are realized.

The relations between things can be causes, grounds, or purposes. Not everything is determined solely by causes. In the *Allgemeine Pathologie* (1842) he teaches that living things are subject to the same natural laws as inanimate nature; only the arrangement of the causally determined parts is different. There is no life force and no natural healing power, yet all life processes function harmoniously as a means toward the goal of survival. Between body and mind there exists a reciprocal cooperation.

In the history of physiology and the interpretation of living matter, Lotze's essay "Leben, Lebenskraft" (1843) played an important role, for no one up to that time had so penetratingly demonstrated the senselessness of the then generally accepted concept of a life force. To him a life force as a single cause of a multitude of consequences was unimaginable. How could it activate or alter the extraordinary number of the most varied mechanisms? The organism is simply a combination of mechanical processes that are in harmony with natural goals. The vital properties, or "life force," arise only from the concatenation of the mechanical properties of the entire organism. Nonetheless, each individual organism emerges not through chance, but through creation. The union of mind and body indicates a higher purposefulness, and the communication between body and soul occurs by means of a psychophysical mechanism with a preestablished occasionalistic harmony. Thus emerges a philosophical physiology which seriously investigates the scientific relation of causality but at the same time only briefly touches upon but does not develop the closely related question of goals.

In the article "Seele und Seelenleben" (1846) Lotze emphasized the limits of mechanism in an organism and discussed the three essential aspects of the concept of the mind: consciousness, unity of experience, and freedom. These go beyond the organic and constitute the separate domain of ethics and values.

In 1851 he discussed again, in a more profound manner, the subject of the interpretation of existence in *Allgemeine Physiologie des körperlichen Lebens*. He stated that we must recognize a kind of ensoulment in all things and repeated the justification of teleological views alongside of mechanical conceptions. He again dismisses vitalism with the observation that irritability of organisms is no "life" force but a phenomenon explaining nothing, which must itself be explained. In the system of ordered existence the means and forces are organized in a particular way characteristic of each organism. The *Medizinische Psychologie* (1852) continues the investigation of 1846 on the limits of mechanism. Lotze had by then assumed a completely spiritualistic view, believing that the central focus of the world was spiritual, with matter secondary and dependent. The mind is independent of all material events; it influences the body, but is not influenced by it. He also considers the fate of the soul and believes that immortality is granted only to the most distinguished souls.

Lotze's three-volume masterpiece, the *Mikrokosmus* (1856–1864), presents everything effectively and skillfully in a unified survey. His structure arches from inanimate nature, through animate, to the mind and to man, and encompasses man's history and culture. Lotze's fundamental idea remains the same, namely, that throughout the inanimate, animate, and spiritual worlds, hidden purposes are active, of which science, with its analysis of causality, investigates and explains only the instrumentation of the causal relations. But the key to the understanding of the world is to be sought in ideas and values, not in these mechanical processes. Even the formation and development of a seed are supramechanical and determined by the immanence of an infinite being.

Lotze, however, had found it necessary to publish *Streitschriften* (1857) in order to offset the impressions that he was a materialist, a misconception which arose from an imperfect understanding of his anti-vitalistic stance. His writings received much attention from the natural scientists of the nineteenth century, especially because of his attack on vitalism and his disavowal of the philosophical uses of deductive reasoning and the dialectic method. This break with tradition stands at the beginning of the debate that was carried on particularly by the students of Johannes Müller, namely Schwann, Emil du Bois-Reymond, Helmholtz, Brücke, and also Ludwig, and which was concluded with a definitive victory about 1850.

Lotze was a small, gaunt man, and exceptionally taciturn. He was very formal, stiff, and inclined to melancholy. His style of lecturing was plain, even dull, and lacking high points, but very precise, logical, and convincing. His industry is evident from his abundant writings. The anti-materialists of the nineteenth century saw in him the defender of a view of the world nobler and more beautiful than that offered by Carl Vogt, Moleschott, Friedrich Büchner, and the monists. Lotze saw his goal as uniting in a consistent fashion the results of scientific research with an ethical and religious world view, and in demonstrating a harmony between natural laws and the world of values. Hence his philosophy bordered on theosophy. As A. Krohn said in his article on Lotze, "He sought in that which should be, the basis of that which is."

BIBLIOGRAPHY

I. ORIGINAL WORKS. Lotze's original works are: *Metaphysik* (Leipzig, 1841; Paris, 1883); *Allgemeine Pathologie und Therapie als mechanische Naturwissenschaften* (Leipzig, 1842; 2nd ed., 1848); *Allgemeine Physiologie des körperlichen Lebens* (Leipzig, 1851); *Medizinische Psychologie oder Physiologie der Seele* (Leipzig, 1852); *Mikrokosmus. Ideen zur Naturgeschichte und Geschichte der Menschheit. Versuch einer Anthropologie*, 3 vols. (Leipzig, 1856–1864); *System der Philosophie*, 2 vols. (Leipzig, 1874–1879); and *Geschichte der deutschen Philosophie seit Kant. Dictate aus den Vorlesungen* (Leipzig, 1882).

Three important articles Lotze wrote are: "Leben und Lebenskraft," in R. Wagner, ed., *Handwörterbuch der Physiologie*, 1 (Brunswick, 1842), ix–lviii; "Instinkt," *ibid.*, 2 (1844), 191–209; and "Seele und Seelenleben," *ibid.*, 3 (1846), 142–264. Lotze's shorter works were edited by D. Peipers, *Kleine Schriften*, 3 vols. (Leipzig, 1885–1891).

II. SECONDARY LITERATURE. Works about Lotze and his works are: R. Falkenberg, *H. Lotze. Teil I. Leben und Entstehung der Schriften nach den Briefen* (Stuttgart, 1906); A. Krohn, "Zur Erinnerung an Hermann Lotze," in *Zeitschrift für Philosophie und Philosophische Kritik*, n.s. **80** (1882), 56–93; L. Seibert, *Lotze als Anthropologe* (Wiesbaden, 1900); M. Wentscher, *Hermann Lotze. I. Band. Lotzes Leben und Werke* (Heidelberg, 1913); E. Wentscher, *Das Kausalproblem in Lotzes Philosophie* (Halle, 1903); and S. Witkowski, "Über den Zusammenhang von Lotzes medizinisch-physiologischer Anschauung mit seiner Auffassung von Entstehen und Fortleben der Seele," Ph.D. diss., Giessen University, 1924.

Short bibliographical sketches of Lotze may be found in: W. G. M. Haberling, F. Hubotter, H. Vierordt, eds., *Biographisches Lexikon der hervorragenden Ärzte aller Zeiten und Völker*, **3** (Berlin–Vienna, 1931), 846–847; *Meyers Grosses Konversations-Lexikon*, 6th ed., **12** (Leipzig–Vienna, 1909), 737–738; and *Allgemeine Deutsche Biographie*, **52** (Leipzig, 1906), 93–97.

K. E. ROTHSCHUH

LOVE, AUGUSTUS EDWARD HOUGH (*b.* Weston-super-Mare, England, 17 April 1863; *d.* Oxford, England, 5 June 1940), *applied mathematics, geophysics.*

Love was one of four children and the second son of John Henry Love, a surgeon of Somersetshire. He was educated at Wolverhampton Grammar School, and his subsequent career owed much to his mathematical master, the Reverend Henry Williams.

He entered St. John's College, Cambridge, in 1882. He was a fellow of St. John's College from 1886 to 1889 and held the Sedleian chair of natural philosophy at Oxford from 1899 on. He was elected a fellow of the Royal Society of London in 1894. Love was secretary of the London Mathematical Society for fifteen years and president in 1912–1913. He was noted as a quiet, unassuming, brilliant scholar, with a logical and superbly tidy mind. He liked traveling, was interested in music, and played croquet. He never married; a sister, Blanche, kept house for him.

Love's principal research interests were the theory of deformable media, both fluid and solid, and theoretical geophysics. He also contributed to the theory of electric waves and ballistics, and published books on theoretical mechanics and the calculus.

Love's first great work, *A Treatise on the Mathematical Theory of Elasticity*, appeared in two volumes in 1892–1893. A second edition, largely rewritten, appeared in 1906 and was followed by further editions in 1920 and 1927. This treatise, translated into several foreign languages, served as the world's standard source on the subject for nearly half a century. It is a masterpiece of exposition and stands as a classic in the literature of mathematical physics. It continues to be much referred to by workers in the field.

While Love's contribution to the pure theory of elasticity rests principally on his expository powers, his excursions into theoretical geophysics led to far-reaching discoveries about the structure of the earth. His second work, *Some Problems of Geodynamics*, won the Adams Prize at Cambridge in 1911. The work

includes contributions on isostasy, tides of the solid earth, variation of latitude, effects of compressibility in the earth, gravitational instability, and the vibrations of a compressible planet. Many of his contributions are basic in current geophysical research, especially Love waves and Love's numbers, the latter being key numbers in tidal theory.

Developing the theory of Love waves was probably his greatest contribution. Formal theory on the transmission of primary (P) and secondary (S) waves in the interior of an elastic body had been worked out by Poisson and Stokes (1830–1850). In 1885 Rayleigh had shown that waves (Rayleigh waves) could be transmitted over the surface of an elastic solid. Rayleigh's theory concerned a semi-infinite, uniform, perfectly elastic, isotropic solid with an infinite plane boundary over which the waves travel.

According to Rayleigh the only permissible surface waves under these conditions are polarized so that the SH component of the particle motions is absent; this is the component which lies in the plane of the surface and is at right angles to the direction of wave advance. A second property of the waves is that for any general initial disturbance they advance unchanged in form: there is no dispersion—no spreading out into sine wave constituents over time.

When surface seismic waves were first detected in studies of earthquake records (some time after 1900), they were found to be discordant with the above two properties of Rayleigh waves. Love set out to investigate a suggestion that the earth's crust is responsible for the discordances. He examined a mathematical model consisting of Rayleigh's uniform medium overlain by a uniform layer of distinct elastic properties and density, and found that this model both permits the transmission of SH waves and requires the waves to be dispersed. These waves are now called Love waves. Love was thus the first to satisfy the general observational requirements of seismology with respect to surface waves.

Love's analysis also supplied a relation between periods and group velocities of surface waves, which became a powerful tool in estimating crustal thicknesses in various geographical regions of the earth; it led *inter alia* to the first evidence of the large differences in crustal structures below continents and oceans.

BIBLIOGRAPHY

Love published forty-five research papers over the period 1887–1929. A full list is given in the *Obituary Notices of Fellows of the Royal Society*, **3** (1939–1941), 480–482.

Love's books are *A Treatise on the Mathematical Theory of Elasticity*, 2 vols. (Cambridge, 1892–1893; 2nd ed., 1906; 3rd ed., 1920; 4th ed., 1927); *Theoretical Mechanics* (Cambridge, 1897; 2nd ed., 1906; 3rd ed., 1921); *Elements of the Differential and Integral Calculus* (Cambridge, 1909); *Some Problems of Geodynamics* (Cambridge, 1911).

K. E. BULLEN

LOVEJOY, ARTHUR ONCKEN (*b.* Berlin, Germany, 10 October 1873; *d.* Baltimore, Maryland, 30 December 1962), *epistemology, history of ideas.*

Lovejoy was the son of an American father, the Reverend W. W. Lovejoy, and a German mother, Sara Oncken. He was educated at the University of California (Berkeley) and did graduate work at Harvard, where he came mainly under the influence of William James. After teaching for brief periods at Stanford, Washington University, and the University of Missouri, he went to Johns Hopkins in 1910 and remained there until his retirement in 1938.

Lovejoy's epistemology was based on the premise that experience is irreducibly temporal. He held that the time series was irreversible and dates absolute. From this premise he argued that if two apparently similar (or for that matter different) objects have different dates, they are existentially dual, whatever their causal relations may be. Therefore, the sensory impressions which presumably arise in the human brain must be existentially different from their "objects." Stars, for instance, are seen at dates later than the date at which the light rays, which cause our vision, left them. The star that we see is thus not the star of the date at which we think we see it. This illustration would be true for any visual object and our impression of it. Lovejoy's epistemological dualism was expounded in detail in *Revolt Against Dualism* (1930), along with critical analyses of various forms of monism. Because of his temporalism, he attempted to refute some of the inferences drawn from the special theory of relativity; later, in conversation with the author, he repudiated the papers in which the refutations appeared.

Lovejoy's epistemological dualism was accompanied by a firm belief in the causal efficacy of ideas. He argued against all forms of anti-intellectualism and favored freedom of speech and conscience. He was one of the organizers of the American Association of University Professors and chairman of its committee on academic freedom for several years. A pronounced intellectualist, he became interested in the history of ideas. In collaboration with Philip Wiener, Lovejoy founded the *Journal of the History of Ideas* in 1940.

His historiographic program consisted in analyzing ideas into their component elements and then looking for a given elemental idea in various fields, regardless of the context in which it first appeared. He argued that a given idea—evolution, for instance—might begin as a theory of biology, but could turn up in theories of art, religion, or social organization.

Lovejoy also believed that ideas often begin as simple descriptive labels but take on eulogistic connotations as time goes on; the historian must become aware of these connotations and of their influence on thought. His most famous example was probably his analysis of the meanings of "nature" and its derivatives. He pointed out that authors are frequently unaware of the ambiguity of their ideas—ambiguities that have accumulated over the centuries—and thus fall into unconscious inconsistencies of thinking. His most influential contribution to the history of ideas is undoubtedly *The Great Chain of Being* (1936), preceded by certain chapters of *Primitivism and Related Ideas in Antiquity* (1935). He realized that to complete a detailed history of any idea would require the collaboration of many scholars.

BIBLIOGRAPHY

I. ORIGINAL WORKS. Lovejoy's works include "The Thirteen Pragmatisms," in *Journal of Philosophy, Psychology and Scientific Methods*, **5** (1908), 1–12, 29–39; "Reflections of a Temporalist on the New Realism," *ibid.*, **8** (1911), 589–599; "Some Antecedents of the Philosophy of Bergson," in *Mind*, **22** (1913), 465–483; "On Some Novelties of the New Realism," in *Journal of Philosophy, Psychology and Scientific Methods*, **10** (1913), 29–43; *Bergson and Romantic Evolutionism* (Berkeley, 1914); "On Some Conditions of Progress in Philosophical Inquiry," in *Philosophical Review*, **26** (1917), 123–163; "The Paradox of the Thinking Behaviorist," *ibid.*, **31** (1922), 135–147; *The Revolt Against Dualism: An Inquiry Concerning the Existence of Ideas* (La Salle, Ill., 1930); *Primitivism and Related Ideas in Antiquity* (Baltimore, 1935), written with G. Boas; *The Great Chain of Being: A Study of the History of an Idea* (Cambridge, Mass., 1936); and *Essays in the History of Ideas* (Baltimore, 1948), which includes a complete bibliography up to 1947.

See also "Buffon and the Problem of Species," in Bentley Glass, Owsei Temkin, and William L. Straus, Jr., eds., *Forerunners of Darwin* (Baltimore, 1959), 84–113; "Kant and Evolution," *ibid.*, 173–206; "Herder: Progressionism Without Transformation," *ibid.*, 207–221; "The Argument for Organic Evolution Before the *Origin of Species*, 1830–1858," *ibid.*, 356–414; "Schopenhauer as an Evolutionist," *ibid.*, 415–437; "Recent Criticism of the Darwinian Theory of Recapitulation: Its Grounds and its Initiator," *ibid.*, 438–458; *Reflections on Human Nature* (Baltimore, 1961); and *The Reason, the Understanding, and Time* (Baltimore, 1961).

II. SECONDARY LITERATURE. See George Boas, "A. O. Lovejoy as Historian of Philosophy," in *Journal of the History of Ideas*, **9**, no. 4 (1948), 404–411; Maurice Mandelbaum, "Arthur O. Lovejoy and the Theory of Historiography," *ibid.*, 412–423; W. P. Montague, "My Friend Lovejoy," *ibid.*, 424–427; Marjorie H. Nicholson, "A. O. Lovejoy as Teacher," *ibid.*, 428–438; Theodore Spencer, "Lovejoy's *Essays in the History of Ideas*," *ibid.*, 439–446; H. A. Taylor, "Further Reflections on the History of Ideas: An Examination of A. O. Lovejoy's Program," in *Journal of Philosophy*, **40** (1943), 281–299; and Philip P. Wiener, "Lovejoy's Role in American Philosophy," in *Studies in Intellectual History* (Baltimore, 1953), 161–173.

GEORGE BOAS

LOVELL, JOHN HARVEY (*b.* Waldoboro, Maine, 21 October 1860; *d.* Waldoboro, 2 August 1939), *botany, entomology, apiology.*

Lovell was the son of Harvey H. Lovell, a sea captain, and of Sophronia Caroline Bulfinch Lovell. An interest in natural history led him to study science at Amherst, where he was elected to Phi Beta Kappa. After graduating in 1882 he taught school for several years, but he resigned when his father became seriously ill. His father died in 1898, leaving him a fine house on the Medomac River and enough wealth to provide him with an income for life.

In 1899 he returned to Amherst and earned a master of arts degree, and in the same year he married Lottie Magune. She took an interest in his work and often assisted in collecting, labeling, and cataloging his insects. They had two sons, Harvey Bulfinch Lovell and Ralph Marston Lovell. Harvey developed interests similar to his father's and received a Ph.D. in zoology from Harvard in 1933. They collaborated on six papers on flower pollination from 1932 to 1939.

The particular focus of John Lovell's researches was established when he read Hermann Müller's *Fertilization of Flowers*. The correlation which Müller had described between the colors of flowers and the kinds of insects that were attracted to them was repudiated by Felix Plateau in 1895. One of the main goals of Lovell's early studies on the colors of flowers and color preferences of insects was to substantiate Müller's findings.

Lovell found that the identification of wild bees was often difficult, and he decided to make a special study of them. He collected over 8,000 Apoidea specimens and described, sometimes with the assistance of Theodore D. A. Cockerell, thirty-two new species.

Lovell's interest in bees and pollination soon led him to the study of apiculture and the photography of flowers. He combined these interests in *The Flower*

and the Bee (1918) and *Honey Plants of North America* (1926), each of which contains more than 100 of his plant photographs.

Many of his photographs were also reproduced with his articles in the *American Bee Journal* and in about a thousand articles on plants which he wrote, beginning in 1926, for the *Boston Globe* and other newspapers.

BIBLIOGRAPHY

I. ORIGINAL WORKS. Lovell's two books are *The Flower and the Bee* (1918) and *Honey Plants of North America* (1926). Beginning in 1913 he wrote seventy-eight articles for the four eds. of Amos Ives Root and E. R. Root, *The ABC and XYZ of Bee Culture* (1923–1940). He wrote forty-one articles and notes for the *American Bee Journal*, which appeared from March 1913 to October 1937 (see indexes). Seventeen botanical articles by Lovell are listed in the Torrey Botanical Club *Index to American Botanical Literature*, 1886–1966, 4 vols., III (Boston, 1969), 111–112.

Eleven articles which he wrote describing Apoidea are listed in the bibliography of Covell (cited below). Of his insect collections, 156 type specimens are now part of the collections of the U. S. National Museum and the remainder are located in the Lovell Insect Museum, University of Louisville.

II. SECONDARY LITERATURE. There is a discussion and summary of his Apoidea descriptions in Charles V. Covell, Jr., "A Catalog of the J. H. Lovell Types of Apoidea (Hymenoptera), with Lectotype Designations," in *Proceedings of the Entomological Society of Washington*, **74** (1972), 10–18. For an outline of the history of apiculture in America, see John E. Eckert, Frank R. Shaw, and Everett F. Phillips, *Beekeeping* (New York, 1960), 7–10, 453–458. For a more recent understanding of pollination ecology, see K. Faegri and L. van der Pijl, *The Principles of Pollination Ecology* (Oxford–New York, 1966). For the history of pollination ecology down to 1873, see Hermann Müller, *The Fertilization of Flowers*, trans. into Eng. by D'Arcy Wentworth Thompson (London, 1883), 1–29. A useful biographical sketch is Frank C. Pellett, "John H. Lovell: Notes on the Life and Writings of the Maine Naturalist," in *American Bee Journal*, **79** (1939), 568–570, which includes two photographs of Lovell.

FRANK N. EGERTON III

LOVÉN, SVEN (*b.* Stockholm, Sweden, 6 January 1809; *d.* near Stockholm, 3 September 1895), *marine biology.*

Lovén was the son of Christian Lovén, the mayor of Stockholm. He received his early education in a private school, then in 1824 entered the University of Lund. His teachers included the botanist Agardh and the zoologist Sven Nilsson, with the latter of whom Lovén made a trip to Norway in 1826. The subject of Lovén's first paper, the geographical distribution of birds, shows Nilsson's influence. Lovén took the M.A. in 1829; in 1830 he went to Berlin for a year's further study. In Germany he learned microscope technique and studied with Ehrenberg and Rudolphi, who, together with the Swedish anatomist Anders Retzius, persuaded him to give up ornithology in favor of marine biology.

In 1835 Lovén published a treatise on the plankton crustacean *Evadne nordmanni* and a work entitled *Contribution to the Knowledge of the Genera Campanularia and Syncoryne*, in which he traced the life-cycles of these genera from the egg to the formation of new colonies. He supplemented his knowledge of marine fauna with a number of field excursions, of which the most important was a seventeen-month trip to Spitsbergen and northern Norway that he undertook in 1836–1837. On this voyage Lovén studied marine life, especially plankton, and assembled a rich collection of specimens. He also recorded significant observations on Paleozoic fossils and Quaternary geological formations.

In 1841 Lovén was appointed curator of the invertebrate section of the Museum of Natural History in Stockholm. At the same time, he was engaged in research on the anatomy and evolution of mollusks; his *Index molluscorum* was published in 1846. Lovén then took up the study of the molluscean radula, noting that this structural detail is useful in classification by genera and species. In 1848, while studying the embryological development of mollusks, Lovén (simultaneously with Friedrich Müller) discovered the polar bodies that appear during the maturation of the egg. He incorporated this discovery, together with several other important results, in his *Contribution to the Knowledge of the Development of Mollusca Acephala Lamellibranchiata*, a study of the metamorphic and embryonic stages in a number of different bivalves which was published the same year.

Lovén's interest in fossil forms led him to take up the question of the evolution of the Scandinavian peninsula, a problem that had also been discussed by Celsius and Swedenborg. Lovén studied shellbanks—deposits of fossil shells at altitudes considerably above sea level—on the west coast of Sweden and found such arctic forms as *Pecten islandicus*. These finds corroborated his theory that an arctic sea had once covered much of the present Scandinavian land; he also found that the proportion of southern fossil forms was significantly higher near the present shore, demonstrating a gradually warming climate. He further investigated the peculiar distribution of certain glacial marine forms which were common in the Baltic Sea and in several large inland lakes, but completely lacking on the west coast of Scandinavia. His *On Several Crustaceans Found in Lakes Vättern and Vänern*, published in 1860, offers a geological explanation of this zoological phenomenon.

Although his work on mollusks was most widely recognized, Lovén also published excellent anatomical studies on other species. His *Études sur les Echinoidées*, published in 1874, is of lasting value to students of the Echinodermata.

Lovén remained active at the Museum of Natural History until his retirement in 1892. He made a further permanent contribution to science in his work toward the foundation of the Kristineberg zoological station on the west coast of Sweden. With Berzelius, he began the series *Summary of the Transactions of the Royal Academy of Science* in 1844. In 1903 the Academy issued a memorial medal in his honor.

BIBLIOGRAPHY

A bibliography of eighty-nine works is supplied by Hjalmar Théel, "Sven Ludwig Lovén," in *Kungliga Svenska vetenskapakademien lefnadsteckning*, **4**, no. 3 (1903), 75–82.

KARL-GEORG NYHOLM

LOVITS (LOWITZ), JOHANN TOBIAS (in Russian, **Tovy Yegorovich**) (*b.* Göttingen, Germany, 25 April 1757; *d.* St. Petersburg, Russia, 17 December 1804), *chemistry*.

Lovits' mother died when he was very young; his father was Georg Moritz Lovits, a cartographer and instrument maker, who was also, from 1762, a professor at Göttingen University. In 1768 father and son went to St. Petersburg and thence on an ill-fated expedition to the Caspian steppes. The elder Lovits was executed there by the Cossack revolutionary Pugachev, and in 1774, following that event, his orphaned son was placed in the Academy Gymnasium in St. Petersburg. Lovits left the Gymnasium after two years and entered the main pharmacy of St. Petersburg as a student. By 1779 he had become a journeyman pharmacist, and the following year he was sent to Göttingen to continue his education. His health had been precarious throughout his school years, and his university career was interrupted by a serious illness. He attempted to regain his strength by a long foot trip throughout Europe, and succeeded so well that by 1784 he was able to return to St. Petersburg, and to his studies at the main pharmacy there. The study of chemistry by that time occupied all his free time. In 1787 Lovits was made court apothecary; in 1790 he was elected an adjunct, and in 1793 a full member of the St. Petersburg Academy of Sciences.

Lovits became known as a talented and inventive experimenter. In 1785, while trying to obtain a crystalline form of tartaric acid, he noticed that powdered charcoal which accidentally contaminated the acid solution effectively removed visible impurities. He thus began his research on adsorption, at first attributing the adsorptive qualities of charcoal to its "dephlogistic action." He set up an extensive program to test the effects of charcoal on a number of different substances, employing carbons of wood, bone, and even pure tartaric acid. Having discovered the efficacy of charcoal for removing color from organic products, he recommended that it be used as a purifying agent for vodka, sugar syrup, and drinking water. He made further investigations of gas adsorption by charcoal, and noted its deodorizing action. In the 1790's, Lovits adapted Lavoisier's theory and explained the phenomenon of adsorption chemically (unlike Klaproth and Green, who remained committed to a mechanical interpretation).

Lovits did further research in the crystallization of substances from solutions, introducing the concepts of supercooling and supersaturation. He obtained the crystal hydrates $NaCl \cdot 2H_2O$ and $KOH \cdot 2H_2O$, and distinguished between forced crystallization and spontaneous crystallization, noting that the same substance could thus yield crystals of different form and composition. He explained the role of seeding in crystal growth, and used this method to obtain Rochelle salt crystals "of unusual size" from hot, lightly saturated solutions. He further employed the seeding technique to separate the crystal forms of salts, which he used in a number of chemical analyses. Lovits was the first to describe convection currents in the crystallization process. He also developed several formulas for cooling mixtures; fabricated 288 wax models of crystals; and used a microscope to observe the crystalline patterns left on glass after evaporation of the mother solution (thereby laying the foundations of microchemical analysis).

In analytical chemistry Lovits investigated strontium, chrome, titanium, manganese, columbium (niobium), and their salts. Independently of A. Crawford, he isolated strontium from barite, examined the properties of its salts in detail, and developed a method of distinguishing it from barium and calcium according to its solubility in alcohol. Independently of Vauquelin, Lovits, in 1798, derived chrome from Siberian lead ore and established its crystalline form.

Lovits designed new methods to use in his ana-

lytical work. He dissolved silicates in heated caustic alkalies, instead of melting them, and in 1794 described a technique for titrating acetic acid with potassium tartrate. (The appearance of sediment consisting of undissolved potassium bitartrate marked the end of the process.) In his research on the intermediate and acid salts of carbonic and sulfuric acids, he obtained crystalline bicarbonates and bisulfates to demonstrate that the excess of acids in acid salts represented a chemical, rather than a mechanical, mixture.

Lovits was also the first to isolate a number of organic substances in the pure state. Through the use of a technique combining the principles of crystallization, distillation, and adsorption, he was able to prepare frozen acetic acid, anhydride alcohol, pure sulfuric ether, and many organic acids. He was the first to isolate glucose from honey, and he obtained two new acids—dichloracetic and trichloracetic—by subjecting acetic acid to the action of chlorine.

Lovits was active scientifically for only twenty years. He was often seriously ill, occasionally as a result of his experiments, and survived a number of accidents. One of the most dedicated of chemists, he found satisfaction and joy only in his research.

BIBLIOGRAPHY

I. ORIGINAL WORKS. A collection is *T. E. Lovits. Izbrannye trudy po khimii i khimicheskoy tekhnologii* ("T. E. Lovits. Selected Works in Chemistry and Chemical Technology"; Moscow, 1955), ed. and with notes by N. Figurovsky. A partial list of individual works is given by Poggendorff.

II. SECONDARY LITERATURE. A biography is Figurovsky, *op. cit.*, 405–514; see also his *Leben und Werk des Chemikers Tobias Lowitz* (Berlin, 1959); A. N. Scherer, *Worte der Erinnerung an das Leben und die Verdienste von Tobias Lowitz* (St. Petersburg, 1820); and P. Walden, "Tobias Lowitz, ein vergessener Physikochemiker," in Diergart, ed., *Beiträge zur Geschichte der Chemie* (Leipzig, 1909), 533–544.

N. FIGUROVSKY

LOWELL, PERCIVAL (*b*. Boston, Massachusetts, 13 March 1855; *d*. Flagstaff, Arizona, 12 November 1916), *astronomy*.

More than any other astronomer of his generation, Percival Lowell had a profound influence on the general public. His thesis that the planet Mars was the abode of intelligent life continued to excite the public mind decades after his death; although the idea never gained the acceptance of his colleagues, it was not until after the Mariner flights to Mars during the late

1960's that it could firmly and finally be banished from all consideration.

Lowell's name is also forever linked with Pluto; although he did not live to see that distant planet (and while subsequent evidence has revealed its discovery to be accidental), there is no doubt that his inspiration advanced the date of its detection by many years. His most important contribution to astronomy, however, was his realization that superior observational work can be conducted only where atmospheric conditions are superior. He was a pioneer in constructing an observatory far from the lights and smoke of civilization.

Lowell was descended from some of the most prominent New England families. His father, Augustus Lowell, was closely identified with the cultural life of Boston. His mother, Katharine Bigelow Lawrence, was the daughter of Abbott Lawrence, sometime United States minister to Great Britain. A great-great-grandfather, John Lowell, was a member of the Continental Congress; his son, Lowell's great-grand-father, also John Lowell, represented Boston in the Massachusetts legislature. Both were actively interested in horticulture, and the younger John Lowell had on his farm some of the first greenhouses in the United States to be built on truly scientific principles. John Amory Lowell, Lowell's grandfather, collected a valuable herbarium and botanical library, the latter now forming an important part of the Gray Herbarium. Lowell's younger brother, Abbott Lawrence Lowell, became president of Harvard University; and his youngest sister, Amy Lowell, was well known as a poet and critic. James Russell Lowell, a first cousin of his father, was the foremost American man of letters of his time.

Lowell's early schooling was at Miss Fette's dame school. He subsequently attended Noble's School, where he developed interests in many fields, including astronomy. He graduated from Harvard University in 1876 with distinction in mathematics. After a year in Europe he went into his grandfather's business (cotton mills and trust and utility companies) and in 1883 traveled to Japan to study its people, customs, and language. While in Japan he was invited to serve as foreign secretary and general counsellor to the first diplomatic mission from Korea to the United States. He subsequently visited Korea and wrote of his experiences there in *Chosön—the Land of the Morning Calm—A Sketch of Korea* (1885). For several years he journeyed throughout the Far East and learned much of the oriental character, which he portrayed in *The Sound of the Far East* (1888). *Noto* (1891) is a straight-forward but exciting account of a trip to a remote part of Japan. An earlier interest in Shintoism was renewed by his visit to the sacred mountain of Ontake, and he described his studies of the Shinto trances in *Occult Japan, or the Way of the Gods* (1895).

But Lowell's thoughts were turning more and more to astronomy, and on his final voyage to Japan he took a small telescope with him. He left the Orient for the last time in 1893. A favorable opposition of Mars was due toward the end of 1894, and Lowell resolved to study that planet then under the best possible conditions. At the 1877 opposition Mars had been extensively studied by Giovanni Schiaparelli, whose widely publicized observations of the "canals" had opened a new era in the investigation of that planet. Lowell took up a suggestion by W. H. Pickering that the steadiest air in North America was to be found in the Arizona Territory, and as a result of tests in the spring of 1894 he selected an observing site on the eastern edge of the mesa to the west of Flagstaff, at an altitude of some 7,000 feet. He acquired an eighteen-inch and a twelve-inch telescope and began observations. In *Mars* (1895) Lowell concluded

> . . . that the broad physical conditions of the planet are not antagonistic to some form of life; secondly, that there is an apparent dearth of water upon the planet's surface, and therefore, if beings of sufficient intelligence inhabited it, they would have to resort to irrigation to support life; thirdly, that there turns out to be a network of markings covering the disk precisely counterparting what a system of irrigation would look like; and, lastly, that there is a set of spots placed where we should expect to find the lands thus artificially fertilized, and behaving as such constructed oases should. All this, of course, may be a set of coincidences, signifying nothing; but the probability points the other way.

By 1896 Lowell had replaced the two borrowed telescopes with a twenty-four-inch telescope and had resumed observations of Mars by night and of Mercury and Venus by day. He had also tested sites in the Sahara and in Mexico and South America. During the winter of 1896–1897 he temporarily transferred his telescope to Tacubaya, Mexico, where it was believed—erroneously, as it turned out—that observing conditions would be better than in Flagstaff.

Overwork and insufficient sleep took their toll, and Lowell's health broke down. He was kept from astronomy for four years, except for his participation in an eclipse expedition to Tripoli in 1900. Observations at the Lowell observatory continued, however, and the first two volumes of the observatory's *Annals* appeared. Lowell was back in Flagstaff observing Mars in 1901, 1903, and 1905, and he expanded his earlier ideas about that planet in *Mars and Its Canals*

(1906) and *Mars as the Abode of Life* (1908). Lowell was not the first to regard the Martian bright areas as deserts and the dark areas as vegetation, but he studied in unprecedented detail the progressive "wave of darkening" of the dark areas, from pole to equator, as the seasons advanced from late winter, through spring, and into summer. As water was released from the melting polar caps, plant life would be revived; the accompanying increased prominence of the canals would indicate that water was flowing through them.

The premise that the dark areas are vegetation was almost universally accepted until the late 1950's. Then astronomers began to suspect that the light and dark areas are equally barren, and that the changes in the latter are simply due to light-colored dust being blown across them by winds. Lowell had himself suggested that the polar caps were due to hoarfrost, although astronomers now believe them to arise more from solid carbon dioxide than from solidified water. Observations from the Mariner flights have confirmed the barren nature of the Martian surface. The canals exist, although not as the fantastic system of hundreds of straight lines depicted by Lowell; most, if not all, of them are in fact merely chance alignments of dark patches.

While it was Mars that received the greatest part of Lowell's attention, he did not ignore the other planets. He "confirmed" Schiaparelli's result that Mercury rotates on its axis in the same time it takes to orbit the sun, although radar studies have revealed the true rotation period to be only two-thirds as long. With V. M. Slipher he made, in 1911, the first reliable determination of the rotation period of Uranus—ten and three-quarter hours. He also made a critical investigation of the structure of Saturn's rings, particularly when they were presented edgewise to the earth in 1907. And he made extensive studies of the "cloud formations" on Jupiter.

A nonresident professor at the Massachusetts Institute of Technology, Lowell gave a series of lectures there in 1902, later published as *The Solar System* (1903). Another series of lectures there led to the publication of *The Evolution of Worlds* (1909). In the latter work, as in *Mars as the Abode of Life*, Lowell adopted the Chamberlin-Moulton hypothesis that the solar system arose as the result of the encounter of the sun and another star. He then discussed various stages in the evolution of a planet; as cooling set in, a crust formed, conditions became suitable for the development of life, and finally the oceans and atmosphere disappeared and life ceased. He supposed that Mars had evolved much more completely than the earth, and that the moon had reached its final

stage. *The Evolution of Worlds* concludes with a vivid description of how life on the earth could end, as its inhabitants became aware of a dark star steadily approaching, finally to collide with the sun.

Lowell was also interested in purely theoretical studies of the solar system, and in particular that of the significance of the resonances among the planets. He maintained that, after each of the planets was formed, there would be a tendency for the next one to collect at a point where its period of revolution bore some simple relationship to that of its predecessor: thus, after the formation of Jupiter, Saturn was formed with a period just two-and-a-half times longer; then Uranus with a period three times that of Saturn; and Neptune with a period twice as long again. There was a similar relationship among the periods of the inner planets.

The planets are not now observed to be exactly at these resonances, and Lowell discussed a mechanism whereby each planet was subsequently perturbed somewhat in toward the sun. Much of this theory is described in Lowell's final book, *The Genesis of the Planets* (1916). The process cannot now be given serious consideration, but it led Lowell to anticipate the existence of another planet orbiting the sun with a revolution period twice that of Neptune. He had previously come to a similar conclusion by studying the distribution of the aphelion distances of the periodic comets; there are a large number of cometary aphelia near the orbit of Jupiter, a few near the orbits of Saturn and Uranus, several near that of Neptune, but apparently none in between.

The concept of "cometary families" has since been largely discredited (except for the Jupiter family), but more distant clusters of cometary aphelia could suggest the presence of at least one planet beyond Neptune. For the last eight years of his life Lowell paid particular attention to the problem of finding a trans-Neptunian planet. Recognizing that the orbit of Neptune was too imperfectly known for his purpose, he analyzed the residuals remaining between the observed and calculated positions of Uranus, as J. C. Adams and Le Verrier had done before him; this time, the perturbations by Neptune were taken into account. Lowell had C. O. Lampland photograph the region of the sky in which the new planet X was expected to lie. Subsequent refinement of the calculations led to considerable changes in the prediction, but X still eluded detection.

The search was continued at the Lowell observatory long after its founder's death, and X was finally identified by Clyde Tombaugh in 1930. Named Pluto, with its symbol ♇ depicting also the initials of Percival Lowell, the new planet was announced to the world on the seventy-fifth anniversary of Lowell's birth. Pluto was found to travel in an orbit remarkably close to that predicted, although with a period only three-halves (not twice) that of Neptune. Pluto was considerably fainter than had been anticipated. Since it has now been established that Pluto has a mass scarcely greater than that of Mars (and possibly no greater than that of Mercury), it is quite clear that the discovery was due to an incredible coincidence.

Lowell married Constance Savage Keith in 1908. He was a brilliant speaker and was always in demand for lecture tours. He enjoyed all nature and derived from his ancestors a great love of botany. He found near Flagstaff a number of plants not previously known to prevail so far north, and he also discovered a new species of ash tree that now bears his name. Lowell was an honorary member of the Royal Astronomical Society of Canada, and he received medals from the national astronomical societies of France and Mexico.

BIBLIOGRAPHY

I. ORIGINAL WORKS. In addition to the books mentioned in the text many of Lowell's writings are contained in the *Annals of Lowell Observatory*, **1–3** (1898–1905) and the *Bulletin of Lowell Observatory*, **1–2** (1903–1916). Other works include "On the Capture of Comets by Jupiter," in *Science*, **15** (1902), 289; "Expedition for the Ascertaining of the Best Location of Observatories," in *Monthly Notices of the Royal Astronomical Society*, **63** (1902), 42–43; "A Standard Scale for Telescopic Observations," *ibid.*, **63** (1902), 40–42; "On the Variable Velocity of Zeta Herculis in the Line of Sight," in *Astronomical Journal*, **22** (1902), 190; "On the Kind of Eye Needed for the Detection of Planetary Detail," in *Popular Astronomy*, **13** (1905), 92–94; and "Chart of Faint Stars Visible at the Lowell Observatory," *ibid.*, 391–392.

See also his "Comparative Charts of the Region Following Delta Ophiuchi," in *Monthly Notices of the Royal Astronomical Society*, **66** (1905), 57; "Planetary Photography," in *Nature*, **77** (1908), 402–404; "The Tores of Saturn," in *Popular Astronomy*, **16** (1908), 133–146; "The Revelation of Evolution: A Thought and Its Thinker," in *Atlantic Monthly*, **104** (1909), 174–183; "Planets and Their Satellite Systems," in *Astronomische Nachrichten*, **182** (1909), 97–100; "The Plateau of the San Francisco Peaks in Its Effect on Tree Life," in *Bulletin of the American Geographical Society of New York* (1909); "On the Limits of the Oblateness of a Rotating Planet and the Physical Deductions From Them," in *Philosophical Magazine*, 6th ser., **19** (1910), 710–712; "Saturn's Rings," in *Astronomische Nachrichten*, **184** (1910), 177–182; "The Hood of a Comet's Head," in *Astronomical Journal*, **26** (1910), 131–134; "On the Action of Planets Upon Neighboring Particles," *ibid.* (1911), 171–174; and "Libration and the Asteroids," *ibid.*, **27** (1911), 41–46.

See also "The Sun as a Star," in *Popular Astronomy*, **19** (1911), 283–287; "The Spectroscopic Discovery of the Rotation Period of Uranus," in *Observatory*, **35** (1912), 228–230; "Sur la Désintégration des Comètes," in *Bulletin astronomique*, **29** (1912), 94–100; "Precession and the Pyramids," in *Popular Science Monthly*, **80** (1913), 449–460; "Precession of the Martian Equinoxes," in *Astronomical Journal*, **28** (1914), 169–171; "Mimas and Enceladus," in *Popular Astronomy*, **22** (1914), 633; "Memoir on a Trans-Neptunian Planet," in *Memoirs of the Lowell Observatory*, **1**, no. 1 (1915); "Memoir on Saturn's Rings," *ibid.*, no. 2 (1915); "Measures of the Fifth Satellite of Jupiter Made at the Lowell Observatory in September 1915," in *Astronomical Journal*, **29** (1916), 133–137; and "Our Solar System," in *Popular Astronomy*, **24** (1916), 419–427.

II. SECONDARY LITERATURE. The most complete biographical information is to be found in A. L. Lowell, *Biography of Percival Lowell* (New York, 1935), and in an account issued by the Lowell Observatory and published in *Popular Astronomy*, **35** (1917), 219–223. L. Leonard, *Percival Lowell: An Afterglow* (Boston, 1921) is a delightful character sketch and contains many extracts from his letters.

For recent information on Mars, see S. Glasstone, *The Book of Mars* (Washington, D.C., 1968) and R. B. Leighton, N. H. Horowitz, B. C. Murray, R. P. Sharp, A. G. Herriman, A. T. Young, B. A. Smith, M. E. Davies, and C. B. Leovy, "Mariner 6 Television Pictures: First Report," in *Science*, **165** (1969), 684–690.

For material on Pluto and its discovery, see E. W. Brown, "On a Criterion for the Prediction of an Unknown Planet," in *Monthly Notices of the Royal Astronomical Society*, **92** (1931), 80–101; P. K. Seidelmann, W. J. Klepczynski, R. L. Duncombe, and E. S. Jackson, "Determination of the Mass of Pluto," in *Astronomical Journal*, **76** (1971), 488–492; and C. W. Tombaugh, "Reminiscences of the Discovery of Pluto," in *Sky and Telescope*, **19** (1960), 264–270.

BRIAN G. MARSDEN

LOWER, RICHARD (*b.* Tremeer, near Bodmin, Cornwall, England, 1631; *d.* London, England, 17 January 1691), *medicine, physiology.*

Lower came from an old, affluent family with an interesting history. His grandmother, Mary Nicholls, was related to Anthony Nicholls, a member of the Long Parliament. His mother, Margery Billing, was of Hengar, the largest house in the district; and when Lower married Elizabeth, daughter of John Billing of Hengar, in 1666, the house came into the Lower family. Lower's father, Humphry, inherited Tremeer, the Lower family estate, and bequeathed it to Edward, Richard's older brother. Richard's younger brother, Thomas, a physician, was later imprisoned with the

Quaker leader George Fox for his religious beliefs. Lower was also related to the dramatist Sir William Lower.

Lower was admitted from Westminster School to Christ Church, Oxford, in 1649. He took his B.A. in February 1653 and his M.A. in June 1655. In April 1663 he wrote to Boyle that he had been put out of his place "above a year and a half since for not being in orders," and in June 1665 he took both the B.M. and doctor of physic degrees by accumulation. By this time Lower had spent several years at Oxford in close association with its famous circle of science devotees. He worked particularly closely with Thomas Willis, appointed Sedleian professor of natural philosophy in June 1660, whom he served for many years as research assistant.

In 1666 Lower moved from Oxford to London, where Willis had recently moved, principally to establish a medical practice. He settled at first in Hatton Garden, but during the next decade moved several times, in each case to a more fashionable location. He was admitted candidate of the Royal College of Physicians on 22 December 1671 and fellow on 29 July 1675. After Willis' death in 1675, Lower's successful medical career flourished even more. According to Anthony Wood he was "esteemed the most noted physician in Westminster and London, and no man's name was more cried up at court than his." Lower, having strong Protestant and anti-Popish sentiments, was closely identified with the Whig party, and his later career followed its fortunes. In the 1680's, with the discreditation under Charles II of the Whigs and the ascendance and accession of James II, Lower fell into some disrepute; he lost his court appointment and steadily lost much of his practice. Nevertheless, he carried on for several years, probably spending much of his time in Cornwall, until his death in 1691. In his will he left money to St. Bartholomew's Hospital in London and to the French and Irish Protestant refugees.

Lower was invited to join the Royal Society early in his residence in London, and for a few years he was closely associated with the society and its various scientific activities. After receiving mention several times in the minutes for 1666, Lower himself was "introduced" to the society by Robert Boyle on 2 May 1667. He was formally admitted on 17 October 1667, and in November, after having been considered as early as June, he was invited to take up the post of curator. Lower refused this offer, but on 21 November he was appointed to a committee to audit the society's accounts.

The sorry state into which the society was falling despite Lower's efforts is reflected in an entry in the minutes for 29 June 1668, in which Lower was "desired . . . to make a list of particulars necessary for the making of anatomical experiments." Lower himself dropped from regular participation in the society's affairs by March 1669, probably to attend more fully to his medical practice; in 1678 he formally resigned his fellowship.

During his few, intensely active years with the Royal Society, Lower did much of the work that established his reputation as perhaps the best seventeenth-century English physiologist after Harvey. He was concerned principally with two areas of investigation: transfusion and cardiopulmonary function. His interest in both problems can be traced to his days at Oxford, but the fame of his investigations and many of his most fruitful results owed a great deal to his association with the Royal Society.

Apparently transfusion was attempted at Oxford in the late 1650's. There, according to later accounts, Christopher Wren tried to convey certain medicinal liquors directly into the bloodstream using quills and special bladders. Familiar with these earlier attempts, Lower in 1661 expressed interest in using similar procedures to transmit broth and other nutritive fluids directly into the bloodstream. In a letter to Boyle dated 18 January 1661, Lower expressed his "fancy to try, how long a dog may live without meat, by syringing into a vein a due quantity of good broth" and described his intended procedure as follows: "I shall try it in a dog, and I shall get a tin pipe made, about two inches long, and about the usual bigness of a jugular vein, and hollow, which I may put into the vein. . . ."[1]

By 8 June 1664, Lower was able to write to Boyle in London about a more daring experiment: he intended to "get two dogs of equal bigness [and] let both bleed into the others vein. . . ."[2] As Lower was to explain retrospectively in his *Tractatus de corde* (1669), he was led from the broth experiment to the transfusion attempt by observing how harmoniously the blood of different animals mixed with various injected substances. It was natural to "try if the blood of different animals would not be much more suitable and would mix together without danger or conflict."[3] It is quite possible that Lower was influenced as well by reports of discussions at the Royal Society late in 1663. At one of these, Timothy Clarke had described his method of infusing certain medicinal preparations directly into the veins of dogs, and an unnamed fellow of the society proposed "to let the blood of a lusty dog into the veins of an old one, by the contrivance of two silver pipes fastened to the veins of such two dogs."[4]

With his ideas crystallized, it took Lower only a few months to perfect the requisite experimental technique.

He performed the first successful transfusion at Oxford late in February 1665, transfusing blood "from an artery of one animal into a vein of a second." The Royal Society soon heard of these results, and in early 1666, after several months' interruption due to plague and the London fire, society members were busy making their own investigations into transfusion. In June 1666 John Wallis, who had been present at Lower's successful experiment at Oxford the previous February, reviewed Lower's success; and the society, through Boyle, requested a full account from Lower. This was officially received in September, replicated at the society in November, and printed in *Philosophical Transactions* (December 1666). By mid-1667 Lower had joined the society.

Meanwhile, in Paris, Denis—without proper citation—had appropriated Lower's techniques and applied them to human transfusion. The Royal Society was outraged and Lower, sensitive to his colleagues' concerns, tried and succeeded at human transfusion. On 12 December 1667 the procedure was firmly established in England with its second successful trial, this a public one before a large crowd.

Lower's second major area of physiological investigation was cardiopulmonary function. Again, his interest can be traced to his Oxford days. Already in 1658 Lower and Willis were looking into the fundamental problem from which, when solved, all of Lower's principal results were to derive: the reason for the perceived difference in color between venous and arterial blood.

Willis formulated his own answer to this problem in his *Diatribae duae* (Oxford, 1659), a two-part essay on fermentation and fevers. Willis assumed that the blood, composed of five chemical principles, is normally in a state of gentle fermentation. But when the blood reaches the chambers of the heart the already fermenting fluid effervesces further. As the blood passes through the heart, "its mixture is very much loosned, so that the Spirits, together with the Sulphureous Particles, being somewhat loosned, and as it were inkindled into a flame, leap forth, and are much expanded, and from thence they impart by their deflagration, a heat to the whole."[5]

Lower himself at first accepted this theory of a sudden, energetic enkindling of the blood in the closed chambers of the heart as an explanation for the lighter, more vivid appearance of arterial blood. He made it the basis of an essay written in defense of Willis, the *Diatribae Thomae Willisii . . . de febribus vindicatio adversus Edmundum De Meara* (1665). A few years after writing the *Vindicatio*, however, Lower's own ideas were to change substantially. The changes derived from certain subtle unorthodoxies he

permitted himself in 1665 and, even more, from his positive, fruitful association with the Royal Society, which allowed his doubts to develop into open disagreement with Willis' ideas.

Lower's early departures were evident in a few scattered passages of the *Vindicatio*. Thus, while elaborately defending Willis' theory of an accension of the blood in the heart, Lower nevertheless introduces an idea nowhere evident in the *Diatribae duae*: that the lungs (which were given no clear role by Willis) serve not only to discharge the soot resulting from the "fire" in the heart, but likewise serve to impregnate the blood passing through them with the "nitrous pabulum" of the air.[6] Willis, like Lower after him, had alluded to a "nitrosulphureous ferment implanted in the heart," but only Lower explicitly referred to a pabulum in the lungs that "impregnated" the blood.

Furthermore, in other passages in the *Vindicatio*, Lower refers in detail to the analogies between accension in the heart and air-controlled combustion.[7] He even mentions an experiment in which the heart of a vivisected animal is revived by blowing in air, with the mouth, through a tube into the chyle vessels or vena cava.[8] Finally, in a slightly different context, Lower describes active expulsion of blood from the heart during cardiac systole;[9] Willis, by contrast, had spoken merely of blood being "wheeled about after a constant manner, as it were in a water Engine."[10]

These minor unorthodoxies apparently played on Lower's mind for several years. Then, at the Royal Society, Lower began to collaborate with Hooke, who for some time had been interested in respiratory physiology. Already in 1664 Hooke had tried to determine whether the efficacy of the lungs depended on their motive effect on the blood or on the role they played in admitting air to the body. In 1667 he perfected an experimental technique that allowed him to keep the lungs motionless and inflated, even with the chest cavity fully exposed. Hooke pricked holes in the lungs and blew a continuous stream of air through the motionless lungs of a dog by a bellows arrangement.

In October 1667 Hooke and Lower began to collaborate on cardiopulmonary experiments. Upon Hooke's suggestion, they attempted together to determine the exact effect on the blood of its passage through the lungs; and to accomplish this by altering the normal route, bypassing the lungs, and transmitting blood directly from the pulmonary artery to the aorta through an air-free channel.

Preliminary results from these experimental techniques had an enormous impact on Lower's thinking. He was now able for the first time to observe closely the appearance of the blood, both as it left the right ventricle of the heart and before it entered the lungs, and as it returned from the inflated lungs via the pulmonary vein. Lower could now see clearly that only exposure to the air in the lungs altered the blood's appearance; whereas blood still appeared venous as it left the right ventricle, it was already arterial as it moved from the lungs to the left ventricle. Thus the bright, scarlet color of arterial blood depended on contact with the air and not on effervescence in the heart (which should have occurred as surely in the right as the left ventricle). Lower could also observe closely the continual, rapid, and vigorous pumping action of the heart, which now seemed clearly to be unrelated to a postulated effervescence in the cardiac chambers.

An intense period of reconceptualization and experimentation followed this work at the Royal Society, and led Lower to the publication of his *Tractatus de corde* (London, 1669), which comprised five chapters. The fourth chapter quickly reviews the history of transfusion and presents Lower's principal results; the fifth surveys Lower's thoughts on chyle and its transformation into blood.

The first three chapters of the *De corde* are exclusively concerned with the heart, the blood, respiration, and circulation. Lower begins with detailed descriptions of the muscular anatomy and nerve supply of the heart, comparisons of the fibrous structure of the human heart with that of other animals, and an account of the heart's contractive and expulsive movements. He now denies that there is any nitrosulfureous ferment in the heart and explains that the blood is "too inert to effervesce so violently and suddenly in the Heart or its Vessels."[11] Lower stresses the movement of the blood by the active cardiac systole (an early emphasis of his) and pointedly asks, "If the blood moves through its own power, why does the Heart need to be so fibrous and so well supplied with Nerves?"[12]

Lower also reports experiments he performed to determine the velocity of circulation. In one of these, by taking the average capacity of the left ventricle, counting the number of beats per hour, and estimating the total quantity of blood in the body, he finds that all the blood passes through the heart thirteen times per hour. In another experiment Lower drains almost all the blood from a dog, through the cervical arteries, within three minutes. Both experiments clearly suggest that there can be no profound difference between venous and arterial blood, since overall circulatory velocity is too great to allow drastic transformation.

Finally, Lower comes to a series of experiments on the influence of the air on blood color. He reports that he once held different views on this matter, confessing that he had "relied more . . . on the authority and preconceived opinion of the learned Dr. Willis than my own experience."[13] Acknowledging his indebtedness to Hooke, Lower presents the new experimental basis for his greatly modified thinking. He reports his observation that blood withdrawn from the pulmonary artery "is similar in all respects to venous blood,"[14] and claims that this would not be so if a cardiac effervescence were responsible—as he once believed—for the different appearance of venous and arterial blood. Exposure of the blood to the air is the crucial occurrence, which, he explains, can be further established by blocking of the trachea and noting the still-venous appearance of blood that passes through the air-blocked lungs. This proves definitively that the bright red color of arterial blood is "due to the penetration of particles of air into the blood"; it is the "nitrous spirit of the air" that normally enters the blood in the lungs.

The *Tractatus de corde* was quickly recognized as a major new work on physiology. Warmly reviewed in the *Philosophical Transactions* for 25 March 1669, it won plaudits both in England and abroad and in a short time dramatically changed the thinking of many about the role of the heart and the lungs. Even Willis was deeply impressed. In 1670 Willis published an essay, *De sanguinius accensione*, in which he abandoned his old views for Lower's new ones and applauded "the most learned Doctor Lower" for making him see the light.

Mayow, whose *Tractatus quinque* of 1674 was to represent the next major breakthrough in respiratory physiology, was also greatly influenced. The favorable reception proved enduring, and for many years Lower's *Tractatus de corde* continued to be cited as an important and authoritative work, clearly in the high Harveian tradition of "anatomical experiment." In the next century, too, Lower continued to receive credit. His accomplishments were enthusiastically acknowledged by Senac in his *Traité de la structure de coeur* (Paris, 1749) and by the influential Boerhaave. The *De corde* itself was published in a Leiden edition as late as 1749.

After the *De corde*, Lower published only one minor work on anatomical physiology, the *Dissertatio de origine catarrhi* (London, 1672). Here Lower codified the ideas and experiments he and Willis had performed to show that no passage existed for discharging serous fluids from the cerebral ventricles through the palate and nose; Willis had already reported similar results in chapter twelve of his *Cerebri anatome* (1664), as had Lower himself in the

Tractatus de corde. Other medical works bearing Lower's name appeared in later years, but none of these can be definitively traced to Lower's pen. It seems clear that after the *De corde* Lower's active interest in physiology gave way to a vigorous cultivation of his medical practice, and it was as a physician that he concluded his career.

NOTES

1. *The Works of the Honourable Robert Boyle*, Thomas Birch, ed., V (London, 1744), 518.
2. *Ibid.*, 525–526.
3. Lower, *Tractatus de corde* (London, 1669), 173.
4. Thomas Birch, *The History of the Royal Society*, I (London 1756–1757), 303.
5. Thomas Willis, *The Remaining Medical Works of . . . Dr. Thomas Willis* (London, 1681), 59.
6. *Diatribae Thomae Willisii . . . de febribus vindicatio adversus Edmundum De Meara* (London, 1665), p. 116.
7. *Ibid.*, 117–119.
8. *Ibid.*, 125–126.
9. *Ibid.*, 59.
10. Willis, *Remaining Medical Works*, 64.
11. Lower, *Tractatus de corde*, 62.
12. *Ibid.*, 64.
13. *Ibid.*, 163.
14. *Ibid.*, 164.

BIBLIOGRAPHY

I. ORIGINAL WORKS. Lower's principal works have been referred to above. Two of the medical works that are variously attributed to him are *Bromographia* (Amsterdam, 1669) and *Receipts* (London, 1700). *Diatribae Thomae Willisii . . . de febribus vindicatio adversus Edmundum De Meara* exists only in contemporary Latin eds. *Tractatus de corde* (London, 1669), however, has been reprinted in facs. and translated by K. J. Franklin as vol. IX in R. T. Gunther, *Early Science in Oxford* (Oxford, 1932). *De origine catarrhi* has also been reproduced in facs. and translated, this by Richard Hunter and Ida Macalpine (London, 1963).

Lower also published several minor papers in *Philosophical Transactions.* Among them are "On Making a Dog Draw His Breath Like a Broken-winded Horse," **2** (1667), 544–546; and "An Observation Concerning a Blemish in an Horses Eye . . .," **2** (1667), 613–614.

Many references to Lower's work and opinions can be found in Thomas Birch, *The History of the Royal Society*, 4 vols. (London, 1756–1757), and in A. Rupert and M. B. Hall, eds., *The Correspondence of Henry Olderling* (Madison, Wisc., 1966–   ). Correspondence between Lower and Boyle is found in Thomas Birch, ed., *The Works of the Honourable Robert Boyle*, V (London, 1744), 517–529.

II. SECONDARY LITERATURE. There is no comprehensive study of Richard Lower, but a number of works are of considerable interest and usefulness. Among these are

John F. Fulton, *A Bibliography of Two Oxford Physiologists: Richard Lower (1631–1691), John Mayow (1643–1679)* (Oxford, 1935), which is much more than a bibliography; Francis Gotch, *Two Oxford Physiologists: Richard Lower and John Mayow* (Oxford, 1908); Ebbe C. Hoff and Phebe M. Hoff, "The Life and Times of Richard Lower, Physiologist and Physician," in *Bulletin of the History of Medicine*, **4** (1936), 517–535; and K. J. Franklin, "Biographical Notice," which accompanies his trans. of Lower's *De corde* (see above).

Of great help for particular aspects of Lower's work are Franklin, "Some Textual Changes in Successive Editions of Richard Lower's *Tractatus de corde*," in *Annals of Science*, **4** (1939), 283–294; "The Work of Richard Lower," in *Proceedings of the Royal Society of Medicine*, **25** (1931), 7–12; Leonard G. Wilson, "The Transformation of Ancient Concepts of Respiration in the Seventeenth Century," in *Isis*, **51** (1960), 161–172; and T. S. Patterson, "John Mayow in Contemporary Setting," *ibid.*, **15** (1931), 47–96, 504–546.

Also worth consulting are Michael Foster, *Lectures on the History of Physiology* (Cambridge, 1901); Marjorie Hope Nicolson, *Pepys' Diary and the New Science* (Charlottesville, Va., 1963); Kenneth Dewhurst, "An Oxford Medical Quartet," in *British Medical Journal*, **2** (1963), 857–860; and Hebbel E. Hoff and Roger Guillemin, "The First Experiments on Transfusion in France," in *Journal of the History of Medicine and Allied Sciences*, **18** (1963), 103–124.

THEODORE M. BROWN

LOWITZ, J. T. See **Lovits, Johann Tobias.**

LUBBOCK, SIR JOHN (LORD AVEBURY) (*b.* London, England, 30 April 1834; *d.* Kingsgate Castle, Kent, England, 28 May 1913), *entomology, anthropology, botany.*

Lubbock was the eldest son of a baronet, Sir John William Lubbock. His father was a banker and mathematician who did work on probability and the theory of tides, and was treasurer of the Royal Society. After three years at Eton, young Lubbock was removed from school before he was fifteen and taken into the family bank, where he shortly assumed the responsibilities of an adult partner. Thereafter his education was largely self-directed according to a rigorous schedule, with emphasis upon natural history. He trained himself to shift from one subject to another at short intervals with entire concentration, a habit he retained through life. Of crucial importance for the development of his interests was the presence at Down

House, close by the Lubbock estate in Kent, of Charles Darwin. From the time of his settlement there in 1842, Darwin gave the boy encouragement and direction, beginning a friendship that continued for forty years. In his treatise on barnacles, Darwin utilized Lubbock's talent for drawing, and Lubbock's earliest scientific papers were on zoological specimens from the *Beagle*. His careful work earned the notice and respect of Lyell, T. H. Huxley, Joseph Hooker, and Tyndall, all of whom became his friends. In 1855 Lyell proposed him for the Geological Society. In the same year Lubbock discovered the first fossil remains of a musk-ox to be unearthed in Britain, evidence of a glacial age. Lubbock's account of the methods of reproduction in *Daphnia*, which Darwin submitted to the Royal Society for him, led to his election as a fellow in 1858; three years later he was made a member of the council. A convinced natural selectionist from the beginning, after the release of the Darwin-Wallace papers Lubbock's work in microanatomy, such as his notice of the irregularity in the central ganglion of *Coccus hesperidum*, pointed to the high degree of variation in nature. Despite his youth Lubbock was one of the handful of men whose opinions mattered to Darwin, and he took a prominent part in the controversy that followed the appearance of the *Origin of Species*.

Lubbock first gained an international reputation by his provision of an evolutionary framework for the accumulated archaeological remains bearing on human beginnings. The tools collected from French river gravels by Boucher de Perthes had long indicated an origin for culture antedating the geologically recent past. The final acceptance of this view by leading British men of science in the late 1850's generated an enthusiasm for the reconstruction of man's prehistory. Lubbock had already taken part in the furtherance of Lyell's search for fossil gaps in the geological record. Between 1860 and 1864, he traveled to the Somme Valley and the Dordogne Caves, the Swiss lake village sites, and the tumuli, kitchen middens, and museums of Denmark. He went over the ground with the investigators, studied the finds, and read the reports and literature, even those in Danish.

The series of articles Lubbock wrote aroused wide interest and formed the basis for a pioneer work, *Pre-Historic Times* (1865), that consolidated the data on the life of prehistoric man in Europe and North America. He coined the terms *Neolithic* and *Paleolithic* to distinguish the later and earlier Stone Age periods. Here and in a sequel, *The Origin of Civilisation* (1871), Lubbock identified prehistoric cultures as evolutionary precursors of modern civilization and contended for the independent origination of cultural inventions as against diffusion or borrowing. He saw in a common creative mind for mankind a promise of the general evolutionary movement toward civilization and happiness. Lubbock rejected Bishop Whately's theory of degeneration and categorized savage tribes as comparable to the opossums of the natural world. By studying contemporary primitives he sought clues to the function of ancient implements. The popularity of these books led to their reissue in new editions for over a generation, even after their simplistic evolutionism had become outmoded. But Lubbock never modified these first conclusions.

Anthropology did not interfere with Lubbock's research on insects, and in 1873 the Ray Society published his standard *Monograph on the Collembola and Thysanura*. Beautifully illustrated with his own plates, this book of over two hundred pages separated the springtails from the bristletails on the basis of the ventral tube, and named the new order Collembola. About this time he began the seminal studies in insect behavior that were reported in *Ants, Bees, and Wasps* (1882) and *On the Senses, Instincts, and Intelligence of Animals* (1888). It was not only the normal habits of his subjects that he set out to investigate, but their powers of sensing, learning, and what seemed to be calculated response. For this purpose he devised the "Lubbock nest," as it became known, in which ant colonies are confined in moistened earth between two panes of glass. Stacked in series and attached to a post, these could be lowered to a platform surrounded by a moat and the ants let out for excursions. Previously, ant nests had never been kept under observation for more than several months, and the life-span of an ant was thought to be a year. Lubbock was able to keep some workers alive for as long as seven years, and two queens for twice that time. No one as yet knew how an ant nest started, but Lubbock watched queens of *Myrmica ruginodis* rear larvae and establish a colony. He observed, and described for the first time, that aphid eggs laid in the fall are taken into ant nests over the winter, and in the spring the newly hatched young are transported out to feed on plant shoots. In the nests Lubbock discovered a new mite, *Uropoda formicariae*, and two parasitic dipterons, *Platyphora Lubbocki* and *Phora formicarum*.

While trying to make ants respond to sounds, Lubbock located in their legs a chordontal organ known until then only in Orthoptera, and suggested correctly that it was a sort of hearing instrument. An imaginative and ingenious experimenter, Lubbock introduced specificity into the study of insect behavior by marking individuals with paint for identification, a practice that later became common. He also used obstacles and mazes to test the intelligence of ants, thus anticipating animal psychologists like Kohler.

Lubbock's experiments on insect vision and color sense were of special significance. On a table with movable concentric rings, designed for him by Francis Galton, Lubbock found that some ants were partly influenced in their sense of direction by the angle of the light, a discovery important for homing. By using colored glass and solutions with spectral light, he established that ants and *Daphnia* could not only distinguish colors, but were especially sensitive to ultraviolet light. After tabulating the color preferences of bees, and training them to return to colors associated with honey after the honey was removed, Lubbock concluded that bees could see colors. He did not test them with spectral light, however, to eliminate the possibility that they were attracted merely by different degrees of brightness. With modifications, Karl von Frisch utilized Lubbock's procedures, but it was not until the 1920's that A. Kühn's use of the spectrum delineated the range of color vision in bees and revealed their sensitivity to ultraviolet light.

In his lifetime Lubbock was one of the best-known men in England. He began a long career as a Liberal in Parliament by sponsoring the famous Bank Holidays Act (1871) which established what came to be called St. Lubbock's Days. He went on to sponsor over two dozen other bills, including acts regulating the health professions, the Wild Birds Protection Act (1880), Open Spaces Act (1880), Ancient Monuments Act (1882), and acts requiring the limitation of shop hours and the provision of seats for employees. In 1900 he was made a peer.

He published some twenty-five books, over a hundred scientific papers, and gave lectures on subjects ranging from free trade to the forces that formed the Alps, the hearing of Crustacea, and the pleasures of life. He was never merely a popularizer; his widely read books on the scenery of Switzerland and Britain were also fascinating treatises on geology by an expert. In volumes on British flowers he dealt with the questions of the relation of a flower's parts to each other and to insects.

Essentially, Lubbock was a great public educator, perhaps the foremost of his time. As an exponent of Darwinism, he was as active as Huxley, without his truculence. A vice-chancellor of London University, head of its Extension Society, and president of the Working Men's College, he helped widen educational opportunities and the spread of scientific literacy. An 1887 address to the college on "The Hundred Best Books" had a far-reaching effect on publishing in both England and the United States. Possessed of charm and a conciliatory manner, he helped smooth the proceedings of the many scientific societies he headed at various times. He married twice, the second time to the daughter of Pitt-Rivers the ethnologist. He presided over a large household, and often drafted family members and servants alike to assist and appreciate his always ongoing investigations of nature. Lubbock's mind was not subtle or deep, but he had an organized intelligence and great energy, and he was a magnificent amateur in the old sense. In the world of politics and commerce he was an arch-representative of science; to the intelligent public, during a transition period in intellectual history, he stood for the harmony of experimental truth with idealism and social progress.

BIBLIOGRAPHY

I. ORIGINAL WORKS. An extensive, though not exhaustive, classified bibliography of Lubbock's works appears in Ursula Grant Duff, ed., *The Life-work of Lord Avebury (Sir John Lubbock, 1834–1913)* (London, 1924), but it does not list the numerous revised eds. of his principal books.

II. SECONDARY LITERATURE. The authorized biography is Horace G. Hutchinson's *Life of Sir John Lubbock, Lord Avebury*, 2 vols. (London, 1914). Uncritical and lacking scientific expertise, it is useful for facts and the many letters and memoirs reprinted. Appreciative yet authoritative assessments of Lubbock's contributions in a number of fields, including anthropology, geology, entomology, zoology, and botany, were made by a group of specialists who collaborated on the Grant Duff volume cited above.

Insight into the difficulties Lubbock's anthropology met with in his later years is provided by Andrew Lang, "Lord Avebury on Marriage, Totemism, and Religion," in *Folklore*, **22** (1911), 402–425. Especially valuable for its updating of Lubbock's results in the light of later experimentation and the excerpts it provides from the relevant literature, particularly from W. M. Wheeler on ants and Karl von Frisch on bees, is the reissue of the seventeenth ed. of *Ants, Bees, and Wasps*, edited and annotated by J. G. Myers (London–New York, 1929).

A vigorous defense of Lubbock's scientific achievements and an explanation for their persistent denigration was presented by a zoologist, R. J. Pumphrey, F.R.S., in "The Forgotten Man—Sir John Lubbock, F.R.S.," in *Notes and Records of the Royal Society of London*, **13**, no. 1 (June 1958), 49–58. One aspect of Lubbock's relation to Darwin is treated in Fred Somkin's "The Contributions of Sir John Lubbock, F.R.S. to the *Origin of Species*: Some Annotations to Darwin," *ibid.*, **17**, no. 2 (Dec. 1962), 183–191.

FRED SOMKIN

LUBBOCK, JOHN WILLIAM (*b*. London, England, 26 March 1803; *d*. High Elms, near Farnborough, England, 20 June 1865), *astronomy*.

By profession a banker, Lubbock spent his leisure hours in scientific pursuits. He was among the first to check theory against extensive observations so as to get better predictions of the tides; and for most of his life he worked on the problem of simplifying and extending Laplace's methods for calculating perturbations of lunar and planetary orbits.

Lubbock was named for his father, from whom he inherited (1840) both his mercantile bank (Lubbock & Co.) and his baronetcy. His mother's maiden name was Mary Entwisle. He attended Eton before enrolling in 1821 at Trinity College, Cambridge, where he received a B.A. in 1825 and an M.A. in 1833. In the latter year he married Harriet Hotham; the eldest of their eleven children was the fourth Sir John Lubbock and first Baron Avebury, who wrote many books on natural history.

Lubbock was introduced to Laplace's powerful mathematical techniques during a visit to Paris in 1822, three years before the final volume of the *Mécanique céleste* had appeared. In 1828 Lubbock wrote an article on annuities, applying Laplace's probability theory. By 1831 he was making progress both with predicting the exact position of the moon in the sky and also—thanks to business connections with the chairman of the London Dock Company— with the assembling of many years of water level readings, from which to determine the average time high tide lagged behind the moon (an interval commonly known as the establishment of the port).

For his work on the tides Lubbock received from the Royal Society one of the two medals awarded in 1833; the other went to the geologist Charles Lyell.

Lubbock joined the Royal Astronomical Society in 1828. He became a fellow of the Royal Society in 1829, and served twice as its treasurer and vicepresident (1830–1835, 1838–1847). Rather late in life (1848) he was elected fellow of the Geological Society and contributed to its *Quarterly Journal* in 1849 a suggestion as to how a change in the axis of the earth might have accounted for the redistribution of water and land areas.

BIBLIOGRAPHY

I. ORIGINAL WORKS. Lubbock's first published work, written in 1828, was "On the Calculation of Annuities, and on Some Questions in the Theory of Chances," in *Transactions of the Cambridge Philosophical Society*, **3** (1830), 141–155. His papers on the tides began with "On the Tides on the Coast of Great Britain," in *Philosophical Magazine*,

9 (1831), 333–335; "On the Tides in the Port of London," in *Philosophical Transactions of the Royal Society*, **121** (1831), 379–416; and "Report on the Tides," in *Report of the British Association for the Advancement of Science* (1831–1832), 189–195. His approach to the problem of the tides is summarized in his Bakerian lecture, "On the Tides at the Port of London," in *Philosophical Transactions of the Royal Society*, **126** (1836), 217–266; with an extension, "On the Tides," *ibid*., **127** (1837), 97–140.

"On Change of Climate Resulting From a Change in the Earth's Axis of Rotation" appeared in *Quarterly Journal of the Geological Society of London*, **5** (1849), 4–7. Lubbock's last published paper, "On the Lunar Theory," in *Memoirs of the Royal Astronomical Society*, **30** (1862), 1–53, provides a summary of his work on the motions of the moon, with comparison to the results of other workers.

The Royal Society *Catalogue of Scientific Papers*, IV, 105–106, lists seventy-four articles by Lubbock, one of which was published jointly with William Whewell. He also wrote, with John Drinkwater Bethune, *A Treatise on Probability* (London, 1835) and at least nine other books or pamphlets; see his entry in *Dictionary of National Biography*, XXXIV, 227–228.

II. SECONDARY LITERATURE. Three obituaries appeared: two unsigned, in *Monthly Notices of the Royal Astronomical Society*, **26** (1866), 118–120; and in *Proceedings of the Royal Society*, **15** (1866–1867), xxxii–xxxvii; and one by William John Hamilton, in *Quarterly Journal of the Geological Society of London*, **22** (1866), xxxi–xxxii.

SALLY H. DIEKE

LUBBOCK, RICHARD (*b*. Norwich, England, 1759[?]; *d*. Norwich, 2 September 1808), *chemistry*.

Lubbock's place in the history of chemistry depends solely on his M.D. dissertation (1784), which embodies one of the earliest examples of the rejection of the phlogiston theory in Britain. He was a pupil of Joseph Black, who, according to Lubbock, had long been teaching the phlogiston theory without confidence. Lubbock implies that Black had recently abandoned it, although Black's acceptance of Lavoisier's theory is not generally thought to have occurred as early as 1784. In a letter to Lavoisier in October 1790 Black mentions his original "aversion to the new system" and says that although the approval by older chemists of the new ideas might be prevented by power of habit, "the younger ones will not be influenced by the same power" (see D. McKie, "Antoine Laurent Lavoisier, 1743–1794," in *Notes and Records. Royal Society of London*, **7** [1950], 1–41). Lubbock said that his own theory was partly met by that of Lavoisier but that the latter left some important points unexplained, such as the nature of heat and light.

Little is known of Lubbock's life. He was educated at Norwich Free School and the University of Edinburgh, practiced medicine in Norwich, and was physician at the Norfolk and Norwich Hospital from 1790 to 1808. His younger son, the Reverend Richard Lubbock, wrote a classic work on the natural history of Norfolk.

In his *Dissertatio . . . de principio sorbili*, Lubbock said that it had long been accepted that the air contained a principle which maintained life and which governed calcination, combustion, and other natural processes. It had been given a variety of names—Priestley's "dephlogisticated air" and Lavoisier's "eminently respirable air"—Lubbock favored the term "pure air," which had also been used. According to him it was a compound of an absorbable part (*principium sorbile*) and of *principium aëri proprium*; the latter was the matter of light and heat and was without mass. Metals and combustible substances such as charcoal, sulfur, and phosphorus were true elements: on calcination or combustion they combined with principium sorbile and thereby gained weight, the principium aëri proprium being liberated as heat and light. The variation in the evolution of the latter depended on the extent to which the principium sorbile was removed; as this increased, so the amount of heat manifested increased; if the removal of the principle was extensive, light appeared. Lubbock contended that Lavoisier's theory did not explain why air in which combustion had taken place was vitiated. His idea was that "phlogisticated air"—Lavoisier's "azotic gas" (nitrogen)—was a compound of principium sorbile with a greater proportion of principium aëri proprium than exists in "pure air."

Lubbock's exposition, which was preceded by a critical examination of Stahl's ideas and some prevailing variants of them, was illustrated by numerous experiments. His work was known in Europe: *principe sorbile* is given as a synonym for *oxigène* in Lavoisier's *Méthode de nomenclature chimique* (1787), and extracts from his dissertation were quoted by Christoph Girtanner in an early textbook based on the antiphlogistic system (1792).

BIBLIOGRAPHY

Lubbock's unique work is *Dissertatio physico-chemica, inauguralis, de principio sorbili, sive communi mutationum chemicarum causa, quaestionem, an phlogiston sit substantia, an qualitas, agitans; et alteram ignis theoriam complectens . . .* (Edinburgh, 1784). His ideas are examined by D. McKie and J. R. Partington, in *Annals of Science*, **3** (1938), 356–361, as part of their "Historical Studies on the Phlogiston Theory," *ibid.*, **2** (1937), 361–404; **3** (1938), 1–58, 337–371 (with portrait of Lubbock); **4** (1940), 113–149. See also J. R. Partington, *A History of Chemistry*, III (London, 1962), 489, 627.

E. L. SCOTT

LUCAS, FRANÇOIS-ÉDOUARD-ANATOLE (*b.* Amiens, France, 1842; *d.* Paris, France, 3 October 1891), *number theory, recreational mathematics.*

Educated at the École Normale in Amiens, he was first employed as an assistant at the Paris Observatory. After serving as an artillery officer in the Franco-Prussian War, he became professor of mathematics at the Lycée Saint-Louis and the Lycée Charlemagne, both in Paris. He was an entertaining teacher. He died as a result of a trivial accident at a banquet; a piece of a dropped plate flew up and gashed his cheek, and within a few days he succumbed to erysipelas.

In number theory his research interest centered on primes and factorization. He devised what is essentially the modern method of testing the primality of Mersenne's numbers, his theorem being as follows: The number $M_p = 2^p - 1$, in which p is a prime, is itself prime if and only if $S_{p-1} \equiv 0 \bmod M_p$, where S belongs to the sequence $S_1 = 4$; $S_n = S_{n-1}^2 - 2$. Using this he was able in 1876 to identify $2^{127} - 1$ as a prime.

The first new Mersenne prime discovered in over a century, it is the largest ever to be checked without electronic help. He loved calculating, wrote on the history of mechanical aids to the process, and worked on plans (never realized) for a large-capacity binary-scale computer. He did some highly original work on the arithmetization of the elliptic functions and on Fibonacci sequences, and he claimed to have made substantial progress in the construction of a proof of Fermat's last theorem.

Lucas' many contributions to number theory were balanced by extensive writings on recreational mathematics, and his four-volume book on the subject remains a classic. Perhaps the best-known of the problems he devised is that of the tower of Hanoi, in which n distinctive rings piled on one of three pegs on a board have to be transferred, in peg-to-peg single steps, to one of the other pegs, the final ordering of the rings to be unchanged.

BIBLIOGRAPHY

I. ORIGINAL WORKS. A comprehensive bibliography of 184 items is appended to Duncan Harkin, "On the Mathematical Works of François-Édouard-Anatole Lucas," in *Enseignement mathématique*, 2nd ser., **3** (1957), 276–288.

Only the 1st vol. of Lucas' projected multivolume *Théorie des nombres* (Paris, 1891) was published. See also *Récréations mathématiques*, 4 vols. (Paris, 1891–1894; repr. Paris, 1960).

II. SECONDARY LITERATURE. Lucas' most important contributions to number theory are synopsized in L. E. Dickson, *History of the Theory of Numbers*, 3 vols. (Washington, 1919–1923)—see esp. vol. I, ch. 17. Harkin's article (see above) is also informative in this respect.

NORMAN T. GRIDGEMAN

LUCAS, KEITH (*b*. Greenwich, England, 8 March 1879; *d*. over Salisbury Plain, near Aldershot, England, 5 October 1916), *physiology*.

Lucas was the second son of Francis Robert Lucas, an inventor and engineer who supervised the laying of the early intercontinental submarine telegraph cables and who ultimately became managing director of the Telegraph Construction and Maintenance Company. Under his father's influence, Lucas early displayed great mechanical ingenuity, remarkable manual dexterity, and a deep interest in science and engineering. His mother was the former Katherine Mary Riddle, granddaughter of Edward Riddle and daughter of John Riddle, successive directors of a school for sons of naval officers in Greenwich and both renowned as teachers of navigation and nautical astronomy.

From the Reverend T. Oldham's preparatory school at Blackheath, Lucas went to Rugby School on a classical scholarship in 1893 and then on a minor classical scholarship to Trinity College, Cambridge, where he matriculated in 1898. Lucas had already decided to study science; and he began at once to read for the natural sciences tripos, in part I of which he took a first class in 1901. In keeping with his interests, and despite two full years of support on a classical scholarship, Lucas had as his director of studies at Trinity the noted physiologist Walter Morley Fletcher. In 1901, under the strain of his studies and the death of an old school friend in the Boer War, Lucas suffered a breakdown in his health and left Cambridge for two years. Part of this period he spent in New Zealand, where he carried out a bathymetric survey of a number of lakes.

By the time he returned to Cambridge in the autumn of 1903, Lucas had decided to devote himself to a career in physiological research. He had in fact already devised, at home and on his own, an impressive photographic recording method for tracing the events of muscle contraction. So clearly had he formulated his research interests that he was allowed to forgo the usual routine of organized course work and examinations for part II of the natural sciences tripos and was immediately given a place in the crowded physiological laboratory at Cambridge, initially in a sort of anteroom passageway and later in a small cellar.

In 1904 Lucas won the Gedge Prize and the Walsingham Medal and was elected fellow of Trinity College. He was appointed additional university demonstrator in physiology in 1907 and lecturer in natural science at Trinity College in 1908. In addition to the B.A. degree in 1901, Lucas received the M.A. from Cambridge in 1905 and the D.Sc. in 1911. He was elected fellow of the Royal Society in 1913, having been Croonian lecturer the year before. From 1906 to 1914 Lucas was a director of the Cambridge Scientific Instrument Company. A member of the Trinity College Council, he also helped to plan the new physiological laboratory built at Cambridge in 1914.

Upon the outbreak of World War I, Lucas enlisted and in September 1914 was assigned to the experimental research department of the Royal Aircraft Factory at Farnborough. There he applied his graphical recording methods to an analysis of roll, pitch, and yaw in airplanes. He also helped to design an accurate bombsight and a new magnetic compass which greatly improved aerial navigation and which was granted a War Office secret patent in July 1915. His contributions in this area were recognized in the published report of the Advisory Committee for Aeronautics. In September 1916, after repeated requests, he was allowed to attend the Central Flying School, where he quickly qualified as a pilot. He was killed, while flying solo, in a midair collision. He was survived by three sons and his wife, the former Alys Hubbard, eldest daughter of the Reverend C. E. Hubbard, whom he had married in 1909. After his death, his wife and sons changed their names by deed poll to "Keith-Lucas."

Lucas' career in physiological research was devoted wholly to investigating the properties of nerve and muscle, especially the characteristics in each of waves of excitation (what Lucas called "propagated disturbances"). The dominant and most valuable features of his work in general were clarity, precision, and enormous methodological originality. To the design of physiological instruments he brought the same basic principle that he had already applied at Rugby to the design of a bicycle and an especially admirable microscope:[1] the design itself should ensure the accurate operation of the device even in the face of shoddy worksmanship and wear and tear. On this basis he designed an instrument for the analysis of photographic curves from the capillary electrometer, a method of drawing fine glass tubes of uniform dimensions for the capillary electrometer, and a photographic time marker along the lines of Einthoven's string galvanometer. To reduce the distortion produced by the inertia of recording levers, he used light levers or photographic methods where feasible. So integral to Lucas' achievements were these and other instruments of his own design that he has been described as "essentially an engineer."[2]

In addition to these important methodological contributions, Lucas produced a series of valuable experimental results and established at least one fundamental principle: the "all or none" law for ordinary skeletal muscle. Since the work of Henry P. Bowditch in 1871, it had been known that cardiac muscle follows an "all or none" rule: a given stimulus either evokes the maximum possible contraction, or it evokes no contraction at all; if a cardiac contraction does occur, its strength is independent of the exciting stimulus. Some indirect evidence existed that this principle applied as well to skeletal muscle, as Francis Gotch had explicitly suggested in 1902; but direct support for the suggestion was lacking. This support was provided by Lucas in two papers published in 1905 and 1909.

In the first paper, Lucas showed that when the frog's *cutaneus dorsi* muscle is stimulated directly by electrical currents, the resulting contraction increases in discrete, discontinuous steps as the stimulus is increased. Whether the preparation is the *cutaneus dorsi* muscle as a whole (consisting of 150 to 200 individual muscle fibers) or only a small section of the muscle, these discrete steps are always fewer than the number of individual muscle fibers in the preparation. This result suggested that the individual muscle fibers fall into distinct groups according to their excitability and that each discrete step of increased contraction marks the excitation of an additional fiber or small group of fibers of similar excitability.

In the paper of 1909, Lucas confirmed these earlier results under more normal conditions, for he now evoked contraction not by direct stimulation of the *cutaneus dorsi* muscle but through stimulation of its motor nerve fibers. Persuasive evidence was thus produced that for each skeletal muscle fiber, as for cardiac muscle, contraction (if evoked at all) is maximal regardless of the strength of the exciting stimulus. A stronger stimulus increases contraction in an ordinary many-fibered muscle only because it activates a larger number of the individual constituent fibers; and the "submaximal" contraction of such a muscle is merely the maximal contraction of less than all of its fibers. The absence of submaximal contrac-

tions in the heart is not to be ascribed to any fundamental differences in the functional capacities of skeletal and cardiac muscle cells but, rather, to the fact that cardiac muscle is functionally continuous, its fibers being in connection with one another, while skeletal muscle fibers are separated by their sarcolemma. By 1914 the "all or none" law had been extended to motor nerve fibers by Lucas' most celebrated student, Edgar Douglas Adrian, later a Nobel laureate in physiology or medicine.

In extending to another tissue a property previously established only for cardiac muscle, Lucas followed a course which is at least implicit in most of his work. Upon determining the temperature coefficient for nerve conduction, for example, Lucas pointed out that his mean value of 1.79 for the ten degrees between 8° and 18° C. was similar to values already obtained for muscle conduction, suggesting to him that the conduction process is fundamentally the same in nerve and muscle. In both kinds of tissue, he believed, conduction takes place in two stages: a preliminary local excitatory process at the seat of stimulation, and the subsequent production of a partially independent "propagated disturbance." His attempt to show that the propagated disturbance in muscle is an electric and not a contractile disturbance[3] probably reflects his search for underlying similarities among all excitable tissues.

Similarly motivated was Lucas' comparison of conduction across the myoneural junction, across the A.V. bundle in the heart, and across the synapse in the central nervous system—in all these cases, he argued, impulses pass through a region of diminished conductivity, a "region of decrement."[4] In general, Lucas considered it folly to ascribe special properties to certain kinds of tissue unless and until every attempt had been made to explain the phenomena in terms of known properties common to all excitable tissues. This attitude is evident in his posthumous monograph, *The Conduction of the Nervous Impulse* (1917), in which the phenomena of the peripheral nerves are offered as a guide to processes in the central nervous system.

With respect to the refractory period, inhibition, and the summation of stimuli, Lucas conceived of them in similar terms and attributed them to similar causes, whether they took place in muscle tissue, peripheral nerves, or the central nervous system. In all excitable tissues, he believed, inhibition results when successive stimuli arrive too frequently for the tissue to recover from the impaired conductivity of the refractory period; summation, on the other hand, results when successive stimuli are so timed as to coincide with a temporary postrecovery phase of supernormal excitability and conductivity. This theory of summation, developed by Lucas in association with Adrian, differed essentially from the prevailing theory of Max Verworn and F. W. Fröhlich.

In addition to the "all or none" law and the Lucas-Adrian theory of summation, Lucas contributed to the physicochemical theory of excitation, although his role in this area was more that of an effective and suggestive critic than of a creative pioneer. His departure point here was Walther Hermann Nernst's influential theory of the local excitatory process, according to which the threshold of excitation is reached when a certain difference of ionic concentration is produced at a semipermeable membrane contained in the excitable tissue. Drawing in part on the work of A. V. Hill, another young Cambridge physiologist and future Nobel laureate, Lucas argued that Nernst's theory, properly conceived and appropriately modified, could account for virtually all the phenomena of local excitation. In his Croonian lecture of 1912, Lucas emphasized in typical fashion that what difficulties the theory did present "seem to dovetail into one another, being probably expressions of a common property of the tissues."[5]

Lucas' last research, published posthumously, dealt with the neuromuscular physiology of the crayfish. Besides discovering that the crayfish claw is innervated by two sets of nerve fibers—one responsible for the slow, prolonged contraction of the claw and the other for a brief twitch—Lucas also found that the phase of supernormal excitability is much more pronounced in the crayfish than in the frog, a circumstance that enabled him to produce further support for the Lucas-Adrian theory of summation.[6] But, as Adrian has suggested,[7] the choice of the crayfish as an experimental animal may reflect a shift of emphasis in Lucas' thought far more significant than any of these immediate results. It may be that Lucas had decided to move explicitly and actively in the direction of comparative and evolutionary physiology, a deep and long-standing interest occasionally evident even during his earlier concentration on the frog's neuromuscular tissue.

Almost from the beginning of his career Lucas had noticed that different excitable tissues do possess a few fundamentally different properties despite all attempts to emphasize their similarities. In particular, he found that the value of optimal exciting stimuli varies for different tissues in the same animal and for the same excitable tissues in different animals. So persistent, distinct, and quantifiable are these differences that Lucas was led to postulate the existence of three distinct "excitable substances." Each of these substances was associated with a particular kind of tissue—one with muscle, one with nerve, and one with a hypothetical myoneural "junctional tissue"—and each responded differently to the same exciting currents, especially those of short duration. Moreover, for any one of these excitable substances, the optimal stimulus differed in different animals. In attaching the term "substances" to these characteristic differences in the excitability of different tissues, Lucas was probably influenced by the theory of "receptive substances" then being developed by John Langley, professor of physiology at Cambridge. Certainly Langley had helped to convince Lucas that the region between nerve and muscle contains something whose physiological properties differ markedly from those of ordinary nerve and muscle.[8] That Lucas supposed this something to be a special kind of tissue, rather than a chemical substance, reminds us forcefully that his work preceded the general adoption of the humoral (or chemical) theory of nervous transmission.

In any case, the concept of "excitable substances" was for Lucas only one of the implications to be drawn from the existence of fundamental differences in the excitability of different tissues. From another point of view, even these very basic differences could be referred to a common principle, for they represented "a point of obvious interest in the evolutionary history of the excitable tissues."[9] According to Adrian, Lucas developed his interest in the evolution of function while studying zoology at Cambridge and, under the impulse of this interest, "gave a course of lectures in the Zoology department on the comparative physiology of muscle."[10] An even more direct expression of this interest is provided in a two-part paper of 1909 on the evolution of function. In this paper Lucas both deplores and seeks to explain the lack of interaction between evolutionary concepts and physiological research. His explanation is historical, tracing the separation between function and evolution to the famous debate in the 1820's between Georges Cuvier and Geoffroy Saint-Hilaire. Under Geoffroy's influence, Lucas argues, physiology was excluded from the problem of animal classification and thereby lost the impetus to become a properly comparative and evolutionary science. In advocating a reunion of physiology and evolutionary concepts, Lucas emphasized that "the primary problem of comparative physiology—a problem whose investigation is wholly necessary for the understanding of the evolutionary process . . . [is] the question to what extent and along what lines the functional capabilities of animal cells have been changed in the course of evolution."[11] Lucas' premature death prevents us from knowing to what extent, and with what success, he might have pursued this line of work. As it is, his work stands as a monument of clarity and precision in that era of neurophysiology which preceded the adoption of the chemical theory of nervous transmission and the development of important new methods of amplifying bioelectrical activity.[12]

NOTES

1. About 1925, Lucas' microscope, an unorthodox arrangement with differential screws, was placed among the exhibits of the South Kensington Science Museum. See Col. F. C. Temple, "At Rugby," in *Keith Lucas*, p. 48, *n.* 1.
2. See H. H. Turner, "Ancestry," *ibid.*, p. 12.
3. "On the Relation Between the Electric Disturbance in Muscle and the Propagation of the Excited State," in *Journal of Physiology*, 39 (1909), 207–227, esp. 208–210.
4. *The Conduction of the Nervous Impulse*, pp. 68–73.
5. "Croonian Lecture," p. 516.
6. "On Summation of Propagated Disturbances in the Claw of Astacus, and on the Double Neuro-Muscular System of the Adductor," in *Journal of Physiology*, 51 (1917), 1–35.
7. See E. D. Adrian, "Cambridge 1904–1914," in *Keith Lucas*, pp. 105–106.
8. *The Conduction of the Nervous Impulse*, pp. 67–68.
9. "Croonian Lecture," p. 517.
10. Adrian, *Keith Lucas*, p. 105.
11. "The Evolution of Animal Function," pt. II, p. 325.
12. On the importance of the new amplifying methods, see J[oseph] B[arcroft], "Keith Lucas," in *Nature*, 134 (1934), 475.

BIBLIOGRAPHY

I. ORIGINAL WORKS. A complete bibliography of Lucas' publications is given in *Keith Lucas* (see below), pp. 129–131. His posthumous monograph, *The Conduction of the Nervous Impulse* (London, 1917), was based on the Page May memorial lectures, delivered by Lucas at University College, London, in 1914. Revised for publication by E. D. Adrian, the monograph emphasizes the work of Lucas and his students, especially Adrian. In addition to this monograph, Lucas published 32 papers, nearly all of them in *Journal of Physiology*. For insight into his general approach and guiding principles, the most valuable are "The Evolution of Animal Function," in *Science Progress*, pt. I, no. 11 (1909), 472–483; pt. II, no. 14 (1909), 321–331; and "Croonian Lecture: The Process of Excitation in Nerve and Muscle," in *Proceedings of the Royal Society*, 85B (1912), 495–524.

Lucas established the "all or none" law for skeletal muscle in "On the Gradation of Activity in a Skeletal Muscle Fibre," in *Journal of Physiology*, 33 (1905), 125–137; and "The 'All-or-None' Contraction of the Amphibian Skeletal Muscle Fibre," *ibid.*, 38 (1909), 113–133. Other important papers by Lucas include those cited in notes 3 and 6; "The Excitable Substances of Amphibian Muscle," in *Journal of Physiology*, 36 (1907), 113–135; "The Temperature Coefficient of the Rate of Conduction in Nerve," *ibid.*, 37 (1908), 112–121; "On the Transference of the Propagated Disturbance From Nerve to Muscle With Special Reference to the Apparent Inhibition

Described by Wedensky," *ibid.*, 43 (1911), 46–90; and "On the Summation of Propagated Disturbances in Nerve and Muscle," *ibid.*, 44 (1912), 68–124, written with E. D. Adrian.

II. SECONDARY LITERATURE. The basic source for Lucas' life is *Keith Lucas* (Cambridge, 1934), a series of sketches by men who knew Lucas well at various stages of his life. Written in 1916, when Walter Fletcher planned to write a memoir of Lucas, these sketches were finally published in their original form after Fletcher's death. The sketches, and their authors, are as follows: H. H. Turner, "Ancestry" and "Earliest Years"; Col. F. C. Temple, "At Rugby"; Sir Walter Fletcher, "Undergraduate Days" and "Return to Cambridge"; G. L. Hodgkin, "New Zealand"; E. D. Adrian, "Cambridge 1904–1914"; and Col. Mervyn O'Gorman, Bertram Hopkinson, and Maj. R. H. Mayo, "Wartime." For an evaluation of Lucas as scientist, the chapters by Fletcher and Adrian are the most valuable.

For other sketches of Lucas' life and work, see Horace Darwin and W. M. Bayliss, "Keith Lucas," in *Proceedings of the Royal Society*, 90B (1917–1919), xxxi–xlii; C[harles] S. S[herrington], "Keith Lucas," in *Dictionary of National Biography*, supp. 1912–1921, p. 347; and John Langley, "Keith Lucas," in *Nature*, 98 (1916), 109. For a very brief attempt to place Lucas' work in historical perspective, with excerpts from his writings, see Edwin Clarke and C. D. O'Malley, *The Human Brain and Spinal Cord: A Historical Study Illustrated by Writings From Antiquity to the Twentieth Century* (Berkeley, 1968), pp. 218–221.

GERALD L. GEISON

LUCIANI, LUIGI (*b.* Ascoli Piceno, Italy, 23 November 1840; *d.* Rome, Italy, 23 June 1919), *physiology*.

Luciani was the son of Serafino Luciani and Aurora Vecchi. In 1860 he completed secondary studies in Ascoli Piceno and then—after a period spent in independently pursuing politics, literature, and philosophy—in 1862 began to study medicine at the University of Bologna. He also studied in Naples for a time, returning to Bologna to graduate in 1868. Following his graduation he remained at the university to work in the physiology laboratory directed by Luigi Vella.

Luciani spent March 1872 to November 1873 in Leipzig, at the physiological institute directed by Carl Ludwig. From that time he regarded Ludwig as his real master and this period of residence in Germany as the main epoch of his scientific life. It did, in fact, leave a deep imprint on his mind. Returning to Bologna Luciani became a lecturer in general pathology; after teaching this subject at Bologna (1873–1874) and Parma (1875–1880), he became professor of physiology in Siena (1880–1882), Florence (1882–1893), and finally Rome (1893–1917), where he died, as professor emeritus, of a urinary disease. Luciani was a Senator of the Kingdom and a member of Italian and foreign academies. He was an excellent teacher (many of his pupils rose to university chairs), a man of vast general and philosophical culture, and an able experimenter.

Luciani not only investigated all phases of physiology—general, human, comparative, and linguistic—but also conducted research in many other fields. (He made observations on silkworms, studied experimental phonetics, and took up the theory of self-intoxication as an effect of experimental removal of the thyroid-parathyroid complex in animals, for example.) His treatise *Fisiologia dell'uomo* went through a number of editions in several languages.

Luciani had made a study of the activity of the cardiac diastole in 1871, before going to Ludwig's laboratory. Once there he took up the work of H. F. Stannius and carried out experimental research on the genesis of the automatic activity of the heart (that is, of the periodic cardiac rhythm, now known as Luciani's phenomenon). To this end he used a graphic method, obtaining tracings of three distinct, characteristic phenomena (access, periodic rhythm, and crisis) which can be interpreted as three different phases of cardiac activity prior to its exhaustion. Luciani subsequently took up the related question of the automatic activity of the respiratory centers. He then carried out studies on cerebral localizations; made contributions to the doctrine of the cortical pathogenesis of epilepsy (1878); performed experimental extirpations of the various regions connected with the sensory functions; and did research on the mixed sensory and motor nature of the cortical excitation.

Luciani also carried out significant research on the physiology of fasting, in which he determined the various changes that, in man, the great organic functions undergo. On the basis of his observations he was able to distinguish three stages in fasting—an initial, or hunger, period; a period of physiological inanition; and a final period of morbid inanition or crisis.

Luciani's most important scientific work, however, was his research on the physiology of the cerebellum (1891). Through skillful vivisection, he succeeded in experimentally removing the cerebellum in the dog and the monkey, thereby making a fundamental contribution to the development of knowledge of the nervous system—and, in fact, illuminating the peculiar function of the cerebellum within the framework of the whole nervous system.

Luciani held that the multiform symptomatology consequent upon decerebellation is a series of discrete phenomena, and distinguished among three clinical stages following decerebellation. The first is characterized by the presence of dynamic signs, the second by motor deficiencies, and the third by compensatory phenomena. The limits between the various stages are not, however, sharply defined. He considered cerebellar ataxy to be based on the triad—atonia, asthenia, astasia—now named for him. Clinical observation largely confirmed this triad as valid in human physiopathology. Luciani also asserted that atonia and asthenia are constant components of cerebellar deficiency in the experimental animal.

BIBLIOGRAPHY

I. ORIGINAL WORKS. Luciani published about seventy works, some of them written with collaborators, which appeared in both Italian and foreign journals, or as separate publications, between 1864 and 1917. Baglioni, cited below, provides a complete list. See also Luciani's posthumously published "Cenni autobiografici," in *Archivio di fisiologia*, **19** (1921), 319–349.

II. SECONDARY LITERATURE. On Luciani's life and work, see esp. Silvestro Baglioni, "Luigi Luciani," in Aldo Mieli, ed., *Gli scienziati italiani dall'inizio del medio evo ai giorni nostri*, I (Rome, 1921), 336–343, with a bibliography of Luciani's publications, works published on the occasion of jubilees, and literature on Luciani. See also Paolo Crepax, "The First Italian Contributions to the Study of Cerebellar Functions and the Work of Luigi Luciani. II. Luigi Luciani," in Luigi Belloni, ed., *Essay on the History of Italian Neurology* (Milan, 1963), 225–236, with bibliography.

BRUNO ZANOBIO
GIANLUIGI PORTA

LUCRETIUS (*b.* Italy, *ca.* 95 B.C.; *d. ca.* 55 B.C.), *natural philosophy.*

Lucretius followed the Epicurean maxim "Live unnoticed" so well that almost nothing is known for certain about him. His "poemata" were known to Cicero and his brother in 54 B.C.[1] St. Jerome reports that he was born in 94 (or 93 or 96, according to other manuscripts), that he was driven mad by an aphrodisiac, that in the intervals between fits of madness he wrote several books, which Cicero afterwards edited or corrected (*emendavit*), and that he took his own life at the age of forty-four.[2] In the life of Vergil attributed to Donatus, it is said that Lucretius died on the same day that Vergil took the *toga virilis*, but the date of this event is stated ambiguously and may be either 55 or 53.

Lucretius was probably a Roman, and probably of aristocratic family, although other views have been advanced. His only work, the poem *De rerum natura*, shows familiarity with Roman life and with Roman literature. It is written for "Memmius," probably C. Memmius, a Roman aristocrat who was praetor in 58 B.C. and later governor of Bithynia. The poem is written in Latin hexameters and divided by the poet into six "books." The title itself is a translation of Περὶ φύσεως, the name of many Greek works of natural philosophy, including a hexameter poem by Empedocles and a long prose treatise by Epicurus, of which only mutilated fragments survive. There is some indication that the poem was not finished—there are repetitious passages (although some may be deliberate), some books are more polished than others, and the end of book VI does not seem to be the intended end of the whole poem.

Books I and II contain an exposition of the elements of the atomic theory. Books III and IV are about the soul. Book V, which is the longest, describes the origin of the cosmos and the natural growth of living creatures and of civilization. Book VI is on sundry natural phenomena of the sky and earth.

The core of Epicurean natural philosophy is given in books I, II, and V, and there are signs that these were the first books in order of composition. There is some correspondence between the order and proportion of these three books and Epicurus' outline of the subject in the extant *Letter to Herodotus*. In the absence of Epicurus' major work, *On Nature*, it is impossible to say how closely Lucretius follows him, but there is perhaps little or nothing in the natural philosophy of Lucretius that was not in that of Epicurus: The poem shows astonishingly little consciousness of such post-Epicurean philosophies as Stoicism. The Italian imagery and the animadversions on Roman life and morality are no doubt Lucretius' own.

The existence of this long poem on the Epicurean world picture is surprising in itself. The extant work of Epicurus shows a prosaic mind; and the rather impoverished utilitarianism that he taught gives little obvious encouragement to a poet, although there is evidence that Epicureans were interested in poetry and music in the fragments of work by Lucretius' contemporary Philodemus. But for all one knows, it was lonely poetic genius that produced this poem—one of the greatest in the Latin language.

If one compares Lucretius' poem with the extant writings of Epicurus and with the general picture of Epicurus' philosophy given by ancient critics, certain changes of emphasis are noticeable. Lucretius devoted two whole books, set in the middle of the exposition of the atomic cosmology, to the structure and functions of the soul—a much higher proportion than in

Epicurus' *Letter to Herodotus*. Theory of knowledge or "canonic" received little attention from Lucretius. Moreover, the moral lessons, although they are certainly not omitted, occur mainly in the introductions to each book, or in the form of satire on Roman life; there is little preaching in the manner of Epicurus' *Letter to Menoeceus*. For all these differences, the *De rerum natura* remains purely Epicurean in that the acknowledged motive is not disinterested scientific curiosity, but peace of mind.

Lucretius' atomic theory can be understood best by comparing it with the world picture of Plato and Aristotle. In contrast with the finite, single world of Platonic and Aristotelian theory, later adopted by Christian philosophers, the atomists argued that the universe is infinitely large and contains an unlimited number of *cosmoi*, past, present, and future.[3] The single Aristotelian cosmos was without beginning or end in time; there was thus no problem for Aristotelians about the origin of its parts and of their order. The atomic theory, on the other hand, was committed to explaining the origin of everything in the world. Atoms and void were ungenerated and indestructible, but the earth, sea, air, and stars were compounds that came into being at a particular time; their origin had to be explained.

Plato and Aristotle preferred teleological explanations in their natural philosophies. Plato's *Timaeus* offers some grounds for this preference in the notion that the cosmos was created by an intelligent craftsman; the Christian world picture was similar in this respect. Aristotle's eternal cosmos had no creator; the evidence of order and design showed that the cosmos is an ordered whole, but did not point to a designer. Epicurean atomism rejected this teleology, and sought to explain everything by mechanical causes.[4] It was therefore necessary to find plausible explanations for apparently purposive or highly ordered phenomena, and some of Lucretius' most earnest arguments were devoted to this end. The hypothesis of the infinity of the universe was a vital premise in these arguments: in infinite time an infinite supply of atoms moving in infinite space will produce everything that atoms can possibly produce by their combinations.[5]

The theory held that all atoms are too small to be perceived individually. They are all made of the same material, and have no properties other than shape, size, and weight; their weight is the cause of their natural motion downward through the void. This motion could be interrupted by two causes: an unexplained swerve (*clinamen*)—postulated by Epicurus to explain the formation of compounds and to free the movements of the soul from "fate"—and collisions with other atoms.[6] The perceptible qualities of compounds were explained by relating them to atomic shapes and to the proportion of void in the compound. Atoms in compounds move continually, with very frequent collisions in dense compounds, but more freely in compounds containing a greater proportion of void.[7]

Lucretius presented a simple causal theory of perception: all compounds throw off "films" of atoms (*simulacra*) from their surfaces, and these somehow mark their pattern on the soul atoms by direct contact.[8] The soul itself is a mixture of atoms of four kinds—something like heat, something like *pneuma*, something like air, and a fourth unnamed kind.[9] All the soul atoms are highly mobile, but they are not themselves alive; like other atoms they possess no properties other than shape, size, and weight.[10] At death they simply disperse into the air (the theory so confidently rebutted in Plato's *Phaedo*, 70a ff.).[11]

Book V of Lucretius' poem puts the elements of the atomic theory into action, so to speak, to show how the cosmos and all things in it originated from atoms moving in the void, without any divine plan or direction. First the world masses were formed, then the earth began to grow vegetation spontaneously, and finally animal species also emerged from the earth. Once having come from earth, a species survived if it were so adapted as to nourish and reproduce itself; otherwise it simply died out as soon as the earth, growing old, ceased to be spontaneously productive. (The theory thus includes the origin of species and the survival of the fittest, but not the evolution of the species.) It was this account of the natural origin of everything, denying Providence and divine creation, that, along with the denial of the survival of the soul, most antagonized Christian philosophers.[12]

The fatal weakness of the ancient atomic theory, considered as a framework on which to build explanations of natural phenomena, was that it could not offer any laws describing the elementary interactions of atoms. The whole theory depended on the effects of shape, size, and weight of atoms when they collided with each other; but the mechanics of the theory relied on simple intuitions and analogies, such as the vague principle of "like to like" taken over from Democritus. In the ancient world the teleological explanation adopted by Platonists, Aristotelians, and Stoics was clearly more satisfying, especially in biology.

During the early part of the Christian era, Lucretius was first attacked for denying Providence, then, later, forgotten except by grammarians and lexicographers. His poem may have been known in Padua in the thirteenth century,[13] but it was Gian Francesco Poggio's rediscovery of a manuscript early in the fifteenth century that began the great revival of interest in his work. Both the anti-Aristotelian cosmology and the beauty of Lucretius' poetry attracted writers of the Italian Renaissance. Ficino studied him, but rejected his doctrines. Bruno found support in Lucretius' doctrine of the infinite universe and plurality of worlds, and wrote Latin poems in imitation of him. With the full revival of atomism in Western Europe, especially as manifested by Gassendi, it became harder to distinguish the influence of Lucretius from that of Democritus, who was known mainly through Aristotle's polemics, and from that of Epicurus.

NOTES

1. Cicero, *Ad Q. Fratrem*, 2, 9, 3.
2. St. Jerome, on Eusebius' *Chronicle*, 94.
3. *De rerum natura*, I, 951–1082; II, 1023–1089.
4. *Ibid.*, IV, 822–876; V, 110–234.
5. *Ibid.*, I, 1021–1051; II, 1058–1063; V, 419–431.
6. *Ibid.*, II, 62–293.
7. *Ibid.*, II, 332–521; 730–864.
8. *Ibid.*, IV, 26–857.
9. *Ibid.*, III, 177–369.
10. *Ibid.*, II, 865–1022.
11. *Ibid.*, III, 417–829.
12. E.g., Lactantius, *De ira dei*, 10.
13. Billanovich, "Veterum vestigia vatum."

BIBLIOGRAPHY

I. ORIGINAL WORKS. The *editio princeps* of *De rerum natura* was that of T. Ferrandus (Brescia, 1473). The best modern English ed. is that of C. Bailey (Oxford, 1947, repr. with corrections, 1949), although the commentary is weak on philosophical matters. Other particularly interesting eds. are those of H. A. J. Munro (Cambridge, 1864) and C. Giussani (Milan, 1896–1898). There is a useful commentary by A. Ernout and L. Robin (Paris, 1925–1926). A reliable but dull English trans. in prose is that of R. E. Latham (Harmondsworth, 1951); a more exciting one, in verse, is by Rolfe Humphries, deplorably entitled *Lucretius: The Way Things Are* (Bloomington, Ind., 1968).

II. SECONDARY LITERATURE. E. Bignone, *Storia della letteratura Latina*, II (Florence, 1945), 456–462; and C. Bailey and D. E. W. Wormell in M. Platnauer, ed., *Fifty Years (and Twelve) of Classical Scholarship* (Oxford, 1968) contain good secondary bibliographies.

On Lucretius as a natural philosopher see V. E. Alfieri, *Atomos Idea* (Florence, 1953); Anne Amory, "*Obscura de re lucida carmina*: Science and Poetry in *De Rerum Natura*," in *Yale Classical Studies*, **21** (1969), 145–168; C. Bailey, *The Greek Atomists and Epicurus* (Oxford, 1928; repr. New York, 1964); and E. Bignone, cited above. Also see G. Billanovich, "Veterum vestigia vatum," in *Italia Medioevale e Umanistica*, **1** (1958), 155–243; P. Boyancè, *Lucrèce et l'Épicurisme* (Paris, 1963); P. De Lacy, "Limit and Variation in the Epicurean Philosophy," in *Phoenix*, **23** (1969), 104–113; and D. R. Dudley, ed., *Lucretius*

(London, 1965; seven essays by different authors). B. Farrington's *Science and Politics in the Ancient World* (London, 1935) was reviewed by A. Momigliano in *Journal of Roman Studies* (1941), 149 ff.

Other studies include D. J. Furley, "Lucretius and the Stoics," in *Bulletin of the Institute of Classical Studies*, **13** (1966), 13–33; and "Variations on Themes From Empedocles in Lucretius' Proem," *ibid.*, **17** (1970), 55–64; G. D. Hadzits, *Lucretius and His Influence* (New York, 1935); Gerhard Müller, *Die Darstellung der Kinetik bei Lukrez* (Berlin, 1959); G. Santayana, *Three Philosophical Poets: Lucretius, Dante and Goethe* (Cambridge, 1910); F. Solmsen, "Epicurus and Cosmological Heresies," in *American Journal of Philology*, **62** (1951), 1 ff.; "Epicurus on the Growth and Decline of the Cosmos," *ibid.*, **64** (1953), 34 ff.; and W. Spoerri, *Späthellenistische Berichte über Welt, Kultur und Götter* (Basel, 1959).

DAVID J. FURLEY

LUDENDORFF, F. W. HANS (*b*. Thunow, near Koszalin, Germany, 26 May 1873; *d*. Potsdam, Germany, 26 June 1941), *astronomy*.

Ludendorff was the youngest son of Wilhelm Ludendorff, a farmer, and his wife, the former Clara von Tempelhof, a descendant of the old Prussian military family. After an elementary education at home from a tutor, Ludendorff attended the Falk Realgymnasium in Berlin, then he qualified for admission to the University of Berlin in 1892. He studied astronomy, mathematics, and physics and received the Ph.D. in 1897. His main teachers were Förster and Bauschinger. After a year at the Hamburg observatory under Rümcker, Ludendorff joined the astrophysical observatory at Potsdam in 1898 and remained there until his retirement in 1939. In 1905 he became observer, and in 1915, chief observer; in 1921–1939 he was director of the famous institute. Ludendorff was elected a member of the Preussische Akademie der Wissenschaften at Berlin in 1921, a position that carried with it the title of professor and the right to lecture at the University of Berlin.

During his student years, at Hamburg, and early in his stay at Potsdam, Ludendorff was active in both theoretical and measurement astronomy. In 1899 the Potsdam part of the *Photographische Himmelskarte* was completed. Ludendorff assisted in this work and also in the evaluation of the plates until 1900. However, from 1901 to 1921 he worked only in spectrography, to some extent with Eberhard. After becoming director of the observatory, Ludendorff could no longer spend the nights observing and gave up that work. At the beginning of his spectroscopic studies Ludendorff investigated the radial velocities of many stars. He later determined the orbits of spectroscopic

binaries, calculated their masses, and regularly published catalogs of their orbital elements. Thus he found that the masses of the B stars are three times greater than the masses of the stars of classes A–K. He was also occupied with the statistics of spectroscopic binaries and classified helium stars. Attempting to treat the δ Cephei and ζ Geminorum variables as binaries, Ludendorff found in 1913 that they could not be double stars. Subsequently he investigated the relationship of these stars and of the planetary nebulae to the helium stars, problems which led him more and more to variable star investigations. Among Ludendorff's spectroscopic work his measurements of radial velocities of the Ursa Major group, especially of star ϵ, should be mentioned.

The last two decades of Ludendorff's life were devoted to the variable stars and to writing. In particular he investigated ϵ Aurigae, R Coronae Borealis, and such long-period variables as o Ceti (Mira). Here he did not carry out observations but did critical sifting. He also proposed a new classification of variable stars. With G. Eberhard and A. Kohlschütter he edited the *Handbuch für Astrophysik*, writing parts of volumes VI and VII. He also helped to revise some popular astronomy books.

From the time of a visit to Mexico to observe a solar eclipse in 1923—he observed the solar corona, photometering its spectrum—and to Bolivia, where he erected a branch observatory for the spectrographic *Durchmusterung* of the southern sky in 1926, Ludendorff was interested in the astronomical knowledge of the older American civilizations, especially of the Mayans. He passionately investigated various Mayan inscriptions, relating them to conspicuous constellations long before the Christian era.

From 1933 to 1939 Ludendorff was president of the Astronomische Gesellschaft and presided over three of its congresses. He was also a member of many scientific societies, including the Royal Astronomical Society.

Ludendorff was the youngest brother of General Erich Ludendorff, well-known for his service during World War I and later for his extremist political ideas, of which Hans never approved. Hans Ludendorff served for only a short time as military meteorologist, and though a lance-corporal, he sometimes dined with Hindenburg and his brother Erich. In 1907 Ludendorff married Käthe Schallehn; they had two sons and one daughter.

BIBLIOGRAPHY

Ludendorff's writings include *Die Jupiter-Störungen der kleinen Planeten vom Hecuba-Typus* (Berlin, 1896), his dissertation; "Untersuchungen über die Kopien des Gitters Gautier No. 42 und über Schichtverzerrungen auf photographische Platten," in *Publikationen des Astrophysikalischen Observatoriums zu Potsdam*, **49**, pt. 15 (1903); "Der grosse Sternhaufen im Hercules Messier 13," *ibid.*, **50**, pt. 15 (1905); "Der Veränderliche Stern R Coronae Borealis," *ibid.*, **57**, pt. 19 (1908); "Erweitertes System des Grossen Bären," in *Astronomische Nachrichten*, **180** (1908), 183; "Verzeichn. d. Bahnelem. spektroskop. Doppelsterne," in *Vierteljahrschrift der Astronomische Gesellschaft*, **45–50, 62** (1910–1915, 1927); "Über die Bezieh. d. verschied. Klass. Veränderl. Sterne," in *Seeliger Festschrift* (Berlin, 1924), pp. 89–93; "Radialgesch. v. ε Aurigae," in *Sitzungsberichte der Preussischen Akademie der Wissenschaften zu Berlin* (1924), 49–69; "Spektroskop. Untersuchungen über d. Sonnenkorona," *ibid.* (1925), 83–113; "Über d. Abhängigkeit d. Form d. Sonnenkorona v. d. Sonnenfleckenhäufigkeit," *ibid.* (1928), 185–214; 13 papers with the general title, "Untersuchungen zur Astronomie der Maya," *ibid.* (1930–1937); and "Über d. Lichtkurven d. Mira-Sterne," *ibid.* (1932), 291–325.

In addition, Ludendorff was editor of *Handbuch der Astrophysik* from 1920 to 1930.

A biography is P. Guthnik, "Hans Ludendorff," in *Vierteljahrschrift der Astronomischen Gesellschaft*, **77** (1942).

H. Christ. Freiesleben

LUDWIG, CARL FRIEDRICH WILHELM (*b.* Witzenhausen, Germany, 29 December 1816; *d.* Leipzig, Germany, 27 April 1895), *physiology.*

Ludwig's father, Friedrich Ludwig, was a cavalry officer during the Napoleonic wars, who in 1816 retired from his military post and entered the civil service of the Electorate of Hessen as a *Landrezeptor* at Witzenhausen; he was promoted to *Rentmeister* in 1821, and in 1825 moved to Hanau. Ludwig completed his schooling at the Hanau Gymnasium in 1834, then enrolled as a medical student at the University of Marburg, where he was a stormy petrel among his fellow-students. (A deep scar on his upper lip bore witness in later years to his youthful turbulence and dueling.) He was compelled to leave the university because of conflicts with its authorities, possibly a result of his political activities. After studying at Erlangen and at the surgical school in Bamberg, he was allowed to return to Marburg. He received his medical degree in 1840 and the following year became prosector of anatomy under his friend Ludwig Fick. In 1842 he obtained the *venia legendi*, the right to teach in the medical faculty, with a dissertation on the mechanism of renal function.

In 1846 Ludwig was appointed associate professor (extraordinarius) at Marburg, where he continued his teaching and research until 1849, when he received an appointment as professor of anatomy and physiology at Zurich. Although most of his time was taken up with dissections and lectures, he continued the investigations of the physiology of secretion that he had initiated earlier, and showed that the secretion of the salivary glands is dependent on nerve stimulation and not on the blood supply (1850). During this time he was also working on his *Lehrbuch der Physiologie*, of which the first volume appeared in 1852 and the second in 1856.

In 1855 Ludwig went to Vienna as professor of anatomy and physiology at the Josephinum, the Austrian military-medical academy, which had been organized the preceding year. At this institution he carried on the work that he had begun in Marburg and Zurich, particularly his investigations of the blood gases. In 1859, in a paper published by his student I. M. Sechenov, he described his invention of the mercurial blood pump. This instrument enabled him to separate the gases from a given quantity of blood taken directly *in vivo*. Over the next three decades, Ludwig and his students, who were growing in number, developed these early researches in a variety of directions, eventually embracing the entire subject of respiratory exchange.

When the new chair of physiology was instituted at Leipzig in 1865, Ludwig was offered the post and accepted it. His first problem was the planning of a physiological institute, and he created a model for others to follow. It is probable that Liebig's chemical laboratory at Giessen and Bunsen's physical laboratory at Marburg served as examples. Ludwig's institute, however, was organized in keeping with his broad concept of physiology. He sought to explain vital phenomena in terms of mechanics, that is, through laws of physics and chemistry. It is clear that a visit to Berlin in 1847, in the course of which he met Helmholtz, Brücke, and du Bois-Reymond—men who were to be his lifelong friends and companions in the creation of modern physiology—was influential in the development of his thought.

Ludwig hoped to elucidate physiological problems by combining the study of the anatomy of an organ with a knowledge of the physicochemical changes that occur in its functioning. To this end he created physical, chemical, and anatomical (including histology) divisions in his laboratory, which was built in the form of a capital "E." One wing was devoted to histology, another to physiological chemistry, and the third, main section was equipped for the physical study of physiological problems.

When Ludwig began his career, there was an almost complete lack not only of physiological laboratories but also of experimental instruments. The circumstances under which he worked, particularly in his earlier years, fixed the direction of his ideas and methods. He was both an anatomist and a student of physics, conversant with the newest methods and developments of his science. Bunsen was his intimate friend and influenced him greatly in regard to chemistry and physics. Ludwig's combination of ingenuity, resourcefulness, and knowledge of physical science enabled him to become one of the greatest experimenters in the history of physiology.

In designing the experiments, Ludwig invented numerous methods and instruments. In 1846, he described the kymograph, which, in its subsequent modification by Marey and Chauveau, became a standard tool for the graphic recording of experimental results. His work on circulation led him to devise the mercurial blood pump (1859), the stream gauge (1867), and the method of maintaining circulation in isolated organs (1865).

Ludwig's teaching was as important as his research achievements. The entire work of the institute was characterized by its complete unity of purpose, a quality well illustrated by his lectures. They were usually given at four in the afternoon, and were addressed to the mature student; all those working under Ludwig's direction at the institute attended them, and the undergraduates often had a difficult time (most of them heard the lectures several semesters before being examined). Ludwig attacked his lectures in the same thorough, enthusiastic manner that characterized all his work. The focal point was the illustrative experiments, often the result of recent work done in the laboratory, which Ludwig prepared each day, assisted only by his laboratory aide, Salvenmoser.

The spirit of the laboratory was compounded of equal shares of hard work and enthusiasm and the students sensed it immediately. Ludwig's capacity to judge the abilities of his students led to a useful division of labor. He found something for each worker to do, and he collaborated in the experimentation as well as in the publication of the final results. His role as a teacher was enhanced still further by his *Lehrbuch*, the first modern text on physiology. The book was meant for students and made no attempt to define life or to elucidate "vital forces" or "biological principles." In accordance with Ludwig's basic approach, all explanations of living processes were given in terms of physics and chemistry and the research results that he presented bore testimony to his use of the methods of these sciences.

Ludwig's desire to investigate and to explain vital processes in physicochemical terms was apparent as early as 1842 in his Marburg dissertation (published the following year as *Beiträge zur Lehre vom Mechanismus der Harnsekretion*). In it Ludwig developed a physical theory of renal secretion, suggested to him by the structure of the kidney glomeruli, whereby the first stage in renal excretion represented a diffusion of liquid through a membrane because of a difference in pressure between the two sides. He sought to support this theory in further experiments published in 1849 and 1856; these researches are fundamental to present knowledge of diffusion through membranes. In 1851 Ludwig discovered through another series of experiments that salivary secretion depends on initiation by the glandular nerves, the pressure of the secretion being independent of the blood pressure.

Ludwig was interested, too, in all the aspects of circulation. He studied the fluidity of the circulating blood and its lateral pressure, as well as the dependence of these functions on cardiac activity, on the muscles, and on various other factors. He investigated the physiology of respiration, including gas exchange in the lungs, the respiratory movements, and tissue respiration. He also worked on the lymphatic system, making quantitative as well as histological determinations. His treatise on the structure of the kidneys is a classic, and a large part of what is now known about the mechanism of cardiac activity is based upon his work.

Ludwig belonged to that remarkable group of German physiologists and teachers who in the latter half of the nineteenth century created modern physiology. In 1874, on the twenty-fifth anniversary of his professorship, students who had worked with him at Marburg, Zurich, Vienna, and Leipzig presented him with a distinguished collection of original papers. On his seventieth birthday, in 1886, a second *Festgabe* was presented to him by former students. At the time of his death, almost every physiologist who was active had at some juncture studied with him.

In 1849 Ludwig married Christiane Endemann, the daughter of a Marburg law professor. They had two children, one of whom, a daughter, survived him, as did his wife. He died at the age of seventy-nine, having been ill with bronchitis for seven weeks.

BIBLIOGRAPHY

I. ORIGINAL WORKS. For an understanding of Ludwig's work, see *Lehrbuch der Physiologie des Menschen*, I (Heidelberg, 1852), II (Heidelberg, 1856). His other publications, including those of his students, are listed in Heinz Schröer, *Carl Ludwig, Begründer der messenden Experimentalphysiologie 1816–1895* (Stuttgart, 1967), 294–312, which also contains a number of Ludwig's letters. For the correspondence between Ludwig and du Bois-Reymond, see Estelle du Bois-Reymond, ed., *Zwei Grosse Naturforscher des 19. Jahrhunderts. Ein Briefwechsel zwischen Emil Du Bois-Reymond und Carl Ludwig* (Leipzig, 1927), with foreword and annotations by Paul Diepgen; other letters are included in E. Ebstein, "Briefe von Du Bois-Reymond, Claude Bernard and Johannes Müller an Karl Ludwig," in *Medizinische Klinik*, **40** (1925), 1517.

II. SECONDARY LITERATURE. For information on Ludwig's life and work, see T. N. Bonner, *American Doctors and German Universities* (Lincoln, Nebraska, 1963), 120–129; J. Burdon-Sanderson, "Carl Friedrich Wilhelm Ludwig," in *Proceedings. Royal Society of London*, **59** pt. 2 (1895–1896), 1–8; Simon Flexner and James Thomas Flexner, *William Henry Welch and the Heroic Age of American Medicine* (New York, 1941), 84 ff.; Morton H. Frank and Joyce J. Weiss, "The 'Introduction' to Carl Ludwig's Textbook of Human Physiology," in *Medical History*, **10** (1966), 76–86; Wilhelm His, "Carl Ludwig and Karl Thiersch," in *Popular Science Monthly*, **52** (1898), 338–353; Hugo Kronecker, "Carl Friedrich Wilhelm Ludwig," in *Berliner klinische Wochenschrift*, **25** (1895), 466; Erna Lesky, "Zu Carl Ludwigs Wiener Zeit, 1855–1865," in *Sudhoffs Archive*, **46** (1962), 178; and Warren P. Lombard, "The Life and Work of Carl Ludwig," in *Science*, **44** (1916), 363–375.

See also N. S. R. Maluf, "Carson, Ludwig, and Donders and the Negative Interpleural Pressure," in *Bulletin of the History of Medicine*, **16** (1944), 417–418; "How a Physiologist Anticipates a Physical Chemist," *ibid.*, **14** (1943), 352–365; George Rosen, "Carl Ludwig and His American Students," *ibid.*, **4** (1936), 609–650; K. E. Rothschuh, "Carl-Ludwig-Portraits in der bildenden Kunst," in *Archiv für Kreislaufforschung*, **33** (1960), 33; William Stirling, "Carl Ludwig, Professor of Physiology at the University of Leipzig," in *Science Progress*, **4** (1895), 155–176; Robert Tigerstedt, "Karl Ludwig, Denkrede," in *Biographische Blätter*, **1**, pt. 3 (1895), 271–279; Gerald B. Webb and Desmond Powell, *Henry Sewall, Physiologist and Physician* (Baltimore, Md., 1946), 46–50.

GEORGE ROSEN

LUEROTH (or LÜROTH), JAKOB (*b.* Mannheim, Germany, 18 February 1844; *d.* Munich, Germany, 14 September 1910), *mathematics.*

Lueroth's first scientific interests lay in astronomy. He began making observations while he was still in secondary school, but since he was hampered by bad eyesight he took up the study of mathematics instead. He attended the universities of Heidelberg, Berlin, and Giessen from 1863 until 1866; he had already, in 1865, written his doctoral dissertation on the Pascal configuration. In 1867 he became *Privatdozent* at the University of Heidelberg, and two years later, when he was still only twenty-five years old, he was

appointed professor ordinarius at the Technische Hochschule in Karlsruhe. From 1880 until 1883 he taught at the Technische Hochschule of Munich, and from the latter year until his death, at the University of Freiburg.

Lueroth's first mathematical publications were concerned with questions in analytical geometry, linear geometry, and theory of invariants, a development of the work of his teachers Hesse and Clebsch. His name is associated with three specific contributions to science. The first of these, a covariant of a given ternary form of fourth degree, is called the "Lueroth quartic," and Lueroth discovered it when he examined, following Clebsch, the condition under which a ternary quartic form may be represented as a sum of five fourth-powers of linear forms. In 1876 he demonstrated the "Lueroth theorem," whereby each uni-rational curve is rational—Castelnuovo in 1895 proved the analogous but more difficult theorem for surfaces. Finally, the "Clebsch-Lueroth method" may be employed in the construction of a Riemann surface for a given algebraic curve in the complex plane.

In addition, Lueroth worked in other areas of mathematics far removed from algebraic geometry. He obtained partial proof of the topological invariance of dimension (proved in 1911 by L. Brouwer) and, following the work of Staudt, did research in complex geometry. He was also involved in the logical researches of his friend Schröder and published two books in applied mathematics and mechanics. These were *Grundriss der Mechanik*, in which he used the vector calculus for the first time, and *Vorlesungen über numerisches Rechnen*. Lueroth collaborated in editing the collected works of Hesse and Grassmann.

BIBLIOGRAPHY

I. ORIGINAL WORKS. A complete bibliography of Lueroth's works may be found in the Brill and Noether obituary (see below). The papers containing his main discoveries are "Einige Eigenschaften einer gewissen Gattung von Kurven 4. Ordnung," in *Mathematische Annalen*, **2** (1869), 37–53; "Das Imaginäre in der Geometrie und das Rechnen mit Würfen," *ibid.*, **8** (1875), 145–214; "Beweis eines Satzes über rationale Kurven," *ibid.*, **9** (1876), 163–165; and "Über die kanonischen Querschnitte einer Riemannschen Fläche," in *Sitzungsberichte der physikalisch-medizinischen Sozietät in Erlangen*, **15** (1883), 24–30. He also published *Grundriss der Mechanik* (Munich, 1881), and *Vorlesungen über numerisches Rechnen* (Leipzig, 1900).

II. SECONDARY LITERATURE. An obituary is A. Brill and M. Noether, "Jacob Lueroth," in *Jahresberichte der Deutschen Mathematikervereinigung*, **20** (1911), 279–299.

WERNER BURAU

LUGEON, MAURICE (*b*. Poissy, France, 10 July 1870; *d*. Lausanne, Switzerland, 23 October 1953), *geology*.

Lugeon was the youngest of the five children of David Lugeon, a sculptor and burgher of Chevilly, Vaud, Switzerland, and Adèle Cauchois, who came from Normandy. The elder Lugeon had been a member of the staff brought together by Viollet-le-Duc to restore the cathedrals of France; the family returned to Switzerland in 1876, when he was commissioned to take part in the restoration of the cathedral in Lausanne. The family had limited means, and Lugeon began studying for a career in banking or industry, entering a bank as an apprentice after six years of school. (It is interesting to note that later in life he served on several boards of directors, continuing his early financial inclination.)

Lugeon's interest in geology was awakened on a school trip to Mt. Salève, near Geneva, when he was ten years old. By the time he was twelve, he was a regular visitor to the geology collections of the Lausanne university museum, where he met Eugene Renevier and his assistant, Théophile Rittener, both of whom took an interest in him. When Lugeon was fifteen, Rittener took him on a summer mapping trip in the mountains of Savoy, and Lugeon succeeded him as Renevier's assistant.

Having attained a monthly salary of seventy-five francs in his new post, Lugeon decided to advance his education by taking final school-leaving examinations. This was only the first step in his aspiration to earn an academic degree, and his circumstances remained difficult. He held a number of different jobs during this period, among them collecting and classifying lichens for the botanical department of the museum and working as a reporter. He also found time to publish several papers on paleontology.

In 1891 Lugeon accompanied Renevier to the mountains of Savoy to do mapping for the Société Géologique de France. On this expedition he received intensive instruction in stratigraphy—Renevier's chief interest—which became the basis for much of his later work. Renevier sent Lugeon to Munich, where there was a center for paleontological research, directed by Zittel, in the winter of 1893–1894; Lugeon thus received further training in this subject. The following spring, Lugeon returned to Savoy and in December 1895 he presented his thesis, "La région de la brèche du Chablais (Haute-Savoie)," to the University of Lausanne. In 1897—the same year in which he married Ida Welti, a grandniece of Oswald Heer—Lugeon became a lecturer at the university; he was made titular professor in 1898, and in 1906 he succeeded Renevier as head of the department of geology.

Lugeon's first inaugural lecture, on drainage and physiographic problems, was an important contribution to alpine geology, but it was overshadowed by the more fundamental (and more decisive to the development of geology) paper that he delivered to the Société Géologique de France in 1901. The latter, entitled "Les grandes nappes de recouvrement des Alpes du Chablais et de la Suisse," was the product of seven years' fieldwork and, more important, exhibited Lugeon's ability to organize a multitude of observations within a new framework—that of the new science of tectonics, for which the memoir became a source book. In it, Lugeon described the macrostructure of the whole Alpine chain, and showed for the first time the interrelationships of a vast series of recumbent folds and successive thrust sheets—the *nappes de charriage* (or *nappes de recouvrement*) or *Decken*—within the historical dynamics of the Alps. His radical view of the enormous overturned folds of the Valais or Pennine Alps was later dramatically confirmed in the building of the Simplon Tunnel, and the tectonic theories set out in his paper have since been applied to all parts of the world.

Lugeon's work opened a new era in the systematic alpine geology that had been developing since the time of Saussure and Buch. The stratigraphic succession of the Alps had gradually been defined, and they had been geologically mapped for the first time in 1853; a new set of sheets, to a scale of 1 : 100,000, was published between 1865 and 1887. With this increasingly detailed data, however, a greater number of irregularities or abnormalities in the stratigraphic succession became apparent, and new explanations were necessary. J. J. Scheuchzer had depicted folds and Escher von der Linth had suspected both recumbent folds and nappes or overthrusts (although he had been afraid to publish such heretical views); Escher's successor Albert Heim had explored and described the famous Glarus double fault, and thereby laid the foundation of the study of rock deformations. In 1883 Marcel Bertrand reinterpreted Heim's findings and provided one of the most important arguments for the unilateral movement that Suess had already proposed in 1875. In 1893 Hans Schardt had recognized the exotic origin of the Prealps, and had explained it by gravity gliding.

But these were exceptional analyses, and the structure of the Alps as a whole was still understood only as a chaos of many different fold directions and interfering faults. The hypotheses then available were inadequate to a satisfactory explanation of the broad range of observations, and the value of Lugeon's pioneering paper lay in the synthesis that it offered. Following the presentation of his memoir in 1901,

Lugeon conducted the annual field meeting of the Société Géologique de France through the Savoy Prealps and convinced many of the participants of the allochthony of those mountains.

Two years later, in 1903, Lugeon, who had never visited the Carpathians, studied published observations of them and pointed out that they, like the Alps, were formed by recumbent folds and thrust masses. His interpretations, drawn as they were from documentary evidence only, were opposed by some geologists, but the results obtained by the Vienna Geological Congress, during an excursion to the Tatras, vindicated his ideas. In 1907 V. Uhlig, the leading authority on Carpathian geology, accepted Lugeon's views, while in 1909 Suess drew upon them in his *Das Antlitz der Erde*. In addition to introducing a whole new interpretative principle, Lugeon was responsible for both the concepts and terminology of such tectonic staples as autochthony, allochthony, window, and involution.

Lugeon had thus attained an international reputation by the time he was thirty. When he became head of the department of geology at the University of Lausanne in 1906, scientists and students came to him from all over the world. Many of the latter became distinguished geologists, most notably, perhaps, Émile Argand, who began to explore the Pennine Alps with his teacher, and who later developed Lugeon's methods further. Lugeon not only helped, but often collaborated directly with his fellow scientists, as in the analysis of the periodic variations of the Swiss glaciers that he carried out with F. A. Forel and the studies of the northern Alps that he made with Emile Haug. In a less direct way, his ideas stimulated Termier to demonstrate windows in the eastern Alps.

Lugeon made numerous scientific trips, on which he made such significant observations as the nappes of Sicily. He generally preferred, however, to remain in France and Switzerland and make more and more detailed studies of areas that he knew well. From 1900 he was engaged in highly refined mapping of the high calcareous Alps between the Sanetsch Pass and the valley of the Kander. This map was published in 1910, with four books of explicative descriptions, sectional maps, and panoramas that brilliantly corroborated his theories. He continued mapping this area for the next several decades; this cartographic work, marked as it is by the careful analysis of local structures and the integration of this analysis into a comprehensive theory, remains a major contribution to the tectonic literature of the first half of the twentieth century.

Lugeon also served as an expert consultant in applied geology, especially in the determination of dam sites. These activities took him and his staff all over the world, and a report of their work was published in 1932. Lugeon's services were in such demand that he soon had to limit himself to taking up only the most difficult problems, although he continued to work as a consultant for the rest of his life. He had once defined the relationship between theoretical and applied geology for his students: "Faites de la bonne géologie, on peut toujours l'appliquer."

Despite his other projects, structural geology in all its facets—from local details to the grand problems of orogeny—remained his chief interest. In 1941 he published, with his successor Gagnebin, a memoir in which he took up the idea of gravity gliding to explain the emplacement of the Prealps and offered demonstrations of many new consequences of this hypothesis. Between 1941 and 1948 he completed a geological relief map, of which several copies are extant, of the high calcareous Alps that embodied his own cartographic results.

Lugeon was witty and ironical, and a lover of practical jokes (about which there are numerous stories, some of them apocryphal, many authentic). In addition to his scientific works, he wrote on food and wines and he was especially proud of his *La fondue Vaudoise*. Although his last years were not untroubled, he maintained a vivid scientific curiosity and interest in the work of his friends and colleagues. He died in his home, "Les Préalpes," and was buried in the cemetery of Chevilly, where his family had lived for generations.

BIBLIOGRAPHY

I. ORIGINAL WORKS. A complete bibliography of Lugeon's works may be found in the biographies by H. Badoux, in *Actes Société helvétique des sciences naturelles*, **133** (1953), 327–341, with a list of his honors and a portrait; P. Fallot, in *Bulletin de la Société géologique de France*, 6th ser., **4** (1954), 303–340, with portrait; trans. into English in *Proceedings. Geological Society of America* (1955), 122–127.

Individual writings include "La région de la brèche du Chablais (Haute-Savoie)," in *Bulletin des Services de la carte géologique de la France et des topographies souterraines*, **7** (1896); "Leçon d'ouverture du cours de géographie physique professé à l'Université de Lausanne. (La loi des vallées transversales des Alpes occidentales; l'histoire de l'Isère; le Rhône était-il tributaire du Rhin?)," in *Bulletin de la Société vaudoise des sciences naturelles*, **33** (1897), 49–78; "Les dislocations des Bauges (Savoie)," in *Bulletin des Services de la carte géologique de la France et des topographies souterraines*, **11**, no. 77 (1900), 359–470; "Réunion extraordinaire de la Société géologique de

France à Lausanne et dans le Chablais. Programme et comptes rendus des excursions et des séances, avec notes diverses," in *Bulletin de la Société géologique de France*, 4th ser., **1** (1901), 678–722; and "Les grandes nappes de recouvrement des Alpes du Chablais et de la Suisse," *ibid.*, **1** (1901), 723–825, with a letter from A. Heim.

See also "Sur la coupe géologique du Simplon," in *Comptes rendus hebdomadaires des séances de l'Académie des sciences*, **134** (1902), and in *Bulletin de la Société vaudoise des sciences naturelles*, **38** (1902), 34–41; "Les nappes de recouvrement de la Tatra et l'origine des klippes des Carpathes," *ibid.*, **39** (1903), and in *Bulletin des laboratoires de géologie, géographie physique, minéralogie, paléontologie, géophysique et du Musée géologique de l'Université de Lausanne*, no. 4; "Sur l'existence, dans le Salzkammergut, de quatre nappes de charriage superposées," in *Comptes rendus hebdomadaires des séances de l'Académie des sciences* (1904), written with E. Haug; "Sur la grande nappe de recouvrement de la Sicile," *ibid.* (1906), written with E. Argand; "La fenêtre de Saint-Nicolas," in *Bulletin de la Société vaudoise des sciences naturelles*, **43** (1907), 57; and "Sur les relations tectoniques des Préalpes internes avec les nappes helvétiques de Morcles et des Diablerets," in *Comptes rendus hebdomadaires des séances de l'Académie des sciences* (1909).

See further "Carte géologique des Hautes-Alpes calcaires entre la Lizerne et la Kander. Échelle 1 : 50,000," in *Beiträge zur geologischen Karte der Schweiz;* "Sur deux phases de plissements paléozoiques dans les Alpes," in *Comptes rendus hebdomadaires des séances de l'Académie des sciences* (1911); "Sur l'existence de grandes nappes de recouvrement dans le bassin du Sebou," *ibid.* (1918), written with L. Gentil and L. Joleaud; and "Observations et vues nouvelles sur la géologie des Préalpes romandes," in *Bulletin des laboratoires de géologie, géographie physique, minéralogie, paléontologie, géophysique et du Musée géologique de l'Université de Lausanne*, no. 72 (1941), and *Mémoires de la Société vaudoise des sciences naturelles*, **47** (1941), 1–90, written with Elie Gagnebin.

II. Secondary Literature. For further information on Lugeon's life, see the obituary notices by C. Jacob, in *Comptes rendus hebdomadaires des séances de l'Académie des sciences*, **237** (1953), 1045–1050; A. Lombard, in *Revue de l'Université de Bruxelles*, **2** (1954); and E. Wegmann, in *Geologische Rundschau*, **42**, no. 2 (1954), 311–314. See also L. Seylaz, *Les Alpes* (1953), pp. 177–178.

Eugene Wegmann

LUGININ, VLADIMIR FEDOROVICH (*b*. Moscow, Russia, 2 June 1834; *d*. Paris, France, 26 October 1911), *chemistry*.

Luginin graduated from the Mikhailov Artillery School in St. Petersburg in 1853 and the Artillery Academy in 1858.

In 1854–1856 Luginin took part in the Crimean War as an artillery officer. In the 1860's he was active in politics. He was a member of Velikoruss, a secret revolutionary-democratic organization, and was in close contact with Alexander Herzen, N. P. Ogarev, and Mikhail Bakunin. At one time Herzen suggested that Luginin should join the staff of the publication *Kolokol* ("The Bell"). In 1867 Luginin abandoned all political activity and devoted himself entirely to science. From 1874 to 1881 he worked in his own laboratory in St. Petersburg, and from 1882 to 1889 in Paris. Between 1889 and 1905 Luginin's scientific and educational activities were centered around Moscow University, where with his own funds he established the first thermochemical laboratory in Russia, which today bears his name.

Luginin's interest in thermochemistry was influenced by Berthelot, with whom he published a number of articles. Their thermochemical research on the heats of neutralization of citric and phosphoric acids (1875) proved these acids to be tribasic. In 1879 he investigated the effect of exchanging the hydrogen atoms with electronegative groups as well as with NH_2 groups at the heat of neutralization of substances belonging to various classes of organic chemistry. From 1880 Luginin engaged in important research to determine the heats of combustion of organic compounds.

In 1894, Luginin published a monograph entitled *Opisanie razlichnykh metodov opredelenia teplot gorenia organicheskikh soedineny* ("Description of Various Methods for Determining the Heats of Combustion of Organic Compounds"). This led the development of methods and techniques in thermochemical research. During 1894–1900, Luginin investigated the specific heats and latent heats of evaporation of various compounds in liquid form. He supplied a significant amount of exact data for the calculation of the heats of formation of organic substances. His work demonstrated the limits of applicability of Trouton's rule.

BIBLIOGRAPHY

Luginin's writings include "Étude thermochimique sur l'effet produit par les substitutions de Cl et de NO_2 et de NH_2 dans les corps de différentes groupes de la chimie organique," in *Annales de chimie et de physique*, 5th ser., **17** (1879), 222–268; "Sur la mesure de chaleur de combustion des matières organiques," *ibid.*, **27** (1882), 347–374; *Opisanie razlichnykh metodov opredelenia teplot gorenia organicheskikh soedineny* (Moscow, 1894); and *Méthodes de calorimétrie, usitées au laboratoire thermique de l'Université de Moscou* (Geneva, 1908), written with A. Shukarev.

A biography is Y. I. Soloviev and P. I. Starosselsky, *Vladimir Fedorovich Luginin* (Moscow, 1963).

Y. I. Soloviev

ŁUKASIEWICZ, JAN (*b.* Lvov, Austrian Galicia [now Ukrainian S.S.R.], 21 December 1878; *d.* Dublin, Ireland, 13 February 1956), *mathematical logic.*

Łukasiewicz' father, Paul, was a captain in the Austrian army; his mother, the former Leopoldine Holtzer, was the daughter of an Austrian civil servant. The family was Roman Catholic, and the language spoken at home was Polish. Young Łukasiewicz studied mathematics and philosophy at the University of Lvov, earning his doctorate *sub auspiciis imperatoris,* a rare honor (1902). At the same institution he received his *Habilitation* (1906) and lectured in logic and philosophy, as *Privatdozent* until 1911, then as extraordinary professor. In 1915 Łukasiewicz accepted an invitation to lecture at the University of Warsaw, then in German-occupied territory.

Between the world wars, as a citizen of independent Poland, Łukasiewicz was minister of education (1919), professor at the University of Warsaw (1920–1939), twice rector of that institution, an active member of scientific societies, and the recipient of several honors. He and Stanislaw Leśniewski founded the Warsaw school of logic, which A. Tarski helped make world famous. Viewing mathematical logic as an instrument of inquiry into the foundations of mathematics and the methodology of empirical science, Łukasiewicz succeeded in making it a required subject for mathematics and science students in Polish universities. His lucid lectures attracted students of the humanities as well.

The sufferings endured by Łukasiewicz and his wife (the former Regina Barwinska) during World War II are poignantly recalled in an autobiographical note. (See Sobociński's "In Memoriam," cited below.) In 1946 Łukasiewicz, then an exile in Belgium, accepted a professorship at the Royal Irish Academy, Dublin, where he remained until his death.

After some early essays on the principles of non-contradiction and excluded middle (1910), Łukasiewicz arrived by 1917 at the conception of a three-valued propositional calculus. His subsequent researches on many-valued logics is regarded by some as his greatest contribution. He viewed these "non-Aristotelian" logics as representing possible new ways of thinking, and he experimented with interpreting them in modal terms and in probability terms. The nonstandard systems he developed have value independently of the philosophy that inspired them or of the usefulness of those interpretations. Łukasiewicz created the elegant "Łukasiewicz system" for two-valued propositional logic and the parenthesis-free "Polish notation."

The metalogic (a term he coined on the model of Hilbert's terminology) of propositional calculi, notably the theory of their syntactic and semantic completeness, owes much to Łukasiewicz and his school. He regarded these studies as a prelude to analogous investigations for the rest of logic, which were then carried out by Tarski.

Using modern formal techniques, Łukasiewicz reconstructed and reevaluated ancient and medieval logic. Through his work in this area, we have changed our view of the history of logic.

During his last years in Ireland, Łukasiewicz published important studies on modal and intuitionistic logic, and he again made logical history with a detailed and novel study of Aristotle's syllogistic. Essentially he interpreted syllogisms in Aristotle to be theorems of logic, not rules of derivations.

BIBLIOGRAPHY

I. Original Works. Most of Łukasiewicz' contributions were first presented in short notes, often in Polish, or in his university lectures. A list of all, or almost all, of his publications is appended to Andrzej Mostowski's "L'oeuvre scientifique de Jan Łukasiewicz dans le domaine de la logique mathématique," in *Fundamenta mathematicae,* **44** (1957), 1–11. His following writings present important results systematically: *Elementy logiki matematycznej* ("Elements of Mathematical Logic"; Warsaw, 1929; 2nd ed., 1958), translated by Olgierd Wojtasiewicz as *Elements of Mathematical Logic* (New York, 1963); "Philosophische Bemerkungen zu mehrwertigen Systemen des Aussagenkalküls," in *Comptes rendus des séances de la Société des sciences et des lettres de Varsovie,* Cl. III, **23** (1930), 51–77, written with Alfred Tarski; "Untersuchungen über den Aussagenkalkül," *ibid.,* 30–50; "Zur Geschichte der Aussagenlogik," in *Erkenntnis,* **5** (1935–1936), 111–131; "A System of Modal Logic," in *Journal of Computing Systems,* **1** (1953), 111–149; and *Aristotle's Syllogistic From the Stand-Point of Modern Formal Logic,* 2nd ed. (Oxford, 1957).

II. Secondary Literature. The following two articles jointly constitute a valuable survey of Łukasiewicz' lifework as a logician, philosopher, and historian of logic: L. Borkowski and J. Słupecki, "The Logical Works of Jan Łukasiewicz," in *Studia logica,* **8** (1958), 7–56; and Tadeusz Kotarbiński, "Jan Łukasiewicz's Works on the History of Logic," *ibid.,* 57–62. Shorter general treatments of Łukasiewicz's work are the Mostowski article cited above; Bolesław Sobociński, "In Memoriam Jan Łukasiewicz," in *Philosophical Studies* (Maynooth, Ireland), **6** (1956), 3–49, which contains an autobiographical note, "Curriculum vitae of Jan Łukasiewicz," and a bibliography; and Heinrich Scholz, "In Memoriam Jan Łukasiewicz," in *Archiv für mathematische Logik und Grundlagenforschung,* **3** (1957), 3–18, which contains an excellent summary of the technical aspects of Łukasiewicz' contributions.

Łukasiewicz' exegesis of Aristotle's syllogistic is disputed in Arthur N. Prior, "Łukasiewicz's Symbolic Logic," in *Australasian Journal of Philosophy*, **30** (1952), 33–46, and is discussed in Gunther Patzig, *Die Aristotelische Syllogistik: Logisch-philologische Untersuchungen über das Buch A der "Ersten Analytiken"* (Göttingen, 1959); English trans. by J. Barnes, *Aristotle's Theory of the Syllogism: A Logico-philological Study of Book A of the Prior Analytics* (Dordrecht, 1968), *passim*, esp. 196–202.

For a general evaluation of Łukasiewicz' philosophical and logical ideas, see Henryk Skolimowsky, *Polish Analytical Philosophy: A Survey and a Comparison with British Analytical Philosophy* (New York, 1967), 56–72.

GEORGE GOE

LULL, RAMON (*b.* Ciutat de Mallorques [now Palma de Mallorca], *ca.* 1232; *d.* Ciutat de Mallorques [?], January/March [?] 1316), *polymathy.*

A Catalan encyclopedist, Lull invented an "art of finding truth" which inspired Leibniz's dream of a universal algebra four centuries later. His contributions to science are understandable only when examined in their historical and theological context. The son of a Catalan nobleman of the same name who participated in the reconquest of Mallorca from the Moors, Lull was brought up with James the Conqueror's younger son (later crowned James II of Mallorca), whose seneschal he became. About six years after his marriage to Blanca Picany (1257) he was converted from a courtly to a religious way of life, following a series of visions of Christ crucified. He never took holy orders (although he may have become a Franciscan tertiary in 1295), but his subsequent career was dominated by three religious resolutions: to become a missionary and attain martyrdom, to establish colleges where missionaries would study oriental languages, and to provide them with "the best book[s] in the world against the errors of the infidel."[1]

Lull's preparations lasted a decade; his remaining forty years (from 1275, when he was summoned by Prince James to Montpellier, where he lectured on the early versions of his Art) were spent in writing, preaching, lecturing, and traveling (including missionary journeys to Tunis in 1292; Bougie, Algeria, in 1307; and Tunis late in 1315), and in attempts to secure support from numerous kings and four successive popes for his proposed colleges. During Lull's lifetime only James II of Mallorca established such a foundation (1276, the year of his accession); when he lost Mallorca to his elder brother, Peter III of Aragon, the college at Miramar apparently was abandoned (*ca.* 1292). In Lull's old age his proposals were finally approved by the Council of Vienne (1311–1312); and colleges for the study of Arabic, Hebrew, and Chaldean were founded in Rome, Bologna, Paris, Salamanca, and Oxford after Lull's death. Pious tradition has it that he died after being stoned by Muslims in Bougie (January 1316[?]), although his actual death is variously said to have occurred in Bougie, at sea, or in Mallorca; modern scholars doubt the historicity of his martyrdom. As for his third resolution, it led to the various versions of Lull's Art—and all his scientific contributions were by-products of this enterprise.

James the Conqueror's chief adviser, the Dominican Saint Ramon de Penyafort, dissuaded Lull from studying in Paris, where his age and lack of Latin would have told against him; he therefore studied informally in Mallorca (1265[?]–1273[?]). His thought was thus not structured at the formative stage by the Scholastic training which molded most other late medieval Christian thinkers; this fostered the development of his highly idiosyncratic system by leaving his mind open to numerous non-Scholastic sources. These included cabalism (then flourishing in learned Jewish circles in both Catalonia and Italy), earlier Christian writers discarded by Scholasticism (for instance, John Scotus Eriugena, whose ninth-century *De divisione naturae* influenced Lullian cosmological works, notably the *Liber chaos*, either directly or indirectly—and hence also his Art), and probably also Arabic humoral medicine and astrology. The Augustinian Neoplatonism of the Victorines also proved important, partly because of its continuing prominence but mainly because its marked coincidences with both Islamic and cabalistic Neoplatonism favored the creation of a syncretistic system which was firmly grounded in doctrines equally acceptable to Christians, Jews, and Muslims.

This fusion occurred after the eight years Lull spent in Mallorca studying Latin, learning Arabic from a slave, reading all texts available to him in either tongue, and writing copiously. One of his earliest works was a compendium of the logic of al-Ghazālī in Arabic (1270[?]); it has since been lost, although two later compendia with similar titles survive—one in Latin, the other in Catalan mnemonic verse. In all, Lull wrote at least 292 works in Catalan, Arabic, or Latin over a period of forty-five years (1270–1315); most of them have been preserved, although no Arabic manuscripts have yet been traced and many Catalan and Latin works remain unpublished. His initial awkwardness in Latin, coupled with his desire that knowledge be made available to non-Latin-speaking sectors of society, made Lull the first person to mold Catalan into a literary medium. He used it not only in important mystical works, poetry, and allegorical novels (none of which concerns us here) but also to deal with every learned subject which engaged his attention: theology and philosophy; arithmetic, geometry, and astronomy (often mainly astrology), which, together with music, formed the quadrivium (the higher division of the seven liberal arts); grammar, rhetoric, and logic (the trivium); law; and medicine. Thus, Lull created a fully developed learned vocabulary in Catalan almost a century before any other Romance vernacular became a viable scholarly medium. Almost all Lull's works in such nonliterary fields were connected in some way with his Art, because the "art of finding truth" which he developed to convert "the infidel" proved applicable to every branch of knowledge. Lull himself pioneered its application to all subjects studied in medieval universities—except for music—and also constructed one of the last great medieval encyclopedias, the *Arbor scientiae* (1295–1296), in accordance with its basic principles.

Yet the Art can be understood correctly only when viewed in the light of Lull's primary aim: to place Christian apologetics on a rational basis for use in disputations with Muslims, for whom arguments *de auctoritate* grounded on the Old Testament—widely used by Dominicans in disputations with the Jews—carried no weight. The same purpose lay behind the *Summa contra gentiles* of Aquinas, written at the request of his fellow Dominican Penyafort, whose concern for the conversion of all non-Christians (but particularly those in James the Conqueror's dominions) thus inspired the two chief thirteenth-century attempts in this direction; the *Summa contra gentiles* was finished during the interval between Lull's discovery of his own calling and his interview with Penyafort. But whereas Aquinas distinguished categorically between what reason could prove and that which, while not contrary to reason, needed faith in revelation, Lull advanced what he called necessary reasons for accepting dogmas like the Trinity and the Incarnation. This gave his Art a rationalistic air that led to much subsequent criticism. Lull himself described his Art as lying between faith and logic, and his "necessary reasons" were not so much logical proofs as reasons of greater or lesser congruence which could not be denied without rejecting generally accepted principles. In this respect they were not appreciably more "rationalistic" than Aquinas's "proofs" that the truths of faith were not incompatible with reason. But the differences between the two apologetic systems are far more striking than their resemblances.

Lull regarded his Art as divinely inspired and hence infallible (although open to improvement in successive

versions). Its first form, the *Ars compendiosa inveniendi veritatem* or *Ars maior*[2] (1273–1274[?]), was composed after a mystical "illumination" on Mount Randa, Mallorca, in which Lull saw that everything could be systematically related back to God by examining how Creation was structured by the active manifestation of the divine attributes—which he called Dignities and used as the absolute principles of his Art. Examining their manifestations involved using a set of relative principles; and both sets could be visualized in combinatory diagrams, known as Figures *A* and *T*. The original Figure *A* had sixteen Dignities, lettered *BCDEFGHIKLMNOPQR*; the original Figure *T* had five triads, only three of which (*EFG* + *HIK* + *LMN*) were strictly principles of relation, the others being sets of subjects (God + Creature + Operation, *BCD*) and possible judgments (Affirmation + Doubt + Negation, *OPQ*). All early versions had a proliferation of supplementary visual aids, which always included diagrams showing the four elements, and—with the obvious exception of Figure *T*—most features of the system were grouped into sets of sixteen items, lettered like the Dignities.

This quaternary base seems to provide the key to the origins of the Art's combinatory aspect, apparently modeled on the methods used to calculate combinations of the sixteen elemental "grades" (four each for fire, air, water, and earth) in both astrology and humoral medicine. A major simplification in the *Ars inventiva* (*ca.* 1289) eliminated the elemental features, reduced the diagrams to four (unchanged thereafter), reduced Figure *T* to the nine actual relative prin-

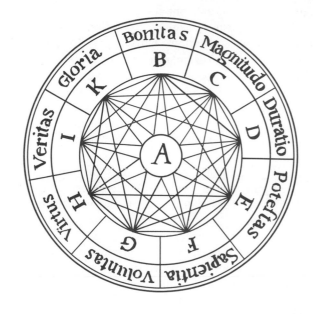

FIGURE 1. The Lullian "Dignities."

	1. Essentia 2. Unitas 3. Perfectio									
	A	B	C	D	E	F	G	H	I	K
Praedicata { Absoluta		Bonitas	Magnitudo	Æternitas seu Duratio	Potestas	Sapientia	Voluntas	Virtus	Veritas	Gloria
T. Relata seu respectus		Differentia	Concordantia	Contrarietas	Principium	Medium	Finis	Maioritas	Æqualitas	Minoritas
Alphabetum seu principia huius artis sunt aut { Q. Quaestiones		Vtrum?	Quid?	De quo?	Quare?	Quantum?	Quale?	Quando?	Vbi?	Quomodo? Cum quo?
S. Subiecta		Deus	Angelus	Coelum	Homo	Imaginatio	Sensitiua	Vegetatiua	Elementatiua	Instrumentatiua
V. Virtutes		Iustitia	Prudentia	Fortitudo	Temperantia	Fides	Spes	Charitas	Patientia	Pietas
V. Vitia		Auaritia	Gula	Luxuria	Superbia	Acidia	Inuidia	Ira	Mendacium	Inconstantia

FIGURE 2. The "alphabet" of Lull's *Ars brevis* (1303).

ciples (Difference + Concordance + Contradiction, Beginning + Middle + End, and Majority + Equality + Minority) and the sixteen original Dignities to the nine shown in Figure 1. In still later versions the symbolic letters *BCDEFGHIK* acquired up to six meanings that were ultimately set out in the gridlike "alphabet" of the *Ars generalis ultima* and its abridgment, the *Ars brevis* (both 1308), from which Figure 2 is reproduced. The traditional seven virtues and seven vices have been extended to sets of nine, to meet the requirements of the ternary system; the last two of ten *quaestiones* (a series connected with the ten Aristotelian categories) had to share the same compartment, since the set of fundamental questions could not be shortened and still be exhaustive.

The most distinctive characteristic of Lull's Art is clearly its combinatory nature, which led to both the use of complex semimechanical techniques that sometimes required figures with separately revolving concentric wheels—"volvelles," in bibliographical parlance (see Figure 3)—and to the symbolic notation of its alphabet. These features justify its classification among the forerunners of both modern symbolic logic and computer science, with its systematically exhaustive consideration of all possible combinations of the material under examination, reduced to a symbolic coding. Yet these techniques taken over from nontheological sources, however striking, remain ancillary, and should not obscure the theocentric basis of the Art. It relates everything to the exemplification of God's Dignities, thus starting out from both the monotheism common to Judaism, Christianity, and Islam and their common acceptance of a Neo-

platonic exemplarist world picture, to argue its way up and down the traditional ladder of being on the basis of the analogies between its rungs—as becomes very obvious in Lull's *De ascensu et descensu intellectus* (1305). The lowest rung was that of the elements, and Lull probably thought that the "model" provided by the physical doctrines of his time constituted a valid "scientific" basis for arguments projected to higher levels. Since this physical basis would be accepted in the scientific field by savants of all three "revealed religions," he doubtless also hoped that the specifically

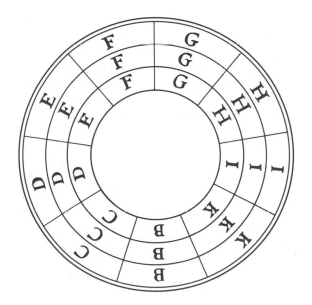

FIGURE 3. The fourth figure of the later Art: the inner wheels rotate independently, allowing all possible ternary combinations of the letters *BCDEFGHIK* to be read off.

Christian conclusions which he drew in the apologetic field would be equally acceptable. It even seems likely that what hit him with the force of a divine "illumination" on Mount Randa was his sudden recognition of such a possibility.

There is no evidence that Lull's Art ever converted anybody, but his application of the combinatory method to other disciplines (begun in the four *Libri principiorum, ca.* 1274–1275) was followed by numerous later Lullists; the Art's function as a means of unifying all knowledge into a single system remained viable throughout the Renaissance and well into the seventeenth century. As a system of logical inquiry (see Lull's *Logica nova* [1303] for the strictly logical implications, disentangled from other aspects), its method of proceeding from basic sets of preestablished concepts by the systematic exploration of their combinations—in connection with any question on any conceivable subject—can be succinctly stated in terms taken from the *Dissertatio de arte combinatoria* (1666) of Leibniz, which was inspired by the Lullian Art: "A proposition is made up of subject and predicate; hence all propositions are combinations. Hence the logic of inventing [discovering] propositions involves solving this problem: 1. given a subject, [finding] the predicates; 2. given a predicate, finding the subjects [to which it may] apply, whether by way of affirmation or negation."[3]

Recent research has concentrated on the clarification of Lull's ideas, the identification of their sources, and the nature of their influence on later thinkers— especially Nicholas of Cusa and Giordano Bruno. Major advances in all these fields have taken place since the 1950's, but much more research is still required. The specific origins of Lull's doctrines regarding the elements, whose importance has been fully recognized only since 1954 (see Yates), are particularly significant. A proper exploration of the antecedents of his *Opera medica* is a prerequisite for establishing Lull's final place in the history of Western science. In this connection it must be mentioned that although Lull himself was opposed to alchemy (but not to astrology, a "science" he sought to improve in the *Tractatus novus de astronomia* [1297]), his methods had obvious applications in the alchemical field—and they were so applied in a host of pseudo-Lullian alchemical works, most of them composed more than fifty years after his death. These works explain the traditional (but false) "scientific" view which made him "Lull the Alchemist."

NOTES

1. *Vida coëtanea.* The Latin (dictated by Lull [?], probably 1311) says "book," which doubtlessly agreed with Lull's

original resolve; the plural, in the fourteenth-century Catalan text (modernized in *Obres essencials*, see I, 36), would better fit the series of "improved" versions of the Art itself, which first took shape almost ten years after Lull's conversion.

2. References to an *Ars magna* in later centuries are usually either to the definitive *Ars magna generalis ultima* (1308) or to Lull's system in general. The alternative title of the first version recalls Roger Bacon's *Opus maius* (1267); the connections between Lull and Bacon have yet to be investigated, but many resemblances may well be due to common Arabic sources.

3. "Propositio componitur ex subiecto et praedicato, omnes igitur propositiones sunt combinationes. Logicae igitur inventivae propositionum est hoc problema solvere: 1. Dato subiecto praedicata. 2. Dato praedicato subiecta invenire, utraque cum affirmative, tum negative" (G. W. Leibniz, *op. cit.* [in text], no. 55, in *Sämtliche Schriften und Briefen*, 2nd ser., I [Darmstadt, 1926], 192).

BIBLIOGRAPHY

I. Original Works. The larger of the standard eds. in Catalan is *Obres de Ramon Lull*, 21 vols., with 9 more planned (Palma de Mallorca, 1901–   ), cited below as *ORL. Obres essencials*, 2 vols. (Barcelona, 1957–1960), cited below as *Ob es*, contains the chief literary works; the modernized text has many errata, but there are excellent general introductions and a select bibliography.

Collections in Latin are Beati Raymundi Lulli, *Opera omnia*, I. Salzinger, ed., vols. I-VI, IX (VII and VIII unpublished) (Mainz, 1721–1742), contains 48 works, repr. Minerva GMBH, cited below as *MOG;* reprint of *Quattuor libri principiorum* from *MOG* I (Paris–The Hague, 1969), cited below as *QLP; Opera parva*, 3 vols. (Palma, 1744–1746), 15 works, 12 of which are not in *MOG;* and *Opera medica* (Palma, 1742)—it and *Opera parva* are to be issued in Gerstenberg Reprints. A modern critical ed. is *Raymundi Lulli Opera latina*, 5 vols., of 30 planned (Palma, 1961–   ), thus far previously unpublished works, cited below as *ORL*.

Major scientific works and versions of the Art are *Ars compendiosa inveniendi veritatem/Ars maior* (1273–1274[?]), *MOG* I; *Ars Universalis* (1274–1275[?]), *MOG* I; *Liber principiorum theologiae, Liber principiorum philosophiae, Liber principiorum juris, Liber principiorum medicinae* (1274–1275[?]), *MOG* I, *QLP; Liber chaos* (1275–1276[?]), *MOG III; Ars compendiosa medicinae* (1275–1276[?]), *Opera medica; Logica Algazalis* (ca. 1281), which is related to the Catalan verse *Logica del Gatzel* (after 1282[?]), *ORL* XIX; *Ars inventiva [veritatis]* (1289[?]), *MOG* V; *De levitate et ponderositate elementorum* (1293), *Opera medica; Arbor scientiae* (29 Sept. 1295–1 Apr. 1296), in various rare eds., in Catalan as *Arbre de ciencia* (simultaneous[?]), *ORL* XI-XIII, *Ob es* I; *Tractatus novus de astronomia* (1297; unpublished), Latin text discussed in Yates (1954; see below), Catalan MS is British Museum, Add. 16434, to appear in *ORL;* and *Liber de geometria [nova et compendiosa]* (1299), ed. by J. M. Millás-Vallicrosa (Barcelona, 1953), considered unreliable—see R. D. F. Pring-Mill, "La geometría luliana," in *Estudios Lulianos*, **2** (1958), 341–342.

Other works by Lull are *Liber de natura* (1301) (Palma, 1744); *Logica nova* (Palma, 1744); *Liber de regionibus sanitatis et infirmitatis* (1303), *Opera medica; De ascensu et descensu intellectus* (1305) (Palma, 1744); *Ars brevis* (1308), *Opera parva* I; *Ars generalis ultima/Ars magna [generalis ultima]* (1305–1308), in L. Zetzner, *Raymundi Lulli opera ea quae ad . . . artem . . . pertinent* (Strasbourg, 1598, 1609, 1617, 1651); and *Vita coëtanea* (dictated [?] 1311), B. de Gaiffier, ed., in *Analecta Bollandiana*, **48** (1930), 130–178, in Catalan as *Vida coëtania, Ob es*.

II. SECONDARY LITERATURE. See E. Colomer, S.J., *Nikolaus von Kues und Raimund Lull* (Berlin, 1961); C. E. Dufourcq, *L'Espagne catalane et le Maghreb aux XIIIᵉ et XIVᵉ siècles* (Paris, 1966); J. N. Hillgarth, *Ramon Lull and Lullism in Fourteenth-Century France* (Oxford, 1971); Erhard-Wolfram Platzeck, O.F.M., *Raimund Lull, sein Leben, seine Werke, die Grundlagen seines Denkens*, 2 vols. (Düsseldorf, 1961–1964), vol. II contains the fullest bibliography of Lull's writings and Lullian studies; and Frances A. Yates, "The Art of Ramon Lull: An Approach to It Through Lull's Theory of the Elements," in *Journal of the Warburg and Courtauld Institutes*, **17** (1954), 115–173; and "Ramon Lull and John Scotus Erigena," *ibid.*, **23** (1960), 1–44; but see R. D. F. Pring-Mill, in *Estudios Lulianos*, **7** (1963), 167–180.

See also *Estudios Lulianos*, which began publication in 1957, and E. W. Platzeck's comprehensive survey of research from 1955 to 1969 in *Antonianum*, **45** (1970), 213–272.

R. D. F. PRING-MILL

LUMMER, OTTO RICHARD (*b.* Gera, Germany, 17 July 1860; *d.* Breslau, Germany [now Wrocław, Poland], 5 July 1925), *optics*.

After completing his dissertation in 1884, Lummer became an assistant to Helmholtz; and in 1887 he followed the latter to the newly founded Physikalisch-Technische Reichsanstalt (PTR) in Berlin. Helmholtz, his revered teacher and his constant model, was for Lummer, as Gehrcke recalled, the "absolute standard as a research worker and as a man." In 1889 Lummer became a member of the PTR, and in 1894 he was given the title of professor. Lummer did not qualify for lecturing until 1901, at the University of Berlin.

As early as 1849 Haidinger had announced the existence of interference fringes that occur on mica plates and that, unlike Newton's rings, "do not move when the plates producing them are displaced." These fringes of equal inclination, caused by interference between rays emerging after multiple internal reflections from a parallel-sided plate, were rediscovered (for the third time, after Haidinger and Mascart) by Lummer in 1884 in Helmholtz' laboratory at the University of Berlin; they became known as Lummer fringes. Helmholtz, who had not perceived the phenomenon because of his nearsightedness, was not willing to accept the existence of the interference effects. He was soon convinced, however, and called Lummer's dissertation "an unusually good work."

Since Lummer fringes are the result of differences in path length of many wavelengths, Lummer arrived at the idea, in 1901, of developing the plane parallel plates into a spectroscope of the highest resolution. This device had the advantage of possessing greater resolving power than the interferometer produced in 1897 by Fabry and Perot. The considerable drawback of low luminous intensity, caused by the glancing incidence of the light, was eliminated in 1902 by Gehrcke, who cemented a prism to the plate with Canada balsam. The new apparatus, for which Lummer proposed the name Lummer–Gehrcke interference spectroscope, proved to be an excellent tool for spectroscopy and superior to the simple line grating.

At the PTR, Lummer had the task of working out the bases for a suitable international primary standard of luminosity. In 1889 he constructed, with Brodhun, an exact photometer, the Lummer-Brodhun cube. The new instrument fulfilled "through optical arrangements all the conditions of an ideal grease spot," something that the previously employed real grease-spot photometer could not do. In photometry it became necessary to hold constant the light sources that were being compared. The existing bolometer was not exact enough for Lummer's needs. In 1892, with F. Kurlbaum, he constructed a surface bolometer, which superseded all the previous types. Lummer thus gradually approached the field in which he was to have his greatest successes: thermal radiation.

In 1898, after preliminary work concerning, among other things, the production of the blackbody, Lummer tackled the problem of determining the Kirchhoff function depending only on wavelength and temperature—that is, he was seeking the emissive power of the blackbody. With Pringsheim he confirmed Wien's displacement law and also, with greater precision, Wien's radiation law, which Wien had stated in 1896 and Paschen had experimentally ascertained. In 1900, however, Lummer and Pringsheim discovered the "nonvalidity" of this law, which they called the Wien-Planck spectral equation: It "is thereby demonstrated that the Wien-Planck spectral equation does not yield the blackbody radiation that we measured in the region of 12μ to 18μ."

The competing team of Rubens and Kurlbaum verified this important result and derived from their measurements a conclusion that went even further:

"The intensity of a monochromatic beam at high temperatures is proportional to the temperature." This was the decisive stimulus leading to Planck's radiation formula, which he communicated on 19 October 1900. Lummer and Pringsheim subsequently confirmed this law with great precision, thereby establishing an unassailable foundation for the emerging quantum theory.

In 1904 Lummer was appointed a full professor at the University of Breslau. At first it was not easy for this specialist in optics to cover the whole field of physics. But his lectures soon became, as Clemens Schaefer wrote, "revelations of a mind in which the divine spark glowed."

BIBLIOGRAPHY

I. ORIGINAL WORKS. Lummer's writings include "Über eine neue Interferenzerscheinung an planparallelen Glasplatten und eine Methode, die Planparallelität solcher Gläser zu prüfen (Inauguraldissertation)," in *Annalen der Physik und Chemie*, n.s. **23** (1884), 49–84; "Über eine neue Interferenzerscheinung," *ibid.*, 513–548; "Photometrische Untersuchungen," in *Zeitschrift für Instrumentenkunde*, **9** (1889), 41–50, 461–465; **10** (1890), 119–133; **12** (1892), 41–50, written with Eugen Brodhun; "Über die Herstellung eines Flächenbolometers," *ibid.*, **12** (1892), 81–89; "Über die Strahlung des absolut schwarzen Körpers und seine Verwirklichung," in *Naturwissenschaftliche Rundschau*, **11** (1896), 65–68, 81–83, 93–95; "Die Vertheilung der Energie im Spectrum des schwarzen Körpers," in *Verhandlungen der Deutschen Physikalischen Gesellschaft*, **1** (1899), 23–41, written with Ernst Pringsheim; "Le rayonnement des corps noirs," in *Rapports présentés au Congrès international de physique réuni à Paris en 1900*, II (Paris, 1900), 41–99; *Die Lehre von der strahlenden Energie (Optik)*, II, pt. 3 of Müller–Pouillet's *Lehrbuch der Physik und Meteorologie*, 10th ed. (Brunswick, 1909); and *Grundlagen, Ziele und Grenzen der Leuchttechnik* (Munich, 1918).

II. SECONDARY LITERATURE. See Ernst Gehrcke, "Erinnerungen an Lummer," in *Physikalische Blätter*, **11** (1955), 315–317; Hans Kangro, *Vorgeschichte des Planckschen Strahlungsgesetzes* (Wiesbaden, 1970), esp. pp. 192–200; Fritz Reiche, "Otto Lummer," in *Physikalische Zeitschrift*, **27** (1926), 459–467; and Clemens Schaefer," Otto Lummer zum 100. Geburtstag," in *Physikalische Blätter*, **16** (1960), 373–381.

ARMIN HERMANN

LUNA, EMERICO (*b.* Palermo, Italy, 6 January 1882; *d.* Palermo, 4 December 1963), *anatomy*.

Born into a socially prominent family, Luna studied at the Institute of Histology of the University of Palermo. He received his degree with honors and became an assistant at the Institute of Normal Human Anatomy. He was made a full professor in 1922. Luna founded the Italian Anatomical Society and served as secretary until his death.

Luna was among the first to suture the heart successfully and to introduce the teaching of radiological anatomy. He was also active in politics and served as a deputy from Palermo and as a city councillor in Palermo. A major interest was expanded medical care for the poor, and he introduced legislation toward this end.

Luna's earliest studies dealt with the morphology of the cerebellum and with the projection on its surface of the cerebellar nuclei, in order to avoid them in the successive experimental extirpation of sections of the lobulus paramedianus, of the formatio vermicularis and of the crus secundum. By applying Marchi's method he demonstrated the course of the degenerated bundles and was able to localize the motor center in the cortex of the internal segment of the anterior lunated lobulus; he further demonstrated that for movements of the neck in the lobulus simplex the fibers follow the cerebrospinal fasciculus, the presence of which he confirmed in the dog.

In later investigations Luna demonstrated the nerve paths which proceed from the intermediate nerve and the vago-glosso-pharyngeal complex to the cerebellum and the spino-olivari fibers that terminate in the reticular substance of the medulla oblongata. He also carried out investigations on the development and morphology of the intercalated nucleus of Staderini, and he described the existence of a nucleus situated ventrally to that of the hypoglossus in *Sus schropha* (1). These studies preceded those of other investigators on the tegmental rhombencephalic centers.

In histology Luna studied the fine structure and nature of the reticular tissue and published a masterly and still authoritative monograph (2). He also studied the relation between the diameter of the capillaries and the size of the subject, the lymphatics of the lung, the morphology of the suprarenals, and muscular and vascular anomalies. He wrote many distinguished books, both literary and scientific, among which are the magnificent volume on the nervous system (3) in Bertelli's *Trattato di anatomia umana* and on regional clinical anatomy (4).

BIBLIOGRAPHY

Luna's writings include (1) "Ricerche istologiche sopra un nucleo riscontrato nel rombencefalo di *Sus schropha*," in *Folia neuro-biologica*, **5**, no. 1 (1911); (2) "Studio sul tessuto reticolare," in *Ricerche di morfologia*, **1** (1921);

(3) vol. V of the *Trattato di anatomia umana*, Bertelli, ed., 2nd ed. (Milan, 1938); (4) *Trattato di anatomia clinica regionale* (Florence, 1948).

IGNAZIO FAZZARI

LUNGE, GEORG (*b.* Breslau, Prussia [now Wrocław, Poland], 15 September 1839; *d.* Zurich, Switzerland, 3 January 1923), *chemistry, chemical technology.*

Lunge was the son of a merchant. At the age of seventeen he graduated at the head of his class from a Gymnasium in Breslau. Subsequently, at the University of Breslau, he studied the natural sciences, especially chemistry, and in 1859 obtained his doctorate *magna cum laude* with a dissertation entitled *De fermentatione alcoholica.* He first studied under Löwig and Cohn, then with Bunsen and Kirchhoff at Heidelberg. In 1860 Lunge joined the chemical industry, initially as a chemist at a Silesian fertilizer factory. In 1862 he opened his own plant for the production of potassium ferrocyanide, ammonia, lead salts, and tartaric acid; but the venture was unsuccessful.

Lunge then went to England, where he first worked in a factory producing coal-tar products. In 1865 he joined the newly founded, small alkali works of Baily, Bowron & Co., in South Shields, first as chemist and subsequently as manager. Lunge married a Miss Bowron, daughter of one of his employers. He participated in the founding and activities of the Newcastle Chemical Society; established contacts with representatives of science and industry; and established a fine reputation as a specialist in chemical technology. On the recommendation of Heinrich Caro, Lunge was invited in 1875 to become professor of technical chemistry at the Eidgenössische Polytechnikum Schule in Zurich. Subsequently he was granted Swiss citizenship. He resigned his teaching post at Zurich in 1907 but continued to write and do laboratory work until 1916. He retired at the age of seventy-seven.

At a time when most chemists worked in organic chemistry, Lunge was among the few who chose inorganic chemistry as a field of concentration. He was eminently pragmatic; Haber said of him that he had awakened spirits and conquered problems in applied science which previously had been dealt with only by technicians. Lunge worked toward the control of manufacturing processes by means of refined technical-chemical investigations and analyses and by the quantitative analysis of synthetic compounds. His vast technical knowledge based on practical experience made him a master in applying scientific results to economic-technical problems.

Lunge published an enormous number of papers. A bibliography he compiled himself—although not complete—lists eighty-six books and pamphlets as well as 590 articles. Practitioners acclaim Lunge's works as particularly dependable, detailed, precise, and practical, the general approach being coupled with the explanation of the scientific principles involved. Lunge's *Handbuch der Sodaindustrie*, his *Steinkohlenteer und Ammoniak*, and his *Chemisch-technische Untersuchungsmethoden* (written with Ernst Berl) were for decades considered standard works for the chemical raw-materials industry.

Experimental work by Lunge and by many of his pupils treated all problems of chemical manufacturing, especially that of soda, sulfuric acid, chlorine, and chloride of lime, nitric acid, phosphates, coal-tar products, explosives, cellulose, and synthetic fibers. It resulted in several inventions, such as Lunge's plate towers (which used countercurrents) for the acid industry and Heumann's synthesis of indigo.

Lunge also personally directed a large chemical laboratory—in addition to his lecturing—in which students learned to test raw materials and to supervise manufacturing processes. The newly constructed chemical laboratory complex (built in 1883 in association with Victor Meyer) became the model for chemical-technical research and teaching facilities.

BIBLIOGRAPHY

I. ORIGINAL WORKS. Lunge's writings include *Handbuch der Sodaindustrie und ihrer Nebenzweige für Theorie und Praxis*, 2 vols. (Brunswick, 1879; 3rd ed., 3 vols., 1903–1909); *Theoretical and Practical Treatise on the Manufacture of Sulfuric Acid and Alkali*, 3 vols. (London, 1879–1880; 3rd ed., 2 vols. in 4 pts., 1903–1911; supp. to vol. I, London, 1917); *Die Industrie der Steinkohlenteer—Destillation und Ammoniakwasser-Verarbeitung* (Brunswick, 1882), also translated into English (London, 1882; 5th ed., 1912); *Die chemischen Laboratorien des Eidgenössischen Polytechnikums* (Zurich, 1889); *Chemisch-technische Untersuchungsmethoden*, 3 vols. (Berlin, 1899–1900; 6th ed., 4 vols., 1910–1911; 8th ed., 5 vols., 1931–1934), also translated into English by C. A. Keane and others, 3 vols. in 5 pts. (London, 1908–1914), written with Berl; *Zur Geschichte der Entstehung und Entwicklung der chemischen Industrien in der Schweiz* (Zurich, 1901); and *Das Zusammenwirken von Chemie und Ingenieurwesen in der Technik* (Vienna, 1907).

II. SECONDARY LITERATURE. See E. Bosshard, "Georg Lunge 1839–1923," in *Verhandlungen der Schweizerischen naturforschenden Gesellschaft*, **104**, pt. 2 (1923), "Anhang, Nekrologe und Biographien," 25–43, with a bibliography; and "Georg Lunge," in Günther Bugge, ed., *Das Buch der grossen Chemiker*, II (Weinheim, 1965); and Poggendorff, III, 843–844; IV, 926–927, VI, pt. 2, 1591.

EBERHARD SCHMAUDERER

LUSITANUS, AMATUS (RODRIGUES, JOÃO) (*b.* Castelo Branco, Portugal, 1511; *d.* Salonika, Greece (then Turkish), 21[?] January 1568), *medicine, botany.*

No more is known of the parents of João Rodrigues than that they were Marranos, probably of Spanish origin, for they sent him to study medicine at Salamanca University, where he graduated in 1529 or 1530. He seems to have studied surgery longer than was common for medical students of the time, possibly after completing his main course, for he stayed in Spain until 1532. He practiced only briefly in his native country, for in 1533 he migrated to Antwerp, then under Spanish rule, which had a large Portuguese colony. He later mysteriously explained his exile as due to an expectation that something would happen which subsequently did. (It was possibly the intensified harassment of the Marranos.) While in Flanders he made the acquaintance of leading humanists and published in 1536 his first book, *Index Dioscoridis*, a commentary on the first book of the *De materia medica*, intended to be eruditely philological as well as useful to apothecaries. In 1540 he was appointed professor of anatomy at the University of Ferrara, where he collaborated with Canano in his dissections. In the course of research they discovered (probably in 1547) the valve in the azygos vein. Amatus points out that "if you blow air into the lower part of the azygos vein, the vena cava will not be inflated because of a valve at the orifice where the two join." His is the first report of this observation, but argument continues as to who was the active partner. Neither appreciated the real significance of their discovery.

In the summer of 1547 Amatus moved to Ancona, where he established an extensive practice, traveling to Florence, Rome, and Venice to treat highly placed patients. While in Ancona he began to write up his case histories; a hundred of these, starting from his brief practice in Portugal, were published in 1551 as *Curationum medicinalium centuria*. Six similar collections appeared over the next decade, the last in 1561. In further commentaries on Dioscorides he concerned himself more with descriptions of plants and included his own opinions on their identification and supposed medicinal properties, claiming his own successful experience; he also added new Asian plants, such as the coconut palm. Unfortunately for him, he criticized Mattioli and made a bitter and dangerous enemy. When, in 1555, the new pope, Paul IV (the previous pope, Julius III, had been his patient), began persecuting the Marranos, Amatus was forced to flee the papal dominion. His papers, including the fifth *centuria*, were retrieved for him by

friends. He escaped first to Pesaro and then in 1556 to Ragusa, perhaps as municipal physician there—he had long had hopes of securing this post. But in 1559 he left Christian territory altogether and went to Salonika, where he returned openly to Judaism. He died there during an outbreak of the plague in 1568, having, it is said, contracted the disease from his patients.

Although his work on Dioscorides includes some interesting observations and information on contemporary economic botany, his lifework is to be found mainly in his *Curationum medicinalium*. For each case history he gives the patient's name or social position, age, physiognomy, and build; outlines the symptoms and course of the disease; and records his diagnosis, prescription, and the result. There is little order, and he ranges over most branches of medicine. Local climate is held responsible for at least the specific characters of epidemics. Amatus is at his best when discussing the social origin of stress diseases and mental disorders, for which he recommended empirically well-founded diets. Although usually concerned, as a good humanist, to show that his treatment was founded on Hippocratic or Galenic principles, he was ready to innovate, especially in surgery. In operating for empyema, for example, he proposed the third intercostal space, rather than higher up, for the puncture site, in order not to damage the diaphragm. He was also a pioneer in the use of such devices as the obturator in cases of cleft palate and the breast reliever.

BIBLIOGRAPHY

I. ORIGINAL WORKS. Amatus' botanical works are *Index Dioscoridis, en, candide lector, historiales Diosocoridis campi exegemataque simplicium* . . . (Antwerp, 1536), the only work to appear under his own name rather than the humanistic nom de plume Amatus Lusitanus; and *In Dioscoridis de materia medica libros quinque enarrationes* (Venice, 1553; illustrated ed., Lyons, 1558). *Curationum medicinalium centuria* (Florence, 1551), was followed by *Curationum medicinalium centuria secunda* (Paris, 1552). Publication history of the remaining five *centuriae* is quite complicated as they usually appeared with reissues of earlier ones. The first complete ed. of all seven was published at Venice from 1565 to 1570. There were also several posthumous eds. (Lyons, 1580; Bordeaux, 1620).

II. SECONDARY LITERATURE. See (listed chronologically) M. Salomon, "Amatus Lusitanus in seine Zeit," in *Zeitschrift für klinische Medizin* 41–2 (1901); M. de Lemos, *Amato Lusitano, a sua vida e a sua obra* (Porto, 1907); H. Friedenwald, "Amatus Lusitanus," in *Bulletin of the Institute of History of Medicine, Johns Hopkins University,* 4 (1937); J. Lopes-Dias, "Dr. João Rodrigues de Castelo Branco. Amato Lusitano. Ensaio Bio-bibliográfico," in

Congresso do mundo português. Publicacões, **13** (1940). A commemorative volume is *IV Centenario de João Rodrigues de Castelo Branco–Amato Lusitano (Estudios Castelo Branco 1968)*.

On the *Curationum*, see J. O. Leibovitz, "A Probable Case of Peptic Ulcer as Described by Amatus Lusitanus," in *Journal of the History of Medicine and Allied Sciences*, **27** (1953), 212–216; "Amatus Lusitanus and the Obturator in Cleft Palates," in *Bulletin of the History of Medicine*, **13** (1958), 492–503; and F. Segret, "Amatus Lusitanus, Témoin de son temps," in *Sefarrad*, **23** (1968), 285–309.

A. G. KELLER

LUSK, GRAHAM (*b.* Bridgeport, Connecticut, 15 February 1866; *d.* New York, N. Y., 18 July 1932), *physiology, nutrition, clinical investigation.*

Lusk was the son of William Thompson Lusk, a prominent New York teacher and practitioner of obstetrics, and Mary Hartwell Chittenden. Partially deaf, Lusk did not pursue a family interest in clinical medicine, but chose instead a laboratory science career. He received a bachelor's degree from the Columbia University School of Mines (1887); then—as his father had a generation before—he traveled to Germany for advanced study. Lusk came under the influence of Voit and in 1891 received a Ph.D. from Munich, with a dissertation on the influence of carbohydrates in protein metabolism. Upon his return to the United States in 1891, Lusk taught physiology at the Yale Medical School, then moved in 1898 to New York City and the Bellevue Hospital–New York University College of Medicine. In 1909, he was appointed professor of physiology at Cornell Medical College, where he remained until his retirement and death in 1932.

Inspired by Voit's work, particularly in nutrition and metabolism, Lusk devoted his career to the illumination of metabolic processes through the use of the calorimeter in the analysis of intake and output, in both normal and pathological states. While at Yale, Lusk began an important series of studies on diabetes. He administered the chemical phlorhizin to dogs to produce glycosuria and demonstrated a constant ratio between the amount of dextrose and nitrogen excreted in the urine. Later experiments indicated a differential yield of carbohydrate from the metabolism of particular amino acids. His demonstration that carbohydrates were not normally formed in the metabolism of fats held important clinical implications. He also did research on the respiratory quotient and the significance of surface area in the determination of basal metabolism rates

(as opposed to those physiologists who emphasized the importance of body weight).

In 1912 Lusk was appointed scientific director of the Russell Sage Institute of Pathology, newly affiliated with the Cornell division of Bellevue. Working in conjunction with Eugene F. DuBois (clinical director of the program) Lusk had, for the first time, adequate financial and clinical resources to utilize and maintain a calorimeter for work in human physiology and pathology. Much of Lusk's most important work resulted from two decades of collaboration with DuBois and other clinicians, resulting in more than 1,400 calorimeter experiments completed before Lusk's retirement. Lusk probably exerted his broadest scientific influence through his synthetic work, *Elements of the Science of Nutrition*, which appeared in four increasingly detailed editions between 1906 and 1928 and which played an important role in popularizing the findings of calorimeter research.

With Atwater and Benedict, Lusk was a leader in metabolism studies. Like Benedict, however, Lusk's scientific view was firmly oriented toward research methods he had learned in the 1890's; measuring energy relationships with the calorimeter was a basic and unquestioned approach to the understanding of nutrition. As late as 1932, he still dismissed vitamin studies briefly in a chapter on dietetics in his work *Nutrition*. Lusk never appreciated the significance of the vitamins and especially their implications for further work in enzymatic and intracellular processes.

Few of his American contemporaries were more active than Lusk in making the medical profession a truly scientific one. When Lusk arrived in New Haven in 1891, suffused with the German research ideal and devoted to the reshaping of clinical medicine in this mold, he found Yale—like almost every American medical school—dominated by clinicians who could not appreciate his laboratory methods. Since his annual salary was $300, only a private income enabled Lusk to pursue the research demanded by his European training. Lusk soon became part of a group of young American scientists and clinical investigators—frequently German-trained—who actively sought to raise standards of medical research and education in the United States. Genuine scientific training, they argued, would have to become part of the medical school curriculum and part of the intellectual equipment and job qualifications of a new type of clinician. Lusk's family background and his interest in pathological phenomena made him an ideal spokesman for such ideas. His collaboration over two decades with DuBois, moreover, and the practical implications of their work on diabetes had a particularly telling effect in the practice-oriented world of American medicine. Family wealth and his marriage to a daughter of Louis C. Tiffany provided the means for Lusk to become part of New York's social and medical establishment.

A member of numerous scientific societies, including the National Academy of Sciences and the Royal Society, Lusk was founder and organizer of the Society for Experimental Biology and Medicine (1903), American Society of Biological Chemists (1906), and New York's Harvey Society (1905). During World War I, Lusk served as adviser in matters of nutrition for the U. S. government.

BIBLIOGRAPHY

I. ORIGINAL WORKS. There is no full-length biography of Lusk and no extensive collection of his papers. Useful in understanding the background of Lusk's calorimeter work are his *Elements of the Science of Nutrition* (Philadelphia, 1906; 2nd ed., 1909; 3rd ed., 1917; 4th ed., 1928), and his *Nutrition* (New York, 1933). This latter work, edited and published after Lusk's death, concludes with a discussion of basal metabolism; vitamins are mentioned briefly in a chapter on dietetics.

II. SECONDARY LITERATURE. For useful biographical sketches of Lusk, see *Addresses Given at a Memorial Meeting for Graham Lusk at the New York Academy of Medicine on December 10, 1932* (Baltimore, 1933); the editorial "Graham Lusk," in *Journal of Biological Chemistry*, **98** (1932), vii; and Russell H. Chittenden, "Graham Lusk," in *Dictionary of American Biography*, supp. I, 517–518. The most detailed sketch is by Eugene F. DuBois, "Biographical Memoir of Graham Lusk, 1886–1932," in *Biographical Memoirs. National Academy of Sciences*, **21** (1941), 95–142; "Graham Lusk," in *Science*, **76** (1932), 113–115; and John R. Murlin, "Graham Lusk. A Brief Review of His Work," in *Journal of Nutrition*, **5** (1932), 527–538. Compare also C. Culotta, "Francis G. Benedict," in *Dictionary of Scientific Biography*, I, 325–326; and C. E. Rosenberg, "Wilbur Olin Atwater," *ibid.*, I, 609–611. For a useful comparison with Lusk's work, see E. V. McCollum, *A History of Nutrition. The Sequence of Ideas in Nutrition Investigations* (Boston, 1957), esp. ch. 10, "Respiration and Calorimetry."

CHARLES E. ROSENBERG

LUSTIG, ALESSANDRO (*b.* Trieste, Austria [now Italy], 5 May 1857; *d.* Marina di Pietrasanta, Lucca, Italy, 23 September 1937), *pathology, bacteriology.*

Lustig received his medical degree at Vienna in 1882, then was an assistant at the Institute of Physiology in Vienna and, in 1884, at the Institute of Physiology at Innsbruck. He next went to Turin, where he obtained an Italian medical degree; soon afterward he started his scientific work in the research laboratory of the Mauriziano Hospital in Turin. In 1886, during a cholera epidemic, Lustig tended the victims in lazarettos; his investigations on the disease carried out at that time are among the earliest contributions to its study after the discovery of *Vibrio cholerae* by Koch (1884). He was appointed professor of general pathology at the University of Cagliari in Sardinia in 1889, and in 1890 at Florence, where he worked until his retirement in 1932.

Lustig began his scientific activity in histology and physiology. He dealt with the nerve ends of smooth muscles, epithelial degeneration of the olfactory membrane after destruction of the olfactory lobe, myocardial changes after section of extracardial nerves, the effects of celiectomy, the etiology of endemic goiter, and experimental acetonuria.

From 1891 Lustig's activity was mainly in bacteriology, immunology, and the prevention of infections. After his investigations on cholera, he devoted further study to the bacteriology of this infection and published an excellent monograph on the detection of water bacteria. In 1897, with his pupil G. Galeotti, Lustig extracted from *Bacterium pestis* a substance having the chemical characteristics of nucleoproteids, and demonstrated its immunizing properties: these investigations stand, in the history of bacteriology and immunology, as one of the first attempts at chemical identification of a bacterial antigen and at using chemically defined antigens to induce active immunity.

These substances were used by Lustig and his coworkers as chemical vaccines to immunize animals and obtain immune sera that were employed for serum therapy in cases of plague. Later, Lustig and his pupils Galeotti and G. Polverini were invited to India to apply the results of their research. In 1897 and 1898 they were in Bombay, where they made epidemiological observations on plague and used a serum prepared in the Laboratory of General Pathology at Florence to treat a considerable number of plague victims. Having verified the efficacy of the serum, they started prophylactic vaccination with nucleoproteids and created in Bombay a laboratory for the preparation of nucleoproteids and antiplague sera. This activity is documented in numerous papers by Lustig and his co-workers, which were published in Italian, English, and German journals from 1897 to 1903. In the Italian medical journal *Morgagni*, Lustig published "I metodi razionali di immunizzazione per mezzo di sostanze chimicamente estratte dai microrganismi patogeni" (1903), in which the premises for future developments of both bacteriological chemistry and immunology are clearly seen.

In 1901 Lustig published *Trattato di patologia generale*, which went through eight editions. Starting with the third edition he had the collaboration of his pupils G. Galeotti, P. Rondoni, and G. Guerrini. While general pathology had until then been considered as the propaedeutic part of morbid anatomy, in that book Lustig and his collaborators clearly indicated the new dimension of this discipline, including in it immunology and physiopathology. This extension proved to be essential for a complete understanding of fundamental pathogenetic mechanisms.

In 1913, with several collaborators, Lustig published *Le malattie infettive dell'uomo e degli animali*. In 1931, in collaboration with G. C. Rovida and G. Ferraloro, he wrote *Fisiopatologia e clinica dei gas da combattimento*, which he dedicated "to the memory of the eight thousand Italian soldiers who died in World War I following the first gas attack on the Austrian front."

Later, Lustig's interest turned more and more to social medicine and hygiene: this is attested by his many papers on combating malaria, tuberculosis, and tumors.

BIBLIOGRAPHY

Lustig's writings include "Studi sul colera asiatico," in *Resoconto sanitario dello Spedale civile di Trieste* (1886); "Ueber die Aetiologie des endemischen Kropfes," in *Verhandlungen des Internationalen Kongresses für Medizin* (1890); *Diagnostik der Bakterien des Wassers* (Jena, 1893); "Risultati delle ricerche fatte in India negli animali e nell'uomo intorno alla vaccinazione preventiva contro la peste bubbonica," in *Pubblicazioni del R. Istituto di studi superiori . . . in Firenze* (1897); "Versuche mit Pestschutzimpfungen bei Thieren," in *Deutsche medizinische Wochenschrift*, **23** (1897), 227, written with G. Galeotti; *Trattato di patologia generale* (Milan, 1901); "I metodi razionali di immunizzazione per mezzo di sostanze chimicamente estratte dai microrganismi patogeni," in *Morgagni*, **45** (1903), 721; "Ueber Bakteriennukleoproteide," in W. Kolle and A. von Wassermann, eds., *Handbuch der pathogenen Mikroorganismen*, II (Jena, 1913), 1362; sections of *Le malattie infettive dell'uomo e degli animali* (Milan, 1913); and *Fisiopatologia e clinica dei gas da combattimento* (Milan, 1931), written with G. C. Rovida and G. Ferraloro.

GIOVANNI FAVILLI

LUTHER, C. ROBERT (*b.* Schweidnitz, Germany [now Swidnica, Poland], 10 April 1822; *d.* Düsseldorf, Germany, 15 February 1900), *astronomy*.

Luther was the son of F. H. A. August Luther and the former Wilhelmine von Ende. In 1831–1841 he attended the secondary school of his native town. From 1841 to 1843 he studied natural sciences, especially astronomy, at the University of Breslau and continued these studies at Berlin in the fall of 1843. As a student of Encke's, Luther soon began doing computations for the *Berliner astronomisches Jahrbuch*, which published his work from 1849 to 1899. From 1847 he was an observer at the Berlin observatory; in 1848 he reduced Encke's meridian circle observations; and beginning in 1850 he succeeded Galle at the nine-inch refractor. In 1851 he followed Brünnow as director of the small observatory at Bilk, a suburb of Düsseldorf, remaining in Düsseldorf until his death.

Luther's lifework was the planetoids; he discovered twenty-four with priority and many others which had been discovered independently about the same time. For several of these planetoids he calculated the ephemerides continuously; these ephemerides are among the best and most accurately calculated ones for planetoids. The work deserves to be appreciated because at first Luther had only a telescope with a six-foot focal length at Bilk (in 1877 he acquired a larger one) and made all his observations with a nonilluminated ring micrometer. In the last years of his life Luther restricted his work to the reduction of observations that, because of his defective vision, were made by his son Wilhelm.

Luther received many honors, including an honorary doctorate from the University of Bonn (1855). The *Astronomische Nachrichten*, from volume 21 (1844) to volume 152 (1900), contains many, mostly short, notes by Luther.

Luther married Caroline Märcker in 1859; they had a son, Wilhelm.

BIBLIOGRAPHY

Luther's writings, besides the notes in *Astronomische Nachrichten*, include *Hora O Berliner akademische Sternkarten* (Berlin, 1857); and "Neuberechnung der Barker'schen Hilfstafel," in Encke's new ed. of Olbers' *Methode eine Kometenbahn zu berechnen* (Weimar, 1847).

An obituary is V. Knorre, in, *Vierteljahrsschrift der Astronomischen Gesellschaft*, **17** (1900), 191–200.

H.-CHRIST. FREIESLEBEN

LUZIN, NIKOLAI NIKOLAIEVICH (*b.* Tomsk, Russia, 9 December 1883; *d.* Moscow, U.S.S.R., 28 February 1950), *mathematics*.

Luzin was the son of a trade official, Nikolai Mitrofanovich Luzin, and Olga Nikolaievna. He completed his secondary schooling at Tomsk in 1901 and entered the mathematics division of the Physics-Mathematics Faculty of Moscow University. Here he became an active member of the circle of science students headed by N. E. Zhukovsky and studied mathematics under the guidance of D. F. Egorov. He spent the winter and spring of 1906 in Paris, where he attended lectures at the Sorbonne and the Collège de France. At the end of 1906 Luzin completed the course at Moscow University and remained there to prepare for a professorship. In 1910, after passing the examinations for the master's degree, he was appointed assistant professor at Moscow University but did not take up his duties there; he was sent to Göttingen and Paris for further study in those fields that had interested him for several years—the theory of functions of a real variable, integration theory, and the theory of trigonometric series. Luzin's first memoirs, published in 1911–1913 in *Matematicheskii sbornik* and the *Comptes rendus* of the Paris Academy of Sciences, immediately attracted the attention of the scientific world. In the spring of 1914, upon his return to Moscow, Luzin started lecturing, one of his courses being on function theory; he also organized a special research seminar on the subject. In 1915 he submitted a monograph entitled *Integral i trigonometrichesky ryad* ("Integrals and the Trigonometric Series"), published in *Matematicheskii sbornik*, and defended it at the Physics-Mathematics Faculty as his master's thesis. On the basis of its outstanding merits, the scientific council awarded Luzin the doctorate in pure mathematics, and in 1917 he became a professor.

During the period 1914–1924 Luzin, a brilliant lecturer and scientific organizer, was the center of a Moscow school of function theory which greatly influenced the subsequent development of mathematics, both in the Soviet Union and abroad. Such outstanding mathematicians as P. S. Alexandrov, A. Y. Khinchin, D. E. Menshov, M. Y. Suslin, A. N. Kolmogorov, N. K. Bari, and P. S. Novikov were his pupils.

Luzin was a member of the Moscow Mathematical Society, of the Moscow Society of Explorers of Nature, and of the Cracow Academy of Sciences; an honorary member of the Calcutta Mathematical Society and of the Belgian Mathematical Society; and was elected vice-president of the International Mathematical Congress held at Bologna in 1928. In 1927 Luzin was elected a corresponding member of the Soviet Academy of Sciences, and in 1929 he became an academician.

After 1930 Luzin devoted less time to teaching and worked mainly at the Soviet Academy of Sciences:

the Mathematical Institute (1929–1936; 1941–1950) and the Institute of Automatics and Telemechanics (1936–1950).

Luzin's mathematical creativity relates mostly to the theory of functions of a real variable in its two branches, metric and descriptive. Insofar as the first is concerned, Luzin's thesis (Moscow, 1915) is paramount, since it contains important results on the structure of measurable sets and functions, on primitive functions, on convergence of trigonometric series, and on representability of functions by trigonometric series. Cited in the thesis are examples of power series with coefficients tending to zero and nevertheless diverging everywhere on the boundary of the circle of convergence (1912), as well as a trigonometric series with coefficients tending to zero that nevertheless diverges almost everywhere (1912). These examples stimulated many later investigations. Luzin later showed that every measurable function can, in a certain sense, be represented as a trigonometric series that may be summable almost everywhere to that function by the methods of Poisson and Riemann.

Another important result obtained by Luzin on absolute convergence resides in the fact that when a trigonometric series converges absolutely at two points, the distance between which is incommensurable with respect to π, this series converges absolutely over an everywhere dense set and therefore will either converge everywhere or diverge everywhere.

The investigation of the structure of measurable sets and functions led Luzin to prove the so-called C property: that is, that every measurable function which is almost everywhere finite over a given segment can be made continuous over the segment by varying its value on a set of arbitrarily small measure (1912). In Luzin's hands this theorem was a most important means of investigation; by resorting to it he managed to solve completely a number of cardinal problems: finding a primitive function, the representability of a function as a trigonometric series, and finding a harmonic function that is holomorphic inside a circle and takes given values on the circumference.

In the theory of integration, Luzin solved the problem of how to distinguish the Lebesgue integral or the Denjoy integral from the other primitives of the given function. For this purpose he introduced a new concept of complete variation of a function for a perfect set. The metric theory of functions was applied by Luzin to the study of boundary properties of analytical functions.

After 1915 Luzin turned to the descriptive theory of functions. Having investigated the so-called B sets studied by Borel, Baire, and Lebesgue, Luzin raised questions concerning the power of *B* sets and the construction of sets that are not *B* sets without resorting to Zermelo's axiom, to which many mathematicians objected. Both of the problems were solved by Luzin's pupils; M. Y. Suslin constructed a more extended class of sets than that of *B* sets, called analytical or *A* sets. Luzin introduced new definitions of both *A* sets and *B* sets, as well as the "sieving process," which became very important in the theory of *A* sets. Through the use of this process, Luzin also showed that a segment may be represented as a sum of pairwise disjoint *B* sets. It is to date the strongest result in the theory of sets that is not based upon Zermelo's axiom. Luzin also created a theory of "projective" sets (1925), which are obtained from *B* sets by successively performing the operation of projection and taking a complement. Through the introduction of this concept, some difficulties of a mathematical and logical nature came to light and were studied by his successors.

Luzin also provided decisive results in the solution of the problem of bending on the main base (1938) that dated back to K. M. Peterson, and the evaluation of the convergence of S. A. Chaplygin's method of approximate solution of differential equations (1932). He also wrote brilliant articles on Euler and Newton (1933, 1943). Luzin's many manuals and textbooks on mathematical analysis and the theory of functions of a real variable went through many editions and are still used by students in the Soviet Union.

BIBLIOGRAPHY

I. ORIGINAL WORKS. Luzin's writings were brought together in *Sobranie sochinenii* ("Collected Works"), 3 vols. (Moscow, 1953–1959). Individual works include *Leçons sur les ensembles analytiques et leurs applications* (Paris, 1930); and *Integral i trigonometrichesky ryad* ("Integrals and Trigonometric Series"), new ed. (Moscow-Leningrad, 1951), with biography of Luzin by V. V. Golubev and N. K. Bari, pp. 11–31; an analysis of his work by Bari and L. A. Lusternik, pp. 32–45; detailed commentary by Bari and D. E. Menshov, pp. 389–537; and a bibliography, pp. 538–547.

II. SECONDARY LITERATURE. See N. K. Bari and L. A. Lusternik, "Raboti N. N. Luzina po metricheskoy teorii funktsy" ("The Works of N. N. Luzin in the Metric Theory of Functions"), in *Uspekhi matematicheskikh nauk*, **6**, no. 6 (1951), 28–46; V. S. Fedorov, "Trudi N. N. Luzina po teorii funktsy kompleksnogo peremennogo" ("The Works of N. N. Luzin in the Theory of Functions of a Complex Variable"), *ibid.*, **7**, no. 2 (1952), 7–16; V. K. Goltsman and P. I. Kuznetsov, "Raboti N. N. Luzina po differentsialnim uravneniam i po vychislitelnim metodam" ("The Works of N. N. Luzin in Differential Equations and

in Computational Methods"), *ibid.*, 17–30; L. V. Keldysh and P. S. Novikov, "Raboti N. N. Luzina v oblasti deskriptivnoy teorii mnozhestv" ("The Works of N. N. Luzin in the Area of the Descriptive Theory of Sets"), *ibid.*, **8**, no. 2 (1953), 93–104; and A. P. Youschkevitch, *Istoria matematiki v Rossii* ("The History of Mathematics in Russia"; Moscow, 1968), 565–577.

A. B. PAPLAUSCAS

LYAPUNOV, ALEKSANDR MIKHAILOVICH (*b.* Yaroslavl, Russia, 6 June 1857; *d.* Odessa, U.S.S.R., 3 November 1918), *mathematics, mechanics.*

Lyapunov was a son of the astronomer Mikhail Vasilievich Lyapunov, who worked at Kazan University from 1840 until 1855 and was director of the Demidovski Lyceum in Yaroslavl from 1856 until 1863; his mother was the former Sofia Aleksandrovna Shilipova. Lyapunov's brother Sergei was a composer; another brother, Boris, was a specialist in Slavic philology and a member of the Soviet Academy of Sciences.

Lyapunov received his elementary education at home and later with an uncle, R. M. Sechenov, brother of the physiologist I. M. Sechenov. With R. M. Sechenov's daughter Natalia Rafailovna (whom he married in 1886), he prepared for the Gymnasium. In 1870 Lyapunov's mother moved to Nizhny Novgorod (now Gorky) with her children. After graduating from the Gymnasium in Nizhny Novgorod in 1876, Lyapunov enrolled in the Physics and Mathematics Faculty of St. Petersburg University, where P. L. Chebyshev greatly influenced him.

Upon graduating from the university in 1880, Lyapunov remained, upon the recommendation of D. K. Bobylev, in the department of mechanics of St. Petersburg University in order to prepare for a professorial career. In 1881 he published his first two scientific papers, which dealt with hydrostatics: "O ravnovesii tyazhelykh tel v tyazhelykh zhidkostyakh, soderzhashchikhsya v sosude opredelennoy formy" ("On the Equilibrium of Heavy Bodies in Heavy Liquids Contained in a Vessel of a Certain Shape") and "O potentsiale gidrostaticheskikh davleny" ("On the Potential of Hydrostatic Pressures").

In 1882 Chebyshev posed the following question: "It is known that at a certain angular velocity ellipsoidal forms cease to be the forms of equilibrium of a rotating liquid. In this case, do they not shift into some new forms of equilibrium which differ little from ellipsoids for small increases in the angular velocity?" Lyapunov did not solve the question at the time, but the problem led him to another that became the subject of his master's dissertation, *Ob ustoychivosti ellipsoidalnykh form ravnovesia vrashchayushcheysya zhidkosti* ("On the Stability of Ellipsoidal Forms of Equilibrium of a Rotating Liquid"; 1884), which he defended at St. Petersburg University in 1885.

In the autumn of that year Lyapunov began to teach mechanics at Kharkov University as a *Privatdozent*. For some time he was completely occupied by the preparation of lectures and by teaching, but in 1888 his papers on the stability of the motion of mechanical systems having a finite number of degrees of freedom began to be published. In 1892 he published the classic *Obshchaya zadacha ob ustoychivosti dvizhenia* ("The General Problem of the Stability of Motion"), and in the same year he defended it as his doctoral dissertation at Moscow University; N. E. Zhukovsky was one of the examiners. Lyapunov studied this field until 1902.

In 1893 Lyapunov became a professor at Kharkov. In addition to mechanics he taught mathematics courses. He was also active in the Kharkov Mathematical Society. From 1891 until 1898 he was its vice-president, and from 1899 until 1902 its president and the editor of its *Soobshchenia* ("Reports").

At Kharkov, Lyapunov conducted investigations in mathematical physics (1886–1902) and the theory of probability (1900–1901) and obtained outstanding results in both. At the beginning of 1901 he was elected an associate member of the St. Petersburg Academy of Sciences, and at the end of that year he became an academician in applied mathematics, a chair which had remained vacant for seven years, since the death of Chebyshev.

In St. Petersburg, Lyapunov devoted himself completely to scientific work. He returned to the problem that Chebyshev had placed before him and, in an extensive series of papers which continued until his death, developed the theory of figures of equilibrium of rotating heavy liquids and of the stability of these figures.

In 1908 Lyapunov attended the Fourth International Congress of Mathematicians in Rome. He was involved in the publication of the complete collected works of Euler *(L. Euleri Opera omnia)* and was an editor of volumes XVIII and XIX of the first (mathematical) series, which appeared in 1920 and 1932. Lyapunov's scientific work received wide recognition. He was elected an honorary member of the universities of St. Petersburg, Kharkov, and Kazan, a foreign member of the Accademia dei Lincei (1909) and of the Paris Academy of Sciences (1916), and a member of many other scientific societies.

In the summer of 1917 Lyapunov went to Odessa

with his wife, who suffered from a serious form of tuberculosis. He began to lecture at the university: but in the spring of the following year his wife's condition rapidly deteriorated and she died on 31 October 1918. On that day Lyapunov shot himself and died three days later, without regaining consciousness. In accordance with a wish stated in a note that he had left, he was buried with his wife.

Lyapunov and A. A. Markov, who had been schoolmates at St. Petersburg University and, later, colleagues at the Academy of Sciences, were Chebyshev's most prominent students and representatives of the St. Petersburg mathematics school. Both were outstanding mathematicians and both exerted a powerful influence on the subsequent development of science. Lyapunov concentrated on three fields: the stability of equilibrium and motion of a mechanical system having a finite number of degrees of freedom; the stability of figures of equilibrium of a uniformly rotating liquid; the stability of figures of equilibrium of a rotating liquid.

Lyapunov's papers on the stability of systems having a finite number of degrees of freedom, among which his doctoral dissertation occupies a central position, belong equally to mathematics and to mechanics. They contain thorough analyses of a great many problems in the theory of ordinary differential equations.

The mathematical formulation of a problem closely related historically to investigations in celestial mechanics of the eighteenth and nineteenth centuries (the problem of the stability of the solar system) is the following: Given a system of n ordinary, first-order differential equations for n functions $x_k(t)$ of the independent variable t (time). It is assumed that the equations are solved with respect to the derivative dx_k/dt on the left side and that the right sides are power series with respect to $x_1, x_2, \cdots, x_n$ without free members, such that the equations have the obvious null solution $x_1 = x_2 = \cdots = x_n = 0$. The coefficients of the series can depend on t. The solution of the system is completely defined by assignment of the values of the unknown functions x_k for some value $t = t_0$. The stability of the null solution, according to Lyapunov, is stability in the infinite time interval $t \geq t_0$, with respect to the initial data. In other words, stability consists in the fact that, for $t \geq t_0$, the solution of the system $x_k(t)$ will be sufficiently small in absolute value for sufficiently small absolute values of the initial data $x_k(t_0)$. The mechanical systems described above, often called dynamic systems, play a fundamental role in dynamics.

When the corresponding system of differential equations is integrated and its solution is found in simple form, the investigation of stability presents no difficulty. As a rule, however, this integration is impracticable. Therefore, mathematicians generally use the approximation method, which consists in replacing the right sides of the equations by the system of linear members of their expansions into power series. In this manner the task devolves into a study of the stability of a linear system of differential equations; this substantially simplifies the problem, especially when the coefficients of the linear system are constants. It remained unclear, however, whether the replacement of the given system by a linear one was valid and, if valid, under what conditions. Use of a second- or somewhat higher-order approximation (that is, the retention of second- or somewhat higher-order members on the right side) enables one to improve the accuracy of knowledge about functions $x_k(t)$ in a finite time interval but gives no new basis for any conclusions about stability in the infinite interval $t \geqslant t_0$. As Lyapunov noted, the only attempt at a rigorous solution of the question had been made by Poincaré a short time earlier in the special cases of second-order and, in part, third-order systems.

With the aid of new methods that he had created, Lyapunov himself solved, for extremely general assumptions, the question of when the first approximation solves the problem of stability. He thoroughly examined the cases, especially important in practice, when the coefficients of the series on the right side of the equations are constants (the "established motion") or are periodic functions of time t, having one and the same period. For example, if, given constant coefficients, the real parts of all the roots of the system's characteristic equation (an nth degree, "secular" algebraic equation) are negative, the solution of the initial system is stable; if, however, there is among the roots one having a positive real part, then the solution is unstable. The first approximation, however, does not permit one to solve the problem of stability if the characteristic equation, while not having roots with positive real numbers, has roots the real parts of which are equal to zero. Here, the cases when the characteristic equation has one root equal to zero, or when it has two purely imaginary conjugate roots, are of special interest; these cases were exhaustively investigated by Lyapunov. In the case of periodic coefficients Lyapunov examined the possibilities arising in two especially interesting instances: when one of the roots of the characteristic equation is equal to unity and when two imaginary conjugate roots have a modulus equal to unity.

Among many other results is the proof of the theorem of the instability of motion if the force function of the forces acting on the system is not a maximum. Several of Lyapunov's articles dealing with a detailed analysis of the solution of homogeneous linear second-order equations having periodic coefficients (1896–1902) have the same orientation.

The ideas of this cycle of papers, especially Lyapunov's doctoral dissertation, are related to Poincaré's investigation. Specific results obtained by both these scholars coincide, but they do not deal with the basic content or the basic methods of their works. In particular, Poincaré made wide use of geometrical and topological concepts, while Lyapunov used purely analytical methods. Both Poincaré's papers and Lyapunov's works are fundamental to the qualitative theory of ordinary differential equations. At first Lyapunov's theory of the stability of mechanical systems did not receive the wide response given to Poincaré's more general ideas. But, from the early 1930's the number of papers directly related to Lyapunov's investigations increased very rapidly, especially with the growth of the significance of problems concerning the stability of motion in modern physics and engineering, primarily because of the study of fluctuations in various mechanical and physical systems. Problems of stability arise in the determination of the work regimen of various machines, in the construction of airplanes, electrical engineering, and ballistics.

Lyapunov studied figures of equilibrium of a uniformly rotating liquid over a period of thirty-six years. In the lecture "O forme nebesnykh tel" ("On the Shape of Celestial Bodies"; 1918) he said:

> According to a well-known hypothesis, each such body was initially in a liquid state; it took its present form before solidification, having previously received an unchanging form as the result of internal friction. Assuming this, the shape of a celestial body must be one of those which can be assumed by a rotating liquid mass, the particles of which mutually attract one another according to Newton's law, or, at least, must differ little from such a figure of equilibrium of a rotating liquid [*Izbrannye trudy*, p. 303].

Lyapunov mentioned the mathematical difficulty of studying equilibrium figures, a study which entails the solution of nonlinear integral equations.

It was Newton, his eighteenth-century successors Maclaurin and d'Alembert, and others who established that ellipsoids of rotation could be figures of equilibrium of homogeneous rotating liquids. Later, Jacobi demonstrated that certain triaxial ellipsoids could also be such figures. Other scholars also studied this problem. When, in 1882, Chebyshev placed before Lyapunov the question concerning the possibility of the existence of other equilibrium figures that are close to ellipsoidal, Lyapunov could solve the problem only in the first approximation. Believing it impossible to judge the existence of new figures according to the first approximation, he put off a definitive solution to the question. In his master's thesis of 1884 he guardedly mentioned that certain algebraic surfaces which were close to earlier-known ellipsoids of equilibrium, satisfy the conditions of equilibrium in the first approximation. On the other hand, in this thesis he examined the problem of the stability of the Maclaurin and Jacobi ellipsoids, injecting clarity and rigor into the statement of the problem, defining for the first time the concept of stability for a continuous medium.

In a series of papers written between 1903 and 1918, Lyapunov moved deeply into the investigation of Chebyshev's problem and related questions. In *Recherches dans la théorie de la figure des corps célestes* and *Sur l'équation de Clairaut* ... he proved the existence of nearly spherical figures of equilibrium for a sufficiently slowly rotating nonhomogeneous liquid, and investigated the solutions to the integraldifferential equations arising from this, which contain the unknown function both under the integral sign and under the sign of the derivatives; the first of these equations is "Clairaut's equation." In *Sur un problème de Tchébycheff* and *Sur les figures d'équilibre peu différentes des ellipsoids* ... it was established that among ellipsoids of equilibrium there are "ellipsoids of bifurcation" and that, in addition to ellipsoidal figures close to these, there also exist close, nonellipsoidal figures of equilibrium. A number of methods are entailed in the consistent determination of the equations of these figures. Finally, in the posthumously published *Sur certaines séries de figures d'équilibre d'un liquide hétérogène en rotation,* it is proved that each Maclaurin and Jacobi ellipsoid differing from the ellipsoids of bifurcation engenders new figures of equilibrium that are close to the Maclaurin and Jacobi ellipsoids in form; their density is not considered constant but, rather, as weakly varying.

In *Problème de minimum dans une question de stabilité des figures d'équilibre d'une masse fluide en rotation,* Lyapunov further developed and made more precise the theory of stability stated in his master's thesis and investigated the stability of the new, nearly ellipsoidal, figures of equilibrium that he had previously found.

In solving all these problems and the corresponding nonlinear integral and integral-differential equations, Lyapunov had to overcome great mathematical difficulties. To this end he devised delicate methods of approximation, the convergence of which he proved

with the rigor of contemporary mathematics; generalized the concept of the integral (in the direction of the Stieltjes-Riemann integral); and proved a number of new theorems on spherical functions.

Lyapunov's works again approach those of Poincaré. At a certain angular velocity, figures of equilibrium that Poincaré called "pear-shaped" branch off from Jacobi ellipsoids. The astronomer G. H. Darwin encountered the problem of the stability of pearshaped forms in his hypothesis concerning the origin of double stars arising from the division of a rotating liquid mass into two bodies. Poincaré, who examined the question within the limits of the second approximation, stated the hypothesis that these forms were stable; and Darwin, using Poincaré's general theory, seemingly confirmed this opinion, which was indispensable to his cosmogonical hypothesis, by calculations. Lyapunov's calculations, which were based on precise formulas and evaluations, led him to the opposite conclusion—that the pear-shaped figures were unstable. In 1911 Poincaré stated that he was not sure of the correctness of his prior opinion, but that to solve the question would require one to begin the very complex computations again. In 1912 Lyapunov published the necessary calculations in the third part of *Sur certaines séries de figures d'équilibre* ..., but no one sought to verify them. In 1917 Sir James Jeans confirmed Lyapunov's results, having discovered the defect in Darwin's computations.

During the period 1886–1902, Lyapunov devoted several works to mathematical physics; *Sur certaines questions qui se rattachent au problème de Dirichlet* (1898) is fundamental among these. Here, for the first time, a number of the basic properties of the potentials of simple and double layers were studied with utter rigor and the necessary and sufficient conditions, under which the function that solves Dirichlet's problem within a given range has normal derivatives over the limiting range of the surface, were indicated. These investigations created the foundation of a number of classic methods for solving boundary-value problems. In addition, Lyapunov's works on mathematical physics brought that area of analysis to the attention of a number of Kharkov mathematicians, especially V. A. Steklov, Lyapunov's student.

Finally, in two works that arose from a course in the theory of probability taught by Lyapunov, he substantially generalized Laplace's limit theorem in application to sums of random independent values. Chebyshev gave the first such generalization of this theorem in 1887, indicating the possibility of its proof, in the form given by him, by the method of moments; and Markov carried out the full proof on this basis in 1898. In "Sur une proposition de la théorie des probabilités" (1900) and "Nouvelle forme du théorème sur la limite de probabilité" (1901), Lyapunov proved the central limit theorem by the method of characteristic functions, which has subsequently assumed a fundamental place in the theory of probability; moreover, he did so under much broader conditions than Markov had used. Some time later, however, Markov proved the central limit theorem under Lyapunov's conditions by using the method of moments. These works by Lyapunov also served as the starting point for many later investigations.

BIBLIOGRAPHY

I. ORIGINAL WORKS. A complete list of Lyapunov's works is in *Aleksandr Mikhailovich Lyapunov. Bibliografia*, compiled by A. M. Lukomskaya, V. I. Smirnov, ed. (Moscow–Leningrad, 1953). Collections of his writings are *A. M. Lyapunov, Izbrannye trudy* ("Selected Works"; Moscow–Leningrad, 1948), with a bibliography compiled by A. M. Lukomskaya; and his *Sobranie sochineny* ("Collected Works"), 5 vols. (Moscow, 1954–1965), which includes Russian translations of all works written in French.

Individual works are *Ob ustoychivosti ellipsoidalnykh form ravnovesia vrashchayushcheysya zhidkosti* ("On the Stability of Ellipsoidal Forms of Equilibrium of a Rotating Liquid"; St. Petersburg, 1884), his master's thesis, translated into French as "Sur la stabilité des figures ellipsoidales d'équilibre d'un liquide animé d'un mouvement de rotation," in *Annales de la Faculté des sciences de l'Université de Toulouse*, 2nd ser., **6** (1904), 5–116; *Obshchaya zadacha ob ustoychivosti dvizhenia* ("The General Problem of the Stability of Motion"; Kharkov, 1902; 2nd ed., Moscow–Leningrad, 1935; 3rd ed., 1950), his doctoral dissertation, translated into French as "Problème générale de la stabilité du mouvement," in *Annales de la Faculté des sciences de l'Université de Toulouse*, 2nd ser., **9** (1907), 203–474, reprinted as no. 17 in the Annals of Mathematics series (Princeton, 1947); *Recherches dans la théorie de la figure des corps célestes* (St. Petersburg, 1903); *Sur l'équation de Clairaut et les équations plus générales de la théorie de la figure des planètes* (St. Petersburg, 1904); *Sur un problème de Tchebycheff* (St. Petersburg, 1905); *Sur les figures d'équilibre peu différentes des ellipsoids d'une masse liquide homogène douée d'un mouvement de rotation*, 4 vols. (St. Petersburg, 1906–1914); and *Problème de minimum dans une question de stabilité des figures d'équilibre d'une masse fluide en rotation* (St. Petersburg, 1908).

Published posthumously were *Sur certaines séries de figures d'équilibre d'un liquide hétérogène en rotation*, 2 vols. (Leningrad, 1925–1927); and *Raboty po teorii potentsiala* ("Papers on the Theory of Potentials"; Moscow–Leningrad, 1949), with a biographical essay by V. A. Steklov.

II. SECONDARY LITERATURE. See Y. L. Geronimus, *Ocherki o rabotakh korifeev russkoy mekhaniki* ("Essays on the Works of the Leading Figures of Russian Mechanics"; Moscow, 1952); A. T. Grigorian, *Ocherki istorii mekhaniki v Rossii* ("Essays on the History of Mechanics in Russia"; Moscow, 1961), 139–148, 219–225; V. I. Smirnov, "Ocherk nauchnykh trudov A. M. Lyapunova" ("Essay on the Scientific Works of A. M. Lyapunov"), in V. I. Smirnov, ed., *A. M. Lyapunov, Izbrannye trudy* (see above), 495–538; "Ocherk zhizni A. M. Lyapunova" and "Obzor nauchnogo tvorchestva A. M. Lyapunova" ("Essay on the Life of A. M. Lyapunov" and "A Survey of the Creative Scientific Work of A. M. Lyapunov"), in *Aleksandr Mikhailovich Lyapunov. Bibliografia* (see above), 469–478, 479–532; and "Iz perepiski P. Appelya, Z. Adamara, G. Burkkhardta, V. Volterra, P. Dyugema, K. Zhordana, A. Puankare i N. Rado s akademikom A. M. Lyapunovym" ("From the Correspondence of P. Appell, J. Hadamard, H. Burckhardt, V. Volterra, P. Duhem, C. Jordan, H. Poincaré, and N. Rado With Academician A. M. Lyapunov"), in *Trudy Instituta istorii estestvoznania i tekhniki. Akademia nauk SSSR*, **19** (1957), 690–719; V. A. Steklov, *Aleksandr Mikhailovich Lyapunov. Nekrolog* (Petrograd, 1919), repr. in *Obshchaya zadacha ustoychivosti dvizhenia*, 2nd ed. (see above), 367–388 and in Lyapunov's *Raboty po teorii potentsiala* (see above), 7–32; and A. P. Youschkevitch, *Istoria matematiki v Rossii do 1917 goda* ("The History of Mathematics in Russia Before 1917"; Moscow, 1968), 448–458.

A. T. GRIGORIAN

LYELL, CHARLES (*b.* Kinnordy, Kirriemuir, Angus, Scotland, 14 November 1797; *d.* London, England, 22 February 1875), *geology, evolutionary biology*.

Charles Lyell was the eldest child of Charles Lyell, Esq., of Kinnordy and the former Frances Smith, daughter of Thomas Smith of Maker Hall, Swaledale, Yorkshire. Both of Lyell's parents had been born in London, where both his grandfathers were connected with the British navy. His paternal grandfather, also Charles Lyell, served as a purser on various ships and in 1770 entered into a partnership to supply His Majesty's ships on the coast of North America. In 1778 he became secretary to Admiral John Byron during the latter's disastrous expedition to America and the West Indies. In 1782 he purchased the estate of Kinnordy at Kirriemuir, in what was then the county of Forfarshire, Scotland, and retired to lead the life of a Scottish laird.

Lyell's father matriculated in 1786 at Saint Andrews University and in 1787 at Peterhouse College, Cambridge, from which he was graduated B.A. in 1791. He thereafter studied law at Lincoln's Inn until he inherited the Kinnordy estate in Scotland on his father's death in 1796. On 4 October 1796 he married Frances Smith at Sidmouth, Devonshire.

When Charles Lyell was less than a year old, his father left Scotland for the south of England, where, in the autumn of 1798, he took a long lease on Bartley Lodge at Lyndhurst, on the border of the New Forest in Hampshire. There Lyell spent his boyhood. Strongly interested in botany, his father collected rare plants in the New Forest and corresponded with James Sowerby, Dawson Turner, William Hooker, and other botanists. He also made regular trips to Scotland to supervise his estate.

In 1805 Lyell, aged seven, was sent to school at Ringwood, Hampshire, and in 1808 at Salisbury. In December 1808 he became severely ill with pleurisy, and during his convalescence at Bartley he began to collect insects and study their habits. In 1810 Lyell and his younger brother Thomas were sent to school at Midhurst, in Sussex. He left Midhurst in June 1815 and in February 1816 matriculated at Exeter College, Oxford, as a gentleman commoner. At Oxford he received the customary classical education based largely on the reading of Aristotle and other ancient authors, but in 1817 he took the course of lectures in mineralogy given by William Buckland and in 1818 attended Buckland's lectures in geology.

Since boyhood Lyell had been an enthusiastic amateur entomologist, and now Buckland aroused his interest in geology. In July 1817 Lyell visited his father's friend Dawson Turner at Yarmouth, Norfolk, where he studied the effects of the interaction of the Yare River with the sea in forming the delta on which Yarmouth stood. In September 1817, while in Scotland with his father, he went with two college friends on horseback through the Highlands, along Loch Awe to Oban and thence by water to the island of Mull and to Staffa, famous for its columnar basalt formation. On Staffa, Lyell confirmed for Buckland that there were the broken ends of basalt columns in the roof of Fingal's Cave, a fact which showed that the cave had not been formed by the erosion of an intrusive dike of softer lava, as had been suggested by Leopold von Buch. During the summer of 1818 Lyell accompanied his parents and sisters on a carriage tour through France, Switzerland, and the north of Italy, crossing the Jura and the Alps. In the Alps he observed the effects of glaciers and the destruction produced by mountain torrents.

On 19 March 1819 Lyell was elected to the Geological Society of London and in the same year to the Linnean Society. He was entered at Lincoln's Inn, where in the autumn of 1819 he began to study law, reading in the office of John Patteson, the pleader. During the spring of 1819, however, when Lyell was studying for his degree examinations at Oxford, his eyes had begun to give him a great deal of pain and

he found that he could not sustain the prolonged and intense reading needed for his legal studies. He got on as best he could with the help of a reading clerk, but in August 1820 set out with his father on a long tour of the Continent. They traveled through Belgium to Cologne and thence up the Rhine valley and south into Italy, where they visited Ravenna and Rome. Along the Adriatic coast of Italy Lyell observed how the rivers descending from the Apennines had created a coastal plain, and cities which were ports during Roman times were now five miles from the sea. After his return to London in November 1820, Lyell continued his legal studies, but in a more relaxed fashion.

During the summer of 1821 Lyell visited his old school at Midhurst, Sussex, and, becoming curious about the geology of Sussex, called on Gideon Mantell, a surgeon in Lewes, who had formed a collection of fossils from the chalk of the South Downs and the underlying strata of the Weald. They became close friends and pursued a common interest in the geology of southeast England. In April 1822 Lyell visited Winchelsea and Romsey, on the southeast coast, to study the series of strata below the chalk, since they were visible in the cliffs along the English Channel. In late June 1822 Lyell also visited the Isle of Wight, where he discovered that the sequence of strata below the chalk was the same on the Isle of Wight as on the coast of Sussex and that the formation on the Isle of Wight called the greensand by Thomas Webster was identical with the Reigate firestone and the marl rock of western Sussex. The formation in England called greensand by G. B. Greenough and W. D. Conybeare was identical, however, with a lower series of beds which Webster had called the ferruginous sand on the Isle of Wight. Lyell outlined the distinction between the formations now known as the upper and lower greensand in a letter to Mantell of 4 July 1822. He did not publish his findings, and the same observations were first published in a general study of the greensand by William Fitton in 1824, after he had seen Lyell's letter to Mantell on the subject.

On 25 June 1823 Lyell arrived in Paris, where he spent the next two months. He studied French and attended free lectures on mining, geology, chemistry, and zoology. He met many French scientists, including Alexandre Brongniart, Georges Cuvier, and Constant Prévost, and the great German scientist and traveler Alexander von Humboldt, who was then living in Paris. With Prévost, Lyell studied the geology of the Paris basin and was influenced by Prévost to believe that the alternation of freshwater and marine formations could be explained naturally, without resort to catastrophes of unknown magnitude or cause. Prévost had found places where marine and freshwater fossils were mixed together, and he suggested that the basin had been at times a freshwater lake and at other times a great bay of the sea into which various rivers had emptied. The change from one state to another would have required only a relatively minor geological change in the barrier separating the Paris basin from the open sea, or in the level of the basin in relation to sea level. Prévost's explanation of geological changes in the Paris basin was radically different from that of Cuvier, who had accounted for the alternation of marine and freshwater formations by suggesting violent incursions of the sea over the land. Prévost, a student of Lamarck, also held to the principle of "induction to deduce what has been from what is."[1]

In Paris, Lyell took a broad and discriminating interest in French culture and institutions, but the scientific influence of Paris on him was most profound. He became aware of the depth and seriousness of French studies on natural history and geology, and in particular he became interested in freshwater formations.

In June 1824 Lyell entertained Constant Prévost when he visited England, and they went together on a geological tour of the southwest of England. During the late summer of 1824 Lyell worked at the geological mapping of his native county of Forfarshire in Scotland and made a detailed study of the marl deposits formed in its small freshwater lakes. This study provided the material for Lyell's first scientific paper, "On a Recent Formation of Freshwater Limestone in Forfarshire . . . ," which he began to read to the Geological Society on 17 December 1824. He found that modern freshwater marls were similar in their physical characteristics and contained the same types of fossils as the ancient freshwater marls studied by Cuvier and Brongniart in the Paris basin. In particular Lyell found that in certain circumstances a hard, dense limestone deposited in the Scottish lakes was exactly like certain ancient freshwater limestones of the Paris basin. Cuvier and Brongniart had believed that under modern conditions only soft, friable deposits formed in lakes; and Lyell showed that the distinction they had drawn between ancient and modern freshwater sediments was not valid.

In 1822 Lyell was called to the bar; and from 1825 to 1827 he was a practicing barrister, traveling on the Western Circuit, which included assizes at Winchester, Salisbury, Dorchester, Taunton, Exeter, and Bodmin. Although Lyell never derived any significant income from his legal practice, he valued his professional status as a lawyer because it freed him from many social demands upon his time. On circuit he had opportunities to study the geology of the southwest of England, and it was while on circuit during the summer of 1827 that he read Lamarck's *Philosophie zoologique.* From 1823 to 1826 Lyell served as one of the secretaries of the Geological Society, and in 1826 he was elected a fellow of the Royal Society. In 1825 he published a paper on a dike of serpentine cutting through sandstone strata in Forfarshire.[2] He also began to write articles for the *Quarterly Review.* His first article, published in December 1825, was a review of Thomas Campbell's *Letter to Mr. Brougham on the Subject of a London University;* and the writing of it aroused Lyell's interest in the state of university education in England. In June 1826 he published his second article, "On Scientific Institutions," in the *Quarterly Review;* and in September 1826 his third article appeared, a review of the first volume of the second series of the *Transactions of the Geological Society of London.* The last article was in effect a review of the state of geology in 1826. Lyell discussed current knowledge of the regular succession of stratified formations and the many recent discoveries of fossils, especially of the skeletons of fossil vertebrates. In considering the forces that had brought about geological change, he thought it possible that, given sufficient time, geological causes now active, such as earthquakes and volcanic action, could have raised sedimentary strata from the bottom of the sea to the places they now occupy in hills and mountains. He thought it premature to consider that any unknown force would have been needed and that to postulate more powerful disturbing forces in earlier geological periods would tend to discourage geologists from studying those changes now going on. Lyell showed that older strata had been deposited during long periods of tranquil and orderly conditions, just as younger strata had, and that the elevation and bending of strata proceeded in much the same way in successive geological periods.

In June 1827 the *Quarterly Review* published Lyell's fourth article, "State of the Universities," an extensive and profound comparison of universities in England with those in Scotland and on the Continent. Lyell described the concentration of teaching in the colleges at Oxford and Cambridge; their attention to classical studies to the exclusion of modern languages, modern history, economics, political science, and natural sciences; and the fact that although the dons taught nothing but classics, they made almost no contribution to classical scholarship. He followed this original and comprehensive analysis of English university education with various suggestions for reform, some of which were implemented much later in the nineteenth century.

During the summer of 1827 Lyell wrote a review of George Scrope's *Memoir on the Geology of Central France* (London, 1827), which was published in the *Quarterly Review* for October 1827. Scrope's book aroused Lyell's interest in the Auvergne district of France. In 1822 the discovery by Gideon Mantell of a river delta formation in the Tilgate forest beds beneath the chalk in Sussex had suggested to Lyell the magnitude of the earth movements which could sink the land surface, represented by the Tilgate forest beds, beneath the deep ocean in which the chalk was deposited, and then elevate it again to form the high ridges of the Weald. He also realized that the outlines of the ancient land surfaces, even those contemporary with the younger Tertiary strata of the Hampshire and London basins, had been completely obliterated. In contrast, the Auvergne, with its succession of ancient volcanic formations, was a geographically definable area since an early period in geological time. In Auvergne there were lava flows from at least three successive periods of volcanic activity. The most recent extinct volcanoes still retained their cones and craters intact, with unbroken sheets of lava extending into the river valleys. Beneath these layers of lava were others which bore no relation to the existing cones. Still older were isolated masses of basalt capping outlying hills. In addition to volcanic rocks of successive ages there were in Auvergne thick formations of freshwater strata containing fossils of extinct animals. Thus, through geological periods long enough for great changes in organic life, the Auvergne had remained a region of volcanic mountains, valleys, and freshwater lakes. In its geological formations was an extraordinarily long and continuous record of geological history.

In May 1828 Lyell set off for Auvergne to see its geology for himself. In Paris he joined Roderick Murchison and Mrs. Murchison, and they traveled south in Murchison's light open carriage. During the next two months they traversed the volcanic mountains and freshwater formations of central France. Lyell was struck by the resemblance of the ancient freshwater sediments of Auvergne to the modern deposits he had studied in Scotland. Both contained such fossils as the seedpods of *Chara* (gyrogonites), *Cypris*, caddis fly larva cases (*Phryganea*), and freshwater shells. But he was also astonished by a Tertiary freshwater limestone in the Cantal, near Aurillac, which at first sight looked exactly like the English chalk, a much older marine formation. Lyell and Murchison observed the action of rivers in Auvergne in reexcavating river valleys after they had been filled by successive lava flows.

From the Auvergne, Lyell and Murchison descended into the Rhone valley at Montélimar and went south. On 9 August they were at Nice, where they paused for some weeks to rest and to allow Murchison to recover from an attack of fever. The effect of the tour thus far had been to suggest to Lyell many analogies between conditions during the geological past and those of the present. His enthusiasm for geology was raised to the highest pitch. Murchison now suggested to Lyell that he go on to the south of Italy and Sicily, where he would see younger strata and many instances of modern changes produced by the volcanoes of Vesuvius and Etna. Before he left London, Lyell had begun the manuscript of a geological book in which he pointed out analogies between ancient and modern conditions. The tour through France had provided him with numerous instances to amplify this work, and he decided to go on to gather even more information.

In Nice, Lyell learned from Giovanni Risso that the fossil seashells in the local marine Tertiary strata included about 18 percent of species still living in the Mediterranean. From Nice, Lyell and Murchison traveled east along the coast to Genoa. They then returned to Savona and crossed the Apennines to Turin, where Franco Bonelli, director of the museum of zoology, told them that the fossil shells of the nearby hill of Superga differed from those of the subapennine beds but corresponded closely to the shells of the Bordeaux Tertiary formation in France. They differed also in the proportion of fossil shells belonging to still-living species. Lyell now formed the idea of classifying Tertiary formations according to the proportion of living species among their fossils. Furthermore, because he considered that volcanoes and earthquakes were associated with the uplift of strata, he thought that as he approached the active volcanoes of Vesuvius and Etna, he would find younger and more recently uplifted strata containing larger proportions of still-living species.

Murchison and Lyell traveled together as far as Padua, where they parted, Lyell going south through Italy while Murchison turned north on his way back to England. Lyell examined collections of fossils at Parma, Bologna, Florence, and Siena and made his own collection of subapennine shells. From Naples he went to the island of Ischia, where he collected some thirty species of fossil shells, all belonging to species living in the Mediterranean, from marl strata at an elevation of 700 feet on the side of the extinct volcano of Epomeo. Up to this point Lyell's discoveries entirely fulfilled his expectations. He thought the strata on Ischia had been elevated very recently and represented more or less contemporary deposits of the Mediterranean sea bottom. He assumed that soft marls containing only living species of shells must be very recent. He had found that the strata in the vicinity of volcanoes, and in an area where earthquakes were frequent, contained fossil shells of the same species as were still living in the Mediterranean. In Naples, Lyell studied Vesuvius and the temple of Serapis at Pozzuoli, which showed evidence of both elevation and subsidence of the land during historic times.

On 16 November 1828 Lyell crossed to Messina, Sicily, and rode on muleback south along the coast to Taormina. He visited the Val del Bove and from Nicolosi climbed Mount Etna. He was deeply impressed by the enormous size and great age of Etna, which he was convinced had been built up by a long series of volcanic eruptions like those still going on. His first doubts about the necessary recentness of strata containing living species of fossils may have arisen from a bed of clay above Catania that contained many modern Mediterranean shells. When he looked back at Etna from the ridge above Primosole, he saw that the enormous mass of the volcano appeared to rest, as though on a platform, on the plateau formed by the clay hills above Catania, so that the clay strata appeared older than the mountain.

In Lentini, Lyell saw for the first time the hard white limestone of the Val di Noto; it puzzled him because, while he thought it ought to be recent, it contained only the casts of shells, like an ancient Secondary limestone. As he rode down the valley of the Anapo River toward Syracuse, Lyell saw the white limestone exposed in the cliffs to a thickness of more than 800 feet. At the foot of the white limestone escarpment at Floridia, near Syracuse, were strata of calcareous sandstone. On the south side of the harbor of Syracuse, Lyell found, apparently beneath the white limestone—and therefore still older—strata of soft marl containing many perfect fossil shells, some still retaining their colors and all belonging to species still living in the surrounding Mediterranean. He was, however, uncertain of the relation of the marl to the white limestone until he reached Girgenti (now Agrigento), where he found strata of blue clay containing shells overlain by strata of calcareous sandstone identical with that at Floridia.

Astonished at what he was finding, and doubting whether he had observed correctly, Lyell explored the interior of Sicily until at Castrogiovanni (now Enna) he found all the strata of the Sicilian formation, from the white limestone of Lentini down through sandstones and marls to the blue clay of Syracuse, containing living species of shells with their original colors, all exposed in order in one immense escarpment. For Lyell the discovery that the white limestone, containing only casts and impressions of shells, was a very recent formation, had the force of revelation. It meant that the characteristics of a rock stratum were determined not by its geological age but by the conditions under which it was laid down, and these conditions had recurred again and again in successive geological periods. In Sicily, Lyell saw too that volcanic activity had gone on gradually and uniformly, interspersed with periods of rest, through an immense extent of time. Finally, he saw that the assemblage of shell species now living in the Mediterranean constituted a very old fauna, which had changed very little during the immense time required to deposit the stratified rocks of Sicily and to elevate them into hills of rounded and worn outline.

Because Lyell saw in Sicily a continuity between the fauna living in the Mediterranean and its fossil ancestors preserved in the rocks, he realized that the conditions under which both lived must be analogous. Therefore conditions during past geological ages must have been essentially similar to modern conditions on the earth's surface, and the forces which brought about geologic changes must have been the result of processes similar to those going on at the present time. Fired with such new ideas, Lyell set out for England in January 1829, determined to rewrite his book to see how far he could "explain the former changes of the earth's surface by causes now in operation." He was now certain that the Tertiary formations represented a much greater period of time than he had dreamed and that the strata of the Paris basin, of the hill of Superga at Turin, of the subapennine hills, and of Sicily were not parallel and contemporary formations but represented different and successive periods of geological time.

In Turin, Lyell discussed his Sicilian results with Bonelli, and in Geneva he obtained from Augustin de Candolle information on the geographical distribution of plants. In Paris, which he reached on 14 February 1829, Lyell called on Jules Desnoyers, who in 1825 had shown that the Tertiary formation of the Loire valley was younger than that of the Paris basin. When Lyell told Desnoyers of his Sicilian discoveries and his opinion that the various Tertiary formations were of different ages and could be arranged according to the proportion of living species among their fossils, Desnoyers said that he himself had come to similar conclusions and that Gérard Paul Deshayes, who possessed a large collection of fossil shells, had also decided that Tertiary formations might be arranged in a chronological series on the basis of differences in their characteristic groupings of fossil shell species. Lyell immediately consulted Deshayes, who told him that on the basis of their fossil shells, Tertiary formations might be distinguished into three successive geological periods. Lyell then asked Deshayes to prepare a catalog of fossil shells from all the Tertiary formations of Europe.

Lyell returned to London on 24 February 1829, and from then until the beginning of June 1830 he wrote and saw through the press the first volume of his *Principles of Geology*. It was published by John Murray in July 1830 (not January, as stated in later editions of the *Principles*) and created an immediate sensation. In it Lyell first discussed the historical development of geology and then treated the principles of geological reasoning. He argued that the order of nature in the past was uniform with that in the present and, therefore, that the geologist should always try to explain geological phenomena by analogy with modern conditions. The greatest difficulty he had to overcome was the clear evidence for a warmer climate during past geological epochs even in high northern latitudes, such as those of Great Britain. To account for the changes in climate which had occurred between past geological epochs and the present, Lyell studied the factors which determine climate in different parts of the world at the present time. He showed how not only local climate, but even worldwide climatic conditions, depend on the pattern of distribution of land and sea and would, therefore, be altered by changes in their distribution. An increase in the proportion of land near the equator, and of ocean area toward the poles, would tend to create a warmer world climate and vice versa.

Lyell surveyed the full range of processes which at present are altering the earth's surface—the eroding effects of running water in streams and rivers and of waves along the seacoast, the accumulation of sediments in deltas and on the sea bottom, and the cumulative effects of earthquakes and volcanoes in elevating the land. He showed that even the largest volcanoes, such as Vesuvius and Etna, were the product of a long series of eruptions distributed through immense periods of time, and the eruptions were never greater nor more frequent than in historic times. Lyell emphasized repeatedly that the magnitude of the geological changes which had occurred during the past was not a reason to postulate extraordinary convulsions or catastrophes. The greatest changes could be accomplished by ordinary geological processes acting gradually, if they were given sufficient time.

Lyell sought to separate geology from cosmology and refused to consider the question of the origin of the earth, or its state when first formed. Furthermore, he considered it unscientific to attempt to explain otherwise puzzling geological phenomena by reference to the origin of the world. In the succession of geological formations and geological changes Lyell saw an unending vista of uniform conditions on the earth's surface, as stable as those that exist today, and of geological processes ceaselessly at work. The principle of the uniformity of the "course of Nature" throughout the history of the earth gave significance to every feature of the present natural world for the understanding of events in the past. The geologist therefore must study all changes now occurring on the earth, because these changes, daily at work, may enable him to understand otherwise puzzling geological phenomena of the past.

During the summer of 1830 Lyell made a geological expedition to the Pyrenees, followed by several weeks of study of Tertiary shells with Deshayes at Paris. When he returned to London on 9 November, half the edition of the first volume of the *Principles* was already sold. During 1831 he wrote the second volume, which was published in January 1832. In this volume Lyell considered the changes which had occurred in the living world through geological time. His studies on Tertiary shells had already shown him that as one proceeded from older to younger strata, the proportion of fossils belonging to extinct species declined gradually while that of living species increased. Thus, throughout the Tertiary period species of shells had become extinct, one by one, to be replaced, one by one, by new species. The continuity thus revealed in the living world, accompanied by gradual change, was in sharp distinction to the apparently abrupt changes in the forms of animal life observed in the secondary strata of France and England. Lyell pointed out that all the species of mammals living when the present assemblage of marine mollusks had become established in the sea had since become extinct. Thus the land mammals, which were subject to many more vicissitudes than marine forms, became extinct more rapidly.

To account for extinction Lyell showed that the life of each species was dependent upon the continuance of a certain set of physical conditions in its environment. Geological processes, however, were steadily tending to alter these conditions, both locally and over wide regions. Thus the possible habitats for a species were steadily shifting and sometimes were obliterated. Lyell also showed that the life of a species was at the same time dependent upon a multitude of relationships with other species living in the same area. There was severe competition between species for living space, so that sometimes a species might become extinct simply because it could not contend successfully with others. And the extinction of one species would drag in its train the extinction of others which were dependent upon it. Similarly, the increase and spread of a successful species would force many others into extinction. Yet the geographical distribution of species showed that every species had tended to spread outward from its geographical center of origin. Lyell thus showed that the living world of plants and animals was in a state of dynamic balance and that the fluctuations of the balance of nature would themselves steadily tend to produce the extinction of species.

Lyell's argument required the assumption that species were real, definite, and stable entities. If species were infinitely plastic, or had no real existence, as Lamarck had supposed, they need never become extinct but could simply adapt themselves endlessly to varying conditions. Lyell therefore began his discussion of species with a systematic examination and criticism of Lamarck's theory.

Lyell also used evidence drawn from the geographical distribution of plants and animals to show that each species appeared to have arisen in a single center, from which it had spread. The area of its distribution was limited by geographical barriers of different kinds. Places with similar altitude and climate on two isolated continents have entirely different sets of species, although the two sets of species may have adapted in similar ways to similar conditions. Lyell showed that each species had arisen at a particular place and at a particular time in geologic history, and had persisted for a certain period, at the end of which it became extinct and was replaced by a new species.

Lyell left the species problem at this point. He had shown that the emergence of new species was a steady process in geologic history that was needed to compensate for the equally steady process of extinction, but he did not attempt to say how new species emerged. His readers were thus left in suspense. Privately, Lyell had pondered the question of the origin of species and was certain that they emerged by some natural process, but he had no explanation to offer. Although he was fascinated by Lamarck's theory, he felt certain, on scientific grounds, that it was false.

In 1831 Lyell was appointed professor of geology at King's College, London, and in May and June 1832 delivered his first course of lectures on geology, a course which was widely attended by members of the public. On 12 July 1832, at Bonn, Germany, Lyell married Mary Elizabeth Horner, aged twenty-three, daughter of Leonard Horner, a fellow of the Geological Society and from 1828 to 1830 warden of London University. On their return to London after a wedding trip up the Rhine valley and through Switzerland and France, Lyell took a house at 16 Hart Street. Mary Lyell, who read German and French fluently, assisted Lyell in his reading and geological work at home and accompanied him on almost all his geological travels abroad. She became an accomplished conchologist and, because of the weakness of his eyes, often wrote Lyell's letters for him.

In the third volume of the *Principles*, published in 1833, Lyell attempted to answer some of the criticisms of his doctrines provoked by the first two volumes. The opening chapter is a splendid defense of the point of view to which William Whewell had already attached the name "uniformitarian." Lyell argued that the natural order of the past was uniform with that of the present; the same physical laws held true and the same kinds of processes occurred. The geologist should, therefore, attempt to explain geological phenomena by analogy with modern processes. The apparent difficulty in doing so was chiefly a result of ignorance of the nature and extent of geological changes now going on. The remainder of the volume was an application of the doctrine of uniformity and the use of modern analogies to the problems of Tertiary geology. Lyell introduced his classification of Tertiary formations into four successive epochs and the terms Eocene (Gr. ἠώς, dawn; καίνος, recent), Miocene (Gr. μειων, less; καίνος, recent), and the older and newer Pliocene (Gr. πλειον, more, larger; καίνος, recent) to designate them. In the coinage of these terms he was assisted by William Whewell, who suggested the common root καινος. Lyell's classification showed that the Tertiary formations made up a series of strata enormously greater than had previously been suspected and represented a period of time correspondingly great. Lyell included, as an appendix to the third volume, Deshayes's tables of more than 3,000 species of Tertiary fossil shells.

Besides establishing a new era in geology, the *Principles* became a lifework for Lyell. He continued to revise it and brought it out in twelve successive editions. The twelfth edition was corrected by him but appeared after his death. The second edition consisted of a corrected version of the first and second volumes, published in May 1832 and January 1833, respectively, before the appearance of the third volume in May 1833. In May 1834 he published a new edition of the whole work, called the third edition, in four small volumes, dividing the material in the three volumes of the first edition into four books but omitting Deshayes's tables of Tertiary shells. While continuing to revise and add to his text, Lyell retained the format of four small volumes for the fourth edition, which appeared in June 1835, and the fifth edition, which appeared in March 1837.

In July 1838 Lyell published his *Elements of Geology* in one volume. Although the *Elements* was intended to be a brief descriptive work and not theoretical, in writing it Lyell took for granted the theoretical viewpoint he had already established in the *Principles*. Thus Lyell's *Elements* was the first modern textbook of geology written on the assumption that geological phenomena could be explained completely in terms of natural and knowable causes.

When Lyell came to prepare the sixth edition of the *Principles*, he removed from it the discussion of Tertiary formations in book IV, in order to transfer all purely descriptive geology to a second edition of the *Elements*. He also transferred four chapters dealing with various theoretical questions from book IV to book I in order to retain them in the *Principles*. Lyell was anxious that the *Principles* and the *Elements* should not overlap in their subject matter. In addition he developed, in chapter 10 of book I, a theory that erratic boulders had been transported by icebergs; and in chapter 11 he presented evidence that volcanic action had occurred in all geological periods with about the same intensity as at present. Lyell thus established in the sixth edition of the *Principles*, published in two volumes in June 1840, the plan of organization to which he would adhere through the seventh edition (February 1847), the eighth edition (May 1850), and the ninth edition (June 1853). The seventh through ninth editions were each a single large octavo volume. After 1853 Lyell did not revise the *Principles* until 1865, when he undertook a major reorganization of the book.

The second edition of the *Elements* appeared in July 1841. With the inclusion of the chapters on Tertiary formations and other additions, it had grown from twenty-five to thirty-six chapters in two volumes. In the third edition, published in January 1851, Lyell changed the title to *A Manual of Elementary Geology* but did not alter the basic plan of the book. It remained the *Manual* in the fourth edition of January 1852 and the fifth edition of February 1855. For the sixth edition, however, published in January 1865, Lyell returned to the original *Elements of Geology*.

Lyell took great trouble to provide both the *Principles* and the *Elements* with maps, diagrams, and illustrations. He had numerous drawings of fossils made and transferred to woodcuts or engravings that were often of unusual beauty. As a rule each new edition of his work contained additional illustrations. Lyell took equal pains with his prose. The *Elements* is a model of simple, lucid exposition, while in the *Principles* he cultivated a disarming and entrancing style of great persuasive power. Lyell used visual images, analogies, and metaphors to help the reader envision the past history of the earth.

From 1834 to 1836 Lyell was president of the Geological Society of London. During June and July 1834 he traveled alone to Sweden to determine whether the rising of the land there, a phenomenon reported by a number of writers, were real or not. Lyell found that the evidence for a gradual and imperceptible, but steady, rise of the land in northern Sweden was clear and inescapable. On 27 November and 18 December 1834 he presented the results of his Swedish tour to the Royal Society of London as the Bakerian lecture.

In October 1836 Charles Darwin returned from the *Beagle* voyage, and a warm friendship soon sprang up between him and Lyell. Darwin had taken Lyell's *Principles* with him on the *Beagle*, and in South America he had discovered that the whole southern part of the continent had undergone a recent elevation in gradual and successive stages. On 7 March 1838 Darwin presented to the Geological Society a paper in which he connected the phenomena of earthquakes and volcanic action in South America to show that the elevation of the Andes and of the whole continent had been brought about gradually by the cumulative effect of repeated earthquakes and volcanic eruptions. Such a large-scale example of the action of modern causes provided Lyell with very welcome support for the theory of geological uniformity, for which he was still contending against catastrophist opponents. Lyell was also deeply impressed by Darwin's theory of the origin of coral reefs and atolls by gradual subsidence. Darwin and Lyell met most frequently from 1836 to 1841, when Darwin was living in London. After Darwin moved to Downe, Kent, he and Lyell corresponded regularly and met occasionally in London. From time to time the Lyells went to Downe to spend several days with the Darwins, and during these visits Lyell usually took work with him.

In 1837 Lyell became involved in a controversy with Edward Charlesworth over the classification of the crag, a Tertiary formation of Norfolk. In 1835 Charlesworth had correctly distinguished the red crag from the older coralline crag; but Lyell had thought that because there were 150 species of shells common to the two formations, they must belong to the same geological period. He suggested that the two deposits had been laid down contemporaneously in different parts of the same sea. Charlesworth then attacked the basis for Lyell's classification of Tertiary formations. He pointed out the uncertainty in the discrimination of species and cited the opinion of some naturalists that almost all species of crag fossils were extinct. Because of the uncertainty whether fossil shells were identical with living forms or belonged to extinct species, Charlesworth argued that Lyell's system of classification based on the proportion of living to extinct species in a formation was unreliable.

To find answers to the questions raised by Charlesworth, Lyell made three geological tours of the crag, in April 1838 to Suffolk and in July 1838 and June 1839 to Suffolk and Norfolk. He found that Charlesworth was right in considering the coralline crag to be an older formation than the red crag, but after an exhaustive study of crag fossil shells he also found that the percentage of living species in the various crag formations confirmed Charlesworth's geological findings instead of contradicting them. The coralline crag contained only 19 percent living species, while the red crag contained 30 percent and the Norwich crag, which Charlesworth considered a still younger formation, contained between 50 and 60 percent living species of shells. Ironically, therefore, Charlesworth's conclusions were upheld by the very system he had attacked. The crag question also caused Lyell to study intensively the range of variation, through time, of species of Tertiary fossil shells and to compare the opinions of the two leading fossil conchologists of Europe, Heinrich Beck and Deshayes, on the identity of crag shell species.

On 20 July 1841 the Lyells sailed for America, where they remained until August 1842. After landing at Boston, Lyell visited the geologists of the New York State Geological Survey at Albany and the Lyells traveled through western New York, accompanied by James Hall. Deeply impressed by Niagara Falls, Lyell collected evidence to show that the falls were receding steadily toward Lake Erie and that the Niagara gorge had been produced by the gradual recession of the falls from the face of the escarpment at Queenston, Ontario. During October and November 1841 Lyell delivered the Lowell lectures in Boston. In December the Lyells traveled to the South, where Lyell studied the Tertiary formations of the coastal plain in Virginia, the Carolinas, and Georgia. On their return northward Lyell gave courses of geological lectures in Philadelphia and New York, attended the meeting of the American Association of Geologists and Naturalists at Boston in April 1842, and then made a tour of the Ohio valley, Lake Erie, Lake Ontario, and the St. Lawrence River valley. He studied the succession of terraces around Lake Erie and Lake Ontario; and in Montreal and Quebec and at Lake Champlain he collected, from deposits of clay several hundred feet above sea level, fossil seashells belonging to living Arctic species. During July and August 1842 Lyell spent a month studying the coal formation of Nova Scotia. He showed that the gypsum-bearing strata were part of the lower Carboniferous formation rather than the upper.

At Pictou, Nova Scotia, Lyell met John William Dawson, then aged twenty-one and newly returned from a year of study at the University of Edinburgh, who accompanied him on several geological expeditions. Lyell encouraged Dawson to prepare papers to send to the Geological Society of London and thereby launched Dawson on his career as a geologist. Lyell was a sympathetic and perceptive observer of the United States and Canada and made a number of warm friends among Americans, who were impressed by Lyell's geological knowledge and universal curiosity but sometimes bewildered by his absentmindedness and odd mannerisms. Invariably they were charmed by the beauty and winning manners of Mary Lyell, who was equally at ease in mansion or log cabin, in steamboat, railway car, or stagecoach, and always cheerful and uncomplaining, whatever mishaps or hardships she might suffer. On her part Mary Lyell developed a strong affection for America. During the Civil War, when the United States was very unpopular in England, she defended the cause of the Union and befriended the United States ambassador, Charles Francis Adams, when he was subjected to social ostracism in London.

In 1845 Lyell published his *Travels in North America*, a work unusual among descriptions of America by British travelers in its fairness and insight, and incorporating much discussion of the geology of North America. He included a geological map of eastern North America from the Gulf of St. Lawrence to Florida and Texas, based on the published works of twenty-six authors as well as on his own travels. In discussing American colleges Lyell was also led to discuss English university education because, he said, in trying to explain it to Americans he himself had become more aware of its unusual nature. Lyell followed up his criticisms of the English universities by helping to obtain the establishment of a royal commission on the universities.

In September 1845 Lyell returned to the United States, again to give the Lowell lectures in Boston. He and his wife first traveled to Maine and through the White Mountains of New Hampshire. After Lyell had delivered his course of lectures, the Lyells set off in December on a long tour through the South, stopping for two weeks in January 1846 with Hamilton Couper at Hopeton plantation, on the Altamaha River in Georgia. From Savannah, Georgia, they went to Claiborne, on the Alabama River, where Lyell collected fossils, then by steamboat to Mobile. From Mobile they went up the Tombigbee River to Tuscaloosa, to visit the Alabama coal field. Returning to Mobile, they continued by steamboat to New Orleans, where Lyell made an expedition to the mouth of the Mississippi River to study the growth of its delta. From New Orleans the Lyells went up the Mississippi and Ohio rivers by steamboat, and overland across Pennsylvania to Philadelphia. On 1 June 1846 they sailed for England. In 1849 Lyell published an account of this tour in his *Second Visit to the United States.*

In October 1846 the Lyells moved from 16 Hart Street to a larger house at 11 Harley Street (now 73 Harley Street). In 1848 Lyell was knighted, and in 1849 he was reelected president of the Geological Society of London. In this capacity he gave evidence before the Oxford University Commission, and by this and other means he was active in the reform of the universities and the introduction of science into university education. His books on America attracted the attention of Prince Albert, and he served as one of the royal commissioners for the Great Exhibition of 1851.

In August 1852 the Lyells sailed for Halifax, Nova Scotia, where Lyell went with J. W. Dawson to study the great fossil cliff at South Joggins. On this occasion they found inside the trunk of one of the upright fossil *Sigillaria* trees of Joggins the skeleton of a reptile, later described by Richard Owen and named *Dendrerpeton acadianum.* Since the first air-breathing animal was discovered in the coal only in 1844, *Dendrerpeton* was one of but three or four fossil reptiles then known from the Carboniferous period. From Nova Scotia the Lyells went to Fredericton, New Brunswick, where they were guests of Sir Edmund Head, the governor, and thence to Boston, where Lyell delivered the Lowell Lectures during the autumn of 1852. In December they returned to London. In June 1853 Lyell made a fourth visit to the United States, to represent, with Lord Ellesmere, the Royal Commission for the Exhibition of 1851 at the New York Industrial Exhibition of 1853; he returned to London at the beginning of August.

In December 1853 the Lyells sailed to Madeira, accompanied by Mr. and Mrs. Charles Bunbury, to spend several months studying the volcanic geology of Madeira and the Canary Islands. On Madeira, Lyell met a young German naturalist, George Hartung, who had come there to recover from consumption. Hartung joined Lyell in his geological expeditions and in the collection of specimens. Lyell was deeply impressed by the distinctive flora of these oceanic islands. On Madeira, at an elevation of about 1,000 feet above sea level, he discovered a bed of lignite containing fossilized leaves of plants similar to those of the modern forests of Madeira. The fossil

plants showed that Madeira had existed as a land surface, and probably as an isolated oceanic island, since the Miocene. In the light of their long geological history as isolated islands, the zoology of the islands was also remarkable. They possessed no native mammals but contained an unusual number of insect species, especially of beetles; and many of the species were peculiar to individual islands. The species of land shells were even more remarkable. There were seventy-seven species on Madeira and fifty-five species on Pôrto Santo, but only nine species were common to the two islands, although they are only thirty miles apart.

The Lyells returned to England in March 1854. Until February 1855 Lyell was occupied in preparing the fifth edition of the *Manual.* He then visited Berlin and during the summer made a long visit to Scotland. In November 1855 Hartung came to London, and Lyell and he began to go over their collections from Madeira and the Canary Islands. The remarkable number of distinct species of insects and land shells —a pattern of geographical distribution of species similar to that which Charles Darwin had observed in the Galápagos Islands twenty years earlier— impressed Lyell as bearing directly on the question of the origin of species. On 26 November 1855 Lyell read an article by A. R. Wallace, "On the Law Which Has Regulated the Introduction of New Species," in the *Annals and Magazine of Natural History* for September 1855. Wallace presented evidence from paleontology and from the geographical distribution of plants and animals to show that "Every species has come into existence co-incident in both space and time with a pre-existing closely allied species." Wallace's paper seemed to express very aptly the meaning of the distribution of both fossil and living species in Madeira and the Canary Islands; and Lyell made extensive notes on it in a notebook devoted solely to the species question, the first of what would ultimately be seven such notebooks. Through the winter of 1856 Lyell continued to study Madeiran and Canary species, and he began to investigate the question of how species might migrate across areas of ocean to colonize islands.

On 13 April 1856 the Lyells went to Downe, Kent, to spend four days with the Charles Darwins. On the morning of 16 April, Darwin explained to Lyell his theory of the origin of species by natural selection. Lyell had been aware for many years that Darwin believed in the transmutation of species; but he now learned, apparently for the first time, the details of Darwin's theory to account for the process of transmutation. Lyell immediately urged Darwin to publish his theory, a step which Darwin was reluctant to take because he thought that it could not be understood, or appreciated fully, except within the framework of a broad array of connected biological and geological evidence. During the summer of 1856, however, Darwin began to write on the relationship of the geographical distribution of species to geological history. In October 1856 Darwin decided that he could not publish a brief sketch of his theory and began to write the large work on which he was still engaged in June 1858, when he received from Alfred Russel Wallace the manuscript of Wallace's paper containing the theory of natural selection.

The species of Madeira and the Canary Islands, together with Darwin's theory of natural selection, caused Lyell to accept at least tentatively the possibility of the transmutation of species. In 1857 a series of discoveries of fossil mammals in the Purbeck strata showed that a rich mammalian fauna had lived during the Secondary period, in what had been considered exclusively an age of reptiles. This caused Lyell again to doubt whether there had been a genuine progressive development of animal life through geological time. In 1858 the publication of the Darwin-Wallace papers on natural selection renewed Lyell's interest in the species question. From 1858 to 1861, when he began to write the *Antiquity of Man*, Lyell made many entries in his species journals and corresponded frequently with Darwin.

In October 1857 Lyell revisited southern Italy and Sicily, where he had not been since 1828, to make a fresh study of the structure of Vesuvius and Etna. In 1853–1854, in his study of Madeira and the Canaries, made with Hartung, Lyell had become convinced that the evidence on which Leopold von Buch had founded his theory of craters of elevation (1825) was completely fallacious. According to Buch's theory, the volcanic rocks forming such islands as Tenerife and Palma had been formed originally as horizontal sheets of lava which had later been upheaved in a great convulsion to create the cones and craters of their modern volcanoes. Buch believed that liquid lavas could not solidify to form sheets of solid rock on the steep slopes where they now occurred. Therefore, they must have been solidified in a horizontal position and later upheaved. In 1834 Élie de Beaumont, in a paper on Mount Etna, argued that the solid beds of lava in the Val del Bove, inclined at angles of 28° and more, resembled portions of modern lavas that flowed over ground almost level or inclined at no more than 3°. Geologists who accepted Élie de Beaumont's conclusions were forced to believe that all modern volcanoes had acquired their conical form by later upheaval of their beds of lava.

In 1853–1854, on Madeira and Palma, Lyell had

seen modern lavas forming sheets of solid rock and inclined at angles of 15° to 20° but showing no sign of any disturbance in position. In 1855 Hartung had also observed on Lanzarote in the Canaries a solid basaltic lava on a slope of 30°. In 1857 Lyell found on Etna lavas which had solidified on steep slopes of from 15° to 40° in inclination. The lavas formed continuous sheets of rock alternating with layers of loose scoriae above and beneath them. Lyell reported these results to the Royal Society on 10 June 1858, and in September and October 1858 he returned to Etna to make a more thorough study of its structure. He found that Etna had neither a linear axis nor a single center of upheaval. Instead, he found two earlier centers of eruption in the Val del Bove. From each center the beds of lava sloped away in all directions, but beds of lava arising from Etna's modern center of eruption had flowed over and buried those from the earlier centers. Lyell considered this to be decisive evidence against the crater-of-elevation theory because "although one cone of eruption may envelope and bury another cone of eruption, it is impossible for a cone of upheaval to mantle round and overwhelm another cone of upheaval so as to reduce the whole mass to one conical mountain."[3] He concluded that the conical form of Etna, as of all volcanoes, was entirely the result of the long-continued process of volcanic eruption.

In June 1858 Charles Darwin consulted Lyell about Alfred Russel Wallace's paper on natural selection, which he had just received, and Lyell and Joseph Hooker together presented Darwin's and Wallace's papers on natural selection to the Linnean Society on 1 July 1858. In May 1859 Joseph Prestwich announced to the Royal Society that he had found, at St. Acheul near Abbeville, France, a flint implement, the product of human workmanship, embedded in place in ancient river gravel. Prestwich's discovery, which established the geological age of the flint implements described earlier from Abbeville by Boucher de Perthes, was clear evidence that man had lived in Europe as far back as the later Pliocene and, therefore, far longer than had previously been thought. In July 1859 Lyell went to Abbeville and Amiens to see for himself the places where flint implements had been found and continued to pursue the question of the antiquity of man, which he saw was related to that of the origin of species.

During 1860 and 1861 Lyell studied evidence of the early existence of man in Europe; and in 1862 he began to write *The Geological Evidences of the Antiquity of Man*, which was published in February 1863. In the *Antiquity of Man* Lyell discussed the state of knowledge concerning the prehistory of man, including the discovery of stone tools, the definition of the Bronze and Stone ages, the shell mounds of Denmark, and the Swiss lake dwellings. He gave a particularly thorough account of the discovery in 1857 of the skeleton of a man in a cave at Neanderthal, Germany, because the skull of the Neanderthal man, although unquestionably human, showed heavy eyebrow ridges like those of apes. In considering the origin of man, Lyell argued that if all races of man were descended from a common ancestry, as he believed they were, then it would have required a very long period of time for the gradual formation of such distinct races as the Caucasian, Mongolian, and Negro. If the different races of man were descended from a common ancestry, however, Lyell thought it equally probable that closely related species of animals and plants were likewise descended from a common parentage. He then reviewed his own 1832 analysis of Lamarck's theory and said that while he had disagreed with Lamarck's view of the transmutation of species, he had agreed with Lamarck "in believing that the system of changes now in progress in the organic world would afford, when fully understood, a complete key to the interpretation of all the vicissitudes of the living creation in past ages."[4] Lyell described Darwin's and Wallace's theory of the indefinite modification of species by natural selection and gave a brief abstract of some of Darwin's arguments in the *Origin of Species*. He accepted Darwin's theory as providing a clear explanation of many biological and geological phenomena previously puzzling, but did not make any declaration of his own adherence to the theory.

In the *Antiquity of Man*, however, Lyell, in the manner of a barrister, presented to the reader a broad array of evidence which indicated that man had evolved gradually from lower animals over an immense period of time, that species had been modified one into another, and that the modification had probably been produced by natural selection. He compared the gradual divergence of the various European languages from a common root language to the gradual divergence of species. By presenting evidence without drawing conclusions from it, Lyell kept the reader's attention on the evidence and required him to draw his own conclusions. Lyell thus made the question of the origin of man and other species one of evidence rather than of doctrine. He kept his readers in suspense to the end of the book and induced them to consider the meaning of the evidence for themselves. Lyell thus gave Darwin powerful support in the controversy following the publication of the *Origin of Species*. Darwin, however, expressed disappointment that Lyell did not make a clear statement of his own opinion on the origin of species.[5]

In reply Lyell said that he had expressed his opinion fully "so far as my reason goes, and farther than my imagination and sentiment can follow."[6] Lyell seems to have felt a particular revulsion toward the idea that man was descended from animals and to have thought that the origin of the human intellect required a special explanation. At Darwin's urging he amended his statements concerning species in a later edition of the *Antiquity of Man* but remained hesitant.

On 30 November 1864, at the anniversary meeting of the Royal Society at which the Copley Medal was awarded to Charles Darwin in absentia, Lyell announced publicly that he had changed his mind concerning species and declared his faith in Darwin's theory of the indefinite modification of species by natural selection. Between 1865 and 1868 Lyell rewrote and revised the *Principles* for the tenth edition, so as to make it conform in every part with Darwin's theory and to express his wholehearted conviction of the truth of the theory of evolution by natural selection. In the second volume of the tenth edition, published in 1868, Lyell devoted the first ten chapters of book III to various aspects of the species question. In chapter 37 he discussed the theory of natural selection and in four succeeding chapters showed how the complex facts of the geographical distribution of species were explicable in terms of natural selection but not by any other hypothesis. The tenth edition of the *Principles* was Lyell's last great feat of scientific writing. The eleventh edition of 1872 and the twelfth edition, published in 1875 after his death, included only minor revisions.

In 1864 Lyell was elected president of the British Association for the Advancement of Science and delivered the presidential address at the annual meeting at Bath. Also in 1864 he was created a baronet by Queen Victoria. Since their marriage in 1832 Lady Lyell had helped her husband with his correspondence, writing many of his letters from dictation; but in 1865 Lyell engaged as his secretary Arabella Buckley, and his letters after that were usually written in her hand. After 1869 Lyell's health began to fail. His eyesight became gradually worse, until he was blind, and his strength diminished. Yet he continued to make geological expeditions to various places in the British Isles; and in April 1872 he and Lady Lyell, accompanied by T. McKenna Hughes, went to the south of France to visit the caves of Aurignac.

On 25 April 1873 Lady Lyell died unexpectedly; and the loss, after forty years of so close and constant a companion, was a severe blow to Lyell. After some months of failing health he died on 22 February 1875 and was buried in Westminster Abbey.

In addition to his knighthood and baronetcy Lyell received many honors. The Royal Society awarded him the Copley Medal and the Royal Medal; the Geological Society, the Wollaston Medal. He was elected a member of the American Philosophical Society and a corresponding member of the Institut de France and of the Royal Academy of Sciences at Berlin, in addition to membership in many other scientific and learned societies.

Lyell established geology as a science. He applied to the subject the strictest discipline of rigorous reasoning and expunged it of all that was merely fanciful and speculative. His criteria for admissible causes in geology stand today more strongly than ever; and the kind of detailed analogy which he drew between ancient and modern conditions in oceans, lakes, streams, and estuaries foreshadowed the modern development of paleoecology. In certain theoretical interpretations Lyell was clearly wrong. Until 1857 he defended the view that erratic boulders had been transported by icebergs, whereas for the most part they had been transported by continental glaciation. Lyell also exaggerated the role of the sea in shaping the form of the land and did not fully appreciate the immense scale of subaerial denudation in determining landforms. For many years he mistakenly upheld the fixity of species. Yet Lyell's theoretical positions, even when wrong, were always carefully reasoned; and he showed an extraordinary capacity even into old age to understand the meaning of new evidence and to change his mind.

After Lyell's death his reputation, together with that of Darwin, suffered a serious decline—principally because, in the controversy over the age of the earth initiated in 1865 by Lord Kelvin, Kelvin and other physicists had asserted that the earth could not be older than 10 to 25 million years. Within these time limits geologists could not account for the long series of geological changes which had occurred, in terms of the uniform action of natural causes. Consequently there was a tendency for geologists to revert to catastrophic interpretations of past geological changes. Lord Kelvin's estimate of the age of the earth was based on calculations of the rate of heat loss by the earth, assuming that it had begun as an incandescent molten mass, approximately at the temperature of the sun, and had gradually cooled according to the laws of radiation. Kelvin had admitted that his calculations would be invalidated if any steady source of heat were to be discovered within the earth.

As early as 1830 Lyell had concluded that the occurrence of volcanic activity throughout all periods of geological history required a steady source of heat within the earth, and he had rejected the concept of a gradually cooling earth. In 1904 Ernest Rutherford pointed out that a steady source of heat within the earth had been found in the discovery of radioactivity. Estimates of the age of the earth were rapidly revised upward and the modern estimates, which are in excess of 4,000 million years, are great enough to allow the uniform action of gradual causes to produce all the geological changes that have occurred, just as they are also adequate to allow the gradual action of natural selection to produce all the results of evolution in biology. Lyell's faith in geological explanation in terms of the uniform action of observable natural processes has been vindicated by the progress of his science.

NOTES

1. C. Prévost, "De l'importance de l'étude des corps organisés vivants pour la géologie positive," in *Mémoires de la Société d'histoire naturelle de Paris*, **1** (1823), 259–268, see 262.
2. "On a Dike of Serpentine, Cutting Through Sandstone, in the County of Forfar," in *Edinburgh Journal of Science*, **3** (1825), 112, 126.
3. "On the Structure of Lavas Which Have Consolidated on Steep Slopes; With Remarks on the Mode of Origin of Mount Etna, and on the Theory of 'Craters of Elevation,' " in *Philosophical Transactions of the Royal Society*, **148** (1858), 703–786, see 761.
4. *The Antiquity of Man*, 2nd ed. (London, 1863), p. 393.
5. Darwin to Lyell, 6 Mar. 1863, in *The Life and Letters of Charles Darwin* (London, 1888), III, 11–13.
6. Lyell to Darwin, 11 Mar. 1863, in *Life, Letters and Journals of Sir Charles Lyell Bart.* (London, 1881), II, 363–364.

BIBLIOGRAPHY

I. ORIGINAL WORKS. There is a fairly complete list of Lyell's scientific papers in the Royal Society's *Catalogue of Scientific Papers* and of all his writings in appendix E to *Life, Letters and Journals of Sir Charles Lyell Bart.*, Katherine M. Lyell, ed., 2 vols. (London, 1881). For Lyell's publications up to 1841, the bibliography in Leonard G. Wilson, *Charles Lyell, the Years to 1841: The Revolution in Geology* (New Haven–London, 1972), contains some items omitted from the other two lists and complete references to his early articles in the *Quarterly Review*.

Selected papers are "On a Recent Formation of Freshwater Limestone in Forfarshire, and on Some Recent Deposits of Freshwater Marl; With a Comparison of Recent With Ancient Freshwater Formations; and an Appendix on the Gyrogonite or Seed Vessel of the Chara" (1824), in *Transactions of the Geological Society of London*, 2nd ser., **2** (1829), 73–96; "The Bakerian Lecture. On the Proofs of a Gradual Rising of the Land in Certain Parts of Sweden," in *Philosophical Transactions of the Royal Society*, **125** (1835), 1–38; "On the Relative Ages of the Tertiary Deposits Commonly Called 'Crag' in the Counties of Norfolk and Suffolk," in *Magazine of Natural History*, n.s. **3** (1839), 313–330; "On the Upright Fossil Trees Found at Different Levels in the Coal Strata of Cumberland, Nova Scotia" (1843), in *Proceedings of the Geological Society of London*, **4** (1842–1845), 176–178; "On Craters of Denudation, with Observations on the Structure and Growth of Volcanic Cones," in *Quarterly Journal of the Geological Society of London*, **6** (1850), 207–234; "The Tertiary Strata of Belgium and French Flanders," *ibid.*, **8** (1852), 277–371; and "On the Structure of Lavas Which Have Consolidated on Steep Slopes; With Remarks on the Mode of Origin of Mount Etna, and on the Theory of 'Craters of Elevation,' " in *Philosophical Transactions of the Royal Society*, **148** (1858), 703–786.

Lyell's books were *Principles of Geology. Being an Attempt to Explain the Former Changes of the Earth's Surface by Reference to Causes Now in Operation*, 3 vols. (London, 1830–1833; 2nd ed., 2 vols., 1832–1833; 3rd ed., 4 vols., 1834; 4th ed., 1835; 5th ed., 1837; 6th ed., 3 vols., 1840; 7th ed., 1 vol., 1847; 8th ed., 1850; 9th ed., 1853; 10th ed., 2 vols., 1867–1868; 11th ed., 1872; 12th ed., 1875); *Elements of Geology* (London, 1838; 2nd ed., 2 vols., 1841; 3rd ed., pub. as *A Manual of Elementary Geology*, 1 vol., 1851; 4th ed., 1852; 5th ed., 1855; 6th ed., 1865); *Travels in North America, in the Years 1841–2; With Geological Observations on the United States, Canada and Nova Scotia*, 2 vols. (London–New York, 1845); *A Second Visit to the United States of North America*, 2 vols. (London, 1849); *The Geological Evidences of the Antiquity of Man With Remarks on Theories of the Origin of Species by Variation* (London, 1863; 2nd ed., 1863; 3rd ed., 1863; 4th ed., 1873); and *The Student's Elements of Geology* (London, 1871).

Many of Lyell's letters and travel diaries were published in the *Life, Letters and Journals of Sir Charles Lyell Bart.*, Katherine M. Lyell, ed., 2 vols. (London, 1881). The original copies of many of Lyell's letters to members of his family, his scientific journals, and his notebooks are the property of Lord Lyell of Kinnordy, Kirriemuir, Angus, Scotland. Lyell's letters to other scientists are scattered among libraries and MS collections, both public and private, throughout the world.

Between 1855 and 1861 Lyell filled seven notebooks with notes and references on the species question; these have been published as *Sir Charles Lyell's Scientific Journals on the Species Question*, Leonard G. Wilson, ed. (New Haven–London, 1972).

II. Secondary Literature. In addition to K. M. Lyell's *Life, Letters and Journals*, three brief popular biographies of Lyell have been published: Sir Edward Bailey, *Charles Lyell* (New York, 1963); Thomas George Bonney, *Charles Lyell and Modern Geology* (London, 1895); and F. J. North, *Sir Charles Lyell* (London). Although all of these biographies are heavily dependent on the *Life, Letters and Journals* and on Lyell's published writings, each was written by a professional geologist who contributed useful insights into Lyell's work.

Leonard G. Wilson, *Charles Lyell, the Years to 1841: The Revolution in Geology* (New Haven–London, 1972), is the first of three volumes of a detailed, large-scale biography of Lyell based on extensive study of both published and MS sources.

There are references to Lyell among the lives and letters of many eminent Victorians, both British and American. Of particular value are Katherine M. Lyell, ed., *Memoir of Leonard Horner, F.R.S., F.G.S., Consisting of Letters to His Family and From Some of His Friends*, 2 vols. (London, 1890); and Frances Joanna Bunbury, ed., *Life, Letters and Journals of Sir Charles J. F. Bunbury Bart.*, 2 vols. (London, 1894).

The intellectual and scientific background to Lyell's thought is discussed in a lively study by Charles Coulston Gillispie, *Genesis and Geology* (Cambridge, Mass., 1951). Various aspects of Lyell's concept of uniformity are discussed in the following: Walter F. Cannon, "The Uniformitarian–Catastrophist Debate," in *Isis*, **51** (1960), 38–55; and "The Impact of Uniformitarianism. Two Letters From John Herschel to Charles Lyell 1836–1837," in *Proceedings of the American Philosophical Society*, **105** (1961), 301–314; R. Hooykaas, *Natural Law and Divine Miracle, A Historical-Critical Study of the Principle of Uniformity in Geology, Biology and Theology* (Leiden, 1959), an attack on the principle of uniformity, inspired by religious doctrines; M. J. S. Rudwick, "A Critique of Uniformitarian Geology: A Letter From W. D. Conybeare to Charles Lyell, 1841," in *Proceedings of the American Philosophical Society*, **111** (1967), 272–287; and "Lyell on Etna, and the Antiquity of the Earth," in Cecil J. Schneer, ed., *Toward a History of Geology* (Cambridge, Mass., 1969), pp. 288–304; and Leonard G. Wilson, "The Development of the Concept of Uniformitarianism in the Mind of Charles Lyell," in *Proceedings of the Tenth International Congress of the History of Science* (Paris, 1964), pp. 993–996; and "The Origins of Charles Lyell's Uniformitarianism," in *Uniformity and Simplicity* (New York, 1967), pp. 35–62.

Leonard G. Wilson

LYMAN, BENJAMIN SMITH (*b.* Northampton, Massachusetts, 11 December 1835; *d.* Philadelphia, Pennsylvania, 30 August 1920), *geology.*

In 1852–1855 Lyman studied law at Harvard University. He spent the field seasons of 1856 and 1857 assisting his uncle, J. P. Lesley, with the geological survey of Pennsylvania. He went to Philadelphia in 1856, and the following year he traveled to the middle Atlantic and southern states to collect statistics on iron manufacturing for the Iron and Steel Association. In 1858 Lyman joined the Geological Survey of Iowa as assistant to James Hall. Under Hall's influence he decided to become a geologist. In September of that year he entered the School of Mines at Paris, and in 1861 he transferred to the Freiberg Mining Academy. Lyman returned to the United States in 1862, subsequently working, again with his uncle, on geological surveys of Pennsylvania, Virginia, Nova Scotia, California, and Alabama. About 1866 Lyman devised the method of representing subsurface geological structure by the use of structural contour lines. In 1870 he was employed by the government of India to carry out a geological survey of oil fields in the Punjab.

The Meiji government of Japan invited experts from the West to assist in transforming Japanese society. The American contingent, led by Horace Capron, included Lyman. In 1872 he contracted with the Hokkaido *kaitakushi* (development board) as geologist and mining engineer. He undertook a geological survey of Yesso (the ancient name for Hokkaido) in 1873–1875. Beginning in 1876 he prospected for oil in Japan, and he returned to America in 1881. He worked as a geologist for the Geological Survey of Pennsylvania from 1887 to 1895.

In 1873–1875 Lyman and his co-workers, to whom he taught mathematics, physics, and geology, undertook the geological survey of the Kayanuma and Poronai coalfields. They published a geological map on a scale of 1:5,000. In the same period Lyman visited other areas on Hokkaido; results of these visits are *Geological Sketch Map of the Island of Yesso, Japan* (1876) and *A General Report of the Geology of Yesso* (1877).

Lyman had hoped to return to America after finishing the geological survey of Hokkaido; but instead he undertook a geological survey for oil for the Ministry of Industry. He visited the Niigata oil field and western Japan in 1876–1881. The article "Geological and Topographical Maps of the Oil Lands in Japan," written during this period, includes a geological map of the Niigata oil field on the scale 1:60,000.

Lyman made lasting contributions to Japan by establishing the first geological map of an extensive area, making structure contour maps of the coalfields and oil fields, and teaching practical American geology to thirteen young Japanese geologists. The future geologists, managers, and administrators of the Japanese mining industry were among Lyman's protégés, for example, E. Yamagiwa and J. Shimada, who found the great coalfield at Ikushumbetsu (1880), and I. Ban, who found the Oyubari coalfield (1888).

Lyman returned to the United States and from 1887 to 1895 Lyman was vice-director of the Pennsylvania Geological Survey. He had a deep knowledge of literature, philosophy, law, art, and archaeology. A lifelong bachelor, Lyman was also a vegetarian.

BIBLIOGRAPHY

I. ORIGINAL WORKS. Lyman's books and papers have been collected at the Forbes Library, Northampton, Mass.,

but there is no complete bibliography of the more than 150 publications attributed to him. His most important writings are the *Geological Survey of Hokkaido*, 5 vols. (Tokyo, 1875–1877); *Geological Sketch Map of the Island of Yesso, Japan (1:2,000,000)* (Tokyo, 1876); and *A General Report on the Geology of Yesso* (Tokyo, 1877). Other of his works on Japanese geology are included in Horace Capron, *Reports and Official Letters to the Kaitakushi* (Tokyo, 1875) and *Geological Survey of Japan, Reports of Progress for 1878, 1879* (Tokyo, 1879). Works on American geology, mostly that of Pennsylvania, are listed in J. M. Nickles, "Geologic Literature on North America, 1785–1918," in *Bulletin of the United States Geological Survey*, no. 746 (1922). See also E. S. Dunkman, "Notes on the Benjamin Smith Lyman Collection," MSS, Forbes Library, Northhampton, Mass.

II. SECONDARY LITERATURE. See M. L. Ames, *Life and Letters of Peter and Susan Lesley* (New York, 1909), which contains correspondence between Lyman and the Lesleys; Gonpei Kuwada, *Biography of Benjamin Smith Lyman* (Tokyo, 1937); and F. B. Sanborn, *Recollections of Seventy Years* (Boston, 1909), which includes recollections of Lyman, with a photograph.

H. KOBAYASHI

LYMAN, CHESTER SMITH (*b.* Manchester, Connecticut, 13 January 1814; *d.* New Haven, Connecticut, 29 January 1890), *astronomy, geology.*

Lyman is credited with being the first person to obtain reliable evidence for an atmosphere surrounding the planet Venus: when the dark side of Venus was toward the earth in 1866, and again in 1874, he saw it surrounded by a complete bright circle, which he correctly attributed to refraction of sunlight in the Cytherean atmosphere.

The son of a miller, Chester Lyman, and his wife Mary Smith, Lyman gave evidence of an interest in astronomy while still quite young. But the career he chose for himself was the ministry, and so, after an elementary education in public schools, he taught school for several years to finance a college education. At age nineteen he entered Yale College; here he helped found the *Yale Literary Magazine* and had access to the astronomical observatory as a perquisite of his job as assistant to the professor of natural philosophy. He graduated B.A. in 1837.

After two years as superintendent of the Ellington Academy, Lyman entered the Union Theological Seminary in 1839, but transferred after a year to the theological school at Yale, from which he graduated B.D.

His first pastorate, that of the First Congregational Church in New Britain, Connecticut, was also his last: in 1845 he resigned, for reasons of health, and set

577

off for the South Seas. He went around Cape Horn to Hawaii (then called the Sandwich Islands), where he worked sporadically as a missionary, schoolteacher, and surveyor. He also visited the volcano of Kilauea and recorded geological details of the surrounding region.

In 1847 Lyman moved on to California, arriving shortly before it was ceded to the United States by Mexico, and just in time to have his surveying activities interrupted by the Gold Rush. In 1850 he returned to Connecticut, married Delia Williams Wood, and settled down in New Haven for the rest of his life.

Lyman was appointed professor of industrial mechanics and physics in the Sheffield Scientific School of Yale College in 1859. It was during this tenure that he made his observations of the planet Venus. His professorship was altered in 1871 to include only astronomy and physics, and again in 1884 to cover only astronomy. He served as president of the Connecticut Academy of Sciences from 1859 to 1877, and was granted an M.A. degree by Beloit College in 1864.

BIBLIOGRAPHY

I. ORIGINAL WORKS. Lyman published almost exclusively in Silliman's *American Journal of Science and the Arts:* letters from him describing California and gold mining—said to have been the first reliable accounts received on the East Coast of this bonanza—appeared in 2nd ser., **6** (1848), 270–271 (includes mention of the discovery of gold at Sutter's Fort on the Sacramento River); 2nd ser., **7** (1849), 290–292 (his first visit to the gold fields); *ibid.*, 305–309 (how he himself dug for gold, and a description of conditions in the mining camps); 2nd ser., **8** (1849), 415–419 (describes the geology of placers); and 2nd ser., **9** (1850), 126–127 (the discovery of gold-bearing veins).

Lyman's description of the volcano Kilauea also appeared in Silliman's *Journal*, 2nd ser., **12** (1851), 75–82; as did his observations of Venus, 2nd ser., **43** (1867), 129–130, and 3rd ser., **9** (1875), 47–48.

The journal that Lyman kept during his travels, *Around the Horn to the Sandwich Islands and California, 1845–50* (New Haven, 1924), was prepared for publication by Frederick John Teggert; it includes a portrait and an introduction by Lyman's daughter, Delia Lyman Porter.

Thirteen articles by Lyman are listed in the *Royal Society. Catalogue of Scientific Papers*, **4** (London, 1870), 141; **8** (London, 1879), 285; and **10** (London, 1894), 665.

II. SECONDARY LITERATURE. Facts about Lyman's early life can be found in the annual *Catalogue of the Officers and Students in Yale College*, for the years 1833–1834 through 1842–1843, and in *Historical Register of Yale University* (New Haven, 1939), p. 367.

For contemporary evaluations, see "Sketch of Chester S. Lyman," in *Popular Science Monthly*, **32** (1887–1888), 116–121, with portrait facing p. 1, and an obituary notice in Silliman's *American Journal of Science and the Arts*, 3rd ser., **39** (1890), 245–246. Both are unsigned.

SALLY H. DIEKE

LYMAN, THEODORE (*b.* Boston, Massachusetts, 23 November 1874; *d.* Brookline, Massachusetts, 11 October 1954), *experimental physics.*

Lyman came from an old and wealthy Massachusetts family. His great-grandfather was a very successful Boston merchant. His father, also Theodore, was a marine biologist who served one term in Congress. His mother, the former Elizabeth Russell, was the granddaughter of a U.S. minister to Sweden. Theodore Lyman never married and spent his life in his grandfather's mansion on a large estate in Brookline.

He received the B.A. degree in 1897 and the Ph.D. in 1900 from Harvard. After a year at the Cavendish Laboratory in Cambridge and a summer at Göttingen he returned to Harvard as an instructor in physics. His entire career was spent at Harvard, where he was director of the Jefferson Physical Laboratory from 1910 to 1947 and held the Hollis professorship (the oldest endowed scientific chair in the United States) from 1921 until he retired.

Lyman's doctoral dissertation was devoted to the problem of applying the concave grating to the measurement of spectral lines in the extreme ultraviolet, a region where the rays cannot pass through air. The technical problems were great and consumed six years. In the work Lyman found false lines in the spectrum which he was able to explain as due to periodic errors in the grating ruling. The clarification of these "Lyman ghosts" in 1900 constituted his doctoral thesis. His first published measurement of wavelengths in the "Lyman region" (1906) gave the first accurate measurements below 2,000 Å. and extended the known extreme ultraviolet region significantly. Viktor Schumann in Germany had used a fluorite prism to disperse the light that did not permit wavelength determination.

Lyman's later scientific work was devoted to measuring various spectra and the optical properties of various materials in the region and to extending the ultraviolet spectrum to the final limit of 500 Å., which he attained in 1917. In 1914 he announced the discovery of the fundamental series of hydrogen, which was an essential part of the foundation on which Bohr developed the quantum theory of the atom.

Never in robust health, Lyman retired from his professorship in 1925 but continued as director of the Jefferson Physical Laboratory until 1947. His last paper was published in 1935, although he continued to direct doctoral dissertations until 1942.

He was a member of the National Academy of Sciences, the American Philosophical Society, the American Academy of Arts and Sciences (president, 1924–1927), the American Physical Society (president, 1921–1922); an honorary member of the Optical Society of America and the Royal Institution of Great Britain; and a fellow of the Royal Geographical Society.

He received the Rumford Medal of the American Academy of Arts and Sciences, the Cresson Medal of the American Philosophical Society, and the Ives Medal of the Optical Society of America.

BIBLIOGRAPHY

I. ORIGINAL WORKS. Lyman published about forty scientific papers. His most important work was *The Spectroscopy of the Extreme Ultra-Violet* (New York, 1914; rev. ed., 1928). Important papers include: "An Explanation of False Spectra From Diffraction Gratings," in *Physical Review*, **16** (1903), 257–266; and "The Spectrum of Helium in the Extreme Ultra-Violet," in *Astrophysical Journal*, **60** (1924), 1–14.

II. SECONDARY LITERATURE. See the discussion of Lyman and his work by P. W. Bridgman, in *Biographical Memoirs*. *National Academy of Sciences*, **30** (1957), 237–250, which includes a complete bibliography.

RALPH A. SAWYER

LYONET, PIERRE (*b*. Maastricht, Netherlands, 21 July 1706; *d*. The Hague, Netherlands, 10 January 1789), *entomology*.

Lyonet's family came originally from northeastern France. They were Calvinists, and their search for religious peace took them to Metz, the Palatinate, and finally Switzerland. Lyonet's father, Benjamin Lyonet, migrated at the beginning of the eighteenth century to Holland, where in 1704 he married Marie le Boucher, the daughter of Huguenot refugees. He was a Presbyterian pastor and was given a parish in Heusden. Lyonet, the elder of two sons (four other children died in infancy), was a frail child. He later wrote: "I was always so quiet that I was thought to be deprived of reason; it was thus with no mild joy that my parents heard me, at two years of age, cry for the first time."

Little is known about Lyonet's early education, but it is likely that he studied Latin, Greek, and Hebrew under the tutelage of his father, who intended his son for the clergy. Lyonet entered Leiden University (1724), accordingly, as a student of theology. In view of the congeniality that existed in those years between science and theology (at least in Protestant countries), it is not suprising that Lyonet studied mathematics, Newtonian physics, military architecture, and anatomy during his first two years at Leiden. In 1728, a year after completing his course, he was admitted to the pastorate. He soon found, however, that he did not have a real vocation, and he persuaded his reluctant father to allow him to return to Leiden to study law (1730). He graduated after a year's work, with a thesis entitled *De justo quaestionis usu* (on the just use of torture), and in the same year set himself up as an *avocat* in The Hague.

Although Lyonet was apparently successful at the bar, he discovered his life's work elsewhere, through two discrete but probably related activities. He began to study insects and became a translator (1738) and then a cipher clerk for the government. As a clerk, working on his own initiative, he broke the code used by the Prussian ambassador to the United Provinces (cracking it took him eighteen months), then other codes used by diplomats in the country, and even those of diplomats in London whose letters passed through The Hague. After convincing his initially skeptical government of the usefulness of decoding, he was allowed to continue the secret work, and did so until his death. He fought for nearly ten years (from 1753) for recognition of his services in the only form acceptable to him: the title of Secretary of Ciphers, which was granted him in 1762.

Lyonet, like Bonnet, first became interested in the study of insects through reading Pluche's *Natural History*, but he was inspired to study them seriously by the first volume (on "chenilles et papillons") of Réaumur's *Mémoires*, which appeared in 1734. Réaumur's influence on Lyonet was decisive, as it had been on Bonnet and Trembley. The magisterial volumes of *Mémoires* served as models to emulate and bases to build upon. Lyonet, who had respect for few naturalists, praised only Swammerdam and Réaumur. From Réaumur he learned method and the importance of being exceedingly careful.

Lyonet began systematic observation on insects in 1736. In 1738 he undertook to correct and expand a translation of F. C. Lesser's *Insectotheologia*. Lyonet's annotations to the translation indicate that he was familiar with the subject and that his ideas on the general biological problems of his time were already formed; his ideas on classification and generation found in the notes to Lesser also appear in the *Traité anatomique* of 1760 and in the posthumously published *Recherches.*

The *Traité anatomique de la chenille qui ronge le bois de saule* was begun in 1745. Lyonet had originally planned a treatise on all the insects in the vicinity of The Hague (and indeed the *Recherches* consist of that part of this project which he was able to complete). When he saw the fame that Trembley and Bonnet had achieved, however (Trembley had created a stir with the demonstration of regeneration of hydras in his *Mémoires pour servir à l'histoire d'un genre de polypes d'eau douce*, largely illustrated by Lyonet, while Bonnet had observed the parthenogenesis of aphids), he decided to establish his own reputation in micro-anatomy. He examined the common goat moth caterpillar (*Cossus ligniperda*) and the anatomy of its chrysalis and imago. He intended to delineate the metamorphosis of the insect in subsequent volumes, but was prevented from doing so by an affliction of the eyes, which after 1767 made it impossible for him to do close work. *Traité anatomique* is devoted wholly to the anatomy of the caterpillar (except for a short initial chapter on its lifecycle), and the plates, drawn and engraved by Lyonet, portray the muscles, nerves, bronchia, heart, viscera, silk vessels, and the internal parts of the head with astonishing precision.

For Lyonet the principal enemies of sound thinking in natural history were *l'esprit de système* and mechanistic ideas, both exemplified by Buffon. Lyonet rejected both animalculist and ovist preformation theories of generation and believed that spontaneous ("equivocal") generation was an illusion fostered by sloppy experimental technique. All animals come from eggs, he said, echoing Harvey (by way of Swammerdam), except those few which reproduce by budding (Trembley's polyps). Lyonet did not formulate a theory of generation, but the logic of his position would have led him to a theory of epigenesis, if he had pursued it. His declarations on generation could have been approved by Aristotle: in reproduction, both the female and male "principles" play a role.

Lyonet considered himself an empiricist, like Swammerdam and Réaumur, who examined insects, to be sure, but who saw only what any unbiased and respectful observer would see. In a way, it was so: the *Traité anatomique* is a triumph of the eye. But his empiricism was less than pure, since two assumptions controlled every line he wrote or drew. He believed, first, that the world and all its creatures are a vast cipher and, second, that the duty of man is to decode it. He found the natural world to be as intricately, precisely, and richly designed as a work by a Dutch artist; and he believed that the more this great design was elucidated, the greater would be man's reverence for the Designer. The tasks of breaking the code by tracing the design to its last perfect detail was therefore perhaps the one supremely worthwhile thing to do.

Beginning about 1767 Lyonet, whose eyesight was still sufficient for everyday purposes, began to collect paintings, including those of Vermeer (widely thought to have been neglected in the eighteenth century). He spent his later years in preparing his notes on insects in the vicinity of The Hague for publication. Although he had a manuscript ready for the printer by 1787, various delays kept it from the presses until 1832, when W. de Haan published it as the *Recherches.*

BIBLIOGRAPHY

I. ORIGINAL WORKS. A complete list of Lyonet's writings and drawings, published and unpublished, may be found in W. H. Van Seters, *Lyonet* (see below), 185–199. A sketchbook of Lyonet's which turned up after the biography was published is described by Van Seters, "Lyonet's Kunstboek," in *Medical and Biological Illustration,* **13** (1963), 255–264. Lyonet's works referred to in the text are *Théologie des insectes ou démonstration des perfections de Dieu dans ce que concerne les insectes, traduit de l'allemand de Mr Lesser avec des remarques de Mr P. Lyonet,* 2 vols. (The Hague, 1742); *Traité anatomique de la chenille qui ronge le bois de saule* (The Hague, 1760); and *Recherches sur l'anatomie et les métamorphoses de différentes espèces d'insectes, ouvrage posthume de Pierre Lyonet, publié par M. W. de Haan . . .* (Paris, 1832).

II. SECONDARY LITERATURE. A complete biographical source is W. H. Van Seters, *Pierre Lyonet, 1706–1789, sa vie, ses collections de coquillages et de tableaux, ses recherches entomologiques* (The Hague, 1962); but see also Émile Hublard, "Le naturaliste hollandais Pierre Lyonet. Sa vie et ses oeuvres 1706–1789," in *Mémoires et publications de la Société des sciences, des arts, et des lettres du Hainaut,* **61** (1910), 1–159, also published separately (Mons, 1910), especially for a number of Lyonet's letters. For the milieu, see J. R. Baker, *Abraham Trembley of Geneva* (London, 1952); R. S. Clay and T. H. Court, *The History of the Microscope* (London, 1932); F. J. Cole, *Early Theories of Sexual Generation* (Oxford, 1930); L. C. Miall, *The Early Naturalists, Their Lives and Work (1530–1789)* (London, 1912); Jean Torlais, *Réaumur* (Paris, 1936; new ed., 1961); Maurice Trembley, ed., *Correspondance inédite entre Réaumur et Abraham Trembley* (Geneva, 1943); Aram Vartanian, "Trembley's Polyp, La Mettrie, and Eighteenth-Century French Materialism," in *Journal of the History of Ideas,* **11** (1950), 259–286, repr. in P. P. Wiener and Aaron Noland, eds., *Roots of Scientific Thought* (New York, 1957), 497–516.

STUART PIERSON

LYOT, BERNARD (*b*. Paris, France, 27 February 1897; *d*. Cairo, Egypt, 2 April 1952), *solar and planetary astronomy, optics*.

Lyot, whose father, a surgeon, died when the boy was seven, studied to be an engineer. After graduating from the École Supérieure d'Électricité in 1917, he obtained a post at the École Polytechnique as assistant to the physicist A. Pérot, with whom he studied maritime and aerial radio guidance devices for the army. Pérot put him in contact with the observatory at Meudon, where he himself was working. Lyot joined this observatory in 1920 and, having earned his *licence ès sciences*, successively became assistant (1925), astronomer (1930), and chief astronomer (1943).

The first problem that Lyot studied—which also was the subject of his doctoral dissertation in 1929—concerned the polarization of light reflected from the surfaces of the planets. In order to detect this polarization he had to construct a polariscope ten times more sensitive than the existing instruments. From 1923 to 1930 he determined, for each planetary surface, the polarization curve as a function of the angle of vision and, by comparison with laboratory measurements of various substances, he obtained information on the structure of the surfaces observed. He showed, notably, that the lunar soil behaves like volcanic dust and that Mars experiences sandstorms.

The polarization of the solar corona could not be studied during eclipses because the latter's duration was too short. The observation of the corona when there was no eclipse—conducted with the aid of a screen masking the image of the disk—was thought to be impossible because of the light diffused by the atmosphere. Lyot showed that the "parasite" light was caused by the apparatus and could be eliminated. Thus in 1930 he invented the coronograph, which has become the classic instrument for observing the solar corona.

In order to be able to use all the information contained in the image given by the coronograph, it was necessary to work in strictly monochromatic light and to avoid introducing absorption. These two apparently contradictory conditions were satisfied in the monochromatic filter that Lyot devised in 1933. He employed a property of birefringent crystalline laminae, which in polarized light produce interferences, the periods of which vary with the thickness of the lamina: by stacking up a suitable series of laminae, one obtains well-separated passbands, the width of which does not exceed one angstrom. This filter is used in the network of automated heliographs that today assure the permanent observation of solar eruptions and rapidly evolving chromospheric phenom-

ena. Conjoined with the coronograph, the filter has permitted the taking of films showing the movements of solar prominences; they are among the most popular astronomical documents. Lyot himself took the first of these films in 1939.

Lyot spent his life studying phenomena which seemed to be impossible to detect. His skill as a physicist was such that no major advance has been made in the types of instruments that he invented. His work was conceived in accordance with an initial overall plan; for instance, as early as 1923 he stated the principle of the photoelectric polarimeter, which the electron multiplier enabled him to realize in 1950. This instrument, which can detect polarized light when it constitutes as little as 1/10,000 of the total flux, has made possible the observation of coronal rays without the coronograph and without the need for high-altitude stations.

Lyot was elected to the Académie des Sciences in 1939 and in the same year received the gold medal of the Royal Astronomical Society. He was awarded the gold medal of the Astronomical Society of the Pacific in 1947. A pleasant and unpretentious person, Lyot divided his time between his laboratory at Meudon, mountain observations, and his family. He enjoyed skiing, swimming, and sailing and appeared astonishingly youthful. He died of a heart attack upon his return from an exhausting mission to Khartoum to observe a solar eclipse.

BIBLIOGRAPHY

I. ORIGINAL WORKS. Lyot's investigations were primarily in four fields.

On polarization he wrote "Recherches sur la polarisation de la lumière des planètes et de quelques substances terrestres," in *Annales de l'Observatoire, Section de Meudon*, **8** (1929), 1–161; and six notes in *Comptes rendus . . . de l'Académie des sciences*, **189** (1929), 425–426; **191** (1930), 703–705, 834–836; **198** (1934), 249–251, 774–777.

On the coronograph and its applications, see three notes, *ibid.*, **191** (1930), 834–836; **193** (1931), 1169–1173; **194** (1932), 443–446; two articles in *Astronomie:* **45** (1931), 248–253; **46** (1932), 272–287; "Études de la couronne solaire en dehors des éclipses," in *Zeitschrift für Astrophysik*, **5** (1932), 73–95; and "A Study of the Solar Corona and Prominences Without Eclipses," in *Monthly Notices of the Royal Astronomical Society*, **99** (1939), 578–596.

The monochromatic filter is the subject of two notes in *Comptes rendus*, **197** (1933), 1593–1595, **212** (1941), 1013–1017; and "Le filtre monochromatique polarisant et ses applications en physique solaire," in *Annales d'astrophysique*, **7** (1944), 31–79.

On the photoelectric polarimeter, see a note in the *Comptes rendus*, **226** (1948), 25–28.

Three other papers should be mentioned: "Une nouvelle méthode d'observation de la couronne solaire," *ibid.*, **231** (1950), 461–464; "Étude spectroscopique de la rotation de la couronne solaire," *ibid.*, **233** (1951), 1529–1532, written with A. Dollfus; and "Étude des défauts d'homogénéité de grands disques de verre," in *Revue d'optique théorique et instrumentale*, **29** (1950), 499–512, written with M. Françon.

II. SECONDARY LITERATURE. See the following, listed chronologically: F. Robbins, "The Gold Medallist of the Royal Astronomical Society," in *Journal of the British Astronomical Association*, **49** (1939), 259–263; A. Chevalier, "Notice nécrologique," in *Comptes rendus*, **234** (1952), 1501–1505; A. Danjon, "Bernard Lyot," in *Annales d'astrophysique*, **15** (1952), 75–78; and L. d'Azambuja, "L'oeuvre de B. Lyot," in *Astronomie*, **66** (1952), 265–277.

JACQUES R. LÉVY

MAANEN, ADRIAAN VAN (*b.* Sneek, Netherlands, 31 March 1884; *d.* Pasadena, California, 26 January 1946), *astronomy.*

Descended from a long line of aristocrats, van Maanen was the son of Johan Willem Gerbrand and Catharina Adriana Visser van Maanen. He received his B.A. (1906), M.A. (1909), and Sc.D. (1911) from the University of Utrecht. From 1908 to 1911 he worked at the University of Groningen, where he met J. C. Kapteyn. In 1911 van Maanen joined the Yerkes Observatory as a volunteer assistant; and in 1912, on Kapteyn's recommendation, he was appointed to the staff of the Mt. Wilson Observatory. His job there —to measure the proper motions and parallaxes of stars—employed the skills he had acquired while working on his thesis, "The Proper Motions of the 1418 Stars in and Near the Clusters h and χ Persei."

From its completion in 1914, van Maanen used the sixty-inch telescope at the eighty-foot Cassegrain focus for parallax determinations, the first such use of a reflector for such delicate measurements. In the 1920's he also began using the 100-inch reflector at the forty-two-foot Newtonian focus. To measure either parallax or proper motion from a photograph, van Maanen employed a stereocomparator. After superimposing sets of comparison stars, he measured the distance separating the two images in question with a movable micrometer thread.

Van Maanen's study of the parallaxes of more than 500 stars can be divided into two parts. He used one group, comprising stars of apparent magnitude +5 to +7 with moderate proper motions, as a distance standard for measuring spectroscopic parallaxes of more distant objects. Another group, made up of faint stars with great proper motions, led to better understanding of the luminosity function. During these observations he discovered the second known white dwarf (now named "van Maanen's star"), which yielded new information about such objects. A skillful determiner of parallaxes, his average probable error in those measurements was given as $\pm 0''.006$.

Van Maanen studied the proper motions of planetary nebulae, globular and open clusters, faint stars in or near the Orion nebula, near bright stars with large proper motions, faint stars in forty-two of Kapteyn's Selected Areas, and spiral nebulae. These studies yielded important fundamental information about several then puzzling phenomena, among them measures of the distances and absolute magnitudes of planetary nebulae, identification of stars as members of the Orion system and of the Pleiades and h Persei clusters, and rudimentary distances to 125 Cepheid variables.

In 1916 van Maanen published the results that he derived from the displacements of eighty-seven nebular points on two pairs of plates of M101. He detected a rotation rate of $0''.02$ per year at a distance of 5' from the nucleus, a finding he checked by having Seth Nicholson, a meticulous observer, measure half the points. All nine of the spirals that van Maanen eventually investigated seemed to show motions outward along their arms. When Knut Lundmark in 1927 measured van Maanen's plates of M33, he found a rotational component only one-tenth as large as van Maanen's; moreover, van Maanen himself later obtained rotations only half as large as his earlier ones. But although other information strongly indicated that spirals are remote (and hence could not be rotating as fast as he had found), he continued to trust his calculations. In the famous Shapley-Curtis debate in 1920, Shapley, van Maanen's lifelong friend, cited van Maanen's findings as proof that spirals are relatively nearby. Fifteen years later, after plates of several spirals had been taken at longer intervals, Edwin Hubble and van Maanen published papers in *Astrophysical Journal* stating that van Maanen's results on rotations had been incorrect, apparently because of systematic errors.

Van Maanen also attempted to measure the general solar magnetic field, an undertaking begun in 1908 by G. E. Hale. The technique involved measuring the weakly polarized components of Zeeman-split lines. Several staff members at Mt. Wilson worked on the project, but the reduction of the observations was specifically van Maanen's responsibility. Initially he found an overall field strength of roughly fifty gauss, which was later revised to about twenty. Recently J. O. Stenflo analyzed van Maanen's plates by computer and found that van Maanen's visual measurements apparently had again involved systematic errors. It should be noted that the field strengths being measured are so slight (about 1 gauss) that no one was able to determine them reliably until new techniques were introduced in about 1952.

Van Maanen's entire career dealt with visually measuring almost imperceptible changes on photographic plates. In parallax observations he ranked high, but his results on the proper motions of spirals and the magnetic field of the sun were largely incorrect. Numerous explanations have been offered as to why he made such errors. Whatever the reason, the fundamental fact remains that the changes he was attempting to measure were at the very limits of precision of his equipment and techniques. Ironically, even though some of his findings caused confusion for over a decade, they also provided a healthy catalyst for research and discussion and demonstrated the ever-present dangers of systematic error, for even a careful observer.

BIBLIOGRAPHY

I. ORIGINAL WORKS. Van Maanen published more than 150 papers, about fifty of them in the *Contributions from the Mount Wilson Solar Observatory*. Aside from research papers he also wrote popular pieces and biographical sketches and collaborated in the publication of *Hemel en Dampkring*. Many of his most important papers appeared in *Astrophysical Journal*, among them "List of Stars With Proper Motion Exceeding 0″50 Annually," **41** (1915), 187–205; "Preliminary Evidence of Internal Motion in the Spiral Nebula Messier 101," **44** (1916), 210–228; and "The General Magnetic Field of the Sun. Apparent Variations of Field-Strength With Level in the Solar Atmosphere," **47** (1918), 206–254, written with G. E. Hale, F. H. Seares, and F. Ellerman.

II. SECONDARY LITERATURE. Obituaries of van Maanen include Dorrit Hoffleit, in *Sky and Telescope*, **5** (1946), 10; Alfred H. Joy, in *Popular Astronomy*, **54** (1946), 107–110; and Frederick H. Seares, in *Publications of the Astronomical Society of the Pacific*, **58** (1946), 88–103, with portrait. Van Maanen's errors in the determination of the rotations of spirals have been discussed by numerous investigators, including Knut Lundmark, in *Uppsala Astron. Obs. Medd.*, no. 30 (1927); Edwin Hubble, "Angular Rotations of Spiral Nebulae," in *Astrophysical Journal*, **81** (1935), 334–335; Walter Baade, in C. Payne-Gaposchkin, ed., *Evolution of Stars and Galaxies* (Cambridge, Mass., 1963), 28–29; Harlow Shapley, *Through Rugged Ways to the Stars* (New York, 1969), 50, 55–57, 80; and J. D. Fernie, "The Historical Quest for the Nature of the Spiral Nebulae," in *Publications of the Astronomical Society of the Pacific*, **82** (1970), 1212–1213, 1218–1219.

Commentaries on the difficulties of measuring the general solar magnetic field and van Maanen's attempts to do so are given by K. O. Kiepenheuer, in G. P. Kuiper, ed., *The Sun* (Chicago, 1953), 361 ff.; C. de Jager, in *Handbuch der Physik*, II (Berlin, 1959), 340 ff.; Einar Tandberg-Hanssen, *Solar Activity* (Waltham, Mass., 1967), 75 ff.; and Jan Olof Stenflo, "Hale's Attempts to Determine the Sun's General Magnetic Field," in *Solar Physics*, **14** (1970), 263–273.

Correspondence with and about van Maanen is contained in "The George Ellery Hale Papers, 1882–1937" (Pasadena, Calif., 1968), microfilm ed., California Institute of Technology.

RICHARD BERENDZEN
CAROL SHAMIEH

MACALLUM, ARCHIBALD BYRON (*b.* Belmont, Ontario, Canada, 1858; *d.* London, Ontario, 5 April 1934), *biochemistry, physiology.*

Macallum was one of several children of Alexander and Annie (née McAlpine) McCallum. His father emigrated from Kilmartin, Argyllshire, Scotland, in the early nineteenth century, settling in southwestern Ontario. The family was of Gaelic-speaking Presbyterian background, and many members achieved distinction in the professions in Canada and the United States.

Macallum graduated in 1880 from the University of Toronto, winning a silver medal in the natural sciences. For some time afterward he taught high school in Cornwall, Ontario, where he married Winifred Isobel Bruce. In 1883 he was appointed lecturer in biology at Toronto. He obtained his Ph.D. from Johns Hopkins in 1888 and his M.B. from Toronto in 1889. He received many other degrees and academic honors and was a member of numerous learned societies and professional groups, serving at various times as an officer in several of these. He was elected a fellow of the Royal Canadian Society in 1901 and fellow of the Royal Society in 1906.

From 1890 to 1916 Macallum was professor of physiology and later of biochemistry at Toronto. After a three-year period devoted to the founding of the National Research Council of Canada, he joined the faculty of McGill University as professor of biochemistry. Under the auspices of the Rockefeller Foundation he was visiting professor in 1921 at the Peking Union College. Upon his retirement in 1928 he returned to London, Ontario, continuing his research on a part-time basis at the Medical School of the University of Western Ontario, of which his son Archibald Bruce became dean (1928–1934).

Macallum is perhaps best known today for his theory that there is a significant relationship between the inorganic composition of vertebrate blood plasma and that of the ancient oceans. He argued that specific concentrations of inorganic ions encountered in modern vertebrate blood plasma constitute an heirloom from primeval sea life, preserved by the emergence of multicellular organisms having closed circulatory systems, and by the evolution of the kidney. In a 1918 paper he ascribed to the kidney the important function of regulating the inorganic composition of the body fluids. His most mature statement on the supposed paleochemistry of the body fluids appeared in 1926. Despite obvious difficulties of conclusive demonstration, this theory is still referred to in modern texts of general physiology.

Some of his other important scientific papers dealt with the microchemical determination and localization of the inorganic constituents of plant and animal tissues. More recent investigations have shown a number of errors in some of his conclusions due to the limitation of techniques available in his time.

Macallum may be considered one of the pioneers of medical and biological science in Canada, both for his own scientific researches and for his many efforts on behalf of higher education, especially the development of the study of the biosciences in the Canadian premedical curriculum.

BIBLIOGRAPHY

I. ORIGINAL WORKS. Macallum's writings include "Contributions to the Morphology and Physiology of the Cell," in *Transactions of the Royal Canadian Institute*, **1** (1891), 247–278; "On the Demonstration of the Presence of Iron in Chromatin by Micro-Chemical Methods," in *Proceedings of the Royal Society*, **50** (1892), 277–286; "On the Absorption of Iron in the Animal Body," in *Journal of Physiology*, **16** (1894), 268–297; "On the Detection and Localisation of Phosphorus in Animal and Vegetable Tissues," in *Proceedings of the Royal Society*, **63** (1898), 467–479; "On the Cytology of Non-nucleated Organisms," in *Transactions of the Royal Canadian Institute*, **6** (1899), 439–506; "On the Inorganic Composition of the Medusae, *Aurelia flavidula* and *Cyanea arctica*," in *Journal of Physiology*, **29** (1903), 213–241; "The Palaeochemistry of the Ocean in Relation to Animal and Vegetable Protoplasm," in *Transactions of the Royal Canadian Institute*, **7** (1904), 535–562; "On the Distribution of Potassium in Animal and Vegetable Cells," in *Journal of Physiology*, **32** (1905), 95–128; "On the Nature of the Silver Reaction in Animal and Vegetable Tissues," in *Proceedings of the Royal Society*, **76B** (1905), 217–229; and "On the Distribution of Chlorides in the Nerve Cells and Fibres," *ibid.*, **77B** (1906), 165–193, written with M. L. Menten.

Later works are "The Scientific Spirit in Medicine," in *Montreal Medical Journal*, **37** (1908), 1–21; "Die Me-

thoden und Ergebnisse der Mikrochemie in der biologischen Forschung," in *Ergebnisse der Physiologie*, **7** (1908), 552–652; "On the Origin of Life on the Globe," in *Transactions of the Royal Canadian Institute*, **8** (1910), 423–441; "The Inorganic Composition of the Blood in Vertebrates and Invertebrates, and its Origin," in *Proceedings of the Royal Society*, **82B** (1910), 602–624; "Oberflächenspannung und Lebenserscheinungen," in *Ergebnisse der Physiologie*, **11** (1911), 598–659; an English trans., "Surface Tension and Vital Phenomena," appears in *University of Toronto Studies. Physiological Series*, no. 8 (1912), 1–82; "*Acineta tuberosa*: A Study on the Action of Surface Tension in Determining the Distribution of Salts in Living Matter," in *Proceedings of the Royal Society*, **86B** (1913), 527–550; "The Ancient Factors in the Relations Between the Blood Plasma and the Kidneys," in *American Journal of the Medical Sciences*, **156** (1918), 1–11; "Paleochemistry of the Body Fluids and Tissues," in *Physiological Reviews*, **6** (1926), 316–357; and "The Significance of Ketogenesis," in *Canadian Medical Association Journal*, **22** (1930), 3–11.

II. SECONDARY LITERATURE. For obituaries of Macallum see *Obituary Notices of Fellows of the Royal Society of London*, **1** (Dec. 1934), 287–291; and *Proceedings and Transactions of the Royal Society of London*, 3rd ser., **28** (1934), xix–xxi.

R. A. RICHARDSON

MACAULAY, FRANCIS SOWERBY (*b.* Witney, England, 11 February 1862; *d.* Cambridge, England, 9 February 1937), *mathematics.*

The son of a Methodist minister, Macaulay was educated at Kingswood School, Bath, a school for the sons of the Methodist clergy, and at St. John's College, Cambridge. After graduating with distinction, he taught mathematics for two years at Kingswood and, from 1885 to 1911, at St. Paul's School, London, where he worked with senior pupils who were preparing to enter a university. He was remarkably successful: two of his many pupils who became eminent mathematicians were G. N. Watson and J. E. Littlewood. In *A Mathematician's Miscellany*, Littlewood gives a vivid picture of Macaulay's methods: there was little formal instruction; students were directed to read widely but thoroughly, encouraged to be self-reliant, and inspired to look forward to pursuing research in mathematics.

In recognition of his own researches, which he had steadily carried on despite his heavy teaching responsibilities, in 1928 Macaulay was elected a fellow of the Royal Society, a distinction very seldom attained by a schoolmaster. Apart from some elementary articles in the *Mathematical Gazette* and a school text on geometrical conics, he wrote some fourteen papers on algebraic geometry and a Cambridge tract on modular systems, otherwise polynomial ideals. The earlier papers concerned algebraic plane curves, their multiple points and intersections, and the Noether and Riemann-Roch theorems. This work led to later papers on the theory of algebraic polynomials and of modular systems. Much of this was pioneering work with an important influence on subsequent research in algebraic geometry, and it was directed toward the construction of a firm and precise basis of algebra on which geometrical theorems could be safely erected.

BIBLIOGRAPHY

I. ORIGINAL WORKS. Macaulay's books are *Geometrical Conics* (Cambridge, 1895); and *The Algebraic Theory of Modular Systems*, Cambridge Mathematical Tracts, no. 19 (Cambridge, 1916). A list of Macaulay's papers follows the obituary notice by H. F. Baker cited below.

II. SECONDARY LITERATURE. See H. F. Baker's notice of Macaulay in *Journal of the London Mathematical Society*, **13** (1938), 157–160; and J. E. Littlewood, *A Mathematician's Miscellany* (London, 1953), 66–83—the paragraphs relevant to Macaulay are quoted in Baker's notice.

T. A. A. BROADBENT

MACBRIDE, DAVID (*b*. Ballymoney, Antrim, Ireland, 26 April 1726; *d*. Dublin, Ireland, 28 December 1778), *medicine, chemistry*.

Macbride's father and grandfather were both Presbyterian ministers; his brother John rose to the rank of admiral in the British navy. Macbride chose a career in medicine and became apprenticed to a local surgeon after leaving the village school. He served as a surgeon in the navy during the War of the Austrian Succession (1740–1748) and then spent some time in Edinburgh and London, learning more about his profession from well-known teachers, before establishing a practice in Ballymoney in 1749. In 1751 he moved to Dublin.

His career seems to have met with only a limited success until after the publication of *Experimental Essays* (1764), which secured him a doctorate from Glasgow (prior to this he had no degree) and a European reputation. The work dealt with various aspects of a theory that Macbride had developed from Stephen Hales's concept of air. Hales's observations of the expulsion of "air" from all kinds of materials, during heating and fermentation, led him to regard air as an essential constituent of all bodies. Its apparently dual nature—elastic in the free state yet capable of fixation in solids—prevented the component particles from coalescing into a "sluggish lump," while at the same time it contributed to their union (Hales, *Vegetable Staticks* [London, 1727], pp. v–vi, 313–314).

Stressing the latter property (air as a "cementing principle"), Macbride attempted to apply the idea to medicine. He believed that it had been supported by Pringle's experiments and confirmed by his own, which appeared to show that "air" freed from fermenting mixtures could counteract putrefaction. He believed that any mixture of animal and vegetable substances with water would ferment, hence the value of a mixed diet. The need for vegetable matter in the diet led to his advocacy of wort (an infusion of malt) in the treatment and prevention of scurvy. This method was favorably reported on by Captain Cook and others.

In one of his essays Macbride established the precipitation of chalk from limewater as a test for "fixed air"—(a phenomenon that confirmed his theory)—but he was unable to decide whether "fixed air" was a substance quite distinct from atmospheric air or simply a part of the latter modified by its fixation in solids.

His experiments with limewater led him to observe that it is more efficacious than plain water in extracting tannin from oak bark; and he petitioned the Irish parliament for recompense if he divulged his "secret" to Irish tanners, claiming that considerable time and money would be saved by his method. There is no record that his petition was successful; but the innovation was reported on favorably by the Dublin Society, and the discovery was eventually published.

Macbride was apparently a skilled surgeon and obstetrician, and his practice became lucrative. His medical treatise was accepted as authoritative and was translated into several European languages.

BIBLIOGRAPHY

I. ORIGINAL WORKS. Macbride's writings include *Experimental Essays* (London, 1764, 1767); and *A Methodical Introduction to the Theory and Practice of Physic* (London, 1772), 2nd ed., enl., *A Methodical Introduction to the Theory and Practice of the Art of Medicine*, 2 vols. (Dublin, 1777). *Some Account of a New Method of Tanning* (Dublin, 1769) gives the advantages but not the secret of the method; the latter is given in "An Improved Method of Tanning Leather," in *Philosophical Transactions of the Royal Society*, **68** (1778), 111–130.

II. SECONDARY LITERATURE. The main biographical source is A. Smith, "David Macbride, M.D.," in *Dublin Quarterly Journal of Medical Science*, **3** (1847), 281–290.

Macbride's theory of air and some of its consequences are dealt with in E. L. Scott, "The 'Macbridean Doctrine' of Air . . .," in *Ambix*, **17** (1970), 43–57.

E. L. SCOTT

MacBRIDE, ERNEST WILLIAM (*b.* Belfast, Ireland, 12 December 1866; *d.* Alton, Hampshire, England, 17 November 1940), *embryology*.

The eldest son of Samuel MacBride and Mary Jane Browne, MacBride was educated at Belfast and Cambridge and in Germany. He graduated from Cambridge in 1891 and worked for a year under Anton Dohrn at the Marine Biological Station in Naples before returning to Cambridge. In 1897 he became the first professor of zoology at McGill University, Montreal, where he built up a strong school before returning in 1909 to the Imperial College of Science and Technology, remaining there until his retirement in 1934. In 1902 he married Constance Harvey; they had two sons. He was elected fellow of the Royal Society in 1905, vice-president of the Zoological Society of London in 1913, and was active on several committees concerned with marine biology and fisheries.

MacBride's *Textbook of Embryology*, Volume I, *Invertebrata* (1914) was the standard work for many years and reflects his wide knowledge and interest in comparative embryology. His particular interest, the development of echinoids, began in Naples and continued throughout his professional life. He studied the problem of metamorphosis from the bilateral larva to the radial adult and used it to elucidate phylogenetic affinities. He found that metamorphosis occurs in Asterina during a previously unnoticed fixed stage, which discovery enabled him to postulate a fixed stage in the phylogeny of this group. There had already been some suggestion by Bateson of affinities between the echinoderms and chordates, for which hypothesis MacBride provided support from embryological evidence, mainly in the origin of the nervous system and coelom, in echinoderms and in amphioxus. His *Textbook* includes the Protochordata and analyzes relationships.

From his earliest years MacBride was increasingly a supporter of some form of Lamarckian inheritance of acquired characters. As he expressed it, ". . . habit is response to environment and inherited structure is nothing but the crystallisation of the habits of past generations."

BIBLIOGRAPHY

I. ORIGINAL WORKS. The Royal Society obituary lists a selected bibliography of thirty items, among them the series of papers on the embryology of echinoderms and his books. Worth noting in supplement to that list are MacBride's contribution of "Zoology" to *Evolution in the Light of Modern Knowledge: A Collective Work* (London, 1924), 211–261; and his intro. to his own trans. of E. Rignano, *Biological Memory* (London, 1926), 1–16. He also wrote the section on larvae of echinoderms for *Natural History Reports. British Antarctic Terra Nova Expedition, 1910. Zoology*, **4**, pt. 3 (1920), 83–94; and contributed numerous letters to *Nature* and *The Times*.

II. SECONDARY LITERATURE. The only comprehensive analysis of MacBride's life and work is by W. T. Calman, in *Obituary Notices of Fellows of the Royal Society of London*, **3** (1940), 747–759, with portrait. An anonymous obituary appeared in *Nature*, **146** (1940), 831–832; and a printed pamphlet was prepared by MacBride, *Application for the Chair of Zoology in University College London, with Testimonials* (1906).

DIANA M. SIMPKINS

McCLUNG, CLARENCE ERWIN (*b.* Clayton, California, 5 April 1870; *d.* Philadelphia, Pennsylvania, 17 January 1946), *cytology, zoology*.

Through his studies on the accessory chromosome in insects, Clarence E. McClung contributed significantly to the establishment of the chromosome theory of inheritance. In 1901 and 1902 he pointed out that the accessory chromosome (or X chromosome as it is sometimes called) was possibly the nuclear element responsible for determining sex. Thus he was among the first to offer evidence that a given chromosome carried a definable set of hereditary traits.

Of Scotch-Irish descent (i.e., Scots who moved to Ireland), McClung's ancestors had come to the United States in 1740 and settled in Lancaster County, Pennsylvania. His father, Charles Livingston McClung, was a civil and mining engineer, and his mother, Annie H. Mackey, the daughter of a physician. Because his father's business required the family to move about (mostly through the West and Midwest), young McClung's schooling was sporadic. By the time he was ready to enter high school, however, the family had settled in Columbus, Kansas (in the mid-1880's) and McClung's intellectual abilities began to show. He became especially interested in science; from his father he learned surveying, and from working in an uncle's drug store, he learned pharmacy. Following this latter interest, he entered the University of Kansas School of Pharmacy in Lawrence (1890), and completed the pharmacy course in two years (receiving his Ph.G. in 1892). For a year he taught chemistry and pharmacy at the university, and in the fall of 1893 enrolled in the College of Liberal Arts.

As an undergraduate his interests shifted from chemistry to zoology, particularly through the influence of S. W. Williston, who encouraged McClung's natural mechanical bent and allowed him to work in the histology laboratory learning special techniques. Williston also entrusted McClung with teaching part of his course in histology during one semester. McClung received his B.A. in 1896, and immediately entered graduate school at Kansas, receiving his M.A. in 1898, and Ph.D. in 1902. During his graduate years he spent one semester at Columbia University with the cytologist Edmund Beecher Wilson, and one summer (1898) working with William Morton Wheeler at the University of Chicago. Both of these men were interested in the nature and behavior of chromosomes, and it was through their influence that McClung's attention was directed to these nuclear elements.

While still a graduate student at Kansas he was appointed assistant professor of zoology, and later of histology and animal morphology (1898–1900); in 1901 he was made associate professor of zoology and head of the zoology department. He served as curator of the university's paleontological collections (1902–1912), and was acting dean of the Medical School (1902–1906). In 1906 he became professor of zoology, a post he held until 1912 when he accepted a call to become head of the zoological laboratories at the University of Pennsylvania, where he remained until his retirement in 1940. During the academic year 1940–1941 he served as acting chairman of the department of zoology at the University of Illinois, and in 1943–1944 was acting chairman of the biology department at Swarthmore College (Pennsylvania). Always interested in teaching, McClung introduced a variety of pedagogical innovations during his career. At Kansas, where he taught introductory biology, he deemphasized memorization and encouraged students to think through problems on their own. And at Pennsylvania, he served on many university committees concerned with curriculum reform and matters of basic educational policy.

McClung's biological work covers several distinct areas of interest: paleontology (on which he wrote some early papers in 1895, 1905, and 1908), technical microscopy and microscopy techniques, and studies on chromosomes. The latter area includes his most important contributions.

By the 1890's it had become clear to most biologists that the chromosomes were somehow involved in the processes of heredity. Both Wilhelm Roux and August Weismann had suggested theoretical roles for the chromosomes as hereditary determiners, while a host of microscopists had carefully detailed the movements of chromosomes in the mitotic and meiotic divisions. The constancy of chromosome number for any species was recognized; and the number of chromosomes for the cells of higher animals and plants was found to be even, suggesting that equal numbers come from the egg and from the sperm. It was also known that the chromosomes divide longitudinally at each somatic division, and that in the formation of gametes (sperm or egg cells) the chromosome number is reduced by one-half (each sperm or egg receiving only half the total number characteristic of the species). Yet there were also a number of facts now part of our common understanding of heredity which were unknown at that time. It was not known until after 1901 or 1902 that the chromosomes exist in definite pairs (homologs). Furthermore, it was thought that when the chromosomes reappear at the end of interphase (just before the cell begins its division cycle), they are linked together end-to-end as one continuous thread (called a spireme). As the division cycle begins, the thread was thought to break up into the number of chromosomes characteristic of the species. The most basic question still unanswered was, in terms of the hereditary information they carry, does each chromosome differ qualitatively from the others, or are they all basically the same, each bearing a full complement of hereditary information? If it were possible to identify a given hereditary trait (or set of traits) with any specific chromosome, this basic question would be answered. The chromosomes would then appear to have individuality, i.e., each would appear to differ from the others, and would control a different trait or traits.

In 1891 Hermann Henking had noted the peculiar meiotic behavior of an unusual chromosome in spermatocytes of the small fire wasp (Hemipteran) *Pyrrhocoris*. This chromosome, which Henking called a "chromatin body" and labeled "X," did not seem to pair up with a partner chromosome at prophase I of meiosis, thus seeming to lead a peculiarly separate existence. Furthermore, Henking noted that the male of the species had an uneven number of chromosomes, while the female had an even number. In spermatogenesis one-half of the sperm received this "X" element (thus ending up with twelve chromosomes), while the other half did not receive it (thus ending up with only eleven chromosomes). Similar "accessory chromosomes" were reported for other species of insects, including the long-horned grasshopper, *Xiphidium fasciatum*, as observed by McClung in 1899. It was not until McClung's suggestive papers of 1901 and 1902, however, that the significance of these unpaired "X" elements was fully realized. Most important, McClung's work had a crucial, though indirect significance for the question of the individuality of the chromosomes.

When McClung was in Chicago in 1898, Wheeler suggested that he study spermatogenesis in the grasshopper *Xiphidium*; Wheeler himself had been working on oogenesis in this species, and wanted someone to do the complementary studies on males. In 1899 McClung published his first set of observations on the "X" element which he observed clearly in grasshopper spermatocytes; because it was unpaired he coined the term "accessory chromosome" to replace Henking's rather vague designation of "X." In two longer papers (1901 and 1902) McClung went beyond the cytological observations of his predecessors. He saw in the behavior of the accessory chromosome a clear mechanism for understanding how sex could be determined. McClung started with two notions (1) that the chromosomes were the bearers of hereditary information, and (2) that sex was to some extent at least determined by heredity. Thus it was logical to conclude that sex must in some way be determined by the chromosomes. The accessory chromosome, McClung pointed out, fits all the requirements for being a sex determiner: it is present in all cells of the organism until they are fully formed, thus serving to control the development of sexual characteristics in the adult; and it is present in one-half the gametes of the sex that bears it (e.g., males). Thus, at fertilization, one-half the zygotes will contain the accessory, and one-half will lack it. Now, McClung reasoned, sex is the only hereditary characteristic which divides a species into two equal groups. It is quite possible, then, that the accessory chromosome is the hereditary element which determines this difference.

Although his theory proposed that sex was determined at the moment of fertilization, McClung did not hold that this was necessarily true for all species, or that the environment did not sometimes influence the development of the hereditary predisposition. In humans, he felt sex was determined at conception, as evidenced by the fact that identical twins are always of the same sex. But in other species this might not be the case. He took a broad (and from today's perspective too indulgent a view of the environmental theory) approach to this question when he wrote in 1902:

> Sex, then, *is* determined sometimes by the fact of fertilization and can not be subsequently altered. But between this extreme and the other of marked instability [*i.e.*, totally dependent on the environment] there may be found all degrees of response to environment. It must accordingly be granted that there is no hard-and-fast rule about the determination of sex, but that specific conditions have to be taken into account in each case.

We know today that environmental factors do have some influence on sex ratios in some species; but they do not have the fundamental role which McClung and some of his contemporaries often assigned to them.

It should be noted that McClung made two additional errors in his theory of sex determination. Because he gave such prominence to the influence of environmental conditions, he believed in a theory popular at the time called "selective fertilization"—the idea that the egg could "choose" whether it was fertilized by a sperm bearing an accessory, or by one lacking the accessory. We know today that the egg is incapable of carrying out any such selectivity. Furthermore, through a miscount of the number of chromosomes in the female of the insects he was studying, McClung thought that a sperm bearing an accessory chromosome (the X) would be male-determining. In fact it is, as we know now, female-determining (a sperm bearing either no accessory or a Y-chromosome is male-determining).

McClung posed his ideas about the role of the accessory only as a working hypothesis, tentative and perhaps suggestive, but not as a proof of the chromosomal nature of sex determination. The evidence was largely circumstantial, resting upon the observed parallelism between the presence or absence of the accessory and the sexual differentiation into males or females. His hypothesis proved to be very stimulating, however. Within a few years (1905) E. B. Wilson and Nettie M. Stevens, independently, showed that for most groups of animals males carried one accessory chromosome (the genotype being designated as X, XO, or XY, "Y" indicating a second element, the Y-chromosome, in many species found associated with the X), and females two accessory chromosomes (the genotype being designated XX). In some species they found that the relationship was just reversed: males had two accessories (XX) and females one (XO or XY). Their work provided a sound and systematic basis for the chromosomal theory of sex determination.

McClung's work, and subsequently that of Wilson and Stevens, substantiated the concept of the individuality of the chromosomes. By associating the inheritance of one set of traits (sexual) with one particular chromosomal element, the McClung theory suggested that each chromosome was different from the others, governing one specific set of characteristics. At just about the same time, the concept of chromosomal individuality received considerable support from other quarters: particularly from the work of Boveri with polyspermy in the sea urchin (1902), and that of T. H. Montgomery (1901) and W. S. Sutton (1902, 1903).

Through the concept of chromosomal individuality, McClung's work led directly to the correlation of the chromosome theory with Mendel's newly publicized laws of heredity (rediscovered in 1900). The parallelism between the separation of maternal and paternal members of each chromosome pair in meiosis and Mendel's postulate of segregation of heritable factors was picked up by both Montgomery (1901) and Sutton (1902, 1903). Sutton had been a graduate student of McClung's at Kansas in 1901, and gained both interest and insight into the chromosome question from his teacher. At the time he wrote his own important papers on Mendelism, however, Sutton had moved on to Columbia University as a student of E. B. Wilson. McClung's studies on the accessory chromosome came at a fortuitous time in the history of genetics. They pulled together disparate information by suggesting a purpose for the otherwise inexplicable movements of the chromosomes in general and of the accessory in particular during spermatogenesis. They gave a new and fruitful means for understanding the inheritance of sex by providing a mechanism for explaining the 1:1 male–female ratio observed for most species. And lastly, they set the stage for relating Mendel's abstract "factors" to real material bodies (chromosomes) in the cell nucleus.

Like many biologists at the time, McClung saw heredity and development as inextricably linked. Heredity operates, he maintained, by controlling the cell's metabolic functioning. And since that functioning depends upon environmental circumstances (for availability of raw materials, for example), it was clear that an individual's ontogeny was molded by hereditary potentialities interacting with specific environmental conditions. This was a consciously epigenetic view, conditioned in part by reaction to the prevalence of particulate theories of heredity in the past (such as those of Haeckel or Weismann) which placed all emphasis on heredity. To McClung, the most important arena in which further understanding of the relationships between heredity and development could be worked out was cytology. Biochemical knowledge was too scanty at the time to make his approach a feasible one for understanding how cells grew and differentiated during embryonic development. But cytology was accessible, and should be used to explore these fundamental questions:

> The apprehension of large principles of organization should therefore be our aim, and I have no doubt that once an understanding of the cytological changes in the body of an animal during its ontogeny is reached, we shall have solved, as far as it is possible for us to do, some of the larger problems of heredity and development that have become our scientific inheritance [1908].

In addition to his studies on chromosomes, McClung also made contributions to techniques of biological staining and to the design of microscopes. Particularly noted was the "McClung model" microscope, which had an improved mechanical design. He was also the author of a series of papers on photomicrography and a *Handbook of Microscopical Technique* (1929), and he pioneered in the use of simple, new designs in laboratory equipment for introductory biology courses.

Besides his teaching and research, McClung served in a number of administrative posts outside the university. In 1913 he was appointed a trustee of the Marine Biological Laboratories, Woods Hole, Massachusetts (he had taught part of the embryology course there in the summer of 1903), and in 1914 a member of the investigative staff. In 1917 he became chairman of the Zoology Committee of the Division of Biology and Medicine of the National Research Council (NRC), and in 1919 the first chairman of its newly created Division of Biology and Agriculture (NRC). In the latter post he initiated plans for a comprehensive biological abstracting service, which eventually led to the publication of *Biological Abstracts* (published by the Union of American Biological Societies, of which McClung became president of the board of trustees, 1925–1933). As chairman of the Division of Biology and Agriculture, he also initiated plans for standardizing biological stains, eventually giving rise to the Biological Stain Commission. He served as the managing editor of the *Journal of Morphology* from 1920 until 1946, and the associate editor of *Cytologia* from 1930 onward.

McClung held memberships in all of the important zoological societies. These include American Morphological Society (1901), American Association for the Advancement of Science (1902; fellow, 1908); American Society of Zoologists (secretary, Central Branch, 1905; president, Central Branch, 1910; president, national organization, 1914); American Philosophical Society (1913); American Society of Naturalists (1913; president, 1927); Philadelphia Academy of Sciences (1914); Wistar Institute of Anatomy and Biology, advisory board (1914); American Association of Anatomists (1914); and the Washington Academy of Sciences (1920).

In addition, he received many honors, including membership in several honorary societies. The latter include Sigma Xi (national president, 1917–1921), Beta Beta Beta (president, 1936), and the National Academy of Sciences (1920). He was also the United States representative at the International Biological Congress in Montevideo, Uruguay, in 1930, a goodwill scientific ambassador (sponsored by the Rockefeller

Foundation) to Japan (1933–1934), a recipient of the Distinguished Service Citation from the University of Kansas (1941), and a D.Sc. from Franklin and Marshall College (1942).

McClung was known as a congenial and friendly person by both his colleagues and students. He had a broad range of interests involving athletics, English literature, music, photography, and dramatics. Noted as a sensitive and meticulous worker, McClung was described by one student as "an artist in everything he does." He was married to Anna Adelia Drake of Lawrence, Kansas, on 31 August 1899; they had two children, Ruth Cromwell and Della Elizabeth.

BIBLIOGRAPHY

I. ORIGINAL WORKS. The most complete bibliography of McClung's writings is at the conclusion to the biographical sketch by Wenrich mentioned below; however, this covers only up until 1940. His most important papers include: "The Spermatocyte Divisions of the Acrididae," in *Kansas University Quarterly*, **9** (1900), 73–100; "Notes on the Accessory Chromosome," in *Anatomischer Anzeiger*, **20** (1901), 220–226; "The Accessory Chromosomes: Sex Determinant?" in *Biological Bulletin*, **3** (1902), 43–84; "Cytology and Taxonomy . . .," in *Kansas University Science Bulletin*, **4** (1908), 199–215; "A Comparative Study of Chromosomes in Orthopteran Spermatogenesis," in *Journal of Morphology*, **25** (1914), 651–749; and "The Cell Theory—What of the Future?" in *American Naturalist*, **74** (1939), 47–53.

II. SECONDARY LITERATURE. The only substantial biographical treatment of McClung was prepared by D. H. Wenrich on the occasion of McClung's seventieth birthday: "Clarence Erwin McClung," in *Journal of Morphology*, **66** (1940), 635–688. Wenrich also prepared several shorter treatments after McClung's death: *American Naturalist*, **80** (1946), 294–296; and *Yearbook. American Philosophical Society* (1946), 322–325. These are all, however, truncated versions of the more complete biographical sketch. Further information can be found in a series of short sketches devoted to McClung in *Bios*, **11** (1940), 141–155, by various colleagues.

GARLAND E. ALLEN

McCOLL, HUGH (*b.* 1837; *d.* Boulogne-sur-Mer, France, 27 December 1909), *mathematical logic.*

McColl's contributions to mathematical logic and its symbolic expression helped to clarify the subject in the particular period which may be said to begin with Boole's *An Investigation of the Laws of Thought. . .* (1854) and reach a climax in the *Principia Mathematica* (1950) of Whitehead and Russell.

The logical calculus of propositions has a certain analogy to that of classes, with implication in the former corresponding to inclusion in the latter. Thus, for propositions p, q, r, we have that if p implies q and q implies r, then p implies r, while for classes A, B, C, the dual statement is that if A is contained in B and B is contained in C, then A is contained in C. But the duality is not complete. If p implies q or r, then p implies q or p implies r, but if A is contained in B or C, with "or" in its usual inclusive sense, then we cannot say that either A is contained in B or A is contained in C. The ambiguity is to be seen in Boole's *Laws of Thought*, where he is aware of the duality but is not always quite clear about which interpretation of his symbolic calculus he is using. Since the duality is not perfect, the question arises as to which calculus is the more basic. In his papers, chiefly in the period 1880–1900, discussing many points of the symbolic logic then in process of formation, McColl takes the view, which has much to commend it, that implication and propositions have a more fundamental character than inclusion and classes. His arguments are forceful; but his logical position would have been clearer had he distinguished between a propositional function containing an indeterminate such as "x is a prime number," and a proposition, which is the form assumed by a propositional function when the indeterminate receives a specific value. The proposition is then a statement which is either true or false, whereas no truth-value can be assigned to a propositional function. The distinction was hinted at by Peano, but seems to have been first clearly drawn by Russell.

BIBLIOGRAPHY

McColl's main writings on symbolic logic are "On the Calculus of Equivalent Statements," in *Proceedings of the London Mathematical Society*, 1st ser. **9, 10, 11, 13**; "Symbolic Reasoning," in *Mind* (1880, 1897, 1900); and "La logique symbolique et ses applications," in *Bibliothèque du Congrès International de Philosophie*, III (Paris, 1901).

T. A. A. BROADBENT

McCOLLUM, ELMER VERNER (*b.* near Fort Scott, Kansas, 3 March 1879; *d.* Baltimore, Maryland, 15 November 1967), *organic chemistry, nutrition.*

Elmer V. McCollum originated the first white rat colony in the United States devoted solely to the purpose of experimentation in nutrition. The outcome of this endeavor was his personal discovery and codiscovery of a number of the vitamins. Although he worked with other aspects of nutrition, the major portion of his professional career was devoted to vitamins and other trace nutrients.

McCollum received his bachelor's degree from the University of Kansas in 1903 and completed his doctorate at Yale University in 1906. Although his primary field was organic chemistry, circumstances led him to work for a period of time under Thomas B. Osborne at the Connecticut Agricultural Experiment Station where he acquired a strong interest in what was then called agricultural chemistry (biochemistry). In 1907 he was employed by the Wisconsin Agricultural Experiment Station to conduct chemical analyses on the food and excreta of dairy cattle, part of an experiment inaugurated a year earlier to determine the effect of various cereal grains upon the health and reproductive capacity of cattle. McCollum, despairing of the long and tedious procedures entailed in the use of such large animals, instituted a study which resulted in his setting up the albino rat colony. Under the most adverse conditions, including the hostility of the dean of the College of Agriculture, he conducted experimental work of such a nature that he was able to report in 1913 that rats fed on a diet deficient in certain fats resumed normal growth when fed "the ether extract of egg or of butter." Furthermore, he was able to transfer this "growth-promoting factor" to otherwise nutritionally inert fat or oil which then exhibited growth-promoting activity in rats.

Within two years McCollum also demonstrated that certain water-soluble substances were necessary for normal health in rats, and he consequently named these substances, present in foods in relatively small quantities, "fat-soluble A" and "water-soluble B," thus initiating the alphabetical nomenclature for vitamins. He at first thought that there existed one fat-soluble A and one water-soluble B, but further work in his laboratory and at other institutions soon indicated that there were numerous chemical entities involved.

In 1917 McCollum left Wisconsin to become the first biochemist of the School of Hygiene and Public Health of Johns Hopkins University, where he continued his studies of the vitamins and where, in collaboration with members of the medical school, he aided in the elucidation of what is now known as vitamin D (the antirachitic factor). Another outcome of McCollum's work both at Wisconsin and at Johns Hopkins was the development of the use of the living animal as an analytical tool. As far as nutrition was concerned, the only means by which the presence of curative or preventive substances could be detected was the animal feeding experiment, that is, biological analysis.

Because of his outstanding contributions in the field of nutrition, McCollum received many awards and he was invited to serve as a member of numerous national and international organizations devoted to public health. He was involved with the World Health Organization and the Nutrition Board of the National Research Council, as well as being an American fellow of the Royal Society of London.

McCollum's interests extended beyond the laboratory to the public domain via lectures, magazine articles, and books. His career indicates he was a man of tenacious character who, even after his retirement in the early 1940's, retained an active interest in nutrition and related health fields, evidenced by the fact that he published his book *A History of Nutrition* in 1957, and maintained an influence upon the science he had pioneered many years before.

BIBLIOGRAPHY

A detailed biography and bibliography of McCollum is in *Biographical Memoirs of Fellows of the Royal Society*, **15** (1969), 159–171. His works include *The Newer Knowledge of Nutrition* (1918; 5th ed. 1939); with E. Simmonds, *Food, Nutrition and Health* (1926); *A History of Nutrition* (1957); and *Text Book of Organic Chemistry for Medical Students*. His autobiography is *From Kansas Farm Boy to Scientist* (Lawrence, Kans., 1964). McCollum also contributed chapters or sections to a number of textbooks such as *Endocrinology and Metabolism* (1922); and *Human Biology and Racial Welfare* (1930). He published over 200 papers in the major scientific periodicals, as well as numerous popular magazine articles.

McCollum's early years of nutritional investigations (1907–1915) are most thoroughly dealt with in Stanley L. Becker, "The Emergence of a Trace Nutrient Concept Through Animal Feeding Experiments" (Ph.D. diss., 1968; Univ. of Wisconsin Microfilms), esp. chaps. 3–5.

STANLEY L. BECKER

MacCULLAGH, JAMES (*b.* near Strabane, County Tyrone, Ireland, 1809; *d.* Dublin, Ireland, 24 October 1847), *physics*.

There is little reliable biographical information concerning MacCullagh. He was the son of a poor farmer and apparently inherited some money from a wealthy grandfather. At any rate, he entered Trinity College, Dublin, as a pensioner in 1824 and went on to take every undergraduate honor in classics and science. In 1833 he became professor of mathematics at Trinity and in 1842 he succeeded Humphrey Lloyd as professor of natural philosophy. MacCullagh developed the school of mathematical physics that Lloyd had founded to such an extent that in 1845 the *Cambridge Mathematical Journal* became the *Cambridge and Dublin Mathematical Journal* as part of the campaign conducted by Kelvin (its editor), Stokes, and others to upgrade mathematical physics in Britain. In 1833 MacCullagh became a member of the Royal Irish Academy. He held successively higher offices, and in 1838 received the Academy's first gold medal. In 1842 he received the Copley Medal of the Royal Society of London; he became a fellow in the following year.

MacCullagh gave seven courses of lectures on mathematical physics. In one he independently duplicated Poinsot's work on rigid bodies; in another he exploited potential theory. His papers on geometry are generally characterized by depth, taste, and elegance, while a paper on curves of the second order was also highly original.

Pursuing the goal of giving rigor to Fresnel's wave optics, MacCullagh contributed valuable geometrical constructions. He worked steadily toward clarifying the problem posed by Fresnel's theory, and by 1837 had settled on four assumptions: (1) the vibrations of the wave are parallel to the plane of polarization; (2) the density of the ether is constant, but the elastic properties vary; (3) the *vis viva* of the wave is preserved at interfaces; and (4) the vibrations are continuous across interfaces. With these as given, and assuming Fresnel's form for the wave surface, in 1837 Mac-Cullagh set out a phenomenological theory in a paper entitled "On the Laws of Crystalline Reflexion and Refraction." (The simultaneous development of a similar theory by F. E. Neumann led to considerable nationalistic controversy.)

William Rowan Hamilton, in presenting the gold medal of the Royal Irish Academy to MacCullagh for this paper, called MacCullagh's method "mathematical induction" as opposed to "dynamical deduction," indicating that MacCullagh had sought and found a mathematical generalization of the phenomena rather than having sought to derive the phenomena from established dynamical principles. John Herschel seconded Hamilton's praise of the paper and predicted that physical optics was "on the eve of some considerable improvement . . . [by] searching among the phenomena for laws simple in their geometrical enunciation, . . . *without (for a while) much troubling ourselves how far those laws may be in apparent accordance with . . . general principles in dynamics.*"

Three theories of physical optics were published in 1839: Cauchy's second theory, Green's elastic solid theory, and MacCullagh's dynamical theory (the first two being read on the same day). Seeking independently to deduce the phenomena from dynamical principles, MacCullagh and Green each proceeded by finding a potential for the presumed luminiferous medium and then deriving a wave equation by means of the Lagrangian variational principle. MacCullagh, in "An Essay Towards a Dynamical Theory of Crystalline Reflexion and Refraction," called this method "dynamical reasoning." Such "dynamical" theories would be "mechanical" if the potential were in turn derived from a complete mechanical structure rather than being postulated from general considerations. MacCullagh, however, admitted failure in his search for such a mechanical basis.

Stokes in 1862 led the way in preferring Green's linear displacement potential to MacCullagh's rotational potential, since the latter involved unbalanced couples. Although both Green's and MacCullagh's theories were more natural than Cauchy's—in that they avoided Cauchy's disposable constants—no theory prevailed until about 1900, when the electromagnetic theory achieved dominance.

In 1880 FitzGerald showed (in "On the Electromagnetic Theory of Reflection and Refraction of Light") that MacCullagh's formulation

$$\delta \int \ddot{\vec{R}} \, d^3r = -\delta \int (\vec{C} \cdot \vec{V} X \vec{R})^2 \, d^3r$$

could be translated into an electromagnetic one,

$$\delta \int \frac{1}{2} \vec{E} \cdot \vec{B} \, d^3r = \delta \int \frac{1}{8\pi} \vec{B} \cdot \vec{H} \, d^3r.$$

(Both MacCullagh's and FitzGerald's formulations are given in vector notation for clarity.) The wave equation studied by MacCullagh, FitzGerald, and later Larmor was for the displacement variable R (which was translated by FitzGerald as being equivalent to $\int \vec{H} \, dt$).

In a set of papers on "A Dynamical Theory of the Electric and Luminiferous Medium" (1893–1897), Larmor attempted with little success to combine MacCullagh's theory, Maxwell's electrodynamics, and Kelvin's rotationally elastic ethers. (The problem is more tractable with a purely electromagnetic approach, which also avoids the search for a mechanical basis for MacCullagh's displacement variable.)

MacCullagh's 1839 paper was a prototype of the techniques of mathematical physics exploited so successfully by the British in the latter half of the nineteenth century. It is an early example of the growing importance of rotational terms in the dynamics of continuous mediums, of which the curl relations in Maxwell's electrodynamics and Kelvin's theories of vortex motion provide prime later illustrations.

MacCullagh was an Irish nationalist and a strict adherent of the doctrines of the Roman Catholic church. He was modest and sternly moral; despite a keen relish for society, he never married. His disappointment at losing a parliamentary election, in which he had stood as a nationalist candidate, coupled with overwork, resulted in severe dyspepsia and an aggravation of earlier mental illness. He committed suicide at the age of thirty-eight.

BIBLIOGRAPHY

I. ORIGINAL WORKS. MacCullagh's writings are gathered in John H. Jellett and Samuel Haughton, eds., *The Collected Works of James MacCullagh* (Dublin, 1880).

II. SECONDARY LITERATURE. Chief biographical sources are *Encyclopaedia Brittanica*, 9th and 11th eds.; *Proceedings of the Royal Irish Academy*, **4** (1847–1850), 103–116; and *Abstracts of the Papers Communicated to the Royal Society*, **5** (1843–1853), 713–718.

On MacCullagh's work and milieu, see especially W. R. Hamilton, "Address of the President," in *Proceedings of the Royal Irish Academy*, **1** (1836–1839), 212–221, on the occasion of the award of the Academy's gold medal to MacCullagh. See also George F. FitzGerald, "On the Electromagnetic Theory of Reflection and Refraction of Light," in *Philosophical Transactions of the Royal Society*, **171** (1880), 691–711; Richard T. Glazebrook, "Report on Optical Theories" in *Report of the British Association for the Advancement of Science* (1885), 157–261, a thorough summary, with references, of the theories of optics available in the late nineteenth century; Joseph Larmor, *Mathematical and Physical Papers*, 2 vols. (Cambridge, 1921), of which the abstract and introduction to the first paper contain valuable historical material and commentary on method consistent with British usage of the period; his *Aether and Matter* (Cambridge, 1900) is a revision of these papers with a greater emphasis on electron theory and relativity; and George G. Stokes, "Report on Double Refraction," in *Report of the British Association for the Advancement of Science* (1862), 253–267 (in his obituary notice of Stokes, in *Scientific Papers*, V [New York, 1964], 180, Rayleigh held that Stokes had treated MacCullagh's theory unjustly). The foregoing represent the main sources for the determination of MacCullagh's place in the historical development of physical optics.

DON F. MOYER

MACCULLOCH, JOHN (*b.* Guernsey, Channel Islands, 6 October 1773; *d.* Poltair, Cornwall, England, 20 August 1835), *geology, chemistry.*

Macculloch was descended from a Scottish family, the Maccullochs of Ardwell, Galloway. His father,

James Macculloch, after being engaged in business in Brittany, retired to Cornwall, where Macculloch attended school. He entered Edinburgh University to study medicine and graduated M.D. in 1793. His interest in geology arose during his stay in Edinburgh, possibly because he attended the lectures of John Walker, professor of natural history, who included geology and mineralogy in his course.

Macculloch's first appointment was as assistant surgeon to the Royal Regiment of Artillery, a branch of the army controlled by the Master General and Board of Ordnance. In 1803 he was appointed chemist to the Board of Ordnance. From 1807 he also practiced at Blackheath, near London. He became a member of the newly formed Geological Society of London in 1808, and its president in 1816.

In 1811 he gave up his medical practice and thereafter was employed by the Board of Ordnance in tasks requiring a knowledge of geology. He spent the summers of 1811 to 1813 in Scotland, investigating what rocks could be used safely in mills for grinding gunpowder. In 1814 the Board of Ordnance appointed him geologist to the Trigonometrical Survey then being carried out in Scotland. This involved two tasks. One was to choose sites geologically suitable for setting up the zenith sector used to determine the meridians; the other was to select a mountain geologically suitable for determining the earth's density (a previous determination made by the astronomer Maskelyne had in 1774 proved unsatisfactory for geological reasons).

While engaged in this work Macculloch used his spare time to record additional geological information with the intention of constructing ultimately a geological map of the whole of Scotland; and he tried to persuade his employers that official support for the preparation of such a map would be in the national interest. His employment in Scotland was terminated in 1820. During this period Macculloch also lectured in chemistry during the winter at the Royal Military Academy at Woolwich and later held a similar post at the East India Company's College at Addiscombe, where he also taught geology. He was elected a fellow of the Royal Society in 1820.

In the next few years Macculloch spent some time in completing for the Board of Ordnance reports on the work he had carried out in Scotland. In 1826 his post as chemist was abolished. He was then informed that for the purpose of completing a geological map of Scotland he could transfer his services to the Treasury, which would pay him a salary and expenses.

From 1826 until about 1832 Macculloch visited Scotland every summer to complete his geological survey. The question of whether his geological map should be published caused some delay, but eventually the Treasury sanctioned publication. Macculloch died as a result of a carriage accident in 1835; the map was published, posthumously, in 1836. He married a Miss White in 1835.

Macculloch was the author of a large number of books and papers of geological, mineralogical, and chemical interest. His most important work was that carried out in Scotland. Here his knowledge of mineralogy and chemistry proved invaluable in studying the igneous and metamorphic rocks, which occur over about three-quarters of the country. He was an acute observer of geological phenomena, and the value of his published work was often enhanced by his careful sketches of the field relations between the different types of rock.

In some respects Macculloch was conservative in outlook. He was unwilling to accept new geological ideas unless supported by evidence acceptable to him. He examined the lithological and mineralogical characteristics of the sediments carefully, and accepted that their contained fossils yielded information about the physical conditions existing at the time they were formed. He believed, however, that contemporaneous knowledge of fossil forms and their distribution was inadequate. He felt that their use as stratigraphical indexes and for correlation was unreliable and likely to cause confusion, even though by about 1820 they were quite widely used for this purpose. Contemptuous of stratigraphical paleontologists, Macculloch once described them as "namby pamby cockleologists and formation men." Nevertheless, in *A Description of the Western Isles of Scotland* (1819), he recorded the occurrence of Jurassic fossils in the islands of Skye and Raasay, and remarked on their similarity to those found in Jurassic rocks in Somerset and Gloucestershire in England.

Macculloch also found for the first time organic remains (*Serpulites maccullochii*) in the Cambrian quartzite in the northwest highlands of Scotland. Though he did not recognize the significance of this discovery, it later proved of great importance in working out the complicated overthrust rock succession in this area.

His *Description of the Western Isles of Scotland* was Macculloch's most important book. The numerous islands described, large and small, many of which had not previously been examined by geologists, contain rocks ranging in age from Precambrian to Tertiary, including many igneous rocks. His descriptions of the igneous rocks and the sketches and maps in the accompanying atlas promoted a true understanding of the nature and origin of igneous rocks at a time

when the mistaken views of Werner on their origin had not yet been eradicated.

Macculloch's *Geological Classification of Rocks . . . Comprising the Elements of Geology* (London, 1821) describes his system of classifying rocks. He divided rocks into two main classes: Primary and Secondary. He subdivided Primary into unstratified (granite) and stratified (mainly gneisses and schists, with some sediments). The secondary included all the younger sediments and a few "unstratified" rocks, which his descriptions clearly indicate were igneous intrusions, although he did not specify them as such. Macculloch also described in detail the occurrences of basalt lava ("trap"), the remains of the extensive Tertiary basalt lava plateau off the west of Scotland. Although he realized they were analogous in appearance and composition to recent lava flows, he seemed unwilling to commit himself to the view that the "trap" rocks were true lava flows. He regarded the problem as an obscure one.

Macculloch's rock classification was based on that of Werner—as a matter of convenience because it was still widely used—but this classification did not imply acceptance of Werner's ideas about the origin of rocks. He omitted Werner's "transition" group, regarding it as an unjustifiable complication.

Macculloch's last geological book was his *System of Geology, With a Theory of the Earth* (London, 1831). His "theory of the earth" was largely Huttonian in concept, modified by the suggestion—perhaps derived from Cuvier—that a succession of revolutions might have brought about the extinction of some forms of life. An unusual feature of the work is the inclusion, in an appendix, of advice on the qualifications required of a geologist; on describing geological observations; on the instruments required; and on constructing geological maps. Much of this information is still useful.

Macculloch's geological map of Scotland, on a scale of four miles to the inch, was the first large-scale geological map of the country. It differentiated eighteen rock types and was largely, if not entirely, based on his own observations. It was a remarkable achievement for one man, especially considering the difficulties of access to the remoter parts of the country and the inaccuracies of the only topographical map available. Though gradually superseded by other maps during the nineteenth century, some of the areas he described had still not received detailed examination even as late as the mid-twentieth century.

Macculloch's observations greatly advanced general knowledge of the varied rock formations in Scotland, especially that of the igneous rocks. Though his work is now largely forgotten, it was appreciated in his time by Lyell, who made several references to it in both his *Principles of Geology* and his *Elements of Geology*. In an obituary notice, Lyell recorded "that as an original observer Macculloch yields to no other geologist of our time, and he is perhaps unrivalled in the wide range of subjects on which he displayed great talent and profound knowledge," and he added that he had "received more instruction from his labours in geology than from those of any living writer."

BIBLIOGRAPHY

I. Original Works. Macculloch's geological works include *A Description of the Western Isles of Scotland . . . Comprising an Account of Their Geological Structure*, 3 vols., with an atlas of plates and maps in one vol. (London, 1819); *A Geological Classification of Rocks . . . Comprising the Elements of Geology* (London, 1821); *A System of Geology, With a Theory of the Earth*, 2 vols. (London, 1831); *A Geological Map of Scotland by Dr. Macculloch, F.R.S. &c.*, published by order of the Lords of the Treasury by S. Arrowsmith (London, 1836). There are four different issues of the map, with different titles, dates, and publishers. The geology is the same in all issues. None is dated 1836, but independent evidence establishes this as the date on which the map was first published. *Memoirs to His Majesty's Treasury Respecting a Geological Survey of Scotland* (London, 1836), published posthumously, accompanied the geological map.

A complete list of Macculloch's scientific papers is in the Royal Society *Catalogue of Scientific Papers* (1800–1863), IV (1870), 153–155. Of the total of seventy-nine, forty-six are of geological or mineralogical interest. The earlier (1811–1824) are in the *Transactions of the Geological Society of London;* later papers (1819–1830) are mainly in the *Quarterly Journal of Literature, Science and the Arts*. Macculloch published several books on subjects other than geology which are listed in the usual reference works.

II. Secondary Literature. There is an obituary notice by Lyell in *Proceedings of the Geological Society*, **2** (1838), 358–359; see also T. G. Bonney, *Dictionary of National Biography*, XII, 461–463; V. A. Eyles, "John Macculloch, F.R.S., and His Geological Map: an Account of the First Geological Survey of Scotland," in *Annals of Science*, **2** (1937), 114–129; and "Macculloch's Geological Map of Scotland: an Additional Note," *ibid.*, **4** (1939), 107.

V. A. Eyles

MACELLAMA. See **Mashallah.**

ERNST MACH (*b.* Chirlitz-Turas near Brno, Moravia [now Chrlice-Tuřany, Czechoslovakia], 18 February 1838; *d.* Vaterstetten, near Haar, Germany, 19 February 1916), *physics, physiology, psychology.*

Ernst Mach spent his entire life, until the final three years, in the Austro-Hungarian empire. It was a time of increasing national self-determination, affirmations of linguistic identity among the non-Germanic peoples, and physical and intellectual emancipation of various ethnic groups. His parents provided an environment which nurtured unrestrained, critical, and stubborn scientific inquisitiveness and skepticism.

Mach was the first of three children of Johann Mach and Josephine Lanhaus. His father had received an excellent classical education that included two years' study in the philosophy faculty of the University of Prague. In 1840 he settled with his family on a farm in Untersiebenbrunn, near Vienna. Johann Mach was a practical and inventive idealist, a stark individualist who, with the collaboration of members of his more or less secluded household, distributed his efforts between improving methods of silkworm cultivation, tending his orchard, observing behavior in animals and children, reading Greek and Latin classics, and private tutoring. Mach's mother was raised within the tradition of a family engaged in law and medicine. She was a woman of tender character and artistic disposition, absorbed in instilling in her children a love of music and poetry.

Except for a year at the Benedictine Gymnasium in Seitenstetten, Mach was instructed at home by his father until he was fourteen. In 1848, at age ten, a year that remained fixed in Mach's memory as one dominated by parental sympathies for the Hungarian revolution against the Hapsburg monarchy, he entered the first class of the Gymnasium. He enjoyed the geography lessons, but he was so turned away by the grammar of ancient languages and pious aphorisms that his religious mentor recommended a handicraft or career in business for the untalented student. Accordingly, Mach's father again assumed the supervision of the boy's education. The mornings were taken up with studies in the prescribed Gymnasium subjects—Greek and Latin grammar and literature, history, algebra, and geometry—liberally punctuated with observational and experimental interludes in house, garden, and woods. The afternoons were devoted in part to manual labor in the father's agricultural ventures and in part to an apprenticeship with a cabinetmaker.

Mach entered the sixth class of the public Piarist Gymnasium in Kremsier (Kroměříž) in 1853 at the age of fifteen. The religious exercises displeased him but were more than compensated for by his enthusiasm for the way in which the natural sciences were presented. In later years Mach at various times paid special tribute to his teacher of natural history and geography, F. X. Wessely. Apparently Wessely presented Lamarck's theory of evolution (before Darwin's *Origin of Species* was published) so convincingly that Mach never managed to rid himself of an underlying evolutionary epistemology grounded in an appeal to the inheritance of acquired characteristics.

After five years of mathematics, physics, and philosophy at the University of Vienna, in 1860 Mach received the doctorate with a dissertation on electrical discharge and induction. While at the university, working as a *Privatdozent* in the laboratory of his teacher, Andreas von Ettingshausen (Doppler's successor in the chair of physics), Mach carried out a series of experimental investigations designed to provide theoretical support for Doppler's controversial law relating changes of musical pitch and optical frequency to the relative motion of signal and receiver. Furthermore, he presented a number of papers to the Academy of Sciences in Vienna in which he employed the idea of intermolecular vibrations to account for gaseous spectra. "Molecular functions" was the term Mach used to explain the phenomena of resonance in mechanically vibrating systems, the behavior of fluids in relation to density and viscosity, capillary phenomena, and the principal radii of curvature of liquid surfaces.

Although Mach derived most of his income in Vienna from popular scientific lectures on optics, musical acoustics, and psychophysics, he also presented formal university lectures on the principles of mechanics and designed a special course in physics for medical students. The latter formed the basis for his *Compendium der Physik für Mediciner* (1863). This work notably demonstrated that early in his career Mach had adopted a thoroughly mechanistic interpretation of natural phenomena and accepted the atomic-molecular theory and the kinetic theory of gases without reservation—at least as a working model and hypothesis.[1] In this instance Mach simply was following the philosophically atomistic account of physics that was then in fashion among physicists. Even so, in the preface and at the end of the *Compendium*, Mach explicitly discusses the inadequacies of the atomic theory. He remarks there that whatever metaphysical conception of matter may be put forward in future, the results obtained according to the atomic theory will always be capable of being translated into another conception—just as formulas in polar coordinates may be expressed in rectangular coordinates.

Before leaving Vienna Mach's scientific interests had begun to shift from physics to the physiology and psychology of sensation and to the new discipline of psychophysics. In the reflections on his life that appear in his *Leitgedanken* (1910) Mach says that he was pressed into the field of the psychology of sensation because he lacked the means for physical investigations. "Here, where I could observe my sensations, and against their environmental circumstances, I attained, as I believe, a natural *Weltanschauung* freed from speculative, metaphysical ingredients."[2] When Mach began to explore psychophysical problems associated with vision, audition, and variations in blood pressure, he gradually but surely reached the conclusion that his mechanistic and atomistic approach had netted him very little. This reorientation of Mach's scientific attention is manifestly visible in the "Vorträge über Psychophysik" that appeared toward the end of 1863. For him this shift represented an escape from metaphysical questions, a retreat from mechanism and physical reductionism, and the intentional avoidance of hypotheses. He wrote: "For the value of a hypothesis consists mainly herein, that by a kind of *regula falsi* it always leads closer and closer to the truth."[3] By 1863 the atomic hypothesis was already for Mach a kind of *regula falsi*.

In 1864 Mach accepted a full professorship in mathematics at the University of Graz. Having received no promise of an institute or resources for scientific equipment, he used his own funds to secure the necessary research facilities. By 1866 he was given the title of professor of physics, although he continued to pursue physiological and psychophysical problems on aural accommodation, the sense of time, and spatial vision. Most important at this juncture was Mach's discovery of what later came to be known as Mach's bands, a phenomenon that relates the physiological effect of spatially distributed light stimuli to visual perception. A Mach band is observed when a spatial distribution of light results in a sharp change in illumination at some point. A negative change corresponds to a band brighter than its surroundings in the region of sharp change. A positive change corresponds to a band darker than its surroundings in the region of sharp change. This phenomenon, a physiological effect that has no physical basis, was the subject of five papers published between 1865 and 1868. A final paper appeared in 1906. The effect was essentially rediscovered in the 1950's and since has been the subject of considerable investigation.[4]

In 1867 Mach married Ludovica Marussig in Graz. He had already accepted the professorship of experimental physics at Charles University in Prague. He produced most of his important work during the twenty-eight years he spent in that chair and saw the publication of over a hundred scientific papers. Although he was deeply involved throughout in the theoretical reformation of his views on mechanics and thermodynamics, his journal publications chiefly reflect his experimental endeavors.

Prominent among the psychophysical investigations during the Prague years are Mach's studies on the changes of kinesthetic sensation and equilibrium associated with physical movement, acceleration, and change of orientation in the human body. To these may be added a steady stream of research papers in which Mach resolutely continued to probe problems already initiated in Vienna and Graz: experiments with spatially distributed retinal stimuli (Mach bands), monocular stereoscopy, the anatomy and function of the organs of auditory perception, and aural accommodation.

Within the discipline of physics proper Mach's output was no less impressive. The more conventional physical studies carried out in Prague conspicuously include a great variety of optical experiments connected with refraction, interference, polarization, and spectra. He investigated the wave motion associated with mechanical, electrical, and optical phenomena and notably clarified the longitudinal-wave propulsion characteristics of stretched and unstretched glass rods and quartz rods. He also studied the mechanical effects resulting from spark discharge within solids and on surfaces.

Between 1873 and 1893 Mach and various collaborators, including his son Ludwig, devised and perfected optical and photographic techniques to study sound waves and the wave propulsion and gas dynamics of projectiles, meteorites, explosions, and gas jets. Stimulated by the remarks of the Belgian artillerist Henri Melsens, in 1881 Mach undertook to study the flight of projectiles by means of photographic techniques that he had already devised for other experiments in his Prague laboratory.[5] His celebrated 1887 paper on supersonics was published jointly with P. Salcher of the Marine Academy of Fiume (now Rijeka, Yugoslavia) in the *Sitzungsberichte* of the Academy of Sciences in Vienna.[6] The experiments described in this classic paper were carried out in Fiume with the support of the Royal Austrian Navy. In this paper, the angle α, which the shock wave surrounding the envelope of an advancing gas cone makes with the direction of its motion, was shown to be related to the velocity of sound v and the velocity of the projectile ω as $\sin \alpha = v/\omega$ when $\omega > v$. After 1907, following the work of Ludwig Prandtl at the Kaiser Wilhelm Institut für Strömungsforschung in Göttingen, the angle α was called the Mach angle.[7]

Recognizing that the value of ω/v (the ratio of the speed of an object to the speed of sound in the undisturbed medium in which the object is traveling) was becoming increasingly significant in aerodynamics

for high-speed projectile studies, J. Ackeret in his inaugural lecture in 1929 as *Privatdozent* at the Eidgenössische Technische Hochschule, Zürich, suggested the term "Mach number" for this ratio.[8] The Mach number was introduced into the literature in English by the late 1930's and since the end of World War II has taken on considerable importance in theoretical and fluid dynamics. The work that has come to be most closely associated with Mach represents, in all probability, contributions that Mach would have conceived to be almost inconsequential when compared with his criticisms of classical mechanics and his experimental innovations in psychophysiology.

Mach also published while in Prague numerous popular scientific lectures and essays of historical and educational import and major treatises and monographs on conservation of energy (1872), spectral and stroboscopic investigations of musical tones (1873), the theory of the sensation of motion (1875), a critical history of mechanics (1883), and a volume on the analysis of sensations (1886). From 1882 to 1884 he was rector of the university during the difficult days when it separated into a German and a Czech faculty. In 1887 Mach and Johann Odstrčil published, with the help of a number of collaborators, the first of a series of physics textbooks, which ran to some twenty editions and were used with varying success in Germany and Austria for about four decades. Similarly, demonstration apparatus designed in Mach's laboratory was in use in Prague, Vienna, and Leipzig.

In 1895 Mach moved to the University of Vienna to assume a teaching position in philosophy, with the title professor of the history and theory of the inductive sciences. His *Popular Scientific Lectures*, a later edition of which was dedicated to William James, was first published in English in 1895. His *Principien der Wärmelehre*, dedicated to J. B. Stallo, appeared in 1896. In 1897 Mach suffered a stroke which left the right side of his body paralyzed. After a period of recuperation, he resumed lecturing and writing. He officially retired from his professorship in 1901, the year of his appointment to the upper chamber of the Austrian parliament. His *Erkenntnis und Irrtum* appeared in 1905 and his *Space and Geometry* in 1906.

In 1913 Mach moved with his wife to the country home of his son Ludwig in Vaterstetten, Germany. His *Kultur und Mechanik* was published in 1915, the year before he died. Mach's *Die Principien der physikalischen Optik* was published posthumously in 1921.

A physicist by training, Mach wished to be recognized as such. All the same, he was deeply engaged for most of his life in investigating problems in physiology, psychology, and the history and philosophy of science. An overall examination of his lifework reveals that he was an inventive experimentalist, an acute and imaginative critic of scientific theory, and was unusually sensitive to the importance of formulating problems in areas where physics, physiology, and psychology intersect. Mach's broad fascination with the phenomenal world of his immediate environment was leavened with an unusual and solicitous curiosity about nature in its pristine form. He recognized a strong desire for self-enlightenment and realized that he wanted to be a physicist, but a physicist unconstrained by the conventional barriers of the specialists with whom he came in contact.

In Einstein's obituary for Mach in 1916 we read: "The unmediated pleasure of seeing and understanding, Spinoza's *amor dei intellectualis*, was so strongly predominant in him that to a ripe old age he peered into the world with the inquisitive eyes of a carefree child taking delight in the understanding of relationships."[9] Einstein believed that even in those cases in which Mach's scientific inquiries were not founded on new principles, his work at all times displayed "extraordinary experimental talent." Even where Mach's philosophy intruded upon his science his colleagues nevertheless praised his intuition and skill in scientific research. In 1927 Wilhelm Ostwald wrote: "So clear and calculated a thinker as Ernst Mach was regarded as a visionary *[Phantast]*, and it was not conceivable that a man who understood how to produce such good experimental work would want to practice nonsense *[Allotria]* which was so suspicious philosophically."[10] Arnold Sommerfeld spoke of Mach as a brilliant experimentalist but a peculiar theoretician who, in seeking to embrace the "physiological" and "psychical" in his physics, had to relegate the "physical" to a less pretentious level than physicists were accustomed to expect from a colleague.[11]

Fundamental among Mach's theoretical contributions and reflections were his explanations of visual, aural, and kinesthetic sensation; his views on mechanics, thermodynamics, optics, and molecular spectroscopy; and the ideas associated with his wave propulsion studies. Generally speaking, at least during his lifetime, Mach's theoretical opinions were judged to be amalgamated with too many hypercritical, obstreperous, and extrascientific remarks. In other instances, either the subject matter of his inquiries or his approach to the problems, or both, were too far afield to interest professional physicists. Mach's uncompromising rejection of the atomic theory, for example, far surpassed that of his contemporaries who,

even when noncommittal about atoms and molecules as existential entities, never questioned its extraordinary usefulness as a powerful hypothesis. Mach became less denunciatory about the theory as he became older, but it is doubtful that he ever abandoned his dogmatic antiatomistic position, even after the discoveries at the turn of the century had furnished rather convincing evidence that he was wrong.

Mach looked upon the atomic theory and "the artificial hypothetical atoms and molecules of physics and chemistry" as "traditional intellectual implements" of the discipline. He wrote: "The value of these implements for their special, limited purposes is not one whit destroyed. As before, they remain economical ways of symbolizing experience. But we have as little right to expect from them, as from the symbols of algebra, more than we have put into them, and certainly not more enlightenment than from experience itself."[12]

The most severe critic of Mach's position on thermodynamics was Max Planck,[13] for whom the principle of conservation of energy was a true law of nature, a reality independent of man's existence. For Mach the principle took the position of a maxim or convention for organizing a large class of natural phenomena and was rooted in an anthropomorphic sanction related to a biologically determined economy of effort conducive to survival. "Energy" was for Mach no more than a plausible and powerful concept like force, space, or temperature. Thus it is wrong to include Mach among energeticists such as Wilhelm Ostwald and Georg Helm—as is often done.[14]

As for the second law of thermodynamics, Boltzmann felt that neither Planck nor Mach had penetrated its statistical essence. After 1900 Planck, but not Mach, accepted Boltzmann's interpretation. In fact, Mach continued to challenge, on philosophical grounds, the atomic-molecular-mechanical explanation of the laws of thermodynamics, preferring characteristically to give them a more simple and purely postulational status.[15] In his *Wärmelehre* (1896) Mach stated,

The mechanical conception of the Second Law through the distinction between *ordered* and *unordered* motion, through the establishment of a parallel between the increase of entropy and the increase of unordered motion at the expense of ordered, seems quite *artificial*. If one realizes that a real analogy of the *entropy increase* in a purely mechanical system consisting of absolutely elastic atoms does not exist, one can hardly help thinking that a violation of the Second Law—and without the help of any demon—would have to be possible if such a mechanical system were the *real* foundation of thermal processes. Here I agree with

F. Wald completely, when he says: "In my opinion the roots of this (entropy) law lie much deeper, and if success were achieved in bringing about agreement between the molecular hypothesis and the entropy law, this would be fortunate for the hypothesis, but not for the entropy law."[16]

While thermodynamics at present enjoys autonomy as a discipline independent of mechanics, at the beginning of the century the statistical interpretation thoroughly permeated thermodynamics because of the great achievements and general reception of the atomic-molecular theory. It is thus even more difficult today to see how Mach could have been so blind to the steady advance of what became one of the most powerful theories for all of the physical sciences.

Mach's critical reflections on mechanics gave rise to a spirited discussion of the scientific, historical, and philosophical foundations of classical physics. His perspicuity in these matters is admirably demonstrated by the richness of the responses elicited from Hertz, Pearson, Boltzmann, Föppl, Love, Stallo, Clifford, Picard, Poincaré, Duhem, Seeliger, Vailati, and Jourdain. Even so, as Einstein wrote in 1916, referring to Mach's *Die Mechanik* of 1883, "There you will find set forth brilliantly ideas which by no means as yet have become the common property of physicists."[17]

According to Mach, Newton possessed the two characteristics necessary for greatness in a scientist: an imaginative grasp of the essential elements of experience of the world and the intellectual power of generalization. In *Die Mechanik*, Mach presented Newton's mechanical views in considerable detail. He offered generous praise for the clarity of presentation of the *Principia* along with some forceful arguments for the rational reformulation of some of its concepts. A case in point was Mach's conception of inertial mass, which he treated not as an intrinsic property of an object but as an entity specified by the dynamical coupling between the object and the rest of the universe. He proposed that Newton's conception of mass, as quantity of matter, be replaced by an "arbitrarily established definition," namely, that "all those bodies are bodies of equal mass, which, mutually acting on each other, produce in each other equal and opposite accelerations."[18] Such a definition, Mach contended, would render superfluous Newton's special enunciation of the principle of reaction, a conclusion favored for reasons of economy of thought.

Newton's views on absolute time, space, and motion were challenged in *Die Mechanik* on the grounds that they could in no way be related to experimental observations. Mach suggested the elimination of all propositions from which observables cannot be deduced and further proposed that the motions of bodies be considered relative to all observable matter in the universe at large: "When we reflect that we cannot abolish isolated bodies..., that is, cannot determine by experiment whether the part they play is fundamental or collateral, that hitherto they have been the sole and only competent means of the orientation of motions and of the descriptions of mechanical facts, then it will be found expedient provisionally to regard all motions as determined by these bodies."[19] On Mach's terms a body in an empty universe has no inertia. The inertia of a system is reduced to a functional relationship between the system and the rest of the universe, including the most distant parts of the interacting material system.

To call attention to this principle, Einstein, in a four-page paper on general relativity (1918), introduced the expression "Mach principle" *(Machsches Prinzip)* to emphasize a generalization of Mach's claim that the inertia of an isolated body can have no meaning;[20] that inertia must be reduced to the reciprocal action of bodies; that the inertial frame is determined by the mass distribution in the universe; and that the inertial force on a body is the interaction of distant matter on the body. What is entailed is the choice, even if it be provisional, of a material system that mathematically approximates absolute space.

Mach's critique of Newtonian mechanics, interpreted by Einstein within the context of Riemannian field theory, served as one of the strongest incentives for the development of Einstein's gravitational theory—although Einstein eventually discovered that the Mach principle did not hold for his new theory. What it did show was that the metric of space-time could be determined by the distribution of matter and energy; that the curvature of space, and from this the motion of bodies, could be determined from matter in space. Thus the motion of bodies was seen to be due to the influence of the surrounding masses (including the stars) and not, as Newton had supposed, to any effort on the part of bodies to maintain their direction of motion in absolute space.

Einstein hoped that he would be able to give mathematical expression to the Mach principle; admittedly he was not completely successful. He found support for the Mach principle by showing that his field equations turned out to have no solution, no metric, in matter-free space. He managed to assimilate the reconcilable aspect of Mach's principle into the general theory of relativity, based on the equivalence principle and the conception of covariance under general transformations of space-time coordinates, but he was not content to accept the qualification of restriction to finite space-time boundary conditions that is implied in the Mach principle. In fact, he discovered that he could write field equations that gave the correct solutions only by adding the so-called cosmological term.[21]

The scientific and philosophical literature on the reinterpretations and formulations of the Mach principle is huge.[22] Demonstrations of its compatibility with gravitational theory and other cosmological models continue to be proposed, reformulated, and rejected. Attempts to show where the principle does or does not make sense continue; as do objections to the principle itself or to parts of a particular formulation of it. Suffice it to say that there is little agreement on the mathematical formulation of the Mach principle. The expression is highly anachronistic as a collective term and has little in common with Mach's original conception of the problem. Still, the logical connection between Mach's views on mechanics and Einstein's theory of relativity, even now, is not a meaningless issue.

In his *Autobiographical Notes* (1946) Einstein saw "Mach's greatness in his incorruptible skepticism and independence." Although he there referred to Mach's epistemological position as one "which today appears to me to be essentially untenable," he also recognized that Mach had influenced his thought during his early years.[23] Einstein on several occasions mentioned that he had drawn inspiration from Mach's *Mechanik*, and it is therefore something of an enigma that Mach so categorically rejected the theory of relativity. In the preface to *Die Principien der physikalischen Optik*, written in 1913 but not published until 1921, Mach complained that he was "gradually becoming regarded as the forerunner of relativity" and that philosophers and physicists were carrying on a crusade against him: "I have repeatedly observed that I was merely an unprejudiced rambler, endowed with original ideas, in various fields of knowledge. I must, however, as assuredly disclaim to be a forerunner of the relativists as I withhold from the atomistic belief of the present day. The reason why, and the extent to which, I reject the present-day relativity theory, which I find to be growing more and more dogmatical, together with the particular reasons which have led me to such a view—the considerations based on the physiology of the senses, the theoretical ideas, and above all the conceptions resulting from my experiments—must remain to be treated in the sequel."[24] The sequel—apparently an attack on Einstein's theory of relativity—never materialized.

In considering Mach's contribution to the history of science, it is helpful to understand that all of his historicocritical writings lend strength to the thesis that the history of a scientific discipline, concept, or theory was for him a means to interpret and illuminate epistemological problems in the philosophy of science that puzzled him as a physicist.[25] Mach never undertook to write history with the intent merely of reconstituting the development of the subject as an end in itself. He wrote no history of areas in which he recognized no problem. By the same token he made no attempt to treat any aspect of the history of science in a systematic fashion. He was not predisposed to examine the nature of scientific revolutions or to relate science to its organizational, institutional, or sociocultural framework. He put forward no systematic philosophy of science.

As a young man Mach was given to considerable introspection and puzzlement about the nature of physics and the obligations of the physicist toward the new branches of science opening up alongside physics. By means of historical studies and the critical examination of the foundations of physics, he hoped to achieve insights into the direction that his own work might take. Mach's writings exerted considerable influence on late nineteenth- and early twentieth-century philosophic thought. The characteristic epistemological questions that Mach formulated were the outgrowth of his preoccupation with physics as seen from within the context of an obstinate inquisitiveness concerning the historical tradition inherited by physics.

Mach was first attracted to the history of science for what it might teach him about physics. In *Die Mechanik* he spelled this out, saying that

> . . . not only a knowledge of the ideas that have been accepted and cultivated by subsequent teachers is necessary for the historical understanding of a science, but also . . . the rejected and transient thoughts of the inquirers, nay even apparently erroneous notions, may be very important and very instructive. The historical investigation of the development of a science is most needful, lest the principles treasured up in it become a system of half-understood prescripts, or worse, a system of *prejudices*. Historical investigation not only promotes the understanding of that which now is, but also brings new possibilities before us, by showing that which exists to be in great measure *conventional* and *accidental*. From the higher point of view at which different paths of thought converge we may look about us with freer vision and discover routes before unknown.[26]

Mach's historical perspective was biased toward the investigation of specific problems and concepts. To this end, history was not conceived chronologically, biographically, or even topically. The documents that formed the basis of his historical analyses were almost exclusively limited to scientific writings. There is ample evidence that Mach had a good command of

Latin, Greek, French, Italian, and English and that he examined the primary sources. In addition he was familiar with a very broad secondary literature and, as his personal correspondence shows, exchanged ideas with an international group of scholars.

In 1863 Mach was already persuaded that his scientific curiosity might be nurtured by a serious study of the history of science, if only as an aid in the teaching of science. For he believed that students should not be expected to adopt propositions as self-evident which had developed over several thousand years. In his first major historical work, *Die Geschichte und die Wurzel des Satzes von der Erhaltung der Arbeit* (1872), he conjectured that there is "only one way to [scientific] enlightenment: historical studies!" The investigation of nature, he believed, should be founded on a special classical education that "consists in the knowledge of the historical development . . . of science." It was not the logical analysis of science but the history of science that would encourage the scientist to tackle problems without engendering an aversion to them. The scientist might follow two paths in order to become reconciled with reality: "Either one grows accustomed to the puzzles and they trouble one no more, or one learns to understand them with the help of history and to consider them calmly from that point of view."[27]

The youthful considerations included in the small (fifty-eight-page) *Geschichte und Wurzel* touched upon themes and points of view that continued to be explored by Mach for the rest of his life: the meaning and function of scientific theories, the epistemological importance of the physiology and psychology of sensation for the natural sciences in general, the principle of economy of thought, the inadequacy of Newtonian mechanics, the sterility of the atomic theory, and the sharp criticism of classical causality, physical reductionism, mechanism, materialism, and all forms of metaphysical speculation. In his historico-critical treatises on mechanics, optics, and heat theory, and in his *Analyse der Empfindungen* (1886) and *Erkenntnis und Irrtum* (1905), Mach returned to these same issues. It is instructive to try to identify some of the recurrent themes and cardinal epistemological questions raised in these works and then to discover how they are formulated within the context of Mach's historical outlook.

The pivotal questions that Mach's historicocritical analyses sought to elucidate may be formulated as follows: How did we inherit our current scientific concepts and theories? Why are they given to us in the way that we have become accustomed to accept them, rather than in some other form that may be logically more plausible or aesthetically more commendable? What factors can we identify as contributory to the adoption of preferred modes of reasoning and analogical adaptation from other domains? At any given time in history, what was considered to constitute evidence, verification, or a conclusive proof for a scientific theory?

With these questions, formulated and elucidated with examples drawn from the history of science, the essential framework of Mach's conception of the scientific enterprise takes on a fairly predictable form: Physics comprises only a small part of the body of scientific knowledge: its intellectual concepts and implements are too specialized. The natural sciences are inexpressibly richer than physics, and their history is inexhaustibly diversified. In any particular science that is being actively cultivated the ideas are generally undergoing metamorphosis. Since scientific concepts, laws, and theories are to some extent perennially obsolete, it is meaningless to harp on their anchored truth status. The conceptual creations of science, always tentative and at best incomplete, take on a configuration at any time that reveals the attendant historical circumstances and the convergence of interest and attention of those scientific investigators at work on the problems—now physicists, now physiologists, now psychologists.

Implied here is the notion that the nature and form given to a scientific construct depend in large part on the whims of history and on the environmentally conditioned process of cognitive organization employed by scientists. The concept of matter, for example, is seen to be bound, in its content, to a particular historically determined state of scientific development rather than to any fixed reality. Necessarily subjoined to this cognitive activity—biologically joined, in fact—is a mandate for abstraction and the exercise of economy of thought. Given that there exists no conceivable rock bottom of information potentially relevant for understanding the ways of nature, and recognizing the many alternatives for relating and organizing the facts, the scientific investigator has no choice but to fall back on drastic abstraction and generalization.

Mach, of course, understood that scientists commonly strive to achieve logical consistency, simplicity and elegance of formulation, inclusiveness, and range of applicability. Actually, scientific concepts, laws, and hypotheses, when studied within the context of their genesis, do not display so prominently the elegant logical traits and clear features that characterize the orthodox image of science. Instead, their most visible feature is their scientific extrinsicness. With the passage of time, that which is historically acquired comes to be philosophically affirmed. Mach underlined the need for scientists to acknowledge and neutralize the subtle way in which scientific constructs take on a status of philosophical necessity rather than historical contingency.

In *Die Mechanik*, for example, Mach sought to demonstrate how the historical study of the development of the principles of statics and dynamics—from historical contingency to philosophical necessity—could furnish the tactics for developing the analytical and methodological desiderata for interpreting and purifying the conceptual components of science. By means of the critical, historical, and psychological exposure of the roots of science, Mach intended, above all, to expose metaphysical obscurities, inherited anthropomorphisms, and ambiguities and to demonstrate the artificiality of the mechanical interpretation of the sciences. To this end he explored the function of instinctive knowledge, the role of memory, the correlation between the origin of an idea and its status in science at a given time, the psychology of discovery in contradistinction to the logic of discovery, and the authority that induction and deduction derive from experience.

The disclosure of the mental steps of proof adopted by different investigators is informative. For what reason, by what authority, did Stevin in his consideration of the principle of the inclined plane (based on the condition of equilibrium of an endless uniform chain on a triangular prism) argue from the general to the specific case? Why did Archimedes, on the other hand, in his treatment of the principle of the lever argue from the specific to the general case? What constituted proof is by no means unambiguously clear in these two cases.

Again, when Daniel Bernoulli purported to have demonstrated that the proposition for composition of forces is a geometrical truth independent of experience, Mach accepted this "proof" as no more than a dubious reduction of what is easier to observe from what is more obscure and difficult to observe, a demonstration in which it is possible to conceal the nature of the so-called proof. The significant feature in this case, as Mach saw it, was to search for the historical reasons why Bernoulli's demonstration might have been accepted as proof. Was it not the case, here as in other examples, that the investigator had built his demonstration on an appeal to instinctive knowledge that is supposed to be self-evident and that claims to be basically different from experiential knowledge? For Mach so-called instinctive knowledge, no matter how heuristically valuable, was assumed to contain important elements of experience hidden in its premises. He tried, wherever possible, to buttress

this experience-oriented point of view with examples drawn from the history of science.

Mach's overall objective, narrow as it may seem, was to rid science of concepts that have no parallel in experience. This emphasis frequently has been characterized in the literature as the "Mach criterion," according to which only those propositions from which statements about observable phenomena can be deduced should be employed in theory. Scientific "proofs" that are not tied to experience, Mach felt, serve either as a cover-up for counterfeit rigor or as an appeal to the so-called higher authority of purely instinctive cognitions. In the case of a family of mechanical principles (exclusion of the *perpetuum mobile*, center of gravity, virtual work, *vis viva*, d'Alembert's principle, Gauss's principle of least constraint, Maupertuis's principle of least action, Hamilton's principle) Mach demonstrated to his own satisfaction that each of these can be derived from any other—given sufficient mathematical ingenuity and perseverance.

Clearly, Mach reasoned, these principles are all related in such a way that, if any one is taken to be true, then all the rest can be deduced by mathematical and logical reasoning. But what affords the rationale for accepting any specific principle as true in the first place? It can only be that the principle provides the right answers to problems in statics and dynamics. If any one of the above principles can be translated by deduction into any other, it nevertheless remains to be shown how the validity of at least one of them can be established. Mach's answer, given historically, was that the roots of the most primitive of such principles derive from experience. An example might be the experimental impossibility of designing a machine that furnishes unlimited quantities of mechanical work without the input of effort. Mach was dogmatic about this point—that the behavior of nature cannot be divined exclusively on the basis of so-called self-evident suppositions, unless the suppositions are themselves drawn from experience.

Mach analyzed at some length the history of the treatment of problems in statics (using both static and dynamic arguments) and in dynamics (using both dynamic and static arguments). Mach found that, historically considered, statics was prior to dynamics; whereas logically or conceptually understood, statics could be reduced to a limiting case of dynamics. Mach hoped in this way to discover by analysis what clear meaning, if any, was to be attached to the statement that one scientific principle is more fundamental than another. The wider generality of one principle compared to another, Mach felt, was not necessarily a sufficient warrant to accept it as more basic. Nor should the historical priority of discovery or enunciation of one principle over that of an alternative formulation dictate logical status. In short, "basic" and "fundamental" had for Mach no fixed significance when severed from the context of the scientific problem. The practical solution to understanding mechanical principles, Mach felt, was to learn by experience in scientific problem solving.[28]

Mach's emphasis in *Die Mechanik* is neatly summarized as follows:

> The most important result of our reflections is . . . *that precisely the apparently simplest mechanical theorems are of a very complicated nature; that they are founded on incomplete experiences, even on experiences that never can be fully completed; that in view of the tolerable stability of our environment they are, in fact, practically safeguarded to serve as the foundation of mathematical deduction; but that they by no means themselves can be regarded as mathematically established truths, but only as theorems that not only admit of constant control by experience but actually require it.*[29]

Mach's position on mechanics was an ambiguous one. On the one hand he played upon the crucial importance of a critical analysis of physical principles. On the other hand, he concluded that from a logical, economical, and practical point of view there is no persuasive rationale for defending either the historical legacy or the relevance of mechanics for the development of other scientific disciplines. While the study of the history of science abundantly demonstrates the prestigious place of mechanics, Mach conjectured that its applicability for other scientific domains was severely limited. While mechanics, Mach thought, offered little means of understanding heat theory, electricity, and light, its application within psychology was unqualifiably pernicious. The resolute thrust that characterized Mach's efforts to exploit experimental physiology and psychology—in part, by means of physical techniques—was indicative of the genuineness with which he was searching for novel problems and perspectives beyond the conventional physics of his day, without ever being able to relinquish his hold on professional physics or to put aside experimental physics as such.

Mach's philosophy of science was governed by the impulse to explore in depth the epistemological roots of science; but he was certain that this exploration could not be undertaken by examining the scientist's work without analyzing his behavior. Hence we recognize Mach's perseverance in demonstrating the relevance of the analysis of sensations and of the importance of psychology and physiology as a corrective to the prevailing mechanistic physicalism.

Mach's philosophical point of view and, in particular, his emphasis on scientific laws as summary statements of observation led to his being identified with the positivists. In 1909 Lenin published, in Moscow, his *Materializm i empirio-kritisizm. Kriticheskie zametki ob odnoy reaktsionnoy filosofii* ("Materialism and Empirio-Criticism; Critical Comments on a Reactionary Philosophy"). In this work—much commented upon since then and essential in the development of Soviet Marxism—Lenin scathingly denounced the young Machists. Along with Mach, Avenarius, and Berkeley, they were accused of supporting a pernicious positivism and subjective idealism antithetical to Marxist dialectial materialism.

In addition to being associated with radical and empirical skepticism, positivism, subjective idealism, and the renunciation of truth in any transcendental sense, Mach is known to have supported a theory of knowledge based on the study of biological behavior. The ideas presented in Mach's *Beiträge zur Analyse der Empfindungen* (1886; rcv. cd., 1900) sprang from the profound conviction, as explained in the preface, "that the foundations of science as a whole, and of physics in general, await their next greatest elucidations from the side of biology, and especially from the analysis of sensations."[30]

In the various revisions of this work, the 1901 edition of which was dedicated to Pearson, Mach explicitly clarified his views on how psychological, physiological, and physical experience, taken as sensations, provide man's sole source of knowledge concerning the world. The so-called elements of sensation that Mach had in mind—colors, sounds, temperatures, pressures, spaces, times, and so forth—are functionally connected in many ways and are associated with mind, feelings, and volition. Some of these associations (adaptations) stand forth more prominently than others, are engraved on our memory, and are expressed in language. Phenomena are represented as a complex of interrelated sensations embracing the object and subject of the sensations, the sensed, and the senser, such that any dualism between subject and object disappears.

The elements of sensation are not entirely independent, but for the sake of analysis can be separated into three groups: The external (*äussere*) elements, $A, B, C, \cdots$, characterize physical bodies and define the discipline of physics; the internal (*innere*) elements $K, L, M, \cdots$, characterize human bodies and define the discipline of physiology; the interior (*innerste*) elements, $\alpha, \beta, \gamma, \cdots$, characterize our ego (memory, volitions) and define the discipline of psychology. Since the properties of one and the same physical object, therefore, appear modified and conditioned by our own bodies, our sense organs under different circumstances produce different sensations and perceptions. The gulf that separates physical from psychological investigation resides not in a difference of subject matter but in different modes of investigation in the two domains. For example, to refer to that which is physical in an object being examined is but to designate one method of cognitive organization of which there are many. It is not the facts but the points of view that distinguish the disciplines.

From a psychophysiological point of view, the process of cognition includes the adaptation of thoughts to facts *(Beobachtung)* and thoughts to other thoughts *(Theorie)*. Mach asserted that the world of the percipient is composed entirely of sensations and not any illusive, protean, pseudophilosophical, Kantian *Ding-an-sich* that is supposed to remain after all of the qualities of a body are taken from it. Things, bodies, matter—the so-called objects of our experience—are thought symbols for combinations of elements and complexes of sensations and therefore are nothing apart from the totality of their attributes. A more or less complete description of phenomena should be accompanied by a more or less complete statement of the relevant functional relationships. To suit his purposes an investigator can analyze that which is given in experience, but he cannot by any manipulation of the empirically given data produce new information about how nature will behave in a new situation. He can, of course, predict how nature will behave in the empirically unknown, but it is always experience that serves as final judge about how nature in fact does behave in the unknown.

Mach's so-called principle of psychophysical parallelism as a guide in the investigation of sensations follows from the assumption that all sensations can be investigated from the point of view of physics, physiology, or psychology. There are no sensations uniquely physical or physiological or psychological. There are only sensations to be investigated from different points of view and according to the choice of connections between elements isolated for examination.

To strengthen his principle of psychophysical parallelism and to encourage the broadest possible interchange within the physical and biological field, Mach condoned the use of provisional teleological motives because of their heuristic value in formulating significant questions. More important for Mach's doctrine of how sensations become the basis for behavior or action are his views on biological evolution. He was convinced that all of science had its origins in the needs of life. The animal body is a relatively constant sum of touch and sight sensations,

and all physical knowledge can only mentally represent and anticipate compounds of the elements of sensation.

Mach's argument can be briefly reconstructed as follows: The external phenomenal world is hopelessly heterogeneous and complex. Biological organisms cannot adapt to this environment, cannot survive, unless the given heterogeneous sensations as stimuli are converted into some focused form of homogeneous behavior that favors self-preservation. Over long periods of time biological organisms have developed a mechanism of accepting (scanning, rejecting) heterogeneous stimuli and correlating them and integrating them into homogeneous, purposeful behavior. How? By a sensor mechanism—tactile, aural, thermal—that excites but one nerve path; this in turn connects with the brain and gives rise to voluntary and, by habituation, involuntary behavior. The net process from unorganized stimuli to anatomically and symmetrically organized response (an example is the need for rapid locomotion) is a movement toward the biological organism's evolutionary acquisition of control over nature's stimuli.

It might be suggested that Mach's principle of economy of thought was also rooted in evolutionary arguments that championed those survival acts that relate to minimizing effort. Mach's views on *Denkökonomie* were first spelled out in his 1868 lecture on "The Form of Liquids" and in *Die Geschichte und die Wurzel* (1872). In the former he compared the principle of least surface for liquids to the miserly but intelligent mercantilist principle of a tailor working with the greatest saving of material, adding: "But why, tell me, should science be ashamed of such a principle? Is science . . . as a maximum or minimum problem . . . itself anything more than—a business? Is not its task to acquire with the least possible work, in the least possible time, with the least possible thought, the greatest possible part of eternal truth?"[31] Elsewhere, in his 1882 lecture "On the Economical Nature of Physical Inquiry" and in a special chapter in *Die Mechanik*, Mach reiterated and reemphasized the principle of *Denkökonomie* and its connection with mathematical reasoning, causality, teleology, evolution, and psychic phenomena.[32] The transparent omnipresence of this principle in Mach's writings led Peirce to say, "Dr. Ernst Mach who has one of the best faults a philosopher can have, that of riding his horse to death, does just this with his principle of Economy in science."[33]

As a physicist given to championing psychophysiology as the science of the future, Mach was not at all persuasive in his obscure position. Was he suggesting that concepts, methods, and distinctive points of view within the domain of psychophysiology might prove effective for investigating problems in the physical sciences that had hitherto been the exclusive concern of professionals in the discipline? Or should the fields of psychology and physiology and their attendant problems be opened up for investigation by the methods developed within the physical sciences? The former position, a rather radical one, calls for an extraordinarily sweeping psychophysiological reconstruction of physical principles—whatever that might entail. The second position, psychology as auxiliary to physics, either approximates physical reductionism, toward which Mach was ill-disposed, or else borders on psychophysics in the style of Fechner, whose approach considerably influenced Mach. In any case, Mach apparently chose to exploit either possibility, as the occasion demanded: psychophysiology to provide new directives for physics, and physics enriched through the focus of attention on psychophysiological problems. He seems to have leaned philosophically toward the former but to have organized his own research according to the latter.

While Mach made no claim to be a philosopher, much has been written about his scientific philosophy; he was more of a scientist's philosopher than a philosopher's philosopher. In 1886 he wrote in his *Analysis of Sensations*, "I make no pretension to the title of philosopher. I only seek to adopt in physics a point of view that need not be changed immediately on glancing over into the domain of another science; for, ultimately, all must form one whole."[34]

In the preface to *Erkenntnis und Irrtum* (1905) Mach remarked that the scientist, without claiming to be a philosopher, has a strong urge to satisfy an almost insatiable curiosity about the origins, structure, process, and conceptual roots of science. Averse to being labeled a philosopher, Mach nevertheless was not timid about raising and discussing methodological and epistemological questions. His progressive drift from physics to the philosophy of science via the history of science is nowhere more clearly evident than in *Erkenntnis und Irrtum*. The most comprehensive analytical and systematic treatment of Mach's philosophical views, the work is seldom read and almost never cited by historians of science. When his critics referred to his writings as *die Machsche Philosophie*, he replied:

Above all there is no Machist philosophy. At most [there is] a scientific methodology and a psychology of knowledge *[Erkenntnispsychologie]*; and like all scientific theories both are provisional and imperfect efforts. I am not responsible for the philosophy which can be constructed from these with the help of extraneous ingredients. . . . The land of the transcendental is closed to me. And if I make the open confession that its inhabitants are not able at all to excite my curiosity, then you may estimate the wide abyss that exists between me and many philosophers. For this reason I already have declared explicitly that I am by no means a philosopher, but only a scientist. If nevertheless occasionally, and in a somewhat noisy way, I have been listed among the former then I am not responsible for this. Of course, I also do not want to be a scientist who blindly entrusts himself to the guidance of a single philosopher in the way that Molière's physician expected and demanded of his patients.[35]

In 1872 Mach wrote, "The object of science is the connection of phenomena; but the theories are like dry leaves which fall away when they have long ceased to be the lungs of the tree of science."[36] Science was for Mach primarily "the compendious representation of the actual." It is on this crucial point that his thought exhibits a gross miscalculation about the strength and reach, especially within recent science, of the highly artificial conceptual tools that scientists employ in their exploration of nature and even more of the exploration of that aspect of nature that is a product of the scientists' own creation.

Superimposed on Mach's ambitious program to relate the sciences to their historical and philosophical implications was his unflinching drive to unmask the theological, animistic, and metaphysical elements of science as he saw them. For this reason (among others that touch upon the long-range implications of his antirealistic, anticausal, antimechanistic, antimaterialistic, and antiatomistic world view) it was virtually impossible for contemporary scientists, philosophers, and historians to avoid taking sides *vis-à-vis* Mach. Positions of neutrality or indifference were rare during his lifetime—and still are. The deeper he delved into his historical studies the more he became engulfed by philosophical questions. Much as he eschewed the title of philosopher, his involvement with such questions ultimately forced him to carve out a scientific metaphysics of his own—although he would have denied that.

If at times Mach's historical position and emphasis seem superficial, erroneous, and misdirected, the caliber and import of his work can still be evaluated against the state of the art of historical and philosophical discussions in the sciences in his day.

As Einstein wrote, in the year of Mach's death, "I even believe that those who consider themselves to be adversaries of Mach scarcely know how much of Mach's outlook they have, so to speak, absorbed with their mothers' milk."[37]

NOTES

1. Erwin Hiebert, "The Genesis of Mach's Early Views on Atomism," in R. S. Cohen and R. J. Seeger, eds., *Ernst Mach: Physicist and Philosopher* (1970), 79–106.
2. "Die Leitgedanken . . .," in *Scientia*, **8** (1910), 234.
3. "Aus Dr. Mach's Vorträgen über Psychophysik," in *Österreichische Zeitschrift für praktische Heilkunde*, **9** (1863), 366.
4. Ratliff, *Mach Bands: Quantitative Studies on Neural Networks in the Retina* (1965).
5. Cf. Mach's 1897 lecture: "On Some Phenomena Attending the Flight of Projectiles," in *Popular Scientific Lectures* (1943).
6. E. Mach and P. Salcher, "Photographische Fixirung der durch Projectile in der Luft eingeleiteten Vorgänge," in *Sitzungsberichte der Akademie der Wissenschaften in Wien*, **95** (1887), 764–780. This paper and four others are conveniently reproduced in Joachim Thiele, ed., *Ernst Mach. Arbeiten über Erscheinungen an fliegenden Projectilen* (Hamburg, 1966).
7. Ludwig Prandtl, "Neue Untersuchungen über die strömende Bewegung der Gase und Dämpfe," in *Physikalische Zeitschrift*, **8** (1907), 23–30.
8. J. Ackeret, "Der Luftwiderstand bei sehr grossen Geschwindigkeiten," in *Schweizerische Bauzeitung*, **94** (1929), 179–183.
9. Albert Einstein, "Ernst Mach," in *Physikalische Zeitschrift*, **17** (1916), 101–104.
10. Wilhelm Ostwald, *Lebenslinien, Eine Selbstbiographie*, II (Berlin, 1927), 171.
11. Arnold Sommerfeld, "Nekrolog auf Ernst Mach," in *Jahrbuch der bayerischen Akademie der Wissenschaften* (1917), 58–67.
12. *Beiträge* (1886), pp. 142–143; English ed. (1959), p. 311.
13. For a discussion and evaluation of the differences in philosophical outlook between Mach and Planck, see Erwin Hiebert (1968).
14. Cf. Erwin Hiebert, "The Energetics Controversy and the New Thermodynamics," in Duane H. D. Roller, ed., *Perspectives in the History of Science and Technology* (Norman, Okla., 1971), 67–86.
15. Cf. Hiebert, *The Conception of Thermodynamics in the Scientific Thought of Mach and Planck* (Freiburg im Breisgau, 1968), pp. 104–107.
16. *Wärmelehre* (1896), p. 364.
17. Einstein, *loc. cit.* (1916), p. 102.
18. *Die Mechanik* (1889), p. 203; English ed. (1960), p. 266.
19. *Ibid.*, pp. 215–216 and 283 resp.
20. Albert Einstein, "Prinzipielles zur allgemeinen Relativitätstheorie," in *Annalen der Physik*, 4th ser., **55** (1918), 241–244.
21. See *Dictionary of Scientific Biography*, IV, 312–333.
22. Cf. Hong-Yee Chiu and W. F. Hoffmann, *Gravitation and Relativity* (New York, 1964).
23. P. A. Schilpp, ed., *Albert Einstein: Philosopher-Scientist* (Evanston, Ill., 1949), p. 21.
24. *Die Principien der physikalischen Optik* (1921), pp. viii–ix; English ed. (1926), p. vii–viii. See also Joseph Petzoldt, "Das Verhältnis der Machschen Gedankenwelt zur Relativitätstheorie," in the 8th ed. (1921) of *Die Mechanik;* and Ludwig Mach's pref. to the 9th ed. (1933).
25. Cf. Erwin Hiebert, "Mach's Philosophical Use of the History of Science," in Roger H. Stuewer, ed., *Historical and Philosophical Perspectives of Science* (Minneapolis, 1970), pp. 184–203.
26. *Die Mechanik* (1889), pp. 237–238; English ed. (1960), pp. 316–317.
27. *Geschichte und Wurzel* (1872), pp. 1–4; English ed. (1911), pp. 15–18.
28. For Mach's conception of the role of physical experiments and thought experiments in scientific problem solving, see Erwin Hiebert, "Mach's Conception of Thought Experi-

ments in the Natural Sciences," in *S. Sambursky Symposium* (in press).
29. *Die Mechanik* (1889), pp. 221–222; English ed. (1960), pp. 289–290.
30. *Beiträge* (1886), p. v; English ed. (1959), pp. xxxv–xxxvi.
31. *Popular Scientific Lectures* (1943), p. 16.
32. *Ibid.* (1943), pp. 186–213; and "Die Oekonomie der Wissenschaft," in *Die Mechanik* (1889), pp. 452–466; English ed. (1960), pp. 577–595.
33. *Collected Papers of Charles Sanders Peirce*, C. Hartschorne and P. Weiss, eds., I (Cambridge, 1931), par. 122.
34. *Beiträge* (1886), p. 21; English ed. (1959), p. 30.
35. *Erkenntnis und Irrtum* (1905), pp. vii–viii.
36. *Geschichte und Wurzel* (1872), p. 46; English ed. (1911), p. 74.
37. Albert Einstein, "Ernst Mach," in *Physikalische Zeitschrift*, **17** (1916), 102.

BIBLIOGRAPHY

I. ORIGINAL WORKS. There is no collected edition of Mach's works. The Royal Society *Catalogue of Scientific Papers* lists 91 papers to the year 1900; Poggendorff is useful but incomplete. The most complete Mach bibliography, for both original works and secondary literature is Joachim Thiele, "Ernst Mach—Bibliographie," in *Centaurus*, **8** (1963), 189–237. The section on original works in this bibliography (without the list of secondary works) was revised and updated in Thiele (see below).

The library of the Ernst-Mach-Institut der Fraunhofer-Gesellschaft zur Förderung der angewandten Forschung, Freiburg im Breisgau, owns the largest collection of correspondence and other Mach documents: about 2,500 letters (mostly addressed to Mach) dated 1860–1916, some MSS, and other personalia and information by and about family members. The institute also houses a large but far from complete collection of Mach's publications and related secondary literature. Other major repositories for Mach correspondence and documents are the Morris Library of Southern Illinois University, Carbondale, Ill.; the Burndy Library, Norwalk, Conn.; the Akademie-Archiv of the Deutsche Akademie der Wissenschaften zu Berlin; and the University Library of the Technische Universität, Berlin-Charlottenburg.

The following chronological list of Mach's published books does not duplicate separately published pamphlets and lectures contained in those volumes.

1. *Compendium der Physik für Mediciner* (Vienna, 1863).
2. *Einleitung in die Helmholtz'sche Musiktheorie. Populär für Musiker dargestellt* (Graz, 1866).
3. *Die Geschichte und die Wurzel des Satzes von der Erhaltung der Arbeit* (Prague, 1872), includes Mach's "Ueber die Definition der Masse," in *Repertorium für physikalische Technik*, **4** (1868), 355–359. 2nd ed. (Leipzig, 1909) unchanged except for added "Bemerkungen zum zweiten Abdruck," pp. 59–60. English trans. and annotations by Philip E. B. Jourdain (Chicago–London), 1911.
4. *Optisch-akustische Versuche. Die spectrale und stroboskopische Untersuchung tönender Körper* (Prague, 1873).
5. *Grundlinien der Lehre von den Bewegungsempfindungen* (Leipzig, 1875); facs. ed. (Amsterdam, 1967).
6. *Die Mechanik in ihrer Entwickelung historisch-kri-*

tisch dargestellt (Leipzig, 1883). The 8th ed. (1921) includes Joseph Petzoldt, "Das Verhältnis der Machschen Gedankenwelt zur Relativitätstheorie." The 9th ed. (1933) contains a pref. by Ludwig Mach; facs. (Darmstadt, 1963). English trans. of 9th German ed. by Thomas J. McCormack (Chicago–La Salle, Ill., 1942). 6th American ed., with new intro. by Karl Menger (La Salle, Ill., 1960).

7. *Beiträge zur Analyse der Empfindungen* (Jena, 1886); 2nd ed., rev. and enl., *Die Analyse der Empfindungen und das Verhältnis des Physischen zum Psychischen* (Jena, 1900); 9th ed., 1922. English trans. of the 1st German ed. by C. M. Williams (Chicago, 1897); rev. and supp. from the 5th German ed. by Sidney Waterlow (Chicago, 1914). Paperback ed., with new intro. by Thomas S. Szasz (New York, 1959).

8. *Popular Scientific Lectures*, Thomas J. McCormack, trans. (La Salle, Ill., 1895); 5th ed., 1943. *Populärwissenschaftliche Vorlesungen* (Leipzig, 1896), 5th ed., 1923.

9. *Die Principien der Wärmelehre. Historisch-kritisch entwickelt* (Leipzig, 1896); 4th ed., with added index of persons, 1923. No known translations to date.

10. *Erkenntnis und Irrtum. Skizzen zur Psychologie der Forschung* (Leipzig, 1905); 2nd ed., 1906. The 3rd (1917) through 5th (1926) eds. contain Friedrich Jodl, "Ernst Mach und seine neueste Arbeit: 'Erkenntnis und Irrtum,' " from *Neue Freie Presse*, 24 Sept. 1905. English trans. in process for *Vienna Circle Collection* to be published by D. Reidel, with intro. and commentary by E. Hiebert.

11. *Space and Geometry in the Light of Physiological, Psychological and Physical Inquiry*, repr. from *Monist* (La Salle, Ill., 1906; 1960).

12. *Kultur und Mechanik* (Stuttgart, 1915).

13. *Die Leitgedanken meiner naturwissenschaftlichen Erkenntnislehre und ihre Aufnahme durch die Zeitgenossen. Sinnliche Elemente und naturwissenschaftliche Begriffe* (Leipzig, 1919), a pamphlet repr. of two essays originally published in *Scientia*, **8** (1910), 227–240; and *Pflügers Archiv für die gesamte Physiologie des Menschen und der Tiere*, **136** (1910), 263–274.

14. *Die Principien der physikalischen Optik. Historisch und erkenntnis-psychologisch entwickelt* (Leipzig, 1921). English trans. by John S. Anderson and A. F. A. Young (London, 1926; London–New York, 1956).

15. *Grundriss der Naturlehre für die unteren Classen der Mittelschulen* (Prague, 1887), written with Johann Odstrčil. Reissued (1887–1913) by Mach, K. Habart, and G. Wenzel in various eds. specifically designed for secondary school instruction in Austria and Germany.

16. *Grundriss der Physik für die höheren Schulen des Deutschen Reiches* (Leipzig, 1890), edited with the help of F. Harbordt and M. Fischer.

17. *Leitfaden der Physik für Studierende* (Prague–Vienna–Leipzig, 1891), written with G. Jaumann. 2nd ed., 1891.

II. SECONDARY LITERATURE.

1. [Maria Mach], *Erinnerungen einer Erzieherin. Nach Aufzeichnungen von ***, mit einem Vorwort herausgegeben von Professor Ernst Mach*, 2nd ed. (Vienna, 1913). Maria Mach was Ernst Mach's sister.

2. Friedrich Herneck, "Ueber eine unveröffentliche Selbstbiographie Ernst Machs," in *Wissenschaftliche Zeitschrift der Humboldt-Universität Berlin*, Math.-nat. Reihe, **6** (1956–1957), 209–220, from a thirteen-page MS of 1913 in the archives of the Deutsche Akademie der Wissenschaften zu Berlin.

3. Joachim Thiele, *Die Bedeutung Ernst Machs für die Wende von der klassischen zur modernen Physik. Ein Beitrag zur vergleichenden Geschichte wissenschaftstheoretischer Systeme* (Hamburg, 1959), an unpublished doctoral diss.

4. Theodor Ackermann Antiquariat, *Bibliothek Ernst Mach*, 2 pts. (Munich, 1959–1960), a list of some 3,700 works from Mach's working library.

5. K. D. Heller, *Ernst Mach. Wegbereiter der modernen Physik. Mit ausgewählten Kapiteln aus seinem Werk* (Vienna–New York, 1964).

6. Floyd Ratliff, *Mach Bands: Quantitative Studies on Neural Networks in the Retina* (San Francisco, 1965), contains in English trans. Mach's six papers on this subject (1865–1906).

7. Frank Kerkhof, ed., *Symposium zum Anlass des 50. Todestages von Ernst Mach* (Freiburg im Breisgau, 1966).

8. Erwin Hiebert, *The Conception of Thermodynamics in the Scientific Thought of Mach and Planck* (Freiburg im Breisgau, 1968).

9. J. Hintikka, ed., "A Symposium on Ernst Mach," in *Synthese*, **18** (1968), 132–301.

10. Joachim Thiele, ed., *Ernst Mach Abhandlungen: Die Geschichte und die Wurzel des Satzes von der Erhaltung der Arbeit (1872). Zur Geschichte des Arbeitbegriffes (1873). Kultur und Mechanik (1915)* (Amsterdam, 1969), a facs. ed. with foreword and bibliography of Mach's works.

11. Robert S. Cohen and R. J. Seeger, eds., *Ernst Mach: Physicist and Philosopher*, Boston Studies in the Philosophy of Science, no. 6 (Dordrecht, 1970).

12. J. Bradley, *Mach's Philosophy of Science* (London, 1971).

13. John T. Blackmore, *Ernst Mach. His Work, Life, and Influence* (Berkeley, Calif., 1972).

ERWIN N. HIEBERT

MACHEBOEUF, MICHEL (*b.* Châtel-Guyon, France, 19 October 1900; *d.* Paris, France, 20 August 1953), *biochemistry*.

Born to a sturdy Auvergnese family and son of Elie Macheboeuf, a distinguished physician, Macheboeuf studied medicine at Clermont-Ferrand and at Paris. He soon entered the Pasteur Institute, working in Gabriel Bertrand's laboratory (he succeeded Bertrand as head of the department of biochemistry in 1942). His teaching abilities were recognized by professorships at the University of Bordeaux and at the Sorbonne. His early scientific work, as Rockefeller fellow, was done under S. P. L. Sørensen in Copenhagen. They jointly investigated the structure of egg albumin and, in 1928, demonstrated that it is a mixture of phosphoproteins to which phosphorus is strongly bound. Shortly afterward Macheboeuf made his fundamental discovery of the linkage between the lipides and the proteins of blood plasma: the protidolipidic "cenapse." Blood plasma contains large amounts of lipides, which, when isolated, are insoluble in water. In the blood plasma they form soluble cenapses or lipide-protein complexes. Lipide and protein molecules are then strongly bound by their homologous carbon chains—that is, by their water-repellent groups. These groups are somewhat mutually neutralized, and thus the lipide-protein cenapse becomes water-soluble. This concept is now universally accepted. It had immediate important clinical application: the lipide-albumin index, the amount of lipides that remain in aqueous solution with 100 grams of albumin. In normal blood this index is about 12, but it reaches 60 or more in cases of lipoidic nephrosis. Macheboeuf also showed that alteration of the normal amount of cenapses modifies the exchange of water and electrolytes between blood and tissues and thus is one of the major causes of edema.

Macheboeuf made a major contribution to the immunochemistry of the tubercle bacillus. He found in this bacillus different groups of important substances: a precipitatory factor which he identified as a specific phosphatidic acid, strong antigens, and toxic substances which cancel out the effect of the strong antigens because they inhibit the activity of the antibody-producing cells. Thus the essential difficulties of antituberculosis vaccine manufacture were precisely defined.

Macheboeuf was among the first to investigate the effect of ultrahigh pressures. He found that bacteria and viruses are permanently inactivated above 6,000 atmospheres, and enzymes resist up to 12,000, while bacterial spores are killed only above 22,000 atmospheres.

Macheboeuf headed an active laboratory that produced fruitful results in many areas: plasma lipoproteins, mitochondrial enzymes, and the effect of antibiotics upon bacterial metabolic enzymes. Thus Macheboeuf was a source of inspiration to biochemists, French and foreign alike, until his untimely death (of lung ailment). He married Simone Bezou; they had three daughters.

BIBLIOGRAPHY

I. ORIGINAL WORKS. Macheboeuf's most important works include "Études sur les effets biologiques des ultrapressions. Résistance des bactéries, des diastases et des toxines aux pressions très élevées," in *Comptes rendus*

hebdomadaires des séances de l'Académie des sciences, **195** (1932), 1431, written with J. Basset; "Études chimiques sur le bacille tuberculeux. I. Essais préliminaires d'extraction et de fractionnement des substances lipoïdiques de corps bacillaires tués par la chaleur," in *Bulletin de la Société de chimie biologique*, **16** (1934), 355, and in *Annales de l'Institut Pasteur*, **52** (1934), 277, written with G. Levy, N. Fethke, J. Dieryck, and A. Bonnefoi; "Études sur les effets biologiques des ultra-pressions. Modification de la spécificité antigénique des sérums sous l'influence des pressions très élevées," in *Comptes rendus hebdomadaires des séances de l'Académie des sciences*, **200** (1935), 496, written with J. Basset and J. Perez; "Sur l'état des lipides et du cholestérol dans le sérum sanguin. Destruction de certaines cénapses lipidoprotéidiques et libération de leurs substances lipoïdiques par un savon," *ibid.*, **206** (1938), 860, written with F. Tayeau; *L'état des lipides dans la matière vivante des cénapses et leur importance biologique*, 7 vols., Hermann and co-editors (1937).

Subsequent works include "Nouvelles recherches sur la nature et la stabilité des liaisons unissant les lipides aux protéides dans le sérum sanguin," in *Bulletin de la Société de chimie biologique*, **23** (1941), 31, written with F. Tayeau; "Recherches sur les phosphoaminolipides du sérum sanguin. Nature des phospholipides liés aux albumines du sérum de Cheval à l'état de cénapses acido-précipitables," *ibid.*, **25** (1943), 358, written with J.-L. Delsal; "Action des savons à cation actif sur les protéines. I. Précipitation de la sérum-albumine par un cation gras. II. Précipitation des protéines du sérum par un cation gras," in *Annales de l'Institut Pasteur*, **74** (1948), 196, written with J. Polonovski; "Recherches biochimiques sur le mode d'action de la streptomycine dans le métabolisme d'une bactérie : *Clostridium sporogenes*," *ibid.*, **75** (1948), 242, written with F. Gros and S. Jaulen; "Action des antibiotiques sur le métabolisme protidique d'une bactérie : *Clostridium sporogenes*. I. Recherche sur le catabolisme des protéines et des peptides," *ibid.*, **75** (1948), 320, written with F. Gros and P. Lacaille; "II. Recherches sur le métabolisme des aminoacides," *ibid.*, 446, written with U. Rambech and F. Gros; "Études des cénapses lipoprotéiques par relargage et électrophorèse," in *Bulletin de la Société de chimie biologique*, **33** (1951), 998, written with P. Rebeyrotte; and "Some Aspects of the Influence of Hydrostatic Pressure on Reactions Catalysed by Enzymes," in *Journal of Colloid Science*, supp. 1 (1954), written with G.-P. Talwar and J. Basset.

II. SECONDARY LITERATURE. See the notice by J. Polonovski, in *Bulletin de la Société de chimie biologique*, **35** (1953), 1279–1286.

A. M. MONNIER

M'INTOSH, WILLIAM CARMICHAEL (*b.* St. Andrews, Scotland, 10 October 1838; *d.* St. Andrews, 1 April 1931), *marine zoology.*

William M'Intosh was the only son of Baillie John M'Intosh, a builder and magistrate in St. Andrews.

He credited his mother, Eliza Mitchell, with an early stimulus toward marine descriptive zoology. His youngest sister, Roberta, who married Albert C. L. Günther (keeper of zoology at the British Museum of Natural History), illustrated many of his works.

He was educated at St. Andrews (1853–1857) and Edinburgh, where he received his M.D. in 1860. He specialized in mental diseases and was superintendent of the Perthshire Asylum at Murthly from 1863 to 1882. During this time, the results of his marine zoological studies appeared regularly in the scientific literature.

Volume I of his *Monograph of the British Marine Annelids* (*The Nemerteans*, published in two parts [1873–1874]) brought him wide recognition; hence the Annelid collections from the *Porcupine* and *Challenger* expeditions were assigned to him for description. The *Monograph* was not continued until 1900, when volume II, *Polychaetes*, appeared; this work was concluded with volume IV in 1923.

M'Intosh assumed the chair of natural history at St. Andrews in 1882; he retired from it in his eightieth year. In 1883 he was appointed to conduct a royal commission scientific inquiry into the effects of beam-trawling on the Scottish sea fisheries. A knowledge of the early life histories of a variety of marine species was needed, and requisite facilities became available when he established the Gatty Laboratory (1884), the first marine laboratory in Great Britain, at St. Andrews. M'Intosh and his co-workers first described in detail the pelagic eggs and larvae of the major British marine food-fishes, a critical aspect of fishery biology.

M'Intosh received the Royal Medal in 1899, the Linnean Medal in 1924, and was president and active in the affairs of the Ray Society in London from 1913 through March 1931. He never married.

BIBLIOGRAPHY

Among M'Intosh's writings are: *Monograph of the British Marine Annelids*, 4 vols. (London, 1873–1923); "On the Annelida of the Porcupine Expeditions of 1869 and 1870," in *Transactions of the Zoological Society of London*, **9** (1876), 395–416; *Report on the Annelida polychaeta collected by H. M. S. Challenger during the years 1873–1876*, Challenger Expedition, Zool., XII (London, 1885); *Report on Cephalodiscus dodecalophus, M'Intosh, a New type of the Polyzoa, procured on the voyage of H. M. S. Challenger during the years 1873–1876*, Challenger Expedition, Zool., XX (London, 1887); with E. E. Prince, "On the Development and Life-Histories of the Teleostean Food- and Other Fishes," in *Transactions of the Royal Society of Edinburgh*, **35** (1890), 665–946; *The Gatty Marine Laboratory* . . . (Dundee, 1896); with A. T. Master-

man, *The Life-Histories of the British Marine Food-Fishes* (London, 1897); and *The Resources of the Sea* . . . (London, 1899).

Obituary notices appeared in the 2 Apr. 1931 issues of *The New York Times* and the *Times* (London); W. T. C., "Prof. W. C. M'Intosh, F. R. S.," in *Nature*, **127** (2 May 1931), 673–674; W. T. C., "William Carmichael M'Intosh—1838–1931," in *Proceedings of the Royal Society*, **110B** (1932), xxiv–xxviii, with portrait. Also see *List of Works, Memoirs, and Papers* (Dundee, n.d.).

DANIEL MERRIMAN

MACLAURIN, COLIN (*b*. Kilmodan, Scotland, February 1698; *d*. Edinburgh, Scotland, 14 January 1746), *mathematics*.

Maclaurin was the youngest of the three sons of John Maclaurin, minister of the parish of Kilmodan and a man of profound learning. John, the eldest son, followed in his father's footsteps and became a noted divine. The father died when Maclaurin was only six weeks old and after the death of his mother nine years later, Maclaurin was cared for by an uncle, Daniel Maclaurin, a minister of Kilfinnan.

In 1709 Maclaurin entered the University of Glasgow where he read divinity for a year. At Glasgow he became acquainted with Robert Simson, professor of mathematics. Simson, who tried to revive the geometry of the ancients, particularly the *Elements* of Euclid, stimulated Maclaurin's interest in this aspect of mathematics.

In 1715 Maclaurin defended the thesis "On the Power of Gravity," for which he was awarded a master of arts degree. It led to his appointment, in 1717, as professor of mathematics at Marischal College, Aberdeen, although he was still only in his teens. This appointment marked the beginning of a brilliant mathematical career which was to continue without interruption until the end of his life.

In 1719 Maclaurin visited London, where he was well received in the scientific circles of the capital and where he met Newton. On a second visit he met and formed a lasting friendship with Martin Folkes, who became president of the Royal Society in 1741, Maclaurin was meanwhile actively working on his *Geometrica organica*, which was published in 1720 with Newton's imprimatur.

Geometrica organica, sive descriptio linearum curvarum universalis dealt with the general properties of conics and of the higher plane curves. It contained proofs of many important theorems which were to be found, without proof, in Newton's work, as well as a considerable number of others which Maclaurin had discovered while at the university. Following traditional geometrical methods, Maclaurin showed that the higher plane curves, the cubic and the quartic, could be described by the rotation of two angles about their vertices. Newton had shown that the conic sections might all be described by the rotation of two angles of fixed size about their vertices S and C as centers of rotation. If the point of intersection of two of the arms lie on a fixed straight line, the intersection of the other two arms will describe a conic section which will pass through S and C.

In 1722 Maclaurin left Scotland to serve as companion and tutor to the son of Lord Polwarth, plenipotentiary of Great Britain at Cambrai. They visited Paris, then went on to Lorraine, where Maclaurin, during a period of intense mathematical activity, wrote *On the Percussion of Bodies*. It won him the prize offered by the French Academy of Sciences in 1724.

In the same year, the sudden death of Maclaurin's pupil caused him to return to Aberdeen. As a result of three years' absence, however, his chair had been declared vacant. Maclaurin then moved to Edinburgh, where he acted as deputy for the elderly James Gregory. There is no doubt that Maclaurin owed his appointment to a strong recommendation from Newton, who wrote to him:

> I am very glad to hear that you have a prospect of being joined to Mr. James Gregory in the Professorship of the Mathematics at Edinburgh, not only because you are my friend, but principally because of your abilities, you being acquainted as well with the new improvements of mathematics as with the former state of these sciences. I heartily wish you good success and shall be very glad of hearing of your being elected.

In a further letter to the lord provost of Edinburgh, Newton wrote:

> I am glad to understand that Mr. Maclaurin is in good repute amongst you, for I think he deserves it very well: And to satisfy you that I do not flatter him, and also to encourage him to accept the place of assisting Mr. Gregory, in order to succeed him, I am ready (if you will please give me leave) to contribute twenty pounds per annum towards a provision for him till Mr. Gregory's place becomes void, if I live so long.

Maclaurin was appointed to the Edinburgh chair when it fell vacant. He assumed its duties in 1725, lecturing on a wide range of topics that included twelve books of Euclid, spherical trigonometry, the conics, the elements of fortification, astronomy, and perspective, as well as a careful exposition of Newton's *Principia*.

Maclaurin was elected a fellow of the Royal Society in 1719. He was also influential in persuading the

members of the Edinburgh Society for Improving Medical Knowledge to widen its scope. The society's name was thus changed to the Philosophical Society and Maclaurin became one of its secretaries. (In 1783 the organization was granted incorporation by George III as the Royal Society of Edinburgh.) In 1733 Maclaurin married Anne, daughter of Walter Stewart, solicitor general for Scotland. Of their seven children, two sons and three daughters survived him.

Maclaurin's *Treatise of Fluxions* (1742) has been described as the earliest logical and systematic publication of the Newtonian methods. It stood as a model of rigor until the appearance of Cauchy's *Cours d'analyse* in 1821. Maclaurin, a zealous disciple of Newton, hoped to silence criticism of the latter's doctrine of "prime and ultimate ratios," which proved something of a stumbling block to even Newton's staunchest supporters. In the *Treatise* Maclaurin tried to provide a geometrical framework for the doctrine of fluxions; in this way he hoped to refute his critics, the most vociferous of whom was George Berkeley, Bishop of Cloyne. In 1734 Berkeley had published *The Analyst. A Letter Addressed to an Infidel Mathematician*, in which he derided Newton's conception of "prime and ultimate ratios." (The "infidel mathematician" himself was Halley, who had piloted the first edition of the *Principia* through the press.) Berkeley maintained that it was not possible to imagine a finite ratio between two evanescent quantities. "What are these fluxions?" he asked. "The velocities of evanescent increments? They are neither finite quantities, nor quantities infinitely small, nor yet nothing. May we not call them the ghosts of departed quantities?"

In the preface to the *Treatise*, Maclaurin gave his reasons for replying to Berkeley:

> A Letter published in the year 1734 under the Title of *The Analyst*, first gave occasion to the ensuing Treatise, and several Reasons concurred to induce me to write on the subject at so great length. The Author of that piece had represented the Method of Fluxions as founded on false Reasoning, and full of Mysteries. His objections seemed to have been occasioned by the concise manner in which the Elements of this method have been usually described, and their having been so much misunderstood by a Person of his abilities appeared to me to be a sufficient Proof that a fuller account of the grounds of this was required.

He took up the question of fluxions almost immediately and defended Newton's methods:

> In explaining the notion of Fluxions I have followed Sir Isaac Newton in the First Book imagining there can be no difficulty in conceiving Velocity wherever there is

motion, nor do I think I have departed from his sense in the Second Book, and in both I have endeavoured to avoid several expressions which though convenient, might be liable to exceptions and perhaps occasion disputes. . . .

There were some who disliked the making much use of infinites and infinitesimals in geometry. Of this number was Sir Isaac Newton (whose caution was almost as distinguishing a part of his character as his invention) especially after he saw that this liberty was growing to so great a height. In demonstrating the grounds of the method of fluxions he avoided them, establishing it in a way more agreeable to the strictness of geometry.

Maclaurin followed Newton in abandoning the view that variable quantities were made up of infinitesimal elements and in approaching the problem from kinematical considerations. Moreover, he consistently followed the Newtonian notation, although the Leibnizian notation was by this time well established on the Continent. Thus he wrote (in the *Treatise*, p. 738), "The fluxion of xy is $x\dot{y} + \dot{x}y$."

The *Treatise* is otherwise noteworthy for the solution of a great number of problems in geometry, statics, and the theory of attractions. It contains an elaborate discussion on infinite series, including Maclaurin's test for convergence, as well as a remarkable investigation of curves of quickest descent and various isoperimetrical problems. It describes his series for the expansion of a function of x, namely,

$$f(x) = f(0) + xf'(0) + \frac{x^2}{2!} f''(0) + \frac{x^3}{3!} f'''(0) + \cdots .$$

Maclaurin also elaborated many of the principles enunciated by Newton in the *Principia* in this work, including problems in applied geometry and physics, founded on the geometry of Euclid.

Maclaurin's discussion of the attraction of an ellipsoid on an internal point is particularly significant. His interest in this subject began in 1740 when he submitted an essay "On the Tides" (*De causa physica fluxus et refluxus maris*) for a prize offered by the Académie des Sciences. Maclaurin shared the award with Daniel Bernoulli and Euler; all three men based their work upon proposition 24 of the *Principia*, on the flux and reflux of the sea. Maclaurin's original essay was hastily assembled, but he developed his ideas much further in the *Treatise* (II, article 686). He showed that a homogeneous fluid mass revolving uniformly about an axis under the action of gravity must assume the form of an ellipsoid of revolution. Clairaut was so impressed with Maclaurin's exposition that in his *Théorie de la figure de la terre* (1743), he abandoned analytical techniques and attacked the problem of the shape of the earth by purely geometrical methods.

In the *Treatise* Maclaurin presented for the first time the correct theory for distinguishing between maximum and minimum values of a function; he further indicated the importance of this distinction in the theory of multiple points of curves. In Chapter IX of Volume I, article 238, "Of the Greatest and Least Ordinates, of the points of contrary flexion and reflexion of various kinds, and of other affections of curves that are defined by a common or by a fluxional equation," he wrote that "There are hardly any speculations in Geometry more useful or more entertaining than those which relate to the *Maximum* and *Minimum*."

Maclaurin's persistent defense of the Newtonian methods was not without harmful consequences for the progress of mathematics in Great Britain. National pride induced Englishmen to follow the geometrical methods which Newton had employed in the *Principia*, and to neglect the analytical methods which were being pursued with such conspicuous success on the Continent. As a result, English mathematicians came to think that the calculus was not really necessary. This unfortunate neglect persisted for a century or more. It was said that during the eighteenth century Maclaurin and Matthew Stewart, who succeeded him in the mathematical chair at Edinburgh, were the only prominent mathematicians in Great Britain. Writing toward the end of the century, J. Lalande, in his *Life of Condorcet*, maintained that in 1764 there was not a single first-rate analyst in the whole of England.

Maclaurin's advice was sought nevertheless on many topics, not all of them mathematical. He was a skilled experimentalist, and he devised a variety of mechanical appliances. He made valuable astronomical observations and did actuarial computations for the use of insurance societies. He also took an active part in improving maps of the Orkney and Shetland Islands, with a view to discovering a northeast polar passage from Greenland to the southern seas, and prepared an extensive memorial upon this subject for the government. (Since the government was at that time primarily interested in finding a northwest passage, the matter was dropped.)

When a Highland army marched upon Edinburgh in the uprising of 1745, Maclaurin wholeheartedly organized the defenses of the city. With tireless energy, he planned and supervised the hastily erected fortifications, and, indeed, drove himself to a state of exhaustion from which he never recovered. The city fell to the Jacobites and Maclaurin was forced to flee to England. He reached York and sought refuge with Thomas Herring, the archbishop. He returned to

Edinburgh once it became clear that the Jacobites were not going to occupy the city, but the rigors he had endured had very severely undermined his health. He died soon after, at the age of forty-eight. Only a few hours before his death he dictated the concluding passage of his work on Newton's philosophy, in which he affirmed his unwavering belief in a future life.

At the meeting of the university following Maclaurin's death, his friend, Alexander Munro, professor of anatomy at the University of Glasgow, paid tribute to him: "He was more nobly distinguished from the bulk of mankind by the qualities of the heart: his sincere love of God and men, his universal benevolence and unaffected piety together with a warmth and constancy in his friendship that was in a manner peculiar to himself."

BIBLIOGRAPHY

I. ORIGINAL WORKS. Maclaurin's works are *Geometrica organica, sive descriptio linearum curvarum universalis* (London, 1720); *The Treatise of Fluxions*, 2 vols. (Edinburgh, 1742); and *A Treatise of Algebra* (1748), a somewhat elementary posthumous work on the application of algebra to geometry, to which is joined a Latin tract, "De linearum geometricarum proprietatibus generalibus" (1756), printed from a manuscript written and corrected in Maclaurin's own hand. *An Account of Sir Isaac Newton's Philosophical Discoveries* (London, 1748) has a prefatory memoir on Maclaurin, "An Account of the Life and Writings of the Author," by Patrick Murdoch.

Maclaurin's papers published in the *Philosophical Transactions of the Royal Society* are: "Of the Construction and Measure of Curves," no. 356 (1718); "A New Universal Method of Describing All Curves of Every Order by the Assistance of Angles and Right Lines," no. 359 (1719); "A Letter . . . to Martin Folkes Esq. Concerning Equations with Impossible Roots (May 1726)," no. 394; "A Second Letter . . . to Martin Folkes Concerning the Roots of Equations, With the Demonstration of Other Rules in Algebra," no. 408 (1729); "On the Description of Curve Lines With an Account of Further Improvements, and a Paper Dated at Nancy, 27 Nov. 1722," no. 439; and "An Abstract of What Has Been Printed Since the Year 1721, as a Supplement to a Treatise Concerning a Description of Curve Lines, Published in 1719, and to Which the Author Proposes to Add to That Supplement," **39**.

Further papers published in the *Philosophical Transactions* are "An Account of the Treatise of Fluxions," no. 467 and continued in no. 469; "A Rule for Finding the Meridional Parts to a Spheroid With the Same Exactness as a Sphere," no. 461 (1711); "A Letter From Mr. Colin Maclaurin . . . to Mr. John Machin Concerning the Description of Curve Lines. Communicated to the Royal Society December 21. 1732"; "An Observation of the Eclipse of the Sun, on February 18, 1737 Made at Edinburgh, in a Letter to Martin Folkes," **40**, 177; "Of the Basis of Cells Wherein Bees Deposit Their Honey," no. 471 (1743).

Maclaurin also left a large number of manuscripts and unfinished essays on a variety of subjects, mathematical and nonmathematical.

II. SECONDARY LITERATURE. Further information on Maclaurin's life and work may be found in W. W. R. Ball, *A Short Account of the History of Mathematics* (1912), 359–363; Florian Cajori, *History of Mathematics* (1919); Moritz Cantor, *Vorlesungen über Geschichte der Mathematik* (1884–1908); J. P. Montucla, *Histoire des Mathématiques*, 4 vols. (1799–1802); H. W. Turnbull, "Colin Maclaurin," in *American Mathematical Monthly*, **54**, no. 6 (1947).

J. F. SCOTT

MACLEAN, JOHN (*b*. Glasgow, Scotland, 1 March 1771; *d*. Princeton, New Jersey, 17 February 1814), *chemistry*.

Maclean's father, John Maclean, a surgeon, and his mother, Agnes Lang Maclean, both died when he was young. He was raised by George Macintosh, the father of Charles Macintosh, the inventor of the waterproofed cloth named after him.

Maclean attended Glasgow Grammar School and entered the University of Glasgow when he was about thirteen. At the university, under the influence of Charles Macintosh, who was four years older, he joined the Chemical Society and presented several papers. In 1787 he left Glasgow to travel and study at Edinburgh, London, and Paris. At Paris he made contact with Lavoisier and Berthollet, who won him over to the antiphlogistic theory of the "new chemistry." He returned to Glasgow in 1790, and on 1 August 1791 he received his diploma authorizing him to practice surgery and pharmacy. The same day he became a member of the faculty of physicians and surgeons.

In April 1795 Maclean left Scotland for America, at least in part because of his sympathy for the United States. Benjamin Rush advised him to settle in Princeton, seat of the College of New Jersey. After delivering a course of lectures in Princeton during the summer of 1795, Maclean was chosen professor of chemistry and natural history at the college. He is recognized as the first professor of chemistry, outside of a medical school, in any American college. He was also appointed professor of mathematics and natural philosophy; such comprehensiveness was necessary since there was only one other professor, who also served as president.

Maclean's *Two Lectures on Combustion*, published at Philadelphia in 1797, was important in the overthrow of the phlogiston theory. Publication of the work led to a discussion by Maclean, Priestley, James Woodhouse, and Samuel Mitchill in the New York *Medical Repository.*

In his teaching at Princeton, Maclean divided chemistry into "dead" and "living" matter, foreshadowing the later division into organic and inorganic. His dead matter was further divided into "simple" and "compound" substances. Of the thirty-seven simple substances he discussed, some twenty are now recognized as elements, including oxygen, hydrogen, aluminum, tungsten, platinum. The rest would now be classified as compounds—lime, soda, potash, and a number of acids.

In 1802 Maclean met with Benjamin Silliman, who, although he was not yet qualified for that role, had been appointed professor of chemistry at Yale. Maclean prepared a reading list for him.

Maclean resigned from the College of New Jersey in 1812 and shortly after joined the faculty of the College of William and Mary in Williamsburg, Virginia. Because of ill health he stayed there only a little over a year. He returned to Princeton, where he died soon after.

Maclean married Phoebe Bainbridge, the sister of Commodore William Bainbridge, on 7 November 1798. They had two daughters and four sons. The eldest son, John, became the tenth president of Princeton.

BIBLIOGRAPHY

Maclean's published work was *Two Lectures on Combustion* (Philadelphia, 1797). The chief source of biographical information is a memoir by his son, John Maclean, *A Memoir of John Maclean, M.D., the First Professor of Chemistry,* printed privately (Princeton, 1876). See also William Foster, "John Maclean—Chemist," in *Science,* **60** (3 Oct. 1924), 306–308; John F. Fulton and Elizabeth H. Thomson, *Benjamin Silliman* (New York, 1947), and Theodore Hornberg, *Scientific Thought in the American Colleges 1638–1800* (Austin, 1945). Princeton University Library has several of Maclean's letters.

VERN L. BULLOUGH

MACLEAR, THOMAS (*b.* Newtown Stewart, Tyrone, Ireland, 17 March 1794; *d.* Mowbray, near Cape Town, South Africa, 14 July 1879), *astronomy.*

Defying his father's wish that he become a clergyman, Maclear studied medicine at Guy's and St. Thomas's hospitals in London. In 1815 he joined the staff of Bedford Infirmary, where his interest in astronomy was aroused by his friendship with Admiral William Henry Smyth. From 1823 he practiced medicine in Biggleswade, Bedfordshire, where he set up a small observatory in his garden; he was lent the Wollaston telescope by the Royal Astronomical Society to observe occultations of Aldebaran which he had himself calculated. In 1833 he was appointed Her Majesty's astronomer at the Cape of Good Hope, where he arrived on 5 January 1834, shortly before John Herschel.

Until his retirement, Maclear devoted himself to the work of the observatory and to matters of public welfare in the colony. From 1837 to 1847 he carried out the remeasurement and extension of Lacaille's arc as a basis for the survey of the colony, and this earned him the Lalande Prize in 1867 and a Royal Medal in 1869. In 1839–1840 and 1842–1848 he observed α Centauri to confirm the parallax derived by Thomas Henderson. He made numerous observations of comets and double stars, and furnished materials for successive Cape Catalogues. His observations of Mars during the opposition of 1862 were used by others in determinations of the sun's distance.

Maclear also promoted a wide range of applied sciences in the colony. He assembled meteorological, magnetic, and tidal data, and in 1860 he established time signals for Port Elizabeth and Simonstown. He sponsored the construction of lighthouses, promoted sanitary improvements, and took part in a commission on weights and measures. He was keenly interested in African exploration and was a friend of Livingstone and Stanley.

Maclear was knighted in 1860. He retired in 1870 and went blind in 1876, but he continued to interest himself in public affairs at the Cape until his death.

BIBLIOGRAPHY

I. ORIGINAL WORKS. Maclear's writings include *The Verification and Extension of Lacaille's Arc of the Meridian at the Cape of Good Hope,* 2 vols. (London, 1866), and numerous papers, mostly in the *Memoirs* and *Monthly Notices* of the Royal Astronomical Society. Lists of these papers are given in the Royal Society *Catalogue of Scientific Papers,* IV (1870), 166–168, and VIII (1879), 299–300; and in Poggendorff, III, 852–853.

II. SECONDARY LITERATURE. The most important memoir on Maclear's astronomical work at the Cape is ch. 7, "Les travaux de Maclear au cap de Bonne-Espérance," of "Tableau de l'astronomie dans l'hémisphère austral et dans l'Inde," by É. Mailly, in *Mémoires couronnés et mémoires publiés par l'Académie royale des sciences, des lettres et des beaux-arts de Belgique,* **23** (1873), 77–109. Extensive biographical sketches are by David Gill in

Monthly Notices of the Royal Astronomical Society, **40** (1880), 200–204, and by Agnes M. Clerke in *Dictionary of National Biography*, XII, 648–649.

MICHAEL A. HOSKIN

MACLEOD, JOHN JAMES RICKARD (*b*. Cluny, near Dunkeld, Perthshire, Scotland, 6 September 1876; *d*. Aberdeen, Scotland, 16 March 1935), *physiology*.

Macleod was a distinguished teacher, author, investigator, and administrator. He was the son of Rev. Robert Macleod, who shortly after the boy's birth was called to Aberdeen; Macleod received his education at the Aberdeen Grammar School and Aberdeen University. He studied medicine at Marischal College, and graduated with distinction as M.B., Ch.B in 1898, winning the Matthews Duncan and Fife Jamieson medals; he was also awarded the Anderson traveling scholarship and spent a year in the Physiology Institute at Leipzig, where he studied biochemistry under Siegfried and Burian. In 1900 Macleod joined the London Hospital Medical College as demonstrator in physiology under Sir Leonard Hill. He became lecturer in biochemistry at the school in 1902 and was also selected as Mackinnon research scholar of the Royal Society. He married Mary Watson McWalter in 1903; there were no children.

During his short stay in London Macleod published an account of experiments on intracranial circulation and on caisson disease, carried out in conjunction with Hill; he retained his interest in the problems of respiration throughout his life, publishing many papers on the control of respiration between 1902 and 1922. In the early years of the twentieth century Macleod continued his postgraduate studies at Cambridge, where he took his diploma in public health. In 1903 he published a text entitled *Practical Physiology*, and in the same year he was appointed professor of physiology at Western Reserve University, Cleveland (now Case Western Reserve University). Here he remained as a teacher and researcher for fifteen years. In 1918 he became professor of physiology at the University of Toronto and not long afterward published, with collaborators, a textbook of nearly 1,000 pages, *Physiology and Biochemistry in Modern Medicine*. This text, which reached its seventh edition the year before Macleod's death, was widely read and consulted. Its title reveals it as one of the last of such broad scope and, at the same time, as the precursor of other, more recent wide-ranging treatises appealing both to the special student and to the clinician.

In his first years at Western Reserve Macleod published a series of papers on the carbamates and one on purine metabolism. In 1907 there appeared the first of a long series of "Studies in Experimental Glycosuria" in the *American Journal of Physiology*, studies on the breakdown of liver glycogen, whether produced by piqûre, stimulation of the splanchnics, reflexly by asphyxia, or by injection of adrenaline. He conceived of the problem as one fundamentally involving the access of the diastatic enzyme to the stored glycogen. In 1913, nearly ten years before the discovery of insulin, Macleod wrote a book on diabetes and its pathological physiology, an expansion of lectures which he had delivered during the summer of 1912 at the University of London. Although he published on surgical shock (1918–1920) and other subjects, his first years in Toronto were devoted chiefly to studying the peculiarities of respiration in decerebrate animals and of the effects of anoxemia and of excess oxygen. Later, in 1921, he made a thorough examination of the control of the blood-sugar level in the normal and in the depancreatized animal and of the roles played by the liver, the muscles, and the pancreas in the metabolism of sugar.

His return to work on carbohydrate metabolism had been stimulated by the initial successes of Banting and Best. As J. B. Collip subsequently observed, Macleod had already attained, by the time of his arrival in Toronto (1918), "an outstanding position in the field of carbohydrate metabolism, and it was both appropriate and fortunate that the discovery of insulin should have been made in his laboratory." It was early in 1921 that Macleod agreed to receive Frederick G. Banting, a young surgeon, into his department to carry out investigations aimed at determining the true function of the pancreatic islets; C. H. Best, a member of the professor's senior class in physiology, was assigned to be Banting's assistant. Banting and Best began their research on 16 May. The general pattern of their work, following Banting's conception of how the islets might be freed from the acinar tissue of the gland and then extracted, was worked out with Macleod; but its first results were obtained in midsummer, when Macleod had gone to Scotland. On his return, he discontinued his work on anoxemia and turned all the resources of his laboratory to the new work. J. B. Collip joined the team; and usable preparations of insulin were ready, and were used with success, early in 1922.

Macleod was president of the American Physiological Society at the time of the discovery of insulin and had received many honors; now they multiplied. In 1923 Banting and Macleod shared the Nobel Prize; Banting divided his share with Best, and

Macleod divided with Collip. Macleod became fellow of the Royal Society in 1923 and was awarded honorary degrees by Toronto, Western Reserve, Aberdeen, and other universities. In 1928 he returned to Scotland as regius professor of physiology at Aberdeen. Productive work there, and at the Rowett Institute, continued to add to knowledge of carbohydrate metabolism. The metabolism of the decerebrate eviscerated animal, with special reference to the respiratory quotient, occupied much of his time until crippling arthritis put an end to his laboratory work; even then he continued to direct the activities of his department. Macleod's last important publication marked his return to an earlier problem, the nervous control of the glycogenic function of the liver.

BIBLIOGRAPHY

I. ORIGINAL WORKS. Macleod's writings include *Practical Physiology* (1903); "Studies in Experimental Glycosuria," in *American Journal of Physiology* (1907); "Teaching and Research Positions in Medical Science," in *Western Reserve University Bulletin*, **11**, no. 6 (1908), 129–150; and *Physiology and Biochemistry in Modern Medicine* (St. Louis, 1918), written with Roy G. Pearce and others.

II. SECONDARY LITERATURE. See C. H. Best, "The Late John James Rickard Macleod, M.B., Ch.B., LL.D., F.R.C.P.," in *Canadian Medical Association Journal*, n.s. **32** (1935), 556; J. B. C[ollip], "John James Rickard Macleod (1876–1935)," in *Biochemical Journal*, **29**, no. 1 (1935), 1253–1256; "John J. R. Macleod, F.R.S., D.Sc., M.D. Aberd., F.R.C.P. Lond.," in *Lancet*, no 228 (1935), 716–717; and L. G. Stevenson, *Sir Frederick Banting*, rev. ed. (Toronto, 1947).

LLOYD G. STEVENSON

MACLURE, WILLIAM (*b.* Ayr, Scotland, 27 October 1763; *d.* St. Angelo, Mexico, 23 March 1840), *geology*.

Maclure, the son of David and Ann Maclure, was educated by private tutors. He came to the United States in 1782 to establish "mercantile arrangements" and returned to London as a partner in the house of Miller, Hart and Company, where he soon amassed a fortune. He traveled back and forth between Europe and America, and spent several years traveling through Europe, including Scandinavia and Russia, observing geological features and seeking instruction from geologists in several countries. In Paris he met Count Volney, who discussed American geology with him.

Returning to the United States in 1796, Maclure examined the geology of the country as he traversed it from New England to the far southeast, "crossing

the dividing lines of the principle formations in 15 or 20 different places." He published his report and colored map, "Observations on the Geology of the United States, Explanatory of a Geological Map" (in *Transactions of the American Philosophical Society*, **6** [1809], 411–428).

In 1815 Maclure visited France and met Lesueur the painter-naturalist, whom he persuaded to return to America with him as his personal cartographer-naturalist. They spent the winter of 1815–1816 examining the geology and natural history of the West Indies, then made repeated traverses of the Allegheny Mountains, collecting specimens and revising the geological map. From December 1817 to April 1818, Maclure organized an expedition to Georgia and Spanish Florida with Lesueur, Thomas Say, Titian Peale, and George Ord.

Maclure developed an estate in Spain and lived there from 1820 to 1824. In 1824, following a revolution and the confiscation of his property, he returned to America. Here he joined Robert Owen in his New Harmony venture, in which he invested $82,000. He visited Mexico in 1827 and later moved there.

Maclure's best known work is the *Observations on the Geology of the United States*. Although preceded by Johann D. Schöpf's work in German (1787) and Volney's in French (1803), Maclure's articles and book are the first connected account originally written in English on the geology of the United States. The expanded and revised work and map were published as a separate volume in 1817 and in the *Transactions of the American Philosophical Society* in 1818. In the text and map, Maclure divided the country into areas of "primitive rocks," "transition rocks," "floetz and secondary rocks," and "alluvial rocks." The primitive rocks are crystalline rocks in the area that extends from New England southwest to Alabama. The transition rocks occur in the folds of the Appalachians; the secondary rocks are the flat-lying strata west of the Appalachians. The alluvial rocks are found in the valley of the Mississippi and in the coastal plain from Cape Cod southeast to the mouth of the Mississippi River.

In 1817 Maclure published a report on his detailed examination of the West Indies (*Journal of the Academy of Natural Sciences of Philadelphia*, **1**, 134–149). In this report he discussed the uplifted coral limestone in some of the islands and the various kinds of volcanic materials, including volcanic breccia, which he interpreted as volcanic mud flows. His "Essay on the Formation of Rocks . . ." (1818) is important for his explanation of his terminology and for his theories of the origin of rocks. In a series of eleven papers (1819–1831) published in the *American*

Journal of Science, Maclure recorded observations on the geology of the United States and other parts of the world and expanded upon his ideas of rock origin and geological processes.

The short paper "Genealogy of the Earth–Geological Observations" (1838) is the most philosophical of his geological writings. In it he espoused Lamarckian evolution and clarified his belief in organic and inorganic development through a gradual series of minute changes, rather than by large jumps or catastrophes.

Maclure is usually regarded as a follower of Werner because he used that terminology, but he specifically disclaimed his belief in that school's theory of crystalline rock origin. He was convinced of the igneous origin of basalt and stated that sedimentary rocks were deposited in separate basins and were therefore not continuous in an "onionskin" fashion around the world. He was uncertain about the origin of primitive rocks, and thought that they might be diverse in origin. From his studies of various areas of the world, he had concluded that sedimentary rocks and lava flows alternated with each other. Thus he speculated that the primitive rocks may have originated as sediments and lava, later becoming "smelted, roasted and liquified," almost the concept of granitization in present-day terminology.

Maclure was convinced that basalt and related rocks developed from lava flows, but he did not discuss granites as intrusive rocks, nor did he mention the explanations of Hutton and Playfair. He urged more attention to the "primitive formations" because of their great age and the changes that they had undergone. He disclaimed support, however, of the aqueous theory of the origin of primitive rocks. "The geology of the United States . . . is a strong argument against the Wernerian system—all these theories have had their day, and are fast going out of fashion" (1822).

Maclure recognized the role of streams in the formation of valleys. Following S. L. Mitchill and many others, he thought that the region west of the Appalachian Mountains had once been the site of a great lake, which had drained out through the Hudson and broken out across the mountains in several other valleys. Maclure was one of the first men in America to notice and speculate on the origin of the granite erratics in the northern part of the country. He stated that the granite erratics between Lake Erie and the Ohio River had been transported southward by "large pieces of floating ice" in the lake that he believed had occupied the trans-Appalachian area (1823).

Maclure's work on metallic deposits and the connection between metals and volcanic regions are of interest. In writing about Mexico (1831), he proposed that "precious metals have been converted into vapor, that would penetrate through chinks that would not permit lava to pass." Thus he realized that lava was intrusive until it reached the surface. This explanation for veins is directly contrary to that of Werner, who supposed that veins had been formed by infilling of cracks from the surface.

Maclure's influence was not only great as an observer and writer on geology and as a maker of important maps, but also through his support of scientists and scientific organizations. One of the founders of the Academy of Natural Sciences of Philadelphia, he was president from 1817 to his death.

BIBLIOGRAPHY

I. ORIGINAL WORKS. Maclure's map and *Observations* of 1817 have been produced in facsimile (New York, 1962). The 1809 map has been reproduced by Merrill (New Haven, 1924). His papers on his travels are in the early volumes of the *American Journal of Science* and the *Journal of the Academy of Natural Sciences of Philadelphia.* Among them are "Essay on the Formation of Rocks . . .," in *Journal of the Academy of Natural Sciences of Philadelphia,* **1** (1818), and published separately (Philadelphia, 1818; New Harmony, 1832).

The three-volume work *Opinions on Various Subjects Dedicated to the Industrious Producers* (New Harmony, 1831–1838) sets forth in detail his ideas on economic, political, and related areas; it contains little science except for one important paper, "Genealogy of the Earth— Geological Observations," *ibid.,* III, 175–178.

II. SECONDARY LITERATURE. There is as yet no full biography of Maclure. S. G. Morton, *A Memoir of William Maclure, Esq.* (Philadelphia, 1841), with a portrait, reprinted in *American Journal of Science,* **47** (1844), 1–17, is the source of the most immediate information. A. E. Bestor, "Education and Reform at New Harmony: Correspondence of William Maclure and Marie Duclos Fretageot, 1820–1833," in *Indiana Historical Society,* **15,** no. 3 (1948), discusses Maclure's association with New Harmony and contains some of the letters from Europe and Mexico preserved at the Working Men's Institute at New Harmony; Charles Keyes, "William Maclure: Father of American Geology," in *Pan-American Geologist,* **44** (1925), 81–94, is a fulsome account with some information; G. P. Merrill, *First One Hundred Years of American Geology* (New Haven, 1924; New York, 1962), 31–37, 46–47, has summarized Maclure's geological contributions; and Jessie Poesch, *Titian Ramsey Peale, 1799–1885 . . .* (Philadelphia, 1961), gives information on Maclure's expedition to Georgia and Florida based on original correspondence.

Lesueur's connection with Maclure is given in some detail by R. W. G. Vail, *The American Sketchbooks of Charles Alexander Lesueur 1816–1837* (Worcester, 1938). A portrait of Maclure and many references to his association with Thomas Say are in H. B. Weiss and G. M. Zeigler, *Thomas Say, Early American Naturalist* (Springfield–Baltimore, 1931). William E. Wilson, *The Angel and the Serpent, the Story of New Harmony* (Bloomington, Indiana, 1964), gives extensive consideration to Maclure at New Harmony.

All of Maclure's geological papers are being prepared for publication in facsimile, edited and annotated by George W. White.

GEORGE W. WHITE

MacMAHON, PERCY ALEXANDER (*b.* Malta, 26 September 1854; *d.* Bognor Regis, England, 25 December 1929), *mathematics.*

MacMahon was the son of Brigadier General P. W. MacMahon. He entered the army in 1871, rising to the rank of major in 1889. He served as instructor in mathematics at the Royal Military Academy from 1882 to 1888, as assistant inspector at Woolwich arsenal to 1891, and as professor of physics at the Artillery college until his retirement in 1898. Afterward, he was deputy warden of standards at the Board of Trade from 1906 to 1920. A fellow of the Royal Society in 1890, he was president of the London Mathematical Society in 1894–1896, and president of the Royal Astronomical Society in 1917.

MacMahon was a master of classical algebra, who had remarkable insight into algebraic form and structure, together with a power of rapid and precise calculation. His early work dealt with invariants, following the studies of Cayley and Sylvester. He noticed that the partial differential equation for semi-invariants is fundamentally the same as that for general symmetric functions. MacMahon made use of the concept of generating functions, and of U. Hammond's symbolic calculus of differential operators in connection with symmetric functions. His power of calculation helped him in the work of tabulation and enumeration.

The study of symmetric functions led to MacMahon's interest in partitions and to the enumeration of Euler's Latin squares. His presidential address to the London Mathematical Society gave a survey of combinatorial analysis, and his two-volume treatise of 1915–1916 is a classic in this field. It identified and clarified the master theorems, and indicated a wealth of applications. An introductory version was published in 1920.

MacMahon's interest in repeating patterns and space-filling solids began in his childhood with observations of piles of shot found in his military environment. He revived this interest in latter years, writing a book on mathematical pastimes.

BIBLIOGRAPHY

I. ORIGINAL WORKS. The presidential address on combinatorial analysis is printed in the *Proceedings of the London Mathematical Society*, 1st ser., **28** (1897). Some ninety research papers are listed in the obituary notice by H. F. Baker, cited below. Works by MacMahon were *Combinatorial Analysis*, I–II (Cambridge, 1915–1916); *An Introduction to Combinatorial Analysis* (Cambridge, 1920); and *New Mathematical Pastimes* (Cambridge, 1921).

II. SECONDARY LITERATURE. The obituary notice by H. F. Baker in the *Journal of the London Mathematical Society*, **5** (1930), 305–318, gives a brief sketch of MacMahon's life and a substantial account and analysis of his mathematical work.

T. A. A. BROADBENT

MACMILLAN, WILLIAM DUNCAN (*b.* La Crosse, Wisconsin, 24 July 1871; *d.* St. Paul, Minnesota, 14 November 1948), *astronomy, mathematics.*

William Macmillan was the son of Duncan D. Macmillan and Mary Jean MacCrea. He attended Lake Forest College, the University of Virginia, and Fort Worth University, from which he received the B.A. in 1898. He then went to the University of Chicago, where he spent most of his working life. He took the M.A. there in 1906 and the Ph.D. in 1908. A pupil of F. R. Moulton, he became a research assistant, first in geology (1907–1908) and then in mathematics and astronomy (1908–1909). He held a succession of posts in astronomy at the university, becoming professor emeritus in 1936.

Macmillan's interests centered around cosmogony and related topics in applied mathematics. Probably his most widely known works were his textbooks of theoretical mechanics. He made a number of original contributions to potential theory, the theory of differential equations with periodic coefficients, and the theory of automorphic functions. He took an active part in the then-controversial discussions of the theory of relativity, contributing to *A Debate on the Theory of Relativity* (New York, 1927) with R. D. Carmichael, H. T. Davis, and others.

One of Macmillan's most influential pieces of work was an attempt to remove the supposed paradox of P. L. de Cheseaux (1744) and H. W. M. Olbers (1823), whereby, with the hypothesis of an infinite and uniform distribution of stars throughout space, the night sky would shine with a brightness corresponding to their average surface brightness. In 1918 and 1925 Macmillan proposed a form of continual material creation (*Astrophysical Journal*, **48** (1918), 35, and *Science*, **62** (1925), 63–72, 96–99, 121–127). His main concern was with the formation of the planets and stars. Among his so-called postulates he included two according to which the universe maintains a steady state, and another according to which the energy of a large region of the universe, supposedly unbounded, is conserved. He acknowledged that matter is converted to energy in stellar interiors, and explained away the De Cheseaux-Olbers paradox as a disappearance or dissipation of the radiation traversing empty space. (This radiation was to reappear in the form of hydrogen atoms.) Subsequently, R. A. Millikan, one of Macmillan's colleagues at Chicago, used his theory to account for the origin of cosmic rays, but by 1935 A. H. Compton proved that it could not account for the high energies of much cosmic radiation. The theory was then abandoned. It should be noted that, unlike more recent steady-state theories, Macmillan's identified a source from which the mass or energy of the created particle was drawn. He did not suggest creation *ex nihilo*.

BIBLIOGRAPHY

Macmillan collaborated with F. R. Moulton, C. S. Slichter, *et al.*, in *Contributions to Cosmogony and the Fundamental Problems of Geology. The Tidal and Other Problems* (Washington, D.C., 1909), and with Moulton, F. R. Longley, *et al.*, in *Periodic Orbits*, Carnegie Institution of Washington publ. no. 161 (Washington, D.C., 1920). His best-known work was *Theoretical Mechanics*, 3 vols. (New York, 1927–1936). On the background to Macmillan's writings on cosmogony, see J. D. North, *The Measure of the Universe* (Oxford, 1965), esp. 18, 198–199, and 260–261.

J. D. NORTH

MACQUER, PIERRE JOSEPH (*b*. Paris, France, 9 October 1718; *d*. Paris, 15 February 1784), *chemistry*.

Best known as the author of a widely read textbook and of the first chemical dictionary, Macquer made no lasting contributions to chemical theory and discovered few new substances. Nevertheless he was an influential member of the Paris scientific community and did much important but unpublished research behind the scenes as a government scientific adviser. The descendant of a Stuart supporter[1] who in 1688 had accompanied James II into exile, he was the elder son of Joseph Macquer and Marie-Anne Caillet. An early interest in science was encouraged by one of his teachers, Charles Le Beau, a well-known historian; and he decided to devote himself to research. However, his parents insisted on his first qualifying in a profes-

sion, and he chose medicine. After graduating from the Paris Faculty of Medicine in 1742 he practiced for only a few years, being at one time doctor for the poor of the parishes of St.-Nicolas and St.-Sauveur,[2] near his home in the rue St.-Sauveur. He studied chemistry under G. F. Rouelle and soon began to do research.

Rouelle had started lecturing at the Jardin du Roi in 1742, and his influence on French chemistry was yet to be felt. Since there were few experienced and able chemists competing for places in the Academy of Sciences, Macquer was elected in 1745, before reading his first published paper, on the solubility in alcohol of different oils. He was hoping to relate the changes that occurred in oils on rectification to the solubilities of various products, but his experiments and theoretical discussion contributed little to this difficult subject. He was on firmer ground in a later investigation of the solubilities of carefully dehydrated inorganic salts in alcohol (1766, 1773); his quantitative results were of value to chemists who used alcohol extraction in the analysis of residues from evaporated mineral waters.

The most important of Macquer's early researches was his study in 1746 and 1748 of white arsenic (arsenious oxide), which he found to react with niter (potassium nitrate) to form a previously unknown crystalline salt (potassium arsenate) that was quite different from the compound (potassium arsenite) obtained by dissolving white arsenic in potash. The new salt formed precipitates with metallic salts, and Macquer recognized that in them the metal was combined with the "arsenical part" of his compound. He did not, however, go so far as to assert that arsenic formed an acid although, by heating white arsenic with oil of vitriol (sulfuric acid), he had, in fact, prepared its anhydride as an "arsenical glass" that gave an acid solution in water. The true nature of arsenic acid and its salts was recognized in 1775 by C. W. Scheele.

Pastel and indigo were the only fast blue dyes used before 1749, when Macquer discovered a method of dyeing with Prussian blue, an insoluble substance used as an artists' pigment. It was prepared by adding potash that had been calcined with animal matter to a solution of alum and green vitriol (ferrous sulfate), and Macquer therefore boiled skeins of flax, cotton, silk, and wool with alum and green vitriol, and dipped them into a solution of the specially treated potash. The specimens were dyed a dull blue, which brightened on rinsing in dilute sulfuric acid and proved to be fast for wool and silk. Macquer then attempted to analyze Prussian blue (1752). Although he did not solve the problem of its constitution, he found that alum was

618

not an essential constituent. Again, his research was later extended by Scheele. These researches on arsenic and Prussian blue were praised by Macquer's contemporaries, but it was through his books that he became widely known and influenced the development of chemistry.

The first textbook, *Élémens de chymie théorique*, appeared in 1749, when there was a real need for an up-to-date book by a French author; Nicolas Lemery's *Cours de chymie* had not been printed in Paris since 1730 (an edition revised by Baron was not published until 1756), and the anonymous *Nouveau cours de chymie* (generally attributed to J. B. Senac) had not been printed since 1737. The *Nouveau cours* included an account of the phlogiston theory, which was being taught by Rouelle in the 1740's, but it is unlikely to have been available to the many people whose interest in chemistry he was stimulating. Macquer wrote his *Élémens* for people with no previous chemical knowledge. He started with an account of the four elements, air, water, earth, and fire (of which phlogiston was a modification), briefly discussed affinity, and then considered compound substances in order of their increasing complexity, mineral, vegetable, and animal. He was careful not to mention any substance before acquainting the reader with it: for example, acids, alkalis, and salts were described before metals, so in the account of acids their power of dissolving metals was not mentioned. This "synthetic" treatment, as Macquer called it, seems to have been popular with beginners but was of little value in laboratory work, where an experimenter would normally be concerned with the analysis of naturally occurring substances that were compounds or mixtures. Macquer gave a thorough account of compound substances in *Élémens de chymie pratique* (1751), which was no mere laboratory manual. The two books were complementary and were reprinted together in 1756, with slight modifications. There were no further editions in France,[3] but the combined work enjoyed a great vogue in Britain, where Andrew Reid's 1758 translation was reprinted as late as 1777—by which time it was badly out of date.

Textbooks are generally written by teachers, but Macquer's teaching experience began only in 1752, when he was elected professor of pharmacy in the Paris Faculty of Medicine for a year.[4] His partnership with Antoine Baumé was more lasting. In 1757 they gave a joint course in chemistry that was attended by fifty or sixty people[5] and proved to be the first of sixteen annual winter courses. The outline in their *Plan d'un cours de chymie . . .* (1757) shows that they followed roughly the same order as in Macquer's *Élémens*, and they demonstrated 2,000 experiments.

Their joint research included a study of one of the first specimens of platinum to reach France (1758); they discovered no new chemical properties but showed that small portions could be melted with the aid of a powerful burning lens.

By 1773, when the joint courses ceased, Macquer had started lecturing at the Jardin du Roi. L. C. Bourdelin had been professor of chemistry since 1743, but his health was poor and up to 1769 the lectures were often given by P. J. Malouin. Buffon, the intendant, then granted Macquer the reversion of the chair. He gave his first course in 1770 and, after Bourdelin's death in 1777, became the titular professor and continued to lecture every summer until 1783. The professor's lectures were always followed by experiments, performed and explained by the demonstrator. H. M. Rouelle (brother of Macquer's chemistry teacher) had been demonstrator since 1768, and Macquer seems to have left him to plan the course, for the vegetable and animal kingdoms were treated before the mineral kingdom, as in Rouelle's own private course. When A. L. Brongniart (1742–1804) succeeded Rouelle, Macquer revised his course and from 1779 taught the mineral kingdom first, as in his *Élémens* and in a private course given by Brongniart. Macquer occasionally introduced new material into his lectures but, surprisingly, said little about the chemistry of gases, explaining in an introductory lecture that he preferred not to deal with modern and controversial topics in a short course intended for beginners. His lectures were praised by Condorcet, who attended them, but his audiences were deprived of an up-to-date account of important new developments.

Macquer's principal book, the *Dictionnaire de chymie* (1766), was one of a series that included J. C. Valmont de Bomare's *Dictionnaire raisonné universel d'histoire naturelle* (1764) and an anonymous *Dictionnaire portatif des arts et métiers* (1766) compiled by Macquer's brother Philippe.[6] Like the latter, Macquer's work also appeared anonymously, because Macquer had been commissioned to write it hastily and was worried about his reputation.[7] Some articles to which he gave cross-references do not, in fact, appear, but he need not have worried, for the *Dictionnaire* was an immediate success. It was reprinted in 1766 and again in 1769, and Macquer soon started work on an enlarged and revised edition which was published—no longer anonymously—in 1778. There were several Swiss editions, and German, English, Danish, and Italian translations.

The *Dictionnaire* contained about 500 articles in alphabetical order, ranging in length from two-line definitions to long essays like that on "salt," which filled more than seventy pages. Most articles were revised in the second edition, and Macquer added some new ones, notably "Gas," a 168-page account of a topic that hardly existed when he was writing the first edition.

In the preface of 1766 Macquer confessed that when asked to write a chemical dictionary—for which there was no precedent—he had misgivings because he thought that all parts of chemistry were interdependent and also that the subject did not seem suited to alphabetical treatment. However, he had come to see certain advantages—the dictionary had taken the form of a collection of essays and therefore could be studied by each reader in the order he preferred; and, while listing topics in alphabetical order, Macquer had thought of some that might not otherwise have occurred to him. Cross-references were freely given in both editions, and the utility of the second was greatly increased by the inclusion of a subject index of more than 600 pages. In his 1778 preface Macquer stated clearly that the book was intended not for beginners but for those who had attended a course of lectures and had read a textbook, and he suggested the order in which such a student should read about 280 of the main articles. Essays on general theoretical topics were to be followed by those on the mineral kingdom, and then by articles on the vegetable and animal kingdoms—the ordering of the *Élémens* and of his later courses.

Like most of his contemporaries, Macquer accepted the four-element theory of matter and expounded on it in his books and lectures, but he constantly tried to reconcile it with new discoveries. He followed Boerhaave in believing that earths such as lime and silica were modifications of the pure elementary earth which, he thought, must be a hard, transparent, crystalline substance. In 1766 he identified it with diamond; but in 1772, in collaboration with Lavoisier and others, he showed that diamond was combustible, and so by 1778 he had concluded that pure rock crystal was the element. A metal was composed of a kind of earth (the calx) combined with phlogiston (which in 1749 he regarded as elementary fire in combination with some other principle) and possibly also with the mercurial earth of Becher and Stahl. But by 1766 he had serious doubts about the mercurial earth, for most calxes could be converted to metal by the addition of phlogiston alone, in the form of charcoal. He therefore concluded that a metal was composed only of calx and phlogiston. It was difficult to expel the last traces of phlogiston by heating, and Macquer thought that if this could be achieved all metals might be found to contain the same earth, which would open up the possibility of transmutation of metals. Macquer also

made the perceptive suggestion that mineral earths like lime and magnesia were of essentially the same nature as metallic calxes[8] and might one day be combined with phlogiston to form new metals. In 1773, with other chemists of the Academy, he used a large burning glass to heat magnesia and alumina with ivory black, a form of charcoal; this experiment may have been an attempt to combine them with phlogiston.

When the second edition of the *Dictionnaire* was written, Lavoisier was challenging the phlogiston theory, but in 1778 the antiphlogistic theory was still far from complete, and Macquer was able to suggest a compromise. In 1773 he had praised Lavoisier's early experiments on gases,[9] and he now agreed that vital air (oxygen) was absorbed during combustion and calcination. He believed this effect to be accompanied by the emission of phlogiston from the combustible or metal. He now identified phlogiston with light and still regarded it as a modification of elementary fire; he did not think of heat as a material substance but preferred the Baconian theory that it was a phenomenon caused by the motion of particles of matter. Lavoisier's discovery of the composition of water in 1783 greatly strengthened the antiphlogistic theory, and his calorimetric researches with Laplace tended to support the material theory of heat. In December 1783, when discussing C. L. Morozzo's experiments on calcination, Macquer said that on this subject Lavoisier had "an absolutely new idea, to which he has already given much probability by many fine experiments."[10] Soon afterward Macquer was reported to be preparing a new edition of the *Dictionnaire*, with some revised articles,[11] and it seems likely that he was very near to accepting the antiphlogistic theory just before his death.

The compromise theory proposed by Macquer in 1778 resembled one advocated by L. B. Guyton de Morveau, with whom he corresponded regularly. He welcomed Guyton's reform of chemical nomenclature in 1782 for he had himself criticized the old unsystematic nomenclature as early as 1749, although he offered only tentative proposals for reform and generally retained the old names in his books. He was, however, responsible for reintroducing Van Helmont's word "gas," for he was reluctant to describe as an "air" any substance that differed from the air of the atmosphere.

Macquer's books helped to spread knowledge of chemical affinity. While admitting that progress in chemistry could have led to its extension, he reprinted E. F. Geoffroy's affinity table of 1718 unaltered in the *Élémens*, arguing that it included all the principal affinities;[12] he did, however, discuss criticisms to which it had been subjected and added some new ones.

In 1749 he believed that there was an affinity between two substances when they resembled each other, but in 1766 he defined affinity simply as the tendency of constituent or integrant parts of substances to combine and as the force that makes them adhere when united. He did not speculate about the causes of affinity but referred his readers to the works of Newton, Keill, and others who had attempted to illuminate this obscure subject. Both the *Élémens* and the *Dictionnaire* contained sets of propositions showing the ways in which affinity could manifest itself: simple affinity, when two parts of the same substance adhered or two substances combined to form a new one; and various kinds of complex affinity, when, for example, a compound of two components was decomposed by a third substance that had a greater affinity for one of them, or when double decomposition took place between two compounds, each of two components. These distinctions had been recognized by Geoffroy and others, but Macquer expressed them systematically for the first time.

A conscientious and respected member of the Academy of Sciences, Macquer served as its director in 1774. Although only briefly a practicing physician, he had become interested in the applications of chemistry to medicine, and in 1776 was a founding member of the Société Royale de Médecine. He prepared many reports on memoirs and books submitted to these learned societies, and from 1750 examined books on chemistry, medicine, and natural history in his capacity as a royal censor. He became even more deeply involved in literary work in 1768, when he succeeded J. H. Macquart as a scientific and medical member of the editorial board of the *Journal des sçavans*, a state-owned monthly journal that published book reviews and occasional original memoirs.[13] Macquer's importance in the scientific life of Paris was therefore greater than is indicated by his few published papers, which were mainly concerned with applications of chemistry; his theoretical discussions and some original experimental work were included in his books.

With J. Hellot and M. Tillet he carefully studied the ancient method of assaying silver and gold by cupellation (1763); they standardized the procedure to obtain consistent results and disproved the old belief that silver was formed during the process by transmutation of lead. He investigated rubber—recently introduced from South America—and found that it dissolved in rectified ether and could be formed into flexible tubes (1768); but he was unsuccessful in his efforts to make flint glass (1773).

Dyeing and porcelain manufacture were the techniques that benefited most from Macquer's researches. After his success with Prussian blue, he was appointed to assist Hellot as government inspector of the dyeing industries. A leading silk dyer who allowed him to visit his workshop explained the processes, and this led to the publication of Macquer's *Art de la teinture en soie* (1763) in the Academy's series, Descriptions des Arts et Métiers. In 1768 he found that cochineal, a scarlet dye previously used only for wool, could be applied to silk with the aid of a mordant of tin dissolved in aqua regia. He also became interested in the theory of dyeing. Hellot advocated a mechanical theory, believing that particles of dye were retained in the pores of the fabric. While not entirely denying this, Macquer concluded in the *Dictionnaire* (1778) that there was adhesion, or perhaps even chemical combination, among the fabric, the mordant, and the dye. This chemical theory was later elaborated by Berthollet.

From 1751 to 1766 Hellot was scientific adviser to the Royal Porcelain Works at Sèvres, and Macquer assisted him for much of that time. Most of his technical research was not published, so there is only fragmentary information about his work on ceramics. With Baumé he examined more than 800 specimens of clay from many parts of France and studied the effect of heating them with various earthy substances in a powerful charcoal furnace of his own design (1758). The much-admired oriental porcelain had been imitated at Meissen in 1715, but the secret eluded the French until after 1765, when the necessary kaolin was found near Limoges. From August to November 1768 Macquer traveled in the southwest[14] and verified the presence of large deposits, and within a year the craftsmen at Sèvres developed the necessary techniques and produced porcelain as good as any in the world.

After Hellot's death in 1766 Macquer succeeded him as inspector of dyeing and, with E. Mignot de Montigny, as a scientific adviser at Sèvres.[15] His influence on French technology may have been considerable through his post as consultant to the government Bureau de Commerce, which controlled French trade and industry.[16] This well-paid post was no sinecure, and in 1781 Macquer told Bergman that much of his time was spent investigating problems, some of them secret, concerning the saltpeter and other industries as well as pottery and dyeing.[17]

Commissioned by the government to write a comprehensive treatise on dyeing,[18] by the end of 1783 he found it necessary to ask for an assistant to relieve him of some of his work for the *Journal des sçavans*.[19] His health was already failing, and he died a few weeks later. He left a widow, whom he had married in 1748, and two daughters.[20]

NOTES

1. In their *éloges* of Macquer (see Bibliography), Condorcet described him as descended from a noble Scottish family, and Vicq d'Azyr said that his great-grandfather accompanied James I (presumably a misprint for James II) to France. Evidence produced by D. McKie, "The Descent of Pierre Joseph Macquer," in *Nature*, **163** (1949), 627, suggests that he was descended from an Irish family, the Maguires, barons of Enniskillen.

2. Macquer disclosed his motives for studying medicine in the draft of a letter to D. F. R. Mesnard de Chousy, 24 Mar. 1774, Bibliothèque Nationale, MS français 9134, fol. 100. He referred to his work as *médecin des pauvres malades* in an unpublished memoir on the accidental poisoning of wine and milk with lead and copper, Bib. Nat., MS français 9132, fol. 112.

3. In a letter to T. O. Bergman, 18 July 1772, Macquer said that he was working on new eds. of both the *Élémens* and the *Dictionnaire;* see F. Carlid and J. Nordström, eds., *Torbern Bergman's Foreign Correspondence*, I (Stockholm, 1965), 243. An incomplete MS of a revised ed. of *Élémens*, which internal evidence shows to have been written after 1768, is Bib. Nat., MSS français 9131, fols. 1–18 (chs. 1–2, pp. 1–36), and 9133, fols. 216–254 (chs. 3–5, pp. 37–113). This rev. ed. was never completed. A 1775 ed. mentioned by J. R. Partington, *A History of Chemistry*, III (London, 1962), 80, seems not to exist.

4. He is named as professor of pharmacy in *Almanach royal* (Paris, 1753), 347. At this time a new professor was elected each year.

5. The attendance is recorded in a note by Macquer, Bib. Nat., MS français 9134, fols. 131–132.

6. For an account of Philippe Macquer (1720–1770), advocate, historian, and man of letters, see the anonymous "Éloge de M. Macquer, avocat en parlement," in *Le nécrologe des hommes célèbres de la France* (Paris, 1771), 187–206. His *Dictionnaire portatif des arts et métiers* is discussed by J. Proust, "Deux encyclopédistes hors de l'Encyclopédie: Philippe Macquer et l'abbé Jaubert," in *Revue d'histoire des sciences*, **11** (1958), 330–336. At one time he edited the scientific part of the weekly *Avant-coureur;* see a letter from P. J. Macquer to Bergman, 22 Feb. 1768, Carlid and Nordström, *op. cit.*, 230.

7. He explained why the *Dictionnaire* was published anonymously in a letter to Bergman, 22 Feb. 1768, in Carlid and Nordström, *op. cit.*, 229.

8. Bergman later suggested that baryta might be the calx of an unknown metal; see W. A. Smeaton, in *Dictionary of Scientific Biography*, II (1970), 8. Lavoisier expressed the same idea in antiphlogistic terms, when he conjectured that all earths might be metals oxidized to a certain degree (Lavoisier, *Traité élémentaire de chimie* [Paris, 1789], 195).

9. See W. C. Ahlers, "P. J. Macquer et le rapport sur les *Opuscules physiques et chimiques de Lavoisier*," in *Actes du XIIᵉ Congrès international d'histoire des sciences*, VI (Paris, 1971), 5–9.

10. Review by Macquer of *Lettre de M. le Comte Morozzo à M. Macquer, sur la décomposition du gas méphitique & du gas nitreux* (Turin, 1783), in *Journal des sçavans* (1783), 864–867 (quoted on p. 867).

11. M. Landriani to Bergman, 13 Feb. 1784, in Carlid and Nordström, *op. cit.*, 201.

12. The affinity table in Macquer's *Élémens* is an exact copy of Geoffroy's; careful comparison shows that it was printed from the same copper plate as that in Geoffroy's posthumous *Traité de matière médicale*, I (Paris, 1743). Perhaps it was because this plate was available that Macquer did not draw up a new table. He included no affinity table in the *Dictionnaire*.

13. Macquer's appointment as editor is mentioned in the anonymous "Éloge de Jacques-Henri Macquart," in *Journal des sçavans* (1768), 635–638. For the history of the *Journal des sçavans*, see E. Hatin, *Histoire politique et littéraire de la presse en France*, II (Paris, 1859), 151–217; a brief account is in Hatin's *Bibliographie historique et critique de la presse française* (Paris, 1866), 28–32.

14. Letters from Macquer to his brother and other correspondents, written from the southwest between 23 Aug. and 4 Nov. 1768, are in Bib. Nat., MSS français 9134, fols. 86–96; 9135, fols. 65–96.

15. Macquer and De Montigny (d. 1782) are described as *commissaires de l'Académie Royale des Sciences, pour les recherches* in the official list of personnel at the Manufacture de Porcelaines de France à Sève [sic] that was published in the *Almanach royal* from 1776 onward. There is no entry under this heading in earlier years.

16. See E. Lelong's, "Introduction," in Pierre Bonnassieux, ed., *Conseil de commerce et Bureau de Commerce. Inventaire analytique des procès-verbaux* (Paris, 1900), xxvii–xxviii.

17. Macquer to Bergman, 7 July 1781, in Carlid and Nordström, *op. cit.*, 253–254.

18. Macquer to Bergman, 7 Mar. 1782, *ibid.*, 255. The proposed work, described in an eight-page prospectus (see below), was never completed.

19. Correspondence concerning Macquer's request is in Bib. Nat., MSS français 9134, fols. 116, 120, and 12306, fols. 66, 78.

20. Macquer's brother Philippe (see note 6) had died in 1770. Another relation, who died in 1782, was a cousin called Macquer (other names unknown). He was coauthor, with H. G. Duchesne, of *Manuel du naturaliste* (Paris, 1770), frequently but incorrectly attributed to P. J. Macquer. Information about the cousin is given by W. C. Ahlers in his doctoral thesis (see Bibliography).

BIBLIOGRAPHY

I. ORIGINAL WORKS. Macquer's *Élémens de chymie théorique* (Paris, 1749) was reprinted with only minor alterations as a new ed. in 1753. *Élémens de chymie pratique*, 2 vols. (Paris, 1751), appeared as a 2nd ed. in 1756, and *Chymie théorique* was again reprinted then. The 1756 eds. were together translated into English by Andrew Reid as *Elements of the Theory and Practice of Chemistry*, 2 vols. (London, 1758). D. McKie, in *Endeavour*, **16** (1957), 135, records 4 subsequent English eds. published in London (1764; 1775) and Edinburgh (1768; 1777). German (1752, 1758), Italian (1781), and Russian (1791) translations are recorded by H. C. Bolton, *A Select Bibliography of Chemistry* (Washington, 1893), 646. Earlier Russian (1774–1775) and later German (1768) eds. and a Dutch trans. (1773, 1775), are mentioned by J. Ferguson, *Bibliotheca chemica*, II (Glasgow, 1906), 60, but he often gives incorrect dates.

Macquer and Antoine Baumé gave a detailed account of their joint lecture course in *Plan d'un cours de chymie, expérimentale et raisonnée, avec un discours historique sur la chymie* (Paris, 1757). Macquer's *Art de la teinture en soie* (Paris, 1763), was published in the series of Descriptions des Arts et Métiers of the Académie Royale des Sciences. An English trans. appeared of *The Art of Dying [sic] Wool, Silk and Cotton. Translated from the French of M. Hellot, M. Macquer and M. Le Pileur d'Apligny* (London, 1789), 263–381, and on pp. 233–339 of the reprint (London, 1901). The book was also translated into Spanish (Madrid, 1771), German (Leipzig, 1779), and Arabic

(Boulāq, 1823). Macquer's method of dyeing silk with cochineal, published in the *Mémoires* of the Academy for 1768 (see below), was also described in a pamphlet, *Méthode pour teindre la soie en plusieurs nuances de rouge vif de cochenille et autres couleurs, par M. Macquer* (Paris, 1769). His projected general treatise on dyeing was described in *Prospectus et plan d'une description générale de l'art de la teinture . . . par M. Macquer* (Paris, 1782).

Macquer was coauthor, with J. M. F. de Lassone, E. Gourley de la Motte, A. L. de Jussieu, J. B. Carburi, and L. C. Cadet, of a short medical work, *Traitement contre le ténia ou ver solitaire, pratiqué à Morat en Suisse, examiné et éprouvé à Paris* (Paris, 1775; repr. 1776); summarized in *Journal des sçavans* (1776), 606–611; English trans. by S. Foart Simmons, *An Account of the Tenia or Long Tape Worm . . .* (London, 1777).

The breadth of Macquer's interests is shown by the full title of his *Dictionnaire de chymie, contenant la théorie & la pratique de cette science, son application à la physique, à l'histoire naturelle, à la médecine & à l'économie animale*, first published anonymously in 2 small octavo vols. (Paris, 1766); a reimpression, with slightly different pagination, appeared later in 1766 and another in 1769. There was also a Swiss printing (3 vols., Yverdon, 1767). The words *à l'économie animale* in the title were replaced by *aux arts dépendans de la chymie* in the 2nd ed., which was published, with Macquer named as author, in both octavo in 4 vols. (Paris, 1778) and quarto in 2 vols. (Paris, 1778). A 3-vol. octavo reprint, incorrectly dated 1777 was not published before 1778. There were also 3 Swiss printings (Yverdon, 1779; "en Suisse," 1779–1780; Neuchâtel, 1789). James Keir's English trans., *A Dictionary of Chemistry*, first appeared in 2 vols. (London, 1771); a 2nd English ed., required before the 2nd French ed. was ready, contains supplementary material by Keir (3 vols., London, 1777). The 1st ed. was also translated into German and Danish; the 2nd ed. into German and Italian. Full details of the translations are given by J. R. Partington, *A History of Chemistry*, III (London, 1962), 81–82.

The following memoirs by Macquer appeared in the *Histoire [H.] et Mémoires [M.] de l'Académie Royale des Sciences* (the date of publication in parenthesis follows the nominal date): "Sur la cause de la différente dissolubilité des huiles dans l'esprit de vin," *M.*, 1745 (1749), 9–25; "Recherches sur l'arsenic. Premier mémoire," *M.*, 1746 (1751), 233–236; "Observations sur la chaux et sur le plâtre," *M.*, 1747 (1752), 678–696; "Second mémoire sur l'arsenic," *M.*, 1748 (1752), 35–50; "Mémoire sur une nouvelle espèce de teinture bleue, dans laquelle il n'entre ni pastel ni indigo," *M.*, 1749 (1753), 255–265; "Examen chymique du bleu de Prusse," *M.*, 1752 (1756), 60–77; "Mémoire sur une nouvelle méthode de M. le Comte de la Garaye pour dissoudre les métaux," *M.*, 1755 (1761), 25–35; "Recherches sur la nature de la teinture mercurielle de M. le Comte de la Garaye. Premier mémoire," *M.*, 1755 (1761), 531–546 (there was no further memoir on this topic); "Mémoire sur un nouveau métal connu sous le nom d'or blanc ou de platine," *M.*, 1758 (1763), 119–133, written with A. Baumé; "Mémoire sur les argiles et sur la

fusibilité de cette espèce de terre avec les terres calcaires," *M.*, 1758 (1763), 155–176; "Examen chimique de l'eau de la rivière d'Yvette," *M.*, 1762 (1764), 376–380, written with J. Hellot; "Mémoire sur les essais des matières d'or et d'argent," *M.*, 1763 (1766), 1–14, written with J. Hellot and M. Tillet; "Mémoire sur l'action d'un feu violent de charbon, appliqué à plusieurs terres, pierres et chaux métalliques," *M.*, 1767 (1770), 298–314; "Sur une source minéral trouvé à Vaugirard," *H.*, 1768 (1770), 69–75, written with S. F. Morand and L. C. Cadet; "Mémoire sur un moyen de teindre la soie en un rouge vif de cochenille et de lui faire prendre plusieurs autres couleurs plus belles et plus solides qu'on a faites jusqu'à présent," *M.*, 1768 (1770), 82–90; "Mémoire sur un moyen de dissoudre la résine caoutchouc connue présentement sous le nom de résine élastique de Cayenne, et de la faire reparoitre avec toutes ses qualités," *M.*, 1768 (1770), 209–217; "Recherches sur la composition du flint-glass, avec des vues pour le perfectionner," *M.*, 1773 (1777), 502–511; "Premier essai du grand verre ardent de M. Trudaine établi au jardin de l'Infante au commencement du mois d'octobre de l'année 1774," *M.*, 1774 (1778), 62–72, written with J. C. P. Trudaine de Montigny, L. C. Cadet, A. L. Lavoisier and M. J. Brisson; and "Analyse de l'eau du lac Asphaltite," *M.*, 1778 (1781), 69–72, written with A. L. Lavoisier and B. G. Sage.

Macquer's research on the solubility of salts in alcohol was published as "Mémoire sur la différente dissolubilité des sels neutres dans l'esprit de vin, contenant des observations particulières sur plusieurs de ces sels," in *Mélanges de philosophie et de mathématique de la Société Royale de Turin*, 3 (1766), 1–30; and "Second mémoire . . . de ces sels," *ibid.*, 5 (1770–1773), 173–190; the first memoir was reprinted in *Introduction aux observations sur la physique*, 1 (1777), 461–472, 559–568; and the second in *Observations sur la physique*, 9 (1777), 182–193. Other memoirs by Macquer include "Lettre . . . au sujet des expériences qui se font au foyer de la grande lentille à liqueur de M. de Trudaine," in *Journal des sçavans* (1776), 561–563; "Observations sur la dissolution des sédimens et incrustations pierreuses que forme l'urine dans les vaisseaux où elle séjourne," *ibid.*, 613–616; "Mémoire sur les savons acides, et sur les avantages qu'on en pourroit retirer dans la pratique de la médecine," in *Mémoires de la Société royale de médecine* (1776), 379–386; "Réflexions sur la magnésie du sel d'Epsom," in *Histoire de la Société royale de médecine* (1779), 235–243. Minor reports written by Macquer jointly with other academicians are not included in this bibliography; details of those of which Lavoisier was a coauthor are in D. I. Duveen and H. S. Klickstein, *A Bibliography . . . of Lavoisier* (London, 1954).

Eleven bound vols. of Macquer's papers are at the Bibliothèque Nationale, Paris: MSS français 9127–9135 contain MSS of published and unpublished books, memoirs, and lecture notes as well as drafts of letters written by him; MSS français 12305–12306 contain letters received by him from many correspondents. An inventory and index of these vols. (except MS 9135, which contains documents relating to porcelain), compiled in 1943 by

Paul M. Bondois, is in Bib. Nat., MS français, nouvelle acquisition 13260; it is useful but not completely accurate. A small collection of Macquer's correspondence is at the library of the Muséum National d'Histoire Naturelle, Paris, MS 283; some of his notebooks and other documents concerning porcelain are in the archives of the Manufacture Nationale de Sèvres, Y 57–60. In a doctoral thesis (see below) W. C. Ahlers lists the principal contents of all these MSS and draws attention to Macquer material in other French archives. The eighteen letters from Macquer to Bergman at the archives of the University of Uppsala are printed with an additional letter in G. Carlid and J. Nordström, eds., *Torbern Bergman's Foreign Correspondence*, I (Stockholm, 1965), 229–255, 437–438.

II. SECONDARY LITERATURE. The best contemporary account of Macquer's life and work is F. Vicq d'Azyr, "Éloge de M. Macquer," in *Histoire de la Société royale de médecine* for 1782–1783 (1787), pp. 69–94, repr., but without the valuable footnotes, in his *Éloges historiques*, I (Paris, 1805), 277–303. Less informative is Condorcet, "Éloge de M. Macquer," in *Histoire de l'Académie Royale des Sciences* for 1784 (1787), pp. 20–30, repr. in his *Oeuvres*, III (Paris, 1847), 125–138. A recent study, containing much information from MS sources, is the unpublished doctoral thesis by Willem C. Ahlers, "Un chimiste du XVIIIe siècle. Pierre Joseph Macquer (1718–1784). Aspects de sa vie et de son oeuvre," Université de Paris, Faculté des Lettres et Sciences Humaines, thèse de troisième cycle, 1969. L. J. M. Coleby, *The Chemical Studies of P. J. Macquer* (London, 1938), is a convenient source of information about Macquer's published work. Useful bibliographical data are given by D. McKie, "Macquer, the First Lexicographer of Chemistry," in *Endeavour*, 16 (1957), 133–136. Macquer's joint lecture course with Baumé is described by R. Davy, *L'apothicaire Antoine Baumé*

(Cahors, 1955), 38–40; and the text of their agreement is printed in J. P. Contant, *L'enseignement de la chimie au Jardin Royal des Plantes de Paris* (Cahors, 1952), 65–69. Contant says little about Macquer's lectures; a short account is given by W. A. Smeaton, "P. J. Macquer's Course of Chemistry at the Jardin du Roi," in *Actes du X*e *Congrès international d'histoire des sciences, Ithaca, 1962* (Paris, 1964), 847–849.

Macquer's views on the nature of the elements are discussed by W. A. Smeaton, "Macquer on the Composition of Metals and the Artificial Production of Gold and Silver," in *Chymia*, 11 (1966), 81–88. A good account of his ideas on affinity is given by A. M. Duncan, "Some Theoretical Aspects of Eighteenth-century Tables of Affinity," in *Annals of Science*, 18 (1962), 177–194, 217–232. His contributions to the reform of nomenclature are discussed by M. P. Crosland, *Historical Studies in the Language of Chemistry* (London, 1962), 120–122, 134–138.

The importance of Macquer and Baumé's research on platinum is assessed by D. McDonald, *A History of Platinum* (London, 1960), 32–34; and the analysis of an iron ore by Macquer and E. Mignot de Montigny is described by R. G. Neville, " 'Observations sur la mine de fer de Bagory': An Unpublished Manuscript by P. J. Macquer," in *Chymia*, 8 (1962), 89–96. Macquer's technical research is set in its historical context by H. Guerlac, "Some French Antecedents of the Chemical Revolution," in *Chymia*, 5 (1959), 73–112; further information is given by W. C. Ahlers, "P. J. Macquer, pionnier de la recherche fondamentale dans le domaine de l'industrie chimique," in *Actes du XIII*e *Congrès international d'histoire des sciences, Moscow/Leningrad, 1971* (in press).

References to additional secondary sources are given in the notes above.

W. A. SMEATON